36. Beta from a simple linear regression
$\beta = [(T \times \sum XY) - (\sum Y \times \sum X)]/[(T \times \sum X^2) - (\sum X)^2]$

37. Alpha from a simple linear regression
$\alpha = [(\sum Y)/T] - [\beta \times (\sum X)/T]$

38. Standard deviation of the random error term from a simple linear regression
$\sigma_e = \{[\sum Y^2 - (\alpha \times \sum Y) - (\beta \times \sum XY)]/[T-2]\}^{1/2}$

39. Standard error of beta from a simple linear regression
$\sigma_\beta = \sigma_e/\{\sum X^2 - [(\sum X)^2/T]\}^{1/2}$

40. Standard error of alpha from a simple linear regression
$\sigma_\alpha = \sigma_e/\{T - [(\sum X)^2/\sum X^2]\}^{1/2}$

41. Correlation coefficient
$\rho = [(T \times \sum XY) - (\sum Y \times \sum X)]/\{[(T \times \sum Y^2) - (\sum Y)^2] \times [(T \times \sum X^2) - (\sum X)^2]\}^{1/2}$

42. Beta of the firm
$\beta_{\text{firm}} = \beta_{\text{debt}}[(1-\tau)D/V_u] + \beta_{\text{equity}}(E/V_u)$

43. Beta of the firm's equity
$\beta_{\text{equity}} = \beta_{\text{firm}} + (\beta_{\text{firm}} - \beta_{\text{debt}})(D/E)(1-\tau)$

44. Adjusted historical beta
$\beta_a = a + b\beta_h$

45. Capitalization-of-income method of valuation
$$V = \sum_{t=1}^{\infty} [C_t/(1+k)^t]$$

46. Zero-growth DDM
$V = D_1/k$

47. Constant-growth DDM
$V = D_1/(k-g)$

48. Multiple-growth DDM
$$V = [\sum_{t=1}^{T} D_t/(1+k)^t] + [D_{T+1}/(k-g) \times (1+k)^T]$$

49. "Normal" price-earnings ratio with constant growth
$V/E_0 = p\{[1 + r(1-p)]/[k - r(1-p)]\}$

50. Lintner dividend payout model
$D_t = ap^*E_t + (1-a)D_{t-1}$

51. Annual earnings as a random walk
$E_t = E_{t-1} + \epsilon_t$

52. Quarterly earnings as an autoregressive process
$QE_t = QE_{t-4} + a(QE_{t-1} - QE_{t-5}) + b + e_t$

53. Intrinsic value of puts and calls
$IV_C = MAX(0, P_S - E)$
$IV_P = MAX(0, E - P_S)$

54. Put-call parity
$P_P + P_S = P_C + E/e^{RT}$

55. Black-Scholes formula for the fair value of a call option
$V_C = N(d_1)P_S - (E/e^{RT})N(d_2)$
$d_1 = [\ln(P_S/E) + (R + .5\sigma^2)T]/\sigma\sqrt{T}$
$d_2 = [\ln(P_S/E) + (R - .5\sigma^2)T]/\sigma\sqrt{T}$
$= d_1 - \sigma\sqrt{T}$

56. Black-Scholes formula for the fair value of a put option
$P_P = (E/e^{RT})N(-d_2) - P_S N(-d_1)$

57. Fair value of a futures contract
$P_f = P_S + I - B + C$

58. Fair value of an index futures contract
$P_f = P_S + RP_S - yP_S$

59. Investment company's net asset value
$NAV_t = (MVA_t - LIAB_t)/NSO_t$

60. Return on an investment company's shares
$r_t = [(NAV_t - NAV_{t-1}) + I_t + G_t]/NAV_{t-1}$

61. Risk tolerance (as implied by a choice of a portfolio)
$\tau = [2(\bar{r}_S - r_f)\sigma_S^2]/(\bar{r}_S - r_f)^2$

62. Certainty equivalent return
$u_i = \bar{r}_p - (1/\tau)\sigma_p^2$

63. Ex post alpha
$\alpha_p = ar_p - ar_{bp}$

64. Ex post alpha based on the CAPM
$\alpha_p = ar_p - [ar_f + (ar_M - ar_f)\beta_p]$

65. Ex post characteristic line
$r_p - r_f = \alpha_p + \beta_p(r_M - r_f)$

66. Reward-to-volatility ratio (Treynor ratio)
$RVOL_p = (ar_p - ar_f)/\beta_p$

67. Reward-to-variability ratio (Sharpe ratio)
$RVAR_p = (ar_p - ar_f)/\sigma_p$

68. Ex post characteristic curve
$r_p - r_f = a + b(r_M - r_f) + c[(r_M - r_f)^2]$

69. Ex post characteristic lines
$r_p - r_f = a + b(r_M - r_f) + c[D(r_M - r_f)]$
where: $D = 0$ if $r_M > r_f$
$D = -1$ if $r_M < r_f$

70. Return on a foreign investment
$r_f = r_d + r_c + r_d r_c$

71. Standard deviation of a foreign investment
$\sigma_f = (\sigma_d^2 + \sigma_c^2 + 2\rho_{dc}\sigma_d\sigma_c)^{1/2}$

A-MacKay

INVESTMENTS

SECOND CANADIAN EDITION

William F. Sharpe
STANFORD UNIVERSITY

Gordon J. Alexander
UNIVERSITY OF MINNESOTA

Jeffery V. Bailey
RICHARDS AND TIERNEY, INC.

David J. Fowler
YORK UNIVERSITY

Prentice Hall Canada Inc.
SCARBOROUGH, ONTARIO

To Kathy
WFS

To my mother and in memory of my father
GJA

To Stephen and Megan
JVB

To Lesley
DJF

Canadian Cataloguing in Publication Data

Investments
2nd Canadian ed.
First ed. by William F. Sharpe, Gordon J. Alexander, and David J. Fowler

ISBN 0-13-260423-X

1. Investments – Canada. 2. Investment analysis. I. Sharpe, William F.

HG4521.S43 1997 332.6'0971 C96–930614-8

Prentice-Hall, Inc., Upper Saddle River, New Jersey
Prentice-Hall International (UK) Limited, London
Prentice-Hall of Australia, Pty, Limited, Sydney
Prentice-Hall Hispanoamericana, S.A., Mexico City
Prentice-Hall of India Private Limited, New Delhi
Prentice-Hall of Japan, Inc., Tokyo
Simon & Schuster Asia Private Limited, Singapore
Editoria Prentice-Hall do Brasil, Ltda., Rio de Janeiro

ISBN: 0-13-260423-X

Acquisitions Editor: Patrick Ferrier
Developmental Editor: Lesley Mann
Copy Editor: Chelsea Donaldson
Production Editor: Mary Ann McCutcheon
Production Coordinator: Deborah Starks
Permissions Research: Marijke Leupen
Cover Design: Pronk&Associates
Art Direction: Kyle Gell
Cover Image: Pronk&Associates
Page Layout: Pronk&Associates

1 2 3 4 5 RRD 01 00 99 98 97

Printed and bound in the USA

Every reasonable effort has been made to obtain permissions for all articles and data used in this edition. If errors or omissions have occurred, they will be corrected in future editions provided written notification has been received by the publisher.

We welcome readers' comments, which can be sent by e-mail to **collegeinfo_pubcanada@prenhall.com**

About the Authors

WILLIAM F. SHARPE William F. Sharpe is currently Professor of Finance at the Stanford University Graduate School of Business. Dr. Sharpe has published articles in a number of professional journals, including *Financial Analysts Journal, Journal of Business, Journal of Finance, Journal of Financial and Quantitative Analysis, Journal of Portfolio Management*, and *Management Science*. Dr. Sharpe is past President of the American Finance Association. In 1990 he received the Nobel Prize in Economics. Dr. Sharpe received his A.B., M.A., and Ph.D. degrees in Economics from the University of California at Los Angeles.

GORDON J. ALEXANDER Gordon J. Alexander is presently the IDS Professor of Finance at the University of Minnesota. Dr. Alexander has published articles in *Financial Management, Journal of Banking and Finance, Journal of Finance, Journal of Financial Economics, Journal of Financial and Quantitative Analysis*, and *Journal of Portfolio Management*. In addition, he has been an Associate Editor of the *Journal of Financial and Quantitative Analysis* and is currently Book Review Editor of the *Journal of Finance*. Dr. Alexander received his Ph.D. in Finance, M.A. in Mathematics, and M.B.A. from the University of Michigan, and his B.S. in Business Administration from the State University of New York at Buffalo.

JEFFERY V. BAILEY Jeffery V. Bailey is a Managing Partner of the firm of Richards & Tierney, Inc., a Chicago-based pension fund consulting organization. He was formerly the Assistant Executive Director of the Minnesota State Board of Investment. Mr. Bailey has published articles in *Financial Analysts Journal* and *Journal of Portfolio Management* as well as having contributed articles to the practitioner handbooks *Managing Institutional Assets* and *Pension Fund Investment Management*. He received his B.A. in Economics from Oakland University and his M.A. in Economics and M.B.A. in Finance from the University of Minnesota.

DAVID J. FOWLER David J. Fowler is an Associate Professor at the Schulich School of Business at York University in Toronto. Dr. Fowler has published two books, *The Drug Industry: A Case Study in Foreign Control* and *Endowed Charitable Foundations in Canada: A Study of Spending and Investment Strategies Under Revenue Canada Regulations*, as well as numerous articles in professional publications such as *Journal of Business Finance and Accounting, Journal of Finance, Journal of Financial Economics*, and *Journal of Financial Research*. Dr. Fowler received his B.Sc (Eng) from the Imperial College of Science & Technology at the University of London, and his M.B.A. and Ph.D. at the University of Toronto.

Brief Contents

Contents

23 FINANCIAL ANALYSIS 767

24 INVESTMENT MANAGEMENT 815

Preface to the Second Canadian Edition

In preparing this Second Canadian Edition of *Investments*, I have followed the same guiding principles that were outlined in the preface to the First Edition. In general, relevant Canadian material has been added, and the results of US empirical studies have been augmented with the corresponding Canadian results when these were available.

This new edition contains the following improvements over the previous edition:

- **Updated material.** Where appropriate, material has been updated to keep students abreast of the latest developments in investments.
- **Institutional issues.** Students want to know how the concepts presented in the text are applied in the "real world." In each chapter, a feature entitled *Institutional Issues* discusses issues that face large institutional investors, such as pension funds and mutual funds. Whenever possible, these features are presented from a Canadian perspective.
- **More international content.** The globalization of the investment industry is proceeding at a rapid pace. It is imperative that students become familiar with an increasingly diverse set of international investing concepts. Chapter 26 deals directly with international securities and security markets.
- **Expanded coverage of options and futures and the introduction of swaps.** The use of these types of derivative securities has become commonplace among institutional investors. Accordingly, Chapters 20 and 21 have been extended to more fully present the basic concepts underlying options and futures. In addition, Chapter 24 contains an introduction to swaps.
- **Redesigned chapter summaries.** To facilitate a quick review of a chapter's highlights, we have rewritten each chapter's summary in an easy-to-read list format.
- **Additional end-of-chapter problems.** The number of questions and problems at the end of each chapter has roughly doubled.
- **CFA examination questions.** To give students a sense of the knowledge required of certified investment professionals, questions from recent Chartered Financial Analyst examinations have been added.
- **Key terms.** To emphasize important concepts, key terms used in the text are set in boldface, and listed at the end of each chapter.
- **Annotated references and Internet addresses.** For those students who are interested in further study of subjects presented in the text, an extensive set of references, including Canadian references, is listed at the end of each chapter. In addition, many chapters contain a list of relevant Internet addresses.

- **Answers to selected problems.** Students often wish to know if they are working in the right direction when solving problems. Answers to selected end-of-chapter problems are therefore included at the end of the text.

A supplements package is also available, both on disk and in hard copy. Included in this package are the following:

- **Instructor's Manual.** Solutions to end-of-chapter problems are presented thoroughly and clearly. Also presented is a set of course outlines that are designed to accommodate a variety of teaching approaches.
- **Test Item File.** The Test Item file gives the instructor access to hundreds of exam questions (true-false, multiple choice, and problems) and their solutions.

In preparing this Second Canadian Edition of Investments, I was pleased to confirm that Canadian academics and some practitioners have continued to be diligent researchers of the Canadian scene. In the preface to the previous edition I expressed my hopes that the *Canadian Investment Review* would prosper under its new owners. It is an invaluable source of information about the application of investment theory in the Canadian environment and has prospered to the extent of expanding from two issues per year to four. Long may it continue to make academic research accessible to practitioners and the latter's work known to academics.

Many others have provided assistance in the preparation of this book. My thanks go to my colleagues at the Schulich School of Business, York University, particularly those in Finance — Elizabeth Maynes, Moshe Milevsky, Eli Prisman, Chris Robinson and Savits Verma, but above all Jamie Carlsen, who covered for me when I was completing this task. I would also like to thank Bernard Augustin, Kim Bueler, Roy Hill, John Kaszel, Daniel Kelly, Fionulla Martin, Melanie Moore, Dawn Scott, Matt Taugher and Shawn Wilcox. I especially appreciate Sebouh Aintablian's help in preparing the statistical tables and helping with the instructor's manual. I am also indebted to Brett Matthews, who provided me with data on and insights into the operations of mutual funds.

It has been pleasant to work with the following people from Prentice Hall Canada: acquisitions editor, Patrick Ferrier; developmental editor, Lesley Mann; production editor, Mary Ann McCutcheon; and freelance editor, Chelsea Donaldson. I would like to thank the following reviewers:

Ben Amoako-Adu, Wilfrid Laurier University
John Benson, University of Guelph
Alex Faseruk, Memorial University
Moon Hoe Lee, University of Saskatchewan
Eben Otuteye, University of New Brunswick

When a manuscript finally goes to press, every author is aware that there may still be undetected errors or omissions. Any corrections and/or constructive comments will, therefore, be gratefully received.

David Fowler
1997

CHAPTER 1

Introduction

This book is about investing in marketable securities. Accordingly, it focuses on the investment environment and process. The **investment environment** encompasses the kinds of marketable securities that exist and where and how they are bought and sold. The **investment process** is concerned with how an investor should proceed in making decisions about marketable securities in which to invest, how extensive the investments should be, and when the investments should be made. Before discussing the investment environment and process in more detail, the term **investment** will be described.

Investment, in its broadest sense, means the sacrifice of certain present value for (possibly uncertain) future value. Two different attributes are generally involved: time and risk. The sacrifice takes place in the present and is certain. The reward comes later, if at all, and the magnitude is generally uncertain. In some cases time predominates (for example, government bonds). In other cases risk is the dominant attribute (for example, call options on common shares). In yet others, both time and risk are important (for example, shares of common stock).

A distinction is often made between investment and **savings**. Savings is defined as foregone consumption; investment is restricted to "real" investment of the sort that increases national output in the future. Although this definition is useful in other contexts, it is not especially helpful here. The distinction between real and financial investments, however, is important.

Real investments generally involve some kind of tangible asset, such as land, machinery, or factories. **Financial investments** involve contracts written on pieces of paper, such as shares and bonds. In primitive economies most investment is of the real variety. However, in a modern economy, much investment is of the financial variety. Highly developed institutions for financial investment greatly facilitate real investment. By and large, the two forms of investment are complementary, not competitive.

The financing of an apartment house provides a good example. Apartments are sufficiently tangible ("bricks and mortar") to be considered real investment. Where are the resources required to pay for the land and the construction of the apartments obtained? Some may come from direct investment—for example, a wealthy doctor who wants to build an apartment house may use some of his or her money to finance the project. The rest of the resources may be provided by a mortgage. In essence, someone loans the doctor money, with repayment promised in fixed amounts on a specified schedule over many years. In the typical case the "someone" is not a person but an institution acting as a financial intermediary. Thus, the doctor has made a real investment in the apartment house, and the institution has made a financial investment in the doctor.

As a second example, consider what happens when Canadian Pacific (CP) finds itself in need of money to pay for plant construction. This real investment may be financed by the sale of new common stock in the **primary market** for securities. The common stock itself represents a financial investment to the purchasers, who may subsequently trade these shares in the **secondary market** — for example, on the Toronto Stock Exchange (TSE). Although transactions in the secondary market do not generate money for CP, the fact that such a market exists makes the common stock more attractive and thus facilitates real investment. Investors would pay less for new shares of common stock if there were no way to sell them quickly and inexpensively.

These examples have introduced the three main elements of the investment environment — securities (also known as financial investments or financial assets), security markets (also known as financial markets), and financial intermediaries (also known as financial institutions). They are discussed in more detail next.

THE INVESTMENT ENVIRONMENT

Securities

When someone borrows money from a pawnbroker, he or she must leave some item of value as security. Failure to repay the loan (plus interest) means that the pawnbroker can sell the pawned item to recover the amount of the loan (plus interest) and perhaps make a profit. The terms of the agreement are recorded via pawn tickets. When a college student borrows money to buy a car, the lender usually holds formal title to the car until the loan is repaid. In the event of default, the lender can repossess the car and attempt to sell it to recover his or her costs. In this case the official certificate of title, issued by the province, serves as the security for the loan.

When someone borrows money for a vacation, he or she may simply sign a piece of paper promising repayment with interest. The loan is unsecured in the sense that there is no collateral, meaning no specific asset has been promised to the lender in the event of default. In such a situation, the lender would have to take the borrower to court to try to recover the amount of the loan. Only a piece of paper, called a promissory note, stands as evidence of such a loan.

When a firm borrows money, it may or may not offer collateral. For example, some loans may be secured (backed) by specific assets (buildings, equipment, and so on). Such loans are registered as mortgage bonds, which indicate the terms of repayment and the particular assets pledged to the lender in the event of default. However, it is much more common for a corporation simply to pledge all its assets, perhaps with some provision for the manner in which the division will take place in the event of default. Such a promise is known as a debenture bond.

Finally, a firm may promise a right to share in the firm's profits in return for an investor's funds. Nothing is pledged, and no irrevocable promises are made. The firm simply pays whatever its directors deem reasonable from time to time. However, to protect against serious malfeasance, the investor is given the right to participate in the determination of who will be members of the board of directors. His or her property right is represented by a share of common stock, which can be sold to someone else who will then be able to exercise that right. The holder of common shares is said to be an *owner* of the corporation and can, in theory, exercise control over its operation through the board of directors.

In general, only a piece of paper represents the investor's rights to certain prospects or property and the conditions under which he or she may exercise those rights. This piece of paper, serving as evidence of property rights, is called a *security*. A security, with all its rights and conditions, may be transferred to another investor. Thus, everything from a pawn ticket to a share of CP common stock is a security. Hereafter the term **security** will be used to refer to *a legal representation of the right to receive prospective future benefits under stated conditions.* One of the objectives of security analysis is to identify mispriced securities by determining their prospective future benefits, the conditions under which they will be received, and the likelihood of their occurring.

By and large the focus here is on securities that may be easily and efficiently transferred from one owner to another. Thus, the concern is with shares and bonds rather than with pawn tickets, although much of the material in this book applies to all three types of instruments.

Figure 1.1 and Table 1.1 show the year-by-year results obtained from investing in four types of securities over the 46-year period from 1950 through 1995. In each case the percentage change in a hypothetical investor's wealth from the beginning to the end of the year is shown. This amount, known as the **rate of return** (or simply the *return*), is calculated as follows:

$$\text{Return} = \frac{\text{end-of-period wealth} - \text{beginning-of-period wealth}}{\text{beginning-of-period wealth}} \tag{1.1}$$

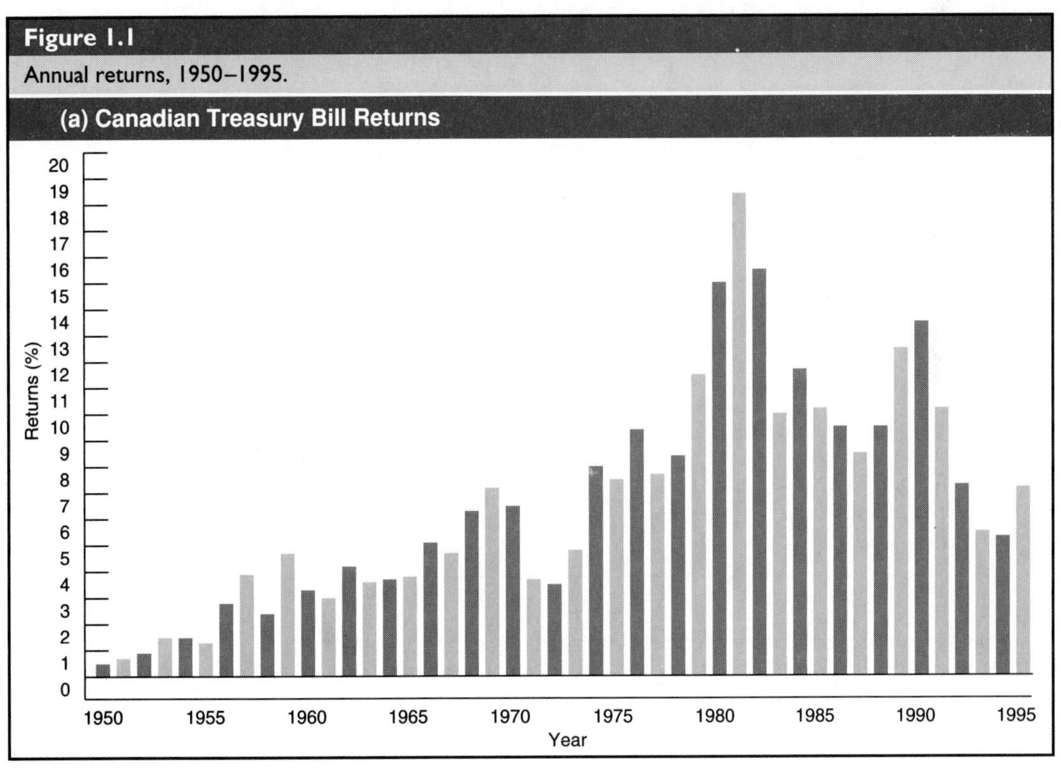

Figure 1.1
Annual returns, 1950–1995.

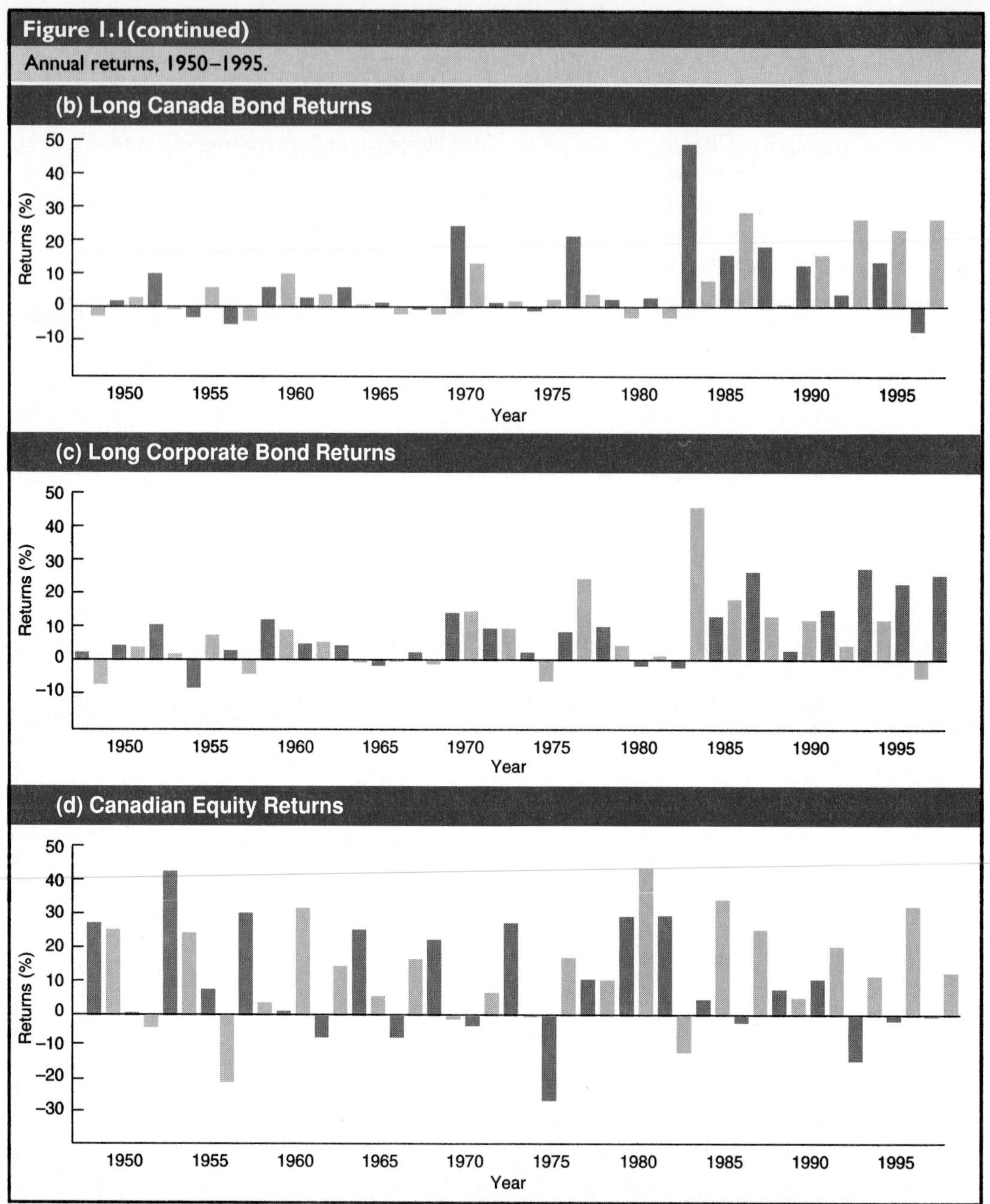

SOURCE: Reprinted, with permission, from James E. Hatch and Robert W. White, *Canadian Stocks, Bonds, Bills, and Inflation: 1950–1987*, Copyright 1988, The Research Foundation of The Institute of Chartered Financial Analysts, Charlottesville, Va.; Melanie Moore, *ScotiaMcLeod's Handbook of Canadian Debt Market Indices: 1947–1995* (Toronto: ScotiaMcLeod Inc., 1995); and Melanie Moore, *Debt Market Indices*, ScotiaMcLeod Inc. (November 30, 1995).

Table 1.1

Annual Returns: Stocks, Bonds, and Treasury Bills and Changes in the Consumer Price Index (CPI), 1950–1995.[a]

		Total Returns			
Year	*Treasury Bills*	*Long Canada Bonds*	*Long Corporate Bonds*	*Equities*	*CPI*
1950	0.51	–0.11	2.68	27.91	6.10
1951	0.71	–3.01	–6.44	25.50	10.73
1952	0.95	2.05	4.49	1.17	–1.73
1953	1.54	3.76	3.99	–8.28	0.00
1954	1.53	9.78	10.34	43.61	0.35
1955	1.36	–0.43	2.18	24.11	0.35
1956	2.75	–3.54	–7.58	8.81	3.15
1957	3.83	6.60	7.58	–20.58	2.03
1958	2.51	–5.82	2.99	31.25	2.66
1959	4.62	–4.44	–4.28	4.59	1.29
1960	3.31	6.88	11.94	1.78	1.28
1961	2.89	9.75	8.91	32.75	0.32
1962	4.22	3.16	4.95	–7.09	1.57
1963	3.63	4.59	5.38	15.60	1.86
1964	3.79	6.74	4.71	25.43	1.82
1965	3.92	1.04	–0.58	6.68	2.98
1966	5.03	1.72	–1.53	–7.07	3.48
1967	4.59	–2.27	–0.34	18.09	4.20
1968	6.44	–0.62	2.43	22.45	4.03
1969	7.09	–2.36	–1.04	–0.81	4.65
1970	6.70	22.70	13.97	–3.57	1.48
1971	3.81	11.79	14.48	8.01	4.87
1972	3.55	1.59	9.51	27.38	5.10
1973	5.11	1.96	2.40	0.27	9.27
1974	7.85	–0.98	–5.86	–25.93	12.32
1975	7.41	2.74	8.35	18.48	9.53
1976	9.27	19.65	23.32	11.02	5.91
1977	7.66	4.68	10.34	10.76	9.46
1978	8.34	2.76	5.00	29.66	8.36
1979	11.41	–3.30	–1.77	44.77	9.80
1980	14.97	3.23	1.41	30.13	11.19
1981	18.41	–3.26	–1.96	–10.25	12.10
1982	15.42	47.39	44.33	5.54	9.26
1983	9.62	8.58	12.75	35.49	4.55
1984	11.59	15.85	17.87	–2.39	3.76
1985	9.88	27.24	25.74	25.07	4.35

Table 1.1
(Continued)

Total Returns					
Year	*Treasury Bills*	*Long Canada Bonds*	*Long Corporate Bonds*	*Equities*	*CPI*
1986	9.33	18.60	13.05	8.95	4.17
1987	8.48	1.26	3.37	5.88	4.15
1988	9.41	10.65	11.77	11.08	3.96
1989	12.36	15.39	14.13	21.37	5.17
1990	13.48	4.64	4.53	−14.80	5.00
1991	9.83	24.52	26.16	12.02	3.78
1992	7.08	11.58	11.61	−1.43	2.14
1993	5.51	21.12	22.25	32.55	1.70
1994	5.35	–8.14	–4.79	–0.18	0.23
1995	7.01	24.36	24.86	12.92	1.90
Mean	6.61	6.96	7.77	11.71	4.45
Std. Dev.	4.14	10.66	10.17	16.35	3.50

[a] to November 30, 1995

SOURCE: Reprinted, with permission, from James E. Hatch and Robert W. White, *Canadian Stocks, Bonds, Bills, and Inflation: 1950–1987*, Copyright 1988, The Research Foundation of The Institute of Chartered Financial Analysts, Charlottesville, Va.; Melanie Moore, *ScotiaMcLeod's Handbook of Canadian Debt Market Indices: 1947–1995* (Toronto: ScotiaMcLeod Inc., 1995); and Melanie Moore, *Debt Market Indices*, ScotiaMcLeod Inc. (November 30, 1995).

In calculating the return on a security, it is assumed that the investor purchases one unit (for example, one bond or one share of common stock) of the security at the beginning of the period. The cost of this investment is the amount entered in the denominator of equation (1.1). The value in the numerator is the answer to a simple question—how much better (or worse) off is the investor at the end of the period?

For example, assume that Widget Corporation's common stock was selling for \$40 per share at the beginning of the year and for \$45 at the end of the year and paid dividends of \$3 per share during the year. The return on Widget for the year would then be calculated as [(\$45 + \$3) – \$40]/\$40 = .20, or 20%.[1]

Treasury Bills

The first type of security listed in Figure 1.1 involves loaning money on a short-term basis (three months to one year) to the Canadian Government. Such a loan carries little (if any) risk that payment will not be made as promised. Moreover, while the rate of return varies from period to period, at the beginning of any single period it is known with certainty. The return on these investments, known as Treasury bills, ranged from a high of 19.09% per

[1] Generally, any cash received during the period is treated as if it were received at the end of the period. However, this assumption typically results in an understatement of the actual return. For example, if the dividends on Widget were received at midyear, the investor could have put them in a bank savings account and earned, for example, 4% interest for the rest of the year. This interest then would have amounted to .04 × \$3.00 = \$.12, resulting in the annual return being equal to [(\$45 + \$3 + \$.12) – \$40]/\$40 = .203, or 20.3%.

year (in 1981) to a low of 0.51% per year (in 1950), with an average value of 6.61% during the entire 46-year period.

Long-Term Bonds

The second and third types of securities shown in Figure 1.1 are bonds and also involve loaning money. Each type of bond represents a long-term commitment on the part of the issuer (that is, the borrower) to the investor (that is, the lender). This commitment is to make cash payments each year (the coupon payment) up to some point in time (the maturity date), when a single final cash payment (the principal) will also be made. The prices at which these bonds can be bought and sold prior to maturity vary from time to time. Thus, while coupon payments are easily predicted, the end-of-period selling price of the security before maturity is uncertain at the beginning of the period, thereby making the return difficult to predict in advance.

The second type of security (Government of Canada bonds, also known as long Canada bonds) involves loans with a maturity of 10 years or more to the Canadian Government. The third type of security (industrial bonds, otherwise known as corporate bonds), involves long-term loans to Canadian industrial corporations. This data series is based on a small sample of bonds that are not controlled as to maturity.

These two kinds of bonds had their highest annual return in 1982, reaching 47.39% for government bonds and 44.33% for industrial bonds. The lowest annual return for each, however, was reached in different years. For government bonds, the lowest return occurred in 1958 (–5.82%) whereas for industrial bonds the minimum was reached in 1956 (–7.58%). Thus, whereas the second and third types of securities have considerable variability, on average they provide somewhat larger returns than Treasury bills.

Common Shares

The fourth and final type of security is common stocks, which represent a commitment on the part of a corporation to pay periodically whatever its board of directors deems appropriate as a cash dividend. Although the amount of cash dividends to be paid in a year is subject to some uncertainty, it is relatively predictable. However, the amount for which a share can be bought or sold varies considerably from time to time, making the annual return highly unpredictable. Figure 1.1 shows the return from a portfolio of stocks that approximately replicates the TSE 300 Composite Index from 1950 to 1995. Returns ranged from an exciting 44.77% in 1979 to a depressing –25.93% in 1974 and averaged 11.71% per year over the entire period. Such investments can provide substantial returns, which are larger, on average, than the returns provided by corporate bonds. However, these returns also have substantial variability, being more volatile than those of either type of long-term bond.

Table 1.1 provides year-by-year returns for the four types of securities shown in Figure 1.1. The table also includes the annual percentage change in the Consumer Price Index (CPI) as an indicator of changes in the cost of living. Average annual returns are shown at the bottom of the table. Below these values are the values of the standard deviations of annual returns, which serve as measures of the variability of the returns on the respective securities.[2]

---

[2] Standard deviation was calculated as being equal to the square root of $\sum_{t=1}^{42}(r_t - \bar{r})^2/45$, where r_t is the return for year t (t = 1 corresponds to 1950, t = 2 to 1951, and so on) and $\bar{r}$ is the average return over the 46-year period. A larger standard deviation means a greater amount of dispersion in the 46 returns and, as discussed in Chapter 6, indicates more risk.

Table 1.2

A Comparison of Average Annual Returns on Stocks, Bonds, and Treasury Bills and Changes in the CPI in Canada and the US, 1950–1993.

	Canada		US	
	Return	*Standard Deviation*	Return	*Standard Deviation*
Treasury bills	6.63%	4.23%	5.22%	3.09%
Long-term government bonds	6.91	10.33	5.92	10.08
Long corporate bonds	7.67	9.90	6.42	10.03
Equities	11.95	16.62	13.59	16.57
Changes in the CPI	4.60	3.50	4.30	3.18

SOURCE: Derived from Table 1.1 above and Table 1.1 in W.F. Sharpe, G.J. Alexander and J.V. Bailey, *Investments* (Englewood Cliffs, N.J.: Prentice Hall, Inc., 1995).

Table 1.2 compares the rates of return on comparable securities in Canada and the US over the period 1950 to 1993. This table shows that average rates of return and standard deviations of returns in the two countries were quite similar, which should not be surprising given the degree to which Canada's economy is related to that of the US. Table 1.3 provides average annual returns and standard deviations for securities from the United States, Japan, Germany, and the United Kingdom during the period from 1970 to 1992.

The historical record revealed in Figure 1.1, Table 1.1, Table 1.2, and Table 1.3 illustrates a general principle: *When sensible investment strategies are compared with one another, risk and return tend to go together.* That is, securities that have higher average returns tend to have greater amounts of risk.

It is important to note that historical variability is not necessarily an indication of prospective risk. The former deals with the record over some past period; the latter has to do with uncertainty about the future. The pattern of returns on Treasury bills provides one example. Although the values have varied from period to period, in any given period the amount to be earned is known in advance and is thus riskless. On the other hand, the annual return on a common stock is very difficult to predict. For such an investment, past variability may provide a fairly good measure of the uncertainty surrounding the future return.[3]

To see how difficult it is to predict common stock returns, cover the portion on Table 1.1 from 1965 on and then try to guess the return in 1965. Having done this, uncover the value for 1965 and try to guess the return for 1966. Proceed in this manner a year at a time, keeping track of your overall predictive accuracy. Unless you are very clever or very lucky, you will conclude that the past pattern of stock returns provides little help in predicting next year's return. It will be seen that this is a characteristic of an **efficient market**—that is, a market where security prices reflect information immediately. At this stage, it is enough to indicate that the past variability of stock returns can be taken as a rough approximation of future risk.

---

[3] Studies have found that (1) stocks have not become more volatile recently and (2) stocks have tended to be more volatile during recessions (particularly during the Great Depression of 1929 to 1939).

Table 1.3

Summary Statistics for US, Japanese, German, and UK Securities, 1970–1992.

	Average Return[a]				Standard Deviation			
	US	*Japan*	*Germany*	*UK*	*US*	*Japan*	*Germany*	*UK*
Short-term interest rates	7.36%	6.71%	6.58%	11.51%	2.67%	2.77%	2.38%	2.52%
Government bonds	9.81	7.32	7.88	12.35	11.45	4.69	4.69	12.81
Common stocks	12.69	14.77	9.40	19.10	16.43	30.76	25.84	34.63
Inflation	5.99	5.31	3.85	9.49	3.31	5.17	2.02	5.50

[a] Foreign returns are calculated in local currencies. Foreign stock returns include dividend income adjusted for the tax rate applicable to US investors. Government bonds include maturities greater than one year.

SOURCE: US financial market data adapted from *Stocks, Bonds, Bills, and Inflation 1993 Yearbook* (Chicago: Ibbotson Associates, 1993). Foreign financial market data provided by Brinson Partners, Morgan Stanley Capital International, International Financial Statistics, and DRI/McGraw-Hill.

Is one of these four types of securities obviously the best? No. To oversimplify, the right security or combination of securities depends on the investor's situation and preferences for returns relative to his or her distaste for risk. There may be right or wrong securities for a particular person or purpose. But it would be surprising indeed to find a security that is clearly wrong for everyone and every purpose. Such situations are simply not present in an efficient market.

Security Markets

Security markets exist in order to bring together buyers and sellers of securities, meaning they are mechanisms that exist in order to facilitate the exchange of financial assets. There are many ways in which they can be categorized. One way has already been mentioned—primary and secondary financial markets. Here the key distinction was whether or not the securities were being offered for sale by the issuer. Interestingly, the primary market itself can be subdivided into seasoned and unseasoned new issues. A seasoned new issue refers to the offering of an additional amount of an already existing security, whereas an unseasoned new issue involves the initial offering of a security to the public. Unseasoned new issues are often referred to as *initial public offerings*, or *ipo*'s.

Another way of distinguishing security markets involves the life span of financial assets. **Money markets** typically involve financial assets that have a maturity of one year or less, whereas **capital markets** typically involve financial assets that have a maturity greater than one year. Thus, Treasury bills are traded in a money market, and long-term bonds are traded in a capital market.

Financial Intermediaries

Financial intermediaries, also known as financial institutions, are organizations that issue financial claims against themselves (meaning that they sell financial assets representing claims on themselves in return for cash) and use the proceeds from these issues to purchase primarily the financial assets of others. Financial claims against an organization simply represent the

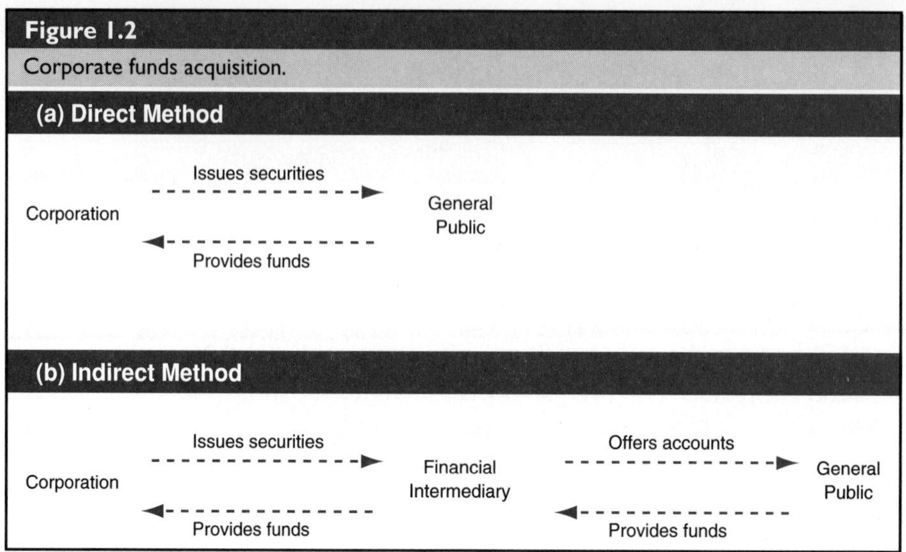

Figure 1.2
Corporate funds acquisition.

right-hand side of its balance sheet; the key distinction between financial intermediaries and other types of organizations involves the items on the left-hand side of the balance sheet.

For example, a chartered bank issues financial claims against itself in the form of debt (for example, chequing and savings accounts) and equity, but then again so does a typical manufacturing firm. However, looking at the assets held by a chartered bank reveals that most of the bank's money is invested in loans to individuals and corporations as well as in government securities such as Treasury bills, whereas the typical manufacturing firm has its money invested mostly in land, buildings, machinery, and inventory. Thus, the bank has invested primarily in financial assets, whereas the manufacturing firm has invested primarily in real assets. Accordingly, banks are classified as financial intermediaries and manufacturing firms are not. Other types of Canadian financial intermediaries include trust companies, caisse populaires, credit unions, life insurance companies, mutual funds, and pension funds.

Financial intermediaries provide an indirect method for corporations to acquire funds. As illustrated in Figure 1.2(a), corporations can obtain funds directly from the general public by the use of the primary market, as mentioned earlier. Alternatively, they can obtain funds indirectly from the general public by using financial intermediaries, as shown in Figure 1.2(b). Here the corporation gives a security to the intermediary in return for funds. In turn, the intermediary acquires funds by allowing the general public to maintain investments such as chequing and savings accounts.

THE INVESTMENT PROCESS

As previously mentioned, the investment process describes how an investor should decide which marketable securities to invest in, how extensive the investment should be, and when the investment should be made. A five-step procedure for making these decisions forms the basis of the investment process:

INSTITUTIONAL ISSUES

Institutional Investors

The past 30 years have witnessed a concentration of financial power in the hands of a relatively few organizations collectively known as *institutional investors*. The economic and social consequences of this consolidation have been enormous. Because this book is about investing, we will discuss not only the basic concepts, but also how they are applied by, and apply to, these immensely influential organizations.

The term *institutional investors* is used nebulously by practitioners. In a very broad sense, institutional investors are simply financial intermediaries of any type. This definition sets them apart from *retail investors*, who are individuals owning portfolios for which they are the direct beneficiaries.

At times, however, practitioners refer to institutional investors in a narrower context. For example, when discussing the consequences of increased institutional investor participation in the common stock market, the focus is primarily on pension funds, mutual funds, insurance companies, and non-pension-fund money invested by bank trust departments. These organizations, in aggregate, own a large fraction of the outstanding market value of Canadian corporations.

Unquestionably, the most dynamic institutional investors today are pension funds and mutual funds. Pension funds are a relatively recent phenomenon. Over the past 40 years, participation in pension funds has mushroomed, with approximately 40% of the working population enrolled in some type of pension plan today.

Until recently, most pension funds were invested conservatively in bonds and common stocks. Since that time these organizations have become the driving force behind many investment industry innovations. They have moved into international stocks and bonds, derivative securities, and various "alternative equity" investments, such as oil and gas, venture capital, and timberland. Furthermore, they have popularized a variety of investment management techniques, such as passive management and market timing.

In terms of sheer growth, mutual funds have been even more impressive than pension funds. As late as 1990, many investors viewed mutual funds skeptically as speculative investments. The industry still suffered a hangover from the collapse of many equity funds in the 1973–1974 recession. Today the mood has changed dramatically.

The financial deregulation of the 1980s led to an explosion of mutual fund products. Mutual fund sponsors expanded their offerings in terms of both types of assets and investment styles. Whereas previously most mutual funds concentrated on investments in Canadian stocks, investors can now own mutual funds investing in foreign stocks, Canadian and foreign bonds, Canadians and foreign short-term fixed-income securities, options, futures, and real estate. Funds may emphasize value or growth stocks, mortgage or Canada bonds, passive or active management. The variations are seemingly endless and continue to grow. Where once the *Globe and Mail* could list mutual fund data on half a page, it now devotes over a page and a half to daily mutual fund activity.

Willie Sutton remarked that he robbed banks because "that's where the money is." Institutional investors command attention because they are now "where the money is," with most of it invested in common stocks and corporate and government bonds. Recently, pension funds (and RRSP holders) were allowed to raise their foreign holdings from 10% to 20% of the portfolio value. This opened up new investment avenues for portfolio investors. By comparison, as the importance of retail investors has declined, the traditional investment services provided to individuals have been reduced in number and increased in price.

INSTITUTIONAL ISSUES (continued)

The growth in institutional investor portfolios has had a bearing on many of the financial instruments and investment management techniques discussed in this text. Consider the following examples:

Security Markets. Institutional investors now dominate security trading. They control over 50% of the daily trading on the Toronto Stock Exchange (TSE). Furthermore, 20 years ago few TSE trades involved share amounts over 5000. Today trades of that magnitude are commonplace. The growth in large common stock trades has threatened to overwhelm the traditional trading systems. In response new mechanisms have been created, such as computerized trading and the formation of block trading specialists (see Chapter 3).

Corporate Control. As a consequence of their size, institutional investors collectively own a significant interest in many large publicly traded corporations. Only in the last 10 years have institutional investors made a concerted effort to exercise their influence on corporations, but that effort had already had a noticeable impact. Numerous corporate boards have been altered and businesses restructured in response to pressure from institutional investors (see Chapter 17).

Futures. Institutional investors have largely avoided commodity futures. However, their involvement with financial futures (which were not even traded 20 years ago) has helped generate effective dollar trading volume in common stock index futures that is frequently larger than the dollar value of trading in the underlying common stocks (see Chapter 21).

Investment Management. Institutional investors have demanded new types of investment management techniques. For example, by allocating large sums to passive management, they single-handedly created a new industry (see Chapter 24).

Portfolio Performance Evaluation. Institutional investors have placed considerable emphasis on understanding how well their investments have performed and identifying the sources of those results. This emphasis has led to the development of sophisticated portfolio monitoring and performance analysis systems (see Chapter 25).

Quantitative Techniques. Institutional investors have pioneered the application of quantitative security valuation techniques, such as dividend discount models (see Chapter 18). They have explicitly sought to maintain adequate portfolio diversification and to control systematic and unsystematic risk using complex risk models (see Chapters 8, 11, and 24).

Fixed-Income Securities. In large part because of the diverse needs of institutional investors, bond trading firms have created an array of complex fixed-income securities. Mortgage-backed securities (MBSs), real return bonds, and floating-rate notes are but a few examples (see Chapter 14).

Given current demographic trends, the growth in assets controlled by institutional investors seems unlikely to abate. For example, as "baby boomers" reach their peak saving years (ages 40–60) over the next two decades, purchases of mutual fund shares and contributions to pension funds will continue to rise. Consequently, the influence of institutional investors on security markets can be expected to increase further in the years ahead.

1. Set investment objectives and policy.
2. Perform security analysis.
3. Construct a portfolio.

4. Revise the portfolio.
5. Evaluate the performance of the portfolio.

Investment Policy

The first step, setting **investment policy**, involves determining the investor's objectives and the amount of his or her investable wealth. Since there is a positive relationship between risk and return for sensible investment strategies, it is not appropriate for an investor to say that his or her objective is to "make a lot of money." What is appropriate for an investor in this situation is to state that the objective is to attempt to make a lot of money while recognizing there is some chance that large losses may be incurred. Investment objectives should be stated in terms of both risk and return.

This step in the investment process concludes with identification of the potential categories of financial assets for consideration in the ultimate portfolio. This identification will be based on, among other things, the investment objectives, amount of investable wealth, and tax status of the investor. For example, as shall be seen later, it does not usually make sense for individual investors in high tax brackets to purchase preferred shares or for tax-exempt investors (such as pension funds) to invest in securities that provide significant tax deferral opportunities.

Security Analysis

The second step of the investment process, performing **security analysis**, involves examining a number of individual securities (or groups of securities) within the broad categories of financial assets previously identified. The principal objectives of security analysis are to identify the expected return and risk characteristics of different securities; to identify securities that fit an investor's tax and liquidity needs and to identify mispriced securities. There are many approaches to security analysis. However, most of these approaches fall into one of two classifications. The first classification is known as **technical analysis** (performed by technicians or technical analysts). The second is known as **fundamental analysis** (performed by fundamentalists or fundamental analysts). In discussing these two approaches to security analysis, the primary focus is on common stocks. The analysis of other financial assets is discussed later.

In its simplest form, technical analysis involves the study of historical stock market prices in an attempt to predict future price movements for the common stock of a particular firm. Initially, past prices are examined in order to identify recurring trends or patterns in price movements. Then, more recent stock prices are analyzed in order to identify emerging trends or patterns that are similar to past ones. This matching of emerging trends or patterns with past ones is done in the belief that these trends or patterns repeat themselves. Thus, by identifying an emerging trend or pattern, the analyst expects to be able to predict future price movements for that particular stock.

When fundamental analysis is used to identify mispriced securities, the starting point is the assumption that the "true" (or "intrinsic") value of any financial asset is equal to the present value of all cash flows that the owner of the asset expects to receive. Accordingly, the fundamental stock analyst will attempt to forecast the timing and size of these cash flows and then will convert them to their equivalent present value by using an appropriate discount factor. More specifically, the analyst must attempt to forecast the stream of dividends that a particular stock will provide in the future, which is equivalent to forecasting the firm's earnings per share and payout ratios. The discount rate must be then be estimated. Once the true value of the common stock of a particular firm has been determined, it is compared to the current market price of the common stock in order to see if the stock is fairly priced or not. Stocks that have a true value less than their current market price are known as overvalued or overpriced stocks, whereas those that have a true value greater than their current market price are known as undervalued or underpriced stocks. The magnitude of the difference between the true value and current market price is also important information, since the strength of the analyst's conviction that a given stock is mispriced will depend, in part, on this difference. Fundamental analysts believe that notable cases of mispricing will be corrected by the market in the future, meaning that prices of undervalued stocks will show unusual appreciation and prices of overvalued stocks will show unusual depreciation.

► Portfolio Construction

The third step of the investment process, **portfolio construction**, involves identifying those specific assets in which to invest as well as determining the proportions of the investor's wealth to put in each one. Here the issues of selectivity, timing, and diversification need to be addressed by the investor. **Selectivity**, also known as microforecasting, refers to security analysis and thus focuses on forecasting price movements of individual securities. **Timing**, also known as macroforecasting, involves the forecasting of price movements of common stocks in general relative to fixed-income securities, such as corporate bonds. **Diversification** involves constructing the investor's portfolio so as to minimize risk, subject to certain restrictions.

► Portfolio Revision

The fourth step of the investment process, **portfolio revision**, concerns the periodic repetition of the previous three steps. That is, over time the investor may change his or her investment objectives, which, in turn, means that the currently held portfolio may no longer be optimal. Instead, perhaps a new portfolio should be formed by selling some securities currently held and purchasing new ones. Another motivation for revising a given portfolio is that over time the prices of securities change, so that some securities initially considered unattractive may become attractive and others that were attractive may no longer be so. Thus, the investor may want to add the former to his or her portfolio while simultaneously deleting the latter. Such a decision will depend upon, among other things, the size of the transactions costs incurred in making these changes as well as the magnitude of the perceived improvement in the investment outlook for the revised portfolio.

▶ Portfolio Performance Evaluation

The fifth step of the investment process, **portfolio performance evaluation**, involves periodically determining how the portfolio performed in terms of not only the return earned but also the risk experienced by the investor. Thus, appropriate measures of return and risk as well as relevant standards (or benchmarks) are needed.

ASSET OWNERSHIP

According to the Toronto Stock Exchange survey carried out in 1994, over 7 million Canadian residents directly or through mutual funds owned preferred and common shares. Table 1.4 shows the percentage of the adult population that owned these shares in 1983, 1986, 1989, and 1994. However, many more residents had indirect ownership of stocks through other financial intermediaries such as pension plans. There has been a continuous increase in the level of share ownership since these surveys started in 1983. The 1989 survey showed that the typical shareholder had an above-average income, at least some college or university education, and a white-collar job.

Table 1.5 shows the financial assets and liabilities of Canadians expressed in dollars and percentage terms. Note that the four largest assets in terms of value are residential buildings, life insurance and pensions, land, and stock holdings. The largest liability is home mortgages. Although some mortgages are held as assets by other individuals, most are held by banks and trust companies, who obtain them by lending money provided by individuals (reflected in the table by the first asset listed). The difference between assets and liabilities is large, reflecting the fact that total liabilities are quite small.

Table 1.4

Shareowners of Public Corporations, 1983–1994.

	Shareholders as a Percentage of the Adult Population		
Year	*Direct Owners*	*Mutual Fund Owners*	*Total*[a]
1983	9.0%	6.0%	13.0%
1986	15.0	6.0	18.0
1989	16.0	11.0	23.0
1994	18.5	20.9	N/A

[a] The total is not the sum of the other two columns because some investors fall into both ownership categories.

SOURCE: The Toronto Stock Exchange, *Canadian Shareowners: Their Profiles and Attitudes* (December 1989); and Toronto Stock Exchange, *1994 Shareowners Study* (mimeo, undated).

Table 1.5

Financial Assets and Liabilities of Canadian Individuals and Unincorporated Businesses, 1993.

Category	*Millions of Dollars*	*Composition*[a]
Assets:		
Bank deposits and currency	$288.4	10.7%
Canada Savings Bonds	32.6	1.2
All other bonds	21.9	0.8
Stock holdings	332.1	12.3
Life insurance and pensions	424.4	15.7
Foreign currency deposits and investments	19.5	0.7
Other financial assets	290.4	10.7
Total financial assets	1399.3	51.7
Residential buildings	599.9	22.2
Non-residential buildings	34.2	1.2
Machinery and equipment	11.5	0.4
Consumer durables	256.2	9.5
Inventories	15.3	0.6
Land	388.0	14.3
Total assets	2704.4	100.0
Liabilities:		
Consumer credit	$103.6	3.8%
Bank loans	17.8	0.7
Other loans	25.7	1.0
Other debt	7.2	0.3
Mortgages	328.9	12.2
Total liabilities	483.2	17.9
Financial assets less liabilities	916.1	33.9

[a] percent of total assets.

SOURCE: Statistics Canada, *National Balance Sheet Accounts, Annual Estimates, 1984–1993* (Ottawa, Ont., 1995), Supplementary Table 1.

Table 1.6 shows the ownership patterns of a variety of financial assets for different age groups and income ranges. Panel (a) shows that common stocks and derivatives are held by higher proportions of those investors aged 45 and over. Panel (b) shows that common stocks and derivatives are held by higher proportions of those in the highest income group.

Table 1.6

Demographics of Ownership of Financial Assets, 1994.

a. Ownership by Age

Type of Investment	*Under 35*	*35–44*	*45–54*	*55–64*	*65 & Over*
Common stocks of Canadian companies	11.8%	14.9%	18.0%	16.8%	14.6%
Preferred stocks of Canadian companies	5.8	8.2	10.6	11.4	9.6
Common stocks of US companies	3.1	4.7	7.4	7.0	4.6
Mutual funds invested in stocks	19.4	24.4	25.6	22.1	13.1
Mutual funds (other)	25.4	29.8	30.5	27.6	16.9
Options or futures	4.1	4.7	4.6	4.8	1.8
Any Canadian stocks	14.9	18.9	22.2	21.8	18.1
Any mutual funds	33.0	38.5	40.2	35.7	22.9
GICs	17.7	22.9	31.4	40.8	42.5
Bonds (includes CSBs & T-Bills)	31.6	36.1	37.0	35.0	34.1
Investment real estate	5.2	6.1	9.3	7.9	3.9
None owned	41.4	35.2	32.8	34.8	39.3

b. Ownership by Income

Type of investment	*Under $20K*	*$20–29K*	*$30–44K*	*$45–59K*	*$60–74K*	*$75K & Over*
Common stocks of Canadian companies	4.3%	7.1%	13.7%	17.5%	22.8%	34.9%
Preferred stocks of Canadian companies	2.5	4.7	7.0	10.6	14.1	20.3
Common stocks of US companies	1.1	2.1	3.9	5.0	7.6	16.4
Mutual funds invested in stocks	4.7	11.3	18.1	27.0	34.3	49.0
Mutual funds (other)	6.9	15.3	24.1	35.3	43.0	51.5
Options or futures	2.8	3.0	3.9	4.9	5.4	5.5
Any Canadian stocks	5.6	10.0	16.9	23.0	28.5	41.4
Any mutual funds	9.8	21.5	32.6	44.8	54.8	66.5
GICs	18.8	27.4	26.0	31.5	34.5	41.3
Bonds (includes CSBs & T-Bills)	18.2	27.9	34.2	41.1	48.9	49.3
Investment real estate	1.2	3.2	6.9	7.1	9.0	14.6
None owned	65.9	46.6	36.3	26.2	15.9	12.5

SOURCE: Toronto Stock Exchange, *1994 Shareowners Study* (mimeo, undated).

Table 1.7

Number of Employees: Finance, Insurance, and Real Estate 1971–1991.

	Number of Employees (thousands)			
Employer	*1971*	*1981*	*1986*	*1991*
Deposit accepting intermediaries	133.3	261.4	272.3	322.3
Consumer and business financing	17.3	20.3	14.2	21.5
Investment intermediaries	20.3	21.6	26.1	26.8
Insurance carriers	70.8	104.6	124.6	177.4
Other financial intermediaries	14.3	22.6	27.6	28.8
Real estate operators	31.8	86.8	79.0	79.4
Insurance and real estate agents	70.2	118.9	147.1	149.4
Total	358.0	636.2	700.9	805.6
Employees in this industry as a percent of total employees in nonagricultural industries	4.15%	5.28%	6.26%	6.45%

SOURCE: Statistics Canada, *Census of Population* (Ottawa, Ont.), various years.

THE INVESTMENT INDUSTRY

Table 1.7 shows the number of people employed in the Finance, Insurance, and Real Estate industry in Canada in recent years. As can be seen, the absolute and relative size of the industry has been increasing. In 1991, approximately 1 out of every 16 nonagricultural workers dealt with investments, broadly defined. Some (known as **investment advisors**) provide advice, some are in sales, some arrange transfers of property or securities from one investor to another, others (known as **professional money managers**) manage investors' funds, and still others handle the record keeping in this most abstract and paper-oriented of industries.

SUMMARY

1. Because this book is about investing, it focuses on the investment environment and the investment process.
2. An investment involves the sacrifice of current dollars for future dollars.
3. Investments may be made in real assets or in financial assets (securities) through either primary markets or secondary markets.
4. The primary task of security analysis is to identify mispriced securities by determining the prospective future benefits of owning those securities, the conditions under which those benefits will be received, and the likelihood of such conditions.
5. The rate of return on an investment measures the percentage change in the investor's wealth due to owning the investment.

6. Studies of the historical rates of return on various types of securities demonstrate that common stocks produce relatively high but variable returns. Bonds generate lower returns with less variability. Treasury bills provide the lowest returns with the least variability.
7. In an efficient market, security prices reflect information immediately. Security analysis will not enable investors to earn abnormally high returns.
8. Security markets exist in order to bring together buyers and sellers of securities.
9. Financial intermediaries (financial institutions) are organizations that issue financial claims against themselves and use the proceeds to purchase primarily the financial assets of others.
10. The investment process describes how an investor makes decisions about what securities to invest in, how extensive these investments should be, and when they should be made.
11. The investment process involves five steps: set investment policy, perform security analysis, construct a portfolio, revise the portfolio, and evaluate portfolio performance.
12. Although the investment industry is of modest importance relative to total employment figures, it has a profound impact on everyone's life.

QUESTIONS AND PROBLEMS

1. Why do secondary security markets not generate capital for the issuers of securities traded in those markets?
2. Following the overthrow of communist regimes in Eastern Europe, many of the fledgling democracies placed the development of security markets near the top of their economic agendas. Why do you think that they did so?
3. Colfax Glassworks stock currently sells for $36 per share. One year ago the stock sold for $33. The company recently paid a $3 per share dividend. What was the rate of return for an investor in Colfax stock over the year?
4. At the beginning of the year, Ray Fisher decided to take $50 000 in savings out of the bank and invest it in a portfolio of stocks and bonds; $20 000 was placed into common stocks and $30 000 into corporate bonds. A year later, Ray's stock and bond holdings were worth $25 000 and $23 000, respectively. During the year $1000 in cash dividends was received on the stocks, and $3000 in coupon payments was received on the bonds. (The stock and bond income was not reinvested in Ray's portfolio.)
   a. What was the return on Ray's stock portfolio during the year?
   b. What was the return on Ray's bond portfolio during the year?
   c. What was the return on Ray's total portfolio during the year?
5. Explain why the rate of return on an investment represents the investor's relative increase in wealth from that investment.
6. Why are Treasury bills considered to be a risk-free investment? In what way do investors bear risk when they own Treasury bills?
7. Why are corporate bonds riskier than Canadian government bonds?

8. The following table shows the annual returns on a portfolio of small stocks during the 20-year period from 1971 to 1990. What is the average return and standard deviation of this portfolio? How do they compare with the 1971–1990 average return and standard deviation of the common stock portfolio whose annual returns are shown in Table 1.1?

1971: 16.50%	1976: 57.38%	1981: 13.88%	1986: 6.85%
1972: 4.43	1977: 25.48	1982: 28.01	1987: –9.30
1973: –30.90	1978: 23.46	1983: 39.67	1988: 22.87
1974: –19.95	1979: 43.46	1984: –6.67	1989: 10.18
1975: 52.82	1980: 39.88	1985: 24.66	1990: –21.56

9. Does it seem reasonable that higher return securities historically have exhibited higher risk? Why?
10. Give an example, outside of the financial markets, in which you commonly face a trade-off between risk and return.
11. Examining Table 1.1, you can find many years in which Treasury bills produced greater returns than common stocks. How can you reconcile this fact with the statements made in the text, citing a positive relationship between risk and return?
12. Calculate the average annual return on common stocks, government bonds, and Treasury bills during the five decades from the 1930s through the 1980s. Which period was clearly the "decade of the financial asset"?
13. Describe how life insurance companies, mutual funds, and pension plans each act as financial intermediaries.
14. Why does it not make sense to establish an investment objective of "making a lot of money"?
15. What factors might an individual investor take into account in determining his or her investment policy?
16. Distinguish between technical and fundamental security analysis.

KEY TERMS

investment environment
investment process
investment
savings
real investment
financial investment
primary market
secondary market
security
rate of return
efficient market
money market
capital market
investment policy
security analysis
technical analysis
fundamental analysis
portfolio construction
selectivity
timing
diversification
portfolio revision
portfolio performance evaluation
investment advisor
professional money manager

REFERENCES

1. The following provide a perspective on Canadian security returns and Canadian holdings of financial assets:

James E. Hatch and Robert W. White, *Canadian Stocks, Bonds, Bills, and Inflation: 1950–1987* (Charlottesville, Va.: The Research Foundation of The Institute of Chartered Financial Analysts, 1988).

Melanie Moore, *Scotia McLeod's Handbook of Canadian Debt Market Indices: 1947–1995* (Toronto, Ont.: ScotiaMcLeod Inc., 1995). ScotiaMcLeod also publishes a monthly bulletin entitled *Debt Market Indices.*

Toronto Stock Exchange, *Canadian Shareowners — Their Profile and Attitudes* (Toronto: TSE, Strategic Research and Planning Division, 1989).

Toronto Stock Exchange, *1994 Shareowners Study* (mimeo, undated).

2. A major source of historical returns on US security markets is contained in either one of the two following publications:

Roger G. Ibbotson and Rex A. Sinquefield, *Stocks, Bonds, Bills, and Inflation: The Past and the Future* (Charlottesville, Va: Financial Analysts Research Foundation, 1983). Note that the Financial Analysts Research Foundation has since been renamed the Research Foundation of the ICFA. It can be contacted by calling (804) 980-3647.

Stocks, Bonds, Bills, and Inflation 1994 Yearbook (Chicago: Ibbotson Associates, 1994). This annual yearbook of monthly and annual data can be purchased by calling (312) 616-1620.

3. Additional historical data on US common stock returns can be found in:

Jack W. Wilson and Charles P. Jones, "A Comparison of Annual Common Stock Returns: 1871–1925 and 1926–85," *Journal of Business* 60, no. 2 (April 1987): 239–258.

4. The historical relative returns of US stocks versus bonds are studied in:

Jeremy J. Siegel, "The Equity Premium: Stock and Bond Returns Since 1802," *Financial Analysts Journal* 48, no. 1 (January/February 1992): 28–38.

5. Comparable Japanese data for a more limited time period are presented in:

Yasushi Hamao, "A Standard Data Base for the Analysis of Japanese Security Markets," *Journal of Business* 64, no. 1 (January 1991): 87–102.

6. Historical data on global market returns are presented in:

Roger G. Ibbotson and Laurence B. Siegel, "The World Bond Market: Market Values, Yields, and Returns," *Journal of Fixed Income* 1, no. 1 (June 1991): 90–99.

7. The volatility of common stocks is examined in:

G. William Schwert, "Why Does Stock Market Volatility Change Over Time?" *Journal of Finance* 44, no. 5 (December 1989): 1115–1153.

Peter Fortune, "An Assessment of Financial Market Volatility: Bills, Bonds, and Stocks," *New England Economic Review* (November/December 1989): 13–28.

8. For a discussion and analysis of US common stock indices, see:

G. William Schwert, "Indexes of US Stock Prices from 1802 to 1987," *Journal of Business* 63, no. 3 (July 1990): 399–426.

CHAPTER **2**

Buying and Selling Securities

When a security is sold, many people are likely to be involved. Although it is possible for two investors to trade with each other directly, the usual transaction employs the services provided by brokers, dealers, and markets.

A **broker** acts as an agent for an investor and is compensated via commission. Many individual investors deal with brokers in large retail houses — firms with many offices that are connected by private wires with their own headquarters and, through the headquarters, with major markets. The people in these brokerage firms with prime responsibility for individual investors are termed **account executives**, or **registered representatives.**

Institutional investors, such as chartered banks, pension funds, and other financial institutions, deal with these large retail brokerage firms and with smaller *boutiques* that specialize in institutional business. Two other types of brokerage firms are **regional brokerage firms** and **discount brokers**. The former concentrate on transactions within a geographic area, meaning the securities being traded have a special following in that area of the country. This may be because the issuers of the securities are located in that area. Discount brokers provide "bare-bones" services at low cost, meaning they provide fewer services than do *full-service brokerage firms* such as CIBC Wood Gundy or RBC Dominion Securities. Investors who simply want to have their orders executed and do not seek investment advice can save a substantial fraction of the commission by using a discount broker.

An account executive's compensation is typically determined in large part by the **commissions** paid by his or her customers — an amount that is directly related to the amount of turnover (that is, trading) in an investor's account. This provides some temptation to recommend frequent changes in investors' holdings. Furthermore, since the commission rates on various types of investments differ, there is some temptation to recommend changes in those types of investments with the highest rates. In the long run, however, account executives who encourage excessive turnover (or "churning") will often lose customers and may even be subjected to lawsuits.[1] Nonetheless, such behaviour may be advantageous for them in the short run.

It is a simple matter to open an account with a brokerage firm: simply appear at (or call) the local office. A registered representative is assigned to you and helps you to fill out a *New Client Application Form.* After this form has been signed, everything else can be done by mail or telephone. Transactions are posted to your account as they are to a bank account. For example, you can deposit money, purchase securities using money from the account, and add the proceeds from security sales to the account. Brokers exist (and charge fees) to

[1] For more on churning, see Seth C. Anderson, Sue L. Visscher, and Donald A. Winslow, "Guidelines for Detecting Churning in an Account," *AAII Journal* 11, no. 9 (October 1989): 12–14.

Table 2.1

Trading Lot Sizes at Four Canadian Exchanges.

	Board Lot		
Share Price	*ME/TSE*	*ASE*	*VSE*
under $0.10	1000	1000	1000
at $0.10 to $0.99	500	500	500
at $1.00 to $100.00	100	100	100
over $100.00	100	100	100

SOURCE: *The Canadian Securities Course* (Toronto: Canadian Securities Institute, 1992).

make security transactions as simple as possible. All that the investor has to do is to provide the broker with what is referred to here as **order specifications**.

In discussing order specifications, it will be assumed that the investor's order involves common stock. In this situation the investor must specify

1. the name of the firm,
2. whether the order is to buy or sell shares,
3. the size of the order,
4. how long the order is to be outstanding, and
5. what type of order is to be used.

The last three specifications are discussed next in more detail.

ORDER SIZE

In buying or selling common stock, the investor places an order involving either a **board lot**, an **odd lot**, or both. The size of a board lot on Canadian stock exchanges varies with the price of the stock, as shown in Table 2.1. Any order less than a board lot is referred to as an odd lot. Orders that are for more than 100 shares but are not multiples of 100 are viewed as a mixture of board and odd lots. Thus an order for 259 shares is viewed as an order for two board lots and an odd lot of 59 shares.

TIME LIMIT

The investor must specify a time limit on his or her order, meaning the time within which the broker should attempt to fill the order. For **day orders**, the broker will attempt to fill the order only during the day in which it was entered. If the order is not filled by the end of the trading session, then it expires. If a time limit is not specified by the investor, the broker will treat an order as a day order. **Good through orders** are valid for a specified number of days and automatically expire if they have not been executed by the expiry date.

Open orders, also known as **good-till-cancelled**, or GTC, **orders**, remain in effect until they are either filled or cancelled by the investor. However, during the time period before the order has been filled, the broker may periodically ask the investor to confirm the order. In contrast to GTC orders are **fill-or-kill orders**, also known as FOK orders. These orders stipulate that if the order can only be partially completed, then any portion unfilled will be cancelled. **All or none orders**, or AON, require the trader to execute the total number of shares specified before it will be accepted. Such an order must specify the minimum number of shares required.

Discretionary orders allow the broker to set the specifications for the order. The broker may have virtually complete discretion, in which case he or she decides on all the order specifications, or limited discretion, in which case he or she decides only on the price and timing of the order.

TYPES OF ORDERS

► At the Market Orders

The most common type of order is the **at the market order** or simply **market order**. Orders that do not specify a price are treated as market orders. Here the broker is instructed to buy or sell a stated number of shares immediately. In this situation the broker is obliged to act on a "best-efforts" basis to get the best possible price (as low as possible for a purchase order, as high as possible for a sell order) at the time the order is placed. Consequently, when placing a market order the investor can be fairly certain that the order will be executed but is uncertain of the price. However, there is generally fairly good information available beforehand concerning the likely price at which such an order will be executed. Not surprisingly, market orders are day orders.

► Limit Orders

A second type of order is a **limit order**. Here, a **limit price** is specified by the investor when the order is placed with the broker. If the order is to purchase shares, then the broker is to execute the order only at a price that is less than or equal to the limit price. If the order is to sell shares, then the broker is to execute the order only at a price that is greater than or equal to the limit price. Thus, for limit orders to purchase shares the investor specifies a ceiling on the price, and for limit orders to sell shares the investor specifies a floor on the price. A **limit order with price discretion** is one in which the client sets some price limits within which the trader may execute the order. In contrast to a market order, an investor using a limit order may not be certain that the order will be executed. Hence, there is a tradeoff between these two types of orders — immediacy of execution at an uncertain price versus uncertain execution within a bounded price range.

For example, assume that the common stock of the ABC Corporation is currently selling for $25 a share. An investor placing a limit order to sell 100 shares of ABC with a limit price of $30 per share and a time limit of one day is not likely to have his or her order executed, since this price is significantly above the current price of $25. Only if today's price becomes much more favourable (meaning in this case that the stock price rises by at least $5 per share) will the limit order be executed.

► Stop Orders

Two special kinds of orders are stop orders (also known as stop-loss orders) and limit stop orders. For a **stop order** the investor must specify what is known as a **stop price**. If it is a sell order, the stop price must be below the market price at the time the order is placed; conversely, if it is a buy order, the stop price must be above the market price at the time the order is placed. If someone else later trades the stock at a price that reaches or passes the stop price, then the stop order becomes, in effect, a market order. Hence, a stop order can be viewed as a conditional market order.

Continuing with the ABC Corporation example, a stop-sell order at $20 would not be executed until a trade involving others had taken place at a price of $20 or lower. Conversely, a stop-buy order at $30 would not be executed until a trade involving others had taken place at a price of $30 or more. If the price did not fall to $20, then the stop-sell order would not be executed. Similarly, if the price did not rise to $30, the stop-buy order would not be executed. In contrast, a limit order to sell at $20 or a limit order to buy at $30 would be executed immediately, since the current market price is $25.

One potential use of stop orders is to "lock in" paper profits. For example, assume an investor had purchased ABC stock at $10 per share two years ago, and thus has paper profits of $25 – $10 = $15 per share. Entering a stop-sell order at $20 per share means that the investor will be sure of making roughly $20 – $10 = $10 per share if the stock falls in price to $20 or less. If, instead of falling, the stock price rises, then the investor's stop-sell order is ignored and the investor's paper profits increase in size. Thus, the stop-sell order will provide the investor with a degree of profit protection.[2]

One of the dangers of stop orders is that the actual price at which the order is executed may be some distance from the stop price. This can occur if the stock price moves very rapidly in a given direction. For example, ABC may have an industrial accident that results in a spate of lawsuits and causes the stock price to fall very rapidly to $12 per share. In this situation a stop-sell order at $20 may be executed at $16, for example, instead of near the stop price of $20.

MARGIN ACCOUNTS

A **cash account** with a brokerage firm is like a regular chequing account: deposits (cash and the proceeds from selling securities) must cover withdrawals (cash and the costs of purchasing securities). A **margin account** is like a chequing account that has overdraft privileges: Within limits, if more money is needed than is in the account, a loan is automatically made by the broker.[3]

When opening a margin account with a brokerage firm, an investor must sign a Margin Account Agreement Form. This agreement grants the brokerage firm the right to pledge the investor's securities as collateral for bank loans, provided the securities were purchased using a margin account. Most brokerage firms also expect investors to allow them to lend their securities to others who wish to "sell them short," a procedure that is described later in this chapter.

In order to facilitate either the pledging or lending of securities, brokerage firms request that securities purchased through a margin account be held in **street name**.[4] This means that the owner of the security, as far as the original issuer is concerned, is the brokerage

2 Stop-buy orders can be used to lock in paper profits for what are known as short sales, which are discussed later in this chapter.

3 There are other types of accounts; it should be noted that an investor may have more than one type of account with a brokerage firm.

4 Investors with cash accounts may voluntarily elect to have their securities held in street name. Reasons offered for doing so include reduced risk of theft and improved record keeping (typically the brokerage firm will send monthly statements detailing the investor's holdings).

firm — that is, the registered owner is the brokerage firm. As a result, in the case of common stock the issuer will send all dividends, annual reports, and voting rights to the brokerage firm, not to the investor. However, the brokerage firm will act merely as a conduit in this situation and simply forward these items to the investor.[5] Accordingly, holding a security in street name will not result in the investor being treated in a substantively different manner from holding the security in his or her own name.[6]

With a margin account, an investor may undertake certain types of transactions that are not allowed with a cash account. These transactions are known as margin purchases and short sales, which are discussed next.

► Margin Purchases

With a cash account, an investor who purchases a security must pay the entire cost of the purchase with cash. However, with a margin account the investor must come up with cash for only a percentage of the cost and can borrow the rest from the broker.[7] The amount borrowed from the broker as a result of such a **margin purchase** is referred to as the investor's **debit balance**. The interest charged on loans advanced by a broker for a margin purchase is usually calculated by adding a service charge (for example, 1%) to the broker's **call loan rate**. In turn, the call loan rate is the rate paid by the broker to the chartered bank that loaned the broker the cash that ultimately went to the investor to pay for part of the purchase.

For example, the bank may loan money to the broker at a rate of 10% and then the broker may loan this money to the investor at a rate of 11%. Note that the call loan rate (10% in this example) can change over time and with it the interest rate that investors are charged.

The securities purchased by the investor serve as collateral on the loan made by the broker. In turn, the broker uses these securities as collateral on the loan made by the bank. Thus, the broker is, in a sense, acting as a go-between in the lending process, facilitating a loan from the bank to the investor.

Minimum Margin Requirement

The minimum percentage of the purchase price that must come from the investor's own funds is known as the **minimum margin requirement**. The minimum margin requirements are established jointly by the stock exchanges and determine the maximum loan that may be extended for long positions in securities (excluding bonds and debentures) listed on any recognized exchange in Canada, the US, the Tokyo Stock Exchange First Section or on the stock list of the Stock Exchange in London, England. Individual brokerage firms,

---

[5] It is possible that the investor will not receive the voting rights if the stock has been loaned to a short seller. This is discussed later in the chapter.

[6] An investor whose securities are held in street name may be concerned about what happens if the brokerage firm goes bankrupt. If this were to happen, the Canadian Investor Protection Fund (CIPF), an industry sponsored contingency fund that insures investors' accounts against brokerage firm insolvency, would step in and cover the investors' losses up to $250 000.

[7] With either a cash or a margin account, the investor who purchases stock has up to three business days after an order is executed to provide the broker with the necessary cash. Accordingly, the third business day after execution is known as the **settlement date**. A shorter time period is allowed for bonds, bills, or options. For margin purchases, the loan value of certain other securities can be used instead of cash as a down payment, in which case these securities must be provided by the settlement date. Sellers of securities must also provide their brokers with their securities by the settlement date. If requested, an investor may be able to get an extension to the settlement date.

Table 2.2

Minimum Margin Requirements on Long and Short Positions in Listed Equities.

On Listed Securities Selling at:	Minimum Credit Balance in Account	
	Long Position[a]	*Short Position*
\$5.00 and over[b]	30% of market	130% of market
\$2.00 and over	50% of market	150% of market
\$1.75 to \$1.99	60% of market	–
\$1.50 to \$1.99	–	\$3.00 per share
\$1.50 to \$1.74	80% of market	–
\$0.25 to \$1.49	–	200% of market
under \$1.50	100% of market	–
under \$0.25	–	100% of market plus \$0.25 per share

[a] These rates apply to the initial transaction. If the share price falls, the investor provides additional margin and the broker's loan is reduced.
[b] This rate applies only to *Option Eligible Securities* (OES), which are those that meet the eligibility criteria as underlying securities for either Canadian or US exchange-traded options. Also included are securities convertible into OES and preferred shares of companies whose equity qualifies.

SOURCE: The Canadian Securities Course (Toronto: Canadian Securities Institute, 1992).

however, are allowed to require margins higher than the minimum. Hypothetically, therefore, the industry could set a minimum margin of 50% and your broker could require 60%. Table 2.2 shows the minimum margin requirements which vary with the share price.[8] In general investors are advised to avoid the practice of margining close to the prevailing price limits (i.e., maintaining a minimum amount of margin in the account) in order to provide some protection against having to respond to a margin call following a minor adverse price change.[9]

Consider, as an example, an investor who purchases on margin 100 shares of Widget Corporation for \$50 per share. With a margin requirement of, say, 60%, the investor must pay the broker $.6 \times 100$ shares $\times \$50$ per share = \$3000. The remainder of the purchase price, $(1 - .6) \times 100$ shares $\times \$50$ per share = \$2000, is funded by a loan from the broker to the investor.[10]

---

[8] Margin requirements for the purchase of most debt securities are significantly lower than those for equities and vary according to the quality of the issue and its time to maturity.

[9] The procedures followed in the US involve slightly more structure. *Initial margin requirements* established by the Federal Reserve Board must be met at the time of the original transaction. Subsequently, the investor must keep the actual margin in the account at or above the *maintenance margin* which is lower than the initial margin. Maintenance margin levels are established by the exchanges and may be raised by the brokers.

[10] Generally, at the end of each month the interest on the loan will be calculated and added to the amount of the loan appearing on the right-hand side of the investor's balance sheet. For ease of exposition, this fact is ignored in the examples given here.

Actual Margin

The **actual margin** in the account of an investor who has purchased stocks can be calculated daily as

$$\text{Actual margin} = \frac{\text{market value of assets} - \text{loan}}{\text{market value of assets}} \tag{2.1}$$

This daily calculation of the actual margin in an investor's account is known as having the account **marked to the market**. Upon examination of equation (2.1), it can be seen that at the time of the margin purchase, the actual margin and initial margin are the same. However, subsequent to the purchase, the actual margin can be either greater than or less than the initial margin. In this example, if Widget stock fell to \$25 per share, then the actual margin would drop (\$2500 – 2000)/\$2500 = 20%. The investor would be subject to a **margin call** and would have to put \$1000 into the account to restore the margin to 60%. This can be done by either depositing cash or securities into the account, or selling some securities currently held in the account and using the proceeds to pay off part of the loan. Any of these actions will raise the numerator or lower the denominator on the right-hand side of equation (2.1), thereby increasing the actual margin.[11] If the investor does not act (or cannot be reached), then in accordance with the terms of the margin agreement, the broker will sell securities from the account to increase the actual margin to (at least) the minimum margin requirement.

If, instead of falling, the share price rises, then the investor can take part of the increase out of the account in the form of cash, since the actual margin in the account will have risen above the minimum margin requirement.[12]

Rate of Return

The use of margin purchases allows the investor to engage in **financial leverage**. That is, by using debt to fund part of the purchase price, the investor can increase the expected rate of return of the investment. However, there is a mitigating factor in the use of margin, and that is the effect on the risk of the investment.

Consider Widget again. If the investor believes the stock will rise by \$15 per share over the next year, the expected rate of return on the cash purchase of 100 shares of Widget will be (\$15 × 100 shares)/(\$50 × 100 shares) = 30%, assuming that no cash dividends are paid and the purchase price is \$50 per share. A margin purchase, where the interest rate on margin loans is 11% and the minimum margin requirement is 60%, on the other hand, would have an expected return of [(\$15 × 100 shares) – (.11 × \$2000)]/\$3000 = (\$1500 – \$220)/\$3000 = 42.7%. Thus, the investor has increased the expected rate of return from 30% to 42.7% by the use of margin.

What will happen, however, to the rate of return if the stock falls by \$10 per share? In this case the investor who made a cash purchase will have a rate of return equal to (–\$10 × 100 shares)/(\$50 × 100 shares) = –20%. The margin purchaser, on the other hand, will have a rate of return equal to [(–\$10 × 100) – (.11 × \$2000)]/\$3000 = (–\$1000 – \$220)/\$3000 = –40.7%. Thus, the margin purchaser will experience a much larger loss than the cash purchaser for a given dollar decline in the price of the stock.

---

[11] The broker may ask the investor immediately (in some cases within the settlement period, but usually sooner) to bring the actual margin up to a level corresponding to the minimum margin requirement or to one that is even higher.

[12] Alternatively, the cash could be used as part of the minimum margin requirement on an additional margin purchase by the investor. In fact, if it was large enough, it could be used to meet the entire requirement.

Margin purchases are usually made in the expectation that the stock price will rise in the near future, meaning that the investor thinks the stock's current price is too low. If an investor thinks that a given stock is not too low but too high, then the investor may engage in what is known as a short sale, which is discussed next.

Short Sales

An old investor's adage is to "buy low, sell high." Most investors hope to do just that by buying securities first and selling them later.[13] However, with a **short sale** this process is reversed: the investor sells a security first and buys it back later. In this case the old adage about investors aspirations might be reworded to "sell high, buy low."

Short sales are accomplished by borrowing share certificates for use in the initial trade and then repaying the loan with certificates obtained in a later trade. Note that the loan here involves certificates, not dollars and cents (although it is true that the certificates at any point in time have a certain monetary value). This means the borrower must repay the lender by returning certificates, not dollars and cents (although it is true that an equivalent monetary value, determined on the date the loan is repaid, can be remitted instead). It also means that there are no interest payments to be made by the borrower.

Rules Governing Short Sales

Any order for a short sale must be identified as such. The exchanges in Canada have ruled that short sales may not be made when the market price for the security is falling. This allows investors with long positions to liquidate before short sellers can profit in a declining market. The precise rule on the TSE is that a short sale must not be made on the Exchange below the price of the last sale of a board lot. This implies that a short sale may be effected on an **uptick** (for a price higher than that of the previous trade) or on a **zero tick** (for a price equal to that of the previous trade).[14]

Within five business days after a short sale has been made, the short-seller's broker must borrow and deliver the appropriate securities to the purchaser. The borrowed securities may come from the inventory of securities owned by the brokerage firm itself or from the inventory of another brokerage firm. However, they are more likely to come from the inventory of securities held in street name by the brokerage firm for investors that have margin accounts with the firm. The life of the loan is indefinite, meaning there is no time limit on it.[15] If the lender wants to sell the securities, then the short seller will not have to repay the loan providing that the brokerage firm can borrow shares elsewhere, thereby transferring the loan from one source to another. If, however, the brokerage firm cannot find a place to borrow the shares, then the short seller will have to repay the loan immediately. Interestingly, the identities of the borrower and lender are known only to the brokerage firm — that is, the lender does not know who the borrower is and the borrower does not know who the lender is.

---

[13] After purchasing a security, an investor is said to have established a *long position* in the security.

[14] The tick rule is not applicable in the over-the-counter (OTC also known as the CDN) market, suggesting that short selling can be done at any time in that market providing that the required shares can be borrowed. (The CDN market is discussed in a later section of this chapter.)

[15] The Toronto Stock Exchange publishes a semi-monthly list of the *short positions* in its securities (a short position refers to the number of shares of a given company that have been sold short where, as of a given date, the loan remains outstanding).

An Example

An example of a short sale is indicated in Figure 2.1. At the start of the day, Mr. Leung owns 100 shares of the XYZ Company, which are being held for him in street name by Brock, Inc., his broker. During this particular day, Ms. Smith places an order with her broker at Brock to short sell 100 shares of XYZ (Mr. Leung believes the price of XYZ stock is going to rise in the near future, whereas Ms. Smith believes it is going to fall). In this situation, Brock takes the 100 shares of XYZ that they are holding in street name for Mr. Leung and sells them for Ms. Smith to some other investor, in this case Mr. Jones. At this point XYZ will receive notice that the ownership of 100 shares of its stock has changed hands, going from Brock (remember that Mr. Leung held his shares in street name) to Mr. Jones. At some later date, Ms. Smith will tell her broker at Brock to purchase 100 shares of XYZ (perhaps from a Ms. Poole) and use these shares to pay off her debt to Mr. Leung. At this point, XYZ will receive another notice that the ownership of 100 shares has changed hands, going from Ms. Poole to Brock, restoring Brock to their original position.

Cash Dividends

What happens when XYZ declares and subsequently pays a cash dividend to its shareholders? *Before the short sale*, Brock would receive a cheque for cash dividends on 100 shares of stock. After depositing this cheque in their own account at a bank, Brock would write a cheque for an identical amount and give it to Mr. Leung. Thus, neither Brock or Mr. Leung has been made worse off by having his shares held in street name. *After the short sale*, XYZ will see that the owner of those 100 shares is not Brock any more but is now Mr. Jones. Thus, XYZ will now mail the dividend cheque to Mr. Jones, not Brock. However, Mr. Leung will still be expecting his dividend cheque from Brock. Indeed, if there was a risk that he would not receive it, he would not have agreed to have his securities held in street name. Brock would like to mail him a cheque for the same amount of dividends that Mr. Jones received from XYZ—that is, for the amount of dividends Mr. Leung would have received from XYZ had he held his shares in his own name. If Brock does this, then they will be losing an amount of cash equal to the amount of the dividends paid. In order to prevent themselves from experiencing this loss, they make Ms. Smith, the short seller, give them a cheque for an equivalent amount!

Consider all the parties involved in the short sale now. Mr. Leung is content, since he has received his dividend cheque from his broker. Brock is content, since their net cash outflow is still zero, just as it was before the short sale. Mr. Jones is content, since he received his dividend cheque directly from XYZ. What about Ms. Smith? She should not be upset with having to reimburse Brock for the dividend cheque given by them to Mr. Leung, since the price of XYZ's common stock can be expected to fall, on the ex-dividend day, by an amount roughly equal to the amount of the cash dividend, thereby reducing the dollar value of her loan from Brock by an equivalent amount.

Financial Reports and Voting Rights

What about annual reports and voting rights? Before the short sale, these were sent to Brock, who then forwarded them to Mr. Leung. After the short sale, Brock no longer received them, so what happened? Annual reports are easily procured by brokerage firms free of charge, so Brock probably got copies of them from XYZ and mailed a copy to Mr. Leung. However, voting rights are different. These are limited to the registered shareholders (in this case, Mr. Jones) and cannot be replicated in the manner of cash dividends by Ms. Smith, the

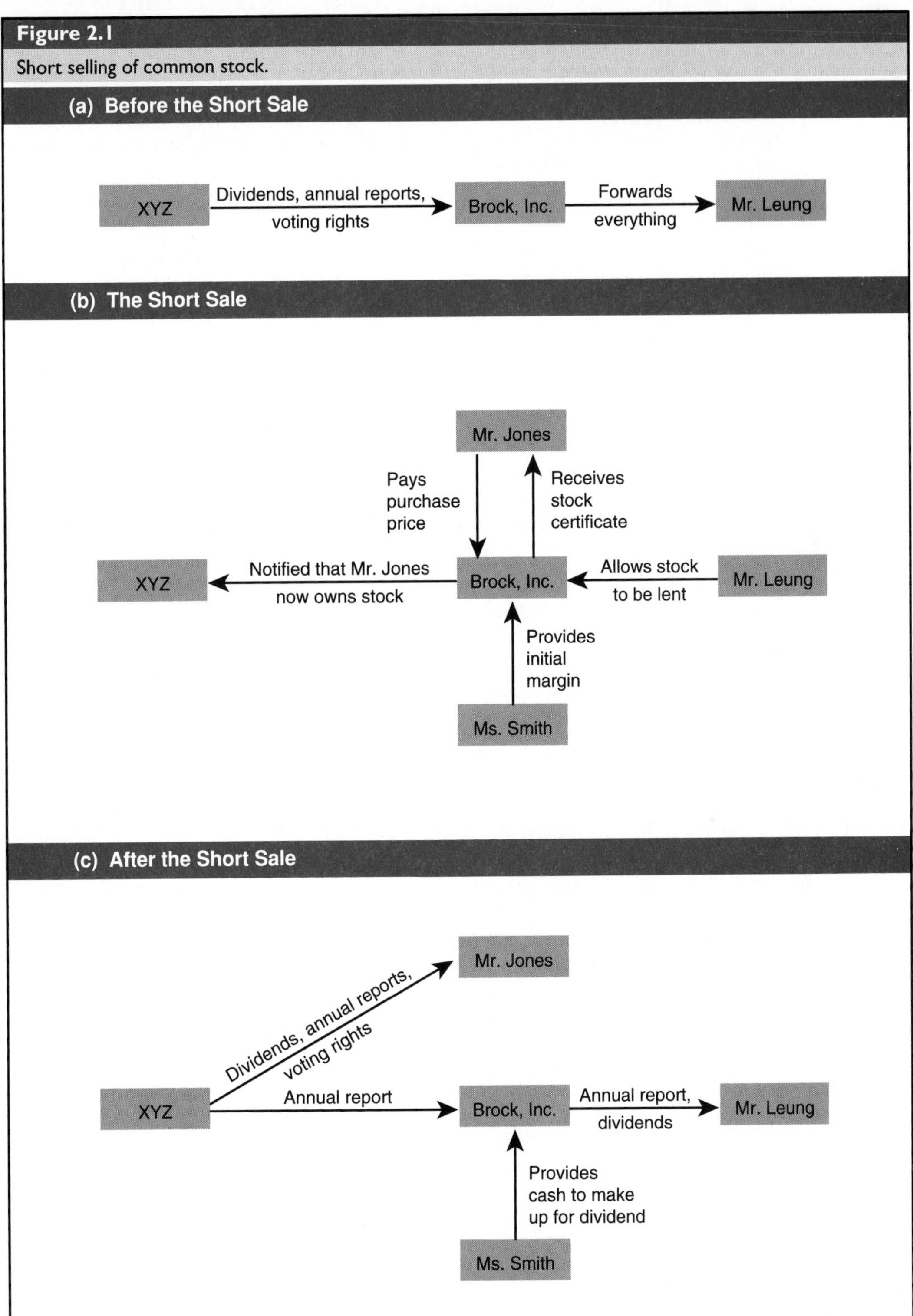
Figure 2.1
Short selling of common stock.
(a) Before the Short Sale
XYZ
Dividends, annual reports, voting rights
Brock, Inc.
Forwards everything
Mr. Leung
(b) The Short Sale
Mr. Jones
Pays purchase price
Receives stock certificate
XYZ
Notified that Mr. Jones now owns stock
Brock, Inc.
Allows stock to be lent
Mr. Leung
Provides initial margin
Ms. Smith
(c) After the Short Sale
Mr. Jones
Dividends, annual reports, voting rights
XYZ
Annual report
Brock, Inc.
Annual report, dividends
Mr. Leung
Provides cash to make up for dividend
Ms. Smith

short seller. Thus, when voting rights are issued, the brokerage firm (Brock, Inc.) will try to find voting rights to give to Mr. Leung (perhaps Brock owns shares or manages a portfolio that owns shares of XYZ and will give these voting rights to Mr. Leung). Unless he is insistent, however, there is a chance he will not get his voting rights once his shares have been borrowed and used in a short sale. In all other matters, he will be treated just as if he were holding the shares of XYZ in his own name.

Margin Requirements

As previously mentioned, a short sale involves a loan. Thus, there is a risk that the borrower (in the example, Ms. Smith) will not repay the loan. In this situation the broker would be left without the 100 shares that the short seller, Ms. Smith, owes him or her. Either the brokerage firm, Brock, is going to lose money or else the lender, Mr. Leung, is going to lose money. To prevent this from happening, the cash proceeds from the short sale, paid by Mr. Jones, are not given to the short seller, Ms. Smith. Instead, they are held in her account with Brock until she repays her loan. Unfortunately this will not assure the brokerage firm that the loan will be repaid.

In the example, assume the 100 shares of XYZ were sold at a price of $100 per share. In this case, the proceeds from the short sale of $10 000 are held in Ms. Smith's account, but she is prohibited from withdrawing it until the loan is repaid. Now imagine that at some date after the short sale, XYZ stock rises by $20 per share. In this situation, Ms. Smith owes Brock 100 shares of XYZ with a current market value of 100 shares × $120 per share = $12 000 but has only $10 000 in her account. If she skips town, Brock will have collateral of $10 000 (in cash) but a loan of $12 000, resulting in a loss of $2000. However, Brock can use margin requirements to protect itself from experiencing losses from short sellers who do not repay their loans. In this example, Ms. Smith must not only leave the short-sale proceeds with her broker, but she must also give her broker sufficient funds to raise the credit balance in her account to the prescribed minimum.[16] Assuming that the minimum credit balance is 150%, she must give her broker .5 × $10 000 = $5000 cash that is referred to as the margin in the account.

The price of XYZ stock would have to rise above $150 per share in order for Brock to be in jeopardy of not being repaid. Thus, the minimum credit balance provides the brokerage firm with a certain degree of protection. However, this protection is not complete, since it is not unheard of for stocks to rise in value by more than 50%. It is vigilance that protects the brokerage firm from losing money in such situations. As soon as the share price rises the broker must issue a margin call in order to maintain the credit balance in the account. The credit balance in a short sale is defined as

$$\text{Actual margin} = (\text{initial credit balance} - \text{loan})/\text{loan}. \tag{2.2}$$

The initial credit balance is the amount in the account when the short sale is executed and the loan is the current market value of the securities borrowed.

In this example, if XYZ stock rises to $130 per share, the margin in Ms. Smith's account will be [($100 × 100) × (1 + .5) – ($130 × 100)]/($130 × 100) = 23% and she will receive a margin call. Just as in margin calls on margin purchases, she will be asked to put up more margin, meaning she will be asked to add cash or securities to her account.

---

[16] Table 2.2 presents the minimum credit balances required for short sales.

If, instead of rising, the share price falls, then the short seller can take a bit more than the drop in the price out of the account in the form of cash, since in this case the actual balance has risen above the minimum balance required.[17]

An interesting question is, what happens to the cash in the short seller's account? When the loan is repaid, the short seller will have access to the cash (actually, the cash is usually used to repay the loan). Before the loan is repaid, however, it may be that the short seller can earn interest on the portion of the cash balance that represents margin (some brokerage firms will accept certain securities, such as Treasury bills, in lieu of cash for meeting margin requirements). What happens to the cash proceeds from the short sale? In some cases the securities may be lent only on the payment of a premium by the short seller; therefore, the short seller not only forgoes interest on the cash proceeds but must pay a fee for the use of the securities. In other cases the lending broker may pay the short seller interest on the cash proceeds that are in his or her margin account. Usually, however, securities are loaned "flat"— the brokerage firm keeps the cash proceeds from the short sale and enjoys the use of this money, and neither the short seller nor the investor who lent the securities receives any direct compensation. In this case, the brokerage firm makes money not only from the commission paid by the short seller but also on the cash proceeds from the sale (they may, for example, earn interest by purchasing Treasury bills with these proceeds).

Rate of Return

The use of short selling results in opposite rates of return to the investor than would be earned if the shares were purchased on margin (assuming that initial margin for the short sale is met by depositing cash and that the short loan is "flat," and ignoring interest on the margin loan). Hence, short sales also involve the use of financial leverage.

Consider XYZ stock once again, which Ms. Smith short sold at a price of $100 per share. If she later repays the short loan when the stock is selling for $75 per share and just after XYZ has paid a $1 per share cash dividend, then her rate of return would be equal to ($100 – $75 – $1)/(.6 × $100) = $24/$60 = 40%. In contrast, note that the return for someone who had purchased the stock of XYZ on margin would be equal to ($75 + $1 – $100)/(.6 × $100) = –$24/$60 = –40%, whereas the rate of return for someone who had purchased the stock without using margin would be equal to ($75 + $1 – $100)/$100 = –$24/$100 = –24%.

However, if Mrs. Smith has incorrectly predicted the future price movement of XYZ and it goes up to $120 per share just after paying as $1 per share cash dividend, then her rate of return would be equal to ($100 – $120 – $1)/(.6 × $100) = –$21/$60 = –35%. Conversely, if the stock had been purchased on margin, her rate of return would have been equal to ($120 + $1 – $100)/(.6 × $100) = $21/$60 = 35%. Without margin, the rate of return on the stock would be equal to ($120 + $1 – $100)/$100 = $21/$100 = 21%.

What happens to these rate of return calculations if interest is earned on both the initial margin and the short proceeds? It increases the rate of return to the short seller. Consider the example where XYZ fell to $75, and assume that the short seller earned 5% on the initial margin deposit and 4% on the short proceeds. In this case the return to the short seller would

[17] Alternatively, the short seller could short sell a second security and not have to put up all (or perhaps any) of the minimum balance requirement.

be equal to $100 – $75 – $1 + (.05 × .6 × $100) + (.04 × $100)/(.6 × $100) = $31/$60 = 51.7%, which is notably higher than the 40% previously calculated. Hence, financial leverage is even more effective when interest is paid to the short seller.

Aggregation

An investor with a margin account may purchase several different securities on margin or may short sell several different securities. Alternatively, he or she may purchase some on margin and short sell others. The determination of whether an account is under or overmargined depends on the total activity in the account. For example, if one stock is undermargined and another is overmargined, then the overmargined stock can be used to offset the undermargined stock, provided it is overmargined to a sufficiently large degree. How these multiple transactions are aggregated in one account in order to see the state of the account on any given day is shown next.

Multiple Margin Purchases

In the case of multiple margin purchases, aggregation is straightforward. The investor's balance sheet is restated by recalculating the market value of all the stocks held using current market prices. Here the current market price of any particular security usually means the price at which the last trade was made in the market involving that security on the previous day. Next, the total amount of the investor's liabilities is carried over from the previous day, since the amounts of the margin loans do not change from day to day. In turn, this allows equation (2.1) to be used in order to recalculate the actual margin in the account.

Multiple Short Sales

In a similar manner, the actual margin of an investor who has short sold more than one stock can be determined. In this case, however, it is not the assets that are reevaluated every day as the account is marked to the market. Instead, it is the liabilities that are reevaluated based on current market prices, since the short seller's liabilities are shares whose market value is changing every day. Once the dollar values of the liabilities are recalculated, the actual margin in the account can be determined using equation (2.2).

Simultaneous Margin Purchases and Short Sales

The situation where the investor has purchased some stocks, perhaps on margin, and has short sold others is more complicated than either of the situations just described. This is because the equation used to calculate actual margin for margin purchases, equation (2.1), and the equation used to calculate actual margin for short sales, equation (2.2), are different. This can be seen by simply noting what is in the denominator in each equation. For margin purchases, the market value of the assets appears in the denominator. However, for short sales, the market value of the loan appears in the denominator. If both kinds of transactions appear in the same account, neither equation can be used to calculate the overall actual margin in the account. However, the account can be analyzed in terms of the dollar amount of assets that are necessary for the account to meet the margin requirement. This can be illustrated with an example.

INSTITUTIONAL ISSUES

Market Neutral Strategies

Institutional investors have traditionally viewed management of common stock portfolios as a one-sided problem: buy underpriced stocks that are likely to appreciate in value relative to an established benchmark. However, that perspective is rapidly changing as these investors explore investment techniques that involve purchases *and* short sales of stocks so as to systematically control portfolio risk and profit from insights into mispriced securities. These techniques are collectively known as "market neutral" strategies.

The logic underlying market neutral strategies is simple. If on average all securities are fairly priced, then mispricing must be a zero-sum game—underpriced securities must be accompanied by overpriced securities. Therefore if an investor can discover mispriced securities, why should he or she restrict himself or herself to buying the underpriced securities? Why not profit by short selling the overpriced securities as well?

The basic process of implementing market neutral strategies is similarly straightforward. The investor holds a portfolio consisting of three investments: short-term risk-free securities (for example, 90-day Treasury bills), long positions in stocks, and short positions in stocks. The market value of each investment is the same. Furthermore, the long and short stock positions have equal exposures to common causes of stock market variability. (See Chapter 11 for a discussion of factors affecting stock returns.) The resulting portfolio, therefore, is fully hedged against any type of stock market movement.

Why should this hedged portfolio be of interest? After all, it should earn only the risk-free return. The answer lies with the stock selection skills of the market neutral investor. If the investor possesses valuable knowledge of mispriced securities, then he or she will purchase underpriced stocks whose unique circumstances will cause them to increase in value relative to the market. Conversely, he or she will short sell overpriced stocks whose unique circumstances will cause them to decrease in value relative to the market. The net result is that the investor benefits from his or her ability to identify mispriced stocks, without exposure to the vagaries of the stock market.

As a simple example, consider an investor who begins the year with $100 in cash. The investor uses the cash to purchase $100 of stocks. At the same time the investor short sells $100 of stocks. These purchases and short sales have been carefully designed to exhibit no net exposure to any industry or other factor influencing stock market returns. (For example, the investor might form long-short pairs within industries—buy $5 of GM stock and short sell $5 of Ford stock.) At the beginning of the year the investor's portfolio appears as follows:

Long	Short	Cash	Total
$100	–$100	$100	$100

Assume that the investor selects wisely and the long portfolio is worth $110 at year-end, for a 10% return. (By comparison, the stock market's return was 8%.) Furthermore, the short portfolio also has risen in value (but not by as much as the long portfolio or the stock market) to $105 (a 5% return), and the cash holdings have earned $2 in interest (a 2% return). At year-end the investor's portfolio appears as follows:

Long	Short	Cash	Total
$110	–$105	$102	$107

This investor has earned $7 on a $100 portfolio, or a 7% return, without assuming any market risk. The only risk the investor has taken lies in his or her ability to identify mispriced stocks. The return from adroit stock selection is known as "alpha" (see Chapter 25). In fact, the market neutral investor earns a "double alpha" by gaining from insights into both underpriced and overpriced stocks.

Of course, the real world, with its unaccommodating nature, makes the implementation of market neutral strategies much more complex than our simple example implies. Consider the following steps that the market neutral investor must follow:

1. **Establish a margin account**. As the text describes, short selling must be conducted in a margin account. Thus, the investor must select a broker to hold the stocks and cash involved in the market neutral strategy.
2. **Make long and short transactions simultaneously**. Long positions must always equal short positions, or the portfolio may be exposed to unintended risks. The Toronto Stock Exchange's uptick rule (see page 29) and the limited availability of appropriate stocks for short selling complicates this task.
3. **Maintain collateral with the broker**. The stocks from the long positions, cash from the short sales, and a small amount of initial cash (to serve as a liquidity reserve for daily marks to market on the short positions) must be deposited with the broker.
4. **Reimburse for dividends paid and substitute for recalled borrowed stocks**. The investor must compensate the stock lender for any dividends paid on the borrowed stocks. Also, if the borrowed securities are sold by the lender and cannot be replaced, the investor must find appropriate substitutes.
5. **Continuously monitor portfolio positions**. Security price movements will affect the long-short balance in the portfolio. Only careful daily monitoring can prevent the portfolio from moving away from a market neutral stance.

Institutional investors pay special attention to selecting a broker for their market neutral strategies. They invariably choose large, established brokers with impeccable credit ratings. These brokers have the best access to securities for short sales, either through their street name holdings or through security lending networks. Institutional investors also consider the interest income rebates provided by the brokers. Unlike small investors, who typically receive no interest on their short sale proceeds, institutional investors can negotiate to receive anywhere from 75% to 90% of the income earned by the broker on the short sale proceeds.

Any investment organization can implement market neutral strategies. However, investors using quantitative investment processes (for example, dividend discount models—see Chapter 18) are the primary purveyors of this approach. Their processes typically rank a large number of stocks from highly attractive to unattractive—a step necessary to develop a diversified collection of long and short opportunities. Moreover, these investors' portfolio construction methods usually are very structured, thus facilitating the intricate design and maintenance of offsetting long and short positions.

Some institutional investors extend the market neutral strategies and "equitize" the cash held in their portfolios—that is, they purchase common stock futures contracts (see Chapter 21), effectively creating stock market exposure equal to the value of their cash holdings. Their portfolio returns then become the return on the stock market plus the returns produced by their insights into attractive long and short stocks.

This "equitization" technique opens up a vast range of investment strategies that permit the market neutral investor to "transport" his or her skills to other markets (see Chapter 21). For example, consider a pension fund with policy requiring investment of a portion of its assets in fixed-income securities. It could simply buy a portfolio of bonds to satisfy the policy guidelines. However, suppose that the pension fund had access to skillful market-neutral stock managers. The pension fund could use those managers' investment talents, while at the same time purchasing Treasury bond futures contracts to give it the required fixed-income market exposure. Thus the pension fund's investment policy is satisfied and, if the market neutral managers are successful, then the pension fund profits from their skill as well. In essence,

INSTITUTIONAL ISSUES (continued)

the pension fund has "transported" the market neutral stock managers' skills to the bond market.

Market neutral strategies offer no guarantee of success, as they rely on the stock selection abilities of the investor. A poor investor can generate substantial transaction costs (see Chapter 3), while adding no "alpha" to the portfolio. Moreover, if the offsetting long-short positions are constructed inaccurately, the portfolio could experience unpleasant surprises.

Despite these caveats, market neutral strategies represent an intriguing combination of portfolio risk control and security selection. These strategies have been employed on a large scale for only a few years. Nevertheless they are rapidly making their influence felt as institutional investors examine the very essence of how value is added to their portfolios through active management.

Consider an investor who short sells 100 shares of Widget on July 1 at $50 per share and purchases 100 shares of XYZ on margin at $100 per share on July 15. The minimum margin requirements for both transactions are 30%. Furthermore, assume Widget and XYZ are selling for $40 and $80 per share respectively on July 31. In this situation, the broker will require the investor to have assets of sufficient value to protect the short sale loan of Widget shares and the cash loan to purchase XYZ on margin. In general, the amount required as collateral against a short sale is equal to the current market value of the shorted shares multiplied by 1 plus the minimum margin requirement. For the short sale loan of Widget shares, this amounts to $4000 × (1 + .3) = $5200, where .3 corresponds to the minimum margin requirement. There is, however, a balance of $6500 in the account pertaining to this transaction.

The amount required as collateral against a margin purchase is, in general, equal to the dollar value of the margin loan divided by 1 minus the maintenance margin requirement. For the cash loan to purchase XYZ, this amounts to $7000/(1 – .3) = $10 000.

The total amount required in this example is, therefore, $10 000 + $5200 = $15 200. Since the assets in the account are currently worth $14 500, the investor will receive a margin call in the amount of $700.

SUMMARY

1. Investors typically buy or sell securities through brokers who are compensated for their services with commissions.
2. When transacting in a security, investors must specify the following: the security's name; buy or sell; order size; time limit; and type of order.
3. The three standard types of orders are market, limit, and stop.
4. Investors may purchase securities with cash or may borrow from brokerage firms to buy securities on margin.
5. Investors must make down payments on their margin purchases, maintain minimum actual margin levels in their margin accounts, and pay interest on margin loans.
6. If an investor's actual margin falls below the minimum required, the investor's account is undermargined. The investor will receive a margin call and must increase the actual margin level in the account.

7. Buying on margin results in financial leverage, thereby magnifying (positively or negatively) the impact of a security's return on the investor's wealth.
8. Short sales involve the sale of securities that are not owned, but rather are borrowed by the sellers. The borrowed securities must ultimately be purchased in the market and returned to the lenders.
9. A short seller must deposit the proceeds of the short sale and the required margin with his or her broker. The short seller must also maintain a minimum actual margin level in his or her margin account or face a margin call.
10. For investors who purchase on margin or short sell several securities, the determination of whether an account is undermargined or overmargined depends on the aggregated activity in their accounts.

QUESTIONS AND PROBLEMS

1. Describe the conflict of interest that typically exists in the investment advisory relationship between a brokerage firm and its clients.
2. How many board lots and what odd lot size are in an order for 511 shares?
3. Discuss the advantages and disadvantages to the investor of the following:
   a. Market order
   b. Limit order
   c. Stop order
4. Why are margin account securities held in street name?
5. Lucille Killefer purchases on margin 200 shares of Landfall Corporation stock at $75 per share. The margin requirement is 55%. Prepare Lucille's balance sheet for this investment at the time of purchase.
6. Buck Ewing opened a margin account at a local brokerage firm. Buck's initial investment was to purchase 200 shares of Woodbury Corporation on margin at $40 per share. Buck borrowed $3000 from a broker to complete the purchase.
   a. At the time of the purchase, what was the actual margin in Buck's account?
   b. If Woodbury stock subsequently rises in price to $60 per share, what is the actual margin in Buck's account?
   c. If Woodbury stock subsequently falls in price to $35 per share, what is the actual margin in Buck's account?
7. Sam Arnovich buys on margin 1000 shares of Rockford Systems stock at $60 per share. The initial margin requirement is 50% but Sam only uses 75% margin. If the Rockford stock falls to $50, will Sam receive a margin call?
8. Avalon Company's stock is currently selling for $15 per share. The initial margin requirement is 60%. Charles Anson buys 100 shares of Avalon stock on 75% margin. To what price must the stock fall for Charles to receive a margin call?
9. Liz Arlington has deposited $15 000 in a margin account with a brokerage firm. If the margin requirement is 50%, what is the maximum dollar amount of stock that Liz can purchase on margin?
10. Penny Bailey bought on margin 500 shares of South Beloit Inc. at $35 per share. The margin requirement is 45% and the annual interest on margin loans is 12%. Over the next year of the stock rises to $40. What is Penny's return on investment?
11. Calculate Buck Ewing's rate of return in parts (b) and (c) Problem 6 under the assumption that the margin loan was outstanding for one year and carried an interest rate of 10%,

and that the prices of $60 and $35 were observed after one year during which the firm did not pay any cash dividends.

12. Ed Delahanty purchased 500 shares of Niagara Corporation stock on margin at the beginning of the year for $30 per share. The margin requirement was 55%. Ed paid 13% interest on the margin loan and never faced a margin call. Niagara paid dividends of $1 per share during the year.
   a. At the end of the year, if Ed sold the Niagara stock for $40 per share, what would Ed's rate of return be for the year?
   b. At the end of the year, if Ed sold the Niagara stock for $20 per share, what would Ed's rate of return be for the year?
   c. Recalculate your answers to parts (a) and (b) assuming that Ed made the Niagara stock purchase for cash instead of on margin.

13. Individual investors are sometimes contacted by their brokers and told that they have "unused buying power" in their brokerage accounts. What do the brokers mean by this statement?

14. Beatrice Bancroft short sells 500 shares of Rockdale Manufacturing at $25 per share. The margin requirement is 50%. Prepare Beatrice's balance sheet as of the time of the transaction.

15. Through a margin account, Cindy Cummings short sells 200 shares of Madison Inc. stock for $50 per share. The margin requirement is 45%.
   a. If Madison stock subsequently rises to $58 per share, what is the actual margin in Cindy's account?
   b. If Madison stock subsequently falls to $42 per share, what is the actual margin in Cindy's account?

16. Daniel Benoit short sells 500 shares of Naperville Products at $45 per share. The margin requirement is 55%, but Daniel provides 70% margin at the time of purchase. If Naperville stock rises to $50, will Daniel receive a margin call?

17. Sun Prairie Foods stock currently sells for $50 per share. The initial margin requirement is $50. If Willie Keeler short sells 300 shares of Sun Prairie stock and provides 60% margin, to what price can the stock rise before Willie receives a margin call?

18. Eddie Gaedel is an inveterate short seller. Is it true that Eddie's potential losses are infinite? Why? Conversely, is it true that the maximum return that Eddie can earn on his investment is 100%? Why?

19. The stock of DeForest Inc. sold at the beginning of the year for $70 per share. At that time David Barclay short sold 1000 shares of the stock. The margin requirement was 50%. DeForest stock has risen to $75 at year-end, and David faced no margin calls in the interim. Further, the stock paid a $2 dividend at year-end. What was David's return on this investment?

20. Calculate Cindy Cummings' rate of return in parts (a) and (b) of Problem 17, assuming that the short loan was flat but the margin deposit earned interest at a rate of 8%, and that the prices of $58 and $42 were observed after one year during which the firm did not pay any dividends.

21. What aspects of short selling do brokerage houses typically find to be especially profitable?

22. Peter Barnhart purchases 100 shares of Batavia Lumber Company stock on margin at $50 per share. Simultaneously, Peter short sells 200 shares of Geneva Shelter stock at $20 per share. With an initial margin requirement of 60%:
   a. What is the initial equity (in dollars) in Peter's account?

b. If Batavia and Geneva rise to $55 and $22 per share, respectively, what is Peter's equity position (in dollars)?

23. On May 1, Ivy Olson sold short 100 shares of Lac Minerals stock at $25 per share and bought on margin 200 shares of St. Louis Park Company stock for $40 per share. The initial margin requirement was 50%. On June 30, Lac stock sold for $36 per share and St. Louis Park stock sold for $45 per share.
   a. Prepare a balance sheet showing the aggregate financial position on Ivy's margin account as of June 30.
   b. Determine whether Ivy's account is subject to a margin call on June 30.

KEY TERMS

broker
account executive
registered representative
regional brokerage firm
discount broker
commission
order specifications
board lot
odd lot
day order
good through order
open order
good-till-cancelled order
fill-or-kill order
all or none order
discretionary order
market order
limit order
limit price
limit order with price discretion
stop order
stop price
cash account
margin account
street name
margin purchase
debit balance
call loan rate
settlement date
minimum margin requirement
actual margin
marked to the market
margin call
financial leverage
short sale
uptick
zero tick

REFERENCES

1. For a discussion of the mechanics of purchasing and selling securities, along with margin purchasing and short selling, see:

   How to Invest in Canadian Securities (Toronto: Canadian Securities Institute, 1994).

   The Canadian Securities Course (Toronto: Canadian Securities Institute, 1992).

   James J. Angel, "An Investor's Guide to Placing Stock Orders," *AAII Journal* 15, no. 4 (April 1993): 7–10.

2. An interesting discussion of margin requirements and their impact on market volatility is contained in:

   David A. Hsieh and Merton H. Miller, "Margin Requirements and Market Volatility," *Journal of Finance* 45, no. 1 (March 1990): 3–29.

3. A recent study that examines levels and changes in short interest is:

Averil Brent, Dale Morse, and E. Kay Stice, "Short Interest: Explanations and Tests," *Journal of Financial and Quantitative Analysis* 25, no. 2 (June 1990): 273–289.

4. Market neutral investment strategies are discussed in:

Bruce I. Jacobs and Kenneth L. Levy, "Long/Short Equity Investing," *Journal of Portfolio Management* 20, no. 1 (Fall 1993): 52–63.

CHAPTER 3

Security Markets

A **security market** can be defined as a mechanism for bringing together buyers and sellers of financial assets in order to facilitate trading. Security markets are **secondary** (as opposed to primary) **markets**, because the financial assets traded on them were issued at some previous point in time. One of their main functions is "price discovery," — that is, to cause prices to reflect currently available information. The quicker this is done, the more efficiently financial markets will see that capital is allocated to its most productive opportunities.

CALL AND CONTINUOUS MARKETS

Call Markets

In **call markets**, trading is allowed only at certain specified times. In such a market, when a security is "called," those individuals who are interested in either buying or selling it are physically brought together.[1] Then there may be an explicit auction in which prices are called out until the quantity demanded is as close as possible to the quantity supplied. Alternatively, orders may be left with a clerk, and periodically an official of the exchange sets a price that allows the maximum number of shares from the previously accumulated orders to be traded.

Continuous Markets

In **continuous markets**, trades may occur at any time. Although only investors are needed for such a market to operate, it generally would not be very effective without intermediaries also being present. In a continuous market without intermediaries, an investor who wants to buy or sell a security quickly might have to either spend a great deal of money searching for a good offer or run the risk of accepting a poor one. Since orders from investors arrive more or less randomly, prices in such a market would vary considerably, depending on the flow of buy orders relative to the flow of sell orders. However, anyone willing to take temporary positions in securities could potentially make a profit by ironing out these transitory variations in supply and demand. This is the role of intermediaries known as dealers (also known as market-makers) and specialists. In the pursuit of personal gain, they generally reduce fluctuations in security prices that are unrelated to changes in value and, in doing so, provide **liquidity** for investors. Here, liquidity refers to the ability of investors to convert securities into cash at a price that is similar to the price of the previous trade, assuming no new information has arrived since the previous trade.

[1] Enough time is allowed to elapse between calls (for example, an hour or more) so that a substantial number of orders to buy and sell will accumulate.

Security markets for common stocks (as well as certain other securities) in Canada typically involve dealers. This chapter provides a detailed description of how these markets function and the role played by the dealers. Although the focus is on markets for common stocks, many of the features of such markets are applicable to the markets for other types of financial assets (such as bonds). **Organized exchanges**, which are central physical locations where trading is done under a set of rules and regulations, are discussed first. Examples of such exchanges for common stocks are the Toronto Stock Exchange, the Montreal Exchange, and various regional exchanges.

MAJOR MARKETS IN CANADA

▶ The Toronto Stock Exchange

The Toronto Stock Exchange (TSE) is a provincially incorporated not-for-profit organization that (as of July 1995) had 91 members. It has a charter and a set of by-laws governing its operation and the activities of its members. A 13-person board of governors elected by the membership supervises the exchange. Ten of the governors are members and two are not members; the latter are known as **public governors**. The president and chief executive officer is the remaining governor.

In order to become a member, an applicant must purchase a **seat** (comparable to a membership card) from a current member and be elected to membership of the exchange. By holding a seat, the member has the privilege of being able to execute trades using the facilities provided by the exchange. Since most trades of common stocks, in both dollar value and number of shares, take place on the TSE, this privilege is valuable.[2] Not surprisingly, many brokerage firms and investment dealers are members, meaning that an officer (if the firm is a corporation), a general partner (if the firm is a partnership), or an employee of the firm is a member. Indeed, many such firms have more than one member. A firm with one or more TSE memberships is often referred to as a **member firm**.

A stock that is available for trading on the TSE is known as a **listed security**. In order for a company's stock to be listed, the company must apply to the TSE and meet the published listing requirements, which include having a large enough number of freely tradeable shares in the hands of at least 300 public holders.[3] Companies that are approved for listing pay an annual fee and provide certain information to the public.[4] After listing, if trading interest in a security declines substantially, it may be **delisted** by the exchange, meaning that it is no longer available for trading on the TSE. (Delistings also occur when a listed company is acquired by another company or is merged into another company.) At other times there may be a **trading halt**, meaning that there is a temporary suspension of trading in that security. Trading halts typically are issued for a given stock when trading in it is due to rumors or a recent news announcement (such as a rumor of a takeover attempt or an announcement

[2] During 1990, trading volume on the TSE averaged, on a daily basis, 22.6 million shares, worth in excess of $250 million. The Montreal Exchange, the second largest organized exchange, had comparable daily values of less than one-quarter of these amounts.

[3] For further details see a current issue of the TSE publication *Listing Requirements*.

[4] In the case of initial public offerings it is usual for these to be underwritten by an investment dealer and to trade initially in the OTC market. Only after a satisfactory trading record has been established will the exchange agree to list the shares.

of unexpectedly low quarterly earnings). The opening of trading can be delayed for similar reasons or if a large imbalance in orders has accumulated since the previous close.

Companies may apply for listing on more than one exchange either within Canada or abroad and these are known as *interlisted issues*. In the case of Canadian stocks that are interlisted in the US, it is usual for these securities to trade directly on both the Canadian and US exchanges (commonly the NYSE, ASE or NASDAQ).

Toronto Stock Exchange Members

Members of the TSE are allowed to have a specified maximum number of **trading representatives** (known as floor attorneys) who operate on the floor of the exchange on behalf of the member firm. Trading representatives fall into two categories depending on the type of trading activity in which they engage.

1. **Order traders**. These representatives take orders that the public has placed with brokerage firms and see to it that they are executed on the exchange; the brokerage firms that they work for are paid commissions by the customers for their services. They are precluded from trading for their employer's account but are permitted to trade for their personal account provided that their orders are entered in the same way as the public's.
2. **Registered traders**. These representatives are allowed to handle customer's orders and also to trade on their firm's behalf. In the latter case they generally share in any trading profits that may be realized. A special sub-group of these traders are known as registered traders responsible for a stock or **designated market makers (DMM)**.

The DMM is required to maintain an orderly market for his or her securities of responsibility. This includes establishing an opening price that, as far as possible, clears all outstanding orders, maintaining posted bid and offer (ask) quotations, maintaining a **minimum guaranteed fill** (MGF) size, assisting other traders in executing orders, and ensuring fair and orderly trading. The principal function of the DMM is to provide liquidity to the market. To this end he or she stands ready to fill any public orders for which there is no other counter-party up to the MGF established. In order to accomplish this the DMM is expected to maintain an inventory (either long or short) of the shares of the stock for which he or she is responsible and may alter the bid-ask spread at any time during trading so as to adjust the size of this inventory.[5] Like the specialist on the NYSE, who performs a similar function, the DMM is a monopolist as there is only one market-maker for each DMM stock. In addition, a given DMM may handle several stocks with any accompanying rights and warrants, but not necessarily preferred shares issued by the same company. In order to become a DMM, a registered trader applies to the TSE and, following a satisfactory review by a selection committee, is allocated the requested stock. Stocks listed on the TSE, however, fall into two categories, Tier A and Tier B, depending on their trading frequency. Tier A consists of about 126 of the most frequently traded stocks with the remainder falling into Tier B.[6] Clearly, from a DMM's point of view, Tier A stocks are much more desirable than Tier B stocks. As a result, it is sometimes difficult to find dealers willing to make a

[5] The DMM must enter an order (either buy or sell) to effect a change in either the level or size of the bid-ask spread.

[6] Tier A stocks are those that trade, on average, 24 or more times per day over a six-month period. The remaining 1500-odd listings fall into Tier B.

market in the latter stocks. In such cases, DMMs with Tier A stocks assume responsibility for Tier B stocks that cannot be allocated by the selection committee. Nonetheless, there are less active Tier B stocks with no DMM that trade with no MGF.[7]

Placing a Market Order

At the time of writing, trading procedures on the Toronto Stock Exchange are in a state of flux in that the classical open outcry auction process is carried on simultaneously with computerized trading. Since the auction process is at the heart of all continuous trading systems it is useful to describe it by using a specific example. Mr. B in Sudbury asks his broker for the current price of Imperial Oil (IO) shares. The broker punches a few buttons on his computer and reads on the screen that the current **bid** and *offer* or **ask prices** on the TSE are as favourable as the prices available on any other market, being equal to 49 and 49.10, respectively. In addition, the quotation machine indicates that the MGF for this stock is 599 shares. This means that the DMM is willing to buy a maximum of 500 shares (plus an odd lot) of IO at a price of $49 (the bid price) and is willing to sell a maximum of 500 shares (plus an odd lot) at $49.10 (the offer price). After being given this information, Mr. B instructs his broker to "buy 300 at market," meaning he wishes to place a market order with his broker for 300 shares of IO.

At this point the broker transmits the order to his or her firm's Toronto headquarters, where the order is subsequently relayed to the brokerage firm's booth on the exchange floor. Upon receiving the order, the firm's order trader goes to the trading post for IO. The existence of an MGF is equivalent to a standing order to buy at 49 and means that no one else is prepared to sell at a lower price, and at the same time the MGF is eqivalent to a standing order to sell at 49.10 which means that no higher price need be paid. This leaves only the spread between the two prices for possible negotiation. If Mr. B is lucky, another trader (for example, one with a market order to sell 300 shares for Ms. S) will "take" the order at a price "between the quotes" (here, at 49.05). Information will be exchanged between the two traders and the sale will be made. Figure 3.1 illustrates the procedure used to fill Mr. B's order.

If the gap between the quoted bid and ask prices is wide enough, an auction may occur among various traders, with sales made at one or more prices between the DMM's quoted values. This auction is known as a **double** (or two-way) **auction,** since both buyers and sellers are participating in the bidding process.

What if no response had been forthcoming from the floor when Mr. B's order arrived? In such a case, the DMM would "take the other side," selling 300 shares to Mr. B's broker at a price of 49.10 per share.

If the **bid-ask spread** (i.e., the difference between the ask and the bid prices) on a share is no larger than the standard unit in which prices are quoted, then market orders are generally executed directly by the DMM.[8] This is because there is no spread for possible

---

[7] As of the third quarter of 1995 there were 126 stocks in this category. The minimum required MGF for all Tier B stocks with a DMM is *one board lot plus an odd lot.* The required MGF for a stock with a board lot size of 100 shares, then, is 199 shares.

[8] The following minimum quotation spreads (between bid and offer prices) are permitted on the TSE:

Price per Share	*Minimum Spread*
Under $0.50	$0.005
Over $0.50 and under $3.00	$0.01
Over $3.00	$0.05

SOURCE: The Canadian Securities Course (Toronto: Canadian Securities Instiiute, 1992), and the Toronto Stock Exchange.

Figure 3.1

Order flow for a typical securities transaction on the OTC market and on the floor of the TSE.

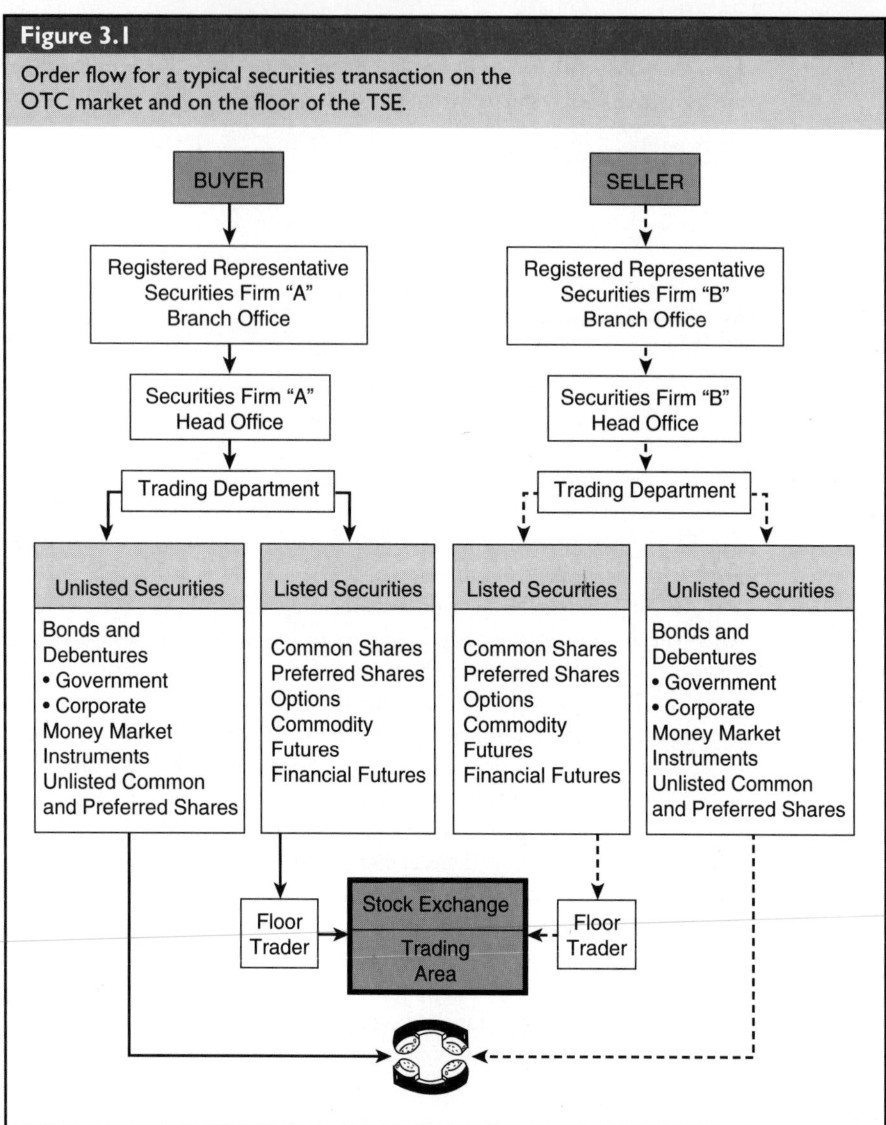

negotiation. In the previous example, if the DMM had quoted bid and ask prices of 49 and 49.05, then there is no incentive for Mr. B's order trader to try to obtain a better price for the purchase order than 49.05, since any seller could obtain a price of 49 from the DMM. That is, to entice someone other than the DMM to sell IO to Mr. B, his order trader would have to offer a better price than 49.05, since this is the price the seller could obtain from the DMM. Given that the next highest price is 49.05 and that the DMM is willing to trade at that price, Mr. B's order trader will deal with the DMM rather than with the "crowd."

Placing a Limit Order

So far, the discussion has been concerned with what would happen to a market order that was placed by Mr. B. What if Mr. B had placed a limit order instead of a market order? There are two situations that can occur with a limit order. First, the limit price may be within the bid and ask prices of the DMM. Second, the limit price may be outside these prices. In the first situation, where the DMM is quoting prices of 49 and 49.10, assume Mr. B has placed a limit order with his broker to buy 300 shares of IO at a price of 49.05 or better. When this order is carried to the trading post, it is possible that it will be executed by the order trader for the limit price of 49.05, since someone in the crowd may be willing to take the other side of the transaction. After all, anyone with a sell order can transact with the DMM at his or her price of 49. To these people, the limit price of 49.05 looks more attractive, since it represents a higher selling price to them. Thus, they would prefer to do business with Mr. B's order trader rather than with the DMM.

In the second situation, assume Mr. B has placed a limit order to buy 300 shares of IO with a limit price of 48. When this order is carried to the trading post, the order trader will not even attempt to fill it, since the limit price is outside the DMM's current bid and offer prices. That is, since anyone with a sell order can deal with the DMM at a price of 49, there is no chance that anyone will want to sell to Mr. B for the limit price of 48. Thus, the order will be given to the DMM to be entered in the limit order book for possible execution in the future. Limit orders in the book are executed in order of price. For example, all purchase orders with limit prices of 48.50 will be executed (if at all) before Mr. B's order is executed. If there are several limit orders in the book at the same price, they are executed in order of arrival (that is, first in, first out).

It may not be possible to fill an entire order at a single price. For example, a broker with a market order to buy 500 shares might obtain 300 shares at 49.05 and have to pay 49.10 for the remaining 200. Similarly, a limit order to buy 500 shares at 49.05 or better might result in the purchase of 300 shares at 49.05 and the entry of a limit order in the limit order book for the other 200 shares.

Computerized Order Handling

The TSE has two computerized systems for handling orders. Routine small market orders for specified Tier A and more actively traded Tier B stocks can be handled by the *Market Order System for Trading* (or MOST). In this context a small market order is defined as one involving the MFG or fewer shares. On receipt of a market order the Toronto office of the customer's brokerage firm may route the market order to the floor of the Exchange, either as described above or by computer through MOST directly to the DMM, whereupon it will be executed instantly at the bid or the offer price, with a confirmation of the execution sent immediately to the brokerage firm for transmittal to the client.[9] Larger market orders are handled in a slightly different way and will be described below.

All orders for the remaining Tier A and Tier B stocks are handled by the *Computer Assisted Trading System* (or CATS). This is a fully automated trading system where all market orders are executed immediately at the current bid or offer price. If there are not sufficient shares available to complete the order at the bid or ask then the balance is treated as a limit order. For those stocks serviced by a market-maker the order is sent directly to the DMM

---

[9] Odd-lot orders are handled by MOST in the same way as board lots with no price premium or discount. The brokerage firm, however, will charge higher transaction costs for handling such an order.

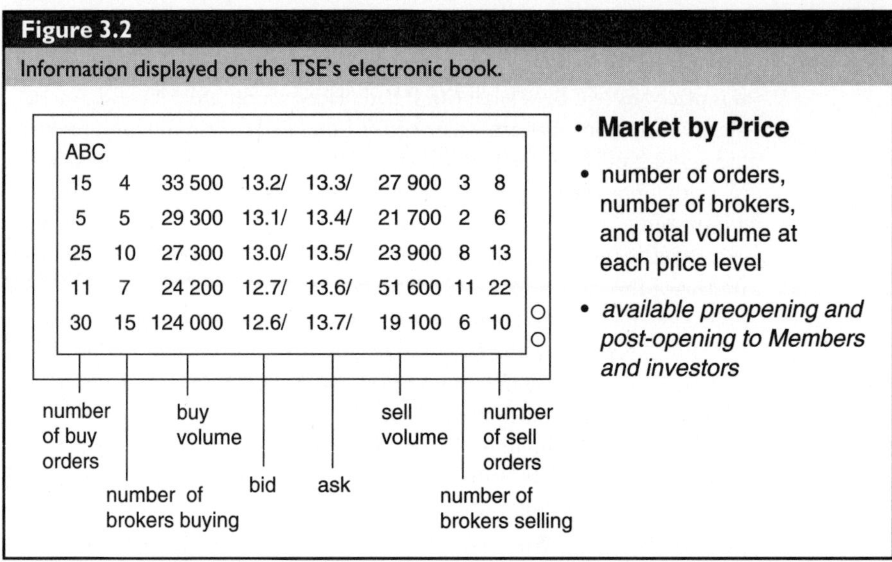

Figure 3.2

Information displayed on the TSE's electronic book.

and executed instantly in the same way as MOST. In the fall of 1995 about 750 stocks traded on CATS and an approximately equal number traded on the floor. CATS, however, only represents about 25% of the trading value on the exchange.

Limit orders entered on CATS are queued according to price and arrival time within each price level and will trade when their price matches the other side of the market.

It is clear that the limit order book contains valuable information as it shows the available supply and demand for shares at different prices. On the NYSE, the market-maker or *specialist* has sole access to this information, which can be profitably used to the specialist's advantage. The TSE differs significantly in this respect in that the book for stocks not traded by CATS (i.e., those traded on MOST) is managed by the *Limit Order Trading System* (LOTS), otherwise known as the *Electronic Book* and all information is electronically displayed and available to investors. Figure 3.2 shows an example of the information displayed. LOTS is a hybrid system in that orders can either be entered electronically or from the floor, unlike CATS, which is fully automated. A market order that exceeds the MGF automatically becomes a limit order, is assigned a limit price, and trades accordingly. The TSE expects to implement fully computerized trading operations by the fall of 1997.

Large Orders

Exceptionally large orders are generally defined as orders involving 10 000 or more shares or a value exceeding $100 000 (whichever is less) and are known as **blocks**. Typically, these orders are placed by institutional customers and may be handled in a variety of ways. One way of handling a block order is to take it directly to the DMM and negotiate a price for it. However, if the block is large enough, it is quite likely that the DMM will lower the bid price (for sell orders) or raise the asked price (for buy orders) by a substantial amount or will not be interested in the offer. This will occur because of the risks involved: taking the order will probably cause the DMM's inventory of the stock to exceed the acceptable long or short position.[10]

Certain investment dealers specialize in handling block trades. Since they are well-known, they are in a position to arrange counter-trades among their customers. These blocks are then crossed on the floor of the exchange at the prevailing market price without involving the DMM or anyone else. Alternatively, the investment dealer may take on the block as a principal and either retain the block in inventory or attempt to distribute it in the market. In such a case the dealer pays a net price that is fractionally below the market. Under TSE rules the maximum spread allowable is specified and is designed to reflect the risks involved.[11]

For example, suppose the CN Pension Fund informs an investment dealer that it wishes to sell 20 000 shares of IO common stock. The dealer then finds three institutional investors that want to buy, say, 5000 shares apiece; the dealer decides that it too will buy 5000 shares of IO stock from CN. Noting that the buyers have said that they would be willing to pay \$70 per share, the block house subsequently informs CN that it will buy the 20 000 shares for \$69.75 each, less a commission of \$8000. Assuming that CN accepts the deal, the dealer now becomes the owner of the shares but must first cross them on the TSE, since the dealer is a member of the exchange. After the cross, the dealer gives 5000 shares to each of the institutional buyers in exchange for \$350 000 (5000 shares × \$70 per share) and hopes that the remaining 5000 shares that it now owns can be sold in the near future at a favourable price. Needless to say, the possibility of not being able to sell them at a favourable price is one of the risks involved in being such a dealer.

► Other Exchanges

Table 3.1 shows the total trading volume of securities listed on each of the active stock exchanges in Canada from 1991 to 1994. The Toronto Stock Exchange dominates the list. Second in importance is the Montreal Exchange (ME), which shares the listing of many companies with the TSE and also lists a number of significant Quebec-based companies exclusively. The Vancouver Stock Exchange has specialized in junior and more speculative issues. The Alberta and Winnipeg stock exchanges are termed **regional exchanges** since, historically, each served as the sole location for trading securities primarily of interest to investors in its region. The trading volume on these regional exchanges is quite small, being comparable to that of the over-the-counter (OTC) market.

These other stock exchanges use procedures similar to those of the Toronto Stock Exchange. The role of the market-maker and the extent of automation differ, but the approach is basically the same.

Options exchanges and futures exchanges utilize some procedures that differ significantly from those employed by stock exchanges. Futures exchanges often have daily price limits instead of having specialists with directions to maintain fair and orderly markets. In Canadian options trading the market-maker is referred to as a specialist, and is charged with responsibility for the book of limit orders and with the maintenance of an orderly market.

---

[10] One alternative for the institution that is thinking of placing the block order is to sequentially place many small orders. However, institutions generally do not want to do this, since it means that their block order will not be executed with due speed.

[11] Currently the maximum spread is limited to 0.25.

Table 3.1

Trading Volumes on Canadian Stock Exchanges.

(a) Trading Volume, 1991 to 1994.[a]

	1991		1992		1993		1994	
	Shares	%	*Shares*	%	*Shares*	%	*Shares*	%
TSE	5 838	49.4	7 326	51.7	14 882	56.0	15 460	58.0
ME	1 350	11.4	1 683	11.9	2 706	10.2	2 487	9.3
VSE	3 681	31.1	3 899	27.5	5 749	21.6	5 303	19.9
ASE/WE	678	5.7	868	6.1	2 228	8.4	2 236	8.4
CDN	281	2.4	405	2.9	1 021	3.8	1 148	4.3

(b) Trading Value, 1991 to 1994.[a]

	1991		1992		1993		1994	
	Dollars	%	*Dollars*	%	*Dollars*	%	*Dollars*	%
TSE	67 750	73.7	76 161	73.5	147 055	71.5	182 202	76.6
ME	18 333	19.9	21 064	20.3	30 331	15.4	32 443	13.6
VSE	3 465	3.8	3 572	3.4	6 781	3.4	5 795	2.4
ASE/WE	568	0.6	982	0.9	2 140	1.1	2 227	0.9
CDN	1 799	2.0	1 801	1.7	10 293	5.2	15 128	6.4

[a] In millions.

SOURCE: Toronto Stock Exchange, *1994 Official Trading Statistics* and information provided by CDN Inc.

The Over-the-Counter Market

In the early days, banks acted as the primary dealers for stocks and bonds, and investors literally bought and sold securities over the counter at the banks. Transactions are more impersonal now, but the designation remains in use for transactions that are not executed on an organized exchange but, instead, involve the use of a dealer. Most bonds are sold over the counter, as are the securities of small (and some not-so-small) unlisted and foreign companies. The large increase in the value traded on the **Canadian Dealing Network Inc.** (CDN) between 1992 and 1993 is a reflection of the introduction of trading in foreign company shares in the fall of 1992.

The over-the-counter market for stocks in Canada is still relatively primitive. In 1986, the Ontario Securities Commission established the *Canadian Over-the-Counter Automated Trading System* (COATS). This provides quotations and trading data for unlisted securities trading in Ontario. In March 1991, the CDN, a subsidiary of the TSE, assumed responsibility for the operation and market regulation of COATS. This is now called the CDN System and provides two kinds of market information: current market bid and offer prices provided by approved market-makers and statistics for the previous trading day (volume, opening, high, low, and closing sale prices, or closing bid and ask quotations, and net changes for the day).

Table 3.2	
Size of a Board Lot on the CDN System.	
Price Range	*Number of Shares*
< $0.10	1000
$0.10 to $0.99	500
$1.00 to $99.875	100
$100 to $199.875	10
$200 or more	1

The CDN System is a quotation system and not a trading system. Actual transactions are made via direct negotiation between broker and dealer.[12] The price paid by a customer buying shares is likely to be higher than the amount paid by the broker to procure the shares (the difference is known as a **markup**). When selling shares, the customer receives a price less than that received by the broker (here the difference is known as a **markdown**). In rare instances the customer may also be charged a commission. The size of these markups and markdowns is expected to be "reasonable" and should reflect the riskless nature of the agency transaction.

Dealers apply to CDN Inc. to become market-makers in CDN securities in the System. They are provided with terminals with which to enter bid and asked prices for the shares of any stock in which they "make a market." Such dealers must be prepared to execute trades for at least one normal trading unit (board lot) at the prices quoted. Table 3.2 shows the size of a board lot that depends on the security's price. As soon as a bid or asked price is entered for a security, it is placed in a central computer file and may be seen by other subscribers (including other dealers) on their own terminals. When new quotations are entered, they replace the dealer's former prices. Market-makers are required to provide uninterrupted bid and ask quotations from 9:30 a.m. to 5:00 p.m. on every day that the CDN System is open for business. There may be more than one market-maker for any given security.

To have quotations displayed on the CDN System, a security must have at least one registered market-maker (that is, one dealer), the firm must meet the OSC reporting requirements, and the application to quote must be approved by the Board of Directors of CDN Inc. Other securities that do not meet these requirements simply have their trading statistics reported daily. Currently there are about 500 securities that have quotations displayed. Brokers with orders to buy or sell securities for which there are no quotations use less formal communication networks to obtain "best execution" for their clients.

► The Third and Fourth Markets

The third and fourth markets are markets in which securities trade off the floor of an organized exchange. Unlike the situation in the United States, the third and fourth markets should not exist in Canada. Under the regulations accompanying the *Ontario Securities Act,* stocks listed on an organized exchange are prohibited from trading in the OTC market.

[12] Generally the order will be a market order, since there is no limit order book in the over-the-counter market. Limit orders will be handled (if at all) in an informal manner by the broker, who will periodically check to see if the order can be executed without violating the limit price; stop and stop limit orders are not allowed in the OTC market. 100% margin is required on all OTC transactions.

These markets are, however, perfectly viable options for large traders wishing to buy or sell foreign securities. Therefore, a brief description of the US situation may be useful.

The term *third market* refers to the trading of any exchange-listed security in the OTC market. The viability of such a market is enhanced today by the fact that their trading hours are not fixed (unlike exchanges) and that they can continue to trade securities even when trading is halted on an exchange. In Canada large volumes of foreign securities have recently started trading on the CDN.

Many institutions have dispensed with brokers and exchanges altogether for transactions in exchange-listed stocks and other securities. Trades of this type, where the buyer and seller deal directly with each other, are sometimes said to take place in the *fourth market.* In the United States, some of these transactions are facilitated by an automated computer-communications system called *Instinet*, which automatically provides quotations and execution.[13] A subscriber can enter a limit order in the computerized "book," where it can be seen by other subscribers, who can, in turn, signal their desire to take it. Whenever two orders are matched, the system automatically records the transaction and sets up the paperwork for its completion. Subscribers can also use the system to find likely partners for a trade and then conduct negotiations by telephone.

► Foreign Markets

The three largest stock markets in the world are in New York, London, and Tokyo. These stock markets each have different rules and operating procedures that offer some interesting contrasts.

New York

Trading on the New York Stock Exchange (NYSE) is all carried out on the floor of the Exchange at 1 Wall Street in New York City. The trading procedure is similar to that followed on the TSE for non-CATS traded securities. The market making process on the NYSE, however, is quite different from that on the TSE.

Specialists are at the heart of the trading activity on the NYSE. Each stock that is listed on the NYSE currently has one specialist assigned to it. There are over 2000 common stocks listed on the NYSE and only 400 specialists, so each specialist is assigned more than one stock.

All orders involving a given stock must be taken physically to a **trading post**, a spot on the floor of the NYSE where the specialist for that stock stands at all times during the hours the NYSE is open. It is here that an order is either executed or left with the specialist.

Any limit order that the commission broker cannot execute immediately because the current market priced is not at or better than the specified limit price will be left with the specialist for possible execution in the future. If this order is subsequently executed, the specialist is paid part of the customer's commission. The specialist keeps these orders in what is known as the **limit order book** (or specialist's book). Stop and stop limit orders are also left with the specialist, who then enters them in the same book. In this capacity the specialist is acting as a broker (that is, agent) for the customer's broker and can be thought of as a "broker's broker."

---

[13] The use of an intermediary such as a computer system makes it difficult to categorize such trades. Some people refer to the market where trades involving a "matchmaker" take place as the 3.5 market. The term fourth market is then used only when referring to the market where no matchmaker is involved.

The specialist also acts as a **dealer** in certain stocks (in particular, for the same stocks in which he or she acts as a broker). This means that the specialist buys and sells certain stocks for his or her own account and is allowed to seek a profit in doing so. However, in acting as a dealer, the specialist is required by the NYSE to maintain a "fair and orderly market" in those stocks in which he or she is registered as a specialist. Thus, the NYSE expects the specialist to buy or sell shares from his or her own account when there is a temporary imbalance between the number of buy and sell orders. (In doing so, specialists are allowed to short sell their assigned stocks.) Even though the NYSE monitors the trading activities of the specialists, this requirement is so ill-defined that it is difficult, if not impossible, to enforce.

The NYSE has developed special procedures to handle both routine small orders and exceptionally large orders. In 1976 the NYSE developed an electronic system known as Designated Order Turnaround (or DOT) to handle small orders, defined at that time as market orders involving 199 or fewer shares and limit orders involving 100 or fewer shares. Subsequent developments led to DOT being replaced by a procedure known as the Super Designated Order Turnaround system (or SuperDOT), which now accepts market orders involving 30 999 or fewer shares and limit orders involving 99 999 or fewer shares. In order to use SuperDOT, the member firm must be a participating subscriber. With this system, the New York office of the customer's brokerage firm can send the customer's order directly to the specialist, whereupon it will be exposed to the crowd and executed immediately (if possible), with a confirmation of the execution sent to the brokerage firm. SuperDOT represents the extent of computerized trading on the NYSE.

London

In October 1986 the "Big Bang" introduced several major reforms to the London Stock Exchange. Fixed brokerage commissions were eliminated, membership was opened up to corporations, and foreign firms were allowed to purchase existing member firms. Furthermore, an automated dealer quotation system known as SEAQ (Stock Exchange Automated Quotations) was introduced. This system involves competing market-makers whose quotes are displayed over a computer network. Small orders can be executed by using SAEF (SEAQ Automated Execution Facility), which functions rather like the TSE's MOST. Large orders are handled over the telephone. Limit orders are not handled centrally but instead are handled by individual brokers or dealers who note when prices have moved sufficiently that they can be executed.

Tokyo

Similar to the London Stock Exchange, the Tokyo Stock Exchange has experienced major reforms. CORES (Computer-Assisted Order Routing and Execution System), a computer system for trading all but the 150 most active securities, was introduced in 1982. Then in 1986 the exchange began to admit foreign firms as members, and in 1990 FORES (Floor Order Routing and Execution System) was introduced as a computer system to facilitate trading in the most active stocks.

Interestingly, the system of trading both the most active and the relatively less active securities is quite different from any system found in North America or the United Kingdom. It is centred on members known as *saitori* who act, in a sense, as auctioneers in that they are neither dealers nor specialists. Instead they are intermediaries who accept orders from member firms and are not allowed to trade in any stocks for their own account.

At the opening of the exchange (because the exchange is open from 9 a.m. to 11 a.m. and 1 p.m. to 3 p.m., there are two openings per day) the *saitori* members follow a method called *itayose*, which operates like a call market in that the *saitori* seeks to set a single price so that the amount of trading is maximized (subject to certain constraints). This involves constructing supply and demand schedules for the market and limit orders that have been received, and noting where the two schedules intersect. (An example of how this is done is described in Chapter 4 and illustrated in Figures 4.1 through 4.4.)

After the opening of the exchange, the *saitori* follows a method known as *zaraba*, where orders are processed continually as they are received—that is, market orders are offset against previously unfilled limit orders. New limit orders are filled, if possible, against previously unfilled limit orders. If these new limit orders cannot be filled, then they are entered in the limit order book for possible future execution. Unlike the limit order book on the TSE, the limit order book in Tokyo is only available for inspection by member firms. Furthermore, unlike the TSE, the Tokyo Stock Exchange prohibits trading at prices outside a given range based on the previous day's closing price. Hence, there can be situations where trading in a stock ceases until the next day (when the price range is readjusted) unless two parties decide to trade within the current range.

INFORMATION-MOTIVATED AND LIQUIDITY-MOTIVATED TRADERS

There are two major reasons for security transactions. An investor may believe that a security has become mispriced — meaning that its value is outside the current bid and asked prices. One who feels this way believes that he or she has information not known to (or understood by) the market in general and may be termed an **information-motivated trader**. On the other hand, an investor may simply want to sell some securities to buy a new car, or buy some securities with recently inherited money, or the like. Such a person may be called a **liquidity-motivated trader**. In making security transactions, he or she does not presume that others in the market have evaluated the prospects for the security incorrectly.[14]

Dealers can make money by trading with liquidity-motivated traders or with inept information-motivated traders. But, on the average, they can only lose money by trading with clever information-motivated traders. The larger a dealer's bid-ask spread, the less business he or she will do; but whatever the spread, when a clever information-motivated investor makes a trade, the dealer may expect to lose. In the absence of unwise investors, the very existence of a dealer depends on investors' desires for liquidity. A dealer must select a bid-ask spread wide enough to limit the number of trades with customers possessing superior information, but narrow enough to attract an adequate number of liquidity-motivated transactions.

---

[14]A similar classification of traders that has often been used by financial economists involves (1) informed speculative traders who possess both public and private information, (2) uninformed speculative traders who possess just public information, and (3) noise traders whose trades are not based on information. Hence the first two types can be viewed as information-motivated traders, the third as liquidity-motivated traders. See Sandford J. Grossman and Joseph E. Stiglitz, "On the Impossibility of Informationally Efficient Markets," *American Economic Review* 70, no. 3 (June 1980): 393–408.

The Stock Exchange of Hong Kong: Another Asian Exchange Switches to Automated Matching

by Ann Guenther Sherman
Hong Kong University of Science and Technology

As the unrelenting march toward integration of the world's security markets continues, the competitive pressures on national stock exchanges to adopt efficient and low-cost trading mechanisms have grown stronger. The Stock Exchange of Hong Kong (SEHK) provides an interesting example of the conflict between entrenched business practices and external competition, and the ultimate resolution of that conflict.

Stock trading has a long history in Hong Kong, with informal trading dating back to 1866 and a formal exchange established in 1891 (the second in Asia, after Japan's). By 1973 four exchanges operated in the tiny city-state, far too many to justify from an economic perspective. Despite considerable controversy, the four exchanges were merged into the SEHK in 1986.

The newly created SEHK had many potential models for a trading system. It could have built on CATS (Computer-Assisted Trading System) of the Toronto Stock Exchange, which for some of its listed stocks is the world's first fully automated trading system. The SEHK could also have learned from CORES (Computer-Assisted Order Routing and Execution System), a modified version of CATS instituted by the Tokyo Stock Exchange. Other models include NASDAQ (National Association of Securities Dealers Automated Quotations), which was used as the basis for the Big Bang reorganization of the London Stock Market. Or, of course, Hong Kong could have followed one of the many auction/modified open-outcry systems in use around the world, including that of the New York Stock Exchange.

Instead, the SEHK chose an unusual way of arranging trades. Each member of the exchange has a booth or a desk on the exchange floor, at which it can have up to two representatives. Each booth has two telephones (an internal and an external line) and up to two computer terminals, only one of which operates in an interactive mode while the other is in display-only mode. Members enter and buy and sell orders into the computer, and the orders are shown on the screen for that stock. The orders include price but not quantity. If another member of the exchange wishes to trade with the person who input the order, then he or she telephones that person. If the lines are full and the call cannot get through, then the trader may choose to get up and go to the other person's booth. The member who input the order is under no obligation to deal with the first person who calls or dashes over, and the quantity of any trade must be negotiated. After a trade has been made, the seller must enter the details into the system within 15 minutes. There is no order-matching facility, no designated market-maker, and no priority assigned to orders at the same price.

One of the system's weaknesses is that a person entering an order has less information than he or she would have in a simple open-outcry system. When a trader standing at a post on the NYSE shouts out an order, he or she can see how many other people at the post are ready to respond to the order and may even be able to judge how anxious they are to trade. When a trader enters an order into a terminal on the SEHK, he or she can only wait for the phone to ring. While talking to the first person who calls, the trader cannot tell how many others are also trying to get through—the only way to learn this is to hang up and wait for the phone to ring again, a method that may prove costly if in fact no one else is interested. This weakness is partially offset by the habit of traders' running over to each other's desks, a feature that was probably not in the original plan.

Another potential problem, especially during busy times, is that each order takes longer to arrange than in an automated order-matching system. Rather than simply entering a limit order into an automated system and receiving confirmation when the order is filled, traders must enter the order, wait for someone to contact them, negotiate a quantity, and then (if they are selling) enter the details into the computer. Most exchanges, such as those in Malaysia and Singapore, experienced sharp rises in turnover after they introduced automated trading systems. Taiwan, with fully automated trading, has handled daily volume levels close to Tokyo's (although Tokyo's market capitalization was then around 30 times larger). In spite of the possible reduction in trading capacity, however, the Hong Kong system may appeal to those who prefer private negotiation when arranging deals, rather than the impersonality of an order-matching system or the open competition of an open-outcry system.

A key disadvantage (or advantage, depending on your outlook) of the Hong Kong system is that it may facilitate manipulation of stock prices. Efficient and cheap price manipulation requires coordination on the part of the manipulators. They create a series of fake trades among themselves in the same stock at ever increasing (or decreasing) prices. In an automated matching system, price manipulators can still buy shares at above-market prices, but they cannot determine who gets those high prices, because orders are filled based on price and time priority. With the Hong Kong system, a price manipulator need only tell an accomplice when he or she plans to enter the order and make sure that the accomplice is ready to dial quickly. If the accomplice is not the first person to call, the manipulator can refuse to trade.

Although the SEHK fell behind many other Asian countries in updating trading methods, its members eventually recognized the necessity for reform. The Hong Kong securities industry was heavily influenced by the October 1987 crash, in which the Hong Kong stock and futures exchanges performed embarrassingly poorly. During the crash, the SEHK closed for 4 days, October 20–23 (the only stock exchange in the world to close for so long), and the chairman of the exchange was later arrested and convicted for accepting bribes in connection with a new listing on the exchange. In the aftermath of the crash, there have been major changes in Hong Kong, including the formation of the Securities and Futures Commission, which has tightened regulation of the market. Among other changes, some forms of insider trading are now illegal, and stock price manipulation is now prosecuted.

At the SEHK a new clearing system was adopted in 1992, and an automated order-matching system began operating on November 1, 1993, although it initially handled only a few stocks on an experimental basis. The order-matching system was originally expected to be introduced two years earlier, but complications in the replacement of the clearing system and the resistance of vested interests delayed its implementation. After automated order matching is fully implemented, members will have a choice between trading on the floor of the exchange and trading from terminals in their offices. Exchange officials expect the trading floor to soon be deserted, as happened in London after the Big Bang. The SEHK also has plans to introduce short selling and stock options, and it may extend trading hours beyond the current 3 1/2 hours a day. Although these changes have taken many years, soon the SEHK will be as technologically advanced as other major exchanges around the world.

After control of Hong Kong switches from Great Britain to the People's Republic of China (PRC) in 1997, it is not clear what will happen to the SEHK. Most of the exchange's plans

INSTITUTIONAL ISSUES (continued)

for expansion involve the listing of mainland companies, which it began in 1993. If the economic opening and development of the PRC continues, Hong Kong may be able to greatly enlarge its position as an international financial center. On the other hand, Hong Kong's stock market has a close rivalry with Singapore's, and Taiwan announced its intention to supplant Hong Kong as an Asian financial center after 1997. There are already signs that the 1997 takeover may affect two of Hong Kong's key advantages, the rule of law and press freedom, in which case Singapore and Taiwan would gain a great competitive advantage.

A dealer can take either a passive or an active role. For example, a bid-ask spread can be established and a tentative price set. As orders come in and are filled, the dealer's inventory (position) will vary and may even become negative when promises to deliver securities exceed promises to accept delivery. But any clear trend suggests that the price should be altered. In effect, a *passive dealer* lets the market indicate the appropriate price.

An *active dealer* tries to get as much information as possible and to alter bid and ask prices in advance to keep the flow of orders more in balance. The better a dealer's information, the smaller the bid-ask spread required to make a profit. Poorly informed dealers will either price themselves out of the market by having too low a bid price or too high an ask price, or go out of business after incurring heavy losses by being picked off by more knowledgeable traders.

PRICES AS INFORMATION SOURCES

The usual description of a market assumes that every trader wishes to purchase or sell a known quantity at each possible price. All the traders come together, and in one way or another a price is found that clears the market — that is, makes the quantity demanded as close as possible to the quantity supplied.

This may or may not be an adequate description of the markets for consumer goods, but it is clearly inadequate when describing security markets. The value of any capital asset depends on its future prospects, which are almost always uncertain. Any information that bears on such prospects may lead to a revised estimate of value. The fact that a knowledgeable trader is willing to buy or sell some quantity of a security at a particular price is likely to be information of just this sort. Offers to trade may thus affect other offers. Prices may, therefore, both clear markets *and* convey information.

The dual role of prices has a number of implications. For example, it behooves the liquidity-motivated trader to publicize his or her motives and thereby avoid an adverse effect on the market. Thus, an institution purchasing securities for a pension fund that intends simply to hold a representative cross section of securities should make it clear that it does not consider the securities underpriced. On the other hand, any firm trying to buy or sell a large number of shares that it considers mispriced should try to conceal either its motives, its identity, or both (and many try). Such attempts may be ineffective, however, as those asked to take the other side of such trades try to find out exactly what is going on (and many succeed).

Most securities are sold the standard way, which requires delivery of certificates within the settlement period (three business days). On rare occasions, a sale may be made as a cash transaction, requiring delivery the same day, or the seller may be given the choice of any delivery day within a specified period (typically, no more than 60 days). On other occasions, such as new issues, extensions to the settlement period are granted.

It would be extremely inefficient if every security transaction had to end with a physical transfer of share certificates from the seller to the buyer. A brokerage firm might sell 500 shares of BCE Inc. stock for one client, Mr. S, and later that day buy 500 shares for Ms. B, another client. Mr. S's 500 shares could be delivered to his buyer, and Ms. B's shares could be obtained by accepting delivery from her seller. However, it would be much easier to transfer Mr. S's shares to Ms. B and instruct B's seller to deliver 500 shares directly to S's buyer. This would be especially helpful if the brokerage firm's clients, Mr. S and Ms. B, held their securities in street name. Then, the 500 shares they traded would not have to be physically moved and their ownership would not have to be changed on the books of BCE.

► Clearing Corporations

The process can be facilitated even more by a *clearing corporation*, the owners of which are brokerage firms, banks, and other financial institutions. Records of transactions made by members during a day are sent there. At the end of the day, both sides of the trades are verified for consistency; then all transactions are netted out. Each member receives a list of the net amounts of securities to be delivered or received along with the net amount of money to be paid or collected. Every day, each member settles with the clearing corporation instead of with various other firms.

In Canada there are two clearing corporations: the Canadian Depository for Securities Limited (CDS), to handle trades made on the Montreal Exchange, the Toronto Stock Exchange, and in the OTC market, and the West Canada Clearing Corporation (WCCC) for Alberta and Vancouver Stock Exchange members. Non-participating financial institutions may use CDS or WCCC services as clients of direct participants. Some banks belong simply to facilitate delivery of securities which, for example, may serve as collateral for secured demand loans.

By holding securities in street name and using clearing corporations, brokers can reduce the costs of transfer operations. But even more can be done with book based systems—certificates can be immobilized almost completely. The WCCC together with the West Canada Depository Trust Company (WCDTC) accomplishes this by maintaining computerized records of the securities "owned" by its member firms (brokers, banks, and so on). Members' share certificates are credited to their accounts at the WCDTC, but the certificates are transferred to the WCDTC on the books of the issuing corporation and remain registered in its name unless a member subsequently withdraws them. Whenever possible, one member will "deliver" securities to another by initiating a simple bookkeeping entry in which one account is credited and the other debited for the shares involved. Dividends paid on securities held by the WCDTC are simply credited to members' accounts based on their holdings and may be subsequently withdrawn in cash.

INSURANCE

When a brokerage firm fails, its clients may discover for the first time that securities and cash balances in their accounts are no longer physically available. This could lead to erosion of investor confidence; therefore, the Toronto, Montreal, Vancouver, and Alberta Stock Exchanges and the Investment Dealers Association of Canada have jointly established the **Canadian Investor Protection Fund** (CIPF) to protect the investing public against losses due to the financial failure of a member of one of the sponsoring organizations. When an investor becomes a customer of a member of any one of the sponsors, that customer's accounts are covered by the CIPF. Each account is insured up to a stated amount ($250 000 per account in 1990).[15] The cost of the insurance is borne by the member firms through regular annual fees and periodic special assessments. Should this be insufficient to settle all claims, the CIPF can borrow through a line of credit provided by two Canadian chartered banks.

COMMISSIONS

► Fixed Commissions

Until 1975, the New York Stock Exchange required its member brokers to charge fixed minimum commissions for stocks, with no "rebates, returns, discounts or allowances in 'any shape or manner,' direct or indirect."[16] Fixed commissions were also charged on the TSE and remained in force until 1983.

In the era of fixed commissions, brokerage firms did not compete with one another over commissions. However, those brokerage firms that belonged to the Toronto Stock Exchange competed with one another in a different manner — namely, by offering a panoply of ancillary services to customers. Large institutions were provided with security analysis, performance measurement services and the like in return for **soft dollars** — brokerage commissions ostensibly paid for having a brokerage firm execute their trades and indirectly designated as payment for services rendered. The US experience indicates that for every $3 in commissions received on large trades, brokerage firms were willing to spend up to approximately $2 to provide ancillary services to the customers. Thus, it follows that it cost brokerage firms roughly $1 per $3 of commission received just to execute a large trade for a customer. Apparently, up to two-thirds of the fixed commission rate ($2 out of $3) on such large orders was pure (marginal) profit.

The existence of fixed commissions has been attributed to the natural monopoly arising from economies of scale in bringing together many people (either physically or via modern communication technology) to trade with one another. The potential profits from such a monopoly are limited by the advantages it confers. The increasing institutionalization of security holdings and progress in communications and computer technology have diminished the advantages associated with a centralized physical exchange. Thus, the removal

---

[15] A given client may have more than one type of account and may, therefore, be able to claim more than the limit shown.

[16] See Wilford J. Eiteman, Charles A. Dice, and David K. Eiteman, *The Stock Market* (New York: McGraw-Hill, 1969): 138.

Figure 3.3

Typical commission rates for selected transactions; dollar commissions as a percentage of the value of the order.

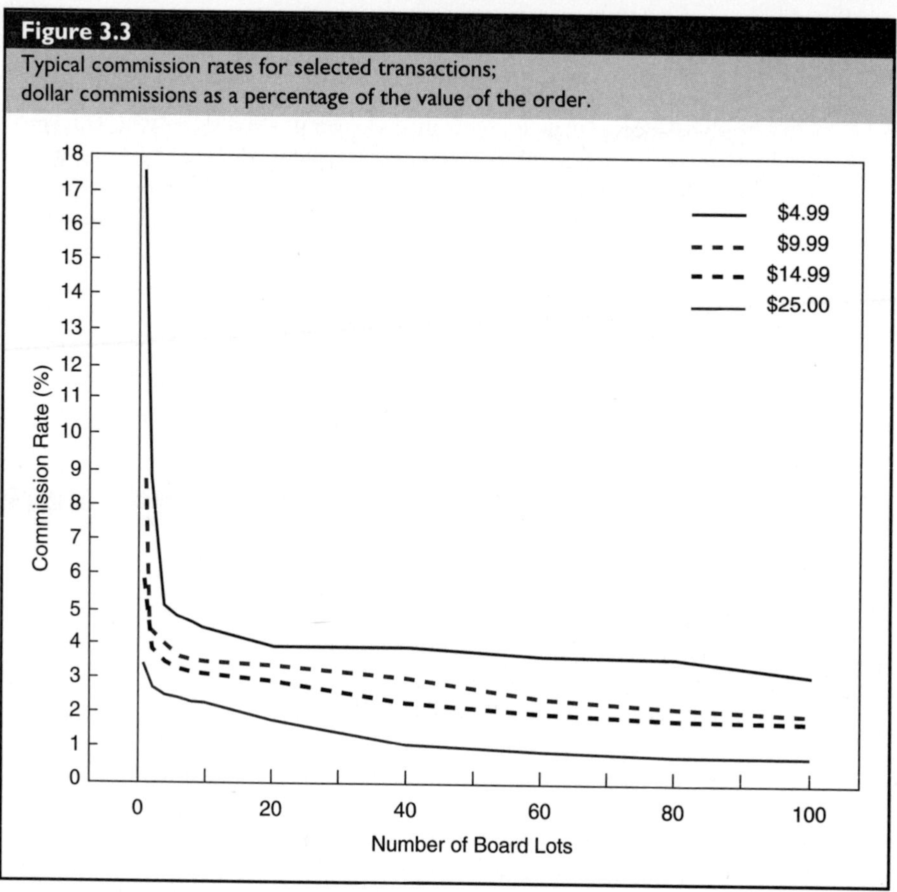

of legal protection for this particular type of price fixing may only have been another example of a response to technological change.

Competitive Commissions

The system of fixed commissions in the US was finally terminated by the *Securities Act Amendments* of 1975 (but only after repeated challenges by the NYSE). Since May 1, 1975 (known in the trade as **May Day**), brokers have been free to set commissions at any desired rate or to negotiate with customers concerning the fees charged for particular trades. The former procedure is more commonly employed in "retail" trades executed for small investors, whereas the latter is used more often when handling large trades involving institutional investors and others.

Prior to May Day, commission rates in Canada were generally higher than those in the US. Following the introduction of negotiated rates in the US, trading in interlisted securities tended to migrate to US exchanges where transactions costs were lower. This forced Canadian dealers to match US commission rates on large trades in order to protect their business. On April 1, 1983 Canada moved to negotiated commission rates.[17]

[17] Even before this date commissions were negotiable for trades in excess of $500 000.

After April 1983, rates for large trades in Canada fell substantially. So did those charged for small trades by firms offering only bare-bones brokerage services. On the other hand, broad-line firms that provided extensive services to small investors for no additional fee continued to charge commissions similar to those specified in the earlier fixed schedules. In succeeding years, as costs have risen, charges for smaller transactions have increased, whereas those for large trades have not.

Increased competition among brokerage firms has resulted in a wide range of alternatives for investors. Following April 1983, some firms *unbundled*, meaning they priced their services separately from their pricing of order execution. Other firms *went discount* meaning they dropped almost all ancillary services and cut commissions accordingly. Still others bundled new services into comprehensive packages. Some of these approaches have not stood the test of time, but just as mail-order firms, discount houses, department stores, and expensive boutiques coexist in retail trade, many different combinations are viable in the brokerage industry.

Figure 3.3 shows typical commission rates charged by retail brokerage firms for small to medium-sized trades. These rates are representative of those charged by full-line retail brokers that provide offices with quotation boards, research reports, account executives available for advice and information, and the like. The rates also apply to trades made by customers whose volume of business is small. Discount firms with little but execution capability typically charge 30% to 70% less.

TRANSACTION COSTS

► The Bid-Ask Spread

Commission costs are only a portion of the total cost associated with buying or selling a security. Consider a "round-trip" transaction, in which shares are purchased and then sold during a period in which no new information causes investors collectively to reassess the value of the shares (more concretely, the bid and asked prices quoted by dealers do not change). The shares will typically be purchased at the dealers' asked price and sold at the bid price, which is lower. The bid-ask spread thus constitutes a portion of the round-trip transaction costs.

According to one study covering US markets, the spread between the bid and asked prices for a typical stock is approximately $.30 per share for the securities of large, actively traded companies. This amounts to less than 1% of the price per share for most stocks of this type — a reasonably small amount to pay for the ability to buy or sell in a hurry.

However, not all securities enjoy this type of liquidity. Shares of smaller firms tend to sell at lower prices but at similar bid-ask spreads. As a result, the percentage transaction cost is considerably larger. This is shown in part (a) of Table 3.3. Stocks were assigned to sectors based on each firm's **market capitalization**, which is equal to the market value of the firm's outstanding equity. For example, if the total market value of the common stock of a company was less than $10 million, it was considered to be in sector 1 (the smallest capitalization sector), and if the market value was greater than $1.5 billion, the company was included in sector 9 (the largest capitalization sector). As the table shows, the larger the capitalization, the greater was the average price per share. Note also that the average spread in dollars was actually greater for the smallest capitalization stocks than for the largest. Most importantly, however, the ratio of the average spread to the average price fell continuously

INSTITUTIONAL ISSUES

Soft Dollars

Suppose that you have decided to build a new home. As your first step you hire a general contractor to oversee the different construction phases. The general contractor, in turn, hires various subcontractors to lay the foundation, frame the house, install wiring, and so on.

You can compensate the general contractor in large part based on the charges billed by the subcontractors. Now assume that the general contractor allowed the subcontractors to charge more than the true costs of their services. The difference between the billed costs and the true costs was then rebated to the general contractor in the form of payments for goods and services only indirectly related to the general contractor's work on your home, such as accounting services or transportation vehicles.

Presumably you would find such an arrangement objectionable. After all, fairness dictates that the general contractor's charges to you include only the actual cost of the subcontractor's labour and materials. The general contractor should pay for accounting services directly out of its own pocket. The efficiency and equity of such an arrangement seems unquestionable, except perhaps in the investment management business, where each year institutional investors pay hundreds of millions of "soft" dollars to brokerage firms in a situation analogous to our hypothetical home-building example.

Soft dollars are brokerage commissions paid by institutional investors in excess of amounts required to compensate brokers for simply executing trades. As the text describes, soft dollars had their origin in the fixed commission rates imposed by exchanges in years past. Large institutional investors paid the same commission rates as small retail investors, despite the obvious economies of scale present in carrying out large trades as opposed to small trades.

Brokerage firms competed with one another, not by lowering commission rates, but by rebating a portion of the commissions to large investors. These brokerage firms did so by offering a plethora of "free" services to the investors. These services typically involved various types of investment research, although on occasion they included such ethically questionable items as airline tickets and lodging for trips abroad.

After the deregulation of commission rates it was widely assumed that soft dollars would disappear. Investors would pay brokers only for executing their trades in the most cost-effective manner. Other services, such as investment research, would be purchased directly from the supplying firms. This decoupling of payments for trade execution from other services is known as "unbundling."

Surprisingly, the soft dollar industry, despite some initial rough going following deregulation, did not wither away. In fact, it flourished. Investment research continued to be paid for out of commissions.

One factor affecting the use of soft dollars was the general trend of institutional investors toward hiring external investment managers to invest their assets. These managers, in a loose sense, act as the general contractor referred to earlier. The managers have discretion over the allocation of their clients' commissions. They are permitted (and, in fact, have a strong incentive) to use soft dollars to pay for various forms of investment research. That research primarily includes fundamental company analyses, data on expected earnings, and economic forecasts. It also includes computer software and hardware, performance measurement, and educational

INSTITUTIONAL ISSUES (continued)

services. By using soft dollars to pay for such research, the costs are effectively shifted to the managers' clients, rather than paid for by the managers themselves.

Establishing the size of the soft dollar industry is difficult, but it is large and lucrative enough to support a number of brokerage firms devoted solely to supplying third-party research services to investors in exchange for soft dollars. These brokerage firms make arrangements with providers of investment research to funnel payments for services rendered to investment managers in exchange for having the managers execute trades through the brokerage firms.

In the investment industry, prices for research services are often quoted on two levels: hard (straight cash payment) or soft (price in commission dollars). The ratio of the two prices implies a conversion rate. Although this conversion rate is negotiable, an approximate figure is two commission dollars paid to receive one dollar in services.

The stated rationale behind managers' use of soft dollars is that their clients benefit from the research services purchased. Presumably, in the absence of soft dollars, managers would raise their fees to enable them to purchase the necessary research directly, yet maintain their current profit margins. However, managers are not required to provide their clients with a detailed accounting of their soft-dollar use.

Thus, it is difficult for clients to assess whether their commission dollars are being wisely allocated by their managers. One is hard-pressed to imagine how clients are better off under a system of unidentified, implicit fees than they would be if commission payments were completely unbundled.

Why don't institutional clients insist that soft-dollar use be prohibited or at least be fully divulged? Inertia and ignorance appear to be two explanations. Another reason is that many institutional investors have themselves become beneficiaries of soft dollars. They use soft dollars by directing their managers to purchase various services for their immediate benefit. (Soft dollars generated in this manner are sometimes called "directed commissions.") For example, a corporate pension fund staff may use their managers' soft dollars to purchase performance measurement services that the corporate budget would not normally allow.

Over the years, soft dollars have been criticized as being inefficient and ripe for abuse. Calls for prohibition of soft dollars have occasionally been heard. However, the soft-dollar industry is powerful and to date has been able to ward off any substantive changes.

from 6.55% for the smallest sector to .52% for the largest sector. This means that the larger the capitalization of the firm, the greater the liquidity of its shares.

The majority of the stocks traded on the TSE tend to fall into the lower market capitalization deciles shown in Table 3.3. Therefore, it is likely that transaction costs are generally higher in Canada than in the US. This conclusion is borne out by a study conducted by Tinic and West in the early 1970s in which they compared bid-ask spreads on TSE listed stocks with those on the NYSE and the OTC.[18] Even after controlling for daily trading volume, average stock price, price volatility, trading frequency, and the number of markets in which the security is listed (but not market capitalization) they found that bid-ask spreads on the TSE are larger than those on either of the US markets. They concluded that the price of liquidity was higher on the TSE and the marketability of TSE-listed stocks was inferior. They attributed this inferior performance to the lack of a well-developed dealer market in Canada. Whereas the specialist on the NYSE and the dealers on the OTC were committed to filling board lot orders, and thereby maintaining an active and continuous market, the registered traders on the TSE were only required to provide bid and offer quotations and to fill odd-lot orders (at a premium or a discount). Both the market-making function on the TSE and the capitalization of member firms have changed significantly, however, in the past 20 years, so these conclusions require updating and confirmation.

The inverse relationship between the amount of trading activity (or market value) and spread size can be explained once it is recognized that the spread is the dealer's compensation for providing investors with liquidity. The smaller the amount of trading, the less frequently the dealer will capture the spread (by buying at the bid and selling at the asked). Hence, the dealer will need a wider spread in order to generate a level of compensation commensurate with more frequently traded securities.

► Price Impact

Brokerage commissions and bid-ask spreads represent transaction costs for small orders (typically 100 shares). For larger orders, the possibility of **price impacts** must be considered. Consider purchase orders. Due to the law of supply and demand, the larger the size of the order, the more likely the investor's purchase price will be higher. Furthermore, the more rapidly the order is to be completed and the more knowledgeable the individual or organization placing the order, the higher is the purchase price charged by the dealer.

Panel (b) of Table 3.3 provides estimates of average costs for transactions in the "upstairs dealer" market. All three sources of costs are included: bid-ask spreads, brokerage commissions, and price impacts. The figures refer to the total cost for a round-trip — a purchase followed by a sale — and reveal that for any capitalization sector, larger block sizes are associated with larger percentage transaction costs. The figures also reveal that for any given dollar-size block, larger capitalization sectors are associated with smaller percentage transaction costs. A similar observation can be made upon examination of panel (a).

Panel (a) of Figure 3.4 plots the percentage transaction costs for blocks of $25 000 each, which corresponds to the values in the third column from the left in panel (b) of

---

[18] Seha M. Tinic and Richard R. West, "Marketability of Common Stocks in Canada and the USA: A Comparison of Agent Versus Dealer Dominated Markets," *Journal of Finance* 29, no. 3 (June 1974): 729–46. Schulman presents evidence that spreads in December 1988 on the TSE 35 stocks were, on average, higher than on the NYSE, as shown below:

	Bid/ask spread	
	TSE 35	*NYSE*
High	1.80%	1.31%
Median	0.65%	0.38%
Low	0.22%	0.08%

SOURCE: E. Schulman, "The 'Global Village' Securities Market: Will Canada be a Participant...or a Bystander?" *Canadian Investment Review* II, no. 2 (Fall 1989): 61–6. For a difference of opinion on the significance of the spread differential, see K. Cachia and E. Schulman, "Comparison of Bid-Offer Spreads on NYSE and TSE: Comment and Response," *Canadian Investment Review* III, no. 1 (Spring 1990): 31.

Table 3.3

Bid-Ask Spreads and Round-Trip Transaction Costs.

(a) Common Stock Bid-Ask Spreads: Small Orders.

	Capitalization						
Sector	*From (millions)*	*To (millions)*	*Number of Issues*	*Percentage of US Market*	*Average Price*	*Average Spread*	*Spread Price*
1 (small)	$ 0	$ 10	1 009	.36%	$ 4.58	$.30	6.55%
2	10	25	754	.89	10.30	.42	4.07
3	25	50	613	1.59	15.16	.46	3.03
4	50	75	362	1.60	18.27	.34	1.86
5	75	100	202	1.27	21.85	.32	1.46
6	100	500	956	15.65	28.31	.32	1.13
7	500	1 000	238	12.29	35.43	.27	.76
8	1 000	1 500	102	8.87	44.34	.29	.65
9 (large)	1 500	99 999	180	57.48	52.40	.27	.52

(b) Percentage Round-Trip Transaction Costs, Common Stock.

	Capitalization								
	Dollar Value of Block ($ thousands)								
Sector	*5*	*25*	*250*	*500*	*1 000*	*2 500*	*5 000*	*10 000*	*20 000*
1 (small)	17.3%	27.3%	43.8%						
2	8.9	12.0	23.8	34.4%					
3	5.0	7.6	18.8	25.9	30.0%				
4	4.3	5.8	9.6	16.9	25.4	31.5%			
5	2.8	3.9	5.9	8.1	11.5	15.7	25.7%		
6	1.8	2.1	3.2	4.4	5.6	7.9	11.0	16.2%	
7	1.9	2.0	3.1	4.0	5.6	7.7	10.4	14.3	20.2%
8	1.9	1.9	2.7	3.3	4.6	6.2	8.9	13.6	18.1
9 (large)	1.1	1.2	1.3	1.7	2.1	2.8	4.1	5.9	8.0

SOURCE: Thomas F. Loeb, "Trading Cost: The Critical Link Between Investment Information and Results," *Financial Analysis Journal* 39, no. 3 (May/June 1983): 41–2.

Table 3.3. Values range from over 27% (for small capitalization stocks) to 1.2% (for large capitalization stocks).

Panel (b) of Figure 3.4 shows the relationship between order size and transaction cost for each of the three largest capitalization sectors, which correspond to the last three rows of panel (b) of Table 3.3. The figure shows that the impact of a very large order on price can be substantial, and the impact is greater for smaller capitalizations.

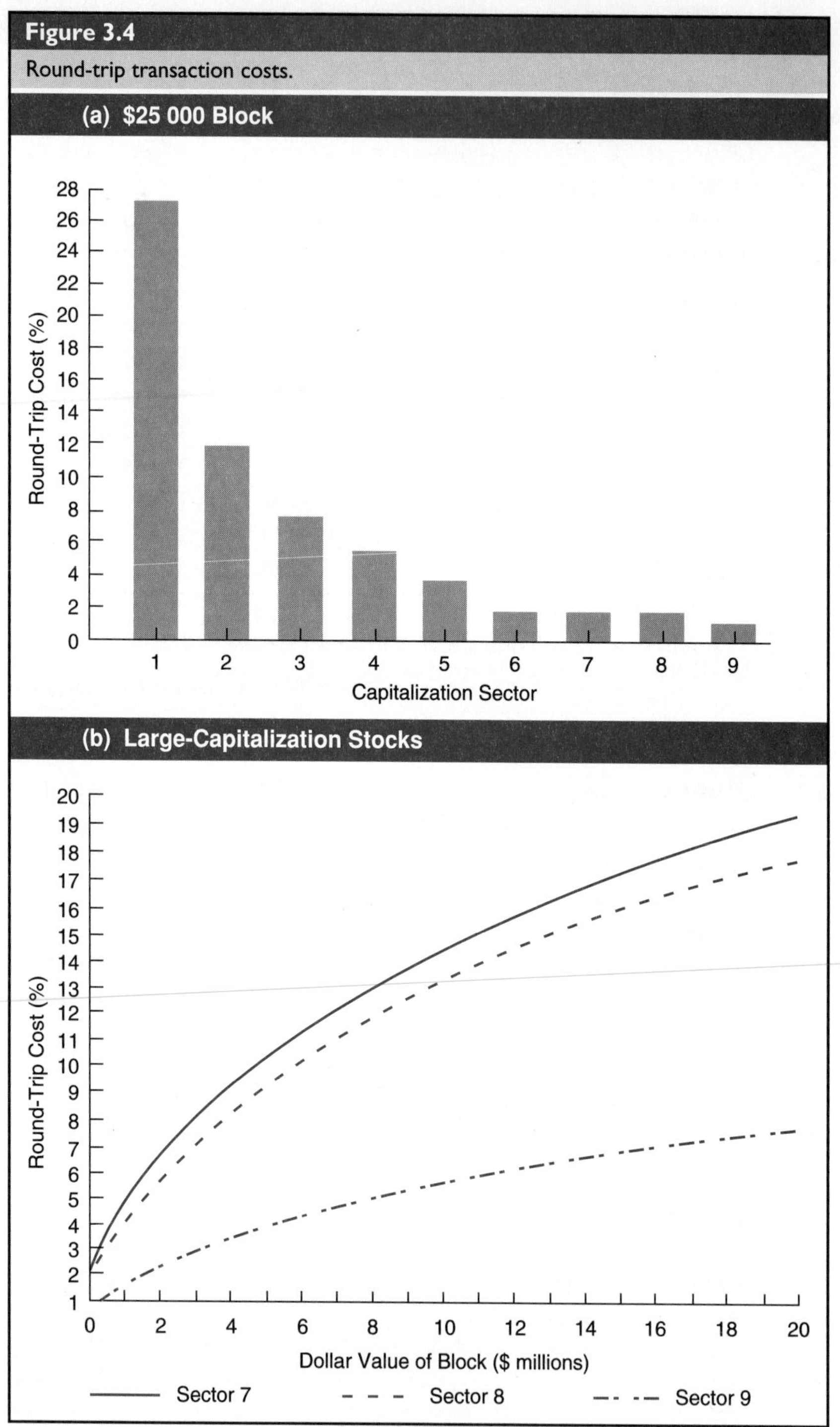
Figure 3.4
Round-trip transaction costs.
(a) $25 000 Block
Round-Trip Cost (%)
28
26
24
22
20
18
16
14
12
10
8
6
4
2
0
1
2
3
4
5
6
7
8
9
Capitalization Sector
(b) Large-Capitalization Stocks
Round-Trip Cost (%)
20
19
18
17
16
15
14
13
12
11
10
9
8
7
6
5
4
3
2
1
0
2
4
6
8
10
12
14
16
18
20
Dollar Value of Block ($ millions)
Sector 7
Sector 8
Sector 9

PRIMARY DISTRIBUTIONS

The discussion so far has focused on secondary markets for securities, where securities that were initially issued at some previous point in time are subsequently traded. The focus now shifts to the primary market for securities, which is the name given to the markets where the initial issuance itself takes place. Some issuers deal directly with purchasers in this market, but many rely on **investment dealers** who act as **underwriters** by serving as intermediaries between issuers and the ultimate purchasers of their securities.[19]

Private Placements

In some instances, issuers decide that only a few large institutional investors should be solicited, and the entire issue is sold to one or more of them. Such **private placements** are frequently used for bond issues, with the dealer acting as an agent for the issuing corporation. As long as the minimum cash value of the issue is greater than $150 000 and relatively few potential buyers are contacted (say, less than 25), requirements for detailed disclosure, public notice, and so on may be waived, thereby considerably reducing the cost of floating an issue. These placements are often announced after the fact, via advertisements in the financial press.

Such investments, however, are illiquid because the investor is typically prohibited from selling the security within two years of the purchase date. This has resulted in few equities being sold in this manner. Instead, most private placements involve fixed-income securities that are purchased by investors who are attracted by their coupon payments, not the prospect of capital gains.

Public Sale

When a public sale is contemplated, much more must be done. Many dealers and brokers may serve as intermediaries in the process. One, acting as the "lead" underwriter, will put together a **banking group** and a **selling group**. The banking group includes firms that purchase the securities from the issuing corporation and thus underwrite part of the offering. The selling group includes firms that contact potential buyers and do the actual selling, usually on a commission basis.

The process begins with discussions between the issuing corporation and one or more investment dealers. Some issuers utilize **competitive bidding** and then select the investment dealer offering the best overall terms. This procedure is used for many government bond issues. Many corporations, however, maintain a continuing relationship with a single underwriter and negotiate the terms of each new offering with that firm. The underwriter is usually heavily involved in the planning of an offering, the terms involved, the amount to be offered, and so on, serving, in effect, as a financial consultant to the corporation.

Once the basic characteristics of an offering have been established, a preliminary **prospectus** disclosing material relevant to the prospective buyer is filed with the provincial

---

[19] Outside Canada underwriters are generally referred to as *investment bankers*. For more on investment banking, see Richard A. Brealey, Stewart C. Myers, Gordon Sick and Robert Gianmarino, *Principles of Corporate Finance*, 2nd Canadian ed. (Toronto: McGraw-Hill Ryerson, 1992); and Stephen Ross, Randolph Westerfield, Jeffrey Jaffe and Gordon Roberts, *Corporate Finance*, 1st Canadian ed. (Toronto: Irwin, 1995). For the US situation see the January/February 1986 issue of the *Journal of Financial Economics*, which contains papers presented at a symposium on investment banking.

securities commission in provinces where these are required. (This prospectus is often referred to as a **red herring**, since it has a disclaimer printed in red ink across the first page that informs the reader that it is not an offer to sell). The actual price of the security is not usually included in the preliminary prospectus, and no final sales may be made until the registration has been approved and a final prospectus issued, indicating the offer price at which the shares will be sold. The final prospectus may be issued about three weeks after all *deficiencies* regarding adequate disclosure have been resolved to the satisfaction of the securities commission. The securities commission, however, does not take a position regarding the investment merits of an offering or the reasonableness of the price.

A security issue may be completely underwritten by an investment dealer and the other members of the syndicate. If it is, the issuing corporation receives the public offering price less a stated percentage spread (although underwriters will occasionally be compensated with some combination of shares and warrants, perhaps in addition to a smaller spread). The underwriters, in turn, sell the securities at the public offering price (or less) and may take some of the securities themselves. Underwriters who provide this sort of **firm commitment** bear all the risk, since the public may not be willing to buy the entire issue.

Not all agreements are of this type. In the case of a **rights offering** (where the current shareholders are given the opportunity to buy the new shares first), an underwriter may agree to purchase, at a fixed price, all securities not taken by current shareholders. This is termed a **standby agreement**. In the case of a non-rights offering (where the shares are offered to the general public first), members of a selling group may serve as agents instead of dealers, agreeing only to handle an offering on a **best-efforts basis.**

During the period when new securities remain unsold, the investment banker is allowed to attempt to "stabilize" the price of the security in the secondary market by standing ready to make purchases at a particular price. Such **pegging** may continue for up to ten days after the official offering date. There is a limit to the amount that can be purchased in this manner, usually stated in the agreement under which the underwriting syndicate is formed, since the members typically share the cost of such transactions. If there is to be any pegging, a statement to that effect must be included in the prospectus.

In any security transaction, there may be explicit and implicit costs. In a primary distribution, the explicit cost is the underwriting spread and the implicit cost is any difference between the public offering price and the price that might have been obtained otherwise. The spread provides the underwriter with compensation for selling the issue and bearing the risk that the issue may not be completely sold to the public, thereby leaving them with ownership of the unsold shares. The lower the public offering price, the smaller the risk that the issue will not be sold quickly at that price. If an issue is substantially underpriced, the selling group can be assured that the securities will sell rapidly, requiring little or no support in the secondary market. Since many corporations deal with only one underwriter and since the larger investment dealers rely on one another for inclusion in syndicates, it has been alleged that issuers pay too much in spreads, given the prices at which their securities are offered. In other words, the returns to underwriting are alleged to be overly large relative to the risks involved, owing to ignorance on the part of issuers or the existence of an informal cartel among investment dealers.

► Underpricing of Ipo's

Whether or not returns to underwriting are overly large, a number of **initial public offerings** (ipo's) appear to be underpriced. Ipo's are the first offerings of shares of a company to the

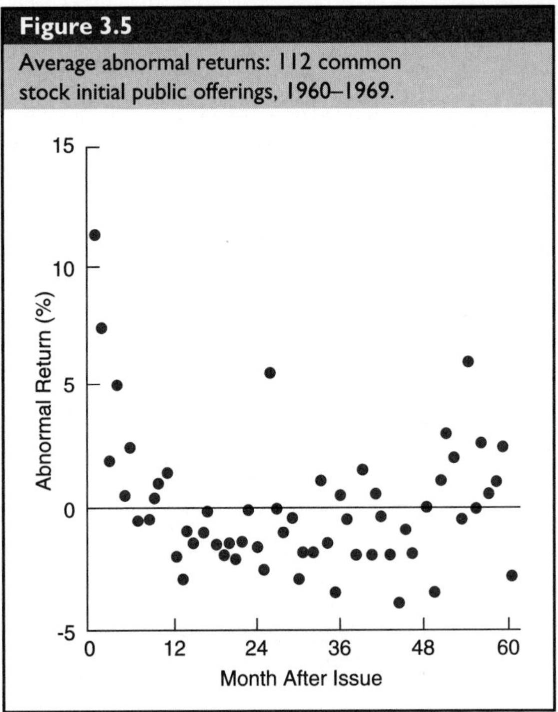

Figure 3.5

Average abnormal returns: 112 common stock initial public offerings, 1960–1969.

SOURCE: Roger G. Ibbotson, "Price Performance of Common Stock New Issues," *Journal of Financial Economics* 2, no. 3 (September 1975): 252.

public and are sometimes referred to as **unseasoned offerings**. The abnormal returns for a sample of ipo's in the US are shown in Figure 3.5. Each one of the first 60 months after the initial offering is shown on the horizontal axis, and the corresponding average abnormal return, meaning the average return over and above that of stocks of equal risk, is shown on the vertical axis. The leftmost point indicates the average abnormal return obtained by an investor who purchased such a stock at its offering price and sold it for the bid price at the end of the month during which it was offered. The average abnormal return was substantial: 11.4%. The remaining points show the average abnormal returns that could have been obtained by an investor who purchased the security in the secondary market at the beginning of the month indicated and then sold it in the secondary market at the end of that particular month. Some of these post-offering abnormal returns were positive, but most were negative.

On the average, offerings of these unseasoned securities appear to have been underpriced. Investors able to purchase a cross-section of such shares at their offering prices might thus expect better performance than those holding other securities of equal risk. It is not surprising that such offerings are often rationed by the members of the selling group to "favoured" customers. It is "not uncommon for underwriters to receive, prior to the effective date, 'public indication of interest' for five times the number of shares available."[20] Unfavoured customers are presumably allowed to buy only the new issues that are not

[20] Securities and Exchange Commission, *Report of Special Study on Security Markets*, 1973.

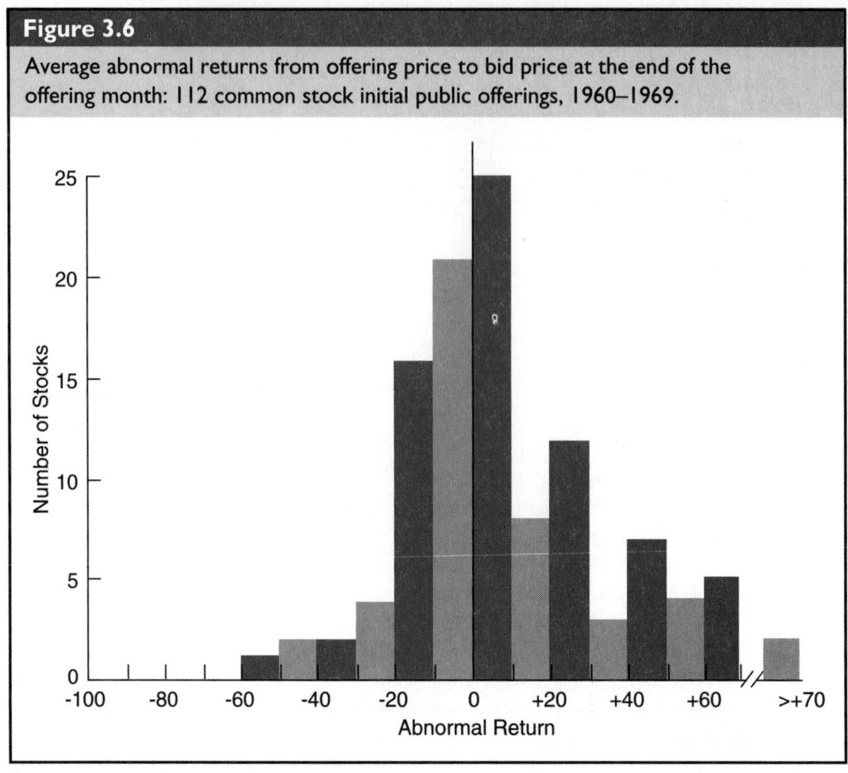

SOURCE: Roger G. Ibbotson, "Price Performance of Common Stock New Issues," *Journal of Financial Economics* 2, no. 3 (September 1975): 248.

substantially underpriced. Since costs may be incurred in becoming a favoured customer, it is not clear that even such an investor obtains abnormally large returns overall.

A subsequent study found that the initial abnormal return, measured over the time period beginning with the offering and ending when the first closing price was reported, was 14.1%.[21] Although there is evidence that the average abnormal returns remained positive over the next two months, the average abnormal return over the three-year period after the first close was –37.4%. Three other interesting observations were that (1) offerings of smaller firms had lower three-year abnormal returns than those of larger firms, (2) firms that had the highest positive initial abnormal return had the worst performance over the subsequent three-year period, and (3) younger firms going public had both higher initial abnormal returns and lower subsequent three-year abnormal returns than older firms going public.

Whereas the return obtained by the purchaser of a new issue may be substantial on average, the amount may be very good or very bad in any particular instance, as Figure 3.6

[21] Investors who quickly sell their shares in order to capture this price spurt are known as "flippers." See Jay R. Ritter, "The Long-Run Performance of Initial Public Offerings," *Journal of Finance* 46, no. 1 (March 1991): 3–27. Also, see Roger G. Ibbotson, Jody L. Sindelar, and Jay R. Ritter, "Initial Public Offerings," *Journal of Applied Corporate Finance* 1, no. 2 (Summer 1988): 37–45. An interesting explanation for the initial underpricing is provided by Kevin Rock, "Why New Issues Are Underpriced," *Journal of Financial Economics* 15, no. 1/2 (January/February 1986): 187–212.

shows. Although the odds may be in the purchaser's favour, a single investment of this type is far from a sure bet.

A Canadian study examined 115 ipo's in the period 1971 to 1983. The average *first trading day* return was 11.6% with a standard deviation of 40.2%. The minimum first day return was –81.7% and the maximum 196.7%. This duplicates the US finding that ipo's are, on average, significantly underpriced but no single investment of this type is a certain winner. The range of first-day returns recorded, however, is surprisingly large.[22]

► Seasoned Offerings

Interestingly, the announcement of a seasoned US stock offering seems to result in a decline of roughly 2% to 4% in the firm's stock price. This could be because managers tend to issue stock when they think it is overpriced in the marketplace. Thus, the announcement of the offering causes investors to revise downward their assessment of the value of the stock, leading to a price decline. A Canadian study that examined seasoned offerings found that the issuing firm's share price declined, on average, by about 1%, but reported finding little support for the theoretical assymetric information models of Myers and Majluf and Lucas and McDonald.[23]

► Shelf Registration

A recent change in Canadian regulations has made it possible for corporations to foster greater competition among underwriters. In May 1991, National Policy 44 came into force to allow firms to register securities in advance of issuance. With such a **shelf registration**, securities may be sold up to two years later. With securities "on the shelf," the corporation can request competitive bids from investment bankers and refuse to sell shares if acceptable bids are not forthcoming. There is not yet any evidence to indicate what effect this change has had on underwriting costs in Canada. Shelf registration has, however, been allowed in the US since 1982, where the evidence suggests that issuing costs have been reduced.[24]

SECONDARY DISTRIBUTIONS

As mentioned earlier, an individual or institution wishing to sell a large block of stock can do so through a secondary distribution. An investment banking group buys the block from the seller and then offers the shares to the public through an organized exchange.

---

[22] I. Krinsky and W. Rotenberg, "The Valuation of Initial Public Offerings," *Contemporary Accounting Research* 5, no. 2 (Spring, 1989): 500–514. See also V. Jog and A. Riding, "Underpricing in Canadian IPOs," *Financial Analysts Journal* (November/December 1987), who reported similar results for a sample of 100 firms. Also see V. Jog and A. Srivastava, "La Sous-evaluation des emissions premières au Canada: Une mise à jour," *Finéco* 4, no. 1 1ere semestre, 1994).

[23] See Stewart C. Myers and Nicholas S. Majluf, "Corporate Financing and Investment Decisions When Firms Have Information That Investors Do Not Have," *Journal of Financial Economics* 13, no. 2 (June 1984): 187–221; Wayne H. Mikkelson and M. Megan Partch, "Valuation Effects of Security Offerings and the Issuance Process," *Journal of Financial Economics* 15, no. 1/2 (January/February 1986): 31–60; D. Lucas and R. McDonald, "Equity Issues and Stock Price Dynamics," *Journal of Finance*, 1990; and V. Jog and H. Schaller, "Share Price Behavior around the Announcement of New Equity Issues: A New Test of the Assymetric Information Models," Carleton University Working Paper, 1991.

[24] See Sanjai Bhagat, M. Wayne Marr, and G. Rodney Thompson, "The Rule 415 Experiment: Equity Markets," *Journal of Finance* 40, no. 5 (December 1985): 1385–1401.

Figure 3.7

Prices for 345 secondary distributions, 1961–1965.

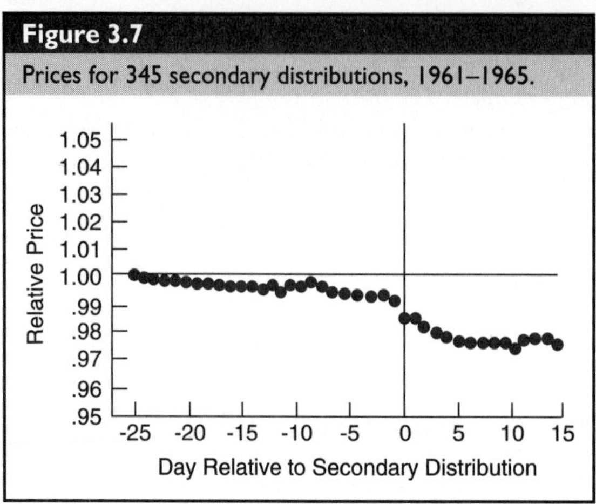

SOURCE: Myron S. Scholes, "The Market for Securities: Substitution versus Price Pressure and the Effects of Information on the Share Prices," *Journal of Business* 45, no. 2 (April 1972): 193.

All the Securities Commissions in Canada (except Quebec) require that the sale of securities from a *control position* be accompanied by a prospectus and an underwriter. A control position is one in which the person offering the shares owns a sufficient number to materially affect control of the company. In most provinces a 20% holding is deemed to represent control, although there are circumstances under which a smaller holding may be ruled to be a control position. The distribution then proceeds in the same way as a primary distribution.

The impact of the sale of a large block on the market price of the shares provides information on the resiliency of the capital market. The results of a US study are described below. Figure 3.7 shows the average price (adjusted for market changes) for 345 secondary distributions, with the price 25 days prior to the distribution taken as 1.0. On the average, a secondary distribution leads to a 2% to 3% decline in price. Since there is no evidence of a subsequent price rebound, this decline is most likely due to the information contained in the fact that someone has decided to sell. Additional analysis of these results, as shown in Table 3.4, supports the assertion. The size of the decline was related to the identity of the seller — being the greatest for sellers likely to be information-motivated and smallest for sellers likely to be liquidity-motivated.[25]

REGULATION OF SECURITY MARKETS

Securities regulation in Canada is a provincial responsibility. The first such legislation was enacted in Manitoba in 1912. Other provinces followed suit and for a considerable period legislation in this country resembled a patchwork quilt. Interprovincial cooperation has increased significantly following recognition of the fact that the Canadian market is national and increasingly becoming international in scope. In 1965, the *Report of the Attorney-General's Committee on Securities Legislation in Canada* (the Kimber Report) recommended significant

---

[25] A more recent study has confirmed these findings; see Wayne H. Mikkelson and M. Megan Partch, "Stock Price Effects and Costs of Secondary Distributions," *Journal of Financial Economics* 14, no. 2 (June 1985): 165–94.

Table 3.4

Average Price Decline Versus Type of Seller: 345 Secondary Distributions, 1961–1965.

Type of Seller	*Percentage Change in Adjusted Price from Ten Days Before the Distribution to Ten Days After the Distribution*
Corporations and officers	2.9%
Investment companies and mutual funds	2.5
Individuals	1.1
Estates	.7
Banks and insurance companies	.3

SOURCE: Myron S. Scholes, "The Market for Securities: Substitution Versus Price Pressure and the Effects of Information on Share Prices," *Journal of Business* 45, no. 2 (April 1972): 202.

revisions to Ontario's securities laws modelled on the US Securities Act of 1933 (sometimes called the truth-in-securities law) and the Securities Exchange Act of 1934. The resulting **Ontario Securities Act, 1966** required registration of new issues, disclosure of relevant information by the issuer, and prohibits misrepresentation and fraud in security sales. It also covers secondary markets by requiring national exchanges, brokers, and dealers to be registered, as well as those who counsel or advise investors and specifying reporting requirements for insider trades. Many of these provisions have been included in securities legislation enacted by other provinces. Subsequent amendments to the Ontario Securities Act have included the extension of corporate reporting requirements and the introduction of regulations governing take-over bids. An example of interprovincial cooperation in this area is the adoption of a number of national policies by all the securities commissions in the country. In this way uniformity of regulation across the country has increased.

The organization of the **Ontario Securities Commission** (OSC) is typical of most provincial commissions. There are ten commissioners consisting of a chair, two vice-chairs and seven members, plus a director who oversees day-to-day operations. Other commissions vary as to the number of members appointed by the provincial governments. The OSC differs from the securities commissions in other provinces in having a larger enforcement branch and a department dealing with derivative securities.

Securities legislation relies heavily on the principle of **self-regulation**. The securities commissions in general delegate part of their authority over trading practices for listed securities to the organized exchanges within their jurisdiction and maintain a watching brief over their activities. Trading in over-the-counter securities has been delegated to the Canadian Dealing Network Inc. (CDN) and the Investment Dealers Association (IDA).

Canadian stocks interlisted on US exchanges fall under the joint jurisdiction of the appropriate provincial body and the US Securities and Exchange Commission (SEC). The SEC imposes more stringent reporting requirements and more extensive information disclosure in prospectuses than is generally required in Canada. On the other hand, the SEC has less strict takeover rules than the OSC; therefore, interlisting may provide a way of avoiding some types of regulatory constraint. In recent years there has been increased cooperation between the SEC and the larger provincial securities commissions in such matters as insider trading, improper trading activity, fraud, and incomplete disclosure.

SUMMARY

1. Security markets facilitate the trading of securities by providing a means of bringing buyers and sellers of financial assets together.
2. In Canada, common stocks are traded primarily on organized security exchanges or in the over-the-counter market.
3. Organized security exchanges provide central physical locations where trading is done under a set of rules and regulations.
4. The primary organized security exchange in Canada is the Toronto Stock Exchange. Various regional exchanges also operate.
5. Trading on organized security exchanges is conducted only by members who transact in a special group of securities.
6. Exchange members fall into one of two categories, depending on the type of trading activity in which they engage. Those categories are order traders and registered traders.
7. Designated market makers are charged with maintaining an orderly market in their assigned stocks. In this capacity they perform two roles. They maintain a limit order book for unexecuted trades, and they act as a dealer, trading in their stocks for their own accounts.
8. In the over-the-counter (OTC) market individuals act as dealers in a manner similar to DMMs. However, unlike DMMs, OTC dealers face competition from other dealers.
9. Most of the trading in the OTC market is done through a computerized system known as the Canadian Dealer Network (CDN).
10. Trading in listed securities may not take place outside the various exchanges.
11. Foreign security markets each have their own particular operating procedures, rules, and customs.
12. Dealers typically make money trading with liquidity-motivated traders and lose money trading with adept information-motivated traders. A dealer must set a bid-ask spread that attracts sufficient revenue from the former group but avoids excessive losses to the latter.
13. Clearinghouses facilitate the transfer of securities and cash between buyers and sellers. Most Canadian security transactions are now cleared electronically.
14. The Canadian Investor Protection Fund (CIPF) is an industry organized agency that insures the accounts of clients of all brokers and members of exchanges against loss due to a brokerage firm's failure.
15. Following deregulation, commissions have been negotiated between brokerage firms and their larger clients. In a competitive environment, commission rates typically vary inversely with the size of the order.
16. Transaction costs are a function of the stock's bid-ask spread, the price impact of the trade, and the commission.
17. The primary market for securities involves the initial issuance of securities.
18. Although some issuers deal directly with purchasers, most hire underwriters to assist them in the sale of the securities.
19. The most prominent security market regulator is the Ontario Securities Commission (OSC), a provincial agency directed by ten commissioners. Regulation of the Canadian security markets involves both federal and provincial laws.
20. The OSC has delegated to the TSE, the CDN, and the IDA the power to control trading practices through a system of self-regulation.

QUESTIONS AND PROBLEMS

1. Differentiate between the role of a DMM on the TSE and the role of a dealer on the CDN system.
2. Give several reasons why a corporation might desire to have its stock listed on the TSE.
3. Describe the functions of order traders and registered traders.
4. Pigeon Falls Fertilizer Company is listed on the TSE. George Hartnett, the DMM handling Pigeon Falls stock, is currently bidding 35.30 and asking 35.40. What would be the likely outcomes of the following trading orders?
   a. Through a broker, Eva Rooney places a market order to buy 100 shares of Pigeon Falls stock. No other broker from the crowd takes the order.
   b. Through a broker, Eva places a limit order to sell 100 shares of Pigeon Falls stock at 36.
   c. Through a broker, Eva places a limit order to buy 100 shares of Pigeon Falls stock at 35.35. Another broker offers to sell 100 shares of Pigeon Falls stock at 35.35.
5. The limit order screen for International Enterprises appears as follows:

Limit-Sell		*Limit-Buy*	
Price	*Shares*	*Price*	*Shares*
$30.250	200	$29.750	100
30.375	500	29.000	100
30.500	300	28.500	200
30.875	800	27.125	100
31.000	200	26.875	200

   The last trade in the stock took place at $30.
   a. If a market order to sell 200 shares arrives, what will happen?
   b. If another market order to sell 100 shares arrives just moments later, what will happen?
6. Because DMMs such as Chuck Goodwin are charged with maintaining a "fair and orderly" market, at times they will be required to sell when others are buying and buy when others are selling. How can Chuck earn a profit when required to act in such a manner?
7. Why is the CDN so important to the success of the OTC market?
8. Why was the deregulation of commissions such an important event for the TSE?
9. What is the purpose of CIPF insurance? Under what conditions might CIPF insurance be expected to be effective? Under what conditions might it fail to accomplish its objectives?
10. After deregulation, why did commission rates fall so sharply for large investors, but decline so little (or even increase) for small investors?
11. Transaction costs can be thought of as being derived from three sources. Identify and describe those sources.
12. What functions does a clearinghouse perform?
13. Fred Basinski is considering an investment in Palmer Lumber Company. Based on an analysis of Palmer's prospects, Fred expects the company's stock to rise from $40 to $45 over the next six months. Using data in Table 3.3(b), Palmer stock is in sector 1. Fred plans to invest $25 000 in the company and then liquidate the investment six months later. Given Fred's price appreciation expectations, is this investment likely to be profitable? Why?

14. Describe the primary conclusions of the results of the trading cost study presented in Table 3.3.
15. Why are liquid and continuous secondary security markets important to the effective functioning of primary security markets?
16. Describe the role of an underwriting syndicate in a public security offering.
17. Distinguish between a competitive bid underwriting and a negotiated underwriting.
18. Investment bankers frequently attempt to stabilize the price of a newly issued security in the secondary market.
    a. How is this stabilization accomplished?
    b. What is the purpose of the stabilization?
    c. What can go wrong with the stabilization attempts?
19. Why must companies that publicly issue securities file a prospectus with the OSC? What does the OSC's acceptance of the prospectus imply?
20. Discuss why ipo's appear to generate abnormal returns for investors. Are these returns a "sure thing"? What are the economic implications of these high returns for ipo issuers?

KEY TERMS

security market
secondary market
call market
continuous market
liquidity
organized exchange
public governor
seat
member firm
listed security
delisted shares
trading halt
trading representative
order trader
registered trader
designated market maker (DMM)
minimum guaranteed fill (MGF)
bid price
ask price
double auction
bid-ask spread
blocks
regional exchange
Canadian Dealing Network (CDN)
markup
markdown
specialist
trading post
limit order book
dealer
information-motivated trader
liquidity-motivated trader
Canadian Investor Protection Fund (CIPF)
soft dollars
May Day
market capitalization
price impacts
investment dealer
underwriter
private placement
banking group
selling group
competitive bidding
prospectus
red herring
firm commitment
rights offering
standby agreement
best-efforts basis
pegging
initial public offering (ipo's)
unseasoned offering
shelf registration
Ontario Securities Act, 1996
Ontario Securities Commission (OSC)
self-regulation

REFERENCES

1. A good reference source for Canadian stock markets is:

   The Canadian Securities Course (Toronto: The Canadian Securities Institute, 1992).

2. Other valuable sources are the following fact books, which are updated annually:

   New York Stock Exchange, *Fact Book.* (To order, write: New York Stock Exchange, Publications Department, 1 Wall St., New York, NY 10005, USA.)

   American Stock Exchange, *American Stock Exchange Fact Book.* (To order, write: American Stock Exchange, Publications Department, 86 Trinity Place, New York, NY 10006, USA.)

   National Association of Security Dealers, *Nasdaq Fact Book & Company Directory.* (To order, write: National Association of Security Dealers, NASD MediaSource, P.O. Box 9403, Gaithersburg, MD 20898–9403, USA.)

   London Stock Exchange, *Stock Exchange Official Yearbook 1992–1993* (1993). (To order, write: The Publicity and Promotions Department, The London Stock Exchange, London EC2N 1HP, UK)

   Toronto Stock Exchange Press, *1994 Official Trading Statistics.* (To order, write: The Toronto Stock Exchange, Strategic Research & Planning, The Exchange Tower, 2 First Canadian Place, Toronto, Ontario M5X 1J2.)

   Tokyo Stock Exchange, *Tokyo Stock Exchange 1993 Fact Book.* (To order, write: Tokyo Stock Exchange, New York Research Office, 45 Broadway, New York, NY 10006, USA.)

3. For a description of various stock markets, see:

   Guiseppe Tullio and Giorgio P. Szego, eds., "Equity Markets—An International Comparison: Part A," *Journal of Banking and Finance* 13, nos. 4/5 (September 1989): 479–782.

   Guiseppe Tullio and Giorgio P. Szego, eds., "Equity Markets—An International Comparison: Part A," *Journal of Banking and Finance* 14, nos. 2/3 (August 1990): 231–672.

   Roger D. Huang and Hans R. Stoll, *Major World Equity Markets: Current Structure and Prospects for Change*, Monograph Series in Finance and Economics 1991–1993, New York University Salomon Center, New York, 1991.

   Roger D. Huang and Hans R. Stoll, "The Design of Trading Systems: Lessons from Abroad," *Financial Analysts Journal* 48, no. 5 (September/October 1992): 49–54.

4. Other useful sources for information on market microstructure are:

   Ian Domowitz, "The Mechanics of Automated Execution System," *Journal of Financial Intermediation* 1, no. 2 (June 1990): 167–194.

   Lawrence E. Harris, *Liquidity, Trading Rules, and Electronic Trading Systems*, Monograph Series in Finance and Economics 1990–1994, New York University Salomon Center, New York, 1990.

   Peter A. Abken, "Globalization of Stock, Futures, and Options Markets," *Federal Reserve Bank of Atlanta Economic Review* 76, no. 4 (July/August 1991): 1–22.

5. For a discussion of the effects of listing and delisting on a firm's stock, see:

John J. McConnell and Gary C. Sanger, "The Puzzle in Post-Listing Common Stock Returns," *Journal of Finance* 42, no. 1 (March 1987): 119–140.

Gary C. Sanger and James D. Peterson, "An Empirical Analysis of Common Stock Delistings," *Journal of Financial and Quantitative Analysis* 25, no. 2 (June 1990): 261–272.

6. Empirical studies that examine the costs of trading include:

Walter Bagehot, "The Only Game in Town," *Financial Analysts Journal* 27, no. 2 (March/April 1971): 12–14, 22.

Larry J. Cuneo and Wayne H. Wagner, "Reducing the Cost of Stock Trading," *Financial Analysts Journal* 31, no. 6 (November/December 1975): 35–44.

Gilbert Beebower and William Priest, "The Tricks of the Trade," *Journal of Portfolio Management* 6, no. 2 (Winter 1980): 36–42.

Jack L. Treynor, "What Does It Take to Win the Trading Game?" *Financial Analysts Journal* 37, no. 1 (January/February 1981): 55–60.

Thomas F. Loeb, "Trading Cost: The Critical Link Between Investment Information and Results," *Financial Analysts Journal* 39, no. 3 (May/June 1983): 39–44.

Stephen A. Berkowitz, Dennis E. Logue, and Eugene E. Noser, Jr., "The Total Cost of Transactions on the NYSE," *Journal of Finance* 43, no. 1 (March 1988): 97–112.

André F. Perold, "The Implementation Shortfall: Paper Versus Reality," *Journal of Portfolio Management* 14, no. 3 (Spring 1988): 4–9.

Lawrence R. Glosten and Lawrence E. Harris, "Estimating the Components of the Bid/Ask Spread," *Journal of Financial Economics* 21, no. 1 (May 1988): 123–142.

Hans R. Stoll, "Inferring the Components of the Bid-Ask Spread: Theory and Empirical Tests," *Journal of Finance* 44, no. 1 (March 1989): 115–134.

Robert W. Holthausen, Richard W. Leftwich, and David Mayers, "Large-Block Transactions, the Speed of Response, and Temporary and Permanent Stock-Price Effects," *Journal of Financial Economics* 26, no. 1 (July 1990): 71–95.

7. For a Canadian perspective on the topics covered in this chapter, see:

Jeffrey G. McIntosh and Ronald J. Daniels, "Capital Markets and the Law: The Peculiar Case of Canada," *Canadian Investment Review* III, no. 2 (Fall 1990).

K. P. Ambachtsheer, "Soft Dollars: The $60 Million Question," *Canadian Investment Review* V, no. 2 (Winter 1992).

R. Daniels, "How 'Broke' is the System of Securities Regulation?" *Canadian Investment Review* V, no. 1 (Spring 1992).

L. A. Sauvé, "L'Ecart Vendeur-Acheteur et L'Information boursière à Toronto," *Finéco* 2, no. 2 (2e semestre 1992).

P. M. Clarkson and J. Merkley, "Ex-Ante Uncertainty and the Underpricing of Initial Public Offerings: Further Canadian Evidence," *Canadian Journal of Administrative Sciences* 11, no. 1 (March 1994).

M. Robinson and R. White, "Sizing Up the Block Trading Market," *Canadian Investment Review* VII, no. 2 (Summer 1994).

N. Ursel, "Deregulation in Investment Banking and Underwriting Fees for Seasoned Common Equity Offerings on the Toronto Stock Exchange," *Proceedings*, Administration Sciences Association of Canada Conference, Windsor (June 1995).

CHAPTER 4

Investment Value and Market Price

Payments provided by securities may differ in both timing and riskiness. Thus, a security analyst must estimate when and under what conditions payments will be received (and, of course, the size of such payments). This typically requires detailed analysis of the firm involved, the industry or industries in which the firm operates, and the economy as a whole.

Once such estimates have been made, the overall investment value of the security must be determined. This generally requires conversion of uncertain future values to certain present values. The current prices of other securities can often be utilized in this process. If it is possible to obtain a similar set of payments in some other way, the market price of doing so provides a benchmark for the investment value of the security being analyzed, since an investor would not want to pay more than this for the security or to sell it for less. In some cases, however, equivalent alternatives may not exist, or the mere act of buying or selling the security in question in the quantities being considered might substantially affect the price. Under these conditions, the preferences of the investor may have to be used explicitly in the process of estimating the security's investment value.

Later chapters discuss in detail the manner in which estimated future payments can be used to determine investment value. Methods for estimating the payments and finding equivalent alternatives will be discussed after the characteristics of the securities have been introduced. In this chapter, some general principles of investment value are presented, leaving procedures designed for specific types of securities for later.

DEMAND AND SUPPLY SCHEDULES

Although there are over 300 million shares of the Royal Bank of Canada common stock outstanding, on an average day less than 350 thousand shares will be traded, despite the fact that this is one of the most actively traded stocks on the TSE. What determines the prices at which such trades take place? A simple (and correct) answer is demand and supply. A more fundamental (and also correct) answer is investors' estimates of the Royal Bank's future earnings and dividends, since such estimates greatly influence demand and supply. Before dealing with such influences, it is useful to examine the role of demand and supply in the determination of security prices.

As shown in the preceding chapter, securities are traded by many people in many different ways. Whereas the forces that determine prices are similar in all markets, they are slightly more obvious in markets using periodic "calls"; one such market, mentioned in Chapter 3, is the Tokyo Stock Exchange, where the *saitori* use the *itayose* method of price determination at the twice-a-day openings.

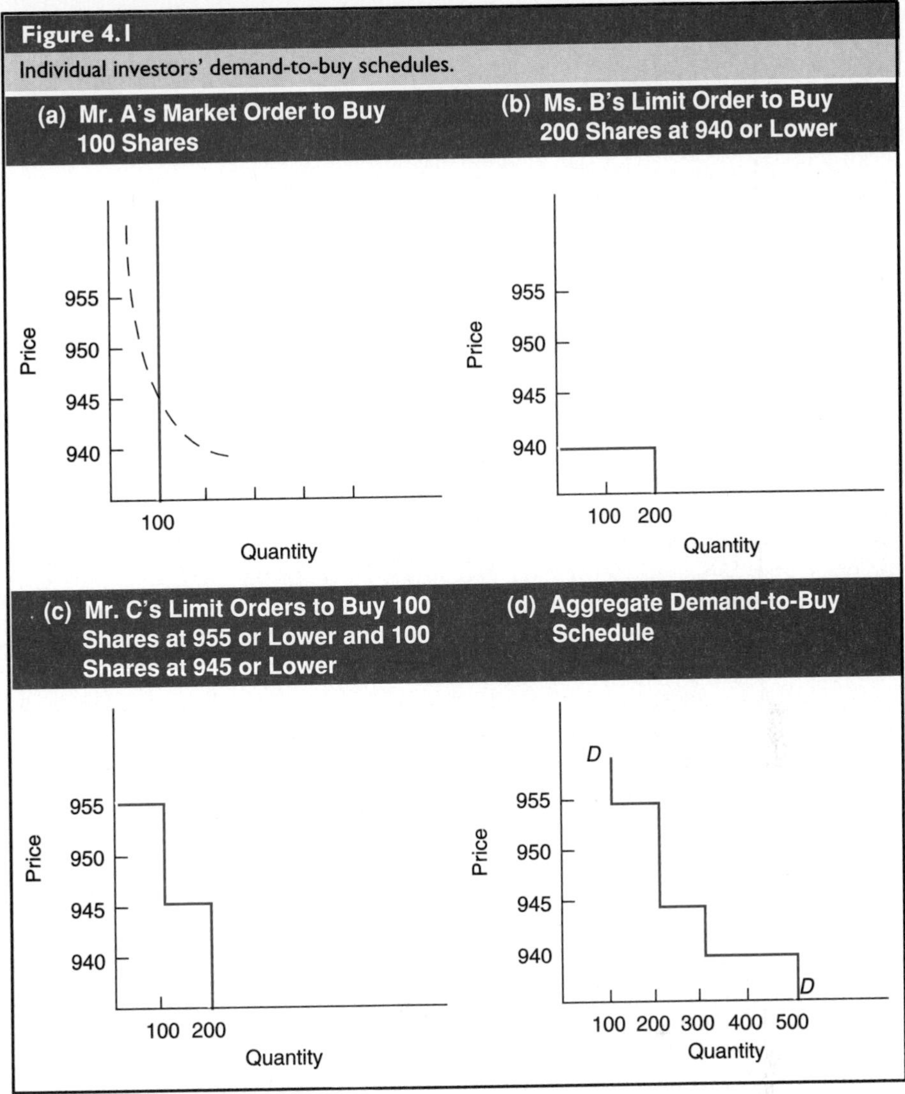

Figure 4.1

Individual investors' demand-to-buy schedules.

The Demand-to-Buy Schedule

At a designated time, all brokers holding orders to buy or sell shares of a given stock for customers gather at a specified location on the floor of the exchange. Some of the orders are market orders. For example, Mr. A may have instructed his broker to buy 100 shares of Minolta at the lowest possible price, whatever it is. His personal **demand-to-buy schedule** at that time is shown in Figure 4.1(a): he wishes to buy 100 shares no matter what the price. Although this schedule captures the contractual nature of Mr. A's market order at a specific point in time, Mr. A undoubtedly has a good idea that his ultimate purchase price will be near the price for which orders were executed just before he placed his order. Thus, his true demand schedule might be sloping downward from the upper-left portion to the lower-right portion of the graph. This is shown by the dashed line in the figure. It indicates his desire to buy more shares if the price is lower. However, to simplify his own tasks as well

Figure 4.2

Individual investors' supply-to-sell schedules.

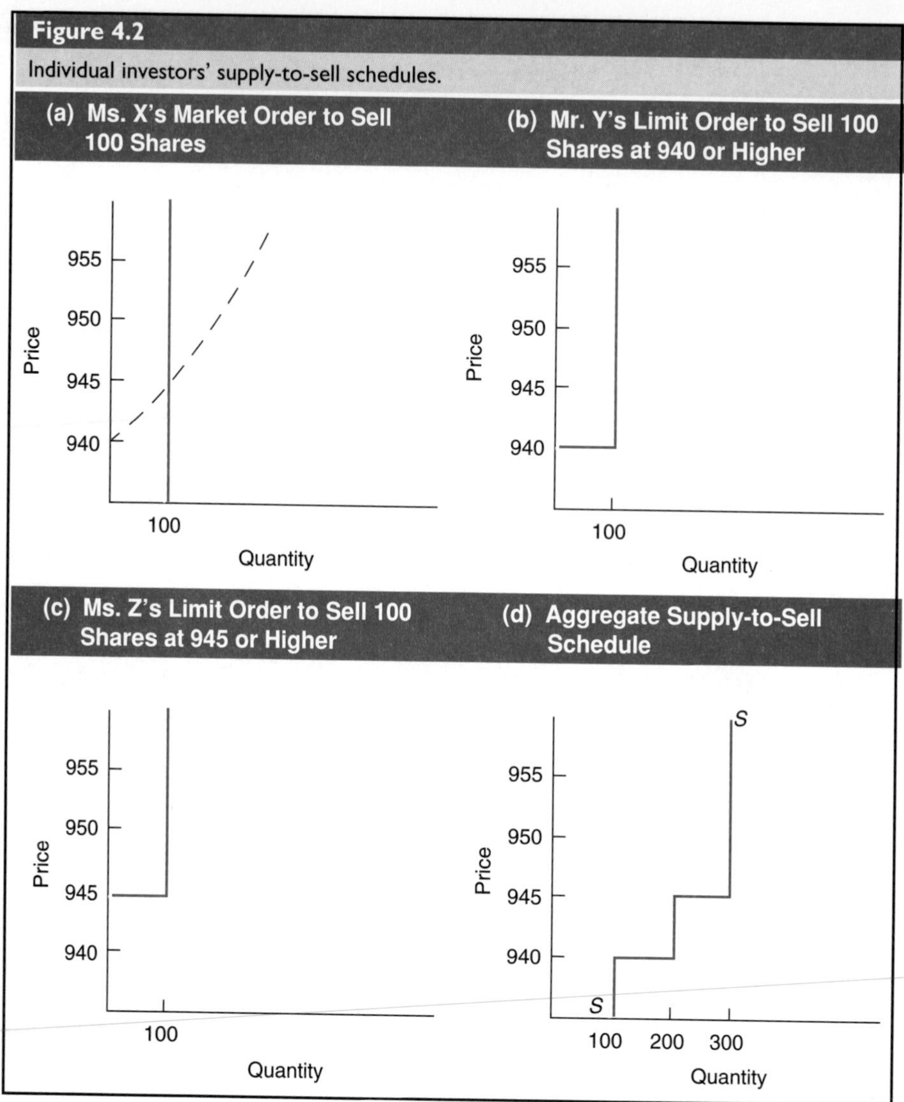

as his broker's tasks, he has estimated that the price for which his order will ultimately be executed will be in the range at which he would choose to hold 100 shares. In the example shown here, this price is 945 yen per share.

Other customers may place limit orders with their brokers. Thus, Ms. B may have instructed her broker to buy 200 shares of Minolta at the lowest possible price if and only if that price is less than or equal to 940 yen per share. Her demand schedule is shown in Figure 4.1(b).

Some customers may give their broker two or more orders for the same security. Thus, Mr. C may wish to buy 100 shares of Minolta at a price of 955 or less, plus an additional 100 shares if the price is at or below 945. To do this, Mr. C places a limit order for 100 shares at 955 and a second limit order for 100 shares at 945. Figure 4.1(c) portrays his demand schedule.

If one could look at all the brokers' books and aggregate all the orders to buy Minolta (both market and limit orders), it would be possible to determine how many shares would be bought at every possible price. Assuming that only Mr. A, Ms. B, and Mr. C have placed buy orders, the resulting aggregate demand-to-buy schedule would look like line *DD* in Figure 4.1(d). Note that at lower prices more shares would be demanded.

The Supply-to-Sell Schedule

Brokers will also hold market orders to sell shares of Minolta. For example, Ms. X may have placed a market order to sell 100 shares of Minolta at the highest possible price. Figure 4.2(a) displays her **supply-to-sell schedule**. As with market orders to buy, customers generally place such orders on the supposition that the actual price will be in the range in which their true desire to sell the stated number of shares would lie. Thus, Ms. X's actual supply schedule might appear more like the dashed line in Figure 4.2(a), indicating her willingness to sell more shares at higher prices.

Customers may also place limit orders to sell shares of Minolta. For example, Mr. Y may have placed a limit order to sell 100 shares at a price of 940 or higher, and Ms. Z may have placed a limit order to sell 100 shares at a price of 945 or higher. Panels (b) and (c) of Figure 4.2 illustrate these two supply-to-sell schedules.

As with the buy orders, if one could look at all the brokers' books and aggregate all the orders to sell Minolta (both market and limit orders), it would be possible to determine how many shares would be sold at every possible price. Assuming that only Ms. X, Mr. Y, and Ms. Z have placed sell orders, the resulting aggregate supply-to-sell schedule would look like line *SS* in Figure 4.2(d). Note that at higher prices more shares would be supplied.

Interaction of the Schedules

The aggregate demand and supply schedules are shown on one graph in Figure 4.3. Generally, no one would have enough information to draw the actual schedules. However, this in no way diminishes the usefulness of the schedules as representations of the underlying forces that are interacting to determine the market-clearing price of Minolta.

What actually happens when all the brokers gather together with their order books in hand? A *saitori* "calls out" a price—for example, 940 yen per share. The brokers then try to complete transactions with one another at that price. Those with orders to buy at that price signify the number of shares they wish to buy. Those with orders to sell do likewise. Some tentative deals will be made, but as Figure 4.3 shows, more shares will be demanded at 940 than will be supplied. In particular, 300 shares will be demanded, but only 200 shares will be supplied. When trading is completed (meaning all possible tentative deals have been made), there will be a number of brokers calling "buy" but nobody will stand ready to sell to them. The price of 940 is too low.

Seeing this, the *saitori* will cry out a different price—for example, 950. Since the previous trades are all cancelled at this point, the brokers will consult their order books once again and signify the extent to which they are willing to buy or sell shares at this new price. In this case, as Figure 4.3 shows, when trading is completed, there will be a number of brokers calling "sell," but nobody will stand ready to buy from them. In particular, 300 shares will be supplied but there will be a demand for only 200 shares. The price of 950 is too high.

Undaunted, the *saitori* will try again, and again, if necessary. Only when there are relatively few unsatisfied brokers will the price (and the associated tentative deals) be declared

Figure 4.3

Determining a security's price by the interaction of the demand-to-buy and supply-to-sell schedules.

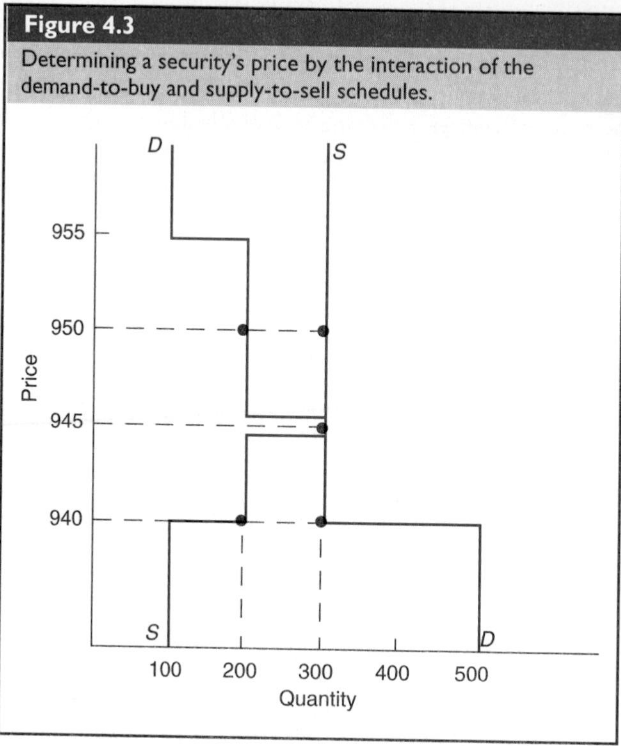

final. As Figure 4.3 shows, 945 is such a price. At 945, customers collectively wish to sell 300 shares. Furthermore, there is a collective demand for 300 shares at this price. Thus, quantity demanded equals quantity supplied. The price is "just right."

Another way to view this process is to focus on the quantity that would actually be traded at any given price. For any particular price, this is the smaller of (1) the quantity people are willing to buy and (2) the quantity others are willing to sell, as shown in Figure 4.4. At the price where the quantity that would be traded is maximized, demand will equal supply. As can be seen in the figure, this occurs at a price of 945.

Trading procedures employed in security markets vary from auction markets to dealer markets and from call markets to continuous markets. However, the similarities are more important than the differences. In Canada, for example, Designated Market-Makers at the Toronto Stock Exchange and dealers in the over-the-counter market provide some of the functions of the *saitori* at the Tokyo Stock Exchange, and trades can take place at any time. Nevertheless, the basic principles of security price determination still operate. In general, market price equates quantity demanded with quantity supplied.

DEMAND-TO-HOLD SECURITIES

For some purposes it is useful to ignore moment-to-moment changes in customers' orders and focus instead on the fundamental forces at work. Instead of asking how many shares an investor wishes to buy or sell at a given price, the number of shares the investor wishes to hold at that price can be determined. There is, of course, a close relationship between the two quantities. If an investor wishes to hold more shares than are currently held, the

Figure 4.4
Aggregate quantity traded.

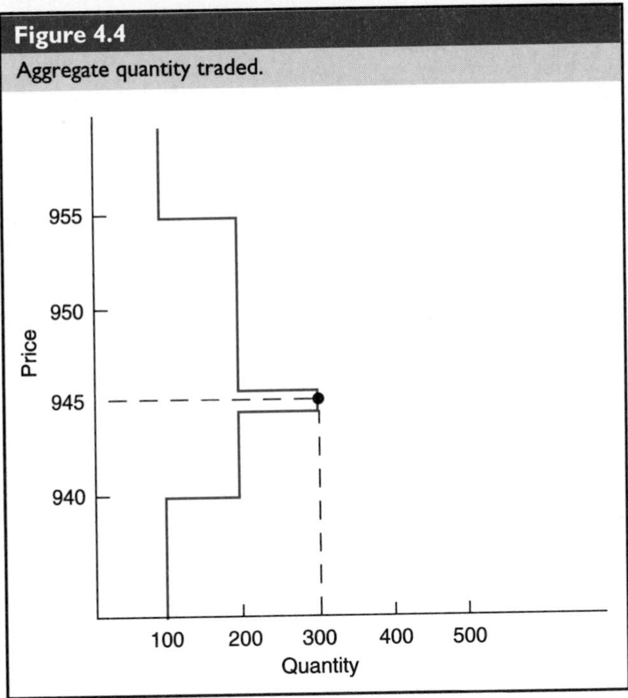

difference is the investor's demand-to-buy schedule. Conversely, if an investor wishes to hold fewer shares than are currently held, the difference is the investor's supply-to-sell schedule.

The Demand-to-Hold Schedule

In Figure 4.5 one investor's **demand-to-hold schedule** for a security is shown by curve *dd*. This simply plots the number of shares that the investor wishes to hold at each possible price. In general, lower prices are associated with larger numbers of shares. Of course, the entire schedule is predicated on the investor's current feelings about the security's future prospects. If something makes the investor more optimistic about the security, he or she will generally wish to hold more shares at any given price. In that case, the entire schedule may shift to the right, as shown by curve $d'd'$. Alternatively, if something makes the investor more pessimistic about the security, the entire curve may shift to the left, as shown by curve $d''d''$.

A factor that complicates an analysis of this type is the tendency for some investors to regard sudden and substantial price changes in a security as indicators of changes in the future prospects of the issuer. In the absence of further information, an investor may interpret such a change as an indication that "someone knows something that I don't know." While exploring the situation, the investor may at least temporarily revise his or her own assessment of the issuer's prospects and, in doing so, may alter the demand-to-hold schedule. For this reason, few investors place limit orders at prices substantially different from the current price, for fear that such orders would be executed only if prospects changed significantly, giving recognition to the idea that a careful reevaluation would be in order before buying or selling shares under such conditions.

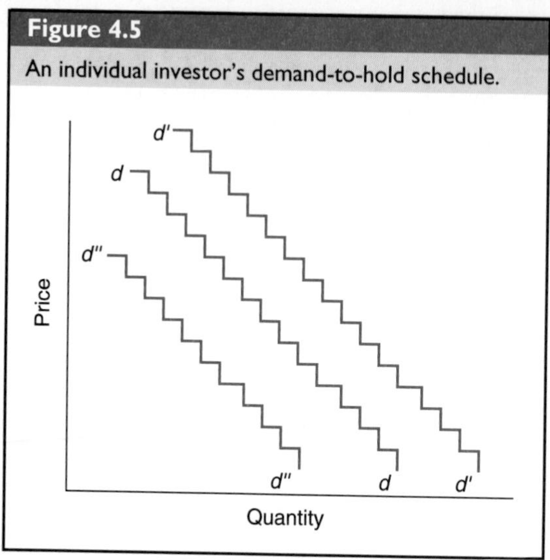

Figure 4.5
An individual investor's demand-to-hold schedule.

Despite this complication, it is possible to construct an aggregate schedule indicating the total number of shares of a given firm that investors will wish to hold at various prices, assuming no change in their views of the relative prospects of the firm. This overall demand-to-hold schedule, obtained by adding the individual investors' demand-to-hold schedules, would look like curve *DD* in Figure 4.6. In the short run, at least, the available number of shares is fixed—for example, at *Q* in the figure. Only one price will equate the aggregate demand-to-hold with the available number of shares. In Figure 4.6, it is *P*. At any higher price, current holders of the security will collectively wish to hold fewer shares than are outstanding. In their attempts to sell such shares, they will drive the price down until they or others are willing to hold all the shares. Conversely, if the price is below *P*, investors will collectively wish to hold more shares than are available. In their attempts to buy shares, they will drive the price up until they no longer want additional shares. Ultimately, the price will settle at *P*, where the aggregate demand equals the available quantity.

► Elasticity of the Schedule

How elastic (that is, flat) will the aggregate demand-to-hold schedule for a security be? The answer depends in part on the extent to which the security is regarded as "unique." Securities are considered "more unique" when they have few close substitutes. Securities are considered "less unique" when they have more close substitutes. This means that the aggregate demand schedule will be more elastic (that is, more flat) for less unique securities. Equivalently, the less unique a security is, the greater the increase in the quantity demanded will be for a given fall in price. This is because these shares will produce a smaller increase in the typical portfolio's risk when substituted for other shares.

► Shifts of the Schedule

If one investor becomes more optimistic about the prospects for a security, while at the same time another investor becomes more pessimistic about the same security, they may very likely trade with one another with no effect on the aggregate demand-to-hold schedule. In this situation there will be no change in the market price for the security. However, if more

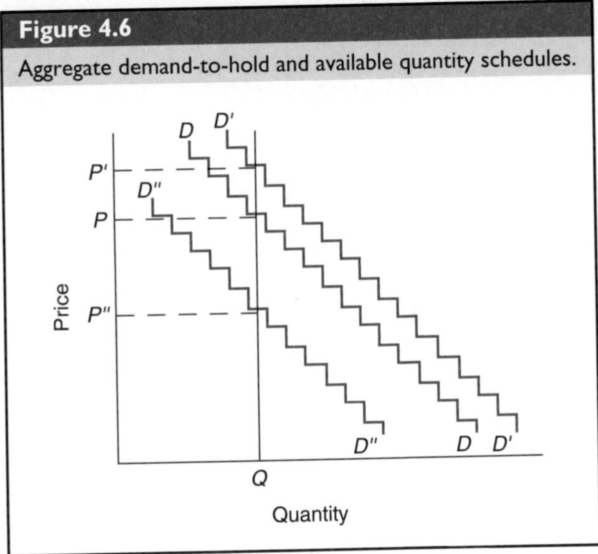

Figure 4.6
Aggregate demand-to-hold and available quantity schedules.

investors become optimistic rather than pessimistic, the schedule will shift to the right (for example, to $D'D'$ in Figure 4.6), causing an increase in price (to P'). Correspondingly, if more investors become pessimistic than optimistic, the schedule will shift to the left (for example, to $D''D''$ in Figure 4.6), causing a decrease in price (to P'').

THE EFFECTS OF PROCEDURES FOR SHORT SALES

Thus far, the individual investor's demand-to-hold schedule has been drawn only in the region of positive quantities. But there is more to it: the higher the price, the smaller the quantity the investor will wish to hold. At some price, the desired amount is zero, and at higher prices, the investor may consider short selling the security.

If short sellers received the proceeds from such sales, an individual investor's demand-to-hold schedule for a given security would look like the curve in Figure 4.7(a). This curve can be thought of in either of two ways: as a demand curve (that is, at price A, the investor wishes to hold quantity B) or as a marginal value curve (that is, if quantity B is held, the marginal value of one share more or less will be the amount A).

In fact, however, short sellers do not receive the proceeds of such sales. Instead, these proceeds are held by the short seller's brokerage firm as collateral. In most instances, the short seller does not even receive interest on this money and, furthermore, short sellers must meet margin requirements on the face amount of the short-sale proceeds. This changes the situation from that shown in Figure 4.7(a). Selling a security one owns generates cash that can be used for other purposes, but selling a security that one does not own requires an investment of cash. Thus, the decision to go short requires a higher price than it would if the short seller got the full use of the proceeds. The effective demand-to-hold schedule would look like the curve in Figure 4.7(b). To the right of the vertical axis the curve is the same as in Figure 4.7(a), but to the left the curve is higher.

INSTITUTIONAL ISSUES

The Arizona Stock Exchange: A Better Mousetrap

So you think that supply and demand curves are merely esoteric figments of ivory-tower thinking. Perhaps a valid concept, you say, but they cannot possibly be of any practical use in establishing security prices. Well, do not tell that to AZX Inc. Since early 1991 that organization (or its predecessor, Wunsch Auction Systems, Inc.) has been conducting regular security auctions among institutional investors for a broad list of common stocks. Market clearing prices in those auctions are determined by the explicit interaction of the investors' supply and demand preferences.

Step back for a moment and recall how prices are set on organized security exchanges or the OTC market (see Chapter 3). Dealers (whether specialists or OTC dealers) "make markets" in particular securities—that is, acting as intermediaries, they buy and sell from other investors for their own accounts. The dealers quote prices (bid-asked) to sellers and buyers on a continuous basis. They adjust prices as they sense supply and demand building and ebbing. It is the competitive efforts of these intermediaries that determine security prices.

AZX has developed a market mechanism quite different from that of the conventional dealer markets. AZX calls this mechanism the Arizona Stock Exchange, although it bears no resemblance to any existing stock exchange. (The name derives from financial support provided to AZX by the state of Arizona.) The concept behind the Arizona Stock Exchange is simple. Auctions are scheduled on a regular basis (currently daily at 5 p.m. EST, after the New York Stock Exchange closes). Prior to a scheduled auction, investors submit orders electronically to buy or sell specified quantities of a security at specified prices (essentially limit orders—see Chapter 2).

At the time of the auction, the orders of all participating investors are aggregated by computer—that is, the computer calculates supply and demand curves for each security being auctioned. The intersection of these curves determines the market clearing price for a security. At that price the maximum number of shares of stock will be exchanged. (All buy orders above and all sell orders below the equilibrium price are matched, whereas orders at the equilibrium price are matched on a time priority basis.)

Investors are able to access the auction order information (in graphic or tabular form) up to the time of the auction through an open limit order book. As opposed to a specialist's proprietary closed limit order book, the Arizona Stock Exchange permits investors to examine the current supply and demand for a stock. This allows investors to raise their bid prices (or lower their asked prices) to adjust to the current market conditions. In order to prevent manipulative behaviour, withdrawn orders incur a penalty charge.

The Arizona Stock Exchange possesses some intriguing advantages over traditional dealer markets:

1. It is simple and fair. All investors have access to the same auction information, and all investors trade at the same price.
2. Investors have direct access to the market. This feature removes the inherent conflicts of interest present in dealer markets.
3. Investors' orders are anonymous. Orders and trade executions are handled by computer.
4. It matches "natural" buyers and sellers (those with an explicit desire to transact), thereby perhaps establishing more robust and stable prices.
5. Transaction costs are low (about 1¢ per share versus 10¢ to 20¢ per share in dealer markets).

This last point warrants elaboration. Traditional dealer markets are continuous—trading can occur at any time during the trading day.

INSTITUTIONAL ISSUES (continued)

Continuous trading mechanisms are expensive and require dealers because the "other side" of a trade is not always immediately available. Dealers provide liquidity to investors who wish to transact immediately. With more frequent large trades having been made by institutional investors in the last decade, the ability of dealer markets to provide continuous liquidity has been severely tested. The market crash of October 1987 was an extreme, but not singular, example.

Many (and perhaps most) institutional investors do not require immediate liquidity. They can wait several hours to trade, particularly if by waiting their transaction costs are reduced significantly. In lieu of the continuous intervention of the dealer, the Arizona Stock Exchange substitutes a periodic call to market. Without the expensive overhead of the dealer, the Arizona Stock Exchange can afford to match buyers and sellers at a small fraction of the cost of the dealer market.

What are the disadvantages of the Arizona Stock Exchange? Conceptually, there are none to investors who do not require immediate liquidity. However, if you throw a party and no one comes, the party is a failure no matter how elaborate the preparations. Likewise, to be successful, AZX must attract enough institutional investors to generate sufficient liquidity and to contribute to the "discovery" of market prices. Consequently, AZX must overcome investor inertia and ignorance. As with any fledgling trading mechanism, the Arizona Stock Exchange faces a catch-22: institutional investors want to see large trading volumes before they will participate, but those large volumes can occur only if institutional investors participate.

An operation like the Arizona Stock Exchange would not be permitted in Canada, where all trades must pass through an organized exchange. However, the process is very similar to the opening procedures on the TSE. In the morning all the trades that have accumulated overnight are analyzed by computer and an opening price established that ensure that the maximum number of shares will be exchanged at the opening bell.

To date traders have not beaten a path to AZX's door. Currently 20 to 25 institutional investors use the system on any given day, and daily volume runs in the range of 300 000 to 700 000 shares traded. While these figures pale in comparison to the activity on the New York Stock Exchanged, participating investors and trading volumes have been growing over the last few years.

The effect of this is shown in Figure 4.7(c). The solid curve is the effective demand-to-hold schedule. The dashed curve is the portion of the original demand curve in Figure 4.7(a) that is to the left of the vertical axis. If the current price of the security is P^*, this investor will go short only Q_1^* shares, not Q_2^* shares. Thus, his or her pessimism about the security will not have as much impact on the market as it would if short sellers got the full use of the short-sale proceeds. In a sense, the person chooses a holding (Q_1^*) at which he or she considers the marginal value (M^*) to be less than the current market price (P^*).

PRICE AS A CONSENSUS

However one chooses to analyze security price determination, it is important to remember that a free market price for a security reflects a kind of consensus. This can be seen in Figure 4.8. Assume that the current market price for this particular security is P^*.

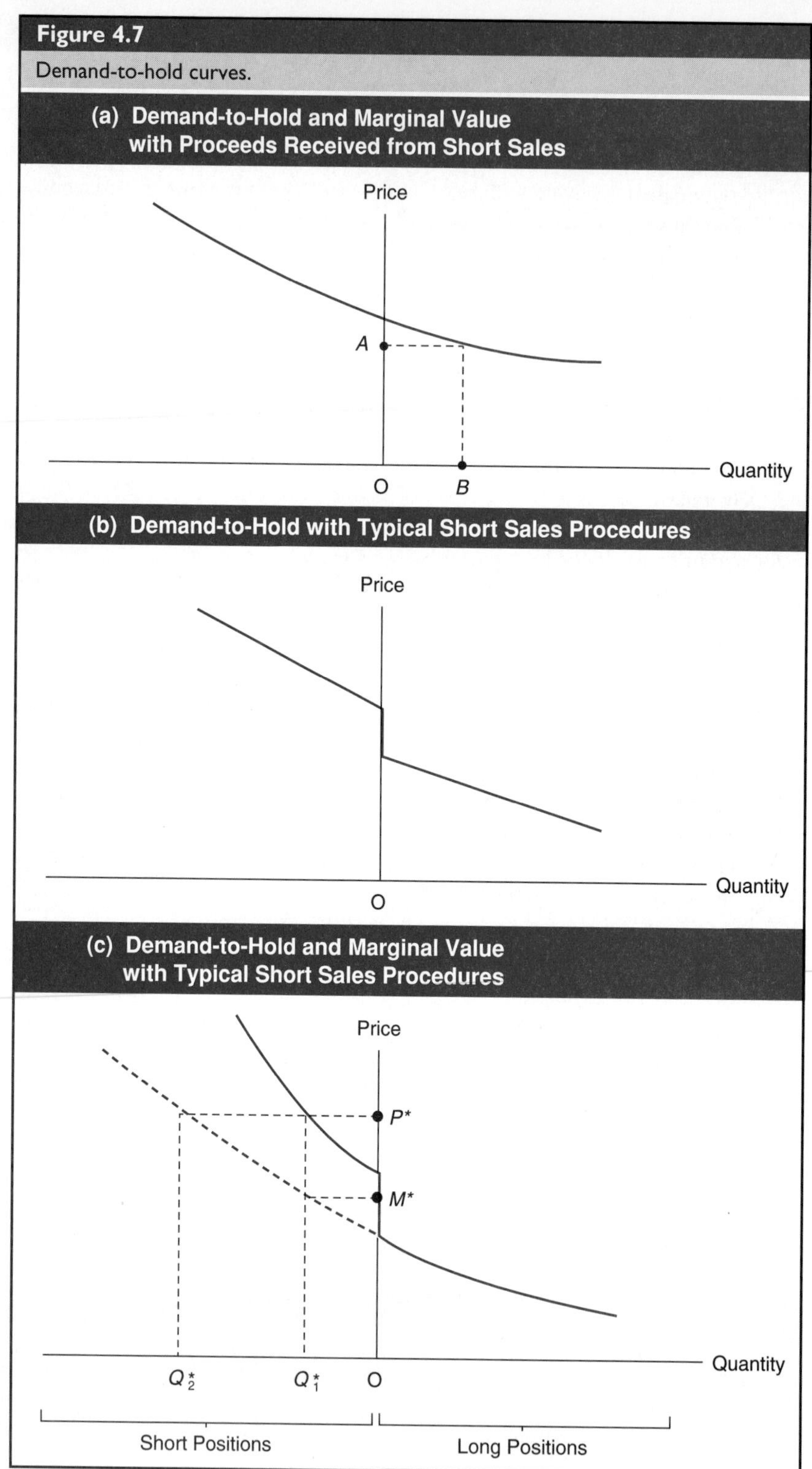
Figure 4.7
Demand-to-hold curves.
(a) Demand-to-Hold and Marginal Value with Proceeds Received from Short Sales
Price
A
O
B
Quantity
(b) Demand-to-Hold with Typical Short Sales Procedures
Price
O
Quantity
(c) Demand-to-Hold and Marginal Value with Typical Short Sales Procedures
Price
P*
M*
Q*2
Q*1
O
Quantity
Short Positions
Long Positions

Some individuals hold the security. For each of them, the situation is like that shown in Figure 4.8(a), where it can be seen that the investor has adjusted his or her portfolio so that the marginal value of a share (M^*) equals its market price.

A few investors may be short sellers. Their situation is like that shown in Figure 4.8(b). Because of the short-sale rule, each short seller will have taken a position at which the marginal value of a share is less than the price. Many investors will choose to hold no shares, and thus their position is neither long nor short. Their situation is shown in Figure 4.8(c). For each of them, the marginal value is equal to or, as in the case shown here, somewhat below the market price.

Were it not for short-selling rules, every investor would adjust his or her portfolio holdings until the marginal value of a security equalled its current market price. Since the market price is the same for everyone, the marginal value would be the same for all investors (assuming all investors pay attention to the market). Price would clearly represent a consensus of investor opinion about value.

Short-selling rules change this situation, but only slightly. Since some investors (primarily pessimists) might choose holdings at which marginal value is below the market price, this market price could be slightly higher than an average of investors' marginal values. Accordingly, securities may be slightly "overpriced."

However, short-sale rules are likely to have a small impact on market prices. Even for the short seller, the disparity between market price and marginal value may be small. For those who hold no shares, it would be smaller yet (or even zero). And, for those who hold shares, it will be zero. Moreover, short positions are typically a small fraction of long positions. For practical purposes, price can be reasonably considered to be equal to a consensus opinion of investors concerning marginal value. For it to be seriously in error as an estimate of that value, many investors must be either poorly informed or poor analysts. Moreover, there must be either (1) a preponderance of such investors with overly optimistic forecasts or (2) a preponderance of such investors with overly pessimistic forecasts. Otherwise, the actions of such investors will offset each other, making price a good estimate of the present value of the security's future prospects.

MARKET EFFICIENCY

Imagine a world in which (1) all investors have costless access to currently available information about the future; (2) all investors are good analysts; and (3) all investors pay close attention to market prices and adjust their holdings appropriately.[1] In such a market, a security's price will be a good estimate of its **investment value**, where investment value is the present value of the security's future prospects as estimated by well-informed and capable analysts.

An **efficient market** can now be defined:

> A (perfectly) efficient market is one in which every security's price equals its investment value at all times.

---

[1] Actually, not all investors need to meet these three conditions in order for security prices to equal their investment values. Instead, what is needed is for marginal investors to meet these conditions, since their trades would correct the mispricing that would occur in their absence.

Figure 4.8

Price of a security as a consensus.

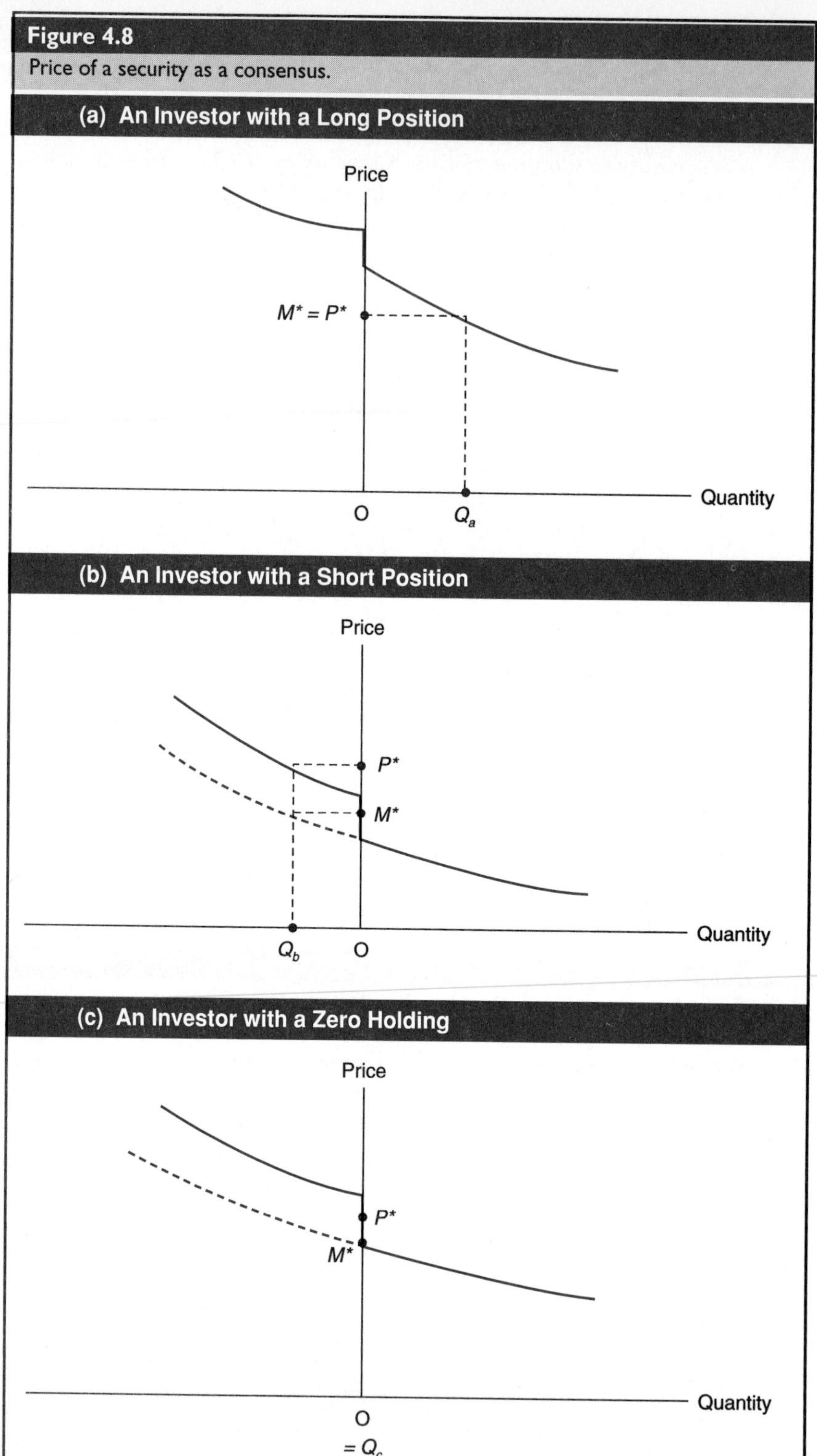

In an efficient market, a set of information is fully and immediately reflected in market prices. But what information? A popular definition is the following:[2]

Form of Efficiency	*Set of Information Reflected in Security Prices*
Weak	Previous prices of securities
Semistrong	All publicly available information
Strong	All information, both public and private

An equivalent definition of an efficient market is the following:

> A market is efficient with respect to a particular set of information if it is impossible, on the average, to make abnormal profits by using this set of information to formulate buying and selling decisions.

For example, a market would be described as having **weak-form efficiency** if it were impossible to make abnormal profits by using past prices to make decisions about when to buy and sell securities. The evidence suggests that major security markets in the United States and Canada are weak-form efficient. However, neither US nor Canadian markets conform quite as well to the definition of **semistrong-form efficiency** (although the lack of a precise meaning for "publicly available" makes this form of efficiency somewhat ambiguous). They conform even less well to the definition of **strong-form efficiency**.

In an efficient market, any new information would be immediately and fully reflected in prices. New information is just that: new, meaning a surprise (anything that is not a surprise is predictable and should have been predicted before the fact). Since happy surprises are about as likely as unhappy ones, price changes in an efficient market are about as likely to be positive as negative. Whereas a security's price might be expected to move upward by an amount that provides a reasonable return on capital (when considered in conjunction with dividend payments), anything above or below this would, in such a market, be unpredictable. In a perfectly efficient market, price changes would be random.[3]

Now consider a crazy market, in which prices never bear any particular relationship to investment value. In such a world, price changes might also appear to be random. However, major security markets in Canada and the United States are certainly not irrational. They may not attain perfect efficiency, but they are certainly much closer to it than to irrationality. To understand financial markets, it is important to understand perfectly efficient markets.

As mentioned earlier, in an efficient market a security's price will be a good estimate of its investment value, where investment value is the present value of the security's future prospects as estimated by well-informed and capable analysts. Any substantial disparity between price and value would reflect market inefficiency. In a well-developed and free market, major inefficiencies are rare. The reason is not hard to find. Major disparities between price and investment value will be noted by alert analysts, who will seek to take advantage of their

[2] Eugene F. Fama, "Efficient Capital Markets: A Review of Theory and Empirical Work," *Journal of Finance* 25, no. 5 (May 1970): 383–417.

[3] In this situation, security prices are said to follow a **random walk**, meaning that security price changes (say, from one day to the next) are independently and identically distributed. That is, the price change from day t to day $t + 1$ is not influenced by the price change from day $t - 1$ to day t, and the size of the price change from one day to the next can be viewed as being determined by the spin of a roulette wheel (with the same roulette wheel being used every day).

discoveries. Securities priced below value (known as underpriced or undervalued securities) will be purchased, creating pressure for price increases due to the increased demand to buy. Securities priced above value (known as overpriced or overvalued securities) will be sold, creating pressure for price decreases due to the increased supply to sell. As investors seek to take advantage of opportunities created by temporary inefficiencies, they will cause the inefficiencies to be reduced, denying the less alert and the less informed a chance to obtain large abnormal profits.

In Canada and the United States there are thousands of professional security analysts and even more amateurs. Not surprisingly, due to their actions the major US and Canadian security markets appear to be much closer to efficiency than to irrationality. As a result it is extremely difficult to make abnormal profits by trading securities in these markets.

SUMMARY

1. The forces of supply and demand interact to determine a security's market price.
2. An investor's demand-to-buy schedule indicates the quantity of a security that the investor wishes to purchase at various prices.
3. An investor's supply-to-sell schedule indicates the quantity of a security that the investor wishes to sell at various prices.
4. The demand and supply schedules for individual investors can be aggregated to create aggregate demand and supply schedules for a security.
5. The intersection of the aggregate demand and supply schedules determines the market clearing price of a security. At that price the quantity traded is maximized.
6. An investor's demand-to-hold schedule indicates the quantity of a security that the investor wishes to own at various prices, assuming no change in the investor's views concerning the relative prospects for the security.
7. The market price of a security can be thought of as representing a consensus opinion about the future prospects for the security.
8. In an efficient market a security's market price will fully reflect all available information relevant to the security's value at that time.
9. The concept of market efficiency can be expressed in three forms: weak, semistrong, and strong.
10. The three forms of market efficiency make different assumptions about the set of information reflected in security prices.

QUESTIONS AND PROBLEMS

1. What is the difference between call security markets and continuous security markets?
2. What is the relationship between the demand-to-hold schedule and the demand-to-buy and supply-to-sell schedules for a particular security?
3. At two separate points of time, Donald Bright drew up the following personal demand-to-hold schedules for an investment in Lisle Bakery stock. Calculate Donald's demand-to-buy schedule at the end of Year 2.

Year 1		Year 2	
Price	*Quantity*	*Price*	*Quantity*
$30	1000	$30	1100
40	900	40	990
50	800	50	880
60	700	60	770
70	600	70	660

4. Using an aggregate demand-to-hold schedule and associated demand-to-buy or supply-to-sell schedules, explain and illustrate the effect of the following events on the equilibrium price and quantity traded of Fairchild Corporation's stock.
   a. Fairchild officials announce that next year's earnings are expected to be significantly higher than analysts had previously forecast.
   b. A wealthy shareholder initiates a large secondary offering of Fairchild stock.
   c. Another company, quite similar to Fairchild in all respects except for being privately held, decides to offer its outstanding shares for sale to the public.
5. Is it true that in the short run the supply schedule for a security is perfectly inelastic, whereas the demand-to-hold schedule is typically elastic? Explain.
6. Short sellers do not receive the proceeds from their short sales, must put up initial margin, and often do not receive interest on these sums held by their brokers. How does this affect the aggregate demand-to-hold schedules for securities?
7. Ian Begley is pondering the statement, "The pattern of security price behaviour might appear the same whether markets were efficient or security prices bore no relationship whatsoever to investment value." Explain the meaning of this statement to Ian.
8. We all know that investors have widely diverse opinions about the future course of the economy and earnings forecasts for various industries and companies. How then is it possible for all these investors to arrive at an equilibrium price for any particular security?
9. Distinguish between the three forms of market efficiency.
10. Does the fact that a market exhibit weak-form efficiency necessarily imply that it is also strong-form efficient? How about the converse statement? Explain.
11. Consider the following types of information. If this information is immediately and fully reflected in security prices, what form of market efficiency is implied?
    a. A company's recent quarterly earnings announcement.
    b. Historical bond yields.
    c. Deliberations of a company's board of directors concerning a possible merger with another company.
    d. Limit orders.
    e. A brokerage firm's published research report on a particular company.
    f. Movements in the TSE 300 Composite Index as plotted in the *Globe and Mail: Report on Business*.

12. Would you expect that fundamental security analysis makes security markets more efficient? Why?
13. Would you expect that TSE Designated Market Makers should be able to earn an abnormal profit in a semistrong efficient market? Why?
14. Is it true that in a perfectly efficient market no investor would consistently be able to earn a profit?
15. Although security markets may not be perfectly efficient, what is the rationale for expecting them to be highly efficient?
16. When a corporation announces its earnings for a period, the volume of transactions in its stock may increase, but frequently that increase is not associated with significant moves in the price of its stock. How can this be explained?
17. What are the implications of the three forms of market efficiency for technical and fundamental analysis (discussed in Chapter 1)?
18. The years 1986 and 1987 will probably be long remembered for the insider trading scandals that were exposed in the United States.
    a. Is successful insider trading consistent with the three forms of market efficiency? Explain.
    b. Play the role of devil's advocate and present a case outline the benefits to financial markets of insider trading.

CFA Exam Question

19. Discuss the role of a portfolio manager in a perfectly efficient market.

Key Terms

demand-to-buy schedule
supply-to-sell schedule
demand-to-hold schedule
investment value
efficient market
weak-form efficiency
semistrong-form efficiency
strong-form efficiency
random walk

References

1. A discussion and examination of the demand curves for stocks is contained in:

   Andrei Shleifer, "Do Demand Curves Slope Down?" *Journal of Finance* 41, no. 3 (July 1986): 579–590.

   Lawrence Harris and Eitan Gurel, "Price and Volume Effects Associated with Changes in the S&P 500: New Evidence for the Existence of Price Pressures," *Journal of Finance* 41, no. 4 (September 1986): 815–829.

   Stephen W. Pruitt and K.C. John Wei, "Institutional Ownership and Changes in the S&P 500," *Journal of Finance* 44, no. 2 (June 1989): 509–513.

2. For articles presenting arguments that securities are "overpriced" due to short sale restrictions, see:

   Edward M. Miller, "Risk, Uncertainty, and Divergence of Opinion," *Journal of Finance* 32, no. 4 (September 1977): 1151–1168.

Douglas W. Diamond and Robert E. Verrecchia, "Constraints on Short-Selling and Asset Price Adjustment to Private Information," *Journal of Financial Economics* 18, no. 2 (June 1987): 277–311.

3. Many people believe that the following articles are the seminal pieces on efficient markets:

   Harry V. Roberts, "Stock Market 'Patterns' and Financial Analysis: Methodological Suggestions," *Journal of Finance* 14, no. 1 (March 1959): 1–10.

   Eugene F. Fama, "Efficient Capital Markets: A Review of Theory and Empirical Work," *Journal of Finance* 25, no. 5 (May 1970): 383–417.

   Eugene F. Fama, "Efficient Capital Markets: II," *Journal of Finance* 46, no. 5 (December 1991): 1575–1617.

4. For an extensive discussion of efficient markets and related evidence, see:

   George Foster, *Financial Statement Analysis* (Englewood Cliffs, NJ: Prentice Hall, 1986), Chapters 9 and 11.

   Stephen F. LeRoy, "Capital Market Efficiency: An Update," *Federal Reserve Bank of San Francisco Economic Review*, no. 2 (Spring 1990): 29–40. A more detailed version of this paper can be found in: Stephen F. LeRoy, "Efficient Capital Markets and Martingales," *Journal of Economic Literature* 27, no. 4 (December 1989): 1583–1621.

   Peter Fortune, "Stock Market Efficiency: An Autopsy?" *New England Economic Review* (March/April 1991): 17–40.

   Richard A. Brealey and Stewart C. Myers, *Principles of Corporate Finance* (New York: McGraw-Hill, 1991), Chapter 13.

   Stephen A. Ross, Randolph W. Westerfield, and Jeffrey F. Jaffe, *Corporate Finance* (Homewood, IL: Richard D. Irwin, 1993), Chapter 13.

5. Interesting overviews of efficient market concepts are presented in:

   Robert Ferguson, "An Efficient Stock Market? Ridiculous!" *Journal of Portfolio Management* 9, no. 4 (Summer 1983): 31–38.

   Bob L. Boldt and Harold L. Arbit, "Efficient Markets and the Professional Investor," *Financial Analysts Journal* 40, no. 4 (July/August 1984): 22–34.

   Fischer Black, "Noise," *Journal of Finance* 41, no. 3 (July 1986): 529–543.

CHAPTER 5

The Valuation of Riskless Securities

A useful first step in understanding security valuation is to consider those fixed-income securities that are certain of making their promised payments in full and on time. The obvious candidates are the securities representing the debt of the Canadian government. Since the government can print money whenever it chooses, the promised payments for such securities are virtually certain to be made on schedule. However, there is a degree of uncertainty as to the purchasing power of the promised payments. While Government of Canada bonds may be riskless in terms of their nominal payments, they may be quite risky in terms of their real (or inflation-adjusted) payments.This issue will be discussed further in Chapter 13.

Despite this concern with inflation risk, it will be assumed hereafter that there are fixed-income securities whose nominal and real payments are certain. Specifically, to the extent that inflation exists, it will be assumed that its magnitude can be accurately predicted. Such an assumption makes it possible to focus on the impact of time on security valuation. Having accomplished this, the influence of other attributes on security valuation can be considered.

YIELD-TO-MATURITY

Interest rates are associated with investments and investments differ in longevity. Therefore, there are many interest rates, not just one. Furthermore, there are many ways that interest rates can be calculated. One such method results in an interest rate that is known as the yield-to-maturity; another results in an interest rate known as the spot rate, which is discussed in the next section.

In describing yields-to-maturity and spot rates, we will assume that three hypothetical riskless securities that are free from default risk (meaning that investors have no doubts about being paid fully and on time) are available. By considering these securities, the impact of differing degrees of default risk on yields-to-maturity and spot rates has been removed. These three securities are referred to as bonds A, B, and C. Bond A matures in one year, at which time the investor will receive \$1000. Similarly, bond B matures in two years, at which time the investor will receive \$1000. Bond C is a coupon bond that pays the investor \$50 one year from now and matures two years from now, paying the investor \$1050 at that time. The prices at which these bonds are currently being sold in the market are:

Bond A (the one-year pure-discount bond):	\$934.58
Bond B (the two-year pure-discount bond):	\$857.34
Bond C (the two-year coupon bond):	\$946.93

The **yield-to-maturity** on any fixed-income security is the single interest rate (with interest compounded at some specified interval) that, if paid by a bank on the amount invested, would enable the investor to obtain all the payments made by the security in question. It is a simple matter to determine the yield-to-maturity on the one-year security, bond A. Since an investment of \$934.58 will pay \$1000 one year later, the yield-to-maturity on this bond is the rate r_A that a bank would have to pay on a deposit of \$934.58 in order for the account to have a balance of \$1000 after one year. Thus, the yield-to-maturity on bond A is the rate r_A that is the solution to the following equation:

$$(1 + r_A) \times \$934.58 = \$1000 \tag{5.1}$$

which is 7%.

In the case of bond B, assuming annual compounding at a rate r_B, an account with \$857.34 invested initially (the cost of B) would grow to $(1 + r_B) \times \$857.34$ in one year. Leaving this total intact, the account would grow to $(1 + r_B) \times [(1 + r_B) \times \$857.34]$ by the end of the second year. The yield-to-maturity is the rate r_B that makes this amount equal to \$1000. In other words, the yield-to-maturity on bond B is the rate r_B that is the solution to the following equation:

$$(1 + r_B) \times [(1 + r_B) \times \$857.34] = \$1000 \tag{5.2}$$

which is 8%.

For bond C, consider investing \$946.93 in an account. At the end of one year, the account would grow in value to $(1 + r_C) \times \$946.93$. Then the investor would remove \$50, leaving a balance of $[(1 + r_C) \times \$946.94] - \$50$. At the end of the second year this balance would have grown to an amount equal to $(1 + r_C) \times \{[(1 + r_C) \times \$946.93] - \$50\}$. The yield-to-maturity on bond C is the rate r_C that makes this amount equal to \$1050:

$$(1 + r_C) \times \{[(1 + r_C) \times \$946.93] - \$50\} = \$1050 \tag{5.3}$$

which is 7.975%.

Equivalently, yield-to-maturity is the discount rate that makes the present value of the promised future cash flows equal to the current market price of the bond.[1] When viewed in this manner, yield-to-maturity is analogous to internal rate of return, a concept used for making capital budgeting decisions that is often described in introductory finance textbooks. This can be seen for bond A by dividing both sides of equation (5.1) by $(1 + r_A)$, resulting in:

$$\$934.58 = \frac{\$1000}{(1 + r_A)}. \tag{5.4}$$

Similarly, for bond B both sides of equation (5.2) can be divided by $(1 + r_B)^2$, resulting in:

$$\$857.34 = \frac{\$1000}{(1 + r_B)^2} \tag{5.5}$$

whereas for bond C both sides of equation (4.3) can be divided by $(1 + r_C)^2$:

[1] This calculation assumes that the bond will not be called prior to maturity. If it is assumed that the bond will be called as soon as possible, then the discount rate that makes the present value of the corresponding cash flows equal to the current market price of the bond is known as the bond's *yield-to-call*.

$$\$946.93 - \frac{\$50}{(1 + r_C)} = \frac{\$1050}{(1 + r_C)^2}$$

or

$$\$946.93 = \frac{\$50}{(1 + r_C)} + \frac{\$1050}{(1 + r_C)^2}. \tag{5.6}$$

Since equations (5.4), (5.5), and (5.6) are equivalent to equations (5.1), (5.2), and (5.3), respectively, the solutions must be the same as before, with $r_A = 7\%$, $r_B = 8\%$, and $r_C = 7.975\%$.

For coupon-bearing bonds, the procedure for determining yield-to-maturity involves trial and error. In the case of bond C, a discount rate of 10% could be tried initially, resulting in a value of $913.22 for the right-hand side of equation (5.6), a value that is too low. This indicates that the number in the denominator is too high, so a lower discount rate, such as 6%, is used next. In this case, the value on the right-hand side is $981.67, which is too high and indicates that 6% is too low. This means the solution is between 6% and 10%, and the search could continue until the answer, 7.975%, is found.

Fortunately, computers are good at trial-and-error calculations. One can describe a very complex series of cash flows to a computer and get an answer concerning yield-to-maturity in short order. In fact, some hand-held calculators come with built-in programs to find yield-to-maturity, where one simply enters the number of days to maturity, the annual coupon payments, and the current market price and then presses the key that indicates yield-to-maturity; then in a few seconds the answer appears.

Yield-to-maturity is the most commonly used measure of a bond's "interest rate," or "return." It can be computed for any bond and it facilitates comparisons among different investments. However, it has some serious drawbacks. In order to understand these drawbacks, the concept of spot rates must be introduced.

SPOT RATES

A **spot rate** is measured at a given time as the yield-to-maturity on a pure-discount security and can be thought of as the interest rate associated with a spot contract. Such a contract, when signed, involves the immediate loaning of money from one party to another. The loan, along with interest, is to be repaid in its entirety at a specific time in the future. The interest rate that is specified in the contract is the spot rate.

Bonds A and B in the previous example were pure-discount securities, meaning an investor who purchased either one would expect to receive only one cash payment from the issuer. Accordingly, in this example the one-year spot rate is 7% and the two-year spot rate is 8%. In general, the t-year spot rate s_t is the solution to the following equation:

$$P_t = \frac{M_t}{(1 + s_t)^t} \tag{5.7}$$

where P_t is the current market price of a pure-discount bond that matures in t years and has a maturity value of M_t. For example, the values of P_t and M_t for bond B would be $857.34 and $1000, respectively, with $t = 2$.

Spot rates can also be determined in another manner if only coupon-bearing bonds are available for longer maturities. Generally the one-year spot rate (s_1) will be known, since there frequently will be a one-year pure-discount Treasury bill available for making this calculation. However, it may be that no two-year pure-discount security exists. Instead, only a two-year coupon-bearing bond may be available for investment, having a current market price of P_2, a maturity value of M_2, and a coupon payment one year from now equal to C_1. In this situation, the two-year spot rate (s_2) is the solution to the following equation:

$$P_2 = \frac{C_1}{(1 + s_1)^1} + \frac{M_2}{(1 + s_2)^2}. \tag{5.8}$$

For example, assume that only bonds A and C exist. In this situation it is known that the one-year spot rate, s_1, is 7%. Now, equation (5.8) can be used to determine the two-year spot rate, s_2, where P_2 = \$946.93, C_1 = \$50, and M_2 = \$1050:

$$\$946.93 = \frac{\$50}{(1 + .07)^1} + \frac{\$1050}{(1 + s_2)^2}.$$

The solution to this equation is $s_2 = .08 = 8\%$. Thus, the two-year spot rate is determined to be the same in this example regardless of whether it is determined directly by analyzing pure-discount bond B or indirectly by analyzing coupon-bearing bond C in conjunction with bond A. Although this will not always be the case, often the differences are insignificant.

DISCOUNT FACTORS

Having determined a set of spot rates, it is a straightforward matter to determine the corresponding set of **discount factors.** A discount factor d_t is equivalent to the present value of \$1 to be received t years in the future from a government security and is equal to:

$$d_t = \frac{1}{(1 + s_t)^t}. \tag{5.9}$$

The set of these factors is sometimes referred to as the **market discount function** that changes from day to day as spot rates change. In the example, $d_1 = 1/(1 + .07)^1 = .9346$ and $d_2 = 1/(1 + .08)^2 = .8573$.

Once the market discount function has been determined, it is fairly straightforward to find the present value of any default-free security. Let C_t denote the cash payment to be made to the investor at year t on the security being evaluated. The multiplication of C_t by d_t is termed **discounting**: converting the given future value into an equivalent present value. The latter is equivalent in the sense that P present dollars can be converted into C_t dollars in year t via available investment instruments, given the currently prevailing spot rates. An investment paying C_t dollars in year t with certainty should sell for $P = d_t C_t$ dollars today. If it sells for more, it is overpriced; if it sells for less, it is underpriced. These statements rest solely on comparisons with equivalent opportunities in the marketplace. Valuation of default-free investments thus requires no assessment of individual preferences, only careful analysis of available opportunities in the marketplace.

The simplest and, in a sense, most fundamental characterization of the structure of the market for default-free bonds is given by the current set of discount factors, referred to earlier as the market discount function. With this set of factors, it is a simple matter to evaluate a default-free bond that provides more than one payment, for it is, in effect, a package of bonds, each of which provides only one payment. Each amount is simply multiplied by the appropriate discount factor, and the resultant present values are summed.

For example, assume that the government is preparing to offer for sale a two-year coupon-bearing security that will pay \$70 in one year and \$1070 in two years. What is a fair price for such a security? It is simply the present value of \$70 and \$1070. This can be determined by multiplying \$70 and \$1070 by the one-year and two-year discount factors, respectively. Doing so results in (\$70 × .9346) + (\$1070 × .8573), which equals \$982.73.

No matter how complex the pattern of payments, this procedure can be used to determine the value of any default-free bond of this type. The general formula for the bond's present value (PV) is:

$$PV = \sum_{t=1}^{n} d_t C_t \tag{5.10}$$

where the bond has promised cash payments C_t for each year t through year n.

At this point, it has been shown how spot rates and, in turn, discount factors can be calculated. However, no link between different spot rates (or different discount factors) has been established. For example, it has yet to be shown how the one-year spot rate of 7% is related to the two-year spot rate of 8%. The concept of forward rates makes the link.

FORWARD RATES

In the example, the one-year spot rate was determined to be 7%. This means that the market has determined that the present value of \$1 to be paid by the government in one year is \$1/1.07, or \$.9346. That is, the relevant discount rate for converting a cash flow one year from now to its present value is 7%. Since it was also noted that the two-year spot rate was 8%, the present value of \$1 to be paid by the government in two years is $\$1/1.08^2$, or \$.8573.

An alternative view of \$1 to be paid in two years is that it can be discounted in two steps. The first step determines its equivalent one-year value. That is, \$1 to be received in two years is equivalent to $\$1/(1 + f_{1,2})$ to be received in one year. The second step determines the present value of this equivalent one-year amount by discounting it at the one-year spot rate of 7%. Thus, its current value is

$$\frac{\$1/(1 + f_{1,2})}{(1 + .07)}.$$

However, this value must be equal to \$.8573, since it was mentioned earlier that according to the two-year spot rate, \$.8573 is the present value of \$1 to be paid in two years. That is,

$$\frac{\$1/(1 + f_{1,2})}{(1 + .07)} = \$.8573 \tag{5.11}$$

which has a solution for $f_{1,2}$ of 9.01%.

The discount rate $f_{1,2}$ is known as the **forward rate** from year 1 to year 2. That is, it is the discount rate for determining the equivalent value of a dollar one year from now if it is to be received two years from now. In the example, \$1 to be received two years from now is equivalent in value to \$1/(1.0901) = \$.9174 to be received one year from now (in turn, note that the present value of \$.9174 is \$.9174/1.07 = \$.8573).

INSTITUTIONAL ISSUES

Almost Riskless Securities

Unless we wish to remain on a purely abstract level, our discussion concerning the valuation of riskless securities requires an actual riskless security to value. Surprisingly, no such financial asset can be found in US and Canadian financial markets.

A riskless security provides the investor with a certain return over the investor's time horizon. As an investor is ultimately interested in the purchasing power of his or her investments, the riskless security's return should be certain on a real (inflation-adjusted) basis.

Although government securities have zero risk of default, even they do not provide riskless real returns. Their principal and interest payments are not adjusted for inflation over the securities' lives. As a result, unexpected inflation may produce real returns different from those expected at the time the securities were purchased.

However, assume that inflation remains low and fairly predictable. Will government securities provide investors with riskless returns? The answer is generally "no."

An investor's time horizon usually will not coincide with the life of a particular security. If that time horizon is shorter than the security's life, then the investor must purchase another equivalent security when the first security matures. If interest rates have changed in the interim, the investor will earn a different return than he or she originally anticipated. (This risk is known as reinvestment-rate risk—see Chapter 9.)

If the government security's life exceeds the investor's time horizon, then the investor will have to sell the security before it matures. If interest rates change prior to the sale, the price of the security will change, thereby causing the investor to earn a different return from the one originally anticipated. (This risk is known as interest-rate risk—see Chapter 9.)

Even if the security's life matches the investor's time horizon, it generally will not provide a riskless return. With the exception of Treasury bills, all government securities make periodic interest payments (see Chapter 14), which the investor must reinvest. If interest rates change over the security's life, then the investor's reinvestment rate will change, causing the investor's return to differ from that originally anticipated at the time of the security's purchase.

Clearly, what investors need are default-free securities that make only one payment (which includes principal and all interest) when those securities mature. Investors could then select a security whose life matched their investment time horizons. These securities would be truly riskless, at least on a nominal basis.

A fixed-income security that makes only one payment at maturity is called a zero coupon bond. Until the 1980s, however, government zero coupon bonds did not exist, except for Treasury bills (which have a maximum maturity of one year). Today, over $200 billion of Treasury zero coupon bonds have been created in the US, and a flourishing market has developed in Canada. The growth of this market has been fueled by the unique advantages of riskless securities and the strong demand for those securities by institutional investors.

A coupon-bearing government security can be viewed as a portfolio of zero coupon bonds. Each interest payment, as well as the principal, can be considered as a separate bond. In 1982, several brokerage firms came to a novel realization: a security's payments could be segregated and sold piecemeal through a process known as coupon stripping.

For example, brokerage firm XYZ could purchase a newly issued 20-year government bond and deposit the bond with a custodian bank. Assuming semiannual interest payments, XYZ can create 41 separate zero coupon

INSTITUTIONAL ISSUES (continued)

bonds (40 interest payments plus one principal repayment). Naturally, XYZ could create larger zero coupon bonds by buying and depositing more securities of the same issue. These zero coupon bonds, in turn, can be sold to investors (for a fee, of course). As the government makes its required payments on the bond, the custodian bank remits the payments to the zero coupon bondholders of the appropriate maturity and effectively retires that particular bond. The process continues until all interest and principal payments have been made and all of the zero coupon bonds associated with this bond have been extinguished.

US brokerage firms have issued zero coupon bonds based on Treasury securities under a number of exotic names, such as LIONs (Lehman Investment Opportunity Notes), TIGRs (Merrill Lynch's Treasury Investment Growth Receipts), and CATs (Salomon Brothers' Certificates of Accrual on Treasury Securities). Not surprisingly, these securities have come to be known in the trade as "animals."

Brokerage firms and investors benefit from coupon stripping. The brokerage firms found that the sum of the parts was worth more than the whole, as the zero coupon bonds could be sold to investors at a higher combined price than could the source government security. Investors benefited from the creation of a liquid market in riskless securities.

In 1985, the US Treasury introduced a program called STRIPS (Separate Trading of Registered Interest and Principal Securities). This program allows purchasers of certain interest-bearing Treasury securities to keep whatever cash payments they want and to sell the rest. The stripped bonds are "held" in the Federal Reserve System's computer (called the *book entry system*), and payments on the bonds are made electronically. Any financial institution that is registered on the Federal Reserve System's computer may participate in the STRIPS program.

Brokerage firms soon found that it was much less expensive to create zero coupon bonds through the STRIPS program than to use bank custody accounts. As a result, virtually all such bonds are now created through the STRIPS program.

The values of zero coupon government securities depend on many factors, including tax rates and regulations, the life of the securities, the relationship of long to short interest rates, and the market demand for certain bonds. Accounting for these valuation factors, the market maintains an equilibrium between the values of underlying government securities and the stripped bonds. Just as financial organizations have found it profitable to produce stripped bonds, those same zero coupon bonds can be bundled to reconstitute the underlying securities if market prices warrant. The inexpensive operation of the STRIPS program has increased the efficiency of the zero coupon government bond market.

In 1991 the Government of Canada issued one series of Real Return Bonds that are inflation index linked and have subsequently been stripped by various investment dealers. These instruments are very close to a true riskless security.

Symbolically, the link between the one-year spot rate, two-year spot rate, and one-year forward rate is:

$$\frac{\$1/(1+f_{1,2})}{(1+s_1)} = \frac{\$1}{(1+s_2)^2} \tag{5.12}$$

which can be rewritten as:

$$(1+f_{1,2}) = \frac{(1+s_2)^2}{(1+s_1)} \tag{5.13}$$

or

$$(1+s_1)(1+f_{1,2}) = (1+s_2)(1+s_2). \tag{5.14}$$

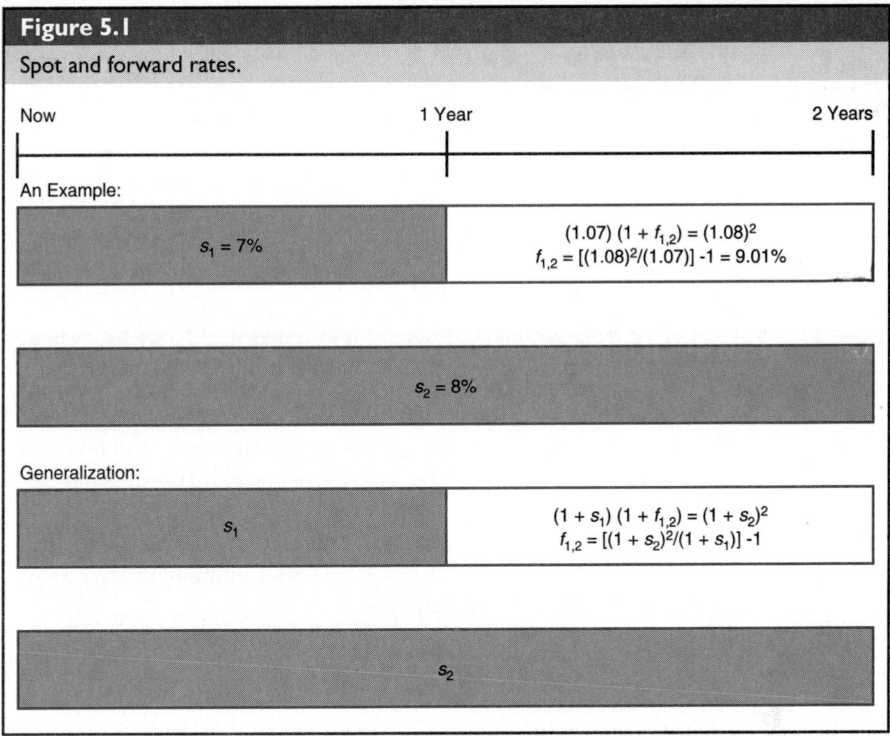

Figure 5.1

Spot and forward rates.

More generally, for year $t - 1$ and year t spot rates, the link to the forward rate between years $t - 1$ and t is:

$$(1 + f_{t-1,t}) = \frac{(1 + s_t)^t}{(1 + s_{t-1})^{t-1}} \tag{5.15}$$

or

$$(1 + s_{t-1})^{t-1} \times (1 + f_{t-1,t}) = (1 + s_t)^t. \tag{5.16}$$

Figure 5.1 illustrates this by referring to the example and generalizing from it.

There is another interpretation that can be given to forward rates. Consider a contract made now, in which money will be loaned a year from now and paid back two years from now. Such a contract is known as a **forward contract**; the interest rate on the one-year loan that is specified in it (note that the interest will be paid when the loan matures in two years) is known as the forward rate.

It is important to distinguish this rate from the rate for one-year loans that will prevail for deals made a year from now (the spot rate at that time). A forward rate applies to contracts made now but relating to a period "forward" in time. By the nature of the contract, the terms are certain now, even though the actual transaction will occur later. If instead one were to wait until next year and sign a contract to borrow money in the spot market at that time, the terms might turn out to be better or worse than today's forward rate, since the future spot rate is not perfectly predictable.

In the example, the marketplace has priced these securities such that a representative investor making a two-year loan to the government would demand an interest rate equal to the two-year spot rate, 8%. Equivalently, the investor would be willing simultaneously to (1) make a one-year loan to the government at an interest rate equal to the one-year spot rate,

7%, and (2) sign a forward contract with the government to loan the government money one year from now, being repaid two years from now, where the interest rate to be paid is the forward rate, 9.01%.

When viewed in this manner, forward contracts are implicit. However, forward contracts are sometimes made explicitly. For example, a contractor might obtain a commitment from a bank for a one-year construction loan a year hence at a fixed rate of interest. Financial futures markets (discussed in Chapter 21) provide standardized forward contracts of this type. For example, in April one could contract to pay $984.70 in September to purchase a 91-day Treasury bill that would pay $1000 in December.

FORWARD RATES AND DISCOUNT FACTORS

In equation (5.9) it was shown that a discount factor for t years could be calculated by adding 1 to the spot rate for t years, raising this sum to the power t, and then taking the reciprocal of the result. For example, it was shown that the two-year discount factor associated with the two-year spot rate of 8% was equal to $1/(1 + .08)^2 = .8573$.

Equation (5.14) suggests an equivalent method for calculating discount factors. In the case of the two-year factor, this method involves multiplying the one-year spot rate by the forward rate and taking the reciprocal of the result:

$$d_2 = \frac{1}{(1 + s_1) \times (1 + f_{1,2})} \tag{5.17}$$

which in the example is

$$d_2 = \frac{1}{(1 + .07) \times (1 + .0901)} = .8573.$$

More generally, the discount factor for year t that is shown in equation (5.9) can be restated as follows:

$$d_t = \frac{1}{(1 + s_{t-1})^{t-1} \times (1 + f_{t-1,t})}. \tag{5.18}$$

Thus, given a set of spot rates, it is possible to determine the market discount function in either of two ways, both of which will provide the same figures. First, the spot rates can be used in equation (5.9) to arrive at a set of discount factors. Alternatively, the spot rates can be used to determine a set of forward rates and then the spot rates and forward rates can be used in equation (5.18) to arrive at a set of discount factors.

COMPOUNDING

Thus far, the discussion has concentrated on annual interest rates by assuming that cash flows are compounded (or discounted) annually. This is often appropriate, but for more precise calculations a shorter period may be more desirable. Moreover, some lenders explicitly compound funds more often than once each year.

Compounding is the payment of interest on interest. At the end of each compounding interval, interest is computed and added to principal. This sum becomes the principal on which interest is computed at the end of the next interval. The process continues until the end of the final compounding interval is reached.

No problem is involved in adapting the previously stated formulas to compounding intervals other than a year. The simplest procedure is to count in units of the chosen interval. For example, yield-to-maturity can be calculated using any chosen compounding interval. If payment of P dollars now will result in the receipt of F dollars ten years from now, the yield-to-maturity can be calculated using annual compounding by finding a value r_a that satisfies the equation

$$P(1 + r_a)^{10} = F, \tag{5.19}$$

since F will be received ten annual periods from now. The result, r_a, is expressed as an annual rate with annual compounding.

Alternatively, yield-to-maturity can be calculated using semiannual compounding by finding a value r_s that satisfies the equation

$$P(1 + r_s)^{20} = F \tag{5.20}$$

since F will be received 20 semiannual periods from now. The result, r_s, is expressed as a semiannual rate with semiannual compounding. It can be doubled to give an annual rate with semiannual compounding; alternatively, the annual rate with annual compounding can be computed for a given value of r_s by using the following equation:

$$1 + r_a = (1 + r_s)^2. \tag{5.21}$$

For example, consider an investment costing \$2315.97 that will pay \$5000 ten years later. Applying equations (5.19) and (5.20) to this security results in

$$\$2315.97(1 + r_a)^{10} = \$5000$$

and

$$\$2315.97(1 + r_s)^{20} = \$5000$$

respectively, where the solutions are $r_a = 8\%$ and $r_s = 3.923\%$. Thus, this security can be described as having an annual rate with annual compounding of 8%, a semiannual rate with semiannual compounding of 3.923%, and an annual rate with semiannual compounding of $2 \times 3.923\% = 7.846\%$.[2]

To reduce the confusion caused by the many different methods that can be used to express interest rates, the US Federal truth-in-lending law requires every lender to compute and disclose the **annual percentage rate** (APR) implied by the terms of a loan. This is simply the yield-to-maturity, computed using the most frequent time between payments on the loan as the compounding interval. Although some complications arise when payments are required at irregular intervals, the use of APRs clearly simplifies the task of comparing lenders' terms. Canadian consumers could benefit from some standardization of reported interest rates.

Semiannual compounding is commonly used to determine the yield-to-maturity for bonds, since coupon payments are usually made twice a year. Most preprogrammed calculators and computers use this approach.

---

[2] Note how, using equation (5.21), $r_a = (1.03923)^2 - 1 = 8\%$, a solution that is the same as the one provided by equation (5.19).

THE BANK DISCOUNT METHOD

Despite the US truth-in-lending law, other methods are still used to determine interest rates. One time-honoured procedure for reporting interest rates is the **bank discount method**. If someone "borrows" $100 from a bank, to be repaid a year later, the bank will discount the interest of, for instance, 8% and give the borrower $92. According to the bank discount method, this is an interest rate of 8%. The borrower only receives $92, for which he or she must pay $8 in interest after one year. The "true" interest rate (APR) must be based on the money the borrower actually gets to use. In this case, the rate is 8.70%, since $8/$92 = .0870.

It is a simple matter to convert an interest rate quoted on the bank discount method to a true interest rate. If the bank discount rate is BDR, then the true rate is simply BDR/(1 – BDR). Substituting the figures from the previous example into this expression gives .08/(1 – .08) = 8.70%, thereby demonstrating that the bank discount rate of 8% understates the true cost of borrowing by .7% in this example.

YIELD CURVES

At any time, fixed income securities will be priced approximately in accord with the existing set of spot rates and their associated discount factors. Although there have been times when all the spot rates were roughly equal in size, generally they have different values. Often the one-year spot rate is less than the two-year spot rate, which in turn is less than the three-year spot rate, and so on (that is, s_t increases as t increases). At other times, the one-year spot rate is greater than the two-year spot rate, which in turn is greater than the three-year spot rate, and so on (that is, s_t decreases as t increases). It is wise for the security analyst to know which case currently prevails, as this is a useful starting point in valuing fixed-income securities.

Unfortunately, this is easier said than done. Only government bonds are clearly free from default risk. However, the features of such bonds may differ from issue to issue. Despite these problems, a summary of the approximate relationship between yields-to-maturity on Government of Canada securities of various terms-to-maturity is presented in the form of a graph illustrating the current yield curve.

A **yield curve** is a graph that shows the yields-to-maturity (on the vertical axis) for government securities of various maturities (on the horizontal axis) as of a particular date. Figure 5.2 provides an example that shows the relationship that existed on January 5, 1996. The curve estimates the current **term structure** of interest rates, and it changes daily as prices (and, hence, yields-to-maturity) change. Current yield curves can be obtained from investment dealers and investment counsellors (for a fee). Many institutional investors produce their own on a regular basis. Figure 5.3 shows some of the commonly observed shapes for the yield curve that have been recorded in the past.

Generally, the relationship between yields and maturities is less than perfect. That is, not all the securities lie exactly on the yield curve. This is largely due to the fact that the yield-to-maturity on a coupon-bearing security is not clearly linked to the set of spot rates currently in existence. Since the set of spot rates is a fundamental determinant of the price of any government security, there is no reason to expect yields to lie exactly on the curve. Indeed, a more meaningful graph would be one where spot rates are measured on the vertical axis instead of yields-to-maturity. With this in mind, two interesting questions to ponder are: why are the spot rates of different magnitudes? And why do the differences in these rates change over time, where sometimes long-term spot rates are greater than short-term spot

Figure 5.2

Yield curve for Government of Canada bonds, January 5, 1996.

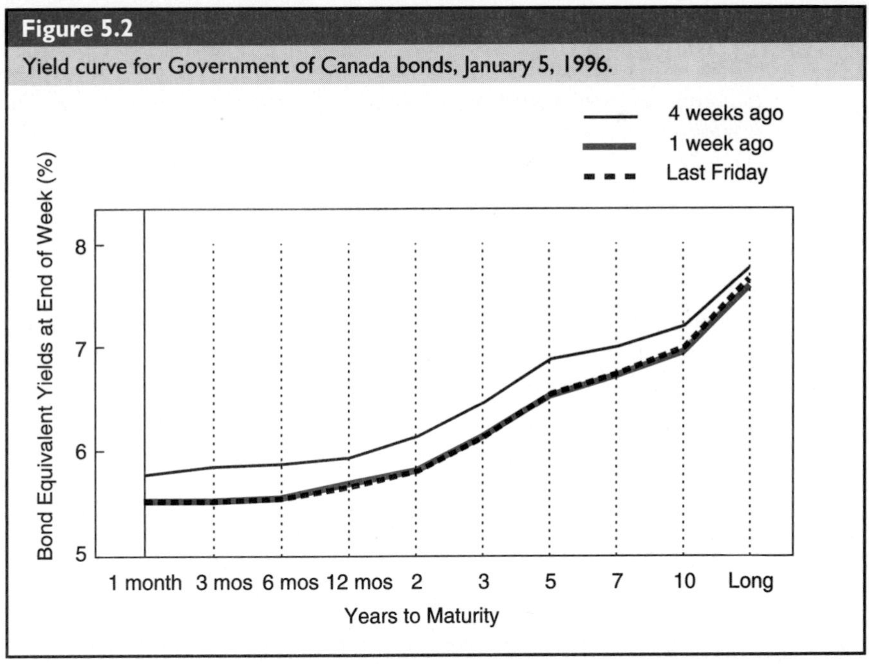

SOURCE: Royal Bank of Canada. Published in the *Globe and Mail: Report on Business*, January 8, 1996.

Figure 5.3

Typical yield curve shapes.

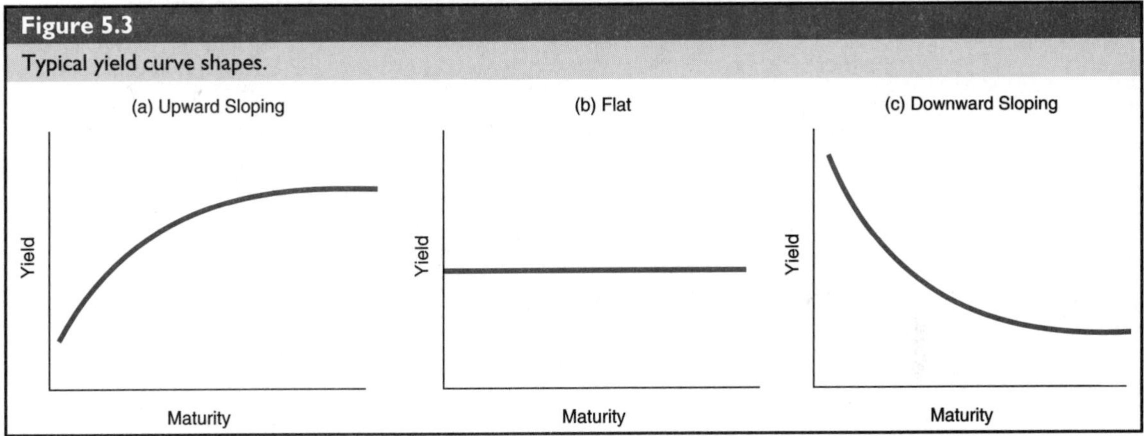

rates and sometimes the opposite occurs? Attempts to answer such questions can be found in various term structure theories.

TERM STRUCTURE THEORIES

Three theories have been generally used to explain the term structure of interest rates. The focus of the discussion is on the term structure of spot rates, since it is these rates and not yields-to-maturity that are critically important in determining the price of any government security.

▸ The Unbiased Expectations Theory

The **unbiased expectations theory** holds that the forward rate represents the average opinion of the expected future spot rate for the period in question. Thus, a set of spot rates that is rising can be explained by arguing that the marketplace (that is, the general opinion of investors) believes that spot rates will rise in the future. Conversely, a set of decreasing spot rates is explained by arguing that the marketplace expects spot rates to fall in the future.[3]

Upward Sloping Yield Curves

In order to understand this theory more fully, consider the earlier example where the one-year spot rate was 7% and the two-year spot rate was 8%. The basic question is, Why are these two spot rates different? Equivalently, why is the term structure upward-sloping?

Consider an investor with \$1 to invest for two years (for ease of exposition, it will be assumed that any amount of money can be invested at the prevailing spot rates). This investor could follow a *maturity strategy*, investing the money now for the full two years at the two-year spot rate of 8%. With this strategy, at the end of two years the dollar will have grown in value to \$1(1.08)(1.08) = \$1.1664. Alternatively, the investor could invest the dollar now for one year at the one-year spot rate of 7%, so that the investor knows that one year from now he or she will have \$1(1.07) = \$1.07 to reinvest for one more year.

Although the investor does not know what the one-year spot rate will be one year from now, the investor has an *expectation* about what it will be (this expected future spot rate will hereafter be denoted by $es_{1,2}$). If the investor thinks it will be 10%, then his or her \$1 has an expected value two years from now of \$1(1.07)(1.10) = \$1.177. In this case, the investor would choose a *rollover strategy*, meaning the investor would choose to invest in a one-year security at 7% rather than in the two-year security, since he or she would expect to have more money at the end of two years by doing so (note that \$1.177 > \$1.1664).

However, an expected future spot rate of 10% cannot represent the general view in the marketplace. If it did, people would not be willing to invest money at the two-year spot rate, since a higher return would be expected from investing money at the one-year rate and using the rollover strategy. Thus, the two-year spot rate would quickly rise, since the supply of funds for two-year loans at 8% would be less than the demand. Conversely, the supply of funds for one year at 7% would be more than the demand, causing the one-year rate to fall quickly. Thus, a one-year spot rate of 7%, a two-year spot rate of 8%, and an expected future spot rate of 10% cannot represent an equilibrium situation.

What if the expected future spot rate is 6% instead of 10%? In this case, according to the rollover strategy, the investor would expect \$1 to be worth \$1(1.07)(1.06) = \$1.1342 at the end of two years. Since this is less than the value the dollar will have if the maturity strategy is followed (\$1.1342 < \$1.1664), the investor would choose the maturity strategy. Again, however, an expected future spot rate of 6% cannot represent the general view in the marketplace because if it did, people would not be willing to invest money at the one-year spot rate.

---

[3] Recently a "modern" expectations theory has been developed that is economically more logical than the "unbiased" expectations theory. However, it provides approximately the same empirical implications and explanations of the term structure as those given by the unbiased expectations theory. Thus, given the similarities between the two theories, only the unbiased expectations theory is presented here.

Earlier, it was shown that the forward rate in this example was 9.01%. What if the expected future spot rate was of this magnitude? At the end of two years the value of $1 with the rollover strategy would be $1(1.07)(1.0901) = $1.1664, the same as the value of $1 with the maturity strategy. In this case, equilibrium would exist in the marketplace because the general view would be that both strategies have the same expected return. Accordingly, investors with a two-year holding period would not have an incentive to choose one strategy over the other.

Note that an investor with a one-year holding period could follow a maturity strategy by investing $1 in the one-year security and receiving $1.07 after one year. Alternatively, a *naive strategy* could be followed, where a two-year security could be purchased now and sold after one year. If so, the expected selling price would be $1.1664/1.0901 = $1.07, for a return of 7% (the security would have a maturity value of $1.1664 = $1(1.08)(1.08), but since the spot rate is expected to be 9.01% in a year, its expected selling price is just the discounted value of its maturity value). Since the maturity and naive strategies have the same expected return, investors with a one-year holding period would not have an incentive to choose one strategy over the other.

Thus, the unbiased expectations theory asserts that the expected future spot rate is equal in magnitude to the forward rate. In the example, the current one-year spot rate is 7% and, according to this theory, the general opinion is that it will rise to a rate of 9.01% in one year. It is this expected rise in the one-year spot rate that is the reason behind the upward-sloping term structure when the two-year spot rate (8%) is greater than the one-year spot rate (7%).

Equilibrium

In equation format, the unbiased expectations theory states that the expected future spot rate is equal to the forward rate:

$$es_{1,2} = f_{1,2}. \tag{5.22}$$

Thus, equation (5.14) can be restated with $es_{1,2}$ substituted for $f_{1,2}$, as follows:

$$(1 + s_2)(1 + s_2) = (1 + s_1)(1 + es_{1,2}) \tag{5.23}$$

which can be conveniently interpreted to mean that the expected return from a maturity strategy must equal the expected return on a rollover strategy.[4]

The previous example dealt with an upward-sloping term structure, where the longer the term, the higher the spot rate. It is a straightforward matter to deal with a downward-sloping term structure, where the longer the term, the lower the spot rate. While the explanation for an upward-sloping term structure was that investors expect spot rates to rise in the future, the reason for the downward-sloping curve is that investors expect spot rates to fall in the future.

Changing Spot Rates and Inflation

An interesting followup question is: Why do investors expect spot rates to change, either by rising or falling, in the future? A possible answer to this question can be found by noting that the spot rates that are observed in the marketplace are nominal rates. That is, they are

---

[4] Equation (5.22) can be expressed more generally as $es_{t-1,t} = f_{t-1,t}$. Thus, using equation (5.16), the unbiased expectations theory states that, in general, $(1 + s_t)^t = (1 + s_{t-1})^{t-1} \times (1 + es_{t-1,t})$.

a reflection of the underlying real rate and the expected inflation rate.[5] If either (or both) of these rates is expected to change in the future, then the spot rate will be expected to change.

For example, assume a constant real rate of 3%. Since the current one-year spot rate is 7%, this means that the general opinion in the marketplace is that the expected rate of inflation over the next year is approximately 4% (the nominal rate is approximately equal to the sum of the real rate and expected inflation rate). Now, according to the unbiased expectations theory, the expected future spot rate is 9.01%, an increase of 2.01% from the current one-year spot rate of 7%. The spot rate is expected to rise by 2.01% because the inflation rate is expected to rise by 2.01%. That is, the expected inflation rate over the next 12 months is approximately 4%, and over the following 12 months it is expected to be higher, at approximately 6.01%.

To recapitulate, the two-year spot rate (8%) is greater than the one-year spot rate (7%) because investors expect the future one-year spot rate to be greater than the current one-year spot rate. They expect it to be greater because of an anticipated rise in the expected rate of inflation, from approximately 4% to approximately 6.01%.

In general, when current economic conditions make short-term spot rates abnormally high (owing, say, to a relatively high current rate of inflation), according to the unbiased expectations theory, the term structure should be downward-sloping. This is because inflation would be expected to abate in the future. Conversely, when current conditions make short-term rates abnormally low (owing say, to a relatively low current rate of inflation), the term structure should be upward-sloping, since inflation would be expected to rise in the future. Examination of historical term structures suggests that this is what has actually happened, since the structure has been upward-sloping in periods of lower interest rates and downward-sloping in periods of higher interest rates.

However, examining historical term structures uncovers a problem. In particular, with this theory, it is logical to expect that over time there will be roughly as many occurrences of upward-sloping term structures as downward-sloping term structures. In reality, upward-sloping structures tend to be more frequent. The liquidity preference theory provides an explanation for this observation.

► The Liquidity Preference Theory

The **liquidity preference theory** (also known as the liquidity premium theory) starts with the notion that investors are primarily interested in purchasing short-term securities. That is, even though some investors may have longer holding periods, there is a tendency for them to prefer short-term securities. This is because these investors realize that they may need their funds earlier than anticipated and recognize that they face less "price risk" (that is, interest rate risk) if they invest in shorter-term securities.

Price Risk

For example, an investor with a two-year holding period would tend to prefer the rollover strategy, since he or she would be certain of having a given amount of cash at the end of one year, when it may be needed. If a maturity strategy had been followed, then the investor would have to sell the two-year security after one year if cash was needed. However, it is not known now what price the investor would get if he or she were to sell the two-year security

---

[5] See Chapter 13 for a discussion of the nature of the relationship between nominal rates, real rates, and expected inflation rates.

in one year. Thus, there is an extra element of risk associated with the maturity strategy that is absent from the rollover strategy.[6]

The upshot is that investors with a two-year holding period will not choose the maturity strategy if it has the same expected return as the rollover strategy, since it is riskier. The only way investors will follow the maturity strategy and buy the two-year security is if its expected return is higher. That is, borrowers are going to have to pay the investors a risk premium in the form of a greater expected return in order to get them to purchase two-year securities.

Will borrowers be inclined to pay such a premium when issuing two-year securities? Yes, they will be so inclined. First, frequent refinancing may be costly in terms of registration, advertising, paperwork, and so on. These costs can be lessened by issuing relatively long-term securities. Second, some borrowers will realize that relatively long-term bonds are a less risky source of funds than relatively short-term bonds, since they will not have to be as concerned about the possibility of refinancing in the future at higher interest rates. Thus, borrowers may be willing to pay more (via higher expected interest costs) for relatively long-term funds.

In the example, the one-year spot rate was 7% and the two-year spot rate was 8%. As mentioned earlier, according to the liquidity preference theory, the only way investors will agree to follow a maturity strategy is if the expected return from doing so is higher than the expected return from following the rollover strategy. This means that the expected future spot rate must be something *less* than the forward rate of 9.01%—perhaps it is 8.6%. If so, then the value of a \$1 investment in two years is expected to be \$1(1.07)(1.086) = \$1.1620, if the rollover strategy is followed. Since the value of a \$1 investment with the maturity strategy is \$1(1.08)(1.08) = \$1.1664, it can be seen that the rollover strategy has a lower expected return for the two-year period, which can be attributed to its smaller degree of price risk.

Liquidity Premium

The difference between the forward rate and the expected future spot rate is known as the **liquidity premium**. It is the extra return given investors in order to entice them to purchase the more risky two-year security. In the example, it is equal to 9.01% − 8.6% = .41%. More generally,

$$f_{1,2} = es_{1,2} + L_{1,2} \tag{5.24}$$

where $L_{1,2}$ is the liquidity premium for the period commencing one year from now and ending two years from now.[7]

How does the liquidity preference theory explain the slope of the term structure? In order to answer this question, note that with the rollover strategy, the expected value of a dollar at the end of two years is $\$1(1+s_1)(1+es_{1,2})$. Alternatively, with the maturity strategy the expected value of a dollar at the end of two years is $\$1(1+s_2)(1+s_2)$. As mentioned earlier, according to the liquidity preference theory there is more risk with the maturity strategy,

---

[6] Unfortunately, this risk is often referred to as *liquidity risk*, when it more appropriately should be called *price risk*, since it is the price volatility associated with longer-term securities that is of concern to investors. Partially offsetting this price risk is a risk that is present in the rollover strategy and absent from the maturity strategy—namely, the risk associated with having an uncertain reinvestment rate at the end of the first year when the rollover strategy is chosen. The liquidity preference theory assumes that this risk is of relatively little concern to investors.

[7] It should be noted that while the forward rate can be determined, neither the expected future spot rate nor the liquidity premium can be observed. All that can be done is estimate their respective values.

which in turn means that it must have a higher expected return. That is, the following inequality must hold:

$$\$1(1 + s_2)(1 + s_2) > \$1(1 + s_1)(1 + es_{1,2}) \tag{5.25}$$

or

$$(1 + s_2)(1 + s_2) > (1 + s_1)(1 + es_{1,2}). \tag{5.26}$$

This inequality is the key to understanding how the liquidity preference theory explains the term structure.[8]

Downward Sloping Yield Curves

Consider the downward-sloping case first, where $s_1 > s_2$. The preceding inequality will hold in this situation only if the expected future spot rate ($es_{1,2}$) is substantially smaller than the current one-year spot rate (s_1).[9] Thus, a downward-sloping term structure will be observed only when the marketplace believes that interest rates are going to decline substantially.

As an example, assume that the one-year spot rate (s_1) is 7% and the two-year spot rate (s_2) is 6%. Since 7% is greater than 6%, this is a situation where the term structure is downward-sloping. Now, according to the previously given inequality,

$$(1 + .06)(1 + .06) > (1 + .07)(1 + es_{1,2})$$

which can hold only if the expected future spot rate ($es_{1,2}$) is substantially less than 7%. Given the one-year and two-year spot rates, the forward rate ($f_{1,2}$) is equal to 5.01%. Assuming the liquidity premium ($L_{1,2}$) is .41%, then according to equation (5.24), $es_{1,2}$ must be 5.01% – .41% = 4.6%. Thus, the term structure is downward-sloping because the current one-year spot rate of 7% is expected to decline to 4.6% in the future.

In comparison, the unbiased expectations theory would also explain the term structure by saying that the reason it was downward-sloping was because the one-year spot rate was expected to decline in the future. However, the unbiased expectations theory would expect the spot rate to decline only to 5.01%, not 4.6%.

Flat Yield Curves

Consider next the case of a flat term structure, where $s_1 = s_2$. The preceding inequality will hold in this situation only if $es_{1,2}$ is less than s_1. Thus, a flat term structure will occur only when the marketplace expects interest rates are going to decline. Indeed, if $s_1 = s_2 = 7\%$ and $L_{1,2} = .41\%$, then $f_{1,2} = 7\%$ and, according to equation (5.24), the expected future spot rate is 7% – .41% = 6.59%, a decline from the current one-year spot rate of 7%. This is in contrast to the unbiased expectations theory, where a flat term structure would be interpreted to mean that the marketplace expected interest rates to remain at the same level.

---

[8] Equation (5.24) can be expressed more generally as $f_{t-1,t} = es_{t-1,t} + L_{t-1,t}$. Thus, using equation (5.14), the liquidity preference theory states that

$$(1 + s_t)^t = (1 + s_{t-1})^{t-1} \times (1 + es_{t-1,t} + L_{t-1,t}).$$

Since $L_{t-1,t} > 0$, it follows that, in general,

$$(1 + s_t)^t > (1 + s_{t-1})^{t-1} \times (1 + es_{t-1,t}).$$

[9] If $es_{1,2}$ were equal to or greater than s_1, then the inequality would not hold in the correct direction, since it was assumed that $s_1 > s_2$.

Upward Sloping Yield Curves

The last case of an upward-sloping yield curve is one where $s_1 < s_2$. If it is slightly upward-sloping, this can be consistent with an expectation that interest rates are going to decline in the future. For example, if $s_1 = 7\%$ and $s_2 = 7.1\%$, then the forward rate is 7.2%. In turn, if the liquidity premium is .41%, then the expected future spot rate is $6.79\% = 7.2\% - .41\%$, a decline from the current one-year spot rate of 7%. Thus, the reason for the slight upward slope to the term structure is that the marketplace expects only a slight decline in the spot rate. In contrast, the unbiased expectations theory would argue that the reason for the slight upward slope was the expectation of a slight increase in the spot rate.

If the term structure is more steeply sloped, then it is more likely that the marketplace expects interest rates to rise in the future. For example, if $s_1 = 7\%$ and $s_2 = 7.3\%$, then the forward rate is 7.6%. Continuing to assume a liquidity premium of .41%, equation (5.24) indicates that the marketplace expects the one-year spot rate to rise from 7% to $7.6\% - .41\% = 7.19\%$. The unbiased expectations theory would also explain this steep slope by saying that the spot rate was expected to rise in the future, but by a larger amount. In particular, the unbiased expectations theory would state that the spot rate was expected to rise to 7.6%, not 7.19%.

In summary, with the liquidity preference theory, downward-sloping term structures are indicative of an expected decline in the spot rate, whereas upward-sloping term structures may indicate either an expected rise or an expected decline, depending on how steep the slope is. Generally, the steeper the slope, the more likely it is that the marketplace expects spot rates to rise. If roughly half the time investors expect spot rates will rise and half the time investors expect spot rates will decline, then the liquidity preference theory suggests that there should be more occurrences of upward-sloping term structures than downward-sloping ones. As mentioned earlier, this is indeed what has happened.

▶ The Market Segmentation Theory

A third explanation for the determination of the term structure rests on the assumption that there is market segmentation: various investors and borrowers are asserted to be restricted by law, preference, or custom to certain maturities. Perhaps there is a market for short-term securities, another for intermediate-term securities, and a third for long-term securities. According to the **market segmentation theory**, spot rates are determined by supply and demand conditions in each market. Furthermore, in its most restrictive form, this theory suggests that investors and borrowers will not leave their market and enter a different one even when the current rates indicate that there is a substantially higher expected return available by making such a move.[10]

With this theory, an upward-sloping term structure exists when the intersection of the supply and demand curves for shorter-term funds is at a lower interest rate than the intersection for longer-term funds. Conversely, a downward-sloping term structure would exist when the intersection for shorter-term funds was at a higher interest rate than the intersection for longer-term funds.

---

[10] A more moderate version is the **preferred habitat theory**, where borrowers and investors will leave their desired maturity segment if there are significant differences in the yields in the various segments.

▸ Empirical Evidence for the Theories

Empirical evidence based on US data provides some insight into the determinants of the term structure, but it is difficult to assess the relative importance of these three theories with a high degree of precision.

The market segmentation theory receives relatively slight empirical validation. This is understandable, given that the theory will not hold if there are some investors and borrowers who are flexible enough to be willing to move into whatever segment has the highest expected return. By their actions, these investors and borrowers will give the term structure a continuity that is linked to expectations of future interest rates.

There does appear to be some evidence that the term structure conveys information about expected future spot rates, as hypothesized by both the unbiased expectations and liquidity preference theories. However, the evidence tends to favour the latter theory, since liquidity premiums also appear to exist.[11] In particular, there appear to be liquidity premiums of increasing size associated with US Treasury securities of up to roughly one year in maturity. However, there do not appear to be any additional premiums beyond one-year maturities. That is, investors seem to demand a premium in order to get them to purchase a one-year security instead of, say, a one-month security. However, no additional premiums are needed in order to get them to purchase two-year securities (even though the two-year security has more price risk than a one-year security).

Two tests of term structure theories show that Canadian data are consistent with the unbiased expectations plus liquidity preference theories in the intermediate maturity range, but the possibility that some market segmentation exists in the long end of the market cannot be rejected.[12]

In summary, it appears that expectations about future spot rates are important determinants of the term structure. Liquidity premiums appear to exist but do not increase in size beyond roughly a year, meaning that investment strategies involving securities with maturities of one year or more will have roughly the same expected return.

Examining the term structure of interest rates is important for determining the current set of spot rates, which can be used as a basis for valuing any fixed-income security. Such an examination is also important because it provides some information about what the marketplace expects regarding the level of future interest rates.

---

[11] The empirical evidence is not without dispute. Fama has argued that the evidence is inconsistent with both the unbiased expectations and liquidity preference theories, but McCulloch refutes Fama's findings and argues in favour of the latter theory. See Eugene F. Fama, "Term Premiums in Bond Returns," *Journal of Financial Economics* 13, no. 4 (December 1984): 529–46 and J. Huston McCulloch, "The Monotonicity of the Term Premium: A Closer Look," *Journal of Financial Economics* 18, no. 1 (March 1987): 185–92 and "An Estimate of the Liquidity Premium, *Journal of Political Economy* 83, no. 1 (February 1975): 95–119. McCulloch's findings are supported by Matthew Richardson, Paul Richardson, and Tom Smith in "The Monotonicity of the Term Premium: Another Look," *Journal of Financial Economics* 31, no. 1 (February 1992): 97–105.

[12] J. S. McCallum, "The Expected Holding Period Return, Uncertainty and the Term Structure of Interest Rates," *Journal of Finance* 30, no. 2 (May 1975): 307–323, and Maureen E. Howe and John S. McCallum, "The Term Structure of Interest Rates in Canada: The Empirical Evidence," *Journal of Business Administration* 12, no. 1 (Fall 1980):137–146.

SUMMARY

1. In order to understand how bonds are valued in the marketplace, it is convenient to examine initially those fixed-income securities that are free from default risk—namely, government securities.
2. The yield-to-maturity of a security is the discount rate that makes the present value of the security's promised future cash flows equal to the current market price of the security.
3. The spot rate is the yield-to-maturity on a pure discount security.
4. Once spot rates (each one associated with a different maturity) have been calculated, they can be used, for example, to value coupon-bearing government securities.
5. A forward rate is the interest rate, established today, that will be paid on money to be borrowed at some specific time in the future, and to be repaid at an even more distant time in the future.
6. The payment of interest on interest is known as compounding.
7. Increasing the number of compounding intervals within a year will increase the effective annual interest rate.
8. A yield curve shows the relationship between yield-to-maturity and term-to-maturity for government securities. This relationship is also known as the term structure of interest rates.
9. Three theories have generally been used to explain the term structure of interest rates: the unbiased expectations theory, the liquidity preference theory, and the market segmentation theory.
10. The unbiased expectations theory states that forward rates represent the consensus opinion about what spot rates will be in the future.
11. The liquidity preference theory states that forward rates represent the consensus opinion about future spot rates by an amount necessary to compensate investors for holding longer-maturity securities.
12. The market segmentation theory states that different spot rates have different values because of the interaction of supply and demand for funds in markets that are separated from each other by maturity.
13. Evidence tends to favour the liquidity preference theory, at least over maturities up to roughly one year.

QUESTIONS AND PROBLEMS

1. Consider two bonds, each with a $1000 face value and each with three years remaining to maturity.
   a. The first bond is a pure-discount bond that currently sells for $816.30. What is its yield-to-maturity?
   b. The second bond currently sells for $949.37 and makes annual coupon payments at a rate of 7% (that is, it pays $70 in interest per year). The first interest payment is due one year from today. What is this bond's yield-to-maturity?
2. Camp Douglas Dirigibles has a bond outstanding with four years to maturity, a face value of $1000, and an annual coupon payment of $100. What is the price of the Camp Douglas bond if its yield-to-maturity is 12%? If its yield-to-maturity is 8%?
3. The concept of yield-to-maturity is based on two crucial assumptions. What are those assumptions? What will happen to the bondholder's return if those assumptions are violated?

4. Patsy Dougherty bought a $1000-face-value bond with a 9% annual coupon and three years to maturity that makes its first interest payment one year from today. Patsy bought the bond for $975.13.

   a. What is the bond's yield-to-maturity?

   b. If Patsy is able to invest the bond's cash flows at only 7%, what is Patsy's actual annual compounded return on the bond investment, assuming that it is held to maturity? (Hint: Think in terms of the cash flows paid to Patsy, the bond's purchase price, and the term of the investment.)

5. Consider three pure-discount bonds with maturities of one, two, and three years and prices of $930.23, $923.79, and $919.54, respectively. Each bond has a $1000 face value. Based on this information, what are the one-year, two-year, and three-year spot rates?

6. What are the discount factors associated with three-year, four-year, and five-year $1000-face-value pure-discount bonds that sell for $810.60, $730.96, and $649.93, respectively?

7. Distinguish between spot rates and forward rates.

8. Given the following spot rates for various periods of time from today, calculate forward rates from years one to two, two to three, and three to four.

Years from Today	*Spot Rate*
1	5.0%
2	5.5
3	6.5
4	7.0

9. Given the following forward rates, calculate the one-, two-, three-, and four-year spot rates.

Forward Time Period	*Forward Rate*
$f_{0,1}$	10.0%
$f_{1,2}$	9.5
$f_{2,3}$	9.0
$f_{3,4}$	8.5

10. Assume that the current one-year spot rate is 6% and the forward rates for one year hence and two years hence are, respectively:

$$f_{1,2} = 9\%$$

$$f_{2,3} = 10\%$$

What should be the market price of an 8% coupon bond, with a $1000 face value, maturing three years from today? The first interest payment is due one year from today. Interest is payable annually.

11. Assume that the government has issued three bonds. The first, which pays $1000 one year from today, is now selling for $909.09. The second, which pays $100 one year from

today and $1100 one year later, is now selling for $991.81. The third, which pays $100 one year from today, $100 one year later, and $1100 one year after that, is now selling for $997.18.

a. What are the current discount factors for dollars paid one, two, and three years from today?

b. What are the forward rates?

c. Helen Wagner, a friend, offers to pay you $500 one year from today, $600 two years from today, and $700 three years from today in return for a loan today. Assuming that Helen will not default on the loan, how much should you be willing to loan?

12. La Banque Nationale offers a passbook savings account that pays interest at a stated annual rate of 6%. Calculate the effective annual interest rate paid by La Banque Nationale if it compounds interest:

a. Semiannually

b. Daily (365 days in a year)

13. Marty MacDonald is considering placing $30 000 in a three-year, default-free fixed-income investment that promises to provide interest at the rate of 8% during the first year, 10% in the second year, and 12% in the third year. Coupon payments can be reinvested at the rate in effect for the following year.

a. Assuming annual compounding and repayment of principal at the end of the third year, to what value is Marty's investment expected to grow after three years?

b. Recalculate your answer to part (a) assuming semiannual compounding.

14. Using the *Globe and Mail* as a data source, turn to the table entitled "Canada Bonds." Find the yield-to-maturity for government securities maturing in approximately one month, three months, one year, five years, ten years, and twenty years. With this information, construct the yield curve as of the paper's publication date.

15. Is it true that an observed downward-sloping yield curve is inconsistent with the liquidity preference theory of the term structure of interest rates? Explain.

16. Assume that the current structure of forward interest rates is upward sloping. Which will have a lower yield-to-maturity:

a. A 15-year pure-discount bond or a 10-year pure-discount bond?

b. A 10-year 5% coupon bond or a 10-year 6% pure-discount bond?

17. How would your answers to question 16 change if the forward interest rate structure were downward sloping?

18. Three theories explaining the term structure of interest rates are described in this chapter. Which theory do you believe best explains the relationship between spot rates and term-to-maturity? Provide supporting arguments for your answer.

19. Assume that the current spot rates are as follows:

Years from Today	*Spot Rate*
1 year	8%
2 years	9%
3 years	10%

If the unbiased expectations theory holds, what should be the yields-to-maturity on one- and two-year pure discount bonds one year from today?

CFA Exam Questions

20. The following are the average yields of US Treasury bonds at two different points in time.

	Yield-to-Maturity	
Term to Maturity	*January 15, 19XX*	*May 15, 19XX*
1 year	7.25%	8.05%
2 years	7.50	7.90
3 years	7.90	7.70
10 years	8.30	7.45
15 years	8.45	7.30
20 years	8.55	7.20
25 years	8.60	7.10

a. Assuming a pure expectations hypothesis, define a forward rate. Describe how you would calculate the forward rate for a three-year US Treasury bond two years from May 15, 19XX, using the actual term structure above.

b. Discuss how each of the three major term structure hypotheses could explain the January 15, 19XX term structure shown above.

c. Discuss what happened to the term structure over the time period and the effect of this change on the US Treasury bonds of two and ten years.

d. Assume that you invest solely on the basis of yield spreads, and in January 19XX acted upon the expectation that the yield spread between one-year and twenty-five-year US Treasuries would return to a more typical spread of 170 basis points. Explain what you would have done on January 15, 19XX, and describe what happened between January 15, 19XX and May 15, 19XX.

21. a. Calculate the two-year spot rate implied by the US Treasury yield curve data given below. Assume that interest is paid annually for purposes of this calculation. Show all calculations.

Years to Maturity	*Current Coupon Yield-to-Maturity*	*Spot Rate*
1	7.5%	7.5%
2	8.0	—

b. Explain why a spot rate curve can be derived entirely from the current coupon (yield-to-maturity) yield curve.

c. Given a US Treasury one-year spot rate of 9.0% and a US Treasury two-year spot rate of 9.5%, calculate the implied one-year forward rate for the two-year US Treasury security with one year remaining to maturity. Explain why a one-year forward rate of 9.6% would not be expected to prevail in a market given these spot rates.

d. Describe one practical application of the spot rate concept and one practical application of the forward rate concept.

KEY TERMS

yield-to-maturity
spot rate
discount factors
market discount function
discounting
forward rate
forward contract
compounding
annual percentage rate (APR)
bank discount method
yield curve
term structure
unbiased expectations theory
liquidity preference theory
liquidity premium
market segmentation theory
preferred habitat theory

REFERENCES

1. Many of the fundamental concepts having to do with bonds are discussed in:

   Homer Sidney and Martin L. Leibowitz, *Inside the Yield Book: New Tools for Bond Market Strategy* (Englewood Cliffs, NJ: Prentice Hall, 1972).

   Marcia Stigum, *The Money Market* (Homewood, IL: Business One Irwin, 3rd ed., 1990).

   Frank J. Fabozzi, ed., *The Handbook of Fixed-Income Securities* (Howewood, IL: Business One Irwin, 3rd ed., 1991).

2. A discussion of the zero coupon government bond market is presented in:

   Deborah W. Gregory and Miles Livingston, "Development of the Market for US Treasury STRIPS," *Financial Analysts Journal* 48, no. 2 (March/April 1992): 68–74.

3. For a thorough review of term structure theories and the associated empirical evidence, see:

   John H. Wood and Norma L. Wood, *Financial Markets* (San Diego, CA: Harcourt Brace Jovanovich, 1985), Chapter 19.

   Frederic S. Mishkin, *The Economics of Money, Banking, and Financial Markets* (Glenview, IL: Scott, Foresman, 1989), Chapter 7.

   Peter A. Abken, "Innovations in Modeling the Term Structure of Interest Rates," Federal Reserve Bank of Atlanta, *Economic Review* 75, no. 4 (July/August 1990): 2–27.

   Frank J. Fabozzi and Franco Modigliani, *Capital Markets: Institutions and Instruments* (Englewood Cliffs, NJ: Prentice Hall, 1992), Chapter 12.

   Steven Russell, "Understanding the Term Structure of Interest Rates: The Expectations Theory," Federal Reserve Bank of St. Louis, *Review* 74, no. 4 (July/August 1992): 36–50.

   James C. Van Horne, *Financial Market Rates and Flows* (Englewood Cliffs, NJ: Prentice Hall, 1994), Chapter 5.

4. For a comparison of the traditional unbiased expectations theory and the modern expectations theory of the term structure of interest rates, see:

   John H. Wood and Norma L. Wood, *Financial Markets* (San Diego, CA: Harcourt Brace Jovanovich, 1985), pp. 645–651.

5. For a discussion of the preferred habitat theory of the term structure of interest rates, see:

   Frank J. Fabozzi and Franco Modigliani, *Capital Markets: Institutions and Instruments* (Englewood Cliffs, NJ: Prentice Hall, 1991), pp. 387–388.

   James C. Van Horne, *Financial Market Rates and Flows* (Englewood Cliffs, NJ: Prentice Hall, 1994), pp. 101, 112–113.

6. For an intriguing tax-based explanation of why the yield curve has usually been upward sloping, see:

   Richard Roll, "After-Tax Investment Results from Long-Term vs. Short-Term Discount Coupon Bonds," *Financial Analysts Journal* 40, no. 1 (January/February 1984): 43–54.

   Ricardo J. Rodriguez, "Investment Horizon, Taxes and Maturity Choice for Discount Coupon Bonds," *Financial Analysts Journal* 44, no. 5 (September/October 1988): 67–69.

7. For a Canadian perspective on the topics covered in this chapter, see:

   Steven Dobson, "The Term Structure of Interest Rates and the Maturity Composition of the Government Debt: The Canadian Case," *Canadian Journal of Economics* (August 1973).

   Clarence L. Barber and John S. McCallum, "The Term Structure of Interest Rates and the Maturity Composition of the Government Debt," *Canadian Journal of Economics* (November 1975).

   James E. Pesando, "The Impact of the Conversion Loan on the Term Structure of Interest Rates in Canada: Some Additional Evidence," *Canadian Journal of Economics* (May 1975).

   G. Lan et E. Otuteye, "L'Evolution des Taux courants et à Terme Sur le Marché de Bons de Trésor (Canada, 1962–1991), *Finéco* 4, no. 1 (1er semestre 1994).

CHAPTER 6

The Valuation of Risky Securities

Payments received from riskless securities can be accurately predicted: neither their amounts nor their timing is uncertain. But many securities do not meet such high standards. Some or all of their payments are *contingent* on events with respect to amount, timing, or both. A bankrupt corporation may not make its promised bond payments in full or on time. A worker who is laid off may pay his or her bills late (or not at all). A corporation may reduce or eliminate its dividend if its business becomes unprofitable, and so on.

The security analyst must try to evaluate the circumstances affecting a risky investment's payments and enumerate the key events upon which such payments are contingent. For example, an aircraft manufacturer's fortunes may depend on whether or not the firm is awarded a major contract by the government, whether or not its recently introduced commercial aircraft is accepted by the airlines, whether or not there is an upturn in the economy with a concomitant increase in demand for airline travel, and so on. To value the stock of such a company properly, the analyst must consider each of these contingencies and estimate the corresponding effect on the firm and its stock.

Identifying important influences and evaluating the impact of each one is exceedingly difficult. Among other things, the appropriate level of detail must be determined. The number of potentially relevant events is almost always very large, and the analyst must attempt to focus on the relatively few that appear to be most important. In some cases it may be best to differentiate only a few alternatives (for example, whether the economy will turn up, turn down, or stay the same). In some cases, finer distinctions may be needed (for example, whether the gross national product will be up 1%, 2%, 3%, and so on).

The process of identifying and evaluating key influences is central to security analysis. The *use* of such estimates is of concern in this chapter. After the contingencies have been identified and the corresponding payments estimated, how can the value of the security be determined?

MARKET VERSUS PERSONAL VALUATION

One approach to the valuation of risky securities focuses on the investor's personal attitudes and circumstances. Given his or her assessment of the likelihood of various contingencies, and feelings about the corresponding risks involved in an investment, an investor might determine the amount he or she would be willing to pay by some sort of introspection. This would be a "personal" valuation of the security.

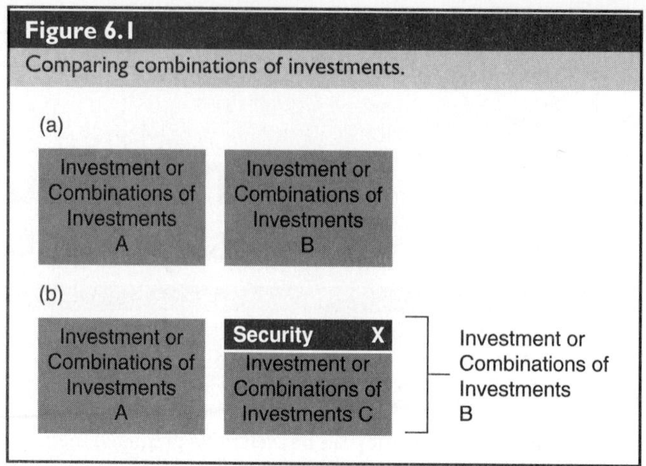

Figure 6.1
Comparing combinations of investments.

Such an approach would be appropriate if there were only one investment in the world. But such is not the case. A security need not and should not be valued without considering available alternatives. Current market values of other securities provide important information, since a security is seldom so unique that nothing else is even comparable. Security valuation should not be done in a vacuum; it should be performed in a market context.

Key to this approach is the comparison of one investment or combination of investments with others having comparable characteristics. For example, assume that A and B in Figure 6.1(a) are similar in this respect; then the two should be equal in value.

Now imagine that alternative B includes a security that an investor wishes to value — call it X. Moreover, assume that all other securities included in A and B are regularly traded and that their market values (prices) are widely reported and easily determined. Combination B can be thought to have two components: security X and the rest, which will be represented by C, as in Figure 6.1(b). Combination C might include many securities, only one, or, as a very special case, none at all.

If people are willing to purchase combination A for a value of V_A, they should be willing to purchase combination B for the same amount, since the two provide comparable prospects. Thus,

$$V_A = V_B.$$

The value of B will, however, be simply the sum of the present values of its components:

$$V_B = V_X + V_C.$$

This implies that the value of security X can be determined solely by reference to market values placed on the securities comprising combinations A and C. Since

$$V_A = V_X + V_C$$

then

$$V_X = V_A - V_C.$$

Therefore, the value of X can be determined by subtracting the value of C from the value of A.

APPROACHES TO SECURITY VALUATION

It is reasonable enough to say that market prices of "comparable investments" should be used to determine the value of a security. But when are two investments truly comparable?

An obvious case arises when investments provide identical payments in every possible contingency. If an investment's outcome is affected by relatively few events, it may be possible to purchase a set of other investments, each of which pays off in only one of the relevant contingencies. A properly selected mix of such investments may thus be completely comparable to the one to be valued. The next section illustrates this approach with an example drawn from the field of insurance.

A much more common approach to valuation is less detailed but more useful. Two alternatives are considered comparable if they offer similar expected returns and contribute equally to portfolio risk. Central to this view is the need to assess the probabilities of various contingencies. The remainder of this chapter and the next four chapters are devoted to this more widely used *risk-return approach*.

EXPLICIT VALUATION OF CONTINGENT PAYMENTS

Insurance

Insurance policies are highly explicit examples of contingent payments. One can buy a \$100 000 one-year "term" life insurance policy on a reasonably healthy 60-year-old for about \$2300. This, of course, can be viewed as an investment (albeit a morbid one): the sum of \$100 000 will be paid by the insurance company if the insured dies within a year; otherwise nothing at all will be paid. Involved is the sacrifice of a present certain value (\$2300) for a future uncertain value. The only relevant event is the possible death of the insured, and the relationship between that event and the amount to be paid is crystal clear.

Now imagine that a reasonably healthy 60-year-old executive asks you for a one-year loan. The executive would like as much as possible now; in return he or she promises to pay you \$100 000 at the end of the year. Your problem is to determine the present value of that promise — that is, how much to advance now. Put somewhat differently, you must determine an appropriate interest rate for the loan.

To keep the example simple, assume that the only source of uncertainty is the borrower's ability to remain in this position and thus earn the requisite money, and that this depends only on his or her continued presence among the living. In other words, if the borrower lives, the \$100 000 will be repaid in full and on time; otherwise, you will receive nothing.

The piece of paper representing the executive's promise to pay \$100 000 is your security X. What is it worth? The answer clearly depends in an important way on the available alternatives. A crucial factor is the current rate of interest.

Assume that the going rate for riskless one-year loans is 8%. If there were no doubt whatever that the executive would repay the loan, it would be reasonable to advance \$92 592.59 (since \$100 000/\$92 592.59 = 1.08). However, the uncertainty connected with the loan makes this inadvisable. The appropriate amount is obviously less. But how much less?

In this case an answer can easily be determined. It would be entirely reasonable to advance at most \$90 292.59, making the *promised* interest rate on the loan approximately 10.75% (since 100 000/90 292.59 = 1.1075). The basis for this calculation is quite simple.

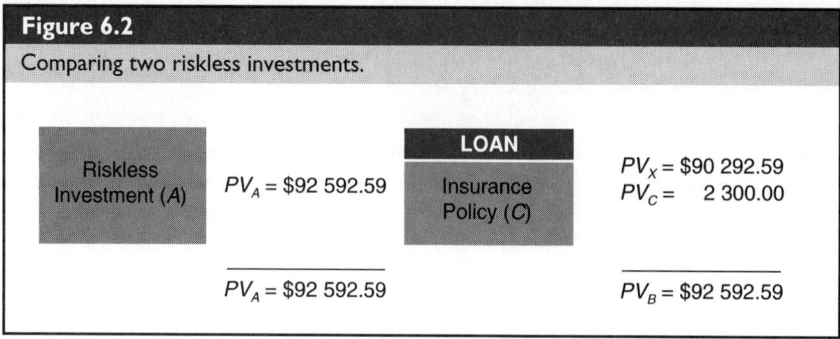

Figure 6.2
Comparing two riskless investments.

It relies on the fact that an investor can insure against the relevant risk, obtaining an overall position that is completely riskless.

Table 6.1 provides the details. The relevant event is whether or not the executive survives the year. The loan is thus a risky investment, paying $100 000 only if the executive lives. The life insurance policy is also a risky investment, paying $100 000 only if the executive dies. But a *portfolio* that includes both investments is totally riskless: Its owner will receive $100 000, no matter what happens! By paying $90 292.59 for the loan and $2300 for the insurance policy, an investor could give up $92 592.59 now for a certain payment of $100 000 a year hence—obtaining a riskless return of 8%, which is the going rate on other riskless ventures.

Table 6.1
Costs and Payments for a Loan and an Insurance Policy.

	Event		
Item	*Executive Dies*	*Executive Lives*	*Cost*
Loan	0	$100 000	$90 292.59
Insurance policy	$100 000	0	2 300.00
Total	$100 000	$100 000	$92 592.59

This is, of course, an application of the general procedure described in the previous section. Figure 6.2 summarizes the details in the format used earlier, for purposes of comparison.

Valuation in a Complete Market

Assume, for the present, that market values can be used to estimate the present value of any contingent payment. A market in which such detailed quotations are available is termed a **complete market**. While no real market conforms to this specification, it is useful to see how valuation would be done in such circumstances.

First, a way to represent the present value of a guaranteed commitment to pay $1 at a specified time if (and only if) a specified event or "state of the world" occurs is needed. The following will suffice:

$$PV(\$1,t,e)$$

where

t = the time at which the dollar is to be paid

e = the event that must occur if the dollar is to be paid.

Armed with this notation, any risky investment can now be analyzed. Every possible contingency could, in theory, be considered separately, giving a (probably very lengthy) list of contingent payments of the following form:

Time of Payment	Event on Which Payment Is Contingent	Amount of Payment
t_1	e_1	D_1
t_2	e_2	D_2
⋮	⋮	⋮

Of course, some of the events might be the same, as might some of the times and amounts.

To find the present value of the investment, the present value of each of its contingent payments must be found and then added together:

(1) Time of Payment	(2) Event on Which Payment Is Contingent	(3) Amount of Payment	(4) Discount Factor	(5) = (3) × (4) Present Value
t_1	e_1	D_1	$PV(\$1,t_1,e_1)$	$D_1 \times PV(\$1,t_1,e_1)$
t_2	e_2	D_2	$PV(\$1,t_2,e_2)$	$D_2 \times PV(\$1,t_2,e_2)$
⋮	⋮	⋮	⋮	⋮
			Total value =	______________

This method of valuation is commonly termed the **state-preference approach**, since it begins with the assumption that people's preferences are for *state-contingent claims* and concludes that securities will be valued on the basis of their payoffs in different "states of the world."

► The Limitations of Insurance

Some believe that Lloyd's of London will insure almost anything. If so, this could ease the security analyst's task considerably. He or she would only (!) have to determine the payments ($D_1,D_2,\ldots$) associated with an investment, the times at which they could be made ($t_1,t_2,\ldots$), and the events on which they were contingent ($e_1,e_2,\ldots$). The analyst could then use the premiums specified for the relevant insurance policies as estimates of appropriate discount factors [$PV(\$1,t_1,e_1),(PV(\$1,t_2,e_2),\ldots$], and perform the required calculations.

But even if Lloyd's will insure anything, the premiums charged for many policies might attract no takers. There are a number of interrelated reasons for this. As a case in point, imagine an aerospace company, the future profits of which depend heavily on whether or not the firm will be awarded a major government contract. Why not buy an appropriate insurance policy from Lloyd's, guaranteed to pay off if the firm loses the contract? Then only Lloyd's and the other firms in the industry would care about the outcome.

The idea is obviously whimsical. If Lloyd's were even willing to issue such a policy, the cost would be more than anyone would be likely to pay. Why? First, because of differences in *information*. Those familiar with the company or the government or both have better information about the likely outcome and can better assess the likelihood of various alternatives. Lloyd's operates at least partly in the dark. To protect itself, it will charge more than otherwise.

Second, there is the likelihood of **adverse selection**. If a policy of this sort is offered at a price low enough to attract anyone at all, the insurer can expect the firms that are least likely to win the contract to buy insurance, whereas those most likely to get the contract will take their chances. This occurs frequently with life insurance. The less healthy an individual, the more likely he or she is to buy a policy; for this reason, the insured is usually required to pass a medical examination as a condition of sale. An examination of the health of a company's bid to win a government award might be much more difficult or expensive, so an insurance company must set its fees for such a policy on the assumption that it would end up insuring the riskiest client or clients.

Another factor is the thoroughly modern phenomenon described by the term **moral hazard**. The purchase of insurance may affect the likelihood of occurence of the event in question. If the manager of a firm is insured against the loss of the contract, he or she may well put less effort into the attempt to win it, increasing the likelihood of its loss and the insurance company's obligation to pay off. This explains the reluctance of an insurance company to insure a house or car for more than its replacement value and the desire of many shareholders to have a corporation's officers own some of the firm's stock and none of its competitors' issues. Here again, the insurance company will account for this effect when setting prices.

Finally, there is the simple matter of *overhead*. Insurance people like to eat, as do investors who provide the capital that insurance companies need. The costs of doing business will, over the long pull, be reflected in the prices charged for that business. No financial service is free, and insurance is no exception.

For all these reasons securities markets do not conform to the specifications of the complete-market state-preference model. Although the approach is helpful for addressing certain theoretical issues, it is less useful for investment purposes than the risk-return (or "mean-variance") approach, to which the discussion now turns.

PROBABILISTIC FORECASTING

Assessing Probabilities

Lacking a plethora of widely available and low-cost insurance policies, it is not possible to value an investment without explicitly considering the likelihood of various outcomes. Instead, the analyst must attempt to assess directly the likelihood of each major event that can affect an investment. In short, he or she must engage in *probabilistic forecasting*.

The idea is simple enough, although its implementation is exceedingly difficult. The analyst expresses his or her assessment of the likelihood of every relevant event as a *probability*. If he or she feels that the chances of an event's taking place are 50-50, a probability of .50 is attached to the event. If the chances seem to be 3 out of 4, the probability is $^3/_4$, or .75 (another way of expressing this is to say that the *odds* are 3 to 1 that the event will take place). If the analyst considers an event to be absolutely *certain*, a probability of 1.0 should be assigned. If he or she feels an event is completely impossible, its probability of occurrence is zero.

It is important, of course, to be consistent in one's estimates. For example, if the events on a list are *mutually exclusive* and *exhaustive* (that is, one of them, but only one, will take place), the probabilities should sum to one.

Probability is, basically, a *subjective* concept. Even simple cases fall under this heading. For example, a gambler may assess the probability of a coin's coming up heads at .5, based on knowledge of coins and observations of the coin in question in the past. But the estimate is still subjective, involving the implicit assumption that the coin really is "fair" and that the past is an appropriate guide to the future. Similar cases arise frequently in security analysis. Relative *frequencies* of various returns in the past are sometimes used as estimates of the *probabilities* of such returns in the future. Clearly this procedure relies on assumptions that require subjective judgment and may in some circumstances be totally inappropriate. Forecasts based on the extrapolation of past relationships are neither wholly objective nor necessarily to be preferred over predictions obtained in more subtle ways.

Probabilistic forecasting entails a decision to confront uncertainty head on, acknowledge its existence, and try to measure its extent. Instead of attempting to answer a question such as "What will Imperial Oil earn next year?" the analyst explicitly considers some of the more likely alternatives and the likelihood of each one. This brings the analysis out in the open, allowing both the estimator and the user or users of such estimates to assess the reasonableness of the values. Insistence on a single number for each estimate, with no measure of associated uncertainty, would suggest naiveté or insecurity on the part of the producer or the consumer of such predictions.

In some organizations analysts engage in explicit probabilistic forecasting, passing on all their detailed assessments to others charged with bringing together the estimates made within the group. In other organizations the analysts make explicit probabilistic forecasts but summarize their evaluations in a relatively few key estimates, sending only the latter to others. In still other organizations analysts do not engage in explicit probabilistic forecasting; instead, they produce estimates that summarize their implicit beliefs about the probabilities of various events. As always, it is not the form but the substance that matters.

► Probability Distributions

It is often convenient to portray probabilistic forecasts graphically. The possible outcomes are represented on the horizontal axis and the associated probabilities on the vertical axis. Figure 6.3 provides an example. In this case the outcomes are qualitatively different in nature and can be listed only on the horizontal axis; the ordering and spacing are arbitrary.

Figure 6.4 shows a somewhat different case. Here the alternative outcomes differ quantitatively and with regard to only one variable: earnings per share next year. In this instance the analyst has chosen to group together all possibilities from \$.90 to \$.99, assess the probability that the actual amount will fall within that range, and then repeat the process for the range from \$1.00 to \$1.09, the range from \$1.10 to \$1.19, and so on.

The analysis could, of course, have been conducted at a more detailed level, with probabilities estimated for outcomes in the ranges from \$.90 to \$.94, \$.95 to \$.99, and so on. An even more detailed analysis would assign a probability to every possible outcome. In this case the bars would be numerous, and each would be very thin, as shown in Figure 6.5. Note that the more numerous the number of bars, the smaller the sizes of associated probabilities.

Figure 6.3

Probabilities of a National or American League team winning the World Series.

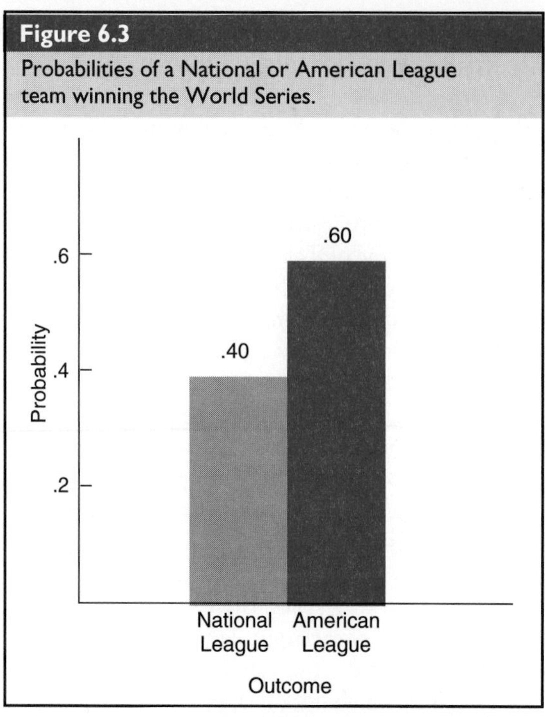

Figure 6.4

Probabilities of next year's earnings per share (using wide ranges).

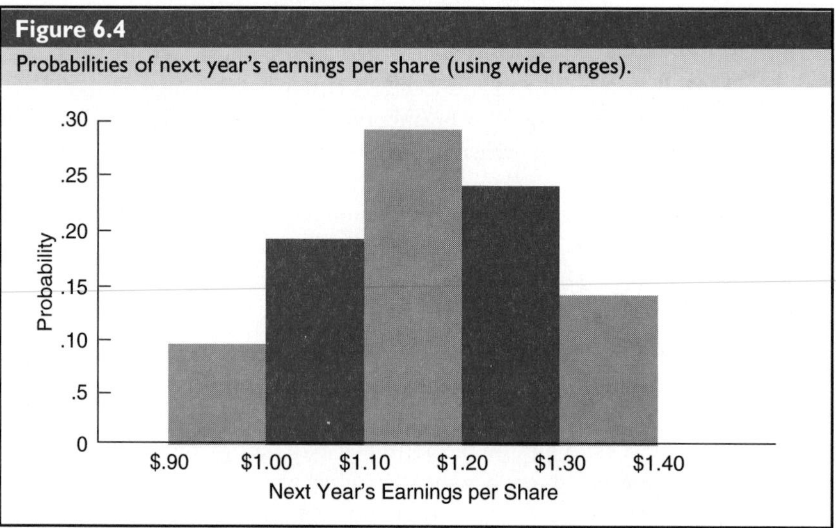

The ultimate in a detailed prediction is represented by a *continuous probability distribution*. Such a curve represents, in effect, the tops of many thin bars. (Technically, the curve represents what happens when there is an infinite number of such bars.) Three examples of curves of this type are shown in Figure 6.6; note that the vertical axis now measures probability density instead of probability. (The terms *mode, median* and *expected value* will be discussed later in the chapter.)

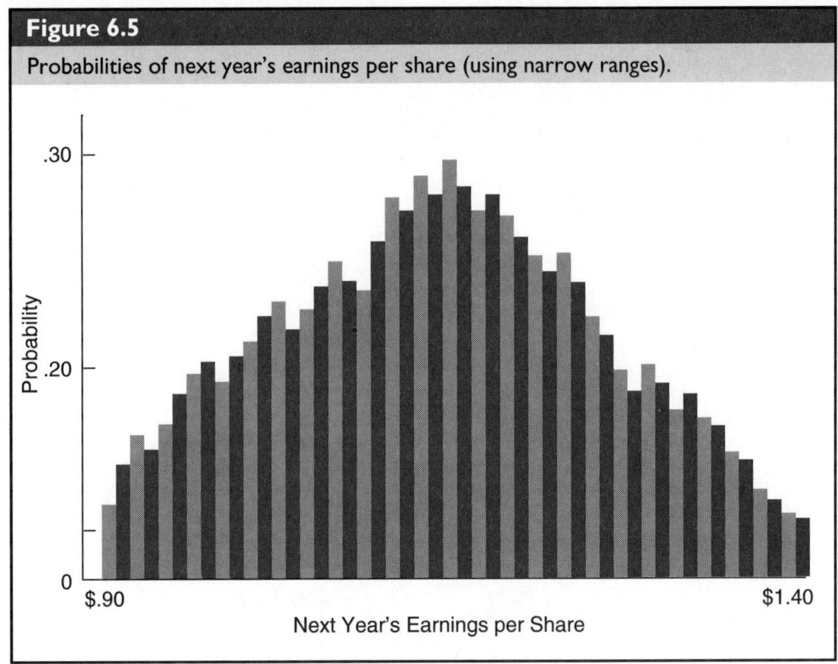

Figure 6.5

Probabilities of next year's earnings per share (using narrow ranges).

If continuous probability distributions are used, the analyst can forgo explicitly assessing particular individual outcomes. Instead, the analyst draws a curve representing the situation as he or she sees it. The relative likelihood of any single outcome (such as earnings per share of $1.035) is zero. However, the relative likelihood of any range of earnings is found by simply finding the size of the area under the curve but above the horizontal axis. Thus, the likelihood of earnings being between $1.03 and $1.04 could be found by measuring the area under the curve between $1.03 and $1.04, which in this case is approximately .07 (that is, there is a chance of 7 out of 100 that earnings will be between $1.03 and $1.04 next year). With a discrete probability distribution such as those shown in Figures 6.4 and 6.5, it was noted that the sum of the probabilities had to be 1. Now, with a continuous probability distribution, the total area under the curve must sum to 1.

Event Trees

When events follow one another over time or are in any sense dependent on one another, it is often useful to describe the alternative sequences with a tree diagram. Figure 6.7 (on page 133) provides an example.

A borrower has promised to pay $15 one year hence and $8 two years hence, if possible. The analyst feels the odds are only 40-60 that the first payment will in fact be made in full. Otherwise, the analyst feels the borrower will be able to pay only $10 one year hence.

As far as the second year is concerned, the likely situation depends, in this analyst's judgment, on the outcome in the first year. If the borrower manages to pay the full $15 in the first year, the analyst feels the odds are only 1 to 9 that the borrower will be able to meet the $8 commitment at the end of two years. Otherwise, the borrower will pay less: $6. On the other hand, if the borrower pays out $10 in the first year, although there appears to be no chance of recovering the $5 shortfall, the analyst feels the odds are about even that the

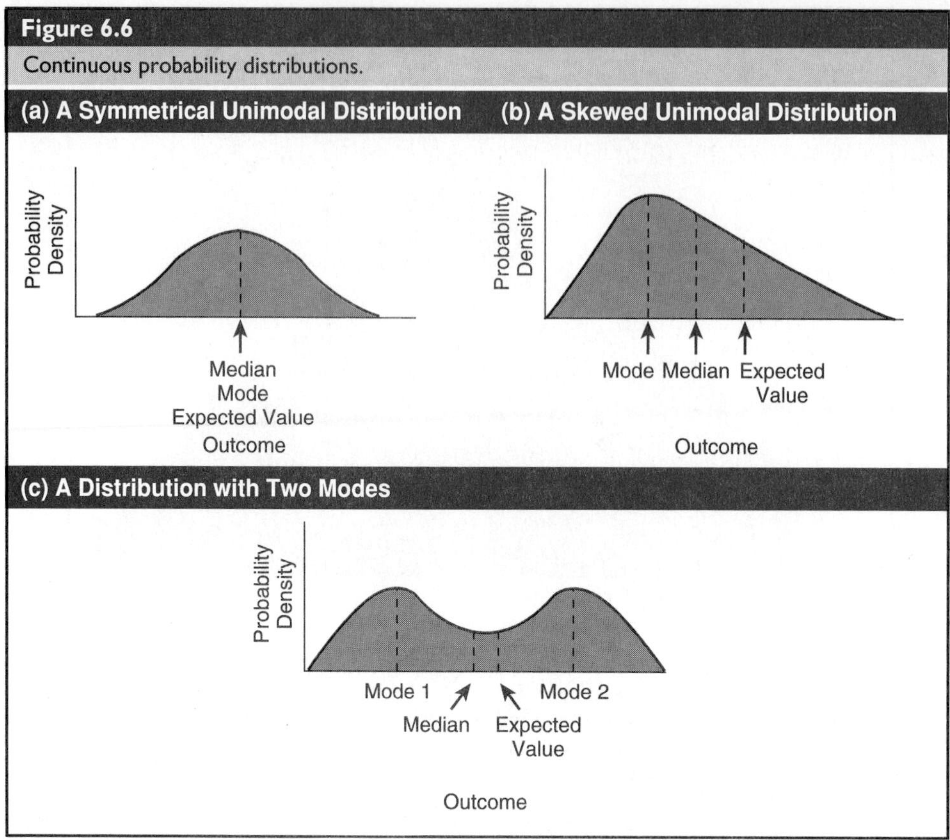

Figure 6.6

Continuous probability distributions.

promised $8 will be paid in the second year. If this does not happen, the analyst feels that $4 will be paid instead.

Figure 6.7 also shows the probability of each of the four possible sequences, or paths, through the tree. For example, the probability that both payments will be made in full is only .04, since there are only 40 chances out of 100 that the first payment will be made, and of those, only 1 out of 10 is expected to be followed by payment in full of the final obligation. This gives 4 out of 100 chances for the sequence: a probability of .04.

► Expected Value

Often an analyst is uncertain about an outcome but wishes (or is required) to summarize the situation with one or two numbers—one indicating the *central tendency* of the distribution of outcomes and one measuring *relevant risk*. Both return and risk are discussed in subsequent chapters; the remainder of this chapter concentrates on central tendencies.

How might a single number intended to summarize a set of possible outcomes be obtained? Obviously no satisfactory way can be found if the alternative outcomes differ qualitatively (for example, the National League versus the American League in winning the World Series). But if the outcomes differ quantitatively, and especially if they differ in only one dimension, a number of possibilities present themselves.

Perhaps the most common procedure is to adopt the *most likely* value. This is known as the **mode** of the probability distribution (for a continuous probability distribution, the

Figure 6.7

An event tree.

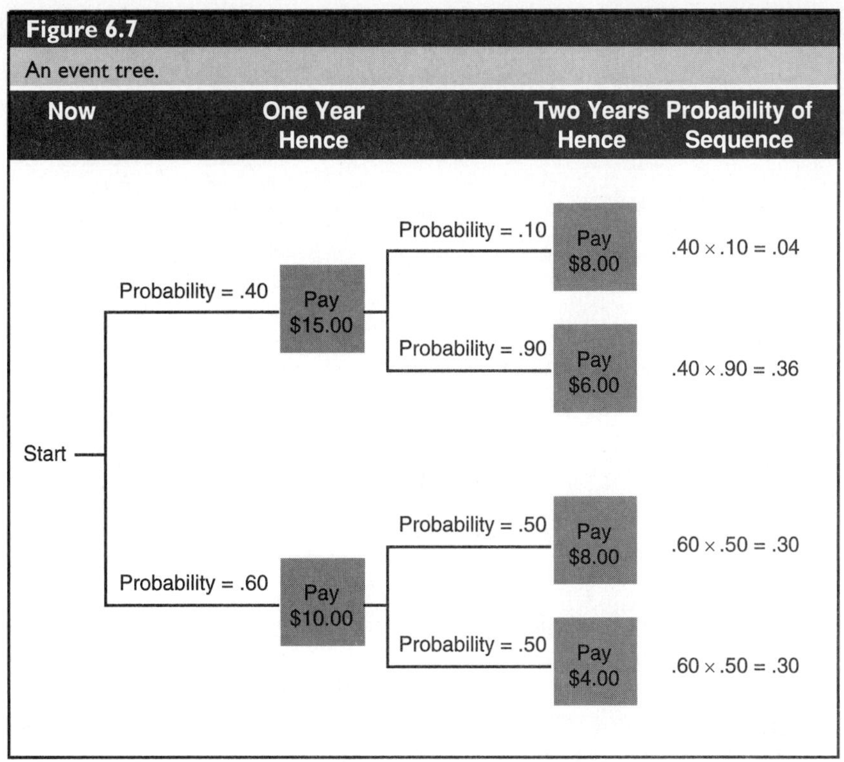

mode is the outcome with the highest probability density). Figure 6.6 shows the mode of each of the distributions. Note that in Figure 6.6(c) there are two modes: In this case, no single number can be used to answer the question in this manner.

Another alternative is to provide a "50-50" number—a value that is as likely to be too low as to be too high. This is called the **median** of the probability distribution. As shown in Figure 6.6, it may differ significantly from the mode(s).

A third alternative is to use an **expected value** (also known as the **mean**), a weighted average of all the possible outcomes, using the associated probabilities as weights. It takes into account all the information expressed in the distribution, both the *magnitude* and the *probability* of occurrence of each possible outcome. Almost any change in an investment's prospects or probabilities will affect the expected value of its outcomes (as it should).

In many instances there are no differences between these three measures. If the distribution is symmetric (each half is a mirror image of the other) and unimodal (there is one most likely value), then the median, mode, and expected value coincide, as in the case shown in Figure 6.6(a). Thus an analyst may choose to think in terms of, say, a 50-50 (median) value, even though the number wanted is the expected value. Only if the underlying probability distribution is highly skewed, as in Figure 6.6 (b), might this procedure lead to difficulties.

In those cases in which the values do differ, there are good reasons to prefer the expected value. As stated earlier, it takes all the estimates into account. But it has another advantage. Estimates about the prospects for securities serve as inputs for the process of portfolio construction or revision. The expected value of the return for a portfolio is related in a straightforward way to the expected values of the returns for its securities, but neither the

Table 6.2

Analysis of Effects of Announcements on Two Securities and a Portfolio of Both Securities.

Announcement	*Probability*	*Predicted Price of Security A*	*Predicted Price of Security B*	*Predicted Value of a Portfolio of A and B*
a	.10	$40.00	$62.00	$102.00
b	.20	42.00	65.00	107.00
c	.10	40.50	60.00	100.50
d	.25	41.00	61.00	102.00
e	.15	38.00	65.00	103.00
f	.10	40.50	59.00	99.50
g	.05	45.00	58.00	103.00
h	.05	40.50	58.00	98.50
	Expected Values:	$40.73	$61.90	$102.63

median nor the mode for a portfolio can, in general, be determined from comparable values for its securities.

Table 6.2 provides an example of the computation of expected values. An analyst is trying to predict the impact on the prices of two securities of a surprise television address scheduled by the President of the United States. The analyst has delineated a number of possible announcements, ranging from changes in the situation in the Middle East through a decision concerning the federal deficit. The alternatives represented in the table have been defined to be mutually exclusive and exhaustive (that is, every possible combination is shown in a different row). After much thought and with some trepidation, the analyst has also estimated the probability of each announcement and the resultant effect on the prices of the two securities. Finally, the analyst has computed the associated values of a portfolio containing one share of each stock.

The expected values are shown at the bottom of the table. Each is obtained by multiplying the probability of every announcement by the associated price, then summing. For example, the expected price of security A is determined by computing $[(.10 \times \$40.00) + (.20 \times \$42.00) + \cdots]$; that of security B by computing $[(.10 \times \$62.00) + (.20 \times \$65.00) + \cdots]$; and that of the portfolio by computing $[(.10 \times \$102.00) + (.20 \times \$107.00) + \cdots]$ Not surprisingly, the expected value of the portfolio equals the sum of the expected values of its component securities. When the expected values for the securities are added together, one is, in effect, adding $(.10 \times \$40.00 + \cdots)$ to $(.10 \times \$62.00 + \cdots)$. Clearly this will give the expected value of the portfolio, which is $.10 \times (\$40.00 + \$62.00) + \cdots$.

► Expected Versus Promised Yield-to-Maturity

If payments from a bond are certain, there is no difference between the expected yield-to-maturity and the promised amount. However, many bonds fail to meet these standards. Two types of risk may be involved. First, the issuer may defer some payments. A dollar received farther in the future is, of course, worth less than a dollar received on schedule; thus the present value of a bond will be smaller, the greater the likelihood that this might happen.

INSTITUTIONAL ISSUES

Cognitive Psychology

The bedrock on which theories of risky security valuation rest is the presumed existence of rational investors who respond in a predictable manner to the opportunities for gain and the risks of loss. As the text discusses, these investors are assumed to assess potential investments on the basis of expected outcomes derived from estimates of the investments' probability distributions of returns. Furthermore, the investors' estimates are assumed to exhibit no systematic biases relative to the "true" probability distributions. That is, investors do not consistently make mistakes in one direction or another when examining potential investments.

If such assumptions of rationality make sense for individual investors then we might reasonably believe that they apply even more appropriately to institutional investors. After all, institutional investors bring to bear extensive analytical resources on the investment management problem. Moreover, the decision-making structures of institutional investors — such as hierarchies of personnel, committees, and performance reviews — are all designed to promote consistent and rational investment choices.

The view of investors as objective decision-makers has traditionally gone unchallenged in the academic world. While many professional investors have argued that investing is dominated by the emotions of fear and greed, their opinions have been dismissed by academics as anecdotal and self-serving. More recently, however, a school of thought has developed among certain academics which argues that investors may not deal with risky choices in a totally rational manner. This line of reasoning is based on a branch of psychology known as *cognitive psychology*, which studies the capacity of human beings for perception and judgment.

Applied to the study of economic decision-making, and investments in particular, cognitive psychology draws some intriguing conclusions. Most fundamentally, people do not appear to be consistent in how they treat economically equivalent choices if the choices are presented in significantly different contexts. These differences are referred to as *framing effects*. Two prominent cognitive psychology researchers, Daniel Kahneman and Amos Tversky, cite a simple example of framing effects (see "The Psychology of Preferences," *Scientific American*, January 1982).

Suppose that you are walking to a Broadway play carrying a ticket that cost \$40. On reaching the theatre you discover that you have lost your ticket. Would you pay another \$40 for a ticket at the door? Now suppose that you were planning to buy the ticket at the door. On arriving you find that you have lost \$40 on the way. Would you still buy a ticket?

The economic consequences of these two situations are identical. You have lost \$40 and now must decide whether to spend another \$40. Interestingly, however, most people buy a ticket in the second case, but not in the first. People therefore appear to "frame" the choices differently. They treat the loss of cash differently from the loss of a ticket.

In terms of investing, these framing effects have been suggested to cause deviations from rational decision-making. For example, it appears that people react differently to situations involving the prospects for large gains as opposed to large losses. That is, investors are assumed to choose a more risky investment over a less risky one only if the expected return of the more risky investment is greater than that of the less risky investment. (This trait is known as risk aversion—see Chapter 7.) Indeed, this assumption seems to hold well for situations involving large gains. For example, consider a situation where you have invested in a start-up company and have a 90% chance of receiving \$1 million and a 10% chance of receiving nothing. Hence the expected payoff is $(.9 \times \$1 \text{ million}) + (.1 \times \$0) = \$900\ 000$. If somebody offered to buy you out for \$850 000, most likely you would accept the offer, since it

INSTITUTIONAL ISSUES (continued)

has nearly the same expected payoff but much less risk. That is, you would be exhibiting risk-aversion behaviour.

Now, however, consider a situation involving large losses. Suppose that you had invested in another start-up company. Things are going poorly, and if nothing changes there is a 90% chance of losing $1 million, but a 10% chance that things might work out well enough not to lose (or gain) anything. Thus the expected loss is (.9 × $1 million) + (.1 × $0) = $900 000. Another investor offers to take over the company if you pay him or her $850 000—a certain $850 000 loss. Most people would reject the offer and choose to remain with the risky option even though it has a lower expected value (–$900 000 versus –$850 000). Thus, in a situation involving large expected losses, people do not seem to exhibit risk-averse behaviour—a framing effect.

People also seem to overestimate the probability of unlikely events occurring and underestimate the probability of moderately likely events occurring. These traits may explain the popularity of lotteries buy may also have direct ramifications for the pricing of investments when the chances of success are low—such as bonds and stocks of bankrupt companies, start-up companies, and options whose strike prices are far above the underlying securities' prices.

Framing effects may also be involved in the observed tendency of investors to overreact to good and bad news. That is, some studies indicate that investors bid up the prices of companies reporting unexpectedly good earnings beyond the amount fairly warranted by the improved earnings. The converse seems to occur for companies reporting unexpectedly poor earnings.

Are the observations of cognitive psychologists relevant to the study of financial markets? Do these framing effects produce market anomalies that create exploitable investment opportunities or even undermine commonly accepted theories of security valuation? Or are these framing effects merely interesting stories whose impacts are overwhelmed by the sophistication and profit motive of avaricious investors? Certainly, investors as a whole are far from irrational, for large and persistent disparities between "fair" values and market values are difficult to find. Nevertheless, the behavioural observations of cognitive psychologists are likely to provide a better understanding of how investors make decisions and help to explain certain apparent market inefficiencies.

The second type of risk is potentially more serious. The borrower may default, in whole or in part, on some of the interest payments or on the principal at maturity. A firm becomes bankrupt when it is clearly unable to meet such obligations; the courts then divide the remaining assets between the various creditors in accordance with provisions agreed upon when the debts were issued.

To estimate the expected yield-to-maturity for a risky debt instrument, all possible outcomes and the probability of each should be considered. The simple example shown in Figure 6.7 can be used to illustrate the procedure. Assume the security in question costs $15; that is, the borrower wants $15 now in return for a commitment to pay $15 one year hence and $8 two years hence. The promised yield-to-maturity is the interest rate that makes the present value of these payments equal $15. In this case it is 38.51% per year, a substantial figure indeed.

But the analyst feels that the probability of actually receiving this yield-to-maturity is only .04. Table 6.3 shows the possible sequences (paths in the event tree), as well as the probability and the yield-to-maturity for each one. The expected yield-to-maturity is simply the weighted average of these values, using the probabilities as weights (for example, (.04 × 38.51%) + (.36 × 30.62%) + (.30 × 13.61%) + (.30 × –5.20%) = 15.09%). The expected yield-to-maturity is considerably less than the promised amount: 15.09% as opposed to 38.51%. And the former is clearly the more relevant figure for investment analysis.

This is an important point. The yield-to-maturity, as normally calculated, is based on promised payments, made at the promised times. If there is any risk that the borrower's commitments will not be paid fully and on time, the expected yield-to-maturity is less than this figure; and the greater the risk, the greater the disparity. This is illustrated in Table 6.4, which shows the (promised) yield-to-maturity values for four groups of bonds classified by Canadian Bond Rating Service, Inc., a major rating service, as having different degrees of risk. Although the *levels* of all four yields reflect general interest rates at the time, the *differences* between them are primarily due to differences in risk. If promised yields of all bonds were the same, the expected yields of high-risk bonds would be less than those of low-risk ones—an unlikely situation indeed. Instead, riskier bonds promise higher yields so that their expected yields can be at least as large as those of less risky ones.

The nature of most debt obligations would be more obvious if contracts were written somewhat differently. At present, a standard bond with no extra features "guarantees" that the borrower will pay the lender, say, \$90 per year for 20 years, then \$1000 twenty years hence. A more appropriate statement would indicate that the borrower guarantees to pay *no more than* \$90 per year for 20 years, and \$1000 twenty years hence.

Table 6.3

Promised Versus Expected Yield-to-Maturity.

Payment One Year Hence	*Payment Two Years Hence*	*Probability*	*Yield-to-Maturity*
\$15	\$8	.04	38.51%
15	6	.36	30.62
10	8	.30	13.61
10	4	.30	–5.20
		Expected yield-to-maturity =	15.09%

Table 6.4

Canadian Bond Rating Service Bond Yields.

Rating	*Yield-to-Maturity*
Canadas	6.80%
AA	7.25%
A	7.59%
BBB	7.81%

SOURCE: Melanie Moore, *Debt Market Indices, ScotiaMcLeod Inc.*, November 30, 1995.

Calculating Holding-Period Return

Yield-to-maturity calculations do not take into account any changes in the market value of a security prior to maturity. This might be interpreted as implying that the owner has no interest in selling the instrument prior to maturity, no matter what happens to its price or his or her situation. The calculation also fails to treat intermediate payments in a fully satisfactory way. If the owner does not wish to spend interest payments, he or she might choose to buy more of these securities. But the number that can be bought at any time depends on the price at that time, and yield-to-maturity calculations fail to take this into account.

While few dispute the value of yield-to-maturity as at least an indicator of a bond's overall return, it should be recognized as no more than this. For some purposes other measures may prove more useful. Moreover, for other types of securities there is no maturity: Common shares provide the most important example.

A measure that can be used for any investment is **holding-period return**. The idea is to specify a holding period of major interest, and then assume that any payments received during the period are reinvested. Although assumptions may differ from case to case, the usual procedure assumes that any payment received from a security (for example, a dividend from a share, a coupon payment from a bond) is used to purchase more units of that security at the then current market price. Using this procedure, the performance of a security can be measured by comparing the value obtained in this manner at the end of the holding period with the value at the beginning. This **value-relative** can be converted to a holding-period return by subtracting 1 from it:[1]

$$r_{hp} = \frac{\text{value at the end of the holding period}}{\text{value at the beginning of the holding period}} - 1.$$

Holding-period return can be converted to an equivalent return per period. Allowing for the effect of compounding, the appropriate procedure would be to find the value that satisfies the relationship

$$(1 + r_g)^N = 1 + r_{hp}$$

or

$$r_g = (\sqrt[N]{1 + r_{hp}}) - 1$$

where:

N = the number of periods in the holding period,
r_{hp} = the holding-period return,
r_g = the equivalent return per period, compounded every period.

Suppose that a stock sold for \$46 per share at the beginning of one year, paid dividends of \$1.50 during that year, sold for \$50 at the end of the year, paid dividends of \$2 during the next year, and sold for \$56 at the end of that year. What was the return over the two-year holding period?

---

[1] The term **price-relative** refers to the ratio of a security's price on a given day to its price on some previous day. Hence, it is the same as the value-relative if there are no cash flows associated with the security between the two days.

To simplify the calculations, assume that all dividend payments are received at year-end. Then the \$1.50 received during the first year could have bought \$1.50/\$50, or .03, shares of the stock at the end of the first year. In practice, of course, this would be feasible only if the money were pooled with other funds similarly invested[2] —for example, in a mutual fund (for example, the dividends from 100 shares could have been used to buy three additional shares). In any event, for each share originally held, the investor would have obtained 1.03 × \$2, or \$2.06, in dividends in the second year, and have had shares with a value of 1.03 × \$56, or \$57.68, at the end of the second year. The ending value would thus have been \$57.68 + \$2.06, giving a value-relative of

$$\frac{\$59.74}{\$46.00} = 1.2987.$$

The holding-period return was thus 29.87% per two years. This is equivalent to $\sqrt{1.2987} - 1 = .1396$, or 13.96% per year.

An alternative method of computation treats the overall value-relative as the product of value-relatives for the individual periods. For example, if V_0 is the value at the beginning, V_1 the value at the end of the first year, and V_2 the value at the end of the second year:

$$\frac{V_2}{V_0} = \frac{V_2}{V_1} \times \frac{V_1}{V_0}.$$

Moreover, there is no need to carry the expansion in number of shares from period to period, since the factor (1.03 in the example) will simply cancel out in the subsequent periods' value-relatives. Each period can be analyzed in isolation, an appropriate value-relative calculated, and the set of such value-relatives multiplied together.

In our example, during the first year, ownership of shares with an initial value of \$46 led to shares and cash with a value of \$50 + \$1.50 at the end of the year. Thus,

$$\frac{V_1}{V_0} = \frac{\$51.50}{\$46.00} = 1.1196.$$

During the second year, ownership of shares with an initial value of \$50 led to shares and cash with a value of \$56 + \$2 at year-end. Thus,

$$\frac{V_2}{V_1} = \frac{\$58}{\$50} = 1.16.$$

The two-year holding-period value-relative was therefore

$$1.1196 \times 1.16 = 1.2987$$

which is exactly equal to the value obtained earlier.

The value-relative for each period can be viewed as 1 plus the return for that period. Thus the return on the stock being analyzed was 11.96% in the first year and 16% in the second. The holding-period value-relative is the product of 1 plus each return. If N periods are involved,

$$\frac{V_N}{V_0} = (1 + r_1)(1 + r_2) \cdots (1 + r_N).$$

---

[2] It is possible to buy fractions of a company's shares through a *Dividend Reinvestment Plan.*

To convert the result to a holding-period return stated as an amount per period, with compounding, one can take the *geometric mean* of the periodic returns:

$$1 + r_g = \sqrt[N]{(1 + r_1)(1 + r_2) \cdots (1 + r_N)}.$$

More sophisticated calculations may be employed within this overall framework. Each dividend payment can be used to purchase shares immediately upon receipt, or, alternatively, allowed to earn interest in a savings account until year-end. Brokerage and other costs associated with reinvestment of dividends can also be taken into account, although the magnitude of such costs will undoubtedly depend on the overall size of the holdings in question. The appropriate degree of complexity will, as always, be a function of the use for which the values are obtained.

Unhappily, the most appropriate holding period is often at least as uncertain as the return over any given holding period. Neither an investor's situation nor his or her preferences can usually be predicted with certainty. Moreover, from a strategic view, an investment manager would like to hold a given security only as long as it outperforms available alternatives. Attempts to identify such periods in advance are seldom completely successful, but managers quite naturally continue to try to discover them. Holding-period return, like yield-to-maturity, provides a useful device for simplifying the complex reality of investment analysis. While no panacea, it allows an analyst to focus on the most relevant horizon in a given instance and offers a good measure of performance over such a period.

► Estimating Expected Holding-Period Return

It is a relatively straightforward matter to calculate holding-period return after the fact. It is quite another thing to estimate it in advance. Any uncertainty surrounding payments by the issuer of a security during the period must be taken into account, but this is usually much simpler than the task of estimating the end-of-period market values, which often constitute a large portion of overall return. For example, it might seem a simple matter to estimate the return over the next year for a share of Alcan stock. Dividends to be paid are relatively easy to predict. But the price at year-end will depend on investors' attitudes toward the company and its stock at that time. To predict even a one-year holding-period return one must consider a much longer period and assess not only the company's future but also investors' future attitudes about that future—a formidable task indeed.

Quite clearly, estimation of holding-period return must account in some way for uncertainty. If a single estimate is required, it should conform to the principles stated earlier. Explicitly, an *expected value* should be provided by considering the various possibilities along with their probabilities. Specifically, a security's expected holding-period return is a weighted average of possible holding-period returns, using probabilities as weights.[3]

EXPECTED RETURN AND SECURITY VALUATION

There is a very simple relationship between expected holding-period return, expected end-of-period value, and current value:

[3] Expected return is also the *mean* of the probability distribution of holding-period returns—hence the "mean" in the term *mean-variance approach*, which is the cornerstone of modern portfolio theory.

$$\text{Expected holding-period return} = \frac{\text{expected end-of-period value}}{\text{current value}} - 1.$$

Thus,

$$\text{Current value} = \frac{\text{expected end-of-period value}}{1 + \text{expected holding-period return}}.$$

In words: To value a security, one needs to estimate the expected value at the end of a holding period and the expected return for the holding period that is appropriate for such a security.

The final phase is crucial. What is the "appropriate" expected return, and on what does it depend? Therein lies the remainder of the theory of valuation.

SUMMARY

1. The valuation of risky securities involves the explicit or implicit analysis of the events on which the securities' payments are contingent.
2. A contingent payment is a guaranteed cash flow that will be made if, and only if, a particular event (or state of the world) occurs.
3. A risky security's value could be calculated by aggregating the premiums corresponding to insurance policies written on each of its contingent payments, if such policies existed.
4. Due to the limitations of the insurance policy approach, for investment purposes the risk-return (mean-variance) approach to risky security valuation is most often employed.
5. Probabilistic forecasting involves identifying various alternative outcomes and the probabilities that those outcomes will occur. These forecasts may be estimated using only past observations or by combining past observations with judgments about the future.
6. Probability distributions express (numerically or graphically) the likelihood of various possible outcomes occurring.
7. Event trees describe the likelihood of alternative sequences of outcomes occurring.
8. The expected value (mean), median, and mode are measures of central tendency of a probability distribution. In general, the expected value is the preferred measure because it takes into account all possible outcomes and their associated probabilities.
9. The expected yield-to-maturity of a bond will differ from the bond's promised yield-to-maturity if any of the bond's payments are uncertain. This difference will vary directly with the uncertainty of those payments.
10. A security's holding-period return compares the expected value of all of the security's cash flows over a given time period (with those cash flows reinvested at an assumed interest rate), relative to the current market price of the security.

QUESTIONS AND PROBLEMS

1. In March, a major bookmaker in Las Vegas accepted bets on the baseball teams that would eventually go to the World Series. For example, one could pay $10 at the time to bet that the Minnesota Twins would represent the American League in the World Series. The payoff on such a bet was set at $1500 if the Twins did go to the World Series, and zero otherwise. Payoffs for bets on all teams in the American League Central Division were (see table on following page):

Team	Payoff per $1 bet
Chicago White Sox	$180
Cleveland Indians	210
Kansas City Royals	60
Milwaukee Brewers	250
Minnesota Twins	150

a. What was the present value of $1 contingent on the event (state of the world) "The Twins go to the World Series?"

b. What was the present value of $1 contingent on the event "The Brewers go to the World Series?"

c. Why did the answers for (a) and (b) differ?

d. If someone had offered to pay you $1 if any team in the American League Central Division went to the World Series, how much would you have paid for this bet ("security")? If you had been virtually certain that one of these teams would go to the World Series, would your answer differ? Why?

2. Franklin Optical is a small business. Its owner, Al Sparks, has requested that the local bank loan the firm $25 000 for two years. The federal government will fully guarantee such a loan for a $1000 fee. If the risk-free two-year interest rate is 5% per annum, what is the interest rate that the bank should charge Franklin?
3. Why is the insurance policy approach to risky security valuation so difficult to implement in practice?
4. From the perspective of an insurance company, provide two examples of adverse selection and two examples of moral hazard.
5. Distinguish between continuous and discrete probability distributions.
6. What are the advantages and disadvantages of using past investment results to assess the probabilities of future investment outcomes?
7. The average annualized return on the S&P 500 index of common stocks from 1926 through 1993 was 12.34%. If, on January 1, 1994, you had been required to provide an estimate of the expected return on the S&P 500 over the coming year, would you have chosen 12.34%? Why or why not?
8. What is the value of event trees for investment decision-making?
9. Consider Fort McLeod Gas Company, whose stock currently sells for $10 per share. Don Paskert, a financial analyst, has estimated the stock's potential year-end prices and associated probabilities over the next two years:

Year 1 — The stock has a 30% chance of rising to $20. It has a 60% chance of rising to $12. It has a 10% chance of falling to $8.

Year 2 — If the stock rises to $20 in Year 1, it has a 50% chance of rising to $25 and a 50% chance of falling to $15. If the stock rises to $12 in Year 1, it has a 70% chance of rising to $15 and a 30% chance of falling to $10. If it falls to $8 in Year 1, it has a 40% chance of falling to $4 and a 60% chance of rising to $12.

a. Draw an event tree for Fort McLeod stock.

b. Based on this event tree, calculate the stock's expected price at the end of Year 2.

10. Calculate the expected return, mode, and median for a stock having the following probability distribution:

Return	Probability of Occurrence
–40%	.03
–10	.07
0	.30
15	.10
30	.05
40	.20
50	.25

11. Dieter Schmidt has estimated the following probability distribution of next year's dividend payments for Manderville Ltd. stock. According to Dieter, what is the expected value of Manderville's dividend?

Dividend	Probability
$1.90	.05
1.95	.15
2.00	.30
2.05	.30
2.10	.15
2.15	.05

12. The probability distribution in Figure 6.6(b) is "skewed to the right." Explain why the distribution's expected value is greater than the median, which in turn is greater than the mode.
13. Amina Shah is a fixed-income analyst who is reviewing a bond issued by Wyeville Company Ltd. The bond has one year to maturity, at which time the company promises to pay $100. It currently sells for $90. Amina believes that Wyeville may not pay the full $100 at year-end. Amina has estimated the following probability distribution of year-end payments. What is the expected yield-to-maturity of the Wyeville bond according to Amina?

Payment	Probability
$ 82	.05
90	.10
95	.30
98	.30
100	.25

14. If an investment returns 7% per year, how long does it take for the investment's value to double?
15. Paul Perritt purchased 100 shares of Westcott Ltd. and held the stock for four years. Paul's holding-period returns over these four years were:

Year	Return
1	+20%
2	+30
3	+50
4	−90

a. What was the value-relative of Paul's investment over the four-year period?
b. What was Paul's geometric mean return for the four-year period?

16. Stoughton Services' stock currently sells for $40. It is expected to pay a dividend of $2 each year for the next several years. It just made its latest dividend payment. Patrick O'Neill expects to sell Stoughton stock two years from today at $50. The reinvestment rate is 5%. If this outcome occurs, what will be the equivalent compound annual return from holding Stoughton stock over this two-year period?
17. Distinguish between expected holding-period return and yield-to-maturity.

KEY TERMS

complete market
state-preference approach
adverse selection
moral hazard
mode
median
expected value
mean
holding-period return
value-relative
price-relative

REFERENCES

1. The state-preference approach to asset pricing was developed by two previous winners of the Nobel prize in economics. See:

   Gerard Debreu, *Theory of Value: An Axiomatic Analysis of Economic Equilibrium* (New York: John Wiley, 1959).

   Kenneth J. Arrow, "The Role of Securities in the Optimal Allocation of Risk-Bearing," *Review of Economic Studies* 31, no. 86 (April 1964): 91–96.

2. For a discussion of the application of the state-preference approach to finance, see:

   Thomas E. Copeland and J. Fred Weston, *Financial Theory and Corporate Policy* (Reading, MA: Addison-Wesley, 1988), Chapter 5.

3. The statistical concepts discussed in this chapter can be found in most introductory statistics textbooks, such as:

   Peter Tryfos, *Business Statistics* (Toronto: McGraw-Hill Ryerson, 1989).

   Thomas H. Wonnacott and Ronald J. Wonnacott, *Introductory Statistics for Business and Economics* (New York: John Wiley and Sons, 1984).

CHAPTER 7

The Portfolio Selection Problem

In 1952, Harry M. Markowitz published a landmark paper that is generally viewed as the origin of the *modern portfolio theory* approach to investing. Markowitz's approach to investing begins by assuming that an investor has a given sum of money to invest at the present time. This money will be invested for a particular length of time, known as the investor's **holding period**. At the end of the holding period, the investor will sell the securities that were purchased at the beginning of the period and then either spend the proceeds on consumption or reinvest the proceeds in various securities (or do some of both). Thus, Markowitz's approach can be viewed as a single-period approach, where the beginning of the period is denoted by $t = 0$ and the end of the period is denoted by $t = 1$. At $t = 0$, the investor must make a decision on what particular securities to purchase and hold until $t = 1$.[1] Since a portfolio is a collection of securities, this decision is equivalent to selecting an optimal portfolio from a set of possible portfolios and is thus often referred to as the *portfolio selection problem.*

In making this decision at $t = 0$, the investor should recognize that security returns (and thus portfolio returns) over the forthcoming holding period are unknown. Nevertheless, the investor could estimate the **expected returns** (or mean returns) on the various securities under consideration and then invest in the one with the highest expected return. (Methods for estimating expected returns are discussed in Chapter 18.) Markowitz notes that this would generally be an unwise decision because the typical investor, while wanting returns to be high, also wants returns to be as certain as possible. This means that the investor, in seeking both to maximize expected return and minimize uncertainty (that is, **risk**), has two conflicting objectives that must be balanced against each other when making the purchase decision at $t = 0$. The Markowitz approach for how the investor should go about making this decision gives full consideration to both of these objectives.

One interesting consequence of having these two conflicting objectives is that the investor should diversify by purchasing not just one security but several. The ensuing discussion of Markowitz's approach to investing begins by defining more specifically what is meant by initial and terminal wealth.

---

[1] Harry M. Markowitz, "Portfolio Selection," *Journal of Finance* 7, no. 1 (March 1952): 77–91. See also his book entitled *Portfolio Selection* (New Haven, Conn.: Yale University Press, 1959). Markowitz recognized in Chapter 13 of *Portfolio Selection* that investing was generally a multiperiod activity, where at the end of each period, part of the investor's wealth was consumed and part was reinvested. Nevertheless, his one-period approach can be shown to be optimal under a variety of reasonable circumstances. See Edwin J. Elton and Martin J. Gruber, *Finance as a Dynamic Process* (Englewood Cliffs, N.J.: Prentice Hall, 1975), particularly Chapter 5.

INITIAL AND TERMINAL WEALTH

In equation (1.1) of Chapter 1 it was noted that the one-period rate of return on a security could be calculated as

$$\text{Return} = \frac{\text{end-of-period wealth} - \text{beginning-of-period wealth}}{\text{beginning-of-period wealth}} \tag{1.1}$$

where beginning-of-period wealth is the purchase price of one unit of the security at $t = 0$ (for example, one share of a firm's common stock), and end-of-period wealth is the market value of the unit at $t = 1$, along with the value of any cash (and cash equivalents) paid to the owner of the security between $t = 0$ and $t = 1$.

Determining the Rate of Return on a Portfolio

Since a portfolio is a collection of securities, its return r_p can be calculated in a similar manner:

$$r_p = \frac{W_1 - W_0}{W_0}. \tag{7.1}$$

W_0 denotes the aggregate purchase price at $t = 0$ of the securities contained in the portfolio. W_1 denotes the aggregate market value of these securities at $t = 1$ as well as the aggregate cash (and cash equivalents) received between $t = 0$ and $t = 1$ from owning these securities. Equation (7.1) can be manipulated algebraically, resulting in

$$W_0(1 + r_p) = W_1. \tag{7.2}$$

From equation (7.2) it can be seen that **initial wealth** (as W_0 is sometimes called), when multiplied by 1 plus the rate of return on the portfolio, is equal to **terminal wealth** (as W_1 is sometimes called).

Earlier, it was noted that the investor must make a decision on which portfolio to purchase at $t = 0$. In doing so, the investor does not know what the value of W_1 will be for most of the various alternative portfolios under consideration, since the investor does not know what the rate of return will be for most of these portfolios.[2] Thus, according to Markowitz, the investor should view the rate of return associated with any one of these portfolios to be what is known in statistics as a **random variable**. A random variable can be "described" by what are known as its *moments*, two of which are its **expected value** (or mean) and **standard deviation.**[3]

Markowitz recommends that investors should base their decisions solely on expected returns and standard deviations. That is, the investor should estimate the expected return and standard deviation of each portfolio and then choose the best one based on the relative magnitudes of these two parameters. The intuition behind this is actually quite

[2] One portfolio that would not have an uncertain rate of return would involve the investor putting all of his or her initial wealth in a government security that matures at $t = 1$. Alternatively, the investor's initial wealth could be put into a term deposit at a bank. However, for almost all other portfolios the rate of return would be uncertain.

[3] A random variable's expected value is, in a sense, its "average" value. Thus, the expected value for the return of a portfolio can be thought of as its expected, or average, return. The standard deviation of a random variable is a measure of the dispersion (or spread) of possible values the random variable can take on. Accordingly, the standard deviation of a portfolio is a measure of the dispersion of possible returns that could be earned on the portfolio. Sometimes **variance** is used as a measure of the dispersion instead of standard deviation. However, since the variance of a random variable is simply the squared value of the standard deviation of the random variable, this distinction is not of importance here. Later these concepts are discussed in more detail.

straightforward. Expected return can be viewed as a measure of the potential reward associated with any portfolio, and standard deviation can be viewed as a measure of the risk associated with any portfolio. Thus, once each portfolio has been examined in terms of its potential rewards and risks, the investor is in a position to identify the one portfolio that appears most desirable to him or her.

An Example

As an example, consider the two alternative portfolios denoted by A and B, shown in Table 7.1. Portfolio A has an expected annual return of 8% and portfolio B has an expected annual return of 12%. Assuming the investor has initial wealth of $100 000 and a one-year holding period, this means that the expected levels of terminal wealth associated with A and B are $108 000 and $112 000, respectively. It would appear, then, that B is the more desirable portfolio. However, A and B have annual standard deviations of 10% and 20%, respectively. Table 7.1 shows that this means there is a 2% chance that the investor will end up with terminal wealth of $70 000 or less if he or she purchases B, whereas there is virtually no chance that the investor's terminal wealth will be less than $70 000 if A is purchased. Similarly, B has a 5% chance of being worth less than $80 000, whereas A again has no chance. Continuing, B has a 14% chance of being worth less than $90 000, whereas A has only a 4% chance. Going on, B has a 27% chance of being worth less than $100 000, whereas A has only a 21% chance. Since the investor has initial wealth of $100 000, this last observation means there is a greater probability of having a negative return if B (27%) is purchased instead of A (21%). Overall, it can be seen from Table 7.1 that A is less risky than B, meaning that on this dimension A would be more desirable. The ultimate decision in regard to whether to purchase A or B will depend on this particular investor's attitude toward risk and return, as is shown next.

Table 7.1

A Comparison of Terminal Wealth Levels for Two Hypothetical Portfolios.

	Percent Chance of Being Below This Level of Terminal Wealth	
Level of Terminal Wealth	*Portfolio A*[a]	*Portfolio B*[b]
$ 70 000	0%	2%
$ 80 000	0%	5%
$ 90 000	4%	14%
$100 000	21%	27%
$110 000	57%	46%
$120 000	88%	66%
$130 000	99%	82%

[a] The expected return and standard deviation of A are 8% and 10%, respectively.
[b] The expected return and standard deviation of B are 12% and 20%, respectively.
Initial wealth is assumed to be $100 000, and both portfolios are assumed to have normally distributed returns.

INDIFFERENCE CURVES

The method that should be used in selecting the most desirable portfolio involves the use of **indifference curves**. These curves represent an investor's preferences for risk and return and thus can be drawn on a two-dimensional figure, where the horizontal axis indicates risk as measured by standard deviation (denoted by σ_p) and the vertical axis indicates reward as measured by expected return (denoted by $\bar{r}_p$).

Figure 7.1 illustrates a "map" of indifference curves that a hypothetical investor might possess. Each curved line indicates one indifference curve for the investor and represents all combinations of portfolios that the investor would find equally desirable. For example, the investor with the indifference curves in Figure 7.1 would find portfolios A and B (the same two portfolios that were shown in Table 7.1) equally desirable, even though they have different expected returns and standard deviations, since they both lie on the same indifference curve, I_2. Portfolio B has a higher standard deviation (20%) than portfolio A (10%) and is therefore less desirable on that dimension. However, exactly offsetting this loss in desirability is the gain in desirability provided by the higher expected return of B (12%) relative to A (8%). This example leads to the first important feature of indifference curves: *all portfolios that lie on a given indifference curve are equally desirable to the investor.*

An implication of this feature is that *indifference curves cannot intersect*. Consider the two intersecting curves that are shown in Figure 7.2. Here the point of intersection is represented by X. Remember that all the portfolios on I_1 are equally desirable. This means they are all as desirable as X, since X is on I_1. Similarly, all the portfolios on I_2 are equally desirable and are as desirable as X, since X is also on I_2. Given X is on both indifference curves, all the portfolios on I_1 must be as desirable as those on I_2. But this presents a contradiction, since I_1 and I_2 are two curves that are supposed to represent different levels of desirability. Thus, in order for there to be no contradiction, these curves cannot intersect.

Figure 7.1

Map of indifference curves for a risk-averse investor.

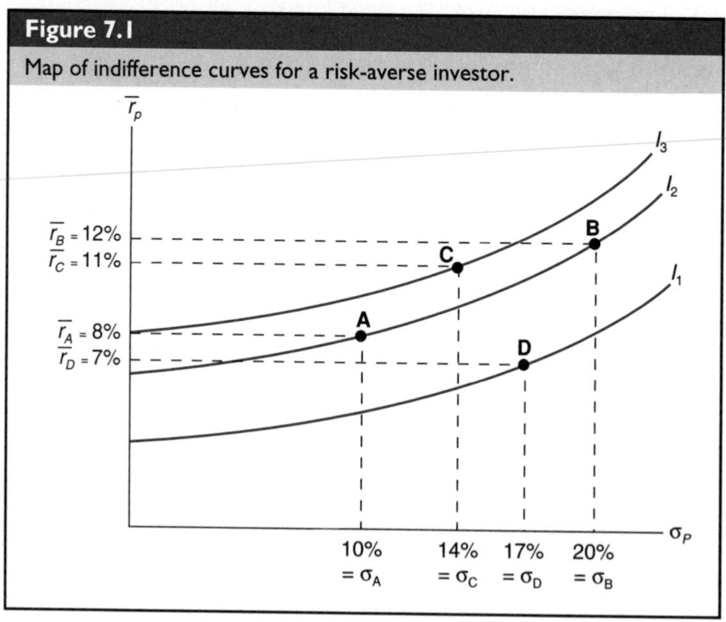

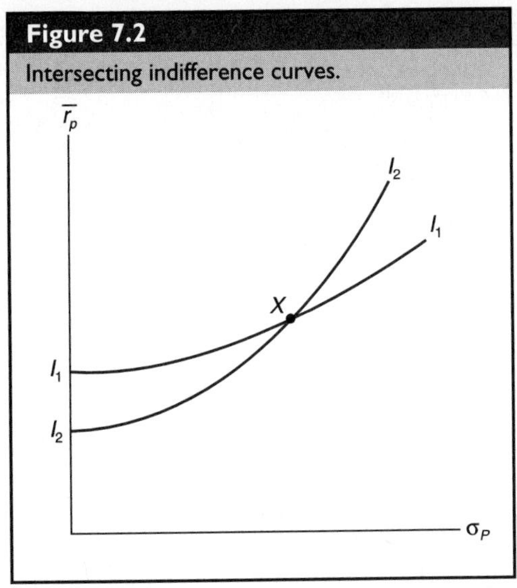

Figure 7.2

Intersecting indifference curves.

Although the investor represented in Figure 7.1 would find portfolios A and B equally desirable, he or she would find portfolio C, with an expected return of 11% and a standard deviation of 14%, to be preferable to both of them. This is because portfolio C happens to be on an indifference curve, I_3, that is located to the northwest of I_2. Now, C has a sufficiently larger expected return relative to A to more than offset its higher standard deviation and, on balance, make it more desirable than A. Equivalently, C has a sufficiently smaller standard deviation than B to more than offset its smaller expected return and, on balance, make it more desirable than B. This leads to the second important feature of indifference curves: *an investor will find any portfolio that is lying on an indifference curve that is "further northwest" to be more desirable than any portfolio lying on an indifference curve that is "not as far northwest."*

Lastly, it should be noted that *an investor has an infinite number of indifference curves.* This simply means that whenever there are two indifference curves that have been plotted on a graph, it is possible to plot a third indifference curve that lies between them. As can be seen in Figure 7.3, given indifference curves I_1 and I_2, it is possible to graph a third curve I^* lying between them. Additional indifference curves can be plotted above I_2 and below I_1.

A good question to ask at this point is, How does an investor determine what his or her indifference curves look like? After all, each investor has a map of indifference curves that, while having the previously noted features, is nevertheless unique to that individual. One method, shown in Chapter 24, involves presenting the investor with a set of hypothetical portfolios, along with their expected returns and standard deviations. Then he or she is asked to choose the most desirable one. Given the choice that is made, the shape and location of the investor's indifference curves can be estimated. This is because it is presumed that the investor acts in accordance with his or her indifference curves in making this choice, even though indifference curves were not explicitly used.[4]

[4] For an alternative procedure, see Ralph O. Swalm, "Utility Theory—Insights into Risk Taking," *Harvard Business Review* 44, no. 6 (November-December 1966): 123–36. Also see footnote 6.

Figure 7.3

Plotting a third indifference curve between two others.

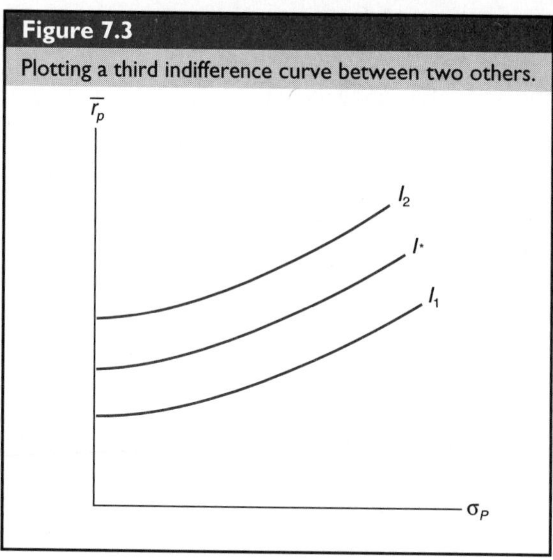

In summary, every investor has an indifference map representing his or her preferences for expected returns and standard deviations.[5] This means the investor should determine the expected return and standard deviation for each potential portfolio, plot them on a graph such as Figure 7.1, and then select the one portfolio that lies on the indifference curve that is furthest northwest. As shown in this example, from the set of the four potential portfolios—A, B, C, and D—the investor should select C.

NONSATIATION AND RISK AVERSION

Nonsatiation

Two assumptions are implicit in this discussion of indifference curves. First, it is assumed that investors, when given a choice between two otherwise identical portfolios, will choose the one with the higher level of expected return. More fundamentally, an assumption of **nonsatiation** is made in utilizing the Markowitz approach, meaning that investors are assumed always to prefer higher levels of terminal wealth to lower levels of terminal wealth. This is because higher levels of terminal wealth allow the investor to spend more on consumption at $t = 1$ (or in the more distant future). Thus, given two portfolios with the same standard deviation,

[5] At some point the reader may wonder why an investor's preferences are based only on expected returns and standard deviations. For example, it may seem logical that the investor's preferences should be based on expected returns, standard deviations, and the probability that a portfolio will lose money. Two reasons are often stated for why an investor's preferences are based on just expected returns and standard deviations. First, if security returns have normal probability distributions, then portfolio returns are completely described by expected returns and standard deviations. Second, if investors have quadratic utility functions, then they will look only at expected returns and standard deviations in evaluating portfolios. See Gordon J. Alexander and Jack Clark Francis, *Portfolio Analysis* (Englewood Cliffs, N.J.: Prentice Hall, 1986), particularly Chapters 2 and 3, for more details. It should be noted that there is some dispute about the validity of using utility theory to describe people's behaviour. The people holding the opposing viewpoints are typically economists and psychologists, and they are often referred to as rationalists and behaviourists, respectively. For a discussion of their views, see the entire second part of the October 1986 issue of the *Journal of Business* and the Institutional Issues section of Chapter 6.

Figure 7.4

Nonsatiation, risk aversion, and portfolio choice.

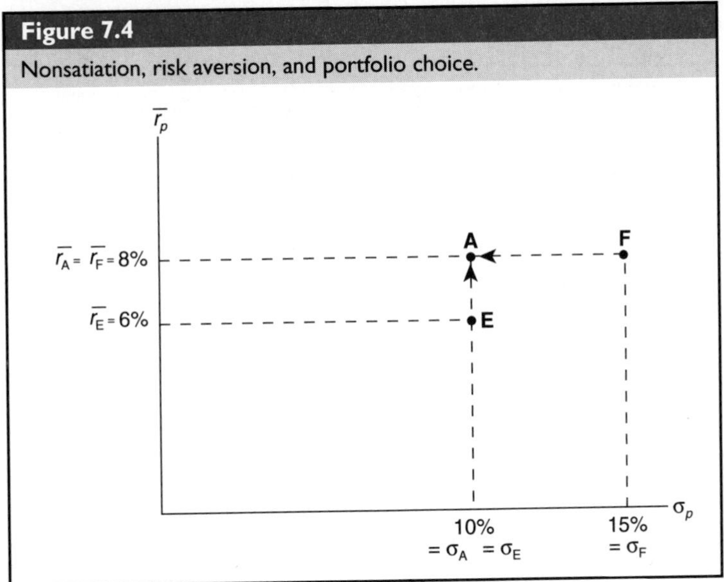

such as A and E in Figure 7.4, the investor will choose the portfolio with the higher expected return. In this case, it is portfolio A.

However, it is not quite so obvious what the investor will do when having to choose between two portfolios with the same level of expected return but different levels of standard deviation, such as A and F. This is where the second assumption enters the discussion.

Risk Aversion

Generally, it is assumed that investors are **risk-averse**, which means that the investor will choose the portfolio with the smaller standard deviation, A.[6] What does it mean to say that an investor is risk-averse? It means that the investor, when given the choice, will not want to take fair gambles, where a fair gamble is defined to be one that has an expected payoff of zero with an equal chance of winning or losing. For example, imagine flipping a coin where heads means you win \$5 and tails means you lose \$5. Since the coin has a 50-50 chance of being heads or tails, the expected payoff is $(.5 \times \$5) + (.5 \times -\$5) = \$0$. Accordingly, the risk-averse investor will choose to avoid this gamble. Intuitively, the investor avoids the gamble because the potential loss represents an amount of "displeasure" that is greater than the amount of "pleasure" associated with the potential gain.

The two assumptions of nonsatiation and risk-aversion are what lead to indifference curves having positive slopes and being convex (convexity means that the slope increases when moving from left to right along the curve).[7] Although it is assumed that all investors are risk-averse, it is not assumed that they have identical degrees of risk aversion. Some investors may be highly risk-averse, and some may be only slightly so. This means that

[6] Investors that are **risk-seeking** would choose F, and investors that are **risk-neutral** would find A and F to be equally desirable. The appendix to this chapter discusses both risk-neutral and risk-seeking investors.

[7] Convexity of indifference curves means that their slopes increase when moving from left to right along any particular one. That is, they bend upwards. The underlying reason for convexity is found in utility theory; see footnote 5.

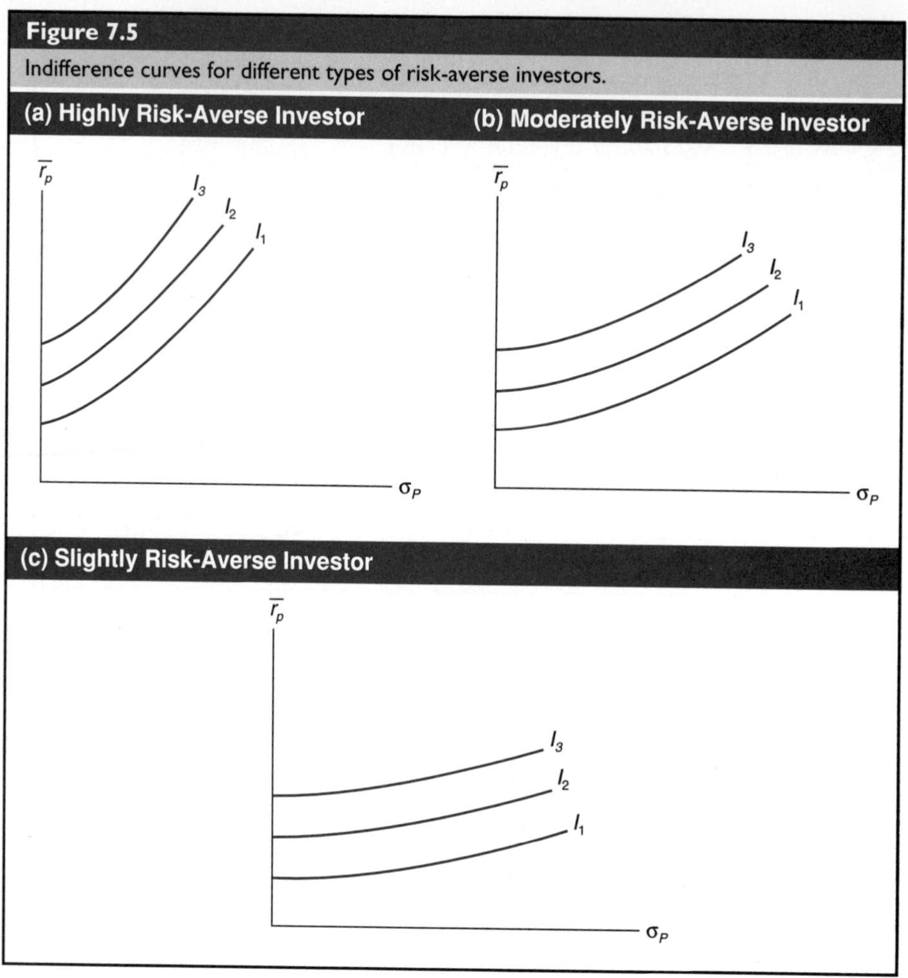

Figure 7.5

Indifference curves for different types of risk-averse investors.

different investors will have different maps of indifference curves. Panels (a), (b), and (c) of Figure 7.5 display maps for investors that are highly risk-averse, moderately risk-averse, and slightly risk-averse, respectively. As can be seen in these figures, a more risk-averse investor has more steeply sloped indifference curves.

CALCULATING EXPECTED RETURNS AND STANDARD DEVIATIONS FOR PORTFOLIOS

The previous section introduced the portfolio-selection problem that every investor faces. It also introduced the investment approach of Harry Markowitz as a method of solving that problem. With this approach, an investor should evaluate alternative portfolios on the basis of their expected returns and standard deviations by using indifference curves. In the case of a risk-averse investor, the portfolio with the indifference curve that is the furthest northwest would be the one selected for investment.

However, certain questions have been left unanswered. In particular, how does the investor calculate the expected return and standard deviation for a portfolio?

Expected Returns

With the Markowitz approach to investing, the focus of the investor is on terminal (or end-of-period) wealth, W_1. That is, in deciding which portfolio to purchase with his or her initial (or beginning-of-period) wealth, W_0, the investor should focus on the effect the various portfolios have on W_1. This effect can be measured by the expected return and standard deviation of each portfolio.

As mentioned previously, a portfolio is a collection of securities. Thus, it seems logical that the expected return and standard deviation of a portfolio should depend on the expected return and standard deviation of each security contained in the portfolio. It also seems logical that the amount invested in each security should be important. Indeed, this is the case.

In order to show how the expected return of a portfolio depends on both the expected return of the individual securities and the amount invested in these securities, consider the three-security portfolio shown in Table 7.2(a). Assume that the investor has a one-year holding period and that for this period he or she has estimated the expected returns on Able, Baker, and Charlie stock to be 16.2%, 24.6%, and 22.8%, respectively. This is equivalent to stating that the investor has estimated the expected end-of-period per-share values of these three stocks to be, respectively, \$46.48 [since (\$46.48 – \$40)/\$40 = 16.2%], \$43.61 [since (\$43.61 – \$35)/\$35 = 24.6%], and \$76.14 [since (\$76.14 – \$62)/\$62 = 22.8%].[8] Furthermore, assume that this investor has initial wealth of \$17 200.

Using End-of-Period Values

The expected return on this portfolio can be calculated in several ways, all of which give the same answer. Consider the method shown in Table 7.2(b). This method involves calculating the expected end-of-period value of the portfolio and then using the formula for calculating rate of return shown in Chapter 1. That is, first the initial portfolio value (W_0) is subtracted from the expected end-of-period value of the portfolio (W_1), and then this difference is divided by the initial portfolio value (W_0), the result of which is the portfolio's expected return. Although the example shown in Table 7.2(b) involves three securities, the procedure can be generalized to any number of securities.

Using Security Expected Returns

An alternative method for calculating the expected return on this portfolio is shown in Table 7.2(c). This procedure involves calculating the expected return of a portfolio as the weighted average of the expected returns of its component securities. The relative market values of the securities in the portfolio are used as weights. In symbols, the general rule for calculating the expected return of a portfolio consisting of N securities is

$$\bar{r}_p = \sum_{i=1}^{N} X_i \bar{r}_i \tag{7.3a}$$

$$= X_1 \bar{r}_1 + X_2 \bar{r}_2 + \cdots + X_N \bar{r}_N \tag{7.3b}$$

where:

[8] The figures given for the expected end-of-period values include both the expected prices and the expected dividends for the period. For example, Able has an expected end-of-period value of \$46.48, which could consist of a hypothetical expected cash dividend of \$2 and share price of \$44.48.

Table 7.2

Calculating the Expected Return for a Portfolio.

(a) Security and Portfolio Values.

Security Name	*Number of Shares Portfolio (1)*	*Initial Market Price per Share (2)*	*Total Investment (3) = (1 × 2)*	*Proportion of Initial Market Value of Portfolio (4) = (3)/W_0*
Able Co.	100	\$40	\$4000	\$4000/\$17 200 = .2325
Baker Co.	200	35	7000	7000/ 17 200 = .4070
Charlie Co.	100	62	6200	6200/ 17 200 = .3605
				Sum of proportions = 1.0000

(b) Calculating the Expected Return for a Portfolio Using End-of-Period Value.

Security Name	*Number of Shares Portfolio (1)*	*Expected End-of-Period Value per Share (2)*	*Aggregate Expected End-of-Period Value (3) = (1) × (2)*
Able Co.	100	\$46.48	\$46.48 × 100 = \$4648
Baker Co.	200	43.61	43.61 × 200 = 8722
Charlie Co.	100	76.14	76.14 × 100 = 7614

Expected end-of-period value of portfolio = $\overline{W}_1$ = \$20 984

$$\text{Portfolio expected return} = \bar{r}_p = \frac{\$20\,984 - \$17\,200}{\$17\,200} = 22.00\%$$

(c) Calculating the Expected Return for a Portfolio Using Security Expected Returns.

Security Name	*Proportion of Initial Market Value of Portfolio (1)*	*Security Expected Returns (2)*	*Contribution to Portfolio Expected Return (3) = (1) × (2)*
Able Co.	.2325	16.2%	.2325 × 16.2% = .77%
Baker Co.	.4070	24.6	.4070 × 24.6 = 10.01
Charlie Co.	.3605	22.8	.3605 × 22.8 = 8.22
			Portfolio expected return = $\bar{r}_p$ = 22.00%

$\bar{r}_p$ = the expected return of the portfolio,
X_i = the proportion of the portfolio's initial value invested in security i,
$\bar{r}_i$ = the expected return of security i,
N = the number of securities in the portfolio.

Thus, an **expected return vector** can be used to calculate the expected return for any portfolio formed from the N securities. This vector consists of one column of numbers, where the entry in row i contains the expected return of security i. In the previous example, the expected return vector was estimated by the investor to be

$$\begin{matrix}\text{Row 1}\\ \text{Row 2}\\ \text{Row 3}\end{matrix} \begin{bmatrix} 16.2\% \\ 24.6\% \\ 22.8\% \end{bmatrix}$$

where the entries in rows 1, 2, and 3 denote the expected returns for securities 1, 2, and 3, respectively.

Since the portfolio's expected return is a weighted average of the expected returns of its securities, *the contribution of each security to the portfolio's expected return depends on its expected return and its proportionate share of the initial portfolio's market value*. Nothing else is relevant. It follows from equation (7.3a) that an investor who simply wants the greatest possible expected return should hold one security: the one he or she considers to have the greatest expected return. Very few investors do this, and very few investment advisors would counsel such an extreme policy. Instead, investors should diversify, meaning that their portfolios should include more than one security. This is because diversification can reduce risk, as measured by the standard deviation.

► Standard Deviations

A useful measure of risk should somehow take into account both the probabilities of various possible bad outcomes and their associated magnitudes. Instead of measuring the probability of a number of different possible outcomes, the measure of risk should somehow estimate the extent to which the actual outcome is likely to diverge from the expected outcome. Standard deviation is a measure that does this, since it is an estimate of the likely divergence of an *actual* return from an *expected* return.

It may seem that any single measure of risk would provide at best a very crude summary of the bad possibilities. But in the more common situation where a portfolio's prospects are being assessed, standard deviation may prove to be a very good measure of the degree of uncertainty. The clearest example arises when the **probability distribution** for a portfolio's returns can be approximated by the familiar bell-shaped curve known as a **normal distribution**. This is often considered a plausible assumption for analyzing returns on diversified portfolios when the holding period being studied is relatively short (say a quarter or less).

A question with standard deviation as a measure of risk is, Why count happy surprises (those above the expected return) at all in a measure of risk? Why not just consider the deviations *below* the expected return? Measures that do so have merit, but if a distribution is symmetric, such as the normal distribution, the results will be the same. Why? Because the left side of a symmetric distribution is a mirror image of the right side. Thus, a list of portfolios ordered on the basis of "downside risk" will not differ from one ordered on the basis of standard deviation if returns are normally distributed.[9]

---

[9] If returns are not normally distributed, the use of standard deviation can still be justified in an approximate sense provided there are small probabilities of extremely high and low returns. See H. Levy and H. M. Markowitz, "Approximating Expected Utility by a Function of Mean and Variance," *American Economic Review* 69, no. 3 (June 1979): 308–17; and Yoram Kroll, Haim Levy, and Harry M. Markowitz, "Mean-Variance versus Direct Utility Maximization," *Journal of Finance* 39, no. 1 (March 1984): 47–61. Some researchers have argued that the best model for a stock's returns is a mixture of normal distributions; for a discussion and references, see Richard Roll, "R2," *Journal of Finance* 43, no. 3 (July 1988): 541–566, particularly footnote 11 on p. 561.

INSTITUTIONAL ISSUES

Alternative Risk Measures

Virtually all investment textbooks (this one being no exception) define a portfolio's investment risk to be its volatility of returns, measured by the standard deviation (or, equivalently, the variance) of the portfolio's return distribution. This definition's pedagogical dominance reflects the practice of academics and, to a lesser extent, those investment professionals steeped in quantitative portfolio management techniques.

Yet ask the average person on the street to define investment risk, and he or she will invariably refer to the chances of something "bad" happening. To suggest to this person that risk also has some association with the possible occurrence of good outcomes will almost certainly draw a disbelieving look.

If, on the surface, the textbook definition of risk appears to have only an indirect relationship with an intuitive sense of risk, why has this "risk as standard deviation" definition so thoroughly dominated investment research? Further, why have alternative risk measures that directly address the likelihood of experiencing undesirable outcomes not been more widely considered and applied?

The straightforward answer to the first question is that standard deviation is computationally easier to work with than any alternative. Proofs and applications of various risk-return investment principles are typically simpler to derive using standard deviation as the measure of risk. For example, Harry Markowitz originally suggested a risk measure involving only negative outcomes when he developed his pioneering work on efficient sets. He rejected that approach in favour of standard deviation in order to simplify the calculations.

As our average person on the street intuitively understands, the biggest problem with standard deviation is that it "discriminates" against investments with volatility on the "upside." As the text describes, we assume that investors dislike risk. Therefore, if we define risk to incorporate both good and bad results, then our risk-reward evaluation of potential investments penalizes investments that might give us positive surprises just as we penalize those investments for the possibility of giving us negative surprises.

All of this concern is moot if investment returns are symmetrically distributed, particularly in the form of a normal distribution (or "bell-shaped" curve). In that case, the chances of a positive outcome a certain distance away from the centre of the distribution are just as great as the chances of a negative outcome an equal distance in the opposite direction. The fact that results above the expected value are included with those below the expected value becomes irrelevant. The standard deviation accurately summarizes the "bad" part of an investment's return distribution.

However, what if investment returns are not normally distributed? For example, we have good reason to believe that common stock returns do not conform to this pattern. Consider that common stock investors face limited liability (see Chapter 17)—the most that they can lose is their original investment. Further, the potential upside gains on their investments are unlimited. Finally, most common stock returns are expected to fall near the market average. What we have just described is a "right-skewed" distribution rather than a normal distribution. Standard deviation insufficiently characterizes the risk of a right-skewed security, ignoring the fact that most of the security's volatility is on the "good" side of the security's expected return.

Interestingly, a simple mathematical transformation can often convert a right-skewed distribution to a normal distribution. If we add 1.0 to a security's return and then compute the natural logarithm of this value, the resulting transformed return distribution may appear to be normally distributed. Consequently, researchers are often concerned with whether security returns are "lognormally" distributed rather than normally distributed. Although the empirical evidence is open to debate, most observers consider lognormality to adequately characterize common stock returns.

Unfortunately, the returns on certain types of securities are neither normally nor lognormally distributed. The most obvious are options (see Chapter 20). For example, a call option allows the owner, for a price, to participate in positive returns on an underlying asset, but avoid the asset's negative returns. Essentially, a call option truncates the underlying asset's return distribution at the point where losses begin. The investor then owns only the "good" or right side of the return distribution. The returns on a call option are definitely not normally distributed.

Moreover, some securities have options embedded in them. For example, callable bonds (see Chapter 14) allow issuers to redeem them at the issuer's discretion. They do so only if interest rates move in their favour. Home mortgages (which are often packaged and sold in pass-through securities—see Chapter 14) have similar prepayment features. Therefore, their returns are also not normally distributed.

If we wish to explicitly focus only on the likelihood of undesirable investment results in defining and measuring risk, what alternatives are available? The simplest answer is called *shortfall probability*. It measures the chances that a security's return will fall short of the expected return. Essentially, it is the proportion of the probability distribution lying to the left of the expected return.

More complex downside risk measures are provided by a family of statistics known as *lower partial moments*, or LPMs. For example, *mean shortfall* measures the average deviation of a security's returns below the expected return. Mean shortfall is more useful than shortfall probability because it takes into account the distance of each downside return from the expected return. That is, shortfall probability tells us only how likely it is that a security's return may fall below the expected return. Mean shortfall tells us how far below the expected return that shortfall is likely to be.

Semivariance is analogous to variance, but only those potential returns below the expected return are used in its calculation. As semivariance is the average squared deviation below the expected return, it penalizes securities with relatively large potential shortfalls.

Applied to securities with non-normal (and non-lognormal) return distributions, these downside risk measures are not only more intuitively appealing but are more flexible in their application than the traditional risk measures. Standard deviation is measured from the mean of the return distribution. However, an investor may want to evaluate investments using some other value as a target, such as the return on a market index or an absolute number such as 0%. Downside risk measures can accommodate these preferences.

However, downside risk measures have their own problems. In particular, they ignore the nature of an investment's possible outcomes above the target return. An alternative to using downside risk measures is to directly bring skewness into the evaluation of an investment. That is, we might assume that investors analyze potential investments not only on the basis of their expected returns and standard deviations, but also on their amount of right-skewness. In essence, risk becomes multidimensional; it includes both standard deviation and skewness. If two investments have the same expected return and standard deviation, the most right-skewed investment would be preferred.

No one risk measure can be expected to function well in all circumstances. Standard deviation has proved effective in the majority of the situations encountered by practitioners. In those cases where it is inadequate, alternatives must be considered not only in light of how well they describe the return distribution, but also in terms of the complexity that they add to the analysis.

Formula for Standard Deviation

For the three-security portfolio consisting of Able, Baker, and Charlie, the formula for the standard deviation is

$$\sigma_p = \left[\sum_{i=1}^{3} \sum_{j=1}^{3} X_i X_j \sigma_{ij} \right]^{1/2} \tag{7.4}$$

where σ_{ij} denotes the **covariance** of the returns between security i and security j.

Covariance

Covariance is a statistical measure of the relationship between two random variables. That is, it is a measure of how two random variables such as the returns on securities i and j "move together." A positive value for covariance indicates that the securities' returns tend to go together—for example, a better-than-expected return for one is likely to occur along with a better-than-expected return for the other. A negative covariance indicates a tendency for the returns to offset one another—for example, a better-than-expected return for one security is likely to occur along with a worse-than-expected return for the other. A relatively small or zero value for the covariance indicates that there is little or no relationship between the returns for the two securities.

Correlation

Closely related to covariance is the statistical measure known as correlation. The covariance between two random variables is equal to the correlation between the two random variables times the product of their standard deviations:

$$\sigma_{ij} = \rho_{ij} \sigma_i \sigma_j \tag{7.5}$$

where ρ_{ij} (the Greek letter rho) denotes the **correlation coefficient** between the return on security i and the return on security j. The correlation coefficient rescales the covariance to facilitate comparison with corresponding values for other pairs of random variables. Correlation coefficients always lie between –1 and +1. A value of –1 represents perfect negative correlation, and a value of +1 represents perfect positive correlation. Most cases lie between these two extreme values.

Figure 7.6(a) presents a scatter diagram for the returns on hypothetical securities A and B when the correlation between these two securities is perfectly positive. Note how all the points lie precisely on a straight upward-sloping line. This means that when one of the two securities has a relatively high return, then so will the other. Similarly, when one of the two securities has a relatively low return, then so will the other.

Alternatively, the returns on the two securities will have a perfectly negative correlation when the scatter diagram indicates that the points lie precisely on a straight downward-sloping line, as shown in Figure 7.6(b). In such a case the returns on the two securities can be seen to move opposite each other. That is, when one security has a relatively high return, then the other will have a relatively low return.

A case of special importance arises when the scatter diagram of security returns shows a pattern that cannot be represented even approximately by an upward-sloping or downward-sloping line. In such an instance, the returns are uncorrelated, meaning the correlation coefficient is zero. Figure 7.6(c) provides an example. In this situation, when one security has a relatively high return, then the other can have either a relatively high, low, or average return.

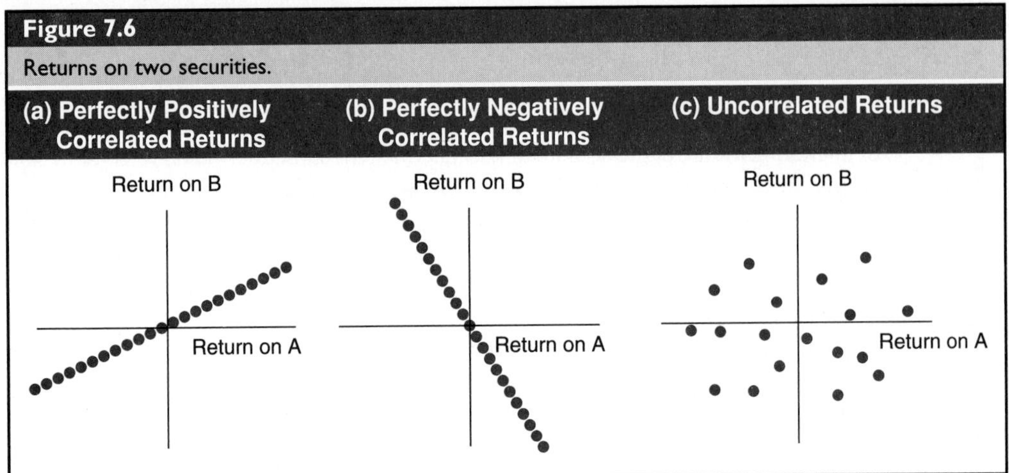

Figure 7.6

Returns on two securities.

Double Summation

Given an understanding of covariance and correlation, it is important to understand how the **double summation** indicated in equation (7.4) is performed. Although there are many ways of performing double summation, all of which lead to the same answer, one way is perhaps more intuitive than the others. It starts with the first summation and sets i at its initial value of 1. Then the second summation is performed for j going from 1 to 3. At this point, i in the first summation is increased by 1, so that now $i = 2$. Again the second summation is performed by letting j go from 1 to 3, except that now $i = 2$. Continuing, i in the first summation is again increased by 1, so that $i = 3$. Then the second summation is again performed by letting j go from 1 to 3. At this point, note that $i = 3$ and $j = 3$, which are the upper limits for both the first and second summations. This means it is time to stop, as the double summation has been finished. This process can be shown algebraically as follows:

$$\sigma_p = \left[\sum_{j=1}^{3} X_1 X_j \sigma_{1j} + \sum_{j=1}^{3} X_2 X_j \sigma_{2j} + \sum_{j=1}^{3} X_3 X_j \sigma_{3j} \right]^{1/2} \tag{7.6a}$$

$$\begin{aligned} &= [X_1 X_1 \sigma_{11} + X_1 X_2 \sigma_{12} + X_1 X_3 \sigma_{13} \\ &\quad + X_2 X_1 \sigma_{21} + X_2 X_2 \sigma_{22} + X_2 X_3 \sigma_{23} \\ &\quad + X_3 X_1 \sigma_{31} + X_3 X_2 \sigma_{32} + X_3 X_3 \sigma_{33}]^{1/2} \end{aligned} \tag{7.6b}$$

Each term in the double sum involves the product of the weights for two securities, X_i and X_j, and the covariance between these two securities. Note how there are nine terms to be added together in order to calculate the standard deviation of a portfolio consisting of three securities. It is no coincidence that the number of terms to be added together (9) equals the number of securities squared (3^2).

In general, calculating the standard deviation for a portfolio consisting of N securities involves performing the double sum indicated in equation (7.4) over N securities, thereby involving the addition of N^2 terms:

$$\sigma_p = \left[\sum_{i=1}^{N} \sum_{j=1}^{N} X_i X_j \sigma_{ij} \right]^{1/2}. \tag{7.7}$$

An interesting feature of the double sum occurs when the subscripts i and j refer to the same security. In equation (7.6b) this occurs in the first ($X_1X_1\sigma_{11}$), fifth ($X_2X_2\sigma_{22}$), and ninth ($X_3X_3\sigma_{33}$) terms. What does it mean to have the subscripts for covariance refer to the same security? For example, consider security one (Able) so that $i = j = 1$. Since σ_{11} denotes the covariance of security 1 (Able) with security 1 (Able), equation (7.5) indicates that

$$\sigma_{11} = \rho_{11}\sigma_1\sigma_1. \tag{7.8}$$

Now the correlation of any security with itself, in this case ρ_{11}, can be shown to be equal to +1.[10] This means that equation (7.8) reduces to

$$\begin{aligned} \sigma_{11} &= +1 \times \sigma_1 \times \sigma_1 \\ &= \sigma_1^2 \end{aligned} \tag{7.9}$$

which is just the square of the standard deviation of security 1, known as the variance of security 1. Thus, the double sum involves both variance and covariance terms.

Variance-Covariance Matrix

As an example, consider the following **variance-covariance matrix** for the stocks of Able, Baker, and Charlie:

	Column 1	Column 2	Column 3
Row 1	146	187	145
Row 2	187	854	104
Row 3	145	104	289

The entry in cell (i, j) denotes the covariance between security i and security j. For example, the entry in (1, 3) denotes the covariance between the first and third securities, which in this case is 145. Also, the entry in cell (i, i) denotes the variance of security i. For example, the variance of security 2 appears in cell (2, 2), and is equal to 854. Using this variance-covariance matrix along with the formula given in equation (7.6b), the standard deviation of the previously mentioned portfolio that had $X_1 = .2325$, $X_2 = .4070$, and $X_3 = .3605$ can now be calculated:

[10] Remember that correlation refers to how two random variables move together. If the two random variables are the same, then they must move exactly together with each other. This can be visualized by graphing the values of the same random variable on both the X-axis and Y-axis. In such a graph, all points would lie on a straight 45° line passing through the origin, thereby implying a correlation of +1.

$$
\begin{aligned}
\sigma_p &= [X_1X_1\sigma_{11} + X_1X_2\sigma_{12} + X_1X_3\sigma_{13} \\
&\quad + X_2X_1\sigma_{21} + X_2X_2\sigma_{22} + X_2X_3\sigma_{23} \\
&\quad + X_3X_1\sigma_{31} + X_3X_2\sigma_{32} + X_3X_3\sigma_{33}]^{1/2} \\
&= [(.2325 \times .2325 \times 146) + (.2325 \times .4070 \times 187) + (.2325 \times .3605 \times 145) \\
&\quad + (.4070 \times .2325 \times 187) + (.4070 \times .4070 \times 854) + (.4070 \times .3605 \times 104) \\
&\quad + (.3605 \times .2325 \times 145) + (.3605 \times .4070 \times 104) + (.3605 \times .3605 \times 289)]^{1/2} \\
&= [277.13]^{1/2} \\
&= 16.65\%.
\end{aligned}
$$

Several interesting features about variance-covariance matrices deserve mention. First, such matrices are square, meaning that the number of columns equals the number of rows and that the total number of cells for N securities equals N^2.

Second, the variances of the securities appear on the diagonal of the matrix, which are the cells that lie on a line going from the upper left-hand corner to the lower right-hand corner of the matrix. In the previous example, the variance of security 1 (146) appears in row 1 of column 1. Similarly, the variances of securities 2 and 3 appear in row 2 of column 2 (854) and row 3 of column 3 (289), respectively.

Third, the matrix is symmetric, meaning the number appearing in row i of column j also appears in row j of column i. That is, the elements in the cells above the diagonal also appear in the corresponding cells below the diagonal. In the previous example, note that 187 appears in row 1 of column 2, and also in row 2 of column 1. Similarly, 145 appears in both row 1 of column 3 and row 3 of column 1, and 104 appears in both row 2 of column 3 and row 3 of column 2. The reason for this feature is quite simple—the covariance between two securities does not depend on the order in which the two securities are specified. This means that, for example, the covariance between the first and second securities is the same as the covariance between the second and first securities. [11]

SUMMARY

1. The Markowitz approach to portfolio selection assumes that investors seek both maximum expected return for a given level of risk and minimum uncertainty (risk) for a given level of expected return.
2. Expected return serves as the measure of potential reward associated with a portfolio. Standard deviation is viewed as the measure of a portfolio's risk.
3. An indifference curve represents the various combinations of risk and return that the investor finds equally desirable.
4. Investors are assumed to consider any portfolio lying on an indifference curve "further to the northwest" more desirable than any portfolio lying on an indifference curve that is "not as far northwest."

[11] For any variance-covariance matrix there is an implied correlation matrix that can be determined by using the data in the variance-covariance matrix and equation (7.5). Specifically, this equation can be used to show that the correlation between any two securities i and j is equal to $\sigma_{ij}/\sigma_i\sigma_j$. The values of σ_{ij}, σ_i, and σ_j can be obtained from the variance-covariance matrix. For example $\rho_{12} = 187/(\sqrt{146} \times \sqrt{854}) = .53$.

5. The assumptions of investor nonsatiation and risk aversion cause indifference curves to be positively sloped and convex.
6. The expected return on a portfolio is a weighted average of the expected returns of its component securities, with the relative portfolio proportions of the component securities serving as weights.
7. Covariance and correlation measure the extent to which two random variables "move together."
8. The standard deviation of a portfolio depends on the standard deviations and proportions of the component securities as well as their covariances with one another.

APPENDIX A

RISK-NEUTRAL AND RISK-SEEKING INVESTORS

Earlier, it was mentioned that the Markowitz approach assumes that investors are risk-averse. Although this is a reasonable assumption to make, it is not necessary to do so. Alternatively, it can be assumed that investors are either risk-neutral or risk-seeking.

Consider the risk-seeking investor first. This investor, when faced with a fair gamble, will want to take the gamble. Furthermore, larger gambles are more desirable than smaller gambles. This is because the "pleasure" derived from winning is greater than the "displeasure" derived from losing. Because there is an equal chance of winning and losing, on balance the risk-seeking investor will want to take the gamble. What this means is that when faced with two portfolios that have the same expected return, this type of investor will choose the one with the higher standard deviation.

For example, in choosing between A and F in Figure 7.4, the risk-seeking investor will choose F. This suggests that the risk-seeking investor will have negatively sloped indifference curves. [12] In addition, risk-seeking investors will prefer to be on the indifference curve that is "furthest northeast." Figure 7.7 illustrates a map of the indifference curves for a hypothetical risk-seeking investor. As shown in the figure, when choosing between A, B, C, and D (the same four portfolios shown in Figure 7.1), this investor will choose B.

The risk-neutral case lies between the risk-seeking and risk-averse cases. While the risk-averse investor does not want to take fair gambles and the risk-seeking investor does want to take such gambles, the risk-neutral investor does not care whether or not the gamble is taken. This means that risk, or more specifically, standard deviation, is unimportant to the risk-neutral investor in evaluating portfolios. Accordingly, the indifference curves for such investors are horizontal lines as shown in Figure 7.8. These investors prefer to be on the indifference curve that is "furthest north." When faced with the choice of A, B, C, and D, such an investor will choose B, because it has the highest expected return.

Whereas investors can be either risk-seeking or risk-neutral, there is evidence to suggest that they are more accurately characterized as being, in general, risk-averse. One piece of evidence is the observation that equities have historically had higher average returns than bonds, suggesting that investors have had to be induced with higher rewards in order to get them to make riskier purchases.

---

[12] It can also be shown that for a risk-seeking investor, these indifference curves will be concave, meaning that their slopes decrease when moving from left to right. The underlying rationale for concavity lies in utility theory; see footnote 5.

Figure 7.7

Map of indifference curves for a risk-seeking investor.

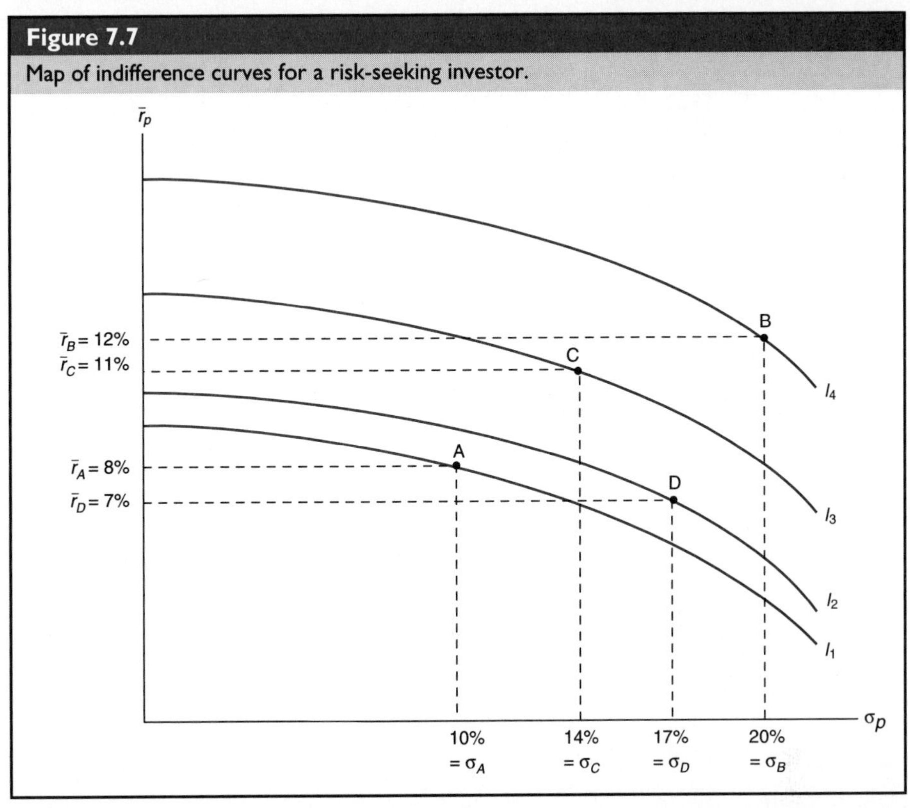

Figure 7.8

Map of indifference curves for a risk-neutral investor.

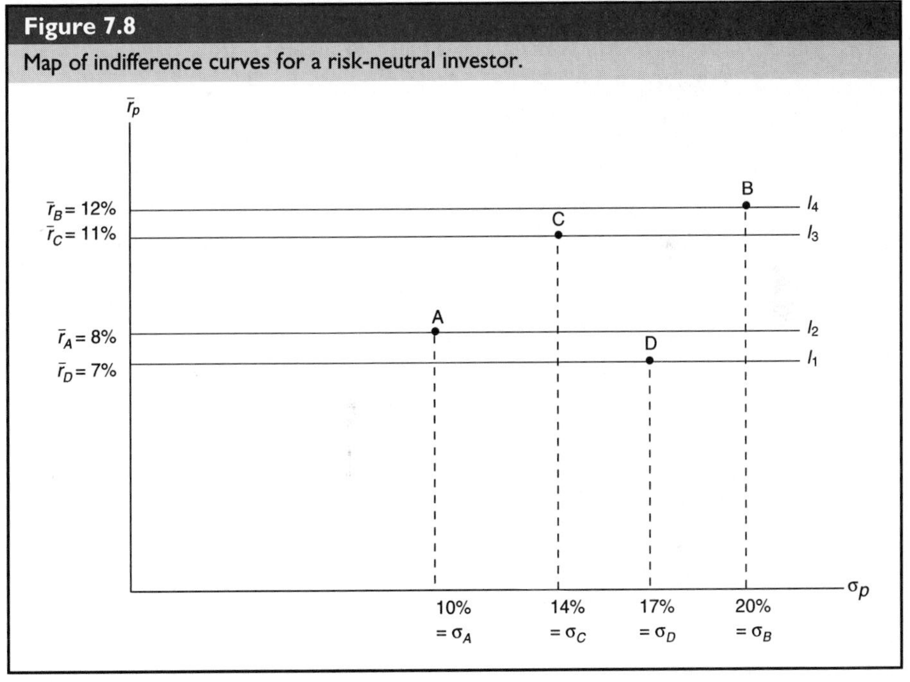

Questions and Problems

1. Listed below are a number of portfolios and expected returns, standard deviations, and the amount of satisfaction (measured in utils) these portfolios provide Art Vaughn. Given this information, graph Art's identifiable indifference curves.

Portfolio	*Expected Return*	*Standard Deviation*	*Utility*
1	5%	0%	10 utils
2	6	10	10
3	9	20	10
4	14	30	10
5	10	0	20
6	11	10	20
7	14	20	20
8	19	30	20
9	15	0	30
10	16	10	30
11	19	20	30
12	24	30	30

2. Why are the indifference curves of typical investors assumed to slope upward to the right?
3. What does a set of convex indifference curves imply about an investor's trade-off between risk and return as the amount of risk varies?
4. Why are typical investors assumed to prefer portfolios on indifference curves lying to the "northwest"?
5. What is meant by the statement that "risk-averse investors exhibit diminishing marginal utility of income"? Why does diminishing marginal utility cause an investor to refuse to accept a "fair bet"?
6. Explain why an investor's indifference curves cannot intersect.
7. Why are the indifference curves of more risk-averse investors more steeply sloped than those of investors with less risk aversion?
8. Consider the following two sets of indifference curves for investors Helen Wilson and Kathy Culver. Determine whether Helen or Kathy:
   a. Is more risk-averse,
   b. Prefers investment A to investment B,
   c. Prefers investment C to investment D.
   Explain the reasons for your answers.

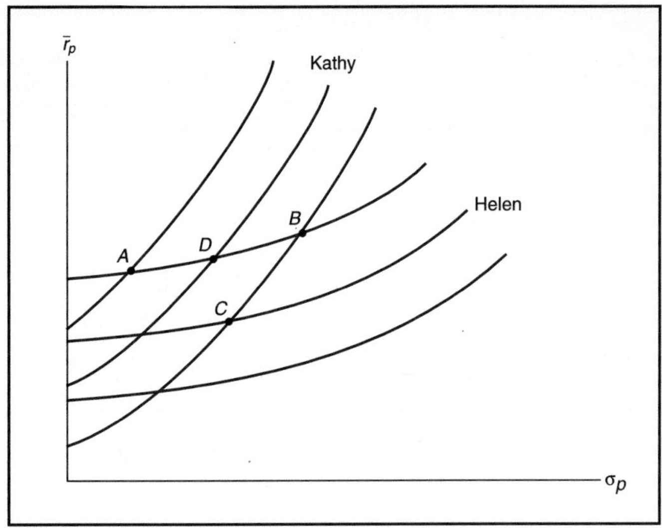

9. Consider four stocks with the following expected returns and standard deviations.

Stock	*Expected Return*	*Standard Deviation*
A	15%	12%
B	13	8
C	14	7
D	16	11

Are any of these stocks preferred over another by a risk-averse investor?

10. Do you agree with the assumptions of nonsatiation and risk aversion? Make a case for or against these assumptions.

11. At the beginning of the year, Chris Bradley owned four securities in the following amounts and with the following current and expected end-of-year prices:

Security	*Share Amount*	*Current Price*	*Expected Year-End Price*
A	100	$50	$60
B	200	35	40
C	50	25	50
D	100	100	110

What is the expected return on Chris's portfolio for the year?

12. Given the following information about four stocks comprising a portfolio, calculate each stock's expected return. Then, using these individual security's expected returns, calculate the portfolio's expected return.

Stock	Initial Investment Value	Expected End-of-Period Investment Value	Proportion of Portfolio Initial Market Value
A	$ 500	$ 700	19.2%
B	200	300	7.7
C	1000	1000	38.5
D	900	1500	34.6

13. Alice Procino has been considering an investment in Oakdale Merchandising. Alice has estimated the following probability distribution of returns for Oakdale stock:

Return	Probability
−10%	.10
0	.25
10	.40
20	.20
30	.05

Based on Alice's estimates, calculate the expected return and standard deviation of Oakdale stock.

14. The expected returns and standard deviations of stocks A and B are:

Stock	Expected Return	Standard Deviation
A	13%	10%
B	5	18

Max McQuarry buys $20 000 of stock A and sells short $10 000 of stock B, using all of the proceeds to buy more of stock A. The correlation between the two securities is .25. What are the expected return and standard deviation of Max's portfolio?

15. Both the covariance and the correlation coefficient measure the extent to which the returns on securities move together. What is the relationship between the two statistical measures? Why is the correlation coefficient a more convenient measure?

16. Give an example of two common stocks that you would expect to exhibit a relatively low correlation. Then give an example of two that would have a relatively high correlation.

17. Nancy Brock has estimated the following joint probability distribution of returns for investments in the stock of Lakeland Halfway Homes and Afton Brewery:

Lakeland	Afton	Probability
−10%	15%	.15
5	10	.20
10	5	.30
20	0	.35

Based on Nancy's estimates, calculate the covariance and correlation coefficient between the two investments.

18. Calculate the correlation matrix that corresponds to the variance-covariance matrix given in the test for Able, Baker, and Charlie.
19. Given the following variance-covariance matrix for three securities, as well as the percentage of the portfolio that each security comprises, calculate the portfolio's standard deviation.

	Security A	*Security B*	*Security C*
Security A	459	−211	112
Security B	−211	312	215
Security C	112	215	179
	$X_A = .50$	$X_B = .30$	$X_C = .20$

20. Ruth Bressler owns three stocks and has estimated the following joint probability distribution of returns:

Outcome	*Stock A*	*Stock B*	*Stock C*	*Probability*
1	−10	10	0	.30
2	0	10	10	.20
3	10	5	15	.30
4	20	−10	5	.20

Calculate the portfolio's expected return and standard deviation if Ruth invests 20% in stock A, 50% in stock B, and 30% in stock C. Assume that each security's return is completely uncorrelated with the returns of the other securities.

21. If a portfolio's expected return is equal to the weighted average of the expected returns of the component securities, why is a portfolio's risk not generally equal to the weighted average of the component securities' standard deviations?
22. When is the standard deviation of a portfolio equal to the weighted average of the standard deviation of the component securities? Show this mathematically for a two-security portfolio. (Hint: Some algebra is necessary to solve this problem. Remember that $\sigma_{ij} = \rho_{ij}\sigma_i\sigma_j$. Try different values of ρ_{ij}.
23. Consider two securities, A and B, with expected returns of 15% and 20%, respectively, and standard deviations of 30% and 40%, respectively. Calculate the standard deviation of a portfolio weighted equally between the two securities if their correlation is:
    a. 0.9
    b. 0.0
    c. –0.9

24. Listed here are estimates of the standard deviations and correlations coefficients for three stocks.

Stock	Standard Deviation	Correlation with Stock: A	B	C
A	12%	1.00	−1.00	0.20
B	15	−1.00	1.00	−0.20
C	10	0.20	−0.20	1.00

a. If a portfolio is composed of 20% of stock A and 80% of stock C, what is the portfolio's standard deviation?
b. If a portfolio is composed of 40% of stock A, 20% of stock B, and 40% of stock C, what is the portfolio's standard deviation?
c. If you were asked to design a portfolio using stocks A and B, what percentage investment in each stock would produce a zero standard deviation? [Hint: Some algebra is necessary to solve this problem. Remember that $X_B = (1 - X_A)$.]

KEY TERMS

holding period
expected returns
risk
initial wealth
terminal wealth
random variable
expected value
standard deviation
variance
indifference curve
nonsatiation
risk-averse investor
risk-seeking investor
risk-neutral investor
expected return vector
probability distribution
normal distribution
covariance
correlation coefficient
double summation
variance-covariance matrix

REFERENCES

1. The seminal work developing the mean-variance model is credited to Harry Markowitz, co-winner of the 1990 Nobel prize in economics, who developed his ideas in a paper and later in a book:

Harry M. Markowitz, "Portfolio Selection," *Journal of Finance* 7, no. 1 (March 1952): 77–91.

Harry M. Markowitz, *Portfolio Selection: Efficient Diversification of Investments* (New York: John Wiley, 1959). A reprint of this book that also contains some new material is available form Basil Blackwell, in Cambridge, MA; its copyright date is 1991.

2. While utility theory can be traced back to the work of Daniel Bernoulli in the early part of the 18th century, the modern notion of utility theory was developed in:

John von Neumann and Oskar Morgenstern, *Theory of Games and Economic Behavior* (New York: John Wiley, 1944).

Kenneth J. Arrow, *Essays in the Theory of Risk-Bearing* (Chicago: Markham, 1971).

3. Significant other work in utility theory is reviewed in:

Paul J. H. Schoemaker, "The Expected Utility Model: Its Variants, Purposes, Evidence and Limitations," *Journal of Economic Literature* 20, no. 2 (June 1982): 529–563.

4. For an introduction to uncertainty and utility theory, see:

Mark P. Kritzman, ". . . About Uncertainty," *Financial Analysts Journal* 47, no. 2 (March/April 1991): 17–21.

Mark Kritzman, ". . . About Utility," *Financial Analysts Journal* 48, no. 3 (May/June 1992): 17–20.

CHAPTER 8

Portfolio Analysis

The previous chapter introduced the portfolio selection problem that every investor faces. It also introduced the investment approach of Harry Markowitz as a method of solving that problem. With this approach, an investor should evaluate alternative portfolios on the basis of their expected returns and standard deviations by using indifference curves. In the case of a risk-averse investor, the portfolio with the indifference curve that is the "furthest northwest" would be the one selected for investment.

However, the previous chapter left certain questions unanswered. In particular, how can Markowitz's approach be used once it is recognized that there are an infinite number of portfolios available for investment? What happens when the investor considers investing in a set of securities, one of which is riskless? What happens when the investor is allowed to buy securities on margin? This chapter will provide the answers to these questions, beginning with the first one.

THE EFFICIENT SET THEOREM

As mentioned earlier, an infinite number of portfolios can be formed from a set of N securities. Consider the situation with Able, Baker, and Charlie companies where N is equal to 3. The investor could purchase just shares of Able or just shares of Baker. Alternatively, the investor could purchase a combination of shares of Able and Baker. For example, the investor could put 50% of his or her money in each company, or 25% in one company and 75% in the other, or 33% in one and 67% in the other, or any percent (between 0% and 100%) in one company with the rest going into the other company. Without even considering investing in Charlie, there are already an infinite number of possible portfolios in which to invest.[1]

Does the investor need to evaluate all these portfolios? Fortunately, the answer to this question is no. The key to why the investor needs to look at only a subset of the available portfolios lies in the **efficient set theorem**, which states that:

> An investor will choose his or her optimal portfolio from the set of portfolios that:
>
> 1. Offer maximum expected return for varying levels of risk, and
> 2. Offer minimum risk for varying levels of expected return.

[1] This can be seen by noting that there are an infinite number of points on the real number line between 0 and 100. If these numbers are thought of as representing the percentage of the investor's funds going into shares of Able, with 100 minus this number going into Baker, it can be seen that there are an infinite number of portfolios that could be formed from just two different securities. In making this assertion, however, it has been assumed that an investor can buy a fraction of a share if he or she so desires. For example, the investor can buy not only one or two or three shares of Able but also 1.1 or 1.01 or 1.001 shares.

The set of portfolios meeting these two conditions is known as the **efficient set**, or *efficient frontier.*

The Feasible Set

Figure 8.1 provides an illustration of the location of the **feasible set**, also known as the *opportunity set*, from which the efficient set can be located. The feasible set simply represents the set of all portfolios that could be formed from a group of N securities. That is, all possible portfolios that could be formed from the N securities lie either on or within the boundary of the feasible set (the points denoted by G, E, S, and H in the figure are examples of such portfolios). In general, this set will have an umbrella-type shape similar to the one shown by the figure. Depending on the particular securities involved, it may be more to the right or left, higher or lower, or fatter or skinnier than indicated here. The point is that its shape will, except in perverse circumstances, look similar to what appears here.

The Efficient Set Theorem Applied to the Feasible Set

The efficient set can now be located by applying the efficient set theorem to this feasible set. First, the set of portfolios that meet the first condition of the efficient set theorem must be identified. Looking at Figure 8.1, there is no portfolio offering less risk than that of portfolio E. This is because if a vertical line were drawn through E, there would be no point in the feasible set to the left of the line. Also, there is no portfolio offering more risk than that of portfolio H. This is because if a vertical line were drawn through H, there would be no point in the feasible set to the right of the line. Thus, the set of portfolios offering maximum expected return for varying levels of risk is the set of portfolios lying on the "northern" boundary of the feasible set between points E and H.

Figure 8.1

Feasible and efficient sets.

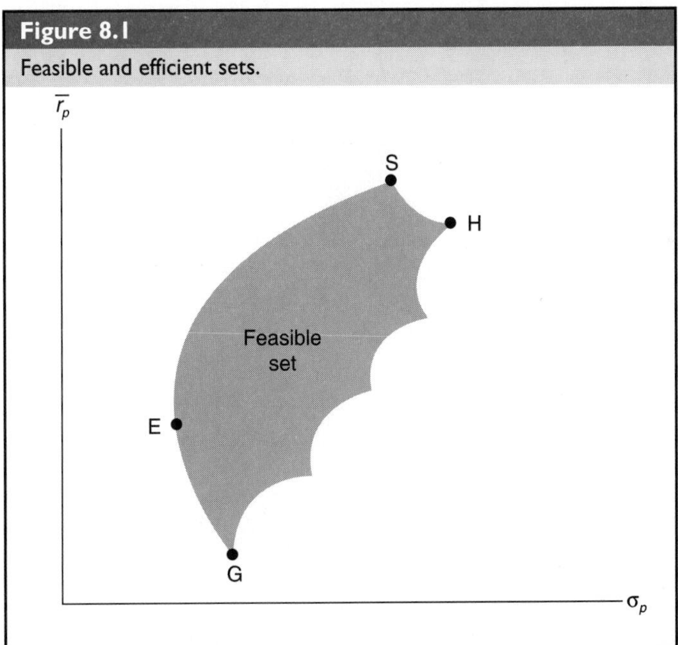

Considering the second condition next, there is no portfolio offering an expected return greater than portfolio S, since no point in the feasible set lies above a horizontal line going through S. Similarly, there is no portfolio offering a lower expected return than portfolio G, since no point in the feasible set lies below a horizontal line going through G. Thus, the set of portfolios offering minimum risk for varying levels of expected return is the set of portfolios lying on the "western" boundary of the feasible set between points G and S.

Remembering that both conditions have to be met in order to identify the efficient set, it can be seen that only those portfolios lying on the "northwest" boundary between points E and S do so. Accordingly, these portfolios form the efficient set, and it is from this set of **efficient portfolios** that the investor will find his or her optimal one.[2] All the other feasible portfolios are **inefficient** and can be safely ignored.

Selection of the Optimal Portfolio

How will the investor select an **optimal portfolio**? As shown in Figure 8.2, the investor should plot his or her indifference curves on the same figure as the efficient set and then choose the portfolio that is on the indifference curve that is furthest northwest. This portfolio will correspond to the point where an indifference curve is just tangent to the efficient set. As can be seen in the figure, this is portfolio O* on indifference curve I_2. Although the investor would prefer a portfolio on I_3, no such portfolio exists, and so wanting to be on this indifference curve is just wishful thinking. In regard to I_1, there are several portfolios

Figure 8.2

Selecting an optimal portfolio.

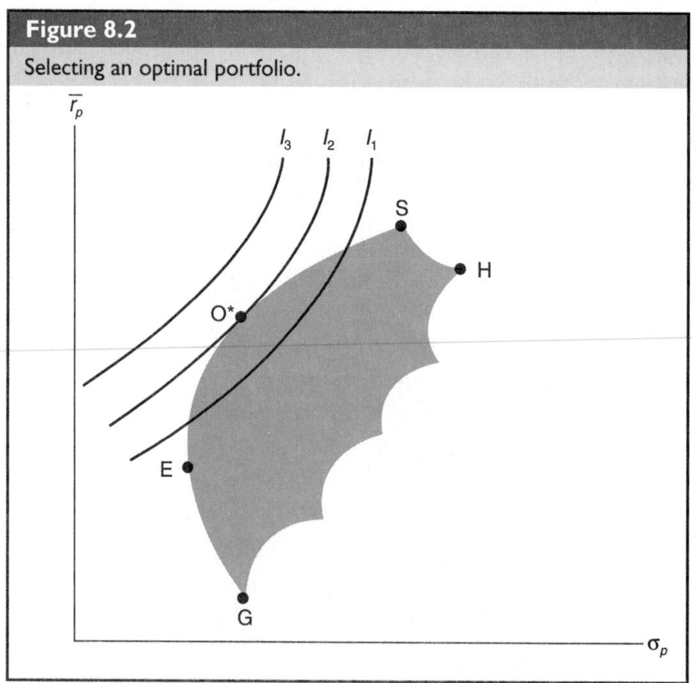

[2] In order to determine the compositions of the portfolios on the efficient set, the investor must solve a quadratic programming problem. See Markowitz's book entitled *Portfolio Selection* (cited at the end of the chapter), particularly pp. 176–185.

INSTITUTIONAL ISSUES

The Trouble with Optimizers

Suppose that the captain of a modern luxury liner chose not to use the ship's state-of-the-art navigational system (a system that employs computers to triangulate off geostationary-orbiting satellites, thereby estimating the ship's position accurately to within a few feet). Instead, suppose that the captain chose to rely on the old-fashioned method of navigating by the stars, an antiquated method fraught with problems and imprecision. Most people would view the captain's choice as, at best, eccentric and, at worst, highly dangerous.

When it comes to constructing portfolios, many investment managers make a choice analogous to that of the ship's captain. They reject computer-based portfolio construction methods in favour of traditional approaches. Are their decisions as foolhardy as the captain's? Or is there a method to their apparent madness?

As this chapter discusses, the concepts of the efficient set and the investor's optimal portfolio are central to modern investment theory. But how can investors actually go about estimating the efficient set and selecting their optimal portfolios? Harry Markowitz first described the solution in the early 1950s. Using a mathematical technique called *quadratic programming*, investors can process expected returns, standard deviations, and covariances to calculate the efficient set. (See Appendix A to this chapter). Given an estimate of their indifference curves (as reflected in their individual risk tolerances — see Chapter 24), they can then select a portfolio from the efficient set.

Simple, right? Certainly not in the 1950s. Given the data processing facilities available to investors at that time, calculating the efficient set for even a few hundred securities was essentially impossible. However, with the advent of low-cost, high-speed computers in the 1980s and the development of sophisticated risk models (see Chapter 11), an efficient set can be created for thousands of securities in a matter of minutes. The necessary computer hardware and software are available to virtually every institutional investor at a relatively low cost. In fact, the process has become so commonplace that it has acquired its own terminology. Using a computer to identify the efficient set and select an optimal portfolio is colloquially known as using an "optimizer." Portfolios are "optimized" and investors are said to apply "optimization techniques."

Despite the technology's widespread availability, relatively few investment managers actually use an optimizer to build portfolios. Instead, they rely for the most part on a series of qualitative rules and judgments.

Why do investment managers resist applying optimization techniques to portfolio building? Ignorance is not the answer. Most investment managers are well aware of Markowitz's portfolio selection concepts and the available technology, having graduated from business schools where these ideas are discussed in detail. Instead, the resistance derives from two sources: territorial concerns and implementation inadequacies.

From a territorial perspective, many investment managers are simply not comfortable with a quantitative approach to investing. Their decision-making emphasizes intuition and complex subjective judgments. The application of optimization techniques to portfolio construction imposes a very systematic and formal decision-making structure. Security analysts must become responsible for generating quantifiable expected return and risk forecasts. Portfolio managers must implement the decisions of a computer. As a result, the optimizer destroys the "artistry and grace" of investment management.

Further, with the introduction of an optimizer, a new breed of investment professional gains influence — the quantitative analyst (derisively called a "quant") — who coordinates the

INSTITUTIONAL ISSUES (continued)

collection and application of risk and return estimates. Authority gained by quantitative analysts diminishes the influence of the traditional security analysts and portfolio managers, much to their consternation.

From the implementation perspective, serious problems have arisen with optimizers in practice. In particular, they tend to produce counterintuitive, uninvestable portfolios. This situation is not so much a problem with optimizers as it is the fault of the human operators supplying inputs to the optimizers. Here the GIGO (garbage in, garbage out) paradigm rules.

By their design, optimizers are attracted to securities with high expected returns, low standard deviations, and low covariances with other securities. Often this information is derived from historical databases covering thousands of securities. Unless the risk and return data are carefully checked, errors (for example, understating a security's standard deviation) can easily lead the optimizer to recommend purchases of securities for erroneous reasons. Even if the data are "clean," extreme historical values for some securities may lead the optimizer astray.

Unless programmed to take transaction costs into account, optimizers also display a nasty habit of generating high turnover and recommending investments in illiquid securities. *High turnover* refers to significant changes in portfolio composition from one period to the next. High turnover can result in unacceptably large transaction costs (see Chapter 3), thereby hindering portfolio performance. *Liquidity* refers to the ability to actually buy the securities selected by the optimizer. Selected securities may possess desirable risk-return characteristics but may not trade in sufficient volume to permit institutional investors to purchase them without incurring sizable transaction costs.

Solutions to these implementation problems do exist, ranging from checking data carefully to placing constraints on maximum turnover or minimum liquidity. In the end, however, nothing can substitute for skillful judgmental forecasts of security returns and risks, balanced by properly applied notions of market equilibrium.

Territorial and implementation problems have given investment managers convenient reasons to avoid optimizers and stick to traditional portfolio construction methods. Nevertheless, the outlook for quantitative portfolio construction techniques is actually quite bright. The increasing efficiency of capital markets has forced institutional investment managers to process more information about more securities more rapidly than ever before. In response, they have generally increased their use of quantitative investment tools. While most do not directly integrate optimizers into their portfolio construction procedures, virtually all have become more sensitive to the objective of creating diversified portfolios that display the highest levels of expected return at acceptable levels of risk.

that the investor could choose (for example, O). However, the figure shows that portfolio O* dominates these portfolios, since it is on an indifference curve that is further northwest. Figure 8.3 shows how the highly risk-averse investor will choose a portfolio close to E. Figure 8.4 shows that the slightly risk-averse investor will choose a portfolio close to S.[3]

Upon reflection, the efficient set theorem is quite rational. In Chapter 7, it was shown that the investor should select the portfolio that puts him or her on the indifference curve furthest northwest. The efficient set theorem, stating that the investor need not be concerned with portfolios that do not lie on the northwest boundary of the feasible set, is a logical consequence.

---

[3] The risk-neutral investor will choose portfolio S, whereas the risk-seeking investor will choose either S or H.

Figure 8.3
Portfolio selection for a highly risk-averse investor.

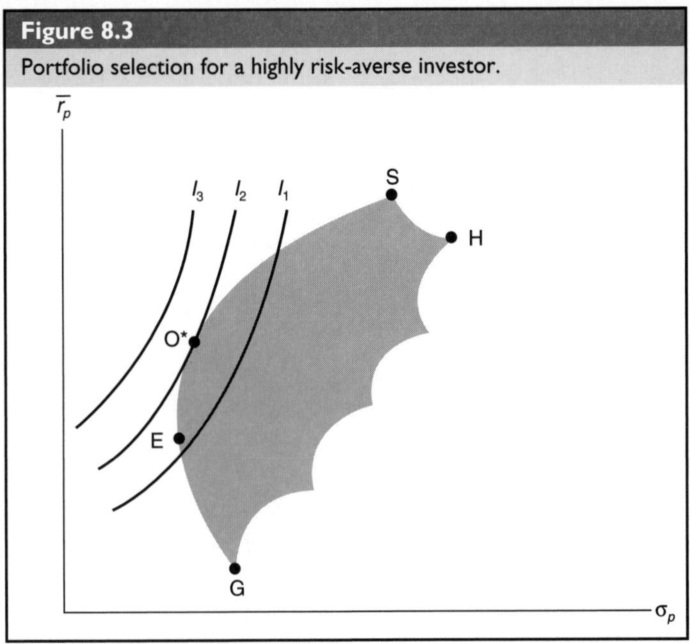

Figure 8.4
Portfolio selection for a slightly risk-averse investor.

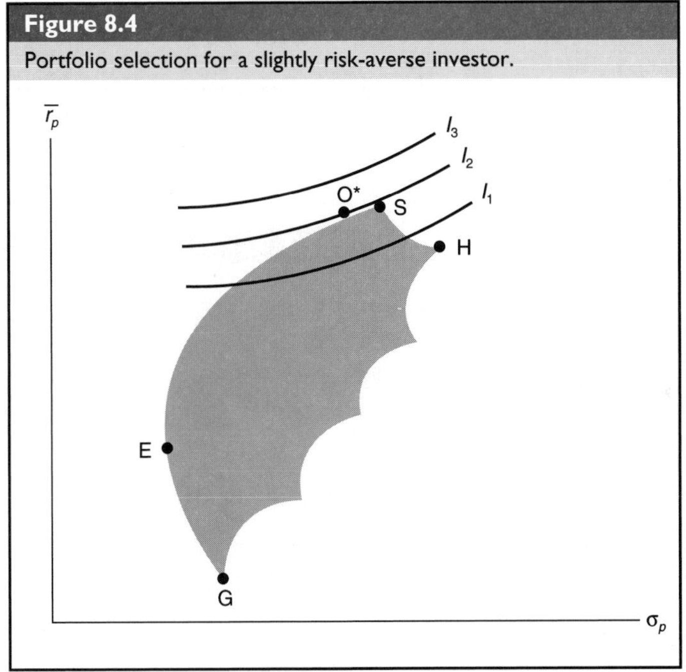

Indifference curves for the risk-averse investor were shown to be positively sloped and convex in Chapter 7. Now it will be shown that the efficient set is generally concave, meaning that if a straight line is drawn between any two points on the efficient set, the straight line will lie below the efficient set. This feature of the efficient set is important because it means

Figure 8.5

Upper and lower bounds to combinations of securities A and G.

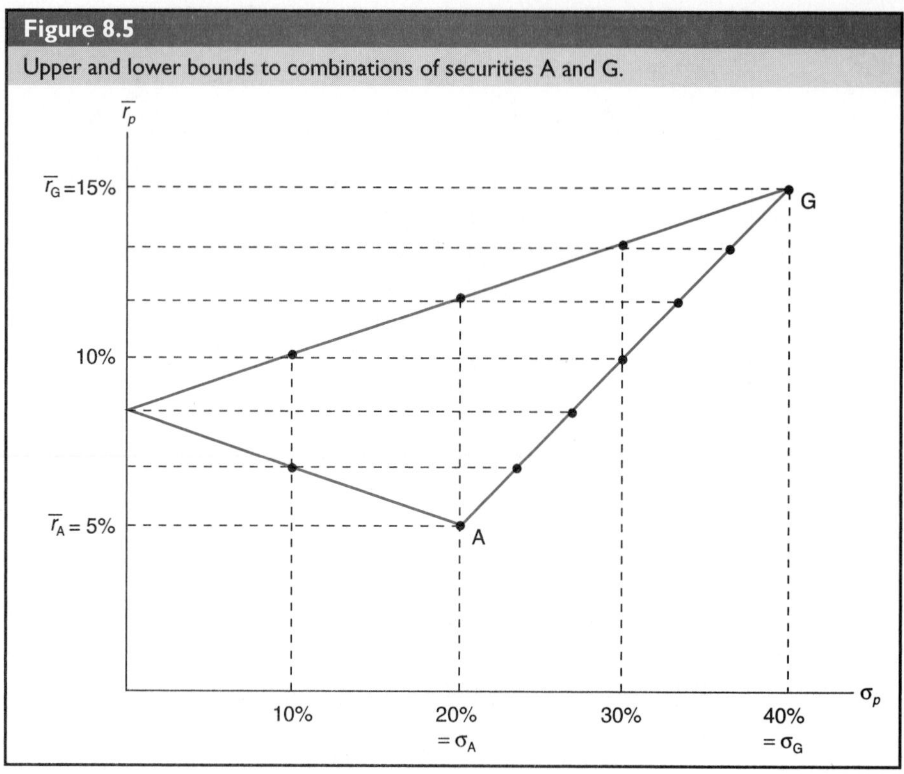

that there will be only one tangency point between the investor's indifference curves and the efficient set.

CONCAVITY OF THE EFFICIENT SET

In order to see why the efficient set is concave, consider the following two-security example. Security 1, the Ark Shipping Company, has an estimated expected return of 5% and standard deviation of 20%. Security 2, the Gold Jewelry Company, has an estimated expected return of 15% and standard deviation of 40%. Their respective locations are indicated by the letters *A* and *G* in Figure 8.5.

Bounds on the Location of Portfolios

Now consider all possible portfolios that an investor could purchase by combining these two securities. Let X_1 denote the proportion of the investor's funds invested in Ark Shipping and $X_2 = 1 - X_1$ denote the proportion invested in Gold Jewelry. Thus, if the investor purchased just Ark Shipping, then $X_1 = 1$ and $X_2 = 0$. Alternatively, if the investor purchased just Gold Jewelry, then $X_1 = 0$ and $X_2 = 1$. A combination of .17 in Ark Shipping and .83 in Gold Jewelry is also possible, as are respective combinations of .33 and .67, and .50 and .50. Although there are many other possibilities, only the following seven portfolios will be considered:

	Portfolio A	Portfolio B	Portfolio C	Portfolio D	Portfolio E	Portfolio F	Portfolio G
X_1	1.00	.83	.67	.50	.33	.17	.00
X_2	.00	.17	.33	.50	.67	.83	1.00

In order to consider these seven portfolios for possible investment, their expected returns and standard deviations must be calculated. All the necessary information to calculate the expected returns for these portfolios is at hand. In doing so, equation (7.3a) must be utilized:

$$\begin{aligned}\bar{r}_p &= \sum_{i=1}^{N} X_i \bar{r}_i \\ &= \sum_{i=1}^{2} X_i \bar{r}_i \\ &= X_1\bar{r}_1 + X_2\bar{r}_2 \\ &= (X_1 \times 5\%) + (X_2 \times 15\%).\end{aligned} \tag{7.3a}$$

For portfolios A and G, this calculation is trivial, since the investor is purchasing shares of just one company. Thus, their expected returns are 5% and 15%, respectively. For portfolios B, C, D, E, and F, the expected returns are, respectively,

$$\begin{aligned}\bar{r}_B &= (.83 \times 5\%) + (.17 \times 15\%) \\ &= 6.70\% \\ \bar{r}_C &= (.67 \times 5\%) + (.33 \times 15\%) \\ &= 8.30\% \\ \bar{r}_D &= (.50 \times 5\%) + (.50 \times 15\%) \\ &= 10\% \\ \bar{r}_E &= (.33 \times 5\%) + (.67 \times 15\%) \\ &= 11.70\% \\ \bar{r}_F &= (.17 \times 5\%) + (.83 \times 15\%) \\ &= 13.30\%.\end{aligned}$$

In calculating the standard deviation of these seven portfolios, equation (7.7) is used:

$$\begin{aligned}\sigma_p &= \left[\sum_{i=1}^{N}\sum_{j=1}^{N} X_i X_j \sigma_{ij}\right]^{1/2} \\ &= \left[\sum_{i=1}^{2}\sum_{j=1}^{2} X_i X_j \sigma_{ij}\right]^{1/2} \\ &= [X_1X_1\sigma_{11} + X_1X_2\sigma_{12} + X_2X_1\sigma_{21} + X_2X_2\sigma_{22}]^{1/2} \\ &= [X_1^2\sigma_1^2 + X_2^2\sigma_2^2 + 2X_1X_2\sigma_{12}]^{1/2} \\ &= [(X_1^2 \times 20\%^2) + (X_2^2 \times 40\%^2) + 2X_1X_2\sigma_{12}]^{1/2}\end{aligned} \tag{7.7}$$

For portfolios A and G, this calculation is trivial, since the investor is purchasing shares of just one company. Thus, their standard deviations are just 20% and 40%, respectively.

For portfolios B, C, D, E, and F, application of equation (7.7) indicates that the standard deviations depend on the magnitude of the covariance between the two securities. As shown in equation (7.5), this covariance term is equal to the correlation between the two securities multiplied by the product of their standard deviations:

$$\begin{aligned}\sigma_{12} &= \rho_{12} \times \sigma_1 \times \sigma_2 \\ &= \rho_{12} \times 20\% \times 40\% \\ &= 800\rho_{12}.\end{aligned} \tag{7.5}$$

This means that the standard deviation of any portfolio consisting of Ark Shipping and Gold Jewelry can be expressed as

$$\begin{aligned}\sigma_p &= [(X_1^2 \times 20\%^2) + (X_2^2 \times 40\%^2) + (2X_1X_2 \times 800\rho_{12})]^{1/2} \\ &= [400X_1^2 + 1600X_2^2 + 1600\%X_1X_2\rho_{12}]^{1/2}.\end{aligned} \tag{8.1}$$

Consider portfolio D first. The standard deviation of this portfolio will be somewhere between 10% and 30%, the exact value depending upon the size of the correlation coefficient. How were these bounds of 10% and 30% determined? First, note that for portfolio D, equation (8.1) reduces to

$$\begin{aligned}\sigma_D &= [(400 \times .25) + (1600 \times .25) + (1600 \times .5 \times .5 \times \rho_{12})]^{1/2} \\ &= [500 + 400\rho_{12}]^{1/2}.\end{aligned} \tag{8.2}$$

Inspection of equation (8.2) indicates that σ_D will be at a minimum when the correlation coefficient, ρ_{12}, is at a minimum. Now, remembering that the minimum value for any correlation coefficient is –1, it can be seen that the lower bound on σ_D is

$$\begin{aligned}\sigma_D &= [500 + (400 \times -1)]^{1/2} \\ &= [500 - 400]^{1/2} \\ &= [100]^{1/2} \\ &= 10\%.\end{aligned}$$

Similarly, inspection of equation (8.2) indicates that σ_D will be at a maximum when the correlation coefficient is at a maximum, which is +1. Thus, the upper bound on σ_D is

$$\begin{aligned}\sigma_D &= [500 + (400 \times 1)]^{1/2} \\ &= (500 + 400)^{1/2} \\ &= (900)^{1/2} \\ &= 30\%.\end{aligned}$$

In general, it can be seen from equation (8.1) that for any given set of weights X_1 and X_2, the lower and upper bounds will occur when the correlations between the two securities are –1 and +1, respectively. Applying the same analysis to the other portfolios reveals that their lower and upper bounds are as follows:

Portfolio	Standard Deviation of Portfolio	
	Lower Bound	*Upper Bound*
A	20%	20.00%
B	10	23.33
C	00	26.67
D	10	30.00
E	20	33.33
F	30	36.67
G	40	40.00

These values are shown in Figure 8.5.

Interestingly, the upper bounds all lie on a straight line connecting points A and G. This means that any portfolio consisting of these two securities cannot have a standard deviation that plots to the right of a straight line connecting the two securities. Instead, the standard deviation must lie on or to the left of the straight line. This observation suggests a motivation for diversifying a portfolio. Namely, *diversification generally leads to risk reduction*, since the standard deviation of a portfolio will generally be less than a weighted average of the standard deviations of the securities in the portfolio.

Also interesting is the observation that the lower bounds all lie on one of two line segments that go from point A to a point on the vertical axis corresponding to 8.30% and then to point G. This means that any portfolio consisting of these two securities cannot have a standard deviation that plots to the left of either of these two line segments. For example, portfolio B must lie on the horizontal line going through the vertical axis at 6.70% but bounded at the values of 10% and 23.33%.

Actual Location of the Portfolios

In sum, any portfolio consisting of these two securities will lie within the triangle shown in Figure 8.5, with its actual location depending on the magnitude of the correlation coefficient between the two securities.

What if the correlation were zero? In this case, equation (8.1) reduces to

$$\begin{aligned}\sigma_p &= [(400X_1^2) + (1600X_2^2) + (1600X_1X_2 \times 0)]^{1/2} \\ &= [400X_1^2 + 1600X_2^2]^{1/2}.\end{aligned}$$

Applying the appropriate weights for X_1 and X_2, the standard deviation for portfolios B, C, D, E, and F can therefore be calculated as follows:

$$\begin{aligned}\sigma_B &= [(400 \times .83^2) + (1600 \times .17^2)]^{1/2} \\ &= 17.94\% \\ \sigma_C &= [(400 \times .67^2) + (1600 \times .33^2)]^{1/2} \\ &= 18.81\% \\ \sigma_D &= [(400 \times .50^2) + (1600 \times .50^2)]^{1/2} \\ &= 22.36\%\end{aligned}$$

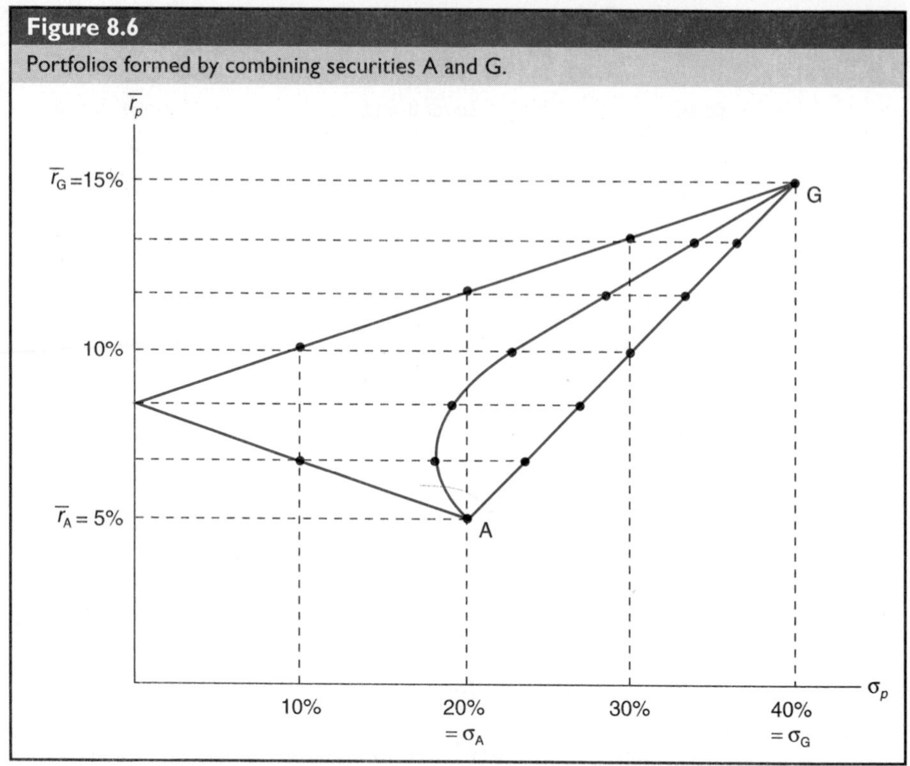

Figure 8.6
Portfolios formed by combining securities A and G.

$$\sigma_E = [(400 \times .33^2) + (1600 \times .67^2)]^{1/2}$$
$$= 27.60\%$$
$$\sigma_F = [(400 \times .17^2) + (1600 \times .83^2)]^{1/2}$$
$$= 33.37\%.$$

Figure 8.6 indicates the location of these portfolios along with the upper and lower bounds that were shown in Figure 8.5. As can be seen, these portfolios—as well as all other possible portfolios consisting of Ark Shipping and Gold Jewelry—lie on a line that is curved or bowed to the left. Although not shown here, if the correlation were less than zero, the line would curve more to the left. If the correlation were greater than zero, it would not curve quite as much to the left. The important point of this figure is that as long as the correlation is less than +1 and greater than –1, the line representing the set of portfolios consisting of various combinations of the two securities will have some degree of curvature to the left. Furthermore, the northwest portion will be concave.

Similar analysis can be applied to a situation where there are more than two securities under consideration. When this is done, as long as the correlations are less than +1 and greater than –1, the northwest portion must be concave, just as it is in the two-security example.[4] Thus, in general, the efficient set will be concave.

[4]This "curvature property" can also be used to explain why the right-hand side of the feasible set has the umbrella shape noted in Figure 8.2. A more rigorous demonstration of concavity is contained in Appendix A.

Figure 8.7
Concavity of the efficient set.

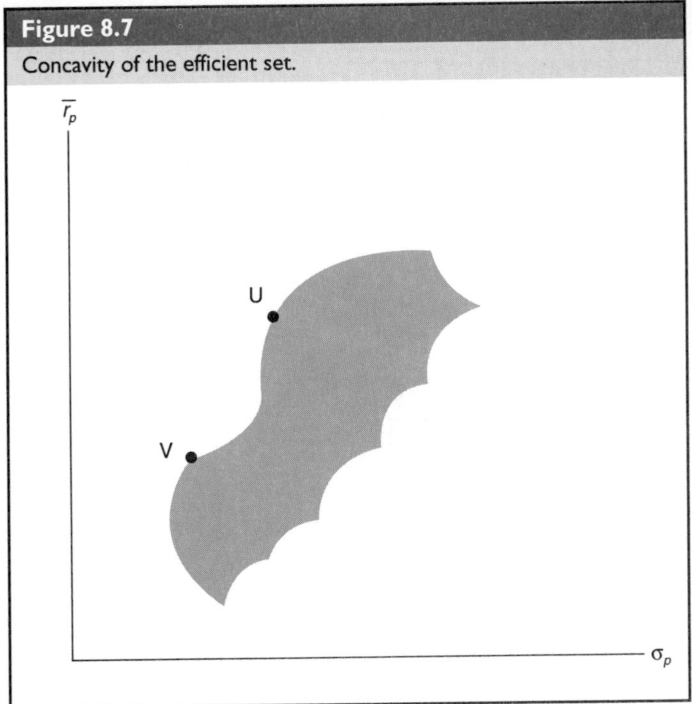

Impossibility of Having "Dents" in the Efficient Set

The previous example used two individual securities, Ark Shipping and Gold Jewelry, and considered all possible portfolios that could be formed by combining them. It is important to recognize that the same principle holds if two portfolios are combined into a third portfolio. That is, point *A* in Figure 8.6 could represent a portfolio of securities with an expected return of 5% and a standard deviation of 20%, and point *G* could represent another portfolio of securities with an expected return of 15% and a standard deviation of 40%. Combining these two portfolios will result in a third portfolio that has an expected return and standard deviation dependent upon the proportion invested in A and G. Assuming the correlation between A and G is zero, the location of the third portfolio will lie on the curved line connecting *A* and *G*.

Recognizing this, it can now be shown why the efficient set is concave. One way to do this is to show that it cannot have any other shape. Consider the efficient set shown in Figure 8.7. Note that there is a "dent" in it between points *U* and *V*. That is, there is a region on it where it is not concave. This cannot be a truly efficient set, since an investor could put part of his or her funds in the portfolio located at *U* and the rest of his or her funds in the portfolio located at *V*. The resulting portfolio, a combination of *U* and *V*, would have to lie to the left of the alleged efficient set. Thus, the new portfolio would be "more efficient" than a portfolio with the same expected return that was on the alleged efficient set between *U* and *V*.

For example, consider the portfolio on the alleged efficient set that lies halfway between *U* and *V*; it is indicated as point *W* in Figure 8.8. If it truly is an efficient portfolio, then it would be impossible to form a portfolio with the same expected return as W but with a lower standard deviation. However, by putting 50% of his or her funds in U and 50%

Figure 8.8

Removing a "dent" from the efficient set.

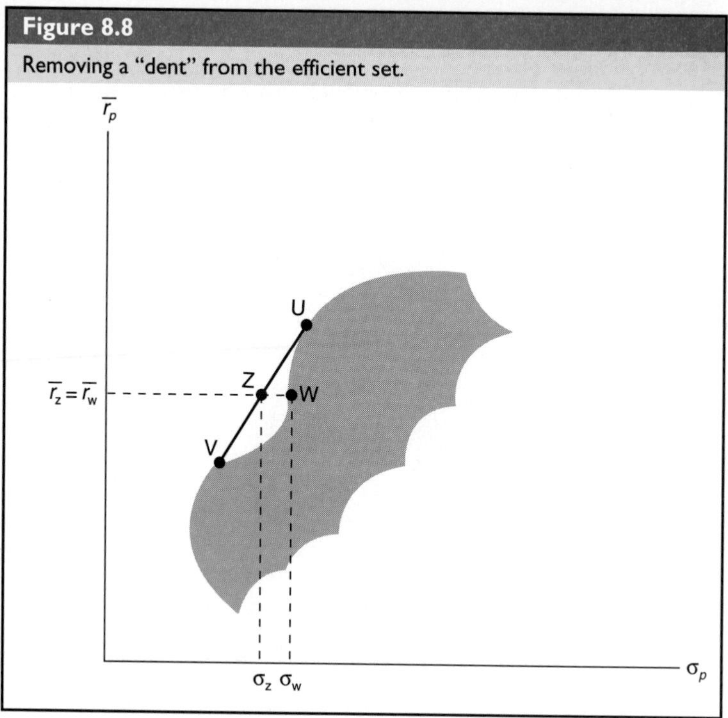

in V, the investor would have a portfolio that dominates W, since it would have the same expected return but a lower standard deviation. Why will it have a lower standard deviation? If the correlation between U and V were +1, this portfolio would lie on the straight line connecting U and V and would thus have a lower standard deviation than W. In Figure 8.8, Z denotes this point. Since the actual correlation is less than +1, it would have a standard deviation even lower than Z's standard deviation. This means that the alleged efficient set was constructed in error, since it is easy to find "more efficient" portfolios in the region where it is not concave.

THE MARKET MODEL

Suppose that the return on a common stock over a given time period (say, a month) is related to the return over the same period that is earned on a market index such as the widely cited TSE 300.[5] That is, if the market has gone up then it is likely that the stock has gone up, and if the market has gone down then it is likely that the stock has gone down. One way to capture this relationship is with the **market model**:

$$r_i = \alpha_{iI} + \beta_{iI} r_I + \epsilon_{iI} \tag{8.3}$$

[5] This is an example of a single-factor model where the factor is the return on a market index (see Chapter 11 for more on factor models; see Chapters 10, 23, and 26 for more on market indices). The model is actually more general than indicated here in that the return need not be on a market index. It can be on any variable that is believed to have a major influence on individual stock returns, such as the predicted rate of increase in industrial production or gross domestic product.

where:

r_i = return on security i for some given period,

r_I = return on market index I for the same period,

α_{iI} = intercept term,

β_{iI} = slope term,

ϵ_{iI} = random error term.

Assuming that the slope term β_{iI} is positive, equation (8.3) indicates that the higher the return on the market index, the higher the return on the security is likely to be. (Note that the expected value of the random error term is zero.)

Consider stock A, for example, which has $\alpha_{iI} = 2\%$ and $\beta_{iI} = 1.2$. This means that the market model for stock A is

$$r_A = 2\% + 1.2r_I + \epsilon_{AI} \tag{8.4}$$

so that if the market index has a return of 10%, the return on the security is expected to be $2\% + (1.2 \times 10\%) = 14\%$. Similarly, if the market index's return is –5%, then the return on security A is expected to be $2\% + (1.2 \times -5\%) = -4\%$.

Random Error Terms

The term ϵ_{iI}, known as the **random error term** in equation (8.3), simply shows that the market model does not explain security returns perfectly. That is, when the market index goes up by 10% or down by 5%, the return on security A is not going to be exactly 14% or –4%, respectively. The different between what the return actually is and what it is expected to be, given the return on the market index, is attributed to the effect of the random error term. Hence, if the security's return were 9% instead of 14%, the 5% difference would be attributed to the random error term (that is, $\epsilon_{AI} = -5\%$; this will be illustrated shortly in Figure 8.11). Similarly, if the security return were –2% instead of –4%, the 2% difference would be attributed to the random error term (that is, $\epsilon_{AI} = +2\%$).

The random error term for a security is a random variable with an expected value of zero and a standard deviation denoted by $\sigma_{\epsilon i}$.[6] It can be thought of as the outcome that will occur when a special kind of roulette wheel is spun. One feature of such a random error term is that its expected outcome is zero.

For example, security A may be thought of as having a random error term corresponding to a roulette wheel with integer values on it that range from –10% to +10%, with the values evenly spaced.[7] This means that there are 21 possible outcomes, each of which has an equal probability of occurring. Given the range of numbers, it also means that the expected outcome of the random error term is zero:

$$[-10 \times \frac{1}{21}] + [-9 \times \frac{1}{21}] + \cdots + [9 \times \frac{1}{21}] + [10 \times \frac{1}{21}] = 0.$$

[6] To be technically correct, the standard deviation of the random error term should be denoted $\sigma_{\epsilon iI}$, because it is measured relative to market index I. The subscript I is not shown here for ease of exposition.

[7] Since the range refers to the possible outcomes and the spacing refers to the probabilities of the various outcomes occurring, it can be seen that the roulette wheel is just a convenient way of referring to the random error term's probability distribution. Typically, it is assumed that the random error term has a normal probability distribution.

INSTITUTIONAL ISSUES

The Active Manager Portfolio Selection Problem

The classic formulation of the portfolio selection problem depicts an investor who must choose a portfolio on the efficient set that exhibits the optimal combination of expected return and standard deviation, given the investor's risk-return preferences. In practice, however, this description inadequately characterizes the situation faced by most organizations that manage money for institutional investors. We want to consider how the portfolio selection problem can be modified to fit the concerns of institutional investors.

Certain types of institutional investors, such as pension and endowment funds (whom we will call the "clients"), typically hire outside firms (whom we will call the "managers") as agents to invest their assets. These managers usually specialize in a particular asset class, such as common stocks or fixed-income securities. The clients establish performance benchmarks for their managers. These benchmarks may be market indices (such as the TSE 300) or specialized benchmarks that reflect specific investment styles (such as small-capitalization growth stocks).

The clients hire some managers to simply match the performance of the benchmarks. These managers are called *passive managers* (see Chapter 24). The clients hire other managers to exceed the returns produced by the benchmarks. These managers are called *active managers*.

In the case of passive managers, the portfolio selection problem is trivial. They simply buy and hold the securities that constitute their assigned benchmarks. Their portfolios are called *index funds*. Passive managers need not refer to the efficient set or risk-return preferences. Those issues must be dealt with by their clients. (Whether the benchmarks chosen by the clients are efficient is a separate, although important, subject that we will not address here.)

Active managers face a much more difficult task. They must create portfolios that produce returns exceeding the returns on their assigned benchmarks in sufficient magnitude and with enough consistency to satisfy their clients.

The greatest obstacle confronting active managers is their lack of omniscience. Even the most capable of them make numerous errors in their security selections. Despite fables about managers who outperform the market's return every year by 10 percentage points, common stock managers who exceed their benchmarks' returns (after all fees and expenses) by 1–2 percentage points per annum are considered exceptional performers. Managers lacking skill (with skill defined in this case as the ability to accurately forecast security returns) will lose to their benchmarks as their fees and trading costs diminish their returns.

We refer to the returns that active managers earn above those of their benchmarks as *active returns*. For example, a manager whose portfolio and benchmark generate returns of 7% and 4%, respectively, has earned a 3% active return (= 7% – 4%). The expected active return for highly skillful managers exceeds that of less talented managers. Nonetheless, in any given period, through sheer chance, the less capable manager's active return may exceed that of the highly skillful manager.

Because the results of active managers' investment decisions are uncertain, their returns relative to their benchmarks exhibit variability over time. We refer to the standard deviation of active return as *active risk*.

Active managers (at least those with some investment forecasting ability) can increase their expected active returns by taking on more active risk. Suppose that Manager X forecasts that Noranda stock will earn a return above that of the benchmark. Noranda constitutes 2% of the benchmark. Manager X could "bet" on

Noranda by holding a portfolio with a 4% position in Noranda stock. The difference between the actual portfolio's position in Noranda and the benchmark's position (4% – 2% = +2%) we call an *active position*. If Noranda does perform well, Manager X's active return will be enhanced by the positive active position in Noranda. However, if Noranda performs poorly, then Manager X's active return will be diminished. The larger Manager X's active position is in Noranda, the greater is his or her expected active return. However, the larger also is Manager X's active risk.

Active risk (and, hence, expected active return) can be eliminated by owning every benchmark security at weights matching those of the same securities in the benchmark. Passive managers follow this approach. Active managers assume active risk when they deviate in their portfolio holdings relative to their benchmarks. Rational and skillful active managers will take on active risk only with the expectation of earning a positive active return.

The outline of the portfolio selection problem for an active manager now becomes clear. The manager is not concerned with the trade-off between portfolio expected return and standard deviation. Rather, the manager chooses between higher expected active return and lower active risk.

This process requires that we make an assumption about the manager's ability to forecast security returns. With that information, we can construct a manager's "efficient set" (based on expected active return and active risk) that exhibits the highest combination of expected active return per unit of active risk and the lowest active risk per unit of expected active return. Managers with greater skill will have efficient sets that lie further to the northwest than managers with less skill.

Indifference curves, analogous to those applied in the classical portfolio selection problem, indicate various combinations of active return and active risk that the manager finds equally desirable. The steepness of these indifference curves reflects the manager's degree of risk aversion, which is directly related to the manager's assessment of how his or her clients will respond to various investment outcomes.

The manager's optimal combination of active return and risk is that point on the efficient set which is tangent to one of the indifference curves. We can view this point as the manager's desired level of aggressiveness in implementing his or her security return forecasts. Managers (and clients) with higher risk aversion will choose portfolios with lower levels of active risk. Conversely, managers (and clients) with lower risk aversion will choose portfolios with higher levels of active risk.

As can be seen, this calculation involves multiplying each outcome by its probability of occurring and then summing up the resulting products. The standard deviation of this random error term can now be shown to be equal to 6.06%:

$$[(-10-0)^2 \times \frac{1}{21}]+[(-9-0)^2 \times \frac{1}{21}] + \cdots + [(9-0)^2 \times \frac{1}{21}] + [(10-0)^2 \times \frac{1}{21}]^{1/2} = 6.06\%.$$

This calculation involves subtracting the expected outcome from each possible outcome, then squaring each one of these differences, multiplying each square by the probability of the corresponding outcome occurring, adding the products, and finally taking the square root of the resulting sum.

Figure 8.9

Security A's random error term.

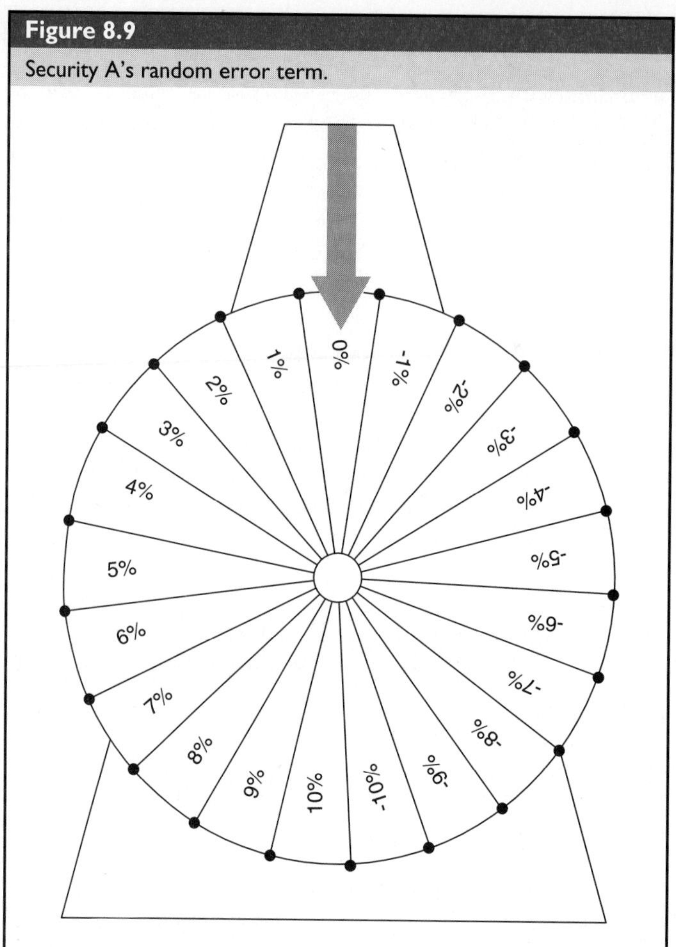

Figure 8.9 illustrates the roulette wheel corresponding to this random error term. In general, securities will have random error terms whose corresponding roulette wheels have different ranges and different forms of uneven spacing. Although all will have an expected value of zero, they will typically have different standard deviations. For example, security B may have a random error term whose expected value and standard deviation are equal to 0 and 4.76%, respectively.[8]

Graphical Representation of the Market Model

The solid line in panel (a) of Figure 8.10 provides a graph of the market model for security A. This line corresponds to equation (8.4), but without the random error term. Accordingly,

[8] This would be the case if security B had a random error term whose roulette wheel had integers from –9% to +9% on it, but the spacing for each integer between –5% and +5% was twice as large as the spacing for each integer from –9% to –6% and +6% to +9%. This means that the probability of any specific integer between –5% and +5% occurring is equal to $^2/_{30}$, whereas the probability of any specific integer from –9% to –6% and +6% to +9% occurring is equal to $^1/_{30}$.

Figure 8.10
Market model.

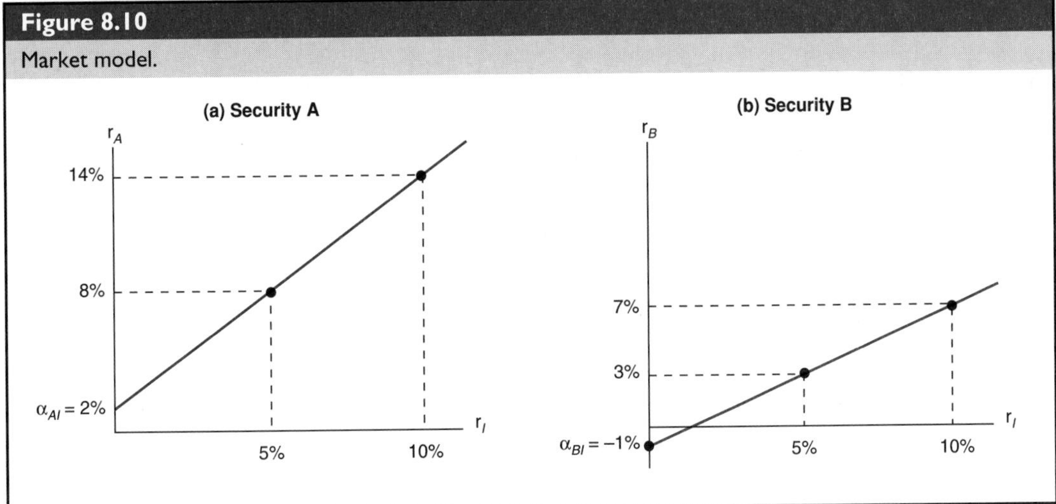

the line that is graphed for security A is

$$r_A = 2\% + 1.2r_I. \tag{8.5}$$

Here, the vertical axis measures the return on the particular security (r_A) whereas the horizontal axis measures the return on the market index (r_I). The line goes through the point on the vertical axis corresponding to the value of α_{AI}, which in this case is 2%. In addition, the line has a slope equal to β_{AI}, or 1.2.

Panel (b) of Figure 8.10 presents the graph of the market model for security B. The line can be expressed as the following equation:

$$r_B = -1\% + .8r_I. \tag{8.6}$$

This line goes through the point on the vertical axis corresponding to the value of α_{BI}, which in this case is –1%. Note that its slope is equal to β_{BI} or .8.

Beta

At this point it can be seen that the slope in a security's market model measures the sensitivity of the security's returns to the market index's returns. Both lines in Figure 8.10 have positive slopes, indicating that the higher the returns of the market index, the higher the returns of the two securities. However, the two securities have different slopes, indicating that they have different sensitivities to the returns of the market index. Specifically, A has a higher slope than B, indicating that the returns of A are more sensitive than the returns of B to the returns of the market index.

For example, assume that the market index's expected return is 5%. If the market index subsequently has an actual return of 10%, it will have returned 5% more than expected. Panel (a) of Figure 8.10 shows that security A should have a return that is 6% (14% – 8%) greater than initially expected. Similarly, panel (b) shows that security B should have a return that is 4% (7% – 3%) greater than initially expected. The reason for the 2% (6% – 4%) difference is that security A has a higher slope than security B—that is, A is more sensitive than B to returns on the market index.

The slope term in the market model is often referred to as **beta**, and is equal to

$$\beta_{iI} = \sigma_{iI} / \sigma_I^2 \tag{8.7}$$

where σ_{iI} denotes the covariance of the returns on stock i and the market index, and σ_I^2 denotes the variance of returns on the market index. A stock that has a return that mirrors the return on the market index will have a beta equal to one (and an intercept of zero, resulting in a market model that is $r_i = r_I + \epsilon_{iI}$). Hence stocks with betas greater than one (such as A) are more volatile than the market index and are known as **aggressive stocks.** In contrast, stocks with betas less than one (such as B) are less volatile than the market index and are known as **defensive stocks.**[9]

Actual Returns

The random error term suggests that for a given return on the market index, the actual return on a security will usually lie off its market model line.[10] If the actual returns on securities A and B turn out to be 9% and 11%, respectively, and the market index's actual return turns out to be 10%, then the actual return on A and B could be viewed as having the following three components:

	Security A	Security B
Intercept	2%	−1%
Actual return on the market index × beta	12% = 10% × 1.2	8% = 10% × .8
Random error outcome	−5% = 9% − (2% + 12%)	4% = 11% − (−1% + 8%)
Actual return	9%	11%

In this case, the roulette wheels for A and B can be thought of as having been spun, resulting in values (that is, random error outcomes) of −5% for A and +4% for B. These values can be viewed as being equal to the vertical distance by which each security's actual return ended up being off its market model line, as shown in Figure 8.11.

DIVERSIFICATION

According to the market model, the total risk of any security i, measured by its variance and denoted σ_i^2, consists of two parts: (1) **market** (or systematic) **risk**; and (2) **unique** (or unsystematic) **risk**. That is, σ_i^2 equals the following:

$$\sigma_i^2 = \beta_{iI}^2 \sigma_I^2 + \sigma_{\epsilon i}^2 \tag{8.8}$$

where σ_I^2 denotes the variance of returns on the market index. Thus $\beta_{iI}^2 \sigma_I^2$ denotes the market risk of security i, and $\sigma_{\epsilon i}^2$ denotes the unique risk of security i as measured by the variance of the random error term, ϵ_{iI}, appearing in equation (8.3).

---

[9] Just how beta is estimated will be addressed in Chapter 17.

[10] If the random error term takes on a value of zero, then the security will lie *on* the line. However, the probability of this occurring is very small for most securities.

Figure 8.11

Market model and actual returns.

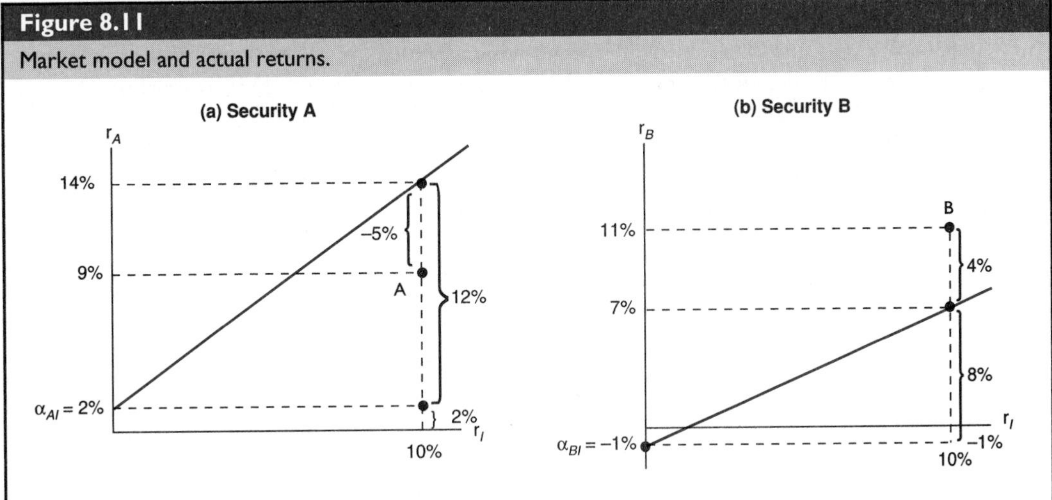

► Portfolio Total Risk

When the return on every risky *security* in a portfolio is related to the return on the market index as specified by the market model, what can be said about the total risk of the *portfolio*? If the proportion of funds invested in security i for a given portfolio p is denoted X_i, then the return on this portfolio will be

$$r_p = \sum_{i=1}^{N} X_i r_i. \tag{8.9}$$

Substituting the right-hand side of equation (8.3) for r_i in equation (8.9) results in the following market model for the portfolio:

$$\begin{aligned} r_p &= \sum_{i=1}^{N} X_i(\alpha_{iI} + \beta_{iI} r_I + \epsilon_{iI}) \\ &= \sum_{i=1}^{N} X_i \alpha_{iI} + \left(\sum_{i=1}^{N} X_i \beta_{iI}\right) r_I + \sum_{i=1}^{N} X_i \epsilon_{iI}) \\ &= \alpha_{pI} + \beta_{pI} r_I + \epsilon_{pI} \end{aligned} \tag{8.10a}$$

where:

$$\alpha_{pI} = \sum_{i=1}^{N} X_i \alpha_{iI} \tag{8.10b}$$

$$\beta_{pI} = \sum_{i=1}^{N} X_i \beta_{iI} \tag{8.10c}$$

$$\epsilon_{pI} = \sum_{i=1}^{N} X_i \epsilon_{iI} \tag{8.10d}$$

In equations (8.10b) and (8.10c), the portfolio's vertical intercept (α_{pI}) and beta (β_{pI}) are shown to be weighted averages of the intercepts and betas of the securities, respectively, using their relative proportions in the portfolio as weights. Similarly, in equation (8.10d), the portfolio's random error term (ϵ_{pI}) is a weighted average of the random error terms of the securities, again using the relative proportions in the portfolio as weights. Thus, the portfolio's market model is a straightforward extension of the market model for individual securities given in equation (8.3).[11]

From equation (8.10a), it follows that the total risk of a portfolio, measured by the variance of the portfolio's returns and denoted σ_p^2, will be

$$\sigma_p^2 = \beta_{pI}^2 \sigma_I^2 + \sigma_{\epsilon p}^2 \qquad (8.11a)$$

where:

$$\beta_{pI}^2 = \left[\sum_{i=1}^{N} X_i \beta_{iI}\right]^2 \qquad (8.11b)$$

and, assuming the random error components of security returns are uncorrelated:

$$\sigma_{\epsilon p}^2 = \sum_{i=1}^{N} X_i^2 \sigma_{\epsilon i}^2 \qquad (8.11c)$$

Equation (8.11a) shows that the total risk of any portfolio can be viewed as having two components, similar to the two components of the total risk of an individual security. These components are again referred to as market risk ($\beta_{pI}^2 \sigma_I^2$) and unique risk ($\sigma_{\epsilon p}^2$).

Next, it will be shown that increased **diversification** can lead to the reduction of a portfolio's total risk. This occurs due to a reduction in the size of the portfolio's unique risk while the portfolio's market risk remains approximately the same size.

Portfolio Market Risk

Generally, the more diversified a portfolio (that is, the larger the number of securities in the portfolio), the smaller will be each proportion X_i. This will not cause β_{pI} either to decrease or to increase significantly unless a deliberate attempt is made to do so by adding either relatively low or high beta securities, respectively, to the portfolio. That is, because a portfolio's beta is an average of the betas of its securities, there is no reason to suspect that increasing the amount of diversification will cause the portfolio beta, and thus the market risk of the portfolio, to change in a particular direction. Accordingly, diversification leads to *averaging* of market risk.

This makes sense because when prospects for the economy turn sour (or rosy), most securities will fall (or rise) in price. Regardless of the amount of diversification, portfolio returns will always be susceptible to such marketwide influences.

Portfolio Unique Risk

The situation is entirely different for unique risk. In a portfolio, some securities will go up as a result of unexpected good news specific to the company that issued the securities (such as an unexpected approval of a patent). Other securities will go down as a result of unexpected company-specific bad news (such as an industrial accident). Looking forward, approximately as many companies can be expected to have good news as bad news, leading

[11] Appendix B shows how the market model can be used to estimate expected returns, variances, and covariances for the securities in the feasible set; with these estimates in hand, the efficient set can subsequently be determined.

to little anticipated net impact on the return of a "well-diversified" portfolio. This means that the more diversified a portfolio becomes, the smaller will be its unique risk and, in turn, its total risk.

This can be quantified precisely if the random error components of security returns are assumed to be uncorrelated, as was done when equation (8.11c) was written. Consider the following situation. If the amount invested in each security is equal, then the proportion X_i will equal $^1/_N$, and the level of unique risk, as shown in equation (8.11c), will be equal to

$$\sigma^2_{\epsilon p} = \sum_{i=1}^{N} \left[\frac{1}{N}\right]^2 \sigma^2_{\epsilon i} \tag{8.12a}$$

$$= \frac{1}{N}\left[\frac{\sigma^2_{\epsilon 1} + \sigma^2_{\epsilon 2} + \ldots \sigma^2_{\epsilon N}}{N}\right]. \tag{8.12b}$$

The value inside the square brackets in equation (8.12b) is simply the average unique risk of the component securities. But the portfolio's unique risk is only one-Nth as large as this, since the term $^1/_N$ appears outside the square brackets. Now, as the portfolio becomes more diversified, the number of securities in it (that is, N) becomes larger. In turn, this means that $^1/_N$ becomes smaller, resulting in the portfolio having less unique risk.[12] That is, diversification can substantially *reduce* unique risk.

Roughly speaking, a portfolio that has 30 or more randomly selected securities in it will have a relatively small amount of unique risk. This means that its total risk will be only slightly greater than the amount of market risk that is present. Thus, such portfolios are "well diversified." Figure 8.12 illustrates how diversification results in the reduction of unique risk but the averaging of market risk.

► An Example

Consider the two securities, A and B, that were referred to earlier. These two securities had betas of 1.2 and .8, respectively; the standard deviations of their random error terms were, respectively, 6.06% and 4.76%. Thus, given that $\sigma_{\epsilon A} = 6.06\%$ and $\sigma_{\epsilon B} = 4.76\%$, it follows that $\sigma^2_{\epsilon A} = 6.06^2 = 37$ and $\sigma^2_{\epsilon B} = 4.76^2 = 23$. Now assume that the standard deviation of the market index, σ_I, is 8%, which implies that the variance of the market index is $8^2 = 64$. Using equation (8.8), this means that the variances of securities A and B are as follows:

$$\sigma^2_A = (1.2^2 \times 64) + 37$$
$$= 129$$
$$\sigma^2_B = (.8^2 \times 64) + 23$$
$$= 64$$

A Two-Security Portfolio

Consider combining securities A and B into a portfolio, with an equal amount of the investor's money going into each security. That is, consider a portfolio that has $X_A = .5 =$

[12] Actually, all that is necessary for this reduction in unique risk to occur is for the maximum amount invested in any one security to decrease continually as N increases.

Figure 8.12

Risk and diversification.

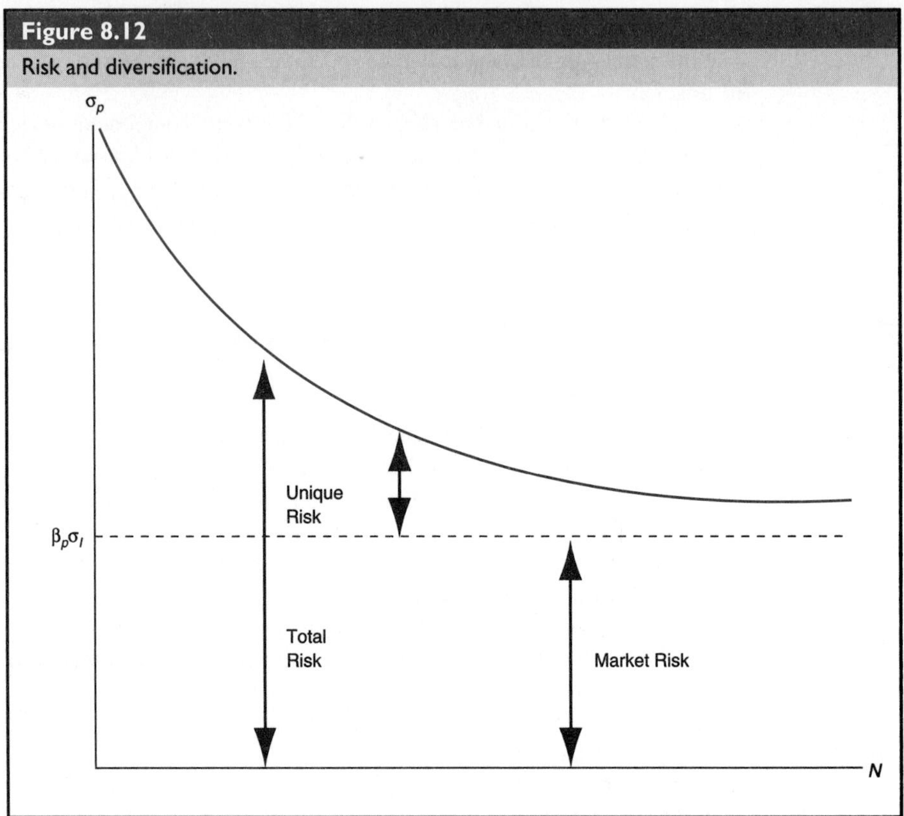

X_B = .5. Since β_{AI} = 1.2 and β_{BI} = .8, the beta of this portfolio can be calculated using equation (8.10c):

$$\beta_{pI} = (.5 \times 1.2) + (.5 \times .8)$$
$$= 1.0$$

Using equation (8.11c), the variance of the portfolio's random error term, $\sigma^2_{\epsilon p}$, equals

$$\sigma^2_{\epsilon p} = (.5^2 \times 37) + (.5^2 \times 23)$$
$$= 15$$

From equation (8.11a), it can be seen that this portfolio will have the following variance:

$$\sigma^2_p = (1.0^2 \times 64) + 15$$
$$= 79$$

This represents the total risk of the two-security portfolio.

A Three-Security Portfolio

Consider what would happen if a third security (C) was combined with the other two to form a three-security portfolio having $X_A = X_B = X_C = .33$. This third security has a beta of

1.0 and a random error term whose standard deviation ($\sigma_{\epsilon c}$) is 5.50%. Thus the variance of the random error term is $\sigma^2_{\epsilon c} = 5.5^2 = 30$, and the security's variance is

$$\sigma^2_c = (1.0^2 \times 64) + 30$$
$$= 94.$$

First of all, note that the three-security portfolio has the same amount of market risk as the two-security portfolio, because both portfolios have a beta of 1.0:

$$\beta_{pI} = (.33 \times 1.2) + (.33^2 \times .8) + (.33 \times 1.0)$$
$$= 1.0$$

Thus, increased diversification has not led to a change in the level of market risk. Instead it has led to an averaging of market risk.

Using equation (8.11c), the variance of the portfolio's random error term equals

$$\sigma^2_{\epsilon p} = (.33^2 \times 37) + (.33^2 \times 23) + (.33^2 \times 30)$$
$$= 10$$

Note that the variance of this three-security portfolio's random error term is less than the variance of the two-security portfolio's random error term (that is, $10 < 15$). Thus, in this example, increased diversification has indeed reduced unique risk.

From equation (8.11a), it can be seen that this three-security portfolio will have the following variance:

$$\sigma^2_p = (1.0^2 \times 64) + 10$$
$$= 74$$

This represents the total risk of the portfolio and is less than the total risk of the two-security portfolio ($74 < 79$). Thus, increased diversification has led to a reduction in total risk.

SUMMARY

1. The efficient set contains those portfolios that offer both maximum expected return for varying levels of risk and minimum risk for varying levels of expected return.
2. Investors are assumed to select their optimal portfolios from among the portfolios lying on the efficient set.
3. An investor's optimal portfolio is identified as the tangency point between the investor's indifference curves and the efficient set.
4. The proposition that the efficient set is concave follows from the definition of portfolio standard deviation and the existence of assets whose returns are not perfectly positively or perfectly negatively correlated.
5. Diversification usually leads to risk reduction, because the standard deviation of a portfolio generally will be less than a weighted average of the standard deviations of the component securities.
6. The relationship between the return on a security and the return on a market index is known as the market model.
7. The market index's return does not completely explain the return on a security. The unexplained elements are captured by the random error term of the market model.

8. The slope in a security's market model measures the sensitivity of the security's return to the market index's return. The slope term is known as the security's beta.
9. According to the market model, the total risk of a security consists of market risk and unique risk.
10. A portfolio's vertical intercept, beta, and random error term are weighted averages of the component securities' intercepts, betas, and random error terms, respectively, with the securities' relative proportions in the portfolio serving as weights.
11. Diversification leads to an averaging of market risk.
12. Diversification can substantially reduce unique risk.

APPENDIX A

THE MARKOWITZ MODEL

DETERMINING THE COMPOSITION AND LOCATION OF THE EFFICIENT SET

Previously, it was noted that there are an infinite number of possible portfolios available to the investor. but that the investor needs to be concerned with only those portfolios that are on the efficient set. However, Markowitz's efficient set is a curved line, which means that there are an infinite number of points along it. This, in turn, means that there are an infinite number of efficient portfolios! How can Markowitz's approach be used if an investor needs to identify the composition of each one of an infinite number of portfolios? Fortunately, there is no need to despair. Markowitz saw this potential problem and, in a major contribution, presented a method for solving it.[13] It involves the use of a quadratic programming algorithm known as the *critical-line method.*

Although the algorithm is beyond the scope of this book, it is important to recognize what it does. To begin with, the investor must estimate the expected return vector and variance-covariance matrix. For example, consider the three-security example presented earlier in the chapter.[14] The expected return vector, denoted by ER, and the variance-covariance matrix, denoted by VC, are estimated to be

$$ER = \begin{bmatrix} 16.2 \\ 24.6 \\ 22.8 \end{bmatrix} \quad VC = \begin{bmatrix} 146 & 187 & 145 \\ 187 & 854 & 104 \\ 145 & 104 & 289 \end{bmatrix}$$

The algorithm then identifies a number of *corner portfolios* that are associated with these securities and completely describe the efficient set. A corner portfolio is an efficient portfolio with the following property: any combination of two adjacent corner portfolios will result in a portfolio that lies on the efficient set between the two corner portfolios. Just what this means is illustrated in the example.

The algorithm begins by identifying the portfolio with the highest expected return. This portfolio corresponds to point S in Figure 8.1 and is an efficient portfolio. It is composed

---

[13] See Harry Markowitz, "The Optimization of a Quadratic Function Subject to Linear Constraints," *Naval Research Logistics Quarterly* 3, nos. 1–2 (March–June 1956): 111–133.

[14] This example is based on one from Markowitz's book entitled *Portfolio Selection* (New Haven, CT: Yale UP, 1959): 176–185.

of just one security—the security with the highest expected return. That is, if the investor wanted to purchase that portfolio, all he or she would have to do is to purchase shares of the company whose stock had the highest expected return. Any other portfolio would have a lower expected return, since at least part of the investor's funds would be placed in shares of other companies that have an expected return lower than S.

In the example, the company whose shares have the highest expected return is the second one, Baker Company. The corresponding efficient portfolio is the first of several corner portfolios that the algorithm will identify. Its composition is given by the following weight vector, denoted by $X(1)$:

$$X(1) = \begin{bmatrix} .00 \\ 1.00 \\ .00 \end{bmatrix}$$

Its expected return and standard deviation correspond to the expected return and standard deviation of Baker, which are equal to 24.6% and $(854)^{1/2} = 29.22\%$ respectively. In Figure 8.13, this corner portfolio is denoted by $C(1)$.

The algorithm then identifies the second corner portfolio. This portfolio is on the efficient set below the first corner portfolio and has a composition given by the following weight vector, denoted by $X(2)$:

$$X(2) = \begin{bmatrix} .00 \\ .22 \\ .78 \end{bmatrix}$$

That is, the second corner portfolio is a portfolio where the investor puts 22% of his or her funds into Baker common stock and the remainder, 78%, into Charlie common stock. Applying these weights to equations (7.3a) and (7.7), the expected return and standard deviation of this corner portfolio can be calculated; they are equal to 23.20% and 15.90%, respectively. In Figure 8.13, this corner portfolio is denoted by $C(2)$.

What is important about the first and second corner portfolios is that they are *adjacent* efficient portfolios, and any efficient portfolio lying on the efficient set between them has a composition that is just a combination of their compositions. For example, the efficient portfolio lying halfway between them has the following composition:

$$[.5 \times X(1)] + [.5 \times X(2)] = .5 \times \begin{bmatrix} .00 \\ 1.00 \\ .00 \end{bmatrix} + .5 \times \begin{bmatrix} .00 \\ .22 \\ .78 \end{bmatrix} = \begin{bmatrix} .00 \\ .61 \\ .39 \end{bmatrix}.$$

That is, the portfolio has weights of .61 in Baker stock and .39 in Charlie stock. Using equations (7.3a) and (7.7), the expected return and standard deviation of this portfolio turn out to be 23.9% and 20.28%, respectively.

Having identified the second corner portfolio, the algorithm then identifies the third one. Its composition is

$$X(3) = \begin{bmatrix} .84 \\ .00 \\ .16 \end{bmatrix}.$$

The weights can now be used to calculate the expected return and standard deviation of this portfolio, which are 17.26% and 12.22%, respectively. As was noted for the previous two corner portfolios, this corner portfolio is an efficient portfolio and is denoted by $C(3)$ in Figure 8.13.

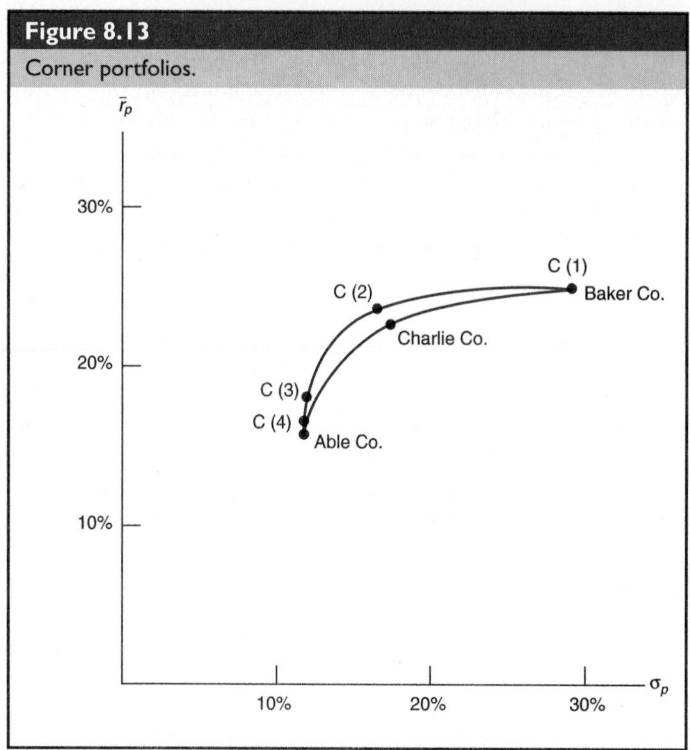

Figure 8.13
Corner portfolios.

Since they are adjacent, combinations of the second and third corner portfolios result in efficient portfolios that lie on the efficient set between them. For example, if the investor puts 33% of his or her money in the second corner portfolio and 67% in the third corner portfolio, then the resulting efficient portfolio has the following composition:

$$[.33 \times X(2)] + [.67 \times X(3)] = .33 \times \begin{bmatrix} .00 \\ .22 \\ .78 \end{bmatrix} + .67 \times \begin{bmatrix} .84 \\ .00 \\ .16 \end{bmatrix} = \begin{bmatrix} .56 \\ .07 \\ .37 \end{bmatrix}$$

Using equations (7.3a) and (7.7), this portfolio can be shown to have an expected return of 19.10% and a standard deviation of 12.88%.

Earlier it was mentioned that only combinations of *adjacent* corner portfolios will be efficient. This means that portfolios formed by combining *nonadjacent* corner portfolios will not lie on the efficient set. For example, the first and third corner portfolios are nonadjacent, which means that any portfolio formed by combining them will not be efficient. For example, if the investor put 50% of his or her funds in the first corner portfolio and 50% in the third corner portfolio, the resulting portfolio would have the following compositions:

$$[.5 \times X(1)] + [.5 \times X(3)] = .5 \times \begin{bmatrix} .00 \\ 1.00 \\ .00 \end{bmatrix} + .5 \times \begin{bmatrix} .84 \\ .00 \\ .16 \end{bmatrix} = \begin{bmatrix} .42 \\ .50 \\ .08 \end{bmatrix}$$

With these weights, the expected return and standard deviation of this portfolio can be shown to be equal to 20.93% and 18.38%, respectively. However, this is an inefficient portfolio. Since its expected return (20.93%) lies between the expected return of the second (23.20%) and third (17.26%) corner portfolios, by combining these two adjacent corner portfolios the investor will be able to form an efficient portfolio that has the same expected return but lower standard deviation.[15]

Table 8.1

Corner Portfolios for a Three-Security Example.

	Weights			Corner Portfolio	
Corner Portfolio	*Able Co.*	*Baker Co.*	*Charlie Co.*	*Expected Return*	*Standard Deviation*
C(1)	.00	1.00	.00	24.60%	29.22%
C(2)	.00	.22	.78	23.20	15.90
C(3)	.84	.00	.16	17.26	12.22
C(4)	.99	.00	.01	16.27	12.08

Continuing, the algorithm now identifies the composition of the fourth corner portfolio:

$$X(4) = \begin{bmatrix} .99 \\ .00 \\ .01 \end{bmatrix}$$

Its expected return and standard deviation can be calculated to be 16.27% and 12.08%, respectively. Having identified this portfolio as the one corresponding to point E in Figure 8.1 (and $C(4)$ in Figure 8.13), meaning that it is the portfolio that has the least standard deviation of all feasible portfolios, the algorithm stops. The four corner portfolios, summarized in Table 8.1, completely describe the efficient set associated with the stock of Able, Baker, and Charlie.

It is a simple matter for the computer, using its capability for graphics, to draw the graph of the efficient set. Perhaps it will find the composition, and in turn the expected return and standard deviation, for each of 20 efficient portfolios that are evenly spaced between the first and second corner portfolios. Then it will "connect the dots," tracing a straight line between each of the twenty successive portfolios. This will give the graph the appearance of a curved line, as shown in Figure 8.13, since these portfolios are located close to each other.

Proceeding in a similar fashion, 20 efficient portfolios between the second and third corner portfolios will be located and the corresponding segment of the efficient set traced. Then the same procedure will be followed for the region between the third and fourth corner portfolios, at which point the graph has been completely drawn.

---

[15] In this example, the efficient portfolio having an expected return of 20.93% can be determined by solving the following equation for Y: $(23.20\% \times Y) + [17.26\% \times (1 - Y) = 20.93\%$. Because this is a linear equation with one unknown, it can easily be solved. The solution, $Y = .62$, indicates that by putting .62 of his or her funds in the second corner portfolio and .38(1.00 – .62) in the third corner portfolio, the investor will have an efficient portfolio with the same expected return but lower standard deviation (specifically, 14.09%) than the portfolio involving a 50-50 combination of the first and third corner portfolios.

DETERMINING THE COMPOSITION OF THE OPTIMAL PORTFOLIO

Once the location and composition of Markowitz's efficient set have been determined, the composition of the investor's optimal portfolio can be determined. This portfolio, indicated by O^* in Figure 8.2, corresponds to the tangency point between the efficient set and one of the investor's indifference curves. The procedure for determining its composition starts by the investor noting graphically the level of its expected return. That is, from the graph the investor can note where O^* is located and then calibrate its expected return simply by using a ruler and extending a line from it to the vertical axis (with computers, more precise ways exist for doing this).

Having done so, the investor can now identify the two corner portfolios with expected returns "surrounding" this level. That is, the investor can identify the corner portfolio with the expected return nearest to but greater than this level (the surrounding corner portfolio that is above O^*) and the corner portfolio with the expected return nearest to but less than this level (the surrounding corner portfolio that is below O^*).

If the expected return of the optimal portfolio is denoted by $\bar{r}^*$ and the expected returns of these two surrounding portfolios are denoted by $\bar{r}^a$ and $\bar{r}^b$, respectively, then the composition of the optimal portfolio can be determined by solving the following equation for Y:

$$\bar{r}^* = (\bar{r}^a \times Y) + [\bar{r}^b \times (1 - Y)]. \tag{8.13}$$

The optimal portfolio will consist of a proportion Y of the "above" surrounding corner portfolio and a proposition $1 - Y$ of the "below" surrounding corner portfolio.

In the example, if the optimal portfolio had an expected return of 20%, then it can be noted that the second and third corner portfolios are the above and below surrounding corner portfolios, since they have expected returns of 23.20% and 17.26%, respectively. Equation (8.13) thus looks like this:

$$20\% = (23.20\% \times Y) = [17.26\% \times (1 - Y)].$$

Solving this equation for Y results in $Y = .46$, meaning that the optimal portfolio consists of a proportion of .46 in the second corner portfolio and .54 in the third corner portfolio. In terms of the amount of investment in the securities of Able, Baker, and Charlie companies, this translates to

$$[.46 \times X(2)] + [.54 \times X(3)] = .46 \times \begin{bmatrix} .00 \\ .22 \\ .78 \end{bmatrix} + .54 \times \begin{bmatrix} .84 \\ .00 \\ .16 \end{bmatrix} = \begin{bmatrix} .45 \\ .10 \\ .45 \end{bmatrix}$$

Thus, the investor should put 45%, 10%, and 45% of his or her funds in shares of Able, Baker, and Charlie, respectively.

More generally, if the weight vectors of the above and below surrounding corner portfolios are denoted by X^a and X^b, respectively, then the weights for the individual securities comprising the optimal portfolio will be equal to $(Y \times X^a) + [(1 - Y) \times X^b]$.

APPENDIX B

DETERMINING THE INPUTS NEEDED FOR LOCATING THE EFFICIENT SET

In order to construct the efficient set, the investor must estimate the expected returns of all the securities under consideration, as well as all of the variances and covariances. Subsequently, the optimal portfolio can be identified by noting where one of the investor's indifference curves is tangent to the efficient set, as shown in Figure 8.2.

Considerable effort is needed to construct this efficient set. First, the expected return for each security must be estimated. Given that there are N risky securities, this means that N parameters must be estimated. Second, the variance for each one of these securities must be estimated. Again, because there are N risky securities, this means that another N parameters must be estimated. Third, the covariance between each pair of risky securities must be estimated. There are $(N^2 - N)/2$ of these parameters to be estimated.[16]

This means that the total number of parameters that need to be estimated is equal to $(N^2 + 3N)/2$, determined as follows:

Expected returns	N
Variances	N
Covariances	$(N^2 - N)/2$
Total	$(N^2 + 3N)/2$

For example, if there were 100 risky securities under consideration, then $[100^2 + (3 \times 100)]/2 = 5150$ parameters would need to be estimated, consisting of 100 expected returns, 100 variances, and 4950 covariances. These parameters can be estimated one by one, a task that will be quite time-consuming, if not impossible. Fortunately, alternatives exist, including one that is based on the market model.[17]

With the market model approach, the expected return on the market index must be estimated initially. Then, the vertical intercept and beta for each security must be estimated. At this point, $(1 + 2N)$ parameters have been estimated (1 for $\bar{r}_I$; $2N$ for the vertical intercept; and beta for each of the N risky securities). In turn, these figures can be used to estimate the expected return for each security using equation (8.3), restated as follows:

$$\bar{r}_i = \alpha_{iI} + \beta_{iI}\bar{r}_I \tag{8.14}$$

[16]This number was arrived at in the following manner. The variance-covariance matrix has N rows and N columns, meaning that there are N^2 cells in it whose corresponding parameters need to be estimated. The cells on the diagonal contain the N variances mentioned earlier, leaving $(N^2 - N)$ covariances to be estimated. Because the variance-covariance matrix is symmetric, only those covariances below the diagonal need to be estimated (this is because they also appear in corresponding locations above the diagonal), leaving a total of $(N^2 - N)/2$ parameters to be estimated.

[17]The market model approach is an approximate one (as are all the other alternatives) because it makes a number of simplifying assumptions. For example, this approach assumes that the random error terms for any two securities are uncorrelated [an assumption that was needed in deriving equation (8.11c) and later in (8.15)]. This means that the outcome from a spin of the roulette wheel for one security (such as Mobil) has no bearing on the outcome from a spin of the roulette wheel for any other security (such as Exxon). It has been argued that this is not true for securities within certain industries. See Benjamin F. King, "Market and Industry Factors in Stock Price Behavior," *Journal of Business* 39, no. 1 (January 1966): 139–170; and James L. Farrell, Jr., "Analyzing Covariation of Returns to Determine Homogeneous Stock Groupings," *Journal of Business* 47, no. 2 (April 1974): 186–207.

Earlier, the expected return on the market index was estimated to be 5%. Given these figures, the expected return for security A was estimated to be 8%, because the vertical intercept and beta of this security were estimated to be 2% and 1.2, respectively:

$$\begin{aligned}\bar{r}_A &= 2\% + (5\% \times 1.2)\\ &= 8\%.\end{aligned}$$

Similarly, the expected return for security B was estimated to be 3%, because its vertical intercept and beta were estimated to be –1% and .8, respectively:

$$\begin{aligned}\bar{r}_B &= -1\% + (5\% \times .8)\\ &= 3\%.\end{aligned}$$

Using the market model approach, the variance of any security i can be estimated by multiplying the squared value of the security's beta by the variance of the market index and then adding the variance of the random error term to the product. The equation for doing this was given earlier:

$$\sigma_i^2 = \beta_{iI}^2 \sigma_I^2 + \sigma_{\epsilon i}^2 \tag{8.8}$$

where σ_i^2 denotes the variance of the market index and $\sigma_{\epsilon i}^2$ denotes the variance of the random error term for security i.

Assuming that the variance on the market index is 49, the respective variances of securities A and B can be estimated as follows:

$$\begin{aligned}\sigma_A^2 &= (1.2^2 \times 49) + 6.06^2\\ &= 107.28\\ \sigma_B^2 &= (.8^2 \times 49) + 4.76^2\\ &= 54.02.\end{aligned}$$

This means that the standard deviations of these securities are estimated to be equal to $10.36\% = \sqrt{107.28}$ and $7.35\% = \sqrt{54.02}$, respectively.

Lastly, the covariance between any two securities i and j can be estimated by the product of the three numbers: the beta of security i, the beta of security j, and the variance of the market index. That is, the following formula can be used:

$$\sigma_{ij} = \beta_{iI} \beta_{jI} \sigma_I^2. \tag{8.15}$$

thus, for securities A and B, the estimated covariance would be

$$\begin{aligned}\sigma_{A,B} &= 1.2 \times .8 \times 49\\ &= 47.04.\end{aligned}$$

In summary, if the market model approach is used to estimate expected returns, variances, and covariances, then the following parameters must first be estimated:

For the market index:	
Expected return ($\bar{r}_I$)	1
Variance (σ_I^2)	1
For each security:	
Vertical intercept (α_{iI})	N
Beta (β_{iI})	N
Variance of random error term ($\sigma_{\epsilon I}^2$)	N
Total	$3N + 2$

Thus, for 100 risky securities $(3 \times 100) + 2 = 302$ parameters need to be estimated when the market model approach is used to determine the efficient set and tangency portfolio. Once these 302 parameters have been estimated, then it is a simple matter to use equations (8.14), (8.8), and (8.15) to estimate the expected returns, variances, and covariances for the risky securities. Alternatively, the expected returns, variances, and covariances could be estimated one by one as noted earlier, in which case 5150 parameters would need to be estimated. As can be seen with this example, the market model approach results in a notable reduction in the number of parameters that need to be estimated.

After the expected returns, variances, and covariances have been estimated, a computer can be given these values. Then, using a "quadratic programming algorithm," the computer can proceed to identify the efficient set.[18] At this juncture, the investor's optimal portfolio can be determined by finding the point at which one of the indifference curves is tangent to the efficient set.

QUESTIONS AND PROBLEMS

1. Why would you expect individual securities to generally lie in the "eastern" portion of the feasible set, whereas only portfolios would lie in the "northwestern" portion?
2. Explain why most investors prefer to hold a diversified portfolio of securities as opposed to placing all of their wealth in a single asset. Use an illustration of the feasible and efficient sets to explain your answer.
3. Why would you expect most US common stocks to have positive covariances? Give an example of two stocks that you would expect to have a very high positive covariance. Give an example of two stocks that you would expect to have a very low positive (or even negative) covariance.
4. Discuss why the concepts of covariance and diversification are closely related.
5. Maya Haas is a portfolio manager. On average, the expected returns on all securities that Maya is researching are positive. Under what conditions might Maya be willing to purchase a security with a negative expected return?
6. In terms of the Markowitz model, explain, using words and graphs, how an investor goes about identifying his or her optimal portfolio. What specific information does an investor need to identify this portfolio?

[18] See Appendix B to Chapter 9 for a description of an algorithm that can be used in conjunction with the market model to determine the composition of the efficient set.

7. David Brinker owns a portfolio of two securities with the following expected returns, standard deviations, and weights:

Security	Expected Return	Standard Deviation	Weight
A	10%	20%	.35
B	15	25	.65

For varying levels of correlation between the two securities, what is the maximum portfolio standard deviation? What is the minimum?

8. Briefly explain why the efficient set must be concave.
9. Lee Kim owns a portfolio whose market model is expressed as:

$$r_p = 1.5\% + 0.90r_I + \epsilon_{pI}.$$

If the expected return on the market index is 12%, what is the expected return on Lee's portfolio?

10. How is beta derived from a security's market model? Why are high beta securities termed "aggressive"? Why are low beta securities termed "defensive"?
11. In the following table you are presented with ten years of return data for the stock of Glenwood City Properties and for a market index. Plot the returns of Glenwood City and the market index on a graph, with the market index's returns on the horizontal axis and Glenwood City's returns on the vertical axis. Draw your best guess of the market model through these points. From this graph only, compute an estimate of the beta of Glenwood City stock.

Year	Glenwood City	Market Index
1	8.1%	8.0%
2	3.0	0.0
3	5.3	14.9
4	1.0	5.0
5	−3.1	−4.1
6	−3.0	−8.9
7	5.0	10.1
8	3.2	5.0
9	1.2	1.5
10	1.3	2.4

12. Consider the stocks of two companies, Woodville Mink Farms and New Richmond Furriers.
    a. If you are told that the slope of Woodville's market model is 1.20 and that the slope of New Richmond's market model is 1.00, which stock is likely to be more risky in a portfolio context? Why?
    b. If you are now also told that the standard deviation of the random error term for Woodville stock is 10.0%, whereas it is 21.5% for New Richmond stock, does your answer change? Explain.

13. The market model specifies a very simple relationship between a security's return and the return on the market index. Discuss some "real world" complexities that might diminish the predictive power of the market model.
14. Two portfolios, one invested in electric utilities and the other in gold mining companies, have the same beta of 0.60. Why would a security analyst be interested to know that the gold portfolio has a much larger standard deviation of the random error term (unique risk) than the utility portfolio?
15. Lyndon Station Ltd. stock has a beta of 1.20. Over five years, the following returns were produced by Lyndon stock and a market index. Assuming a market model intercept term of 0%, calculate the standard deviation of the market model random error term over this period.

Year	*Lyndon Return*	*Market Index*
1	17.2%	14.0%
2	−3.1	−3.0
3	13.3	10.0
4	28.5	25.0
5	9.8	8.0

16. Why does diversification lead to a reduction in unique risk, but not in market risk? Explain both intuitively and mathematically.
17. Stephan Picovich owns a portfolio composed of three securities with the following characteristics:

Security	*Beta*	*Standard Deviation Random Error Term*	*Proportion*
A	1.20	5%	.30
B	1.05	8	.50
C	0.90	2	.20

If the standard deviation of the market index is 18%, what is the total risk of Stephan's portfolio?
18. Consider two portfolios, one composed of four securities and the other of ten securities. All the securities have a beta of one and unique risk of 30%. Each portfolio distributes weight equally among its component securities. If the standard deviation of the market index is 20%, calculate the total risk of both portfolios.
19. (Appendix Question) What is a corner portfolio? Why are corner portfolios important for identifying the composition of the efficient set?
20. (Appendix Question) Why is the market model approach a simpler technique than the original Markowitz approach for constructing the efficient set?
21. (Appendix Question) If the variance of the market index is 490 and the covariance between securities A and B is 470, what is the beta of security B, knowing that security A's beta is 1.20?

22. (Appendix Question) How many parameters must be estimated to analyze the risk-return profile of a 50-stock portfolio using (a) the original Markowitz approach and (b) the market model approach?

KEY TERMS

efficient set theorem
efficient set
feasible set
efficient portfolio
inefficient portfolio
optimal portfolio
market model
random error term
beta
aggressive stock
defensive stock
market risk
unique risk
diversification

REFERENCES

1. As mentioned at the end of Chapter 7, the seminal work developing the mean-variance model is credited to Harry Markowitz, who presented his ideas in a paper and later in a book:

   Harry M. Markowitz, "Portfolio Selection," *Journal of Finance* 7, no. 1 (March 1952): 77–91.

   Harry M. Markowitz, *Portfolio Selection: Efficient Diversification of Investments* (New York: John Wiley, 1959). (A reprint of this book that also contains some new material is available from Basil Blackwell, in Cambridge, MA; its copyright date is 1991.)

2. The technique used for determining the location of the efficient set, along with the composition of the "corner portfolios" that lie on it, was developed in:

   Harry M. Markowitz, "The Optimization of a Quadratic Function Subject to Linear Constraints," *Naval Research Logistics Quarterly* 3, nos. 1–2 (March-June 1956): 111–133.

3. The market model, initially mentioned by Markowitz in a footnote on p. 100 of his book, was developed in:

   William F. Sharpe, "A Simplified Model for Portfolio Analysis," *Management Science* 9, no. 2 (January 1963): 277–293.

4. An extensive discussion of the market model can be found in Chapters 3 and 4 of:

   Eugene F. Fama, *Foundations of Finance* (New York: Basic Books, 1976).

5. For discussions of how diversification reduces market risk, see:

   John L. Evans and Stephen H. Archer, "Diversification and the Reduction of Dispersion: An Empirical Analysis," *Journal of Finance* 23, no. 5 (December 1968): 761–767.

   W. H. Wagner and S. C. Lau, "The Effect of Diversification on Risk," *Financial Analysts Journal* 27, no. 6 (November-December 1971): 48–53.

   Meir Statman, "How Many Stocks Make a Diversified Portfolio?" *Journal of Financial and Quantitative Analysis* 22, no. 3 (September 1987): 353–363.

Gerald D. Newbould and Percy S. Poon, "The Minimum Number of Stocks Needed for Diversification," *Financial Practice and Education* 3, no. 2 (Fall 1993): 85–87.

6. A discussion of some statistical problems that are encountered in partitioning total risk is contained in:

Bert Stine and Dwayne Key, "Reconciling Degrees of Freedom When Partitioning Risk: A Teaching Note," *Journal of Financial Education* 19 (Fall 1990): 19–22.

7. Some of the statistical problems encountered in using optimization techniques to manage portfolios (specifically, the problem of how to cope with *estimation risk*) are discussed in:

J. D. Jobson and Bob Korkie, "Putting Markowitz Theory to Work," *Journal of Portfolio Management* 7, no. 4 (Summer 1981): 70–74.

Gordon J. Alexander and Jack Clark Francis, *Portfolio Analysis* (Englewood Cliffs, NJ: Prentice Hall, 1986), Chapter 6.

Peter A. Frost and James E. Savarino, "Portfolio Size and Estimation Risk," *Journal of Portfolio Management* 12, no. 4 (Summer 1986): 60–64.

Peter A. Frost and James E. Savarino, "For Better Performance: Constrain Portfolio Weights," *Journal of Portfolio Management* 15, no. 1 (Fall 1988): 29–34.

Richard O. Michaud, "The Markowitz Optimization Enigma: Is 'Optimized' Optimal?" *Financial Analysts Journal* 45, no. 1 (January/February 1989): 31–42.

Philippe Jorion, "Portfolio Optimization in Practice," *Financial Analysts Journal* 48, no. 1 (January/February 1992): 68–74.

Vijay K. Chopra and William T. Ziemba, "The Effects of Errors in Means, Variances, and Covariances on Optimal Portfolio Choice," *Journal of Portfolio Management* 19, no. 2 (Winter 1993): 6–11.

CHAPTER 9

Risk-free Lending and Borrowing

The previous two chapters focus on how an investor should go about determining what portfolio to select for investment. With Markowitz's approach, the investor is assumed to have a certain amount of initial wealth (W_0) to invest for a given holding period. Of all the portfolios that are available, the optimal one is shown to correspond to the point where one of the investor's indifference curves is tangent to the efficient set. At the end of the holding period, the investor's initial wealth will have either increased or decreased depending on the portfolio's rate of return. The resulting end-of-period wealth (W_1) can then be either completely reinvested, completely spent on consumption, or partially reinvested and partially consumed.

The Markowitz approach assumes that the assets considered for investment are individually risky—that is, each one of the N risky assets has an uncertain return over the investor's holding period. Because none of the assets has a perfectly negative correlation with any other asset, all the portfolios also have uncertain returns over the investor's holding period and thus are risky. Furthermore, the investor is not allowed to use borrowed money along with his or her initial wealth to purchase a portfolio of assets. This means that the investor is not allowed to use financial leverage, or margin.

In this chapter, the Markowitz approach to investing is expanded by first allowing the investor to consider investing not only in risky assets but also in a risk-free asset. This means there will now be N assets available for purchase, consisting of $N - 1$ risky assets and one risk-free asset. Second, the investor is allowed to borrow money but has to pay a given rate of interest on the loan. The next section considers the effect of adding a risk-free asset to the set of risky assets.

DEFINING THE RISK-FREE ASSET

What exactly is a **risk-free asset** in the context of Markowitz's approach? As this approach involves investing for a single holding period, it means that the return on the risk-free asset is certain. That is, if the investor purchases this asset at the beginning of the holding period, then he or she knows exactly what the value of the asset will be at the end of the holding period. Since there is no uncertainty about the terminal value of the risk-free asset, the standard deviation of the risk-free asset is, by definition, zero.

In turn, this means that the covariance between the rate of return on the risk-free asset and the rate of return on any risky asset is zero. This is so because the covariance between the returns on any two assets i and j is equal to the product of the correlation coefficient between the assets and the standard deviations of the two assets: $\sigma_{ij} = \rho_{ij}\sigma_i\sigma_j$. Given that $\sigma_i = 0$, if i is the risk-free asset, it follows that $\sigma_{ij} = 0$.

As a risk-free asset has, by definition, a certain return, this type of asset must be some kind of fixed-income security with no possibility of default. Since all corporate securities have some chance of default, the risk-free asset cannot be issued by a corporation. Instead, it must be a security issued by the federal government. However, not just any security issued by the Canadian government qualifies as a risk-free asset.

Consider an investor with a three-month holding period who purchases a long Canada Bond maturing in 20 years. Such a security is risky, since the investor does not know what this security will be worth at the end of his or her holding period. That is, interest rates very likely will have changed in an unpredictable manner during the investor's holding period, meaning that the market price of the security will have changed in an unpredictable manner. Since the presence of such **interest-rate risk** makes the value of the bond uncertain, it cannot qualify as a risk-free asset. Indeed, no government bond with a maturity date greater than the investor's holding period can qualify as a risk-free asset.

Next, consider a bond that matures before the end of the investor's holding period, such as a 30-day Treasury bill in the case of an investor with the three-month holding period. In this situation, the investor does not know at the beginning of the holding period what interest rates will be in 30 days. This means that the investor does not know the interest rate at which the proceeds from the maturing Treasury bill can be reinvested (that is, "rolled over") for the remainder of the holding period. The presence of such **reinvestment-rate risk** in all government securities of shorter maturity than the investor's holding period means that these securities do not qualify as a risk-free asset.

This leaves only one type of government security to qualify as a risk-free asset — one with a maturity that matches the length of the investor's holding period. For example, the investor with a three-month holding period would find that a Treasury bill with a three-month maturity date had a riskless return. Since this security matures at the end of the investor's holding period, it provides the investor with an amount of money at the end of the holding period that is known for certain at the beginning of the holding period when an investment decision has to be made.[1]

Investing in the risk-free asset is often referred to as **risk-free lending**, since such an investment involves the purchase of Treasury bills, and thus involves a loan by the investor to the federal government.

ALLOWING FOR RISK-FREE LENDING

With the introduction of a risk-free asset, the investor is now able to put part of his or her money in this asset and the remainder in any of the risky portfolios that are in Markowitz's feasible set. Adding these new opportunities expands the feasible set significantly and, more importantly, changes the location of part of Markowitz's efficient set. The nature of these

[1] To be truly risk-free, the security must not provide the investor with any coupon payments during the holding period. Instead, it must provide the investor with only one cash inflow, and that inflow must occur at the end of the investor's holding period. Any intervening coupon payments would subject the investor to reinvestment-rate risk, since he or she would not know the rate at which the coupon payments could be invested for the remainder of the holding period. It should also be noted that the discussion has focused on an asset that is risk-free in nominal terms, since the presence of inflation means that virtually all government securities are risky in real terms. These points are explored further in the *Institutional Issues* section of Chapter 5.

changes needs to be analyzed, since investors are concerned with selecting a portfolio from the efficient set. In doing so, consideration is given initially to determining the expected return and standard deviation for a portfolio that consists of combining an investment in the risk-free asset with an investment in a single risky security.

Investing in Both the Risk-free Asset and a Risky Asset

In Chapter 7, the companies of Able, Baker, and Charlie were assumed to have expected returns, variances, and covariances as indicated in the following expected return vector and variance-covariance matrix:

$$ER = \begin{bmatrix} 16.2 \\ 24.6 \\ 22.8 \end{bmatrix} \qquad VC = \begin{bmatrix} 146 & 187 & 145 \\ 187 & 854 & 104 \\ 145 & 104 & 289 \end{bmatrix}.$$

Defining the risk-free asset as security number 4, consider all portfolios that involve investing in both the common shares of Able and the risk-free asset. Let X_1 denote the proportion of the investor's funds invested in Able, and $X_4 = 1 - X_1$ denote the proportion invested in the risk-free asset. If the investor put all his or her money in the risk-free asset, then $X_1 = 0$ and $X_4 = 1$. Alternatively, the investor could put all his or her money in just Able, in which case $X_1 = 1$ and $X_4 = 0$. A combination of .25 in Able and .75 in the risk-free asset is also possible, as are respective combinations of .50 and .50, and .75 and .25. Although there are other possibilities, the focus here will be on these five portfolios:

	Portfolio A	Portfolio B	Portfolio C	Portfolio D	Portfolio E
X_1	.00	.25	.50	.75	1.00
X_4	1.00	.75	.50	.25	.00

Assuming that the risk-free asset has a rate of return (often denoted by r_f) of 4%, all the necessary information for calculating the expected returns and standard deviations for these five portfolios is at hand. Equation (7.3a) can be used to calculate the expected returns for these portfolios:

$$\bar{r}_P = \sum_{i=1}^{N} X_i \bar{r}_i \tag{7.3a}$$

$$= \sum_{i=1}^{4} X_i \bar{r}_i.$$

Now, portfolios A, B, C, D, and E do not involve investing in the second and third securities (that is, Baker and Charlie companies), meaning that $X_2 = 0$ and $X_3 = 0$ in these portfolios. Thus, the previous equation reduces to

$$\bar{r}_p = X_1 \bar{r}_1 + X_4 r_4$$

$$= (X_1 \times 16.2\%) + (X_4 \times 4\%)$$

where the risk-free rate is now denoted r_4.

For portfolios A and E this calculation is trivial, since all the investor's funds are being placed in just one security. Thus, their expected returns are just 4% and 16.2%, respectively. For portfolios B, C, and D, the expected returns are, respectively,

$$\begin{aligned}\bar{r}_B &= (.25 \times 16.2\%) + (.75 \times 4\%)\\ &= 7.05\%\\ \bar{r}_C &= (.50 \times 16.2\%) + (.50 \times 4\%)\\ &= 10.10\%\\ \bar{r}_D &= (.75 \times 16.2\%) + (.25 \times 4\%)\\ &= 13.15\%.\end{aligned}$$

The standard deviations of portfolios A and E are simply the standard deviations of the risk-free asset and Able, respectively. Thus, $\sigma_A = .00$ and $\sigma_E = 12.08\%$. In calculating the standard deviations of portfolios B, C, and D, equation (7.7) must be used:

$$\sigma_p = \left[\sum_{i=1}^{N}\sum_{j=1}^{N} X_i X_j \sigma_{ij}\right]^{1/2} \tag{7.7}$$

$$= \left[\sum_{i=1}^{4}\sum_{j=1}^{4} X_i X_j \sigma_{ij}\right]^{1/2}.$$

Remembering that $X_2 = 0$ and $X_3 = 0$ in these portfolios, this equation reduces to

$$\begin{aligned}\sigma_p &= [X_1X_1\sigma_{11} + X_1X_4\sigma_{14} + X_4X_1\sigma_{41} + X_4X_4\sigma_{44}]^{1/2}\\ &= [X_1^2\sigma_1^2 + X_4^2\sigma_4^2 + 2X_1X_4\sigma_{14}]^{1/2}.\end{aligned}$$

This equation can be reduced even further, since security 4 is the risk-free security that, by definition, has $\sigma_4 = 0$ and $\sigma_{14} = 0$. Accordingly, it reduces to

$$\begin{aligned}\sigma_p &= [X_1^2\sigma_1^2]^{1/2}\\ &= [X_1^2 \times 146]^{1/2}\\ &= X_1 \times 12.08\%.\end{aligned}$$

Thus, the standard deviations of portfolios B, C, and D are

$$\begin{aligned}\sigma_B &= .25 \times 12.08\%\\ &= 3.02\%\\ \sigma_C &= .50 \times 12.08\%\\ &= 6.04\%\\ \sigma_D &= .75 \times 12.08\%\\ &= 9.06\%\end{aligned}$$

In summary, the five portfolios have the following expected returns and standard deviations:

Portfolio	X_1	X_4	Expected Return	Standard Deviation
A	.00	1.00	4.00%	0.00%
B	.25	.75	7.05	3.02
C	.50	.50	10.10	6.04
D	.75	.25	13.15	9.06
E	1.00	.00	16.20	12.08

These portfolios are plotted in Figure 9.1. In this figure, it can be seen that the portfolios lie on a straight line connecting the points representing the location of the risk-free asset and Able. Although only five particular combinations of the risk-free asset and Able have been examined here, it can be shown that any combination of the risk-free asset and Able will lie somewhere on the straight line connecting them; the exact location will depend on the relative proportions invested in each asset. Furthermore, this observation can be generalized to combinations of the risk-free asset and any risky asset. That is, any portfolio that consists of a combination of the risk-free asset and a risky asset will have an expected return and standard deviation such that it plots on a straight line connecting them.

Investing in Both the Risk-free Asset and a Risky Portfolio

Next, consider what happens when a portfolio consisting of more than just one risky security is combined with the risk-free asset. For example, consider the risky portfolio that consists

Figure 9.1

Combining risk-free lending with investing in a risky asset.

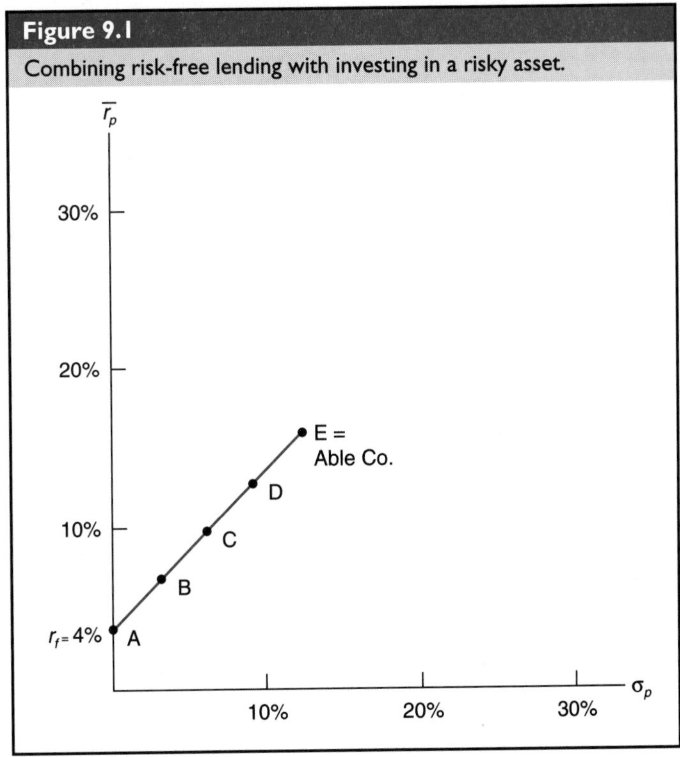

of Able and Charlie in proportions of .80 and .20, respectively. Its expected return (denoted by $\bar{r}_{PAC}$) and standard deviation (denoted by σ_{PAC}) are equal to

$$\begin{aligned} \bar{r}_{PAC} &= (.80 \times 16.2\%) + (.20 \times 22.8\%) \\ &= 17.52\% \\ \sigma_{PAC} &= [(.80 \times .80 \times 146) + (.20 \times .20 \times 289) + (2 \times .80 \times .20 \times 145)]^{1/2} \\ &= 12.30\%. \end{aligned}$$

Any portfolio that consists of an investment in both *PAC* and the risk-free asset will have an expected return and standard deviation that can be calculated in a manner identical to that previously shown for combinations of an individual asset and the risk-free asset. A portfolio that has the proportion X_{PAC} invested in the portfolio *PAC*, and the proportion $X_4 = 1 - X_{PAC}$ in the risk-free asset will have an expected return and standard deviation that are equal to, respectively,

$$\begin{aligned} \bar{r}_p &= (X_{PAC} \times 17.52\%) + (X_4 \times 4\%) \\ \sigma_p &= X_{PAC} \times 12.30\%. \end{aligned}$$

For example, consider investing in a portfolio that consists of *PAC* and the risk-free asset in proportions of .25 and .75, respectively.[2] This portfolio will have an expected return of

$$\begin{aligned} \bar{r}_p &= (.25 \times 17.52\%) + (.75 \times 4\%) \\ &= 7.38\% \end{aligned}$$

and a standard deviation of

$$\begin{aligned} \sigma_p &= (.25 \times 12.30\%) \\ &= 3.08\%. \end{aligned}$$

Figure 9.2 shows that this portfolio lies on a straight line connecting the risk-free asset and *PAC*. Its exact location is indicated by the point *P* on this line. Other portfolios consisting of various combinations of *PAC* and the risk-free asset will also lie on this line, with their exact locations depending on the relative proportions invested in *PAC* and the risk-free asset. For example, a portfolio that involves investing a proportion of .50 in the risk-free asset and a proportion of .50 in *PAC* lies on this line exactly halfway between the two end points.

In summary, combining the risk-free asset with any risky portfolio can be viewed as being no different from combining the risk-free asset with an individual risky security. In both cases, the resulting portfolio has an expected return and standard deviation such that it lies on a straight line connecting the two endpoints.

► The Effect of Risk-free Lending on the Efficient Set

As mentioned earlier, the feasible set is changed significantly as a result of the introduction of risk-free lending. Figure 9.3 shows how it changes the feasible set for the example at hand. Here, all risky assets and portfolios, not just Able and *PAC*, are considered in all possible combinations with the risk-free asset. In particular, note that there are two boundaries that are straight lines emanating from the risk-free asset. The bottom line connects the risk-free

[2] Note that investing the proportion .25 in portfolio *PAC* is equivalent to investing the proportion .20 (.25 × .80) in Able and the proportion .05 (.25 × .20) in Charlie.

Figure 9.2

Combining risk-free lending with investing in a risky portfolio.

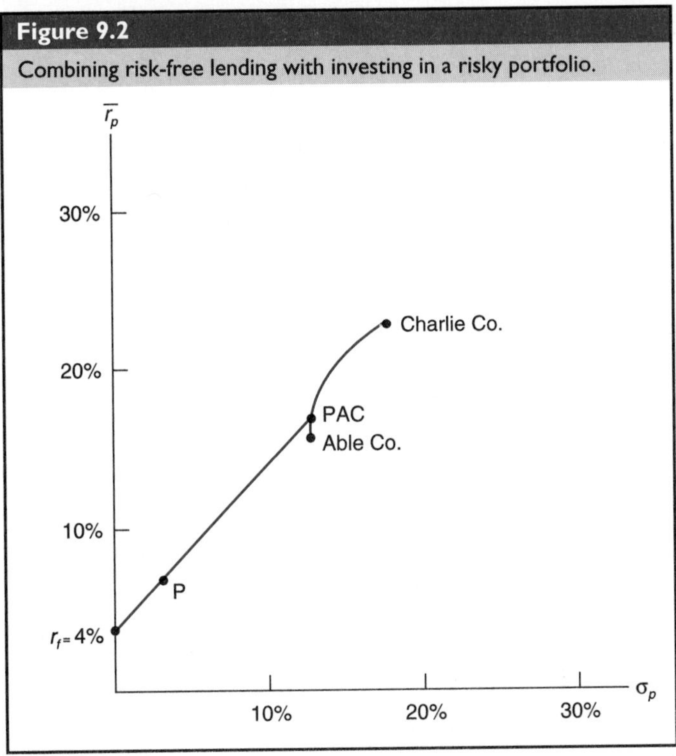

asset with Baker. Thus, it represents portfolios formed by combining Baker and the risk-free asset.

The other straight line emanating from the risk-free asset represents combinations of the risk-free asset and a particular risky portfolio on the efficient set of the Markowitz model. It is a line that is just tangent to the efficient set of the Markowitz model, with the tangency point being denoted by T. This tangency point represents a risky portfolio consisting of Able, Baker, and Charlie in proportions equal to, respectively, .12, .19, and .69. Substituting these proportions into equations (7.3a) and (7.7) indicates that the expected return and standard deviation of T are 22.4% and 15.2%, respectively.

Although other risky efficient portfolios from the Markowitz model can also be combined with the risk-free asset, portfolio T deserves special attention because there is no other portfolio consisting purely of risky assets that, when connected by a straight line to the risk-free asset, lies northwest of it. In other words, of all the lines that can be drawn emanating from the risk-free asset and connecting with either a risky asset or a risky portfolio, none has a greater slope than the line that goes to T.

This is important, since part of the efficient set of the Markowitz model is dominated by this line. In particular, the portfolios on the Markowitz model efficient set going from the minimum risk portfolio, denoted by V, to T are no longer efficient when a risk-free asset is made available for investment. Instead, the efficient set now consists of a straight-line segment and a curved segment. The straight-line segment is the straight line going from the risk-free asset to T and thus consists of portfolios made up of various combinations of the risk-free asset and T. The curved segment consists of those portfolios to the northwest of T on the Markowitz model efficient set.

Figure 9.3

Feasible and efficient sets when risk-free lending is introduced.

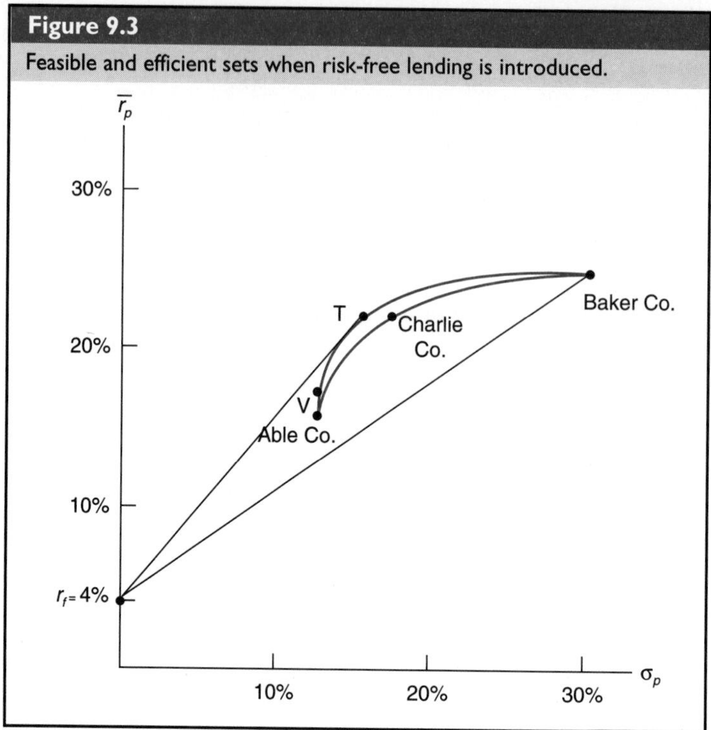

The Effect of Risk-free Lending on Portfolio Selection

Figure 9.4 shows how an investor would go about selecting an optimal efficient portfolio when there is a risk-free asset available for investment in addition to a number of risky assets. If the investor's indifference curves look like those shown in panel (a), then the investor's optimal portfolio O* will involve investing part of his or her initial wealth in the risk-free asset and the rest in T, because O^* lies on the straight-line segment of the efficient set.[3] Alternatively, if the investor is less risk-averse and has indifference curves that look like those shown in part (b), then the investor's optimal portfolio O* will not involve any risk-free investing because O^* lies on the curved segment of the efficient set that lies to the northeast of T.

ALLOWING FOR RISK-FREE BORROWING

The analysis presented in the previous section can be expanded by allowing the investor to borrow money. This means that the investor is no longer restricted to his or her initial wealth when it comes time to decide how much money to invest in risky assets.[4] However, if the investor borrows money, then interest must be paid on the loan. Since the interest

[3] A more risk-averse investor (meaning an investor whose indifference curves have greater slopes) would choose an optimal portfolio that is closer to the risk-free asset on the line that connects the risk-free asset to T. Ultimately, if the investor is infinitely risk-averse, the optimal portfolio will consist of an investment in just the risk-free asset.

[4] Allowing for borrowing can be viewed as giving the investor the opportunity to engage in margin purchases if he or she so desires. That is, with borrowing the investor is allowed to use financial leverage.

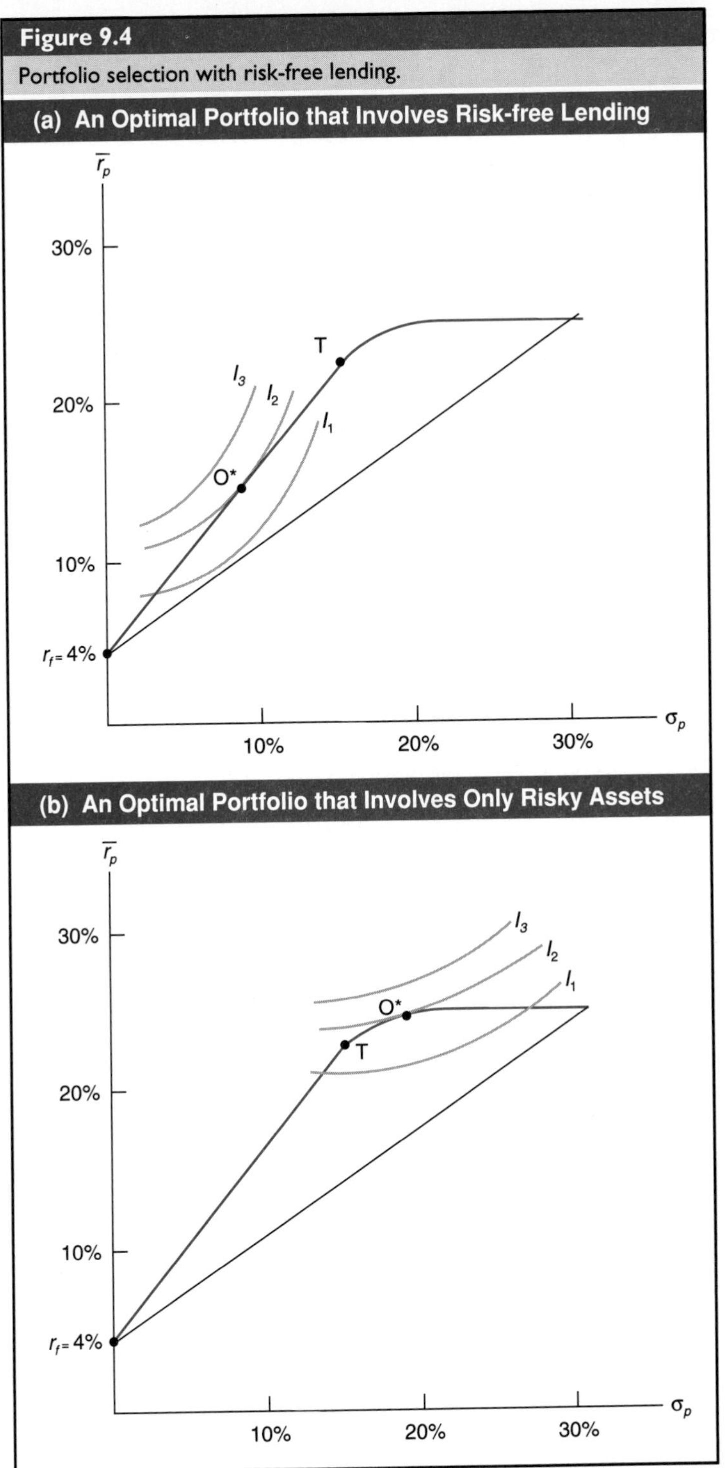
Figure 9.4
Portfolio selection with risk-free lending.
(a) An Optimal Portfolio that Involves Risk-free Lending
$\bar{r}_p$
30%
20%
10%
r_f = 4%
T
I_3
I_2
I_1
O*
10%
20%
30%
σ_p
(b) An Optimal Portfolio that Involves Only Risky Assets
$\bar{r}_p$
30%
20%
10%
r_f = 4%
I_3
I_2
I_1
O*
T
10%
20%
30%
σ_p

rate is known and there is no uncertainty about repaying the loan, this is often referred to as **risk-free borrowing**.

It will be assumed that the rate of interest charged on the loan is equal to the rate of interest that could be earned from investing in the risk-free asset.[5] Using the earlier example, this means that the investor not only has the opportunity to invest in a risk-free asset that earns a rate of return of 4%, but also may borrow money, for which the investor must pay a rate of interest equal to 4%.

Earlier, the proportion invested in the risk-free asset was denoted by X_4, and this proportion was constrained to be a nonnegative number between 0 and 1. Now, with the opportunity to borrow at the same rate, X_4 will no longer be so constrained. In the earlier example, the investor had initial wealth of $17 200. If the investor borrows money, then he or she will have in excess of $17 200 to invest in the risky securities of Able, Baker, and Charlie.

For example, if the investor borrows $4300, then he or she will have a total of $17 200 + $4300 = $21 500 to invest in these securities. In this situation, X_4 can be viewed as being equal to –$4300/$17 200 = –.25. However, the sum of the proportions must still equal 1. This means that if the investor has borrowed money, the sum of the proportions invested in risky assets would be greater than 1. For example, borrowing $4300 and investing $21 500 in Able means that the proportion in Able, X_1, is $21 500/$17 200 = 1.25. Note how in this case $X_1 + X_4 = 1.25 + (-.25) = 1$.

Borrowing and Investing in a Risky Security

In order to evaluate the effect that the introduction of risk-free borrowing has on the efficient set, the example presented in the previous section will be expanded. In particular, consider portfolios F, G, H, and I, where the investor borrows a proportion of his or her initial wealth equal to .25, .50, .75, and 1.00, respectively. In all four portfolios, the investor will invest all the borrowed funds as well as his or her own funds in Able. Thus, the proportions for these portfolios can be summarized as follows:

	Portfolio F	*Portfolio* G	*Portfolio* H	*Portfolio* I
X_1	1.25	1.50	1.75	2.00
X_4	–.25	–.50	–.75	–1.00

The expected returns of these portfolios are calculated in the same manner as was shown in the previous section. Equation (7.3a) is still used:

$$\begin{aligned}\bar{r}_p &= \sum_{i=1}^{N} X_i \bar{r}_i \\ &= \sum_{i=1}^{4} X_i \bar{r}_i \qquad (7.3a) \\ &= X_1 \bar{r}_1 + X_4 \bar{r}_4 \\ &= (X_1 \times 16.2\%) + (X_4 \times 4\%).\end{aligned}$$

[5] Appendix A discusses what happens to the efficient set when the investor is able to borrow, but at a rate that is greater than the rate that can be earned by investing in the risk-free asset.

Thus, portfolios F, G, H, and I have the following expected returns:

$$\begin{aligned}\bar{r}_F &= (1.25 \times 16.2\%) + (-.25 \times 4\%) \\ &= 19.25\% \\ \bar{r}_G &= (1.50 \times 16.2\%) + (-.50 \times 4\%) \\ &= 22.30\% \\ \bar{r}_H &= (1.75 \times 16.2\%) + (-.75 \times 4\%) \\ &= 25.35\% \\ \bar{r}_I &= (2.00 \times 16.2\%) + (-1.00 \times 4\%) \\ &= 28.40\%.\end{aligned}$$

Similarly, the standard deviations of these portfolios are calculated by using equation (7.7), as in the previous section:

$$\sigma_p = \left[\sum_{i=1}^{N}\sum_{j=1}^{N} X_i X_j \sigma_{ij}\right]^{1/2} \tag{7.7}$$

$$= \left[\sum_{i=1}^{4}\sum_{j=1}^{4} X_i X_j \sigma_{ij}\right]^{1/2}$$

which was shown to reduce to

$$\sigma_p = X_1 \times 12.08\%.$$

Thus, the standard deviations of the four portfolios are

$$\begin{aligned}\sigma_F &= 1.25 \times 12.08\% \\ &= 15.10\% \\ \sigma_G &= 1.50 \times 12.08\% \\ &= 18.12\% \\ \sigma_H &= 1.75 \times 12.08\% \\ &= 21.14\% \\ \sigma_I &= 2.00 \times 12.08\% \\ &= 24.16\%.\end{aligned}$$

In summary, these four portfolios, as well as the five portfolios that involve risk-free investing, have the following expected returns and standard deviations:

Portfolio	X_1	X_4	*Expected Return*	*Standard Deviation*
A	.00	1.00	4.00%	0.00%
B	.25	.75	7.05	3.02
C	.50	.50	10.10	6.04
D	.75	.25	13.15	9.06
E	1.00	.00	16.20	12.08
F	1.25	− .25	19.25	15.10
G	1.50	− .50	22.30	18.12
H	1.75	− .75	25.35	21.14
I	2.00	−1.00	28.40	24.16

In Figure 9.5, it can be seen that the four portfolios that involve risk-free borrowing (F, G, H, and I) all lie in the same straight line that goes through the five portfolios that involve risk-free investing (A, B, C, D, and E). Furthermore, the larger the amount of borrowing, the further out on the line the portfolio lies (equivalently, the smaller the value of X_4, the further out on the line the portfolio lies).

Although only four particular combinations of borrowing and investing in Able have been examined here, it can be shown that any combination of borrowing and investing in Able will lie somewhere on this line, with the exact location depending on the amount borrowed. Furthermore, this observation can be generalized to combinations of risk-free borrowing and an investment in any particular risky asset. This means that borrowing at the risk-free rate and investing all the borrowed money plus the investor's own money in a risky asset results in a portfolio that has an expected return and standard deviation that lies on the extension of the straight line connecting the risk-free rate and the risky asset.

Borrowing and Investing in a Risky Portfolio

Next, consider what happens when a portfolio of more than one risky asset is purchased with both the investor's own funds and borrowed funds. Earlier it was shown that the portfolio having proportions invested in Able and Charlie equal to .80 and .20, respectively, had an expected return of 17.52% and a standard deviation of 12.30%. This portfolio was referred to as *PAC*. Any portfolio that involves borrowing money at the risk-free rate and then investing these funds and the investor's own funds in *PAC* will have an expected return and standard deviation that can be calculated in a manner identical to the one previously shown

Figure 9.5

Combining risk-free borrowing and lending with investing in a risky asset.

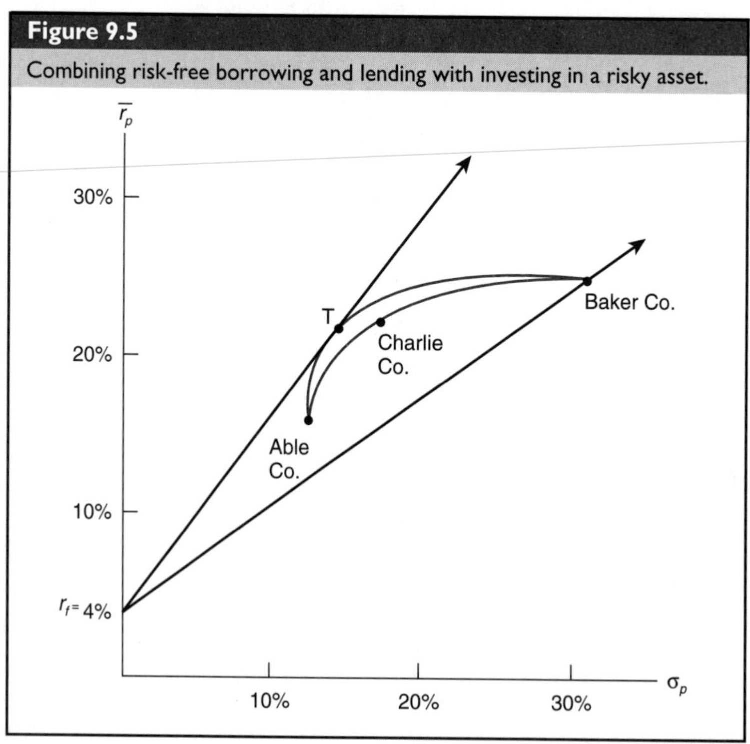

when borrowing was incurred and Able was purchased. A portfolio that involves borrowing the proportion X_4 and investing these funds and all the investor's own funds in *PAC* will have an expected return and standard deviation that are equal to, respectively,

$$\bar{r}_p = (X_{PAC} \times 17.52\%) + (X_4 \times 4\%)$$
$$\sigma_p = X_{PAC} \times 12.30\%.$$

For example, consider borrowing an amount of money equal to 25% of the investor's initial wealth and then investing all the investor's own funds plus these borrowed funds in *PAC*. Thus, $X_{PAC} = 1 - X_4 = 1 - (-.25) = 1.25$.[6] This portfolio will have an expected return of

$$\bar{r}_p = (1.25 \times 17.52\%) + (-.25 \times 4\%)$$
$$= 20.90\%$$

and a standard deviation of

$$\sigma_p = (1.25 \times 12.30\%)$$
$$= 15.38\%.$$

In Figure 9.6, it can be seen that this portfolio (denoted by *P*) lies on the extension of the line that connects the risk-free rate with *PAC*. Other portfolios consisting of *PAC* and borrowing at the risk-free rate will also lie on this extension, with their exact locations

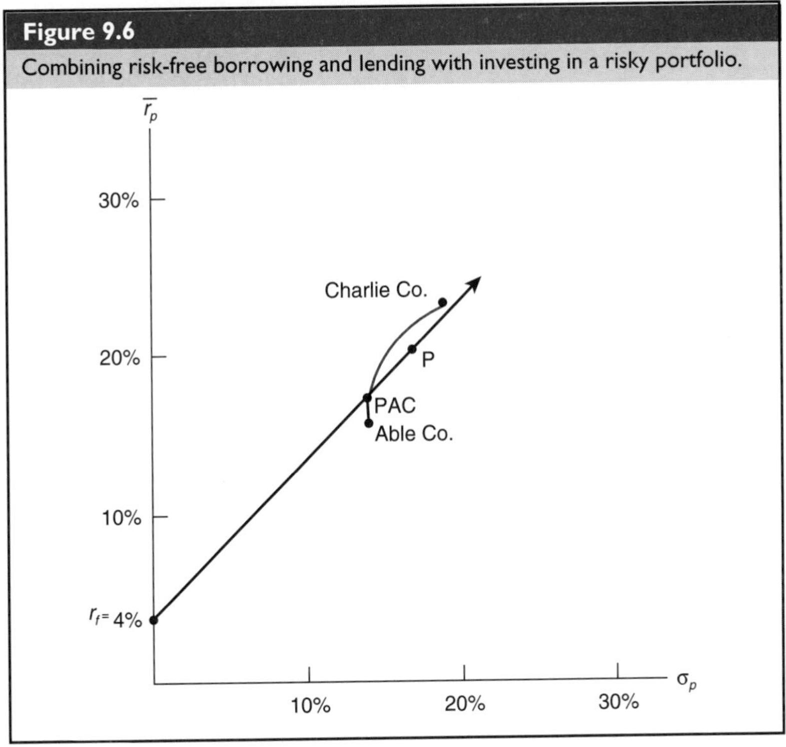

[6] Note that investing the proportion 1.25 in portfolio *PAC* is equivalent to investing the proportion 1.00 (1.25 × .80) in Able and the proportion .25 (1.25 × .20) in Charlie.

depending on the amount borrowed. Thus, borrowing in order to purchase a risky portfolio is no different from borrowing in order to purchase an individual risky asset. In both cases, the resulting portfolio lies on an extension of the line connecting the risk-free rate with the risky investment.

ALLOWING FOR BOTH RISK-FREE LENDING AND RISK-FREE BORROWING

The Effect of Risk-free Lending and Borrowing on the Efficient Set

Figure 9.7 shows how the feasible set is changed when both risk-free lending and borrowing at the risk-free rate are allowed. Here, all risky assets and portfolios, not just Able and *PAC*, are considered. The feasible set is the entire area between the two lines emanating from the risk-free rate that go through the location of Baker and the portfolio denoted by T. These two lines extend indefinitely to the right if it is assumed that there is no limit to the amount of borrowing that the investor can incur.

The straight line that goes through the portfolio T is of special importance, since it represents the efficient set. That is, it represents the set of portfolios that offer the investor the best opportunities, since it represents the set of feasible portfolios lying furthest northwest. Portfolio T, as was mentioned earlier, consists of investments in Able, Baker, and Charlie in proportions of .12, .19, and .69, respectively.[7]

Figure 9.7

Feasible and efficient sets when risk-free borrowing and lending are introduced.

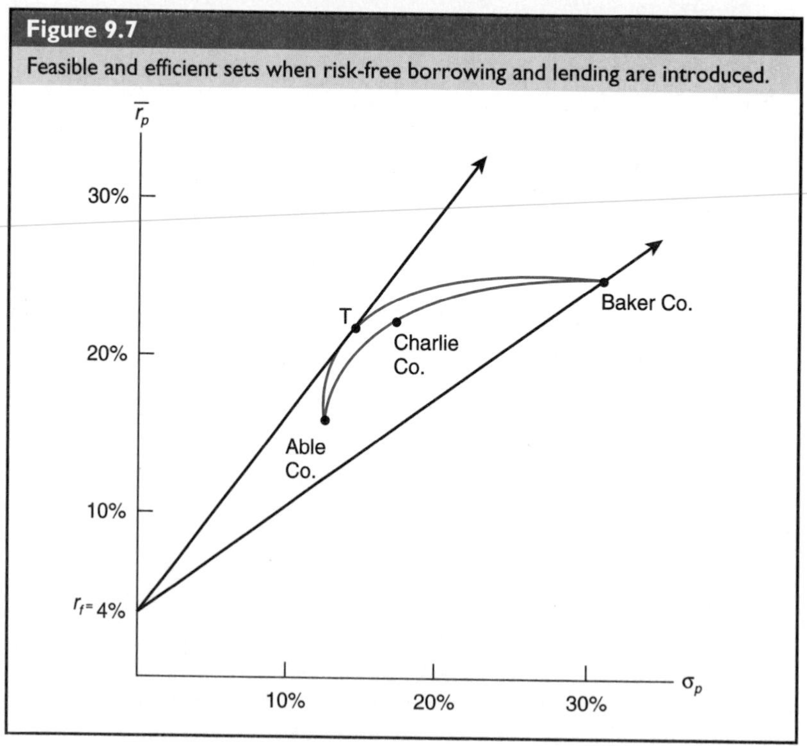

[7] Appendix B illustrates how the composition of the tangency portfolio T is determined.

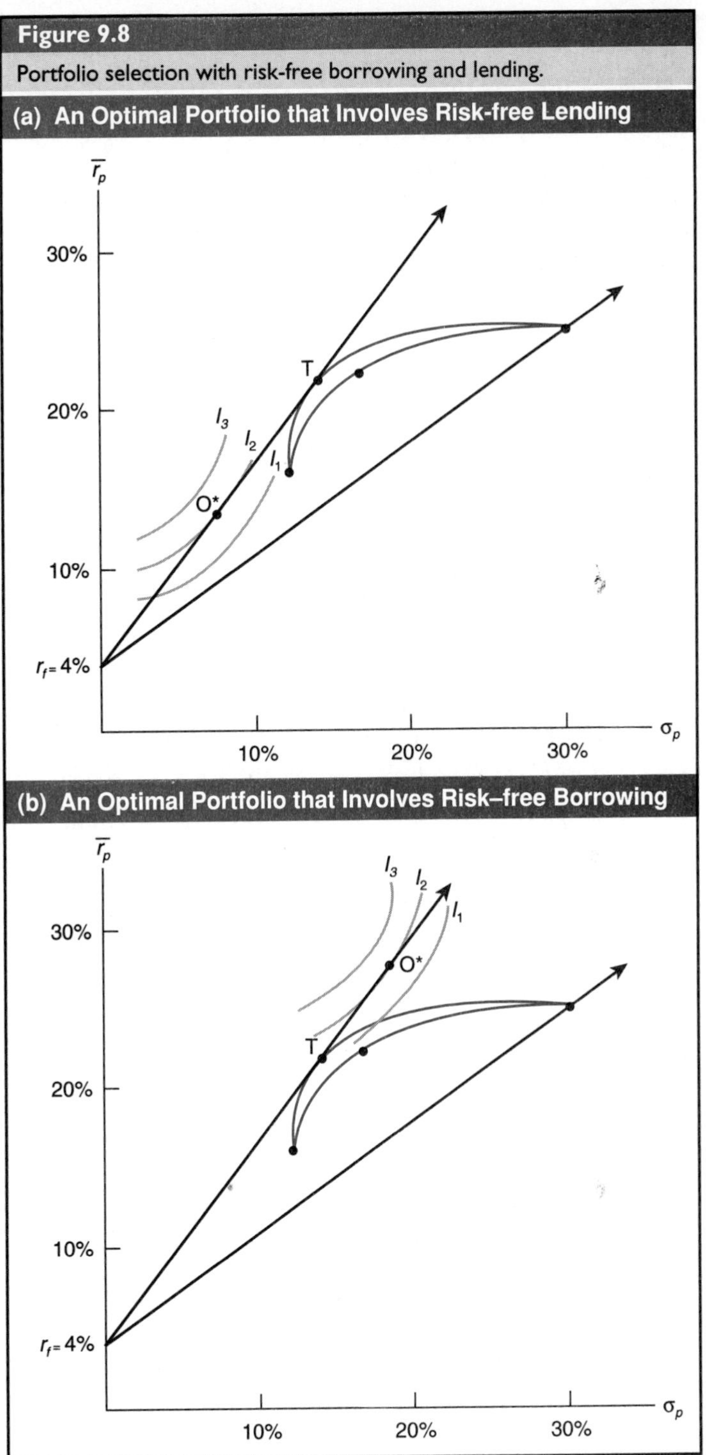
Figure 9.8
Portfolio selection with risk-free borrowing and lending.
(a) An Optimal Portfolio that Involves Risk-free Lending
$\bar{r}_p$
30%
20%
10%
r_f= 4%
T
I_3
I_2
I_1
O*
10%
20%
30%
σ_p
(b) An Optimal Portfolio that Involves Risk–free Borrowing
$\bar{r}_p$
30%
20%
10%
r_f= 4%
I_3
I_2
I_1
O*
T
10%
20%
30%
σ_p

INSTITUTIONAL ISSUES

The Cost of Short-Term Borrowing

The extension of the Markowitz model to incorporate borrowing and lending assumes that investors can borrow or lend at the risk-free rate. Certainly, every investor has the opportunity to lend at the risk-free rate by simply purchasing government securities with maturities corresponding to the length of his or her investment holding period.

Borrowing at the risk-free rate is another matter. In reality, only one entity has the option to borrow at the risk-free rate: the Canadian government. Other investors, be they individuals or institutional investors, must borrow at interest rates exceeding those paid by the government.

Just what level of interest rates do investors pay to borrow? To provide some perspective on this issue, we briefly survey some of the interest rates available in the market for short-term financial assets, known as the *money market.*

The standard of comparison for all money market interest rates is the rate paid on short-term Canadian securities called Treasury bills (see Chapter 1). The return on Treasury bills is completely certain over the short term because the federal government will never default on its obligations. It always has the option to print money or raise taxes to pay off its debts.

Other borrowers, no matter how strong their current financial position, run at least some risk of defaulting on their short-term debts. Largely due to this fact, virtually all non-government borrowers must pay interest rates exceeding those paid by the federal government. The difference between what the government pays to borrow money and what other borrowers pay is known as the *spread.* How large is the spread for non-government borrowers?

If you as an individual investor wish to finance your investment in securities, you typically purchase them on margin from your broker. The same holds true for institutional investors. In such transactions the broker actually borrows money elsewhere in the money market (usually drawing down a line of credit at a bank and pledging securities as collateral). The interest rate paid by the broker is known as *call money* (see Chapter 3). Brokers add anywhere from 1% to 2% to the call money rate to determine the interest rate charged their margin purchase customers. Larger investors can usually negotiate more favourable borrowing terms than smaller investors.

On December 18, 1995 the call money rate was 5.75%. By comparison, the three-month Treasury bill rate was 5.86%. The call money spread, therefore, was –.11 percentage points. Assuming a one percentage point markup over the call money rate, margin investors could expect to pay about .89 percentage points over the Treasury bill rate.

Large, financially strong corporations usually borrow in the money market through an instrument known as *commercial paper.* Commercial paper represents the negotiable, short-term unsecured promissory notes of finance, industrial, utility, insurance, and bank holding companies. On December 18, 1995 three-month commercial paper interest rates were 5.97%, a spread of .11 percentage points over three-month Treasury bills.

Corporations without the size and financial strength to borrow in the commercial paper market must obtain their short-term financing from banks. The interest rate officially quoted by banks on short-term unsecured loans to their best customers is known as the *prime rate.* The prime rate is not always an accurate measure of short-term borrowing costs, as banks often discount from it on loans to their financially strong borrowers. Financially weaker clients, on the other hand, may be charged a premium above the prime rate. In 1992, the prime rate averaged 7.75%, a 1.89 percentage point spread over three-month Treasury bills.

Banks also borrow in the money market in large quantities at wholesale rates. Although

INSTITUTIONAL ISSUES (continued)

these borrowings are unsecured and not insured under federal deposit insurance, the strong financial standing of the chartered banks means that they pay little more than the government for these borrowings. The Bank of Canada rate is an indication of the maximum rate the banks would have to pay. On December 18, 1995 the Bank of Canada rate was 6.22%, indicating that banks would have to pay a maximum spread of .36 percentage points over three-month Treasury bills.

From this brief money market survey, it is apparent that the Treasury bill rate is relevant to investor borrowing only as a base of comparison. Investors actually have to pay more, sometimes much more, to borrow in the money market, but then, of course, such borrowing is not considered risk-free, at least by the lenders.

As before, the line going through T is just tangent to the Markowitz model efficient set. None of the portfolios, except for T, that were on the Markowitz model efficient set are efficient when risk-free lending and borrowing are introduced. Every portfolio (except T) that lies on the Markowitz model efficient set is dominated by a portfolio on this straight line having the same standard deviation along with a higher expected return.

► The Effect of Risk-free Lending and Borrowing on Portfolio Selection

Given the opportunity to either lend or borrow at the risk-free rate, an investor would identify the optimal portfolio by plotting his or her indifference curves on the graph and noting where one of them is tangent to the linear efficient set.[8] Figure 9.8 (on page 221) shows two alternative situations. If the investor's indifference curves look like the ones in panel (a), then the investor's optimal portfolio O* will consist of an investment in the risk-free asset as well as in T. Alternatively, if the investor is less risk-averse and has indifference curves that look like those in part (b), then the investor's optimal portfolio O* will consist of borrowing at the risk-free rate and investing these funds as well as his or her own funds in T.[9]

SUMMARY

1. The return on a risk-free asset is certain. The risk-free asset's standard deviation is zero, as is its covariance with other assets.
2. In extending the Markowitz feasible set to include risk-free lending, investors are assumed to allocate their funds among a risk-free asset and a portfolio of risky assets.
3. With risk-free lending, the efficient set becomes a straight line from the risk-free rate to a point tangent to the curved Markowitz efficient set, in addition to the portion of the Markowitz efficient set that lies northeast of this tangency point.

---

[8] Appendix C illustrates how the composition of the investor's optimal portfolio O* is determined.

[9] The less risk-averse the investor is, the smaller the proportion in the risk-free rate (X_f) and the larger the proportion in T (X_T).

4. Introducing risk-free borrowing permits an investor to engage in leverage. The investor may use all of his or her money, plus money borrowed at the risk-free rate, to purchase a portfolio of risky assets.
5. With risk-free lending and borrowing, the efficient set becomes a straight line from the risk-free rate through a point tangent to the curved Markowitz efficient set.
6. With risk-free lending and borrowing, the efficient set consists of combinations of a single risky portfolio and various proportions of risk-free lending or borrowing.
7. The investor's optimal portfolio is determined by plotting his or her indifference curves against the efficient set.
8. The investor's optimal portfolio will include an investment in the risky portfolio and borrowing or lending at the risk-free rate.
9. Investors with higher levels of risk aversion will engage in less borrowing (or more lending) than investors with less risk aversion.

APPENDIX A

ALLOWING FOR DIFFERENT BORROWING AND LENDING RATES

In this chapter it was assumed that the investor could borrow funds at the same rate that could be earned on an investment in the risk-free asset. As a result, the feasible set became the area bounded by two straight lines emanating from the risk-free rate. The upper line represented the efficient set and had one portfolio in common with the curved efficient set of the Markowitz model. This portfolio was located where the straight line from the risk-free rate was tangent to the curved efficient set. But what happens if the investor can only borrow at a rate that is greater than the rate earned by an investment in the risk-free asset? The rate on the risk-free asset will be denoted r_{fL}, where L indicates lending (because, as mentioned earlier, an investment in the risk-free asset is equivalent to lending money to the government). The rate at which the investor can borrow money will be denoted r_{fB} and is of a magnitude such that $r_{fB} > r_{fL}$.

One way to understand the effect on the efficient set of assuming that these two rates are different is as follows. First, consider what the efficient set would look like if risk-free borrowing and lending were possible at the same rate, r_{fL}. The resulting efficient set would be the straight line shown in Figure 9.9 that goes through the points r_{fL} and T_L.

Second, consider what the efficient set would look like if risk-free borrowing and lending were possible at the higher rate, r_{fB}. The resulting efficient set would be the straight line shown in Figure 9.9 through the points r_{fB} and T_B. Note that the portfolio T_B lies on Markowitz's efficient set above the portfolio T_L because it corresponds to a tangency point associated with a higher risk-free rate.

Third, as the investor cannot borrow at r_{fL}, that part of the line emanating from r_{fL} that extends to the right of T_L is not available to the investor and can thus be removed from consideration.

Fourth, as the investor cannot lend at the risk-free rate r_{fB}, that part of the line emanating from r_{fB} and going through T_B but lying to the left of T_B is not available to the investor and can thus be removed from consideration. The northwest boundary of what remains, shown in Figure 9.10, is the resulting efficient set.

This efficient set consists of three distinct but connected segments. The first segment is the straight line going from r_{fL} to T_L that represents various amounts of risk-free lending

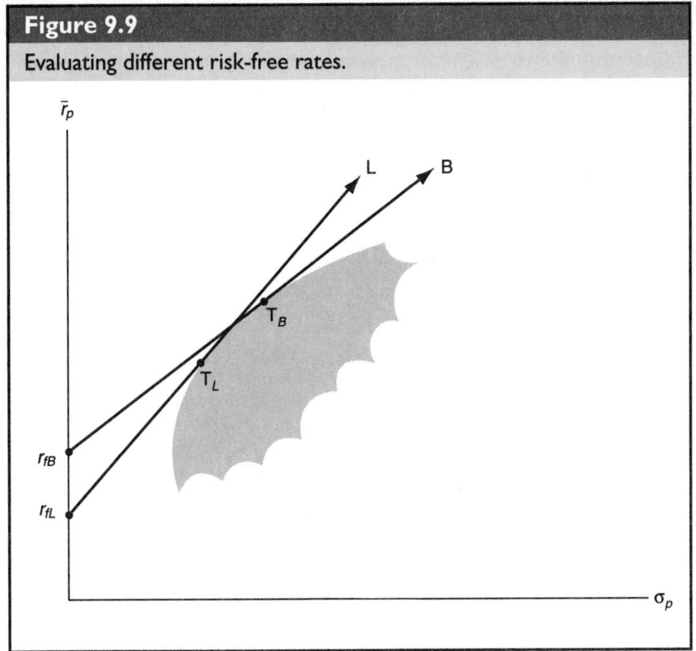

Figure 9.9
Evaluating different risk-free rates.

combined with investing in the portfolio of risky assets denoted T_L. The second segment is the curved line going from T_L to T_B that represents various risky portfolios that were also on Markowitz's curved efficient set. The third segment is the straight line extending outward from T_B that represents various amounts of borrowing combined with an investment in the risky portfolio denoted T_B.

The optimal portfolio for an investor will be, as before, the portfolio that corresponds to the point where an indifference curve is tangent to the efficient set. Depending on the investor's indifference curves, this tangency point could be on any one of the three segments that comprise the efficient set.

APPENDIX B

DETERMINING THE COMPOSITION OF THE TANGENCY PORTFOLIO T

CORNER PORTFOLIOS AND T

When risk-free opportunities are added to the Markowitz model, the efficient set is a straight line going through portfolio T. This portfolio is known as the tangency portfolio as it lies at the point on the curved efficient set of Markowitz that is tangent to a straight line emanating from the risk-free rate.

Determining the composition of portfolio T (and hence its location) involves the same procedures that were presented in Appendix A to Chapter 8. In the example presented earlier in Figure 9.7, portfolio T was shown to lie on the curved efficient set of the Markowitz model. Specifically, it lies between the second and third corner portfolios that are shown in Figure 8.13, where they are denoted $C(2)$ and $C(3)$, respectively. Since T lies between these

Figure 9.10

Efficient set when the risk-free rates are different.

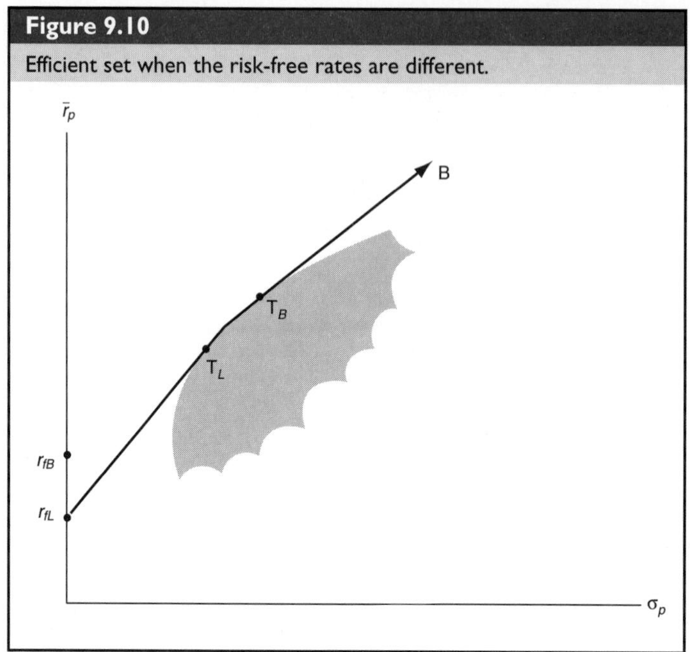

two corner portfolios, its composition is a weighted average of the compositions of $C(2)$ and $C(3)$ that are shown in Table 8.1. These weights [.86 in $C(2)$ and .14 in $C(3)$] can be determined graphically by drawing a horizontal line from T to the vertical axis where the expected return of T can then be measured.

In this example, the expected return of T is 22.4%. Since T lies between $C(2)$ and $C(3)$, its expected return must be a weighted average of the expected returns of $C(2)$, the above surrounding portfolio, and $C(3)$, the below surrounding portfolio. Thus its composition in terms of $C(2)$ and $C(3)$ can be determined by using equation (8.13) with $\bar{r}^* = 22.4\%$, $\bar{r}^a = 23.20\%$, and $\bar{r}^b = 17.26\%$:

$$22.4\% = (23.20\% \times Y) + [17.26\% \times (1 - Y)].$$

The solution to this equation is $Y = .86$. Thus portfolio T consists of $C(2)$ and C(3) in the proportions of .86 and .14, respectively.

In terms of the amount of investment in Able, Baker, and Charlie, this translates to

$$[.86 \times X(2)] + [.14 \times X(3)] = .86 \times \begin{bmatrix} .00 \\ .22 \\ .78 \end{bmatrix} + .14 \times \begin{bmatrix} .84 \\ .00 \\ .16 \end{bmatrix} = \begin{bmatrix} .12 \\ .19 \\ .69 \end{bmatrix}.$$

That is, portfolio T consists of an investment of 12% in Able, 19% in Baker, and 69% in Charlie.

The Market Model and T

There is another method of determining the composition of T that does not involve the identification of corner portfolios and consequently is much simpler than the one just described. Indeed all that is needed to use this method is some basic knowledge of how to use a spreadsheet. It assumes that security returns can be described by the market model and that there is a risk-free borrowing and lending rate r_f available. The method, developed by Elton, Gruber, and Padberg (hereafter EGP), can be described by use of an example.[10]

Imagine that the investor wishes to locate the tangency portfolio T that is associated with the following ten securities.

Security Number (i)	*Expected Return* ($\bar{r}_i$)	*Beta* (β_{iI})	*Unsystematic Risk* ($\sigma^2_{\epsilon i}$)
1	15.0%	1.0	50
2	17.0	1.5	40
3	12.0	1.0	20
4	17.0	2.0	10
5	11.0	1.0	40
6	11.0	1.5	30
7	11.0	2.0	40
8	7.0	0.8	16
9	7.0	1.0	20
10	5.6	0.6	6

Furthermore, assume that the variance of the market index portfolio σ_I^2 is 10 and that the risk-free rate r_f is 5%.

The EGP algorithm begins by noting that the slope of a line emanating from r_f and going through any specific portfolio p will have a slope equal to the value of theta (Θ):

$$\Theta = \frac{\bar{r}_p - r_f}{\sigma_p}. \tag{9.1}$$

The algorithm recognizes that the portfolio p that has the maximum value of Θ is the tangency portfolio T and hence seeks to identify the portfolio that maximizes Θ. This is accomplished by using a five-step procedure.

1. Rank the securities in descending order based on the magnitude of the reward-to-volatility ratio:

$$RVOL_i = (\bar{r}_i - r_f)/\beta_{iI}. \tag{9.2}$$

   (Note that the numerator represents the expected "reward" for buying the security and the denominator represents the security's beta. This ratio is sometimes known as the *Treynor Ratio*.)

   In column (2) of the following table it can be seen that the ten securities are ranked in descending order of $RVOL_i$.

[10] See Edwin J. Elton, Martin J. Gruber, and Manfred D. Padberg, "Simple Criteria for Optimal Portfolio Selection," *Journal of Finance* 31, no. 5 (December 1976): 1341–1357. The example is taken from Edwin J. Elton and Martin J. Gruber, *Modern Portfolio Theory and Investment Analysis* (New York: John Wiley, 1991): 158–165.

2. Starting at the top of the ranking, add securities one by one in calculating the following values of Φ_i:

$$\Phi_i = \sigma_I^2 \frac{\sum_{j=1}^{i} \frac{\overline{r}_j - r_f}{\sigma_{\epsilon j}^2} \beta_{jI}}{1 + \sigma_I^2 \sum_{j=1}^{i} \frac{\beta_{jI}}{\sigma_{\epsilon j}^2}}. \tag{9.3}$$

Column (3) of the following table displays these values.

Security Number (i) (1)	$RVOL_i$ (2)	Φ_i (3)	Z_i (4)	X_i (5)
1	10	1.67	.0910	.2346
2	8	3.69	.0956	.2464
3	7	4.42	.0775	.1998
4	6	5.43	.1100	.2836
5	6	5.45*	.0138	.0356
6	4	5.30	.0000	.0000
7	3	5.02	.0000	.0000
8	2.5	4.91	.0000	.0000
9	2	4.75	.0000	.0000
10	1	4.52	.0000	.0000

3. Compare the values of Φ_i to the corresponding values of $RVOL_i$ one by one while moving down the ranked list of securities. Initially Φ_i will be the smaller of the two values but at some point it will become the larger one. Using k to denote the number of the last security before this happens, securities 1 through k will have non-zero weights in T whereas the other will have weights of zero. Hence Φ_k is the "cutoff rate" for $RVOL_i$. In column (3), note how $RVOL_i$ is larger than Φ_i for the first five rows and then becomes smaller in the sixth row and remains smaller thereafter. This indicates that for this example, $k = 5$ and the cutoff rate [denoted by "*" in column (3)] is 5.45. This means that securities must have a reward-to-volatility ratio larger than 5.45 in order to have a non-zero weight in T.
4. Calculate the following values of Z_i in order to determine the size of the weights for the first k securities:

$$Z_i = \frac{\beta_{iI}}{\sigma_{\epsilon i}^2} \left[\frac{\overline{r}_i - r_f}{\beta_{iI}} - \Phi_k \right]. \tag{9.4}$$

The values of Z_i for $i = k + 1, k + 2, \ldots, N$ are set equal to zero.
The values of Z_i are shown in the fourth column. Because $k = 5$, note how the values of Z_6 through Z_{10} are equal to zero while those for the first five securities are positive numbers.

5. Divide each Z_i by the sum of the Z_i terms to transform them into the weights X_i for each security:

$$X_i = Z_i / \sum_{i=1}^{N} Z_i \tag{9.5}$$

This is necessary because the sum of the Z_i terms typically will not equal one.[11]

In the example, this sum equals .3879. Hence the weight of security one is simply $X_1 = .0910/.3879 = .2345$. This weight and the others are shown in the fifth column in the above table.

APPENDIX C

DETERMINING THE COMPOSITION OF THE INVESTOR'S OPTIMAL PORTFOLIO O*

Once the investor has determined the location of the straight line efficient set by locating the tangency portfolio, he or she can move on to determine the composition of his or her optimal portfolio. This portfolio, denoted O^* in Figure 9.8, corresponds to the tangency point between the efficient set and one of the investor's indifference curves. The procedure for determining its composition is similar to that for the Markowitz model that was described in Appendix A of Chapter 8. It starts by the investor noting graphically the level of O^*'s expected return—that is, the investor locates O^* on the graph and then calibrates its expected return by simply using a ruler and extending a horizontal line from O^* to the vertical axis.

If the expected return of the optimal portfolio is denoted by $\bar{r}^*$ and the risk-free rate and the expected return of the tangency portfolio are r_f and r_T, respectively, then the composition of the optimal portfolio can be determined by first solving the following equation for Y:

$$\bar{r}^* = (\bar{r}_T \times Y) + [r_f \times (1 - Y)]. \tag{9.6}$$

The optimal portfolio will consist of a proportion Y of the tangency portfolio and a proportion $1 - Y$ of the risk-free rate. Thus, the proportions to be invested in each risky security can be calculated by taking their proportions in T and multiplying them by Y.

In the example, if the optimal portfolio of the investor corresponds to the one shown in part (a) of Figure 9.8, then $\bar{r}^* = 14\%$. Thus, equation (9.6) would be

$$14\% = (22.4\% \times Y) + [4\% \times (1 - Y)] \tag{9.7}$$

because $r_T = 22.4\%$ and $r_f = 4\%$. The solution to equation (9.5) is $Y = .54$, meaning that the optimal portfolio consists of a proportion of .54 in the tangency portfolio and .46 in the risk-free asset.

---

[11] By iteratively determining the composition of T for various risk-free rates, it is possible to determine the composition of many portfolios along the curved efficient set of the Markowitz model. Hence this algorithm can also be used to identify the efficient set when a risk-free rate is not present (as in Chapter 8) or when the risk-free borrowing rate is greater than the risk-free lending rate (as in Appendix A). It can also be used when short selling is permitted. See Gordon J. Alexander, "Short Selling and Efficient Sets," *Journal of Finance* 48, no. 4 (September 1993): 1497–1506.

In terms of the amount of investment in Able, Baker, and Charlie companies, this translates to

$$[.54 \times X(T)] = .54 \times \begin{bmatrix} .12 \\ .19 \\ .69 \end{bmatrix} = \begin{bmatrix} .07 \\ .10 \\ .37 \end{bmatrix}.$$

Thus, the investor should invest an amount of money that is equal to 7%, 10%, and 37% of his or her initial wealth in shares of Able, Baker, and Charlie, respectively. Furthermore, 46% of the investor's initial wealth should be used to buy Treasury bills, the risk-free asset.

Alternatively, if the optimal portfolio of the investor corresponds to the one shown in part (b) of Figure 9.8, then $\bar{r}^* = 27\%$. Thus, using equation (9.6):

$$27\% = (22.4\% \times Y) + [4\% \times (1 - Y)] \tag{9.8}$$

and the solution would by $Y = 1.25$, meaning that the optimal portfolio consists of borrowing an amount of money equal to 25% of the investor's initial wealth and then investing the borrowed money and the initial wealth in T. In terms of the amount of investment in the securities of Able, Baker, and Charlie companies, this translates to

$$[1.25 \times X(T)] = 1.25 \times \begin{bmatrix} .12 \\ .19 \\ .69 \end{bmatrix} = \begin{bmatrix} .15 \\ .24 \\ .86 \end{bmatrix}.$$

Thus, the investor should invest an amount of money that is equal to 15%, 24%, and 86% of his or her initial wealth in shares of Able, Baker, and Charlie, respectively.

QUESTIONS AND PROBLEMS

1. Why is a pure discount government security (that is, one that does not make coupon payments, pays interest at maturity, and hence sells at a discount from par) with no risk of default still risky to an investor whose holding period does not coincide with the maturity date of the security?
2. Distinguish between reinvestment-rate risk and interest-rate risk.
3. The covariance between a risk-free asset and a risky asset is zero. Explain why this is the case and demonstrate it mathematically.
4. Lindsay Brown owns a risky portfolio with a 15% expected return. The risk-free return is 5%. What is the expected return on Lindsay's total portfolio if Lindsay invests the following proportions in the risky portfolio and the remainder in the risk-free asset?
   a. 120%
   b. 90%
   c. 75%
5. Consider a risky portfolio with an expected return of 18%. With a risk-free return of 5%, how could you create a portfolio with a 24% expected return?
6. Harriet Baker owns a risky portfolio with a 20% standard deviation. If Harriet invests the following proportions in the risk-free asset and the remainder in the risky portfolio, what is the standard deviation of Harriet's total portfolio?
   a. –30%
   b. 10%
   c. 30%

7. Oswald Burns's portfolio is composed of an investment in a risky portfolio (with a 12% expected return and a 25% standard deviation) and a risk-free asset (with a 7% return). If Oswald's total portfolio has a 20% standard deviation, what is its expected return?
8. Vivian Chao argues that buying a risky portfolio with risk-free borrowing is equivalent to a purchase of the risky portfolio on margin. Patsy Cahill contends that such an investment can be viewed as selling the risk-free asset short and using the proceeds to invest in the risky portfolio. Who is correct? Explain.
9. How does the efficient set change when risk-free borrowing and lending are introduced into the Markowitz model? Explain with words and graphs.
10. Why does the efficient set with the Markowitz model extended to include risk-free borrowing and lending have only one point in common with the efficient set of the Markowitz model without risk-free borrowing and lending? Why are the other points on the "old" efficient set no longer desirable? Explain with words and graphs.
11. Based on the assumptions developed in this chapter, is it true that all investors will hold the same risky portfolio? Explain.
12. How does the feasible set change when risk-free borrowing and lending are introduced into the Markowitz model? Explain with words and graphs.
13. With the Markowitz model extended to include risk-free borrowing and lending, draw the indifference curves, efficient set, and optimal portfolio for an investor with high risk aversion and an investor with low risk aversion.
14. Given the following expected return vector and variance-covariance matrix for three assets:

$$ER = \begin{bmatrix} 10.1 \\ 7.8 \\ 5.0 \end{bmatrix} \qquad VC = \begin{bmatrix} 210 & 60 & 0 \\ 60 & 90 & 0 \\ 0 & 0 & 0 \end{bmatrix}$$

    and given the fact that Peter Traynor's risky portfolio is split 50-50 between the two risky assets:
    a. Which security of the three must be the risk-free asset? Why?
    b. Calculate the expected return and standard deviation of Peter's portfolio.
    c. If the risk-free asset makes up 25% of Peter's total portfolio, what is the portfolio's expected return and standard deviation?
15. What does the efficient set look like if risk-free borrowing is permitted but no lending is allowed? Explain with words and graphs.
16. What will be the effect on total portfolio expected return and risk if you borrow money at the risk-free rate and invest in the optimal risky portfolio?
17. Suppose that your level of risk aversion decreased as you grew richer. In a world of risk-free borrowing and lending, how would your optimal portfolio change? Would the types of risky securities you hold change? Explain with words and graphs.
18. (Appendix Question) How does the efficient set change when the condition of borrowing and lending at the same risk-free rate is changed to borrowing at a rate greater than the rate at which risk-free lending can be conducted? Explain with words and graphs.

19. (Appendix Question) Using the EGP algorithm, find the tangency portfolio associated with the following securities.

Security	*Expected Return*	*Beta*	*Unsystematic Risk* ($\sigma^2_{\epsilon i}$)
1	15.0%	1.50	500
2	11.0	1.10	625
3	10.0	1.00	600
4	9.0	0.90	800
5	7.0	0.70	600

The risk-free rate is 4.0%, and the variance of the market index is 400. (Use of a computer spreadsheet is recommended.)

KEY TERMS

risk-free asset
interest-rate risk
reinvestment-rate risk
risk-free lending
risk-free borrowing

REFERENCES

1. Credit for extending Markowitz's model to include risk-free lending and borrowing belongs to:

James Tobin, "Liquidity Preference as Behavior Towards Risk," *Review of Economic Studies* 26, no. 1 (February 1958): 65–86.

James Tobin, "The Theory of Portfolio Selection," in *The Theory of Interest Rates*, ed. F. H. Hahn and F. P. R. Brechling (London: Macmillan and Co., 1965).

2. For a discussion of various mean-variance models that involve different sets of assumptions regarding risk-free lending and borrowing, margin purchasing, and short selling, see:

Eugene F. Fama, *Foundations of Finance* (New York: Basic Books, 1976), Chapters 7 and 8.

Gordon J. Alexander and Jack Clark Francis, *Portfolio Analysis* (Englewood Cliffs, NJ: Prentice Hall, 1986), Chapter 4.

3. For a discussion of how to determine the composition of portfolios on the efficient set under a variety of different assumptions, see:

Edwin J. Elton, Martin J. Gruber, and Manfred D. Padberg, "Simple Criteria for Optimal Portfolio Selection," *Journal of Finance* 31, no. 5 (December 1976): 1341–1357.

Edwin J. Elton and Martin J. Gruber, *Modern Portfolio Theory and Investment Analysis* (New York: John Wiley, 1991), Chapters 4 and 7.

Gordon J. Alexander, "Short Selling and Efficient Sets," *Journal of Finance* 48, no. 4 (September 1993): 1497–1506.

CHAPTER 10

The Capital Asset Pricing Model

Chapters 7, 8, and 9 presented a method for identifying an investor's optimal portfolio. With this method, the investor needs to estimate the expected returns and variances for all securities under consideration. Furthermore, all the covariances among these securities need to be estimated and the risk-free rate needs to be determined. Once this is done, the investor can find out the composition of the tangency portfolio as well as its expected return and standard deviation. At this juncture the investor can identify the optimal portfolio by noting where one of his or her indifference curves touch but do not intersect the efficient set. This portfolio will involve investing in the tangency portfolio, along with a certain amount of either risk-free borrowing or lending, since the efficient set is linear (that is, a straight line).

Such an approach to investing can be viewed as an exercise in **normative economics**, where investors are told what they should do. Thus, the approach is prescriptive in nature. In this chapter we enter the realm of **positive economics**, and provide a descriptive model of how assets are priced. The model assumes, among other things, that all investors use the approach to investing given in Chapters 7, 8, and 9. The major implication of the model is that the expected return of an asset will be related to a measure of risk for the asset that is known as beta. The exact manner in which expected return and beta are related is specified by the **Capital Asset Pricing Model** (CAPM).

Since many current practices in the investment industry are based on various extensions and modifications of the CAPM, a sound understanding of the original version is important. Accordingly, this chapter presents the original version of the CAPM.[1]

ASSUMPTIONS

In order to see how assets are priced, a model (that is, a theory) must be constructed. This requires simplification, in that the model builder must abstract from the full complexity of the situation and focus only on the most important elements. The way this is achieved is by making certain assumptions about the environment. These assumptions need to be simplistic in order to provide the degree of abstraction that allows for some success in building the model. The *reasonableness* of the assumptions (or lack thereof) is of little concern. Instead, the test of a model is in its ability to help the user understand and predict the process being modeled. As Milton Friedman, recipient of the 1976 Nobel Memorial Prize in Economics, has stated in a famous essay:

[1] Some extended versions of the CAPM are discussed in Appendix A.

> [T]he relevant question to ask about the "assumptions" of a theory is not whether they are descriptively "realistic," for they never are, but whether they are sufficiently good approximations for the purpose in hand. And this question can be answered only by seeing whether the theory works, which means whether it yields sufficiently accurate predictions.[2]

Some of the assumptions that underlie the CAPM also underlie the normative approach to investing that was described in previous chapters. These assumptions are as follows:

1. Investors evaluate portfolios by looking at the expected returns and standard deviations of the portfolios over a one-period horizon.
2. Investors are never satiated, so when given a choice between two otherwise identical portfolios, they will choose the one with the higher expected return.
3. Investors are risk-averse, so when given a choice between two otherwise identical portfolios, they will choose the one with the lower standard deviation.
4. Individual assets are infinitely divisible, meaning that an investor can buy a fraction of a share if he or she so desires.
5. There is a risk-free rate at which an investor may either lend (that is, invest) or borrow money.
6. Taxes and transaction costs are irrelevant.

To these assumptions the following are added:

7. All investors have the same one-period horizon.
8. The risk-free rate is the same for all investors.
9. Information is freely and instantly available to all investors.
10. Investors have **homogeneous expectations**, meaning that they have the same perceptions in regard to the expected returns, standard deviations, and covariances of securities.

As can be seen by examining these assumptions, the CAPM reduces the situation to an extreme case. Everyone has the same information and agrees about the future prospects for securities. Implicitly, this means that investors analyze and process information in the same way. The markets for securities are **perfect**, meaning there are no *frictions* to impede investing; potential impediments such as finite divisibility, taxes, transaction costs, and different risk-free borrowing and lending rates have been assumed away. This allows the focus to be changed from how an individual should invest to what would happen to security prices if everyone invested in a similar manner. By examining the collective behaviour of all investors in the marketplace, we can describe the nature of the resulting equilibrium relationship between each security's risk and return.

THE CAPITAL MARKET LINE

► The Separation Theorem

What are the implications of these ten assumptions? First, investors would analyze securities and determine the composition of the tangency portfolio. In doing so, *everyone would obtain the same tangency portfolio*. This is not surprising, since there is complete agreement among investors on the estimates of the securities' expected returns, variances, and covariances as

[2] Milton Friedman, *Essays in the Theory of Positive Economics* (Chicago: The University of Chicago Press, 1953), p.15.

well as on the size of the risk-free rate. This also means that the linear efficient set (described in Chapter 9) is the same for all investors because it simply involves combinations of the agreed-upon tangency portfolio and risk-free rate.

As all investors face the same efficient set, the only reason they will choose different portfolios is because they have different indifference curves. Thus, different investors will choose different portfolios from the same efficient set because they have different preferences toward risk and return. For example, as was shown in Figure 9.8, the investor in part (a) will choose a different portfolio from the investor in part (b). Note, however that although the chosen portfolios will be different, *each investor will choose the same combination of risky securities*, denoted by T in Figure 9.8. That is, each investor would spread his or her funds among risky securities in the same relative proportions, adding risk-free borrowing or lending in order to achieve a personally preferred overall combination of risk and return. This feature of the CAPM is often referred to as the **separation theorem**:

> The optimal combination of risky assets for an investor can be determined without any knowledge about the investor's preferences toward risk and return.

In other words, the determination of the optimal combination of risky assets can be made separately from the determination of the shape of an investor's indifference curves.

The reasoning behind the separation theorem involves a property of the linear efficient set that was introduced in Chapter 9. There, it was shown that all portfolios located on the linear efficient set involved an investment in a tangency portfolio combined with varying degrees of risk-free borrowing or lending. With the CAPM, each person faces the same linear efficient set, meaning that each person will be investing in the same tangency portfolio (combined with a certain amount of either risk-free borrowing or lending that depends upon that person's indifference curves). It therefore follows that the risky portion of each person's portfolio will be the same.

In the example from Chapter 9, three securities were considered, corresponding to the shares of Able, Baker, and Charlie companies. With a risk-free rate of return of 4%, the tangency portfolio T was shown to consist of investments in Able, Baker, and Charlie in proportions equal to .12, .19, and .69, respectively. If the ten assumptions of the CAPM are made, then the investor shown in part (a) of Figure 9.8 would invest approximately half of his or her money in the risk-free asset and the remainder in T. The investor shown in part (b), on the other hand, would borrow an amount of money equal to approximately half of the value of his or her initial wealth and proceed to invest these borrowed funds as well as his or her own funds in T.[3] Thus, the proportions invested in the three stocks for the investors of parts (a) and (b) would equal[4]

$$(.5) \times \begin{bmatrix} .12 \\ .19 \\ .69 \end{bmatrix} = \begin{bmatrix} .060 \\ .095 \\ .345 \end{bmatrix} \quad \text{for the investor in part (a),}$$

$$(1.5) \times \begin{bmatrix} .12 \\ .19 \\ .69 \end{bmatrix} = \begin{bmatrix} .180 \\ .285 \\ 1.035 \end{bmatrix} \quad \text{for the investor in part (b).}$$

---

[3] If the investor had initial wealth of $40 000, this means that he or she would borrow $20 000 and then invest $60 000 ($40 000 + $20 000) in T.

[4] Note that the proportions in these three stocks sum to .5 for the panel (a) investor and 1.5 for the panel (b) investor. Since the respective proportions for the risk-free rate are .5 and –.5, the aggregate proportions for the stocks and risk-free rate sum to 1.0 for each investor.

While the proportions to be invested in each of these three risky securities for the panel (a) investor (.060, .095, .345) can be seen to be different in size from those invested for the panel (b) investor (.180, .285, 1.035), note that the relative proportions are the same, being equal to .12, .19, and .69, respectively.

► The Market Portfolio

Another important feature of the CAPM is that, in equilibrium, each security must have a non-zero proportion in the composition of the tangency portfolio.[5] That is, no security could, in equilibrium, have a proportion in T that was zero. The reasoning behind this feature lies in the previously mentioned separation theorem, in which it was asserted that the risky portion of every investor's portfolio would be independent of the investor's risk-return preferences. The justification for the theorem was that the risky portion of each investor's portfolio would simply be an investment in the tangency portfolio. If every investor is purchasing T and T does not involve an investment in each security, then nobody is investing in those securities with zero proportions in T. This means that the prices of these zero-proportion securities must *fall*, thereby causing the expected returns of these securities to *rise* until the resulting tangency portfolio has a non-zero proportion associated with them.

In the previous example, Charlie had a current price of \$62 and an expected end-of-period price of \$76.14. This meant that the expected return for Charlie was (\$76.14 – \$62)/\$62 = 22.8%. Now imagine that the current price of Charlie is \$72, not \$62, meaning that its expected return is (\$76.14 – \$72)/\$72 = 5.8%. If this were the case, the tangency portfolio associated with a risk-free rate of 4% would involve just Able and Baker in proportions of .90 and .10, respectively.[6] As Charlie has a proportion of zero, nobody would want to hold shares of Charlie. Consequently, orders to sell would be received in substantial quantities, with virtually no offsetting orders to buy being received. As a result, Charlie's price would fall. However, as Charlie's price falls, its expected return would rise, since the same end-of-period price of \$76.14 is forecast for Charlie as before and it would now cost less to buy one share. Eventually, as the price falls, investors would change their minds and want to buy shares of Charlie. Ultimately, at a price of \$62, investors will want to hold shares of Charlie so that, in aggregate, the number of shares demanded will equal the number of shares outstanding. Thus, in equilibrium, Charlie will have a non-zero proportion in the tangency portfolio.

Another interesting situation could also arise. What if each investor concludes that the tangency portfolio should involve a proportionate investment in the stock of Baker equal to .40, but at the current price of Baker there are not enough shares outstanding to meet the demand? In this situation orders to buy Baker will flood in, and brokers will raise the price in search of sellers. This will cause the expected return of Baker to fall, making it less attractive and thereby reducing its proportion in the tangency portfolio to a level where the number of shares demanded equals the number of shares outstanding.

---

[5] Securities that have zero net amounts outstanding will not appear in the tangency portfolio. Options and futures, discussed in Chapters 20 and 21, are examples of such securities.

[6] Although the expected return of Charlie has been changed, all the variances and covariances as well as the expected returns for Able and Baker are assumed to have the same values that were given in Chapter 7, 8, and 9. The singular change in the expected return of Charlie alters not only the composition of the tangency portfolio but, more generally, the location and shape of the efficient set.

Ultimately, everything will balance out. When all the price adjusting stops, the market will have been brought into equilibrium. First, each investor will want to hold a certain amount of each risky security. Second, the current market price of each security will be at a level where the number of shares that are demanded equals the number of shares that are outstanding.[7] Third, the risk-free rate will be at a level where the total amount of money borrowed equals the total amount of money lent. As a result, the proportions of the tangency portfolio will correspond to the proportions of what is known as the **market portfolio**, defined as follows:

> The market portfolio is a portfolio consisting of an investment in all securities where the proportion to be invested in each security corresponds to its relative market value. The relative market value of a security is simply equal to the aggregate market value of the security divided by the sum of the aggregate market values of all securities.[8]

The reason the market portfolio plays a central role in the CAPM is because the efficient set consists of an investment in the market portfolio, coupled with a desired amount of either risk-free borrowing or risk-free lending. Thus, it is common practice to refer to the tangency portfolio as the market portfolio and to denote it as M instead of T. In theory, M consists of not only common stocks but also other kinds of investments such as bonds, preferred shares, and real estate. However, in practice many people restrict M to common stocks.

► The Efficient Set

In the world of the CAPM, it is a simple matter to determine the relationship between risk and return for efficient portfolios. Figure 10.1 portrays it graphically. Point M represents the market portfolio and r_f represents the risk-free rate of return. Efficient portfolios plot along the line starting at r_f and going through M and consist of alternative combinations of risk and return obtainable by combining the market portfolio with risk-free borrowing or lending. This linear efficient set of the CAPM is known as the **Capital Market Line** (CML). All portfolios other than those employing the market portfolio and risk-free borrowing or lending would lie below the CML, although some might plot very close to it.

The slope of the CML is equal to the difference between expected return of the market portfolio and that of the riskless security, $\bar{r}_M - r_f$, divided by the difference in their risks, $\sigma_M - 0$, or $(\bar{r}_M - r_f)/\sigma_M$.[9] The vertical intercept of the CML is r_f, the straight line characterizing the CML has the following equation:

$$\bar{r}_p = r_f + \left[\frac{\bar{r}_M - r_f}{\sigma_M}\right]\sigma_p \tag{10.1}$$

where $\bar{r}_p$ and σ_p refer to the expected return and standard deviation of an efficient portfolio.[10]

---

[7] In this situation the market for the security is said to have *cleared.*

[8] The aggregate market value for the common stock of a company is equal to the current market price of the shares times the number of shares outstanding.

[9] The slope of a straight line can be determined if the location of two points on the line are known. It is determined by rise over run, meaning it is determined by dividing the vertical distance between the two points by the horizontal distance between the two points. In the case of the CML, two points are known, corresponding to the risk-free rate and the market portfolio, so its slope can be determined in this manner.

[10] The equation of a straight line is of the form $y = a + bx$, where a is the vertical intercept and b is the slope. Since the vertical intercept and slope of the CML are known, its equation can be written as shown here by making the appropriate substitutions for a and b.

Figure 10.1

The capital market line.

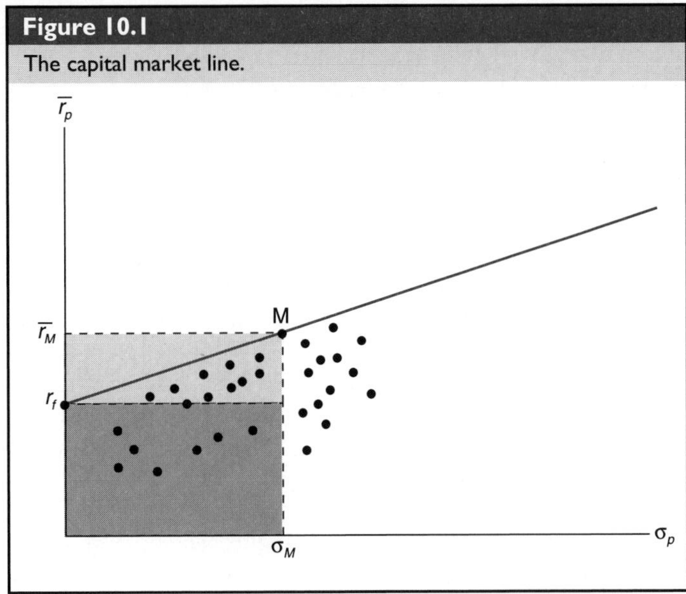

In the previous example, the market portfolio associated with a risk-free rate of 4% consisted of Able, Baker, and Charlie in the proportions of .12, .19, and .69, respectively. It was shown in Chapter 9 that the expected return and standard deviation for a portfolio with these proportions was 22.4% and 15.2%, respectively. Therefore, the equation for the resulting CML is

$$\bar{r}_p = 4 + \left[\frac{22.4 - 4}{15.2}\right]\sigma_p$$
$$= 4 + 1.21\sigma_p.$$

Equilibrium in the security market can be characterized by two key numbers. The first is the vertical intercept of the CML (that is, the risk-free rate), which is often referred to as the *reward for waiting*. The second is the slope of the CML, which is often referred to as the *reward per unit of risk borne*. In essence, the security market provides a place where time and risk can be traded, with their prices determined by the forces of supply and demand. Thus, the intercept and slope of the CML can be thought of as the "price of time" and the "price of risk," respectively. In the example, they are equal to 4% and 1.21, respectively.

THE SECURITY MARKET LINE

► Implications for Individual Risky Assets

The CML represents the equilibrium relationship between the expected return and standard deviation for efficient portfolios. Individual risky securities will always plot below the line, since a single risky security, when held by itself, is an inefficient portfolio. The CAPM does not imply any particular relationship between the expected return and the standard deviation (that is, total risk) of an individual security. To say more about the expected return of an individual security, deeper analysis is necessary.

INSTITUTIONAL ISSUES

The Elusive Market Portfolio

The market portfolio holds a special place in modern investment theory and practice. It is central to the CAPM, which assumes that the market portfolio lies on the efficient set and that all investors hold the market portfolio in combination with a desired amount of risk-free borrowing and lending. Furthermore, the market portfolio represents the ultimate in diversification. Consequently, passive investors (or index fund managers — see Chapter 24), who do not *bet* on the performance of particular securities but rather desire broad diversification, seek to hold the market portfolio. The market portfolio also serves as a universal performance evaluation standard. Investment managers and their clients often compare the manager's results against the returns on the market portfolio.

Despite its widespread application, the market portfolio is surprisingly ill defined. In theory, the composition of the market portfolio is simple: all assets are weighted in proportion to their respective market values. In reality, actually identifying the *true* market portfolio (or even a close approximation) is beyond the capability of any individual or organization.

Consider how we might go about specifying the market portfolio. The process would involve two steps: enumerating the assets to be include and calculating the market values of those assets.

First, we must list the various types of assets that constitute the market portfolio. These days we should think globally by considering assets held by investors both here at home and in foreign countries. Of course we want to include all securities representing the assets of businesses. Therefore, we should include common stocks, preferred stocks, and corporate bonds. In that vein we should also consider the value of proprietorships and partnerships. How about government debt? This should be considered if the debt is backed by real assets such as buildings. (Due to deficit spending, much of the government's debt is actually backed by future taxes and thus does not represent current wealth — a technical matter often overlooked.) We should also include real estate, cash holdings, monetary metals (primarily gold), and art. But we have not finished yet. We should also include consumer durable assets, such as autos, furniture, and major appliances. Last but certainly not least, we should include the largest asset of all, the training and education in which people have invested vast sums, called *human capital.*

Simply listing the composition of the market portfolio is a complex undertaking. Measuring its value is even more problematic. Given the sophistication of Canadian capital markets, the values of domestic publicly traded assets are relatively easy to collect. (We should be careful, however, to avoid double-counting — for example, when one corporation owns part of another corporation.) Data availability in foreign markets varies from country to country. In some markets, such as those in the United Kingdom and Japan, security data collection systems are very sophisticated. In other markets, such as those in Third World countries, comprehensive security valuation data are difficult to acquire.

A similar situation exists with respect to non-publicly traded asset values. In some countries, the government attempts to make accurate estimates of a myriad of asset values from real estate to consumer durable goods. In other countries, little or no effort is made to compile these data.

Finally, with respect to estimating the value of human capital — well, good luck.

The difficulties involved in determining the composition and value of the true market portfolio have led to the use of market portfolio proxies. In dealing with common stocks, for example, most researchers and practitioners arbitrarily define the market portfolio to be a broad stock market index, such as the TSE 300.

What are the ramifications of not knowing the market portfolio's true composition? From a

INSTITUTIONAL ISSUES (continued)

theoretical perspective, the potential problems are significant. In two controversial articles (*Journal of Financial Economics*, May 1977, and *Journal of Finance*, September 1978), Richard Roll argued that the ambiguity of the market portfolio leaves the CAPM untestable. He contended that only if one knows the true market portfolio can one test whether it actually lies on the efficient set. Considering that the CAPM linear relationship between expected return and beta depends on the efficiency of the market portfolio, Roll's argument should not be taken lightly. Furthermore, Roll argues that the practice of using proxies for the market portfolio is loaded with problems. Different proxies, even if their returns are highly correlated, could lead to different beta estimates for the same security. Roll's arguments, it should be noted, were strongly contested by prominent CAPM defenders.

From a practical perspective, investors have generally been willing to overlook the market portfolio's ambiguity. Passive managers typically segment the market into various asset classes, such as stocks and bonds. They then define somewhat arbitrarily a market portfolio for each of those asset classes and construct portfolios to track the performance of the respective asset class market portfolios. Similarly, active managers frequently refer to a designated market portfolio when they devise their investment strategies. Performance evaluators employ market proxies in their CAPM-risk-adjusted return calculations (see Chapter 25).

In Chapter 7 the following equation was given for calculating the standard deviation of any portfolio:

$$\sigma_p = \left[\sum_{i=1}^{N} \sum_{j=1}^{N} X_i X_j \sigma_{ij} \right]^{1/2} \tag{7.7}$$

where X_i and X_j denoted the proportions invested in securities i and j, respectively, and σ_{ij} denoted the covariance of returns between securities i and j. Now consider using this equation to calculate the standard deviation of the market portfolio:

$$\sigma_M = \left[\sum_{i=1}^{N} \sum_{j=1}^{N} X_{iM} X_{jM} \sigma_{ij} \right]^{1/2} \tag{10.2}$$

where X_{iM} and X_{jM} denote the proportions invested in securities i and j in the market portfolio, respectively. It can be shown that another way to write equation (10.2) is as follows:

$$\sigma_M = \left[X_{1M} \sum_{j=1}^{N} X_{jM} \sigma_{1j} + X_{2M} \sum_{j=1}^{N} X_{jM} \sigma_{2j} + X_{3M} \sum_{j=1}^{N} X_{jM} \sigma_{3j} + \cdots + X_{NM} \sum_{j=1}^{N} X_{jM} \sigma_{Nj} \right]^{1/2} \tag{10.3}$$

At this point a property of covariance can be used: The covariance of security i with the market portfolio (σ_{iM}) can be expressed as

$$\sum_{j=1}^{N} X_{jM} \sigma_{ij} = \sigma_{iM}. \tag{10.4}$$

This property, as applied to each one of the N risky securities in the market portfolio, results in the following:

$$\sigma_M = [X_{1M}\sigma_{1M} + X_{2M}\sigma_{2M} + X_{3M}\sigma_{3M} + \cdots + X_{NM}\sigma_{NM}]^{1/2} \tag{10.5}$$

where σ_{1M} denotes the covariance of security 1 with the market portfolio, σ_{2M} denotes the covariance of security 2 with the market portfolio, and so on. Thus, the standard deviation of the market portfolio is equal to the square root of a weighted average of the covariances of all the securities within it, where the weights are equal to the proportions of the respective securities in the market portfolio.

At this juncture an important point can be observed. Under the CAPM each investor holds the market portfolio and is concerned with its standard deviation, since that will influence the magnitude of his or her investment in the market portfolio. The contribution of each security to the standard deviation of the market portfolio can be seen in Equation (10.5) to depend on the size of its covariance with the market portfolio. Accordingly, each investor will note that *the relevant measure of risk for a security is its covariance with the market portfolio,* σ_{iM}. This means that securities with larger values of σ_{iM} will be viewed by investors as contributing more to the risk of the market portfolio. It also means that securities with larger standard deviations should not be viewed as necessarily adding more risk to the market portfolio than those securities with smaller standard deviations.

From this analysis it follows that securities with larger values for σ_{iM} will have to provide proportionately larger expected returns in order for investors to be interested in purchasing them. To understand why, consider what would happen if such securities did not provide investors with proportionately larger levels of expected return: they would contribute to the risk of the market portfolio without contributing proportionately to the expected return of the market portfolio. This means that deleting such securities from the market portfolio would cause the expected return of the market portfolio, relative to its standard deviation, to rise. Since investors would view this as a favourable change, the market portfolio would no longer be the optimal risky portfolio to hold. Thus, security prices would be out of equilibrium.

The exact form of the equilibrium relationship between risk and return can be written as follows:

$$\bar{r}_i = r_f + \left[\frac{\bar{r}_M - r_f}{\sigma_M^2}\right]\sigma_{iM}. \tag{10.6}$$

As can be seen in part (a) of Figure 10.2, equation (10.6) represents a line having a vertical intercept of r_f and a slope of $[(\bar{r}_M - r_f)/\sigma_M^2]$. Since the slope is positive, the equation indicates that securities with larger covariances (σ_{iM}) will be priced so as to have larger expected returns ($\bar{r}_i$). This relationship between covariance and expected return is known as the **Security Market Line** (SML).[11]

Interestingly, a risky security with $\sigma_{iM} = 0$ will have an expected return equal to the rate on the risk-free security, r_f. Intuitively, the reason for this is that the risky security, just like the risk-free security, does not contribute to the risk of the market portfolio. This is so even though the risky security has a positive standard deviation, whereas the risk-free security has a standard deviation of zero.

It is even possible for some risky securities (meaning securities with positive standard deviations) to have expected returns less than the risk-free rate. According to the CAPM,

[11] A more rigorous derivation of the SML is provided in Appendix B.

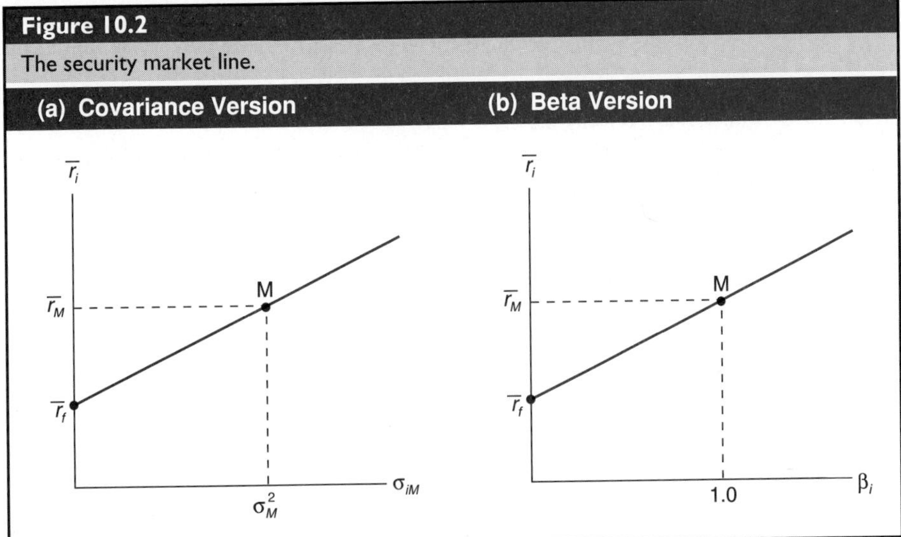

Figure 10.2
The security market line.

this will occur if $\sigma_{iM} < 0$, thereby indicating that they contribute a negative amount of risk to the market portfolio (meaning that they cause the risk of the market portfolio to be lower than it would be if less money were invested in them).

Also of interest is the observation that a risky security with $\sigma_{iM} = \sigma_M^2$ will have an expected return equal to the expected return on the market portfolio, $\bar{r}_M$. This is because such a security contributes an average amount of risk to the market portfolio.

Another way of expressing the SML is as follows:

$$\bar{r}_i = r_f + (\bar{r}_M - r_f)\beta_i \tag{10.7}$$

where the term β_i is defined as

$$\beta_i = \frac{\sigma_{iM}}{\sigma_M^2}. \tag{10.8}$$

The term β_i is known as the **beta coefficient** (or simply the beta) for security i, and is an alternative way of representing the covariance risk of a security. Equation (10.7) is a different version of the SML, as can be seen in part (b) of Figure 10.2. While having the same intercept as the earlier version shown in equation (10.6), r_f, it has a different slope. The slope of this version is $\bar{r}_M - r_f$, whereas the slope of the earlier version was $(\bar{r}_M - r_f)/\sigma_M^2$.

One property of beta is that *the beta of a portfolio is simply a weighted average of the betas of its component securities, where the proportions invested in the securities are the respective weights*. That is, the beta of a portfolio can be calculated as

$$\beta_p = \sum_{i=1}^{N} X_i \beta_i. \tag{10.9}$$

Earlier it was shown that the expected return of a portfolio is a weighted average of the expected returns of its component securities, where the proportions invested in the securities are the weights. This means that since every security plots on the SML, so will every portfolio. More broadly:

> Not only every security but also every portfolio must plot on an upward-sloping straight line in a diagram with expected return on the vertical axis and beta on the horizontal axis.

This means that efficient portfolios plot on both the CML and the SML, whereas inefficient portfolios plot only on the SML.

Also of interest is that the SML must go through the point representing the market portfolio itself. Its beta is 1, and its expected return is $\bar{r}_M$, so its coordinates are $(1,\bar{r}_M)$. Since risk-free securities have beta values of 0, the SML will also go through a point with an expected return of r_f and with coordinates of $(0,r_f)$. This means that the SML will have a vertical intercept equal to r_f and a slope equal to the vertical distance between these two points, $\bar{r}_M - r_f$, divided by the horizontal distance between these two points, $1 - 0$, or $(\bar{r}_M - r_f)/(1 - 0) = \bar{r}_M - r_f$. Thus, these two points suffice to fix the location of the SML, indicating the *appropriate* expected returns for securities and portfolios with different beta values.

The equilibrium relationship shown by the SML comes to exist through the combined effects of investors' adjustments in holdings and the resulting pressures on security prices (as shown in Chapter 4). Given a set of security prices, investors calculate expected returns and covariances and then determine their optimal portfolios. If the number of shares of a security collectively desired differs from the number available, there will be upward or downward pressure on its price. Given a new set of prices, investors will reassess their desire for the various securities. The process will continue until the number of shares collectively desired for each security equals the number available.

For the individual investor, security prices and prospects are fixed, whereas the quantities held can be altered. For the market as a whole, however, these quantities are fixed (at least in the short run) and prices are variable. As in any competitive market, equilibrium requires the adjustment of each security's price until there is consistency between the quantity desired and the quantity available.

It may seem logical to examine historical returns on securities in order to determine whether or not they have been priced in equilibrium, as suggested by the CAPM. However, the issue of whether or not such testing of the CAPM can be done in a meaningful manner is controversial. For at least some purposes, affirmative test results may not be necessary in order to make practical use of the CAPM.

► An Example

In the example that was used earlier, Able, Baker, and Charlie were shown to form the market portfolio in proportions equal to .12, .19, and .69, respectively. Given these proportions, the market portfolio had an expected return of 22.4% and a standard deviation of 15.2%. The risk-free rate in the example was 4%. Thus, for this example, the SML as indicated in equation (10.6) is

$$\bar{r}_i = r_f + \left[\frac{\bar{r}_M - r_f}{\sigma_M^2}\right]\sigma_{iM} \qquad (10.6)$$

$$= 4 + \left[\frac{22.4 - 4}{(15.2)^2}\right]\sigma_{iM}$$

$$= 4 + .08\sigma_{iM}. \qquad (10.10)$$

The following expected return vector and variance-covariance matrix were used in the examples shown in Chapters 7, 8, and 9, and are also used here

$$ER = \begin{bmatrix} 16.2 \\ 24.6 \\ 22.8 \end{bmatrix} \quad VC = \begin{bmatrix} 146 & 187 & 145 \\ 187 & 854 & 104 \\ 145 & 104 & 289 \end{bmatrix}.$$

The covariances of each security with the market portfolio can be calculated by using equation (10.4). More specifically, the covariances for the market portfolio for Able, Baker, and Charlie are equal to

$$\begin{aligned}\sigma_{1M} &= \sum_{j=1}^{3} X_{jM}\sigma_{1j} \\ &= (.12 \times 146) + (.19 \times 187) + (.69 \times 145) \\ &= 153\end{aligned}$$

$$\begin{aligned}\sigma_{2M} &= \sum_{j=1}^{3} X_{jM}\sigma_{2j} \\ &= (.12 \times 187) + (.19 \times 854) + (.69 \times 104) \\ &= 257\end{aligned}$$

$$\begin{aligned}\sigma_{3M} &= \sum_{j=1}^{3} X_{jM}\sigma_{3j} \\ &= (.12 \times 145) + (.19 \times 104) + (.69 \times 289) \\ &= 236.\end{aligned}$$

Note how the SML as given in equation (10.10) states that the expected return for Able should be equal to $4 + (.08 \times 153) = 16.2\%$. Similarly, the expected return for Baker should be $4 + (.08 \times 257) = 24.6\%$ and the expected return for Charlie should be $4 + (.08 \times 236) = 22.8\%$. Each one of these expected returns corresponds to the respective value given in the expected return vector.

Alternatively, equation (10.8) can be used to calculate the betas for the three companies. More specifically, the betas for Able, Baker, and Charlie are equal to

$$\begin{aligned}\beta_1 &= \frac{\sigma_{1M}}{\sigma_M^2} \\ &= \frac{153}{(15.2)^2} \\ &= .66\end{aligned}$$

$$\begin{aligned}\beta_2 &= \frac{\sigma_{2M}}{\sigma_M^2} \\ &= \frac{257}{(15.2)^2} \\ &= 1.11\end{aligned}$$

$$\beta_3 = \frac{\sigma_{3M}}{\sigma_M^2} = \frac{236}{(15.2)^2} = 1.02.$$

Now, equation (10.7) indicated that the SML could be expressed in a form where the measure of risk for an asset was its beta. For the example under consideration, this reduces to

$$\begin{aligned} \bar{r}_i &= r_f + (\bar{r}_M - r_f)\beta_i \\ &= 4 + (22.4 - 4)\beta_i \\ &= 4 + 18.4\beta_i. \end{aligned} \tag{10.11}$$

Note how the SML as given in this equation states that the expected return for Able should be equal to $4 + (18.4 \times .66) = 16.2\%$. Similarly, the expected return for Baker should be $4 + (18.4 \times 1.11) = 24.6\%$ and the expected return for Charlie should be $4 + (18.4 \times 1.02) = 22.8\%$. Each one of these expected returns corresponds to the respective value given in the expected return vector.

It is important to realize that if any other portfolio is assumed to be the market portfolio, meaning that if any set of proportions other than .12, .19, and .69 is used, then such an equilibrium relationship between expected returns and betas (or covariances) will not hold. Consider a hypothetical market portfolio with equal proportions (that is, .333) invested in Able, Baker, and Charlie. Since this portfolio has an expected return of 21.2% and a standard deviation of 15.5%, the hypothetical SML would be as follows:

$$\begin{aligned} \bar{r}_i &= r_f + \left[\frac{\bar{r}_M - r_f}{\sigma_M^2}\right]\sigma_{iM} \\ &= 4 + \left[\frac{21.2 - 4}{(15.5)^2}\right]\sigma_{iM} \\ &= 4 + .07\sigma_{iM}. \end{aligned}$$

Able has a covariance with this portfolio of

$$\begin{aligned} \sigma_{1M} &= \sum_{j=1}^{3} X_{jM}\sigma_{1j} \\ &= (.333 \times 146) + (.333 \times 187) + (.333 \times 145) \\ &= 159 \end{aligned}$$

which means that Able's expected return according to the hypothetical SML should be equal to $4 + (.07 \times 159) = 15.1\%$. However, since this does not correspond to the 16.2% figure that appears in the expected return vector, a portfolio with equal proportions invested in Able, Baker, and Charlie cannot be the market portfolio.[12]

---

[12] Baker and Charlie have covariances of 382 and 179, respectively, which means that their expected returns should be equal to $30.74\% = 4 + (.07 \times 382)$ and $16.53\% = 4 + (.07 \times 179)$. However, these figures do not correspond to the respective figures (24.6% and 22.8%) appearing in the expected return vector, indicating there are discrepancies for all three securities. While this example has used the covariance version of the SML, the analysis is similar for the beta version of SML shown in equation (10.7).

THE MARKET MODEL

Chapter 8 introduces the market model, where the return on a common stock was assumed to be related to the return on a market index in the following manner:

$$r_i = \alpha_{iI} + \beta_{iI} r_I + \epsilon_{iI} \tag{8.3}$$

where:

r_i = return on security i for some given period,

r_I = return on market index for the same period,

α_{iI} = intercept term,

β_{iI} = slope term,

ϵ_{iI} = random error term.

It is natural to think about the relationship between the market model and the Capital Asset Pricing Model. After all, both models have a slope term called "beta" in them, and both models somehow involve the market. However, there are two significant differences between the models.

First, the market model is a *factor model*, or to be more specific, a single-factor model where the factor is a market index. Unlike the CAPM, however, it is not an equilibrium model that describes how prices are set for securities.

Second, the market model uses a *market index* such as the TSE 300, whereas the CAPM involves the *market portfolio*. The market portfolio is a collection of all the securities in the marketplace, whereas a market index is in fact based on a sample of the market broadly construed (for example, 300 in the case of the TSE 300). Therefore, conceptually the beta of a stock based on the market model, β_{iI}, differs from the beta of the stock according to the CAPM, β_{iM}. This is because the market model beta is measured relative to a market index while the CAPM beta is measured relative to the market portfolio. In practice, however, the composition of the market portfolio is not precisely known, so a market index is used. Thus, while conceptually different, betas determined with the use of a market index are treated as if they were determined with the use of the market portfolio. That is, β_{iI} is used as an estimate of β_{iM}.

In the example, only three securities were in existence—the common stocks of Able, Baker, and Charlie. Subsequent analysis indicated that the CAPM market portfolio consisted of these stock in the proportions of .12, .19, and .69, respectively. It is against this portfolio that the betas of the securities should be measured. However, in practice they are likely to be measured against a market index (for example, one that is based on just the stocks of Able and Charlie in proportions of .20 and .80, respectively).

Market Indices

One of the most widely known indices is Standard & Poor's 500 Stock Price Index (generally referred to as the S&P 500), a value-weighted average of the market prices of 500 large stocks.

Complete coverage of the stocks listed on the New York Stock Exchange is provided by the NYSE Composite Index, which is like the S&P 500 in that it is a value-weighted index of share prices but is broader in that it considers more stocks. The American Stock Exchange computes a similar index for the stocks it lists, and the National Association of Security Dealers provides a value-weighted index of the prices of over-the-counter stocks traded on the NASDAQ system. The Russel 300 and the Wilshire 5000-stock index are the most comprehensive indices of common stock prices that is published regularly in the United States and is thus closer than the others to representing the overall performance of American common stocks.[13]

In Canada there are two widely quoted indices — the TSE 300 and the Toronto 35 — both based on TSE-traded securities. The former is a broadly based index of 300 of the more representative stocks listed on the exchange. It is a unique value-weighted index in that the weights are based on the total number of shares outstanding minus the number of shares in any control blocks. The weights therefore, are representative of the trading float. Thirty-five of Canada's larger publicly listed companies make up the Toronto 35 Index, which was developed primarily for the trading of derivative securities. This is a modified value-weighted index: Although the weights are based on the number of shares outstanding, no one stock is permitted to represent more than 10% of the index. The Toronto 35 is also designed to track the TSE 300. Therefore, all industry groups except real estate and construction are included. The composition of both these indices is altered periodically to reflect changing economic conditions and fluctuating company fortunes.

Without question the most widely quoted market index is the Dow Jones Industrial Average (DJIA). Although based on the performance of only 30 stocks listed on the New York Stock Exchange and utilizing a less satisfactory averaging procedure, the DJIA provides at least a fair idea of what is happening to stock values.[14]

Market and Non-Market Risk

In Chapter 8 it was shown that the total risk of security σ_i^2 could be partitioned into two components as follows:

$$\sigma_i^2 = \beta_{iI}^2 \sigma_I^2 + \sigma_{\epsilon i} \tag{8.8}$$

where the components are:

$$\beta_{iI}^2 \sigma_I^2 = \text{market risk, and}$$

$$\sigma_{\epsilon i}^2 = \text{unique risk.}$$

Because beta, or covariance, is the relevant measure of risk for a security according to the CAPM, it is only appropriate to explore its relationship to the total risk of the security. It turns out that the relationship is identical to that given in equation (8.8) *except that the market portfolio is involved instead of a market index:*

$$\sigma_i^2 = \beta_{iM}^2 \sigma_M^2 + \sigma_{\epsilon i} \tag{10.12}$$

As with the market model, the total risk of security i measured by its variance and denoted σ_i^2, is shown to consist of two parts. The first component is the portion related to moves of the market portfolio. It is equal to the product of the square of the beta of the stock and the variance of the market portfolio, and also often referred to as the **market risk** of the

[13] There are a variety of other indices of common stock prices that are commonly reported in the daily press. Many of these are components of the major indices. For example, *The Wall Street Journal* reports on a daily basis not only the level of the S&P 500 but also the levels of the Standard & Poor's Industrials, Transportations, Utilities, and Financials. These last four indices reflect the performance of particular sectors of the stock market. Their components, 500 stocks in total, make up the S&P 500. See Chapters 23 and 26 for a more thorough discussion of stock market indices.

[14] Charles Dow started this index in 1884 by simply adding the prices of 11 companies and then dividing the sum by 11. In 1928, securities were added to bring the total number up to 30, and since then the composition of these 30 has been changed periodically. Due to factors such as stock dividends and splits, the divisor is no longer simply equal to the number of stocks in the index.

security. The second component is the portion not related to moves of the market portfolio. It is denoted $\sigma_{\epsilon i}^2$ and can be considered **non-market risk**. Under the assumptions of the market model, it is also unique to the security in question and hence is termed *unique risk*. Note that if β_{iI} is treated as an estimate of β_{iM}, then the decomposition of σ_i^2 is the same in equations (8.8) and (10.12).

An Example

From the earlier example, the betas of Able, Baker, and Charlie were calculated to be .66, 1.11, and 1.02, respectively. As the standard deviation of the market portfolio was equal to 15.2%, this means that the market risk of the three firms is equal to $(.66^2 \times 15.2^2) = 100$, $(1.11^2 \times 15.2^2) = 285$, and $(1.02^2 \times 15.2^2) = 240$, respectively.

The non-market risk of any security can be calculated by solving equation (10.12) for $\sigma_{\epsilon i}^2$:

$$\sigma_{\epsilon i} = \sigma_i^2 - \beta_{iM}^2 \sigma_M^2 \qquad (10.13)$$

Thus, equation (10.13) can be used to calculate the non-market risk of Able, Baker, and Charlie, respectively:

$$\sigma_{\epsilon i}^2 = 146 - 100$$

$$\sigma_{\epsilon 2}^2 = 854 - 285$$
$$= 569$$

$$\sigma_{\epsilon 3}^2 = 289 - 240$$
$$= 49.$$

Non-market risk is sometimes expressed as a standard deviation. This is calculated by taking the square root of $\sigma_{\epsilon i}^2$ and would be equal to $\sqrt{46} = 6.8\%$ for Able, $\sqrt{569} = 23.9\%$ for Baker, and $\sqrt{49} = 7\%$ for Charlie.

Motivation for the Partitioning of Risk

At this point one may wonder: why partition total risk into two parts? For the investor, it would seem that risk is risk—whatever its source. The answer lies in the domain of expected returns.

Market risk is related to the risk of the market portfolio and to the beta of the security in question. Securities with larger betas will have larger amounts of market risk. In the world of the CAPM, securities with larger betas will have larger expected returns. These two relationships together imply that securities with larger market risks should have larger expected returns.

Non-market risk is not related to beta. This means that there is no reason why securities with larger amounts of non-market risk should have larger expected returns. Thus, according to the CAPM, investors are rewarded for bearing market risk but not for bearing non-market risk.

SUMMARY

1. The Capital Asset Pricing Model (CAPM) is based on a specific set of assumptions about investor behaviour and the existence of perfect security markets.
2. Based on these assumptions, all investors will hold the same efficient portfolio of risky assets.

3. Investors will differ only in the amounts of risk-free borrowing or lending they undertake.
4. The risky portfolio held by all investors is known as the market portfolio.
5. The market portfolio consists of all securities, each weighted in proportion to its market value relative to the market value of all securities.
6. The linear efficient set of the CAPM is known as the Capital Market Line (CML). The CML represents the equilibrium relationship between the expected return and standard deviation of efficient portfolios.
7. Under the CAPM the relevant measure of risk for a security is its covariance with the market portfolio.
8. The linear relationship between market covariance and expected return is known as the Security Market Line (SML).
9. The beta of a security is an alternative way of measuring the risk that a security adds to the market portfolio. Beta is a measure of covariance relative to the market portfolio's variance.
10. The beta from the CAPM is similar in concept to the beta from the market model. However, the market model is not an equilibrium model of security prices as is the CAPM. Furthermore, the market model uses a market index, which is a subset of the CAPM's market portfolio.
11. Under the CAPM, the total risk of a security can be separated into market risk and non-market risk. Under the market model, each security's non-market risk is unique to that security and hence is termed its unique risk.

APPENDIX A

SOME EXTENDED VERSIONS OF THE CAPM

The original capital asset pricing model makes strong assumptions and gives strong implications. In the years since it was developed, more complex models have been proposed. These models generally involve relaxing some of the assumptions associated with the original CAPM, and are often referred to as *extended versions of the CAPM* (or extended capital asset pricing models). Some of them are described in this appendix.

EFFICIENT INVESTMENT POLICIES WHEN BORROWING IS RESTRICTED OR EXPENSIVE

The Capital Market Line

The original CAPM assumes that investors can lend or borrow at the same risk-free rate of interest. In reality, such borrowing is likely to be either unavailable or restricted in amount. What impact might the relaxation of this risk-free borrowing assumption have on the CAPM?

A useful way to answer the question makes the following alternative assumptions: (1) investors can lend money risklessly — that is, they can purchase assets that provide a risk-free return of r_{fL}; or (2) investors can borrow money without limit at a higher rate of interest,

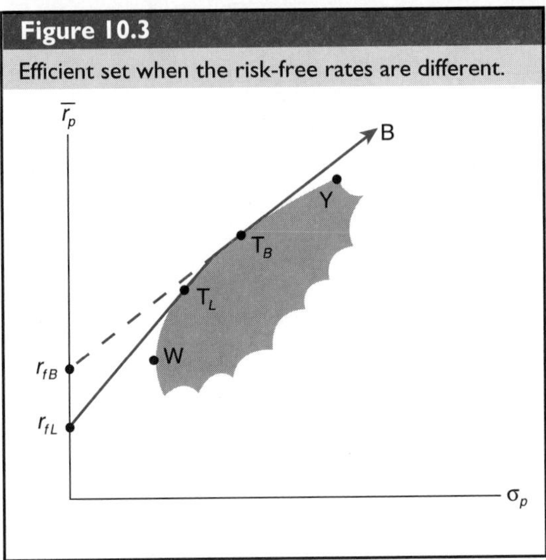

Figure 10.3
Efficient set when the risk-free rates are different.

r_{fB}. These risk-free rates are shown on the vertical axis of Figure 10.3; the "umbrella area" represents risk-return combinations available from investment solely in risky assets.[15]

If there are no opportunities to borrow or lend at the risk-free rate, the efficient set would be the curve $WT_L T_B Y$, and many combinations of risky securities would be efficient. However, the availability of risk-free lending at the rate r_{fL} makes the risky portfolios between W and T_L inefficient, since combinations of risk-free lending and the portfolio plotting at T_L provide more return for the same risk.

Similarly, the ability to borrow money at rate r_{fB} makes another portfolio, denoted by T_B, of special interest. Risky portfolios between T_B and Y are now inefficient, since levered holdings of T_B dominate them by providing more return for the same risk.

Investors with attitudes toward risk that suggest neither borrowing nor lending should hold efficient combinations of risky securities plotting along curve $T_L T_B$. Accordingly, their holdings should be tailored to be consistent with differences in their degrees of aversion to risk.

In this situation the CML is now two lines and a curve, corresponding to the line going from r_{fL} to T_L, then the curve from T_L to T_B, and then the line from T_B on out to the northeast in Figure 10.3.

► The Security Market Line

What becomes of the Security Market Line when the risk-free borrowing rate exceeds the risk-free lending rate? The answer depends on whether or not the market portfolio is in fact one of the efficient combinations of risky securities along the boundary between T_L and T_B in Figure 10.3.[16] If it is not, little more can be said. If it is, a great deal can be said.

Figure 10.4 shows a case in which the market portfolio (shown by point M) is efficient. In part (a) a line has been drawn that is tangent to the efficient set at point M. When this

[15] A more rigorous development of this figure is presented in Appendix A to Chapter 9.

[16] If investors could obtain the proceeds from short sales and there were no restrictions on such sales, then the market portfolio would definitely plot on the efficient set between T_L and T_B.

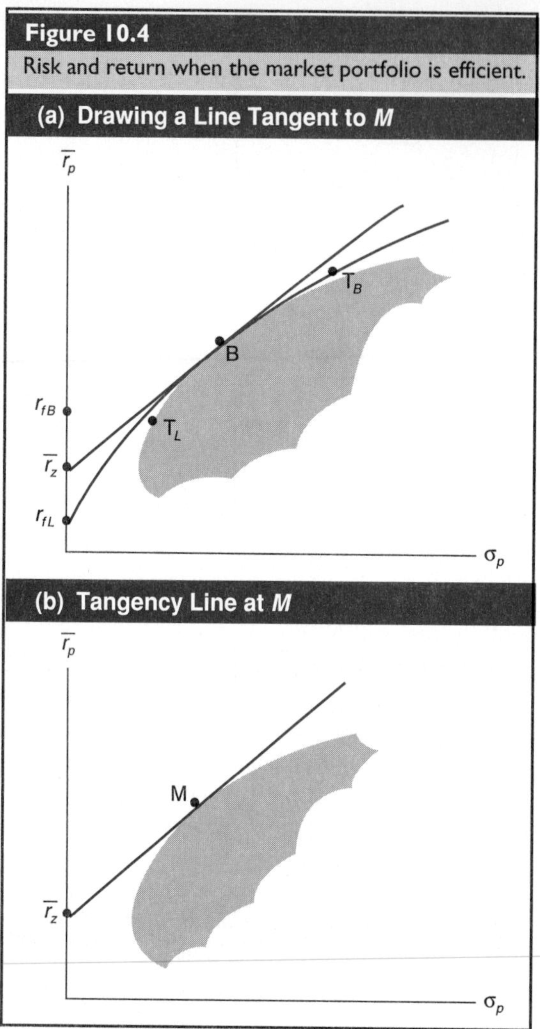

Figure 10.4
Risk and return when the market portfolio is efficient.

line is extended to the vertical axis, the resulting intercept is denoted $\bar{r}_z$. In part (b) only this tangency line is shown.

A striking characteristic of Figure 10.4(b) is that it is precisely the same picture that would be produced in a market in which investors could borrow and lend without limit at a hypothetical risk-free rate equal in value to $\bar{r}_z$. Whereas only point M along the line emanating from $\bar{r}_z$ would be attainable, the expected returns of risky securities would be the same as they would be in a hypothetical market with borrowing and lending at $\bar{r}_z$. That is, all risky securities (and portfolios consisting of these securities) would plot along an SML going through point $\bar{r}_z$, as shown in Figure 10.5.

The vertical intercept of the SML indicates the expected return on a security or portfolio with a beta of zero. Accordingly, this extension of the CAPM is termed the *zero-beta capital asset pricing model.* This version of the CAPM implies that the SML will be flatter than implied by the original version, since $\bar{r}_z$ will be above r_{fL}. As a practical matter, it means that $\bar{r}_z$ must be inferred from the prices of risky securities, since it cannot simply be found in

Figure 10.5

The "zero-beta" security market line.

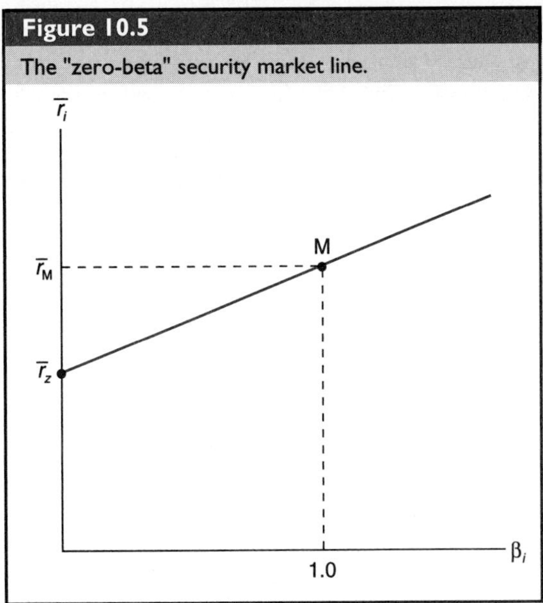

the quotations of current prices on, for example, Treasury bills. Many organizations both in Canada and the United States that estimate the SML generally find that it conforms more to the zero-beta CAPM than to the original CAPM.

Cases in which borrowing is either impossible or costs more as one borrows larger amounts lead to only minor modifications in the conclusions. As long as the market portfolio is efficient, all securities will plot along an SML, but the "zero-beta return" will exceed the risk-free rate at which funds can be invested.

INTRODUCING HETEROGENEOUS EXPECTATIONS

A number of researchers have examined the implications of assuming that different investors have different perceptions about expected returns, standard deviations, and covariances. More specifically, the assumption of homogeneous expectations has been replaced by these researchers with an assumption of ***heterogeneous expectations***.

In one such study, it was noted that each investor would face an efficient set that was unique to him or her.[17] This means that the tangency portfolio (denoted by T in Chapter 9) is unique to each investor, since the optimal combination of risky assets for an investor depends on that investor's perceptions about expected returns, standard deviations, and covariances. Furthermore, an investor will likely determine that his or her tangency portfolio does not involve an investment in some securities (that is, certain securities may have zero proportions in the tangency portfolio). Nevertheless, the SML will still exist. This was shown by aggregating the holdings of all investors, and remembering that in equilibrium each security's price has to be at a level where the amount of the security demanded equals the supply of the security. Now, however, the equilibrium expected return for each security

---

[17] John Lintner, "The Aggregation of Investors' Diverse Judgements and Preferences in Purely Competitive Security Markets," *Journal of Financial and Quantitative Analysis* 4, no. 4 (December 1969): 347–400.

will be a complex weighted average of all investors' perceptions of its expected return. That is, from the viewpoint of a representative, or average, investor, each security will be priced fairly, so its expected return (as perceived by this investor) will be linearly and positively related to its beta.

LIQUIDITY

The original CAPM assumes that investors are concerned only with risk and return. However, other characteristics may also be important to investors. For example, *liquidity* may be important. Here, liquidity refers to the cost of selling or buying a security "in a hurry." For example, a house is regarded as a relatively illiquid investment, since usually a "fair" price for it cannot be obtained quickly. In terms of securities, liquidity may be measured by the size of the spread between the bid and ask prices, with smaller spreads suggesting greater liquidity. Furthermore, it is reasonable to assume that many investors would find more liquid portfolios to be more attractive, keeping everything else the same. However, investors undoubtedly differ in their attitudes toward liquidity. For some it is very important; for others, somewhat important; and for yet others, of little importance.

Under these conditions, security prices would adjust until, overall, investors would be content to hold the outstanding securities. The expected return of a security would be based on two characteristics of the security:

1. The marginal contribution of the security to the risk of an efficient portfolio. This would be measured by the familiar beta (β_i) of the security.
2. The marginal contribution of the security to the liquidity of an efficient portfolio. This would be measured by the liquidity (L_i) of the security.

Now, other things equal, investors dislike large values of β_i but like large values of L_i. This means that two securities with the same beta but different liquidities would not have the same level of expected return. To understand why they would have different levels of expected return, consider what would happen if they had the same level of expected return. In such a situation investors would buy the security with the greater liquidity and sell the one with the lesser liquidity. This would push the price of the first security up and the second one down. Ultimately, in equilibrium the quantity demanded would equal the quantity supplied and the security with the greater liquidity would have a relatively lower expected return. Similarly, two securities with the same liquidity but different betas would not have the same level of expected return. Instead, the security with the higher beta would have a higher expected return.[18]

Figure 10.6 shows the equilibrium relationship one might expect among $\bar{r}_i$, β_i, and L_i. For a given level of β_i, more liquid securities have lower expected returns. And for a given

[18] Investors possess completely illiquid assets in the form of human capital. This means that the ability that an investor has to produce a stream of income by working shows that the investor possesses an asset known as human capital and that different investors have different amounts of human capital. As slavery is outlawed, this asset cannot be sold and hence is non-marketable. Nevertheless, because human capital is an asset, certain researchers have argued that it is relevant to each investor in identifying his or her optimal portfolio. Accordingly, the market portfolio should consist of all marketable and non-marketable assets (like human capital), and each security's beta should be measured relative to it. See David Mayers, "Nonmarketable Assets and Capital Market Equilibrium under Certainty," in *Studies in the Theory of Capital Markets*, ed. Michael C. Jensen (New York: Praeger Publishers, 1972), and "Nonmarketable Assets and the Determination of Capital Asset Prices in the Absence of a Riskless Asset," *Journal of Business* 46, no. 2 (April 1973): 258–267.

Figure 10.6

Security market plane.

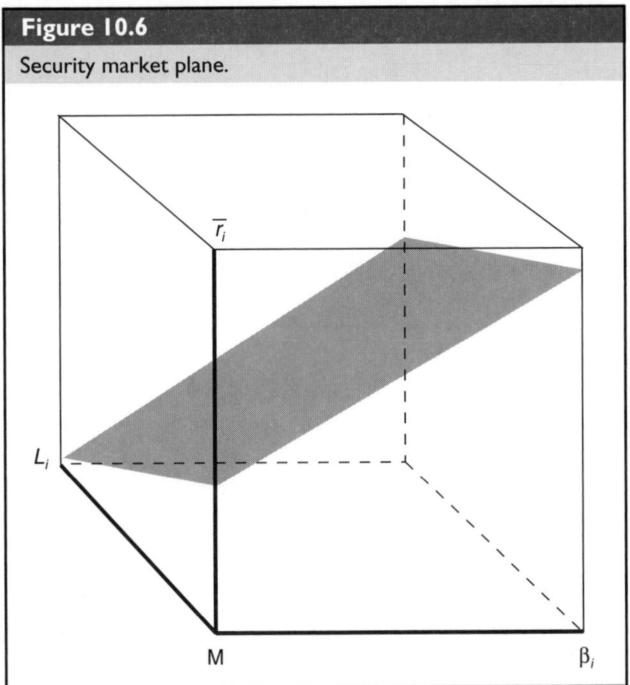

level of L_i, more risky securities have higher expected returns as in the original CAPM. Lastly, there are securities with various levels of β_i and L_i that provide the same level of $\bar{r}_i$. The figure is three-dimensional, since now expected returns are related to two characteristics of securities. Accordingly, it is sometimes referred to as a *Security Market Plane*.[19]

If expected returns are based on beta, liquidity, and a third characteristic, then a four-dimensional CAPM would be necessary to describe the corresponding equilibrium. Whether or not liquidity is an important characteristic of securities has not been demonstrated in a Canadian context. Taxes, however, have been shown to affect before-tax returns on Canadian stocks in a similar way to that found in the United States.[20] Although a diagram cannot be drawn for this type of extended CAPM, an equation can be written for it. Such an equation, by analogy to the three-dimensional plane, is termed a *hyperplane*.

---

[19] The term Security Market Plane is a trademark of Wells Fargo Bank. For more on the relationship between liquidity and stock returns, see Yakov Amihud and Haim Mendelson, "Liquidity and Stock Returns," *Financial Analysts Journal* 42, no. 3 (May/June 1986): 43–48, and "Asset Pricing and the Bid-Ask Spread," *Journal of Financial Economics* 17, no. 2 (December 1986): 223–49.

[20] In the United States taxes were thought to be such a characteristic before the *Tax Reform Act* of 1986, when the tax rate on income from capital gains was less than the tax rate on dividend income. In considering such taxes, one study found that the before-tax expected return of a security was a positive linear function of its beta and its dividend yield. That is, the higher a security's beta or dividend yield, the higher its before-tax expected return. The reason securities with higher dividend yields would have had higher before-tax expected returns was because they would be taxed more heavily. See M. J. Brennan. "Taxes, Market Valuation and Corporate Financial Policy," *National Tax Journal* 23, no. 4 (December 1970): 417–27. The issue of whether or not dividends influence before-tax expected returns has been contentious; it is discussed in Chapters 15 and 16 of Thomas E. Copeland and J. Fred Weston, *Financial Theory and Corporate Policy* (Reading, Mass.: Addison-Wesley, 1988). See I.G. Morgan, "Dividends and Stock Price Behavior in Canada," *Journal of Business Administration* 12 (Fall 1980): 91–106.

In equilibrium, all securities will plot on a *Security Market Hyperplane*, where each axis measures the contribution of a security to a characteristic of efficient portfolios that matter (on average) to investors.

The relationship between the expected return of a security and its contribution to a particular characteristic of efficient portfolios depends on the attitudes of investors to the characteristic:

If, on the average, a characteristic (such as liquidity) is liked by investors, then those securities that contribute more to that characteristic will, other things equal, offer lower expected returns. Conversely, if a characteristic (such as beta) is disliked by investors, then those securities that contribute more to that characteristic will offer higher expected returns.

In a capital market with many relevant characteristics, the task of tailoring a portfolio for a specific investor is more complicated, since only an investor with average attitudes and circumstances should hold the market portfolio. In general:

If an investor likes a characteristic more (or dislikes it less) than the average investor, he or she should generally hold a portfolio with relatively more of that characteristic than is provided by holding the market portfolio. Conversely, if an investor likes a characteristic less (or dislikes it more) than the average investor, he or she should generally hold a portfolio with relatively less of that characteristic than is provided by holding the market portfolio.

For example, consider an investor who likes having a relatively liquid portfolio. Such an investor should hold a portfolio consisting of relatively liquid securities. Conversely, an investor who has relatively little need for liquidity should hold a portfolio of relatively illiquid securities.

The right combination of "tilt" away from market proportions will depend on the extent of the differences between the investor's attitudes and those of the average investor and on the added risk involved in such a strategy. A complex capital market requires all the tools of modern portfolio theory for managing the money of any investor who is significantly different from the "average investor." On the other hand, in such a world, investment management should be relatively passive: after the selection of an initial portfolio, there should be minor and infrequent changes.

APPENDIX B

A Derivation of the Security Market Line

Figure 10.7 shows the location of the feasible set of the Markowitz model, along with the risk-free rate and the associated efficient set that represents the capital market line. Within the feasible set of the Markowitz model lies every individual risky security. An arbitrarily chosen risky security, denoted by I, has been selected for analysis and is shown on the figure.

Consider any portfolio, p, that consists of the proportion X_i invested in security i and the proportion $1 - X_i$ invested in the market portfolio M. Such a portfolio will have an expected return equal to

$$\bar{r}_p = X_i\bar{r}_i + (1 - X_i)\bar{r}_M \tag{10.14}$$

and a standard deviation equal to

$$\sigma_p = [X_i^2\sigma_i^2 + (1 - X_i)^2\sigma_M^2 + 2X_i(1 - X_i)\sigma_{iM}]^{1/2}. \tag{10.15}$$

All such portfolios will lie on a curved line, such as the one shown in Figure 10.7 connecting I and M.

Of concern is the slope of this curved line. Since it is a curved line, its slope is not a constant. However, its slope can be determined with the use of calculus. First, using equation (10.14), the derivative of $\bar{r}_p$ with respect to X_i is taken:

$$\frac{d\bar{r}_p}{dX_i} = \bar{r}_i - \bar{r}_M. \tag{10.16}$$

Second, using equation (10.15), the derivative of σ_p with respect to X_i is taken:

$$\frac{d\sigma_p}{dX_i} = \frac{X_i\sigma_i^2 - \sigma_M^2 + X_i\sigma_M^2 + \sigma_{iM} - 2X_i\sigma_{iM}}{[X_i^2\sigma_i^2 + (1 - X_i)^2\sigma_M^2 + 2X_i(1 - X_i)\sigma_{iM}]^{1/2}}. \tag{10.17}$$

Third, the slope of the curved line iM, $d\bar{r}_p/d\sigma_p$, can be written as

$$\frac{d\bar{r}_p}{d\sigma_p} = \frac{d\bar{r}_p/dX_i}{d\sigma_p/dX_i} \tag{10.18}$$

Finally, the slope of iM can be calculated by substituting equations (10.16) and (10.17) into the numerator and denominator of equation (10.18), respectively:

$$\frac{d\bar{r}_p}{d\sigma_p} = \frac{[\bar{r}_i - \bar{r}_M][X_i^2\sigma_i^2 + (1 - X_i)^2\sigma_M^2 + 2X_i(1 - X_i)\sigma_{iM}]^{1/2}}{X_i\sigma_i^2 - \sigma_M^2 + X_i\sigma_M^2 + \sigma_{iM} - 2X_i\sigma_{iM}}. \tag{10.19}$$

Figure 10.7

Deriving the security market line.

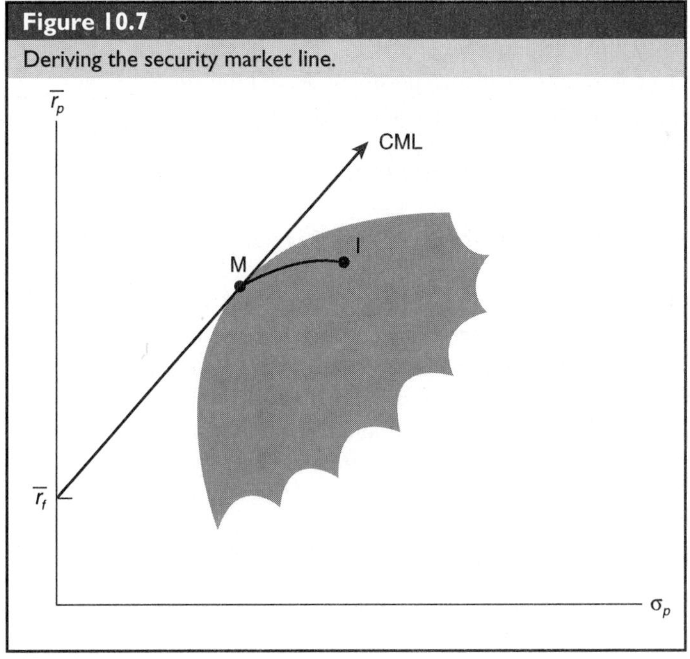

Of interest is the slope of the curved line iM at the endpoint M. Since the proportion X_i is zero at this point, the slope of iM can be calculated by substituting zero for X_i in equation (10.19). After doing so, many terms drop out, leaving

$$\frac{d\bar{r}_p}{d\sigma_p} = \frac{[\bar{r}_i - \bar{r}_M][\sigma_M]}{\sigma_{iM} - \sigma_M^2}. \quad (10.20)$$

At M, the slope of the CML, $(\bar{r}_M - r_f)/\sigma_M$, must equal the slope of the curved line iM. This is because the slope of the curved line iM increases when moving from the endpoint i, converging to the slope of the CML at the endpoint M. Accordingly, the slope of the curve iM at M, as shown on the right-hand side of equation (10.20), is set equal to the slope of the CML:

$$\frac{[\bar{r}_i - \bar{r}_M][\sigma_M]}{\sigma_{iM} - \sigma_M^2} = \frac{\bar{r}_M - r_f}{\sigma_M}. \quad (10.21)$$

Solving equation (10.21) for r_i results in the covariance version of the SML:

$$\bar{r}_i = r_f + \left[\frac{\bar{r}_M - r_f}{\sigma_M^2}\right]\sigma_{iM}. \quad (10.6)$$

The beta version of the SML is derived by substituting β_i for σ_{iM}/σ_M^2 in equation (10.6).

QUESTIONS AND PROBLEMS

1. Describe the key assumptions underlying the CAPM.
2. Many of the underlying assumptions of the CAPM are violated to some degree in the "real world." Does that fact invalidate the model's conclusions? Explain.
3. What is the separation theorem? What implications does it have for the optimal portfolio of risky assets held by investors?
4. What constitutes the market portfolio? What problems does one confront in specifying the composition of the true market portfolio? How have researchers and practitioners circumvented these problems?
5. In the equilibrium world of the CAPM, is it possible for a security not to be part of the market portfolio? Explain.
6. Describe the price adjustment process that equilibrate the market's supply and demand for securities. What conditions will prevail under such an equilibrium?
7. Will an investor who owns the market portfolio have to buy and sell units of the component securities every time the relative prices of those securities change? Why?
8. Given an expected return of 12% for the market portfolio, a risk-free rate of 6%, and a market portfolio standard deviation of 20%, draw the Capital Market Line.
9. Explain the significance of the Capital Market Line.
10. Assume that two securities constitute the market portfolio. Those securities have the following expected returns, standard deviations, and proportions:

Security	Expected Return	Standard Deviation	Proportion
A	10%	20%	.40
B	15	28	.60

Based on this information, and given a correlation of .30 between the two securities and a risk-free rate of 5%, specify the equation for the Capital Market Line.

11. Distinguish between the Capital Market Line and the Security Market Line.

12. The market portfolio is assumed to be composed of four securities. Their covariances with the market and their proportions are shown below:

Security	*Covariance with Market*	*Proportion*
A	242	.20
B	360	.30
C	155	.20
D	210	.30

Given these data, calculate the market portfolio's standard deviation.

13. Explain the significance of the slope of the SML. How might the slope of the SML change over time?

14. Why should the expected return for a security be directly related to the security's covariance with the market portfolio?

15. The risk of a well-diversified portfolio to an investor is measured by the standard deviation of the portfolio's returns. Why shouldn't the risk of an individual security be calculated in the same manner?

16. A security with a high standard deviation of returns is not necessarily highly risky to an investor. Why might you suspect that securities with above-average standard deviations tend to have above-average betas?

17. Oliver Smith, an investments student, argued, "A security with a positive standard deviation must have an expected return greater than the risk-free rate. Otherwise, why would anyone be willing to hold the security?" Based on the CAPM, is Oliver's statement correct? Why?

18. Kitty Bransfield owns a portfolio composed of three securities. The betas of those securities and their proportions in Kitty's portfolio follow. What is the beta of Kitty's portfolio?

Security	*Beta*	*Proportion*
A	.90	.30
B	1.30	.10
C	1.05	.60

19. Assume that the expected return on the market portfolio is 15% and its standard deviation is 21%. The risk-free rate is 7%. What is the standard deviation of a well-diversified (no non-market-risk) portfolio with an expected return of 16.6%?

20. Given that the expected return on the market portfolio is 10%, the risk-free rate of return is 6%, the beta of stock A is .85, and the beta of stock B is 1.20:

a. Draw the SML.

b. What is the equation for the SML?

c. What are the equilibrium expected returns for stock A and B?

d. Plot the two risky securities on the SML.

21. You are given the following information on two securities, the market portfolio, and the risk-free rate:

	Expected Return	*Correlation with Market Portfolio*	*Standard Deviation*
Security 1	15.5%	0.90	20.0%
Security 2	9.2	0.80	9.0
Market Portfolio	12.0	1.00	12.0
Risk-free Rate	5.0	0.00	0.0

a. Draw the SML.
b. Identify the betas of the two securities.
c. Plot the two securities on the SML.

22. The SML describes an equilibrium relationship between risk and expected return. Would you consider a security that plotted above the SML to be an attractive investment? Why?
23. Assume that two securities, A and B, constitute the market portfolio. Their proportions and variances are .39, 160, and .61, 340, respectively. The covariance of the two securities is 190. Calculate the betas of the two securities.
24. The CAPM permits the standard deviation of a security to be segmented into market and non-market risk. Distinguish between the two types of risk.
25. Is an investor who owns any portfolio of risky assets other than the market portfolio exposed to some non-market risk? Explain.
26. Based on the risk and return relationships of the CAPM, supply the missing values in the following table.

Security	*Expected Return*	*Beta*	*Standard Deviation*	*Non-market Risk* ($\sigma^2_{\epsilon i}$)
A	_______%	0.8	_______%	81
B	19.0	1.5	_______	36
C	15.0	_______	12	0
D	7.0	0	8	_______
E	16.6	_______	15	_______

27. (Appendix Question) Describe how the SML is altered when the risk-free borrowing rate exceeds the risk-free lending rate.

KEY TERMS

normative economics
positive economics
Capital Asset Pricing Model (CAPM)
homogeneous expectations
perfect market
separation theorem
market portfolio
Capital Market Line (CML)
Security Market Line (SML)
beta coefficient
market risk
non-market risk

REFERENCES

1. Credit for the initial development of the CAPM is usually given to:

   William F. Sharpe, "Capital Asset Prices: A Theory of Market Equilibrium Under Conditions of Risk," *Journal of Finance* 19, no. 3 (September 1964): 425–442.

   John Lintner, "The Valuation of Risk Assets and the Selection of Risky Investments in Stock Portfolios and Capital Budgets," *Review of Economics and Statistics* 47, no. 1 (February 1965): 13–37; and "Security Prices, Risk, and Maximal Gains from Diversification," *Journal of Finance* 20, no. 4 (December 1965): 587–615.

   Jan Mossin, "Equilibrium in a Capital Asset Market," *Econometrica* 34, no. 4 (October 1966): 768–783.

2. The Sharpe and Lintner papers were compared in:

   Eugene F. Fama, "Risk, Return, and Equilibrium: Some Clarifying Comments," *Journal of Finance* 28, no. 1 (March 1968): 29–40.

3. Some extended versions of the CAPM are described in:

   Gordon J. Alexander and Jack Clark Francis, *Portfolio Analysis* (Englewood Cliff, NJ: Prentice Hall, 1986), Chapter 8.

   Edwin J. Elton and Martin J. Gruber, *Modern Portfolio Theory and Investment Analysis* (New York: John Wiley, 1991), Chapter 12.

4. For a comparison of the market model and CAPM betas, see:

   Harry M. Markowitz, "The 'Two Beta' Trap," *Journal of Portfolio Management* 11, no. 1 (Fall 1984): 12–20.

5. It has been argued that the CAPM is virtually impossible to test because (a) the only testable hypothesis of the CAPM is that the "true" market portfolio lies on the efficient set (when this happens securities' expected returns and betas have a positive linear relationship) and (b) the "true" market portfolio cannot be meaningfully measured. See:

   Richard Roll, "A Critique of the Asset Pricing Theory's Tests: Part I. On Past and Potential Testability of the Theory," *Journal of Financial Economics* 4, no. 2 (March 1977): 129–176.

6. In spite of Roll's critique, several tests of the CAPM have been conducted. Some of them are summarized in:

   Gordon J. Alexander and Jack Clark Francis, *Portfolio Analysis* (Englewood Cliffs, NJ: Prentice Hall, 1986), Chapter 10.

   Edwin J. Elton and Martin J. Gruber, *Modern Portfolio Theory and Investment Analysis* (New York: John Wiley, 1991), Chapter 13.

7. Recently some people have concluded that the CAPM is no longer relevant based on the following test results that show that the relationship between beta and average stock returns is flat:

   Eugene F. Fama and Kenneth R. French, "The Cross-Section of Expected Stock Returns," *Journal of Finance* 47, no. 2 (June 1992): 427–465.

   Eugene F. Fama and Kenneth R. French, "Common Risk Factors in the Returns on Stocks and Bonds," *Journal of Financial Economics* 33, no. 1 (February 1993): 3–56.

8. However, these test results have been challenged by others, such as those listed below. For example, the third study shows that average returns and betas have a positive linear relationship when the market portfolio includes human capital and betas are allowed to vary over the business cycle:

   Louis K. C. Chan and Josef Lakonishok, "Are the Reports of Beta's Death Premature?", *Journal of Portfolio Management* 19, no. 4 (Summer 1993): 51–62.

   Fischer Black, "Beta and Return," *Journal of Portfolio Management* 20, no. 1 (February 1993): 8–18.

   Ravi Jagannathan and Zhenyu Wang, "The CAPM is Alive and Well," unpublished paper, Carlson School of Management, University of Minnesota, Minneapolis, MN, November 22, 1993.

9. For an assertion that the use of modern portfolio theory does not depend upon successful testing of the CAPM, see:

   Harry M. Markowitz, "Nonnegative or Non Nonnegative: A Question about CAPMs," *Journal of Finance* 38, no. 2 (May 1983): 283–295.

10. For a Canadian perspective on the topics covered in this chapter, see:

    Roger Morin, "Market Line Theory and the Canadian Equity Market," *Journal of Business Administration: Capital Markets in Canada* 12, no. 1 (Fall 1980).

    M. J. Brennan and E. S. Schwartz, *Canadian Estimates of the Capital Asset Pricing Model*, Corporate Finance Division, Department of Finance (July 1982).

    A. L. Calvet and J. Lefoll, "Risk and Return in Canadian Capital Markets," *Canadian Journal of Administrative Sciences* 5, no. 1 (March 1988).

    M. J. Robinson, "Univariate Canadian CAPM Tests," in M. J. Robinson and B. F. Smith, eds., *Canadian Capital Markets* (London, Ont: Western Business School, 1993).

CHAPTER 11

Factor Models

The objective of modern portfolio theory is to provide a means by which the investor can identify his or her optimal portfolio when there are an infinite number of possibilities. The investor needs to estimate the expected return and standard deviation for each security under consideration for inclusion in the portfolio, along with all the covariances between securities. With these estimates the investor can derive the curved efficient set of Markowitz. Then for a given risk-free rate the investor can identify the tangency portfolio and determine the location of the linear efficient set. Finally, the investor can proceed to invest in this tangency portfolio and borrow or lend at the risk-free rate, with the amount of borrowing or lending depending on the investor's risk-return preferences.

FACTOR MODELS AND RETURN-GENERATING PROCESSES

The task of identifying the curved Markowitz efficient set can be greatly simplified by introducing a **return-generating process**. A return-generating process is a statistical model that describes how the return on a security is produced. Chapter 8 presented a type of return-generating process known as the market model. The market model states that a security's return is a function of the return on a market index. However, there are many other types of return-generating processes for securities.

► Factor Models

Factor models or index models assume that the return on a security is sensitive to the movements of various factors or indices. The market model assumes that there is one factor— the return on a market index. However, in attempting to accurately estimate expected returns, variances, and covariances for securities, multiple-factor models are potentially more useful than the market model. They have this potential because it appears that actual security returns are sensitive to more than movements in a market index. This means that there is probably more than one pervasive factor in the economy that affects security returns.

As a return-generating process, a factor model attempts to capture the major economic forces that systematically move the prices of all securities. Implicit in the construction of a factor model is the assumption that the returns on two securities will be correlated— that is, will move together—only through common reactions to one or more of the factors specified in the model. Any aspect of a security's return unexplained by the factor model is assumed to be unique or specific to the security and therefore uncorrelated with the unique elements of returns on other securities. As a result, a factor model is a powerful tool for portfolio management. It can supply the information needed to calculate expected returns, variances, and covariances for every security—a necessary condition for determining the curved Markowitz efficient set. It can also be used to characterize a portfolio's sensitivity to movements in the factors.

► Application

As a practical matter, all investors employ factor models, whether they do so explicitly or implicitly. It is impossible to consider separately the interrelationship of every security with every other. The problem of calculating covariances among securities rises exponentially as the number of securities analyzed increases.[1]

Conceptually, thinking about the tangled web of security variances and covariances becomes mind-boggling even when dealing with just a few securities, let alone hundreds or thousands. Even the vast data processing capabilities of high-speed computers are strained when they are called upon to construct efficient sets from a large number of securities.

Abstraction is therefore essential in identifying the curved Markowitz efficient set. Factor models supply the necessary level of abstraction. They provide investment managers with a framework to identify important factors in the economy and the marketplace and to assess the extent to which different securities and portfolios will respond to changes in these factors.

Given the belief that one or more factors influence security returns, a primary goal of security analysis is to determine these factors and the sensitivities of security returns to movements in these factors. A formal statement of such a relationship is termed a *factor model of security returns*. The discussion begins with the simplest form of such a model, a one-factor model.

ONE-FACTOR MODELS

Some investors argue that the return-generating process for securities involves a single factor. For example, they may contend that the returns on securities respond to the predicted growth rate in the gross domestic product (GDP).[2] Table 11.1 and Figure 11.1 illustrate one way of providing substance for such statements.

Table 11.1

Factor Model Data.

Year	*Growth Rate In GDP*	*Rate of Inflation*	*Return on Widget Stock*
1	5.7%	1.1%	14.3%
2	6.4	4.4	19.2
3	7.9	4.4	23.4
4	7.0	4.6	15.6
5	5.1	6.1	9.2
6	2.9	3.1	13.0

[1] See Appendix B to Chapter 8.

[2] GDP is similar to gross national product (GNP) in that it is a measure of a country's total output of goods and services. However, GDP treats imports and exports slightly differently than GNP and, as a result, requires fewer revisions after it is initially reported. Furthermore, international comparisons are straightforward with GDP, as most countries report GDP instead of GNP.

Figure 11.1

A one-factor model.

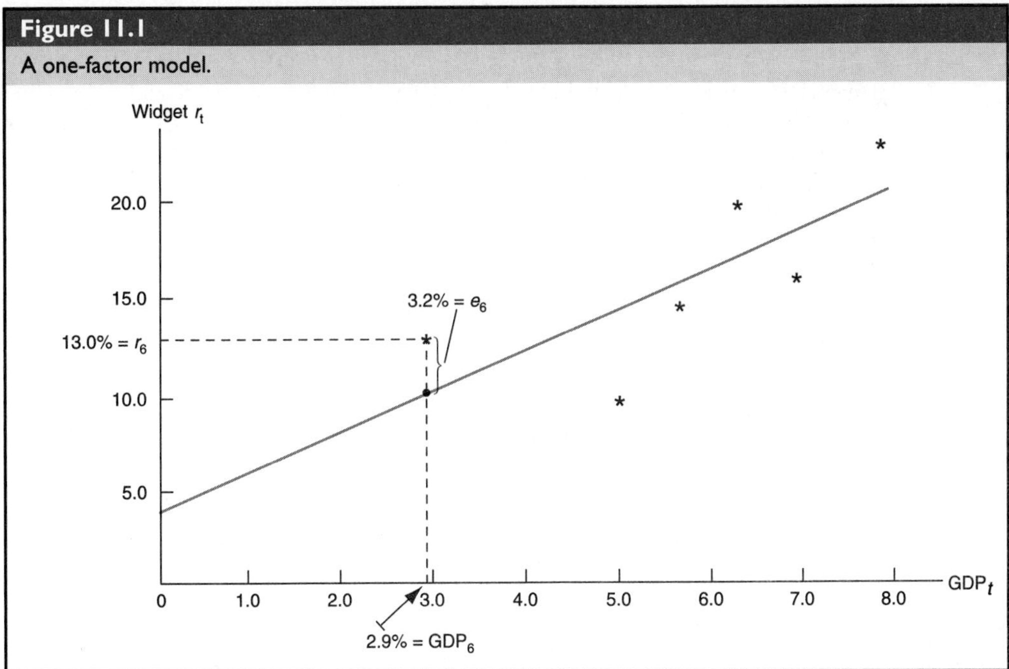

An Example

The horizontal axis of Figure 11.1 shows the predicted growth rate in GDP, while the vertical axis measures the return on Widget's stock. Each point in the graph represents the combination of Widget's return and GDP growth rate for a particular year as reported in Table 11.1. A line has been statistically fitted to the data by using a technique known as *simple-regression analysis.* (*Simple* refers to the fact that there is one variable—GDP in this example—on the right-hand side of the equation).[3] This line has a positive slope of 2, indicating that there exists a positive relationship between GDP growth rates and Widget's returns. Higher rates of GDP growth are associated with higher returns.

In equation form, the relationship between predicted GDP growth and Widget's return can be expressed as follows:

$$r_t = a + b\text{GDP}_t + e_t \tag{11.1}$$

where:

r_t = the return on Widget in period t,

GDP_t = the predicted rate of growth in GDP in period t,

e_t = the unique or specific return on Widget in period t,

b = the **sensitivity** of Widget to predicted GDP growth,[4]

a = the zero factor for GDP.

[3] Only six data points are shown in the figure for ease of exposition. The standard statistical procedure of simple linear regression is discussed in Chapter 17 and in Mark Kritzman, ". . . About Regression," *Financial Analysts Journal* 47, no. 3 (May/June 1991): 12–15. It can be found in most statistics books, such as Thomas H. Wonnacott and Ronald J. Wonnacott, *Introductory Statistics for Business and Economics* (New York, N.Y.: John Wiley and Sons, 1984).

[4] Sometimes b is referred to as the **factor loading**, or **attribute**, of the security.

In Figure 11.1 the zero factor is 4% per period. This is the return that would be expected for Widget if predicted GDP growth equalled zero. The sensitivity of Widget to predicted GDP growth b is 2, and is the same as the slope of the line in Figure 11.1. This value indicates that, in general, higher predicted growth in GDP is associated with higher returns for Widget. If predicted GDP growth equalled 5%, Widget should generate a return of 4% + (2 × 5%) = 14%. If predicted GDP growth were 1% higher — that is, 6% — Widget's return should be 2% higher, or 16%.

In this example, predicted GDP growth in year 6 was 2.9%, and Widget actually returned 13%. Therefore Widget's unique return (given by e_t) in this particular year was +3.2%. This was determined by subtracting an amount that represents Widget's expected return, given that GDP was predicted to grow by 2.9%, from Widget's actual return of 13%. In this case, Widget would have an expected return of 4% + (2 × 2.9%) = 9.8%, thereby resulting in a unique return of 13% – 9.8% = +3.2%.

In effect, the one-factor model presented in Figure 11.1 and equation (11.1) attributes Widget's return in any particular period to three elements:

1. An effect common in any period (the term a)
2. An effect that differs across periods depending on the predicted growth rate of GDP (the term $b\text{GDP}_t$)
3. An effect specific to the particular period observed (the term e_t)

Generalizing the Example

This example of a one-factor model can be generalized in equation form for any security i in period t:

$$r_{it} = a_i + b_i F_t + e_{it} \tag{11.2}$$

where F is the predicted value of the factor in period t and b_i is the sensitivity of security i to this factor. If the predicted value of the factor were zero, the return on the security would equal $a_i + e_{it}$. Note that e_{it} is a random error term just like the random error term discussed in Chapter 8. This means that it is a random variable with an expected value of zero and a standard deviation σ_{ei}. It can be thought of as the outcome occurring from a spin of a roulette wheel.

Expected Return

According to the one-factor model, the expected return on security i can be written as

$$\overline{r}_i = a_i + b_i \overline{F} \tag{11.3}$$

where $\overline{F}$ denotes the expected value of the factor.

This equation can be used to estimate the expected return on the security. For example, if the expected growth rate in GDP is 3%, then the expected return for Widget equals 4% + (2 × 3%) = 10%.

Variance

With the one-factor model, it can also be shown that the variance of any security i is equal to

$$\sigma_i^2 = b_i^2 \sigma_F^2 + \sigma_{ei}^2 \tag{11.4}$$

where σ_F^2 is the variance of the factor F and σ_{ei}^2 is the variance of the random error term e_i. Thus if the variance of the factor σ_F^2 equals 3 and the residual variance σ_{ei}^2 equals 15.2, then according to this equation Widget's variance equals

$$\begin{aligned}\sigma_i^2 &= (2^2 \times 3) + 15.2\\ &= 27.2\end{aligned}$$

Covariance

With a one-factor model the covariance between any two securities i and j can be shown to equal

$$\sigma_{ij} = b_i b_j \sigma_F^2 \tag{11.5}$$

In the example of Widget, equation (11.5) can be used to estimate the covariance between Widget and another hypothetical security, such as the stock of Whatever Company. Assuming that the factor sensitivity of Whatever is 4.0, the covariance between Widget and Whatever equals

$$\begin{aligned}\sigma_{ij} &= 2 \times 4 \times 3\\ &= 24\end{aligned}$$

Assumptions

Equations (11.4) and (11.5) are based on two critical assumptions. The first assumption is that the random error term and the factor are uncorrelated. This means that the outcome of the factor has no bearing on the outcome of the random error term.

The second assumption is that the random error terms of any two securities are uncorrelated. This means that the outcome of the random error term of one security has no bearing on the outcome of the random error term of any other security. In other words, the returns of two securities will be correlated—that is, will move together only through common responses to the factor. If either of these two assumptions is invalid, then the model is an approximation, and a different factor model (perhaps one with more factors) will theoretically be a more accurate model of the return-generating process.

► The Market Model

The market model can now be shown to be a specific example of a one-factor model where the factor is the return on a market index. In Chapter 8, the market model appeared as

$$r_i = \alpha_{iI} + \beta_{iI} r_I + \epsilon_{iI} \tag{8.3}$$

The similarity between equation (8.3) and the general form of the one-factor model in equation (11.2) is readily apparent. The intercept term α_{iI} from the market model equation corresponds to the zero factor term a_i from equation (11.2). Furthermore, the slope term β_{iI} from the market model equates to the sensitivity term b_i from the generalized one-factor model. Each equation has a random error term: e_{it} in the factor model and ϵ_{iIt} in the market model.[5] Finally, the market index return plays the role of the single factor.

However, as mentioned earlier, the concept of a one-factor model does not restrict the investor to using a market index as the factor. Many other factors are plausible, such as predicted GDP or industrial production.

---

[5] The time subscript t was deleted from the market model simply for ease of exposition. Technically speaking, the random error term should be written as ϵ_{iIt}.

Two Important Features of One-Factor Models

Two features of one-factor models are of particular interest.

The Tangency Portfolio

First, the assumption that the returns on all securities respond to a single common factor greatly simplifies the task of identifying the tangency portfolio. To determine the composition of the tangency portfolio, the investor needs to estimate all the expected returns, variances, and covariances. This can be done with a one-factor model by estimating a_i, b_i, and σ_{ei} for each of the N risky securities.[6]

Also needed are the expected value of the factor $\overline{F}$ and its standard deviation, σ_F. With these estimates, equations (11.3), (11.4), and (11.5) can be used to calculate expected returns, variances, and covariances for the securities. Using these values, the curved efficient set of Markowitz can be derived. Finally, the tangency portfolio can be determined for a given risk-free rate.

The common responsiveness of securities to the factor eliminates the need to estimate directly the covariances between the securities. Those covariances are captured by the securities' sensitivities to the factor and the factor's variance.

Diversification

The second interesting feature of one-factor models has to do with diversification. Earlier it was shown that diversification leads to an averaging of market risk and a reduction in unique risk. This feature is true of any one-factor model, except that instead of market and unique (or non-market) risk, the words factor and nonfactor risk are used. In equation (11.4) the first term on the right-hand side ($b_i^2\sigma_F^2$) is known as the **factor risk** of the security, and the second term (σ_{ei}^2) is known as the **nonfactor** (or idiosyncratic) **risk** of the security.

With a one-factor model, the variance of a portfolio is given by

$$\sigma_P^2 = b_P^2\sigma_F^2 + \sigma_{ep}^2 \tag{11.6a}$$

where:

$$b_P = \sum_{i=1}^{N} X_i b_i \tag{11.6b}$$

$$\sigma_{ep}^2 = \sum_{i=1}^{N} X_i \sigma_{ei}^2. \tag{11.6c}$$

Equation (11.6a) shows that the total risk of any portfolio can be viewed as having two components similar to the two components of the total risk of an individual security shown in equation (11.4). In particular, the first and second terms on the right-hand side of equation (11.6a) are the factor risk and nonfactor risk of the portfolio, respectively.

As a portfolio becomes more diversified (meaning that it contains more securities), each proportion X_i will become smaller. However, this will not cause b_p to either decrease or increase significantly unless a deliberate attempt is made to do so by adding securities with values of b_i that are either relatively low or high. As equation (11.6b) shows, this is because b_p is simply a weighted average of the sensitivities of the securities b_i with the values of X_i serving as the weights. Thus, *diversification leads to an averaging of factor risk.*

---

[6] This is shown in more detail in Appendix B to Chapter 8.

However, as a portfolio becomes more diversified, there is reason to expect σ_{ep}^2, the nonfactor risk, to decrease. This can be shown by examining equation (11.6c). Assuming that the amount invested in each security is equal, then this equation can be rewritten by substituting $1/N$ for X_i:

$$\sigma_{ep}^2 = \sum_{i=1}^{N} \left(\frac{1}{N}\right)^2 \sigma_{ei}^2$$

$$= \left(\frac{1}{N}\right)\left[\frac{\sigma_{e1}^2 + \sigma_{e2}^2 + \ldots + \sigma_{eN}^2}{N}\right].$$

The value inside the square brackets is the average nonfactor risk for the individual securities. But the portfolio's nonfactor risk is only one-Nth as large as this because the term $1/N$ appears outside the brackets. As the portfolio becomes more diversified, the number of securities in it, N, becomes larger. This means that $1/N$ becomes smaller, which in turn reduces the nonfactor risk of the portfolio. Simply stated, *diversification reduces nonfactor risk.*[7]

MULTIPLE-FACTOR MODELS

The health of the economy affects most firms. Thus, changes in expectations concerning the future of the economy can be expected to have profound effects on the returns of most securities. However, the economy is not a simple, monolithic entity. Several common influences with pervasive effects can be identified.

1. The growth rate of GDP
2. The level of interest rates
3. The inflation rate
4. The level of oil prices

Two-Factor Models

Instead of a one-factor model, a multiple-factor model for security returns that considers these various influences may be more accurate. As an example of a multiple-factor model, consider a two-factor model. This assumes that the return-generating process contains two factors.

In equation form, the two-factor model for period t is

$$r_{it} = a_i + b_{i1}F_{1t} + b_{i2}F_{2t} + e_{it} \tag{11.7}$$

where F_{1t} and F_{2t} are the two factors that are pervasive influences on security returns and b_{i1} and b_{i2} are the sensitivities of security i to these two factors. As with the one-factor model, e_{it} is a random error term and a_i is the expected return on security i if each factor has a value of zero.

Figure 11.2 provides an illustration of Widget Company's stock, whose returns are affected by expectations concerning both the growth rate in GDP and the rate of inflation. As was the case in the one-factor example, each point in the figure corresponds to a particular

[7] Actually, all that is necessary for this reduction in nonfactor risk to occur is for the maximum amount invested in any one security to continually decrease as N increases. An example based on the market model is given in Chapter 8.

year. This time, however, each point is a combination of Widget's return, the rate of inflation, and the growth of GDP in that year, as given in Table 11.1. To this scatter of points is fitted a two-dimensional plane using the statistical technique of *multiple-regression analysis.* (*Multiple* refers to the fact that there are two predicted variables — GDP and inflation in this example — on the right-hand side of the equation.) The plane for a given security is described by the following adaptation of equation (11.7):

$$r_t = a + b_1 \text{GDP}_t + b_2 \text{INF}_t + e_t.$$

The slope of the plane in the GDP growth-rate direction (the term b_1) represents Widget's sensitivity to changes in GDP growth. The slope of the plane in the inflation rate direction (the term b_2) is Widget's sensitivity to changes in the inflation rate. Note that the sensitivities b_1 and b_2 in this example are positive and negative, respectively, having

Figure 11.2

A two-factor model.

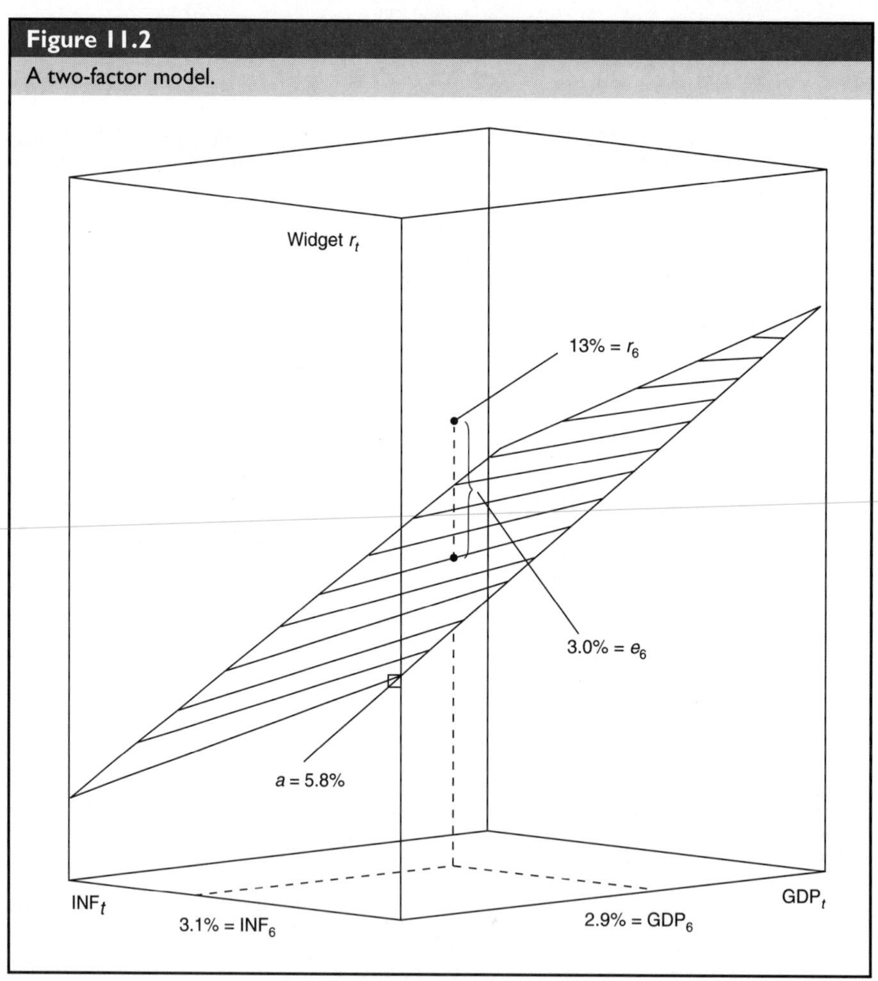

corresponding values of 2.2 and –.7.[8] This indicates that as predicted GDP growth or inflation rises, Widget's return should increase or decrease, respectively.

The intercept term (the zero factor) of 5.8% in Figure 11.2 indicates Widget's expected return if both GDP growth and inflation are zero. Finally, in a given year the distance from Widget's actual point to the plane indicates its unique return (e_{it}), the portion of Widget's return not attributed to either GDP growth or inflation. For example, given that GDP grew by 2.9% and inflation was 3.1%, Widget's expected return in year 6 equals (5.8% + (2.2 × 2.9%) – (.7 × 3.1%) =)10%. Hence its unique return for that year is equal to +3% (13% – 10%).

Four parameters need to be estimated for each security with the two-factor model: a_i, b_{i1}, b_{i2}, and the standard deviation of the random error term denoted σ_{ei}. For each of the factors, two parameters need to be estimated. These parameters are the expected value of each factor ($\overline{F}_1$ and $\overline{F}_2$) and the variance of each factor (σ^2_{F1} and σ^2_{F2}). Finally, the covariance between the factors [COV(F_1, F_2)] needs to be estimated.

Expected Return

With these estimates, the expected return for any security i can be determined by using the following formula:

$$\overline{r}_i = a_i + b_{i1}\overline{F}_1 + b_{i2}\overline{F}_2. \tag{11.8}$$

For example, the expected return for Widget equals 8.9% (5.8% + (2.2 × 3%) – (.7 × 5%)) provided that the expected increases in GDP and inflation are 3% and 5%, respectively.

Variance

According to the two-factor model, the variance for any security i is

$$\sigma^2_i = b^2_{i1}\sigma^2_{F1} + b^2_{i2}\sigma^2_{F2} + 2b_{i1}b_{i2}\text{COV}(F_1, F_2) + \sigma^2_{ei}. \tag{11.9}$$

If, in the example, the variances of the first (σ^2_{F1}) and second (σ^2_{F2}) factors are equal to 3 and 2.9, respectively, and their covariance COV(F_1, F_2) equals .65, then the variance of Widget equals (2.2^2 × 3) + ($-.7^2$ × 2.9) + (2 × 2.2 × –.7 × .65) + 18.2 = 32.1, since its two sensitivities and random error term variance are 2.2, –.7, and 18.2, respectively.

Covariance

Similarly, according to the two-factor model the covariance between any two securities i and j can be determined by

$$\sigma_{ij} = b_{i1}b_{j1}\sigma^2_{F1} + b_{i2}b_{j2}\sigma^2_{F2} + (b_{i1}b_{j2} + b_{i2}b_{j1})\text{COV}(F_1, F_2). \tag{11.10}$$

Thus, continuing with the example, the covariance between Widget and Whatever is estimated to equal (2.2 × 6 × 3) + (–.7 × –5 × 2.9) + [(2.2 × –5) + (–.7 × 6)] × .65 = 39.9 because the sensitivities of Whatever to the two factors are 6 and –5, respectively.

The Tangency Portfolio

As with the one-factor model, once the expected returns, variances, and covariances have been determined using these equations, the investor can proceed to use an *optimizer* (a special kind of mathematical routine) to derive the curved efficient set of Markowitz. Then

---

[8] These values were arrived at by applying multiple regression (see Wonnacott and Wonnacott, *Introductory Statistics for Business and Economics*) to the data given in Table 11.1.

the tangency portfolio can be identified for a given risk-free rate, after which the investor can determine his or her optimal portfolio.

Diversification

Everything said earlier regarding one-factor models and the effects of diversification applies here as well.

1. Diversification leads to an averaging of factor risk.
2. Diversification can substantially reduce nonfactor risk.
3. For a *well-diversified portfolio*, nonfactor risk will be insignificant.

As with a one-factor model, the sensitivity of a portfolio to a particular factor in a multiple-factor model is a weighted average of the sensitivities of the securities where the weights are equal to the proportions invested in the securities. This can be seen by remembering that the return on a portfolio is a weighted average of the returns of its component securities:

$$r_{pt} = \sum_{i=1}^{N} X_i r_{it}. \tag{11.11}$$

Substituting the right-hand side of equation (11.7) for r_{it} on the right-hand side of equation (11.11) results in

$$\begin{aligned} r_{pt} &= \sum_{i=1}^{N} X_i(a_i + b_{i1}F_{1t} + b_{i2}F_{2t} + e_{it}) \\ &= \left[\sum_{i=1}^{N} X_i a_i\right] + \left[\sum_{i=1}^{N} X_i b_{i1} F_{1t}\right] + \left[\sum_{i=1}^{N} X_i b_{i2} F_{2t}\right] + \left[\sum_{i=1}^{N} X_i e_{it}\right] \\ &= a_p + b_{p1}F_{1t} + b_{p2}F_{2t} + e_{pt} \end{aligned} \tag{11.12}$$

where:

$$a_p = \sum_{i=1}^{N} X_i a_i$$

$$b_{p1} = \sum_{i=1}^{N} X_i b_{i1}$$

$$b_{p2} = \sum_{i=1}^{N} X_i b_{i2}$$

$$e_{pt} = \sum_{i=1}^{N} X_i e_{it}.$$

Note that the portfolio sensitivities b_{pl} and b_{p2} are weighted averages of the respective individual sensitivities b_{i1} and b_{i2}.

► Sector-Factor Models

The prices of securities in the same industry or economic sector often move together in response to changes in prospects for that sector. Some investors acknowledge this by using a special kind of multiple-factor model referred to as a **sector-factor model**. To create a sector-factor model, each security under consideration must be assigned to a sector. For a two-sector-factor model, there are two sectors and each security must be assigned to one of them.

For example, let sector-factor 1 consist of all industrial companies and sector-factor 2 consist of all non-industrial companies (such as utility, transportation and financial companies). Thus, F_1 and F_2 can be thought of as representing the returns on an industrial stock index and a non-industrial stock index, respectively. (They could, for example, be components of the TSE 300.) Keep in mind, however, that both the number of sectors and what each sector consists of is an open matter that is left to the investor to decide.[9]

With this two-sector-factor model, the return-generating process for securities is of the same general form as the two-factor model given in equation (11.7). However, with the two-sector-factor model, F_1 and F_2 now denote sector-factors 1 and 2, respectively. Furthermore, any particular security belongs to either sector-factor 1 and sector-factor 2 but not both. By definition, a value of zero is given to the sensitivity term corresponding to the sector-factor to which the security is not assigned. This means that either b_{i1} or b_{i2} is set equal to zero, depending on the sector-factor to which security i is not assigned. The value of the other sensitivity term must be estimated. (To make matters simple, some people simply give it a value of one.)

As an illustration, consider Alcan (AL) and Air Canada (AC). The two-sector-factor model for AL (the time subscript t has been deleted for ease of exposition here) would be

$$r_{AL} = a_{AL} + b_{AL1}F_1 + b_{AL2}F_2 + e_{AL} \qquad (11.13)$$

However, because AL belongs to sector-factor 1 as an industrial security, the coefficient b_{AL2} is assigned a value of zero. Once this assignment is made, equation (11.13) reduces to

$$r_{AL} = a_{AL} + b_{AL1}F_1 + e_{AL} \qquad (11.14)$$

Thus only the values of a_{AL}, b_{AL1}, and σ_{eAL} need to be estimated for AL with the two-sector-factor model. In comparison with the two-factor model, values of a_{AL}, b_{AL2}, and σ_{eAL} need to be estimated.

Similarly, as AC belongs to the non-industrial sector, it would have the following two-sector-factor model:

$$r_{AC} = a_{AC} + b_{AC1}F_1 + b_{AC2}F_2 + e_{AC} \qquad (11.15)$$

which would reduce to

$$r_{AC} = a_{AC} + b_{AC2}F_2 + e_{AC} \qquad (11.16)$$

as b_{AC1} would be assigned a value of zero. Thus only the values of a_{AC1}, b_{AC2}, and σ_{eAC} need to be estimated with the two-sector-factor model.

In general, whereas four parameters need to be estimated for each security with a two-factor model (a_i, b_{i1}, b_{i2}, and σ_{ei}), only three parameters need to be estimated with a two-sector-factor model (a_i, σ_{ei}, and either b_{i1} or b_{i2}). With these estimates in hand, along with estimates of F_1, F_2, σ_{F1}, and σ_{F2}, the investor can use equations (11.8) and (11.9) to estimate expected returns and variances for each security. Pairwise covariances can be estimated using

---

[9] Attempts have been made to identify stock groups, or clusters, where stocks within any group have returns that are more highly correlated with one another than the returns of stocks from different groups. See, for example, Benjamin F. King, "Market and Industry Factors in Stock Price Behavior," *Journal of Business* 39, no. 1 (January 1966): 139–170; James L. Farrell, Jr., "Analyzing Covariation of Returns to Determine Stock Groupings," *Journal of Business* 47, no. 2 (April 1974): 186–207; "Homogeneous Stock Groupings: Implications for Portfolio Management," *Financial Analysts Journal* 31, no. 3 (May/June 1975): 50–62; and Robert D. Arnott, "Cluster Analysis and Stock Price Co-movement," *Financial Analysts Journal* 36, no. 6 (November/December 1980): 56–62.

equation (11.10). This will then enable the investor to derive the curved efficient set of Markowitz from which the tangency portfolio can be determined for a given risk-free rate.

Extending the Model

Once the discussion is extended to more than two factors, diagrams are no longer useful, as the analysis moves beyond three dimensions. Nevertheless, the concepts are the same. If there are k factors, the multiple-factor model can be written as

$$r_{it} = a_i + b_{i1}F_{1t} + b_{i2}F_{2t} + \ldots + b_{ik}F_{kt} + e_{it} \tag{11.17}$$

where each security has k sensitivities, one for each of the k factors.

It is possible to have both factors and sector factors represented in equation (11.17). For example, F_1 and F_2 could represent GDP and inflation as in Table 11.1, whereas F_3 and F_4 could represent the returns on industrial stocks and non-industrial stocks, respectively. Hence, each stock would have three sensitivities: b_{i1}, b_{i2}, and b_{i3} for industrials and b_{i1}, b_{i2}, and b_{i4} for non-industrials.[10]

ESTIMATING FACTOR MODELS

Methods of estimating factor models can be grouped into three primary approaches:

1. Time-series approaches
2. Cross-sectional approaches
3. Factor-analytic approaches

Time-Series Approaches

Time-series approaches are perhaps the most intuitive.[11] The model builder begins with the assumption that he or she knows in advance the factors that influence security returns. Identification of the relevant factors typically proceeds from an economic analysis of the firms involved. Aspects of macroeconomics, microeconomics, industrial organization, and fundamental security analysis will play a major role in the process.

For example, as discussed earlier, certain macroeconomic variables might be expected to have a pervasive impact on security returns, including such things as predicted growth in GDP, inflation, interest rates, and oil prices. With these factors specified, the model builder collects information concerning the values of the factors and security returns from period to period. Using these data, the model builder can calculate the sensitivities of the securities' returns to the factors, the securities' zero factors and unique returns, and the standard deviations of the factors and their correlations. In this approach, accurate measurement of factor values is crucial. In practice, this can be quite difficult.

---

[10] Another example of such a model expands the market model to include sector factors where the sectors are selected to represent "industries." Hence each stock has two sensitivities that indicate how the stock responds to returns on the stock index and an industry index to which the stock belongs. See Gordon J. Alexander and Jack Clark Francis, *Portfolio Analysis* (Englewood Cliffs, NJ: Prentice Hall): 83–92.

[11] The examples given earlier in the chapter are examples of this approach.

INSTITUTIONAL ISSUES

The Barra US and Canadian Equity Multiple-Factor Models

For the quantitatively inclined investment professional, multiple-factor models are intuitively appealing tools. They capture the essence of the fundamental economic and financial forces that affect security returns in a concise and readily testable form. However, moving from abstract discussions to the development of factor models that are sufficiently comprehensive and robust to serve the varied needs of institutional investors is a difficult task. An overview of the BARRA US equity multiple-factor model offers insights into the complex elements of factor model implementation.

The BARRA model is based on the pioneering work of Barr Rosenberg, and econometrician and former finance professor. In the early 1970s, while at the University of California at Berkeley, he and Vinay Marathe formulated a sophisticated factor model. The model related common stock returns to a variety of factors derived primarily from the underlying companies' business operations.

Rosenberg is more than your typical ivory tower academic. Instead of being content to publish his results and receive the accolades of his colleagues, he recognized the commercial applications of his model. He formed a firm, now called BARRA, to enhance and sell the model to institutional investors.

Both the model and the firm proved successful beyond anyone's imagination. BARRA has grown into a worldwide consulting organization with annual revenues exceeding $40 million. Its stock is publicly traded and today has a market capitalization of over $50 million. Although Rosenberg left the firm in 1985 to pursue his own investment management ambitions, BARRA has continued to leverage off of its factor-model expertise by designing additional factor models for the global equity market and various foreign stock markets. The firm has also built factor models for the US and several foreign bond markets.

Rosenberg's original US equity multiple-factor model underwent a major revision in 1982 and is referred to by factor-model aficionados as the *E2 model.* Currently, 630 institutional investors (over 50% of them outside of the United States) subscribe to the E2 model service. These investors range from large investment managers to pension funds, and in total they manage over one trillion dollars of US common stocks.

All factor models are based on the assumption that securities with similar exposures to specific factors will exhibit similar investment behaviour. The factor model builder must translate this basic concept into practice. The process of constructing factor models is far from an exact science. While certain statistical tests can be applied to gauge the explanatory power of a particular factor model, the model builder retains wide latitude to include or exclude potential factors.

It is instructive, therefore, to review how BARRA developed the E2 model. The process by which the model was specified is summarized by five steps.

1. Data collection and checking
2. Factor selection
3. Creation of composite factors
4. Estimation of factor returns and the factor variance-covariance matrix
5. Model testing

The E2 model's construction began with the collection of relevant security data. BARRA gathered monthly components of security returns, such as prices, dividends, and shares outstanding, for the largest 1400 common stocks (the "HICAP estimation universe") over an extended period of time. BARRA also acquired a wide array of income and balance sheet information on the underlying companies. This financial data came largely from the annual and quarterly financial statements issued by the companies.

INSTITUTIONAL ISSUES (continued)

As part of this collection process, BARRA checked the data for quality. Although this task may seem mundane, it was a critical step, as a small amount of bad data can produce a disproportionately large impact on a factor model's accuracy.

The second step involved factor selection. Literally hundreds of potential factors were available for inclusion in the model. BARRA sought to identify those factors that had a pervasive influence on the returns and risks of individual securities. Using historical security return data, BARRA isolated 70 market-related, income statement, and balance sheet factors that demonstrated statistically significant relationships with security prices.

The particular factors selected by BARRA ranged from the obvious to the novel. Examples included a company's historical equity beta, its consensus forecasted earnings growth, its historical variability in earnings, its debt to total assets, the number of security analysts covering a company's stock, and the proportion of a company's operating income derived from foreign sources.

The third step in the E2 model's construction entailed creating a set of composite factors from the 70 individual factors. BARRA employed 13 composite factors: Variability in Markets; Success; Size; Trading Activity; Growth; Earnings/Price; Book/Price; Earnings Variation; Financial Leverage; Foreign Income; Labour Intensity; Yield; and Low Capitalization. The individual factors were assigned to and weighted within the composite factors based on both judgment and statistical analyses.

The purpose of creating these composite factors was largely statistical convenience. As the text describes, a factor model builder must estimate the variance of each factor and the covariances among all the factors. The number of variances and covariances grows exponentially as the number of factors increases. Therefore, instead of having to calculate variances and covariances for dozens of factors, BARRA's task was considerably reduced by combining the individual factors into a handful of composite factors.

To these 13 composite factors, BARRA added 55 industry factors. (In the E2 model, a security can be assigned to as many as six industries, with total weights summing to 1, based on analysis of the company's sales, earnings, and assets.) Thus, in its final form, the BARRA E2 factor model contains 68 fundamental and industry factors.

The fourth step involved estimating factor returns for each of the 68 factors and developing forecasts of nonfactor risk. Given return data on the model's estimation universe, for every month in its test period BARRA effectively estimated the returns on 68 portfolios that each had unit exposure to one particular factor and zero exposure to all other 67 factors. The returns to these unit-exposure portfolios represented the monthly returns to the respective factors. At this point, a forecasting model of nonfactor risk was developed, allowing BARRA to calculate the variance-covariance matrix for the 68 factors.

The last step involved testing the performance of the E2 model. BARRA was concerned with how effective its forecasts of security risk were outside of the test period. Cutting through the statistical jargon, BARRA found that the model performed well.

The BARRA E2 model is applied by institutional investors in a variety of situations. Investment managers use the model to forecast the variability of their portfolio's returns, both in an absolute sense and relative to a benchmark. The model allows the managers to dissect this forecasted risk into factor and nonfactor components. Managers can make informed judgments about the expected rewards offered by their particular portfolio strategies relative to the forecasted risks.

Managers and their clients also use the E2 model for performance attribution (see Chapter 25). Here, an analyst uses the model to calculate a portfolio's historical exposure

INSTITUTIONAL ISSUES (continued)

to the various factors. Then, using BARRA's calculated factor returns, the contribution of each of those exposures to the portfolio's total return is computed. Finally, comparing the portfolio's exposures and the contributions of those exposures to the portfolio's performance against a relevant benchmark provides clues to the success or failure of the manager's strategies.

Institutional investors also use the E2 model to characterize the investment styles of their managers. Similar investment styles tend to exhibit similar E2 factor exposures. For example, large capitalization growth managers typically have large Size and Growth exposures and low Book/Price exposures. By analyzing a series of past returns for various portfolios with the E2 model, a client can more accurately identify the investment styles of its current and potential managers. This process aids in both performance evaluation and manager structuring (see Chapters 24 and 25).

The BARRA US equity multiple-factor model has contributed to the rigour and sophistication with which institutional investors approach the task of managing large pools of US common stocks. Perhaps the most impressive testament to the model's utility and robustness is that in the highly competitive and fickle world of investments, no alternative factor model has gained the widespread acceptance that the E2 model has achieved.

BARRA has also developed the *Canadian Equity Risk Model*, an analogue of the US E2 Multiple Factor Risk Model. The Canadian model uses 11 composite risk indices: Variability in Markets, Momentum, Size, Liquidity, Profitability, Growth, Value, Yield, US Sensitivity, and a non-TSE indicator. The last of these captures the behaviour of smaller firms that are not in the model's estimation universe. The composite indices, in turn, consist of linear combinations of anywhere from two to five fundamental factors. All told, 29 fundamental factors are required to develop the model.

It is interesting to note that not all the risk indices correspond to those used in the E2 model, although the index named "US Sensitivity" presumably includes many of the US factors not included in the Canadian model. In addition, BARRA adds 19 industry factors that are composites constructed from the 40 TSE industry classes, for a total of 30 variables. The model is then applied in the same way as the US model. Tests of an earlier version of this model showed that it explained equity returns better than either a single-factor CAPM or an industry sectoral model.

The Importance of Expectations

Security prices reflect investors' estimates of the present values of firms' future prospects. At any given time the price of Widget stock is likely to depend on the projected growth rate of GDP, the projected rate of inflation, and other factors. If investors' projections of such fundamental economic conditions change, so to will the price of Widget. Because the return on a stock is influenced heavily by changes in its price, stock returns are expected to be more highly correlated with changes in expected future values of fundamental economic variables than with the actual changes that occur contemporaneously.

For example, a large increase in inflation that was fully anticipated might have no effect on the stock price of a company whose earnings are highly sensitive to inflation. However, if the consensus expectation was for a low inflation rate, then the subsequent large increase would have a large effect on the company's stock price.

For this reason, whenever possible it is desirable to select factors that measure changes in expectations rather than realizations, as the latter typically include both changes that were anticipated and those that were not. One way to accomplish this goal is to rely on variables that involve changes in market prices. Thus, the difference in the returns on two portfolios—one consisting of stocks thought to be unaffected by inflation and the other consisting of stocks thought to be affected by inflation—can be used as a factor that measures revisions in inflation expectations. Those who construct factor models using the time-series approach often rely on market-based surrogates for changes in forecasts of fundamental economic variables in this manner.

An Example

Table 11.1 and Figure 11.2 presented an example of how to use the time-series approach to estimate a factor model. In this example, returns on individual stocks such as Widget were related to two factors—gross domestic product and inflation—by comparing over time each stock's returns to the predicted values of the factors.

Recently, Fama and French conducted a study that used a time-series approach to identify the factors that explain stock and bond returns.[12] In their study, monthly stock returns were found to be related to three factors: a market factor, a size factor, and a book-to-market equity factor. In equation form, their factor model for stocks appears as

$$r_{it} - r_{ft} = a_i + b_{i1}(r_{Mt} - r_{ft}) + b_{i2}\text{SMB}_t + b_{i3}\text{HML}_t + e_{it} \tag{11.18}$$

The first factor $(r_{Mt} - r_{ft})$ is simply the monthly return on a broad stock market over and above the return on one-month Treasury bills on a broad stock index. The size factor (SMB_t) can be thought of as the difference in the monthly return on two stock indices—a small-stock index and a big-stock index. (Here a stock's size is measured by its share price at the end of June each year times the number of shares it has outstanding at that time. The small-stock index consists of stocks that are below the median NYSE size and the big-stock index consists of stocks that are above the median.) The book-to-market equity factor (HML_t) is also the difference in the monthly return on two stock indices—an index of stocks with high book-to-market equity ratios and an index of stocks with low book-to-market equity ratios. (Here book equity is shareholders' equity taken from the firm's balance sheet and market equity is the same as the stock's size used in determining the previous factor. The high ratio index consists of stocks that are in the top third, and the low ratio index consists of stocks that are in the bottom third.)

Fama and French also identified two factors that seem to explain monthly bond returns. In equation form, their factor model for bonds appears as

$$r_{it} - r_{ft} = a_i + b_{i1}\text{TERM}_t + b_{i2}\text{DEF}_t + e_{it} \tag{11.19}$$

These two factors are a term-structure factor and a default factor.[13] The term-structure factor (TERM_t) is simply the difference in the monthly returns on long-term Treasury bonds and

[12] Eugene F. Fama and Kenneth R. French, "Common Risk Factors in the Returns on Stocks and Bonds," *Journal of Financial Economics* 33, no. 1 (February 1993): 3–56. Other time series examples are presented in Chapter 12.

[13] Speculative-grade bonds were also found to be related to the three stock factors.

one-month Treasury bills. The default factor (DEF_t) is the difference in the monthly returns on a portfolio of long-term corporate bonds and long-term Treasury bonds.[14]

Cross-Sectional Approaches

Cross-sectional approaches are less intuitive than time-series approaches but can often be just as powerful a tool. The model builder begins with estimates of securities' sensitivities to certain factors. Then, in a particular time period, the values of the factors are estimated based on securities' returns and their sensitivities to the factors. This process is repeated over multiple time periods, thereby providing an estimate of the factors' standard deviations and their correlations.

Note that the cross-sectional approach is entirely different from the time-series approach. With the latter approach, the values of the factors are known and the sensitivities are estimated. Furthermore, the analysis is conducted for one security over multiple time periods, then another security, then another, and so on. With the former approach the sensitivities are known and the values of the factors are estimated. Accordingly, the sensitivities in the cross-sectional approach are sometimes referred to as **attributes**. Furthermore, the analysis is conducted over one time period for a group of securities, then another time period for the same group, then another, and so on. Examples of one-factor and two-factor models will be shown next to illustrate the cross-sectional approach.[15]

One-Factor Models

Figure 11.3 provides a hypothetical example of the relationship between the returns for a number of different stocks in a given time period and one security attribute—dividend yield—for each stock. Each point represents one particular stock, showing its return and dividend yield for the time period under evaluation. In this case, stocks with higher-dividend yields tended to do better—that is, have higher returns—than those with lower-dividend yields. Figure 11.3 (an example of the cross-sectional approach) is based on many stocks for one time period, whereas Figure 11.1 (an example of the time-series approach) is based on one stock for many time periods.

To quantify the relationship shown in Figure 11.3, a straight line has been fitted to the diagram by using the statistical technique of simple-regression analysis. The equation of the line in Figure 11.3 is

$$\overline{r}_{it} = 4 + .5b_{it} \tag{11.20}$$

or, more generally,

$$\overline{r}_{it} = a_t + b_{it}F_t \tag{11.21}$$

---

[14] Interestingly, Fama and French also found that the market factor ($r_{Mt} - r_{ft}$) was related to these two bond factors. In light of this, they constructed a revised market factor that basically consisted of the market factor less the influence of the two bond factors and the two other stock factors, and they found that stock returns were related to five factors: the revised market factor, SML_t, HML_t, $TERM_t$, and DEF_t. Bond returns continued to be related to just the two bond factors.

[15] Note that in the time-series approach, a security's sensitivity to a factor is its "attribute," and the factor is a given macroeconomic variable. Hence the attribute's value is unknown and must be estimated, whereas the value of the factor is known. In the cross-sectional approach, a security's attribute is usually some microeconomic variable measuring the security's exposure to the factor (a stock's dividend yield and market capitalization can be thought of as examples of attributes). Hence the attribute's value is known whereas the factor is unknown and must be estimated.

Figure 11.3

A cross-sectional one-factor model.

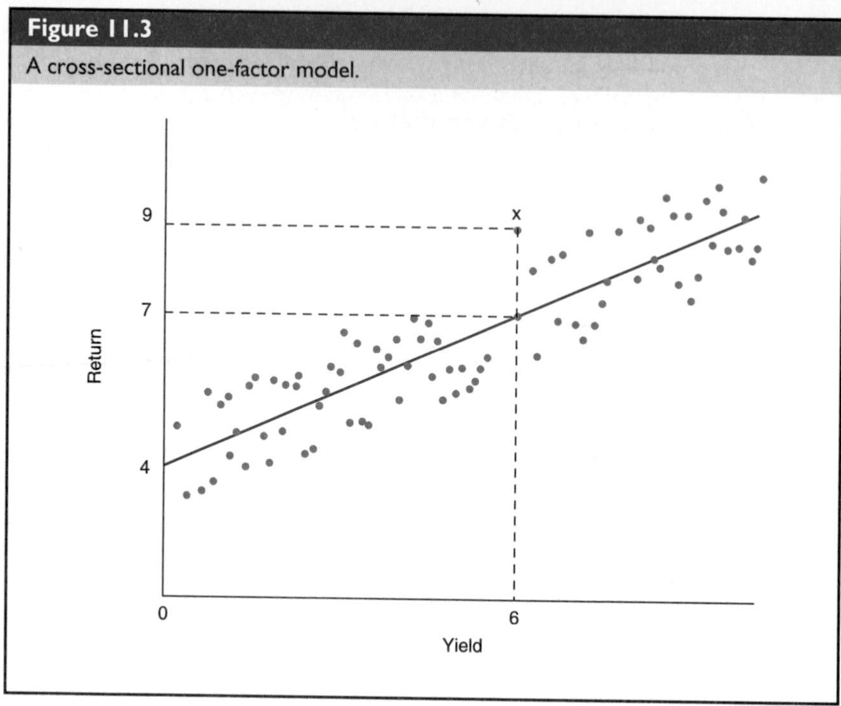

where:

$\bar{r}_{it}$ = the expected return on stock i in period t, given that the factor had an actual value of F_t,

a_t = the zero factor in period t,

b_{it} = the dividend yield of stock i in period t,

F_t = the actual value of the factor in period t.

The vertical intercept a_t indicates the expected return on a typical stock with a dividend yield of zero. Hence, it is called the zero factor, as in equation (11.1). In Figure 11.3 it is equal to 4%. The slope of .5 indicates the increase in expected return for each percent of dividend yield. Hence, it represents the actual value of the dividend yield factor (F_t) in this time period.

From this example it can be seen that the cross-sectional approach uses sensitivities to estimate the values of the factors. Hence, these factors are known as *empirical factors*. In comparison, it was shown earlier that the time-series approach uses known values of factors to provide estimates of a security's sensitivities. These factors are known as *fundamental factors*.

The actual return on any given security may lie above or below the line due to its nonfactor return. A complete description of the relationship for this one-factor model is

$$r_{it} = 4 + .5b_{it} + e_{it} \tag{11.22}$$

where e_{it} denotes the nonfactor return during period t on security i. In Figure 11.3, security x had a dividend yield of 6%. Hence, from equation (11.18), it had an expected return during this time period of 7% (4 + (.5 × 6)). Because it actually had a return of 9%, its nonfactor return was 9% – 7% = +2%.

In periods such as the one shown in Figure 11.3, high-yield stocks tended to outperform low-yield stocks. This indicates that the yield factor F_t was positive at this time. However, in another time period it is possible that low-yield stocks will tend to outperform high-yield stocks. The regression line in the corresponding diagram will be downward-sloping, and the yield factor will be negative. In still other time periods, there will be no relationship between yield and return, resulting in a flat regression line and a yield factor of zero.

A Two-Factor Example

In some time periods small stocks tend to outperform large stocks. In other months the converse is true. Hence, many cross-sectional models use a *size attribute* that is often computed by taking the logarithm of the total market value of the firm's outstanding equity measured in millions, which is, in turn, calculated by taking the firm's share price, multiplying it by the number of shares outstanding, and then dividing the resulting figure by one million.[16] Thus, a \$1-million stock would be assigned a size attribute value of zero; a \$10-million stock a size attribute value of one; a \$100-million stock a size attribute value of two, and so on. This convention is based on the empirical observation that the impact of the size factor on a security with a large total market value is likely to be twice as great as that on a security with one-tenth the value. More succinctly, the size effect appears to be *linear in the logarithms*.

To estimate the size factor in a given month, the procedure used in Figure 11.3 to estimate the yield factor can be employed. The size attributes of securities can be plotted on the horizontal axis and their returns for the given time period plotted (as in Figure 11.3) on the vertical axis. The slope of the resultant regression line provides an estimate of the size factor for the time period.

This procedure has drawbacks, however. Large stocks tend to have high yields. Thus, differences in returns between large and small stocks may be due to some extent to differences in yield, not size. The estimated size factor may be in part a reflection of a true yield factor. The problem is symmetrical in that the estimated yield factor may also be in part a reflection of the true size factor.

To mitigate this problem, returns can be compared with both size and yield attributes simultaneously by using the statistical technique of multiple regression. Figure 11.4 provides an illustration. Each security is represented by a point in a three-dimensional graph with return during the time period shown on the vertical axis, dividend yield for the time period shown on one of the bottom axes, and size for the period shown on the other.

Multiple-regression analysis is typically used to fit a plane to the data. In the example shown in Figure 11.4, this results in the following regression equation:

$$r_{it} = 7 + .4b_{i1t} - .3b_{i2t} + e_{it} \tag{11.23}$$

where b_{i1t} and b_{i2t} denote, respectively, the dividend yield and size of stock i in time period t. In general, the regression equation for a two-factor model is

$$r_{it} = a_t + b_{i1t}F_{1t} + b_{i2t}F_{2t} + e_{it} \tag{11.24}$$

where a_t denotes the zero factor in time period t and the two factors are denoted F_{1t} and F_{2t}.

---

[16] Size has also been used as a factor in the time-series approach but in a different manner. See the previous discussion of the Fama and French study that is mentioned in footnote 12.

Figure 11.4

A cross-sectional two-factor model.

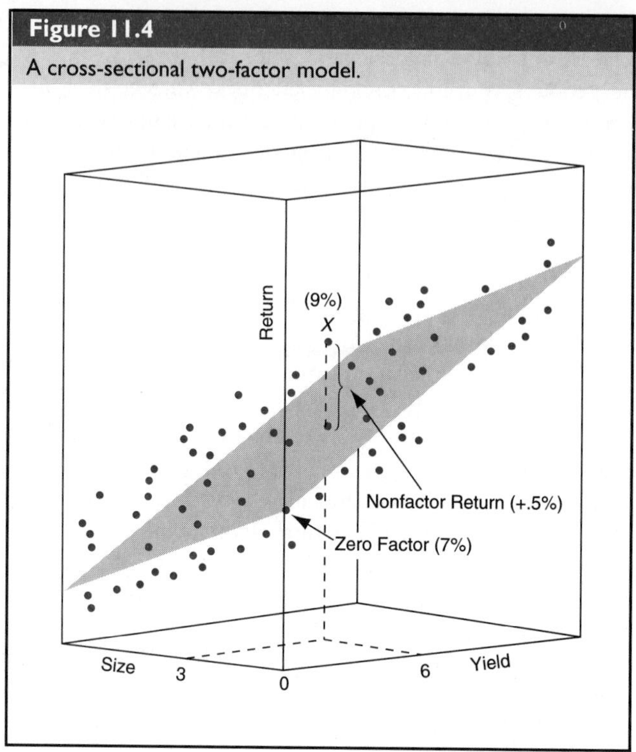

The equation of the plane shown in Figure 11.4 is

$$\bar{r}_{it} = 7 + .4b_{i1t} - .3b_{i2t} \tag{11.25}$$

or, more generally,

$$\bar{r}_{it} = a_t + b_{i1t}F_{1t} + b_{i2t}F_{2t} \tag{11.26}$$

This means that the zero factor a_t was 7%, indicating that a stock with zero-dividend yield and zero size (meaning a market value of $1 million) would have been expected to have a return of 7%. Note that the estimated values of the dividend yield-factor (F_{1t}) and size factor (F_{2t}) are .4 and –.3, respectively. Thus, during this time period, higher-dividend yields and smaller sizes were both associated with larger returns.

Using equations (11.23) and (11.25), a given security X with a dividend yield of 6% and a size of 3 would have been expected to have a return of $7 + (.4 \times 6) - (.3 \times 3) = 8.5\%$. With an actual return of 9%, its nonfactor return e_{it} is thus +.5% (9% – 8.5%) during this time period, as shown in Figure 11.4.

The inclusion of size and dividend yield along with the use of multiple-regression analysis can help sort out the effects of differences in yield and size on differences in security returns. It cannot deal adequately with influences that are not represented at all, nor can it guarantee that the included attributes are not simply serving as *proxies* for other, more fundamental attributes. Statistical tests can indicate the ability of the variables included in the analysis to explain or predict past security returns. But judgment and luck are required to identify variables that can help predict future security returns, risks, and covariances. The extension to more than two variables follows in a straightforward manner from what has been indicated in equations (11.23) through (11.26).

An Example

Sharpe conducted a study that used a cross-sectional approach to identify the factors that explain stock returns.[17] In his study, stock returns were related monthly to five security sensitivities (and eight sector-factors) that were measured for each stock. These sensitivities consisted of firm size (measured like Fama and French), the stock's historic beta when measured against a stock market index, the stock's dividend yield, the stock's historic beta when measured against a bond market index, and a measure of how much of the stock's historical return was due to mispricing.

Over the period 1931 to 1979, Sharpe collected monthly data for over 2000 common stocks. Among other results, his analysis produced a value of .237 (annualized) for the dividend yield factor. By implication, then, a stock with a 5% dividend yield outperformed a stock with a 4% dividend yield (but with similar exposures to all the other factors) by almost .24% per year.

► Factor-Analytic Approaches

Finally, with factor-analytic approaches the model builder knows neither the factor values nor the securities' sensitivities to those factors. A statistical technique called *factor analysis* is used to extract the number of factors and securities' sensitivities based simply on a set of securities' past returns. Factor analysis takes the returns over many time periods on a sample of securities and attempts to identify one or more statistically significant factors that could have generated the covariances of returns observed within the sample. In essence, the return data tell the model builder about the structure of the factor model. Unfortunately, factor analysis does not specify what economic variables the factors represent.

► Limitations

There is no reason to assume that a good factor model for one period will be a good one for the next period. Key factors change, as in the effect of energy prices on security markets in the 1970s and, more recently, during the war in the Persian Gulf. The risks and returns associated with various factors and the sensitivities of securities to factors can change over time.[18]

It would be convenient if neither the relevant factors nor their magnitudes were to change from period to period. If this were so, mechanical procedures could be applied to security returns over an extended past period and the factor model inferred along with all the needed magnitudes. As it is, statistical estimation methods should be tempered by the judgment of the model builder to account for the dynamic nature of the investment environment.

---

[17] William F. Sharpe, "Factors in New York Stock Exchange Security Returns, 1931–1979," *Journal of Portfolio Management* 8, no. 4 (Summer 1982): 5–19. An application is presented in Blake R. Grossman and William F. Sharpe, "Financial Implications of South African Divestment," *Financial Analysts Journal* 42, no. 4 (July- August 1986): 15–29.

[18] One study found that the factors that appear to explain security returns on even dates generally do not explain security returns on odd dates. See Dolores A. Conway and Marc R. Reinganum, "Stable Factors in Security Returns: Identification Using Cross Validation," *Journal of Business and Economics* 6, no. 1 (January 1988): 1–15.

It should be kept in mind that a factor model is not an equilibrium model of asset pricing. Compare, for example, the expected return on a stock using a one-factor model from equation (11.3) with that of the Capital Asset Pricing Model (CAPM) from equation (10.7):[19]

$$\overline{r}_i = a_i + b_i\overline{F} \tag{11.3}$$

$$\overline{r}_i = r_f + (\overline{r}_M - r_f)\beta_{iM} \tag{10.7}$$

Both equations show that the expected return on the stock is related to a characteristic of the stock, b_i or β_{iM}. Assuming that the expected return on the factor $\overline{F}$ and $\overline{r}_M - r_f$ is positive, the larger the size of the characteristic, the larger the security's expected return. Hence, at this point there appears to be little to differentiate these two equations of expected return.

The key is in the other term on the right-hand side of each equation: a_i and r_f. The only characteristic of the stock that determines its expected return according to the CAPM is β_{iM}, as r_f denotes the risk-free rate and is the same for all securities. However, with the factor model there is a second characteristic of the stock that needs to be estimated to determine the stock's expected return—namely, a_i. As the size of a_i differs from one stock to another, it prevents the factor model from being an equilibrium model.

Stated differently, two stocks with the same value of b_i can have dramatically different expected returns according to a factor model. For example, if GDP is expected to rise by 5%, then the expected return on Widget is 14% because a_i and b_i for Widget are 4 and 2 (14% = 4% + (2 × 5%)). In comparison, even though ABC has the same sensitivity to GDP as Widget (b_i = 2), it has an expected return of only 8% because its value of a_i is −2% + (2 × 5%) = −2%.

In contrast, two stocks with the same value of β_{iM} will have the same expected return according to the equilibrium-based CAPM. If Widget and XYZ both have a beta of 1.2, then they both will have an expected return of 14%, given that the risk-free rate is 8% and the expected return on the market is 13% (8% + 13% − 8%) × 1.2).

Having established that a factor model is not an equilibrium model, it seems appropriate to investigate the relationship between the parameters a_i and b_i of the one-factor model and the single parameter β_{iM} of the CAPM.

For example, if actual returns can be viewed as being generated by a one-factor model where the factor F is the return on the market portfolio r_M, then according to equation (11.3), expected returns will be equal to

$$\overline{r}_i = a_i + b_i\overline{r}_M \tag{11.27}$$

because $\overline{F} = \overline{r}_M$. But if equilibrium exists according to the CAPM, then equation (10.7) can be rewritten to state that expected returns will also be equal to

$$\overline{r}_i = (1 - \beta_{iM})r_f + \overline{r}_M\beta_{iM}. \tag{11.28}$$

This means that the parameters of the one-factor model and the CAPM must have the following relationships:

$$a_i = (1 - \beta_{iM})r_f \tag{11.29}$$

$$b_i = \beta_{iM}. \tag{11.30}$$

[19] Time subscripts have been removed for ease of exposition.

This means that if expected returns are determined according to the CAPM and actual returns are generated by the one-factor market model, then a_i and b_i must be equal to $(1 - \beta_{iM})r_f$ and β_{iM}, respectively.[20]

SUMMARY

1. A factor model is a return-generating process that relates returns on securities to the movement in one or more common factors.
2. Any aspect of a security's return unexplained by the factor model is assumed to be unique to the security and therefore uncorrelated with the unique element of returns on other securities.
3. The market model is a specific example of a factor model where the factor is the return on a market index.
4. The assumption that the returns on securities respond to common factors greatly simplifies the task of calculating the curved Markowitz efficient set.
5. The sensitivity of a portfolio to a factor is the weighted average of the sensitivities of the component securities, with the securities' proportions in the portfolio serving as weights.
6. The total risk of a security is composed of factor risk and nonfactor risk.
7. Diversification leads to an averaging of factor risk.
8. Diversification reduces nonfactor risk.
9. Three basic methods are used to estimate factor models: the time-series approach, the cross-sectional approach, and the factor-analytic approach.
10. A factor model is not an equilibrium model of asset prices as is the CAPM. However, if equilibrium exists, certain relationships will hold between the factor model and the equilibrium asset-pricing model.

QUESTIONS AND PROBLEMS

1. Included among the factors that might be expected to be pervasive are expectations regarding growth in real GNP, real interest rates, inflation, and oil prices. For each factor, provide an example of an industry that is expected to have a high (either positive or negative) sensitivity to the factor.
2. Why do factor models greatly simplify the process of deriving the curved Markowitz efficient set?
3. Many investment management firms assign each of their security analysts to research a particular group of stocks. (Usually these assignments are organized by industry.) How are these assignments an implicit recognition of the validity of factor-model relationships?
4. What are two critical assumptions underlying any factor model? Cite hypothetical examples of violations of those assumptions.
5. Mary Childs, a wise investment statistician, once said with respect to factor models, "Similar stocks should display similar returns." What did Mary mean by this statement?

---

[20] If the factor in a one-factor world is the return on the market portfolio (as shown here), then technically the random error term for any security cannot be completely uncorrelated with the factor. This is because the market portfolio consists of all securities and hence is influenced by the nonfactor return of each security. See Eugene F. Fama, *Foundations of Finance* (New York: Basic Books, 1979), Chapter 3.

6. Based on a one-factor model, consider a security with a zero-factor value of 4% and a sensitivity to the factor of .50. The factor takes on a value of 10%. The security generates a return of 11%. What portion is related to nonfactor elements?

7. Based on a one-factor model, consider a portfolio of two securities with the following characteristics:

Security	Factor Sensitivity	Nonfactor Risk (σ_{ei}^2)	Proportion
A	.20	49	.40
B	3.50	100	.60

 a. If the standard deviation of the factor is 15%, what is the factor risk of the portfolio?
 b. What is the nonfactor risk of the portfolio?
 c. What is the portfolio's standard deviation?

8. Recalculate the answers to Problem 7 assuming that the portfolio is also invested in the risk-free asset so that its investment proportions are:

Security	Proportion
Risk-free	.10
A	.36
B	.54

9. Based on a one-factor model, security A has a sensitivity of –.50, whereas security B has a sensitivity of 1.25. If the covariance between the two securities is –312.50, what is the standard deviation of the factor?

10. Based on a one-factor model, for two securities A and B:

$$r_A = 5\% + .8F + e_A$$

$$r_B = 7\% + 1.2F + e_B$$

$$\sigma_F = 18\%$$

$$\sigma_{eA} = 25\%$$

$$\sigma_{eB} = 15\%.$$

Calculate the standard deviation of each security.

11. Based on a one-factor model, if the average nonfactor risk (σ_{ei}^2) of all securities is 225, what is the nonfactor risk of a portfolio with equal weights assigned to its 10 securities? 100 securities? 1000 securities?

12. Based on the discussion of factor and nonfactor risk and given a set of securities that can be combined into various portfolios, what might be a useful measure of the relative diversification of each of the alternative portfolios?

13. With a five-factor model (assuming uncorrelated factors) and a 30-stock portfolio, how many parameters must be estimated to calculate the expected return and standard deviation of the portfolio? How many additional parameter estimates are required if the factors are correlated?

14. Beyond the factors discussed in the text, speculate as to other factors that could reasonably be expected to pervasively affect security returns.

15. Based on a three-factor model, consider a portfolio composed of three securities with the following characteristics:

Security	Factor 1 Sensitivity	Factor 2 Sensitivity	Factor 3 Sensitivity	Proportion
A	−.20	3.60	.05	.60
B	.50	10.00	.75	.20
C	1.50	2.20	.30	.20

What are the sensitivities of the portfolio to factors 1, 2, and 3?

16. Len Murray, a quantitative security analyst, remarked, "The structure of any factor model concerns surprise, in particular the nature of correlations between surprises in different securities' returns." What does Len mean by this statement?

17. Filippo Cesario owns a portfolio of two securities. Based on a two-factor model, the two securities have the following characteristics:

Security	Zero Factor	Factor 1 Sensitivity	Factor 2 Sensitivity	Nonfactor Risk (σ_{ei}^2)	Proportion
A	2%	.30	2.0	196	.70
B	3	.50	1.8	100	.30

The factors are uncorrelated. Factor 1 has an expected value of 15% and a standard deviation of 20%. Factor 2 has an expected value of 4% and a standard deviation of 5%. Calculate the expected return and standard deviation of Filippo's portfolio. [Hint: Think about how equation (11.6a) could be extended to a two-factor model by considering equation (11.9).]

18. Compare the three approaches to estimating factor models.

19. Consider a factor model with earnings yield (or earnings/price ratio) and book-price (or book value/market price ratio) as the two factors. Stock A has an earnings yield of 10% and a book-price of 2. Stock B's earnings yield is 15% and its book-price is .90. The zero factors of stocks A and B are 7% and 9%, respectively. If the expected returns of stocks A and B are 18% and 16.5%, respectively, what are the expected earnings-yield and book-price factor values?

20. Based on a two-factor model, consider two securities with the following characteristics:

Characteristic	Security A	Security B
Factor 1 sensitivity	1.5	.7
Factor 2 sensitivity	2.6	1.2
Nonfactor risk (σ_{ei}^2)	25.0	16.0

The standard deviations of factor 1 and factor 2 are 20% and 15%, respectively, and the factors have a covariance of 225. What are the standard deviations of securities A and B? What is their covariance?

21. Are the factor models consistent with the CAPM? If returns are determined by a one-factor model (where that factor is the return on the market portfolio) and the CAPM holds, what relationships must exist between the two models?

Key Terms

return-generating process
factor models
sensitivity
factor loading (attribute)
factor risk
nonfactor risk
sector-factor model
attributes

References

1. General discussions of factor models can be found in:

William F. Sharpe, "Factors in New York Stock Exchange Security Returns, 1931- 1979," *Journal of Portfolio Management* 8, no. 4 (Summer 1982): 5-19; and "Factor Models, CAPMs, and the ABT [sic]," *Journal of Portfolio Management* 11, no. 1 (Fall 1984): 21–25.

Mark Kritzman, "...About Factor Models," *Financial Analysts Journal* 49, no. 1 (January/February 1993): 12–15.

2. Empirical papers that attempt to identify relevant factors and estimate the magnitudes of the associated values include:

Benjamin F. King, "Market and Industry Factors in Stock Price Behavior," *Journal of Business* 39, no. 1 (January 1966): 139–170.

George J. Feeney and Donald D. Hester, "Stock Market Indices: A Principal Components Analysis," in Donald D. Hester and James Tobin, eds., *Risk Aversion and Portfolio Choice* (New York: John Wiley, 1967).

Edwin J. Elton and Martin J. Gruber, "Estimating the Dependence Structure of Share Prices — Implications for Portfolio Selection," *Journal of Finance* 28, no. 5 (December 1973): 1203–1232.

James J. Farrell, Jr., "Analyzing Covariation of Returns to Determine Homogeneous Stock Groupings," *Journal of Business* 47, no. 2 (April 1974): 186–207.

Barr Rosenberg and Vinay Marathe, "The Prediction of Investment Risk: Systematic and Residual Risk," in *Proceedings of the Seminar on the Analysis of Security Prices* (Center for Research in Security Prices, Graduate School of Business, University of Chicago, November 1975).

Robert D. Arnott, "Cluster Analysis and Stock Price Movement," *Financial Analysts Journal* 36, no. 6 (November/December 1980): 56–62.

Tony Estep, Nick Hanson, and Carl Johnson, "Sources of Value and Risk in Common Stocks," *Journal of Portfolio Management* 9, no. 4 (Summer 1983): 5–13.

Nai-Fu Chen, Richard Roll, and Stephen A. Ross, "Economic Forces and the Stock Market," *Journal of Business* 59, no. 3 (July 1986): 383–403.

Robert D. Arnott, Charles M. Kelso, Jr., Stephen Kiscadden, and Rosemary Macedo, "Forecasting Factor Returns: An Intriguing Possibility," *Journal of Portfolio Management* 16, no. 1 (Fall 1989): 28–35.

Eugene F. Fama and Kenneth R. French, "Common Risk Factors in the Returns on Stocks and Bonds," *Journal of Financial Economics* 33, no. 1 (February 1993): 3–56.

3. Fixed-income factor models are discussed in:

Ronald N. Kahn and Deepak Gulrajani, "Risk and Return in the Canadian Bond Market," *Journal of Portfolio Management* 19, no. 3 (Spring 1993): 86–92.

4. For a Canadian perspective on the topics discussed in this chapter, see:

L. Kryzanowski and M.C. To, "General Factor Models and the Structure of Security Returns," *Journal of Financial and Quantitative Analysis* 18, no. 1 (March 1983).

Peter Muller, "Building a Canadian Equities Risk Model," *Canadian Investment Review* II, no. 1 (Spring 1989).

M.J. Robinson, "An Empirical Examination of the Market Model," in M.J. Robinson and B.F. Smith, eds., *Canadian Capital Markets* (London, Ont.: Western Business School, 1993).

B.F. Smith, "An Analysis of the Usefulness of Multi-Index Models in Explaining Canadian Equity Returns," in M.J. Robinson and B.F. Smith, eds., *Canadian Capital Markets* (London, Ont.: Western Business School, 1993).

CHAPTER 12

Arbitrage Pricing Theory

The Capital Asset Pricing Model (CAPM) is an equilibrium model that describes why different securities have different expected returns. In particular, this positive economic model of asset pricing asserts that securities have different expected returns because they have different betas. However, there exists an alternative model of asset pricing that was developed by Stephen Ross. It is known as **Arbitrage Pricing Theory** (APT), and in some ways it is less complicated than the CAPM.

The CAPM requires a large number of assumptions, including those initially made by Harry Markowitz when he developed the basic mean-variance model. For example, each investor is assumed to choose his or her optimal portfolio by the use of indifference curves based on portfolio expected returns and standard deviations. In contrast, APT makes fewer assumptions. One primary APT assumption is that each investor, when given the opportunity to increase the return of his or her portfolio without increasing its risk, will do so. The mechanism for doing so involves the use of arbitrage portfolios.

FACTOR MODELS

APT starts out by making the assumption that security returns are related to an unknown number of unknown factors.[1] For ease of exposition, imagine that there is only one factor and that factor is the predicted rate of increase in industrial production. In this situation, security returns are related to the following one-factor model:

$$r_i = a_i + b_i F_1 + e_i \tag{12.1}$$

where:

r_i = rate of return on security i,

F_1 = the value of the factor, which in this case is the predicted rate of growth in industrial production,

e_i = random error term.

In this equation, b_i is known as the **sensitivity** of security i to the factor. (It is also known as the factor loading for security i or the attribute of security i.)[2]

---

[1] Factor models are discussed in detail in Chapter 11.

[2] There are other ways to write the equation for a factor model. Note that from equation (12.1) it follows that $\bar{r}_i = a_i + b_i\overline{F}$, where $\bar{r}_i$ and $\overline{F_1}$ are the expected return for security i and the expected value of the factor, respectively. Substituting $\bar{r}_i - b_i\overline{F_1}$ for a_i in equation (12.1) results in the following alternative formulation of a one-factor model: $r_i = \bar{r}_i + b_i(F_1 - \overline{F_1}) + e_i$. Letting $f_1 = F_1 - \overline{F_1}$, a third formulation of a one-factor model is: $r_i = \bar{r}_i + b_i f_1 + e_i$ where f_1 can be interpreted as the unexpected change in the value of the factor.

Imagine that an investor owns three stocks and the current market value of his or her holdings in each one is \$4 000 000. In this case, the investor's current investable wealth (W_0) is equal to \$12 000 000. Everyone believes that these three stocks have the following expected returns and sensitivities:

i	$\bar{r}_i$	b_i
Stock 1	15%	.9
Stock 2	21	3.0
Stock 3	12	1.8

Do these expected returns and factor sensitivities represent an equilibrium situation? If not, what will happen to stock prices and expected returns to restore equilibrium? The answers to these questions will be addressed in the next sections.

Principle of Arbitrage

In recent years, baseball card conventions have become commonplace events. Collectors gather to exchange baseball cards with one another at negotiated prices. Suppose that Ms. A attends such a gathering where in one corner she finds S offering to sell a 1951 Mickey Mantle rookie card for \$400. Exploring the convention further, she finds B bidding \$500 for the same card. Recognizing a financial opportunity, Ms. A agrees to sell the card to B, who gives her \$500 in cash. She races back to give \$400 to S, receives the card, and returns with it to B, who takes possession of the card. Ms. A pockets the \$100 in profit from the two transactions and moves on in search of other opportunities. Ms. A has engaged in a form of arbitrage.

Arbitrage is the earning of riskless profit by taking advantage of differential pricing for the same physical asset or security. As a widely applied investment tactic, arbitrage typically entails the sale of a security at a relatively high price and the simultaneous purchase of the same security (or its functional equivalent) at a relatively low price.

Arbitrage activity is a critical element of modern, efficient security markets. Because arbitrage profits are by definition riskless, all investors have an incentive to take advantage of them whenever they are discovered. Granted, some investors have greater resources and inclination to engage in arbitrage than others. However, it takes relatively few of these active investors to exploit arbitrage situations and, by their buying and selling actions, eliminate these profit opportunities.

The nature of arbitrage is clear when discussing different prices for an individual security. However, "almost arbitrage" opportunities can involve "similar" securities or portfolios. That similarity can be defined in many ways. One interesting way is the exposure to pervasive factors that affect security prices.

A factor model implies that securities or portfolios with equal-factor sensitivities will behave in the same way except for nonfactor risk. Therefore, securities or portfolios with the same factor sensitivities should offer the same expected returns. If not, then "almost arbitrage" opportunities exist. Investors will take advantage of these opportunities, causing their elimination. That is the essential logic underlying APT.

► Arbitrage Portfolios

According to APT, an investor will explore the possibility of forming an **arbitrage portfolio** substantially to increase the expected return of his or her current portfolio without increasing its risk. Just what is an arbitrage portfolio? First of all, it is a portfolio that does not require any additional funds from the investor. If X_i denotes the *change* in the investor's holdings of security i (and hence the weight of security i in the arbitrage portfolio), this requirement of an arbitrage portfolio can be written as

$$X_1 + X_2 + X_3 = 0. \tag{12.2}$$

Second, an arbitrage portfolio has no sensitivity to any factor. Because the sensitivity of a portfolio to a factor is just a weighted average of the sensitivities of the securities in the portfolio to that factor, this requirement of an arbitrage portfolio can be written as

$$b_1X_1 + b_2X_2 + b_3X_3 = 0 \tag{12.3a}$$

or, in the current example,

$$.9X_1 + 3.0X_2 + 1.8X_3 = 0. \tag{12.3b}$$

Thus, in this example, an arbitrage portfolio will have no sensitivity to industrial production.

Strictly speaking, an arbitrage portfolio should also have zero nonfactor risk. However, the APT assumes that such risk is small enough to be ignored. In its terminology, an arbitrage portfolio has "zero factor exposures."

At this point, many potential arbitrage portfolios can be identified. These candidates are simply portfolios that meet the conditions given in equations (12.2) and (12.3b). Note that there are three unknowns (X_1, X_2, and X_3) and two equations in this situation, which means that there is an infinite number of combinations of values for X_1, X_2, and X_3 that satisfy these two equations.[3] As a way of finding one combination, consider arbitrarily assigning a value of .1 to X_1. Doing so results in two equations and two unknowns:

$$.1 + X_2 + X_3 = 0 \tag{12.4a}$$

$$.09 + 3.0X_2 + 1.8X_3 = 0. \tag{12.4b}$$

The solution to equations (12.4a) and (12.4b) is $X_2 = .075$ and $X_3 = -.175$. Hence, a potential arbitrage portfolio is one with these weights.

In order to see if this candidate is indeed an arbitrage portfolio, its expected return must be determined. If it is positive, then an arbitrage portfolio will have been identified.[4] Mathematically, this third and last requirement for an arbitrage portfolio is

$$X_1\bar{r}_1 + X_2\bar{r}_2 + X_3\bar{r}_3 > 0 \tag{12.5a}$$

[3] There will always be an infinite number of solutions whenever there are more unknowns than equations. For example, consider a situation where there is one equation with two unknowns: $Y = 3X$. Note that there is an infinite number of paired values of X and Y that solve this equation, such as (1, 3), (2, 6), and (3, 9).

[4] If its expected return is negative, then simply changing the signs of the weights will cause the expected return to become positive. Note that the new weights will also sum to zero and will still represent a portfolio that has zero sensitivity to the factor. Thus, the new weights will represent an arbitrage portfolio.

or, for this example,

$$15X_1 + 21X_2 + 12X_3 > 0. \tag{12.5b}$$

Using the solution for this candidate, it can be seen that its expected return is (15% × .1) + (21% × .075) + (12 × –.175) = .975%. Because this is a positive number, an arbitrage portfolio has indeed been identified.

The arbitrage portfolio just identified involves buying \$1 200 000 of stock 1 and \$900 000 of stock 2. How were these dollar figures arrived at? The solution comes from taking the current market value of the portfolio (W_0 = \$12 000 000) and multiplying it by the weights for the arbitrage portfolio of X_1 = .1 and X_2 = .075. Where does the money come from to make these purchases? It comes from selling \$2 100 000 of stock 3. (Note that $X_3 W_0$ = –.175 × \$12 000 000 = –\$2 100 000.)

In summary, this arbitrage portfolio is attractive to any investor who desires a higher return and is not concerned with nonfactor risk. It requires no additional dollar investment, it has no factor risk, and it has a positive expected return.

► The Investor's Position

At this juncture the investor can evaluate his or her position from either one of two equivalent viewpoints: (1) holding both the old portfolio and the arbitrage portfolio or (2) holding a new portfolio. Consider, for example, the weight in stock 1. The old portfolio weight was .33 and the arbitrage portfolio weight was .10, with the sum of these two weights being equal to .43. Note that the dollar value of the holdings of stock 1 in the new portfolio rises to \$5 200 000 (\$4 000 000 + \$1 200 000), so its weight is \$5 200 000/\$12 000 000 = .43, equivalent to the sum of the old and arbitrage portfolio weights.

Similarly, the portfolio's expected return is equal to the sum of the expected returns of the old and arbitrage portfolios, or 16% + .975% = 16.975%. Equivalently, the new portfolio's expected return can be calculated using the new portfolio's weights and the expected returns of the stocks, or (.43 × 15%) + (.41 × 21%) + (.16 × 12%) = 16.975%.

The sensitivity of the new portfolio is (.43 × .9) + (.41 × 3.0) + (.16 × 1.8) = 1.9. This is the same as the sum of the sensitivities of the old and arbitrage portfolios (= 1.9 + 0.0).

What about the risk of the new portfolio? Assume that the standard deviation of the old portfolio was 11%. The variance of the arbitrage portfolio will be small because its only source of risk is nonfactor risk. Similarly, the variance of the new portfolio will differ from that of the old only as a result of changes in its nonfactor risk. Thus, it can be concluded that the risk of the new portfolio will be approximately 11%.[5] Table 12.1 summarizes these observations.

---

[5] The APT ignores nonfactor risk. Because the total risk of a portfolio σ_p^2 is equal to $b_p^2\sigma_F^2 + \sigma_{\epsilon p}^2$ according to the one-factor model [see equation (11.6a) in Chapter 11], and given that the arbitrage portfolio has no factor risk by design, meaning that $b_p^2\sigma_F^2 = 0$ because $b_p = 0$, this means that the arbitrage portfolio must be sufficiently diversified so as to have insignificant nonfactor risk and, consequently, insignificant total risk.

Table 12.1					
How an Arbitrage Portfolio Affects an Investor's Position.					
	Old Portfolio	+	*Arbitrage Portfolio*	=	*New Portfolio*
Weights					
X_1	.333		.100		.433
X_2	.333		.075		.408
X_3	.333		−.175		.158
Properties:					
$\bar{r}_p$	16.000%		.975%		16.975%
b_p	1.900		.000		1.900
σ_p	11.000%		small		approx. 11.000%

PRICING EFFECTS

What are the consequences of buying stocks 1 or 2 and selling stock 3? As everyone will be doing this, their market prices will be affected and, accordingly, their expected returns will adjust. Specifically, the prices of stocks 1 and 2 will rise because of increased buying pressure. In turn, this will cause their expected returns to fall. Conversely, the selling pressure put on stock 3 will cause its stock price to fall and its expected return to rise.

This can be seen by examining the equation for estimating a stock's expected return:

$$\bar{r} = \frac{\bar{P}_1}{P_0} - 1 \tag{12.6}$$

where P_0 is the stock's current price and $\bar{P}_1$ is the stock's expected end-of-period price. Buying a stock such as stock 1 or 2 will push up its current price P_0 and thus result in a decline in its expected return $\bar{r}$. Conversely, selling a stock such as stock 3 will push down its current price and result in a rise in its expected return.

This buying-and-selling activity will continue until *all* arbitrage possibilities are significantly reduced or eliminated. At this point there will exist an approximately linear relationship between expected returns and sensitivities of the following sort:

$$\bar{r}_i = \lambda_0 + \lambda_1 b_i \tag{12.7}$$

where λ_0 and λ_1 are constants. This equation is the asset pricing equation of the APT when returns are generated by one factor.[6] Note that it is the equation of a straight line, meaning that in equilibrium there will be a linear relationship between expected returns and sensitivities.

In the example, one possible equilibrium setting could have $\lambda_0 = 8$ and $\lambda_1 = 4$.[7] Consequently, the pricing equation is

$$\bar{r}_1 = 8 + 4b_i. \tag{12.8}$$

---

[6] Technically, this pricing equation is only approximately true and may be significantly wrong for a small number of assets.

[7] Why choose 3 and 4 for λ_0 and λ_1, respectively? The magnitudes that these two parameters assume in equilibrium will depend on many things, such as investors' relative degrees of risk aversion, wealth, and time preferences.

This would result in the following equilibrium levels of expected returns for stocks 1, 2, and 3:

$$\bar{r}_1 = 8 + (4 \times .9) = 11.6\%$$

$$\bar{r}_2 = 8 + (4 \times 3.0) = 20.0\%$$

$$\bar{r}_3 = 8 + (4 \times 1.8) = 15.2\%.$$

As a result, the expected returns for stock 1 and 2 will have fallen from 15% and 21%, respectively, to 11.6% and 20%, because of increased buying pressure. Conversely, increased selling pressure will have caused the expected return on stock 3 to rise from 12% to 15.2%. The bottom line is that the expected return on any security is, in equilibrium, a linear function of the security's sensitivity to the factor b_i.

A Graphical Illustration

Figure 12.1 illustrates the asset pricing equation of equation (12.7). Any security that has a factor sensitivity and expected return such that it lies off the line will be mispriced according to the APT and will present investors with the opportunity of forming arbitrage portfolios. Security B is an example. If an investor buys security B and sells security S in equal dollar amounts, then the investor will have formed an arbitrage portfolio.[8] How can this be?

Figure 12.1

APT asset pricing line.

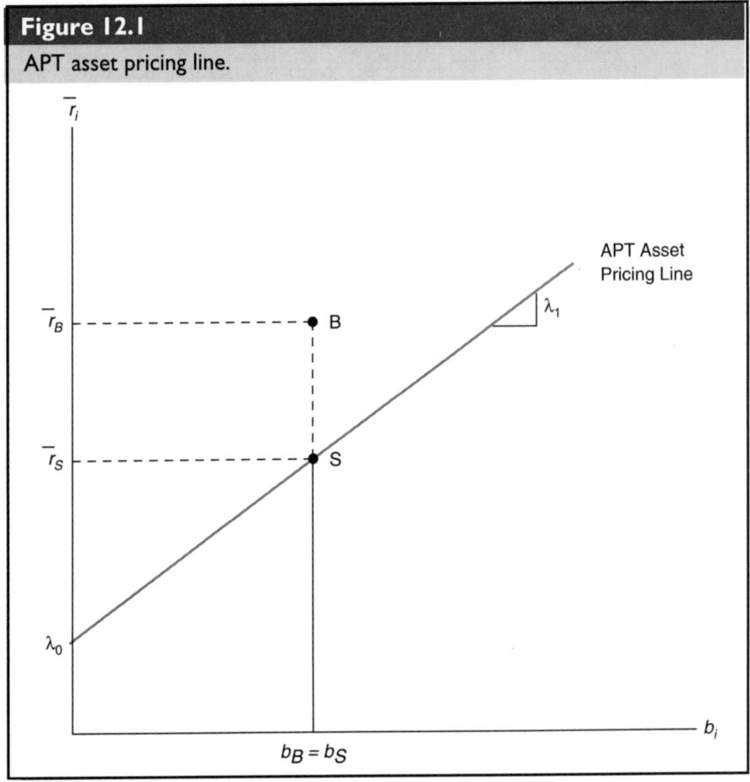

[8] If B were to plot below the APT asset pricing line, then investors would do just the opposite of what is described here. This means that they would buy S and sell B.

First of all, by selling an amount of security S to pay for the long position in security B the investor will not have committed any new funds. Second, because securities B and S have the same sensitivity to the factor, the selling of security S and buying of security B will constitute a portfolio with no sensitivity to the factor. Finally, the arbitrage portfolio will have a positive expected return because the expected return of security B is greater than the expected return of security S.[9] As a result of investors buying security B, its price will rise and, in turn, its expected return will fall until it is located on the APT asset pricing line.[10]

Interpreting the APT Pricing Equation

How can the constants λ_0 and λ_1 that appear in the APT pricing equation (12.7) be interpreted? Assuming that there is a risk-free asset in existence, such an asset will have a rate of return that is a constant. Therefore, this asset will have no sensitivity to the factor. From equation (12.7) it can be seen that $\bar{r}_i = \lambda_0$ for any asset with $b_i = 0$. In the case of the risk-free asset, it is also known that $\bar{r}_i = r_f$, implying that $\lambda_0 = r_f$. Hence the value of λ_0 in equation (12.7) must be r_f, allowing this equation to be rewritten as

$$\bar{r}_i = r_f + \lambda_1 b_i. \tag{12.9}$$

In terms of λ_1, its value can be seen by considering a **pure factor portfolio** (or pure factor play), denoted p^*, that has unit sensitivity to the factor, meaning $b_{p^*} = 1.0$. (If there were other factors, such a portfolio would be constructed so as to have no sensitivity to them.) According to equation (12.9), such a portfolio will have the following expected return:

$$\bar{r}_{p^*} = r_f + \lambda_1. \tag{12.10a}$$

Note that this equation can be rewritten as

$$\bar{r}_{p^*} - r_f = \lambda_1. \tag{12.10b}$$

Thus, λ_1 is the expected excess return (meaning the expected return over and above the risk-free rate) on a portfolio that has unit sensitivity to the factor. Accordingly, it is known as a **factor risk premium** (or factor-expected return premium). Letting $\delta_1 = \bar{r}_{p^*}$ denote the expected return on a portfolio that has unit sensitivity to the factor, equation (12.10b) can be rewritten as

$$\delta_1 - r_f = \lambda_1. \tag{12.10c}$$

Inserting the left-hand side of equation (12.10c) fo λ_1 in equation (12.9) results in a second version of the APT pricing equation:

$$\bar{r}_1 = r_f + (\delta_1 - r_f)b_i. \tag{12.11}$$

In the example, because $r_f = 8\%$ and $\lambda_1 = \delta_1 - r_f = 4\%$, it follows that $\delta_1 = 12\%$. This means that the expected return on a portfolio that has unit sensitivity to the first factor is 12%.

---

[9] A simpler way of viewing this transaction is as a stock swap where S is being swapped for B. Because it is a swap, no new funds are needed. Furthermore, because both B and S have the same factor sensitivity, the swap will not alter the sensitivity of the currently held portfolio. Finally, the replacement of S and B will increase the currently held portfolio's expected return because B has a higher level of expected return than S.

[10] Technically, the APT asset pricing line would shift upward a bit due to the selling of S.

In order to generalize the pricing equation of APT, the case where security returns are generated by more than one factor needs to be examined. This is done by considering a two-factor model next and then expanding the analysis to k factors where $k > 2$.

TWO-FACTOR MODELS

In the case of two factors, denoted F_1 and F_2 and representing predicted industrial production and inflation, each security will have two sensitivities, b_{i1} and b_{i2}. Thus, security returns are generated by the following factor model:

$$r_i = a_i + b_{i1}F_1 + b_{i2}F_2 + e_i. \tag{12.12}$$

Consider a situation where there are four securities that have the following expected returns and sensitivities.

i	$\bar{r}_i$	b_{i1}	b_{i2}
Stock 1	15%	.9	2.0
Stock 2	21	3.0	1.5
Stock 3	12	1.8	.7
Stock 4	8	2.0	3.2

In addition, consider an investor who has \$5 000 000 invested in each of the securities. (Thus, the investor has initial wealth W_0 of \$20 000 000.) Are these securities priced in equilibrium?

Arbitrage Portfolios

To answer this question, the possibility of forming an arbitrage portfolio must be explored. First of all, an arbitrage portfolio must have weights that satisfy the following equations:

$$X_1 + X_2 + X_3 + X_4 = 0 \tag{12.13}$$

$$.9X_1 + 3X_2 + 1.8X_3 + 2X_4 = 0 \tag{12.14}$$

$$2X_1 + 1.5X_2 + .7X_3 + 3.2X_4 = 0. \tag{12.15}$$

This means that the arbitrage portfolio must not involve an additional commitment of funds by the investor and must have zero sensitivity to each factor.

Note that there are three equations that need to be satisfied and that each equation involves four unknowns. Because there are more unknowns than equations, there are an infinite number of solutions. One solution can be found by setting X_1 equal to .1 (an arbitrarily chosen amount) and then solving for the remaining weights. Doing so results in the following weights: $X_2 = .088$, $X_3 = -.108$, and $X_4 = -.08$.

These weights represent a potential arbitrage portfolio. What remains to be seen is if this portfolio has a positive expected return. Calculating the expected return of the portfolio reveals that it is equal to $(.1 \times 15\%) + (.088 \times 21\%) + (-.108 \times 12\%) + (-.08 \times 8\%) = 1.41\%$. Hence, an arbitrage portfolio has been identified.

This arbitrage portfolio involves the purchase of stocks 1 and 2, funded by selling stocks 3 and 4. Consequently, the buying-and-selling pressures will drive the prices of stocks 1 and 2 up and stocks 3 and 4 down. In turn, this means that the expected returns of stocks 1 and 2 will fall and stocks 3 and 4 will rise. Investors will continue to create such arbitrage portfolios until equilibrium is reached. This means that equilibrium will be attained when any portfolio that satisfies the conditions given by equations (12.13), (12.14), and (12.15) has an expected return of zero. This will occur when the following linear relationship between expected returns and sensitivities exists:

$$\bar{r}_i = \lambda_0 + \lambda_1 b_{i1} + \lambda_2 b_{i2}. \tag{12.16}$$

As in equation (12.7), this is a linear equation except that it now has three dimensions, $\bar{r}_i$, b_{i1}, and b_{i2}. Hence, it corresponds to the equation of a two-dimensional plane.

In the example, one possible equilibrium setting is where $\lambda_0 = 8$, $\lambda_1 = 4$, and $\lambda_2 = -2$. Thus the pricing equation is

$$\bar{r}_i = 8 + 4b_{i1} - 2b_{i2}. \tag{12.17}$$

As a result, the four stocks have the following equilibrium levels of expected returns:

$$\bar{r}_1 = 8 + (4 \times .9) - (2 \times 2) = 7.6\%$$

$$\bar{r}_2 = 8 + (4 \times 3) - (2 \times 1.5) = 17.0\%$$

$$\bar{r}_3 = 8 + (4 \times 1.8) - (2 \times .7) = 13.8\%$$

$$\bar{r}_4 = 8 + (4 \times 2) - (2 \times 3.2) = 9.6\%$$

The expected returns of stocks 1 and 2 have fallen from 15% and 21% while the expected returns of stocks 3 and 4 have risen from 12% and 8%, respectively. Given the buying-and-selling pressures generated by investing in arbitrage portfolios, these changes are in the predicted direction.

One consequence of equation (12.17) is that a stock with higher sensitivity to the first factor than another stock will have a higher expected return if the two stocks also have the same sensitivity to the second factor, because $\lambda_1 > 0$. Conversely, since $\lambda_2 < 0$, a stock with higher sensitivity to the second factor will have a lower expected return than another stock with a lower sensitivity to the second factor, provided that both stocks have the same sensitivity to the first factor. However, the effect of two stocks having different sensitivities to both factors can be confounding. For example, stock 4 has a lower expected return than stock 3, even though both of its sensitivities are larger. This is because the advantage of having a higher sensitivity to the first factor ($b_{41} = 2.0 > b_{31} = 1.8$) is not of sufficient magnitude to offset the disadvantage of having a higher sensitivity to the second factor ($b_{42} = 3.2 > b_{32} = .7$).

Pricing Effects

Extending the one-factor APT pricing equation (12.7) to this two-factor situation is relatively uncomplicated. As before, λ_0 is equal to the risk-free rate. This is because the risk-free asset has no sensitivity to either factor, meaning that its values of b_{i1} and b_{i2} are both zero. Hence it follows that $\lambda_0 = r_f$. Thus equation (12.16) can be rewritten more generally as

$$\bar{r}_i = r_f + \lambda_1 b_{i1} + \lambda_2 b_{i2}. \tag{12.18}$$

In the example given in equation (12.16), it can be seen that $r_f = 8\%$.

Next, consider a well-diversified portfolio that has unit sensitivity to the first factor and zero sensitivity to the second factor. As mentioned earlier, such a portfolio is known as a pure factor portfolio or pure factor play because it has: (1) unit sensitivity to one factor, (2) no sensitivity to any other factor, and (3) zero nonfactor risk. Specifically, $b_1 = 1$ and $b_2 = 0$.

It can be seen from equation (12.18) that the expected return on this portfolio, denoted δ_1, will be equal to $r_f + \lambda_1$. As it follows that $\delta_1 - r_f = \lambda_1$, equation (12.18) can be rewritten as

$$\bar{r}_i = r_f + (\delta_1 - r_f)b_{i1} + \lambda_2 b_{i2}. \tag{12.19}$$

In the example given in equation (12.16), it can be seen that $\delta_1 - r_f = 4$. This means that $\delta_1 = 12$, because $r_f = 8$. In other words, a portfolio that has unit sensitivity to predicted industrial production (the first factor) would have an expected return of 12%, or 4% more than the risk-free rate of 8%.

Finally, consider a portfolio that has zero sensitivity to the first factor and unit sensitivity to the second factor, meaning that $b_1 = 0$ and $b_2 = 1$. It can be seen from equation (12.18) that the expected return on this portfolio, denoted δ_2, will be equal to $r_f + \lambda_2$. Accordingly, $\delta_2 - r_f = \lambda_2$, thereby allowing equation (12.19) to be rewritten as

$$\bar{r}_i = r_f + (\delta_1 - r_f)b_{i1} + (\delta_2 - r_f)b_{i2}. \tag{12.20}$$

In the example given in equation (12.16), it can be seen that $\delta_2 - r_f = -2$. This means that $\delta_2 = 6$ since $r_f = 8$. In other words, a portfolio that has zero sensitivity to predicted industrial production (the first factor) and unit sensitivity to predicted inflation (the second factor) would have an expected return of 6%, or 2% less than the risk-free rate of 8%.

MULTIPLE-FACTOR MODELS

When returns were generated by a two-factor model instead of a one-factor model, APT pricing equations (12.7) and (12.11) were simply expanded to accommodate the additional factor in equations (12.16) and (12.20). What happens to these APT pricing equations when returns are generated by a multiple-factor model where the number of factors k is greater than two? It turns out that the basic pricing equations are expanded once again in a relatively straightforward manner.

In the case of k factors ($F_1, F_2, \ldots, F_k$) each security will have k sensitivities ($b_{i1}, b_{i2}, \ldots, b_{ik}$) in the following k-factor model:

$$r_i = a_i + b_{i1}F_1 + b_{i2}F_2 + \ldots + b_{ik}F_k + e_i. \tag{12.21}$$

In turn, this suggests that securities will be priced by the following equation, which is similar to equations (12.7) and (12.16):

$$\bar{r}_i = \lambda_0 + \lambda_1 b_{i1} + \lambda_2 b_{i2} + \ldots + \lambda_k b_{ik}. \tag{12.22}$$

As before, this is a linear equation, except now it is in $k + 1$ dimensions with the dimensions being $\bar{r}_i, b_{i1}, b_{i2}, \ldots$, and b_{ik}.

Extending the APT pricing equations (12.11) and (12.20) to this situation is relatively uncomplicated. As before, λ_0 is equal to the risk-free rate as the risk-free asset has no sensitivity to any factor. Each value of δ_j represents the expected return on a portfolio of stocks that has unit sensitivity to factor j and zero sensitivity to all the other factors. As a result, equations (12.11) and (12.20) can be expanded as follows:

$$\bar{r}_i = r_f + (\delta_1 - r_f)b_{i1} + (\delta_2 - r_f)b_{i2} + \ldots + (\delta_k - r_f)b_{ik}. \tag{12.23}$$

Hence, a stock's expected return is equal to the risk-free rate plus k risk premiums based on the stock's sensitivities to the k factors.

A SYNTHESIS OF THE APT AND THE CAPM

Unlike the APT, the CAPM does not assume that returns are generated by a factor model. However, this does not mean that the CAPM is inconsistent with a world in which returns are generated by a factor model. Indeed, it is possible to have a world where returns are generated by a factor model, where the remaining assumptions of the APT hold, and where all the assumptions of the CAPM hold. This situation will now be examined.

One-Factor Models

Consider what happens if returns are generated by a one-factor model and that factor is the **market portfolio**. In such a situation, δ_1 will correspond to the expected return on the market portfolio and b_i will represent the beta stock i measured relative to the market portfolio. Hence the CAPM will hold.

What if returns are generated by a one-factor model and that factor is *not* the market portfolio? Now δ_1 will correspond to the expected return on a portfolio with unit sensitivity to the factor, and b_i will represent the sensitivity of stock i measured relative to the factor.[11] However, if the CAPM also holds, then security i's expected return will be related to both its beta *and* its sensitivity:

$$\bar{r}_i = r_f + (\bar{r}_M - r_f)\beta_{iM} \quad (12.24)$$

$$\bar{r}_i = r_f + (\delta_1 - r_f)b_i. \quad (12.25)$$

This suggests that betas and sensitivities must somehow be related to each other; just how they are related is shown next.

Beta Coefficients and Factor Sensitivities

How can expected returns be linearly related to both betas and sensitivities? Because betas and sensitivities will be related to each other in the following manner:

$$\beta_{iM} = \frac{\text{COV}(F_1, r_M)}{\sigma_M^2} b_i \quad (12.26)$$

where $\text{COV}(F_1, r_M)$ denotes the covariance between the factor and the market portfolio and δ_M^2 denotes the variance of the return on the market portfolio.[12] Because the quantity $\text{COV}(F_1, r_M)/\sigma_M^2$ is a constant and does not change from one security to another, equation (12.26) is equivalent to saying that β_{iM} will be equal to a constant times b_i when equations (12.24) and (12.25) both hold. Hence, if the factor is industrial production, then equation (12.26) states that each security's beta is equal to a constant times the security's sensitivity to industrial production. The constant will be a positive number if industrial production and the return on the market portfolio are positively correlated, as then $\text{COV}(F_1, r_M)$ will

---

[11] If the factor is a market index (instead of the market portfolio) such as the TSE 300, then δ_1 will correspond to the expected return on the index and b_i will represent the beta of stock i measured relative to the index, denoted previously in Chapter 8 as β_{i1}.

[12] This can be seen by noting that $\text{COV}(r_i, r_M) = \text{COV}(a_i + b_i F_1 + e_i, r_M)$, which simplifies to $\text{COV}(r_i, r_M) = b_i\text{COV}(F_1, r_M) + \text{COV}(e_i, r_M)$. As the last term is approximately zero, this equation reduces to $\text{COV}(r_i, r_M) = b_i\text{COV}(F_1, r_M)$. Dividing both sides by σ_M^2 and recognizing from Chapter 10 that $\text{COV}(r_i, r_M)/\sigma_M^2 = \beta_{iM}$ produces equation (12.26).

be positive.[13] Conversely, the constant will be negative if the correlation is negative because then $\text{COV}(F_1, r_M)$ will be negative.

Factor Risk Premiums

Note what happens if the right-hand side of equation (12.26) is substituted for β_{iM} on the right-hand side of equation (12.24):

$$\bar{r}_i = r_f + \left[(\bar{r}_M - r_f) \frac{\text{COV}(F_1, r_M)}{\sigma_M^2} \right] b_i. \tag{12.27}$$

Comparing this equation with equation (12.9) reveals that if the assumptions of both APT (with one factor) and the CAPM hold, then the following relationship must hold:

$$\lambda_1 = (\bar{r}_M - r_f) \frac{\text{COV}(F_1, r_M)}{\sigma_M^2}. \tag{12.28}$$

By itself, APT says nothing about the size of the factor risk premium λ_1. However, if the CAPM also holds, it can provide some guidance. This guidance is given in equation (12.28), which has been shown to hold if the assumptions of both APT and CAPM are taken as given.

Imagine that the factor moves with the market portfolio, meaning that it is positively correlated with the market portfolio so that $\text{COV}(F_1, r_M)$ is positive.[14] As σ_M^2 and $(\bar{r}_M - r_f)$ are both positive, it follows that the right-hand side of equation (12.28) is positive, and hence λ_1 is positive. Furthermore, because λ_1 is positive, it can be seen in equation (12.9) that the higher the value of b_i, the higher will be the expected return of the security.[15] To generalize, if a factor is positively correlated with the market portfolio, then a security's expected return will be a positive function of the security's sensitivity to that factor.

Using the same kind of argument, if the factor moves against the market portfolio, meaning that F_1 is negatively correlated with $\bar{r}_M$, then λ_1 will be negative. This means that the higher the value of b_i, the lower will be the expected return on the security. Generalizing, if a factor is negatively correlated with the market portfolio, then a security's expected return will be a negative function of the security's sensitivity to that factor.

A Market Index as the Factor

What if returns are generated by a one-factor model and instead of industrial production, the factor is the return on a market index such as the TSE 300? Consider a situation where the following two conditions are met: (1) the returns on the index and market portfolio are perfectly correlated, and (2) the variance of the returns on the market portfolio and the market index are identical.

First of all, a stock's beta will be equal to its sensitivity. This can be seen by examining equation (12.26). Given the two conditions just described, $\text{COV}(F_1, r_M) = \sigma_{F1}\sigma_M = \sigma_M^2$ so that $\text{COV}(F_1, r_M)/\sigma_M^2 = 1$. Hence, equation (12.26) would reduce to $\beta_{iM} = b_i$.

---

[13] $\text{COV}(F_1, r_M)$ will be positive if the correlation is positive because it is equal to the product of the correlation and the standard deviations of F_1 and r_M.

[14] See footnote 13.

[15] The greater the extent to which the factor moves with the market portfolio (meaning the higher the correlation between F_1 and r_M), the greater will be the associated expected return premium λ_1.

INSTITUTIONAL ISSUES

Applying APT

Since its inception in the mid-1970s, Arbitrage Pricing Theory (APT) has provided researchers and practitioners with an intuitive and flexible framework through which to address important investment management issues. As opposed to the Capital Asset Pricing Model (CAPM), with its specific assumptions concerning investor preferences as well as the critical role played by the market portfolio, APT operates under relatively weaker assumptions. Because of its emphasis on multiple sources of systematic risk, APT has attracted considerable interest as a tool for better explaining investment results and more effectively controlling portfolio risk.

Despite its attractive features, APT has not been widely applied by the investment community. The reason lies largely with APT's most significant drawback: the lack of specificity regarding the multiple factors that systematically affect security returns as well as the long-term return associated with each of these factors. Rightly or wrongly, the CAPM unambiguously states that a security's covariance with the market portfolio is the only systematic source of its investment risk within a well-diversified portfolio. APT, conversely, is conspicuously silent regarding the particular systematic factors affecting a security's risk and return. Investors must fend for themselves in determining those factors.

The number of institutional investors actually using APT to manage assets is small. The most prominent organization is Roll & Ross Asset Management Corporation (R&R). As Stephen Ross invented the APT, it is interesting to briefly review how R&R translates this theory into practice.

R&R begins with a statement of the systematic sources of risk (or factors) that it believes are *currently* relevant in the capital markets. Specifically, R&R has identified five factors that pervasively affect common stock returns:

- The business cycle,
- Interest rates,
- Investor confidence,
- Short-term inflation,
- Long-term inflationary expectations.

R&R quantifies these factors by designating certain measurable macroeconomic variables as proxies. For example, the business-cycle factor is represented by real (inflation-adjusted) percentage changes in the index of industrial production, whereas short-term inflation is measured by monthly percentage changes in the Consumer Price Index.

At the heart of the R&R approach are several assumptions. First, each source of systematic risk has a certain current volatility and reward. Factor volatilities and rewards, and even the factors themselves, may change over time. Second, individual securities and portfolios possess different sensitivities to each factor. These sensitivities may also vary through time. Third, a well-diversified portfolio's exposures to the factors will determine its expected return and total risk. Fourth, a portfolio should be constructed that offers the most attractive total reward-to-risk ratio, given the current rewards and volatilities exhibited by the factors.

R&R has developed a security database (updated monthly) that covers roughly 15 000 individual common stocks across 17 countries. For each country's stock market, R&R applies the database to create a pure factor portfolio (discussed in this chapter) for each of the five factors. R&R uses the historical returns on these pure factor portfolios not only to estimate the sensitivity of every security in its database to each of the factors, but also to estimate factor standard deviations, correlations, and risk premiums as well as calculate nonfactor returns and risk for every security.

Attention at this point turns to a client's benchmark. Typically, a US institutional investor

INSTITUTIONAL ISSUES (continued)

will select a market index such as the S&P 500 as its common stock benchmark. R&R's standard assignment is to devise a more efficient portfolio that exceeds the benchmark's expected return by a prespecified (reasonable) amount, yet maintains a similar standard deviation. R&R does this by employing portfolio optimization techniques (see Chapter 8) that combine securities in a way that attempts to set portfolio standard deviation near that of the benchmark; reduce nonfactor risk to minimal levels; emphasize stocks with high nonfactor reward-to-risk; increase exposure to risk factors with attractive reward-to-risk; and minimize buying and selling of securities (to control transaction costs). The process is repeated monthly to keep the portfolio aligned with the benchmark.

The R&R approach is highly quantitative and, intriguingly, involves no judgmental forecasts of factor returns or risks. Rather, historical data on the factors and securities' factor sensitivities is mechanically manipulated to determine the desired portfolio composition. This approach may prove effective if the future mimics the past, but it can produce disappointing results if past factor data display no stable relationship with future values.

R&R has captured considerable institutional investor interest since the firm was organized in 1986. Furthermore, the firm has expanded to take on foreign partners who now apply its techniques abroad. Thus R&R provides an interesting example of converting theoretical investment concepts into practical investment products.

Second, λ_1 will equal $\bar{r}_M - r_f$ under these two conditions. This can be seen by again noting that $\text{COV}(F_1, r_M)/\sigma_M^2 = 1$, which in turn means that equation (12.28) reduces to $\lambda_1 = \bar{r}_M - r_f$. Because equation (12.10c) states that $\delta_1 - r_f = \lambda_1$, this means that $\delta_1 = \bar{r}_M$. Hence the expected return on a portfolio that has unit sensitivity to the returns on the TSE 300 will be equal to the expected return on the market portfolio.

In summary, if a proxy for the market portfolio could be found such that the two conditions given previously were met, then the CAPM would hold where the role of the market portfolio could be replaced by the proxy. Unfortunately, because the market portfolio is unknown, it cannot be verified whether or not any proxy meets the two conditions.

▶ Multiple-Factor Models

It is possible for the CAPM to hold even though returns are generated by a multiple-factor model such as a two-factor model. Again, equations (12.24) and (12.25) can be extended to show that security i's expected return will be related to its beta and two sensitivities:

$$\bar{r}_i = r_f + (\bar{r}_M - r_f)\beta_{iM} \tag{12.29}$$

$$\bar{r}_i = r_f + (\delta_1 - r_f)b_{i1} + (\delta_2 - r_f)b_{i2}. \tag{12.30}$$

In this situation, equation (12.26) can be extended to show that betas will be linearly related to sensitivities in the following manner:

$$\beta_{iM} = \frac{\text{COV}(F_1, r_M)}{\sigma_M^2} b_{i1} + \frac{\text{COV}(F_2, r_M)}{\sigma_M^2} b_{i2} \tag{12.31}$$

where $\text{COV}(F_1, r_M)$ and $\text{COV}(F_2, r_M)$ denote the covariance between the first factor and the returns on the market portfolio and the covariance between the second factor and the returns on the market portfolio, respectively. As the quantities $\text{COV}(F_1, r_M)/\sigma_M^2$ and $\text{COV}(F_2, r_M)/\sigma_M^2$ are constants, it can be seen from equation (12.31) that β_{iM} will be a function of b_{i1} and b_{i2} when equations (12.29) and (12.30) hold. Thus, a stock's beta will be a linear combination of its sensitivities to the two factors, which means that, in this example, the size of a stock's beta will be dependent on the size of its sensitivities to predicted industrial production and inflation.

Note what happens if the right-hand side of equation (12.31) is substituted for β_{iM} on the right-hand side of equation (12.29):

$$\bar{r}_i = r_f + (\bar{r}_M - r_f)\left[\frac{\text{COV}(F_1, r_M)}{\sigma_M^2}b_{i1} + \frac{\text{COV}(F_2, r_M)}{\sigma_M^2}b_{i2}\right] \tag{12.32a}$$

which can be rewritten as

$$\bar{r}_i = r_f + \left[(\bar{r}_M - r_f)\frac{\text{COV}(F_1, r_M)}{\sigma_M^2}\right]b_{i1} + \left[(\bar{r}_M - r_f)\frac{\text{COV}(F_2, r_M)}{\sigma_M^2}\right]b_{i2}. \tag{12.32b}$$

Comparing this equation with equation (12.18) reveals that if the assumptions of both APT (with two factors) and the CAPM hold, then the following relationships must hold:

$$\lambda_1 = (\bar{r}_M - r_f)\frac{\text{COV}(F_1, r_M)}{\sigma_M^2} \tag{12.33a}$$

$$\lambda_2 = (\bar{r}_M - r_f)\frac{\text{COV}(F_2, r_M)}{\sigma_M^2} \tag{12.33b}$$

Hence the size of λ_1 and λ_2 will be dependent upon both the market premium $(\bar{r}_M - r_f)$, a positive number, and the covariance of the factor with the market portfolio, which may be positive or negative. This means that λ_1 and λ_2 will have positive values if the factors are positively correlated with the returns on the market portfolio.[16] However, if either factor is negatively correlated with the returns on the market portfolio, then the corresponding value of λ will be negative (as was the case with λ_2 in the example).

IDENTIFYING THE FACTORS

Left unanswered by APT are the number and identity of the factors that are "priced"—that is, have values of lambda (λ) that are sufficiently positive or negative in magnitude that they need to be included when estimating expected returns. Several researchers have investigated stock returns and estimated that there are anywhere from three to five factors. Subsequently, various people attempted to identify these factors.[17] In one paper by Chen, Roll, and Ross, the following factors were identified:

1. Growth rate in industrial production,
2. Rate of inflation (both expected and unexpected),

[16] For the reasoning behind this assertion, see footnote 13.

[17] In Chapter 11 a three-factor model that was developed by Fama and French was described. In their model, the factors represented returns on (1) a general market index, (2) the difference between small and large stock indices, and (3) the difference between high and low book-to-market equity ratio stock indices.

3. Spread between long-term and short-term interest rates,
4. Spread between low-grade and high-grade bonds.[18]

Another paper by Berry, Burmeister, and McElroy identifies five factors. Of these five factors, three correspond closely to the last three identified by Chen, Roll, and Ross. The other two are the growth rate in aggregate sales in the economy and the rate of return on the S&P 500.[19]

In a series of tests using Canadian data, Otuteye found that two distinct models using different macroeconomic factors performed equally well. The first model included the same factors used by Chen, Roll, and Ross plus a value-weighted market index. The second included the value-weighted market index; the yield spread between high- and low-grade corporate bonds; the growth rate of unemployment; and the Canada/US exchange rate.

Finally, consider the five factors used by Salomon Brothers in what they refer to as their Fundamental Factor Model. Only one factor, inflation, is in common with the factors identified by the others. The remaining factors are as follows:

1. Growth rate in gross national product,
2. Rate of interest,
3. Rate of change in oil prices,
4. Rate of growth in defence spending.[20]

In summary, it is interesting to note that the three sets of factors have some common characteristics. First, they contain some indication of aggregate economic activity (industrial production, aggregate sales, and GNP). Second, they contain inflation. Third, they contain some type of interest rate factor (either spreads or a rate itself). Considering the fact that stock prices can be thought of as being equal to the discounted value of future dividends, the factors make intuitive sense.[21] Future dividends will be related to aggregate economic activity, and the discount rate used to determine present value will be related to inflation and interest rates.

SUMMARY

1. Arbitrage Pricing Theory (APT) is an equilibrium model of security prices, as is the Capital Asset Pricing Model (CAPM).
2. APT makes fewer assumptions about investor preferences than does the CAPM.
3. APT assumes that security returns are generated by a factor model, but does not identify the factors.
4. An arbitrage portfolio includes long and short positions in securities. It must have a net market value of zero, no sensitivity to any factor, and a positive expected return.

---

[18] Note that the third factor can be interpreted as a measure of the term structure of interest rates, and the fourth factor can be interpreted as a measure of the default risk premium that investors demand for holding risky corporate bonds instead of Treasury bonds.

[19] Technically, they used the part of the rate of return of the S&P 500 that could not be attributed to the other four factors.

[20] Technically, they used inflation-adjusted figures for all the variables except the rate of interest.

[21] Dividend discount models are discussed in depth in Chapter 18.

5. Investors will invest in arbitrage portfolios, driving up the prices of the securities held in long positions and driving down the prices of securities held in short positions, until all arbitrage possibilities are eliminated.
6. When all arbitrage possibilities are eliminated, the equilibrium-expected return on a security will be a linear function of its sensitivities to the factors.
7. A factor-risk premium is the equilibrium return over the risk-free rate expected to be generated by a portfolio with a unit sensitivity to the factor and no sensitivity to any other factor.
8. APT and the CAPM are not necessarily inconsistent with each other. If security returns are generated by a factor model and the CAPM holds, then a security's beta will depend on the security's sensitivity to the factors and the covariances between the factors and the market portfolio.
9. APT does not specify the number or identity of the factors that affect expected returns. Most research into factors focuses on indicators of aggregate economic activity, inflation, and interest rates.

QUESTIONS AND PROBLEMS

1. In what significant ways does APT differ from the CAPM?
2. Why would an investor wish to form an arbitrage portfolio?
3. What three conditions define an arbitrage portfolio?
4. Assuming a one-factor model of the form:

$$r_i = 4\% + b_i F + e_i$$

consider three well-diversified portfolios (zero nonfactor risk). The expected valued of the factor is 8%.

Portfolio	Factor Sensitivity	Expected Return
A	0.80	10.4%
B	1.00	10.0
C	1.20	13.6

Is one of the portfolio's expected returns not in line with the factor model relationship? Which one? Can you construct a combination of the other two portfolios that has the same factor sensitivity as the "out-of-line" portfolio? What is the expected return of that combination? What action would you expect investors to take with respect to these three portfolios?

5. Gunnar Seybold owns a portfolio with the following characteristics. (Assume that returns are generated by a one-factor model.)

Security	Factor Sensitivity	Proportion	Expected Return
A	2.0	.20	20%
B	3.5	.40	10
C	0.5	.40	5

Gunnar decides to create an arbitrage portfolio by increasing his holdings of security A by .20 (Hint: Remember, X_B must equal $-X_C - X_A$.)

a. What must be the weights of the other two securities in Gunnar's arbitrage portfolio?

b. What is the expected return on the arbitrage portfolio?

c. If everyone follows Gunnar's buy-and-sell decisions, what will be the effects on the prices of the three securities?

6. Assume that security returns are generated by a one-factor model. Hap Morse holds a portfolio whose component securities have the following characteristics:

Security	Factor Sensitivity	Proportion	Expected Return
A	.60	.40	12%
B	.30	.30	15
C	1.20	.30	8

Specify an arbitrage portfolio in which Hap might invest. (Remember that there are an infinite number of possibilities—choose one.) Demonstrate that this portfolio satisfies the conditions of an arbitrage portfolio.

7. Why must the variance of a well-diversified arbitrage portfolio be small?

8. Why is the concept of arbitrage central to the asset-pricing mechanism of the APT?

9. Based on a one-factor model, Wyeville Labs' stock has a factor sensitivity of 3. Given a risk-free rate of 5% and a factor risk premium of 7%, what is the equilibrium expected return on Wyeville stock?

10. According to the APT, why must the relationship between a security's equilibrium return and its factor sensitivities be linear?

11. Based on a one-factor model, two portfolios, A and B, have equilibrium expected returns of 9.8% and 11.0%, respectively. If the factor sensitivity of portfolios A and B is 0.80 and 1.00, respectively, what must be the risk-free rate?

12. What is a pure factor portfolio? How may such a portfolio be constructed?

13. Based on a one-factor model, assume that the risk-free rate is 6% and the expected return on a portfolio with unit sensitivity to the factor is 8.5%. Consider a portfolio of two securities with the following characteristics:

Security	Factor Sensitivity	Proportion
A	4.0	.30
B	2.6	.70

According to the APT, what is the portfolio's equilibrium expected return?

14. Assume that security returns are generated by a factor model in which two factors are pervasive. The sensitivities of two securities and of the risk-free asset to each of the two factors is shown below, along with the expected return on each security.

Security	b_{i1}	b_{i2}	Expected Return
A	0.50	0.80	16.2%
B	1.50	1.40	21.6
r_f	0.00	0.00	10.0

a. If Dorothy Miller has \$100 to invest and sells short \$50 of security B and purchases \$150 of security A, what is the sensitivity of Dorothy's portfolio to the two factors? (Ignore margin requirements.)
b. If Dorothy now borrows \$100 at the risk-free rate and invests the proceeds of the loan along with the original \$100 in securities A and B in the same proportions as described in Part (a), what is the sensitivity of this portfolio to the two factors?
c. What is the expected return on the portfolio created in Part (b)?
d. What is the expected return premium of factor 2?

15. Claus Pfeffer owns a portfolio with the following characteristics:

Security	Factor 1 Sensitivity	Factor 2 Sensitivity	Proportion	Expected Return
A	2.50	1.40	.30	13%
B	1.60	0.90	.30	18
C	0.80	1.00	.20	10
D	2.00	1.30	.20	12

Assume that the returns are generated by a two-factor model. Claus decides to create an arbitrage portfolio by increasing the holding of security B by .05.
a. What must be the weights of the other three securities in Claus's portfolio?
b. What is the expected return on the arbitrage portfolio?

16. Is it true if one believes that the APT is a correct theory of asset pricing, then the risk-return relationship derived from the CAPM is necessarily incorrect? Why?
17. If the CAPM and APT both hold, why must it be the case that the factor-risk premium is negative for a factor that is negatively correlated with the market portfolio? Explain both mathematically and intuitively.
18. Some people have argued that the market portfolio can never be measured and that the CAPM is therefore untestable. Other have argued that the APT specifies neither the number of factors nor their identity and, hence, is also untestable. If these views are correct, does this mean that the theories are of no value? Explain.
19. Although the APT does not specify the identity of the relevant factors, most empirical APT research has focused on certain types of factors. What are some of the common characteristics of those factors?
20. Assume that the CAPM holds and that returns on securities are generated by a single-factor model. You are given the following information:

$\sigma_M^2 = 400 \qquad b_A = 0.70 \qquad b_B = 1.10 \qquad \text{COV}(F, r_M) = 370$

a. Calculate the beta coefficients of securities A and B.
b. If the risk-free rate is 6% and the expected return on the market portfolio is 12%, what is the equilibrium expected return on securities A and B?

21. Assume that the CAPM holds and that returns are generated by a two-factor model. You are given the following information:

$$\sigma_M^2 = 324 \qquad b_{A1} = .80 \qquad b_{B1} = 1.00 \qquad \text{COV}(F_1, r_M) = 156$$
$$b_{A2} = 1.10 \qquad b_{B2} = .70 \qquad \text{COV}(F_2, r_M) = 500.$$

Calculate the beta coefficients of securities A and B.

CFA Exam Question

22. As the manager of a large, broadly diversified portfolio of stocks and bonds, you realize that changes in certain macroeconomic variables may directly affect the performance of your portfolio. You are considering using an arbitrage pricing theory (APT) approach to strategic portfolio planning and want to analyze the possible impacts of the following four factors:
    - industrial production,
    - inflation,
    - risk premiums or quality spreads,
    - yield curve shifts.

    a. Indicate how each of these four factors influences the cash flows and the discount rates in the traditional discounted cash flow valuation model. Explain how unanticipated changes in each of these four factors could affect portfolio returns.

    b. You now use a constant-proportion allocation strategy of 60% stocks and 40% bonds, which you rebalance monthly. Compare and contrast an active portfolio approach that incorporates macroeconomic factors, such as the four factors listed above, to the constant-proportion strategy currently in use.

Key Terms

Arbitrage Pricing Theory (APT)
sensitivity
arbitrage
arbitrage portfolio
pure factor portfolio
factor risk premium
market portfolio

References

1. Credit for the initial development of the APT belongs to:

   Stephen A. Ross, "The Arbitrage Theory of Capital Asset Pricing," *Journal of Economic Theory* 13, no. 3 (December 1976): 341–360 and "Risk, Return, and Arbitrage," in *Risk and Return in Finance*, Vol. I, ed. Irwin Friend and James L. Bicksler (Cambridge, MA: Ballinger Publishing, 1977), Section 9.

2. Ross's initial presentation of the APT was clarified in:

   Gur Huberman, "A Simple Approach to Arbitrage Pricing Theory," *Journal of Economic Theory* 28, no. 1 (October 1982): 183–191.

3. The fundamental asset pricing equation of Ross's APT is approximately correct for all but a small number of assets. By making additional assumptions all assets will be priced with, at most, negligible error. Some of the papers (also see the papers cited in References 7 and 8) that address this issue are:

Nai-fu Chen and Jonathan E. Ingersoll, Jr., "Exact Pricing in Linear Factor Models with Finitely Many Assets: A Note," *Journal of Finance* 38, no. 3 (June 1983): 985–988.

Gary Chamberlain and Michael Rothschild, "Arbitrage, Factor Structure, and Mean-Variance Analysis on Large Asset Markets," *Econometrica* 51, no. 5 (September 1983): 1281–1304.

Gary Chamberlain, "Funds, Factors, and Diversification in Arbitrage Pricing Models," *Econometrica* 51, no. 5 (September 1983): 1305–1323.

Philip H. Dybvig, "An Explicit Bound on Individual Assets' Deviations from APT Pricing in a Finite Economy," *Journal of Financial Economics* 12, no. 4 (December 1983): 483–496.

Mark Grinblatt and Sheridan Titman, "Factor Pricing in a Finite Economy," *Journal of Financial Economics* 12, no. 4 (December 1983): 497–507.

Gregory Connor, "A Unified Beta Pricing Theory," *Journal of Economic Theory* 34, no. 1 (October 1984): 13–31.

4. Nontechnical descriptions of the APT can be found in:

Richard W. Roll and Stephen A. Ross, "Regulation, the Capital Asset Pricing Model, and the Arbitrage Pricing Theory," *Public Utilities Fortnightly* 111, no. 11 (May 26, 1983): 22–28.

Richard Roll and Stephen A. Ross, "The Arbitrage Pricing Theory Approach to Strategic Portfolio Planning," *Financial Analysts Journal* 40, no. 3 (May-June 1984): 14–26.

Dorothy H. Bower, Richard S. Bower, and Dennis E. Logue, "A Primer on Arbitrage Pricing Theory," *Midland Corporate Finance Journal* 2, no. 3 (Fall 1984): 31–40.

5. Some of the attempts to identify the number of factors that are priced are:

Richard Roll and Stephen A. Ross, "An Empirical Investigation of the Arbitrage Pricing Theory," *Journal of Finance* 35, no.5 (December 1980): 1073–1103.

Stephen J. Brown and Mark I. Weinstein, "A New Approach to Testing Asset Pricing Models: The Bilinear Paradigm," *Journal of Finance* 38, no. 3 (June 1983): 711–743.

Phoebus J. Dhyrmes, Irwin Friend, and N. Bulent Gultekin, "A Critical Reexamination of the Empirical Evidence on the Arbitrage Pricing Theory," *Journal of Finance* 39, no. 2 (June 1984): 323–346.

Richard Roll and Stephen A. Ross, "A Critical Reexamination of the Empirical Evidence on the Arbitrage Pricing Theory: A Reply," *Journal of Finance* 39, no. 2 (June 1984): 347–350.

Charles Trzcinka, "On the Number of Factors in the Arbitrage Pricing Model," *Journal of Finance* 41, no. 2 (June 1986): 347–368.

Dolores A. Conway and Marc R. Reinganum, "Stable Factors in Security Returns: Identification Using Cross Validation," *Journal of Business and Economic Statistics* 6, no. 1 (January 1988): 1–15.

Bruce N. Lehmann and David M. Modest, "The Empirical Foundations of the Arbitrage Pricing Theory," *Journal of Financial Economics* 21, no. 2 (September 1988): 213–254.

Gregory Connor and Robert A. Korajczyk, "Risk and Return in an Equilibrium APT: Application of a New Test Methodology," *Journal of Financial Economics* 21, no. 2 (September 1988): 255–289.

Stephen J. Brown, "The Number of Factors in Security Returns," *Journal of Finance* 44, no. 5 (December 1989): 1247–1262.

Eugene F. Fama and Kenneth R. French, "Common Risk Factors in the Returns on Stocks and Bonds," *Journal of Financial Economics* 33, no. 1 (February 1993): 3–56.

Gregory Connor and Robert A. Korajczyk, "A Test for the Number of Factors in an Approximate Factor Model," *Journal of Finance* 48, no. 4 (September 1993): 1263–1291.

6. A few of the previous papers also identified factors. Some other papers that identified factors are:

Tony Estep, Nick Hansen, and Cal Johnson, "Sources of Value and Risk in Common Stocks," *Journal of Portfolio Management* 9, no. 4 (Summer 1983): 5–13.

Nai-fu Chen, Richard Roll, and Stephen A. Ross, "Economic Forces and the Stock Market," *Journal of Business* 59, no. 3 (July 1986): 383–403.

Marjorie B. McElroy and Edwin Burmeister, "Arbitrage Pricing Theory as a Restricted Nonlinear Multivariate Regression Model," *Journal of Business and Economic Statistics* 6, no. 1 (January 1988): 29–42.

Michael A. Berry, Edwin Burmeister, and Marjorie B. McElroy, "Sorting Out Risks Using Known APT Factors," *Financial Analysts Journal* 44, no. 2 (March-April 1988): 29–42.

7. It has been argued that the APT cannot be meaningfully tested and hence is of questionable practical use by:

Jay Shanken, "The Arbitrage Pricing Theory: Is It Testable?" *Journal of Finance* 37, no. 5 (December 1982): 1129–1140.

Christian Gilles and Stephen F. LeRoy, "On the Arbitrage Pricing Theory," *Economic Theory* 1, no. 3 (1991): 213–229.

Jay Shanken, "The Current State of Arbitrage Pricing Theory," *Journal of Finance* 47, no. 4 (September 1992): 1569–1574.

8. For a discussion of the relationships between the APT and the CAPM, see:

William F. Sharpe, "Factor Models, CAPMs and the ABT," *Journal of Portfolio Management* 11, no. 1 (Fall 1984): 21–25.

Jay Shanken, "Multi-Beta CAPM or Equilibrium-APT?: A Reply," *Journal of Finance* 40, no. 4 (September 1985): 1189–1196.

K.C. John Wei, "An Asset-Pricing Theory Unifying the CAPM and APT," *Journal of Finance* 43, no. 4 (September 1988): 881–892.

9. For a Canadian perspective on the topics covered in this chapter, see:

Patricia J. Hughes, "A Test of the Arbitrage Pricing Theory," *Canadian Journal of Administrative Sciences* 1, no. 2 (December 1984).

Eben Otuteye, "How Economic Forces Explain Canadian Stock Returns," *Canadian Investment Review* IV, no. 1 (Spring 1991).

B.F. Smith, "A Study of the Arbitrage Pricing Theory Using Daily Returns of Canadian Stocks," in M.J. Robinson and B.F. Smith, eds., *Canadian Capital Markets* (London, Ont.: Western Business School, 1993).

CHAPTER 13

Taxes and Inflation

Neither taxation nor inflation should be regarded as an unmitigated evil. Each provides benefits to some individuals that may outweigh the associated costs that others have to bear. Regardless of whether or not the benefits outweigh the costs, both taxes and inflation have an impact on investment decisions and investment results and they are sufficiently important in present-day societies to warrant considerable discussion.

Federal and provincial tax laws play a major role in the way securities are priced in the marketplace, since, understandably, investors are concerned with after-tax returns, rather than before-tax returns. Accordingly, the investor should determine the tax rate applicable to him or her before making any investment decision. This tax rate is not the same for all securities for a given individual investor; when both federal and provincial taxes are considered it can be as low as 6.8% in the case of certain stocks and in excess of 54% for corporate bonds. After determining the applicable tax rate, the investor can estimate a security's expected after-tax return and risk.

TAXES IN CANADA

In Canada, personal and corporate taxes are levied by the federal, the ten provincial, and two territorial governments. In all provinces except Quebec, the federal government acts as a collection agency for personal income taxes; individuals file a single tax return with the federal government, which then distributes the appropriate amount to the provinces. Residents of Quebec must file two separate tax returns, one with Revenue Canada and one with the Quebec Ministry of Finance.

Many of the specific tax rates and provisions cited in this chapter are contained in the amendments to the *Income Tax Act* that were passed in September 1988. Changes do occur from year to year, and current regulations should, of course, be consulted when preparing tax returns or considering major investment decisions. However, the material given here can be considered broadly representative of current taxation in Canada.

Generally speaking, the most important taxes for investment decision making are personal and corporate income taxes. The essential elements of each will be described, and the manner in which they influence the pricing of securities will be considered.

► Corporate Income Taxes

There are three forms of business organizations in Canada and in many other countries— corporations, partnerships, and single proprietorships. The corporate form of organization is the largest in terms of the dollar value of assets owned, even though there are more firms organized as partnerships or single proprietorships. Legally, a corporation is regarded as a

Table 13.1

Federal and Provincial Corporate Tax Rates, 1995.

	Small Cdn.-Controlled Corporations[a]		Other Cdn. Corporations	
Jurisdiction	*Mfg.*	*Non-mfg.*	*Mfg.*	*Non-mfg.*
Federal[b]	13.12%	13.12%	22.12%	29.12%
Provincial:				
Alberta	6.0	6.0	14.5	15.5
British Columbia	10.0	10.0	16.5	16.5
Manitoba	9.0	9.0	17.0	17.0
New Brunswick	7.0	7.0	17.0	17.0
Newfoundland	5.0	5.0	5.0	14.0
Northwest Terr.	5.0	5.0	14.0	14.0
Nova Scotia	5.0	5.0	16.0	16.0
Ontario	9.5	9.5	13.5	15.5
Quebec	5.75	5.75	8.9	8.9
Prince Edward I.	7.5	7.5	7.5	15.0
Saskatchewan	8.0	8.0	17.0	17.0
Yukon Terr.	2.5	6.0	2.5	15.0

[a] Certain Canadian-controlled private corporations are eligible for these rates.
[b] Includes the 4% surtax.

SOURCE: KPMG, Peat, Marwick, Thorne, *Tax Facts, 1995–96* (Toronto, 1995), p. 40.

separate entity, whereas a proprietorship or partnership is considered an extension of its owner or owners. Income earned by proprietorships and partnerships is taxed primarily through the personal income tax levied on their owners. Income earned by a corporation may be taxed twice—once when it is earned, via the corporate income tax, and again when it is received as dividends by holders of the firm's securities, via the personal income tax.[1]

This double taxation of corporate income may at first seem inefficient, if not unfair. It also raises questions about the efficiency of the corporate form of organization. Suffice it to say that limited liability and the ability to subdivide ownership and to transfer shares of that ownership appear to be of sufficient value to more than offset the tax law disadvantages. Moreover, without the corporate income tax, personal tax rates would have to be increased if the level of government expenditures were to remain constant without increasing the national debt.

Corporate Tax Rates (Federal and Provincial)

The corporate income tax is relatively simple in one respect. There are only a few basic rates applicable to all taxable income. The rates vary depending on the size of the corporation and the nature of its operations. Table 13.1 shows the federal and provincial tax rates that came into effect on February 28, 1995.

---

[1] The Income Tax Act attempts to minimize the effects of double taxation on dividends—an issue to be discussed in more detail later.

The federal and provincial rates are additive. Thus, a large Manitoba non-manufacturing corporation pays 46.12% of all its reported income in combined taxes. As demonstrated in Table 13.1 the tax system favours firms in the manufacturing sector. This is intended to stimulate employment. The system of tax rates is also simple in the sense that the **marginal tax rates** and **average tax rates** are equal because there is a single rate applicable to a given corporation. The marginal tax rate is the tax rate it would pay on an additional dollar of income. The average tax rate is equal to the total amount of taxes paid divided by the total income subject to tax. The average rate measures the overall impact of taxes, but the marginal rate is more relevant for most decisions.

Defining Income

Corporate income is partly a philosophic concept, partly an artifact of legal requirements, partly a result of accounting conventions, partly an indication of the hopes of the firm's management, and sometimes only incidentally related to underlying economic factors.

For tax purposes, corporate income is defined as revenues minus expenses. However, a problem arises in measuring these two elements. Simply put, this problem involves determining when to recognize revenues and expenses as having occurred. If a company sells an airplane this year but payment is to be made in instalments over the next 5 years, when is the sales price to be considered taxable revenue? If a new plant is to be built and paid for this year but is to be used to produce goods for the next 20 years, when is the outlay to be considered as an expense? Accountants have a set of procedures, known as generally accepted accounting principles (GAAP), that can be used to handle these and many more subtle cases. However, there is extremely wide latitude within these principles.

The government has prescribed certain limits on the procedures that can be used to calculate income when determining a corporation's income tax liability. In some cases, the firm is required to use the same procedures when reporting its income to its shareholders; in other cases it can (and often does) use different procedures, sometimes resulting in a noticeably different income figure.[2]

Deductibility of Interest Payments

In Canada, interest is regarded as a business expense and can be deducted from revenue when calculating taxable income. For example, consider two firms, each with revenues of $25 000 and noninterest expenses of $15 000. Firm A is financed by both debt and equity and pays $5000 in interest to its creditors. As shown in Table 13.2, its net income after taxes is $4250, which is available to be paid as dividends, if desired. Thus, a total amount of $9250 ($5000 + $4250) can be paid to those who provided the firm's capital.

The other part of the table shows the results for firm B, which differs only with respect to financing. All its capital was provided by common stock financing. Thus, the entire $10 000 of income is subject to tax, leaving only $8500 for distribution to those who provided the firm's capital.

The deductibility of interest payments provides an apparent tax advantage for the use of debt over equity funds. For this reason, it may seem surprising that firms do not choose to obtain more of their capital by issuing bonds. Indeed, the dramatic difference in tax treatment raises substantial questions about the definition of debt and interest, on the one hand, and stocks and dividend payments, on the other. Revenue Canada pays considerable

[2] Differences of this sort are usually described in the firm's annual report.

Table 13.2
The Effect of Deducting Interest Payments.

	Firm A	Firm B
Revenue	$25 000	$25 000
Cost of goods sold	15 000	15 000
Revenue minus expense	10 000	10 000
Interest paid	5 000	0
Taxable income	5 000	10 000
Tax (at 15%)	750	1 500
Available for dividends	$ 4 250	$ 8 500

attention to any arrangement designed to provide the tax characteristics of debt with the financial characteristics of equity. To qualify as debt, there must be a definite lender, a definite borrower, a definite ascertainable obligation (a specific amount), and a time of maturity (date when the debt must be repaid). That is, debt should be represented by an instrument (a legal document such as a contract) that contains an unconditional legal obligation to pay a certain sum either on demand or on a specific date, with interest. Payments made under any other arrangement are not likely to be deductible for purposes of income taxation.

Failure to make interest payments may have serious consequences for the firm and its management. In many cases bankruptcy results, with mandatory and costly corporate reorganization. The greater the magnitude of interest payments in relation to dividend payments, the greater the probability of this type of unfortunate event. This risk of bankruptcy, along with the associated costs of bankruptcy, provides a constraint on the use of debt financing, despite its obvious tax advantage.

Corporate Income from Dividends, Interest, and Capital Gains

The full amount of the dividends *received* by a corporation can be excluded from income when calculating the corporation's income tax liability. The recipient corporation is regarded as a *conduit* between the issuing corporation and individual investors. This special treatment of dividends avoids the partial triple taxation of income. Consider how dividends would be taxed if this exclusion did not exist. Corporation A is taxed on its income and then pays dividends to one of its shareholders, corporation B. Corporation B then pays taxes on its income, which includes the dividends received from A. Finally, the shareholders of B pay income taxes on the dividends received from B. Thus, a dollar of income earned by A would be taxed three times (a tax on A, then a tax on B, then a tax on the shareholders of B) if the dividend exclusion did not exist. With the dividend exclusion, a dollar of income earned by A is taxed, for all practical purposes, only twice. Despite the existence of the dividend tax credit that applies to dividends received by individual investors in Canada, some degree of double taxation still exists.

No deduction is allowed for interest received by a corporation; it is simply added to income and taxed at the regular rate. This means that the effective tax rate on interest received from bonds is substantially greater than the rate on common and preferred shares. This differential tax treatment has an effect on the relative prices that corporate investors are willing to pay for these securities, since their concern is with relative after-tax yields. That is, since preferred shares are generally viewed as being riskier than bonds, the after-tax yield on preferred shares needs to be higher in order for investors to be interested in purchasing them. Given the favourable tax treatment on preferred shares for corporate investors, it is possible for preferred shares to have a lower before-tax yield than bonds while still enabling the corporate investor who buys the more risky preferred shares to be rewarded by earning, a higher after-tax yield relative to bonds.

Tax-Exempt Organizations

Many organizations are wholly or partly exempt from federal income taxes. Non-profit religious, charitable, or educational foundations generally qualify. Such foundations are required to pay out to their beneficiaries a minimum percentage of the value of their assets (3.5% in 1995). Failure to do so can result in a punitive and confiscatory tax.

Investment companies, often called *mutual funds*, may elect to be treated as regulated investment companies for tax purposes. This privilege is granted if certain conditions are met. For example, the funds of the investment company must be invested primarily in securities, without undue concentration in any one. Thus, its income takes the form of dividends and interest received on its investments, as well as capital gains from price appreciation realized when investments are sold at a price that is higher than their purchase price. A regulated investment company pays income tax only on income and capital gains not distributed to its shareholders. As a result of this tax treatment, such companies distribute substantially all income and gains and, in doing so, end up not having to pay any taxes.

Employee pension, profit-sharing, and share-ownership plans may also qualify for tax-exempt status. Such a plan may entrust its assets, which are usually securities, to a *fiduciary* (for example, a trust company). The fiduciary receives new contributions, makes required payments, and manages the investments owned by the plan. A fiduciary under a qualified plan (that is, a plan that meets all the requirements of applicable legislation) pays no taxes on either income or capital gains.

Another example of a tax-exempt entity is the *personal trust*. Here, funds are provided for the benefit of one or more individuals by another individual or individuals with a fiduciary serving as a trustee. Some trusts are created by wills, others by a contract among living persons. Whatever the origin, trusts generally pay taxes only on income that is not distributed to the designated beneficiaries. It is important, however, to have adequate legal and tax advice when establishing these trusts to avoid Revenue Canada's *income attribution rules*, which will be discussed later in this chapter.

Income and capital gains earned by investment companies, pension funds, and personal trusts do not go untaxed forever. Payments made to investment company shareholders, pension fund beneficiaries, and the beneficiaries of personal trusts are subject to applicable personal income tax rules. The exemptions apply only to taxes that might otherwise be levied at the previous stage.

► Personal Income Taxes

Although the corporate income tax is an important feature of the investment scene, its impact on most individuals is indirect. This is not so for the personal income tax. Few investors can avoid dealing with it in detail, at both an economic and an emotional level. Its provisions have major and direct effects on investment behaviour.

Table 13.3

Personal Federal Income Tax Rates, 1995.

Taxable Income	*Tax Rate*
$29 590 or less	$0 + 17% on next $29 590
29 590 to 59 180	50 303 + 26% on next $29 590
59 180 or more	12 377 + 29% on remainder

Personal Tax Rates (Federal)

Taxes must be paid on an individual's world-wide income as defined in the Income Tax Act.[3] Capital gains were not included in income for tax purposes until the Income Tax Act of 1972 came into force. Certain items may be deducted from income before computing the tax due and capital gains and losses are subject to special procedures which are described in a later section. Deductions of special importance for investment purposes are described in this section as well as in later sections.

Three definitions are relevant for tax purposes. *Total income* is the sum of income received from all sources including self-employment (reported as gross income less expenses). *Net income* is total income less certain allowable expenses (for example, contributions to certain retirement funds, union and/or professional dues, alimony payments). *Taxable income* is net income less other specified deductions.

Despite the 1988 changes to the Income Tax Act, many people are still of the opinion that little is simple about personal income taxes in Canada. Table 13.3 shows the federal tax rates in effect in 1995.

These figures are used to calculate the *gross federal tax*. Each taxpayer is entitled to a non-refundable tax credit which is subtracted directly from the gross federal tax to obtain the *basic federal tax*. Finally, the following surtaxes must be added to arrive at the *total federal tax payable:*

3% of the basic federal tax on the first $12 500,
plus 8% on any amount over $12 500.

Provincial and Territorial Income Taxes

All provinces levy personal income taxes which, except for those in Quebec, are calculated as a percentage of the basic federal tax. These rates vary from 45% in the Northwest Territories to 69% in Newfoundland. Ontario's rate of 58% falls between these two extremes and will be used in subsequent examples. In addition, all provinces also levy provincial surtaxes on high income taxpayers.

In any investment decision, the important figure to know is the total federal plus provincial tax payable. Table 13.4 shows the detailed tax calculation for an unmarried resident of Ontario (or a married resident with a spouse earning more than $6456 per year

---

[3] For more details see S. B. Fisher and P. B. Hickey, eds., "KPMG Personal Tax Planning Guide 1996" (Scarborough, Ont.: Thomson Canada Ltd.), 1995.

Table 13.4

Detailed Tax Calculation for an Ontario Resident in 1995.

Taxable Income	$90 000	
On the first	$59 180 tax is	$12 724.00
On the remaining	$30 820 tax at 29% is	8 937.80
Gross federal tax		21 661.80
Less non-refundable tax credit		1 100.00
Basic federal tax		20 561.80
Federal surcharge:		
on first $12 500 of basic tax (3%)		375.00
on the remaining $8 061.80 (8%)		644.94
Total federal tax payable		21 581.74
Provincial tax calculation:		
Basic tax – 58% of basic federal tax		11 925.84
Surcharge – (1) 20% of basic tax over $5 500		1 285.17
– (2) 10% of basic tax over $8 000		392.58
Total provincial tax payable		13 603.89
Total tax collected		$35 185.33
Marginal tax rate		53.19%
Average tax rate		39.09%

and with no children) with a taxable income of $90 000 derived from employment and interest bearing securities and with a non-refundable tax credit of $1100.[4]

Some taxpayers may be able, in addition, to claim a marriage allowance of $ 5382 and other amounts for dependent children, disability allowance, tuition fees, etc. The non-refundable tax credit is 17% of the sum of all these allowances. It is referred to as non-refundable because it can be used to reduce the tax bill to zero but not to generate a refund.

The combined federal and Ontario provincial tax rates are plotted in Figure 13.1. The top line shows the marginal tax (i.e., the tax rate payable on any additional dollar earned). The lower line shows the average tax rate, which is the ratio of total tax paid to total taxable income.

As can be seen in Figure 13.1, the average rate, a measurement of the overall impact of taxes, is below the marginal rate. The latter, however, is more relevant for most investment decisions. The larger an investor's taxable income, the closer the average tax rate comes to the marginal tax rate. Consider an investor with a taxable income of $90 000 who is evaluating an investment opportunity that is expected to increase his or her taxable income by $3000. Using the figures for the combined federal and provincial tax rates, this opportunity will have the following effect on the taxes payable:

[4] Dividends are subject to a different tax treatment from interest payments, as described in a later section. In 1995, *all* taxpayers were allowed to claim a basic personal allowance of $6456 in order to calculate their non-refundable tax credit.

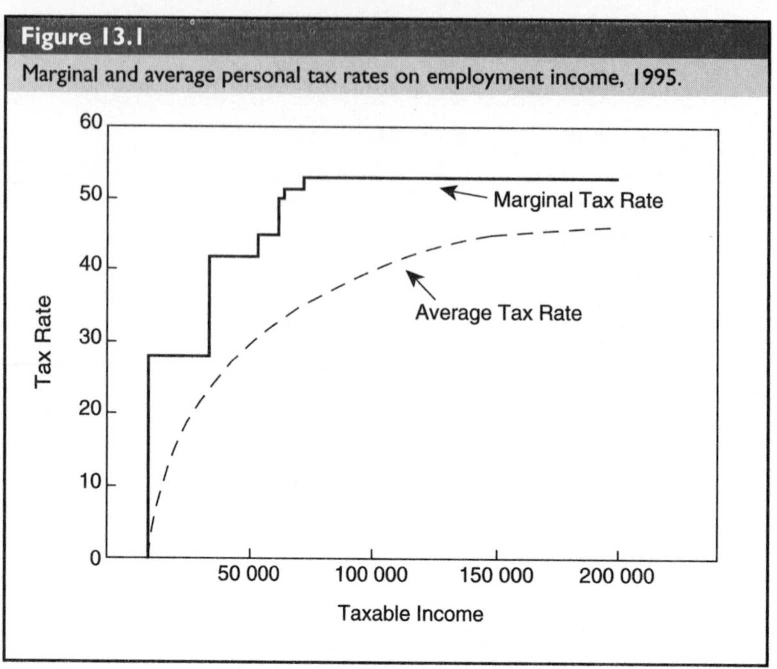

Figure 13.1
Marginal and average personal tax rates on employment income, 1995.

	Before Increase	*After Increase*	*Difference*
Taxable income	$90 000	$93 000	$3 000
Tax payable	35 185	36 781	1 596
Spendable income	$54 815	$56 219	$1 404

Marginal tax rate = ($36 781 – $35 185)/$3000 = $1596/$3000 = 53.2%

As shown in this table, the increase of $3000 in taxable income will result in an increase of $1596 in taxes, leaving a net increase in spendable income of $1404. The calculations for this particular example are simple because the change in taxable income left the taxpayer in the same bracket. Thus, 53.2% of the additional income will be taxed away, leaving 46.8% to be spent. The fact that the average tax rate is 39.09% ($35 185/$90 000) before the increase and 39.55% ($36 781/$93 000) after the increase is irrelevant to this individual in deciding whether or not to make the investment.

When a decision moves income into a higher bracket (a situation that generally applies to taxpayers in lower tax brackets) the computations are more complex. The effective marginal tax rate on such an investment is a weighted average of the two (or more) applicable rates.

Dividend Tax Credit

The **dividend tax credit** (DTC) has a long and honourable history in Canadian tax law. It is designed to mitigate the effects of double taxation (corporate plus personal) on dividend

Table 13.5	
Sample Calculation of the Dividend Tax Credit.	
Dividend received	$1 000.00
Grossed-up dividend	1 250.00
Gross federal tax payable @ 29%	362.50
Less: DTC—0.133333 of $1250	166.63
Basic federal tax	195.87
Federal surtax—8% of basic tax	15.67
Provincial tax and surtax—75.4% of basic tax	147.69
Extra tax payable on the dividend	359.23
Marginal tax rate on dividend income	35.92%

income from taxable Canadian corporations.[5] Prior to the 1972 tax reforms, application of the DTC was simple. The full amount of the dividend was included in taxable income and the gross tax payable computed accordingly. The net tax was then the gross tax less 20% of the dividend.

Since 1972 the system has been more complicated. The following steps must be followed: first, the dividend is *grossed up* by a factor, g; second, the grossed up dividend is included in taxable income and the gross federal tax payable is calculated; third, a factor, q, of the grossed up dividend is allowed as a tax credit and subtracted from gross tax to arrive at the basic federal tax; fourth and fifth, the federal surtax and provincial tax (including surtax, where applicable) is then computed as a fraction of the basic federal tax. The fractions, g and q, are prescribed in the Income Tax Act and its amendments and, therefore, may change from year to year. Table 13.5 shows a sample calculation of the DTC for an Ontario investor in the highest tax bracket of 53.19% who receives a dividend of $1000. For 1995, g is 0.25 and q is 0.1333.

The DTC system can be expressed algebraically as follows:

$$T = (1 + g)(t_f - q)(1 + t_p + t_s) \tag{13.1}$$

where:

T is the total tax payable per dollar of dividend,
g is the gross-up factor,
t_f is the marginal federal tax rate net of surtax,
q is the DTC factor,
t_p is the provincial tax rate (including any surtax) as a fraction of the basic federal tax, and
t_s is the federal surtax rate.

Substituting the figures used in the table into equation (13.1) results in a tax payable of $0.3592 per dollar of dividend that agrees with the marginal tax rate on dividend income of 35.92% obtained above in Table 13.4. This marginal tax rate is substantially smaller than the rate that the same investor would pay on interest income (53.19%). It is clear that, in the

[5] Investors who receive dividends from foreign corporations are generally permitted to deduct any foreign tax paid from their Canadian tax payable but may not claim the DTC. These provisions do not mitigate any double taxation that may occur in the source country.

absence of any risk considerations, a dividend yield of 7.305% provides the above investor with the same after-tax return as an interest payment of 10%. The relationship between dividend yield and interest payment, however, varies according to the investor's tax bracket.

When both corporate and individual taxes are considered it becomes evident that the DTC offers only a partial mitigation of the double taxation problem. A large corporation in Ontario need earn only $100 in order to provide our investor with a before-tax interest payment of $100, but must earn $113.47 if it is in manufacturing and $131.91 if it is a non-manufacturing concern in order to provide the same investor with a dividend payment of $73.05. In the absence of the DTC even more would have to be earned: $155.33 and $180.57 respectively. The situation is different for a small Canadian-controlled corporation, which needs to earn only $94.40 in order to provide the investor with the same after-tax return as an interest payment of $100. In this case there is some over-compensation for double taxation.

Stock dividends are treated in the same way as cash dividends. The cash equivalent of the shares received is grossed up and added to taxable income, and the tax calculation is completed as before, even though the investor has received no cash. This procedure is followed in order to prevent stock dividends from escaping taxation completely because of the lifetime capital gains exemption to (be discussed below).

Capital Gains and Losses

Prior to the 1972 tax reform, the situation was simple — capital gains were not taxed and capital losses were not deductible.

The provisions of the personal income tax laws, introduced in 1972, dealing with the treatment of capital gains and losses have had a great impact on investor behaviour. The taxation of capital gains is now an extremely complex topic. For this reason only the basic elements of these tax provisions will be described here.

A change in the market value of a capital asset is not relevant for tax purposes until it is **realized** as a **capital gain** (or loss) by sale or exchange. If a security purchased for $50 appreciates to a value of $100 in a year, no tax is due on the **unrealized capital gain**. But if it is sold for $120 two years after purchase, the difference of $70 must be declared as a capital gain realized at the time of sale and tax must be paid at the applicable rate.

This rule makes the end of the year an interesting time for stockbrokers. Depending on their situations, their taxpayer-clients may be either anxious or reluctant to realize capital gains or losses before a new tax year begins.

Consider, for example, a taxpayer who earlier in the year sold 1000 shares of stock A for $50 per share, having purchased them three years previously for $20 per share. This investor is liable for taxes on a capital gain of $30 000 (1000 × ($50 – $20)). In December, the investor considers the 1000 shares of stock B, purchased four years ago for $95 per share, now selling for $65 per share. The investor has an unrealized loss of $30 000 (1000 × ($65–$95)) on the investment in B. The investor believes that stock B will rebound in the near future and, therefore, wants to continue owning it. It might seem that the investor should sell B on December 31 and then buy it back January 1, thereby establishing a capital loss of $30 000 on B to offset the capital gain on A. This would remove the tax liability while essentially maintaining his or her position in B. The tax laws, however, preclude a deduction associated with a **superficial loss** on a **wash sale** where a security is sold and a "substantially identical" one is bought within 30 days.

Brokerage firms publish lists pairing similar stocks for those investors who wish to sell a particular stock for tax purposes; by selling a stock and simultaneously purchasing the matching stock, the investor will continually be able to maintain a portfolio with similar investment characteristics. In the previous example, a brokerage firm may have stocks B and C matched together. These two stocks have different issuers but may be in the same industry and, in the opinion of the brokerage firm, be poised for a similar rebound next year. Accordingly, the investor might sell B and purchase C.

End-of-year sales and purchases motivated by tax considerations are fairly common. At this time, securities that experienced substantial price changes during the year tend to have large numbers of trades as holders sell to realize gains or losses. If buyers recognize that the sellers are motivated by knowledge of the tax laws and not some previously unrecognized bad news affecting the company in question, such "selling pressure" should not seriously depress the company's stock price.

Capital gains and losses are those realized on **capital property**, but the Income Tax Act has a specific definition of capital property. For tax purposes, four different kinds of assets are included in capital property: the taxpayer's *principal residence, personal use property, listed personal property*, and *investment and fixed assets in a business*. Gains or losses on current assets that are an integral part of a taxpayer's business (for example, inventories) are considered regular income. The tax treatment of the four kinds of assets is described below.

The capital gain or loss realized when an asset is sold or exchanged is the difference between the value received and the asset's **adjusted cost base** (ACB). For an asset purchased outright, the (initial) ACB is equal to the actual cost of the asset plus any costs or commissions incurred in making the acquisition. Any costs associated with the disposal of the asset simply reduce the size of the capital gain. The treatment of assets received as a gift or inheritance is described below.

While an asset is held, improvements may be made and their costs added to the ACB. On the other hand, any return of capital must be deducted from the ACB, as must depreciation. The accounting required can become complicated. When identical properties such as common shares are purchased at different times and at different prices, these must be pooled in order to determine the ACB. For example, if an investor buys 100 shares at $40 each, then buys another 100 at $50, and later sells 100 shares at $60, what is the realized capital gain? As an adequate identification of the lots is not possible, the ACB used is the average acqusition cost of the shares — $45 — and the gain is $15 per share.

The ability to control the realization of capital gains and losses has obvious advantages. Most important, tax can be paid at the most opportune time. The clearest case involves the realization of capital gains around the time of retirement. Shortly before retirement is usually a time when the taxpayer's income is relatively high, which in turn means that the taxpayer's marginal tax rate is relatively high. After retirement the taxpayer's income and, in turn, marginal tax rate are usually substantially lower. Accordingly, it is generally advantageous for the taxpayer who is near retirement to wait until after retirement to realize any capital gains.

Tax Treatment of Capital Gains and Losses

The tax treatment on disposal of each of the four types of assets included in capital property will be discussed next.

The taxpayer's family home or *principal residence* is not subject to capital gains tax during the owner's lifetime. Unmarried individuals may own a family home that is tax exempt, but married couples are entitled to only one principal residence per family unit. A vacation home (unless it is the only property the family owns) is, therefore, not exempted from capital gains tax and is treated as *personal use property*. This is any asset that is primarily for the personal use or enjoyment of the taxpayer and would not normally be considered an investment asset. If the ACB of personal use property is less than $1000 then, for tax purposes, it is deemed to be $1000. If the selling price of the asset is less than $1000 then no tax is payable. If, on the other hand, the selling price exceeds $1000 then three-quarters of the difference between that price and the ACB must be included in taxable income. Losses may not be claimed on the disposal of personal use property.

The third category, *listed personal property* consists predominantly of collectibles (works of art, rare books, jewelry, etc.). Capital gains realized on the disposal of listed personal property are treated in the same manner as gains on investment assets. Capital losses may only be used to offset gains realized from the sale of other listed personal property.

The final category is *investment and fixed assets in a non-incorporated business*. All capital gains and losses are brought together to obtain a net capital gain or net capital loss figure. If there are net gains, three-quarters of these are included in taxable income whereas three-quarters of net losses (referred to as allowable capital losses) may be used to reduce capital gains in the three immediately preceeding years.[6] As a net result, capital gains are taxed at a preferential rate. In the case of an investor in the maximum marginal tax bracket of 53.19%, the capital gains are taxed at an effective rate of 39.89%. Capital losses may be used to offset capital gains.

Reporting on Capital or Income Account

The gain or loss on the disposition of an investment asset can be taxed either as a gain or loss of income, or as a capital gain or loss at the taxpayer's option. In other words, the taxpayer must choose whether any gains or losses incurred will receive "income or capital treatment." Once the decision has been made, all current and subsequent gains and losses must receive the treatment selected. Certain taxpayers (security dealers, professional traders, and financial institutions) can only report on their income account. The regulations further specify that certain security transactions *must* receive income treatment regardless of the taxpayer's election. Most of these are specialized transactions; however, two of them are noteworthy:

1. The appreciation of a fixed-income security issued at a significant discount (for example, a 91-day Treasury bill) is considered to be income, since it is more akin to interest than to a capital gain.
2. The gain or loss on the short sale of a security is considered to be income.

If Revenue Canada rules that a taxpayer's actions are such that he or she could be considered to be "in the business" of trading securities then all transactions must be reported on the income account. Table 13.6 shows a list of some of the factors that Revenue Canada considers in determining whether or not a taxpayer should be deemed to be carrying on such a business.

---

[6] If any allowable losses are left after extinguishing all prior capital gains then the residue may be carried forward indefinitely.

Table 13.6

Factors Used by Revenue Canada to Determine a Taxpayer's Status.

(a) frequency of transactions—a history of extensive buying and selling of securities or of a quick turnover of properties.
(b) period of ownership—securities are usually owned only for a short period of time.
(c) knowledge of securities markets—the taxpayer has some knowledge or experience in the securities market.
(d) security transactions form a part of a taxpayer's ordinary business.
(e) time spent—a substantial part of a taxpayer's time is spent studying the securities markets and investigating potential purchases.
(f) financing—security purchases are financed primarily on margin or by some other form of debt.
(g) advertising—the taxpayer has advertised or otherwise made it known that he is willing to purchase securities, and
(h) shares owned are normally speculative in nature or of a non-dividend type.

SOURCE: Revenue Canada, *Interpretation Bulletin IT-479R, Transactions in Securities* (Ottawa, February 24, 1984, revised February 21, 1985).

Investors who undertake frequent transactions or who regularly trade in "exotic" securities should recognize that the proceeds of their trading activities may receive income treatment.

Deductible Expenses

Certain interest payments may be deducted from an individual's income to determine taxable income. As a general rule, interest paid on funds borrowed in order to earn business or investment income is tax deductible. This deduction significantly lowers the effective cost of financing an investment by borrowing. To qualify for this deduction, the investment does not have to be profitable, but it must have a reasonable expectation of generating a profit. Borrowing money at 10% in order to buy Canada Savings Bonds paying 7.5% has no reasonable expectation of producing a profit and, therefore, a portion of the interest payment will be disallowed as a deduction. Other expenses associated with investing may be deducted from income if they are ordinary and necessary, and in line with reasonable expectations of a profitable return. Thus, fees paid for investment advice or safekeeping of securities (e.g., a safety deposit box) may be deducted.

Investments that habitually produce financial losses but non-financial pleasure may be considered hobbies by Revenue Canada and may, therefore, not qualify for some or all of the associated deductions. This possibility should concern the racehorse owner, for example, but not the serious investor.

Alternative Minimum Tax

There has long been a suspicion that certain wealthy individuals are able to use tax shelters and other legitimate deductions to pay out only a small fraction of their income in taxes. An *Alternative Minimum Tax* (AMT) has, therefore, been introduced. The calculation of AMT is complicated. As a rule of thumb, a taxpayer may be liable for the AMT if the following condition holds:

$$\text{Tax Payable} < 0.17 \times (\text{Total Income} - \$40\ 000)$$

One tax advisor has put forward the following advice for those in the top tax bracket: One, if you are pleased with the small amount of tax that you calculate this year, you may have an AMT problem. Two, if you think you may be subject to the AMT, then get professional advice.[7]

Tax Reduction Techniques

Tax avoidance is a legitimate activity, whereas tax evasion is illegal. Legal procedures for reducing immediate taxes fall into the following classifications: tax deferrals and tax shelters. As the name implies, the former are methods for delaying the payment of taxes to a time when the taxpayer expects to face a lower marginal tax rate. The latter, on the other hand, purportedly provide methods for shielding income from taxation.

Tax Deferrals

The two principally used forms of tax deferral will be described here.

The best known and most popular tax deferral technique in Canada is the **Registered Retirement Savings Plan** (RRSP). In any year, taxpayers are permitted to contribute a specified fraction (18% in 1996) of *earned income* (to a specified maximum, $13 500 in 1996) to an RRSP established at a financial institution and to deduct the amount from that year's taxable income.[8] Furthermore, the investment returns can accumulate within the plan tax-free. Withdrawals from the plan are permitted at any time, but the amount withdrawn must be added to that year's taxable income.

Full withdrawal, usually on retirement, must occur by age 69 and can receive different tax treatment. For example, the retiree may remove the full amount from the RRSP and purchase an *annuity* that pays the proceeds out over a number of years. Only the annual annuity payment need be included in taxable income. This procedure significantly reduces the overall tax burden on retirement.

An RRSP is a vehicle for accumulating investment returns at a before-tax rate. Suppose that an individual, in the highest tax bracket of 53.19%, wishes to put aside $1200 per year for the next 30 years in an investment that will earn 9% per year. In the absence of an RRSP the investment returns will be taxed each year so that the effective rate of interest will be 4.6071%. At the end of 30 years the individual will have $74 553 on which no further tax is payable. By utilizing an RRSP, the individual can contribute $2344.15 each year to the plan and maintain the same annual disposable income. After 30 years the amount in the plan is $319 525. If this is withdrawn as a lump sum and full tax paid, the net receipt is $163 569, a gain of almost 120%. It is not surprising, therefore, that many Canadians have established RRSPs.

A similar device is a *Deferred Profit Sharing Plan*. This is essentially the same as an RRSP except that the employer makes the contributions directly into the employee's plan.

---

[7] Richard Birch, *The Canadian Price Waterhouse Personal Tax Advisor, 1990* (McClelland-Bantam, Inc.), 1989.

[8] Earned income is defined to include employment income, business income, rental income, and some others. The upper contribution limit is expected to remain unchanged until the year 2001. The upper limit is less for taxpayers whose employer provides a pension plan. This reduction is consistent with the stated objectives of an RRSP, which is to provide retirement income.

The upper contribution limit in 1996 was \$6750. The employer's contribution reduces the amount that the employee can contribute to an RRSP.

Tax Shelters

Income splitting between spouses is an effective way to shelter a portion of investment income and thereby reduce the family's aggregate tax payments. The idea is simple and consists of transferring ownership of income-producing assets from the higher tax bracket family member to the lower tax bracket member or members. Revenue Canada has, however, established a number of rules which must be observed if the income is not to be **attributed** back to the original owner, thereby negating the purpose of the exercise. It pays to read the regulations carefully if income splitting is contemplated. One relatively straightforward way to split income is to establish a **spousal RRSP**. The higher tax bracket family member makes the contributions to the plan in the normal way, but ownership of the plan is vested in the lower tax bracket family member. The benefits of such a plan will be evident at retirement, providing that the plan owner is then in a lower tax bracket than the contributor.

Other tax shelters are also available. Many advertisements exhort high tax-bracket investors to put their money in frontier oil and gas exploration, multiple unit real estate, films and videos produced in Canada, and other investments with purportedly attractive tax characteristics. Such "tax shelters" are devised to take advantage of tax provisions allowing large deductions to create a "tax loss" in the present, to be followed by a subsequent profit, generally in the form of a capital gain. The higher the taxpayer's marginal tax rate, the more attractive these investments become. Therefore, only those in the highest brackets should find such investments interesting. These enterprises are generally formed as limited partnerships. A promoter, or general partner, puts together the operation, with individual investors as limited partners. The hoped-for results are tidy profits for the promoter and the investors, at the expense of the tax collector.

► Estate and Gift Taxes

As of December 1995, there are neither explicit federal nor provincial estate or gift taxes in Canada. Some gifts and estate bequests are taxed as capital gains and losses.

A gift of cash or securities to a spouse incurs no tax liability at the time of transfer; the recipient assumes the asset at the donor's ACB. If the spouse disposes of the asset while the donor is still alive then any capital gain or loss must be reported by the donor in the year of its disposal. For example, in 1987 an investor purchases 500 shares at a price of \$6.25 per share plus commissions of \$0.25 per share making a total ACB of \$6.50 per share. In 1991, she makes a gift of these shares, currently priced at \$12.00 per share, to her husband. In 1996, he sells the shares at \$15.00 per share, realizing a capital gain of $500 \times (15 - 6.5) = \$4250$ that his wife must report in her 1996 tax return. If instead he waits until 1998 (after his wife's demise) to sell the shares for \$15.00 per share then he must report the capital gain of \$4250.

Gifts to other people, including children, are deemed to have taken place at the fair market value at the time of transfer. The donor, therefore, must report, in the year in which the gift is made, the difference between the fair market value and the ACB, and the recipient must use the fair market value as his or her ACB. If, in the example above, the investor had given the shares to her daughter instead of to her husband she would report an immediate capital gain of $500 \times (12 - 6.5) = \$2750$ in 1991 and the daughter would report a capital gain of $500 \times (15 - 12) = \$1500$ in the year in which she sells them for \$15.00.

INSTITUTIONAL ISSUES

Taxing Pension Funds and RRSPs

The battle over reducing the federal budget deficit continues unabated. Two of the last unexploited sources of significant tax revenue are private pension plans and RRSPs. Virtually all such pension plans conform to specific government regulations and as a result offer their sponsors and participants several important tax advantages:

1. Employers may treat pension fund contributions as tax-deductible expenses.
2. Employees defer paying taxes on contributions that their employers make to the pension funds on their behalf.
3. Pension fund investment earnings are not taxed until they are withdrawn.

Under present laws, employers (and in some cases employees) make tax-deductible contributions to a pension plan to prefund pension benefits that are to be paid upon employees' subsequent retirements. These employer contributions clearly represent a form of income to employees. After all, employers could just as easily increase the employees' paycheques by the amount of the contributions and let the employees invest those dollars for themselves. Moreover, this income is invested and grows untaxed over the employees' working lives. Eventually, the employees pay taxes on their invested pension contributions, but not until they receive their pension benefits during their retirement years. Private individuals derive similar benefits from their RRSP contributions.

Proponents of taxing pension plans contend that the costs of exempting pension plans from taxation far exceed the benefits. Their primary argument is that pension funds do not increase national savings significantly. This contention may seem counterintuitive at first. Pension fund taxation proponents believe that employees save less outside of their pension funds because of the savings that accumulate inside the pension funds. That is, pension savings offset other personal savings. Proponents estimate that this offset, while not dollar-for-dollar, effectively reduces net savings from pension plans to about the same amount that Revenue Canada forgoes in lost tax revenues each year.

Taxation proponents also contend that exempting pension funds from taxation violates fundamental tax fairness principles. Not all of the Canadian working population is covered by pension plans. Moreover, those persons covered tend to be in the higher income categories. Further, as these higher income persons are subject to higher marginal tax rates, the benefit of tax-exempt pension funds is greatest for them. (The existence of RRSPs, however, weakens this argument as an employee not covered by a pension plan can design a "homemade" pension plan within an RRSP.)

Most proposals to tax pension funds involve levying a tax on each pension plan expressed as a percentage of the plan's annual contributions and investment earnings. Benefits would then not be subject to tax. As a transition to the tax scheme, a one-time tax on the plans' assets would be charged, thus taxing employees who have already accrued benefits tax-free.

Opponents of taxing pension funds take issue with the crowding-out theory of taxation proponents. That theory is difficult to substantiate empirically, and the crowding-out effect may be much less than proponents contend.

They go on to argue that, as savings ultimately have a multiplier effect on national income, accepting a \$1 revenue loss for \$1 of additional savings may be a sound long-term trade-off.

As for the equity issue, taxation opponents point out that higher income persons in all economies always provide the bulk of the economies' savings. It may be unrealistic and counterproductive to add to the existing disincentives to save in the name of wealth equity.

INSTITUTIONAL ISSUES (continued)

Opponents also point to the technical difficulties of taxing pension plans. A large fraction of pension assets are held by provincial and local pension plans. The employers get no tax benefit from contributions, while taxing the employees would be politically tricky.

Taxation of pension funds, if and when it ever occurs, may not take the form of radical legislation. Rather, it may begin with seemingly innocuous dips into pension fund coffers, such as taxes on pension fund holdings of foreign securities above a certain threshold, or taxes on pension funds' security transactions as well as on their capital gains.

When a taxpayer dies, he or she is deemed to have sold all assets immediately prior to death. A capital gains tax liability will exist against the estate except in the case of assets willed to the spouse, which carry the original ACB and, therefore, attract no immediate tax.

The estate must file an income tax return for a deceased taxpayer. This will be a terminal settlement of all unpaid taxes.

INFLATION IN CANADA

The story is told of the modern-day Rip Van Winkle, who awoke in the year 2010 and immediately called his broker. (Fortunately, pay phones at the time permitted a call of up to three minutes without charge.) He first asked what had happened to the $10 000 he had instructed the broker to put in short-term Treasury bills, continually reinvesting the proceeds. The broker promptly informed him that due to high interest rates and the power of compounding, his initial $10 000 investment had grown to be worth over $1 million. Stunned, Mr. Van Winkle inquired about his stocks, which were also worth about $10 000 when he dozed off. The broker told him that he was in for an even more pleasant surprise: they were now worth $2.5 million. "In short, Mr. Van Winkle," said the broker, "you are a millionaire 3.5 times over."

At this point an operator cut in: "Your three minutes are over, please deposit $100 for an additional three minutes." While this clearly overstates the case, there is no doubt that **inflation** is a major concern for investors. By and large, people have come to fear significant inflation, particularly when it is unpredictable.

► Measuring Inflation

There is no completely satisfactory way to summarize the price changes that have occurred over a given time period for the large number of goods and services available in Canada. Nevertheless, Statistics Canada has attempted to do so by measuring the cost of a specific mix of major items (a "basket of goods") at various points in time. The "overall" price level computed for this representative combination of items is termed a **cost-of-living index**. The percentage change in this index over a given time period can then be viewed as a measure of the inflation (or deflation) that took place from the beginning of the period to the end of the period.

Whether or not this measure of inflation is relevant for a given individual depends to a major extent on the similarity of his or her purchases to the mix of items used to construct the index. Even if an individual finds the mix to be appropriate at the beginning of a period, the rate of increase in the mix over the time period is likely to overstate the increase in the cost of living for the individual. There are two reasons for this. First, improvements in the quality of the items in the mix are seldom taken adequately into account. This means the end-of-period price for a good is not comparable to the beginning-of-period price, since the good is different. For example, a new Toyota may have a 5% higher sticker price than a similar model had the previous year, but the newer model may have better tires on it than the older model. Hence, it would be inaccurate to conclude that the price of this particular model rose by 5% over the year.

Second, and perhaps more important, little or no adjustment is made in the mix as relative prices change. The rational customer can reduce the cost of attaining a given standard of living as prices change by substituting relatively less expensive goods for those that have become relatively more expensive. For example, if the price of beef rises 20% over a given year while the price of chicken rises only 10% over the same year, then the customer may start to eat more chicken and less beef. Failure to take into account this change in the mix will result in an overstatement in the rate of inflation. Despite these two drawbacks, cost-of-living indices provide at least rough estimates of changes in prices.

► Price Indices

As mentioned earlier, no price index can prove totally satisfactory as an indicator of the cost of living for all consumers. Most indices are likely to overstate the extent to which the cost of attaining a given level of satisfaction actually increases during any inflationary period, even for the people whose purchases the index was intended to reflect. Although this is fairly well understood and most governments compute a number of alternative indices to provide a wider choice for analysis, many people tend to focus on one index as an indicator of the price level.

In Canada, the **Consumer Price Index** (CPI) often fills this role, despite attempts to discourage its widespread use.[9] Recognizing its importance, Statistics Canada has changed the composition of the market basket of goods used to make up the CPI from time to time in order to provide a more representative index. Furthermore, the process by which the relevant data are gathered and verified has periodically been improved.

In Chapter 1, Table 1.1 provided some historical perspective on the rate of inflation in Canada. It showed the annual rate of increase in the CPI from 1950 through 1987. As an aid to interpretation, these rates are plotted on a graph, shown in Figure 13.2(a). As can be seen in the figure, the CPI did not grow at a constant rate over the period of 1950 to 1987. However, prices increased in almost every year. Generally speaking, there were four subperiods with different rates of inflation: high inflation in 1950 and 1951, mild inflation from 1952 to 1966, fairly rapid (but uneven) inflation from 1967 to 1982, followed by moderate inflation for 1983 to 1987.

Table 13.7 shows the average annual rate of growth of the CPI for each of these subperiods, measured by what is known as the **geometric mean** growth rate of the CPI. This growth rate, when compounded over the subperiod and applied to the beginning index value, results in the ending index value. For example, at the end of 1977, the CPI was 53.3, and at the end of 1991, it was at 126.4 (the CPI was adjusted so that its average monthly

---

[9] A number of authorities prefer "deflators" derived from gross national product figures, but such indices have not received the publicity accorded the CPI.

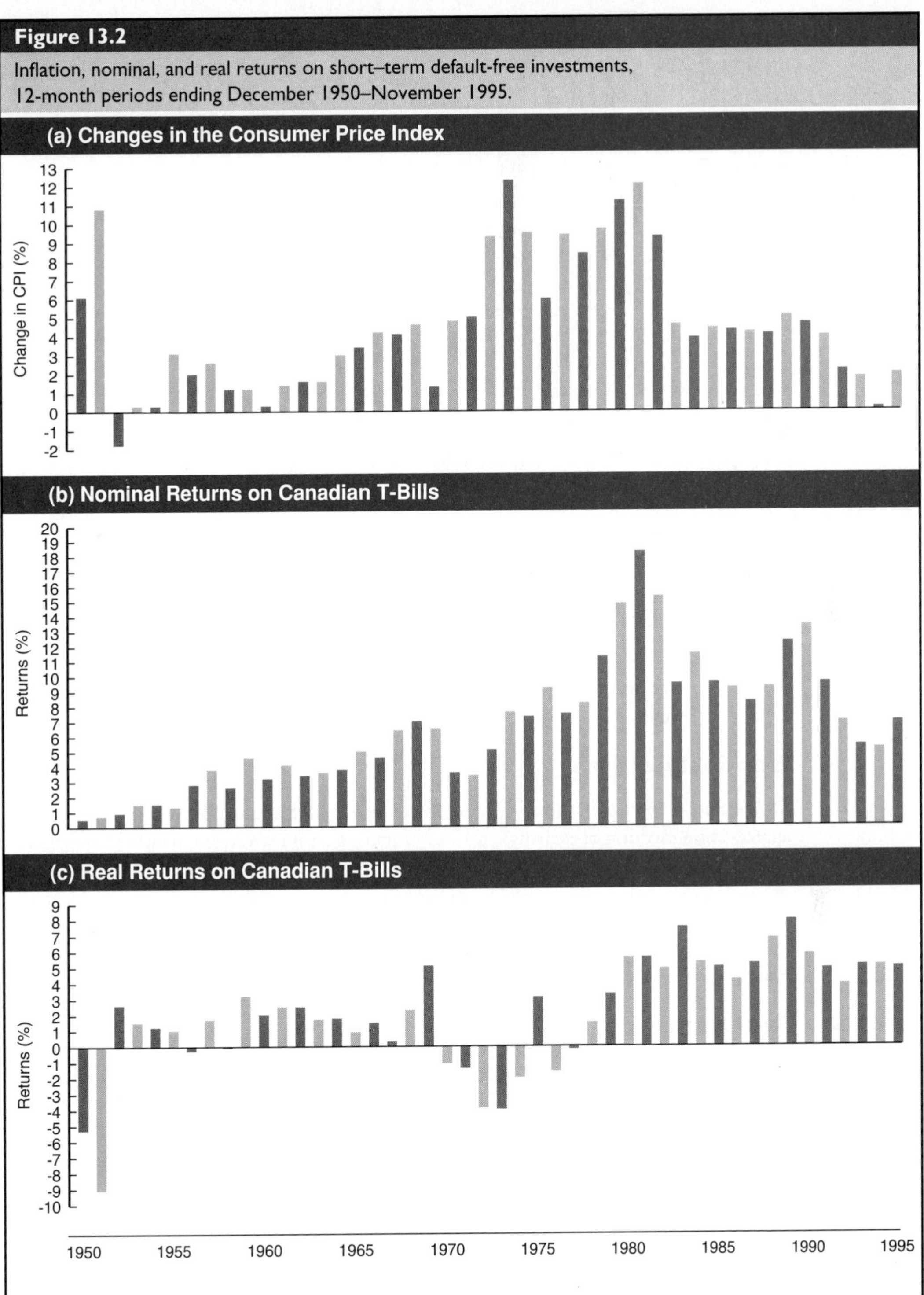
Figure 13.2
Inflation, nominal, and real returns on short–term default-free investments, 12-month periods ending December 1950–November 1995.
(a) Changes in the Consumer Price Index
Change in CPI (%)
(b) Nominal Returns on Canadian T-Bills
Returns (%)
(c) Real Returns on Canadian T-Bills
Returns (%)
1950
1955
1960
1965
1970
1975
1980
1985
1990
1995

SOURCE: See Table 1.1.

Table 13.7

Growth Rates of the Canadian Consumer Price Index.

From	*To*	*Rate of Growth (% Per Year)*
1950	1951	8.4
1952	1965	1.3
1966	1982	7.3
1983	1990	4.4
1992	1995[a]	2.0

[a] to November 30, 1995.

value in 1986 was 100). Thus, the geometric mean growth rate was 6.36%, since 53.3, when compounded at this rate over 14 years, equals 126.4:

$$126.4 = 53.3 \times (1 + .0636)^{14}.$$

More generally, the geometric mean (g) can be calculated by solving the following equation for g:

$$C_e = C_b(1 + g)^y \tag{13.2}$$

which results in

$$g = \left(\frac{C_e}{C_b}\right)^{1/y} - 1 \tag{13.3}$$

where y denotes the number of years and C_e and C_b denote the ending and beginning CPI values, respectively.

Nominal Returns

Modern economies gain much of their efficiency through the use of money—a generally agreed-upon medium of exchange. Instead of trading corn for a stereo to be delivered in one year, as in a barter economy, the citizen of a modern economy can trade his or her corn for money and then trade this "current" money for "future" money by investing it. Later, the "future" money can be used to buy a stereo. The rate at which the citizen can trade current money for future money depends on the investment he or she makes and is known as the **nominal return** (also known as the nominal rate).

Real Returns

In times of changing prices, the nominal return on an investment may be a poor indicator of the **real return** (also known as the real rate) obtained by the investor.[10] This is because part of the additional dollars received from the investment may be needed to recoup the citizen's lost purchasing power due to inflation that has occurred over the investment period. As a result, the nominal return needs to be adjusted to remove the effect of inflation in order to determine the real return. Frequently, the CPI is used for this purpose.

---

[10] Here, real return refers to the increase in purchasing power that the citizen has received as a result of making a particular investment.

For example, assume that at the start of a given year the CPI is at a level of 121 and that at the end of the year it is at a level of 124. This means that it costs $124 at the end of the year to buy the same amount of the CPI market basket of goods that at the start of the year could have been purchased for $121. Assuming the nominal return is 8% for this year, the individual who started the year with $121 and invested it would have $121 × 1.08 = $130.68 at year-end. At this point, the individual could purchase ($130.68/$124) – 1 = .0539 = 5.39% more of the CPI market basket of goods than at the beginning of the year. Thus, the real return for this investment was 5.39%, after allowing for inflation.

These calculations can be summarized in the following formula:

$$\left(C_0 \times \frac{1 + NR}{C_1}\right) - 1 = RR \tag{13.4}$$

where:

C_0 = CPI at the beginning of the year,
C_1 = CPI at the end of the year,
NR = the nominal return,
RR = the real return.

Alternatively, the individual could note that an increase in the CPI from 121 to 124 can be translated into an inflation rate of (124/121) – 1 = .0248, or 2.48%. Denoting this inflation rate as I, the real return can be calculated using the following formula:

$$\left(\frac{1 + NR}{1 + I}\right) - 1 = RR. \tag{13.5}$$

Note that for the example, $RR = (1.08/1.0248) - 1 = .0539$, or 5.39%.

For quick calculation, the real return can be estimated by simply subtracting the inflation rate from the nominal return:

$$NR - I \cong RR \tag{13.6}$$

where $\cong$ means "is approximately equal to." In this example, the quick method results in an estimate of the real return of .08 – .0248 = .0552, or 5.52%. Thus, the error resulting from use of this method is .0552 – .0539 = .0013, or .13%.[11] This relationship between real and nominal rates is known as the Fisher model, named after Irving Fisher, its originator.

► The Effect of Investor Expectations

The simplest view of investors' attitudes toward inflation is that they are concerned with real returns, not nominal returns, and that a single price index is adequate to characterize the difference. Looking to the future, investors do not know what the rate of inflation will be, nor do they know what the nominal return on an investment will be. However, in both cases they have expectations, which are denoted as EI (expected rate of inflation) and ENR (expected nominal return), respectively. Thus, the expected real return on an investment can be approximated by

$$ERR = ENR - EI. \tag{13.7}$$

[11] This error will be larger for higher rates of inflation. Thus, in those countries with "hyperinflation," the quick method will have a substantial amount of error associated with it. For example, if the nominal return is 110% and the inflation rate is 100%, then the true real return is 5%, but the quick method will indicate it is twice as large, 10%.

If a security is to provide a given expected real return, the expected nominal return must be larger by the expected rate of inflation for the relevant holding period. This can be seen by rearranging equation (11.6):

$$ENR = ERR + EI. \tag{13.8}$$

For example, if the expected rate of inflation is 4% and a given security is to provide investors with an expected real return of 6%, then the security must be priced in the marketplace so that its expected nominal return is 10%. In summary, if investors are concerned with real returns, all securities will be priced by the actions of the marketplace so that expected nominal returns incorporate the expected rate of inflation.

► Interest Rates and Inflation

At the start of a given investment holding period, nominal interest rates for securities having no risk of default should cover both a requisite expected real return and the expected rate of inflation for the period in question. At the end of the period, the real return actually received will be the difference between the nominal return and the rate of inflation actually experienced. Only when actual inflation equals expected inflation will the actual real return equal the expected real return on such securities.

As mentioned earlier, Figure 13.2(a) indicates the annual rate of inflation, as measured by changes in the CPI, over the 38-year period 1950–1987. Part (b) shows how short-term nominal interest rates varied over this time period; Treasury bill rates, taken from Table 1.1, are used for this purpose. Part (c), obtained by subtracting part (a) from part (b), represents real returns.

One cannot help being struck by the fact that those who invested in short-term securities over this period frequently ended up with less purchasing power than they started with, since the real return was negative in 11 of the 38 years. Perhaps even more surprising, the average real return over the period 1950 to 1979 was close to zero.

Although expected real returns may vary from year to year, the variation is relatively small. Otherwise investors would not be willing to invest in short-term, highly liquid securities even though they expected to earn close to nothing in real terms. If they are currently willing to do so, such securities will be priced to give a very low expected real return.[12]

If this assumption is made, the "market's" predicted rate of inflation over the near future can be estimated by simply subtracting the estimated expected real rate, say 1%, from the nominal interest rate (also known as the yield) on short-term government securities, namely, Treasury bills. In a sense, this Treasury bill rate represents a consensus prediction of inflation—a prediction that an average investor in this market would make and one that is likely to be more accurate than the predictions of any single forecaster.

► The Effect of Inflation on Borrowers and Lenders

Although deviations of actual inflation from expected inflation may have relatively little effect on the real return on investments in general, they may have a significant effect on

[12]However, there apparently are periods of time when such securities have an expected real return that is positive. For example, in the 1980–1987 period, Treasury bill returns actually exceeded the rate of change in the CPI by over 5%. This suggests that investors probably expected a positive real return over the latter part of the period.

specific investments. In fact, one would expect a direct impact on the real returns associated with investments whose payments are fixed in terms of dollars to be received.

A simple example will illustrate the relationship. Assume that everyone currently expects the rate of inflation to be 5% over the next year and that a lender has agreed to make loans at a nominal rate of 5% (that is, the lender is content with having an expected real return of zero). Thus, one can borrow $100 now and, one year later, pay back $100 × 1.05 = $105 for a one-year loan. That is, if actual inflation equals expected inflation, a one-year loan would require a payment equivalent to $100 in constant (current) dollars a year hence. In this case, the real rate of interest would turn out to be zero.

Now, imagine that an individual takes advantage of the lender's offer, borrowing $100 for one year. How will the borrower and lender be affected if the actual rate of inflation differs from the expected rate of inflation?

Assume that in the first year, prices rise by 9% instead of the expected 5%, meaning that unexpected inflation is 4% = 9% – 5%. In this situation, the short-term borrower gains at the expense of the lender because the borrower still must repay $105, but this is only $105/1.09 = $96.33 in constant-dollar terms, less than the amount of the loan. As a result, the lender receives a real rate of interest of ($96.33 – $100)/$100 = –3.67%, instead of the anticipated rate of 0%.

What if first-year prices had risen by only 3%, meaning that unexpected inflation is –2% = 3% – 5%? In this situation, the short-term lender gains at the expense of the borrower. Although the borrower must repay $105, in constant-dollar terms this amounts to $105/1.03 = $101.94, greater than the amount of the loan. As a result, the lender receives a real rate of interest of ($101.94 – $100)/$100 = 1.94% instead of the anticipated rate of 0%.

These results can be generalized: when the actual rate of inflation exceeds the expected rate of inflation, those with commitments to make payments that are fixed in nominal terms (debtors) gain in real terms at the expense of those to whom payments are to be made (creditors). Conversely, when actual inflation is less than expected inflation, creditors gain and debtors lose.[13] This uncertainty in the real return on fixed-income securities that is due to uncertain inflation is frequently referred to as **purchasing-power risk**.

► Indexation

The previous section suggests that in a world of uncertain inflation, even default-free bonds are subject to purchasing power risk. Contractual nominal interest rates can cover expected inflation, but the subsequent real return from any investment with fixed nominal payments will depend on the actual amount of inflation. As long as the two differ, the expected real return will be uncertain. However, there is a way to design a bond so that its expected real return is certain. This involves the use of **indexation**.

If a specified price index can adequately measure purchasing power, there is no reason why a contract cannot be written with specified real payments instead of specified nominal payments. Thus, if the CPI currently stands at C_0 and will be C_1 one year later, C_2 two years later, and so on, in return for a ten-year loan of $100 a borrower might promise

[13] More specifically, it can be shown that long-term borrowers are likely to gain somewhat more than short-term borrowers when actual inflation exceeds expected inflation and lose somewhat more when actual inflation falls below expectations. Similarly, long-term lenders are likely to lose somewhat more than short-term lenders when actual inflation exceeds expectations and gain somewhat more when actual inflation falls below expectations.

to pay \$10 × C_1 one year later, \$10 × C_2 two years later, …, and \$110 × C_{10} ten years later. To convert these payments to constant real dollars, each one must be divided by the corresponding price level:

Time	Amount in Nominal Dollars	Price Level (CPI)	Amount in Real Dollars
1	$10 \times C_1$	C_1	10
2	$10 \times C_2$	C_2	10
⋮	⋮	⋮	⋮
10	$110 \times C_{10}$	C_{10}	110

The real value of each payment is the amount shown in the final column, regardless of what happens to prices (that is, regardless of the actual values of C_1, C_2, and so on). Thus, the loan is said to be fully indexed, since all amounts are tied to a stated price index on a one-for-one basis. This means that when the price index goes up by 10%, for example, all the subsequent payments go up by 10%.

In some countries, a great many contracts are tied to standard price indices (two notable examples are Israel and Brazil). Government bonds, returns on savings accounts, wage contracts, pension plans, insurance contracts—all have been indexed at various times and places. In Canada, Canada Pension Plan benefits are indexed, as are the pension plans of civil servants, MPs, and some employees. Some of these are fully indexed, while others are only partially indexed, meaning that payments might be increased by, for example, 75% of the price index increases. Since the mid-1970s, personal income tax brackets have been indexed to the CPI of the preceding year. In December 1991, the Canadian government introduced its first indexed bonds, known as Real Return Bonds. They are described in some detail in the next chapter.

The key advantage of indexation is its role in reducing or eliminating purchasing power risk. Typically, higher expected inflation is accompanied by increased uncertainty about the actual rate of inflation. This increased uncertainty means that the potential gains and losses to both non-indexed borrowers and non-indexed lenders are larger. Since both borrowers and lenders dislike the prospect of losses more than they like the prospect of gains, there will be increased pressure for indexation by both borrowers and lenders when a country moves into periods of high inflationary expectations.

Thus, when uncertainty about inflation is substantial, one would expect indexation to become widespread. However, laws regulating interest rates frequently prevent the issuance of fully indexed debt, since these laws usually place a ceiling on the nominal rate but not the real rate. This leads to predictable inefficiencies when expected inflation increases, since rationing of credit that is subject to such ceilings would be required. Rationing would be necessary because a ceiling on the nominal rate means that the real rate declines as inflationary expectations increase, which in turn makes this type of credit attractive to borrowers.[14]

[14] Actually, rationing might not occur, since lenders may simply refuse to make those kinds of loans that are subject to ceilings when inflationary expectations are high.

INSTITUTIONAL ISSUES

The Taxation of Investment Returns

Economists agree that taxing any commodity or activity reduces the output of that commodity or activity. Taxing gains on capital assets, therefore, reduces the amount of capital assets "produced." Other things remaining the same (always a tenuous assumption), lower tax rates will encourage saving, increase investment, and thus enhance economic productivity. However, as the vast proportion of taxable capital assets is directly or indirectly held by a minority of relatively affluent people, proponents of wealth redistribution view capital gains taxes as symbolic of their effort to create a more egalitarian society.

Certain general features of the Canadian tax system lead to movements of wealth from the private sector to the federal government that increase with the rate of inflation. Thus, one of the potential beneficiaries of inflation is the federal government.

Consider a one-year security with an expected real pre-tax return of 7% that is held by someone in a 30% marginal tax bracket. In the absence of inflation, the investor would expect to receive a real return of $(1 - .3) \times 7\% = 4.9\%$. Now, assume that the expected rate of inflation is 2%, so that the expected pre-tax nominal return on the security is $(1.07 \times 1.02) - 1 = 9.14\%$. In this case, the investor's expected after-tax nominal return is $(1 - .3) \times 9.14\% = 6.40\%$, but in real terms this is $(1.0640/1.02) - 1 = 4.31\%$. Similarly, if expected inflation is 4%, then the expected pre-tax nominal return will be 11.28%, the investor's expected after-tax nominal return will be 7.90%, and his or her expected after-tax real return will be 3.75%.

Since it is reasonable to assume that, over time, actual inflation rates will approximately equal expected inflation rates, it can be seen that the higher the actual inflation rate, the lower the actual real after-tax return. In this example, the after-tax real return decreased from 4.9% with no inflation to 4.31% with 2% inflation and to 3.75% with 4% inflation. Thus, taxation of interest income can be viewed as being equivalent to an effective tax rate on real returns that increases with inflation; that is, the higher the inflation rate, the larger the portion of the real pre-tax return that is being allocated to the government. This phenomenon could be avoided by levying taxes on real returns instead of nominal returns.

The tax assessed on your capital, as distinguished from the tax imposed on the profits from your capital, is more akin to a property tax than an income tax. Moreover, the level of that tax changes with the inflation rate, producing an arbitrary and capricious tax structure. Over some holding periods, a capital asset's value may actually suffer a decline in real terms, yet inflation boosts its nominal value sufficiently to generate a gain for tax reporting purposes. An investor selling this asset could find himself or herself paying capital gains taxes on an inflation-adjusted capital loss.

The solution to this inequity involves indexing the base value (that is, the original cost) of the capital asset to the inflation rate. The base value is adjusted upward by the inflation rate experienced over the period the capital asset is held. Only gains above this adjusted base are subject to tax.

Pension funds and RRSPs are big businesses that pay no taxes until the funds are withdrawn by the beneficiaries. In 1993 pension funds held assets worth $257.4 billion and individuals held $188 billion in their RRSPs. Allowing a quite conservative investment return of 6% and an average tax rate across beneficiaries of 45% this represents an immediate tax loss to Revenue Canada of $12 billion — more if the tax deductibility of contributions is also ended. This sum is enough to make a sizable dent in the federal deficit. It must be conceded that taxes will ultimately be paid on these funds but that only occurs later and probably at a reduced tax rate.

INSTITUTIONAL ISSUES (continued)

The fairness and simplicity of adjusting capital gains taxes for inflation seems indisputable. Why has such a proposal not received popular support? Several explanations are plausible. First, in periods of relatively low inflation, such as we have seen since the early 1980s, the inflation-compensation component of capital gains is relatively small, making the issue less pressing. Second, in periods of large budget deficits, any cut in taxes, even in the name of equity and increased long-term investment, causes short-term problems. Current government spending would have to be reduced or other taxes increased if the budget deficit were not to grow in the short term due to the effective capital gains tax cut. Finally, if one accepts the argument for adjusting capital gains for inflation, should not the same logic apply to interest income as well? After all, this investment income has its own inflation-compensation component. However, the tax revenue lost from such a change in the taxation of interest income is unthinkable in these days of large budget deficits.

A notable example occurred in Canada in the 1960s. At that time, ceilings placed on nominal rates paid by banks, coupled with increased inflationary expectations, caused a substantial outflow of funds from such companies and a corresponding reduction in the amount of money made available by them for home mortgages. On the other side were those issuers of securities that were not subject to rate ceilings and who offered an appropriate nominal rate and, thus, had little difficulty in attracting funds. The term **disintermediation** was invented to describe this pattern of funds' flow.

Since inflation is generally harder to predict for longer time periods relative to shorter time periods, uncertainty about inflation often leads to a reduction in the average term-to-maturity of newly issued fixed-income securities. Here term-to-maturity refers to the length of time from the date of issue of the security until the date that last payment is to be made. For example, the average term-to-maturity of fixed-coupon debt issued in periods of great inflationary uncertainty is usually shorter than in more stable times.

Alternatively, debt with long maturities can be written with **variable rates** (also known as floating rates) of interest. Such instruments provide long-term debt at short-term rates. Interest payments are allowed to vary, with each one determined by adding a fixed number of percentage points (say, 2%) to a specified base rate that changes periodically. Two base rates frequently used are the prime rate and the yield on 91-day Treasury bills. If short-term interest rates anticipate inflation reasonably well, such a variable rate security is a reasonable substitute for a fully indexed bond.

► Stock Returns and Inflation

Long-Term Historical Relationships

It is reasonable to assume that investors are more concerned with real returns than with nominal returns because real returns reflect how much better off they are after adjusting for inflation. Accordingly, real returns of securities need to be analyzed. This is done in Table 13.8 for US common stocks and Treasury bills for the long-term period of 1802 to 1993 and five relatively long subperiods.

Table 13.8

Rates of Return on Stocks, Bills, and the Equity Premium.

Period (1)	Real Return on Stocks (2)	Real Return on Bills (3)	Equity Premium (2) – (3) = (4)
1802–1990[1]	7.81%	3.19%	4.62%
1802–1888[1]	7.52	5.62	1.90
1889–1978[1]	7.87	.91	6.96
1979–1990[1]	9.44	2.73	6.71
1926–1993[2]	9.09	.49	8.60
1950–1993[2]	9.29	.92	8.37

[1] *SOURCE:* Andrew B. Abel, "The Equity Premium Puzzle," *Federal Reserve Bank of Philadelphia Business Review* (September-October 1991), p. 8.

[2] *SOURCE:* Table 1.1.

Column (2) of the table shows that, on average, the rate of return on common stocks in the US has substantially exceeded the rate of inflation, providing a real return of nearly 8% for the entire period examined and in excess of 7% in all of the subperiods. In comparison, the rate of return on Treasury bills exceeded the rate of inflation by over 3% in the entire period. However, the subperiods show substantial variation, as the real return ranged from .49% over the period from 1926 to 1993 to 5.62% in the period from 1802 to 1888. Also of interest is the **equity premium** shown in column (4), which is simply the difference between the real rates of return on stocks and bills. Although less than 2% from 1802 to 1888, it has since then been nearly 7%, an amount that some researchers believe is inexplicably large. In summary, Table 13.8 shows that common stocks have historically returned substantially more than the rate of inflation and Treasury bills. That is, in the long run, common stocks have had a large positive real return.

Short-Term Historical Relationships

Another interesting question to investigate is the relationship between the short-term rate of return on stocks and the rate of inflation. Conventional wisdom suggests that stock returns should be relatively high when inflation is relatively high and relatively low when inflation is relatively low. Why? Because stocks represent claims on real assets that should increase in value with inflation.

Figure 13.3 displays the relationship between annual stock returns and rates of inflation in the US from 1926 to 1993. The figure shows that there is no discernible relationship between the rate of inflation and stock returns. Indeed, the correlation coefficient between these two variables is –.02, which for all practical purposes is equal to zero and indicates that there is no significant statistical relationship between the rate of inflation and stock returns.[15] That is, when inflation is relatively high, there is no tendency for stock returns to be either relatively high or relatively low. Similarly, when inflation is relatively low, there

[15] The correlation coefficient for the period from 1950 to 1993 is equal to –.3. Similar results occur when monthly data are used. Hence, some people argue that there is an inverse relationship between historical rates of inflation and stock returns.

Figure 13.3

Annual stock returns and rates of inflation (1926–1993).

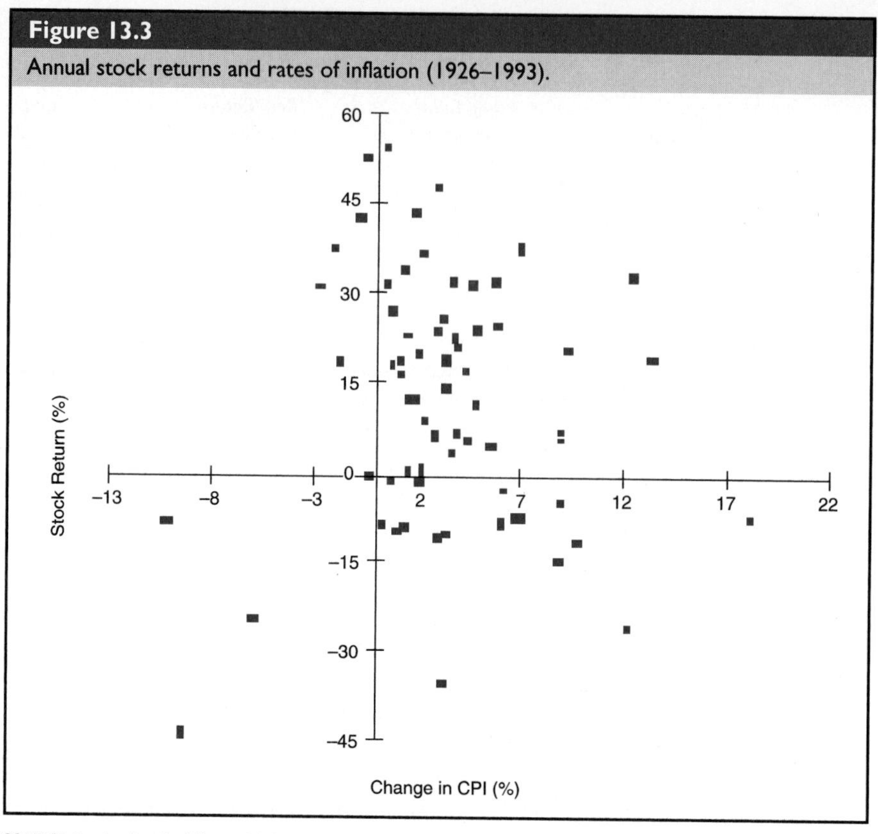

SOURCE: *Stocks, Bonds, Bills, and Inflation 1994 Yearbook* (Chicago: Ibboston Associates, 1994).

is no tendency for stock returns to be either relatively high or relatively low.[16] Accordingly, stocks are not good hedges against inflation in the short term.

Relationships Involving Expected Inflation

The previous results used historical (or *ex post*) rates of inflation and stock returns. Also of interest are tests of the relationship between expected (or *ex ante*) rates of inflation and stock returns. For example, if expected inflation for the forthcoming year is relatively high, what effect does that have on stock returns over the forthcoming year?

One recent study explored this relationship by using time horizons of one and five years.[17] The major difficulty in performing such a test is that expected inflation rates are not observable—only subsequent actual inflation rates are observed. This was overcome by constructing and testing four models for arriving at estimates of expected inflation. These

[16] Interestingly, there appears to be a significantly negative relationship between the real return on stocks and the rate of inflation. That is, higher rates of inflation seem to be accompanied by lower real stock returns. A number of explanations (some of them conflicting) have been offered to account for this observation. For a survey, see David P. Ely and Kenneth J. Robinson, "The Stock Market and Inflation: A Synthesis of the Theory and Evidence," *Federal Reserve Bank of Dallas Economic Review* (March 1989): 17–29.

[17] Jacob Boudoukh and Matthew Richardson, "Stock Returns and Inflation: A Long-Horizon Perspective," American Economic Review 83, no. 5 (December 1993): 1346–1355.

Table 13.9

Testing the Relationships Between Expected Inflation Rates and US Stock Returns, 1802–1990.

Instrumental Variables Used		Estimated Value of β	
One-Year	*Five-Year*	*One-Year*	*Five-Year*
ST int rates	LT int rates	–2.781	1.394
ST inf rates	LT inf rates	–.048[a]	1.820
ST int rates	ST, LT int rates	–2.531	2.072
ST inf rates	ST, LT inf rates	.061[a]	.380

Notes: ST = past year; LT = past five years; int = interest; inf = inflation.
[a] Denotes number is significantly different from 1.0 at .10 level of significance.

SOURCE: Jacob Boudoukh and Matthew Richardson, "Stock Returns and Inflation: A Long-Horizon Perspective," *American Economic Review* 83, no. 5 (December 1993): 1352.

models used past inflation rates and interest rates as "instrumental variables" to estimate expected inflation.

To simplify, the tests involved the following model:

$$r_t = \alpha + \beta\pi_t + e_t \tag{13.9}$$

wherer_t and π_t denote, respectively, the rate of return on stocks and the expected inflation rate over time period t. In this equation the variable of interest is the coefficient β. If there is a one-for-one relationship between expected inflation and stock returns, then the estimated value of β will be approximately equal to 1.0. In such a situation, an increase of 1% in the expected inflation rate would result in a 1% increase in stock returns.

Equation (13.9) was first tested using one-year stock returns and inflation rates from 1802 to 1990 and then tested again using overlapping five-year returns and rates.[18] Table 13.9 presents the results. In two of the four cases involving one-year expectations, the value of β appears to be significantly less than 1.0. This suggests that, in the short term, stock returns do not respond to changes in expected rates of inflation. However, in all four cases involving five-year expectations, the value of β is not significantly different from 1.0, suggesting that stock returns do respond to changes in expected rates of inflation over long horizons.

Hence, the Fisher model appears to be validated when applied over long horizons but not when applied over short horizons.[19] That is, there appears to be a positive relation between expected rates of inflation and stock returns over long periods of time but not over short periods. These findings are consistent with those observed when actual rates of inflation were compared with stock returns.

---

[18] Equation (13.9) was also tested using actual inflation rates and stock returns from 1802 through 1990. The estimated value of [catch math] when one-year rates were used was .07, which was significantly less than 1.0 and not significantly different from zero. When five-year rates were used, its estimated value was .52, which was not significantly different from 1.0. These results are consistent with the earlier results about the observed short-term and long-term relationship between inflation rates and stock returns.

[19] Similar results were obtained when both subperiods and UK data were analyzed.

SUMMARY

1. Because investors concern themselves with after-tax returns, federal and provincial tax laws play a major role in the way securities are priced.
2. Income earned by a corporation may be taxed twice—once when it is earned, via the corporate income tax, and again when it is received as dividends by the stockholders, via the personal income tax. The dividend tax credit, however, mitigates the effect of this double taxation.
3. In the case of both individuals and corporations, the marginal tax rate is more relevant than the average tax rate for making investment decisions.
4. Capital gains need only be included in taxable income when they are realized.
5. The Income Tax Act identifies four kinds of assets to be included in capital property—the taxpayer's personal residence, personal use property, listed personal property, and investment and fixed assets in a business. Capital gains on a taxpayer's personal residence are not taxable and losses are not deductible.
6. The calculation of capital gains taxes involves netting all gains and losses for each kind of asset included in the definition of capital property. Each asset type must be treated separately.
7. Some tax shelters, such as RRSPs, permit the deferment of taxes on the investor's wage income and investment earnings.
8. Inflation measures the percentage change in a specific cost-of-living index at various points in time.
9. Whether a measure of inflation is relevant for a given individual depends to a large extent on the similarity of his or her purchases to the composition of the Consumer Price Index.
10. An investor's real return is a function of the difference between the investor's nominal return and the inflation rate.
11. Real returns are important to an investor because they represent how much the investor's purchasing power has increased (or decreased) and thus how much better (or worse) off the investor is.
12. If investors are concerned with real returns, securities will be priced so that expected nominal returns incorporate the expected inflation rate.
13. When the actual inflation rate exceeds the expected inflation rate, debtors gain in real terms at the expense of creditors. The opposite is the case when actual inflation is less than expected inflation.
14. Investment returns can be indexed by tying security payments to changes in the price level. Indexation reduces or removes an investment's purchasing-power risk.
15. Over long periods of time, common stocks have generated large, positive real returns. Treasury bills have produced much lower, but still positive, real returns.
16. Over short periods of time, stock returns are not positively related to either actual or expected rates of inflation. However, over long periods of time, stock returns are positively related to both actual and expected rates of inflation.

QUESTIONS AND PROBLEMS

1. Why is the marginal tax rate more relevant to investment decision-making than the average tax rate?

2. Given the following income tax schedule, draw a graph illustrating the marginal and average tax rates as a function of income level.

Income	*Tax Rate*
$ 0 – $10 000	10%
$10 001 – $20 000	13
$20 001 – $30 000	15
$30 001 – $50 000	20
$50 001 and above	25

3. Why would a corporation report one annual income figure to their shareholders and another to the tax authorities?
4. Given that interest payments are tax deductible for a corporation while dividend payments are not, why don't corporations finance all of their operations with debt?
5. Preferred shares have several fixed-income characteristics, yet generally provide lower after-tax yields to individual investors than do straight-debt securities. However, corporations seem to find preferred-share investments particularly attractive. Why?
6. Heinz Groh expects consumer prices to rise at a 7% rate next year, and has negotiated a 9.5% pay increase. Given a 35% marginal income tax bracket, will this pay increase cause Heinz's real income (that is, purchasing power) to grow? Explain.
7. Is the following statement true or false? Dividends from taxable Canadian corporations are subject to the dividend tax credit. Therefore, shares of these corporations are more attractive investments for inclusion in an RRSP than the bonds of the same corporations. Explain your answer.
8. A corporate bond is selling for $950. It matures in a year, at which time the holder will receive $1000. In addition, the bond will pay $50 in interest during the year. What would be the after-tax return on the bond to an investor in the 50% marginal income tax bracket if capital gains do not receive preferential tax treatment? Recalculate the return assuming that only 75% of any capital gain is taxable.
9. Consider a stock in a taxable Canadian corporation that provides a dividend yield of 6%. To an investor in the following marginal tax brackets, what is the equivalent before-tax yield on a taxable bond? Use the values for g and q given in the text.
   a. 17%
   b. 26%
   c. 34%
10. What is a wash sale? Why does Revenue Canada prohibit such transactions for tax calculation purposes?
11. Jean Lalonde lives in a province where the tax payable is 60% of the basic federal rate. Jean's marginal basic federal tax rate is 26%. There is a federal surtax of 5% but none provincially.
    a. What is Jean's effective provincial marginal tax rate?
    b. What is Jean's effective federal marginal tax rate?
    c. What is Jean's effective combined marginal tax rate?
12. Given the following beginning and ending values for a particular price index, and the respective number of years between the measurement of the two values, calculate the annual compounded (geometric mean) inflation rate.

	Price Index Beginning Value	Price Index Ending Value	Years Covered
a.	100	115	1
b.	115	170	3
c.	170	150	2

13. Why do cost-of-living indices frequently overstate the true economic impact of inflation on typical consumers?
14. Distinguish between the nominal and the real rate of return on an investment.
15. Ken Higgins started 1991 with investments valued at $10 500. At the end of 1991 those same investments were worth $12 000. During the same time period the price index rose from 210 to 230. What was Ken's real rate of return during 1991?
16. Why is it reasonable to assume that rational investors will build an expected inflation premium into the returns they require from their investments?
17. In the late 1970s and early 1980s, a period of unexpectedly high inflation, Harry Fell referred to long-term bonds issued by corporations and the government as "certificates of confiscation." Why would Harry make such a comment?
18. Why is it often argued that the federal government is the greatest beneficiary of inflation?
19. Many economists contend that during periods of inflation, taxes on investment income reflect, in part, a tax on the return of capital and, hence, are inequitable. Explain the reasoning behind this argument.
20. Explain why the returns on bonds are found to be negatively correlated with unexpected inflation. Why does this relationship become progressively more negative as one considers longer lived bonds?
21. Ciara Karpertian bought a two-year 12% coupon Canada bond at the beginning of 1989. The bond was bought at its face value of $10 000. Over the first year, inflation ran at a semiannual rate of 8%. Investors' inflation expectations at the end of 1989 rose to a 7% semiannual rate.
    - **a.** At the beginning of 1990, what price would the bond have to sell at in order to offer investors a 7% semiannual return over the last year of the bond's life?
    - **b.** If the bond were priced at the figure calculated in part (a), what return would Ciara have earned over the year 1989?
22. Common stocks, somewhat surprisingly, do not appear to be effective hedges against either expected or unexpected inflation. Explain why the stocks of some companies might be better hedges against inflation than others.

KEY TERMS

marginal tax rate
average tax rate
dividend tax credit (DTC)
realized capital gain
unrealized capital gain
superficial loss
wash sale
capital gains and losses
capital property
adjusted cost base (ACB)
Registered Retirement Savings Plan (RRSP)
attributed income
spousal RRSP
inflation
cost-of-living index
Consumer Price Index (CPI)
geometric mean
nominal return
real return
purchasing power risk
indexation
disintermediation
variable rates
equity premium

REFERENCES

1. For a valuable book that provides a framework for analyzing how tax rules affect decision-making, see:

   Myron S. Scholes and Mark A. Wolfson, *Taxes and Business Strategy* (Englewood Cliffs, NJ: Prentice Hall, 1992).

2. Portfolio management and taxation are discussed in:

   Robert H. Jeffrey and Robert D. Arnott, "Is Your Alpha Big Enough to Cover Its Taxes?" *Journal of Portfolio Management* 19, no. 3 (Spring 1993): 15–25.

3. The seminal work linking interest rates and inflationary expectations is:

   Irving Fisher, *The Theory of Interest* (New York: Macmillan, 1930).

4. For a review article and test of this linkage, see, respectively:

   Herbert Taylor, "Interest Rates: How Much Does Expected Inflation Matter?" *Federal Reserve Bank of Philadelphia Business Review* (July/August 1982): 3–12.

   Jacob Boudoukh and Matthew Richardson, "Stock Returns and Inflation: A Long-Horizon Perspective," *American Economic Review* 83, no. 5 (December 1993): 1346–1355.

5. The relationship between real interest rates and inflation is discussed in:

   George G. Pennachi, "Identifying the Dynamics of Real Interest Rates and Inflation: Evidence Using Survey Data," *Review of Financial Studies* 4, no. 1 (1991): 53–86.

6. The following papers present an analysis of the effect of inflation on the accounting treatment of corporate earnings:

   Franco Modigliani and Richard A. Cohn, "Inflation and the Stock Market," *Financial Analysts Journal* 35, no. 2 (March/April 1979): 24–44.

   Kenneth R. French, Richard S. Ruback, and G. William Schwert, "Effects of Nominal Contracting on Stock Returns," *Journal of Political Economy* 91, no. 1 (February 1983): 70–96.

William H. Beaver, Paul A. Griffin, and Wayne R. Landsman, "How Well Does Replacement Cost Income Explain Stock Return [sic]?" *Financial Analysts Journal* 39, no. 2 (March/April 1983): 26–30, 39.

William C. Nordby, "Applications of Inflation-Adjusted Accounting Data," *Financial Analysts Journal* 39, no. 2 (March/April 1983): 33–39.

Charles G. Callard and David C. Kleinman, "Inflation-Adjusted Accounting: Does It Matter?" *Financial Analysts Journal* 41, no. 3 (May/June 1985): 51–59.

7. For a discussion of the relationship of the inflation rate to the returns on stocks, bonds, and real estate, see:

Eugene F. Fama and G. William Schwert, "Asset Returns and Inflation," *Journal of Financial Economics* 5, no. 2 (November 1977): 115–146.

8. Other papers dealing with the relationship between inflation and stock returns can be found at the end of the following survey articles:

David P. Ely and Kenneth J. Robinson, "The Stock Market and Inflation: A Synthesis of the Theory and Evidence," *Federal Reserve Bank of Dallas Economic Review* (March 1989): 17–29.

Andrew B. Abel, "The Equity Premium Puzzle," *Federal Reserve Bank of Philadelphia Business Review* (September/October 1991): 3–14.

9. The equity premium has also been reviewed and analyzed in:

Jeremy J. Siegel, "The Equity Premium: Stock and Bond Returns Since 1802," *Financial Analysts Journal* 48, no. 1 (January/February 1992): 28–38, 46.

10. The tendency of certain types of common stocks to offer better inflation hedges is discussed in:

Douglas K. Pearce and V. Vance Roley, "Firm Characteristics, Unanticipated Inflation, and Stock Returns," *Journal of Finance* 43, no. 4 (September 1988): 965–981.

Christopher K. Ma and M. E. Ellis, "Selecting Industries as Inflation Hedges," *Journal of Portfolio Management* 15, no. 4 (Summer 1989): 45–48.

Yaman Asikoglu and Metin R. Ercan, "Inflation Flow-Through and Stock Prices," *Journal of Portfolio Management* 18, no. 3 (Spring 1992): 63–68.

11. International evidence on the relationship between stock returns and inflation is provided by:

Bruno Solnik, "The Relation Between Stock Prices and Inflationary Expectations: The International Evidence," *Journal of Finance* 38, no. 1 (March 1983): 35–48.

N. Bulent Gultekin, "Stock Market Returns and Inflation: Evidence From Other Countries," *Journal of Finance* 38, no. 1 (March 1983): 49–65.

12. For a Canadian perspective on the topics covered in this chapter, see:

I. G. Morgan, "Dividends and Stock Price Behaviour in Canada," *Journal of Business Administration: Capital Markets in Canada* 12, no. 1 (Fall 1980).

J. Pesando, "Inflation-Indexed Pensions: Investment Policy Implications," *Canadian Investment Review I*, no. 1 (Fall 1988).

B. Amoako-Adu, M. Rashid, and M. Stebbins, "Capital Gains Taxes and Equity Values: An Empirical Test of Stock Price Reactions to the Introduction and Reduction of a Capital Gains Tax Exemption," *Journal of Banking and Finance* 16, no. 2 (April 1992).

F. Adjaoud and D. Zéghal, "Fiscalité et Politique de Dividend Au Canada: Nouveaux Résultats," *Finéco 3*, no. 2 (2e semestre 1993).

S. Brian Fisher and Paul B. Hickey, eds., *KPMG Personal Tax Planning Guide, 1996* (Scarborough, Ont.: Carswell, Thomson Professional Publishing Company, 1995).

INTERNET RESOURCES

The following investment information sources can be accessed at these Internet addresses:

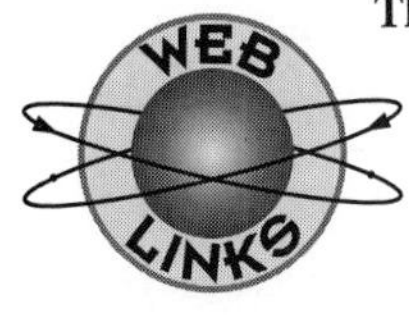

Canadian Tax Discussion Group	**USENET: can.taxes**
Canadian Tax Tip of the Day	**http://www.kpmg.ca/tax_tip.html**
Deloitte & Touche TaxBreaks	**http://www.ftn.net/DT/index.html**

CHAPTER 14

Fixed-Income Securities

This chapter provides a broad survey of the major types of fixed-income securities, with an emphasis on those currently popular in Canada. A security is a contract giving the investor certain rights to the future prospects of the issuer. These rights can differ from one security to another and the future prospects of issuers can also differ substantially; therefore, the number of different types of fixed-income securities is too high to allow a complete survey to be included.

The term *fixed-income* is commonly used to cover the types of securities discussed in this chapter, but it can be misleading. Typically, these securities promise the investors that they will receive certain specified cash flows at certain specified times in the future. If a security provides only a single cash flow, it is known as a **pure-discount security**. Alternatively, it may involve multiple cash flows. If all these cash flows (except for the last one) are of the same size, they are generally referred to as **coupon payments**. The specified date beyond which the investor will no longer receive cash flows is known as the **maturity date**. On this date the investor receives the **principal** (also known as the *par value* or *face value*) associated with the security, along with the last coupon payment. All the cash flows promised, however, may not be received. That is, there is some risk, however small, that a promised payment will not be made in full and on time.

SAVINGS DEPOSITS

Perhaps the most familiar type of fixed-income investment is the personal savings account at a chartered bank, trust company, credit union, or caisse populaire. Such an account provides substantial (if not complete) safety of principal, low probability of failure to receive interest, high liquidity, and a relatively low return.

Chartered Banks

Many people maintain a chequing account in a chartered bank. Formally, these accounts are termed **demand deposits**, since money can be withdrawn on demand by the depositors. While the bookkeeping required to keep track of withdrawals and deposits is costly to the bank, the balance in such an account is available to support interest-earning loans made by the bank. Banks offer an array of chequing accounts with different terms and conditions. Figure 14.1 shows the different types of demand deposits offered by a chartered bank. In general, customers with small balances who write many cheques pay the bank, whereas those with large balances who write few cheques are paid by the bank. This is because the bank pays interest on the customer's deposit (either on the daily closing balance or on the minimum balance maintained in the account over a specified period) and at the same time

Figure 14.1

Typical chartered bank deposit accounts.

INTEREST RATE CHANGES

Investment Builder™ Accounts

On portion of daily closing balance in excess of $150,000	4.590%
On portion of daily closing balance of $100,000 to less than $150,000	4.560%
On portion of daily closing balance of $60,000 to less than $100,000	4.510%
On total daily closing balances of $25,000 to less than $60,000	3.400%
On total daily closing balances of $10,000 to less than $25,000	3.260%
On total daily closing balances of $5,000 to less than $10,000	3.100%
On total daily closing balances of $0 to less than $5,000	3.000%

Moneybuilder Accounts

On total daily closing balance when $5,000 or more	0.750%
On total daily closing balance when $3,000 to $4,999	0.500%
On total daily closing balance when $1,000 to $2,999	0.250%
On total daily closing balance less than $1,000	0.250%

Money Manager Accounts

Balances of $2,000 or more	0.250%
Balances under $2,000	0.250%

(Calculated on daily closing balance; paid each month)

Daily Interest Savings Accounts

(Calculated on daily closing balance; paid each month)	0.250%

My First Account

(Calculated on daily closing balance; paid each month)	0.500%

Premium Savings Accounts

(Calculated on minimum monthly balance; paid semi-annually)	0.500%

Chequing Savings

(Calculated on minimum semi-annual balance; paid semi-annually)	0.250%

Client Trust Accounts

	1.000%

U.S. Dollar Daily Interest Chequing Accounts

On portion of daily closing balance $25,000 or more	2.875%
On amount between $5,000 and $25,000	2.500%
On the first $5,000 of daily closing balance	1.750%

(Calculated on daily closing balance; paid each month)

Daily Interest Savings RSP

On portion of daily closing balance in excess of $60,000	4.250%
On amount in excess of $25,000 up to $60,000	3.750%
On amount in excess of $5,000 up to $25,000	3.500%
On the first $5,000 of daily closing balance	2.750%

(Calculated on daily closing balance; paid monthly)

Savings Account RIF

On total daily closing balance when $50,000 or more	3.750%
On total daily closing balance when $10,000 to less than $50,000	3.500%
On total daily closing balance when less than $10,000	3.250%

(Calculated on total daily closing balance; paid semi-annually)

Self-Directed RSP (Cash Balance)

	3.750%

Self-Directed RIF (Cash Balance)

	3.750%

SOURCE: Toronto-Dominion Bank (December 2, 1995).

charges for handling the customer's cheques and for other services. In some cases accounts with larger minimum balances are paid higher interest rates.

An alternative to a chequing account is a savings account. This type of account typically earns a higher rate of interest than a chequing account but offers no chequing privileges. Cash withdrawals may be made at any time. Service charges and interest are determined in the same manner as for a chequing account. Almost any amount may be invested in a savings account. No security is issued; instead, the current balance plus interest earned is either posted to the depositor's passbook or recorded in a monthly statement.

Credit unions offer accounts similar to those described above, and many investment companies (described in Chapter 22) provide at least limited cheque-writing services.

Time deposits, also known as **guaranteed investment certificates** (GICs) or *term deposits*, have a stated maturity date (for example, one year after the initial deposit), with interest paid at maturity on short-term (less than one year) deposits and either annually or semi-annually on long-term deposits. In practice, such deposits can be withdrawn at any time. A penalty must be paid, however, when this is done prior to maturity. Often, the penalty takes the form of recomputing the interest earned using a lower rate. Most types of time deposits require a minimum investment; for example, $1000 each.

► Trust and Mortgage Loan Companies

In general, trust and mortgage loan companies accept demand and shorter-term deposits (up to five years), then use the money primarily to make longer-term loans, often for home mortgages. Trust companies offer accounts and services that are very similar to those provided by chartered banks and are therefore referred to as *near banks*.

The interest rates and maturities on deposits offered by these institutions are generally similar to those offered by the chartered banks. Figure 14.2 shows the short- and medium-term retail rates offered by various financial institutions, as reported weekly in *The Globe and Mail: Report on Business*.

► Credit Unions

A credit union accepts deposits from members of the credit union (membership is limited to individuals sharing some kind of common bond, often a common employer) and uses them to make loans to other members. Typically, loans are relatively small and relatively short-term (for example, to finance the purchase of an automobile). Excess funds are invested in highly liquid short-term assets.

Each credit union is owned by its members, who elect a board of directors. The interest rates and maturities on deposits are generally similar to those on savings accounts in banks or trust companies, but earn dividends instead of interest. Many credit unions also offer GICs and chequing accounts to their members.

► Other Types of Personal Savings Accounts

A number of institutions similar to those described above also exist. In some countries, the government-run post office accepts savings deposits. In Canada, some provincial governments operate savings banks, such as *The Province of Ontario Savings Office*. Certain kinds of life insurance policies include a savings component — payments often exceed the amount strictly required to pay for the insurance involved. The cash value of such a policy may be obtained by cancellation; alternatively, some or all of it may be borrowed without

Figure 14.2

Short- and mid-term interest rates offered by various financial institutions.

Interest Rates

This survey of rates offered by a sample group of companies was prepared by Cannex Financial Exchanges, Jan. 5, 1996, at 5:01 p.m. Savings rates are non-redeemable except where indicated by an 'r'. Rates are for information purposes only and should be confirmed by the company quoted.

SAVINGS RATES

Company	($1,000 balance) Savings account	Chequing account	(Interest paid at maturity) Minimum deposit	30 days	60 days	90 days	120 days	180 days	270 days	(Interest paid annually) Minimum deposit	One year	Two years	Three years	Four years	Five years
BANKS															
Banca Com. Ital. Canada, Toronto	2.25	2.00	5,000	r 4.75	r 4.75	r 4.75	r 4.75	r 4.88	r 4.88	1,000	5.00	5.50	5.88	6.13	6.50
Bank of Montreal, Toronto	3.00	0.50	5,000	4.75	4.75	4.75	4.75	4.88	4.88	1,000	5.00	5.50	5.88	6.13	6.50
Bank of Nova Scotia, Toronto	0.25	0.25	5,000	4.75	4.75	4.75	4.75	4.88	4.88	500	5.00	5.50	5.88	6.13	6.50
CIBC, Toronto	0.50	0.25	5,000	4.50	4.50	4.50	4.50	4.50	4.50	1,000	4.50	4.75	5.13	5.50	5.75
Citibank, Toronto	0.50	0.25	5,000	r 4.75	r 4.75	r 4.75	r 4.75	r 4.88	r 4.88	5,000	r 5.00	r 5.50	r 5.88	r 6.13	r 6.50
HongKong Bank, Vancouver	0.50	0.50	5,000	4.75	4.75	4.75	4.75	4.88	4.88	1,000	5.00	5.50	5.88	6.13	6.50
Laurentian Bank, Montreal	0.25	-	10,000	4.75	4.75	4.75	4.75	5.00	5.00	1,000	5.00	5.50	5.88	6.13	6.50
National Bank of Greece, Montreal	-	-	5,000	4.50	4.50	4.75	4.75	5.00	5.00	1,000	5.25	5.75	6.00	6.38	6.63
National Bank, Montreal	0.20	0.10	1,000	4.50	4.50	4.63	4.63	4.75	4.75	1,000	5.00	5.50	5.88	6.13	6.50
Republic National Bk NY, Montreal	-	-	50,000	4.80	4.75	4.75	4.70	4.70	4.70	50,000	5.10	5.25	5.50	5.75	5.95
Royal Bank of Canada, Montreal	0.50	0.25	5,000	4.50	4.50	4.50	4.50	4.50	4.50	500	4.50	4.75	5.13	5.38	5.75
Toronto-Dominion Bank, Toronto	3.00	0.25	5,000	4.50	4.50	4.50	4.50	4.63	4.63	1,000	4.75	5.00	5.38	5.63	6.00
TRUST COMPANIES															
AGF Trust Co., Toronto	-	-	10,000	r 5.00	r 5.00	r 5.00	r 5.00	r 5.00	r 5.00	5,000	5.45	5.75	6.05	6.30	6.60
Bayshore Trust, Toronto	2.50	2.50	5,000	4.75	4.75	5.00	5.00	5.00	5.00	1,000	5.00	5.13	5.75	5.75	6.13
Bonaventure Trust, Montreal	-	-	5,000	4.38	4.38	4.38	4.38	4.63	4.75	1,000	5.38	5.75	6.13	6.25	6.50
Canada Trust, Toronto	3.25	0.25	5,000	r 4.25	r 4.25	r 4.25	r 4.25	r 4.38	r 4.38	1,000	4.63	5.00	5.38	5.63	6.00
Co-Operative Trust, Saskatoon	-	-	5,000	4.25	4.25	4.25	4.25	4.50	4.50	500	4.50	4.75	5.13	5.38	5.75
Community Trust, Toronto	-	-	5,000	r 4.63	r 4.63	r 4.75	r 5.13	r 5.00	r 4.88	5,000	5.00	5.50	5.88	6.13	6.50
Effort Trust, Hamilton	1.00	1.00	5,000	4.25	4.25	4.50	4.50	4.50	4.50	5,000	5.38	5.75	6.00	6.25	6.63
Equitable Trust, Toronto	-	-	5,000	5.15	5.25	5.30	5.30	5.30	5.30	5,000	5.55	6.00	6.15	3.00	6.50
Family Trust, Markham	1.25	1.25	5,000	r 4.88	r 5.00	r 5.00	r 5.00	r 5.13	r 5.13	1,000	5.38	5.63	5.88	6.38	6.63
FirstLine Trust, Toronto	-	-	5,000	4.88	4.88	4.88	5.00	5.13	5.13	1,000	5.38	5.50	5.85	6.10	6.30
Investors Group Trust, Winnipeg	-	-		-	-	-	-	-	-	1,000	5.00	5.50	5.88	6.13	6.50
Metropolitan Trust, Edmonton	-	-	5,000	r 4.75	r 4.75	r 4.75	r 4.75	r 4.88	r 4.88	1,000	5.00	5.63	5.88	6.13	6.50
Montreal Trust, Montreal	0.25	0.25	5,000	4.75	4.75	4.75	4.75	4.88	4.88	500	5.00	5.50	5.88	6.13	6.50
Municipal Trust, Barrie	1.25	0.75	5,000	r 4.75	r 4.75	r 4.75	r 4.75	r 4.88	r 4.88	500	5.00	5.50	5.88	6.13	6.50
National Trust, Toronto	0.50	0.50	1,000	r 4.75	r 4.75	r 4.75	r 4.75	r 4.88	r 4.88	500	5.00	5.50	5.88	6.13	6.50
North American Trust, Toronto	3.00	3.00	5,000	4.75	4.75	4.75	4.75	5.00	5.00	500	5.00	5.50	5.88	6.13	6.50
Peace Hills Trust, Edmonton	2.50	0.75	1,000	4.25	4.25	4.50	4.50	4.50	4.50	1,000	5.40	5.65	5.70	5.90	6.40
Peoples Trust, Vancouver	-	-	5,000	4.50	5.00	5.00	5.00	5.40	5.40	5,000	5.50	5.75	6.00	6.00	6.25
Royal Trust, Toronto	0.50	0.50	5,000	r 4.50	r 4.50	r 4.50	r 4.50	r 4.50	r 4.50	1,000	4.50	4.75	5.13	5.38	5.75
Sun Life Trust, Toronto	-	-	10,000	4.63	4.63	4.63	4.75	4.75	4.88	1,000	5.38	5.63	6.00	6.13	6.50
Trust General, Montreal	-	-	1,000	4.50	4.50	4.63	4.63	4.75	4.75	1,000	5.00	5.50	5.88	6.13	6.50
OTHER INSTITUTIONS															
Alberta Treasury Branch, Edmonton	-	-	1,000	4.75	4.75	4.75	4.75	5.00	5.00	1,000	5.00	5.50	5.88	6.13	6.50
Avestel Credit Union, Hamilton	-	-	5,000	4.00	-	4.13	-	4.13	-	500	4.50	4.75	5.13	5.50	6.00
CS COOP Credit Union, Ottawa	-	-	5,000	4.75	4.75	4.75	4.75	4.88	4.88	1,000	5.00	5.50	5.88	6.13	6.50
Canada Life, Toronto	-	-	1,000	r 4.00	r 4.00	r 4.00	r 4.00	r 4.25	r 4.25	1,000	r 5.00	r 5.25	r 5.63	r 6.00	r 6.25
Capital City Savings, Edmonton	0.25	0.25	1,000	4.50	4.50	4.50	4.50	4.63	4.63	1,000	5.00	5.50	5.88	6.13	6.50
Commercial Union Life, Scarborough	-	-		-	-	-	-	-	-	10,000	r 4.50	r 4.90	r 5.25	r 5.55	r 5.75
Empire Life, Kingston	-	-		-	-	-	-	-	-	2,500	r 5.00	r 5.25	r 5.75	r 6.00	r 6.38
Equitable Life, Waterloo	3.50	-		-	-	-	-	-	-	500	r 4.60	r 5.00	r 5.35	r 5.60	r 6.05
Fede Des Caisses De Mtl, Montreal	0.25	0.25	2,000	-	-	-	-	4.88	4.88	1,000	5.00	5.50	5.88	6.13	6.50
Home Savings & Loan, St. Catharines	-	-	5,000	4.50	5.00	5.00	5.00	5.25	5.25	5,000	5.40	5.75	6.00	6.00	6.50
Industrial Alliance, Sillery	-	-	1,000	-	-	r 3.65	r 3.65	r 3.75	r 3.80	1,000	r 4.40	r 4.80	r 5.00	r 5.05	r 5.75
Laurier Life, Etobicoke	-	-		-	-	-	-	-	-	15,000	4.63	r 4.75	r 5.00	r 5.63	r 5.88
London Life, London	-	-	2,500	-	-	-	-	-	r 4.34	10,000	5.00	5.50	5.88	6.13	6.50
ManuLife Financial, Waterloo	-	-		-	-	-	-	-	-	1,000	r 4.75	r 5.25	r 5.63	r 5.88	r 6.25
Maritime Life, Halifax	-	-		-	-	-	-	-	-	5,000	r 4.75	r 5.13	r 5.50	r 5.75	r 6.00
Metropolitan Life, Ottawa	-	-		-	-	-	-	-	-	1,000	r 5.00	r 5.38	r 5.75	r 6.00	r 6.38
Mutual Group, Toronto	-	-		-	-	-	-	-	-		-	-	-	-	-
NN Financial, Don Mills	-	-		-	-	-	-	-	-	10,000	4.88	5.13	5.38	5.50	6.25
National Life, Toronto	-	-		-	-	-	-	-	-	500	r 4.50	r 4.90	r 5.30	r 5.50	r 6.00
Prov Ont Savings Office, Oshawa	-	1.25	5,000	r 4.75	r 4.75	r 4.75	r 4.75	r 4.88	r 4.88	500	5.00	5.50	5.88	6.13	6.50
Prudential Insurance, Scarborough	-	-		-	-	-	-	-	-	300	4.38	4.63	5.13	5.38	5.75
Royal Life, Oakville	-	-		-	-	-	-	-	-	10,000	r 4.88	r 5.13	r 5.38	r 5.75	r 6.13
Security Home Mortgage, Calgary	-	-	10,000	4.75	4.75	4.75	4.88	4.88	4.88	5,000	5.00	5.50	5.88	6.00	6.38
Standard Life, Montreal	-	-	5,000	4.25	-	4.25	-	4.50	-	1,000	4.88	5.25	5.63	5.88	6.25
SunLife of Canada, Toronto	-	-		-	-	-	-	-	-	1,000	r 4.63	r 5.00	r 5.38	r 5.75	r 6.00
Transamerica Life, Scarborough	-	-		-	-	-	-	-	-	25,000	r 5.00	r 5.30	r 5.65	r 5.90	r 6.05
Westbury Canadian Life, Hamilton	-	-		-	-	-	-	-	-	5,000	r 3.88	r 4.38	r 4.88	r 5.25	r 5.38

SOURCE: Reprinted by permission of *The Globe and Mail: Report on Business* (January 8, 1996).

cancelling the policy. The implicit rate of return on the cash value of an insurance policy is typically low, reflecting the extremely low risk to the policyholder and the length of the insurance company's commitment.

► Deposit Insurance

In 1967, the *Canadian Deposit Insurance Corporation* (CDIC) was created by the federal government to guarantee deposits in all federally incorporated chartered banks, and trust and loan companies and all provincially incorporated trust and loan companies, with the exception of those in the Province of Quebec. The Quebec Deposit Insurance Board (QDIB) was established to insure deposits of all deposit-accepting institutions in Quebec as well as deposits accepted outside Quebec by institutions incorporated in that province. In 1990, the CDIC had 151 insured member institutions — 116 federally and 35 provincially incorporated.

The CDIC was created to achieve several objectives:

1. protection of small depositors,
2. provision of last resort facilities,
3. improvement in the minimum financial standards of deposit-taking institutions across the country, and
4. maintenance of confidence and stability in the financial system.

The deposit insurance system was designed to operate much like a casualty insurance company. The premiums collected from the insured member institutions, together with income from investments, are used to cover operating expenses and losses, with any excess contributing to an increase in reserves. In a properly functioning deposit insurance system the premium plus investment income should be sufficient to cover expenses and anticipated losses together with an amount budgeted for unforeseen losses.

The insured limit under the Canada Deposit Insurance Act on Canadian dollar deposits with an original term to maturity of five years or less was set at $60 000 in 1983 and has remained at that level since. Judicious use of multiple accounts in different financial institutions makes it possible to increase the total amount covered by deposit insurance. Member institutions were originally required to pay an annual insurance premium of 1/30th of 1% of insured deposits, but this was raised to 0.1% in 1988. All member institutions pay the same premium with no risk differential.

Claims were minimal prior to 1983. There was, however, a dramatic increase in claims in the period 1983 to 1986 as several financial institutions became insolvent and were declared bankrupt. The Deposit Insurance Fund's surplus of $253 million at the end of 1982 became a deficit of $1245 million in 1986 and stood at $643 million at the end of 1991.

MONEY MARKET INSTRUMENTS

Certain types of short-term (meaning, arbitrarily, one year or less), highly marketable loans play a major role in the investment and borrowing activities of industrial corporations and financial intermediaries. Individual investors with substantial funds may invest in such

money market instruments directly or indirectly via money market accounts at various financial institutions.[1]

Some money market instruments are negotiable and are traded in active secondary dealer markets; others are not. Some may be purchased by anyone with adequate funds, others only by particular types of institutions. Many are sold on a discount basis; for example, a 91-day Treasury bill with a face value of $100 000 might be sold for $98 000—where the face value of $100 000 is to be paid to the investor at maturity and the difference of $2000 represents interest income.

Interest rates on such money market instruments are often reported on an **annualized rate basis.** This means that in the example above, the T-bill will be described in the media as providing a rate of 8.19% per year calculated as follows:

$$(\$2000/\$98\ 000) \times (365/91) \times 100 = 8.19\%$$

Over the 91-day period the investor receives a return of $2000/$98 000, or 2.04%. If, however, the proceeds were reinvested at the same rate four times over, the actual return or **annual percentage rate** (APR) would be $1.0204^4 - 1 = 8.41\%$. Both *The Globe and Mail: Report on Business* and *The Financial Post* publish a daily list of the current interest rates on a number of Canadian, US and international money market instruments. Figure 14.3 presents samples of these lists. Table 14.1 shows the size of the Canadian money market broken down by type of instrument. Most of these are described in the next section.

Table 14.1

Money Market Instruments Held Outside the Bank of Canada, December 1993.

Type of Instrument	*Amount (in millions)*	
Treasury bills:		
Government of Canada	$148 898	
Provincial governments	18 760	
Municipal governments	1 915	
Sub-total Treasury bills		$169 573
Short-term paper:		
Bankers' acceptances	$ 26 171	
Finance paper	5 996	
Commercial paper	25 246	
Sub-total short-term paper		57 413
Total Money Market		$226 986

SOURCE: Bank of Canada Review, Autumn 1995.

[1] Short-term obligations and bonds of the Government of Canada and its agencies that mature in less than three years are also considered to be money market instruments. Useful descriptions of the various types of money market instruments are contained in W. T. Hunter, *Canadian Financial Markets* (Peterborough, Ont.: Broadview Press Ltd., 1988) ; and James E. Hatch and Robert W. White, *Canadian Stocks, Bonds, Bills, and Inflation: 1950–1987*, (Charlottesville, Va.: The Research Foundation of The Institute of Chartered Financial Analysts), 1988.

Figure 14.3

Canadian and US money market rates quoted in the financial press.

Money Rates

ADMINISTERED RATES

Bank of Canada	5.79%
Canadian prime	7.50%

MONEY MARKET RATES
(for transactions
of $1-million or more)

3-mo. T-bill(when-issued)	5.56%
1-month treasury bills	5.51%
2-month treasury bills	5.52%
3-month treasury bills	5.55%
6-month treasury bills	5.61%
1-year treasury bills	5.74%
10-year Canada bonds	7.06%
30-year Canada bonds	7.58%
1-month banker's accept.	5.70%
2-month banker's accept.	5.70%
3-month banker's accept.	5.70%
Commercial Paper (R-1 Low)	
1-month	5.73%
2-month	5.72%
3-month	5.71%
Call money	5.75%

Supplied by Dow Jones Telerate Canada

UNITED STATES

NEW YORK (AP) — Money rates for Friday as reported by Dow Jones Telerate:

Telerate interest rate index: 5.460

Prime Rate: 8.50

Discount Rate: 5.25

Broker call loan rate: 7.25

Federal funds market rate: High 6.00; low 5.00; last 5.50

Dealers commercial paper: 30-180 days: 5.84-5.38

Commercial paper by finance company: 30-270 days: 5.56-5.14

Bankers acceptances dealer indications: 30 days, 5.55; 60 days, 5.50; 90 days, 5.45; 120 days, 5.40; 150 days, 5.35; 180 days, 5.30

Certificates of Deposit Primary: 30 days, 4.64; 90 days, 4.90; 180 days, 4.93

Certificates of Deposit by dealer: 30 days, 5.56; 60 days, 5.53; 90 days, 5.50; 120 days, 5.47; 150 days, 5.44; 180 days, 5.41

Eurodollar rates: Overnight, 5.50-5.75; 1 month, 5.5625-5.625; 3 months, 5.50-5.5625; 6 months, 5.375-5.4375; 1 year, 5.25-5.3125

London Interbank Offered Rate: 3 months, 5.625; 6 months, 5.50781; 1 year, 5.42578

Treasury Bill auction results:average discount rate: 3-month as of Dec. 26: 4.91; 6-month as of Dec. 26: 5.04; 52-week as of Dec. 7: 5.06

Treasury Bill annualized rate on weekly average basis, yield adjusted for constant maturity, 1-year, as of Dec. 26: 5.30

Treasury Bill market rate, 1-year: 4.89-4.87

Treasury Bond market rate, 30-year: 5.94

SOURCE: Reprinted by permission of *The Globe and Mail: Report on Business* (December 30, 1995).

Finance and Commercial Paper

Finance paper is an unsecured short-term promissory note issued in either Canadian dollars or other currencies (usually US dollars) by sales finance and consumer loan companies. Commercial and industrial corporations issue **commercial paper** with characteristics similar to that of finance paper but offering slightly higher rates.[2] Finance paper is secured by the pledge of the installment obligations that the company will receive. Commercial paper is often backed by either a standby line of credit at a bank or a guarantee from a parent company or affiliate to insure that the loan will be paid off when it comes due. The interest rates on finance and commercial paper reflect this low risk, being relatively low compared to other corporate fixed-income securities and slightly higher than Treasury bills.

Finance and commercial paper is issued in minimum denominations of $50 000, with maturities of 30 to 365 days for the former and one to 365 days for the latter (but typically less than 90 days). The secondary market for both types of paper is limited. Therefore, they are usually held to maturity. Commercial paper often has a 24-hour prepayment provision, whereby the company can repay the note on one day's notice.

Bankers' Acceptances

In Canada, a **bankers' acceptance** is a pure-discount security that is a substitute for commercial paper as a source of financing. It can be regarded as a negotiable, certified

[2] About 25% of all finance and commercial paper outstanding at the end of 1995 was denominated in a foreign currency.

cheque made out to the bearer. The firm seeking financing must write a bill for $100 000 or a multiple thereof payable to itself within 180 days or less for acceptance by its bank. *Acceptance* means that the bank will guarantee payment. Once accepted, the company can endorse the bill to the bearer and sell it (at a discount) in the money market. At maturity the bank is obliged to redeem the bill and it collects the necessary funds from the issuing company. The effective rate of interest is only slightly higher than that on T-bills, reflecting the high credit-worthiness of the company and the bank's guarantee. In addition to the interest, the issuing corporation must also pay the bank a fee for accepting the bill.

In the United States, banker's acceptances were created to finance goods in transit, but currently they are generally used to finance foreign trade. A company buying goods imported from abroad makes out a bill payable to itself as described above, then has it accepted by its bank and turns it over to the seller. The seller of the goods, having received the accepted bill, need not wait until it is due in order to receive payment. It can be sold in the money market at a discount.

▶ Term Deposits Issued by Financial Institutions

Negotiable Deposits

Bearer Deposit Notes (BDNs) are the only short-term instruments issued by the Canadian chartered banks that are traded in the money market. These **negotiable deposits** are issued in multiples of $100 000 with maturities ranging from 30 to 365 days. They are transferable but not redeemable before maturity and, therefore, marketable. US banks issue similar securities, known as **Certificates of Deposit** (CDs) (or Jumbo CDs when they are in large denominations).

Non-Negotiable Deposits

The chartered banks also issue Certificates of Deposit that are similar to BDNs but are neither transferable nor negotiable. These are also called *Term Deposit Receipts* or *Term Notes* and are issued in denominations ranging from $5000 to $100 000 with maturities ranging from one day to five years.

Trust and mortgage loan companies issue similar instruments under a variety of names (Deposit Receipts, Guaranteed Trust Certificates, Guaranteed Investment Certificates and Guaranteed Investment Receipts). In general, term deposits have a minimum denomination of $5000 with one-day to one-year maturities, and receipts or certificates have a minimum denomination of $500 with one- to five-year maturities.

▶ Eurodollars

In the world of international finance, large short-term CDs denominated in dollars and issued by banks outside North America (most often in London) are known as **Eurodollar CDs** (or simply Euro CDs). Dollar-denominated time deposits in banks outside North America are known as **Eurodollar deposits**. A key distinction between Euro CDs and Eurodollar deposits is that Euro CDs are negotiable, meaning they can be traded, whereas Eurodollar deposits are non-negotiable, meaning they cannot be traded.

The demand and supply conditions for such instruments may differ from the conditions for other Canadian and US money market instruments, owing to restrictions imposed (or likely to be imposed) by the Canadian and US governments. Enough commonality exists, however, to keep interest rates from markedly diverging from those available in North

America. Euro CDs are not covered by deposit insurance as are deposits issued by Canadian financial institutions.

Repurchase Agreements

Sometimes one investor (often a financial institution) will sell another investor (often another financial institution) a money market instrument and agree to repurchase it for an agreed-upon price at a later date. For example, investor A might sell investor B, for a price of $10 million, a number of Treasury bills that mature in 180 days. Investor A signs a **repurchase agreement** with investor B specifying that after 30 days, investor A will repurchase these Treasury bills for $10.1 million. Thus, investor A will be paying investor B $100 000 in interest for a 30-day loan of $10 million. Investor B is, in essence, purchasing a money market instrument that matures in 30 days. The annualized interest rate is known as the **repo rate**, which in this case is equal to ($100 000/$10 000 000) × (365/30) = 12.17%.

Note how this repurchase agreement is like a collateralized loan from B to A, with the Treasury bills serving as the collateral. Such loans involve very little risk to the lender (B), because the money market instruments typically used in repurchase agreements are of high quality.

CANADIAN GOVERNMENT SECURITIES

It should come as no surprise that the Canadian government relies heavily on debt financing. In recent years revenues have seldom covered expenses, and the difference has been financed primarily by issuing debt instruments. Moreover, new debt must be issued in order to raise the necessary funds to pay off old debts that mature, an operation known as **debt refunding**. In addition to issuing its own debt, the Canadian government implicitly guarantees the debts of certain federal agencies such as the Export Development Corporation, the Farm Credit Corporation, and the Federal Business Development Bank. The bonds of these agencies are generally regarded as being of high quality but low liquidity. In the past, the government has also unconditionally guaranteed the principal and interest of debt securities of certain Crown Corporations.

Some idea of the magnitude and ownership of Canadian government marketable term debt (one year or more) can be gained by examining Table 14.2. The federal government, through the Bank of Canada, is a moderately large debt holder, as are provincial and local governments. The vast majority of these bonds, however, are held by the private sector; notably by foreign investors and trusteed pension funds. The remainder are fairly uniformly distributed amongst the various Canadian institutions and individuals. Over 97% of these bonds are denominated in Canadian dollars with the remainder issued predominantly in Eurodollars or Japanese yen. Nearly 90% of the total public debt is marketable, meaning it is represented by securities that can be sold at any time by the original purchaser through investment dealers. The major non-marketable issues are held by individuals in the form of Canada Savings Bonds. Marketable issues include Treasury bills and bonds of different maturities. Table 14.3 shows the amounts in each category and the maturity structure of the marketable securities in December 1993.

The Bank of Canada has considerable latitude in selecting maturities for new issues and makes a practice of providing bonds of different maturities with each issue — presumably to appeal to investors with different horizons. At the end of 1993 more than 56% of the

Table 14.2

Ownership of Outstanding Government of Canada Marketable Term Debt, December 1993.[a]

Held By	*Amount (in millions)*	*Percentage of Total*
Chartered banks	$ 30 341	14.9%
Thrift institutions	1 969	1.0
Life insurance companies	16 705	8.2
Property and casualty insurance companies	8 400	4.1
Trusteed pension funds	37 228	18.3
Mutual funds	9 690	4.8
Investment dealers	100	neg.
Non-financial private corporations	404	0.2
Misc. private financial institutions	425	0.2
Foreign investors	72 218	35.4
Individuals and non-incorporated business	1 891	0.9
Sub-total—privately held federal bonds	$179 371	88.0%
Non-financial government enterprise	$ 136	neg.
Public financial institutions	4 946	2.4
Social security funds	3 500	1.7
Provincial and local governments	9 262	4.6
Bank of Canada	6 622	3.3
Federal government	87	neg.
Sub-total publicly held federal bonds	$ 24 553	12.0%
Total federal marketable bonds	$203 924	100.0%

[a] Excludes Treasury bills but includes federal government guaranteed issues.

SOURCE: Statistics Canada, *National Balance Sheet Accounts: System of National Accounts, Annual Estimates, 1984–1993*, Ottawa, March 1995.

total debt was short-term, maturing in three years or less, and about 64% had a maturity date within five years.[3]

The three principal types of debt issued by the Canadian government as well as two derivative securities are discussed next.

Government of Canada Treasury Bills

Treasury bills are issued on a discount basis, with maturities of up to 52 weeks, in denominations of $5000, $25 000, $100 000, and $1 million (although at times denominations as small as $1000 have been offered). All are issued in **bearer form** only. This means that the buyer's name is neither recorded in the Bank of Canada's books nor on the security itself. The face value is payable at maturity to the current holder of the security. Although Treasury bills are sold at a discount, their dollar yield (that is, the difference

[3] The effective maturity of the non-marketable debt is not easy to determine because Canada Savings Bonds are redeemable by the buyer on demand at any time.

Table 14.3

Maturity Structure of Marketable Interest-Bearing Government of Canada Debt, December 1993.

Type and Maturity	*Amount (in millions)*	*Percentage of Total*
Non-marketable issues:		
Canada Savings Bonds	$ 31 814	7.8%
Foreign series	6 573	1.6
Other[a]	3 499	0.9
Total Non-marketable Debt	$ 41 892	10.3%
Marketable issues:		
Treasury bills	$165 900	40.6%
Under 3 years	64 470	15.8
3–5 years	32 448	8.0
5–10 years	57 669	14.1
10 years and over	45 837	11.2
Total Marketable Debt	$408 216	100.0%
Total Debt	$296 617	100.0%

[a] All of these bonds are held by the Canada Pension Plan Investment Fund.

SOURCE: Bank of Canada Review, Autumn 1995.

between the purchase price and face value if the bill is held to maturity) is treated as interest income for tax purposes.

Offerings of 91-day and 182-day bills are made once each week, 364-day bills are offered most weeks, and occasionally shorter maturities are also offered. All are sold at auction every Tuesday at noon (Monday if Tuesday is a holiday) by the Bank of Canada acting as an agent of the Minister of Finance. The Bank of Canada itself and **primary distributors** (specified chartered banks and investment dealers) are eligible to bid on bills intended for resale, but others may bid on their own account. Bids may be entered on either a competitive or non-competitive basis. With a competitive bid, the investor states a price he or she is willing to pay. For example, an investor might enter a bid for a stated number of 91-day bills at a price of 98.512. If the bid is accepted, the investor will pay $98 512.00 for each $100 000 of face value, meaning that an investment of $98 512.00 will generate a receipt of $100 000 if held to maturity 91 days later. With a non-competitive bid, the investor agrees to pay the average price of all bids that will be accepted by the Bank of Canada.

The results of the auction are announced by the Bank of Canada at about 2:00 p.m. on Tuesday. Generally, bids are received for more bills than are being offered, so some bidders are not successful. All non-competitive bids are accepted, with the balance of the issue allocated between the highest competitive bidders. Every Wednesday *The Globe and Mail* publishes the results of the auction that took place on the previous day and the amounts to be offered the following week. Figure 14.4 presents the results of the auction that took place on January 9, 1996.

Individuals may purchase Treasury bills indirectly from a bank or investment dealer, or through a mutual fund, all of whom offer them at a slightly higher price than that paid

Figure 14.4

Treasury bill auction results for January 9, 1996.

Federal bill yields

The average yield at this week's auction of $3.7-billion of 91-day Government of Canada treasury bills was 5.532 per cent, up from 5.483 per cent last week.

Accepted yields for the bills ranged from a high of 5.538 per cent for a price equivalent of 98.63810 to a low of 5.510 per cent for a price equivalent of 98.64489. The average yield of 5.532 per cent provided a price equivalent of 98.63960.

For an offering of $1.6-billion of 182-day bills, accepted yields ranged from a high of 5.625 per cent for a price equivalent of 97.27173 to a low of 5.580 per cent for a price equivalent of 97.29296. The average yield of 5.618 per cent provided a price equivalent of 97.27514. Last week's average yield was 5.571 per cent.

For an offering of $1.3-billion of 364-day bills, accepted yields ranged from a high of 5.679 per cent for a price equivalent of 94.64011 to a low of 5.665 per cent for a price equivalent of 94.65262. The average yield of 5.673 per cent provided a price equivalent of 94.64587. Last week's average yield was 5.691 per cent.

SOURCE: Reprinted by permission of *The Globe and Mail: Report on Business* (January 10, 1996).

at the auction (i.e., at a lower yield). Figure 14.5 shows the yields quoted by an investment dealer to his retail customers for different amounts and maturities of Treasury bills.

There is an active secondary market where institutions may trade Treasury bills with investment dealers. The bid-ask spread on these transactions varies between 1 and 5 basis points (for example, a dealer may quote bid 7.36% and ask 7.32%, meaning that the dealer is willing to pay a price that will earn him an annualized rate of 7.36%) depending on the size of the transaction and the volatility of the market.

► Government of Canada Short-Term Bonds

These consist of bonds and government guaranteed bonds with a residual maturity of three years or less and may consist of either medium-term (maturity between three and ten years) or long-term bonds that are approaching maturity, or newly issued short-term bonds. Short-term bonds are traded in the money market, although the characteristics and marketing of newly issued bonds with a maturity of three years are more like those of medium-term and long-term bonds, discussed on the next page.

Figure 14.5

Treasury bill quotations, October 30, 1995.

Rate Report

All Rates Subject to Change

Treasury Bills

TERM	RATE
30 Day	6.30%
60 Day	6.40%
90 Day	6.50%
180 Day	6.55%
364 Day	6.55%

SOURCE: Reprinted with the permission of Dylan Rogers, Richardson-Greenshields of Canada Limited.

Prices and yields on short-term bonds are quoted in the newspapers along with other Government of Canada bonds. The following is a typical bond quotation, reported in *The Globe and Mail* on December 30, 1995.

Dec. 29 1995	Coupon Rate %	Maturity Date	Mid-Point Price $	Yield
Canada	8.00	Nov 1 98	104.765	6.133

This indicates that this short-term bond maturing on November 1, 1998 carries a coupon rate of 8% and a quoted price of $104.765. This quoted price is the mid-point between the bid and the ask. The effective yield to maturity based on the quoted price is approximately 6.133%. A purchaser of this bond could expect to pay the ask price while a seller would receive the bid price. As the bid-ask spread is generally $0.10 to $0.15 for government bonds, the seller could expect to receive $104.69 and the buyer could expect to pay $104.84.

In practice, the situation facing a potential buyer (or seller) is somewhat more complicated. The buyer is required to pay the seller not only the ask price (say, $104.84) but also any **accrued interest**. For example, on December 29, 59 days have elapsed since the last coupon payment and 123 days remain until the next. Therefore, an amount equal to $59/182 = 0.3242$ of the semiannual coupon ($0.3242 \times 40 = \$12.968$) is added to the ask price to arrive at the settlement price (in this case, $104.84 + 12.97 = \$117.81$). Similarly if an investor were to sell this bond the dealer would pay the bid price plus accrued interest ($\$104.69 + \$12.97 = \$117.66$). This procedure is commonly followed with all bonds.

► Government of Canada Medium- and Long-Term Bonds

Medium-term bonds have maturities from three to ten years at the time of issue. Long-term bonds are those with initial maturities greater than ten years. Interest or coupon payments are generally made semiannually at a set rate. Bonds may be issued in either **bearer** or **registered form**, commonly in denominations of $1000, $5000, $25 000, $100 000 or $1 million. Bonds issued in bearer form have numbered and dated coupons attached to the **bond certificate** that may be detached and cashed on the due date (but not before). The name of the owner of a **registered bond** is recorded at the Bank of Canada in Ottawa and also appears on the bond certificate. Interest is paid by cheque directly to the owner. Transfer of ownership of a registered bond is somewhat more complicated than for a bearer bond, although the former provides security in the event of a theft.[4]

Some issues may have a *call* or *redemption feature* that allows them to be "called" on specified notice (thirty to sixty days typically). The Bank of Canada has the right to force the investor to sell the bonds back to the government at a pre-determined price (par or slightly above). These issues usually provide **call protection**, in that the call provision does not come into effect for several years after the date of issue.

For callable issues, the yield-to-maturity is calculated using the stated price. If this price is greater than par, then the calculation of yield-to-maturity is based on an assumption that the bond will be called at the earliest allowable date.

Several issues also include a **purchase fund**, under whose provisions the Government of Canada undertakes to retire a specified fraction of the issue prior to maturity by purchasing the bonds in the open market at prices not exceeding a specified value (usually par or slightly below).

Many Government of Canada bonds trade in an active secondary market. Prices and yields of more heavily traded Government of Canada, provincial, and corporate bonds are quoted daily in *The Globe and Mail* and *The Financial Post*. Figure 14.6 illustrates typical information provided in the former publication.

► Canada Savings Bonds

Once a year, generally for about two weeks ending on November 1, non-marketable *Canada Savings Bonds* (CSBs) are offered—only to individuals, estates, and specified trusts. No more than a specified amount may be purchased by any one person in a single year, but the amount may vary from year to year (for example, $20 000 in 1987, $75 000 in 1991). Term to maturity varies from issue to issue. In the early 1980s 7-year terms prevailed, but the 1991 series had a 12-year term. Term to maturity is not an important feature, because the valuable option CSBs provide is the possibility of redemption, at face value plus accrued interest, at any time prior to maturity by presenting the bonds at any financial institution.

Two types of CSBs are available. Simple interest bonds pay interest annually on November 1 each year. Compound interest bonds are essentially pure-discount bonds, meaning that no interest is paid on them prior to maturity, at which time a lump sum representing principal plus interest is paid.

All CSBs are floating-rate bonds with an annual adjustment period. The interest rate payable is announced for the first year at the time of issue. In subsequent years the interest rate is equal to the rate paid on the newly issued CSBs. In any given year, therefore, all CSB series pay the same interest rate.[5] Both types are fully registered and may be neither transferred nor assigned, although some banks will accept CSBs as collateral for loans. These bonds are available in denominations from $100 to $10 000, and may be purchased from

---

[4] Some bonds currently in existence are registered as to principal only. These carry coupons like a bearer bond but the owner's name is recorded on the bond certificate. Such bonds are no longer issued.

[5] In times of rapidly rising interest rates the Bank of Canada has been forced to change rates during the year in an effort to stem the flood of redemptions, but has not always been successful. In 1990, redemptions exceeded the new issue by over $8 billion.

Figure 14.6

Price quotations for actively traded Canadian Bonds.

Canadian Bonds

Provided by RBC Dominion Securities

Selected quotations, with changes since the previous day, on actively traded bond issues. Yields are calculated to full maturity, unless marked C to indicate callable date. Price is the midpoint between final bid and ask quotations Dec. 29, 1995.

Issuer	Coupon	Maturity	Price	Yield	$ Chg
GOVERNMENT OF CANADA					
CANADA	7.75	15 SEP 96	101.375	5.693	-0.010
CANADA	8.00	15 MAR 97	102.595	5.716	NC
CANADA	7.00	15 SEP 97	101.815	5.854	+0.010
CANADA	6.25	1 FEB 98	100.525	5.975	+0.020
CANADA	8.00	1 NOV 98	104.765	6.133	+0.010
CANADA	5.75	1 MAR 99	98.625	6.233	+0.020
CANADA	7.75	1 SEP 99	104.525	6.340	+0.030
CANADA	8.50	1 MAR 00	107.335	6.456	-0.012
CANADA	7.50	1 SEP 00	103.775	6.543	-0.010
CANADA	7.50	1 MAR 01	103.913	6.590	-0.011
CANADA	9.50	1 OCT 01	113.175	6.694	-0.050
CANADA	9.75	1 DEC 01	114.736	6.687	-0.016
CANADA	8.50	1 APR 02	108.787	6.748	-0.001
CANADA	7.25	1 JUN 03	101.836	6.927	+0.006
CANADA	7.50	1 DEC 03	103.125	6.978	+0.002
CANADA	10.25	1 FEB 04	119.808	6.996	-0.002
CANADA	6.50	1 JUN 04	96.682	7.028	+0.003
CANADA	9.00	1 DEC 04	112.700	7.054	NC
CANADA	8.75	1 DEC 05	111.815	7.070	-0.007
CANADA	10.00	1 JUN 08	121.823	7.295	+0.036
CANADA	9.50	1 JUN 10	118.464	7.394	+0.039
CANADA	9.00	1 MAR 11	114.279	7:414	+0.041
CANADA	10.25	15 MAR 14	127.148	7.491	+0.048
CANADA	9.75	1 JUN 21	124.371	7.574	+0.055
CANADA	8.00	1 JUN 23	104.850	7.577	+0.050
CANADA	9.00	1 JUN 25	116.554	7.585	+0.055
CMHC	8.80	1 MAR 00	108.072	6.546	-0.012
REAL RETURNS	4.25	1 DEC 21	97.875	4.388	+0.250
PROVINCIAL					
ALBERTA	7.75	4 FEB 98	103.356	6.009	+0.017
ALBERTA	8.00	1 MAR 00	105.268	6.529	-0.010
ALBERTA	7.50	1 DEC 05	101.897	7.227	-0.005
B C	7.00	9 JUN 99	102.203	6.274	+0.029
B C	9.00	9 JAN 02	110.485	6.844	+0.025
B C	8.00	23 AUG 05	105.107	7.252	-0.005
B C	8.50	23 AUG 13	107.430	7.720	-0.010
B C	8.00	8 SEP 23	101.905	7.829	-0.010
B C MUN FIN	7.75	1 DEC 05	103.393	7.262	-0.005
HYDRO QUEBEC	9.25	2 DEC 96	103,025	5.778	-0.050
HYDRO QUEBEC	10.88	25 JUL 01	117.125	7.091	+0.020
HYDRO QUEBEC	7.00	1 JUN 04	96.350	7.594	+0.030
HYDRO QUEBEC	11.00	15 AUG 20	128.175	8.295	+0.150
HYDRO QUEBEC	9.63	15 JUL 22	113.975	8.312	+0.150
MANITOBA	7.00	19 APR 99	101.982	6.319	+0.028
MANITOBA	7.75	14 SEP 00	104.215	6.685	-0.010
MANITOBA	9.38	15 NOV 04	113.759	7.242	+0.000
MANITOBA	7:75	22 DEC 25	98.175	7.910	-0.009
NEW BRUNSWIC	7.00	17 MAR 98	101.875	6.071	+0.100
NEW BRUNSWIC	8.38	26 AUG 02	107.350	6.971	NC
NEW BRUNSWIC	8.50	28 JUN 13	106.700	7.792	+0.300
NEWFOUNDLAND	10.13	22 NOV 14	117.575	8.268	NC
NOVA SCOTIA	9.60	30 JAN 22	115.800	8.130	NC
ONTARIO HYD	7.25	31 MAR 98	102.366	6.096	+0.020
ONTARIO HYD	9.38	31 JAN 00	109.754	6.602	-0.013
ONTARIO HYD	9.00	24 JUN 02	110.320	6.989	-0.029
ONTARIO HYD	7.75	3 NOV 05	102.841	7.337	-0.005
ONTARIO HYD	8.50	26 MAY 25	106.145	7.955	-0.010
ONTARIO	9.00	15 SEP 04	111.046	7.261	+0.001
ONTARIO	8.50	2 DEC 25	106.147	7.957	-0.010
P E I	9.75	30 APR 02	112.975	7.158	+0.050
P E I	11.00	19 SEP 11	126.200	8.032	-0.100
QUEBEC	8.00	30 MAR 98	103.815	6.141	+0.060
QUEBEC	10.25	7 APR 98	108.425	6.184	+0.050
QUEBEC	10.25	15 OCT 01	114.550	7.129	NC
QUEBEC	9.38	16 JAN 23	111.245	8.323	-0.110
SASKATCHEWAN	9.88	6 JUL 99	110.480	6.485	+0.026
SASKATCHEWAN	7.50	19 DEC 05	101.027	7.352	-0.004
SASKATCHEWAN	8.75	30 MAY 25	108.825	7.967	-0.050
TORONTO -MET	7.75	1 DEC 05	102.613	7.372	-0.005
CORPORATE					
AGT LIMITED	9.50	24 AUG 04	113.500	7.358	NC
AGT LIMITED	8.80	22 SEP 25	107.875	8.094	NC
AVCO FIN	8.75	15 MAR 00	106.875	6.833	NC
BELL CANADA	9.20	1 JUN 99	108.000	6.539	NC
BELL CANADA	8.80	17 AUG 05	108.750	7.504	NC
BELL CANADA	9.70	15 DEC 32	117.875	8.160	+0.125
BC TELEPHONE	9.65	8 APR 22	117.000	8.078	+0.125
BANK OF MONT	8.80	13 SEP 10/05	109.250	7.441C	NC
BANK OF N S	8.90	20 JUN 25	109.125	8.083	NC
CENTRA GAS	8.85	1 SEP 05	107.875	7.678	NC
CDN IMP BANK	8.65	22 AUG 05	108.500	7.398	NC
CDN UTIL	8.43	1 JUN 05	107.375	7.329	NC
CDN UTIL	9.40	1 MAY 23	115.625	7.984	NC
INTERPRV PIP	8.20	15 FEB 24	101.250	8.085	+0.125
MOLSON BREW	8.20	11 MAR 03	104.250	7.423	NC
NVA SCOT PWR	9.75	2 AUG 19	116.000	8.204	NC
NOVA GAS	8.30	15 JUL 03	105.125	7.399	NC
PANCDN PETE	8.75	9 NOV 05	109.375	7.391	-0.125
ROYAL BANK	10.50	1 MAR 02	117.000	7.045	NC
TALISMAN	9.45	22 DEC 99	109.250	6.750	NC
TALISMAN	9.80	22 DEC 04	113.750	7.651	NC
THOMSON CORP	7.95	15 NOV 05	103.125	7.494	NC
TRANSCDA PIP	9.45	20 MAR 18	112.875	8.181	NC
UNION GAS	8.65	10 NOV 25	105.500	8.154	+0.125
WSTCOAST ENE	9.50	10 JAN 00	109.250	6.827	NC
WSTCOAST ENE	9.70	15 NOV 04	113.625	7.560	NC
WSTCOAST ENE	8.50	23 NOV 15	103.375	8.153	+0.125

MAPLE LEAF WARRANTS

Underlying issue	Type	Expiry	Strike	Price	$ Chg
CAN 9.00 DEC 04	C	14 FEB 96	101.800	9.435	NC

ScotiaMcLeod Indexes

Index	Close	% chg	Yield	Chg	52 wk High	52 wk Low
Short	261.53	0.02	6.238	-0.00	261.53	224.45
Mid	291.04	-0.02	6.961	0.01	291.10	233.47
Long	318.53	-0.04	7.699	0.01	318.67	242.74
Universe	290.83	-0.01	6.857	0.00	290.87	236.00

Benchmarks

Issuer	Coupon	Maturity	Price	Yield	$ chg
U.S. Treasury	6 7/8	Aug/25	112 27/32	5.94	+18/32
British gilt	8.5	Jul/05	107 16/32	7.41	+3/32
German	6.5	May/05	103.43	6.02	+0.13
Japan #174	4.5	Dec/05	111.78	2.900	-0.12

SOURCE: Reprinted by the permission of *The Globe and Mail: Report on Business* (December 30, 1995).

chartered banks and other financial institutions. Some employers allow their employees to obtain them through payroll savings plans.

Income from CSBs is taxed in the same manner as any other fixed income security—payments from simple interest bonds must be reported in the year in which they are received and accrued interest on compound interest bonds must be reported, despite the fact that no interest has actually been received. Each year the Bank of Canada publishes tables showing the amount of accrued interest that must be reported for compound interest bonds.

Zero-Coupon or Strip Bonds

A non-callable Government of Canada bond is, in effect, a portfolio of pure-discount or **zero-coupon** bonds. That is, each coupon payment, as well as the principal, can be viewed as a bond in itself; the investor who owns the bond can therefore be viewed as holding a number of individual pure-discount bonds. In 1982, a number of brokerage firms began separating these components, using a process known as **coupon stripping**, described in Chapter 5.

Figure 14.7 shows typical market prices for a set of stripped default-free securities, where price is expressed as a percent of maturity value. As the figure shows, the longer the investor has to wait until maturity, the lower the price of the security. In Canada, strip bonds are derived from federal and provincial securities and trade in the OTC market, but prices are not quoted in the business press. Investors wishing to trade these securities may approach the chartered banks or dealers who specialize in them to obtain quotes. Figure 14.8 shows a typical investment dealer's quotation for stripped coupons (generally based on Government of Canada or provincial bonds).

Figure 14.7

Typical market prices for a set of stripped default-free securities.

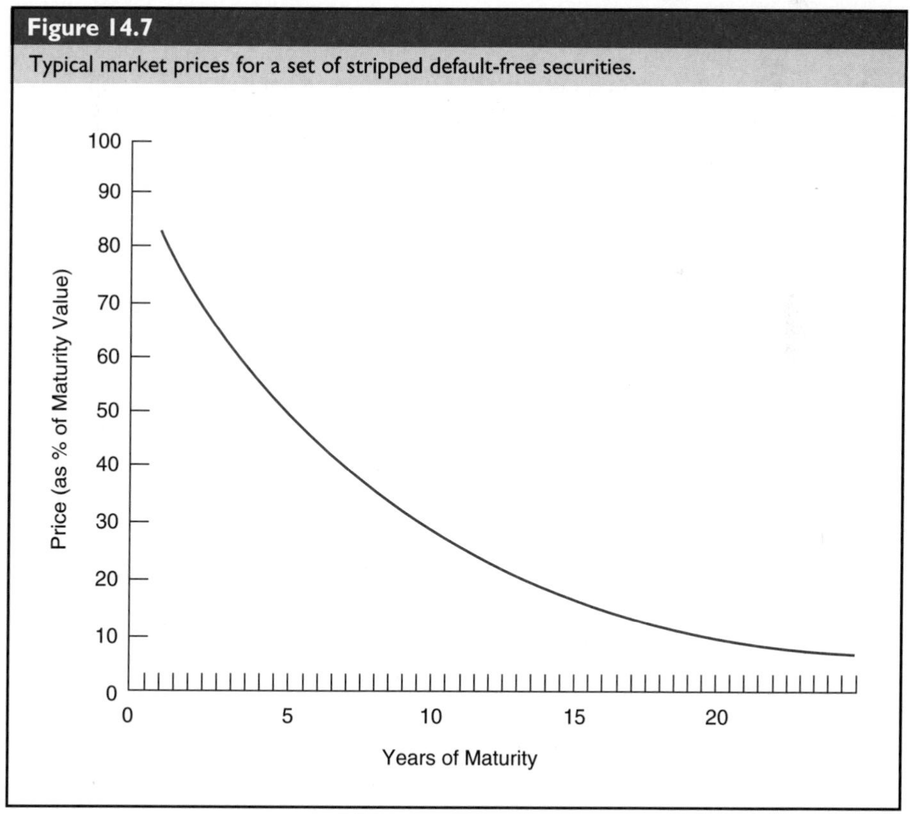

Figure 14.8

Quotations for stripped coupons, October 30, 1995.

Rate Report

All Rates Subject to Change

Strip Coupons

Term	Rate	Cost	Maturity Value
3 Year	7.25%	$850	
5 Year	7.52%	$694	$1000
10 Year	8.27%	$452	
15 Year	8.71%	$299	$1000
20 Year	8.77%	$184	

Real Return Strip Coupons

Term	Yield	Inflation
3 Year	4.35%	2.30%
5 Year	4.40%	
10 Year	4.45%	
15 Year	4.50%	
20 Year	4.50%	

SOURCE: Reprinted with the permission of Dylan Rogers, Richardson Greenshields of Canada Ltd.

▶ Real Return Bonds

Real Return Bonds are designed to provide a specified real return over their lifetime; that is, they are indexed so as to offer an inflation protected return. On December 10, 1991, the Government of Canada issued $700 million of non-callable 4.25% Real Return Bonds that mature on December 1, 2021. These are the first example of their kind in North America, although index-linked bonds have been issued by other governments, notably in the UK and Israel.

While the nominal yield to maturity and nominal cash flows are known in advance for conventional bonds (for example, an 8% Government of Canada bond purchased at par has a nominal yield of 8% per annum), the real yield depends on the rate of inflation throughout the term of the bonds. Even though the nominal amount due on maturity is known in advance, the purchasing power of that amount is uncertain and may be more or less than the purchasing power of the original principal.

In the case of Real Return Bonds the real yield to maturity and real cash flows are known in advance. The nominal yield, however, depends on the rate of inflation throughout the term of these bonds and, while the purchasing power of the amount due at maturity is known in advance, the actual nominal amount due at maturity is uncertain and may be more or less than the nominal amount of the original principal.

A Real Return Bond offers investors the following advantages:

- guaranteed real yield to maturity
- preservation of purchasing power of principal and coupons
- automatic reinvestment of inflation compensation, thereby reducing reinvestment risk
- better matching of inflation-indexed liabilities
- improved portfolio risk/return characteristics

For a more detailed description of the Government of Canada's Real Return Bond offering see the Institutional Issues section.

INSTITUTIONAL ISSUES

Real Return Bonds

Summary of the Offering

Issue: 4.25% Real Return Bonds due 2021 (the "Bonds"), with a rate of return linked to the Consumer Price Index for Canada.

Issue Amount: $700 000 000

Issue Price: 100%

Real Yield: 4.25%

Rank: The Bonds constitute direct, unsecured, unconditional obligations of Her Majesty in right of Canada. Principal and interest on the Bonds (interest consisting of coupon interest and inflation compensation) are direct charges on, and payable out of, the Consolidated Revenue Fund of Canada.

Date of Maturity: December 1, 2021 ("Maturity")

Date of Closing: December 10, 1991 ("Date of Closing")

Consumer Price Index: The Consumer Price Index for purposes of the Bonds is the All-items Consumer Price Index for Canada (1986 = 100), not seasonally adjusted, as published by Statistics Canada.

Indexing Process: An index ratio (the "Index Ratio") is applied to calculate both Coupon Interest and Inflation Compensation. The Index Ratio for any date ("Date") is defined as the ratio of the reference CPI ("Ref CPI_{Date}") applicable to such date divided by the reference CPI applicable to the Date of Closing ("Ref CPI_{Base}").

$$\text{Index Ratio}_{\text{Date}} = \left[\frac{\text{Ref CPI}_{\text{Date}}}{\text{Ref CPI}_{\text{Base}}}\right]$$

The reference CPI for the first day of any calendar month is the CPI for the third preceding calendar month. For example, the reference CPI for January 1, 1992 will be the CPI for October 1991. The reference CPI for any other day in a month is calculated by linear interpolation between the reference CPI applicable to the first day of the month in which such day falls and the reference CPI applicable to the first day of the month immediately following.

Interest and Final Payment: The Bonds bear interest adjusted in relation to the Consumer Price Index for Canada ("CPI") which interest consists of both an inflation compensation component ("Inflation Compensation") calculated based on Principal and payable at Maturity and a cash entitlement ("Coupon Interest") calculated based on Principal and accrued Inflation Compensation, which Coupon Interest is payable in semi-annual instalments on June 1 and December 1 (the "Coupon Payment Dates"), commencing June 1, 1992. Coupon Interest is calculated by multiplying one-half of the coupon of 4.25% per annum by the sum of the Principal and the Inflation Compensation which has accrued from the date of issue of the Bonds to the relevant Coupon Payment Date. At Maturity, in addition to Coupon Interest payable on such date, a final payment (the "Final Payment") equal to the sum of Inflation Compensation accrued from the date of issue of the Bonds to Maturity (whether positive or negative) and Principal will be made.

Final Payment = Principal + Inflation Compensation

Calculation of Interest: Inflation Compensation accrued to any Date is calculated by first multiplying the Principal by the Index Ratio applicable to that Date ("Index $\text{Ratio}_{\text{Date}}$") and then subtracting the Principal.

$$\text{Inflation Compensation}_{\text{Date}} = \left\{[\text{Principal} \times \text{Index Ratio}_{\text{Date}}] - \text{Principal}\right\}$$

or

$$\text{Inflation Compensation}_{\text{Date}} = \left\{\left[\text{Principal} \times \frac{\text{Ref CPI}_{\text{Date}}}{\text{Ref CPI}_{\text{Base}}}\right] - \text{Principal}\right\}$$

Coupon Interest is calculated by multiplying one-half of the coupon of 4.25% per annum by the sum of the Principal and the Inflation Compensation accrued from the date of issue of the Bonds to the relevant Coupon Payment Date.

$$\text{Coupon Interest}_{\text{Date}} = \frac{4.25\%}{2} \times [\text{Principal} + \text{Inflation Compensation}_{\text{Date}}]$$

Sample Calculation

Assumptions for purposes of illustration:

Issue Date:	December 1, 1991	$\text{Ref CPI}_{\text{Base}}$:	126.7000 ($\text{Ref CPI}_{\text{December 1991}}$)
Maturity Date:	March 1, 2021	$\text{Ref CPI}_{\text{December 1, 1991}}$:	$\text{CPI}_{\text{September 1991}}$
Annual Coupon:	4.25%	Principal:	100

Coupon Interest—June 1, 1992

$\text{Ref CPI}_{\text{June 1, 1992}}$ = 127.5000 (or $\text{CPI}_{\text{March 1992}}$)

$$\text{Index Ratio}_{\text{September 1, 1991}} = \left[\frac{127.5000}{126.7000}\right] = 1.00631$$

$$\text{Inflation Compensation}_{\text{June 1, 1992}} = \left\{\left[\text{Principal} \times \frac{\text{Ref CPI}_{\text{June 1, 1992}}}{\text{Ref CPI}_{\text{December 1991}}}\right] - \text{Principal}\right\}$$

$$\text{Inflation Compensation}_{\text{June 1, 1992}} = [100 \times 1.00631] - 100 = 0.631$$

$$\text{Coupon Interest}_{\text{Date}} = \frac{4.25\%}{2} \times [\text{Principal} + \text{Inflation Compensation}_{\text{Date}}]$$

$$\text{Coupon Interest}_{\text{June 1, 1992}} = \frac{4.25\%}{2} \times [100 + 0.631] = \$2.1384$$

INSTITUTIONAL ISSUES (continued)

Final Payment—March 1, 2021:

Ref $CPI_{March\ 1,\ 2021} = 395.8500 = CPI_{December\ 2020}$

$$\text{Index Ratio}_{March\ 1,\ 2021} = \left[\frac{395.8500}{126.7}\right] = 3.1243$$

$$\text{Inflation Compensation}_{March\ 1,\ 2021} = [100 \times 3.1243] - 100 = 212.4309$$

$$\text{Final Payment} = \text{Principal} + \text{Inflation Compensation}$$

$$\text{Final Payment}_{March\ 1,\ 2021} = 100 + 212.4309 = 312.4309$$

SOURCE: Excerpts from the original *Offering Circular*, October 1991 and material provided by Daniel Kelly, CIBC Wood Gundy.

▶ Mortgage Backed Securities

Technically, *mortgage-backed securities* are not Government of Canada securities but they are guaranteed by the government and so are described here. A mortgage-backed security (MBS) is a flow-through security that represents an ownership interest in a pool of residential first mortgages with similar terms to maturity (usually five years) and similar interest rates. The mortgages must be individually guaranteed under the National Housing Act (NHA). They are assembled by a financial institution (such as a bank, trust company, credit union, etc.), into an MBS that is underwritten by the Canada Mortgage and Housing Corporation (CMHC)—a federal government agency—then sub-divided into individual units and sold to the general public in minimum denominations of $5000.

Unlike most bonds, MBSs pay investors, on a monthly basis, an amount that represents a *pro rata* return of principal as well as interest on the underlying mortgages. For example, a holder of a $25 000 certificate from a $1 million pool would indirectly "own" 2.5% of each mortgage in the pool. Each month the homeowners make mortgage payments that are part principal and part interest. In turn, each month the investor receives 2.5% of the aggregate amount paid by the homeowners, less a small service charge. The mortgages are free from default risk because timely payment to the investor is guaranteed by CMHC, whether or not the issuer receives payment from the homeowner.

Two types of MBS are available—those consisting of non-prepayable mortgages and those consisting of prepayable mortgages.

There is a risk associated with the latter. When interest rates fall, homeowners prepaying or paying off their mortgages reduce the investor's return because both the term to maturity and the interest payments are reduced. MBSs based on prepayable mortgages would, therefore, be expected to sell at lower prices (higher yields) than those based on non-prepayable mortgages. The quoted prices and yields presented in Figure 14.9 show that this is the case. However, the yield differences are quite small, suggesting that prepayment risk is not perceived to be high.

Figure 14.9

Quoted prices and yields of mortgage-backed securities.

Mortgage-Backed Securities

Mortgage-backed securities are investments in pools of residential mortgages guaranteed by the Canadian government under the National Housing Act. This representative list of actively traded pools is provided by CIBC Wood Gundy Securities Inc. and shows the gross bid price for transactions of at least $1-million at Friday's close. The list is divided between open mortgages that are prepayable, and are likely to produce accelerated return of principal, and closed mortgages, on which unscheduled principal payments are not permitted. Indicated yields assume no prepayments. All MBS are priced to their weighted average maturity date.

Prepayable

Pool	Issuer	Maturity	Coupon	Price	Yield
96404645	Shoppers	Jan.97	8.250	101.80573	6.05
96405642	Canada Trust	Jul.97	7.750	101.90525	6.09
96407549	SunLife Trust	Jan.98	7.875	102.53891	6.24
96407978	Mackenzie	Apr.98	7.375	101.89735	6.32
96410170	FirstLine	May.99	6.250	98.87789	6.62
96411004	MUTUAL	Oct.99	8.750	105.55786	6.67
96411178	CIBC	Oct.99	8.875	105.89488	6.68
96411582	Household	Jun.00	8.100	103.60867	6.86
96500194	Sec Home Mort	Jul.98	7.125	101.19403	6.48

Nonprepayable

Pool	Issuer	Maturity	Coupon	Price	Yield
96600200	Peoples Trust	Jun.99	8.000	104.00881	6.52
99001752	Maritime Life	Mar.96	9.000	100.22525	5.73
99003139	Royal Bank	Jan.97	7.875	101.66957	5.80
99003915	CIBC	Sep.97	7.000	101.22395	6.00
99004640	CIBC	Mar.03	8.250	105.60934	7.10
99004657	Met. Trust	Feb.98	7.500	102.33001	6.12
99005308	Met. Trust	Jul.00	7.625	103.12319	6.70
99005597	FirstLine	Aug.98	6.625	100.62471	6.24
99005928	CIBC	Jan.97	4.750	98.81270	5.80
99006678	Bk Of Montre	Dec.00	8.000	104.55282	6.75

SOURCE: Reprinted by the permission of *The Globe and Mail: Report on Business* (January 8, 1996).

PROVINCIAL, TERRITORIAL, AND LOCAL GOVERNMENT SECURITIES

Provincial, territorial, and municipal governments all borrow money to finance their investments and operations. In aggregate, the provincial and territorial governments have more term debt outstanding than the federal government. The securities issued by the first two are collectively referred to as **provincial bonds** or "provincials," while those of the third group are called **municipal bonds**, or simply "municipals" (the securities of the Canadian government are referred to as "Canadas"). Table 14.4 shows the distribution of ownership of provincial, territorial, and municipal term debt as of the end of 1993.

Provincial and Territorial Bonds

Provincials are issued to finance public works and, recently, social welfare programs. The payments on these securities are supported by provincial tax revenues. Many provinces also guarantee the bonds issued by provincial authorities and commissions, notably their hydro-electric commissions. As Figure 14.6 indicates, Hydro-Quebec and Ontario Hydro bonds are listed among the more actively traded issues. The three principal holders of provincials are the trusteed pension plans, social security funds (notably the Canada Pension Plan) and foreign investors. The provinces have, in general, been more aggressive than the federal government in tapping foreign markets for funds, which provide better borrowing rates and conditions. Close to one-third of the outstanding issues are denominated in foreign currencies, predominantly US dollars, but also Eurodollars, Swiss francs, and Japanese yen. At the time of issue their coupon rates were significantly below those prevailing in the domestic market. As a result, the provinces have assumed a significant degree of foreign exchange risk.

Table 14.4

Ownership of Outstanding Provincial, Territorial, and Municipal Term Debt, December 1993.[a]

Held by	Provincials Amount[b]	Provincials Percentage of Total	Municipals Amount[b]	Municipals Percentage of Total
Chartered banks	$ 5 349	1.9%	$ 514	1.4%
Thrift institutions	2 644	1.0	176	0.5
Life insurance companies	13 669	4.9	2 909	7.9
Property and casualty insurance companies	5 641	2.0	1 372	3.7
Trusteed pension funds	53 666	19.1	2 879	7.8
Mutual funds	5 041	1.8	391	1.1
Investment dealers	1 320	0.5	156	0.4
Non-financial private corporations	164	neg.	—	—
Misc. private financial institutions	288	0.1	—	—
Foreign investors	117 951	42.0	5 025	13.7
Individuals and non-incorporated business	8 254	3.0	9 235	25.2
Sub-total—privately held term debt	$ 213 987	76.3%	$ 22 657	61.7%
Non-financial government enterprise	3 041	1.1	8	neg.
Public financial institutions	9 440	3.4	1 189	3.2
Social security funds	34 595	12.3	—	—
Provincial and local governments	19 351	6.9	12 876	35.1
Federal government	13	neg.	3	neg.
Sub-total publicly held term debt	$ 66 440	23.7%	$14 074	38.3%
Total term debt	$280 427	100.0%	$ 36 731	100.0%

[a] Excludes Treasury bills but includes provincial government guaranteed issues.
[b] in millions of dollars.

SOURCE: Statistics Canada, *National Balance Sheet Accounts: System of National Accounts, Annual Estimates, 1984–1993*, Ottawa, March 1995.

To assist municipalities, the provinces raise funds through government agencies such as the Alberta Municipal Financing Corporation and the Ontario Municipal Improvements Corporation. These agencies float large bond issues (guaranteed by the province) at advantageous rates and then distribute the proceeds to small municipalities that would otherwise have difficulty raising funds. An investor purchasing these bonds is effectively investing in a portfolio of municipal bonds that are guaranteed by the provincial government.

► Municipal Bonds

Municipals are usually issued by larger cities as **installment debentures**, where specified groups of debentures mature in each succeeding year. The largest cities, such as Montreal, Toronto, and Vancouver may issue **term debentures** (that is, debentures that all mature on the same date) or a mixture of serial and term bonds. These issues are generally underwritten by an investment dealer who specializes in municipals or they are sold through a private placement. Table 14.4 indicates that the holders of municipal bonds are more widely varied than those of federal and provincial bonds. It should be noted, however, that no municipals appear in Figure 14.6 where actively traded issues are listed.

In recent years municipalities have, more frequently, been using non-market sources of capital such as the provincial agencies mentioned above, senior levels of government, and the Canada Pension Plan and provincial pension plan funds. Foreign sources, predominantly in the US, have also been used, but these represented only about 8% of the total at the end of 1993.

CORPORATE BONDS

Corporate bonds are similar to other kinds of fixed-income securities in that they carry the promise of specified payments at specified times and provide legal remedies in the event of default. Restrictions are often placed on the activities of the issuing corporation in order to provide additional protection for bondholders (for example, there may be restrictions on the amount of additional bonds that can be issued in the future).

From the viewpoint of the issuing corporation, debt differs from equity in two crucial respects. First, principal and interest payments are obligatory. Failure to make any payment in full and on time can expose the issuer to expensive, time-consuming, and potentially disruptive legal actions. Second, unlike dividend payments, interest payments are considered expenses to the corporation, and hence can be deducted from earnings before calculating the corporation's income tax liability. As a result, each dollar paid in interest reduces earnings before taxes by a dollar, thereby reducing corporate taxes by $0.40 for a firm in the 40% marginal tax bracket. This leads to less than a dollar decline in earnings after taxes (in the 40% tax bracket example, the decline in earnings is $0.60).

► The Indenture

An issue of bonds is generally covered by a **trust indenture** or **trust deed**, in which the issuing corporation promises a specified **trustee** that it will comply with a number of stated provisions. Chief among these is the timely payment of required coupons and principal on the issue. Other terms are often included to control the sale of pledged property, the issuance of other bonds, and the like.

The trustee for a bond issue, usually a trust company, acts on behalf of the bondholders. Some actions may be required by the indenture, whereas others, such as acting in response to a request from specific bondholders, may be done at the trustee's discretion.

If the corporation defaults on an interest payment, after a relatively short period of time (perhaps one to six months) the entire principal typically becomes due and payable—a procedure designed to enhance the bondholders' status in any forthcoming bankruptcy or related legal proceedings.

Types of Bonds

An exhaustive list of the names used to describe bonds would be intolerably long. Different names are often used for the same type of bond, and occasionally the same name will be used for two quite different bonds. A few major types do predominate, however, with relatively standard nomenclature.

Mortgage Bonds

Bonds of this type represent debt that is secured by the pledge of specific property. In the event of default, the bondholders are entitled to obtain the property in question and sell it to satisfy their claims on the firm. In addition to the property itself, the holders of mortgage bonds have an unsecured claim or **floating charge** on all the other assets of the corporation.

Mortgage bondholders are usually protected by terms included in the bond indenture. The corporation may be constrained from pledging property for other bonds (or such bonds, if issued, must be "junior," or "second," mortgages, with only a secondary claim on the property). Certain property acquired by the corporation after the bonds were issued may also be pledged to support the bonds.

Collateral Trust Bonds

These bonds are backed by other securities that are usually held by the trustee. A common situation of this sort arises when the securities of a subsidiary firm are pledged as collateral by the parent firm.

Equipment Obligations

These securities (also known also as equipment trust certificates) are backed by specific pieces of equipment; for example, railway cars or commercial aircraft. If necessary, the equipment can be readily sold and delivered to a new owner. The legal arrangements used to facilitate the issuance of such bonds can be very complex. The most popular procedure uses the *Philadelphia plan*, in which the trustee initially holds the equipment, issues obligations, and leases the equipment to a corporation. Money received from the lessee is subsequently used to make interest and principal payments to the holders of the obligations; ultimately, if all payments are made on schedule, the leasing corporation takes title to the equipment.

Debentures

These are general obligations of the issuing corporation and thus represent unsecured credit. To protect the holders of such bonds, the indenture will usually limit the future issuance of secured debt as well as any additional unsecured debt.

Subordinated Debentures

When more than one issue of debentures is outstanding, a hierarchy may be specified. For example, subordinated debentures are junior to unsubordinated debentures, meaning that in the event of bankruptcy, junior claims are to be considered only after senior claims have been fully satisfied.

Other Types of Bonds

Income bonds are more like preferred shares (described in a later section) than bonds. Payment of interest in full and on schedule is not absolutely required, and failure to do so need not send the corporation into bankruptcy. Since 1978, interest on such bonds has qualified as a tax deductible expense in Canada for the issuing corporation. Except in reorganizations, this type of bond is rarely used.

Guaranteed bonds are issued by one corporation but backed in some way by another (for example, by a parent firm). **Participation bonds** require stated interest payments and provide additional amounts if earnings exceed some stated level. In **serial bonds**, different portions of the issue mature at different dates.

Convertible bonds may, at the holder's option, be exchanged for other securities, often common shares. Such bonds, which have become very popular in recent years, are discussed in more detail in Chapter 20.

Extendible bonds give the bondholder the option of extending the term to maturity of the bond on a specific date. For example, a five-year extendible bond may allow the investor, within six months of maturity, to extend the maturity by five years at the same or a slightly higher interest rate.

Retractable bonds give the bondholder the option of reducing the term to maturity of the bond on a specified date.

► Call Provisions

Management would like to have the right to pay off the corporation's bonds at par at any time prior to maturity. Reducing debt or altering maturity by refunding provides desirable flexibility. Most important, expensive high-coupon debt issued during a time of high interest rates can be replaced with cheaper low-coupon debt if rates decline.

Not surprisingly, investors hold a different opinion on the matter. The issuer's ability to redeem an issue at par at any time virtually precludes a rise in price over par and robs the holder of potential gains from the price appreciation associated with declining interest rates; moreover, it introduces a new form of uncertainty. A bond with such a feature will almost certainly sell for less than one without it.

Despite the cost of obtaining this sort of flexibility, many corporations include call provisions in their bond indentures that give the corporation the option to call some or all of the bonds from their holders at stated prices during specified periods prior to maturity. In a sense, the firm sells a bond and simultaneously buys an option from the holders. The net price of the bond, therefore, is the difference between the value of the bond and the option. (Note that retractable bonds give the investor the option of forcing the issuer to call the security.)

Investors are often given some call protection: during the first few years after being issued, a bond may not be callable. When a bond is callable, a **call premium** may be specified in the call provision. If the issue is called when a call premium is specified then the issuer must pay the bondholders a **call price** that is a stated amount above par. Generally, the call premium declines as the maturity date approaches.

An entire issue may be called, or only specific bonds that are chosen randomly by the trustee may be called. In either case, a notice of redemption will appear in advance in the financial press.

Call features are not popular with Canadian institutional investors, probably because the relative illiquidity of the corporate bond market makes it difficult to replace a called bond with one having similar characteristics. For many years an alternative form of call protection was used that included a provision stating that the issue was non-refundable for financial advantage. This meant that the corporation could not call the bonds in order to replace them with bonds carrying a lower coupon rate but could call them to retire the issue without replacing them. This provision proved to be unenforceable so it was replaced with the **Canada Call**. The Canada Call required the issuer to pay a call premium such that the investor could enter the long Canada market to replace the bond with one that provided an equivalent cash flow. It soon became evident, however, that the investors benefitted from this provision because they were able to obtain higher quality bonds as replacements. Currently the **Canada plus x** call feature is standard on practically all corporate bonds issued. Under this provision the call premium is calculated using the corresponding Canada bond yield plus x basis points to reflect the quality differential.

► Sinking Funds

A bond indenture will often require the issuing corporation to make annual payments into a **sinking fund**. Each payment covers part of the principal as well as the interest, thereby reducing the amount outstanding at maturity.

Sinking funds operate by having the corporation transfer cash to the trustee, who then purchases bonds in the open market. Alternatively, the corporation may obtain the bonds, by either purchase or call, and deposit them with the trustee. Call prices for sinking fund purchases may differ from those specified when the entire issue is to be repaid prior to maturity.

Required contributions to a sinking fund may or may not be the same each year. In some cases, the required amount may depend on earnings or output; in others, the goal is to make the annual payments equal.

► Private Placements

Bonds intended for eventual public sale are usually issued in denominations of $1000 each. Both bearer and registered forms may be utilized. Often, however, a single investor (or a small group of investors) will buy an entire issue. Such *private placements* are typically purchased by large financial institutions.

► Bankruptcy

When a corporation fails to make a scheduled coupon or principal payment on a bond, the corporation is said to be in default on that obligation. If the payment is not made within a relatively short period, litigation will usually follow.

A corporation unable to meet its obligatory debt payments is said to be technically insolvent (or insolvent in the equity sense). If the value of the firm's assets falls below its liabilities, it is said to be insolvent (or insolvent in the bankruptcy sense).

If voluntary agreements with creditors cannot be obtained, bankruptcy—usually "voluntary"—is filed by the corporation itself. Subsequent developments involve, among others, courts, court-appointed officials, representatives of the firm's creditors, and the management of the firm.

Liquidation

A question that arises in many bankruptcies is whether or not the firm's assets should be liquidated (that is, sold) and the proceeds divided among the creditors. Such an action is taken only if the court feels the resulting value would exceed that likely to be obtained if the firm continued in operation (perhaps after substantial reorganization).

If the firm's assets are liquidated in a *straight bankruptcy*, secured creditors receive either the property pledged for their loans or the proceeds from the sale of the secured property. If this amount falls short of their claims, the difference is considered an unsecured debt of the firm; on the other hand, any excess is made available for other creditors. Next, assets are used to pay the claims of priority creditors to the extent possible. These include claims for such items as administrative expenses, wages (up to a stated limit per person), uninsured pension claims, taxes, and rents. Anything left over is used to pay unsecured creditors in proportion to their claims on the firm.

Reorganization in Lieu of Bankruptcy

If the value of a firm's assets, when employed as part of a going concern, appears to exceed their value in liquidation, a reorganization of the firm and its liabilities may be undertaken. Such proceedings, conducted under the provisions of The Bankruptcy and Insolvency Act, may be voluntary (initiated by the firm) or involuntary (initiated by three or more creditors). A number of parties must concur in the proposed reorganization, including the holders of two-thirds of the value in each general class of creditor that is affected by the reorganization.

Among the goals of reorganization are "fair and equitable" treatment of various classes of securities and the elimination of "burdensome" debt obligations. Typically, creditors are given new claims on the reorganized firm, with the amounts of the new claims intended to be at least equal in value to the amounts that the creditors would have received in liquidation. For example, holders of debentures might receive bonds of longer maturity, holders of subordinated debentures might become shareholders, and shareholders might be left without any claims on the firm.

Some Financial Aspects of Bankruptcy

Although the subject is far too complex for detailed treatment here, two aspects of bankruptcy deserve some discussion. First, the choice between continuation of a firm and liquidation of its assets should be unrelated to the reasons for its bankruptcy. If an asset can be sold for more than the present value of its future earnings, it should be. Management may have to be taken to court to be forced to do this, but the issue is not one of solvency or lack thereof.

Second, the definition of insolvency is rather vague. Assume, for example, that assets can be adequately valued at liquidating or going-concern value, whichever is greater. A firm is said to be insolvent if this value is less than that of the firm's liabilities. How should these liabilities be valued? Their current market value will frequently be less than the value of the assets, whereas their book value may be greater than the value of the assets.

► Ownership of Corporate Bonds

At the end of 1993, investors held more than $153 billion of corporate and foreign bonds. As can be seen in Table 14.5, the largest investors were life insurance companies, pension funds, and foreign investors. Over 50% of these bonds were issued in foreign currencies, the principal ones being US dollars, Eurodollars, Swiss francs and Japanese yen.

Some firms use foreign denominated bond issues in order to hedge their foreign exchange exposure in the product market. For example, a Canadian pulp and paper company with substantial US sales, whose product prices are quoted in US dollars, loses revenue when the Canadian dollar rises vis-à-vis the US dollar. If its debt is US-dollar denominated then

Table 14.5

Ownership of Outstanding Corporate and Foreign Bonds, December 1993.

Held by	*Amount (in millions)*	*Percentage of Total*
Chartered banks	$ 5 581	3.5%
Thrift institutions	1 644	1.0
Life insurance companies	34 321	21.6
Property and casualty insurance companies	4 448	2.8
Trusteed pension funds	14 384	9.1
Mutual funds	4 524	2.9
Investment dealers	902	0.6
Non-financial private corporations	2 517	1.6
Misc. private financial institutions	2 445	1.5
Foreign investors	71 250	44.9
Individuals and non-incorporated business	11 779	7.4
Sub-total—privately held corporate bonds	$153 795	96.9%
Non-financial government enterprise	116	0.1
Public financial institutions	1 149	0.7
Provincial and local governments	3 650	2.3
Federal government	25	–
Sub-total—publicly held bonds	$ 4 940	3.1%
Total corporate bonds	$158 735	100.0%

SOURCE: Statistics Canada, *National Balance Sheet Accounts: System of National Accounts, Annual Estimates, 1984–1993*, Ottawa, March 1995.

the Canadian-dollar value of its interest payments will also fall providing at least a partial off-set.

► The Secondary Bond Market

Most trading in corporate bonds takes place through dealers in the over-the-counter market. A small number of debentures are listed on the Alberta, Vancouver, and Toronto Stock Exchanges. About 100 dealers and a few banks and trust companies are active in the OTC market. The major dealers and large institutional clients are electronically linked—bid and offer prices for a wide range of bonds are displayed on video screens located in their offices. Some dealers issue periodic quotation sheets that are reported in the daily business press.

FOREIGN BONDS

The foreign bond market refers to bonds issued and denominated in the currency of a country other than the one in which the issuer is primarily located. For example, the Mexican government has issued bonds that are denominated in US dollars, mature in 1997, and carry an 8 1/8% coupon rate. Foreign bonds that are issued in the United States and are denominated in US dollars are referred to as Yankee bonds, and foreign (that is, non-Japanese) bonds that are issued in Japan are referred to as Samurai bonds.

In issuing foreign bonds, the issuer must abide by the rules and regulations imposed by the government of the country in which the bonds are issued. This may be relatively easy or difficult, depending on the countries involved.

One of the main advantages of purchasing foreign bonds is the opportunity to obtain international diversification of the default risk of a bond portfolio while not having to be concerned about foreign exchange fluctuations. For example, a Canadian investor might be able to buy a Toyota bond in Japan that is denominated in yen, but in doing so would have to worry about the yen-dollar exchange rate. This is because the coupon payments and ultimately the principal would be paid to the investor in yen, which would then have to be converted into dollars at a currently unknown exchange rate. However, the investor could avoid such worries by purchasing a Toyota bond that is denominated in Canadian dollars.

EUROBONDS

Owing in part to government restrictions on investment in foreign securities, a number of borrowers have found it advantageous to sell securities in other countries. The term **Eurobond** is loosely applied to bonds that are offered outside the country of the borrower and usually outside the country in whose currency the securities are denominated. Thus, a bond issued by a Canadian corporation that is denominated in Japanese yen and sold in Germany and Switzerland would be referred to as a Eurobond.[6]

Since the Eurobond market is neither regulated nor taxed, it offers substantial advantages for many issuers and buyers of bonds. For example, a foreign subsidiary of a Canadian corporation may issue a Eurobond in "bearer" form. No tax is withheld by the corporation, and the tax (if any) paid by the purchaser depends on his or her country of residence. Because of these regulatory and tax advantages, interest rates on Eurobonds tend to be somewhat lower than those on domestic bonds denominated in the same currency.

A recent development has been the appearance of **global issues**. These are large issues that appear simultaneously in several countries and are underwritten by investment dealers in those countries. For example, a recent Ontario Hydro issue of $1.5 billion was issued in Canadian dollars and underwritten in the US, the UK, Japan, several European countries, and Australia, among other markets. With world-wide distribution of this kind it is possible to maintain a 24-hour market in these securities, thereby enhancing their liquidity.

TAX TREATMENT OF FIXED-INCOME SECURITIES

The tax treatment of coupon-bearing securities is not complicated — the coupon payment must be reported as income in the year that it is received and tax is payable at the regular rate.

Coupon-bearing securities bought at either a discount or a premium in the marketplace, if held to maturity, affect the investor's income tax because the difference between the purchase price and the par value must be treated as a capital gain or loss at maturity.

Revenue Canada also requires that taxes be paid annually on the accrued interest on zero-coupon or pure-discount securities.

---

[6] There are also fixed-income securities of this nature that have shorter lives; they are sometimes referred to as Euronotes or Euro-commercial paper. The market where they (and Eurobonds) are issued and traded is known as the Eurocredit market.

For example, a stripped bond that matures in two years for $1000 can be purchased currently for $850. Thus, the investor will earn $150 in interest over two years, realizing it only when the bond matures. Revenue Canada, however, requires that the investor pay taxes on a portion of the $150 each year, but has no specific rules as to how the accrual should be calculated as long as the method used is "reasonable." One simple alternative is to allocate an equal fraction of the implied interest to each year to maturity. The investor would then report $75 ($150/2) per year as interest income. An alternative is to use the **economic accrual method**. In this method the yield is calculated, which in this case is $(\$1000/\$850)^{1/2} - 1 = 8.46\%$. This means that the implied value of the bond at the end of the first year is $\$850 \times 1.0846 = \$921.91$; thus, the amount of interest income to be recognized that year is $\$921.91 - \$850 = \$71.91$ or $\$850 \times 0.0846$. The amount of interest income to be recognized in the second year, assuming the bond is held to maturity, will be $\$1000 - \$921.91 = \$78.09$ or 921.21×0.0846 (note that $\$1000 = \$921.91 \times 1.0846$). This method results in a lower reported interest income in the first year and a larger one in the second and, therefore, reduces the present value of the investor's two tax bills.

With zero-coupon bonds the investor has a cash outflow when purchasing the bond and also has to pay tax on the accrued interest every year until it matures. The investor only receives a cash inflow at maturity. As a result, such securities are attractive primarily for tax-exempt or low tax-bracket investors (for example, as RRSP investments).

The taxation of Real Return bonds presents some special features. Adjusted coupon payments must be reported in the normal manner in the year they are received. In addition, the inflationary adjustment to the principal that accrues during the year must be included in taxable income. Thus, for taxation year T, the amount Principal $\times [IR_T - IR_{T-1}]$ must be reported as income. The taxation of these bonds resembles that of strip bonds in that tax must be paid on an amount that has not yet been received, a factor that makes them less attractive to taxed investors.

PREFERRED SHARES

In some respects, **preferred shares** are like perpetual bonds. A given annual dollar amount is promised by the issuer to the investor. This amount may be stated as a percent of the stock's par value (for example, 8% of $100, meaning $8 per year), or directly as a dollar figure (for example, $2.75 per year). Since the security is a stock, such payments are called dividends rather than interest. They do not qualify as a tax-deductible expense for the issuing corporation, but do qualify for the personal dividend tax credit. Furthermore, failure to make such payments does not constitute grounds for bankruptcy proceedings.

A recent innovation is variable or **floating rate preferred shares** (known as adjustable rate preferred stock, or ARPS, in the US), where the dividend is reset periodically in terms of an established market rate with an underlying floor (or minimum payment). For example, the annualized "percent of par" for the minimum payment may be set at 8% and the quarterly dividends reset every three months to equal half the prevailing Bank of Canada rate plus 1.5%. Any difference between 8% and the actual dividends paid must be made up in the final quarter.

Related to variable rate preferred are money market or **auction preferred shares** (known as **dutch auction rate** preferred stock, DARPS, in the US).[7] The price of these shares is fixed but the dividend is reset periodically (usually every calendar month) at a level that is determined at an auction between current and potential owners. If the auction is not successful, then a minimum dividend rate is triggered. This rate is predetermined in relation to an established market-based rate such as the prime rate or the current bankers' acceptance yield.

Preferred shares are generally "preferred as to dividends." Specified payments must be made on the preferred shares before any dividends may be paid to holders of the firm's common stock. Failure to pay a preferred dividend in full does not constitute default, but unpaid dividends are usually cumulative. This means that all previously unpaid preferred share dividends must be paid (but seldom with interest) before any dividends may be paid on the common stock.

No indenture is provided with a preferred share issue. Various provisions protecting the preferred shareholders against potentially harmful actions, however, may be written into the corporation's charter. For example, one provision may limit the dollar amount of senior securities that can be issued in the future. Although preferred shareholders typically do not have voting rights, there may be another provision that gives them voting rights when the corporation is in arrears on its preferred dividends.

Many issues of preferred shares are callable, often at a premium; such stock is sometimes said to be redeemable at a stated redemption price. *Retractable preferred* provide the investor with an option to force the redemption of the issue by the company at a specified date and price. *Participating preferred* shares entitle the holder to receive extra dividends when earnings permit. *Convertible preferred* shares may, at the option of the holder, be converted into another security (usually the firm's common stock) on stated terms. Some firms issue more than one class of preferred shares, with preference accorded the various classes in a specified order.

In the event of a dissolution of the firm, preferred shares take precedence over common stock in the liquidation of assets. Generally this means that preferred shareholders are entitled to receive the share's par value before any payment is made to common shareholders.

Since preferred shares have many features of a bond without the substantial tax advantage that bonds give to the issuer, they are used less often than debt. In 1990, \$0.942 billion of such shares were issued, compared with \$8.6 billion of publicly offered corporate debt.[8]

As indicated in Chapter 13, interest income from bonds held by a corporate investor is subject to corporate income tax at an effective rate in excess of 40%, while dividend income is generally tax exempt. For this reason, preferred shares tend to sell at prices that give lower before-tax returns than long-term bonds, even though the latter may be considerably lower in risk. As a result, preferred shares are generally unattractive holdings for tax-exempt non-corporate investors.

Many preferred shares are traded on major exchanges in a manner similar to common stocks. Typically, they are assigned to the market-maker responsible for the firm's common

---

[7] Presumably these are referred to as dutch auction preferred because the lowest bidder is the winner. For a discussion of ARPS and DARPS, see Michael J. Alderson, Keith C. Brown, and Scott L. Lummer, "Dutch Auction Rate Preferred Stock," *Financial Management* 16, no. 2 (Summer 1987): 68–73.

[8] *Bank of Canada Review*, November 1991.

stock. Trading prices are reported in the financial press in the same format as that used for common stocks.

SUMMARY

1. The most familiar types of fixed-income securities are personal savings deposits. These include demand deposits, time deposits, and guaranteed investment certificates issued by chartered banks, trust companies, caisses populaires, and credit unions.
2. Highly marketable, short-term securities are referred to as money market instruments. These securities include commercial paper, large-denomination certificates of deposit, bankers' acceptances, repurchase agreements, and Eurodollars CDs.
3. The Bank of Canada issues debt securities to finance the government's borrowing needs. These securities are issued in various maturities—from short-term Treasury bills to intermediate-term and long-term bonds. The Bank of Canada also issues Canada Savings Bonds to individual investors.
4. Canada bonds can be converted into a set of pure-discount bonds by issuing marketable receipts entitling the holder to a specific coupon payment or the bond's principal payment. Separating a bond into its component payments is known as coupon stripping.
5. Government agencies also issue securities to finance their operations. In some cases this debt is explicitly backed by the federal or provincial governments. In other cases the government guarantee is implicit.
6. The Government of Canada has issued a series of index-linked Real Return bonds that are inflation protected.
7. Provincial governments issue a wide variety of fixed-income securities, generally backed solely by the full faith and credit of the issuer.
8. Municipal bonds, especially for smaller municipalities, are issued by provincial municipal finance corporations.
9. Corporate bonds, such as mortgage bonds or equipment obligations, may be backed by specific assets. Alternatively, corporate bonds, such as debentures, may represent general obligations of the issuing corporation.
10. Corporate bonds (and some federal government and municipal bonds) may contain call provisions, giving the issuer the right to redeem the security prior to maturity under specified terms.
11. Corporations entering bankruptcy may undergo liquidation or reorganization, or enter into arrangements.
12. Foreign bonds are those that are issued and denominated in the currency of a country other than that of the issuer.
13. Eurobonds are those that are issued in a country other than that of the issuer and in a currency different from that of the country where they are offered.
14. Preferred share dividends are generally fixed but do not represent legal obligations of the issuers. Most preferred share dividends are cumulative, requiring payment of all unpaid preferred dividends before common stock dividends can be paid.

QUESTIONS AND PROBLEMS

1. What is the annual equivalent yield on a 13-week Treasury bill selling at a price of 96?
2. Consider a 13-week Treasury bill, issued today, which is selling for $9675. (Its face value is $10 000.)
   a. What is the annual discount based on the selling price of the security?
   b. What is the annual equivalent yield of the security?
3. If a three-month Treasury bill sells for a price of 98, whereas a six-month Treasury bill sells for 96, is the equivalent yield (unannualized) for the six-month bill twice that of the three-month bill? Why?
4. Rank the various money market instruments discussed in the text in terms of default risk. Explain the reasoning behind your rankings. Find the latest interest rates for these securities. Do they correspond with your default-risk rankings?
5. Bonds may be issued in either bearer or registered form. Given the characteristics of bearer and registered bonds, discuss the relative merits of each.
6. Using the *Globe and Mail* as a data source, identify a particular Canada bond. What is its coupon rate? What is its maturity date? What is the security's yield-to-maturity?
7. Describe the standard practice by which sellers of government and corporate bonds are compensated for accrued interest.
8. What is the rationale for including a call provision in the indenture of a bond issue? How do bond investors typically respond to the inclusion of a call provision?
9. How do zero-coupon fixed-income securities provide returns to investors?
10. Consider a ten-year zero-coupon Treasury security selling for a price of $300, with a face value of $1000. What is the before-tax annual rate of return to an investor who buys and holds this security to maturity?
11. Why does Revenue Canada treat the difference between the price of a strip bond purchased at a discount and its face value as ordinary income to the investor, as opposed to treating it as a capital gain?
12. Bonds issued by federal agencies carry an explicit or implicit promise that the federal government will ensure payment of interest and principal. Why then are these securities usually priced by the market to offer yields above Canada securities?
13. What is a mortgage-backed security? What is the primary risk that such securities present to investors?
14. Cary Dolan, an amateur investor, said "I prefer investing in mortgage-backed securities. Their government guarantee gives me a risk-free return." Comment on Cary's remark.
15. Labrador Airlines was in difficult financial shape owing to ongoing recession and labour problems. To this point the firm had issued no debt, but management believed that borrowing in the bond market was the only way to get through the tough times. Because of its poor financial condition, Labrador's investment bankers advised management that a debenture issue would not be well received. What other bond issuance options might Labrador pursue?
16. Is any mortgage bond necessarily a more secure investment than any debenture? Explain.
17. A callable bond is sometimes described as a combination of a non-callable bond and an option. Explain why this description is appropriate. Further, explain the impact of these two features on the price of a callable bond.
18. Chris Dolan is considering purchasing one of two bonds: a corporate bond with a 9% coupon interest rate, selling at par, or a preferred share, with a 6% dividend rate. Given that Chris lives in Ontario, is in the 26% federal tax bracket, and assuming that all other

relevant factors are the same between the two securities, which should Chris select? (Ignore any surtaxes and use the dividend tax credit factors given in Chapter 13.)

19. Is it true that most corporations that default on their debt eventually enter bankruptcy and see their assets liquidated to repay creditors? Explain.

20. Eurobonds have become very popular forms of financing in recent years. What features of the Eurobond market make Eurobonds attractive to issuers and bondholders?

21. In trying to explain the concept of preferred shares to a novice investor, Lisa Mototsune referred to it as a "hybrid" security. What did Lisa mean by this term?

22. What is the purpose of the cumulative restriction of most preferred shares?

23. The preferred shares of Clinton Foods carry a dividend of $8 per share. The stock currently sells for $50. If one year from today the Clinton preferred share price remains unchanged, what is the return from holding the stock for:

a. A corporation in the 35% tax bracket?

b. An individual in the 35% tax bracket?

CFA Exam Question

25. A portfolio manager at Superior Trust Company is structuring a fixed-income portfolio to meet the objectives of a client. The client plans to retire in 15 years and wants a substantial lump sum at that time. The client has specified the use of AAA-rated securities.

The portfolio manager compares coupon Canadas with zero-coupon stripped Canadas and observes a significant yield advantage for the stripped bonds.

Maturity	*Coupon Canadas*	*Zero-Coupon Stripped Canadas*
3 year	5.50%	5.80%
5 year	6.00	6.60
7 year	6.75	7.25
10 year	7.25	7.60
15 year	7.40	8.80
30 year	7.75	7.75

Briefly discuss two reasons why zero-coupon stripped Canadas could yield more than coupon Canadas with the same final maturity.

Key Terms

pure-discount security
coupon payment
maturity date
principal
demand deposit
time deposit
guaranteed investment certificate (GIC)
money market instrument
annualized rate basis
annual percentage rate (APR)
finance paper
commercial paper
bankers' acceptance
negotiable deposit
Certificate of Deposit (CD)
Eurodollar CDs
Eurodollar deposit
repurchase agreement
repo rate
debt refunding

bearer form
primary distributor
accrued interest
registered form
bond certificate
registered bond
call protection
purchase fund
zero-coupon bond
coupon stripping
Real Return Bond
provincial bond
municipal bond
installment debenture
term debenture
trust indenture
trust deed
trustee
floating charge
income bond
guaranteed bond
participation bond
serial bond
convertible bond
extendible bond
retractable bond
call premium
call price
Canada Call
Canada plus x
sinking fund
Eurobond
global issue
economic accrual method
preferred share
floating rate preferred share
auction preferred share
dutch auction rate

REFERENCES

1. A concise summary description of the various types of money market instruments is contained in:

Timothy Q. Cook and Timothy D. Rowe, *Instruments of the Money Market* (Federal Reserve Bank of Richmond, 1986).

2. The following contain thorough descriptions of the various types of fixed-income securities discussed in this chapter:

Frank J. Fabozzi and Franco Modigliani, *Capital Markets: Institutions and Instruments* (Englewood Cliffs, NJ: Prentice Hall, 1992), Chapters 13–18.

Frank J. Fabozzi, Franco Modigliani, and Michael G. Ferri, *Foundations of Financial Markets and Institutions* (Englewood Cliffs, NJ: Prentice Hall, 1994), Chapters 16, 17, 20–24.

3. For a discussion of coupon stripping in the US, see:

Miles Livingston and Deborah Wright Gregory, *The Stripping of US Treasury Securities*, Monograph Series in Finance and Economics #1989–1, New York University Salomon Center, Leonard N. Stern School of Business.

Deborah W. Gregory and Miles Livingston, "Development of the Market for US Treasury STRIPS," *Financial Analysts Journal* 48, no. 2 (March/April 1992): 68–74.

Phillip R. Daves, Michael C. Ehrhardt, and John M. Wachowicz, Jr., "A Guide to Investing in US Treasury STRIPS," *AAII Journal* 15, no. 1 (January 1993): 6–10.

Phillip R. Daves and Michael C. Ehrhardt, "Liquidity, Reconstitution, and the Value of US Treasury STRIPS," *Journal of Finance* 47, no. 1 (March 1993): 315–329.

4. For a discussion of the market for securities issued by the US Treasury, see:

Peter Wann, *Inside the US Treasury Market* (New York: Quorum Books, 1989).

5. For discussion of mortgage-backed securities, see:

   Earl Baldwin and Saundra Stotts, *Mortgage-Backed Securities: A Reference Guide for Lenders & Issuers* (Chicago: Probus Publishing, 1990).

   Eduardo S. Schwartz and Walter N. Torous, "Prepayment, Default, and the Valuation of Mortgage Pass-through Securities," *Journal of Business* 65, no. 2 (April 1992): 221–239.

   Frank J. Fabozzi and Franco Modigliani, *Mortgage & Mortgage-Backed Securities Markets* (Boston: Harvard Business School Press, 1992).

6. For a discussion of the foreign bond and Eurobond markets, see:

   J. Orlin Grabbe, *International Financial Markets* (New York: Elsevier Science Publishing, 1991), Chapters 16–18.

   Bruno Solnik, *International Investments* (Reading: MA: Addison-Wesley, 1991), Chapters 6–7.

7. For a discussion of the Eurocredit market, see:

   Arie L. Melnik and Steven E. Plaut, *The Short-Term Eurocredit Market*, Monograph Series in Finance and Economics #1991–1, New York University Salomon Center, Leonard N. Stern School of Business.

8. For a discussion of how government bond markets function in the United Kingdom, Japan, and Germany, see:

   Thomas J. Urich, *UK, German and Japanese Government Bond Markets*, Monograph Series in Finance and Economics #1991–2, New York University Salomon Center, Leonard N. Stern School of Business.

9. The accuracy of reported prices for corporate bonds is analyzed in:

   Kenneth P. Nunn, Jr., Joanne Hill, and Thomas Schneeweis, "Corporate Bond Price Data Sources and Risk/Return Measurement," *Journal of Financial and Quantitative Analysis* 21, no. 2 (June 1986): 197–208.

   Oded Sarig and Arthur Warga, "Bond Price Data and Bond Market Liquidity," *Journal of Financial and Quantitative Analysis* 24, no. 3 (September 1989): 367–378.

   Arthur D. Warga, "Corporate Bond Price Discrepancies in the Dealer and Exchange Markets," *Journal of Fixed Income* 1, no. 3 (December 1991): 7–16.

10. The market for preferred shares is discussed in:

    Arthur L. Houston, Jr., and Carol Olson Houston, "Financing with Preferred Stock," *Financial Management* 19, no. 3 (Autumn 1990): 42–54.

11. An extensive discussion of the private placement market for corporate debt is contained in:

    Mark Carey, Stephen Prowse, John Rea, and Gregory Udell, "The Economics of Private Placements: A New Look," *Financial Markets, Institutions & Instruments* 2, no. 3 (1993).

12. For a Canadian perspective on the topics covered in this chapter, see:

    C. R. Dipchand and R. J. Hanrahan, "Exit and Exchange Option Values on Government of Canada Retractable Bonds," *Financial Management* 8, no. 3 (Autumn 1979).

A. L. Ananthanarayanan and E. Schwartz, "Retractable and Extendible Bonds: The Canadian Experience," *Journal of Finance* 35, no. 1 (March 1980).

J. Cooperman, M. Gagnon, H. Hinkle, P. Kearns and V. Rao, "Canadian Mortgage Securities: A Primer," *Journal of Fixed Income* 4, no. 3 (Dec. 1994).

INTERNET RESOURCES

The following investment information sources can be accessed at these Internet addresses:

Altamira Investment Services	**http://www.altamira.com**
Quote.Com Financial Market Data	**http://www.quote.com**

CHAPTER 15

Bond Analysis

Consider an investor who believes that there are situations where public information can be used to identify mispriced bonds (i.e., one who believes the bond market is not semistrong-efficient). To translate that belief into action about which bonds to buy and sell, an analytical procedure is needed. One procedure involves comparing a bond's yield-to-maturity with a yield-to-maturity that the investor feels is appropriate, based on the characteristics of the bond as well as current market conditions. If the yield-to-maturity is higher than the appropriate yield-to-maturity, then the bond is said to be underpriced (or undervalued) and is a candidate for buying. Conversely, if the yield-to-maturity is lower than the appropriate one, then the bond is said to be overpriced (or overvalued) and is a candidate for selling (or even short selling).

Alternatively, the investor could estimate the bond's "true," or "intrinsic," value, and compare it with the bond's current market price. Specifically, if the current market price is less than the bond's intrinsic value, then the bond is underpriced, and if it is greater, then the bond is overpriced.

Both procedures for analyzing bonds are based on the capitalization of income method of valuation. The first procedure, involving yields, is analogous to the internal rate of return method that is discussed in most introductory finance textbooks, whereas the second procedure, involving intrinsic value, is analogous to the net present value method that also appears in such books. Although the focus in those books is on making an investment decision involving some type of real asset (such as whether or not a new piece of machinery should be purchased), the focus here is on making an investment decision involving a particular type of financial asset—bonds.

APPLYING THE CAPITALIZATION OF INCOME METHOD TO BONDS

An investor who believes the bond market is efficient would question the ability of other investors to identify mispriced situations. However, if an investor believes such situations exist, then an economically sensible and logical approach to valuation is needed to identify them. One such approach is the **capitalization of income method of valuation**.

This method of valuation states that the intrinsic value of any asset is based on the discounted value of the cash flows that the investor expects to receive in the future from owning the asset. As mentioned earlier, one way that this method has been applied to bond valuation is to compare the bond's yield-to-maturity (y) with the yield-to-maturity the investor deems appropriate (y^*). Specifically, if $y > y^*$, then the bond is underpriced, and if $y < y^*$, then the bond is overpriced. However, if $y = y^*$, then the bond is said to be fairly priced.

Promised Yield-to-Maturity

Letting P denote the current market price of a bond with a remaining life of n years and promising cash flows to the investor of C_1 in year 1, C_2 in year 2, and so on, the yield-to-maturity (more specifically, the **promised yield-to-maturity**) of the bond is the value of y that solves the following equation:

$$P = \frac{C_1}{(1+y)^1} + \frac{C_2}{(1+y)^2} + \frac{C_3}{(1+y)^3} + \cdots + \frac{C_n}{(1+y)^n}.$$

Using summation notation, this equation can be rewritten as

$$P = \sum_{t=1}^{n} \frac{C_t}{(1+y)^t}. \tag{15.1}$$

For example, consider a bond that is currently selling for \$900 and has a remaining life of three years. For ease of exposition, assume it makes annual coupon payments amounting to \$60 per year and has a par value of \$1000. That is, $C_1 = \$60$, $C_2 = \$60$, and $C_3 = \$1060 = \$1000 + \$60$. Using equation (15.1), the yield-to-maturity on this bond is the value of y that solves the following equation:

$$\$900 = \frac{\$60}{(1+y)^1} + \frac{\$60}{(1+y)^2} + \frac{\$1060}{(1+y)^3}$$

which is $y = 10.02\%$. If subsequent analysis indicates that the yield-to-maturity should be 9.00%, then this bond is underpriced, since $y = 10.02\% > y^* = 9.00\%$.

Intrinsic Value

Alternatively, the intrinsic value of a bond can be calculated using the following formula:

$$V = \frac{C_1}{(1+y^*)^1} + \frac{C_2}{(1+y^*)^2} + \frac{C_3}{(1+y^*)^3} + \cdots + \frac{C_n}{(1+y^*)^n}.$$

or, using summation notation,

$$V = \sum_{t=1}^{n} \frac{C_t}{(1+y^*)^t}. \tag{15.2}$$

Since the purchase price of the bond is its market price P, the **net present value** (NPV) to the investor is equal to the difference between the value of the bond and the purchase price:

$$\begin{aligned} NPV &= V - P \qquad (15.3) \\ &= \left[\sum_{t=1}^{n} \frac{C_t}{(1+y^*)^t}\right] - P. \end{aligned}$$

The NPV of the bond in the previous example is the solution to the following equation:

$$\begin{aligned} NPV &= \left[\frac{\$60}{(1+.09)^1} + \frac{\$60}{(1+.09)^2} + \frac{\$1060}{(1+.09)^3}\right] - \$900 \\ &= \$24.06. \end{aligned}$$

Since this bond has a positive NPV, it is underpriced. This will always be the case when a bond has a yield-to-maturity that is more than appropriate (earlier, it was shown that this bond's yield-to-maturity was 10.02%, which is more than 9.00%, the appropriate yield-to-maturity). That is, in general, any bond with $y > y^*$ will always have a positive NPV and vice versa, so that under either method it would be underpriced.[1]

Alternatively, if the investor had determined that y^* was equal to 11.00%, then the bond's NPV would have been –\$22.19. This would suggest the bond was overpriced, just as would have been noted when the yield-to-maturity of 10.02% was compared with 11.00%. This will always be the case—a bond with $y < y^*$ will always have a negative NPV and vice versa, so that under either method it would be found to be overpriced.

It should also be pointed out that if the investor had determined that y^* had a value of approximately the same magnitude as the bond's yield-to-maturity of 10%, then the NPV of the bond would be approximately zero. In such a situation, the bond would be viewed as being fairly priced.

Note that in order to use the capitalization of income method of valuation, the values of C_t, P, and y^* must be determined. It is generally quite easy to determine the values for C_t and P, since they are the bond's promised cash flows and current market price, respectively. However, determining the value of y^* is difficult, since the investor must estimate an appropriate value for the bond. Such a decision will depend on the characteristics of the bond, as well as on current market conditions. Given that the key ingredient in bond analysis is determining the appropriate value of y^*, the next section discusses the attributes that should be considered in making such a determination.

BOND ATTRIBUTES

Five primary attributes of a bond are important in bond valuation: (1) length of time until maturity; (2) coupon rate; (3) call provisions; (4) taxation; (5) marketability; and (6) likelihood of default. At any time, the structure of market prices for bonds differing in these dimensions can be examined and described in terms of yields-to-maturity. This underlying structure is sometimes referred to as the **yield structure**. Often, attention is confined to differences along a single dimension, holding the other attributes constant. For example, the set of yields of bonds of different maturities constitutes the **term structure** (discussed in Chapter 5), and the set of yields of bonds of different default risk is referred to as the **risk structure**.

Most bond analysts consider the yields-to-maturity for default-free bonds to form the term structure. "Risk differentials" are then added to obtain the relevant yields-to-maturity for bonds of lower quality. While subject to some criticism, this procedure makes it possible to think about a complicated set of relationships sequentially.

The differential between the yields of two bonds is usually called a **yield spread**. Most often, it involves a bond that is under analysis and a comparable default-free bond (that is, a government security of similar maturity and coupon rate). Yield spreads are sometimes

[1] A more accurate method of determining a bond's intrinsic value involves the use of spot rates. That is, in determining the NPV of this bond, the investor might have determined that the relevant spot rates for the one-year, two-year, and three-year cash flows are 8.24%, 8.69%, and 9.03%, respectively. Using these values, the bond's intrinsic value would be equal to $\$60/1.0824 + \$60/1.0869^2 + \$1060/1.0903^3 = \$924.06$. Although V is the same in this example when either spot rates or y^* are used in the calculations, this need not always be the case.

measured in **basis points**, where one basis point equals .01%. If the yield-to-maturity for one bond is 8.50% and that of another is 8.90%, the yield spread is 40 basis points.

Coupon Rate and Length of Time Until Maturity

These attributes of a bond are important because they determine the size and timing of the cash flows that are promised to the bondholder by the issuer. Given a bond's current market price, these attributes can be used to determine the bond's yield-to-maturity, which will subsequently be compared with what the investor thinks it should be. More specifically, if the market for Canada bonds is viewed as being efficient, then the yield-to-maturity on a Canada bond that is similar to the bond under evaluation can form a starting point for the analysis.

Consider the previously mentioned bond selling for $900 that has promised cash flows over the next three years of $60, $60, and $1060, respectively. Suppose there is a Canada bond that provides a cash flow over the next three years of $50, $50, and $1050 and is selling for $912.89. The yield-to-maturity on this second security is 8.5%, information that can be used to determine what the yield-to-maturity should be on the $900 bond. In this situation, the yield spread between the bond and the government security is 10.02%–8.50% = 1.52% and the analyst must then consider whether or not this spread is appropriate. Figure 15.1 shows the yield spreads between indexes of bonds of three different qualities (AAA, AA, and BBB) from January 1985 to December 1994. Note that these spreads can vary dramatically through time.[2]

Call Provisions

At first glance, bonds issued when yields-to-maturity are relatively high may appear to be unusually attractive investments. However, this is not necessarily the case because many corporate bonds have a **call provision** that enables the issuer to redeem the bonds prior to maturity, usually for a price somewhat above par. This price is known as the **call price**, and the difference between it and the par value of the bond is known as the **call premium**. An issuer will often find it financially advantageous to call the existing bonds if yields drop substantially after the bonds were initially sold, since the issuer will be able to replace them with lower yielding securities that are less costly.[3]

For example, consider a ten-year bond issued at par ($1000) that has a coupon rate of 12% and is callable at $1050 any time after it has been outstanding for five years.[4] If, after five years, yields on similar five-year bonds were 8%, the bond would probably be called. This means that an investor who had planned on receiving annual coupon payments of $120 for ten years would instead actually receive the call price of $1050 after five years. At this time, the investor could take the $1050 and reinvest it in the 8% bonds, thereby receiving $84 per year in coupon payments over the last five years (it is assumed here that

---

[2] The yield spread series for AAA bonds is truncated in October 1993. This was the month that the last AAA corporate bond in Canada was downgraded to AA.

[3] Many corporate bonds have, in addition to a call provision, a provision for a sinking fund where each year the issuer retires a pre-specified portion of the original bond issue.

[4] In this example, the **yield-to-call** (or, to be more specific, the yield-to-first-call) is 12.78%. That is, 12.78% is the discount rate that makes the present value of $120 received after each of the first four years and $1170 ($1050 + $120) at the end of five years equal to the issue price of the bond, $1000. Note that the yield-to-first-call is greater than the bond's promised yield-to-maturity at the time of issue (12%).

Figure 15.1

Yield spreads, 1985–1994 (long-term monthly averages).

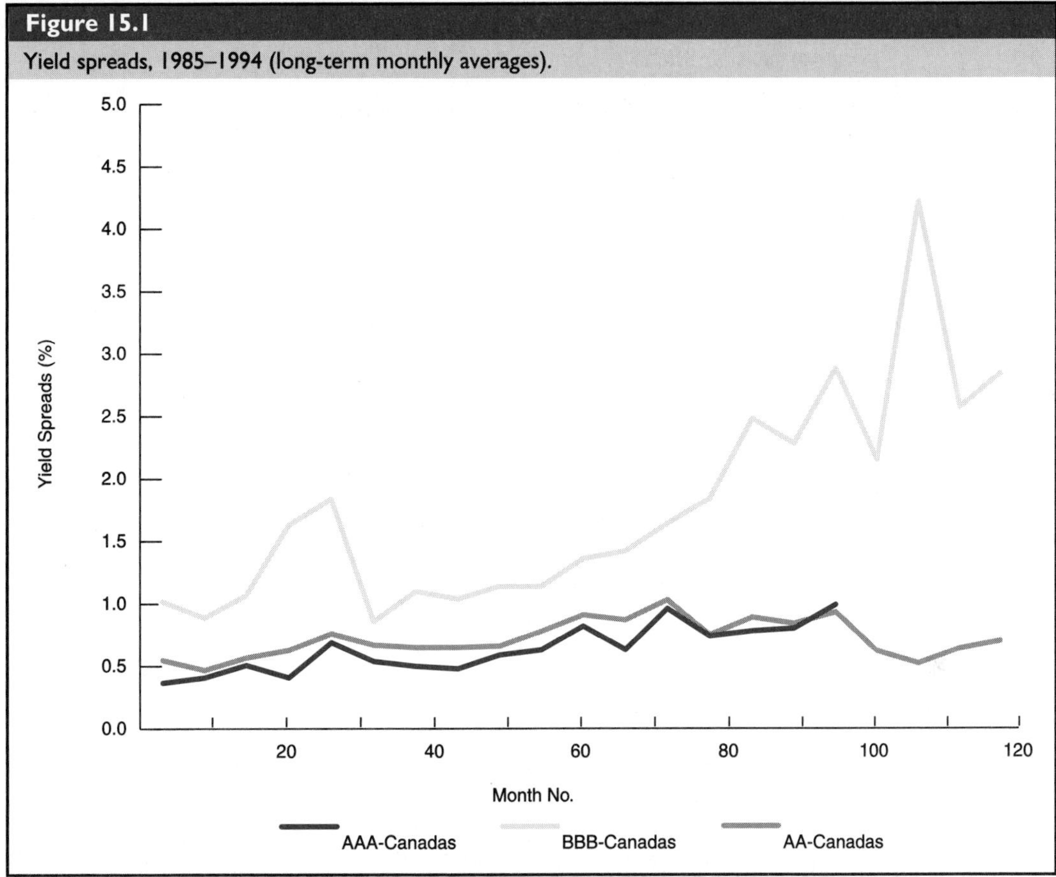

SOURCE: Prepared with data from Melanie Moore, *Scotia McLeod's Handbook of Canadian Debt Market Indices: 1947–1995* (Toronto: Scotia McLeod Inc.), February 1995; Melanie Moore, *Debt Market Indices*, November 30, 1995, Scotia McLeod Inc.

the investor can purchase a fraction of a bond, so that the full \$1050 can be invested in the 8% bonds), and \$1050 at the end of the tenth year as a return of principal. Given this pattern of cash flows, the actual yield-to-maturity (otherwise known as the *realized return*) over the ten years would be 10.96%.

This example suggests that the higher the coupon rate of a callable bond, the greater is the likely divergence between actual and apparent yields. This is borne out by experience. Figure 15.2 plots the coupon rate, set at time of issue, on the horizontal axis. Since most bonds are initially sold at (or very close to) par, the coupon rate is also a measure of the yield-to-maturity that an investor may have thought was obtainable by purchasing one of the newly issued bonds.

The vertical axis in this figure plots the actual yield-to-maturity obtained up to the original maturity date by an investor, assuming that the payments received in the event of a call were reinvested in non-callable bonds with appropriate maturities. The curve is based on experience for a group of callable bonds issued by utility companies during a period of fluctuating interest rates. As can be seen, the coupon rate and actual yield are quite similar in magnitude until the coupon rate approaches 5%. At this point, higher coupon rates are no longer associated with higher actual yields, since these coupon rates were relatively high

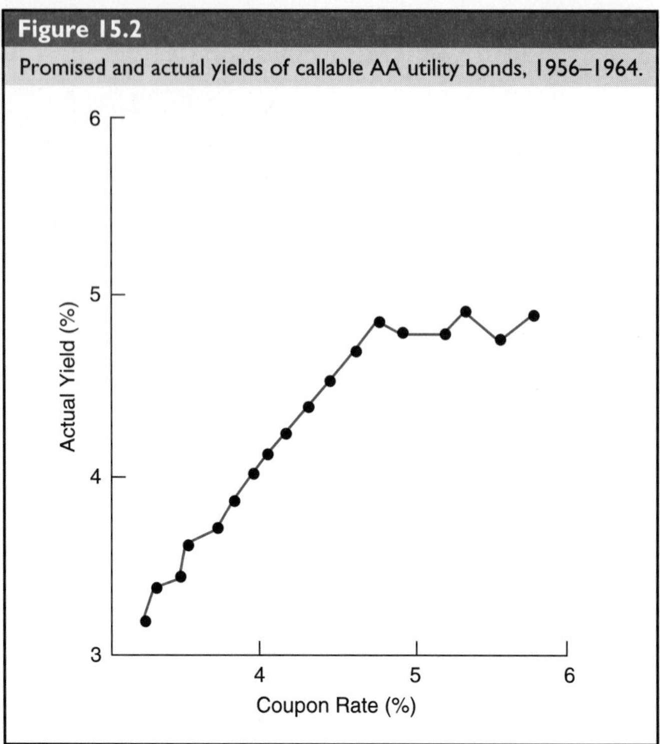

Figure 15.2

Promised and actual yields of callable AA utility bonds, 1956–1964.

SOURCE: Frank C. Jen and James E. Wert, "The Effect of Call Risk on Corporate Bond Yields," *Journal of Finance* 22, no. 4 (December 1967): 646.

during the time period examined; as a consequence, most of the bonds with coupon rates above 5% were ultimately called.

The upshot is that bonds with a greater likelihood of being called should have a higher yield-to-maturity. That is, the higher the coupon rate or the lower the call premium, the higher the yield-to-maturity should be. Equivalently, bonds with higher coupon rates or lower call premiums will have lower intrinsic values, all else being equal.

Taxation

Taxation affects bond prices and yields in other ways. For example, low-coupon bonds selling at a discount provide returns in two forms: coupon payments and capital gains. In Canada, coupon payments are taxed as ordinary income, and capital gains are taxed at a reduced rate. Furthermore, taxes on the latter may be deferred until the bond is either sold or matures. This means that such **deep discount bonds** have a double tax advantage. Other things being equal they should, therefore, have lower before-tax yields than high-coupon bonds. That is, low-coupon bonds have a higher intrinsic value than high-coupon bonds.

Marketability

Marketability (sometimes also referred to as liquidity) refers to the ease with which an investor can sell an asset quickly without having to make a substantial price concession. An example of an illiquid asset is a *collectible*, such as a piece of artwork. An investor who owns a Van Gogh painting may have to settle for a relatively low price if he or she has to sell it within an hour. If the sale can be postponed for a length of time in order to set up a public auction, a much higher price could probably be obtained. Alternatively, an investor with $1 000 000 worth of BCE common stock who has to sell these shares within an hour will probably be able to receive a price close to that previously paid for them. Furthermore, it is unlikely that waiting would increase the expected selling price of such securities.

Since most bonds are bought and sold in dealer markets, one measure of a bond's marketability is the bid-ask spread that the dealers are quoting on the bonds. Bonds that are actively traded tend to have lower bid-ask spreads than bonds that are inactive. This is because the dealer is more exposed to risk when making a market in an inactive security than when making a market in an active security. The source of this risk is the inventory that the dealer holds and the fact that interest rates in general may move in a way that causes the dealer to lose money on his or her inventory. Accordingly, bonds that are actively traded should have a lower yield-to-maturity and a higher intrinsic value than bonds that are inactive, everything else being equal.

▶ Likelihood of Default

In Canada, two corporations — the Canadian Bond Rating Service (CBRS) and Dominion Bond Rating Service (DBRS) — provide ratings of the creditworthiness of many corporate, municipal, and provincial bonds. In the US, Standard & Poor's Corporation and Moody's Investors Service, Inc. provide similar information.[5] These **bond ratings** are often used by investors as an indication of the likelihood of default by the issuer. Figures 15.3 and 15.4 provide details of the CBRS and DBRS ratings.[6]

A broader categorization is often employed, with bonds classified as being of either **investment grade** or **speculative grade**. Typically, investment-grade bonds are bonds that have been assigned to one of the top four ratings (AAA through BBB by DBRS; A++ through B++ by CBRS). In contrast, speculative-grade bonds are bonds that have been assigned to one of the lower ratings (BB and below by DBRS; B+ and below by CBRS). Sometimes these low-rated securities are called **junk bonds**. Investment-grade bonds whose quality has fallen to junk levels are referred to as **fallen angels**.

Certain regulated financial institutions (such as trust companies, insurance companies, and pension plans) are prohibited from purchasing bonds that are not of investment grade. Because an important group of investors is encouraged or forced to purchase them, investment grade bonds are believed to command "superpremium" prices, and hence disproportionately low yields. If this were true, a major disparity in yields would attract many new issuers, thereby increasing the supply of such bonds and causing the prices to fall and yields to rise. For a significant superpremium to persist, substantial market segmentation on both the buying and the selling side would be required. Since there is no clear evidence that segmentation exists, it seems likely that the differences in yields between investment-grade bonds and speculative-grade bonds are roughly proportional to differences in default risk.

---

[5] Both Moody's and Standard & Poor's have made a practice of rating Canadian government bonds as well as selected Canadian corporate bonds.

[6] Both rating agencies use finer gradations than those shown in the figures. The ratings may be augmented by the addition of the qualifiers "high" or "low" to indicate both the relative ranking and the trend within a classification.

Figure 15.3

Canadian Bond Rating Service's rating definitions of long-term debt.

Highest Quality A++

This category encompasses bonds of outstanding quality. They possess the highest degree of protection of principal and interest. Companies with debt rated A++ are generally large national and/or multinational corporations whose products or services are essential to the Canadian economy.

These companies are the acknowledged leaders in their respective industries and have clearly demonstrated their ability to best withstand adverse economic or trade conditions either national or international in scope. Characteristically, these companies have had a long and creditable history of superior debt protection, in which the quality of their assets and earnings has been constantly maintained or improved, with strong evidence that this will continue.

Very Good Quality A+

Bonds rated A+ are similar in characteristics to those rated A++ and can also be considered superior in quality. These companies have demonstrated a long and satisfactory history of growth with above-average protection of principal and interest on their debt securities.

These bonds are generally rated lower in quality because the margin of assets or earnings protection may not be as large or as stable as those rated A++. In both these categories the nature and quality of the assets and earnings coverages are more important than the numerical values of the ratios.

Good Quality A

Bonds rated A are considered to be good quality securities and to have favorable long-term investment characteristics. The main feature that distinguishes them from the higher rated securities is that these companies are more susceptible to adverse trade or economic conditions. Consequently, the protection is lower than for the categories of A++ and A+.

In all cases the A rated companies have maintained a history of adequate asset and earnings protection. There may be certain elements that may impair this protection sometime in the future. Confidence that the current overall financial position will be maintained or improved is slightly lower than for the securities rated above.

Medium Quality B++

Issues rated B++ are classified as medium or average grade credits and are considered to be investment grade. These companies are generally more susceptible than any of the higher rated companies to swings in economic or trade conditions that would cause a deterioration in protection should the company enter a period of poor operating conditions.

There may be factors present either from within or without the company that may adversely affect the long-term level of protection of the debt. These companies bear closer scrutiny but in all cases both interest and principal are adequately protected at the present time.

Figure 15.3

(Continued)

Lower Medium Quality B+

Bonds which are rated B+ are considered to be lower medium grade securities and have limited long-term protective investment characteristics. Assets and earnings coverage may be modest or unstable.

A significant deterioration in interest and principal protection may occur during periods of adverse economic or trade conditions. During periods of normal or improving economic conditions, assets and earnings protection are adequate. However, the company's ability to continually improve its financial position and level of debt protection is at present limited.

Poor Quality B

Securities rated B lack most qualities necessary for the long-term fixed income investment. Companies in this category have a general history of volatile operating conditions, and the assurance has been in doubt that principal and interest protection will be maintained at an adequate level. Current coverages may be below industry standards and there is little assurance that debt protection will significantly improve.

Speculative Quality C

Securities in this category are clearly speculative. The companies are generally junior in many respects and there is little assurance that the adequate coverage of principal and interest can be maintained uninterruptedly over a period of time.

Default D

Bonds in this category are in default of some provisions in their trust deed and the companies may or may not be in the process of liquidation.

Rating Suspended

A company which has its rating currently suspended is experiencing severe financial or operating problems of which the outcome is uncertain. The company may or may not be in default but at present there is uncertainty as to the company's ability to pay off its debt.

Note: (High) and (Low) designations after a rating indicate an issuer's relative strength within a rating category.

SOURCE: The CBRS Method of Rating: Corporate and Government Securities (Canadian Bond Rating Service Inc., 1989): 16,17.

Ratings are designed "to provide investors with a readily identifiable measure of the financial strength of a debt issue. In this way its relative level of risk and hence the required return may be compared to other types of securities throughout a diversified portfolio."[7] Moreover:

> Ratings involve judgments about the future on the one hand, and they are used by investors as a means of protection on the other, therefore, an effort is made when assigning ratings to

[7] *The CBRS Method of Rating* (Montreal: Canadian Bond Rating Service, Inc., 1989): 6.

Figure 15.4

Dominion Bond Rating Service's bond rating scale.

AAA "Near Perfection"

Bonds which are rated AAA are of the highest investment quality. The degree of protection afforded principal and interest is of the highest order. Earnings are relatively stable, the structure of the industry in which the Company operates is very strong, and the outlook for future profitability is extremely favorable. There are few qualifying factors present which would detract from the performance of the Company, and the strength of liquidity ratios is unquestioned for the industry in which the Company operates.

AA Well Above Average

Bonds rated AA are of superior investment quality, and protection of interest and principal is considered high. In many cases, they differ from bonds rated AAA to a small degree.

A Up to High Average, Upper Medium Grade

Bonds rated A are upper medium grade securities. Protection of interest and principal is still substantial, but the degree of strength is less than with AA rated companies. Companies in this category may be more susceptible to adverse economic conditions.

BBB Up to Low Average, Medium Grade

Bonds rated BBB are medium grade securities. Protection of interest and principal is considered adequate, but the Company may be more susceptible to economic cycles, or there may be other adversities present which reduce the strength of these bonds.

BB Mildly Speculative

Bonds rated BB are lower medium grade obligations, and are considered mildly speculative and below average. The degree of protection afforded interest and principal is uncertain, particularly during periods of economic recession, and the size of the Company may be relatively small.

B Middle Speculative

Bonds rated B are "middle" speculative. Uncertainty exists as to the ability of the Company to pay interest and principal on a continuing basis in the future, especially in periods of economic recession.

CCC Highly Speculative

Bonds rated CCC are considered highly speculative and are in danger of default of interest and principal. The degree of adverse elements present is more severe than bonds rated B.

CC In Default

Bonds rated CC are in default of either interest or principal, and other severe adverse elements are present.

Figure 15.4

(Continued)

C Second Tier of Debt of a Company in Default

C is the lowest rating provided. Bonds rated C differ from bonds rated CC with respect to the relative liquidation values.

"NR"

For certain companies, we may complete the editorial, yet not rate the Company formally, in which case we would rate it NR, or "not rated".

High or Low

In addition to the above, our ratings may be modified by the quotation "high" or "low" to indicate the relative standing within a rating classification.

Highest Rating

Please note: the rating quoted at the top left of the front page of a report indicates the rating of the highest order or securities issued by the Company.

SOURCE: DBRS, Dominion Bond Rating Service Limited, 1992: 7.

> look at the "worst" potential outcomes in the "visible" future, as well as the past record and the present status. Investors using the ratings should not expect to find in them a reflection of statistical factors alone. They are an appraisal of long-term risks, including the recognition of many non-statistical factors.[8]

Despite this disclaimer, the influence of "statistical factors" on the ratings is apparently significant. Several studies have investigated the relationship between historical measures of a firm's performance and the ratings assigned its bonds. Many of the differences in the ratings accorded various bonds can, in fact, be attributed to differences in the issuers' situations, measured in traditional ways. For corporate bonds, better ratings are generally associated with lower financial leverage (that is, debt to total assets); smaller past variation in earnings over time; larger asset base (firm size); more profitable operations; and lack of subordination to other debt issues. The results obtained by Canadian studies are similar to those of US studies. One use of these findings is in the development of models for predicting the initial ratings that will be given to forthcoming bond issues as well as for predicting changes in the ratings of outstanding bonds.

Default Premiums

Since common stocks do not "promise" any cash flows to the investor, they are not subject to default. To assess the investment prospects for a common stock, all possible holding-period returns might be considered. By multiplying each return by its perceived probability of occurrence and then adding up the products, an estimate of the expected holding-period return can be determined.

---

[8] *Moody's Bond Record* (New York: Moody's Investors Service, Inc., January 1988): 1.

INSTITUTIONAL ISSUES

Are Canadian Bond Raters Biased?

by Greg Ip

Investors may be taking on too much risk in the Canadian bond market by accepting credit ratings from Canadian agencies that often are more lenient than those issued by US agencies, some market observers say.

An increasing number of Canadian companies are being rated by Standard & Poor's Corp. or Moody's Investors Service Inc., both of New York, which have initiated major pushes into the Canadian market.

Their ratings are regularly lower than those assigned to the same issuers by Montreal-based Canadian Bond Rating Service Inc. and Dominion Bond Rating Service Ltd. of Toronto.

Indeed, a *Globe and Mail* analysis of 55 Canadian-controlled companies whose debt is rated by at least one US and one Canadian agency shows that on average the Canadian rating is one notch higher than the US rating.

The Canadian ratings are higher on 45 issuers, lower on four and the same on six.

While the average difference in ratings is small, on some it is substantial and enough to make the difference between classifying a company's debt as "investment grade" instead of "junk."

That distinction can make a half-percentage-point difference in the yield—the interest rate a company would have to pay on its bond—demanded by investors (as shown in Figure 15.5).

A notch separates one rating from the one directly below. For example, A1 is one notch above A2, two notches above A3 and three notches above triple-B1. Triple-A is the highest available, followed by double-A, single-A, triple-B, etc. Each letter category is divided into three subcategories, such as A1, A2, and A3. This article uses a standardized rating system instead of the agencies' four different systems.

For example, Moody's rates PanCanadian Petroleum Ltd. at A2 while S&P rates the Calgary-based company at A3, but both DBRS and CBRS rate it three notches higher at double-A2. Vancouver-based West Fraser Timber Co. Ltd. is rated triple-B3 by Moody's and S&P and A3 by CBRS.

But while the split clearly exists, opinion is divided on why and what it means for the market.

"Investors may feel a (false) sense of comfort from the Canadian ratings," Greg Foss, a trader and analyst at Midland Walwyn Capital Inc., said in a report to clients. "However, the facts are that S&P and Moody's offer a much more global perspective to their ratings. Our question to investors is: Are you being adequately compensated for your true credit risk?"

Mr. Foss, who specializes in trading riskier, high-yield bonds sometimes referred to as junk bonds, which are generally shunned by predominantly conservative Canadian investors, believes ratings bias enables many Canadian companies to receive investment-grade status in Canada when they wouldn't elsewhere and thus borrow at unrealistically low yields from Canadian investors hungry for investment-grade securities. Meanwhile, below-investment-grade companies are denied capital unless they offer punitively high yields or go to the United States.

A credit rating assesses the likelihood an issuer will be able to pay its interest and principal on time. Agencies look at financial ratios like debt to equity and the number of times interest is covered by earnings before interest, tax, depreciation and amortization.

"The [financial] ratios you need to maintain a double-A are much more stringent in the US than in Canada," Mr. Foss said.

But Brian Neysmith, president of CBRS, said it's the US, not Canadian, agencies that are biased.

"We feel not that we're high; we say they're low-balling the ratings." He said that before CBRS and DBRS started up in the early 1970s, the Canadian companies rated by US agencies were usually subsidiaries of US companies and automatically received a lower rating than their parent.

"That impression still remained, that from the US point of view, the Canadian companies and foreign companies were one less than whatever the comparable US company was. We go back 20 years with a lot of these companies. We've seen them develop over the years, so we have a very good understanding of what makes the company tick."

DBRS president Walter Schroeder said US agencies are biased by size. "We have the same standards and ratios. It's just that we don't adjust for size. To us, $1-billion is a reasonable size. To the United States, it's low."

Mr. Schroeder said the discrepancy disappears for issuers other than Canadian companies. Canadian agencies have been quicker to downgrade Canadian governments than have US agencies, and on Japanese banks, DBRS's ratings are generally lower than those assigned by US agencies. On US companies, DBRS's ratings are similar to those of US agencies, he said.

But John Tysall, director of corporate ratings for S&P in Toronto, said S&P does not discriminate against small companies except in an industry where size matters, such as in consumer goods where a strong brand name is a valuable asset. Even then, size usually matters only if the firm ranks first or second.

He said S&P's ratings tend to be lower than those of Canadian agencies because its "comparisons tend to be broader and much more international. We are comparing a Canadian company to other companies in the same industry in the US, or Europe or wherever it is appropriate."

Hilary Parkes, representative director with Moody's Canada Inc., declined to comment on rating comparisons.

Some observers believe the Canadian agencies also have an inherent self-interest in rating Canadian companies higher, because without an investment-grade rating, a company generally cannot issue bonds in Canada and therefore has no incentive to pay an agency a rating fee.

Most Canadian pension funds, for example, will not buy bonds rated below A3, the cutoff in Canada between investment grade and junk or "high-yield" grade, which forces companies rated triple-B1 and lower to go to the United States for capital. US investors generally demand a US agency rating on a bond before they buy it. The increased number of companies seeking capital in the United States is one of the reasons US ratings are increasingly sought.

"If you're triple-B or below, you must issue in the US," said Doug Knight, a partner in Vancouver-based Deans Knight Capital Management Ltd.

That means a Canadian company will usually only hire a Canadian agency if it expects to get an A3 or higher rating, he said.

"Who would bother to pay them for a credit rating if they're not going to get what they want?"

Another manager agreed. "Why would you even bother [asking for a rating] if it's going to deny you access to the capital market?"

But CBRS president Mr. Neysmith said it would be "suicidal" for an agency to risk its credibility with investors by slanting a rating for the sake of fees.

"One thing that keeps us honest in this business is every decision we make is public. And because it's all financial [markets], you know in a relatively short period of time whether you're right or wrong. The market knows the difference between a double-B and triple-B. Markets are great equalizers."

A Canadian company's debt tends to trade in Canada according to the Canadian rating but in the United States according to the US rating. That can save a Canadian company money when borrowing in Canada. For example, Talisman Energy Inc.'s 12-year US-dollar bond issued in June, and rated triple-B1 by both S&P and Moody's, trades at a yield of about 100 basis points (one percentage point) above the equivalent US federal government bond. Its nine-year Canadian dollar bond is rated A2 by both DBRS and CBRS and trades at about 50 basis points above the equivalent Government of Canada bond.

If Talisman were rated triple-B in Canada, its borrowing costs would probably climb to at least 100 basis points over Canada bonds, if it could borrow at all, said Midland trader Mr. Foss.

"People in Canada believe, correctly or not, that [Talisman] is single-A," Mr. Foss said. "And if it's single-A, you have the 'too many people chasing too few bonds' scenario," which drives in spreads.

DBRS president Mr. Schroeder said the reason for Talisman's different Canadian and US ratings "is strictly the size."

But S&P's Mr. Tysall disagreed, saying Talisman is a large independent oil and gas producer even by US standards. He said Occidental Petroleum Corp. and Phillips Petroleum Co. are US companies with three and five times, respectively, the reserves of Talisman but they carry the same rating.

A more extreme split-rating case is Winnipeg-based Russell Metals Inc. (formerly Federal Industries Ltd.). Its senior debt is rated B3 in the United States and trades at 550 basis points above US Treasuries. But its subordinated debt, whose holders stand behind senior debt holders in the event of default, is rated three to five notches higher in Canada—double-B1 by DBRS, double-B3 by CBRS—and trades at between 300 and 350 basis points above Government of Canada bonds. Canadian investors are thus getting less return for more risk than US investors.

Opinion is divided on whether the difference in spreads generally reflects the different ratings or simply inefficiencies in the bond market.

Mr. Knight thinks the market makes its own assessment regardless of rating. "It is still in the end a demand and supply marketplace. There are often issues rated single-A that trade at 50 [basis points above Canada bonds] and another will trade at 150."

But when a US agency rates a bond lower than the Canadian agency, "I think it's a red flag of caution," one fund manager said. "You have to think about why it is that way. You might not buy the 20-year security, but you'll buy the three-year security."

It is also difficult to assess the success of rating agencies in Canada because of the lack of detailed studies of how companies were rated when they defaulted. US agencies regularly produce such studies.

Mr. Schroeder attributes that to the relatively small number of defaults in Canada outside the real estate industry.

"Defaults are lower in Canada because we don't have a high-yield market. And the question after default is, do you get your money back? Even though Royal Trust failed, everyone got paid back. You don't get that many pure, unadulterated bankruptcies."

Mr. Foss said steel maker Stelco Inc. is an example of how Canadian agencies misinformed investors about the quality of a bond. CBRS rated Stelco double-A3 until 1989, and eventually downgraded it several times to single-B by 1992 as the company's fortunes darkened. In the 18 months after its rating fell below single-A, Stelco's bond prices tumbled from about 90 cents on the dollar to 35 cents as Canadian institutions unloaded the debt. US investors then snapped up the deeply discounted bonds. As the company rebounded, its credit rating was upgraded to triple-B and its bonds have recovered to $1.05.

"The guys that won were US guys, the guys that lost were the Canadians," Mr. Foss said.

But Mr. Neysmith said a credit rating is not like a stock recommendation. "Ratings are not leading indicators. They are meant to determine if a company is able to continue paying its debt service. [Stelco's rating] matched the decline in its business."

INSTITUTIONAL ISSUES (continued)

Mr. Foss, however, criticized the Canadian agencies not so much for acting slowly but for rating Stelco too high to start with. He said Stelco's interest-coverage ratio would not have earned it higher than a triple-B from S&P. (S&P does not rate Stelco.)

Many bond experts said investors should treat credit ratings as simply an additional input into their own analysis.

John Carswell, a manager at Toronto-based investment management company Foyston Gordon & Payne, said: "A credit rating is an extremely subjective and qualitative process. You have to use your own investment analysis. No one should buy a corporate bond unless you do your own credit analysis on that bond, because even the US agencies get that wrong from time to time."

SOURCE: Reprinted with permission of *The Globe and Mail* (December 13, 1995).

Figure 15.5

Corporate bond yields by ratings, 1977–1994 (long-term monthly averages).

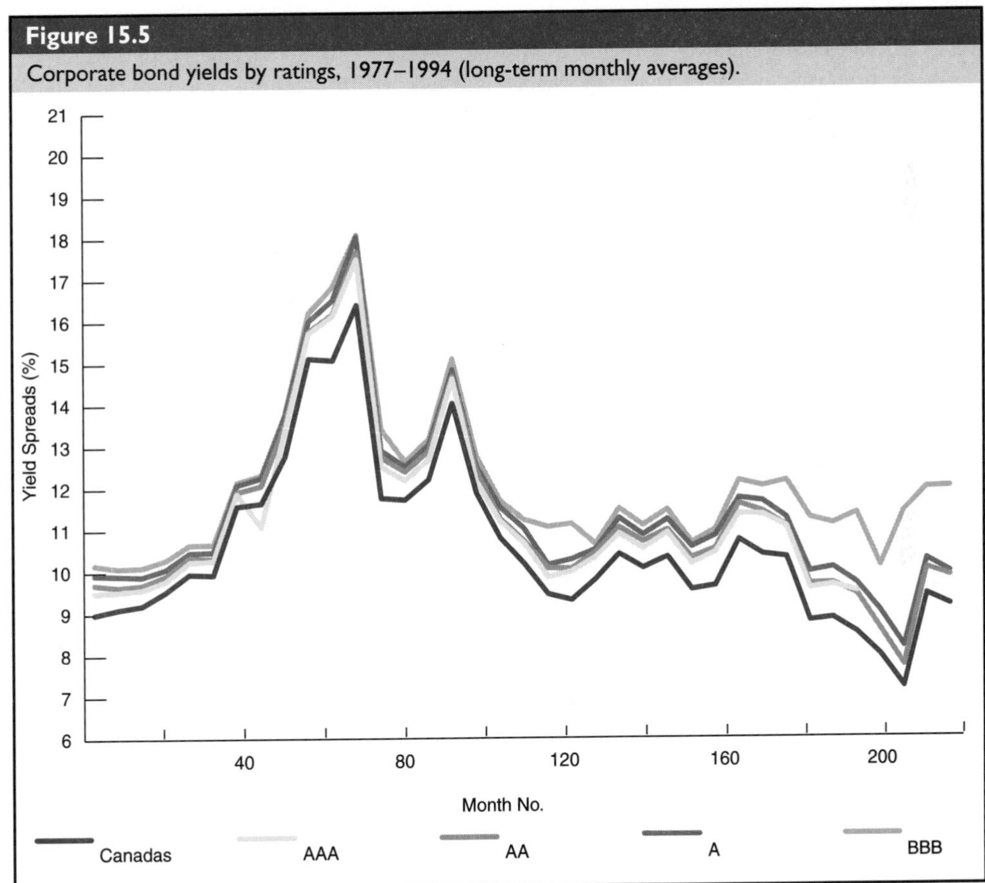

SOURCE: Adapted from Melanie Moore, *ScotiaMcLeod's Handbook of Canadian Debt Market Indices: 1947–1994* (ScotiaMcLeod Inc., 1995).

Figure 15.6

Yield-to-maturity for a risky bond.

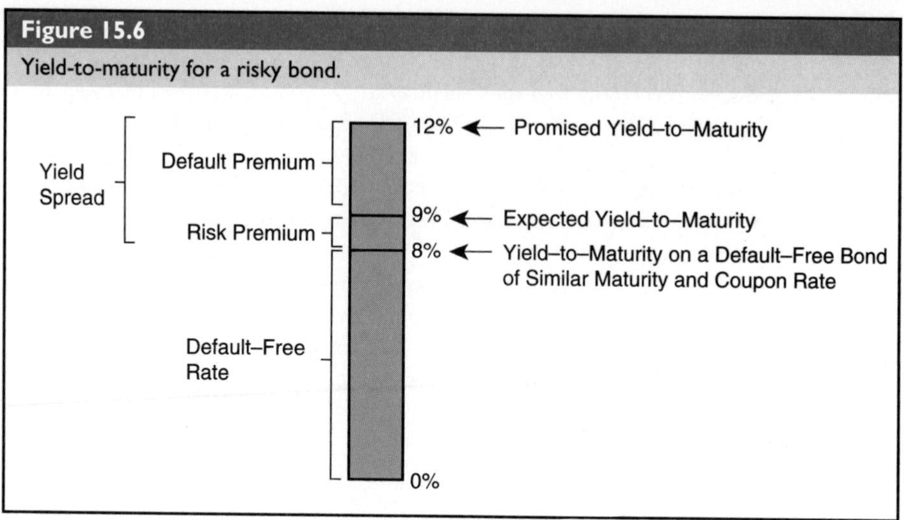

A similar procedure can be employed with bonds, with the analysis usually focusing on yield-to-maturity. Formally, all possible yields are considered, along with their respective probabilities, and a weighted average is computed to determine the **expected yield-to-maturity**. As long as there is any possibility of default or late payment, the expected yield will fall below the promised yield. In general, the greater the risk of default and the greater the amount of loss in the event of default, the greater will be this disparity.

This is illustrated in Figure 15.6 for a hypothetical risky bond. Its promised yield-to-maturity is 12% but, owing to a high default risk, the expected yield is only 9%. The 3% difference between the promised and expected yields is the **default premium**. Any bond that has some probability of default should offer such a premium, and the greater the probability of default, the larger the premium should be.

Just how large should a bond's default premium be? According to one model, the answer depends on both the probability of default and the likely financial loss to the bondholder in the event of default.[9]

Consider a bond that is perceived to be equally likely to default in each year (given it did not default in the previous year), with the probability that it will default in any given year denoted by p_d. Assume that if the bond does default, a payment equal to $(1 - \lambda)$ times its market price a year earlier will be made to the owner of each bond. According to this model, a bond will be fairly priced if its promised yield-to-maturity (y) is

$$y = \frac{\bar{y} + \lambda p_d}{1 - p_d} \tag{15.4}$$

where $\bar{y}$ denotes the bond's expected yield-to-maturity. The difference (d) between a bond's promised yield-to-maturity (y) and its expected yield-to-maturity ($\bar{y}$) was referred to earlier

[9] The model was developed by Gordon Pye in "Gauging the Default Premium," *Financial Analysts Journal* 30 no. 1 (January/February 1974): 49–52.

as the bond's default premium. Using equation (15.4), this difference for a fairly priced bond will be equal to

$$
\begin{aligned}
d &= y - \bar{y} \\
&= \left[\frac{\bar{y} + \lambda p_d}{1 - p_d}\right] - \bar{y}
\end{aligned}
\tag{15.5}
$$

As an example, consider the bond illustrated in Figure 15.6. Assume that this bond has a 6% annual default probability and that it is estimated that if the bond does default, each bondholder will receive an amount equal to 60% of the bond's market price a year earlier (meaning that $1 - \lambda = .60$, which in turn means that $\lambda = .40$). Using equation (15.5), this bond would be fairly priced if its default premium were equal to

$$
\begin{aligned}
d &= \left[\frac{.09 + (.40 \times .06)}{1 - .06}\right] - .09 \\
&= .0313
\end{aligned}
$$

or 3.13%. Since the actual default premium earlier was estimated to be 3%, it can be seen that the two figures are similar. This suggests the actual default premium is appropriate, according to this model.

What sort of default experience might the long-run bond investor anticipate? And how is this experience likely to be related to the ratings of the bonds held? In a massive US study of all large bond issues and a sample of small bond issues, Hickman attempted to answer these questions.[10] He analyzed investor experience for each bond from 1900 through 1943 to determine the actual yield-to-maturity, measured from the date of issuance to the date on which the bond matured, defaulted, or was called—whichever came first. He then compared this actual yield with the promised yield-to-maturity based on the price at time of issue. Every bond was also classified according to the ratings assigned at time of issue. Part (a) of Table 15.1 shows the major results.

As might be expected, Hickman found that, in general, the riskier the bond, the higher the promised yield at time of issue and the higher the percentage of bonds that subsequently defaulted. However, a surprise was uncovered when the actual yields-to-maturity were compared with promised yields-to-maturity. As the last column on the right of the table shows, in four out of five rating classifications, the actual yield was found to *exceed* the promised yield. Fortunately, a convenient explanation exists for this finding—the period studied by Hickman was one where a substantial drop in interest rates occurred. This is important because the drop made it attractive for issuers to call their outstanding bonds, paying the bondholders a call premium in the process and resulting in an actual yield above the promised yield.

To see what might have happened had this not been the case, Fraine and Mills reanalyzed the data for large investment-grade issues.[11] Their results are shown in part (b) of Table 15.1. The initial columns differ from those in part (a) because smaller issues were excluded. The major difference between the parts appears in the right-hand column, where Fraine and Mills substituted a bond's promised yield for its actual yield whenever the latter was larger,

---

[10] W. Braddock Hickman, *Corporate Bond Quality and Investor Experience* (Princeton, N.J.: Princeton University Press, 1958).

[11] Harold G. Fraine and Robert H. Mills, "The Effect of Defaults and Credit Deterioration on Yields of Corporate Bonds," *Journal of Finance* 16, no. 3 (September 1961): 423–34.

Table 15.1

Actual and Realized Bond Yields-to-Maturity, 1900–1943.

(a) All Large and a Sample of Small Issues

Composite Rating	*Comparable Moody's Rating*	*Promised Yield-to-Maturity at Issue*	*Percent Defaulting Prior to Maturity*	*Actual-Yield-to-Maturity*
I	Aaa	4.5%	5.9%	5.1%
II	Aa	4.6	6.0	5.0
III	A	4.9	13.4	5.0
IV	Baa	5.4	19.1	5.7
V-IX	below Baa	9.5	42.4	8.6

(b) All Large Issues

Composite Rating	*Comparable Moody's Rating*	*Promised Yield-to-Maturity*	*Actual Yield-to-Maturity*	*Modified Actual Yield-to-Maturity*
I	Aaa	4.5%	5.1%	4.3%
II	Aa	4.5	5.1	4.3
III	A	4.9	5.0	4.3
IV	Baa	5.4	5.8	4.5

SOURCE: (a) W. Braddock Hickman, *Corporate Bond Quality and Investor Experience* (Princeton, N.J.: Princeton University Press, 1953):10. (b) Harold G. Fraine and Robert H. Mills, "The Effect of Defaults and Credit Deterioration on Yields of Corporate Bonds," *Journal of Finance* 16, no. 3 (September 1961): 433.

thereby removing the effects of most calls. Unlike Hickman, their results suggest that there was little difference in actual yields within the highest rating classifications.

More recently, Edward Altman examined the default experience of corporate bonds over the period from 1971 through 1990.[12] His methodology was somewhat different from Hickman's in that for each bond he noted its rating when it was originally issued and then how many years later it went into default (if at all). From this he compiled "mortality tables," such as Table 15.2, which shows the percentage of bond issues that went into default within various numbers of years after issuance.

There are several interesting observations that can be made upon inspection of this table. First, in looking down any particular column, it can be seen that the cumulative rate of default increases as one moves further from the date of issuance. Second, with the exception of those bonds originally rated AA, lower rated bonds had higher default rates. Third, the default rates for the speculative grades of bonds are strikingly high. Indeed, it raises the question of whether or not such bonds make good investments, as their higher yields might not make up for their higher default rates. This question will be addressed shortly.

---

[12] Edward I. Altman, "Defaults and Returns on High-Yield Bonds Through the First Half of 1991," *Financial Analysts Journal* 47, no. 6 (November/December 1991): 67–77.

Table 15.2

Default Rates of US Bonds, 1971–1990.

Years After Issuance	Original Rating						
	AAA	AA	A	BBB	BB	B	CCC
1	.00%	.00%	.00%	.03%	.00%	.87%	1.31%
2	.00	.00	.30	.57	.93	3.22	4.00
3	.00	1.11	.60	.85	1.36	9.41	19.72
4	.00	1.42	.65	1.34	3.98	16.37	36.67
5	.00	1.70	.65	1.54	5.93	20.87	38.08
6	.14	1.70	.73	1.81	7.38	26.48	40.58
7	.19	1.91	.87	2.70	10.91	29.62	NA
8	.19	1.93	.94	2.83	10.91	31.74	NA
9	.19	2.01	1.28	2.99	10.91	39.38	NA
10	.19	2.11	1.28	3.85	13.86	40.86	NA

SOURCE: Edward I. Altman, "Defaults and Returns on High-Yield Bonds Through the First Half of 1991," *Financial Analysts Journal* 47, no. 6 (November/December 1991): Table X, pp. 74–75.

Risk Premiums

It is useful to compare the expected return of a risky security with the certain return of a default-free security. In an efficient market, the difference in these returns will be related to the relevant risk of the security. Consider common stocks, where the investor has a holding period of one year or less. In this situation, the expected return on a share is typically compared with the yield of a Treasury bill having a maturity date corresponding with the end of the holding period (note that the yield on such a Treasury bill is equal to its holding-period return).

Traditionally, a risky bond's expected yield-to-maturity is compared with that of a default-free bond of similar maturity and coupon rate. The difference between these yields is known as the bond's **risk premium**. In the example shown in Figure 15.6, default-free bonds of similar maturity and coupon rate offer a certain 8% yield-to-maturity. Since the risky bond's expected yield-to-maturity is 9%, its risk premium is 1% (that is, 100 basis points).

Every bond that might default should offer a default premium. But the risk premium is another matter. Any security's expected return should be related only to its contribution to the risk of a well-diversified portfolio (i.e., its systematic risk); its total risk is not directly relevant.

For example, if a group of companies all faced the possibility of bankruptcy, but from totally unrelated causes, a portfolio that included all their bonds would subsequently provide an actual return very close to its expected return. This is because the default premiums earned on the bonds that did not default would offset the losses incurred from those bonds that did default. Consequently, there would be little reason for this expected return to differ significantly from that of a default-free bond, since there is little doubt concerning what its actual return will be. Accordingly, each bond should be priced to offer little or no risk premium (but each bond should have a substantial default premium).

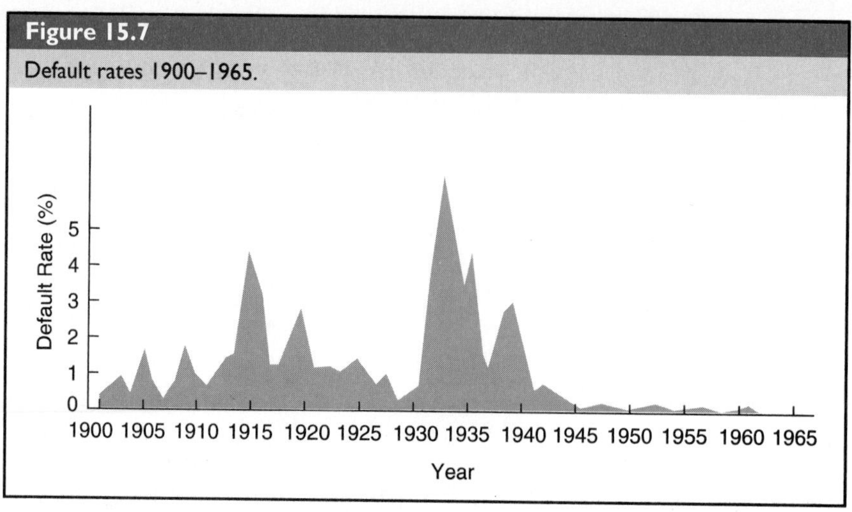

Figure 15.7

Default rates 1900–1965.

SOURCE: Adapted from Thomas R. Atkinson and Elizabeth T. Simpson, *Trends in Corporate Bond Quality* (Columbia University Press, 1967): 5.

However, the risks associated with bonds are not unrelated. Figure 15.7 shows for each year from 1900 to 1965 the ratio of the par value of corporate bonds defaulting during the year to the par value outstanding at the beginning of the year. Not surprisingly, the peaks coincide with periods of economic distress.[13] When business is bad, most firms are affected. The market value of a firm's common stock will decline when an economic downturn is anticipated. If the likelihood of default on its debt also increases, the market value of its outstanding bonds will follow suit. Thus, the holding-period return on a bond may be correlated with the returns of other bonds and with those of stocks. Most important, a risky bond's holding-period return is likely to be correlated to at least some extent with the return on a widely diversified market portfolio that includes both corporate bonds and stocks. This part of the risk of a bond should command a risk premium in the form of a higher expected return, since it is not diversifiable.

The riskier a bond is, the greater its likelihood of default and, in turn, the greater its potential sensitivity to market declines representing lowered assessments of prospects for the economy as a whole. This is illustrated in Table 15.3, which summarizes the investment performance of three portfolios of US bonds, known as bond funds, in the Keystone group.[14] All values shown in the table are based on annual returns earned over a 24-year period by each portfolio. As might be anticipated, the most risky bond portfolio (fund B4) had the

[13] See Marshall E. Blume and Donald B. Keim, "Realized Returns and Defaults on Low-Grade Bonds: The Cohort of 1977 and 1978," *Financial Analysts Journal* 47, no. 2 (March/April 1991): 63–72; Marshall E. Blume, Donald B. Keim, and Sandeep A. Patel, "Returns and Volatility of Low-Grade Bonds, 1977–1989," *Journal of Finance* 46, no. 1 (March 1991): 49–74; and Marshall E. Blume and Donald B. Keim, "The Risk and Return of Low-Grade Bonds: An Update," *Financial Analysts Journal* 47, no. 5 (September/October 1991). A similar observation has been made for municipal bonds. See George H. Hempel, *The Post-war Quality of State and Local Debt* (New York: Columbia University Press, 1971).

[14] For an in-depth analysis of such bond portfolios, see Bradford Cornell and Kevin Greene, "The Investment Performance of Low-Grade Bond Funds," *Journal of Finance* 46, no. 1 (March 1991): 29–48; and Bradford Cornell, "Liquidity and the Pricing of Low-Grade Bonds," *Financial Analysts Journal* 48, no. 1 (January/February 1992): 63–67, 74.

Table 15.3

Risk and Return, Keystone Bond Funds, 1968–1991.

	Fund B1	Fund B2	Fund B4
	Conservative Bonds	*Investment Grade Bonds*	*Discount Bonds*
Average return (% per year)	7.84	8.53	8.64
Standard deviation of return (% per year)	8.27	9.35	13.68
Beta value, relative to S&P 500	.26	.38	.54
Proportion of variance explained by S&P 500	.28	.45	.42

highest average return and highest standard deviation of return, whereas the least risky bond portfolio (fund B1) had the lowest average return and lowest standard deviation.

To estimate each portfolio's sensitivity to changes in stock prices, each portfolio's returns were compared with those of Standard & Poor's 500. Specifically, a beta was calculated for each portfolio in order to measure the sensitivity of each portfolio to swings in the stock market. As can be seen, the riskier the portfolio, the higher the estimated beta, indicating that riskier bonds moved more with stocks and thus should have had higher average returns.

The final row in the table shows the proportion of the year-to-year variation in bond portfolio returns that were associated with stock market swings. As indicated, relatively more of the risky portfolio's variation was associated with the stock market than was the case with the less risky portfolio. Thus, for less-risky bonds, interest-rate risk appears to be more important than stock market risk.[15]

THE RISK STRUCTURE OF INTEREST RATES

The greater a bond's risk of default, the greater its default premium. This alone will cause a bond with a higher default risk to offer a higher promised yield-to-maturity. If it is also true that the greater a bond's risk of default, the greater its risk premium, then the promised yield-to-maturity will have to be even higher. Bonds with lower agency ratings should have higher promised yields-to-maturity if these ratings in fact reflect the risk of default.

Figure 15.5 shows that this is indeed the case. Each of the curves plots the promised yield-to-maturity for a group of corporate bonds assigned the same ratings. It is clear that bonds are priced so that higher promised yields are associated with lower ratings. Figure 15.1, however, shows that the yield differences between rating categories vary considerably over time, suggesting that agency ratings indicate *relative* levels of risk instead of *absolute* levels of risk.

If an absolute level of risk were indicated by a rating classification, then each classification would be associated with a particular probability of default (or, more accurately, a range of probabilities of default). Consequently, as the economy became more uncertain (for example,

[15] In a study of preferred shares, it was found that the price movements of low-rated preferred shares were related more to the price movements of common stocks than to the price movements of bonds; for high-rated preferred shares, the findings were just the opposite. See John S. Bildersee, "Some Aspects of the Performance of Non-Convertible Preferred Stocks," *Journal of Finance* 28, no. 5 (December 1973): 1187–1201.

an increased probability of a recession), bonds would be reclassified as necessary, with most moving to lower ratings. In this situation, yield spreads between classifications would change only slightly, since each classification would still reflect bonds having the same probability of default. However, Figure 15.1 shows that these spreads change considerably over time, an observation that can be interpreted as evidence that the bond market does not believe that the ratings reflect absolute levels of risk.

Rating agencies appear to prefer to avoid making a large number of rating changes as the economy becomes more uncertain. Instead, they prefer to use the classifications to indicate relative levels of risk. This means that an overall increase in economic uncertainty does not result in a significant number of reclassifications. Thus, the probability of default associated with bonds in a given rating classification is greater at such a time. In turn, the yield spreads between classifications of corporate bonds and the yield spreads between corporate and government bonds both increase. Indeed, there is evidence that the spread between the promised yields of bonds of different rating classifications increases when uncertainty about the economy increases.

Some models have attempted to take advantage of this observation in order to predict the amount of economic uncertainty. In particular, these models use the size of the yield spread between, say, bonds rated AAA and those rated BBB as an indication of the degree of economic uncertainty. For example, if this spread is widening, then that might be taken as an indication that the near-term future of the economy was becoming more uncertain. There are also models that look not at yield spreads but at differences in the holding-period returns of AAA and BBB bonds.

DETERMINANTS OF YIELD SPREADS

As mentioned previously, when bond analysts refer to a corporate bond's yield spread, they are typically referring to the difference between the corporate bond's promised yield-to-maturity and that of another bond (often a default-free government security) having similar maturity and coupon rate. The greater the risk of default, the greater this spread should be. Moreover, bonds that have more marketability might command an additional "premium" in price and hence offer a lower yield-to-maturity with a corresponding lower spread. Given a large enough sample of bonds, it should be possible to see if these relationships really do exist.

A US study of corporate bond prices did this.[16] Four measures were used to assess the probability of default:

1. The extent to which the firm's net income had varied over the preceding nine years (measured by the coefficient of variation of earnings — that is, the ratio of standard deviation of earnings to average earnings),
2. The length of time that the firm had operated without forcing any of its creditors to take a loss,
3. The ratio of the market value of the firm's equity to the par value of its debt, and
4. The market value of the firm's outstanding debt.

[16] Lawrence Fisher, "Determinants of Risk Premiums on Corporate Bonds," *Journal of Political Economy* 67, no. 3 (June 1959): 217–37.

INSTITUTIONAL ISSUES

Matrix Bond Pricing

Many institutional investors must periodically determine the market values of their bond portfolios. For example, a pension fund may wish to keep beneficiaries abreast of the value of their fixed-income investments. Further, the pension fund needs accurate market valuations to evaluate fixed-income managers' investment results and to compute their compensation. (Managers' fees are typically based on the market values of their portfolios.)

In some cases, valuing a bond portfolio is a straightforward matter. Prices of most government bonds, many government agency bonds, and certain actively traded corporate bonds are available through real-time electronic quotation systems and the print media. Unlike common stocks, however, where an active market usually exists for all but the smallest issues, many bond issues (even some with large face values outstanding) do not trade frequently. It is not uncommon to find entire bond issues held to maturity by investors. The limited trading of these securities inhibits efforts to accurately determine their current market prices.

How can an institutional investor establish market prices for thinly traded fixed-income securities in its possession? It could ask its fixed-income managers to supply their best estimates of the bonds' market prices. After all, these managers constantly compare their perceptions of the bonds' intrinsic values to the bonds' estimated market prices as part of their portfolio management processes. However, a manager has an inherent conflict of interest in providing such valuations because his or her financial well-being is directly related to those values.

Alternatively, the pension fund might canvass bond dealers who trade the bonds under question (or similar securities) and solicit representative bid prices. Unfortunately, this procedure is too time-consuming to conduct on a regular basis for hundreds of bonds. Furthermore, the dealers have no incentive to participate.

In response to this dearth of pricing data, institutional investors have turned to various commercial bond valuation services. For a fee, these organizations provide third-party security valuations for tens of thousands of fixed-income securities on a daily, weekly, or monthly basis.

Some bond pricing services "lever off" of their own trading operations. They use their bond traders to submit bid-side valuations daily for any securities that the traders regularly see traded in the market. This "hand pricing" by traders offers perhaps the best estimate that institutional investors can readily obtain of the "true" market price, or liquidation value, of their bonds. Note, however, that the pricing services do not offer to transact at their price quotations. An actual bid for an institutional investor's fixed-income portfolio would involve an assessment by the trader of many factors, including the trader's current inventory, the price risk of the portfolio, and available hedges on the portfolio.

Oftentimes, however, a bond pricing service does not have immediate access to current prices for certain securities, either because it does not maintain a trading desk or because its traders do not deal in the securities. In those cases, various mechanical procedures, generally known as *matrix pricing*, are used to estimate market prices. The particular matrix pricing formulas vary among the pricing services and among the types of bonds valued by the services. Nevertheless, the pricing of corporate bonds provides a good example of the essential aspects of matrix bond pricing.

The price matrix for investment-grade corporate bonds is typically three-dimensional, with sector, quality, and term-to-maturity as the three primary variables. Each cell in the matrix represents a unique three-way combination of these variables. For example, one cell might contain industrial bonds with A ratings and three years to maturity. Each cell in the matrix is assigned an incremental yield (or "spread") over

INSTITUTIONAL ISSUES (continued)

comparable maturity Treasury securities, based on an analysis of current market conditions. (For example, three-year, A-rated industrial bonds might be assigned a 100-basis-point spread over Canadas.) These spreads may change over time at the discretion of the pricing service.

Once the matrix spreads are established, a corporate bond is priced by finding the cell in which it resides and using the associated yield to discount the bond's promised cash flows and thereby compute an estimated price. Adjustments may be made for special factors, such as coupon rates, call features, and sinking fund provisions.

As one might expect, the accuracy of matrix bond pricing depends on the comparability of the security under analysis. Those securities that do not deviate significantly in terms of investment characteristics from their actively traded counterparts are relatively easy to price accurately. Securities with unique or relatively complicated features are more difficult to price accurately, and their matrix prices are often considered suspect by fixed-income managers.

First, these measures were calculated, along with the yield spread, for each one of 366 bonds. Second, the logarithm of every yield spread and measure was calculated. Third, statistical methods were used to analyze the relationship between a bond's yield spread and these measures. The one that was found to describe this relationship most accurately was:

$$\begin{aligned}\text{Yield spread} = .987 &+ .307 \text{ (earnings variability)} \\ &- .253 \text{ (time without default)} \\ &- .537 \text{ (equity/debt ratio)} \\ &- .275 \text{ (market value of debt).}\end{aligned} \tag{15.6}$$

This form of the relationship accounted for roughly 75% of the variation in the bonds' yield spreads.

The advantage of an equation such as this is that the coefficients can be easily interpreted. Since all yield spreads and values had been converted to logarithms, the effect is similar to that of using ratio scales on all axes of a diagram. This means that a 1% increase in a bond's earnings variability can be expected to bring about an increase of .307% in the bond's yield spread, other things being equal. Similarly, a 1% increase in a bond's time without default can be expected to cause a decrease of approximately .253% in the bond's yield spread, and so on. Each coefficient is an elasticity, indicating the percentage change in a bond's yield spread likely to accompany a 1% change in the associated measure. Since every measure was found to be related in the expected direction to the yield spread, the study provides substantial support for the notion that bonds with higher default risk and less marketability have higher yield spreads.

FINANCIAL RATIOS AS PREDICTORS OF DEFAULT

For years, security analysts have used accounting ratios to indicate the probability that a firm will fail to meet its financial obligations. Specific procedures have been developed to predict default with such ratios. Univariate analysis attempts to find the best single predictor for this purpose, whereas multivariate analysis searches for the best combination of two or more predictors.

Univariate Methods

Cash inflows can be viewed as contributions to the firm's cash balance, and cash outflows can be viewed as drains on this balance. When the balance falls below zero, default is likely to occur. This means that the probability of default will be greater for the firm when (1) the existing cash balance is smaller; (2) the expected net cash flow (measured before payments to creditors and shareholders) is smaller; and (3) the net cash flow is more variable.

In an examination of various measures used to assess these factors, it was found that the ratio of net cash flow (income before depreciation, depletion, and amortization charges) to total debt was particularly useful.[17] Figure 15.8(a) shows the mean value of this ratio for a group of firms that defaulted on a promised payment and for a companion group that did not. As early as five years before default the two groups' ratios diverged, and the spread widened as the year of default approached.

This changing spread suggests that the probability of default may not be constant through time. Instead, warning signals may indicate an increase in the probability, which should, in turn, cause a fall in the market price of the firm's bonds along with a fall in the market price of its common stock. Figure 15.8(b) shows that such signals are indeed recognized in the marketplace. The median market value of common stock in the firms that did not default went up, while that of the firms that subsequently defaulted went down as the date of default approached.

Canadian stock market data were used to compare the characteristics of a sample of 25 firms that failed with those of a matched sample of firms that did not fail. This showed that impending failure was characterized by: decreasing common stock returns starting about 12 months prior to failure; increasing total risk (increasing variance of returns) also starting about 12 months prior to failure; and a shift from systematic to unsystematic risk as evidenced by a decrease in beta starting about 24 months prior to failure. They concluded that market participants could use their techniques to anticipate failure, on average, 15 months before its occurrence.[18]

Multivariate Methods

Combinations of certain financial ratios have been considered as possible predictors of default.[19] Statistical analysis has indicated that the most accurate method of predicting default has been to calculate a firm's *Z score* from some of its financial ratios as follows:

$$Z = 1.2X_1 + 1.4X_2 + 3.3X_3 + .6X_4 + .99X_5 \tag{15.7}$$

where the following ratios are calculated from information contained in the firm's most recent income statement and balance sheet:

X_1 = (current assets − current liabilities)/total assets
X_2 = retained earnings/total assets

---

17 William H. Beaver, "Market Prices, Financial Ratios and the Prediction of Failure," *Journal of Accounting Research* 6, no. 2 (Autumn 1968): 1979–92. For a more recent study, see James M. Gahlon and Robert L. Vigeland, "Early Warning Signs of Bankruptcy Using Cash Flow Analysis," *Journal of Commercial Bank Lending* 71, no. 4 (December 1988): 4–15.

18 Vijay M. Jog and Allan L. Riding, "Canadian Stock Market Reactions to Impending Corporate Failure," *Proceedings*, Administrative Sciences Association of Canada Conference, Whistler, B.C. (June 1988): 226–40.

19 Edward I. Altman, "Financial Ratios, Discriminant Analysis and the Prediction of Corporate Bankruptcy," *Journal of Finance* 23, no. 4 (September 1968): 589–609.

Figure 15.8

Financial ratios and market prices for firms that defaulted and those that did not.

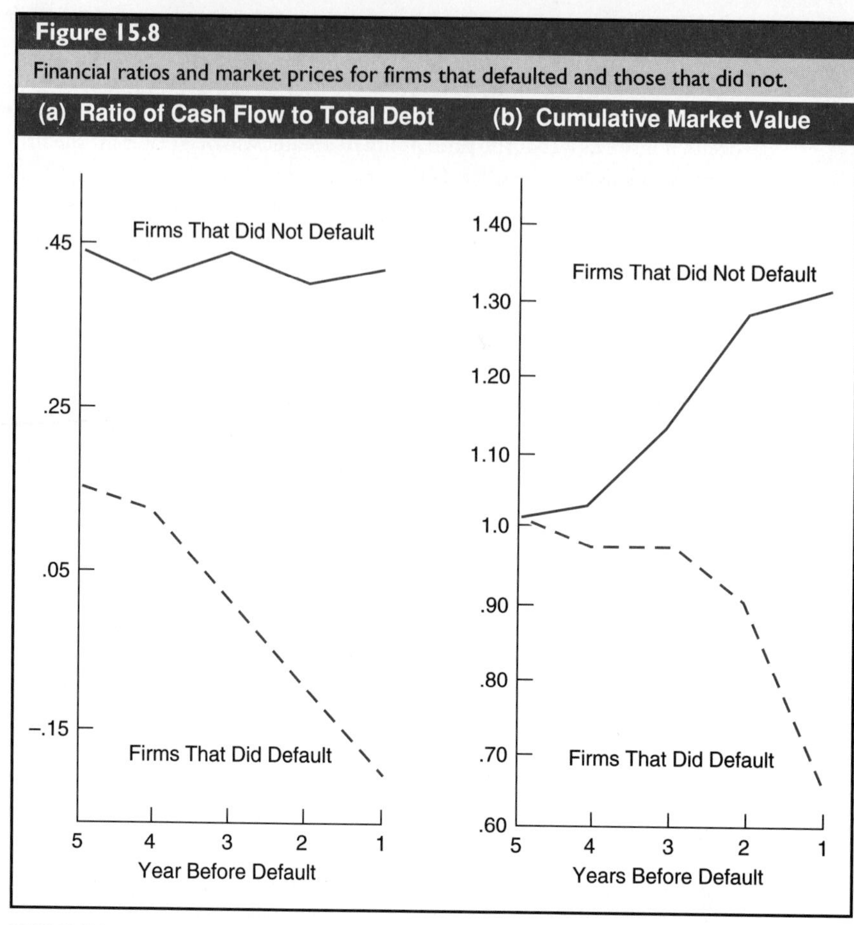

SOURCE: William H. Beaver, "Market Prices, Financial Ratios and the Prediction of Failure," *Journal of Accounting Research* 6, no. 2 (Autumn 1968): 182, 185.

X_3 = earnings before interest and taxes/total assets
X_4 = market value of equity/book value of total debt
X_5 = sales/total assets.

Any firm with a Z-score below 1.8 is considered a likely candidate for default, and the lower the score, the greater the likelihood.

A corresponding Canadian study found that the following financial ratios were significant:[20]

X_1 = sales/total assets
X_2 = total debt/total assets
X_3 = current assets/current liabilities

[20] Edward I. Altman and Mario Y. Lavallee, "Business Failure Classification in Canada, *Journal of Business Administration: Capital Markets in Canada* 12, no. 1 (Fall 1980): 147–64. Subsequent refinements to this model have been made, leading to a revised procedure known as *zeta analysis*. See Edward I. Altman, Robert G. Haldeman, and P. Narayanan, "Zeta Analysis: A New Model to Identify Bankruptcy Risk of Corporations," *Journal of Banking and Finance* 1, no. 1 (June 1977): 29–54.

X_4 = net profits after tax/total debt
X_5 = rate of growth of equity – rate of asset growth.

In this case a critical score of –0.33 indicates a significant probability of default.

► Investment Implications

The preceding discussion does not mean that securities of firms whose cash-flow-to-total-debt ratio or Z-score had declined should be avoided. It should be remembered that the firms represented by the dashed lines in Figure 15.8 were chosen because they eventually defaulted. Had all firms with declining ratios been selected, corresponding decreases in their market price would undoubtedly have been observed, reflecting the increased probability of future default. However, only some of these firms would have ultimately defaulted, whereas the others would have recovered. Consequently, the gains on the firms that recovered might well have offset the losses on the firms that defaulted. In summary, the net result from purchasing a portfolio of stocks with declining ratios or Z-scores is that the investor would have received an average return.

What about purchasing bonds of companies that have just had their ratings increased and selling (or avoiding) bonds of companies that have just had their ratings decreased? After all, such changes in ratings should be related to a change in the default risk of the issuer. In a US study that looked at the behaviour of bond prices around the time of ratings changes, some evidence was found that the bond price adjustment to a rating change occurred in the period from 18 to 7 months *before* the rating change.[21] Little or no evidence of a substantive price change was found either during the month of the rating change or in the period from six months before to six months after the rating change. These findings are consistent with the notion that the bond market is semistrong-form efficient, since bond ratings are predictable from publicly available information.

SUMMARY

1. The capitalization of income method of valuation is a commonly used approach to identifying mispriced bonds. It is based on the discounted value of the cash flows that the investor expects to receive from owning a bond.
2. Given the bond's current market price and promised cash flows, the investor can calculate the bond's promised yield-to-maturity and compare it to an appropriate discount rate.
3. Alternatively, the investor can use an appropriate discount rate to discount the bond's promised cash flows. The sum of the present value of these cash flows is compared to the bond's market price.
4. Six primary attributes are of significance in bond valuation: length of time to maturity, coupon rate, call provisions, tax status, marketability, and likelihood of default.

---

[21] Mark I. Weinstein, "The Effect of a Rating Change Announcement on Bond Price," *Journal of Financial Economics* 5, no. 3 (December 1977): 329–350. Another study that examined rating change announcements that were "noncontaminated by other news releases found a small but statistically significant upward movement in daily bond prices around upgrades; downgrades produced no significant movements," See John R. M. Hand, Robert W. Holthausen, and Richard W. Leftwich, "The Effect of Bond Rating Agency Announcements on Bond and Stock Prices," *Journal of Finance* 47, no. 2 (June 1992): 733–752.

5. Time to maturity, call provisions, tax status, and likelihood of default tend to be directly related to promised yield-to-maturity. Coupon rate and marketability tend to be inversely related to promised yield-to-maturity.
6. Several organizations provide ratings of the creditworthiness of corporate and municipal bonds. These ratings are often interpreted as an indication of the issuer's likelihood of default.
7. Bond ratings indicate relative levels of risk instead of absolute levels of risk.
8. A bond's promised yield-to-maturity can be subdivided into a default-free yield-to-maturity and a yield spread. Furthermore, the yield spread can be subdivided into a risk premium and a default premium.
9. Various statistical models have been developed to predict the probability that a bond issuer will default. These models typically use financial ratios derived from the issuer's balance sheet and income statement.

QUESTIONS AND PROBLEMS

1. Philip Wong owns a $1000 face-value bond with three years to maturity. The bond makes annual interest payments of $75, the first to be made one year from today. The bond is currently priced at $975.48. Given an appropriate discount rate of 10%, should Philip hold or sell the bond?
2. A broker has advised Jane Ens to purchase a ten-year $10 000 face-value bond that makes 8% annual coupon payments. The appropriate discount rate is 9%. The first interest payment is due one year from today. If the bond currently sells for $8560, should Jane follow the broker's advice?
3. Pierre Thibeau is considering investing in a bond currently selling for $8785.07. The bond has four years to maturity, a $10 000 face value, and an 8% coupon rate. The next annual interest payment is due one year from today. The appropriate discount rate for investments of similar risk is 10%.
   a. Calculate the intrinsic value of the bond. Based on this calculation, should Pierre purchase the bond?
   b. Calculate the yield-to-maturity of the bond. Based on this calculation, should Pierre purchase the bond?
4. Consider two bonds with $1000 face values that carry coupon rates of 8%, make annual coupon payments, and exhibit similar risk characteristics. However, the first bond has five years to maturity whereas the second has ten years to maturity. The appropriate discount rate for investments of similar risk is 8%. If this discount rate rises by two percentage points, what will be the respective percentage price changes of the two bonds?
5. Why is it convenient to use Government of Canada securities as a starting point for analyzing bond yields?
6. Bond A's yield-to-maturity is 9.80%; bond B's yield-to-maturity is 8.73%. What is the difference in yields stated in basis points?
7. Eli Falk recently purchased a bond with a $1000 face value, a 10% coupon rate, and four years to maturity. The bond makes annual interest payments, the first to be received one year from today. Eli paid $1032.40 for the bond.
   a. What is the bond's yield-to-maturity?
   b. If the bond can be called two years from now at a price of $1100, what is its yield-to-call?

8. Beverly Grimaldi purchased at par a bond with a face value of $1000. The bond had five years to maturity and a 10% coupon rate. The bond was called two years later for a price of $1200, after making its second annual interest payment. Beverly then reinvested the proceeds in a bond selling at its face value of $1000, with three years to maturity and a 7% coupon rate. What was Beverly's actual yield-to-maturity over the five-year period?
9. Nellie Fox acquired at par a bond for $1000 that offered a 9% coupon rate. At the time of purchase, the bond had four years to maturity. Assuming annual interest payments, calculate Nellie's actual yield-to-maturity if she reinvested all the interest payments in an investment earning 15% per year. What would Nellie's actual yield-to-maturity be if she spent all the interest payments upon receipt?
10. Distinguish between yield-to-first-call and yield-to-maturity.
11. What is the effect of a call provision on a bond's potential for price appreciation?
12. What is the purpose of bond ratings? Given the importance attached to bond ratings by bond investors, why don't common stock investors focus on quality ratings of entire companies in making their investment decisions?
13. According to Dave Cross, "Agency ratings indicate *relative* levels of risk instead of ***absolute*** levels of risk." Explain the meaning of Dave's statement.
14. Based on the default premium model presented in the text, what is the fair value default premium for a bond with an expected yield-to-maturity of 8.5%, a 10% annual default probability, and an expected loss as percent of market value of 60%?
15. Corporate default appears to be an event specific to an individual company. Yet despite the apparently diversifiable nature of corporate default (meaning that relatively few bonds would default in a well-diversified portfolio), the bond market systematically adds default premiums when valuing corporate bonds. Explain why.
16. Junk bonds are often viewed by investors as having financial characteristics much more akin to common stocks than to high-grade corporate bonds. Why?
17. Examine equation (15.6) and explain the rationale underlying the observed relationship (positive or negative) between each of the variables and the yield spread.
18. How would you expect yield spreads to respond to the following macroeconomics events: recession, high inflation, tax cuts, stock market decline, improved trade balance? Explain the reasoning behind each of your answers.
19. Ursula Schmidt has noted that the spread between yield-to-maturity on BBB-rated bonds and that on AAA-rated bonds has recently widened considerably. Explain to Ursula what this change might indicate.

CFA Exam Question

20. [In 1990,] Barney Gray, CFA, is Director of Fixed-Income Securities at Piedmont Security Advisors. In a recent meeting, one of his major endowment clients suggested investing in corporate bonds yielding 9%, rather than US government bonds yielding 8%. Two bond issues—one US Treasury and one corporate—were compared to illustrate the point.

US Treasury bond	8% due 6/15/2010	Priced at 100
AJAX Manufacturing	9.5% due 6/15/2015	Priced at 105
Rated AAA		
Callable @ 107.5 on 6/15/1995		

Gray wants to prepare a response based upon his expectation that long-term US Treasury interest rates will fall sharply (at least 100 basis points) over the next three months. Evaluate the return expectations for each bond, and support your evaluation of which bond would be the superior performer. Discuss the price-yield measures that affected your conclusion.

KEY TERMS

capitalization of income method of valuation
promised yield-to-maturity
net present value
yield structure
term structure
risk structure
yield spread
basis points
call provisions
call price
call premium
yield-to-call
deep discount bond
marketability
bond ratings
investment-grade bond
speculative-grade bond
junk bond
fallen angel
expected yield-to-maturity
default premium
risk premium

REFERENCES

1. For a detailed discussion of bond valuation and the attributes of bonds that are important in their pricing, see:

   Karlyn Mitchell, "The Call, Sinking Fund, and Term-to-Maturity Features of Corporate Bonds: An Empirical Investigation," *Journal of Financial and Quantitative Analysis* 26, no. 2 (June 1991): 201–222.

   James C. Van Horne, *Financial Market Rates and Flows* (Englewood Cliffs, NJ: Prentice Hall, 1994).

   Frank J. Fabozzi, *Valuation of Fixed-Income Securities* (Summit, NJ: Frank J. Fabozzi Associates, 1994).

2. Some of the many studies that have investigated the relationship between historical measures of a firm's performance and its bond ratings are:

   Thomas F. Pogue and Robert M. Soldofsky, "What's in a Bond Rating?" *Journal of Financial and Quantitative Analysis* 4, no. 2 (June 1969): 201–228.

   R. R. West, "An Alternative Approach to Predicting Corporate Bond Ratings," *Journal of Accounting Research* 8, no. 1 (Spring 1970): 118–125.

   George E. Pinches and Kent A. Mingo, "A Multivariate Analysis of Industrial Bond Ratings," *Journal of Finance* 30, no. 1 (March 1975): 201–206.

   Robert S. Kaplan and Gabriel Urwitz, "Statistical Models of Bond Ratings: A Methodological Inquiry," *Journal of Business* 52, no. 2 (April 1979): 231–261.

   Ahmed Belkaoui, *Industrial Bonds and the Rating Process* (Westport, CT: Quorum Books, 1983).

3. Changes in bond ratings have been studied in:

Steven Katz, "The Price Adjustment Process of Bonds to Rating Reclassification: A Test of Bond Market Efficiency," *Journal of Finance* 29, no. 2 (May 1974): 551–559.

Paul Grier and Steven Katz, "The Differential Effects of Bond Rating Changes Among Industrial and Public Utility Bonds by Maturity," *Journal of Business* 49, no. 2 (April 1976): 226–239.

Mark I. Weinstein, "The Effect of a Rating Change Announcement on Bond Price," *Journal of Financial Economics* 5, no. 3 (December 1977): 329–350.

Douglas J. Lucas and John G. Lonski, "Changes in Corporate Credit Quality 1970–1990," *Journal of Fixed Income* 1, no. 4 (March 1992): 7–14.

Edward I. Altman and Duen Li Kao, "Rating Drift in High-Yield Bonds," *Journal of Fixed Income* 1, no. 4 (March 1992): 15–20.

Edward I. Altman, "The Implications of Bond Ratings Drift," *Financial Analysts Journal* 48, no. 3 (May/June 1992): 64–75.

John R. M. Hand, Robert W. Holthausen, and Richard W. Leftwich, "The Effect of Bond Rating Agency Announcements on Bond and Stock Prices," *Journal of Finance* 47, no. 2 (June 1992): 733–752.

4. Default premiums and risks are discussed in:

W. Braddock Hickman, *Corporate Bond Quality and Investor Experience* (Princeton, NJ: Princeton University Press, 1958).

Harold G. Fraine and Robert H. Mills, "The Effects of Defaults and Credit Deterioration on Yields of Corporate Bonds," *Journal of Finance* 16, no. 3 (September 1961): 423–434.

Thomas R. Atkinson and Elizabeth T. Simpson, *Trends in Corporate Bond Quality* (New York: Columbia University Press, 1967).

Gordon Pye, "Gauging the Default Premium," *Financial Analysis Journal* 30, no. 1 (January/February 1974): 49–52.

Ricardo J. Rodriguez, "Default Risk, Yield Spreads, and Time to Maturity," *Journal of Financial and Quantitative Analysis* 23, no. 1 (March 1988): 111–117.

Edward I. Altman, "Measuring Corporate Bond Mortality and Performance," *Journal of Finance* 44, no. 4 (September 1989): 909–922.

Jerome S. Fons and Andrew E. Kimball, "Corporate Bond Defaults and Default Rates 1970–1990," *Journal of Fixed Income* 1, no. 1 (June 1991): 36–47.

Edward I. Altman, "Defaults and Returns on High-Yield Bonds Through the First Half of 1991," *Financial Analysts Journal* 47, no. 6 (November/December 1991): 67–77.

Edward I. Altman, "Revisiting the High-Yield Bond Market," *Financial Management* 21, no. 2 (Summer 1992): 79–92.

5. The classic study on yield spreads is:

Lawrence Fisher, "Determinants of Risk Premiums on Corporate Bonds," *Journal of Political Economy* 67, no. 3 (June 1959): 217–237.

6. Predicting bankruptcy has been a subject of much research; see the following papers and their citations:

William H. Beaver, "Financial Ratios as Predictors of Failure," *Empirical Research in Accounting: Selected Studies, 1966*, supplement to *Journal of Accounting Research*: 71–111.

William H. Beaver, "Market Prices, Financial Ratios and the Prediction of Failure," *Journal of Accounting Research* 6, no. 2 (Autumn 1968): 179–192.

Edward I. Altman, "Financial Ratios, Discriminant Analysis and the Prediction of Corporate Bankruptcy," *Journal of Finance* 23, no. 4 (September 1968): 589–609.

Edward B. Deakin, "A Discriminant Analysis of Predictors of Business Failure," *Journal of Accounting Research* 10, no. 1 (Spring 1972): 167–179.

R. Charles Moyer, "Forecasting Financial Failure: A Re-examination," *Financial Management* 6, no. 1 (Spring 1977): 11–17.

Edward I. Altman, Robert G. Haldeman, and P. Narayanan, "Zeta Analysis: A New Model to Identify Bankruptcy Risk of Corporations," *Journal of Banking and Finance* 1, no. 1 (June 1977): 29–54.

James A. Ohlson, "Financial Ratios and the Probabilistic Prediction of Bankruptcy," *Journal of Accounting Research* 18, no. 1 (Spring 1980): 109–131.

Joseph Aharony, Charles P. Jones, and Itzhak Swary, "An Analysis of Risk and Return Characteristics of Corporate Bankruptcy Using Capital Market Data," *Journal of Finance* 35, no. 4 (September 1980): 1001–1016.

Edward I. Altman and Mario Y. Lavallee, "Business Failure Classification in Canada," *Journal of Business Administration* 12, no. 1 (Fall 1980): 147–64.

Edward I. Altman, "The Success of Business Failure Prediction Models: An International Survey," *Journal of Banking and Finance* 8, no. 2 (June 1984): 171–198.

Cornelius Casey and Norman Bartczak, "Using Operating Cash Flow Data to Predict Financial Distress: Some Extensions," *Journal of Accounting Research* 23, no. 1 (Spring 1985): 384–401.

James A. Gentry, Paul Newbold, and David T. Whitford, "Classifying Bankrupt Firms with Funds Flow Components," *Journal of Accounting Research* 23, no. 1 (Spring 1985): 146–160.

James A. Gentry, Paul Newbold, and David T. Whitford, "Predicting Bankruptcy: If Cash Flow's Not the Bottom Line, What Is?" *Financial Analysts Journal* 41, no. 5 (September/October 1985): 47–56.

Ismael G. Dambolena and Joel M. Shulman, "A Primary Rule for Detecting Bankruptcy: Watch the Cash," *Financial Analysts Journal* 44, no. 5 (September/October 1988): 74–78.

James M. Gahlon and Robert L. Vigeland, "Early Warning Signs of Bankruptcy Using Cash Flow Analysis," *Journal of Commercial Bank Lending* 71, no. 4 (December 1988): 4–15.

Abdul Aziz and Gerald H. Lawson, "Cash Flow Reporting and Financial Distress Models: Testing of Hypothesis," *Financial Management* 18, no. 1 (Spring 1989): 55–63.

7. For a Canadian perspective on the topics covered in this chapter, see:

A. Thibeault and L. Wynant, "Investor Reaction to the Political Environment in Quebec," *Canadian Public Policy* (Spring 1979).

Halim Bishara, "Determinants of Canadian Corporate Bond Ratings: A Multivariate Analysis," *Proceedings*, Administrative Sciences Association of Canada Conference, Halifax, June 1988.

T. Barnes and T. Byng, "The Prediction of Corporate Bond Ratings: The Canadian Case," *Canadian Journal of Administrative Sciences* 5, no. 3 (September 1988).

M. Brennan, J. Detemple et A. Kalay, "Une Nouvelle Optique D'Evaluation de la Dette Contractuelle," *Finéco* 2, no. 2 (2e *Semestre 1992*).

R.N. Kahn and D. Gulrajani, "Risk and Return in the Canadian Bond Market," *Journal of Portfolio Management* 19, no. 3 (Spring 1993).

D. Gulrajani and B. Chui, "Measuring Risk in the Canadian Bond Market," *Canadian Investment Review* VI, no. 3 (Fall 1993).

CHAPTER 16

Bond Portfolio Management

The methods currently in use for managing bond portfolios can be divided into two general categories — passive and active. Methods in the passive category rest on the basic assumption that bond markets are semistrong-form efficient. That is, current bond prices are viewed as accurately reflecting all publicly available information. Thus, bonds are felt to be priced fairly in the marketplace, providing a return that is commensurate with the risk involved. In addition to believing that individual bonds are not mispriced, passive investors also believe that attempting to predict interest rates is, in general, futile. In summary, passive management rests on the belief that attempts at both security selection (that is, identifying mispriced bonds) and market timing (for example, buying long-term bonds when interest rates are predicted to fall and replacing them with short-term bonds when interest rates are predicted to rise) will be unsuccessful in providing the investor with above-average returns.

Active methods of bond portfolio management are based on the assumption that the bond market is not so efficient, thereby giving some investors the opportunity to earn above-average returns. Active management is based on the ability of the portfolio manager either to identify mispriced bonds or to "time" the bond market by accurately predicting interest rates.

This chapter discusses these two general approaches to bond portfolio management. It begins by reviewing some of the findings regarding the efficiency of the bond market.

BOND MARKET EFFICIENCY

In assessing the efficiency of the bond market, a sample of the major US studies and the few Canadian studies available are mentioned. The impression obtained from reading them is that US bond markets appear to be highly, but not perfectly, semistrong-form efficient. That is, bond prices tend to reflect almost all publicly available information. Not surprisingly, this impression is similar to the one obtained from studies of the efficiency of stock markets.

Canadian markets are less active. Therefore, some inefficiencies which may not be economically significant appear to exist. These are discussed below.

► Price Behaviour of Treasury Bills

An early study of bond market efficiency focused on the price behaviour of Treasury bills. In particular, the prices of Treasury bills were analyzed on a weekly basis from October 1946 through December 1964, a total of 796 weeks. The study found that knowledge of how Treasury bill prices changed in the past was of little use in trying to predict how they would change in the future. Consequently, the results from this study are consistent with the notion that the market for Treasury bills is weak-form efficient.[1]

Experts' Predictions of Interest Rates

Bond market efficiency has also been studied by examining the accuracy of interest rate predictions made by experts. These people use a wide range of techniques and a number of different sources of information. Since it is reasonable to assume their information is publicly available, such studies can be viewed as tests of semistrong-form efficiency.

One way these tests have been conducted involves the building of statistical models that are based on what the experts have said in regard to how interest rates should be predicted. Once these models have been constructed, their predictive accuracy can be evaluated. In one study, six different models were constructed and then their one-month ahead predictions were tested over the two-year period of 1973 to 1974. Consistent with the notion of efficient markets, it was found that a simple model of "no change" was more accurate in predicting interest rates than any of the six statistical models.[2]

Another way these tests have been conducted involves comparing a set of explicit predictions with what subsequently actually occurred. One source of such predictions is the quarterly survey of interest rate expectations that appears in the *Goldsmith-Nagan Bond and Money Market Newsletter*, published by Goldsmith-Nagan, Inc. Specifically, this survey reports the predictions made by a number (roughly 50) of "money market professionals" regarding three-month ahead and six-month ahead levels of 10 different interest rates. In one study, the predictions made from September 1969 through December 1972 (that is, 14 sets of quarterly predictions) were compared with those of a "no-change" model — that is, a model that forecasts no change from the current level of interest rates.[3] Interestingly, the professionals seemed to forecast better than the no-change model for short-term interest rates (such as forecasting what the three-month Treasury bill rate will be three months in the future) but did worse than the no-change model for longer-term interest rates (such as forecasting what the intermediate-term Treasury note rate will be three months in the future).

A subsequent study examined the Goldsmith-Nagan predictions of three-month Treasury bill rates six months in the future during the time period from March 1970 through September 1979 (39 predictions).[4] These predictions were compared with those of three "simple" models, the first one being the no-change model. The second simple model was based on the liquidity preference theory of the term structure of interest rates (discussed

---

[1] For details, see Richard Roll, *The Behavior of Interest Rates* (New York: Basic Books, Inc., 1970). Interestingly, this study also produced evidence rejecting the unbiased expectations theory of the term structure of interest rates (see Chapter 5).

[2] J. Walter Elliott and Jerome R. Baier, "Econometric Models and Current Interest Rates: How Well Do They Predict Future Rates?" *Journal of Finance* 34, no. 4 (September 1979): 975–86. It should be noted that the models used by major economic forecasting firms tend to have similar amounts of accuracy. See Stephen K. McNees, "Forecasting Accuracy of Alternative Techniques: A Comparison of US Macroeconomic Forecasts," *Journal of Business & Economic Statistics* 4, no. 1 (January 1986): 5–15, particularly Table 6 where 90-day Treasury bill rate forecasts are evaluated.

[3] Michael J. Prell, "How Well Do the Experts Forecast Interest Rates?" Federal Reserve Bank of Kansas City *Monthly Review* (September-October 1973): 3–13.

[4] Adrian W. Throop, "Interest Rate Forecasts and Market Efficiency," Federal Reserve Bank of San Francisco *Economic Review* (Spring 1981): 29–43. This article contains a useful reference list of other studies concerning the prediction of interest rates.

in Chapter 5). According to this theory, the forward rate implicit in current market rates should be equal to the expected future interest rate plus a liquidity premium. Thus, the expected future interest rate can be forecast by subtracting an estimate of the liquidity premium from the forward rate. The third simple model was what statisticians refer to as an autoregressive model. Basically, a forecast of the future Treasury bill rate was formed from the current Treasury bill rate as well as what the Treasury bill rate was one, two, three, and six quarters ago. The study found that the professionals were more accurate than both the no-change model and the liquidity premium model but were less accurate than the autoregressive model.

Another study evaluated the six-month-ahead predictions of three-month Treasury bill rates that were made by nine economists and reported semiannually in *The Wall Street Journal.* Evaluating the forecasts published from December 1981 through June 1986, it was found that the no-change model was more accurate.[5]

An extensive Canadian study was triggered by the observation that October 1979 ushered in a regime of high and volatile interest rates that lasted several years. The hypothesis that forecasters might perform better in such an environment was tested. The study went on to compare the performance of the simple no-change model with consensus forecasts of short- and long-term interest rates provided by three institutions (McLeod, Young, Weir and Company [now ScotiaMcLeod Inc.]; The Conference Board of Canada; and Data Resources Incorporated of Canada) over the second quarter of 1975 to the third quarter of 1979 and the fourth quarter of 1979 to the fourth quarter of 1984.[6] These institutions report interest rate forecasts for each of the following two quarters as part of their regular quarterly macroeconomic forecasts. The McLeod, Young, Weir forecasts perform as well or slightly better than the simple model in both time periods, but both the Conference Board and Data Resources forecasts deteriorate noticeably in the second period. A significant observation is the deterioration of the accuracy of all short-term interest rate forecasts (including the simple model) in the second period.

It appears from this evidence that the no-change model sometimes provides the most accurate forecasts of future interest rates, while occasionally the experts are more accurate. On balance, a reasonable interpretation of these results is that the bond market is nearly semistrong-form efficient. While the bond market may not be perfectly efficient, the evidence clearly suggests that it is hard to consistently forecast interest rates with greater accuracy than a no-change model.[7]

---

[5] Forecasts implicit in the futures market (discussed in Chapter 21) for Treasury bills were also found to be more accurate than those of the economists but less accurate than those of the no-change model over this time period. For a longer time period, the futures market and no-change model forecasts were of comparable accuracy. See Michael T. Belognia, "Predicting Interest Rates: A Comparison of Professional and Market-Based Forecasts," Federal Reserve Bank of St. Louis *Review* 69, no. 3 (March 1987): 9–15.

[6] James E. Pesando and Andre Plourde, "The October 1979 Change in the US Monetary Regime: Its Impact on the Forecastability off Canadian Interest Rates," *Journal of Finance* 43, no.1 (March 1988): 217–39.

[7] The reported accuracy of macroeconomic forecasters in regard to Treasury bill rates (see the Early Quarter results for a two-quarter horizon in Table 6 of McNees, "Forecast Accuracy") can be compared to the reported accuracy of the no-change model (see Table 1 of Belognia, "Predicting Interest Rates"). While such a comparison should be done with caution, it does suggest that the no-change model is of similar, and in some cases, superior, accuracy. There is also indirect evidence of the superiority of the no-change model in that bond portfolio managers apparently have not been able to generate returns exceeding those of bond market indices. See Christopher R. Blake, Edwin J. Elton, and Martin J. Gruber, "The Performance of Bond Mutual Funds," *Journal of Business* 66, no. 3 (July 1993): 371–403. It also appears that the record of the experts in predicting the level of the stock market is of little value. See Werner F. De Bondt, "What Do Economists Know About the Stock Market?" *Journal of Portfolio Management* 17, no. 2 (Winter 1991): 84–91.

Price Reaction to Bond Rating Changes

A different type of test of market efficiency concerned the reaction of bond prices to rating changes. If ratings are based on public information, then any rating change would follow the release of such information. This suggests that in a semistrong-form efficient market, a bond's price would react to the release of the public information rather than the subsequent announcement of the rating change. Thus, an announcement of a rating change should not trigger a subsequent adjustment in the associated bond's price.

In a study that examined 100 rating changes that took place during the period of 1962 through 1974, no significant changes in bond prices were detected in the period from six months before through six months after the announcement of the change. However, a significant change was observed in the period from 18 months through 7 months before the announcement. Specifically, rating increases were preceded by price increases, and rating decreases were preceded by price decreases.[8]

No comparable Canadian study is available, but the similarity between the bond rating processes in the two countries suggests that Canadian investors are also likely to anticipate bond rating changes.

Money Supply Announcements

Every week, generally on Thursday, the Federal Reserve Board announces the current size of the money supply in the US economy. Now, it is known that interest rates are related to, among other things, the availability of credit and that the money supply affects this availability. This means that if the money supply figures are surprisingly high or low, then the announcement should trigger adjustments in the levels of various interest rates.[9] Furthermore, such adjustments should take place rapidly in a semistrong-form efficient market. Past studies indicate that such adjustments are indeed rapid, generally taking place within a day after the announcement.[10]

---

[8] See Mark I. Weinstein, "The Effect of a Rating Change Announcement on Bond Price," *Journal of Financial Economics* 5, no. 3 (December 1977): 329–50. A study of the prices of the common stocks associated with bonds that had rating changes reported similar results — share prices tended to change several months prior to the announcement dates of the rating changes. See George E. Pinches and J. Clay Singleton, "The Adjustment of Stock Prices to Bond Rating Changes," *Journal of Finance* 33, no. 1 (March 1978): 29–44. Another study that examined rating change announcements that were "noncontaminated" by other news releases found a small but statistically significant upward movement in daily bond prices around upgrades; downgrades produced no significant movements. Oddly, these findings were reversed when stock prices were examined in that no significant movements were found around upgrades but marginally significant downward movements were observed around downgrades. See John R. M. Hand, Robert W. Holthausen, and Richard W. Leftwich, "The Effect of Bond Rating Agency Announcements on Bond and Stock Prices," *Journal of Finance* 47, no. 2 (June 1992): 733–752. Further analysis revealed that one type of downgrade — namely, "downgrades associated with deteriorating financial prospects" — resulted in a significant downward movement in the price of the associated firm's stock. See Jeremy C. Goh and Louis H. Ederington, "Is a Bond Downgrade Bad News, Good News, or No News for Stockholders?" *Journal of Finance* 48, no. 5 (December 1993): 2001–2008.

[9] For an explanation of this adjustment process, see Richard G. Sheehan, "Weekly Money Announcements: New Information and Its Effects," Federal Reserve Bank of St. Louis *Review* 67, no. 7 (August/September 1985): 25–34; and Anthony M. Santomero, "Money Supply Announcements: A Retrospective," *Journal of Economics and Business* 43, no. 1 (February 1991): 1–23.

[10] See, for example, Thomas Urich and Paul Wachtel, "Market Response to Weekly Money Supply Announcements in the 1970s," *Journal of Finance* 36, no. 5 (December 1981): 1063–72; "The Effects of Inflation and Money Supply Announcements on Interest Rates," *Journal of Finance* 39, no. 4 (September 1984): 1177–88; Bradford Cornell, "Money Supply Announcements and Interest Rates: Another View," *Journal of Business* 56, no. 1 (January 1983): 1–23.

In October 1979, the US Federal Reserve set monetary growth as one of its principal macroeconomic targets and started controlling the money supply. Given the interrelationship of the US and Canadian economies, changes in the US money supply should also affect Canadian interest rates. A study by Bailey reports that, since that date, Canadian short-term interest rates and bond prices (as well as share prices) respond to unanticipated changes in the level of the US money supply.[11] This result is consistent with semistrong-form efficiency.

A Direct Test of Bond Market Efficiency

A direct test of the efficiency of both the US and Canadian bond markets was carried out by Appelt and Schulman.[12] They calculated zero-coupon yield curves for both markets on the same days using the prices of available coupon bonds. Figure 16.1 (a) shows the US term structure for March 31, 1988 and Figure 16.1 (b) shows the Canadian term structure on the same day. Using these data they calculated "revealed spot rates" by following a simple arbitrage procedure that can be applied when there is more than one bond issue with the same maturity but different coupon rates. For example, consider the following two bonds:

	Coupon	*Maturity*	*Price*	*Principal*
Bond 1:	10.5 %	95.02.15	$110.78	$100.00
Bond 2:	11.25%	95.02.15	$114.63	$100.00

Shorting bond 1 and buying bond 2 in the correct proportions results in an arbitrage portfolio with a zero net coupon income. This can be achieved by selling $1125 of face value of bond 1 and buying $1050 of face value of bond 2 with the following result:

	Coupon Stream	*Current Investment*	*Receipt at Maturity*
Bond 1:	$–118.125	$–1246.48	$–1125.00
Bond 2:	$ 118.125	$ 1203.62	$ 1050.00
Net	$ 0.000	$ 42.66	$ –75.00

The net result is the same as borrowing $42.66 on March 31, 1988 and repaying $75.00 on February 15, 1995. The implied interest rate is 8.37% (neglecting transaction costs)—about 21 basis points lower than the risk-free spot rate for a 6.88 year bond. By examining all possible combinations in both markets, the revealed spot rates across the maturity spectrum could be calculated. Figures 16.2 (a) and (b) show these revealed rates for US Treasury securities and Canadas respectively. Figure 16.2 (a) shows that there are

[11] W. Bailey, "The Effect of US Money Supply Announcements on Canadian Stock, Bond, and Currency Prices," *Canadian Journal of Economics* 22, no. 3 (August 1989):607–18.

[12] T. Appelt and E. Schulman, "The Government of Canada Bond Market: Is it Efficiently Priced?" *Canadian Investment Review* I, no.1 (Fall 1988):63–70.

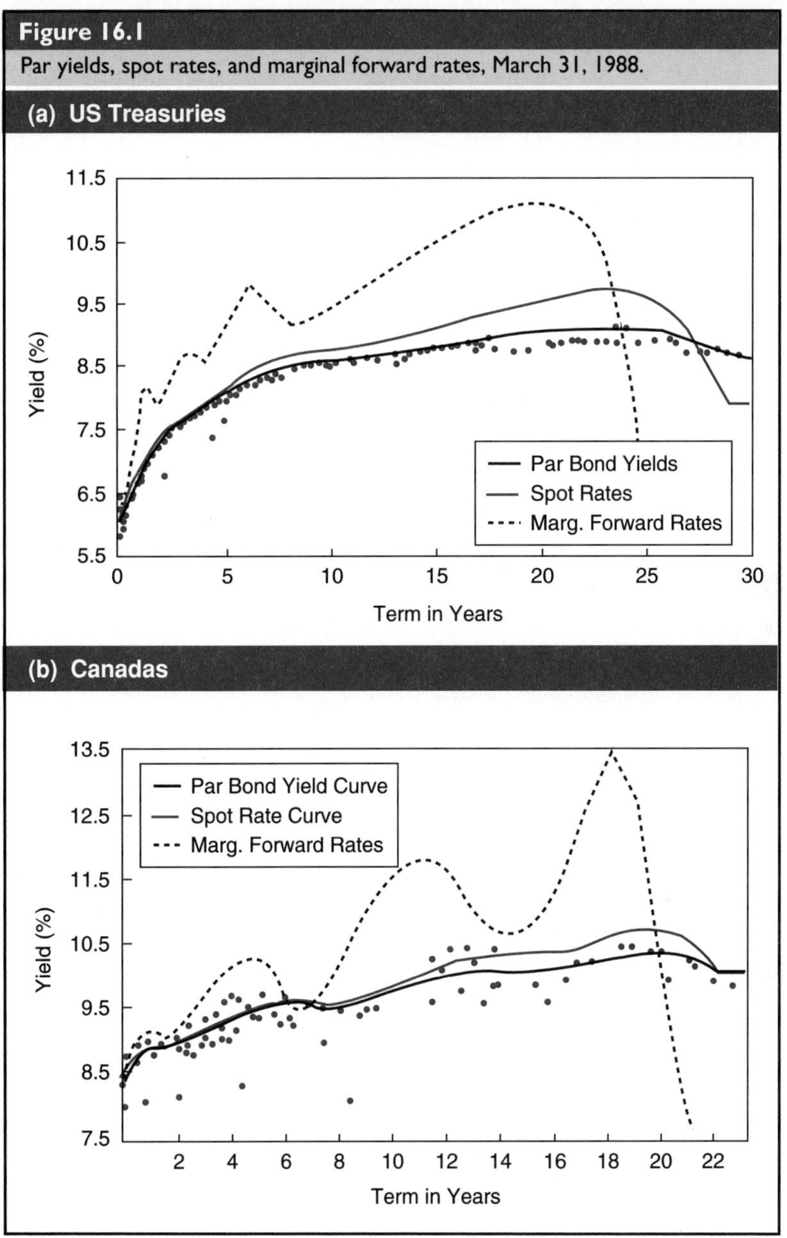

Figure 16.1

Par yields, spot rates, and marginal forward rates, March 31, 1988.

SOURCE: T. Appelt and E. Schulman, "The Government of Canada Bond Market: Is It Efficiently Priced?" *Canadian Investment Review* I, no. 1 (Fall 1988): 63–72.

some arbitrage opportunities to be exploited in the US market, especially at the longer end of the maturity spectrum, but these are relatively small. Figure 16.2 (b) shows that there are substantially larger arbitrage opportunities in the Canadian market. Two factors may explain the differences: first, transactions costs in Canada are higher than those in the US and second, the returns on low-coupon bonds receive more favourable tax treatment in Canada than in the US. The authors argue that the transaction costs in Canada would have to be

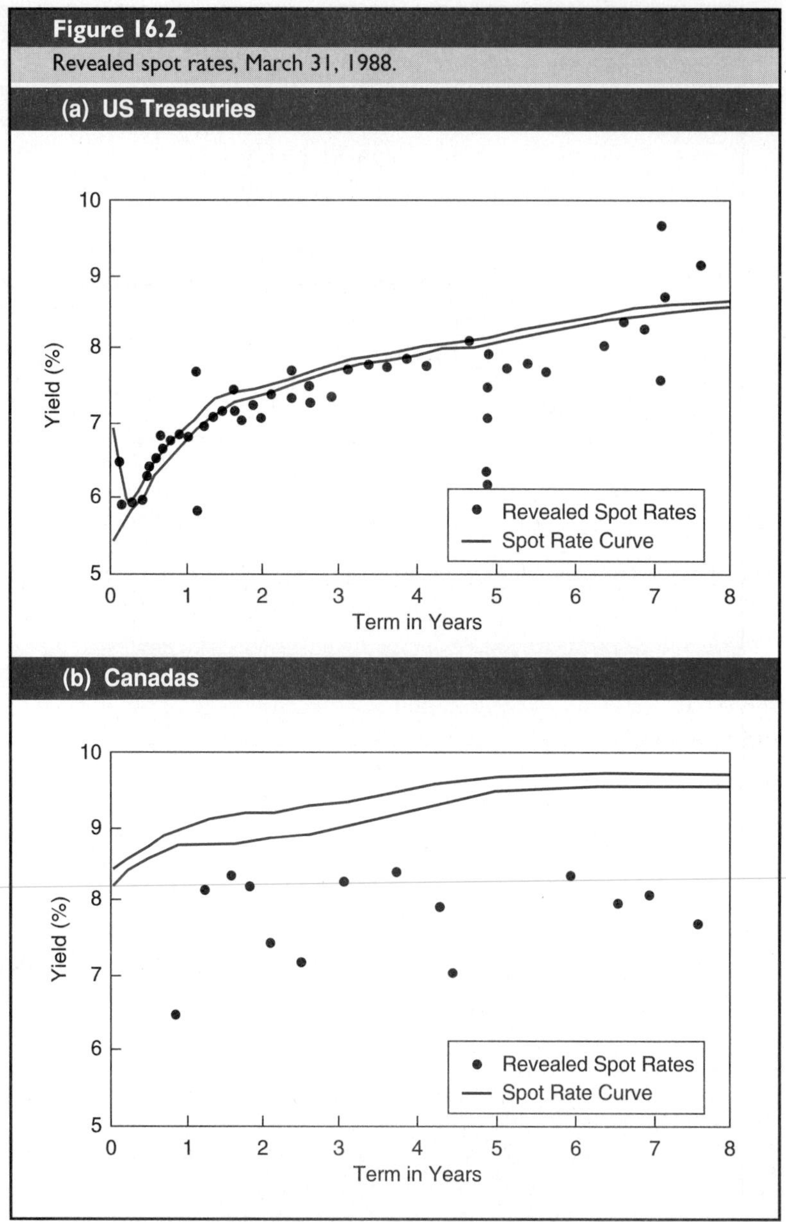

SOURCE: T. Appelt and E. Schulman, "The Government of Canada Bond Market: Is It Efficiently Priced?" *Canadian Investment Review* I, no. 1 (Fall 1988): 63–72.

two to three times the levels observed in the US to explain the differences and that taxation alone cannot explain the degree of mispricing of low-coupon bonds. They conclude that there are arbitrage opportunities in both markets but more so in Canada. For these to be exploitable, however, it must be possible to borrow the securities (with margin requirements that are not onerous) that should be sold short.

Summary

In summary, the evidence on the efficiency of the bond market is consistent with the notion that it is highly, but not perfectly, semistrong-form efficient.[13] Statistical tests of past prices of Treasury bills suggest it is efficient. It appears that corporate bonds reflect the information leading to a rating change in a timely fashion and that interest rates change rapidly when there is a surprise in the announced size of the money supply, observations that are also consistent with the notion of efficiency.

There is some evidence, however, suggesting that certain professionals are occasionally able to make accurate interest rate forecasts. It also appears that there are some limited arbitrage opportunities available. With this in mind, it is not surprising that some bond managers have opted to follow a passive approach to investing, while others have decided to be more active. These two approaches are presented next, beginning with a discussion of some bond pricing theorems. In turn, these theorems will be related to a concept known as duration, which is the basis for one method of passively managing a bond portfolio.

BOND-PRICING THEOREMS

Bond-pricing theorems deal with how bond prices move in response to changes in their yields-to-maturity. Before presenting the theorems, a brief review of some terms associated with bonds will be useful.

The typical bond is characterized by a promise to pay the investor two types of cash flows. The first involves the payment of a fixed dollar amount periodically (usually every six months), with the last payment being on a stated date. The second type of cash flow involves the payment of a lump sum on this stated date. The periodic payments are known as **coupon payments**, and the lump sum payment is known as the bond's principal (or par value or face value). A bond's **coupon rate** is calculated by dividing the dollar amount of the coupon payments a bondholder would receive over the course of a year by the principal of the bond. Lastly, the amount of time left until the last promised payment is made is known as the bond's **term-to-maturity**, whereas the discount rate that makes the present value of all the cash flows equal to the market price of the bond is known as the bond's **yield-to-maturity** (or, simply, yield).

Note that if a bond has a market price that is equal to its par value, then its yield-to-maturity will be equal to its coupon rate. However, if the market price is less than par value (a situation where the bond is said to be selling at a discount), then the bond will have a yield-to-maturity that is greater than the coupon rate. Conversely, if the market price is greater than par value (a situation where the bond is said to be selling at a premium), then the bond will have a yield-to-maturity that is less than the coupon rate.

With this in mind, five theorems that deal with bond pricing have been derived.[14] For ease of exposition, it is assumed that there is one coupon payment per year (that is, coupon payments are made every 12 months). The theorems are as follows:

---

[13] Like the stock market, the bond market has some anomalies. However, they are fewer in number and less pronounced. These anomalies are briefly discussed in the Appendix.

[14] Burton G. Malkiel, "Expectations, Bond Prices, and the Term Structure of Interest Rates," *Quarterly Journal of Economics* 76, no. 2 (May 1962): 197–218. Also see Frank J. Fabozzi and T. Dessa Fabozzi, *Bond Markets, Analysis and Strategies* (Englewood Cliffs, N.J.: Prentice Hall, 1989), particularly Chapter 4.

Figure 16.3

Changes in a bond's price over its life.[a]

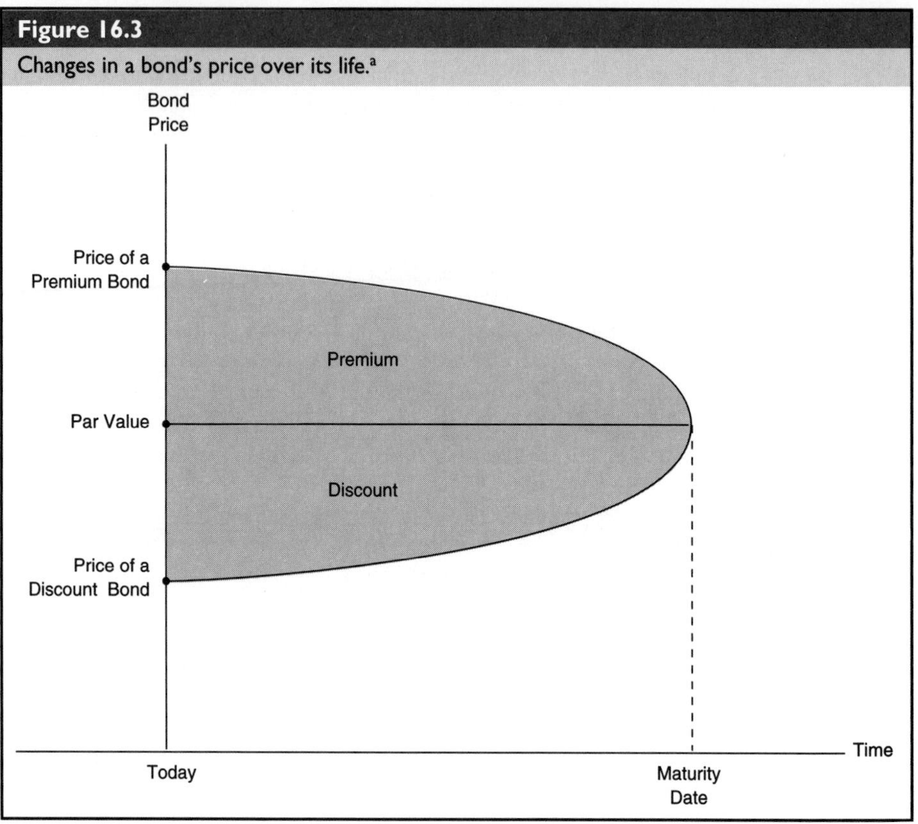

[a] Assuming that the bond's yield-to-maturity remains constant through time.

1. *If a bond's market price increases, then its yield must decrease; conversely, if a bond's market price decreases, then its yield must increase.*

As an example, consider bond A that has a life of five years and a par value of \$1000 and pays coupons annually of \$80. Its yield is 8%, since it is currently selling for \$1000. However, if its price increases to \$1100, then its yield will fall to 5.76%. Conversely, if its price falls to \$900, then its yield will rise to 10.68%.

2. *If a bond's yield does not change over its life, then the size of its discount or premium will decrease as its life gets shorter.*

This can be seen by examining Figure 16.3. Note how the price of a bond that is selling at either a premium or a discount today will converge over time to its par value. Ultimately the premium or discount will completely disappear at the maturity date.

As an example, consider bond B that has a life of five years and a par value of \$1000 and pays coupons annually of \$60. Its current market price is \$883.31, indicating it has a yield of 9%. After one year, if it still has a yield of 9%, it will be selling for \$902.81. Thus, its discount has decreased from \$1000 – \$883.31 = \$116.69 to \$1000 – \$902.81 = \$97.19, for a change of \$116.69 – \$97.19 = \$19.50.

An equivalent interpretation of this theorem is that if two bonds have the same coupon rate, par value, and yield, then the one with the shorter life will sell for a smaller discount or premium. Consider two bonds, one with a life of five years and the other with a life of four years. Both bonds have a par value of $1000, pay annual coupons of $60, and yield 9%. In this situation, the one with a five-year life has a discount of $116.69, whereas the one with a four-year life has a smaller discount of $97.19.

3. *If a bond's yield does not change over its life, then the size of its discount or premium will decrease at an increasing rate as it approaches maturity.*

Figure 16.3 can also be used to illustrate this theorem. Note that, at first, the premium or discount does not change much with time. In contrast, however, the size changes much more rapidly with time as the maturity date approaches.

As an example, consider bond B again. After two years, if it still has a yield of 9%, it will be selling for $924.06. Thus, its discount has decreased to $1000 – $924.06 = $75.94. Now, the amount of the change in the discount from five years to four years was $116.69 – $97.19 = $19.50, for a percentage change from par of 1.95%. However, the amount of the change from four years to three years is larger, going from $97.19 to $75.94, for a dollar change of $21.25 and a percentage change from par of 2.125%.

4. *A decrease in a bond's yield will raise the bond's price by an amount that is greater in size than the corresponding fall in the bond's price that would occur if there were an equal-sized increase in the bond's yield.*

As an example, consider bond C that has a life of five years and a coupon rate of 7%. Since it is currently selling at its par value of $1000, its yield is 7%. If its yield rises by 1% to 8%, then it will be selling for $960.07, a change of $39.93. Alternatively, if its yield falls by 1% to 6%, then it will be selling for $1042.12, a change of $42.12, which is of greater magnitude than the $39.93 associated with the 1% rise in the bond's yield.

5. *The percentage change in a bond's price due to a change in its yield will be smaller if its coupon rate is higher.* (*Note*: This theorem does not apply to bonds with a life of one year or to bonds that have no maturity date, known as consols, or perpetuities.)

As an example, compare bond D with bond C. Bond D has a coupon rate of 9%, which is 2% larger than C's. However, bond D has the same life (five years) and yield (7%) as C. Thus, D's current market price is $1082.00. If the yield on both C and D increases to 8%, then their prices will be $960.07 and $1039.93, respectively.

This represents a decrease in the price of C equal to $1000 – $960.07 = $39.93, or 3.993% (*note*: $39.93/$1000 = 3.993%). For D, the decrease in price is equal to $1082 – $1039.93 = $42.07, or 3.889% (*note*: $42.07/$1082 = 3.889%). Since D has the higher coupon rate, it has the smaller percentage change in price.

It is important for a bond analyst to understand thoroughly these properties of bond prices, since they are valuable in forecasting how bond prices will respond to changes in interest rates.

CONVEXITY

The first and fourth bond pricing theorems have led to the concept in bond valuation known as **convexity**. Consider what happens to the price of a bond if its yield increases or decreases. According to Theorem 1, bond prices and yields are inversely related. However, this relationship is not linear, according to Theorem 4: the size of the rise in a bond's price

Figure 16.4
Bond convexity.

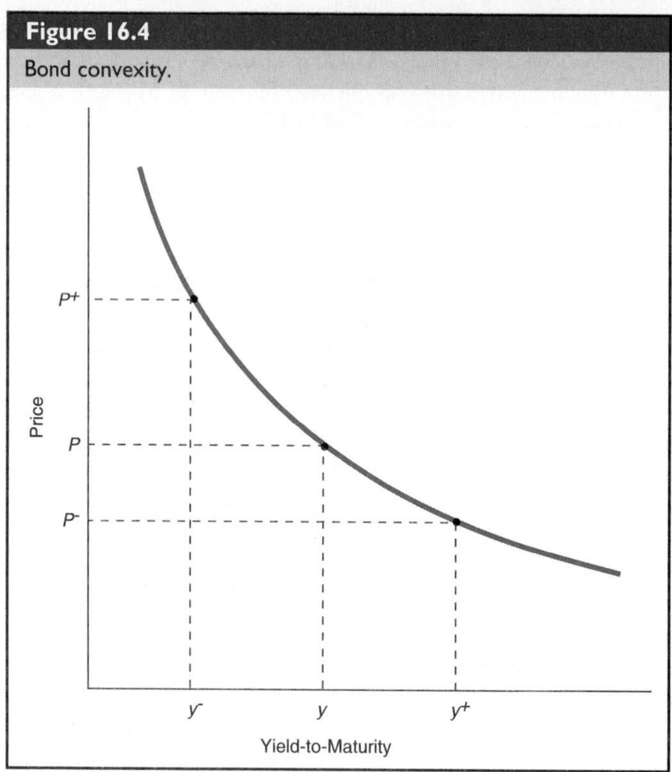

associated with a given decrease in its yield is greater than the drop in the bond's price for a similar-sized increase in the bond's yield.

This can be seen by examining Figure 16.4. The current yield-to-maturity and the price for the bond are denoted by y and P, respectively. Consider what would happen to the bond's price if the yield increased or decreased by a fixed amount (for example, 1%), denoted y^+ and y^-. The associated bond prices are denoted by P^- and P^+, respectively.

Two observations can be made about this figure. First, an increase in the yield to y^+ is associated with a drop in the bond's price to P^-, and a decrease in the yield to y^- is associated with a rise in the bond's price to P^+. This is in accord with the first bond theorem. (Hence, the symbols + and – are paired inversely so that, for example, y^+ is associated with P^-.) Second, note that the size of the rise in the bond's price ($P^+ - P$) is greater than the size of the drop in the bond's price ($P - P^-$). This is in accord with the fourth bond theorem.

The curved line in the figure that shows the relationship between bond prices and yields is convex because it opens upward. Accordingly, the relationship is frequently referred to as convexity. Although this relationship is true for standard types of bonds, it should be mentioned that the degree of curvature (or convexity) is not the same for all bonds. Instead, it depends on the size of the coupon payments, the life of the bond, and its current market price, among other things.

Duration is a measure of the "average maturity" of the stream of payments associated with a bond. More specifically, it is a weighted average of the lengths of time until the remaining payments are made. Consider, for example, a bond with annual coupon payments of \$80, a remaining life of three years, and a par value of \$1000. Since it has a current market price of \$950.25, it has a yield-to-maturity of 10.00%. As shown in Table 16.1, its duration is 2.78 years. This is calculated by taking the present value of each cash flow, multiplying each one by the respective amount of time until it is received, summing the resulting figures up, and then dividing this sum (\$2639.17) by the market price of the bond (\$950.25).

The Formula

Specifically, the formula for a bond's duration (D) is

$$D = \frac{\sum_{t=1}^{T} PV(C_t) \times t}{P_0} \tag{16.1}$$

where $PV(C_t)$ denotes the present value of the cash flow to be received at time t, calculated using a discount rate equal to the bond's yield-to-maturity; P_0 denotes the current market price of the bond; and T denotes the bond's remaining life.[15]

Table 16.1

Calculation of Duration.

Time Until Receipt of Cash Flow	*Amount of Cash Flow*	*Present Value Factor*	*Present Value of Cash Flow*	*Present Value of Cash Flow × Time*
1	\$ 80	.9091	\$ 72.73	\$ 72.73
2	80	.8264	66.12	132.23
3	1080	.7513	811.40	2434.21
			\$950.25	\$2639.17

$$\text{Duration} = \frac{\$2639.17}{\$950.25} = 2.78 \text{ years}$$

[15]There are other methods of calculating a bond's duration. For example, instead of using the bond's yield to calculate $PV(C_t)$, the appropriate current spot rate could be used. The concept of duration was initially developed in 1938 by Frederick R. Macaulay, a Canadian actuary, in *Some Theoretical Problems Suggested by the Movements of Interest Rates, Bond Yields, and Stock Prices in the United States Since 1856* (New York: National Bureau of Economic Research). For an interesting article describing the development of the concept of duration (as well as immunization), see Roman L. Weil, "Macaulay's Duration: An Appreciation," *Journal of Business* 46, no. 4 (October 1973): 589–92.

Why is duration thought of as the "average maturity of the stream of payments associated with a bond?" The current market price of the bond, P_0, is equal to the sum of the present values of the cash flows, $PV(C_t)$, where the discount rate is the bond's yield-to-maturity:

$$P_0 = \sum_{t=1}^{T} PV(C_t). \tag{16.2}$$

Thus, there is an equivalent method for calculating a bond's duration that can be seen by rewriting equation (16.1) in a slightly different manner:

$$D = \sum_{t=1}^{T} \left[\frac{PV(C_t)}{P_0} \times t \right]. \tag{16.3}$$

First, the present value of each cash flow $[PV(C_t)]$ is expressed as a proportion of the market price (P_0). Second, these proportions are multiplied by the respective amount of time until the cash flows are received. Third, these figures are added, with the sum being equal to the bond's duration.

In the example shown in Table 16.1, note that $72.73/$950.25 = .07653 of the bond's market price is to be received in one year. Similarly $66.12/$950.25 = .06958 is to be received in two years, and $811.40/$950.25 = .85388 is to be received in three years. Note how these proportions sum to one, which means that they can be interpreted as weights in calculating a weighted average. Thus, to calculate the average maturity of the payments associated with a bond, each weight needs to be multiplied by the respective amount of time until the corresponding cash flow is to be received, and then the products need to be summed up: (1 × .07653) + (2 × .06958) + (3 × .85388) = 2.78 years.

A zero-coupon bond will have a duration equal to its remaining life, T, since there is only one cash flow associated with such a bond. That is, since $P_0 = PV(C_T)$ for such bonds, equation (16.3) reduces to

$$\begin{aligned} D &= \frac{PV(C_T)}{P_0} \times T \\ &= 1 \times T \\ &= T. \end{aligned}$$

For any coupon-bearing bond, its duration will always be less than the amount of time to its maturity date, T. Again, examination of equation (16.3) indicates why this is so. Since the largest value that t can have is T, and each value of t is multiplied by a weight equal to $PV(C_t)/P_0$, it follows that D must be less than T.

Relationship to Bond Price Changes

One implication of Theorem 5 is that bonds having the same maturity date but different coupon sizes may react differently to a given change in interest rates. That is, the prices of these bonds may adjust by notably different amounts when there is a given change in interest rates. However, bonds with the same duration will react quite similarly. Specifically, the percentage change in a bond's price is related to its duration in the following fashion:

$$\text{Percentage change in price} \cong -D \times \text{percentage change in}(1 + \text{the bond's yield}) \tag{16.4a}$$

where the symbol $\cong$ means "is approximately equal to." This formula implies that when the yields of two bonds having the same duration change by the same percentage, then the prices of the two bonds will change by approximately equal percentages. Equivalently, equation (16.4a) is written as

$$\frac{\Delta P}{P} \cong -D\left(\frac{\Delta y}{1+y}\right) \tag{16.4b}$$

where ΔP denotes the change in the bond's price, P is the bond's initial price, Δy is the change in the bond's yield-to-maturity, and y is the bond's initial yield-to-maturity.

As an example, consider a bond that is currently selling for \$1000 with a yield-to-maturity of 8%. Given that the bond has a duration of ten years, by how much will the bond's price change if its yield increases to 9%? Using equation (16.4b), it can be seen that $\Delta y = 9\% - 8\% = 1\% = .01$, so that $\Delta y/(1 + y) = .01/1.08 = .00926 = .926\%$ and $-D[\Delta y/(1 + y)] = -10[.926\%] = -9.26\%$. Hence the one-percentage-point rise in the yield will cause approximately a 9.26% drop in the bond's price to $\$1000 - (.0926 \times \$1000) = \$926$.

Relationship Between Convexity and Duration

At this point it is useful to consider just what kind of relationship the concepts of convexity and duration have to each other. After all, both have something to do with measuring the association of the change in a bond's price with a change in the bond's yield-to-maturity. Figure 16.5 shows the nature of the relationship.

Like Figure 16.4, this figure represents a bond that is currently selling for P and has a yield-to-maturity of y. Note the straight line that is tangent to the curve at the point associated with the current price and yield.

Figure 16.5

Bond convexity and duration.

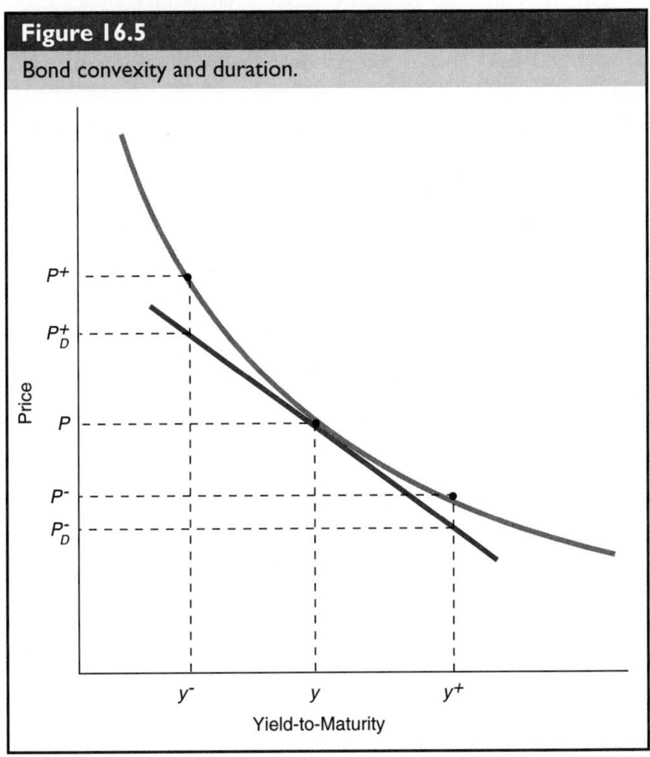

If the bond's yield increases to y^+ then the associated price of the bond will fall to P^-. Conversely, if the bond's yield decreases to y^-, then the associated price of the bond will rise to P^+. However, by using equation (16.4b), the estimated prices will be P_D^- and P_D^+, respectively. This is because the equation, as mentioned earlier, is not exact. Instead, it is an approximation that states that the percentage change in the bond's price is a linear function of its duration. Hence the equation approximates the new price in a linear fashion represented by the straight line and leading to an error that is a consequence of convexity. [In the example, the sizes of the respective errors are $(P^- - P_D^-)$ and $(P^+ - P_D^+)$.] That is, because the relationship between yield changes and bond price changes is convex, not linear, the use of equation (16.4b) will underestimate the new price associated with either an increase or a decrease in the bond's yield.[16] However, for small changes in yields the error is relatively small, and thus, as an approximation, equation (16.4b) works reasonably well. Figure 16.5 shows that the size of the pricing error becomes smaller as the size of the yield change gets smaller. (Note that the distance between the linear approximating line and the convex curve will be smaller for smaller changes in yields from y.)

Changes in the Term Structure

As mentioned earlier, when yields change, most bond prices also change, but some react more than others. Even bonds with the same maturity date can react quite differently to a given change in yields. However, it was shown in equations (16.4a) and (16.4b) that the percentage change in a bond's price is related to its duration. Hence, the prices of two bonds that have the same duration will react similarly to a given change in yields.

For example, the bond shown in Table 16.1 has a duration of 2.78 and a yield of 10%. If its yield changes to 11%, then the percentage change in (1 + the bond's yield) is $(1.11-1.10)/1.10 = .91\%$. Thus its price should change by approximately $-2.78 \times .91\% = -2.53\%$. Using a discount rate of 11%, its price can be calculated to equal \$926.69, for an actual price change of \$926.69 – \$950.25 = –\$23.56 and a percentage change of –\$23.56/\$950.25 = –2.48%. Any other bond having a duration of 2.78 years will experience a similar price change if it has a similar percentage change in its yield.

Consider a bond with a maturity of four years that also has a duration of 2.78 years. When there is a shift in interest rates, and the yields on the three-year and four-year bonds change by the same amount, then their prices will change similarly. For example, if the yield on the four-year bond goes from 10.8% to 11.81% and at the same time the yield on the three-year bond goes from 10% to 11%, then the percentage change in the present value of the four-year bond will be approximately $-2.78 \times (1.1181-1.108)/1.108 = 2.78 \times .91\% = -2.53\%$, which is the same percentage as the three-year bond.

What if the percentage change in (1+the bond's yield) is different? That is, what happens if the term structure shifts in a manner so that the percentage change in (1+the bond's yield) is not the same for all bonds? Perhaps when the three-year bond goes from a yield of 10% to a yield of 11% (a percentage change of $(1.11 - 1.10)/1.10 = .91\%$), the four-year bond will go from a yield of 10.8% to a yield of 11.5% (a percentage change of $(1.115-1.108)/1.108 = .63\%$). In this case the percentage change in price for the four-year

[16] It follows that if there are two bonds that are identical in all aspects except that one has "more convexity," then the one with more convexity would be more desirable. This is because if yields rise, its price will drop by a smaller amount than the other bonds. Conversely, if yields drop, its price will rise by a larger amount than the other bonds. In either case, the investor is better off with the bond having more convexity.

bond will be approximately $-2.78 \times [(1.115 - 1.108)/1.108] = 1.75\%$, which is a smaller change than the -2.53% associated with the three-year bond. Accordingly, even though the two bonds have the same duration, it does not automatically follow that their prices will react identically to any change in yields, as these yield changes can be different for two bonds having the same duration.

IMMUNIZATION

The introduction of the concept of duration has led to the development of the technique of bond portfolio management known as **immunization**.[17] Specifically, this technique allegedly allows a bond portfolio manager to be relatively certain of being able to meet a given promised stream of cash outflows. Thus, once the portfolio has been formed, it is "immunized" from any adverse effects associated with future changes in interest rates.

► How Immunization Is Accomplished

Immunization is accomplished by calculating the duration of the promised outflows and then investing in a portfolio of bonds that have an identical duration. In doing so, this technique takes advantage of the observation that *the duration of a portfolio of bonds is equal to the weighted average of the durations of the individual bonds in the portfolio*. For example, if one-third of a portfolio's funds are invested in bonds having a duration of six years and two-thirds of its funds are in bonds having a duration of three years, then the portfolio itself has a duration of $[(1/3) \times 6] + [(2/3) \times 3] = 4$ years.

Consider a simple situation where a portfolio manager has one and only one cash outflow to make from his or her portfolio—an amount equal to \$1 000 000 that is to be paid in two years. Since there is only one cash outflow, its duration is simply two years. Now, the bond portfolio manager is considering investing in two different bond issues. The first bond issue is the one shown in Table 16.1, where the bonds have a maturity of three years. The second bond issue involves a set of bonds that mature in one year, providing the holder of each bond with a single payment of \$1070 (consisting of a single coupon payment of \$70 and a par value of \$1000). Since these bonds are currently selling for \$972.73, their yield-to-maturity is 10%.

Consider the choices open to the portfolio manager. All the portfolio's funds could be invested in the one-year bonds, with the notion of reinvesting the proceeds from the maturing bonds one year from now in another one-year issue. However, doing so would entail risks. In particular, if interest rates were to decline over the next year, then the funds from the maturing one-year bonds will have to be reinvested at a lower rate than the currently available 10%. Thus, the portfolio manager faces reinvestment-rate risk due to the possibility that the funds one year from now can only be reinvested at a lower rate.[18]

---

[17] For the initial development, see F. M. Redington, "Review of the Principles of Life-Office Valuations," *Journal of the Institute of Actuaries* 78, no. 3 (1952): 286–315. A useful book that discusses duration-based investment strategies is Gerald O. Bierwag, *Duration Analysis* (Cambridge, Mass: Ballinger Publishing Company, 1987).

[18] If there were two-year coupon-bearing bonds available for investment, then there would be no reinvestment-rate risk associated with the principal. However, the investor would still face reinvestment-rate risk in terms of the coupon payments received after one year. Although such risk appears to be relatively minor in this example, it becomes much more substantial in situations involving promised cash outflows that are more than two years into the future.

A second alternative would be for the portfolio manager to invest all the funds in the three-year issue. However, this also entails risks. In particular, the three-year bonds will have to be sold after two years in order to come up with the \$1 000 000. The risk is that interest rates will have risen before then, meaning that bond prices, in general, will have fallen and the bonds will not have a selling price that is equal to or greater than \$1 000 000. Thus, the portfolio manager faces interest-rate risk with this strategy.

One proposed solution is to invest part of the portfolio's funds in the one-year bonds and the rest in the three-year bonds. How much should be placed in each issue? If immunization is to be used, the solution can be found by simultaneously solving a set of two equations involving two unknowns:

$$W_1 + W_3 = 1 \tag{16.5}$$

$$(W_1 \times 1) + (W_3 \times 2.78) = 2. \tag{16.6}$$

Here, W_1 and W_3 denote the weights (or proportions) of the portfolio's funds that are to be invested in the bonds with maturities of one and three years, respectively. Note how equation (16.5) states that the sum of the weights must equal 1, whereas equation (16.6) states that the weighted average of the durations of the bonds in the portfolio must equal the duration of the cash outflow, which is two years.

The solution to these two equations is easily found. First, equation (16.5) is rewritten as

$$W_1 = 1 - W_3. \tag{16.7}$$

Then, $1 - W_3$ is substituted for W_1 in equation (16.6), resulting in

$$[(1 - W_3) \times 1] + (W_3 \times 2.78) = 2. \tag{16.8}$$

Since this is one equation with one unknown, W_3, it can be easily solved. Doing so results in $W_3 = .5618$. Inserting this value into equation (16.7) indicates that $W_1 = .4382$. Thus, the portfolio manager should put 43.82% of the portfolio's funds in the one-year bonds and 56.18% in the three-year bonds.

In this case, the portfolio manager would need \$1 000 000/(1.10^2) = \$826 446 in order to purchase bonds that would create a fully immunized portfolio. With this money, .4382 × \$826 446 = \$362 149 would be used to buy one-year bonds and .5618 × \$826 446 = \$464 297 would be used to buy three-year bonds. Since the current market prices of the one-year and three-year bonds are \$972.73 and \$950.25, respectively, this means that 372 (= \$362 149/\$972.73) one-year bonds and 489 (= \$464 297/\$950.25) three-year bonds would be purchased.

What does immunization accomplish? According to theory, if yields rise, then the portfolio's losses due to the selling of the three-year bonds at a discount after two years will be exactly offset by the gains from reinvesting the maturing one-year bonds (and first-year coupons on the three-year bonds) at the higher rate. Alternatively, if yields fall, then the loss from being able to reinvest the maturing one-year bonds (and first-year coupons on the three-year bonds) at a lower rate will be exactly offset by being able to sell the three-year bonds after two years at a premium. Thus, the portfolio is immunized from the effect of any movements in interest rates in the future.

Table 16.2 shows more explicitly what would happen to the portfolio. The second column shows what the portfolio would be worth at the end of two years if yields remained at 10% over the next two years. As can be seen, the value of the portfolio of one-year and three-year bonds would be approximately equal to the promised cash outflow of \$1 000 000.

Table 16.2

An Example of an Immunized Portfolio.

	Yield-to-Maturity at the End of One Year		
	9%	*10%*	*11%*
Value at t = 2 from reinvesting one-year bond proceeds: [\$1070 × 372.3 × (1 + y)] =	\$ 434 213	\$438 197	\$ 442 181
Value at t = 2 of three-year bonds:			
Value from reinvesting coupons received at t = 1: [\$80 × 488.6 × (1 + y)] =	42 606	42 997	43 388
Coupons received at t = 2: [\$80 × 488.6] =	39 088	39 088	39 088
Selling price at t = 2: [\$1080 × 488.6/(1 + y)] =	484 117	479 716	475 395
Aggregate portfolio value at t = 2	\$1 000 024	\$999 998	\$1 000 052

Alternatively, if yields fell to 9% or rose to 11% before one year had passed and remained at the new level, then the value of the portfolio would be slightly more than the needed \$1 000 000.[19]

Problems with Immunization

The previous paragraph described what immunization accomplishes in theory. This leaves open the possibility that it might not work quite as well in practice. What can cause it to work less than perfectly? In terms of the example, what can cause the value of the portfolio to be less than \$1 000 000 at the end of two years?

Default and Call Risk

To begin with, immunization is based on the belief that all the bonds' promised cash flows will be paid in full and on time. This means that immunization is based on the assumption that the bond will not default and will not be called before maturity—that is, the bonds are assumed to be free from both call risk and default risk. Consequently, if a bond in the portfolio either enters into default or is called, the portfolio will not be immunized.

Multiple Nonparallel Shifts in a Nonhorizontal Yield Curve

Immunization is also based on the assumption that the yield curve is horizontal and that any shifts in it will be parallel and will occur before any payments are received from the bonds that were purchased. In the example, both the one-year and three-year bonds had the same 10% yield-to-maturity at the start, and the shift of 1% in yields was assumed to be the same for both bond issues. Furthermore, this shift was assumed to occur sometime before one year had passed.

[19] The value is more than \$1 000 000 due to the cenvexity property of bonds, discussed earlier.

In reality, the yield curve will not be horizontal at the start, and shifts in it are not likely to be either parallel or restricted as to when they occur. Perhaps the one-year and three-year bonds will have initial yields of 10% and 10.5%, respectively, with the yields on the one-year and three-year bonds falling by 1% and .8%, respectively, after one year. Indeed, there is evidence that there is greater volatility in yields of shorter-term securities.[20] If these kinds of shifts occur, then it is possible that the portfolio will not be immunized.

If the bond portfolio manager followed a special kind of immunization known as **cash matching**, then frequent nonparallel shifts in a nonhorizontal yield curve would have no adverse effect on the portfolio. This is because cash matching involves the purchase of bonds so that the cash received each period from the bonds is identical in size to the promised cash outflow for that period.

Such a cash-matching portfolio of bonds is often referred to as a **dedicated portfolio**. Note that there is no need to reinvest any cash inflows in the future with a dedicated portfolio, so there is no reinvestment rate risk. Furthermore, since bonds do not have to be sold prior to maturity, there is no interest rate risk either.

In the simplest situation where there is one promised cash outflow, the dedicated portfolio would consist of zero-coupon bonds, where each bond has a life corresponding to the date of the promised cash outflow. In the previous example where there was a promised cash outflow of $1 000 000 after two years, this would be accomplished by purchasing the requisite number of zero-coupon bonds having a maturity of two years.

However, cash matching is often not so easily accomplished because the promised cash outflows may involve an uneven stream of payments for which no zero-coupon bonds exist. It can be difficult (if not impossible) and expensive to match cash inflows exactly with promised outflows.

Another potential way around the problem of having nonhorizontal yield curves that have nonparallel shifts is to use one of a variety of more complicated immunization models. These models involve various other assumptions about the current shape of the yield curve and how it will shift in the future. Consequently, the bond portfolio manager must choose the one that he or she deems most accurate. Interestingly, various studies have found that the best performer was the version of immunization that has been described in this chapter, and not the more complicated models. For this reason, some researchers argue that the portfolio manager interested in immunization would be well advised to use this version.[21]

Regardless of the model being used, the bond portfolio manager must recognize that there is a risk being incurred — the risk that the yield curve will shift in a way that does not correspond with the way assumed by the model. For example, if the model presented here is used, then the bond portfolio is facing the risk that the yield curve may not shift in

---

[20] See the articles by Jeffrey Nelson and Stephen Schaefer, "The Dynamics of the Term Structure and Alternative Portfolio Immunization Strategies," pp. 61–101; and Jonathan E. Ingersoll, Jr., "Is Immunization Feasible? Evidence from the CRSP Data," pp. 163–182 in George G. Kaufman, G.O. Bierwag, and Alden Toevs, eds., *Innovations in Bond Portfolio Management: Duration Analysis and Immunization* (Greenwich, CT: JAI Press 1983); and Robert R. Reitano, "Non-Parallel Yield Curve Shifts and Spread Leverage," *Journal of Portfolio Management* 17, no. 3 (Spring 1991): 82–87.

[21] For a summary and set of references, see G. O. Bierwag, George G. Kaufman, Robert Schweitzer, and Alden Toevs, "The Art of Risk Management in Bond Portfolios," *Journal of Portfolio Management* 7, no. 3 (Spring 1981): 27-36; G. O. Bierwag, George G. Kaufman, and Alden Toevs, "Duration: Its Development and Use in Bond Portfolio Management," *Financial Analysts Journal* 39, no. 4 (July-August 1983): 15–35; and Stephen M. Schaefer, "Immunization and Duration: A Review of Theory, Performance and Applications," *Midland Corporate Finance Journal* 2, no. 3 (Fall 1984): 41–58.

a parallel manner. Consequently, some people have argued that none of the immunization models are useful.[22] Others have argued that there are ways to use immunization in the presence of such risk, which has been called **stochastic process risk.**[23]

Rebalancing

Another problem with the use of immunization is the effect of the passage of time on the duration of the bonds held and on the duration of the promised cash outflows. As time passes and yields change, these durations can change at different rates so that the portfolio is no longer immunized. This means that the portfolio may need to be rebalanced fairly often.

Here, rebalancing refers to selling some bonds currently held and replacing them with others so that afterward, the duration of the portfolio matches the duration of the promised cash outflows. However, since rebalancing causes the portfolio manager to incur transaction costs, the manager might not want to rebalance whenever the durations do not match, since the costs might outweigh the perceived gains from rebalancing. Ultimately, the bond portfolio manager will have to decide how frequently to rebalance the portfolio, taking into consideration the risk of being unbalanced along with the transaction costs associated with rebalancing.

Choosing Among Many Candidates

Usually, many portfolios have a duration of the requisite length. Which one is the bond portfolio manager to choose? In the example, imagine that in addition to the one-year and three-year bonds, there is a zero-coupon bond having a life of four years (thus, its duration is also four years) that the manager is considering. Now the manager faces a choice of which portfolio to hold, since there are many with the requisite duration of two years. In addition to the one previously described that consisted of just one-year and three-year bonds, there is also one where two-thirds and one-third of the portfolio's funds are invested in one-year bonds and four-year bonds, respectively. (Note how the duration of this portfolio is also two years: $(^2/_3 \times 1) + (^1/_3 \times 4) = 2$.) Furthermore, there are many other candidate portfolios.

One solution is to choose the portfolio with the highest average yield-to-maturity. Here, the yield of each issue is multiplied by the percentage of the portfolio's funds that are invested in that issue. Another solution is to choose the portfolio that most closely resembles a "bullet," or "focused," portfolio, since it has been argued that such a portfolio has less stochastic process risk than any other. Such a portfolio is one where the bonds in it have durations (or, alternatively, terms-to-maturity) most closely matching the duration of the promised outflows. In the example, the portfolio consisting of just one-year and three-year bonds is more focused than the one consisting of the one-year and four-year bonds.

---

[22] See N. Bulent Gultekin and Richard J. Rogalski, "Alternative Duration Specifications and the Measurement of Basis Risk," *Journal of Business* 57, no.2 (April 1984): 241–264. For rebuttals and responses, see G.O. Bierwag, George G. Kaufman, Cynthia M. Latta, and Gordon S. Roberts, "Duration: Response to Critics," *Journal of Portfolio Management* 13, no. 2 (Winter 1987): 48–52; N. Bulent Gultekin and Richard J. Rogalski, "Duration: Response to Critics: Comment," *Journal of Portfolio Management* 15, no. 3 (Spring 1989): 83–87; G.O. Bierwag, George G. Kaufman, Cynthia M. Latta, and Gordon S. Roberts, "Duration as a Measure of Basis Risk: The Wrong Answer at Low Cost—Rejoinder," *Journal of Portfolio Management* 15, no.4 (Summer 1989): 82–85; and N. Bulent Gultekin and Richard J. Rogalski, "Duration as a Measure of Basis Risk: The Wrong Answer at Low Cost—Answer to Rejoinder," *Journal of Portfolio Management* 15, no. 4 (Summer 1989): 86–87.

[23] G. O. Bierwag, George G. Kaufman, and Alden Toevs, "Bond Portfolio Immunization and Stochastic Process Risk," *Journal of Bank Research* 13 (Winter 1983): 282–291; and G.O. Bierwag, George G. Kaufman, and Cynthia M. Latta, "Duration Models: A Taxonomy," *Journal of Portfolio Management* 15, no.1 (Fall 1988): 50–54.

INSTITUTIONAL ISSUES

Surplus Management

Corporate pension funds are established to secure the funding of retirement benefits promised to corporate employees. Therefore, the primary investment objective of these funds is to accumulate sufficient assets, through contributions and investment income, to satisfy all pension obligations on a timely basis.

The management of corporate pension funds has traditionally focused solely on the asset side of the asset-liability equation. Those organizations charged with the oversight of pension funds (often referred to as "plan sponsors") have typically defined their investment policies in terms of seeking maximum returns subject to their tolerance for volatility of returns (see Chapter 24). This philosophy has led many plan sponsors to invest heavily in equity assets, particularly common stocks, based on their perceived superior long-run risk-return characteristics (see Chapter 1).

The foundation of this investment philosophy received a jolt in 1986 when the US Financial Accounting Standards Board issued FAS 87, a directive requiring US corporations to more fully disclose pension obligations on their financial statements beginning in 1989. Prior to FAS 87, corporate reporting on pension obligations was consigned to annual report footnotes. This level of disclosure seemed inadequate, given that pension assets and liabilities would represent the largest items on many corporations' balance sheets if they were reported there, and that annual pension expenses often represent a large portion of a corporation's earnings. FAS 87 was designed to address this deficiency.

FAS 87 requires that US companies report any negative difference between their pension assets and their pension liabilities on their balance sheets as liabilities. (There is no corresponding balance sheet asset if pension assets exceed pension liabilities.) Moreover, the way in which companies state pension expenses on their income statements was redefined. The expense includes costs associated with pension benefits earned in the current year, plus interest on past obligations, plus the amortization of any unfunded liabilities (that is, liabilities not offset by pension assets), less the expected earnings on the pension fund's assets.

As a result of FAS 87, the earnings of US corporations have become sensitive to changes in their pension fund's surplus, which is the difference in value between the fund's assets and liabilities. A significant decrease in pension surplus will result in an earnings reduction, whereas a significant increase can boost earnings. Thus, FAS 87 created for the first time a source of reported earnings variability directly attributable to changes in a pension fund's assets and liabilities.

This new source of earnings variability has caused some companies to emphasize control of pension surplus volatility through a process known as *surplus management*. How does a plan sponsor manage pension surplus? By developing an investment strategy that causes the value of the pension fund's assets to move more closely with the pension fund's liabilities. That is, the plan sponsor tries to "immunize" the pension fund's liabilities by creating an appropriately structured portfolio of assets. In this way, the variability of changes in pension surplus will be reduced, thereby lowering the pension fund's impact on the variability of the corporation's earnings.

To specify the appropriate composition of the pension fund's portfolio that will immunize the fund's pension liabilities, the plan sponsor must determine what factors can cause the value of these liabilities to change. In the short run, when promised pension benefits can be viewed as fixed, only movements in interest rates will alter the value of pension liabilities. FAS 87 mandates that the value of pension liabilities be calculated as the discounted value of pension benefits earned to date by the company's employees (plus, in some cases, projected salary increases for

INSTITUTIONAL ISSUES (continued)

current employees). The discount rate applied to these earned pension benefits is related to current market interest rates. Therefore, as those interest rates fluctuate, so too does the value of a company's pension liabilities. Interest-rate increases reduce the value of pension liabilities, whereas interest-rate declines increase pension liabilities.

As described in the text, a simple means of at least partially immunizing a set of interest-sensitive liabilities is to create a portfolio of bonds whose duration equals that of the liabilities. As interest rates change, the value of the assets will rise and fall more or less in line with the value of the liabilities, maintaining a relatively constant pension surplus.

FAS 87 has given rise to numerous sophisticated strategies designed to reduce pension surplus volatility. To implement these strategies, some plan sponsors have significantly reduced their pension funds' allocations to equity assets and purchased fixed-income securities.

Such shifts in asset allocation have led critics of surplus management to argue that by maintaining large fixed-income investments, pension plans are sacrificing the superior returns available from equity assets. These critics contend that surplus management is shortsighted. If one views pension liabilities on a longer term basis, they are not fixed. Rather, they grow with inflation and worker productivity (which translate into pay raises and higher benefits). Thus, in the long run, equity assets may be more effective in hedging against these changes in pension liabilities than fixed-income investments.

To date, no legislation similar to FAS 87 has been proposed in Canada. However, many observers feel it is only a matter of time before the issue arises here as well.

Two Canadian studies have found that the simple Macauley measure of duration, despite stochastic process risk, explains about 80% of the variability in Government of Canada bond returns. Furthermore, a simple portfolio construction procedure worked as effectively as the bullet portfolio. The simple procedure consisted in first choosing a bond with a maturity equal to the horizon date and then adding a second bond with a longer duration in the appropriate proportions to make the portfolio duration equal to the horizon.[24]

ACTIVE MANAGEMENT

As mentioned earlier, active management of a bond portfolio is based on the belief that the bond market is not perfectly efficient. Such management can involve security selection, where attempts are made at identifying mispriced bonds. Alternatively, it can involve market timing, i.e., attempts to forecast general movements in interest rates. It is also possible for an active portfolio manager to be involved in both security selection and market timing. While there are a large number of methods of actively managing a bond portfolio, some general types of active management can be described.

---

[24] For a discussion of how to select the best immunizing portfolio, see Alexander and Resnick, "Using Linear and Goal Programming to Immunize Bond Portfolios," *Journal of Banking and Finance* 9, no.1 (March 1985): 35–54; I. Fooladi and G. Roberts, "How Effective are Duration-based Bond Strategies in Canada?" *Canadian Investment Review*, II, no. 1 (Spring 1989): 57–62; G.O. Bierwag, I. Fooladi and G. Roberts, "Designing an Immunized Portfolio: Is M-Squared the Key?" Dalhousie University Working Paper, October 1988.

▶ Horizon Analysis

The return on a bond over any given holding period depends on its price at the beginning of the period and its price at the end of the period, as well as its coupon rate. Thus, the return on a bond over a one-year period will depend on the yield structure at the beginning of the year and the yield structure at the end of the year, since the price of the bond at these two points in time will depend on these structures. It follows that possible changes to the beginning-of-period yield structure must be analyzed in order to analyze possible bond returns over a given holding period. Bond portfolio managers who believe they (or their staffs) are able to identify such changes will want to translate their beliefs into action.

One way of doing this is known as **horizon analysis**, where a single holding period is selected for analysis and possible yield structures at the end of the period (that is, at the "horizon") are considered.[25] The possible returns for two bonds—one currently held and one candidate to replace it—are then analyzed. In doing so, neither bond is assumed to default up to the horizon date. In the process of the analysis, the sensitivities of the returns to changes in key assumptions regarding yields are estimated, allowing at least a rough assessment of some of the relevant risks.

Horizon analysis can be viewed as another way of implementing the capitalization-of-income method of valuation that was discussed in Chapter 15. By focusing on the estimated end-of-period price of a bond, it seeks to determine if the current market price is relatively high or low. That is, for a given estimated end-of-period price, a bond will have a relatively high expected return if its current price is relatively low. Conversely, a bond will have a relatively low expected return if its current price is relatively high.

Figure 16.6 represents a page from a standard yield book for bonds with a 4% coupon. As indicated, a 4% bond with ten years remaining to maturity that is currently priced at $67.48 (for ease of exposition, a par of $100 is used here) will have a 9% promised annual yield-to-maturity (or 4.5% semiannually). Five years into the future, such a bond's term-to-maturity will have decreased and the relevant promised yield-to-maturity will probably have changed. Thus, as time passes, the bond might follow a path through the table such as that shown by the dashed line. If so, it would end up at a price of $83.78 at the *horizon* (five years hence), with an 8% promised annual yield-to-maturity (or 4% semiannually).

Over any holding period, a bond's return typically will be affected by both the passage of time and a change in yields. Horizon analysis breaks this into two parts: one due solely to the passage of time, with no change in yields, and the other due solely to a change in yield, with no passage of time. This is illustrated in Figure 16.6. The total price change from $67.48 to $83.78 (or $16.30) is broken into a change from $67.48 to $80.22 (or $12.74), followed by an instantaneous change from $80.22 to $83.78 (or $3.56). The intermediate value is the price the bond would command at the horizon if its promised yield-to-maturity had remained unchanged at its initial level of 9%. The actual price is that which it commands at its actual yield-to-maturity of 8%. In summary, the total price change can be broken into two parts, representing the two effects:

$$\text{Price change} = \text{time effect} + \text{yield change effect.} \tag{16.9}$$

---

[25] See Martin L. Leibowitz, "Horizon Analysis for Managed Bond Portfolios," *Journal of Portfolio Management* 1, no. 3 (Spring (1975): 23–34; and "An Analytic Approach to the Bond Market," in *Financial Analyst's Handbook*, ed. Sumner N. Levine (Homewood, Ill.: Dow Jones-Irwin, Inc., 1975), pp. 226–77.

Figure 16.6

The effect of time and yield change on a 4% coupon bond.
Note: Y_0 and P_0 denote the bond's yield-to-maturity and price at the beginning of the period; Y_H and P_H denote the bond's yield-to-maturity and price at the horizon (that is, at the end of the period); P_A denotes the bond's price at the horizon if its yield had remained at Y_0 = 9%; yields are compounded semiannually.

Yield to Maturity (%)	10 Yrs	9 Yrs	...	5 Yrs	...	1 Yr	0 Yrs
7.00	78.68	80.22		87.53		97.15	100.00
7.50	75.68	77.39		85.63		96.69	100.00
y_H (8.00)	72.82	74.68		(83.78) ← P_H		96.23	100.00
8.50	70.09	72.09		81.98		95.77	100.00
y_O (9.00) P_O	(67.48)	69.60		(83.78) → P_A		95.32	100.00
9.50	64.99	67.22		78.51		94.87	100.00
10.00	62.61	64.92	...	76.83	...	94.42	100.00
10.50	60.34	62.74		75.21		93.98	100.00
11.00	58.17	60.64		73.62		93.54	100.00

SOURCE: William L. Leibowitz, "Horizon Analysis for Managed Bond Portfolios," *Journal of Portfolio Management* 1, no. 3 (Spring 1975): 26.

So far, no account has been taken of the coupon payments to be received before the horizon date. In principle, one should consider all possible uses of such cash flows or at least analyze possible alternative yield structures during the period to determine likely reinvestment opportunities. In practice, this is rarely done. Instead, a single reinvestment rate is assumed and the future value of all coupon payments at the horizon date is determined by compounding each one using this rate.[26]

For example, if $2 is received every six months (as in Figure 16.6) with the first payment occurring six months from now and the last one occurring five years from now, and each payment is reinvested at 4.25% per six months, then the value at the end of five years will be approximately $24.29. Of this amount, $20 can be considered interest (coupon payments of $2 for 10 six-month periods) with the remaining $4.29 being interest on interest.

[26]The longer the horizon, the greater the importance of the size of the reinvestment rate in determining a bond's return. This means that if the investor's horizon is greater than ten years, for example, then alternative reinvestment rates should be considered.

In summary, a bond's overall dollar return has four components—the time effect, the yield change effect, the coupons, and the interest from reinvesting the coupons. In the example, the overall dollar return is

$$\begin{aligned}
\begin{matrix}\text{Overall}\\ \text{dollar return}\end{matrix} &= \begin{matrix}\text{time}\\ \text{effect}\end{matrix} + \begin{matrix}\text{yield}\\ \text{change effect}\end{matrix} + \text{coupons} + \begin{matrix}\text{interest}\\ \text{on coupons}\end{matrix}\\
&= (\$80.22 - \$67.48) + (\$83.78 - \$80.22) + \$20.00 + \$4.29\\
&= \$12.74 + \$3.56 + \$20.00 + \$4.29\\
&= \$40.59.
\end{aligned}$$

This overall dollar return can be converted into an overall rate of return by dividing it by the market price of the bond at the beginning of the period, \$67.48. In doing so, it can be seen that a bond's overall rate of return consists of four components:

$$\begin{aligned}
\begin{matrix}\text{Overall}\\ \text{dollar return}\end{matrix} &= \frac{\$12.74}{\$67.48} + \frac{\$3.56}{\$67.48} + \frac{\$20.00}{\$67.48} + \frac{\$4.29}{\$67.48}\\
&= .1888 + .0528 + .2964 + .0635\\
&= .6015
\end{aligned}$$

or 60.15%. The first term is the return due to the passage of time, the second term is the return due to yield change, the third term is coupon return, and the fourth term is the return due to the reinvestment of the coupon payments.

Since the second term is uncertain, it is important to analyze it further. In the example, a change in yield from 9.0% to 8.0% will result in a change in the market price from \$80.22 to \$83.78. Given 8.0% was the expected yield at the horizon, an expected overall rate of return of 60.15% was computed. By using different end-of-period yields, different overall rates of return can be calculated. Then, with estimates of the probabilities of these yields occurring, a feel for the bond's risk can be obtained. Indeed, it can now be seen why bond portfolio managers devote a great deal of attention to making predictions of future yields.

► Bond Swaps

Given a set of predictions about future bond yields, holding-period returns over one or more horizons for one or more bonds can be estimated. The goal of **bond swapping** is to manage a portfolio actively by exchanging bonds to take advantage of any superior ability to predict such yields.[27] In making a swap, the portfolio manager believes that an overpriced bond is being exchanged for an underpriced bond. Some swaps are based on the belief that the market will correct for its mispricing in a short period of time, whereas other types of swaps are based on a belief that corrections will either never take place or will take place over a long period of time.

There are a large number of categories for classifying swaps, and the distinctions between the categories are often blurred. Nevertheless, many bond swaps can be placed in one of four general categories:

---

[27] Bond swaps should not be confused with interest-rate swaps, where two issuers of debt keep the respective amounts raised but make each other's coupon payments. That is, issuer *A* makes the coupon payments on issuer *B*'s debt, and issuer *B* makes the coupon payments on issuer *A*'s debt, perhaps because *A* has fixed-rate debt and *B* has floating-rate debt. See, for example, Stuart M. Turnbull, "Swaps: A Zero Sum Game?" *Financial Management* 16, no. 1 (Spring 1987):15–21. and Clifford W. Smith, Jr., Charles W. Smithson, and D. Sykes Wilford, *Managing Financial Risk* (New York: Harper & Row, 1990), Chapters 9–12.

1. **Substitution swap:** Ideally, this swap is an exchange of a bond for a perfect substitute or "twin" bond. The motivation here is temporary price advantage, presumably resulting from an imbalance in the relative supply and demand conditions in the marketplace.
2. **Intermarket spread swap:** This type of swap involves a more general movement out of one market component and into another with the intention of exploiting a currently advantageous yield relationship. The idea here is to benefit from a forecasted changing relationship between the two market components. Although such swaps will almost always have some sensitivity to the direction of the overall market, the idealized focus of this type of swap is the spread relationship itself.
3. **Rate anticipation swap:** Such swaps, on the other hand, are geared toward profiting from an anticipated movement in overall market rates.
4. **Pure yield pickup swap:** These swaps are oriented toward yield improvements over the long term, with little heed being paid to interim price movements in either the respective market components or the market as a whole.[28]

Consider a hypothetical portfolio manager who holds some of a 30-year, AA utility bond issue that has a 7% coupon rate. Since these bonds are currently selling at par, their yield-to-maturity is 7%. Now, imagine that there is another 30-year, AA utility bond issue with a 7% coupon rate that is being made available to the manager at a price so that its yield-to-maturity is 7.10%. The manager could exchange a given dollar amount of the currently held bonds for an equivalent dollar amount of the second bond issue in a substitution swap, thereby picking up 10 basis points in yield.

Alternatively, the manager might note that there is a 10-year, AA utility bond issue outstanding that carries a 6% coupon and is priced at par; thus, its yield is 6%. In this case, there is a 100-basis-point yield spread between the currently held 30-year bonds and the 10-year bonds. If the manager feels this spread is too low, then he or she might initiate an intermarket spread swap by exchanging some of the 30-year bonds for an equivalent dollar amount of the 10-year bonds. Since the manager expects the spread to increase in the future, he or she believes the yield on the 10-year bonds will fall. This means the price on these bonds should rise by an abnormal amount, resulting in an abnormally high holding-period return.

Another possibility is that the manager feels that yields in general are going to rise. In such a situation, the manager will recognize that the currently held portfolio is very risky because longer-term bonds generally move downward further in price for a given rise in yields than do shorter-term bonds. Accordingly, the manager might use a rate anticipation swap to exchange a given dollar amount of the 30-year bonds for an equivalent amount of some short-term bonds.

Lastly, the manager might not want to make any predictions about future yields or yield spreads. Instead, he or she might simply note that some 30-year, AA industrial bonds are currently priced to yield 8%. In this case, the manager might want to enter a pure-yield pickup swap, where some of the 7% utility bonds are exchanged for an equivalent dollar amount of the 8% industrial bonds, the motivation being to earn the extra 100 basis points in yield from the industrials.

---

[28] See Sidney Homer and Martin L. Leibowitz, *Inside the Yield Book* (Englewood Cliffs, N.J.: Prentice Hall, 1972) and Chapter 16 in Marcia Stigum and Frank J. Fabozzi, *The Dow Jones-Irwin Guide to Bond and Money Market Investments* (Homewood, Ill.: Dow Jones-Irwin, Inc., 1987).

Contingent Immunization

One method of bond portfolio management that has both passive and active elements is **contingent immunization**. In the simplest form of contingent immunization, the portfolio is actively managed as long as favourable results are obtained. However, if unfavourable results occur, then the portfolio is immediately immunized.

As an illustration, consider the earlier example where the portfolio manager had to come up with $1 000 000 at the end of two years, and the current yield curve was horizontal at 10%. It was explained that the portfolio manager could immunize the portfolio by investing $826 446 in one-year and three-year bonds. However, the portfolio manager may convince the client that the portfolio should be *contingently* immunized with $841 680. This means that the portfolio manager must be certain that the portfolio will be worth at least $1 000 000 at the end of the two years, with any excess going to the client and the manager being compensated accordingly. Equivalently, the portfolio manager must earn a minimum average return of 9% (note that $\$841\ 680 \times 1.09^2 = \$1\ 000\ 000$) over the two years. Here, the client is willing to settle for a return as low as 9% but hopes that the portfolio manager will be able to exceed the 10% return that could have been locked in with an immunized portfolio.

The manager would proceed to manage the portfolio actively by attempting to engage either in selectivity or timing (or both). Perhaps the arrangement with the client is that the status of the portfolio will be reviewed weekly, and yields that are currently available will be determined.

Consider how the review would be conducted after one year has elapsed and the yield curve is still horizontal, but at 11%. First of all, $1 000 000/(1.11) = $900 901 would be needed to immunize the portfolio at that point. Second, the market value of the current portfolio is determined to be $930 000. Now, in this example, the arrangement between the client and portfolio manager is that the manager can continue to manage the portfolio actively as long as it is worth at least $10 000 more than the amount needed for immunization. Since it is worth $930 000, an amount greater than $900 901 + $10 000 = $910 901, the portfolio manager can continue being active. However, if the portfolio were worth less than $910 901, then, according to the agreement, the manager would have immediately immunized the portfolio.

Riding the Yield Curve

Riding the yield curve is a method of bond portfolio management sometimes used by people who, having liquidity as a primary objective, invest in short-term fixed-income securities. One way of investing is simply to purchase these securities, hold them until they mature, and then reinvest them. An alternative way is to ride the yield curve, provided certain conditions exist.

One condition is that the yield curve be upward-sloping, indicating that longer-term securities have higher yields. Another condition is that the investor believes that the yield curve will remain upward-sloping. Given these two conditions, the investor who is riding the yield curve will purchase securities that have a somewhat longer term-to-maturity than desired and then sell them before they mature, thereby capturing some capital gains.

For example, consider an investor who prefers investing in 91-day Treasury bills. Currently, such bills are selling for $98.25 per $100 of face value, yielding 7.14% (($100 – 98.25)/98.25) × (100 × 365/91))) = 7.14%. However, 182-day Treasury bills are currently selling for $96.20, providing a higher yield of 7.92% (($100 – 96.2)/96.2) ×

(100 × 365/182))) = 7.92%. If this investor believes that the yield curve will remain upward-sloping over the next three months, he or she may choose to ride the yield curve for a higher return than would be possible from simply buying and holding 91-day Treasury bills.

If the investor buys and holds the 91-day Treasury bills, then the resulting annualized rate of return will be 7.14% (as calculated above). Alternatively, if the investor buys 182-day Treasury bills and subsequently sells them after 91 days, then the expected selling price will be \$98.25 (note that this is the same as the current price of 91-day bills, since it is assumed that the yield curve will not have changed after 90 days have elapsed). This means that the expected return is

$$((\$98.25 - \$96.20)/\$96.00) \times (100 \times 365/91) = 8.55\%$$

The expected return from riding the yield curve, therefore, is higher. This is because the investor expects to benefit from a decline in yield that is due to the shortening of the maturity of the Treasury bills that were initially purchased and not to a shift in the yield curve.

It should be kept in mind that if the yield curve changes adversely, then this strategy can reduce the investor's return.[29] That is, riding the yield curve is riskier than simply buying securities that mature at the appropriate time. Similarly, there are two transactions necessary (buying and then selling the security) when riding the yield curve, whereas a maturity strategy has only one transaction (buying the security). Thus, there will be larger transaction costs associated with riding the yield curve.

BONDS VERSUS STOCKS

Bonds and stocks are different kinds of securities, with quite different characteristics. Making an investment decision between them should not be based on some simple one-dimensional comparison. In many cases this decision, known as **asset allocation**, will involve investing in both bonds and stocks.[30]

While historical relationships may not be useful for accurately predicting future relationships, it is instructive to examine the average values, standard deviations, and correlations of past stock and bond returns. The US statistics presented in Table 16.3 are based on quarterly excess returns during one time period, 1926–1985, and two subperiods, 1926–1945 and 1946–1985. The Canadian results cover a single time period, 1950–1989. The similarity in the results obtained in both countries is notable with the exception of the correlation coefficient. Based on average returns, stocks appear to have a substantial advantage for the investor with a reasonably long horizon.[31] However, there is good reason

[29] According to the unbiased expectations theory (discussed in Chapter 5), the yield curve would be expected to shift in such a manner that the expected return on both strategies (in the example, buy and hold the 91-day Treasury bills versus buy and sell the 182-day Treasury bills 91 days later) would be the same.

[30] Chapter 24 presents some methods for making the asset allocation decision. For a model of how to measure the interest rate sensitivity of a portfolio consisting of both stocks and bonds, see Martin L. Leibowitz, "Total Portfolio Duration: A New Perspective on Asset Allocation," *Financial Analysts Journal* 42, no. 5 (September/October 1986): 18–29.

[31] Another US study involving simulation found that, based on historical returns, an investor with a 20-year horizon had about a 5% probability of earning less when investing in a common stock index as opposed to investing in a long-term Treasury bond index. For a ten-year horizon the probability was 11%. See Kirt C. Butler and Dale L. Domian, "Risk, Diversification, and the Investment Horizon," *Journal of Portfolio Management* 17, no. 3 (Spring 1991): 42–47.

Table 16.3

Historical Relationships Between Bonds and Stocks in the United States and Canada.

	Stocks	*Bonds*	*Correlation*
1. US Data			
A. 1926–1985:			
Average quarterly excess return	2.20%	0.41%	
Standard deviation	12.39	3.98	
Correlation			0.30
B. 1926–1945:			
Average quarterly excess return	2.94%	1.11%	
Standard deviation	18.68	1.99	
Correlation			0.45
C. 1946–1985:			
Average quarterly excess return	1.83%	0.06%	
Standard deviation	7.54	4.65	
Correlation			0.40
2. Canadian Data[a]			
D. 1950–1989:			
Average quarterly excess return	1.52%	–0.05%	
Standard deviation	8.96	4.48	
Correlation			0.00

[a] Based on annual data.

SOURCES: US data adapted from Meir Statman and Neal L. Ushman, "Bonds Versus Stocks: Another Look," *Journal of Portfolio Management* 13, no. 2 (Winter 1987): 33–38. Canadian data adapted from Melanie Moore, *ScotiaMcLeod's Handbook of Canadian Debt Market Indices: 1947–1990*, ScotiaMcLeod Inc., February 1991.

to believe that the average returns on long-term bonds are not representative of investors' expectations for future returns. The returns show the results obtained by purchasing a long-term bond, holding it for a period of time, and then replacing it with another long-term bond. The total returns include both income and capital gains or losses. During this period, in both countries, bond price changes were negative more often than positive, averaging roughly –1% per year.[32] A better estimate of investors' expectations might be obtained by assuming that the expected price would be as likely to increase as decrease. Expected future returns on bonds might then have been roughly 1% per year (.25% per quarter) higher than shown in the table.

For an investor concerned with month-to-month variation (such as an investor with a possible need for liquidity or with a short horizon), bonds look relatively more attractive than stocks. This can be seen by examining the standard deviation of returns. In this sense, stocks were riskier than bonds during the period and both subperiods. Note that the increased uncertainty concerning the rate of inflation during the postwar subperiod has increased the variability of bond returns.

---

[32] The observation is based on US data through 1985, as reflected in Table 16.3(a). More recent data indicates that bond price changes have more often been positive than negative.

The correlation between stock and bond returns has been low, and during various periods it has had negative values. This indicates that portfolios combining both stocks and bonds can benefit considerably from the resulting diversification. More recently, however, correlations in the US have been positive, due in part to common reactions to changes in inflationary expectations (a phenomenon that does not appear to have occurred in Canada). Consequently, the gains from diversification have recently been reduced. Nevertheless, from the historical record, it seems reasonable to expect that, in the future, bonds will again offer the benefits of diversification.

SUMMARY

1. Like the common stock markets, Canadian and US bond markets appear to be highly, but not perfectly, semistrong-form efficient.
2. For a typical bond, making periodic interest payments and a final principal repayment on a stated date, five bond pricing theorems apply:
   a. If a bond's market price increases, then its yield must decrease; conversely, if a bond's market price decreases, then its yield must increase.
   b. If a bond's yield does not change over its life, then the size of its discount or premium will decrease as its life gets shorter.
   c. If a bond's yield does not change over its life, then the size of its discount or premium will decrease at an increasing rate as its life gets shorter.
   d. A decrease in a bond's yield will raise the bond's price by an amount that is greater in size than the corresponding fall in the bond's price that would occur if there were an equal-sized increase in the bond's yield. (That is, the price-yield relationship is convex.)
   e. The percentage change in a bond's price owing to a change in its yield will be smaller if its coupon rate is higher.
3. Duration is a measure of the "average maturity" of the stream of payments associated with a bond. It is a weighted average of the length of time until the bond's remaining payments are made, with the weights equal to the present value of each cash flow relative to the price of the bond.
4. The duration of a portfolio of bonds is equal to the weighted average of the durations of the individual bonds in the portfolio.
5. A bond portfolio manager can be fairly confident of being able to meet a given promised stream of cash outflows by creating a bond portfolio with a duration equal to the liabilities. This procedure is known as immunization.
6. Problems with immunization include default and call risk, multiple nonparallel shifts in a nonhorizontal yield curve, costly rebalancings, and a wide range of candidate bond portfolios.
7. Active bond management may involve security selection, market timing (where attempts are made to forecast general movements in interest rates), or combinations of the two.
8. Active management strategies include horizon analysis, bond swaps, contingent immunization, and riding the yield curve.

APPENDIX A

EMPIRICAL REGULARITIES IN THE BOND MARKET

Certain empirical regularities in the stock market are well known among investment professionals.[33] The principal regularities observed are the January effect and the day-of-the-week effect. It has been noted in the stock market that returns are higher in January than in any other month and that returns on Mondays are generally negative, while returns on Fridays are generally positive. Because these regularities cannot be explained by any of the currently known asset pricing models, they are referred to as "anomalies." An interesting question to ponder is this: do such regularities also exist in the bond market? One study looked at this question by examining the daily performance from January 1963 through December 1986 of the Dow Jones Composite Bond Average. (This bond index consists of 20 investment-grade US corporate bonds, divided evenly between industrials and utilities.)[34]

THE JANUARY EFFECT

Table 16.4 presents evidence that, as with common stocks, there is a January effect in bonds—that is, on average, corporate bonds have a notably higher return during the month of January than during the other 11 months of the year. Furthermore, this table also shows that this observation was true across all investment-grade (Aaa to Baa) and two speculative-grade (Ba and B) risk classes. Interestingly, the effect is extremely pronounced for the speculative classes.

Table 16.4

Seasonality in Bond Returns.

	Average Return in January	*Average Monthly Return in Other Months*
(a) 1963–1986	4.34%	–.56%
(b) 1963–1979		
Aaa	1.15%	.22%
Aa	1.21	.29
A	1.18	.30
Baa	1.55	.30
Ba	3.32	.27
B	5.09	.36

SOURCE: Susan D. Jordan and Bradford D. Jordan, "Seasonality in Daily Bond Returns," *Journal of Financial and Quantitative Analysis* 26, no. 2 (June 1991): Table 5, p. 281; Eric C. Chang and Roger D. Huang, "Time-Varying Return and Risk in the Corporate Bond Market," *Journal of Financial and Quantitative Analysis* 25, no. 3 (September 1990): Table 1, p. 331.

---

[33] Some of these regularities are discussed in the Appendix to Chapter 17.

[34] Susan D. Jordan and Bradford D. Jordan, "Seasonality in Daily Bond Returns," *Journal of Financial and Quantitative Analysis* 26, no. 2 (June 1991): 269–285. Note that this study did not examine the bond market in order to see whether the "size effect" (observed for common stocks) was present. Hence, only two of the anomalies discussed in the Appendix to Chapter 17 are discussed here.

THE DAY-OF-THE-WEEK EFFECT

Table 16.5 presents US average daily returns for each business day of the week over the period from 1963 to 1986. As with common stocks, the average return on Monday is negative. However, it is also negative for every day except Thursday, and the average returns for all five days are not statistically significantly different from one another.[35] Hence, in contrast to common stocks, the day-of-the-week effect does not appear to exist for corporate bonds.

Table 16.5

Analysis of Daily Return.

Day of Week	*Average Daily Return*
Monday	–.20%
Tuesday	–.93
Wednesday	–.00
Thursday	.44
Friday	–.00

SOURCE: Susan D. Jordan and Bradford D. Jordan, "Seasonality in Daily Bond Returns," *Journal of Financial and Quantitative Analysis* 26, no. 2 (June 1991): Table 5, p. 281.

QUESTIONS AND PROBLEMS

1. A $10 000 face-value pure-discount bond with a ten-year term-to-maturity currently sells so as to produce an 8% yield-to-maturity. What is the bond's price? Calculate the bond's price if its yield rises to 10%; if its yield falls to 5%.
2. Both bonds A and B have $10 000 face values, have 10% coupon rates, and sell with yields-to-maturity of 9%. However, bond A has a 20-year term-to-maturity while bond B has a five-year term-to-maturity. Calculate the prices of the two bonds. Despite having the same yields, why is one bond's price different from the other's?
3. Consider three pure-discount bonds, each with a $1000 face value; 7% yield-to-maturity; and terms-to-maturity of 5, 10, and 20 years, respectively. Calculate each bond's price. Graph the bond's discounts versus their terms-to-maturity. Is the relationship linear? Why?
4. Consider two bonds with 10% coupon rates and $1000 face values. One of the bonds has a term-to-maturity of 4 years, whereas the other has a term-to-maturity of 15 years. Both make annual interest payments. Assuming that yields on the two bonds rise from 10% to 14%, calculate the intrinsic values of the two bonds before and after the change in interest rates. Explain the difference in percentage price changes.
5. Consider a five-year term-to-maturity bond with a $1000 face value and $100 annual coupon interest payments. The bond sells at par. What is the bond's percentage price change if the yield-to-maturity rises to 12%; if it falls to 8%?
6. Consider two bonds, one with 5 years to maturity and the other with 20 years to maturity. Both have $1000 face values and 8% coupon rates (with annual interest payments), and

[35] The returns on Wednesday and Friday are shown to be zero, but this is only because of rounding, as they are slightly negative.

both sell at par. Assume that the yields of both bonds fall to 6%. Calculate the dollar increases in the bonds' prices. What percentage of this increase in each case comes from a change in the present value of the bonds' principals, and what percentage comes from a change in the present value of the bonds' interest payments?

7. Both bonds A and B have $10 000 face values, 8% yields-to-maturity, and ten-year terms-to-maturity. However, bond A has a 10% coupon rate whereas bond B sells at par. (Both make annual interest payments.) If the yields on both bonds decline to 6%, calculate the percentage price changes of the two bonds.
8. Consider a bond selling at its par value of $1000, with six years to maturity and a 7% coupon rate (with annual interest payments). Calculate the bond's duration.
9. If the yield-to-maturity on the bond in Problem 8 increases to 8%, what happens to the bond's duration? Why does this change occur?
10. Why must the duration of a coupon-bearing bond always be less than the time to its maturity date?
11. Liz Fiorello owns a portfolio of four bonds with the following durations and proportions:

Bond	Duration	Proportion
A	4.5 years	.20
B	3.0	.25
C	3.5	.25
D	2.8	.30

What is the duration of Liz's bond portfolio?

12. Rank order the following bonds in terms of duration. Explain the rationale behind your rankings. (You do not have to actually calculate the bonds' durations. Logical reasoning will suffice.)

Bond	Term-to-Maturity	Coupon Rate	Yield-to-Maturity
1	30 years	10.0%	10.0%
2	30	0.0	10.0
3	30	10.0	7.0
4	5	10.0	10.0

13. What impact would you expect the option features of callable bonds and mortgage-backed securities to have on the expected durations of such bonds as opposed to the durations calculated based on the bonds' stated maturity dates?
14. Consider a bond with a 3.5-year duration. If its yield-to-maturity increases from 8.0% to 8.3%, what is the expected percentage change in the price of the bond?
15. The price-yield relationship for a typical bond is convex, opening upward as shown in Figure 16.4. Investment professionals often describe the price-yield relationship of mortgage pass-through securities as being "negatively convex" — that is, a graph of the relationship opens downward. What features of these securities could produce such a relationship?

16. Explain why immunization permits a bond investor to be confident of meeting a given liability on a predetermined future date.
17. What are the advantages and disadvantages of meeting promised cash outflows through cash matching as opposed to duration matching?
18. Why can nonparallel shifts in the yield curve cause problems for an investor seeking to construct an immunized bond portfolio?
19. Beatrice Richardson is planning to offset a single-payment liability with an immunized bond portfolio. Beatrice is considering buying either bonds with durations close to that of the liability (a "bullet" strategy) or bonds with durations considerably above and below that of the liability (a "barbell" strategy). Why is the "bullet" strategy a lower risk strategy for Beatrice? What are its disadvantages relative to the "barbell" strategy?
20. Describe the four components of return on a bond investment over a given holding period.
21. Consider a bond with a $1000 face value, ten years to maturity, and $80 annual coupon interest payments. The bond sells so as to produce a 10% yield-to-maturity. That yield is expected to decline to 9% at the end of four years. Interest income is assumed to be invested at 9.5%. Calculate the bond's four-year holding period return and the four components of that return.
22. Distinguish between a substitution swap and an intermarket swap.
23. Compare contingent immunization to the strategy of using stop orders (discussed in Chapter 2) to protect a portfolio's value.

CFA Exam Questions

24. Bill Peters is the investment officer of a $60 million pension fund. He has become concerned about the big price swings that have occurred lately in the fund's fixed-income securities. Peters has been told that such price behaviour is only natural given the recent behaviour of market yields. To deal with the problem, the pension fund's fixed-income money manager keeps track of exposure to price volatility by closely monitoring bond duration. The money manager believes that price volatility can be kept to a reasonable level as long as portfolio duration is maintained at approximately seven to eight years. Discuss the concepts of duration and convexity and explain how each fits into the price/yield relationship. In the situation described above, explain why the money manager should have used both duration and convexity to monitor the bond portfolio's exposure to price volatility.
25. You have been asked to evaluate two specific bond issues held in your company's pension fund. The characteristics of these are shown in the table on the next page. Note that these bonds are both issued by the same firm.
    a. Using the duration and yield information in the table, compare the price and yield behaviour of the two bonds under each of the following two scenarios:
        - Scenario 1—strong economic recovery with rising inflation expectations; and
        - Scenario 2—economic recession with reduced inflation expectations.
    b. Using the information in the table, calculate the projected price change for Bond B if the yield-to-maturity for this bond falls by 75 basis points.
    c. Describe the shortcoming of analyzing Bond A strictly to call or to maturity. Explain an approach to remedy this shortcoming.

	Bond A (Callable)	Bond B (Noncallable)
Maturity	2002	2002
Coupon	11.50%	7.25%
Current price	125.75	100.00
Yield-to-maturity	7.70%	7.25%
Modified duration to maturity	6.20	6.80
Convexity to maturity	0.50	0.60
Call date	1996	—
Call price	105	—
Yield-to-call	5.10%	—
Modified duration to call	3.10	—
Convexity to call	0.10	—

KEY TERMS

coupon payment
coupon rate
term-to-maturity
yield-to-maturity
convexity
duration
immunization
cash matching
dedicated portfolio
stochastic process risk
horizon analysis
bond swapping
substitution swap
intermarket spread swap
rate anticipation swap
pure yield pickup swap
contingent immunization
riding the yield curve
asset allocation

REFERENCES

1. There have been many tests of efficiency in the bond market. Footnotes 1 through 9 contain citations of several of them. Some of the others are cited in:

   Frank J. Fabozzi and T. Dessa Fabozzi, *Bond Markets, Analysis and Strategies* (Englewood Cliffs, NJ: Prentice Hall, 1989): 300–303. Chapter 4 also contains an extensive discussion of the concepts of convexity and duration.

2. A book that discusses convexity, duration, and many related investment strategies is:

   Gerald O. Bierwag, *Duration Analysis* (Cambridge, MA: Ballinger Publishing, 1987).

3. A method for measuring convexity is given by:

   Robert Brooks and Miles Livingston, "A Closed-Form Equation for Bond Convexity," *Financial Analysts Journal* 45, no. 6 (November/December 1989): 78–79.

4. The concept of duration and its use to measure interest-rate risk was initially developed by:

   Frederick R. Macaulay, *Some Theoretical Problems Suggested by the Movement of Interest Rates, Bond Yields, and Stock Prices in the United States Since 1856* (New York: National Bureau of Economic Research, 1938).

   J. R. Hicks, *Value and Capital* 2d ed. (Oxford, England: Clarendon Press, 1946; the first edition was published in 1939).

Michael H. Hopewell and George G. Kaufman, "Bond Price Volatility and Term to Maturity: A Generalized Respecification," *American Economic Review* 63, no. 4 (September 1973): 4749–4753.

5. For interesting articles describing the development of the concept of duration (as well as immunization), see:

Roman L. Weil, "Macauley's Duration: An Appreciation," *Journal of Business* 46, no. 4 (October 1973): 589–592.

Frank K. Reilly and Rupinder S. Sidhu, "The Many Uses of Bond Duration," *Financial Analysts Journal* 36, no. 4 (July/August 1980): 58–72.

G. O. Bierwag, George G. Kaufman, and Alden Toevs, "Duration: Its Development and Use in Bond Portfolio Management," *Financial Analysts Journal* 39, no. 4 (July/August 1983): 15–35.

6. For alternative methods of calculating duration, see:

Jess H. Chua, "A Generalized Formula for Calculating Bond Duration," *Financial Analysts Journal* 44, no. 5 (September/October 1988): 65–67.

Sanjay K. Nawalkha and Nelson J. Lacey, "Closed-Form Solutions of Higher-Order Duration Measures," *Financial Analysts Journal* 44, no. 6 (November/December 1988): 82–84.

7. For the initial development and subsequent supportive tests of immunization, see:

F. M. Redington, "Review of the Principles of Life-Office Valuations," *Journal of the Institute of Actuaries* 78, no. 3 (1952): 286–315.

Lawrence Fisher and Roman L. Weil, "Coping with the Risk of Interest-Rate Fluctuations: Returns to Bondholders from Naive and Optimal Strategies," *Journal of Business* 44, no. 4 (October 1971): 408–431.

G. O. Bierwag and George G. Kaufman, "Coping with the Risk of Interest-Rate Fluctuations: A Note," *Journal of Business* 50, no. 3 (July 1977): 364–370.

Charles H. Gushee, "How to Immunize a Bond Investment," *Financial Analysts Journal* 37, no. 2 (March/April 1981): 44–51.

G. O. Bierwag, George G. Kaufman, Robert Schweitzer, and Alden Toevs, "The Art of Risk Management in Bond Portfolios," *Journal of Portfolio Management* 7, no. 2 (Spring 1981): 27–36.

Gerald O. Bierwag, *Duration Analysis* (Cambridge, MA: Ballinger Publishing, 1987), Chapter 12.

Donald R. Chambers, Willard T. Carleton, and Richard W. McEnally, "Immunizing Default-Free Bond Portfolios with a Duration Vector," *Journal of Financial and Quantitative Analysis* 23, no. 1 (March 1988): 89–104.

Iraj Fooladi and Gordon S. Roberts, "Bond Portfolio Immunization," *Journal of Economics and Business* 44, no. 1 (February 1992): 3–17.

8. For some interesting articles on the relationship of duration and convexity, see:

Mark L. Dunetz and James M. Mahoney, "Using Duration and Convexity in the Analysis of Callable Bonds," *Financial Analysts Journal* 44, no. 3 (May/June 1988): 53–72.

Bruce J. Grantier, "Convexity and Bond Portfolio Performance: The Benter the Better," *Financial Analysts Journal* 44, no. 6 (November/December 1988): 79–81.

Jacques A. Schnabel, "Is Benter Better: A Cautionary Note on Maximizing Convexity," *Financial Analysts Journal* 46, no. 1 (January/February 1990): 78–79.

Robert Brooks and Miles Livingston, "Relative Impact of Duration and Convexity on Bond Price Changes," *Financial Practice and Education* 2, no. 1 (Spring/Summer 1992): 93–99.

Mark Kritzman, "... About Duration and Convexity," *Financial Analysts Journal* 48, no. 6 (November/December 1992): 17–20.

Gerald O. Bierwag, Iraj Fooladi, and Gordon S. Roberts, "Designing an Immunized Portfolio: Is M-Squared the Key?" *Journal of Banking and Finance* 17, no. 6 (December 1993): 1147–1170.

9. Some of the research that is critical of the use of duration, convexity, and immunization is mentioned in footnote 22. Other critical research includes:

Jonathan E. Ingersoll, Jr., Jeffrey Skelton, and Roman L. Weil, "Duration Forty Years Later," *Journal of Financial and Quantitative Analysis* 13, no. 4 (November 1977): 627–650.

Ronald N. Kahn and Roland Lochoff, "Convexity and Exceptional Return," *Journal of Portfolio Management* 16, no. 2 (Winter 1990): 43–47.

Antti Ilmanen, "How Well Does Duration Measure Interest Rate Risk?" *Journal of Fixed Income* 1, no. 4 (March 1992): 43–51.

10. For a discussion of how to use non-default-free bonds in an immunized portfolio, see:

Gordon J. Alexander and Bruce G. Resnick, "Using Linear and Goal Programming to Immunize Bond Portfolios," *Journal of Banking and Finance* 9, no. 1 (March 1985): 35–54.

G. O. Bierwag and George G. Kaufman, "Durations of Nondefault- Free Securities," *Financial Analysts Journal* 44, no. 4 (July/August 1988): 39–46, 62.

Gerald O. Bierwag, Charles J. Corrado, and George G. Kaufman, "Computing Durations for Bond Portfolios," *Journal of Portfolio Management* 17, no. 1 (Fall 1990): 51–55.

Gerald O. Bierwag, Charles J. Corrado, and George G. Kaufman, "Duration for Portfolios of Bonds Priced on Different Term Structures," *Journal of Banking and Finance* 16, no. 4 (August 1992): 705–714.

11. For a discussion of the effect of call risk on duration (and immunization), see:

Kurt Winkelmann, "Uses and Abuses of Duration and Convexity," *Financial Analysts Journal* 45, no. 5 (September/October 1989): 72–75.

12. For a discussion of how to use duration to measure the risk of foreign bonds, see:

Steven I. Dym, "Measuring the Risk of Foreign Bonds," *Journal of Portfolio Management* 17, no. 2 (Winter 1991): 56–61.

Steven Dym, "Global and Local Components of Foreign Bond Risk," *Financial Analysts Journal* 48, no. 2 (March/April 1992): 83–91.

13. Dedicated bond portfolios and contingent immunization are discussed in:

Martin L. Leibowitz and Alfred Weinberger, "Contingent Immunization—Part I: Risk Control Procedures," *Financial Analysts Journal* 38, no. 6 (November/December 1982): 17–31.

Martin L. Leibowitz and Alfred Weinberger, "Contingent Immunization—Part II: Problem Areas," *Financial Analysts Journal* 39, no. 1 (January/February 1983): 39–50.

Martin L. Leibowitz, "The Dedicated Bond Portfolio in Pension Funds—Part I: Motivations and Basics," *Financial Analysts Journal* 42, no. 1 (January/February 1986): 69–75.

Martin L. Leibowitz, "The Dedicated Bond Portfolio in Pension Funds—Part II: Immunization, Horizon Matching, and Contingent Procedures," *Financial Analysts Journal* 42, no. 2 (March/April 1986): 47–57.

14. For a discussion of horizon analysis and bond swaps, see:

Sidney Homer and Martin L. Leibowitz, *Inside the Yield Book* (Englewood Cliffs, NJ: Prentice Hall, 1972), Chapters 6–7.

Martin L. Leibowitz, "Horizon Analysis for Managed Bond Portfolios," *Journal of Portfolio Management* 1, no. 3 (Spring 1975): 23–34.

Martin L. Leibowitz, "An Analytic Approach to the Bond Market," in *Financial Analyst's Handbook*, ed. Sumner N. Levine (Homewood, IL: Dow Jones-Irwin, 1975), pp. 226–277.

Marcia Stigum and Frank J. Fabozzi, *The Dow Jones-Irwin Guide to Bond and Money Market Investments* (Homewood, IL: Dow Jones-Irwin, 1987), Chapter 16.

15. For discussion of various yield curve strategies, see:

Jerome S. Osteryoung, Gordon S. Roberts, and Daniel E. McCarty, "Ride the Yield Curve When Investing Idle Funds in Treasury Bills?" *Financial Executive* 47, no. 4 (April 1979): 10–15.

Edward A. Dyl and Michael D. Joehnk, "Riding the Yield Curve: Does It Work?" *Journal of Portfolio Management* 7, no. 3 (Spring 1981): 13–17.

Marcia Stigum and Frank J. Fabozzi, *The Dow Jones-Irwin Guide to Bond and Money Market Investments* (Homewood, IL: Dow Jones-Irwin, 1987), pp. 270–272.

Frank J. Jones, "Yield Curve Strategies," *Journal of Fixed Income* 1, no. 2 (September 1991): 43–51.

Robin Grieves and Alan J. Marcus, "Riding the Yield Curve: Reprise," *Journal of Portfolio Management* 18, no. 4 (Summer 1992): 67–76.

16. More on bond investment strategies is contained in:

Ehud I. Ronn, "A New Linear Programming Approach to Bond Portfolio Management," *Journal of Financial and Quantitative Analysis* 22, no. 4 (December 1987): 439–466.

Michael C. Ehrhardt, "A New Linear Programming Approach to Bond Portfolio Management: A Comment," *Journal of Financial and Quantitative Analysis* 24, no. 4 (December 1989): 533–537.

Randall S. Hiller and Christian Schaack, "A Classification of Structured Bond Portfolio Modeling Techniques," *Journal of Portfolio Management* 17, no. 1 (Fall 1990): 37–48.

Frank J. Fabozzi, *Bond Markets, Analysis and Strategies* (Englewood Cliffs, NJ: Prentice Hall, 1993), in particular Chapters 20–22.

17. For an interesting discussion of what mix of bonds and stocks is appropriate for investors, see:

Martin L. Leibowitz and William S. Krasker, "The Persistence of Risk: Stocks Versus Bonds Over the Long Term," *Financial Analysts Journal* 44, no. 6 (November/December 1988): 40–47.

Paul A. Samuelson, "The Judgment of Economic Science on Rational Portfolio Management: Indexing, Timing and Long-Horizon Effects," *Journal of Portfolio Management* 16, no. 1 (Fall 1989): 4–12.

Martin L. Leibowitz and Terence C. Langetieg, "Shortfall Risk and the Asset Allocation Decision: A Simulation Analysis of Stock and Bond Profiles," *Journal of Portfolio Management* 16, no. 1 (Fall 1989): 61–68.

Keith P. Ambachtscheer, "The Persistence of Investment Risk," *Journal of Portfolio Management* 16, no. 1 (Fall 1989): 69–71.

Kirt C. Butler and Dale L. Domian, "Risk, Diversification, and the Investment Horizon," *Journal of Portfolio Management* 17, no. 3 (Spring 1991): 41–47.

18. Pension fund management is discussed in:

Martin L. Leibowitz, "Total Portfolio Duration: A New Perspective on Asset Allocation," *Financial Analysts Journal* 42, no. 5 (September/October 1986): 18–29, 77.

Martin L. Leibowitz and Roy D. Henriksson, "Portfolio Optimization Within a Surplus Framework," *Financial Analysts Journal* 44, no. 2 (March/April 1988): 43–51.

William F. Sharpe, "Liabilities—A New Approach," *Journal of Portfolio Management* 16, no. 2 (Winter 1990): 4–10.

19. Empirical regularities in the bond market have been investigated by:

Eric C. Chang and J. Michael Pinegar, "Return Seasonality and Tax-Loss Selling in the Market for Long-Term Government and Corporate Bonds," *Journal of Financial Economics* 17, no. 2 (December 1986): 391–415.

Eric C. Chang and Roger D. Huang, "Time-Varying Return and Risk in the Corporate Bond Market," *Journal of Financial and Quantitative Analysis* 25, no. 3 (September 1990): 323–340.

Susan D. Jordan and Bradford D. Jordan, "Seasonality in Daily Bond Returns," *Journal of Financial and Quantitative Analysis* 26, no. 2 (June 1991): 269–285.

20. For a Canadian perspective on the topics covered in this chapter, see:

I.J Fooladi, G.S. Roberts and F. Skinner, "Duration for Corporate and Provincial Bonds with Default Risk," *Proceedings*, Administrative Sciences Association of Canada Conference, Lake Louise, June 1993.

E. Z. Prisman and Y. Tian, "Immunization in Markets with Tax-Clientele Effects: Evidence from the Canadian Market," *Journal of Financial and Quantitative Analysis* 29, no. 2 (June 1994).

G. Athanassakos and Y. Tian, "Seasonality in Canadian Government Bond Returns: An Institutional Explanation," *Proceedings*, Administrative Sciences Association of Canada Conference, Halifax, June 1994.

CHAPTER 17

Common Shares

Common shares are easier to describe than fixed-income securities such as bonds but are harder to analyze. Fixed-income securities almost always have a limited life and an upper dollar limit on cash payments to investors. Common shares have neither. Although the basic principles of valuation apply to both, the role of uncertainty is larger for common shares, so much so that it often dominates all other elements in their valuation.

Common shares represent equity, or an ownership position, in a corporation. It is a residual claim, in the sense that creditors and preferred shareholders must be paid as scheduled before common shareholders can receive any payments. In bankruptcy, common shareholders are in principle entitled to any value remaining after all other claimants have been satisfied. (However, in practice courts sometimes violate this principle.)

The great advantage of the corporate form of organization is the **limited liability** of its owners. Common stocks are generally "fully paid and nonassessable," meaning that common shareholders may lose their initial investment, but no more. That is, if the corporation fails to meet its obligations, the shareholders cannot be forced to give the corporation the funds that are needed to pay off the obligations. However, as a result of such a failure, it is possible that the value of a corporation's shares will be negligible. This will result in the shareholders having lost an amount equal to the price previously paid to buy the shares.

THE CORPORATE FORM

A corporation exists only when it has been granted a **charter**, or certificate of incorporation, by the federal government or a provincial government. This document specifies the rights and obligations of shareholders. It may be amended with the approval of the shareholders, perhaps by a majority or two-thirds vote, where each share of stock generally entitles its owner to one vote. Both the initial terms of the charter and the terms of any amendment must also be approved by the jurisdiction in which the corporation is chartered.

Share Certificates

The ownership of a firm's stock has typically been represented by a single certificate, with the number of shares held by the particular investor noted on it. Such a share certificate is usually registered, with the name, address, and holdings of the investor included on the corporation's books. Dividend payments, voting material, annual and quarterly reports, and other mailings are then sent directly to the investor, taking into account the size of his or her holdings.

Shares of stock held by an investor may be transferred to a new owner with the assistance of either the issuing corporation or, more commonly, its designated **transfer agent**. This agent cancels the old share certificate and issues a new one in its place, made out to the new owner. Frequently a **registrar** will make sure that the cancellation and issuance of certificates has been done properly. Usually banks and trust companies act as transfer agents and registrars. Many shareholders have chosen to avoid these rather cumbersome procedures. Instead, clearing arrangements (discussed in Chapter 3) are used to substitute computerized records for embossed certificates.

► Voting

Since an owner of a share of common stock is one of the owners of a corporation, he or she is entitled to vote on matters brought up at the corporation's annual meeting and to vote for the corporation's directors. Any owner may attend and vote in person, but most choose instead to vote by **proxy**. That is, the incumbent directors and senior management typically solicit all the shareholders, asking each one to sign a proxy statement. Such a statement is a power of attorney authorizing the designated party listed on the statement to cast all of the investor's votes on any matter brought up at the meeting. Occasionally, desired positions on specific issues may be solicited on the proxy statement. However, most of the time the positions held by the incumbents are made known with the proxy solicitation. Since the majority of votes are generally controlled by the incumbents via proxy statements, the actual voting turns out to be perfunctory, leaving little if any controversy or excitement.[1]

► Proxy Fight

Once in a while, however, a **proxy fight** develops. Insurgents from outside the corporation solicit proxies to vote against the incumbents, often in order to effect a takeover of some sort. Shareholders are deluged with literature and appeals for their proxies. The incumbents often win, but the possibility of a loss in such a skirmish tends to curb activities clearly not in the shareholders' best interests.

When proposals are to be voted on, the number of votes given an investor equals the number of shares held. Thus, when a yes or no vote is called for, anyone controlling a majority of the shares can ensure that the outcome he or she favours will receive a majority of the votes. When directors are to be elected, however, there are two types of voting systems that can be used, one of which does not give a majority owner complete control of the outcome. This type of voting system is known as a **cumulative voting system**, whereas the type of voting system that does allow a majority owner to control the outcome completely is known as a **majority voting system**.

Under both systems, the winners of the election are those candidates who have received the highest vote totals. Thus, if six candidates were running for the three directorships, the three receiving the largest number of votes would be elected.

Majority Voting System

With both voting systems, a shareholder receives a total number of votes that is equal to the number of directors to be elected times the number of shares owned. However, with the majority voting system, the shareholder may only give any one candidate, as a maximum, a number of votes equal to the number of shares owned. This means that in a situation where three directors are to be elected, a shareholder with 400 shares would have 1200 votes but

---

[1] For more information on proxies, see Paul Jessup and Mary Bochnak, "Exercising Your Rights: How to Use Proxy Material," *AAII Journal* 14, no. 9 (October 1992): 8–11.

could give no more than 400 of these votes to any one candidate. Note that if there are a total of 1000 shares outstanding and one shareholder owns (or has proxies for) 501 shares, then he or she can give 501 votes to each of the three candidates he or she favours. In doing so, this shareholder will be certain they are elected, regardless of how the remaining 499 shares are voted. The majority shareholder's candidates would each have 501 votes, whereas the *most* any other candidate could receive is 499 votes. Thus, with a majority voting system, a shareholder owning (or controlling with proxies) one share more than 50% can be certain of electing all the candidates he or she favours.

Cumulative Voting System

The cumulative voting system differs from the majority voting system in that a shareholder can cast his or her votes in any manner. As a result, a minority shareholder can be certain of having some representation on the board of directors, provided the number of shares owned is sufficiently large. In the previous example, the minority owner of the 400 shares could cast all his or her 1200 votes for one candidate. Imagine that this owner wanted director A to be elected, but the majority owner of 501 shares wanted candidates B, C, and D to be elected. In this situation, the minority shareholder could give all 1200 votes to A and be certain that A would be one of the three directors elected, regardless of what the majority shareholder did. If the majority owner held the remaining 600 shares, he or she would have 1800 votes. There is no way that candidate A, favoured by the minority shareholder, can come in lower than second place in the vote totals. This is because A will receive 1200 votes, and there is no way that the 1800 votes of the majority shareholder can be cast to give more than one of his or her favoured candidates a vote total in excess of 1200. Thus, the minority shareholder can be certain that A will be elected, whereas the majority shareholder can be certain that only 2 of his or her favourites will be elected.

In general, the formula for determining the minimum number of shares a shareholder must own in order to be able to elect a certain number of candidates under a cumulative voting system is

$$n = \left(\frac{ds}{D + 1}\right) + 1 \tag{17.1}$$

where:

n = the minimum number of shares that must be owned,

d = the number of directors the shareholder wants to be certain of electing,

s = the number of shares outstanding, and

D = the number of directors to be elected.

Thus, the minimum number of shares a shareholder needs in order to be certain of electing one director when three are to be elected and there are 1000 shares outstanding is $[(1 \times 1000)/(3 + 1)] + 1 = 251$. Since the minority shareholder in the example owned 400 shares, he or she is certain of being able to elect one director. Note that the minimum number of shares that must be owned in order to be certain of electing two directors is $[(2 \times 1000)/(3 + 1)] + 1 = 501$. The minimum number owned to be certain of electing all three directors is $[(3 \times 1000)/(3 + 1)] + 1 = 751$.

In summary, the cumulative voting system gives minority shareholders the right to have some representation on the board of directors, provided the number of shares owned is sufficiently large. In contrast, the majority voting system does not give the minority shareholder the right to such representation, even if he or she owns 49.9% of the shares.

The voting system that a corporation decides to use depends not only on the desires of the corporate founders but also on the jurisdiction in which the firm is incorporated. Under Alberta, British Columbia, Ontario or federal incorporation, cumulative voting is permitted providing there are specific provisions in the company's articles or bylaws.

► Takeovers

Periodically, a firm or a wealthy individual who is convinced that the management of a corporation is not fully exploiting its opportunities will attempt a **takeover**. This is frequently done with a **tender offer** being made by a **bidder** to a **target firm**.[2] Before this offer is announced, a small number of the target firm's shares are usually acquired by the bidder in the open market through the use of brokers (if the firm's shares are traded in Ontario then once 10% of the stock has been acquired, the bidder becomes an "insider" under the Ontario Securities Act and must report all further trades to the Ontario Securities Commission).

Then, in the bidder's quest to acquire a substantial number of the target's shares, the bid is announced to the public. Advertisements to purchase shares are placed in the financial press, and material describing the bid is mailed to the target's shareholders. The bidder generally offers to buy, at a stated price, some or all shares offered ("tendered") by the current shareholders of the target. This buying offer is usually contingent on the tender of a minimum number of shares by the target's shareholders by a fixed date. When the buying offer is first made, the offered price ("tender price") is generally set considerably above the current market price, although the offer itself usually leads to a subsequent price increase.

Management of the target firm frequently responds to tender offers with advertisements, mailings, and the like, urging its shareholders to reject the bidder's offer. Sometimes a **white knight** will be sought: another firm that is favourably inclined towards current management will be invited to make a better offer to the target's shareholders. Another type of response by management is to pay **greenmail** to the bidder, meaning that any shares held by the bidder will be bought by the target firm at an above-market price. Still another type of response is for management of the target firm to issue a tender offer of its own, known as a **repurchase offer**, where the firm offers to buy back some of its own stock. (Occasionally repurchase offers are made by firms that have not received tender offers from outside bidders.) Other types of corporate defences include the **Pac-Man defence**, where the initial target turns around and makes a tender offer for the initial acquirer, the **crown jewel defence**, where the target sells its most attractive assets to make the firm less attractive, and the use of **poison pills**, where the target gives its shareholders certain rights that can be exercised only in the event of a subsequent takeover and that, once exercised, will be extremely onerous to the acquirer.

---

[2] Another form of a takeover is a **merger**. A merger occurs when two firms combine their operations, the result being that only one firm exists. Mergers usually are negotiated by the management of the two firms. Tender offers differ in that the management of the bidder makes a direct appeal to the shareholders of the target firm for their shares. Tender offers also differ in that afterward both firms will still exist, because most tender offers are not for all the shares of the target. **Management buyouts** are a special kind of tender offer, where the current management of the firm uses borrowed funds to buy the company. (Hence they are a type of **leveraged buyout**. LBOs can be executed by anyone, including incumbent management.)

Ownership Versus Control

Much has been written about the effects of the separation of ownership and control of the modern corporation.[3] This separation gives rise to what is known as a principal-agent problem. In particular, shareholders can be viewed as principals who hire management to act as their agents. The agent is to make decisions that maximize shareholder wealth as reflected in the firm's stock price. No problem would exist if shareholders could monitor the managers without cost, since the shareholders would then be capable of determining for certain whether or not management had acted in their best interests. However, monitoring is not costless, and complete monitoring of every decision is, practically speaking, impossible.[4] As a result some, but not complete, monitoring is done. This gives management a certain degree of latitude in making decisions and leaves open the possibility that some decisions will be made that are not in the shareholders' best interests.[5] However, the possibility of a proxy fight or tender offer provides at least some check on such decisions.

To align the interests of management with their own, shareholders frequently offer certain incentives to management. An example is the use of stock options. These options are given to certain high-level managers and allow them to purchase a specified number of shares at a stated price (often above the market price when the options are initially issued) by a stated date. This motivates managers to make decisions that will increase the stock price of the firm as much as possible. Furthermore, given their relatively long initial lifespan (in comparison with listed options, discussed in Chapter 20), stock options implicitly exert pressure on management to take a long-term view in making decisions.

Corporate Governance

Conflicts between corporate managements and shareholders surfaced as a major public policy issue in the 1980s. The potentially adversarial principal-agent relationship between corporation owners and managers has long been recognized. In the last decade, however, two major developments brought this issue to greater prominence.

First, corporate managements, responding to a wave of hostile corporate takeovers, instituted various defensive strategies such as poison pill provisions, the sale of key corporate assets, and staggered board of directors terms. These defences were designed to prevent the target companies from being acquired easily, thereby protecting the jobs of existing management. Indeed, they appear to have had the intended result of making those companies worth less to prospective acquirers. However, they also reduced the value of the companies to their existing shareholders.

---

[3] See, for example, Michael C. Jensen and William H. Meckling, "Theory of the Firm: Managerial Behavior, Agency Costs and Ownership Structure," *Journal of Financial Economics* 3, no. 4 (October 1976): 305–360; Eugene F. Fama, "Agency Problems and the Theory of the Firm," *Journal of Political Economy* 88, no. 2 (April 1980): 288–307; Eugene F. Fama and Michael C. Jensen, "Separation of Ownership and Control," *Journal of Law and Economics* 26 (June 1983): 301–325; Eugene F. Fama and Michael C. Jensen, "Agency Problems and Residual Claims," *Journal of Law and Economics* 26 (June 1983): 327–349; the entire issues of vol. 11 (April 1983) and vol. 20 (January/March 1988) of the *Journal of Financial Economics*; and Michael C. Jensen, "Eclipse of the Public Corporation," *Harvard Business Review* 89, no. 5 (September-October 1989): 61–74.

[4] An example of monitoring is having the firm's financial statements independently audited.

[5] For example, management may decide to procure lavishly furnished offices and an executive jet when the conduct of business suggests that these actions are not merited. Furthermore, management may invest in negative net present value investment projects when the firm has "free cash flow" instead of paying it to the shareholders. See Michael C. Jensen, "Agency Costs of Free Cash Flow, Corporate Finance and Takeovers," *American Economic Review* 76, no. 2 (May 1986): 323–329.

Second, large shareholders came to realize that they wielded considerable corporate voting power. The growth of institutional investors has concentrated corporate ownership in the hands of a relatively few organizations. (See the Institutional Issues discussion in Chapter 1.) The resources of these large organizations enabled them to actively oppose management decisions that diminished the value of their investments. *Corporate governance*, a particularly bureaucratic sounding term, has become the catchall description for institutional investor efforts to influence the fundamental business policies of corporate managements.

Until recently, the attitude of most company managements toward shareholders was simply, "If you don't like the way we run the company, then sell our stock and quit complaining." Institutional investors, however, came to realize that they had nowhere else to go. For example, they place hundreds of billions of dollars in portfolios designed to track major stock markets (see Chapter 24). As a result, they effectively hold permanent positions in all large corporations. Corporate governance (or "shareholder rights") activities expressed institutional investors' desire to stand and fight for their interests.

► Shareholders' Equity

Par Value

When a corporation is first chartered, it is authorized to issue up to a stated number of shares of common stock, each of which will often carry a specified **par value**. Legally, a corporation may be precluded from making payments to common shareholders if doing so would reduce the balance sheet value of shareholders' equity below the amount represented by the par value of outstanding stock. For this reason the par value is typically low relative to the price for which the stock is initially sold. Some corporations issue no-par shares (if so, a stated value must be recorded in place of the par value).

When shares are initially sold for more than their par value, the difference may be carried separately on the corporation's books under shareholders' equity. Frequently, the entry is for "capital contributed in excess of par value" or "paid-in capital." The par value of the stock is carried in a separate account, generally entitled "common stock," with the amount equal to the number of shares outstanding times the par value per share (for no-par shares, the stated value).

Book Value

With the passage of time, a corporation will generate income, much of which is paid out to creditors (as interest) and shareholders (as dividends). Any remainder is added to the amount shown as cumulative retained earnings on the corporation's books. The sum of the cumulative retained earnings and other entries (such as "common stock" and "capital contributed in excess of par value") under shareholders' equity is the **book value of the equity**. The **book value per share** is obtained by dividing the book value of the equity by the number of shares outstanding.

Treasury Shares

Typically, a corporation issues only a part of its authorized stock. Some of the remainder may be specifically reserved for outstanding options, convertible securities, and so on. If a corporation wishes to issue new stock in excess of the amount originally authorized, the charter must be amended. This requires approval by both the chartering jurisdiction and the shareholders.

INSTITUTIONAL ISSUES

Corporate Governance in Canada

By Jeffrey MacIntosh

Corporate governance seems to have blossomed into the fashion of the decade. Weighty reports on corporate governance have been issued in the United Kingdom, the United States and now, with the Toronto Stock Exchange's report "Where Were the Directors?", in Canada as well. Yet, the curious thing about all this interest is that there doesn't seem to be any compelling evidence that reform is necessary. Actually, Canada's corporate governance system has never functioned more effectively than it does today.

While there are always improvements that can be made, it is more likely that these improvements will come from the market than from regulators, or even from blue chip panels like the TSE Committee on Corporate Governance, which released a draft report, commonly referred to as the "Dey Report," after committee chairman Peter Dey. In fact, it is possible the report will do more harm than good.

The only solid piece of empirical evidence that appears to have inspired current concerns about corporate governance is the number of well-publicized failures of large public, mainly financial, companies.[6] I use the word "appeared" because it is not at all clear that the current popular interest in corporate governance is anything more than a passing fad that will soon disappear once again into the catacombs of law and management school lecture halls.

But suppose these failures do lie at the root of current interest. Are they evidence of a systemic problem? Characterizing the entire corporate governance system by its failures is wrong. No human system has yet been invented where the rate of failure is zero. For example, it would obviously be desirable to eliminate bank robbery completely. Regulators might be able to do this by requiring that every bank branch be built like Fort Knox, with armed guards at the ready and bomb-proof vaults. But could we afford to do this? The answer is obviously no. Carrying on the business of banking would become horrendously expensive.

Regulation that seeks to completely eliminate corporate failure is not cost-effective regulation. All regulation is costly, due to either the direct or opportunity costs of compliance. The question must then always be whether additional regulation produces at least as much wealth as it costs to implement.

Regrettably, regulators have not always pursued the goal of cost-effective regulation because they almost always have an incentive to err on the side of too much regulation. When a well-publicized scandal or failure occurs, particularly in the financial arena, in which public understanding of institutions and processes is poor, they are often perceived by the press and the public as the product of systemic failure. The blame is laid squarely at the foot of the regulators, who are presumed to have been lax, ineffective and incompetent, even though the scandal could have been caused by determinedly dishonest individuals pulling the wool over the eyes of perfectly capable regulators. Small wonder that regulators like to play it safe with financial markets.

But is the system of corporate governance in need of repair? A good starting place in answering this question is to examine historical returns to shareholders in Canadian companies. Between 1926 and 1987, investors holding all stocks in the

---

[6] It is not at all clear the special problems of governing financial companies have tremendous relevance for commercial companies. Colin Carlton, "Risk and Return in Canada's Capital Markets: A Historical Perspective," *Canadian Investment Review* 2, no. 1 (1989).

TSE 300 Total Return Index realized compound annual (nominal) returns of 10.6%, compared to 9.6% per annum from holding securities in the S&P 500 Index in the United States.[7] From 1950 to 1987, investors holding all TSE 300 firms realized 11.15% per annum.[8] In both countries, smaller capitalization firms have done even better.[9]

These returns certainly do not tell us that all companies in Canada perform well or that management has never acted stupidly. What they suggest is that the system is not fundamentally broken. Investing in Corporate Canada has been highly profitable. Buy-and-hold investors in common stocks have historically earned enviable returns, both on a nominal and a real basis. Therefore, those who claim to have bright new ideas about how to improve Corporate Canada must meet a high standard of proof.

These results also suggest the power of capital markets in protecting shareholder interests. Investors in Canadian companies have done somewhat better than investors in US companies, despite important differences that might lead us to believe that Canadian companies should be more poorly managed. These include:

CONTROL BY A FEW. While the vast majority of US publicly held companies are widely held, the vast majority in Canada have a controlling shareholder. Where there is a controlling shareholder, there is both the incentive and the means to divert wealth from the minority to the controller, whether by transfer pricing arrangements or sweetheart deals with related companies (or the controllers themselves), discriminatory treatment of minority shareholders or other means. In Canada this danger is further exacerbated by the small number of wealthy families like the Bronfmans, who control an astonishingly large share of publicly traded equity.

THE HAROLD BALLARD SYNDROME. Hostile takeovers are viewed by many economists as perhaps the most important control over management's poor performance. An acquirer of a poorly performing company has an opportunity to displace the old managers, install more efficient ones, and reap handsome gains. Clearly, when there is a controlling shareholder unwilling to sell a hostile takeover becomes difficult or impossible. However, controlling shareholders have a greater incentive and ability to discipline managers when performance is poor. So a real difference arises only when we run into the "Harold Ballard Syndrome," in which an inefficient controlling shareholder rejects offers simply to wield power. While it is unclear how many Harold Ballards there are in Canada, the prevalence of public companies with controlling shareholders suggests that corporate control markets are a less effective tool for disciplining managers in Canada than in the United States.

WORK FOR KEEPS. Product markets may also discipline managers, if only because managers typically lose their jobs in bankruptcy. There is a lot of evidence that Canadian product markets are less competitive and, therefore, create less managerial discipline.

COMPETITIVE MANAGERIAL LABOUR MARKETS. Managers will tend to manage more capably for fear of being fired or of diminishing their future prospects at other firms. It's difficult to know whether the pool of managerial talent is far less deep in Canada than in the United States on a per capita basis, but various world competitiveness reports have ranked Canadian managers below those in the United States. Less

---

[7] James E. Hatch and Robert W. White, *Canadian Stocks, Bonds, Bills and Inflation: 1950–1987* (Toronto: The Research Foundation of The Institute of Chartered Financial Analysts, 1989).

[8] For example, between 1973 and 1967, small cap issuers earned 6.1% per annum while TSE 300 firms earned only 2.9% per annum. See footnote 6.

[9] This is likely true for stocks listed on other exchanges. See Carlton in footnote 6.

competition for managerial jobs in Canada will, therefore, force less discipline on management than in the United States.

Therefore, assuming that the risk of investing in Canadian companies is higher than that of investing in US companies (although evidence for TSE companies suggests otherwise),[10] investors have apparently been compensated with higher returns for holding these risky investments.

That's not to suggest that all risks are always appropriately discounted. Studies on particular phenomena, such as the issuance of non-voting shares and stock splits, indicates there are a larger number of inefficiencies in specific areas of Canadian capital markets than in the United States. Nonetheless, the point is that higher risks of opportunistic behaviour by those running a company do not necessarily require regulation if the risks can be priced by the market.

Consider that while tremendous changes in regulation have been adopted over the past three decades — always in the interests of protecting investors — real returns have steadily declined since the 1950s. The average real return of Canadian equities was 8.34% during the 1950s, 6.27% in the 1970s, 4.88% in the 1980s and 3.85% between 1980 and 1987. Over the past 20 years, an abundance of regulations have been implemented from takeover bid and insider trading legislation to more mandatory disclosure. Of course, other factors, such as unexpected inflation, have likely played a role in the falling off of real returns. But it is, at the very least, interesting to note that investors in the 1950s appear to have done very nicely without all of these regulatory reforms.

At the heart of the Dey Report is the recommendation that a majority of directors on a company's board be "unrelated" to the company, and that the majority (and in some cases all) of the directors on various committees be unrelated. This is based on the premise that objective guidance on the running of a company can improve overall performance.

Yet the report presents no systematic evidence to suggest that this, or any other proposal for reform, is necessary. In fact, studies on the role of independent directors over the past three decades, both in Canada and the United States, have cast considerable doubt on the effectiveness of independent directors. There is some recent US evidence that independent directors may improve decision-making in crisis situations but this evidence falls considerably short of supporting the Dey Report recommendation. Indeed, performance may be at risk. Genuinely unrelated directors will not, for obvious reasons, be in the same line of business as the company whose board the directors sit on. This will eliminate conflicts of interest, but how much useful knowledge will these individuals bring to the table? Will they understand, as well as the insiders, what is optimal or even feasible for the company? There is a very real concern about whether ceding to such individuals a primary role in the stewardship of the company is a wise thing to do.

And, with Canada's small pool of directorial talent, is it even possible for a majority of public companies to comply with the recommendation without exhausting the pool of qualified candidates? Implementing the recommendation, therefore, is not without its cost.

The irony is that calls for reform, whether in the UK Cadbury Report, the US Wheat Report or Canada's Dey Report, come at a time when the system of corporate governance has never functioned better, and will continue to improve, for seven reasons:

1. The increasing activism of institutional investors has meant that direct shareholder oversight of management has greatly increased. As markets further institutionalize, this trend will continue.

[10] See footnote 6.

INSTITUTIONAL ISSUES (continued)

2. With advances in information technology, information about various companies can be collected, pooled, and analyzed at a far lower cost than ever before. The cost of monitoring managers will continue to decline.
3. Corporate control markets are increasingly international in scope, due in part to the comparative ease with which acquirers may obtain information about foreign targets, as well as the easing of regulatory restrictions.
4. Product markets are also becoming increasingly global, putting much greater competitive pressure on managers.
5. Market segmentation is declining, which exposes domestic securities issuers to greater competition for funding.
6. It is likely that the managerial labour markets will also become less segmented, putting more pressure on domestic managers.
7. Over the past 20 years, financial economists have developed sophisticated techniques for assessing corporate performance, particularly "event study methodology," which enables economists to investigate the effects of particular corporate events or transactions on share price. These new techniques allow for a better assessment of managerial performance.

The future of corporate governance in Canada is a bright one. Increasing regulatory involvement will only tend to dampen, rather than enliven, the evolution of corporate monitoring mechanisms. This is not to argue that markets should be completely unregulated; only that further regulation should be adopted with caution, based on proper evidence. At the end of the day, the driving force behind the modern public company has much more to do with Adam Smith's invisible hand than with the visible and often clumsy hand of regulation.

SOURCE: Jeffrey MacIntosh, "If It Ain't Broke ...," *Canadian Investment Review VII*, no. 4 (Winter 1994/95). Reprinted with permission of the *Canadian Investment Review*.

When a corporation repurchases some of its own shares, either in the open market through the services of a broker or with a tender offer, the shares may be "held in the treasury." Such **treasury shares** do not carry votes or receive dividends and are equivalent economically (though not legally) to unissued shares.

A major US study of over 1300 stock repurchases found that nearly 90% of the repurchases analyzed were executed in the open market, with the remainder being "self-tender offers."[11] Two types of self-tender offers occurred with approximately equal frequency. The first type was a "fixed-price" self-tender offer, where the corporation makes an offer to repurchase a stated number of shares at a set, predetermined price. The second type was a "Dutch-auction" self-tendered offer, where the corporation again makes an offer to repurchase a stated number of shares, but at a price that is determined by inviting existing shareholders to submit offers to sell. The ultimate repurchase price is the lowest offered price at which the previously stated number of shares can be repurchased from those shareholders that have submitted offers.[12]

---

[11] Robert Comment and Gregg A. Jarrell, "The Relative Signalling Power of Dutch-Auction and Fixed-Price Self-Tender Offers and Open-Market Share Repurchases," *Journal of Finance* 46, no. 4 (September 1991): 1243–1271.

[12] It should be noted that whereas there were similar numbers of fixed-price and Dutch-auction tender offers, the Dutch-auction method is becoming increasingly popular, particularly among larger corporations.

Figure 17.1

Abnormal stock price behaviour around repurchase announcements.

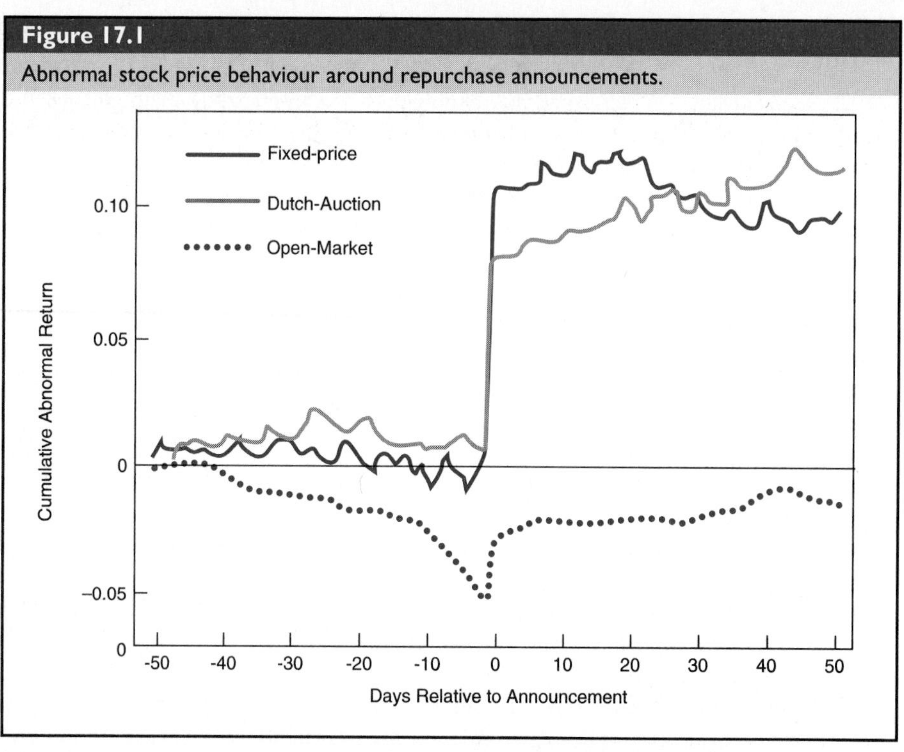

SOURCE: Robert Comment and Gregg A. Jarrell, "The Relative Signalling Power of Dutch-Auction and Fixed-Price Self-Tender Offers and Open-Market Share Repurchases," *Journal of Finance* 46, no. 4 (September 1991): 1254.

Figure 17.1 shows the average stock price behaviour surrounding the announcement date for the three types of stock repurchases just mentioned. For each repurchase, the stock's "abnormal" return was determined by relating daily returns on the stock to the corresponding returns on the stock market index. This was done for the 50-day period immediately prior to the repurchase announcement and the 50-day period immediately following it. These abnormal returns were averaged across firms for each day relative to the announcement and then cumulated across time. The figure shows that open-market repurchases are typically made after the stock price has had an abnormal decline. However, fixed-price and Dutch-auction repurchases are made after a period of fairly normal returns. Also of interest is the observation that the stock price jumped upward on the announcement of the repurchase offer for all three types. (The average size of the abnormal return on the announcement date was 11% for fixed-price, 8% for Dutch-auction, and 2% for open-market repurchases.) Finally, after the repurchase offer expired, the stock price did not tend to fall back to its preannouncement level.

Interestingly, another study found that investors could form profitable investment strategies to take advantage of the observed abnormal return associated with the announcement of a stock repurchase.[13] Specifically, the strategy involves fixed-price self-

---

[13] Such findings are inconsistent with the notion of efficient markets, and hence can be considered an "anomaly." See Josef Lakonishok and Theo Vermaelen, "Anomalous Price Behavior Around Repurchase Tender Offers," *Journal of Finance* 45, no. 2 (June 1990): 455–477. The Appendix discusses several other anomalies uncovered by researchers.

tender offers where the stock is purchased by the investor in the open market shortly before the offer's expiration date if it is selling at least 3% below the repurchase price. Then the investor tenders the stock to the firm on the expiration date. If the repurchase is oversubscribed (meaning that more shares are submitted for repurchase than the corporation has indicated it will buy), then the number of shares that the corporation does not buy are sold in the marketplace shortly after the expiration date. The result is that for an investment of less than a week, this strategy will generate an abnormal return of more than 9%.

Why do firms repurchase their stock? Previously it was mentioned that one motive was to repel a takeover attempt. Two other explanations have been offered. First, management may be attempting to send a signal to the shareholders (and the public) that the corporation's stock is undervalued in the marketplace. Second, it may be beneficial taxwise to the current shareholders for the firm to use excess cash to repurchase stock instead of using it to pay a cash dividend.

For example, consider a shareholder who bought 10 shares of stock at $40 per share that are now worth $50 per share, resulting in an unrealized capital gain of $10 per share, or $100 in total. Furthermore, the shareholder could receive a $10 per share cash dividend from the firm as part of a general disbursement of excess cash. As a result, the stock price will drop $10 per share, removing the capital gain, but all of this dividend will be treated as taxable income to the shareholder. Alternatively, the corporation could spend the same amount to repurchase its stock. If the shareholder tenders his or her *pro rata* share, then the investor will receive $100 for two shares of stock (= $100 cash dividend/$50 share price, assuming perfect markets) and have to pay capital gains on only the amount of $100 that exceeds the $80 (= 2 shares x $40) cost of the two shares that were repurchased. Hence the shareholder would have to pay capital gains taxes on only $20 or the $100 at that time but would have unrealized capital gains of $10 per share on the eight shares still owned (as the stock price would remain at $50 per share), upon which capital gains taxes will have to be paid at some later date when they are sold. Thus, the shareholder benefits from a repurchase in two ways, in that a *smaller* amount is taxed at a capital gains tax rate, which is potentially a *lower* rate than the ordinary income tax rate.

Restricted Shares

Some corporations issue two or more classes of common shares, one or more of which may be restricted. **Restricted shares** are defined under the Ontario Securities Act as equity shares that are not common shares. Equity shares, in turn, are defined as shares of a company that carry a residual right to participate to an unlimited degree in the earnings of the issuing corporation and in its assets upon liquidation. The important feature of this definition is the fact that they participate in the earnings and assets. Common shares are those with unrestricted voting rights per share that are not less than the voting rights of any other outstanding issue.

The Act goes on to recognize three types of restricted shares:

i. Restricted voting shares are those that carry a right to vote that is subject to some restriction on the number or percentage of shares that may be voted by the owner.
ii. Subordinate voting shares are those that carry a right to vote, where there is another class of shares outstanding that carry a greater right to vote.
iii. Non-voting shares are those that carry no right to vote (or a right to vote in certain limited circumstances).

Subordinate and non-voting shares frequently have a preferred position over the voting shares in regard to dividends (and sometimes in liquidation). These shares are unlike preferred shares in that they participate in the earnings of the corporation and do not have a prescribed dividend.

At the end of 1995, there were 160 issues listed on the Toronto Stock Exchange that involved restricted shares. Of these, 86 were subordinate voting, 63 were non-voting, 10 were restricted or limited voting, and one was not classified. Ownership of Canadian corporations is closely held, so the issuance of restricted or non-voting shares is seen as a means of raising additional equity capital without diluting control. Their existence has raised concerns that concentrated voting power with a low investment in the corporation could lead to abuse of other shareholders by the owners of the control block(s). One area of particular concern has been the distribution of the control premium in the event of a takeover. In the absence of any specific provisions, a potential acquirer need only negotiate with the holders of voting or superior voting shares, ignoring the other shareholders. Following considerable controversy, most issuers of restricted voting shares have incorporated *coattail* provisions in their bylaws to allow the holders of restricted voting shares to participate in the takeover premium.

A typical example of subordinate voting shares is Ivaco Inc., which has 22.0 million Class A shares that are entitled to one vote each and 6.7 million Class B shares entitled to 10 votes each. The Class A shares will receive 120% of the dividend declared on Class B shares and are protected against any sub-division or consolidation (but not stock dividends). The coattail provision described in the 1990 *Annual Report* reads as follows:

> In the event an offer is made to holders of Class B shares and a similar offer is not made to Class A shareholders then each Class A share will, for the purposes of such an offer only, be deemed to have been converted to Class B shares in order that the Class A shares will be treated equally with the Class B shares.

In Ivaco's case the Ivanier family plus the company's officers and directors hold over 60% of the votes primarily through holdings of Class B shares. Furthermore, the Class B shares may be freely converted into Class A shares on a one-for-one basis. Absolute control of Ivaco can be secured by owning 4.5 million Class B shares or about 15.5% of the total equity.[14]

The valuation of restricted voting shares presents some interesting challenges given the existence of dividend preferences and coattail provisions. Considerable research has been undertaken that indicates that the value of a vote is worth between 1% and 16% of the equity value. The value of a vote is manifested in a premium paid for the voting over the non-voting or restricted voting shares. This voting premium, however, is sometimes obscured by the effect of the dividend preference. In the case of Ivaco, for example, the Class A shares closed at $4.90 and the Class B at $4.60 on November 30, 1995. On the face of it there appears to be no voting premium. In similar circumstances, Robinson and White estimated that the expected net present value of the dividend difference is larger than the price difference; therefore, the existence of a premium cannot be ruled out.[15]

---

[14] Ivaco is not an extreme example; absolute control of Canadian Tire Corporation can be secured with ownership of about 2.1% of the equity.

[15] C. Robinson and A. White, "Empirical Evidence on the Relative Valuation of Voting and Restricted Voting Shares," *Canadian Journal of Administrative Sciences* 7, no. 4 (December 1990): 9–18. For a summary of the issues and a comprehensive literature review, see E. Maynes, C. Robinson and A. White, "How Much Is A Share Vote Worth?" *Canadian Investment Review* III, no. 1 (Spring 1990): 49–55. It is worth noting that on November 30, 1995 the Canadian Tire voting shares closed at $16.25 while the non-voting shares closed at $15.50.

Stripped Common Shares

These securities are designed to allow investors to separate the dividend portion of a return on a common share from the capital gain. They can be described most easily with an example.

An underwriter floats a new investment corporation and issues two types of securities: *preferred shares* and *capital shares*. The latter are also known as instalment receipts. The proceeds from the sale of these securities are used to purchase the shares of a large and creditworthy company, such as the Bank of Nova Scotia (BNS). The investment corporation is designed to be unwound or liquidated at the end of a specified period.

The owner of preferred shares is entitled to all cash dividends that the company pays the underwriter plus a proportion of any price appreciation that has accrued on the liquidation date of the investment corporation. The owner of an instalment receipt is entitled to all the remaining (if any) price appreciation on the underlying shares. The price of the underlying security is divided between the two classes of shares. The preferred shares, therefore, receive the full dividend but pay a lower price than the underlying shares, thereby obtaining a higher yield. The capital shares, on the other hand, receive the bulk of the capital gains (and no income) but pay a lower price than the underlying security, thereby enhancing any return.

After the original issue, an investor can buy or sell either of these securities through a broker and can find each listed on the Toronto Stock Exchange under the name of the investment corporation. The company that issues the underlying securities has nothing to do with either the creation or subsequent trading of these shares.

An example involved BNS shares as the underlying securities. The investment corporation was known as SNT and the BNS shares were divided into preferred shares listed as XNT.E and capital shares listed as XNT. When BNS stock was selling for $20.75 the preferred shares sold for $12.38 and the capital stock for $8.38. The preferred shares received all dividends declared by BNS and participated in 25% of any capital gain over $27 on BNS shares at the liquidation date, February 8. 1996. The full capital gain up to $27, plus 75% of any capital gain over $27, accrued to the capital shares on February 8, 1996.

Since the first issue of these securities in 1986 a number of dealers have floated issues of stripped common shares using bank stocks as the underlying securities in most cases. In the US similar securities are issued by the Americus Shareowner Service Corporation. The preferred shares are referred to as primes and the instalment receipts as scores.

CASH DIVIDENDS

Payments made in cash to shareholders are termed **dividends**. These are typically declared quarterly by the board of directors and paid to the shareholders of record at a date, known as the **date of record**, specified by the board. The dividends may be of almost any size, subject to certain restrictions contained in the charter or in documents given to creditors. Dividends may even be larger than the current earnings of the corporation, although this is unusual. (If so, they are usually paid out of past earnings.)

Compiling a list of shareholders to receive the dividend is not as simple as it may initially seem, since for many firms the list changes almost constantly as shares are bought and sold. The way of identifying those shareholders who are to receive the dividend is by use of an **ex-dividend date**. Because of the time required to record the transfer of ownership of common stock, major stock exchanges specify an ex-dividend date that is three business days before the date of record. Shares purchased before an ex-dividend date are entitled to receive the dividend in question; those purchased on or after the ex-dividend date are not entitled to the dividend.

For example, a dividend may be declared on April 15 with a date of record of Friday, May 15. In this situation Tuesday, May 12, is the ex-dividend date. If an investor bought shares on Friday, May 8, he or she would subsequently receive the cash dividend (unless the shares were sold later in the day on the 8th). However, if the shares were bought on Tuesday, May 12, the investor would not receive the cash dividend. Besides a declaration date (April 15), an ex-dividend date (May 12), and a date-of-record (May 15), there is also a fourth date, the payment date. On this date (perhaps May 25) the cheques for the cash dividends are put in the mail.

STOCK DIVIDENDS AND STOCK SPLITS

Occasionally, the board of directors decides to forgo a cash dividend and declares a **stock dividend** instead. For example, if a 5% stock dividend is declared, the owner of 100 shares receives 5 additional shares issued for this occasion. The accounting treatment of a stock dividend is to increase the "common stock" and "capital contributed in excess of par" accounts by an amount equal to the market value of the stock at the time of the dividend times the number of new shares issued (the "common stock" account would increase by an amount equal to the par value times the number of new shares; the remainder of the increase would go into the "capital contributed in excess of par" account). In order to keep the total book value of shareholders' equity the same, the "retained earnings" account is reduced by a equivalent amount.

A **stock split** is similar to a stock dividend in that the shareholder owns more shares afterward. However, it differs in both magnitude and accounting treatment. With a stock split, all the old shares are destroyed and new ones are issued with a new par value; afterward, the number of new shares outstanding is usually larger than the previous number of old shares by 25% or more, with the exact amount depending on the size of the split. In contrast, a stock dividend usually results in an increase of less than 25%. While a stock dividend results in adjustments to the dollar figures in certain shareholders' equity accounts, no adjustments are made for a split. For example, if a stock with par value $1 is split 2-for-1, the holder of 200 old shares will receive 400 new shares with par value $0.50, and none of the dollar figures in shareholders' equity would change.

A **reverse stock split** or consolidation reduces the number of shares and increases the par value per share. For example, in a reverse 2-for-1 split, the holder of 200 shares with par value $1 would exchange them for 100 shares with par value $2. Again, there would not be any change in the dollar figures in shareholders' equity.

Stock dividends and splits must be taken into account when following the price of a company's shares. For example, a fall in price per share may be due solely to a large stock dividend. To reduce confusion, most financial services provide data adjusted for at least some of these changes. Thus, if a stock split 2-for-1 on a particular date, prices prior to that date might be divided by 2 to facilitate comparison.

Reasons for Stock Dividends and Splits

Why do corporations issue stock dividends and split their stocks? Nothing of importance would appear to be changed, since such actions do not increase revenues or reduce expenses. All that changes is the size of the units in which ownership may be bought and sold.

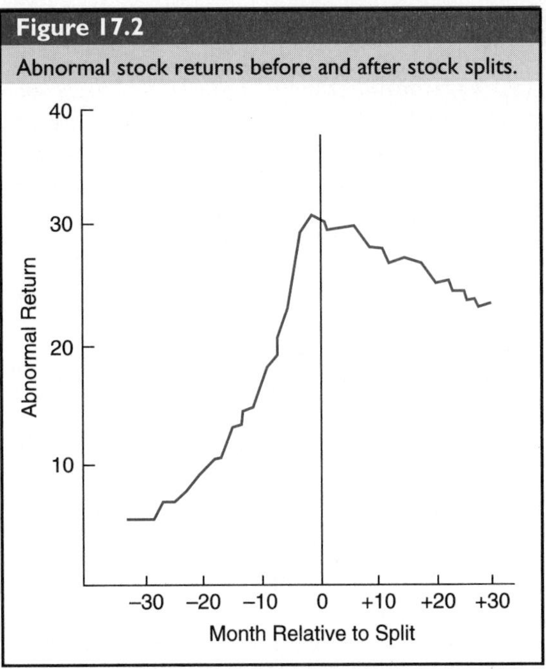

Figure 17.2

Abnormal stock returns before and after stock splits.

SOURCE: Sasson Bar-Yosef and Lawrence D. Brown, "A Re-examination of Stock Splits Using Moving Betas," *Journal of Finance* 32, no. 4 (September 1977):1074.

Moreover, since the process involves administrative effort and costs something to execute, one wonders why it is done.

It is sometimes argued that shareholders respond positively to "tangible" evidence of the growth of their corporation. Another view holds that splits and stock dividends, by decreasing the price per share, may bring the stock's price into a more desirable trading range and hence increase the total value of the amount outstanding.[16]

Figure 17.2 presents the average behaviour of stock returns for 219 stock splits that occurred between 1945 and 1965. For each split, the stock's "abnormal" return was determined by relating monthly returns on the stock to the corresponding returns in the stock market. This was done month by month for the 54-month period immediately prior to the split and the 54-month period immediately following it. These abnormal returns were averaged across firms for each month relative to the firm's split and then cumulated across time.

As the figure shows, the stocks tended to have a positive cumulative abnormal return of about 30% during the 54 months prior to splitting. This was probably not due to anticipation of the coming split, since these splits are not announced until roughly two months before the effective date (denoted by 0 in the figure). The causal relationship could well be just the reverse: stocks split after unusual price increases. That is, unexpected positive developments (such as unexpected large increases in earnings) caused abnormal increases in the share prices of these firms, after which the firms decided to split their stock. The

---

[16] Some evidence in support of this view is provided by Josef Lakonishok and Baruch Lev, "Stock Splits and Stock Dividends: Why, Who, and When," *Journal of Finance* 42, no. 4 (September 1987): 913–932.

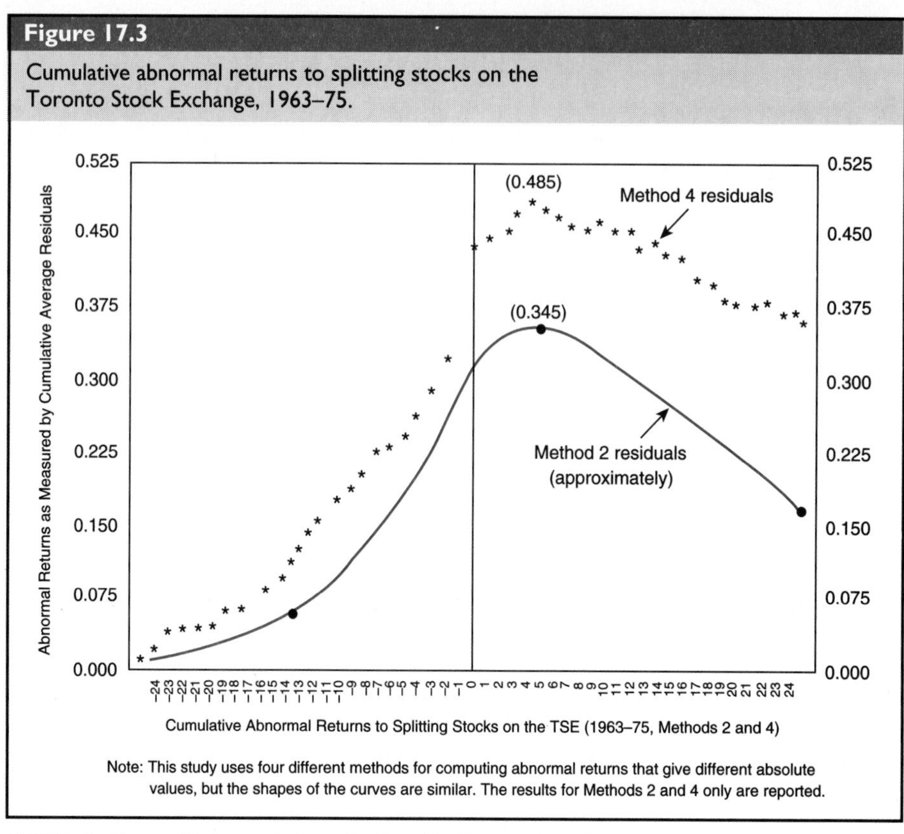

Figure 17.3

Cumulative abnormal returns to splitting stocks on the Toronto Stock Exchange, 1963–75.

SOURCE: G. Charest, "Returns to Splitting Stocks on the Toronto Stock Exchange," *Journal of Business Administration* 12, no. 1 (Fall 1980): 28.

behaviour of prices after the split indicates that investors did not continue to receive positive abnormal returns. In the study shown in Figure 17.2, investors actually lost some ground. Other studies, using different stocks and time periods, found either no abnormal returns or slightly positive abnormal returns after the split.

A comparable Canadian study of 177 stock splits that occurred between 1963 and 1975 shows a similar but not identical pattern of abnormal returns. A disturbing feature of this study, however, is the finding that the maximum abnormal return is recorded about six months *after* the announcement, as shown in Figure 17.3. A further study of 241 stock splits recorded between 1977 and 1985 using weekly data produced results closer to Figure 17.2, with the maximum abnormal return occurring at week minus one.[17] The overall effect of stock splits in Canadian markets is an unresolved issue.

US evidence also suggests that rather than *decreasing* transaction costs, stock splits actually *increased* them. A study of pre-split and post-split behaviour showed that after

[17] See Eugene F. Fama, Lawrence Fisher, Michael C. Jensen, and Richard Roll, "The Adjustment of Stock Prices to New Information," *International Economic Review* 10, no. 1 (February 1969): 1–21; and Guy Charest, "Split Information, Stock Returns and Market Efficiency—I," *Journal of Financial Economics* 6, no. 2/3 (June/September 1978): 265–96; Guy Charest, "Returns to Splitting Stocks on the Toronto Stock Exchange," *Journal of Business Administration* 12, no. 1 (Fall 1980): 19–37; Halim Bishara, "Stock Splits, Stock Returns and Trading Benefits on Canadian Stock Markets," *Akron Business and Economic Review* 19, no. 3 (Fall 1988): 57–65.

splits, trading volume rose less than proportionately, and both commission costs and bid-ask spreads, expressed as a percentage of value, increased — hardly reactions that are favourable to shareholders.[18] For example, after a 2-for-1 stock split, there will be twice as many shares outstanding, so it is reasonable to expect the daily number of shares that are traded to double and also to expect the commission for buying 200 shares after the split to be the same as the commission for buying 100 shares before the split. Instead, it was found that after the split the number of shares traded daily was less than twice as large and the commission was larger.

Another study of stock splits and stock dividends uncovered an apparent market inefficiency.[19] This study examined the performance of stocks around the "ex" dates associated with their stock splits and dividends. If an investor bought shares of a firm the day before its ex date and sold them the day after the ex date, then on average the investor would make an abnormal return of roughly 2% for stock dividends and 1% for stock splits. Such an observance appears to violate the notion of efficient markets because it suggests that an investor can make abnormal returns by trading stocks using a simple strategy based on publicly available information.

PREEMPTIVE RIGHTS

Under common law (and most provincial laws), a shareholder has an inherent right to maintain his or her proportionate ownership of the corporation. The existence of these **preemptive rights** means that when new shares are to be sold, the current shareholders must be given the right of first refusal in regard to the purchase of the shares.[20] This is accomplished by issuing a certificate to each shareholder that indicates the number of new shares he or she is authorized to purchase. This number will be proportional to the number of existing shares currently owned by the shareholder. Usually, the new shares will be priced below the current market price of the stock, making such *rights* valuable. The shareholder can exercise the rights by purchasing his or her allotted amount of new shares, thereby maintaining his or her proportional ownership in the firm, but at the cost of providing additional capital. Alternatively, the rights can be sold to someone else.[21]

For example, if a firm needs $10 000 000 for new equipment, it may decide to sell new shares in order to raise the capital. Given that the current market price of the stock is $60 per share, a *rights offering* may be used to raise the capital, in which the **subscription price** is set at $50 per share.[22] Accordingly, $10 000 000/$50 = 200 000 new shares are to be sold. Assuming the firm has 4 000 000 shares outstanding, this means that the owner

---

[18] See Thomas E. Copeland, "Liquidity Changes Following Stock Splits," *Journal of Finance* 34, no. 1 (March 1979): 115–141; and Robert M. Conroy, Robert S. Harris, and Bruce A. Benet, "The Effects of Stock Splits on Bid-Ask Spreads," *Journal of Finance* 45, no. 4 (September 1990): 1285–1295.

[19] Mark S. Grinblatt, Ronald W. Masulis, and Sheridan Titman, "The Valuation Effects of Stock Splits and Stock Dividends," *Journal of Financial Economics* 13, no. 4 (December 1984): 461–490.

[20] Current shareholders may not be given this right if there is a provision in the charter denying it or if it is denied by the shareholders at the annual meeting.

[21] The investor could simply let the rights expire, causing that investor's proportion in the corporation to decline as others are given ownership in the expanded firm in return for the provision of new capital. Sometimes there is an **oversubscription privilege** given to the subscribing shareholders. This means that those shareholders who have exercised their rights will be given an opportunity to buy the shares that were not purchased.

[22] The subscription price is usually set at roughly 80% of the current market price of the stock.

of one share will receive the right to buy 200 000/4 000 000 = 1/20 of a new share. Since the number of rights received is equal to the number of shares owned, 20 shares must be owned in order to be able to buy one new share. Thus, if a shareholder owns 100 shares, he or she will receive 100 rights, allowing him or her to buy (1/20) × 100 = 5 new shares. These rights are valuable because the owner of them can buy stock at $50 a share when the market price is significantly higher. The current owner of 100 shares can either use the 100 rights by coming up with cash equal to 5 × $50 = $250 or sell the 100 rights to someone else. But this raises a question: what is a fair price for the rights?

Rights are distributed in a manner similar to cash dividends. That is, there is a date of record and, four business days earlier, an **ex-rights date**. Before the ex-rights date, the value of a right can be calculated by using the following equation:

$$C_o - (RN + S) = R \tag{17.2}$$

where:

C_o is the "rights-on" market price of the stock,
R is the value of a right,
N is the number of rights needed to buy one share, and
S is the subscription price.

This equation can be interpreted in the following manner. If an investor purchases one share before the ex-rights date, by definition he or she pays the market price of C_o, shown on the left-hand side of the equation. Alternatively, the investor could purchase the number of rights necessary to buy one share of the new stock at a cost of RN and set aside an amount of money equal to the subscription price S. The total cost of doing this is $RN + S$. The only difference between the two alternatives is that the first one gives the investor not only one share of stock but also one right. Thus, the difference in the cost of the two alternatives, $C_o - (RN + S)$, must equal the value of a right, R, as shown in equation (17.2).

Equation (17.2) can be rewritten as

$$R = \frac{C_o - S}{N + 1}. \tag{17.3}$$

Thus, in the previous example, the value of a right when a share is selling for $60 would be equal to approximately ($60 – $50)/(20 + 1) = $.48.

On or after the ex-rights date, the value of a right can be calculated by using the following equation:

$$C_e - (RN + S) = 0 \tag{17.4}$$

where C_e is the ex-rights market price of a share. The reasoning behind this equation is similar to the reasoning behind equation (17.2). That is, an investor can purchase one share by either buying it in the open market at a cost of C_e or by purchasing the requisite number of rights and setting aside the subscription price, for a total cost of $RN + S$. Since the purchase of one share ex-rights means the investor does not receive a right, the two alternatives provide the investor with the same item. Thus, the cost of these two alternatives should be equivalent, so the difference in their cost should be zero.

Equation (17.4) can be rewritten as

$$R = \frac{C_e - S}{N}. \tag{17.5}$$

In the previous example, if a share is selling for $56 after the ex-rights date, then the value of a right at that time would be approximately ($56 – $50)/20 = $.30.

SHARE PRICE QUOTATIONS

Figures 17.4 and 17.5 provide examples of quotations summarizing a day's transactions in stocks traded over the counter and on the TSE.

Active stocks that traded on the previous day, reported by the Canadian Dealing Network, Inc., are shown in the top section of Figure 17.4. After the security's name, the trading volume, highest, lowest, and closing prices recorded the previous day are shown together with the change in price from the prior trading day. Bid and asked offers for issues that did not trade in the past five days are shown in the bottom section of Figure 17.4 following the security's name.

Regular activity in shares traded on the Toronto Stock Exchange, reported daily (except Mondays), is shown in Figure 17.5. The accompanying instructions in the table, entitled *How to Read the Stock Tables*, describe the information that is provided. The Saturday report presents the same information but includes a weekly summary.

The Globe and Mail: Report on Business also provides share price quotations for companies listed on the Montreal and Vancouver exchanges in Canada and on NASDAQ, which lists the New York and other US stock exchanges.

INSIDER TRADING

The Ontario Securities Commission requires the officers and directors of a corporation whose securities are traded on an organized exchange in Ontario to report any transactions they have made in the firm's shares within 10 days after the end of the month in which the transaction(s) occurred. Shareholders who own 10% or more of the firm's shares, known as *beneficial owners*, must also report their trading activities. Such shareholders, officers, and directors are often referred to as **insiders**. The information they provide about their trading activity is subsequently reported in the Ontario Securities Commission's weekly *Ontario Securities Commission Bulletin.*[23] Almost two months may elapse before knowledge of these trades becomes widespread. For example, the information about trades made in January must be reported by early February and will appear in the late February issue of the OSC Bulletin. When a person first acquires 10% of a firm's shares he or she is subject to the OSC's *early warning disclosure*. This requires them to make an immediate public announcement and report the transaction to the OSC within one day.

The business press reports information about insider trading obtained from the *OSC Bulletin*. In addition, some investment dealers use insider trading activity as part of the information employed to develop buy and sell recommendations.

It is illegal for anyone to enter into a security transaction if they have taken advantage of "inside" information about the corporation that is unavailable to other people involved in the transaction. This proscription includes not only insiders but also those to whom they give such secret information (the recipient of such a tip is termed the *tipee*).

Legal issues aside, two questions of relevance to outside investors may be posed: (1) Do insiders make unusual profits on transactions in their own stocks? (2) If they do, can others profit by following their example as soon as it becomes public knowledge?

---

[23] In some provinces, notably Quebec and Alberta, insiders are required to report their activity within 10 days of executing a trade.

Figure 17.4

Summary of shares quoted on the CDN network.

CDN Unlisted

A-K

52-week high	52-week low	Stock	Sym	High	Low	Close	Chg	Vol (100s)
0.85	0.07	AVL Info	AVLI	0.14	0.14	0.14	+.005	225
0.70	0.06	Afton Food	AFTN	0.12	0.10	0.10	-0.02	2250
0.65	0.25	Ambrex	AMBX	0.45	0.42	0.42		554
1.30	0.47	Amer Teles	ATIL	1.10	0.95	1.05		666
1.30	0.47	Amer Teles	ATIL	1.10	0.95	1.05		666
0.12	0.04	Amertek	AMRT	0.12	0.12	0.12	+0.07	100
1.10	0.26	Anglo Swi	ASWC	0.31	0.31	0.31		50
2.30	1.00	Applied I	AIMC.A	2.15	2.00	2.15		46
0.87	0.10	Aronos	ARMI	0.15	0.15	0.15	+0.05	100
0.55	0.16	Arrowlink	ARKC	0.33	0.30	0.30		80
1.60	0.45	Asia Media	ASIA	0.45	0.45	0.45	-0.20	100
0.45	0.10	Asquith	ASQH	0.45	0.44	0.44	+0.03	450
4.45	0.50	Atapa Min	ATAP	3.95	3.85	3.95		577
1.15	0.40	Band-Ore	BNDR	0.55	0.55	0.55	+0.02	40
6½	**0.50**	**Banro Intl**	**BANR**	**6¼**	**5½**	**5½**	**-¾**	**62**
2.00	**0.50**	**Beauford**	**BFEA**	**1.00**	**1.00**	**1.00**	**+0.25**	**20**
2.80	0.37	Birim Gold	BIRM	2.55	2.35	2.50		1217
0.45	0.15	Black Prl	BLKP	0.18	0.15	0.18		113
0.85	0.15	Blue Moun	BMBI	0.21	0.19	0.21	-0.01	115
4.25	**1.50**	**Borealis**	**BSXC**	**3.00**	**2.50**	**2.80**	**-0.20**	**44**
7	5¾	CAGC	CAGC	6½	5¾	6⅛	+⅛	1921
1.00	0.60	CRSS	CRSS	0.70	0.70	0.70	-0.05	40
0.35	0.25	Cabot Cr	CABT	0.30	0.30	0.30	+0.05	10
0.31	0.05	Cdn Arrow	CAML	0.31	0.31	0.31	+0.12	50
3.70	1.85	Canfibre Gr	CFGL	1.95	1.85	1.85	-0.05	103
0.13	0.03	Canuc Res	CNUC	.075	.075	.075	-0.01	13
1.85	**0.07**	**Castello Bus**	**CSIO**	**1.80**	**1.50**	**1.50**	**-0.25**	**376**
2.30	0.94	Cd Rom Ne	CDRN	1.21	1.07	1.21		902
2.80	**0.62**	**Cdn State**	**CSRS**	**1.30**	**1.15**	**1.28**	**+0.08**	**809**
0.55	0.15	Century Cir	CTCR	0.15	0.15	0.15	-0.05	15
5½	3.70	Certicom	CERT	4.10	4.00	4.10	+0.10	213
0.14	0.03	Cimatec	CIMA	0.13	0.13	0.13	+0.02	500
0.40	0.08	Citadel Gld	CIGD	0.31	0.31	0.31	-0.03	50
0.27	0.15	Clavos Por	CLPM	0.27	0.27	0.27	+0.04	20
0.55	0.08	Cong Inds	CNGI	0.32	0.24	.285	+.045	13097
0.17	0.03	Conquest Y	CQYR	0.11	0.11	0.11	+0.01	100
1.20	0.40	Continti Ca	CNCC	1.20	1.05	1.10	+0.05	610
0.70	0.15	Continti Cp	CTNC	0.60	0.60	0.60		32
1.85	0.10	Cyber Digit	CDVS	0.10	0.10	0.10		120
1.40	0.65	Delayed Dat	DDCI	1.25	1.25	1.25	+0.05	100
1.82	0.40	Dimension	DMMD	0.60	0.60	0.60	+0.10	70
1.50	0.75	Dimethaid	DIME	1.05	1.00	1.00	-0.03	165
26½	15	Drn	DMTX.PR.B	19½	19½	19½		10
0.95	0.45	Eastmain	ESTR	0.50	0.50	0.50		145
17¾	**2.75**	**Eu-N**	**ERNM.WT.A**	**13½**	**13**	**13**	**-¾**	**59**
4.50	1.45	Exxadon Tc	EXDN	4.50	4.10	4.20	+0.15	2175
0.15	0.05	FTCL da	FTCL.PR.A	0.15	0.15	0.15		200
3.50	2.90	Far East	FEGI	3.00	2.90	3.00		231
45	**29**	**Fidelity Partn**	**FIDN**	**43**	**43**	**43**	**+3**	**1**
12½	10	Fidelity Partn	FIDP	10⅞	10⅞	10⅞	+⅛	3
0.42	0.06	Fincore Min	FNDR	0.16	0.16	0.16	-0.01	100
0.15	0.05	Flagship	FLSR	0.05	0.05	0.05		8
1.10	0.10	Foodquest	FDQI	0.45	0.45	0.45		20
2.60	0.75	Footmax	FMAX	1.15	1.00	1.05		818
8¾	0.95	Fortun Min	FORM	8¾	8¼	8⅜	-¼	64
2.45	**0.25**	**Future Av**	**FAVC.A**	**2.45**	**2.25**	**2.45**	**+0.17**	**919**
1.60	0.85	Gran Colo	GCRI	1.40	1.35	1.40		656
0.25	0.21	Grandfield	GFPI	0.23	0.22	0.23	-0.02	249
0.03	.005	Graph/Max	GRFI	0.01	0.01	0.01	-.005	1000
2.15	0.30	Greenlight	GCIX	1.50	1.40	1.45		310
0.58	0.35	Greenshie	GREX	0.55	0.55	0.55	+0.05	500
1.25	0.15	Harte	HTRC	0.40	0.40	0.40		250
0.75	0.60	Heartland	HRTL	0.75	0.75	0.75		1100
1.20	0.30	Hilldale E	HDHL	0.50	0.50	0.50		24
0.40	0.05	Huntington	HINT	0.20	0.20	0.20		30
2.10	**1.25**	**Image Proc**	**IMPS**	**1.40**	**1.35**	**1.35**	**-0.10**	**70**
1.40	**0.01**	**Immedi**	**IMDA.WT**	**1.20**	**1.20**	**1.20**	**-0.20**	**20**
1.37	0.37	Impact Cap	IPCT	0.46	0.46	0.46	-0.04	10
0.21	0.04	Innovdent T	INND	0.07	0.07	0.07	+0.02	100
11⅜	3.00	Instant Publis	TIPI	5⅝	5⅝	5⅝		73
0.65	0.26	Intermune Lif	INLI	0.50	0.41	0.50	+0.07	2119
0.19	0.07	Intl Larder	LRDR	0.09	0.08	0.08	-0.02	930
4.50	**0.75**	**Intl Precio**	**IPMC**	**3.25**	**3.15**	**3.15**	**-0.20**	**178**
0.88	0.25	Intl Telepres	ITLP	0.65	0.65	0.65	+0.04	10
5.92	1.20	Interquest	IQIT	1.30	1.30	1.30	+0.05	103
0.40	0.15	Intex Mining	INXS	0.25	0.25	0.25		60
1.05	0.75	Jetcom	JTCM	1.05	1.05	1.05		14
2.50	**1.20**	**Kafus Ca**	**KFSS**	**2.10**	**1.95**	**2.10**	**+0.10**	**98**
0.55	0.20	Kinbauri	KNBR	0.35	0.35	0.35	-0.05	100
6	**1.00**	**King Prods**	**KINK**	**3.15**	**2.90**	**3.15**	**+0.25**	**249**
1.35	**0.83**	**Kyrgoil**	**KYRG**	**1.20**	**1.13**	**1.13**	**-0.07**	**414**

L-Z

52-week high	52-week low	Stock	Sym	High	Low	Close	Chg	Vol (100s)
4.50	.067	Lakefield Mi	LKFD	2.80	2.60	2.80		60
0.25	0.10	Langis Silvr	LSCM	0.12	0.12	0.12	-0.03	10
4.50	0.50	Latin Amr	LAGD	0.90	0.90	0.90	+0.05	100
0.60	0.10	Laverty	LIDL	0.10	0.10	0.10		50
5.40	2.00	Le Print Expr	LPEI	2.10	2.00	2.10	-0.10	45
0.55	0.25	Lef Intl	LEFI	0.30	0.30	0.30	+0.05	365
5	3.00	Leisure Can	LCAN	3.75	3.75	3.75		65
4.85	1.85	Lenox Poly	LENP	3.35	3.25	3.35		40
7¾	1.05	Lifetech	LFTK	1.85	1.85	1.85	+0.05	8
10⅛	1.60	Luminart	LUMN	2.80	2.55	2.65	+0.05	227
2.20	1.20	Lyndex Expl	LYDX	1.50	1.50	1.50		5
0.75	0.13	Madisn Par	MASN	0.10	0.10	0.10	-0.12	9
1.10	0.80	Manitex Ca	MNTX	1.00	1.00	1.00		8
9¼	**7¾**	**Mrt T**	**MRTT.PR.A**	**9**	**9**	**9**	**+½**	**z 65**
0.23	0.05	Materials Pr	MTLP	0.18	0.15	0.15	-0.05	1500
0.12	0.01	Medyx	MDYX	0.07	0.07	0.07	-0.02	150
1.35	0.05	Meranto Tc	MERA	0.30	0.26	0.26	+0.01	405
0.45	0.06	Mercana In	MRCN	0.09	0.09	0.09		94
1.40	0.80	Midswana	MDSW	1.00	0.80	0.80	-0.20	141
1.63	**0.80**	**Mobile Com**	**MBIL**	**1.50**	**1.50**	**1.50**	**+0.10**	**30**
1.20	1.00	Mosaic Gr	TILE	1.00	1.00	1.00		100
0.30	0.10	Mount Wrgh	MTWI	0.30	0.30	0.30	+0.15	50
0.60	0.01	Multime	MWTM	0.55	0.55	0.55		200
0.30	0.01	NWKI	NWKI	0.12	0.12	0.12	+0.11	65
0.06	0.01	Natl Petrol	NPCL	0.01	0.01	0.01	-.005	20
0.48	0.02	Naturally Ni	NATU	0.11	0.10	0.10	-0.03	860
3.60	1.70	Navitrak Intl	NVTK	2.35	2.35	2.35	+0.05	50
3.00	0.50	Network Da	NKDS	2.50	2.50	2.50		80
1.35	0.45	Newchild In	NCCX	0.80	0.80	0.80		100
0.04	.015	Nova Beau	NBAM	.015	.015	.015		260
2.30	1.01	Olympic Ro	ORWI	1.24	1.14	1.24		234
3.20	0.30	Optimal Ro	OPMR	2.20	2.10	2.10	-0.05	115
1.85	1.10	Oroperu	OROP	1.85	1.75	1.80		1408
0.69	0.10	Ottawa Stru	OSSL	0.10	0.10	0.10		250
1.92	0.25	Pan Pacific	PPSC	1.91	1.65	1.91		82
0.32	0.08	Panthco	PHCO	0.13	0.13	0.13	+0.01	200
0.35	0.10	Perlite Cana	PRLT	0.19	0.17	0.19	+0.09	150
1.10	0.26	Pinetree Ca	PCAP	0.36	0.36	0.36	-0.04	359
1.91	**1.26**	**Planetsafe**	**PLNT**	**1.26**	**1.26**	**1.26**	**-0.22**	**2**
18	0.90	Polyphalt	PLYF	6¼	5¾	6	+⅛	234
2.00	**0.75**	**Primenet**	**PMNT**	**1.00**	**1.00**	**1.00**	**+0.25**	**30**
1.90	1.40	Raw Cree	RAWR	1.90	1.85	1.90		92
0.65	0.35	Regional	REGC	0.43	0.43	0.43		36
4.25	2.00	Rex Diam	REXD	2.25	2.15	2.25	+0.05	230
2.90	1.35	Romarco	RMCM	2.35	1.40	2.30		1300
2.00	0.55	Roma	RMCM.WT	1.40	1.30	1.35	+0.05	1125
0.49	0.05	Romfield Bl	RFDB	0.11	0.10	0.10	-0.01	580
0.40	0.10	Root Inds	RUTE	0.15	0.15	0.15	-0.05	17
0.40	0.20	Sand River	SRIV	0.32	0.32	0.32	-0.03	20
0.75	0.40	Santa Crz	SCGI	0.60	0.57	0.60	+0.02	1430
0.50	0.20	Sharpe En	SHGP	0.27	0.25	0.27	+0.02	640
0.85	0.30	Sirit Techs	SIRT	0.35	0.30	0.35		117
1.45	0.05	Skygame	SKGM	0.75	0.70	0.75		1295
0.34	0.07	Solex Capit	SOLX	0.11	0.11	0.11	-0.01	66
0.70	0.20	Spanex Cap	SPAX	0.53	0.50	0.50	-0.03	250
0.20	0.10	Sparton	SPTN	0.13	0.12	0.13		55
0.35	0.15	Spruce Res	SPRG	0.25	0.20	0.25		150
0.50	0.20	Stackpal Intl	STAX	0.25	0.20	0.25		800
0.37	0.02	Star Gp Nw	STRG	0.11	0.10	0.10		650
1.55	1.00	Starrex Mi	STXX	1.05	1.05	1.05		3
1.30	0.45	Stef Intl	STEF	0.50	0.50	0.50		25
2.00	1.00	Stockguard	SGRD	1.35	1.20	1.35		576
0.80	0.45	Strike Minrl	STRK	0.60	0.58	0.60	+0.02	100
1.62	0.35	Tnk Res	TNKR	0.65	0.60	0.64	-0.11	645
0.10	0.02	Trac Inds	TRAC	0.09	.085	0.09	+.005	610
0.05	0.01	Transpacific	TRNP	0.02	0.02	0.02		24
1.90	1.20	Tropika Intl	TPIL	1.85	1.60	1.85		509
0.40	0.12	Tyranex Gld	TXGI	0.22	0.22	0.22	-0.03	45
1.80	0.90	♣ Vasogen	VASO	1.20	1.10	1.10	-0.05	166
0.88	0.12	Vedron Gold	VDGI	0.58	0.56	0.58	-0.02	110
0.03	0.01	Venga Ae	VAAV	0.02	0.02	0.02	+.005	1165
2.70	0.75	Virtek Visi	VRTK	1.00	0.98	0.98	-0.02	357
1.55	**1.25**	**WIN Ga**	**WNGM**	**1.55**	**1.40**	**1.40**	**-0.10**	**175**
12⅜	8	Warp 10	WARP	10⅝	10⅜	10⅝	+⅛	285
0.75	0.15	Waseco Re	WSCO	0.70	0.70	0.70		15
1.40	0.70	Win	WDMM.PR.B	1.40	1.40	1.40		56
1.40	1.00	Woodvie	WODV	1.18	1.18	1.18		276
2.00	0.40	World Wise	WWTI	0.75	0.72	0.72	+0.02	69
0.37	0.06	Worldtec	WTSI	0.07	0.07	0.07		100
0.60	0.50	Young-Davi	YDVM	0.50	0.50	0.50		6
1.15	0.37	Zamora Go	ZMRA	0.48	0.43	0.43		272

U.S. funds

52-week high	52-week low	Stock	Sym	High	Low	Close	Chg	Vol (100s)
9	3.25	Kazak a	KMCO	8⅝	8⅝	8⅝		18
2.15	0.60	Seven Sea a	SVSE	0.80	0.65	0.80	+0.10	30

UNLISTED BID AND ASKED

Selected quotes for stocks traded in past five days

A-K

Stock	Sym	Bid	Ask	Last
Adrian R	ARCO	1.35	1.45	1.40
Alarmforc	ALRM	0.60	0.85	0.75
Allied Lyo	ALYN	10⅝	11⅜	11
Amteleco	AMTL	4.50	4.90	4.90
Ansil	ANSL	0.70	0.90	0.70
Areq	AQPA.WT	3.90	4.10	2.00
Arjon Ent	ARJG	0.65	0.80	0.65
Awg Am	AWGA	0.10	0.20	0.15
Border	BDRC	4.50	6½	4.50
Brazilian Rs	BZIN	0.45	0.52	0.45
Century Enr	CTEY	0.02	0.07	0.02
Commstar	COMM	0.45	0.48	0.45
Complex	COPX	0.40	0.60	0.50
C da	CMER.PR.A	0.05		0.05
Davidson Ti	DDTS	0.04	0.08	0.07
Eli Eco	ELII.WT.A	1.00	2.00	1.50
Empir	EMPC.PR.B	20⅝		20⅝
Enghouse	ENGX	5¼	5⅞	5¼
Envirotreat S	ETSI	0.04	0.06	0.04
Euro Disney/	EDIS	3.25	3.30	3.05
Eur-N	ERNM.WT.B	6¾	7¾	7¾
Fidelity Pt 91	FIDM	35		35
Fidelity Pa	FIDQ	12½		12½
Fire River	FIRE	0.10	0.30	0.10
First Capi	FRCP.A	0.54	0.69	0.54
Flanagan	FMRI	0.07	0.09	0.09
Floorco	FLRL	.005	0.03	.015
Flowerman	FLWG	0.15	0.45	0.15
Foster's Br	FOST	2.00	2.25	2.00
Franc	FRNV.WT.B	7¾	8¾	8½
Franc	FRNV.WT.A	20½	21½	20½
Future Av	FAVC.B	1.45	1.60	1.40
Gene Scree	GEAN	0.75	0.90	0.75
Glen Aud	GAUR	0.05	0.06	0.06
Goldn Hark	GNHE	0.20	0.25	0.20
Golden	GHMC	0.80	0.95	0.85
Granite C	GRNT.A	3.00	3.50	3.00
Guyana Gld	GGFI	0.60	0.80	0.60
Hall Train	HTRN	0.13	0.17	0.13
Hendricks	HNDX.A	0.30	0.40	0.35
IBI Corp	IBIC	0.03	0.04	0.03
Independent	IDMC	0.05	0.07	0.05
Interqu	IQIT.WT	0.15	0.40	0.15
Islan Tl	ISLT.PR.C	13¼		13⅞
Islan Tl	ISLT.PR.E	20½		20⅝
Islan Tl	ISLT.PR.F	20½	22	20⅝

L-Z

Stock	Sym	Bid	Ask	Last
Lakota Res	LAKO	0.25	0.35	0.25
Legcy Ex	LGCY	0.75	0.85	0.75
Lifetec	LFTK.WT	0.55	0.65	0.60
Magn	MTII.PR.A	0.40	0.65	0.70
Marlat Res	MLAR	0.15	0.25	0.19
Maude Lak	MAUD	0.05	0.14	0.14
Mill Stream	MLSM	0.10	0.13	0.13
Modico	MDCO.A	2.25		2.75
Money Wo	MNWK	0.01	.015	.015
NTH Tl	NRTT.PR.A	14	14¾	13⅞
NTH Tl	NRTT.PR.C	14	14¾	13⅞
NTH Tl	NRTT.PR.D	14		13⅞
New Bidl	NBGM	1.00	1.50	1.10
Nfld Goldbr	NFGB	0.17	0.22	0.20
Onda	VOCO.WT	0.90	1.05	1.00
Pace	PACL	0.48	0.53	0.50
Penstar	PSTR	0.50	0.70	0.67
Placer Pacifi	PPFC	2.85	3.05	2.85
Platin	PNVA.WT.C	0.02	0.07	0.04
Quartz Mo	QZMG	0.03	0.05	0.03
RTO	RTOE.WT	1.35	1.55	1.45
Regal Goldf	REGL	1.15	1.50	1.40
Res Intl	RESZ	0.26	0.35	0.30
Rolls Royce	ROLS	3.70	3.95	3.70
San Paulo	SANP	0.13	0.18	0.13
Sheldn Lar	SLDM	0.20	0.30	0.20
Silver Circl	SCDB	0.49	0.57	0.57
Snow Leopa	SLRI	2.10	2.50	2.50
Spruce Fll	SPRC.B	6	7	6½
Sunburst	SNBR	.005	.015	0.01
Sundust Rs	SDST	0.28	0.33	0.30
Taylor Rand	TRND	0.09	0.12	0.09
Transway	TWYC	0.35	0.45	0.43
Univrsl 92	UNVS	40		40
Van Ollie	VANO	0.03	0.04	0.04
WIMR	WIMR.WT	0.25	0.50	0.50
White St	WSCM	0.13	0.18	0.13
Windigo	WPEL	1.25	2.25	1.30
York Bay	YBAY	0.16	0.25	0.16
Zlin Aeros	ZLIN.A	0.40	0.65	0.40

SOURCE: Reprinted with permission of *The Globe and Mail: Report on Business* (January 10, 1996).

Figure 17.5

Summary of activity in shares traded on the Toronto Stock Exchange.

How to read the stock tables

1	2	3	4	5	6	7	8	9	10	11	12
↑↓	52-week high low	Stock	Sym	Div	High	Low	Close	Chg	Vol (100s)	Yield	P/E ratio

Bold-faced stocks closed yesterday at least 5 per cent higher or lower in price than the previous close. Stocks must close at a minimum $1.

Underlined stocks traded yesterday 500 per cent or more above their 13-week average daily volume (on Canadian exchanges only).

1. (Arrow up or down) - New 52-week high or low in day's trading.
2. 52-week high/low - Highest and lowest intra-day price in past 52 weeks.
3. Stock - Abbreviated company name.
4. Sym - Ticker symbol assigned to issue by exchange; .PR is preferred share, .WT is warrant, .UN is unit, .S means stocks are subject to regulation of the SEC Act, .W means when issued, .RT is right.
5. Div - Indicated annual dividend (excluding special dividends).
6. High - Highest intra-day trading price.
7. Low - Lowest intra-day trading price.
8. Close - Closing price.
9. Chg - Change between closing price and previous closing board lot price.
10. Vol - Number of shares traded in 100s; z preceding figure indicates sales are reported in full.
11. Yield - Expressed as percentage, calculated by dividing the dividend by current market price.
12. P/E ratio - Price/earnings ratio; current stock price divided by the company's earnings per share from continuing operations for the latest 12 months. The P/E ratio is not shown if greater than 100.

To comment or make suggestions about our stock or commodity quotations, please call 416-585-5500. You can also reach us on the Internet at stocks@GlobeAndMail.ca

Footnotes

a - in U.S. dollars (on Canadian exchanges)
au - in Australian dollars
b - in British pounds or pence
c - in Canadian dollars (on U.S. exchanges)
cl - commercial/industrial stock (on the Vancouver Stock Exchange)
da - dividend in arrears
dc - dividend paid in Canadian dollars, but stock trades in U.S. funds
g - coming capital gains distribution will be paid to the current owner
in - inactive stock (on the VSE)
j - subject to special reporting rules
n - stock is new issue
nl - mutual fund with no front-end load or contingent deferred sales load
nv - non-voting
rc - in bankruptcy or receivership or being reorganized under the Bankruptcy Act, or securities assumed by such companies
rf - redemption fee or contingent deferred sales load may apply
rs - resource stock (VSE)
rv - shareholders' voting is restricted
s - indicates 52-week high-low range has been adjusted to reflect stock split or consolidation
sv - subordinate-voting
x - stock is trading ex-dividend
y - in Japanese yen.

Data supplied by Dow Jones Telerate Canada Inc.

A-B

	52-week high	low	Stock	Sym	Div	High	Low	Close	Chg	Vol (100s)	Yield	P/E ratio
	3.90	1.00	ABL Cda	ABL		2.52	2.50	2.50	-0.02	44		
	8	4.00	AFM Hospit	AFM		6¼	6¼	6¼		40		
	20	14⅛	AGF nv	AGF.PR.B	0.60	20	19⅝	19⅝	-⅛	157	3.1	10.1
	9½	6	◆AGRA	AGR.A	0.14	9¼	9¼	9¼		20	1.5	10.9
	9¾	5⅝	◆AGR nv	AGR.B	0.16	9⅛	9	9⅛	+⅛	107	1.8	10.7
	17	8	AIT Advancd	AIV		17	16½	17	+½	14		20.0
	.135	.035	AJ Perron	AJP		.085	0.08	.085	+.005	650		
	0.85	0.50	AQM Auto	AOV		0.56	0.56	0.56	+0.05	50		
	1.29	0.45	ARC Resin	ASR		1.05	1.05	1.05		41		
	14½	10	◆AT Plasti	ATP	0.18	11⅞	11⅞	11⅞		148	1.5	5.5
	11⅝	6½	ATI Techs	ATY		10½	10¼	10⅜	-½	183		30.5
	24	6¾	ATS Autom	ATA		22¾	21½	22¼	-¾	61		21.4
	6	**2.62**	**◆Abacan**	**ABC**		**4.20**	**3.85**	**3.95**	**-0.30**	**2378**		
	11¼	6⅛	Aber j	ABZ		10¾	10½	10¾	+⅛	2672		
	25⅞	17½	Abitibi-Price	A	0.40	20⅞	20⅝	20¾		2068	1.9	
	3.00	2.00	Accord Fina	ACD	0.08	2.76	2.76	2.76	-0.09	z 67	2.9	8.9
	9¾	**3.10**	**Accugrph**	**ACU.A**		**3.35**	**3.15**	**3.15**	**-0.25**	**631**		**23.1**
	13¼	9¾	Acklands	ACK		10½	10½	10½	-⅛	10		10.9
	0.42	.185	Adex Minin	AMG		0.27	0.26	0.26	-0.01	962		
	6¾	3.25	◆Adrian Rs	ADL		4.75	4.50	4.70	-0.05	144		16.8
	1.89	0.35	Advancd G j	AED		1.04	0.94	0.96	+0.01	475		
	0.85	0.14	Advantex	ADX		0.65	0.58	0.60		242		
	5½	3.75	◆Advntre	AVN	0.22	4.00	3.90	4.00		71	5.5	5.2
	20	12¾	Agnico Eagl	AGE	a 0.10	19⅝	19½	19½		752	0.7	37.5
	21⅛	12½	◆Agrium	AGU	0.15	20½	19⅝	19⅝	-⅞	3403	0.8	9.0
	13⅞	**6⅞**	**Aim Safety**	**AIM**		**9¾**	**9⅝**	**9¾**	**-⅛**	**20**		
	13⅝	6⅛	Ainsworth L	ANS		7½	7¼	7¼	-¼	45		7.9
	8¾	4.30	Air Canada	AC		4.85	4.75	4.75	-0.05	1134		9.1
	6⅛	3.85	Air Canad	AC.A		4.35	4.25	4.30		537		8.3
	0.57	0.22	AirBoss	BOS		0.27	0.27	0.27	-0.03	115		
	5¾	2.30	Akita nv	AKT.A		5⅜	5	5¼	-⅛	351		6.6
	6	2.60	◆Akita	AKT.B		5½	5⅜	5⅜	-⅛	58		6.8
	23¼	16⅝	Alberta Enr	AEC	0.40	23¼	22⅞	23	-⅛	1532	1.7	22.5
	24	14⅛	Alta Nat Gs	ANG	0.68	20⅜	20	20⅛	-⅛	632	3.4	12.2
	49⅝	33½	◆Alcan	AL	0.60	41¾	40⅛	40½	-1	12816	2.0	27.3
	25½	21¼	Alcan	AL.PR.E	1.88	25¼	25	25¼		158	7.4	
	22⅞	17¾	Alcan E	AL.PR.F	1.46	22⅝	22⅜	22⅝	+⅛	17	6.5	
	0.65	0.30	Algo Gp sv	AO.A		0.38	0.38	0.38	-0.02	z 5		
	11⅛	4.30	Algoma Stl	ALG		5⅝	5⅜	5½	-⅛	736		1.0
	6¾	3.25	Algonquin	AM	0.40	5½	5½	5½		10	7.3	10.6
↑	**20**	**5½**	**◆Allelix Bi**	**AXB**		**20**	**18½**	**18¾**	**+1**	**3501**		
	17	13	◆Alliance	AAC.A		14⅜	14¼	14¼		21		15.8
	16¼	12½	◆Allia rv	AAC.B		14	13¾	14		15		15.6
	29½	22¼	Alliance Fo	ALP		24½	24⅛	24¼		16		6.2
	25	7	◆AlphaNet	FAX		19½	19½	19½		44		
	1.69	**0.65**	**Alpine Oil**	**ASL**		**1.01**	**1.00**	**1.00**	**+0.05**	**401**		**14.3**
↑	**1.01**	**.375**	**Altai Res**	**ATI**		**1.01**	**0.80**	**1.01**	**+0.26**	**1625**		
	17¼	12½	Amber Enr	AMB		17⅛	17	17		130		30.4
↑	**7**	**2.35**	**Amer Eco**	**ECX**		**7**	**6⅝**	**6⅞**	**+⅝**	**204**		**22.9**
	25¾	**5**	**Amer Sensr**	**ASZ**		**5⅞**	**5½**	**5⅝**	**+¼**	**140**		
	4.50	1.90	Amer Gem	GEM		2.45	2.45	2.45		13		
	7⅛	4.75	◆Anchor	AKC	0.14	5¼	5⅛	5¼		123	2.7	8.9
	16⅞	10¾	Anderson	AXL		14½	14¼	14¼		3764		
	12½	10⅝	Andre nv	ADW.A	0.60	11½	11½	11½		16	5.2	
	9⅝	**2.90**	**Andyne Cm**	**ADY**		**5**	**4.40**	**4.40**	**-0.55**	**83**		
↑	46	40⅞	AngCd	ACT.PR.D	3.15	46	46	46	+1	3	6.8	
	1.10	0.15	Antares Min	ANZ		0.83	0.75	0.79	-0.03	1026		
	8¾	4.40	◆Anvil Rng	ARO		5⅞	5⅞	5⅞	+⅛	16		
	1.84	1.15	Anvil R	ARO.UN		1.84	1.80	1.80	-0.04	79		
	0.18	0.06	Applied Crb	APN		0.10	0.10	0.10		1100		
	25⅞	16	Arbor Me	ABO.A	0.07	21⅞	21¾	21⅞	-⅛	3	0.3	26.0
	24⅞	15½	Arbor nv	ABO.B	0.07	20½	20½	20½	-½	30	0.3	24.4
	11⅞	4.05	Archer Res	ARC		6¼	5⅝	5⅝		3027		

	52-week high	low	Stock	Sym	Div	High	Low	Close	Chg	Vol (100s)	Yield	P/E ratio
	2.90	1.50	◆Breakw j	BWR		1.65	1.61	1.63		180		
	0.04	.005	Break	BWR.RT		0.01	005	0.01		1153		
	1.60	1.01	Brigdon	BRG.A		1.40	1.40	1.40	+0.04	30		15.6
	25½	19¾	◆Bruncor	BRR	1.28	22	21¾	21⅞	-⅛	56	5.8	12.2
	1.55	1.10	◆Buhler	BUI.A	0.05	1.45	1.45	1.45	-0.05	27	3.5	8.1
	11½	9⅝	Bulls Offerin	BUL		11½	11⅜	11⅜	-⅛	5		

C-E

	52-week high	low	Stock	Sym	Div	High	Low	Close	Chg	Vol (100s)	Yield	P/E ratio
	4.85	2.90	C-MAC Ind	CMS		4.20	4.15	4.15	+0.05	25		13.0
	10⅞	6¾	CAE	CAE	0.16	10⅞	10⅝	10⅝	-¼	1361	1.5	21.7
	14¼	9¾	CCL nv	CCQ.B	0.28	11	10⅞	10⅞		203	2.6	11.3
	17¼	10	CFCF sv	CF	0.20	15¾	15⅝	15⅝	+⅛	307	1.3	
	10	6¾	CFM Intl	CFM		9⅝	9⅝	9⅝	+¼	1		17.5
	10⅛	6⅞	◆CGC	GYP	0.20	7	6⅞	7		9	2.9	15.2
	6½	3.50	◆CHC sv	FLY.A	0.10	5⅜	5⅜	5⅜	+⅛	72	1.9	
	13¾	8⅞	CI Fund Man	CIX	0.16	11¾	11⅝	11⅝	+⅛	7700	1.4	17.9
	5⅝	**1.05**	**CIC Canola**	**CCJ**		**1.45**	**1.25**	**1.45**	**+0.20**	**1540**		
	16½	12½	CRS	CWO.UN		16½	16½	16½		6		
	25⅞	21⅝	CRS	CRD	1.49	24¾	24¾	24¾	-⅛	47	6.0	
	7½	6	CRS Robot	ROB		6½	6½	6½	-⅛	1		54.2
	11	6½	CS Res	CRZ		10⅞	10⅞	10⅞		692		30.4
	3.20	0.93	CS Res	CRZ.WT		3.15	2.90	2.94	-0.01	1103		
	14⅞	4½	CSA nv	CSA.A		13½	13	13⅛	-½	105		65.6
	24¾	18	CT Finan	CFS	0.80	24½	24⅛	24¼	+⅛	14	3.3	
	28½	24⅛	CT Fin	CFS.PR.B	1.84	28	27¾	27¾	-⅛	21	6.6	
	1.60	0.26	Cabish sv	CSH.A		1.41	1.41	1.41	+0.01	50		
	16	11	Cabre	CBE		15⅞	15¾	15⅞		1028		27.4
	12¾	4¾	Caldwell	CWL.A	0.50	12¾	12¼	12½		61	4.0	22.7
	11½	5	Caledonia	CAL		8¾	8⅝	8⅝	-⅛	570		
	6½	3.40	Calian Tech	CTY		5¼	5⅛	5¼		40		15.0
	12⅞	5½	Call-Net rv	CN.B		11⅝	11½	11⅝	+⅛	39		
	12¼	6⅞	Call-Net	CN		11¾	11⅜	11½		106		
	1.60	**0.95**	**Camberly**	**CEL**		**1.40**	**1.35**	**1.35**	**+0.13**	**342**		**27.0**
	19	12¾	Cambior	CBJ	0.14	16⅞	16¼	16½	-⅛	2090	0.8	75.0
	2.10	0.40	Cambi	CBJ.WT.A		0.55	0.50	0.52	-0.08	265		
	13⅞	9⅞	Cambridge	CBG	0.32	12	11⅞	11⅞	-⅛	722	2.7	
	5⅞	**2.25**	**◆Camdev**	**CVO**		**3.40**	**3.10**	**3.40**	**+0.40**	**46**		**2.7**
↑	53¾	29⅞	Cameco	CCO	0.50	53¾	52⅝	53¾	+¾	1016	0.9	31.6
	1.79	0.80	Campbl Rs	CCH		1.78	1.61	1.75	+0.05	3914		19.4
	2.30	**1.60**	**Camvec**	**CV**		**2.15**	**2.00**	**2.10**	**-0.20**	**126**		**6.0**
	2.30	**1.60**	**Camvec**	**CV**		**2.15**	**2.00**	**2.10**	**-0.20**	**126**		**6.0**
	26⅛	25⅞	Can Tr	CT.PR.D		26⅛	26	26	-⅛	146		
	2.20	1.32	Can Tungst	CTG		1.50	1.45	1.45	-0.05	124		
	9¼	5⅜	Can-Banc	XCN	0.08	9⅛	8¾	8¾	-¼	441	1.0	
	11	9⅝	Can Banc	XCN.E	0.69	10⅞	10¾	10¾		198	6.4	
	10¼	6	Cda Sthr rv	CSW		8¼	8⅛	8⅛	-¼	7		
	8⅞	2.95	Cdn Airlines	CA		3.20	3.10	3.10	-0.10	201		
	105	.025	Cdn Air	CA.WT.R		0.03	.025	0.03	+.005	12041		
	6	3.40	Cdn Bnk No	CBK	0.20	4.00	3.95	4.00	-0.10	76	5.0	30.8
↑	**1.25**	**0.55**	**Cdn Congst**	**CCN**		**1.25**	**1.07**	**1.25**	**+0.20**	**6649**		
	0.10	0.05	Cdn Cn	CCN.RT		0.15	0.08	0.11	+0.03	34915		
	3.55	0.90	Cdn Crew	KNC		1.80	1.75	1.75	-0.03	98		
	2.38	1.30	Cdn 88 Ener	EEE		2.35	2.30	2.30		894		
	8¾	4.70	Cdn Fracma	CFC	0.40	5⅞	5⅞	5⅞	+⅛	16	6.8	45.2
	33½	26½	◆Cdn Genrl	CGI	0.68	32½	31¾	32½	+⅞	28	2.1	60.2
	6½	**3.05**	**Cdn Gen**	**CGI.WT**		**5¾**	**5⅜**	**5⅞**	**-½**	**2**		
	0.60	0.35	Cdn Hydro	KHD		0.45	0.45	0.45		50		
	42¼	31⅞	CIBC	CM	1.60	41⅞	41⅛	41⅛	-⅝	8663	3.9	9.8
	24	22¼	CIBC	CM.PR.E	1.32	23½	23½	23½		49	5.6	
	97½	91	CIBC	CM.PR.F	5.44	96½	96½	96½	-1	2	5.6	
	29½	27⅛	CIBC	CM.PR.I	2.28	28⅝	28½	28½	-⅛	195	8.0	
	28	26⅞	CIBC	CM.PR.J	2.21	27¼	27⅛	27⅛	-⅛	29	8.2	
	27⅞	24⅛	CIBC	CM.PR.K	1.75	27⅞	27⅛	27⅞		30	6.4	

SOURCE: Reprinted with permission of *The Globe and Mail: Report on Business* (January 10, 1996).

Insiders trade their shares for many reasons. For example, some purchases result from the exercise of options and some sales result from the need for cash. Moreover, it is not unusual to find some insiders purchasing shares during a month in which other insiders are selling. However, when a major piece of inside information suggests that a stock's value differs significantly from its current market price, it would be reasonable to expect a preponderance of insider trades on one side of the market (that is, either purchases or sales).

One way to search for such situations is to examine the *OSC Bulletin* and count the number of times during a month that insiders traded their firm's shares (excluding the exercise of options). If the number of purchases exceeds the number of sales, it might be inferred that favourable inside information motivated the insider trades during the month. If the number of sales exceeds the number of purchases, this can be regarded as an unfavourable signal.

Different cutoff levels could be used in this process to reflect the intensity of insider trading. A cutoff of 1 would require a simple majority of trades of one type, whereas a cutoff of 5 would require a "supermajority" of trades of one type.

Such a procedure was used in a detailed US study of insider transactions during the 1950s and 1960s.[24] Table 17.1 summarizes the key results. The two columns on the right-hand side of the table indicate the abnormal returns over an eight-month period on securities that exceeded the cutoff level for insider trading. For example, during the 1960s, if an investor purchased every stock in the sample for which there were three or more net purchasers and sold every stock for which there were three or more more net sellers during a month, more or less coincident with the transactions of the insiders themselves, then the investor would have earned, on average, an abnormal return of 5.07% over the subsequent eight months. If the transactions had been made instead at roughly the time the information was published in the SEC's *Official Summary*, an average abnormal return of 4.94% would have been earned over the next eight months.

Table 17.1

Abnormal Returns Associated with Insider Trading.

Sample			Average Abnormal Return over Eight Months Following	
Cutoff (No. of Net Purchasers or Sellers)	*No. of Cases*	*Period*	*Month of Transaction*	*Month Information Became Publicly Available*
1	362	1960s	1.36%	.70%
3	861	1960s	5.07	4.94
4	293	1950s	5.14	4.12
5	157	1950s	4.48	4.08

SOURCE: Jeffrey F. Jaffe, "Special Information and Insider Trading," *Journal of Business* 47, no. 3 (July 1974): 421, 426.

As the first row in the table shows, a bare majority of insider trades does not appear to isolate possible effects of insider information. But a majority of three, four, or five does seem to do so. The figures shown are gross of any transaction costs, but even so it appears that insiders can and do make money from their special knowledge of their companies. This is not surprising, since if anyone can know the true value of a firm, it should be the

[24] Jeffrey F. Jaffe, "Special Information and Insider Trading," *Journal of Business* 47, no. 3 (July 1974): 410–428. Also see Joseph E. Finnerty, "Insiders and Market Efficiency," *Journal of Finance* 31, no. 4 (September 1976): 1141–1148; and Aaron B. Feigen, "Information Opportunities from Insider Trading Laws," *AAII Journal* 11, no. 8 (September 1989): 12–15.

insiders. Since the information these insiders presumably are using is nonpublic in nature, these findings suggest that markets are not strong-form efficient.

On the other hand, the abnormal returns associated with transactions that could have been made by outsiders, using only publicly available information on insider trading, are quite surprising. Moreover, those associated with cutoffs of three, four, or five pass statistical tests designed to see if they might be simply due to chance. After transaction costs, trades designed to capitalize on such information would still appear to produce abnormal returns (although not highly so), suggesting that markets are not even semistrong-form efficient. However, more recent studies have found that outsiders cannot use the publicly available information about insider trading to make abnormal profits; these studies thus support the notion that markets are semistrong-form efficient.[25] Whether or not insider trading information can be profitably used by outsiders is an open question given the conflicting evidence. It is also possible that the inefficiency has disappeared as a result of the publicity it has received.

The Canadian situation is less contradictory. Figure 17.6 shows the cumulative average residuals (CAR), based on monthly data, for both buy and sell signals derived from an examination of some 17 000 insider trades executed between 1967 and 1977. Period 0 on the graph represents the publication date of the *OSC Bulletin* and, therefore, indicates the time when outsiders would become aware of inside trading activity. The CARs for month minus one (when the insiders traded) indicate that insiders, on average, are able to buy low and sell high, that outsiders can profit from observing the actions of insiders, and that abnormal returns persist for about 12 months after the original signal. None of these conclusions are consistent with semistrong-form market efficiency. These results have been confirmed by a number of other studies. Some of these also find that not all insiders are equal. Directors of firms who are also bank directors appear to have access to better inside information than other insiders.[26]

EX ANTE AND EX POST VALUES

Equilibrium theories such as the capital asset pricing model and arbitrage pricing theory imply that in the opinion of well-informed investors, securities with certain attributes will, other things being equal, have large expected returns, whereas those with other attributes

---

[25] See Herbert S. Kerr, "The Battle of Insider Trading and Market Efficiency," *Journal of Portfolio Management* 6, no. 4 (Summer 1980): 47–58; Wayne Y. Lee and Michael E. Solt, "Insider Trading: A Poor Guide to Market Timing," *Journal of Portfolio Management* 12, no. 4 (Summer 1986): 65–71; H. Nejat Seyhun, "Insiders' Profits, Costs of Trading, and Market Efficiency," *Journal of Financial Economics* 16, no. 2 (June 1986): 189–212; Michael S. Rozeff and Mir A. Zaman, "Market Efficiency and Insider Trading: New Evidence," *Journal of Business* 61, no. 1 (January 1988): 25–44; and Ji-Chai Lin and John S. Howe, "Insider Trading in the OTC Market," *Journal of Finance* 45, no. 4 (September 1990): 1273–1284.

[26] D. J. Fowler and C. H. Rorke,"Insider Trading Profits on the Toronto Stock Exchange, 1967–1977," *Canadian Journal of Administrative Sciences* 5, no. 1 (March 1988): 13–24. This study also found that the abnormal returns were higher for thinner stocks than for those more frequently traded. See also J. Baesel and G. Stein, "The Value of Information: Inferences from the Profitability of Insider Trading," *Journal of Financial and Quantitative Analysis* 14 (September 1979): 553–69; M. H. Lee and H. Bishara, "Recent Canadian Experiences on the Profitability of Insider Trades," *Financial Review* 24, no. 2 (May 1989): 235–49; J-M. Suret and E. Cormier, "Insiders and the Stock Market," *Canadian Investment Review* III, no. 2 (Fall 1990): 87–90. This study finds that abnormal returns persist after insider trading information has been distributed to a brokerage firm's clients. R. Heinkel and A. Kraus, "The Effect of Insider Trading on Average Rates of Return," *Canadian Journal of Economics* 20, no. 3 (August 1987): 588–611 examined insider trades on the Vancouver Stock Exchange and found weak evidence of superior insider profits.

Figure 17.6

Cumulative abnormal returns to insider trades.

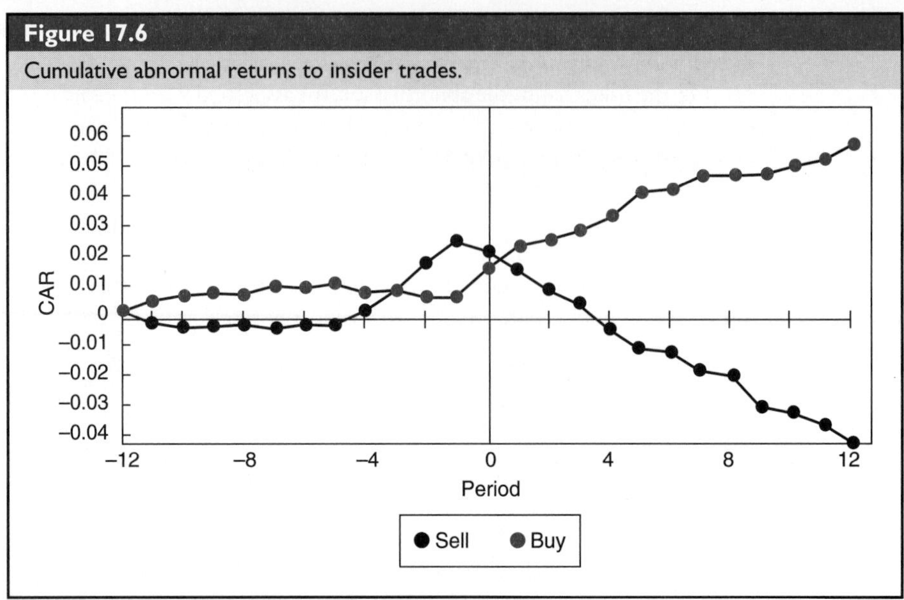

SOURCE: D. Fowler and H. Rorke, "Insider Trading Profits on the Toronto Stock Exchange: 1967–1977," *Canadian Journal of Administrative Sciences* 5, no. 1 (March 1988): 20.

will have small expected returns. Thus, the focus of these theories is on future, or ***ex ante*** (Latin for "before the fact"), expected returns. However, only historical, or ***ex post*** (Latin for "after the fact"), returns are subsequently observed. These historical returns are undoubtedly different from the expected returns, making it extremely difficult to tell whether security attributes and expected returns do, in fact, go together in the manner implied by either the CAPM or APT. Moreover, such theories are relatively silent concerning simple ways in which a security's future, or *ex ante*, attributes and expected returns might be estimated by examining historical, or *ex post*, returns.

To bridge this gap, a number of investigators have used the average historical return of a security as an estimate of its expected return. This requires an assumption that the expected return did not change over some arbitrary time period and that this time period contains a sufficient number of historical returns to make a reasonably accurate estimate of the expected return. However, expectations almost certainly would have changed over the time period needed to obtain a reasonably useful estimate of the expected return for any given security.[27] Despite this objection, it is worthwhile examining historical returns to see

[27] It has been argued that roughly 300 months (25 years) of historical returns are needed in order for a simple averaging technique to produce reasonably useful estimates of expected returns, provided that the "true" but unobserved expected return is constant during this entire period. See J. D. Jobson and Bob Korkie, "Estimation for Markowitz Efficient Portfolios," *Journal of the American Statistical Association* 75, no. 371 (September 1980): 544–54 and "Putting Markowitz Theory to Work," *Journal of Portfolio Management* 7, no. 4 (Summer 1981): 70–74.

how they can be used to come up with meaningful predictions about the future.[28] The next section explores the prediction of a firm's beta. It begins by discussing the estimation of the firm's historical beta by use of the market model.

COMMON STOCK BETAS

For purposes of portfolio management, the relevant risk of a security concerns its impact on the risk of a well-diversified portfolio. In the world of the CAPM, such portfolios would be subject primarily to market risk. This suggests the importance of a security's beta, which measures its sensitivity to future market movements. To estimate beta, in principle the possible sources of such movements should be considered. Then, the reaction of the security's price to each of these sources should be estimated, along with the probability of each reaction. In the process, the economics of the relevant industry and firm, the impact of both operating and financial leverage on the firm, and other fundamental factors should be taken into account.

But what about investigating the extent to which the security's price moved with the market in the past? Such an approach ignores the myriad possible differences between the past and the future. However, it is easily done and provides a useful starting point.

As shown in Chapter 10, a security's beta can be regarded as the slope of the security's market model. If this line were constant over time, meaning it did not change from period to period, then the **historical beta** for a security could be estimated by examining the historical relationship between the excess returns on the security and on the market portfolio. The statistical procedure used for making such estimates of *ex post* betas is **simple linear regression**, also known as ordinary least squares (OLS).[29]

As an example, consider estimating the *ex post* beta for Widget Manufacturing (WM) using a hypothetical market index. Table 17.2 presents the most recent 16 quarterly returns on both WM and the index, and the calculations necessary to determine WM's *ex post* beta and alpha, as well as certain other statistical parameters. As can be seen, WM's beta and alpha were equal to .63 and .79%, respectively, over this period.[30]

Given these values for alpha and beta, the market model for WM is

$$r_{WM} = .79\% + .63r_I + \epsilon_{WM}. \quad (17.6)$$

[28] In doing so, a number of researchers have uncovered certain "empirical regularities" in common stock returns; Appendix A discusses a number of them. For a more detailed summary, see Donald B. Keim, "The CAPM and Equity Return Regularities," *Financial Analysts Journal* 42, no. 3 (May/June 1986): 19-34; Douglas K. Pearce, "Challenges to the Concept of Market Efficiency," Federal Reserve Bank of Kansas City *Economic Review* 72, no. 8 (September/October 1987): 16-33; and Robert A. Haugen and Josef Lakonishok, *The Incredible January Effect* (Homewood, Ill.: Dow Jones-Irwin, 1988).

[29] For an discussion of regression, see Peter Tryfos, *Business Statistics* (Toronto, Ont.: McGraw-Hill Ryerson, 1989).

[30] WM's beta and alpha would have been equal to .63 and .17%, respectively, if excess returns (that is, returns less the risk-free rate) had been used in the calculations instead of returns. Using returns or excess returns (as well as including or ignoring dividends in calculating returns) appears to make little difference in the estimated size of beta. However, there is a substantive difference in the estimated size of alpha. See William F. Sharpe and Guy M. Cooper, "Risk-Return Classes of New York Stock Exchange Common Stocks, 1931–1967," *Financial Analysts Journal* 28, no. 2 (March/April 1972): 46–54.

Table 17.2

Market Model for Widget Manufacturing.

(A) Data

Quarter		*WM Returns = Y (1)*	*Index Returns = X (2)*	Y^2 *(3)*	X^2 *(4)*	$Y \times X$ *(5)*
1	1	−13.38%	2.52%	178.92	6.35	−33.71
	2	16.79	5.45	282.00	29.71	91.54
	3	−1.67	0.76	2.77	0.57	−1.26
	4	−3.46	2.36	11.99	5.58	−8.18
2	5	10.22	8.56	104.53	73.36	87.57
	6	7.13	8.67	50.79	75.19	61.80
	7	6.71	10.80	45.07	116.59	72.49
	8	7.84	3.33	61.47	11.08	26.10
3	9	2.15	−5.07	4.62	25.66	−10.89
	10	7.95	7.10	63.22	50.42	56.46
	11	−8.05	−11.57	64.74	133.87	93.09
	12	7.68	4.65	58.97	21.58	35.67
4	13	4.75	14.59	22.55	212.97	69.29
	14	7.55	2.66	57.03	7.05	20.05
	15	−2.36	3.81	5.58	14.54	−9.01
	16	4.98	7.99	24.78	63.85	39.78
Sum(Σ) =		54.84 = ΣY	66.62 = ΣX	1039.03 = ΣY^2	848.38 = ΣX^2	590.80 = ΣXY

(B) Calculations

1. Beta:

$$\frac{(T \times \Sigma XY) - (\Sigma Y \times \Sigma X)}{(T \times \Sigma X^2) - (\Sigma X)^2} = \frac{(16 \times 590.80) - (54.84 \times 66.62)}{(16 \times 848.38) - (66.62)^2} = .63$$

2. Alpha:

$$[\Sigma Y]/T] - [\text{Beta} \times (\Sigma X/T)] = [54.84/16] - [.63 \times (66.62/16)] = .79\%$$

3. Standard Deviation of Random Error Term:

$$\{[\Sigma Y^2 - (\text{Alpha} \times \Sigma Y) - (\text{Beta} \times \Sigma XY)]/[T-2]\}^{1/2}$$
$$= \{[1039.03 - (.79 \times 54.84) - (.63 \times 590.80)]/[16-2]\}^{1/2} = 6.67\%$$

4. Standard Error of Beta:

$$\text{Standard Deviation of Random Error Term}/\{\Sigma X^2 - [(\Sigma X)^2/T]\}^{1/2}$$
$$= 6.67/\{848.38 - [(66.62)^2/16]\}^{1/2} = .28$$

5. Standard Error of Alpha:

$$\text{Standard Deviation of Random Error Term}/\{T - [(\Sigma X)^2/\Sigma X^2]\}^{1/2}$$
$$= 6.67/\{16 - [(66.62)^2/848.38]\}^{1/2} = 2.03$$

6. Correlation Coefficient:

$$\frac{(T \times \Sigma XY) - (\Sigma Y \times \Sigma X)}{\{[(T \times \Sigma Y^2) - (\Sigma Y)^2] \times [(T \times \Sigma X^2) - (\Sigma X)^2]\}^{1/2}}$$
$$= \frac{(16 \times 590.80) - (54.84 \times 66.62)}{\{[(16 \times 1039.03) - (54.84)^2] \times [(16 \times 848.38) - (66.62)^2]\}^{1/2}} = .52$$

7. Coefficient of Determination:

$$(\text{Correlation Coefficient})^2 = (.52)^2 = .27$$

8. Coefficient of Nondetermination:

$$1 - \text{Coefficient of Determination} = 1 - .27 = .73$$

NOTE: All summations are to be carried out over *t* where *t* goes from 1 to *T* (in this example, *t* = 1, 2, …, 16).

Figure 17.7

Market model for Widget.

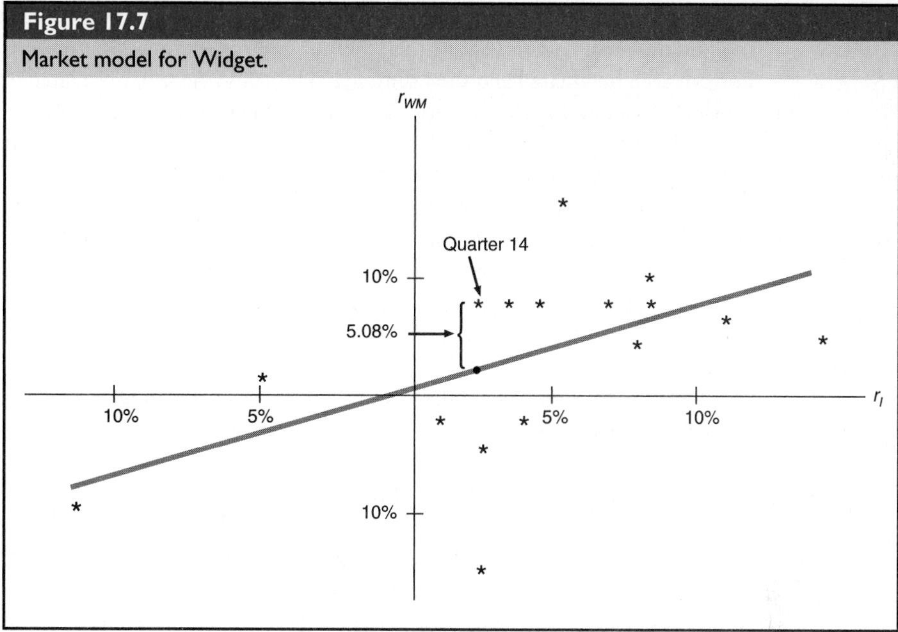

Figure 17.7 presents a scatter diagram of the returns on WM(r_{WM}) and the index r_I. Also shown in the figure is a graph of the market model with the random error term deleted — that is, the figure has a graph of the following line:

$$r_{WM} = .79\% + .63r_I. \tag{17.7}$$

The vertical distance of each point in the scatter diagram from this line represents an estimate of the size of the random error term for the corresponding quarter. The exact distance can be found by rewriting equation (17.6) as

$$r_{WM} - (.79\% + .63r_I) = \epsilon_{WM}. \tag{17.8}$$

For example, looking at part (A) of Table 17.2, three quarters ago (quarter 14) the return on WM and the index were 7.55% and 2.66%, respectively. The value of ϵ_{WM} for that quarter can be calculated by using equation (17.8) as follows:

$$7.55\% - [.79\% + (.63 \times 2.66\%)] = 5.08\%.$$

The values of ϵ_{WM} can be similarly calculated for the other 15 quarters of the estimation period. The standard deviation of the resulting set of 16 numbers is an estimate of the **standard deviation of the random error term** (or residual standard deviation), and is shown in Table 17.2 to be equal to 6.67%. This number can be viewed as an estimate of the historical unique risk of WM.

The market model for WM that is shown in Figure 17.7 corresponds to the regression line for the scatter diagram. Recalling that a straight line is defined by its intercept and slope, it can be shown that there are no other values for alpha and beta that will define a straight line that fits the scatter diagram any better than the regression line. This means that there is no line that could be drawn that would result in a smaller standard deviation of the random error term. Thus, the regression line is often referred to as the line of "best fit."

Equivalently, the line of best fit is the line that has the smallest sum of squared values of the random error terms. That is, the 16 random error terms associated with the regression line can each be squared and then summed. This sum (the sum of squared errors) is smaller for the line of best fit than the sum associated with any other line.

For example, in equation (17.8) if alpha equalled 1.5% and beta equalled .8, then the random error term ϵ_{WM} could be calculated for each of the 16 quarters. With these 16 values, the standard deviation of the random error term could be calculated by squaring each value, summing up the squared values, and dividing the sum by 14 (16 – 2). The standard deviation of the random error term would then be the squared root of this number. However, it would be larger than 6.67%, which is the standard deviation of the random error term associated with the line of best fit—that is, the line with an alpha of .79% and a beta of .63.

It should be remembered that a security's "true" historical beta cannot be observed. All that can be done is to estimate its value. Thus even if a security's "true" beta remained the same forever, its estimated value, obtained in the manner shown in Table 17.2, would still change from time to time because of mistakes (known as sampling errors) in estimating it. For example, if a different set of 16 quarters were examined, the resulting estimated beta for WM would almost certainly be different from .63, the estimated value for the set of 16 quarters given in Table 17.2. The **standard error of beta** shown in Table 17.2 attempts to indicate the extent of such estimation errors. Given a number of necessary assumptions (for example, the "true" beta did not change during the 16-quarter estimation period), the chances are roughly two out of three that the "true" beta is within a standard error, plus or minus, of the estimated beta. Thus, Widget's "true" beta is likely to be larger than .35 (= .63 –.28) and smaller than .91 (= .63 + .28). Similarly, the **standard error of alpha** provides an indication of the magnitude of the possible sampling error that has been made in estimating alpha.

The **correlation coefficient** that is shown in Table 17.2 provides an indication of how closely the returns on Widget were associated with the returns on the index. Because its range is between –1 and +1, the value for WM of .52 indicates a mildly strong positive relationship between WM and the index. This means that larger returns for Widget seem to be associated with larger returns on the index.

The **coefficient of determination** represents the proportion of variation in the return on WM that is related to the variation in the return on the index. That is, it shows how much of the movements in Widget's returns can be explained by movements in the returns on the index. The table shows that 27% of the movements in the return on Widget during the 16-quarter estimation period can be attributed to movements in the return on the index.

Because the **coefficient of nondetermination** is 1 minus the coefficient of determination, it represents the proportion (73%) of movements in the return on Widget that is not due to movements in the return on the index.

Figure 17.8 shows a page from the Security Risk Evaluation report prepared by Merrill Lynch, Pierce, Fenner & Smith Inc. Percentage price changes for many stocks, calculated for each of 60 months (when available), were compared by means of the corresponding percentage changes in the Standard & Poor's 500 using the market model in Table 17.2. Seven of the resulting values from this analysis are of interest for each stock.

The values shown under *Beta* and *Alpha* indicate the slope and intercept, respectively, of the straight line that is the best fit for the scatter diagram of the percentage price changes

Figure 17.8

Sample page from security risk evaluation by Merrill Lynch, Pierce, Fenner & Smith Inc.

Ticker Symbol	Security Name	92/04 Close Price	Beta	Alpha	R-Sqr	Resid Std Dev-n	–Std. Err.– of Beta	–Std. Err.– of Alpha	Adjusted Beta	Number of Observ
AOI	AOI COAL CO	0.500	1.11	−1.79	0.07	19.23	0.49	2.51	1.07	60
APAT	APA OPTICS INC	4.875	0.60	0.80	0.08	9.66	0.25	1.26	0.73	60
APIE	API ENTERPRISES INC	0.688	1.00	2.51	0.02	26.90	0.69	3.51	1.00	60
ASKI	ASK COMPUTER SYS INC	14.875	1.65	−0.06	0.37	10.82	0.28	1.41	1.43	60
ATV	ARC INTL CORP	0.813	1.22	−1.38	0.07	20.71	0.53	2.70	1.15	60
ASTA	AST RESEARCH INC	16.750	1.47	1.66	0.16	16.75	0.43	2.19	1.31	60
ARX	ARX INC	1.875	1.02	−1.90	0.07	17.02	0.43	2.22	1.01	60
ASAA	ASA INTL LTD	1.875	0.79	−1.03	0.01	23.55	0.60	3.07	0.86	60
RCH	ARCO CHEM CO	45.375	1.33	0.03	0.47	7.35	0.19	1.00	1.22	55
ANBC	ANB CORP	36.375	−0.02	1.80	0.10	1.90	0.13	0.56	0.32	12
ATCE	ATC ENVIRONMENTAL INC	2.813	−0.02	0.68	0.02	21.22	0.75	3.22	0.32	46
ATI	ATI MED INC	3.750	0.26	0.07	0.01	19.11	0.49	2.49	0.51	60
ATCIC	ATC INC	1.750	0.61	0.38	0.00	26.63	0.68	3.47	0.74	60
ATNN	ATNN INC	0.219	1.38	1.51	0.00	50.89	1.30	6.64	1.25	60
ATTNF	ATTN AVECA ENTERTAINMENT COR	1.750	2.81	0.39	0.05	42.49	1.59	6.97	2.20	39
AVSY	AVTR SYS INC	0.203	−0.54	6.23	0.06	55.49	3.33	14.41	−0.02	18
AWCSA	AW COMPUTER SYS INC CLASS A	5.875	1.23	7.08	0.01	71.41	1.85	9.29	1.15	60
ARON	AARON RENTS INC	13.125	0.92	−0.23	0.16	10.30	0.26	1.34	0.95	60
ABIX	ABATIX ENVIRONMENTAL CORP	1.750	0.00	0.36	0.03	17.54	0.67	2.96	0.34	37
ABT	ABBOTT LABS	66.000	0.87	0.87	0.51	4.31	0.11	0.56	0.92	60
ABERF	ABER RES LTD	0.969	1.53	3.52	0.02	29.18	1.11	4.93	1.35	37
AANB	ABIGAIL ADAMS NATL BANCORP I	11.000	−1.50	1.81	0.14	12.61	0.70	2.80	−0.66	24
ABBK	ABINGTON BANCORP INC	5.875	1.37	−0.15	0.09	20.09	0.51	2.62	1.24	60
ABD	ABIOMED INC	13.000	1.08	1.04	0.07	18.21	0.47	2.43	1.05	57
ABY	ABITIBI PRICE INC	12.625	0.65	−1.42	0.23	6.00	0.15	0.80	0.77	57
ABRI	ABRAMS INDS INC	4.313	1.28	1.90	0.07	20.91	0.53	2.73	1.18	60
ACAP	ACAP CORP	0.500	0.05	0.88	0.02	13.80	0.35	1.80	0.37	60
ACLE	ACCEL INTL CORP	6.750	1.12	−0.66	0.20	11.10	0.28	1.45	1.08	60
AKLM	ACCLAIM ENTHT INC	6.375	1.29	0.02	0.03	23.62	0.84	3.58	1.19	46
ACCU	ACCUHEALTH INC	5.438	0.53	0.60	0.00	13.47	0.49	2.17	0.69	41

Based on S&P 500 Index. Using Straight Regression Page 3

SOURCE: Reprinted by permission. Copyright © Merrill Lynch, Pierce, Fenner & Smith Incorporated.

for the stock and index. For example, during the 60-month period covered, the stock of Ask Computer had a beta and alpha of 1.65 and −.06%, respectively.

The value of *R-Sqr*, short for **R-squared**, is equivalent to the coefficient of determination shown in Table 17.2.[31] Having a value of .37 means that 37% of the variation in Ask Computer's price changes could be attributed to changes in the market index over the 60-month period.

The value of *Resid Std Dev-n* (**residual standard deviation**) corresponds to the standard deviation of the random error term in Table 17.2. Ask Computer can be seen to have a residual standard deviation of 10.82%.

Std. Err. of Beta (standard error of beta) indicates that there is roughly a two out of three chance that the "true" beta for Ask Computer is between 1.37 (= 1.65 – .28) and 1.93 (= 1.65 + .28). Similarly, the value under *Std. Err. of Alpha* indicates that there is

[31] R is used here to denote the correlation coefficient; sometimes (as in Chapter 8) the Greek letter rho (ρ) is used instead. Thus R-squared is equivalent to ρ-squared, or the square of the correlation coefficient.

roughly a two out of three chance that the "true" alpha for Ask Computer lies between −.147 (= −.06 − 1.41) and 1.35 (= −.06 + 1.41).

The seventh value in Figure 17.8 that is of particular interest is the **adjusted beta** value, which is discussed next.

Adjusting Beta

Without any information at all, it would be reasonable to estimate the beta of a stock to be equal to 1.0, the average size of beta. Given a chance to see how the stock moved relative to the market over some time period, a modification of this prior estimate would seem appropriate. Such a modification would sensibly produce a final estimate of beta that would lie between the value of 1.0 and its estimated value based purely on historical price changes.

Formal procedures for making such modifications have been adopted by most investment firms that estimate betas. The specific adjustments made may differ from time to time and, in some cases, from stock to stock. For example Merrill Lynch calculates *adjusted beta* values by giving approximately 66% weight to the historical estimate of beta and approximately 34% weight to the prior value of beta of 1.0 for each stock. More generally,

$$\beta_a = (.66 \times \beta_h) + (.34 \times 1.0) \tag{17.9}$$

where β_a and β_h are the adjusted and historical betas, respectively.[32] Examination of equation (17.9) indicates that this procedure takes the historical beta for a security and adjusts it by giving it a value closer to 1.0. Thus, historical betas less than 1.0 are made larger but are still less than 1.0, and historical betas greater than 1.0 are made smaller but are still greater than 1.0. The adjustments are in this direction because the weights (.66 and .34) are positive and add up to 1.0, indicating the adjustment procedure is an averaging technique.

Table 17.3 shows the extent to which this procedure anticipates differences between historical and future betas. The second column lists the unadjusted historical betas for eight portfolios of 100 securities each, based on monthly price changes from July 1947 through June 1954 (the portfolios were designed to have significantly different betas during this period). The third column of the table shows the values obtained when an adjustment of the type used by Merrill Lynch was applied. The betas in the fourth column are based on price changes over the subsequent seven years. For a majority of the portfolios, the adjusted betas are closer in magnitude to the subsequent historical betas than are the unadjusted betas. This suggests that the adjusted historical beta is a more accurate estimate of the future beta than the unadjusted historical beta.

The fifth column of Table 17.3 shows the historical betas estimated using data from a third seven-year period. Comparing the unadjusted betas in columns 2, 4, and 5, it can be seen that there is a continuing tendency for betas to shrink toward the mean value of 1.0 over time. Thus, adjustment procedures seem to have some usefulness when it comes to estimating betas for a future time period.

It seems plausible that true betas not only vary over time but have a tendency to move back toward average levels, since extreme values are likely to be moderated over time. A firm

---

[32] Adjusted betas are also published in the *Value Line Investment Survey* and the *Value Line Investment Survey: Canadian Edition*; their adjusted beta is equal to $(.67 \times \beta_h) + (.35 \times 1.0)$. Thus, the adjustment procedures of Value Line and Merrill Lynch are quite similar. See Meir Statman, "Betas Compared: Merrill Lynch vs. Value Line," *Journal of Portfolio Management* 7, no. 2 (Winter 1981): 41–44.

Table 17.3

Ex Ante and *Ex Post* Beta Values for Portfolios of 100 Securities Each.

	July 1947–June 1954			
Portfolio (1)	*Unadjusted* (2)	*Adjusted* (3)	*July 1954–June 1961* (4)	*July 1961–June 1968* (5)
1	.36	.48	.57	.72
2	.61	.68	.71	.79
3	.78	.82	.88	.88
4	.91	.93	.96	.92
5	1.01	1.01	1.03	1.04
6	1.13	1.10	1.13	1.02
7	1.26	1.21	1.24	1.08
8	1.47	1.39	1.32	1.15

SOURCE: Marshall E. Blume, "Betas and Their Regression Tendencies," *Journal of Finance* 30, no. 3 (June 1975): 792.

whose operations or financing make the risk of its equity considerably different from that of other firms is more likely to move back toward the average than away from it. Such changes in betas are due to real economic phenomena, not simply an artifact of overly simple statistical procedures. There is, however, no reason to expect every stock's true beta to move to the same average in the same manner at the same speed. In this regard, some fundamental analysis of the firm may prove more useful than the adoption of more sophisticated statistical methods for processing past price changes in estimating beta.

Although historical betas for portfolios can provide useful information about future betas, historical betas for individual securities are subject to great error and should be treated accordingly. Note the magnitude of the standard errors of the betas shown earlier in Figure 17.8.

Table 17.4 provides another view. Every stock listed on the New York Stock Exchange was assigned to one of ten classes in each year from 1931 through 1967, based on the magnitude of its historical beta calculated using data from the preceding five years. The stocks in the top 10% of each January's ranking were assigned to class 10, the next 10% to class 9, and so on. The table shows the percent of the stocks that were in the same class and within one risk class five years later. Also shown are the entries that would be expected if there were no relationship between such past and future beta classes. Examination of the table reveals that individual security betas have some but not a great deal of predictive value.

Figure 17.9 shows that the predictive ability of historical portfolio betas improves with the amount of diversification in a portfolio. The vertical axis plots the percentage of the differences in (measured) portfolio betas (based on weekly price changes) in one year that can be attributed to differences in their (measured) betas in the prior year. The horizontal axis indicates the number of securities in each portfolio. It can be seen in the figure that the historical betas for portfolios containing roughly 10 to 20 securities or more have a high degree of predictive ability. Thus, individual security betas are worth estimating even though they are rather inaccurate when viewed by themselves. This is because their

Table 17.4

Movement of Stocks Among Beta Classes.

	Percentage of Stocks in the Same Beta Class Five Years Later		Percentage of Stocks in the Same Beta Class or Within One Risk Class Five Years Later	
Risk Class	*Actual*	*Expected If There Were No Relationship*	*Actual*	*Expected If There Were No Relationship*
10 (highest beta values)	35.2%	10%	69.3%	20%
9	18.4	10	53.7	30
8	16.4	10	45.3	30
7	13.3	10	40.9	30
6	13.9	10	39.3	30
5	13.6	10	41.7	30
4	13.2	10	40.2	30
3	15.9	10	44.6	30
2	21.5	10	60.9	30
1 (lowest beta values)	40.5	10	62.3	20

SOURCE: William F. Sharpe and Guy M. Cooper, "Risk-Return Classes of New York Stock Exchange Common Stocks, 1931–1967," *Financial Analysts Journal* 28, no. 2 (March/April 1972): 53.

Figure 17.9

Percentage of differences in beta values attributable to differences in prior year's betas.

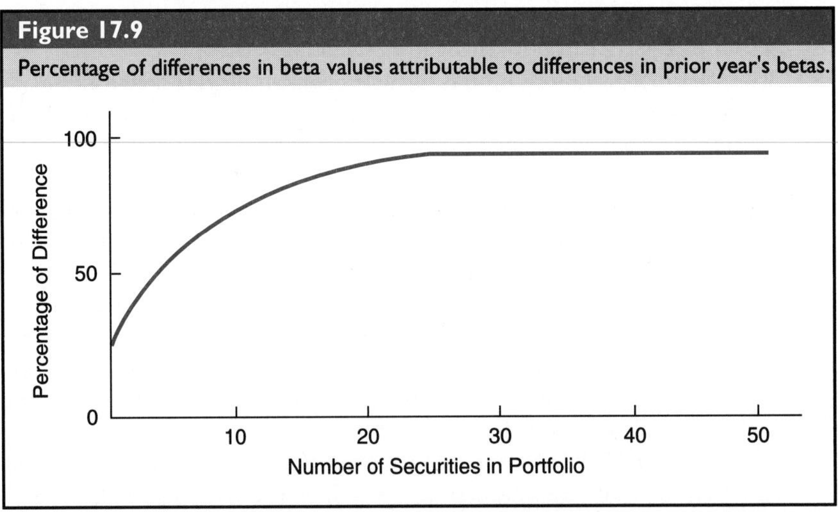

SOURCE: Robert A. Levy, "On the Short-term Stationarity of Beta Coefficients," *Financial Analysis Journal* 27, no. 6 (November/December 1971): 57.

individual inaccuracies seem to cancel out one another when the beta of a diversified portfolio is calculated, resulting in quite an accurate estimate of the portfolio's beta.

► Leverage and Beta

The beta of a *firm* represents the sensitivity of the aggregate value of the firm to changes in the value of the market portfolio. It depends on both the demand for the firm's products and the firm's operating costs. However, most firms have both debt and equity outstanding. This means that the beta of a firm's *equity* (that is, stock) depends on the beta of the firm and the firm's financial leverage. For example, imagine that there are two firms that are identical in every way except that firm A has debt while firm B is free of debt. This means that even though they have the same earnings before interest and taxes (EBIT), they will have different earnings after taxes (EAT) because A, unlike B, has to make interest payments. In this situation, the firm betas for A and B are the same, but the stock beta for A will be greater than the stock beta for B. The difference in their debt levels is the reason for the difference in their stock betas. This is because the debt makes the earnings available to common shareholders more variable for A than for B. Thus, the stock beta for A could be viewed as being equal to the stock beta it would have if it had no debt (that is, the beta of B) plus an adjustment for the amount of debt it actually has outstanding.

One method that has been suggested for determining the influence of debt on the beta of the stock of a firm involves a four-step procedure.[33] First, the current market values of the firm's outstanding debt D and equity E must be determined. Once this is done, the current market value of the levered firm V_L can be determined:

$$V_L = D + E. \tag{17.10}$$

Second, the market value of the firm *if it were unlevered* must be determined, using the following formula:

$$V_u = V_L - \tau D \tag{17.11}$$

where:

V_u is the market value of the firm if it was unlevered,

τ is the average corporate tax rate for the firm,

D is the market value of the firm's debt.

Third, the beta of the firm can be calculated after estimating the betas of the firm's debt β_{debt} and equity β_{equity} by using the following formula:

$$\beta_{\text{firm}} = \beta_{\text{debt}} \frac{(1-\tau)D}{v_u} + \beta_{\text{equity}} \frac{E}{V_u}. \tag{17.12}$$

Fourth, the effect of any degree of leverage on the equity beta of the firm can be determined by restating equation (17.12). Specifically, solving the equation for β_{equity} results in[34]

$$\beta_{\text{equity}} = \beta_{\text{firm}} + (\beta_{\text{firm}} - \beta_{\text{debt}}) \left(\frac{D}{E}\right)(1-\tau). \tag{17.13}$$

---

[33] The method is developed more fully in Richard A. Brealey and Stewart C. Myers, *Principles of Corporate Finance* (New York: McGraw-Hill, 1991), pp. 191–192, 468–469; and Thomas E. Copeland and J. Fred Weston, *Financial Theory and Corporate Policy* (Reading, MA: Addison-Wesley, 1988), Chapter 13.

[34] To derive equation (17.13), note that equation (17.11) can be written as $V_u = D + E - \tau D$ since $V_L = D + E$. Hence the quantity $D + E - \tau D$ can be substituted for V_u in equation (17.12), and then the altered equation can be solved for β_{equity} and simplified, resulting in equation (17.13).

In evaluating equation (17.13), it should be noted that the value of β_{firm} does not change as the firm's debt-equity ratio (D/E) is changed. Assuming that the value of β_{debt} also does not change, then increasing the firm's debt-equity ratio will increase the beta of the firm's equity. This makes intuitive sense, because a higher debt-equity ratio will make a firm's EAT more volatile. Conversely, lowering a firm's debt-equity ratio should lower the firm's equity beta because it makes EAT less volatile.

This property of beta can be useful in estimating the beta of a firm's equity if the firm has recently altered its debt-equity ratio (or is contemplating increasing the ratio). For example, imagine that until last month ABC Inc. had $60 000 000 of equity and $40 000 000 of debt outstanding for a total firm value of $100 000 000; its tax rate is 30%. Using the market model shown in Table 17.2, but applied to data before the recent equity issuance, it is determined that the equity beta and debt beta of ABC are 1.40 and .20, respectively. However, ABC has just issued $20 000 000 of equity and used the proceeds to retire some of the debt so that the current values of ABC's debt and equity are $74 000 000 and $20 000 000, respectively. (The $74 000 000 value of equity represents the sum of $20 000 000 in new equity and $54 000 000 in old equity, which has decreased in value by $6 000 000 due to the loss of tax shields resulting from the $20 000 000 reduction in ABC's debt.) What is the equity beta of ABC likely to be in the immediate future?

The previously described four-step procedure can be used to answer this question. First, it is noted from equation (17.10) that the value of ABC before the new equity issuance was $100 000 000. Second, it is noted from equation (17.11) that the value of ABC if the firm were unlevered would be equal to ($100 000 000 – (.3 × $40 000 000) =) $88 000 000. Third, the beta of the firm can be estimated using equation (17.12):

$$\beta_{\text{firm}} = .20\left[\frac{(1-.3)\$40\ 000\ 000}{\$88\ 000\ 000}\right] + 1.40\left(\frac{\$60\ 000\ 000}{\$88\ 000\ 000}\right)$$

$$= 1.02$$

Lastly, the current equity beta (that is, the equity beta after the recent issuance of $20 000 000 of equity) can be estimated by using equation (17.13).

$$\beta_{\text{equity}} = 1.02 + 91.02 - .20)\left(\frac{\$20\ 000\ 000}{\$74\ 000\ 000}\right)(1-.3)$$

$$= 1.17$$

Hence, the reduction in the amount of debt that ABC has outstanding has reduced the beta of the equity from 1.40 to 1.17.[35]

Industry Beta Values

Firms in industries having highly cyclical demand or large fixed costs might be expected to have higher firm betas than those in industries with more stable demand or greater variable costs, since the former will have greater variability in EBIT. Differences in financial leverage could wholly offset such factors, leaving few, if any, differences among the stock betas of firms in different industries. However, this does not seem to be the case. Firms in certain

[35] It is assumed here that ABC's bond beta and average tax were unaffected by the new issuance of equity. More complex analyses are sometimes utilized to take into account the possible impact of capital structure changes upon them.

Table 17.5

Predicted Betas by Industry in Canada, December 1995.

Industry	*Beta*	*Industry*	*Beta*
Integrated Mines	1.16	Mining	1.16
Gold & Precious Minerals	1.40	Integrated Oils	0.91
Oil & Gas Producers	0.91	Oil & Gas Services	0.91
Paper & Forest Products	1.01	Food Processing	0.79
Tobacco	0.79	Distilleries	0.79
Breweries & Beverages	0.79	Household Goods	0.79
Autos & Parts	0.79	Biotech & Pharmaceutical	0.69
Steel	1.25	Fabrication & Engineer.	0.98
Transportation Equipment	0.98	Technology—Hardware	1.06
Building Materials	0.98	Chemicals & Fertilizers	0.98
Business Services	0.98	Technology—Software	1.06
Real Estate	0.84	Transport & Environment	0.81
Pipelines	0.63	Telephone Utilities	0.63
Gas & Electric Utilities	0.65	Broadcasting	0.84
Cable & Entertainment	0.84	Publishing & Printing	0.84
Wholesale Distributors	0.84	Food Stores	0.84
Department Stores	0.84	Specialty Stores	0.84
Hospitality	0.84	Banks & Trusts	0.99
Investment Co. & Funds	0.99	Insurance	0.99
Financial Management	0.99	Conglomerates	1.08

SOURCE: Data provided by *BARRA International*, Dorval, Quebec, December, 1995.

industries do tend to have higher stock betas than those in other industries, and, by and large, the classifications agree with prior expectations.

Table 17.5 shows the predicted average values of beta for stocks in various industry classifications. Stock prices of firms whose products are termed necessities tend to respond less than the stock prices of most other firms when expectations about the future health of the economy are revised. That is, firms producing necessities (such as utilities or food) tend to have lower betas because they tend to have more stable earnings. On the other hand, stock prices of firms that manufacture luxuries tend to respond more than most others when expectations about the future health of the economy are revised. That is, firms in luxuries (such as travel or electronics) tend to have high betas, because they tend to have cyclical earnings. The mining industries also have high betas reflecting the cyclical nature of their earnings.

Forecasting Beta

Information of the type shown in Table 17.5 can be used to adjust historical equity betas. For example, the knowledge that a corporation is in the steel industry suggests that a reasonable prior estimate of its equity beta is 1.25. Thus, it makes more sense to adjust its historical equity beta toward a value of 1.25 than 1.0, the average for all stocks, as was suggested in equation (17.9).

The procedure used to adjust historical betas involves an implicit prediction equation for future betas. Equation (17.9) can be written more generally as:

$$\beta_a = a + b\beta_h \tag{17.14}$$

where a and b are constants. One way to consider the differences in industry betas is to alter equation (17.14) as follows:

$$\beta_a = a\beta_{\text{ind}} + b\beta_h \tag{17.15}$$

where β_{ind} denotes the average equity beta of the industry to which the stock belongs.

For example, consider the values of .33 and .67 for a and b, respectively. Biopharm is a pharmaceutical firm whose historical beta is 0.93. What is its adjusted beta? Noting that the average equity beta for stocks in the pharmaceutical industry is 0.69, its adjusted beta can be calculated by using equation (17.15) as follows:

$$\begin{aligned}\beta_a &= (.33 \times 0.69) + (.67 \times 0.93)\\ &= 0.85.\end{aligned}$$

Thus, Air Express has an adjusted beta of 0.85, which lies between its historical beta of 0.93 and the average beta in its industry of 0.69. Indeed, this is what equation (17.15) accomplishes: it alters a historical beta to give an adjusted beta lying between β_h and β_{ind}.

Multiple-Industry Firms

What happens if the firm has divisions that are in different industries? When there are two industries involved, equation (17.15) is modified as follows:

$$\beta_a = a(E_{\text{ind1}}\beta_{\text{ind1}} + E_{\text{ind2}}\beta_{\text{ind2}}) + b\beta_h \tag{17.16}$$

where E_{ind1} and E_{ind2} denote the percentages of the firm's earnings that are from industries 1 and 2, respectively, and β_{ind1} and β_{ind2} are the betas for industries 1 and 2, respectively.[36]

As an example, consider United Industries, a firm that has half of its earnings coming from a division that is in the gold mining industry and half coming from a division that is in the oil and gas industry. Assuming that a and b are equal to .33 and .67, respectively, and that the historical beta for United Industries is 1.3, its adjusted beta can be calculated in two steps.

First, the value of $E_{\text{ind1}}\beta_{\text{ind1}} + E_{\text{ind2}}\beta_{\text{ind2}}$ needs to be calculated. Doing so produces a value of $(.5 \times 1.4) + (.5 \times 0.91) = 1.16$. This can be interpreted as the average equity beta for any stock whose firm has equal business interests in the electronics and aerospace industries.

Second, the adjusted beta of United Industries can be calculated using equation (17.16) as $(.33 \times 1.16) + (.67 \times 1.3) = 1.25$. Note that this value lies between the firm's historical beta of 1.3 and its "industry" beta of 1.16.

Adjustments Based on Financial Characteristics

Various financial characteristics can also be used to estimate an adjusted beta. For example, stocks with high dividend yields might have lower betas because more of their value is associated with near-term than far-term dividends. Equation (17.16) could thus be augmented to

$$\beta_a = a(E_{\text{ind1}}\beta_{\text{ind1}} + E_{\text{ind2}}\beta_{\text{ind2}}) + b\beta_h + cY \tag{17.17}$$

[36] The term $(E_{\text{ind1}}\beta_{\text{ind1}} + E_{\text{ind2}}\beta_{\text{ind2}})$ would simply be expanded if more than two industries were involved.

where c is a constant and Y is the dividend yield of the firm's stock.

Table 17.6 shows a beta prediction equation of this form, using US historic data from 1928 through 1982.[37] To estimate the beta of a security using this prediction equation, start with a constant based on the industry (referred to as the "sector") in which the security is classified. Add to this constant an amount equal to the security's historical beta times 0.576. Note that this is similar to the historical beta shown in equation (17.9). Finally, add (1) the security's dividend yield times –.019, and (2) the security's "size attribute" times –.105.[38] Algebraically, the model is:

$$\beta_a = a_s + (.576 \times \beta_h) + (-.019 \times Y) + (-.105 \times S) \qquad (17.18)$$

where a_s denotes the constant associated with the sector to which the stock belongs, β_h is the historical beta, Y is the dividend yield, and S is the size of the firm. With this formula, securities having higher yields are predicted to have lower betas, as are those with larger market values of equity outstanding.

Table 17.6

A Beta Prediction Equation Derived from a Factor Model.

Constant Term	
Sector	*Value*
Basic industry	.455
Capital goods	.425
Consumer staple	.307
Consumer cyclical	.443
Credit cyclical	.429
Energy	.394
Finance	.398
Transportation	.255
Utilities	.340
Variable Term	
Attribute	*Coefficient*
Beta	.576
Yield	–.019
Size	–.105

SOURCE: Blake Grossman and William F. Sharpe, "Factors in Security Returns," paper presented at the Center for the Study of Banking and Financial Markets, University of Washington, March 1984.

[37] In this method, both historical and adjusted betas are calculated relative to a value-weighted index of the returns on all stocks listed on the New York Stock Exchange. All attributes were calculated using data available a full month prior to the beginning of the month in which stock returns are measured. This avoids statistical problems and provides results that can be used for actual portfolio management.

[38] The dividend yield is measured in percent per year. The "size attribute" is calculated by taking the logarithm (to the base 10) of the total market value of equity outstanding (that is, price per share times shares outstanding), expressed in billions of dollars.

An Example

As an example, consider a stock that is classified as belonging to "basic industry." It has a historical beta of 1.2, a dividend yield over the previous 12 months of 4%, and an aggregate market value of $7 billion (that is, the firm has 100 million shares outstanding and the stock is selling for $70 per share). Using equation (17.18), its adjusted beta is

$$\begin{aligned}\beta_a &= .455 + (.576 \times 1.2) + (-.019 \times 4) + [-.105 \times (\log 7)] \\ &= .455 + .69 - .08 - .09 \\ &= .98.\end{aligned}$$

Such prediction equations, based on multifactor models, fit historical data considerably better than those that use only historical betas. One study reported an improvement of 86% over the more simple adjusted beta approach.[39] However, such figures describe only the extent to which the equations fit a given set of data. Since the true test of a prediction equation is its ability to *predict*, only extensive experience with such approaches can, in the final analysis, determine how well various factor models can predict beta values.

► Beta Services

Services providing betas on a regular basis in published form are available in several countries. Many use only past price changes to form estimates. Some derive their estimates from more general factor models. One service uses weekly data for two years; another, monthly data for five years. One estimates betas for US securities relative to Standard & Poor's 500; another, relative to the New York Stock Exchange Composite Index; and so on. In each case, estimates for individual securities are subject to error. Thus, it is hardly surprising that estimated values for a given security obtained by different services using different procedures are not the same. This does not indicate that some are useless, only that they should be used appropriately and with caution.

In Canada, betas are provided by *The Polymetric Report, The Value Line Investment Survey: Canadian Edition* and the *Beta Book* published by Barra International, Ltd.

GROWTH VERSUS VALUE

Common stocks are often divided into two categories—**growth stocks** and **value stocks**. Although there are no hard-and-fast rules on how they are divided and disagreement exists among investment professionals as to what category certain stocks belong to, there are two financial measures that are often used to distinguish growth stocks from value stocks. These are the book-value-to-market-value ratio (BV/MV) and the earnings-to-price ratio (E/P).[40]

---

[39] Barr Rosenberg and Vinay Marathe, "The Prediction of Investment Risk: Systematic and Residual Risk," *Proceedings of the Seminar on the Analysis of Security Prices*, University of Chicago, November 1975. Also see Barr Rosenberg, "Prediction of Common Stock Investment Risk," *Journal of Portfolio Management* 11, no. 1 (Fall 1984): 44–53, and "Prediction of Common Stock Betas," *Journal of Portfolio Management* 11, no. 2 (Winter 1985): 5–14.

[40] In general, growth stocks are stocks having rapid increases in earnings whereas value stocks are stocks whose market price seems to be low relative to measures of their worth. Hence, other ratios (such as dividend yield and P/E ratios) are sometimes used in sorting out these two types of stocks.

Book-Value-to-Market-Value Ratio

This ratio is typically calculated as follows. First, the book value of the firm's common stock is determined by using the most recent balance sheet data and calculating the total value of shareholders' equity. Second, the market capitalization of the firm's common stock is determined by taking the most recent market price for the firm's common stock and multiplying it by the number of shares outstanding. Lastly, the book value of shareholders' equity is divided by the market capitalization to arrive at their BV/MV ratio. Relatively low values of this ratio characterize growth stocks, and relatively high values characterize value stocks.[41]

An interesting question is whether there is a relationship between stock returns and their BV/MV ratios. Fama and French examined this issue and found that there was such a relationship.[42] Specifically, they found that on average the larger the size of the BV/MV ratio, the larger the rate of return. Table 17.7 presents their findings.

Panel (a) of Table 17.7 was constructed as follows. First, at the end of June 1963, the book value was determined for each stock on the NYSE, AMEX, and NASDAQ using the annual financial statements for the fiscal year ending in 1962. This value was then divided by the market capitalization for each firm, based on the market price for each firm at the end of December 1962. Second, using these BV/MV ratios, the firms were ranked from smallest to largest and formed into 12 portfolios. Third, the return on each portfolio was tracked monthly from July 1963 through June 1964. Fourth, the entire process was updated by a year so that returns were calculated from July 1964 to June 1965 on 12 BV/MV-ranked portfolios that were formed based on data as of the end of 1963. The process was repeated until a set of monthly returns was available from July 1963 through December 1990 for each of the 12 portfolios.

Table 17.7 (a) shows a clear relationship between average monthly return and the BV/MV ratio—higher values of the ratio are associated with higher average returns. Remembering that growth stocks tend to have low BV/MV ratios and value stocks tend to have high BV/MV ratios, this suggests that over the period analyzed, value stocks tended to outperform growth stocks.

Earning-to-Price Ratio

This ratio is typically calculated as follows. First, the accounting value of the firm's earnings per share is determined by using the most recent income statement and dividing the firm's earnings after taxes by the number of shares outstanding. Second, the market price of the firm's common stock is determined by taking the most recent price at which the firm's common stock was traded. Lastly, the earnings-per-share figure is divided by the market price of the stock to arrive at the E/P ratio. Relatively low values of this ratio characterize growth stocks, and relatively high values characterize value stocks.

---

[41] The S&P/BARRA Value Stock Index and the S&P/BARRA Growth Stock Index involve dividing the S&P 500 stocks into two groups based on the size of their BV/MV ratios every six months. The stocks in each group are then used to form these two market-capitalization-weighted indices. The construction of market indices is discussed in more detail in Chapter 23.

[42] Eugene F. Fama and Kenneth R. French, "The Cross-Section of Expected Stock Returns," *Journal of Finance* 47, no. 2 (June 1992): 427–465. Also see Barr Rosenberg, Kenneth Reid, and Ronald Lanstein, "Persuasive Evidence of Market Inefficiency," *Journal of Portfolio Management* 11, no. 3 (Spring 1985): 9–16.

Table 17.7

Growth Versus Value Stocks.

	Portfolio Number[a]											
	1	2	3	4	5	6	7	8	9	10	11	12
(a) Portfolios Based on BV/MV Ratio:												
Return	.30	.67	.87	.97	1.04	1.17	1.30	1.44	1.50	1.59	1.92	1.83
BV/MV	.11	.22	.34	.47	.60	.73	.87	1.03	1.23	1.52	1.93	2.77
(b) Portfolios Based on E/P Ratio[b]												
Return	1.04	.93	.94	1.03	1.18	1.22	1.33	1.42	1.46	1.57	1.74	1.72
E/P	.01	.03	.05	.06	.08	.09	.11	.12	.14	.16	.20	.28
(c) Portfolios Based on Size:												
Return	1.64	1.16	1.29	1.24	1.25	1.29	1.17	1.07	1.10	.95	.88	.90
ln(MV)	1.98	3.18	3.63	4.10	4.50	4.89	5.30	5.73	6.24	6.82	7.39	8.44

[a] Portfolios formed based on rankings of indicated financial measure for stocks from smallest (1) to largest (12); return indicates the average monthly return, in percent, from July 1963 through December 1990.

[b] The portfolio of stocks that had negative earnings had an average monthly return of 1.46.

SOURCE: Eugene F. Fama and Kenneth R. French, "The Cross-Section of Expected Stock Returns," *Journal of Finance* 47, no. 2 (June 1992): Table II, pp. 436–437; Table IV, pp. 442–443.

Is there a relationship between stock returns and their E/P ratios? Fama and French examined this issue and discovered such a relationship does exist.[43] Specifically, they found that, on average, the larger the size of the E/P ratio, the larger the rate of return. Their results are shown in Table 17.7(b), which was constructed in the same manner as part (a) except that at the end of each June, firms were ranked and assigned to portfolios on the basis of their E/P ratios.

Except for portfolio 1, part (b) shows a clear relationship between average monthly returns and the E/P ratio—higher values of the ratio are associated with higher average returns. Since growth stocks tend to have low E/P ratios and value stocks tend to have high E/P ratios, this data reinforces the conclusions drawn from the BV/MV data—namely, that value stocks tended to outperform growth stocks over the period analyzed.

There is one other interesting feature of this panel. When Fama and French assigned stocks to portfolios based on their E/P ratios, they assigned those stocks that had negative earnings and hence a negative E/P ratio to a separate portfolio. This portfolio had an average monthly return of 1.46%. Thus, if one considers a portfolio with a negative E/P ratio to be the lowest E/P portfolio, then it can be seen from the table that as E/P gets larger, average returns at first decline and then rise. This has led Fama and French to refer to the relationship between average returns and the E/P ratio as being "U-shaped."

[43] Also see S. Basu, "Investment Performance of Common Stocks in Relation to Their Price-Earnings Ratios: A Test of the Efficient Market Hypothesis," *Journal of Finance* 32, no. 3 (June 1977): 663–682; and "The Relationship Between Earnings' Yield, Market Value and Return for NYSE Common Stocks: Further Evidence," *Journal of Financial Economics* 12, no. 1 (June 1983): 129–156.

Size

Although firm size is not generally used as a criterion for distinguishing growth from value stocks, it is often used to sort stocks. For example, many investment professionals think of stocks in terms of two dimensions, as follows:

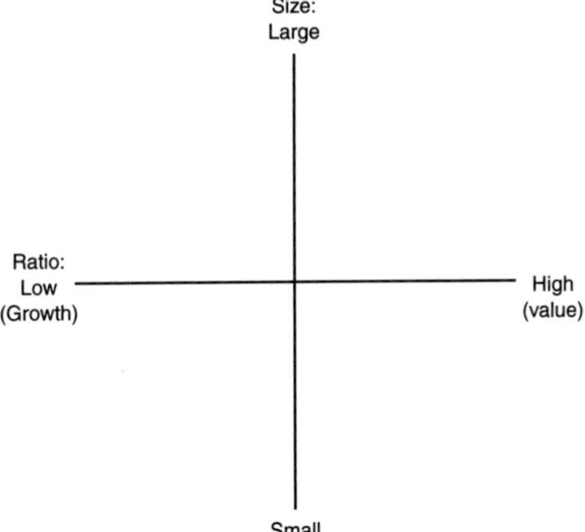

Hence, stocks could be classified as growth or value using the BV/MV ratio and as larger or small using their size. The result is that each stock could be located in a scatter diagram like the one shown.

Typically a stock's market capitalization is used as the measure of its size. This is what Fama and French did when they assigned stocks to one of 12 portfolios after ranking them at the end of each June based on size. Proceeding in a manner analogous to that discussed previously, they tracked the monthly returns for these 12 size-based portfolios from July 1963 to December 1990. Table 17.7(c) displays the average returns and sizes of these portfolios.

In contrast to parts (a) and (b), it can be seen that there is a clear inverse relationship between size and average return. That is, stocks of smaller firms tend to have higher returns than stocks of larger firms. Even more notable is the average return for the smallest portfolio (1). This return is significantly higher than for the next smaller portfolio (2) or for any other. Hence, when some people refer to a **size effect** in stock returns, they are really referring to a "small firm effect."[44]

Interrelationships

The existence of a relationship between any one of three financial variables (BV/MV ratio, E/P ratio, and firm size) and stock returns suggests that at least one missing factor is needed to explain the differences in returns.[45] Hence, it is of interest to examine the interrelationships

---

[44] Other studies of the size effect include Rolf Banz, "The Relationship Between Return and Market Value of Common Stocks," *Journal of Financial Economics* 9, no. 1 (March 1981): 3–18; and Marc R. Reinganum, "Misspecification of Capital Asset Pricing: Empirical Anomalies Based on Earnings Yields and Market Values," *Journal of Financial Economics* 9, no. 1 (March 1981): 19–46.

[45] The missing variable apparently is not beta, as the relationship between these variables and stock returns has been found to exist independent of differences in beta. See Fama and French, "The Cross-Section of Expected Stock Returns."

between the BV/MV ratio, the E/P ratio, firm size, and average returns. The joint effect of E/P ratio and firm size on stock returns is examined next.

E/P, Size, and Average Returns

In order to examine the joint effect of these two financial variables on stock returns, one study noted at each year-end the breakpoints formed by sorting NYSE and AMEX stocks in quintiles based on just size and then on just the E/P ratio.[46] Then, using both of these sets of breakpoints, stocks were assigned to one of 25 size-E/P portfolios for the next year. That is, each stock in the smallest size quintile was assigned to one of five E/P portfolios, then each stock in the next-to-smallest quintile was assigned to one of five E/P portfolios, and so on until there were 25 (= 5 sizes × 5 E/P ratios) size-E/P portfolios. The process was repeated year after year until a set of daily returns was available for each one of the 25 portfolios from 1963 through 1977.

When average returns for the 25 portfolios were compared, it was found that there was a clear inverse relationship between size and average returns for any E/P quintile. For example, consider the five size-ranked portfolios that were formed from the lowest E/P quintile. It was found that when comparing these five portfolios, the larger the size, the smaller the average return.

However, there was no clear relationship between E/P ratios and average returns for any size quintile. For example, consider the five E/P-ranked portfolios that were formed from the smallest size quintile. In this case the largest and third-largest average returns were associated with the lowest and next-to-lowest E/P portfolios. This was contrary to previous observations of the relationship between E/P ratios and average returns. As a consequence, it appears that there is a missing factor that is needed to explain differences in stock returns, and that this factor is more closely related to size than to the E/P ratio.[47]

BV/MV, Size, and Average Returns

Fama and French were interested in the join effect of the BV/MV ratio and firm size on stock returns.[48] Accordingly, they formed 100 portfolios annually based on the rankings of stocks using size and the BV/MV ratio. Monthly returns on these portfolios were then recorded for the period from July 1963 through the end of 1990.

When average returns for the 100 portfolios were compared, it was found that there was an inverse relationship between size and average return for almost every BV/MV decile. For example, comparing the ten size-ranked portfolios that were formed from the largest BV/MV decile, it was found that, in general, the larger the size, the smaller the average return. The only exceptions were the two smallest BV/MV deciles, in which there was no apparent relationship between size and return.

Furthermore, there was a clear direct relationship between BV/MV ratios and average returns for any size quintile. For example, a comparison of the ten BV/MV-ranked portfolios

---

[46] Marc R. Reinganum, "Misspecification of Capital Asset Pricing." Also see Rolf W. Banz and William J. Breen, "Sample Dependent Results Using Accounting and Market Data: Some Evidence," *Journal of Finance* 41, no. 4 (September 1986): 779–793.

[47] It should be noted that this view is not universally held. See Jeffrey Jaffe, Donald B. Keim, and Randolph Westerfield, "Earnings Yields, Market Values, and Stock Returns," *Journal of Finance* 44, no. 1 (March 1989): 135–138.

[48] Fama and French, "The Cross-Section of Expected Stock Returns."

that were formed from the smallest size decile showed that the larger the BV/MV ratio, the larger the average return. Fama and French concluded that at least two missing factors are needed to explain differences in stock returns, and that those factors are closely related to size and the BV/MV ratio.

SUMMARY

1. Common stock represents an ownership position in a corporation. Common shareholders possess a residual claim on the corporation's earnings and assets. Furthermore, their liability for the corporation's obligations is limited.
2. Common shareholders elect the corporation's directors through either a majority or a cumulative voting system.
3. Corporations may at times repurchase some of their outstanding shares either in the open market or through a tender offer. Such actions may involve an attempt to repel a takeover, a signal to shareholders that the shares are undervalued, or a taxwise distribution of cash to shareholders.
4. Stock dividends and splits involve the issuance of additional shares of common stock to current shareholders, proportional to their ownership positions. No change in the total value of the corporation is caused by a stock dividend or split.
5. Preemptive rights give existing shareholders the right of first refusal to purchase new shares. Such shares are purchased in a rights offering.
6. Daily information regarding transactions in publicly traded shares can be found in business newspapers and the business sections of most local newspapers.
7. Trading on inside information is illegal in North American public security markets. However, defining inside information is difficult.
8. A security's beta can be estimated using historical return data for the security and a market index. The beta is the slope of the security's market model, calculated by using simple linear regression.
9. Beta estimates based on historical return data are sometimes adjusted to account for a tendency of betas to drift toward an average value of 1.0 over time.
10. Estimates of betas are generally more accurate for diversified portfolios than for individual securities.
11. Forecasts of a security's beta can be improved by accounting for certain characteristics of the corporation, such as the industry (or industries) in which it operates, its financial leverage, and its market capitalization.
12. Firms that have either low book-value-to-market-value or earnings-to-price ratios, or both, are generally referred to as growth stocks, whereas firms that have either high book-value-to-market-value or earnings-to-price ratios, or both, are generally referred to as value stocks.
13. Firms that have either high book-value-to-market-value ratios, high earnings-to-price ratios, or are of smaller firm size historically have had higher stock returns.
14. When viewed jointly, there seems to be a relationship between stock returns and both firm size and the book-to-value-to-market-value ratio.

APPENDIX A

EMPIRICAL REGULARITIES IN THE STOCK MARKET

Researchers have uncovered certain **empirical regularities** in common stocks. That is, certain cross-sectional differences among stock returns have been found to occur with regularity. Some regularities should occur according to certain asset pricing models. For example, the CAPM asserts that different stocks should have different returns because different stocks have different betas. What makes the regularities that are about to be discussed of special interest is that they are not predicted by any of the traditional asset pricing models. Accordingly, they are sometimes also referred to as **anomalies**.

Earlier it was mentioned that returns were related to a firm's size as well as its book-value-to-market-value and earnings-to-price ratios. Hence these relationships are often used as examples of anomalies.[49] This appendix will examine some calendar anomalies and present some international evidence that indicates that such anomalies also exist in other countries.

SEASONALITY IN STOCK RETURNS

The desire of individuals for liquidity may be thought to change from day to day and from month to month. If so, there may be seasonal patterns in stock returns. One might presume that such patterns would be relatively unimportant. Indeed, according to the notion of efficient markets, such patterns should be quite minor (if they exist at all), because they are not suggested by traditional asset pricing models. However, the evidence indicates that at least two are significant: the **January effect** and the **day-of-the-week effect**.[50]

► January Effect

There is no obvious reason to expect stock returns to be higher in certain months than in others. However, in a study that looked at average monthly returns on NYSE-listed common stocks, significant seasonalities were found.[51] In particular, the average return in January was higher than the average return in any other month. Table 17.8 indicates the average stock return in January and the other 11 months for various time periods. Although the difference in returns was minor in the early part of the century, more recently it appears that the average return in January has been approximately 3% higher than the average monthly returns in February through December.[52]

---

[49] Another anomaly involves financial leverage. More specifically, the stocks of firms with larger debt-to-equity ratios have, on average, larger stock returns. See Laxmi Chand Bhandari, "Debt/Equity Ratio and Expected Common Stock Returns: Empirical Evidence," *Journal of Finance* 43, no. 2 (June 1988): 507–528.

[50] There is also evidence of a "weather effect" in that NYSE stock returns appear to be related to the amount of cloud cover in New York City. More specifically, the average daily return was .13% when the cloud cover was 0–20% and .02% when the cloud cover was 100%. This has been interpreted to mean that investor psychology influences asset prices. See Edward M. Saunders, Jr., "Stock Prices and Wall Street Weather," *American Economic Review* 83, no. 5 (December 1993): 1337–1345.

[51] Michael S. Rozeff and William R. Kinney, Jr., "Capital Market Seasonality: The Case of Stock Returns," *Journal of Financial Economics* 3, no. 4 (October 1976): 379–402. For an argument that the market does not have a January effect, see Jay R. Ritter and Navin Chopra, "Portfolio Rebalancing and the Turn-of-the-Year Effect," *Journal of Finance* 44, no. 1 (March 1989): 149–166.

[52] Interestingly, it appears that the returns over the first half of any month (defined to include the last day of the previous month) are significantly higher than the returns over the second half of the month. See Robert A. Ariel,

Table 17.8

Seasonality in Stock Returns.

Time Period	Average Stock Return in January	Average Stock Return in Other Months	Difference in Returns
1904–1928	1.30%	.44%	.86%
1929–1940	6.63	–.60	7.23
1941–1974	3.91	.70	3.21
1904–1974	3.48	.42	3.06

SOURCE: Michael S. Rozeff and William R. Kinney, Jr., "Capital Market Seasonality: The Case of Stock Returns," *Journal of Financial Economics* 3, no. 4 (October 1976): 388.

► Day-of-the-Week Effect

It is often assumed that the expected daily returns on stocks are the same for all days of the week. That is, the expected return on a given stock is the same for Monday as it is for Tuesday as it is for Wednesday as it is for Thursday as it is for Friday. However, a number of studies have uncovered evidence that refutes this belief. Two early studies looked at the average daily return on NYSE-listed securities and found that the return on Monday was quite different.[53] In particular, the average return on Monday was found to be much lower than the average return on any other day of the week. Furthermore, the average return on Monday was negative, whereas the other days of the week had positive average returns. Table 17.9 displays these findings.

Table 17.9

Analysis of Daily Returns.

	Monday	Tuesday	Wednesday	Thursday	Friday
A. French Study					
January 1953–December 1977	–.17%	.02%	.10%	.04%	.09%
B. Gibbons & Hess Study					
July 1962–December 1978	–.13%	.00%	.10%	.03%	.08%

SOURCE: Kenneth R. French, "Stock Returns and the Weekend Effect," *Journal of Financial Economics* 8, no. 1 (March 1980): 58; and Michael R. Gibbons and Patrick Hess, "Day of the Week Effects and Asset Returns," *Journal of Business* 54, no. 4 (October 1981): 582–583.

The rate of return on a stock for a given day of the week is typically calculated by subtracting the closing price on the previous trading day from the closing price on that day, adding any

"A Monthly Effect in Stock Returns," *Journal of Financial Economics* 18, no. 1 (March 1987): 161–174. Another study found this effect to be concentrated in the first three trading days (plus the last trading day of the previous month) and labelled it the **turn-of-the-month effect**. See Josef Lakonishok and Seymour Smidt, "Are Seasonal Anomalies Real? A Ninety-Year Perspective," *Review of Financial Studies* 1, no. 4 (Winter 1988): 403–425.

[53] Kenneth R. French, "Stock Returns and the Weekend Effect," *Journal of Financial Economics* 8, no. 1 (March 1980): 55–69; and Michael R. Gibbons and Patrick Hess, "Day of the Week Effects and Asset Returns," *Journal of Business* 54, no. 4 (October 1981): 579–596. For an argument that this effect disappeared in the mid 1970s, see Robert A. Connolly, "An Examination of the Robustness of the Weekend Effect," *Journal of Financial and Quantitative Analysis* 24, no. 2 (June 1989): 133–169.

dividends for that day to the difference, and then dividing the resulting number by the closing price as of the previous trading day:

$$r_t = \frac{(P_t - P_{t-1}) + D_t}{P_{t-1}} \tag{17.19}$$

where P_t and P_{t-1} are the closing prices on days t and $t - 1$, and D_t is the value of any dividends paid on day t. This means that the return for Monday uses the closing price on Monday as P_t and the closing price on Friday as P_{t-1}. Thus, the change in price of a stock for Monday $(P_t - P_{t-1})$ actually represents the change in price *over the weekend*, as well as during Monday. This observation has caused some people to refer to the day-of-the-week effect as the *weekend effect*. Other people use the *weekend effect* to refer to price behaviour from Friday close to Monday open, and the *Monday effect* to refer to price behaviour from Monday open to Monday close.

A refinement of the day-of-the-week effect involved an examination of NYSE stock returns over 15-minute intervals during trading hours over the period of December 1, 1981, through January 31, 1983.[54] Figure 17.10 displays the results when these returns were cumulated and examined on a day-of-the-week basis. Several observations can be made. First, the negative returns during trading hours on Monday occurred within an hour of the opening. Afterward, the behaviour of stock prices on Monday was similar to the other days of the week. Second, on Tuesdays through Fridays there was a notable upward movement in prices in the first hour of trading. Third, on all days of the week there was a notable upward movement in prices during the last hour of trading.[55] Hence, most of the daily price movement in a stock typically comes near the open and close.

Somewhat related to the day-of-the-week effect is the **holiday effect**. A study of this effect found that average stock returns on trading days immediately before federal holidays (the market is closed on these holidays; there are eight per year) are 9 to 14 times higher than the average daily returns during the rest of the year.[56] Furthermore, this abnormally high return is spread out from the closing price two days before the holiday to the opening price on the day after the holiday. Tests indicate that it is unrelated to the size, January, or day-of-the-week effects.

INTERRELATIONSHIPS

Researchers have attempted to see whether there are any interrelationships among these regularities. For example, is the January effect more pronounced for small firms? A brief discussion of this interrelationship follows.[57]

---

[54] Lawrence Harris, "How to Profit from Intradaily Stock Returns," *Journal of Portfolio Management* 12, no. 2 (Winter 1986): 61–64; and "A Transaction Data Study of Weekly and Intradaily Patterns in Stock Returns," *Journal of Financial Economics* 16, no. 1 (May 1986): 99–117.

[55] This rise in prices at the end of the day appears to be primarily due to a large price rise between the next-to-last and last trades; this observation appears to be widespread over firms and days of the week. See Lawrence Harris, "A Day-End Transaction Price Anomaly," *Journal of Financial and Quantitative Analysis* 24, no. 1 (March 1989): 29–45.

[56] Robert A. Ariel, "High Stock Returns Before Holidays: Existence and Evidence on Possible Causes," *Journal of Finance* 45, no. 5 (December 1990): 1611–1626. The holiday effect also exists in Japan and the UK. See Chan-Wang Kim and Jinwoo Park, "Holiday Effects and Stock Returns: Further Evidence," *Journal of Financial and Quantitative Analysis* 29, no. 1 (March 1994): 145–157.

[57] Other interrelationships are discussed in the previous edition of this book; see pp. 437–440.

Figure 17.10

Cumulated 15-minute intra-day returns.

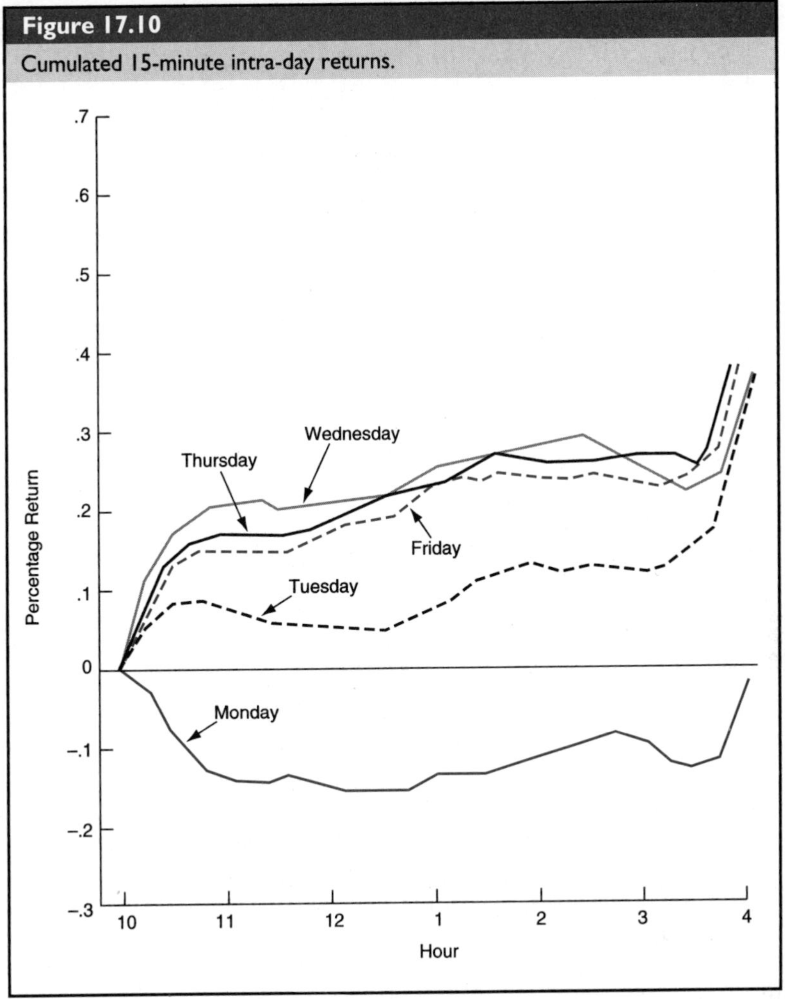

SOURCE: Lawrence Harris, "How to Profit from Intraday Stock Returns," *Journal of Portfolio Management* 12, no. 2 (Winter 1986): 63.

Size and January Effects

Having observed that small firms have higher returns than large firms, and that returns are higher in January than in any other month of the year, it is interesting to ponder whether or not these two effects are somehow interrelated. One study that examined this issue found that the two effects were strongly interrelated.[58] All NYSE-listed and AMEX-listed stocks over the 17-year period of 1963 to 1979 were examined in this study. At the end of each year, each firm was ranked by the size of the aggregate market value of its equity (that is, the year-end market price per share times the number of shares outstanding). Ten portfolios

---

[58] Donald B. Keim, "Size-related Anomalies and Stock Returns Seasonality: Further Empirical Evidence," *Journal of Financial Economics* 12, no. 1 (June 1983): 13–32.

Figure 17.11

Interrelationship between the size effect and the January effect.

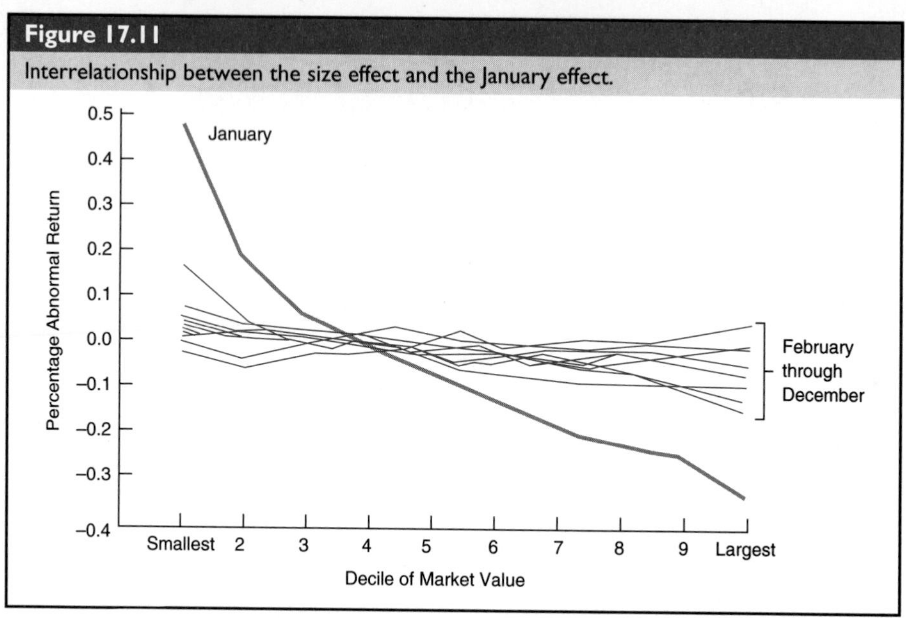

SOURCE: Donald B. Keim, "Size-Related Anomalies and Stock Return Seasonality: Further Empirical Evidence," *Journal of Financial Economics* 12, no. 1 (June 1983): 21.

were then formed based on size, with portfolio 1 containing the smallest 10% of the firms, portfolio 2 the next smallest 10%, and so on.

Abnormal returns were calculated subsequently for each portfolio on a monthly basis over the 17-year period and averaged for each month. Figure 17.11 displays the results.

It can be seen from this figure that the size effect was most pronounced in January because the line for this month slopes down sharply from left to right. The other 11 months of the year appear to be quite similar to each other. Generally, each one of these months displays a slight downward slope, indicating that the size effect also existed for these months, but only to a minor degree. Also of interest is the observation that large firms had a negative abnormal return in January. Thus, the January effect has been due primarily to the behaviour of small firms, and the size effect has been concentrated mainly in the month of January.

Further examination of this interrelationship between the size effect and the January effect has revealed that it is concentrated in the first five trading days of January.[59] In particular, the difference in returns between the smallest firm portfolio and the largest firm portfolio over these five days was 8.0%, whereas over the entire year it was 30.4%. Thus, 26.3% (= 8.0%/30.4%) of the annual size effect occurred during these five days. (If the size effect had been spread evenly over the year, then .4% of it would have been attributed to these five days.)

---

[59] Rogalski also finds that the anomalous price behaviour of stocks in January mostly occurs in the first five trading days. Roll has observed that the largest daily differences in the returns between small firms and large firms occur over the last trading day of the year and the first four days of the year. Furthermore, eight of the subsequent ten trading days also have notably large differences in returns. See Richard Rogalski, "New Findings Regarding Day-of-the-Week Returns Over Trading and Non-Trading Periods: A Note," *Journal of Finance* 39, no. 5 (December 1984): 1603–1614; and Richard Roll, "Vas ist das?" *Journal of Portfolio Management* 9, no. 2 (Winter 1983): 18–28.

Attempts have been made to explain this interrelationship between the January effect and the size effect. One explanation that appears to have some merit has to do with "tax selling." This explanation beings by arguing that stocks that have declined during the year have downward pressure on their prices near year-end as investors sell them to realize capital losses in order to minimize tax payments. After the end of the year, this pressure is removed and the prices jump back to their "fair" values. A related argument asserts that some professional money managers wish to sell those stocks that have performed poorly during the past year in order to avoid their appearance on year-end reports. Such activity is often referred to as "window dressing." Note that these arguments fly in the face of the notion of efficient markets. (The notion of efficient markets would suggest that this cannot be true, because if investors sensed that stocks were becoming undervalued at year-end, they would flood the market with buy orders, thereby preventing any substantive undervaluation from occurring.) Nevertheless, it does appear to have some merit, in that those stocks that declined during the previous year had the largest appreciation in January.[60] However, this association between January returns and the previous year's stock-price declines does not appear to be attributable solely to such downward tax-selling price pressure, because the biggest "losers" during a year appear to have abnormally high returns for as long as five Januaries thereafter.[61] In addition, the January effect exists in Japan (as will be shown later), yet Japan has no capital gains tax and disallows any deduction for capital losses.[62] Rebutting this evidence is the observation that the January effect apparently did not exist prior to the imposition of income taxes in the United States.[63]

A second possible explanation is that small stocks may be relatively riskier in January than during the rest of the year. If this is true, then they should have a relatively higher average return in January. A study finding that the betas of small stocks tend to increase at the beginning of the year lends support to this explanation.[64]

---

[60] See Roll, "Vas ist das?"; Edward A. Dyl, "Capital Gains Taxation and Year-End Stock Market Behavior," *Journal of Finance* 32, no. 1 (March 1977): 165–175; Ben Branch, "A Tax Loss Trading Rule," *Journal of Business* 50, no. 2 (April 1977): 198–207; Dan Givoly and Arie Ovadia, "Year-End Tax-Induced Sales and Stock Market Seasonality," *Journal of Finance* 38, no. 1 (March 1983): 171–185; Marc R. Reinganum, "The Anomalous Stock Market Behavior of Small Firms in January: Empirical Tests for Tax-Loss Selling Effects," *Journal of Financial Economics* 12, no. 1 (June 1983): 89–104; Josef Lakonishok and Seymour Smidt, "Capital Gain Taxation and Volume of Trading," *Journal of Finance* 41, no. 4 (September 1986): 951–974; Jay R. Ritter, "The Buying and Selling Behavior of Individual Investors at the Turn of the Year," *Journal of Finance* 43, no. 3 (July 1988): 701–717; Joseph P. Ogden, "Turn-of-Month Evaluations of Liquid Profits and Stock Returns: A Common Explanation for the Monthly and January Effects," *Journal of Finance* 45, no. 4 (September 1990): 1259–1272; and Greggory A. Brauer and Eric C. Chang, "Return Seasonality in Stocks and Their Underlying Assets: Tax-Loss Selling versus Information Explanations," *Review of Financial Studies* 3, no. 2 (1990): 255–280.

[61] See K. C. Chan, "Can Tax-Loss Selling Explain the January Seasonal in Stock Returns?" *Journal of Finance* 41, no. 5 (December 1986): 1115–1128; Werner F. M. DeBondt and Richard Thaler, "Does the Stock Market Overreact?" *Journal of Finance* 40, no. 3 (July 1985): 793–805; and "Further Evidence on Investor Over-reaction and Stock Market Seasonality," *Journal of Finance* 42, no. 3 (July 1987): 557–581.

[62] A similar observation has been made regarding Canada. See Angle Berges, John J. McConnell, and Gary G. Schlarbaum, "The Turn-of-the-Year in Canada," *Journal of Finance* 39, no. 1 (March 1984): 185–192.

[63] See Steven L. Jones, Winson Lee, and Rudolf Apenbrink, "New Evidence on the January Effect Before Personal Income Taxes," *Journal of Finance* 46, no. 5 (December 1991): 1909–1924.

[64] Richard J. Rogalski and Seha M. Tinic, "The January Size Effect: Anomaly or Risk Mismeasurement?" *Financial Analysts Journal* 42, no. 6 (November-December 1986): 63–70. See also Avner Arbel, "Generic Stocks: An Old Product in a New Package," *Journal of Portfolio Management* 11, no. 4 (Summer 1985): 4–13; and K. C. Chan and Nai-fu Chen, "Structural and Return Characteristics of Small and Large Firms," *Journal of Finance* 46, no. 4 (September 1991): 1467–1484.

EMPIRICAL REGULARITIES IN CANADIAN EQUITY MARKETS

The Canadian situation with respect to the study of empirical regularities is similar to that in the US — many observations but little explanation. This section will briefly discuss those anomalies that have been identified in Canada and list references so that interested readers may pursue the subject further.[65]

► The Size Effect in Canada

Data presented by Hatch and White, reproduced in Table 17.10, strongly suggests the existence of a small-firm effect in Canada. A rigorous study examined this phenomenon in considerable detail. The study, which included adjustments for the effects of non-synchronous trading, discovered the existence of a significant size effect. Other studies (described below) that examine interrelationships between the size effect and other regularities also confirm its existence. Mittoo, however, argues that the small firm effect disappeared from both US and Canadian markets after published research documented its existence and institutions started offering small capitalization investment funds. Table 17.11 shows that the differential returns to small firms effectively disappeared from both US and Canadian markets after May 1982.[66]

Table 17.10

Small- and Large-Stock Performance, 1950–1987.

	Small Stocks	*Large Stocks*
Value Weighted		
Average monthly return	1.30%	0.98%
Monthly standard deviation	5.05%	4.45%
Equally Weighted		
Average monthly return	1.69%	1.07%
Monthly standard deviation	5.40%	4.47%

SOURCE: Reprinted, with permission, from J. E. Hatch and R. W. White, *Canadian Stocks, Bonds, Bills and Inflation: 1957–1987*. Copyright 1988, The Research Foundation of The Institute of Chartered Financial Analysts, Charlottesville, Va.

► Seasonality in Canadian Stock Returns

Several time-related effects have been identified in Canadian stock markets, the best known of which is the January or turn-of-the-year effect. This empirical regularity has been investigated

[65] For an excellent summary, marred only by the lack of an adequate bibliography, see V. M. Jog, "Stock Pricing Anomalies: Canadian Experience," *Canadian Investment Review* I, no.1 (Fall 1988): 55–62.

[66] I. G. Morgan, A. L. MacBeth and D. J. Novak, "The Relationship Between Equity Value and Abnormal Returns in the Canadian Stock Market," Kingston: Queen's University School of Business Working Paper; U. R. Mittoo, "Do Financial Markets Learn from Academic Research?" *Canadian Investment Review* IV, no. 1 (Spring 1991): 83–6.

Table 17.11

Change in the Size Effect.

(a) US Market

Period	Pre-Information July 62–April 82	Post-Information May 82–Sept 87
Annual Size Effect	9.4%	–3.0%
T-statistics	5.5	–0.8

(b) Canadian Market

Period	Pre-Information Jan 53–April 82	Post-Information May 82–May 90
Size Effect	4.5%	–0.8%
T-statistics	3.7	–0.3

SOURCE: U. R. Mittoo, "Do Financial Markets Learn from Academic Research?" *Canadian Investment Review* IV, no. 1 (Spring 1991).

and documented by several researchers. The results of a typical study are summarized in Table 17.12 and show that there is a pronounced January effect in all stocks, large and small, but smaller stocks earn higher returns in January than other firms. Morgan *et al.* report that the January return accounts for practically all the annual abnormal returns earned by small firms. They conclude that there are no abnormal returns to small firms except in January.

Evidence on the tax loss selling hypothesis, however, is mixed. Canada should provide an excellent testing ground for this hypothesis because the capital gains tax was only introduced in 1972. It would be reasonable to expect, therefore, that there should be no January effect prior to 1972. The results presented in Table 17.12, however, clearly show that this effect predates the introduction of the capital gains tax.[67]

Table 17.12

Average Monthly Returns on the TSE 300, on the Market-Value-Weighted Laval Index (MVWI), and on the Equally-Weighted Laval Index (EWI).

	TSE 300		MVWI		EWI	
Period	January	Other Months	January	Other Months	January	Other Months
1963–71	9.98%	0.58%	2.64%	0.92%	3.66%	0.91%
1972–86	3.13%	0.82%	3.51%	1.54%	5.90%	0.97%

SOURCE: V. M. Jog, "Stock Pricing Anomalies: Canadian Experience," *Canadian Investment Review* I, no.1 (Fall 1988): 56.

[67] A. J. Berges, J. J. McConell and G. Schlarbaum, "The Turn-of-the-Year in Canada," *Journal of Finance* 39, no. 1 (March 1984): 185–92; S. M. Tinic, G. Barone-Adessi and R. R. West, "Seasonality in Canadian Stock Prices: A Test of the 'Tax-Loss-Selling' Hypothesis," *Journal of Financial and Quantitative Research* 22, no.1 (March 1987): 51–63.

Unlike the US, however, the turn-of-the-year effect in Canada should manifest itself during the last week of December rather than in January. In Canada, share ownership must be transferred from seller to buyer before a capital gain or loss may be reported for tax purposes. This means that a trade must be executed five trading days before year-end in order to qualify. In most years, the cut-off date is December 20 or 21 (in contrast, in the US simple execution is sufficient to qualify). Stock prices should, therefore, "rebound" during the last week in December if tax loss selling is a significant factor. Two studies have found that this is, in fact, the case.[68]

The day-of-the-week effect has also been reported by several Canadian researchers, as shown in Table 17.13. Returns are significantly negative on Mondays and positive on Fridays with positive but insignificant returns on other days. Despite the existence of these regularities it is probable that transaction costs would eliminate any profit from a trading rule based on these results. Discretionary traders, however, may find it useful to postpone purchases from Monday to Tuesday and to advance sales from Monday to the previous Friday.[69]

Table 17.13

Average Percentage Returns by Day of the Week.

Researchers	*Index*	*Period*	*Mon.*	*Tues.*	*Wed.*	*Thurs.*	*Fri.*
(a) Canada							
Jaffe & Westerfield	TSE 300[b]	1976–83	–.14	.02	.12	.11	.14
Chamberlain et al.	TSE 300[b]	1978–85	–.15	.07	.13	.11	.14
	TSE 300[c]	1978–85	–.10	.05	.08	.07	.11
Bishara	TSE 300[b]	1968–87[d]	–.49	.01	.06	.24	.21
(b) International							
Jaffe & Westerfield	US	1962–83[a]	–.13	.02	.11	.03	.08
	Japan	1970–83[a]	–.02	–.09	.15	.03	.06
	UK	1950–83[a]	–.14	.09	.08	.05	.06
	Australia	1973–83[a]	–.05	–.13	.04	.17	.13

[a] - Close-to-close
[b] - Close-to-open
[c] - Open-to-close
[d] - Only till March 1987

SOURCE: V. M. Jog, "Stock Pricing Anomalies: Canadian Experience," *Canadian Investment Review* I, no.1 (Fall 1988): 56.

[68] C. B. Cadsby, "Canadian Calendar Anomalies and the Capital Asset Pricing Model," in *A Reappraisal of the Efficiency of Financial Markets*, eds. R. M. C. Guimarães, B. G. Kingsman and S. J. Taylor (Berlin: Springer-Verlag; 1989) reports that the turn-of-the-year effect in Canada lasts from December 21 to January 5. See also M. D. Griffiths, "Systematic Changes in Investor Trading Behavior at the Turn-of-the-Year: An Intraday Study," Milwaukee: University of Wisconsin-Milwaukee School of Business Administration Working Paper, 1991. Griffiths also reports that informed investors not subject to capital gains also engage in year-end trading; see M. D. Griffiths, "The Role of Informed Traders in the Canadian Turn-of-the-Year Effect," *Proceedings*, Administrative Sciences Association of Canada, Whistler, B.C., 1990.

[69] T. Chamberlain, C. S. Cheung and C. Kwan, "Day of the Week patterns in Stock Returns: The Canadian Evidence," *Canadian Journal of Administrative Sciences* 5, no.4 (December 1988); H. Bishara, "Stock Returns and the Weekend Effect in Canada," *Akron Business and Economic Review* 20, no. 2 (Summer 1989): 62–71; J. F. Jaffe and R. Westerfield, "A Twist on the Monday Effect in Stock Prices: Evidence from the US and Foreign Stock Markets," *Journal of Banking and Finance* 13, no. 4/5 (September 1989): 641–50.

Table 17.14

Average Wealth Relatives and Tests of Deviations from the Mean.

Day in Trading Month	*Average Daily Wealth Relative*	*T Test Statistic*[a]
−9	0.075%	0.68
−8	0.019	−0.65
−7	0.026	−0.41
−6	0.084	0.33
−5	0.022	−0.51
−4	0.006	−1.88
−3	0.033	−0.36
−2	0.040	−0.23
−1	0.041	−0.19
1	0.160	1.70[b]
2	0.159	1.27
3	0.230	2.16[b]
4	0.012	−0.70
5	0.015	−0.56
6	0.000	−1.02
7	0.014	−0.58
8	0.061	0.01
9	0.110	1.77

[a] Test: H_0: Average return for trading day = overall average daily return, against
H_1: Average return for trading day < overall average daily return.

[b] Statistically significant at the 5% level.

SOURCE: V. Jog and A. L. Riding, "The Month-End Effect in Canadian Stock Prices: Some Anomalous Findings," *Canadian Journal of Administrative Sciences* 6, no. 4 (December 1989): 7–17.

Jog and Riding have reported a month-end effect similar to that reported in US markets, shown in Table 17.14. They find that abnormally high returns are recorded on the last trading day of the calendar month and the first two trading days of the subsequent month. The returns from these three days of each month account for about 60% of the total returns on the TSE 300 for the period 1976–1984. A subsequent study indicates that a strategy based on this regularity would probably not be profitable because of transaction costs. An international study finds that the turn of the month effects are significant in Canada, the UK, Australia, Switzerland and West Germany, whereas pre-holiday effects (similar to the Friday anomaly) are only found in Canada, Japan, Hong Kong and Australia.[70] The next section deals with other international evidence of systematic regularities primarily in the Japanese market.

---

[70] V. Jog and A. L. Riding, "The Month-End Effect in Canadian Stock Prices: Some Anomalous Findings," *Canadian Journal of Administrative Sciences* 6, no. 4 (December 1989): 7–17; V. Jog and A. L. Riding, "Lunar Cycles in Stock Prices," *Financial Analysts' Journal* 45, no. 2 (March/April 1989): 63–8; C. B. Cadsby and M. Ratner, "Turn-of-the-month and Pre-holiday Effects on Stock Returns: Some International Evidence," *Journal of Banking and Finance* 16, June 1992.

INTERNATIONAL EVIDENCE

Several people have investigated foreign stock markets in order to see whether similar anomalies exist.[71] Because the Tokyo Stock Exchange is the largest non-US exchange, evidence concerning anomalies there will be discussed next. Overall, the anomalies that have been observed in the United States also appear, for the most part, in Japan.

► Size Effect

Table 17.15 presents evidence that suggests that the size effect also exists in Japan.[72] The data marked (A) were based on all stocks in the first section of the Tokyo Stock Exchange. (The Tokyo Stock Exchange has two "sections"; the second is less than 10% of the size of the first, measured by the market value of the securities traded on it.) Two indices were prepared and examined over the period from 1952 to 1980; they include the same stocks but are compiled differently. The EW index weights all the stocks equally, and the VW index weights the stocks by market value. Hence the EW index is influenced much more by the performance of small stocks. As the table indicates, the EW index returned 5.1% more, suggesting the presence of a size effect.

The data labelled (B) on Table 17.15 also indicates the presence of a size effect between 3.4% and 8.4% for the period from 1973 to 1987. Here, the performance of small firms is measured with two indices. (Large stocks are measured by the TOPIX index, which is computed in a manner similar to the VW index in (A).) First, the smallest quintile of

Table 17.15

Size Effect on the Tokyo Stock Exchange.

	Small Stocks	*Large Stocks*	*Difference*
A. 1952–1980: EW vs. VW[a]	22.7%	17.6%	5.1%
B. 1973–1987: TSEsmall vs. TOPIX[b]	21.7	13.3	8.4
TSE2 vs.TOPIX[b]	16.7	13.3	3.4

[a] Adapted from Kiyoshi Kato and James S. Schallheim, "Seasonal and Size Anomalies in the Japanese Stock Market," *Journal of Financial and Quantitative Analysis* 20, no. 2 (June 1985): 248.

[b] Adapted from Yasushi Hamao, "Fifteen-Year Performance of Japanese Capital Markets," in *Japanese Capital Markets*, Edwin J. Elton and Martin J. Gruber, eds. (New York: Ballinger, 1990), p. 10.

---

[71] The BV/MV ratio anomaly was found to exist in other countries, particularly France, Switzerland, and Japan, suggesting that value stocks have outperformed growth stocks outside the United States. See Carlo Capaul, Ian Rowley, and William F. Sharpe, "International Value and Growth Stock Returns," *Financial Analysts Journal* 49, no. 1 (January/February 1993): 27–36.

[72] See Kiyoshi Kato and James S. Schallheim, "Seasonal and Size Anomalies in the Japanese Stock Market," *Journal of Financial and Quantitative Analysis* 20, no. 2 (June 1985): 243–260; and Yasushi Hamao, "Fifteen-Year Performance of Japanese Capital Markets," in *Japanese Capital Markets*, Edwin J. Elton and Martin J. Gruber, eds. (New York: Ballinger, 1990), pp. 3–26.

stocks in the first section is formed into a value-weighted index denoted *TSE small.* Second, the stocks in the second section are formed into a value-weighted index denoted *TSE2.* Interestingly, over the same time period the difference in the returns on the S&P 500 (a large-stock value-weighted index) and the returns on the smallest quintile of NYSE-listed stocks was 7.8%, comparable to the differences in Tokyo.

January Effect

Table 17.16 shows the presence of a January effect in the Tokyo Stock Exchange.[73] The first two rows involve the same indices used in row (A) of Table 17.15; row (C) uses a value-weighted index prepared by *Morgan Stanley Capital International Perspective.* In all three cases the average return in January is clearly higher than the average monthly return in the remaining 11 months. Interestingly, June also has an unusually high average return, but not nearly as dramatic as January's.

Table 17.16

January Effect on the Tokyo Stock Exchange.

		Jan.	*Feb.-Dec.*	*Difference*	*June*	*Feb.-May and July-Dec.*	*Difference*
A.	1952–1980: EW[a]	7.1%	1.4%	6.7%	2.8%	1.3%	1.5%
B.	1952–1980: VW[a]	4.5	1.2	3.3	2.5	1.1	1.4
C.	1959–1979: VW[b]	3.5	.7	2.8	2.1	.5	1.6

[a] Adapted from Kiyoshi Kato and James S. Schallheim, "Seasonal and Size Anomalies in the Japanese Stock Market," *Journal of Financial and Quantitative Analysis* 20, no. 2 (June 1985): 248.
[b] Adapted from Mustafa N. Gultekin and N. Bulent Gultekin, "Stock Market Seasonality: International Evidence," *Journal of Financial Economics* 12, no. 4 (December 1983): 475.

Day-of-the-Week Effect

Evidence regarding the day-of-the-week effect is provided in Table 17.17.[74] It should be noted that the Tokyo Stock Exchange was open on Saturday mornings during the periods examined; hence, there is an average return reported for Saturday as well as for Monday through Friday. Two indices are involved. The first is the TOPIX index, which is a value-weighted index based on 225 large, well-established companies on the Tokyo Stock Exchange and is a price-weighted index like the Dow Jones Industrial Average.

[73] See Kato and Schallheim, "Seasonal and Size Anomalies"; and Mustafa N. Gultekin and N. Bulent Gultekin, "Stock Market Seasonality: International Evidence," *Journal of Financial Economics* 12, no. 4 (December 1983): 469–481.

[74] See Jeffrey Jaffe and Randolph Westerfield, "Patterns in Japanese Common Stock Returns: Day of the Week and Turn of the Year Effects," *Journal of Financial and Quantitative Analysis* 20, no. 2 (June 1985): 261–272; "The Weekend Effect in Common Stock Returns: The International Evidence," *Journal of Finance* 40, no. 2 (June 1985): 433–454; and Kiyoshi Kato, Sandra L. Schwartz, and William T. Ziemba, "Day of the Week Effects in Japanese Stocks," in *Japanese Capital Markets* : 249–281.

Table 17.17

Day-of-the-Week Effect on the Tokyo Stock Exchange.

		Monday	Tuesday	Wednesday	Thursday	Friday	Saturday
A.	1970–1983:						
	Nikkei Dow[a]	–.02%	–.09%	.15%	.03%	.06%	.12%
B.	1970–1983:						
	Topix[a]	–.01	–.06	.12	.03	.06	.10
C.	1978–1987:						
	Topix[b]	.00	–.09	.14	.06	.10	.14

[a] Adapted from Jeffrey Jaffe and Randolph Westerfield, "Patterns in Japanese Common Stock Returns: Day of the Week and Turn of the Year Effects," *Journal of Financial and Quantitative Analysis* 20, no 2 (June 1985): 263.
[b] Kiyoshi Kato, Sandra L. Schwartz, and William T. Ziemba, "Day of the Week Effects in Japanese Stocks," in *Japanese Capital Markets*, Edwin J. Elton and Martin J. Gruber, eds. (New York: Ballinger, 1990), p. 253.

The table indicates that Monday returns are, in general, negative, as in Canada and the United States.[75] Furthermore, Wednesday returns are the largest, again similar to the United States. Second largest is Saturday, the last trading day of the week in Japan. This is similar to Canada and the United States in that the last trading day of the week is the second largest. What is surprising is that Tuesday is negative, and even more so than Monday. Otherwise the day-of-the-week effect in Japan is similar to that observed in North America.[76]

Size and January Effects

Examination of Table 17.16 reveals that the size effect in Japan occurs for the most part in January. Hence these two effects are interconnected in a manner similar to that in the United States, as can be seen by examining the average returns indicated in rows (A) and (B).

These data show that there is a pronounced difference in the average returns between the equal-weighted and value-weighted indices of (7.1% – 4.5% =) 2.6% in January, but a relatively small difference of (1.4% – 1.2% =) .2% during the other 11 months of the year. This is notable because the EW index gives much larger weights to small stocks than the VW index, suggesting that the difference between the two indices can be attributed to the performance of the small stocks. In summary, it would appear that in Japan the size effect is primarily a January effect.

---

[75] More recently there has been some evidence that the day-of-the-week effect has become much less noticeable in both the United States and Japan. See Robert Connolly, "An Examination of the Robustness of the Weekend Effect"; and Eric C. Chang, J. Michael Pinegar, and R. Ravichandron, "International Evidence on the Robustness of the Day-of-the-Week Effect," *Journal of Financial and Quantitative Analysis* 28, no. 4 (December 1993): 497–513.

[76] Additional patterns have been discovered. Imagine splitting the set of Mondays in two where one set corresponds to Mondays that follow a week where the market declined and the second set corresponds to Mondays that follow a week where the market rose. Interestingly, in both the United States and Japan, the average return for the first set of Mondays is significantly negative (–.39% in the United States and –.18% in Japan) whereas the average return for the second set of Mondays is slightly positive (.06% in the United States and .11% in Japan). See Jeffrey F. Jaffe, Randolph Westerfield, and Christopher Ma, "A Twist on the Monday Effect in Stock Prices: Evidence from the US and Foreign Stock Markets," *Journal of Banking and Finance* 13, no. 4/5 (September 1989): 641–650.

SUMMARY OF EMPIRICAL REGULARITIES

On balance, what do these regularities suggest that the investor should do? First, investors who want to buy stocks should avoid doing so late on Friday or early on Monday. Conversely, investors who want to sell stocks should try to sell late on Friday or early on Monday. Second, if the stocks of small firms are to be purchased they should be purchased in late December or somewhat earlier. If the stocks of small firms are to be sold, they should be sold in mid-January or somewhat later. Third, if the stocks of large firms are to be purchased, they should be purchased in early February or somewhat later. If the stocks of large firms are to be sold, they should be sold in late December or somewhat earlier.[77]

Two words of caution are in order here. First, none of these empirical regularities is of a sufficient magnitude to suggest that riches are to be made by exploiting them. Indeed, transaction costs would devour most if not all of any profits that might be made.[78] All that they suggest is that if, for whatever reason, a buy or sell order is to be placed, there are some times when it may be more advantageous to do so. Second, although these regularities have been found to exist in the past, and in some instances for long periods of time and in several foreign markets, there is no guarantee that they will continue to exist in the future.[79] It may be the case that as more investors become aware of them and time their trades accordingly, such regularities will cease to exist.

QUESTIONS AND PROBLEMS

1. What is the significant advantage of the corporate form of business organization? Why would you expect that this advantage would be important to the success of a capitalist economy?
2. Fall Creek is conducting the annual election for its five-member board of directors. The firm has 1 500 000 shares of voting common stock outstanding.
   a. Under a majority voting system, how many shares must a shareholder own to ensure being able to elect his or her choices to each of the five director seats?
   b. Under a cumulative voting system, how many shares must a shareholder own to ensure being able to elect his or her choices to two of the director seats?
   c. Andy Latham holds 20% of Fall Creek's outstanding shares. How many directors can Andy elect under a cumulative voting system?
3. The issue of corporate ownership versus control has become quite controversial. Discuss the principal-agent problem as it relates to shareholder-management relations. Specifically, why is there a potential conflict between the two groups? What steps can be taken to mitigate this problem?

---

[77] These recommendations are based on studies that typically involved exchange-listed stocks. For over-the-counter stocks, Richard D. Fortin and O. Maurice Joy ["Buying and Selling OTC Stock: Fine-Tuning Your Trade Date," *AAII Journal* 15, no. 3 (March 1993): 8–10] recommend (1) buying just before and selling just after the end of the month, (2) buying on Tuesday and selling on Friday, and (3) buying within two days on either side of a holiday and avoiding selling during this period.

[78] See Donald B. Keim, "Trading Patterns, Bid-Ask Spreads, and Estimated Security Returns: The Case of Common Stocks at Calendar Turning Points," *Journal of Financial Economics* 25, no. 1 (November 1989): 75–97.

[79] The Appendix to Chapter 16 discusses regularities in the bond market.

4. When a bidder makes a tender offer for a target firm, what types of defences are often applied to fend off the bidder? Do these defences generally seem to be in the best interests of the target firm's shareholders? Why?
5. Why might a corporation wish to issue more than one class of common shares?
6. With respect to the payment of corporate dividends, distinguish between declaration date, ex-dividend date, and date of record.
7. Theoretical arguments and empirical research support the case that stock dividends and splits do not enhance shareholder wealth. However, corporations continue to declare stock dividends and splits. Summarize the arguments for and against stock dividends and splits from the perspective of the shareholder.
8. Menomonie Publishing stock currently sells for $40 per share. The company has 1 200 000 shares outstanding. What would be the effect on the number of shares outstanding and on the share price of the following:
   a. 15% stock dividend
   b. 4-for-3 stock split
   c. Reverse 3-for-1 stock split
9. St. Paul Corporation is planning to raise $35 000 000 through the sale of new common stock under a rights offering. The subscription price is $70 per share while the stock currently sells for $80 per share, rights on. Total outstanding shares equal 10 000 000. Of this amount, Annie Joss owns 100 000 shares.
   a. How many shares will each right permit its owner to purchase?
   b. What will be the total value of Annie's rights a day before the ex-rights date, assuming that the market price of St. Paul stock remains $80?
   c. After the ex-rights date, if the market value of each St. Paul right equals $20, what must be the ex-rights market price of St. Paul's shares?
10. Pete Van Vleet owns stock in DeKalb Dairy. DeKalb is planning a rights offering in which seven shares must be owned to buy one additional share at a price of $15. DeKalb shares currently sell for $63.
    a. What is the value of a DeKalb right?
    b. At the time of the offering announcement, Pete's assets consisted of $1500 in cash and 490 shares of DeKalb. List and show the value of Pete's assets prior to the ex-rights date.
    c. List and show the value of Pete's assets on the ex-rights date if DeKalb stock sells for $60 on that date.
    d. List and shown the value of Pete's assets if Pete sells the DeKalb rights on the ex-right date.
11. Using a recent *Globe and Mail: Report on Business* as a data source, select a TSE-listed stock whose name begins with the same letter as the first letter of your last name. For this stock, calculate its rate of return for that day of the week. What was the stock's trading volume that day?
12. From the perspective of an efficient market proponent, why is it surprising that trades based on insider trading data found in the OCS's *Monthly Bulletin* appear to produce significant abnormal profits?
13. Tomah Electronics' stock price at the end of several quarters, along with the market index value for the same periods, is shown below. Tomah pays no dividends. Calculate the beta of Tomah's stock over the eight quarters.

Quarter	Quarter-End Tomah Share Price	Quarter-End Market Index Value
0	60.000	210.00
1	62.500	220.50
2	64.375	229.87
3	59.875	206.88
4	56.875	190.33
5	61.500	209.36
6	66.500	238.67
7	69.750	257.76
8	68.375	262.92

14. Using the data from Problem 9 in Chapter 1, calculate the beta of the small stock portfolio over the 20-year period. Use the common stock returns from Table 1.1 as the returns on the market index.

15. Shown here are ten quarters of return data for Baraboo Associates stock, as well as return data over the same period for a broad stock market index. Using this information, calculate the following statistics for Baraboo Associates stock.

a. beta

b. alpha

c. standard deviation of random error term

d. coefficient of determination

Quarter	Baraboo Return	Market Return
1	3.8%	2.7%
2	5.3	3.1
3	–7.2	–4.9
4	10.1	9.9
5	1.0	2.7
6	2.5	1.2
7	6.4	3.8
8	4.8	4.0
9	6.0	5.5
10	2.2	2.0

16. What is the rationale for calculating "adjusted" betas, as described in the text?

17. Sugar Grove Technologies has debt and equity with total market values of $120 million and $230 million, respectively. With a 35% corporate tax, what is the firm's unlevered value?

18. The market value of Oswego Computers' total debt outstanding is $10 million. Further, the unlevered market value of Oswego is $40 million. The firm's average corporate tax rate is 35%.

a. If the beta of the firm's debt is .40 and the beta of its equity is 1.20, what is the firm's beta?

b. If the firm borrows another $10 million and uses the proceeds to purchase an equivalent amount of its own equity, what will be the effect on the beta of its equity?

19. Why would one expect that the betas of companies within industries should be more similar than the betas of companies across industries?

20. Necedah Power is an electric utility company. Its historical beta is .70. Its stock offers a dividend yield of 7.6%. The market value of its outstanding equity is currently $140 million. Based on the data from Table 17.6, calculate Necedah's beta.

21. Explain the primary differences between multiple-factor models of beta and historical models of beta. In particular, why might you expect that the multiple-factor models would do a better job of forecasting betas than do the historical models?

22. Generally, stocks with relatively low price per share (roughly $5 per share or less) have higher betas than stocks with a higher price per share. What attributes of low-price stocks might you expect to be correlated with higher beta values?

23. (Appendix Question) The empirical regularities cited in this chapter have potentially troubling implications for the Capital Asset Pricing Model and the concept of highly efficient markets. Discuss some of these implications.

24. (Appendix Question) Benita Del Vecchio, an astute investment observer, wrote, "Testing for empirical regularities is conceptually difficult because it is really a two-hypothesis test. One test relates to the validity of the underlying asset pricing model, and the other test relates to the existence of the empirical regularity." What does Benita mean by this statement?

CFA Exam Questions

25. You ask John Statdud, your research assistant, to analyze the relationship between the return on Coca-Cola Enterprises (CCE) common stock and the return on the market using the Standard & Poor's 500 Stock Index as a proxy for the market. The data include monthly returns for both CCE and S&P 500 over a recent five-year period. The results of the regression are indicated below:

$$R_{CCE,t} = .59 + .94(R_{S\&P,t}) + e_{CCE,t}$$

$$(.81) \quad (3.10)$$

where: $R_{CCE,t}$ is the return on CCE common shares in month t,

$R_{S\&P,t}$ is the return on S&P 500 stock index in month t,

$e_{CCE,t}$ is the residual error in month t.

The numbers in parentheses are the t-statistics (the .01 critical value is 2.66). The coefficient of determination R^2 for the regression is .215.

Statdud wrote the following summary of the regression results:

a. The regression statistics indicate that during the five-year period under study, when the annual return on the S&P 500 was zero, CCE had an average annual return of 0.59%.

b. The alpha value of .59 is a measure of the variability of the return on the market.

c. The coefficient of .94 indicates CCE's sensitivity to the return on the S&P 500 and suggests that the return on CCE's common stock is less sensitive to market movements than the average stock.

d. The t-statistic of 3.10 for the slope coefficient indicates that the coefficient is not statistically significant at the .01 level.
e. The R^2 for the regression of .215 indicates that the average estimate deviates from the actual observation by an average of 21.5%.
f. There is no concern that the slope coefficient lacks statistical significance since beta values tend to be less stable (and therefore less useful) than alpha values.
g. The regression should be rerun using ten years of data. This would improve the reliability of the estimated coefficients while not sacrificing anything.

Identify which of the seven statements made by Statdud are incorrect and justify your answer(s).

26. You are a portfolio manager meeting a client. During the conversation that followed your formal review of her account, your client asked the following question: "My granddaughter, who is studying investments, tells me that one of the best ways to make money in the stock market is to buy the stocks of small-capitalization firms on a Monday morning late in December and to sell the stocks one month later." What is she talking about?
    a. Identify the apparent market anomalies (empirical regularities) that would justify the proposed strategy.
    b. Explain why you believe such a strategy might or might not work in the future.

KEY TERMS

common shares
limited liability
charter
transfer agent
registrar
proxy
proxy fight
cumulative voting system
majority voting system
takeover
tender offer
bidder
target firm
white knight
greenmail
merger
management buyout
leveraged buyout
repurchase offer
Pac-Mac defence
crown jewel defence
poison pill defence
par value
book value of the equity
book value per share
treasury shares
restricted shares
dividends
date of record
ex-dividend date
stock dividend
stock split
reverse stock split
preemptive rights
oversubscription privilege
subscription price
ex-rights date
insiders
ex ante
ex post
historical beta
simple linear regression
standard deviation of the random error term
standard error of alpha
standard error of beta
correlation coefficient
coefficient of determination
coefficient of nondetermination
R-squared
residual standard deviation

adjusted beta
growth stocks
value stocks
size effect
empirical regularities
anomalies
January effect
day-of-the-week effect
turn-of-the-month effect
holiday effect

REFERENCES

1. For a discussion of the motivations for takeovers and the associated consequences, see:

   Michael C. Jensen and Richard S. Ruback, "The Market for Corporate Control: The Scientific Evidence," *Journal of Financial Economics* 11, nos. 1–4 (April 1983): 5–50.

   Richard Roll, "The Hubris Hypothesis of Corporate Takeovers," *Journal of Business* 59, no. 1, pt. 2 (April 1986): 197–216

   J. Fred Weston, Kwang S. Chung, and Susan E. Hoag, *Mergers, Restructuring, and Corporate Control* (Englewood Cliffs, NJ: Prentice Hall, 1990).

   Michael C. Jensen, "Corporate Control and the Politics of Finance," *Journal of Applied Corporate Finance* 4, no. 2 (Summer 1991): 13–33.

   Andrei Shleifer and Robert W. Vishny, "The Takeover Wave of the 1980s," *Journal of Applied Corporate Finance* 4, no. 3 (Fall 1991): 49–56.

   Jack Treynor, "The Value of Control," *Financial Analysts Journal* 49, no. 5 (July/August 1993): 6–9.

2. For a study of how risk arbitrageurs (investors who buy and sell shares of firms involved in takeovers and divestitures) are able to earn substantial returns, see:

   David F. Larcker and Thomas Lys, "An Empirical Analysis of the Incentives to Engage in Costly Information Acquisition: The Case of Risk Arbitrage," *Journal of Financial Economics* 18, no. 1 (March 1987): 111–126.

3. Three interesting studies of stock repurchases are:

   Josef Lakonishok and Theo Vermaelen, "Anomalous Price Behavior Around Repurchase Tender Offers," *Journal of Finance* 45, no. 2 (June 1990): 455–477.

   Robert Comment and Gregg A. Jarrell, "The Relative Signalling Power of Dutch-Auction and Fixed-Price Self-Tender Offers and Open-Market Share Repurchases," *Journal of Finance* 46, no. 4 (September 1991): 1243–1271.

   Laurie Simon Bagwell, "Dutch Auction Repurchases: An Analysis of Shareholder Heterogeneity," *Journal of Finance* 47, no. 1 (March 1992): 71–105.

4. Americus Trust Securities are discussed in:

   Robert A. Jarrow and Maureen O'Hara, "Primes and Scores: An Essay on Market Imperfections," *Journal of Finance* 44, no. 5 (December 1989): 1263–1287.

   P. C. Venkatesh, "Trading Costs and Ex-Day Behavior: An Examination of Primes and Scores," *Financial Management* 20, no. 3 (Autumn 1991): 84–95.

5. Stock splits and stock dividends are examined in:

Eugene F. Fama, Lawrence Fisher, Michael C. Jensen, and Richard Roll, "The Adjustment of Stock Prices to New Information," *International Economic Review* 10, no. 1 (February 1969): 1–21.

Sasson Bar-Yosef and Lawrence D. Brown, "A Re-examination of Stock Splits Using Moving Betas," *Journal of Finance* 32, no. 4 (September 1977): 1069–1080.

Guy Charest, "Split Information, Stock Returns, and Market Efficiency-I," *Journal of Financial Economics* 6, no. 2/3 (June/September 1978): 265–296.

Thomas E. Copeland, "Liquidity Changes Following Stock Splits," *Journal of Finance* 34, no. 1 (March 1979): 115–141.

J. Randall Woolridge, "Ex-Date Stock Price Adjustment to Stock Dividends: A Note," *Journal of Finance* 38, no. 1 (March 1983): 247–255.

Mark S. Grinblatt, Ronald W. Masulis, and Sheridan Titman, "The Valuation Effects of Stock Splits and Stock Dividends," *Journal of Financial Economics* 13, no. 4 (December 1984): 461–490.

Josef Lakonishok and Baruch Lev, "Stock Splits and Stock Dividends: Why, Who, and When," *Journal of Finance* 42, no. 4 (September 1987): 913–932.

Robert S. Conroy, Robert S. Harris, and Bruce A. Benet, "The Effects of Stock Splits on Bid-Ask Spreads," *Journal of Finance* 45, no. 4 (September 1990): 1285–1295.

David A. Dubofsky, "Volatility Increases Subsequent to NYSE and AMEX Stock Splits," *Journal of Finance* 46, no. 1 (March 1991): 421–431.

6. Insider trading has been examined in a number of studies. Some of the major ones are:

Jeffrey F. Jaffe, "Special Information and Insider Trading," *Journal of Business* 47, no. 3 (July 1974): 410–428.

Joseph E. Finnerty, "Insiders and Market Efficiency," *Journal of Finance* 31, no. 4 (September 1976): 1141–1148.

Herbert S. Kerr, "The Battle of Insider Trading and Market Efficiency," *Journal of Portfolio Management* 6, no. 4 (Summer 1980): 47–58.

Wayne Y. Lee and Michael Solt, "Insider Trading: A Poor Guide to Market Timing," *Journal of Portfolio Management* 12, no. 4 (Summer 1986): 65–71.

H. Nejat Seyhun, "Insiders' Profits, Costs of Trading, and Market Efficiency," *Journal of Financial Economics* 16, no. 2 (June 1986): 189–212.

J. Nejat Seyhun, "The Information Content of Aggregate Insider Trading," *Journal of Business* 61, no. 1 (January 1988): 1–24.

Michael S. Rozeff and Mir A. Zaman, "Market Efficiency and Insider Trading: New Evidence," *Journal of Business* 61, no. 1 (January 1988): 25–44.

Ji-Chai Lin and John S. Howe, "Insider Trading in the OTC Market," *Journal of Finance* 45, no. 4 (September 1990): 1273–1284.

Lisa K. Meulbroek, "An Empirical Analysis of Illegal Insider Trading," *Journal of Finance* 47, no. 5 (December 1992): 1661–1699.

Mustafa Chowdhury, John S. Howe, and Ji-Chai Lin, "The Relation between Aggregate Insider Transactions and Stock Market Returns," *Journal of Financial and Quantitative Analysis* 28, no. 3 (September 1993): 431–437.

7. The behaviour of beta coefficients has been extensively studied. See, for example:

Marshall Blume, "On the Assessment of Risk," *Journal of Finance* 26, no. 1 (March 1971): 1–10.

Robert A. Levy, "On the Short-Term Stationarity of Beta Coefficients," *Financial Analysts Journal* 27, no. 6 (November/December 1971): 55–62.

William F. Sharpe and Guy M. Cooper, "Risk-Return Classes of New York Stock Exchange Common Stocks, 1931–1967," *Financial Analysts Journal* 28, no. 2 (March-April 1972): 46–54.

Robert S. Hamada, "The Effect of the Firm's Capital Structure on the Systematic Risk of Common Stocks," *Journal of Finance* 27, no. 2 (May 1972): 435–452.

Marshall Blume, "Betas and Their Regression Tendencies," *Journal of Finance* 30, no. 3 (June 1975): 785–795.

Barr Rosenberg and Vinay Marathe, "The Prediction of Investment Risk: Systematic and Residual Risk," *Proceedings of the Seminar on the Analysis of Security Prices*, Center for Research in Security Prices, Graduate School of Business, University of Chicago, November 1975.

Barr Rosenberg and James Guy, "Prediction of Beta from Investment Fundamentals," *Financial Analysts Journal* 32, no. 3 (May–June 1976): 60–72, and no. 4 (July–August 1976): 62–70.

Meir Statman, "Betas Compared: Merrill Lynch vs. Value Line," *Journal of Portfolio Management* 7, no. 2 (Winter 1981): 41–44.

Diana R. Harrington, "Whose Beta is Best?" *Financial Analysts Journal* 39, no. 5 (July/August 1983): 67–73.

Barr Rosenberg, "Prediction of Common Stock Investment Risk," *Journal of Portfolio Management* 11, no. 1 (Fall 1984): 44–53.

Barr Rosenberg, "Prediction of Common Stock Betas," *Journal of Portfolio Management* 11, no. 2 (Winter 1985): 5–14.

Gordon J. Alexander and Jack Clark Francis, *Portfolio Analysis* (Englewood Cliffs, NJ: Prentice Hall, 1986): 185–192.

George Foster, *Financial Statement Analysis* (Englewood Cliffs, NJ: Prentice Hall, 1986), Chapter 10.

Frank K. Reilly and David J. Wright, "A Comparison of Published Betas," *Journal of Portfolio Management* 14, no. 3 (Spring 1988): 64–69.

Thomas E. Copeland and J. Fred Weston, *Financial Theory and Corporate Policy* (Reading, MA: Addison-Wesley, 1988), Chapter 13.

Richard A. Brealey and Stewart C. Myers, *Principles of Corporate Finance* (New York: McGraw-Hill, 1991): 191–192, 468–469.

8. The characteristics of value and growth stocks are described in:

   Ken Gregory, "Fund Investment Strategies: Growth vs Value Investing," *AAII Journal* 11, no. 9 (October 1989): 22–25.

   David E. Tierney and Kenneth J. Winston, "Using Generic Benchmarks to Present Manager Styles," *Journal of Portfolio Management* 17, no. 4 (Summer 1991): 33–36.

   John Bajkowski, "A Question of Style: Growth and Value Investing," *AAII Journal* 14, no. 5 (June 1992): 33–37.

   John Bajkowski, "Creating Stock Screens That Make Practical Sense," *AAII Journal* 15, no. 6 (July 1993): 34–37.

9. Many of the studies conducted concerning various empirical regularities are cited in the footnotes. Also see:

   Donald B. Keim, "The CAPM and Equity Return Regularities," *Financial Analysts Journal* 42, no. 3 (May/June 1986): 19–34.

   Michael Smirlock and Laura Starks, "Day-of-the-Week and Intraday Effects in Stock Returns," *Journal of Financial Economics* 17, no. 1 (September 1986): 197–210.

   Richard H. Thaler, "Anomalies: The January Effect," *Journal of Economic Perspectives* 1, no. 1 (Summer 1987): 197–201; and "Anomalies: Seasonal Movements in Security Prices — Weekend, Holiday, Turn-of-the-Month, and Intraday Effects," *Journal of Economic Perspectives* 1, no. 2 (Fall 1987): 169–177.

   Douglas K. Pearce, "Challenges to the Concept of Market Efficiency," Federal Reserve Bank of Kansas City *Economic Review* 72, no. 8 (September/October 1987): 16–33.

   Elroy Dimson, ed., *Stock Market Anomalies* (Cambridge, England: Cambridge University Press, 1988).

   Robert A. Haugen and Josef Lakonishok, *The Incredible January Effect* (Homewood, IL: Dow Jones-Irwin, 1988).

   Burton G. Malkiel, *A Random Walk Down Wall Street* (New York, W.W. Norton, 1990), Chapter 8.

   Eugene F. Fama, "Efficient Capital Markets: II," *Journal of Finance* 46, no. 5 (December 1991): 1575–1617.

   Narasimhan Jegadeesh, "Does Market Risk Really Explain the Size Effect?" *Journal of Financial and Quantitative Analysis* 27, no. 3 (September 1992): 337–351.

   Mark D. Griffiths and Robert W. White, "Tax-Induced Trading and the Turn-of-the-Year Anomaly: An Intraday Study," *Journal of Finance* 48, no. 2 (June 1993): 575–598.

10. For a tongue-in-cheek article on anomalies that shows that market returns are influenced by superstition because returns on Friday the 13th are, on average, abnormally low, see:

    Robert W. Kolb and Ricardo J. Rodriguez, "Friday the Thirteenth: 'Part VII' — A Note," *Journal of Finance* 42, no. 5 (December 1987): 1385–1387.

11. For a Canadian perspective on the topics covered in this chapter, see:

    D. J. Fowler and C. H. Rorke, "Thin Trading and Beta Estimation Problems on the Toronto Stock Exchange," *Journal of Business Administration: Capital Markets in Canada* 12, no. 1 (Fall 1980).

B. Smith and A. Amoako-Adu, "Financing Canadian Corporations with Restricted Voting Shares," *NCMRD Working Paper*, London, Ont. 1991.

G. Athanassakos, "Portfolio Rebalancing and the January Effect," *Financial Analysts Journal* 48, no. 6 (Nov./Dec. 1992).

J. B. Berk, "A Critique of Size-Related Anomalies," *Review of Financial Studies* 8, no. 1 (Summer 1993).

S. R. Foerster and D. C. Porter, "Calendar and Size-Based Anomalies in Canadian Stock Returns," in M. J. Robinson and B. F. Smith, eds., *Canadian Capital Markets* (London, Ont.: Western Business School, 1993).

D. C. Porter, "Stock Splits and Changing Betas," in M. J. Robinson and B. F. Smith, eds., *Canadian Capital Markets* (London, Ont.: Western Business School, 1993).

W. J. McNally, "Le Rachat D'Actions Signale-t-il Une Variation Du Risque," *Finéco* 4, no. 1 (1er semestre 1994).

G. Athanassakos and M. J. Robinson, "The Day-of-the-Week Anomaly: The Toronto Stock Exchange Experience," *Journal of Business Finance and Accounting* 21, no. 6 (Sept. 1994).

G. Athanassakos, "How to Predict the Likelihood of the January Effect," *Canadian Investment Review* VIII, no. 1 (Spring 1995).

V. Jog and B. Li, "Price Related Anomalies on the Toronto Stock Exchange," *Proceedings*, Administrative Sciences Association of Canada Conference, Windsor, June 1995.

G. F. Tannous, "Management Compensation and Shareholder Value," *Proceedings*, Administrative Sciences Association of Canada Conference, Windsor, June 1995.

INTERNET RESOURCES

The following investment information sources can be accessed at these Internet addresses:

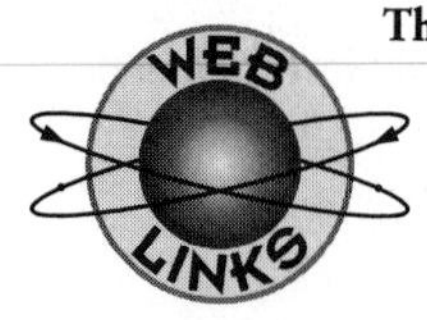

Altamira Investment Services	**http://www.altamira.com**
Annual Report Source	**http://www.annualreport/CyberPlex/ARS/AnnualreportSource.html**
InvestNet Canada	**http://islandnet.com/invest**
Quote.Com Financial Market Data	**http://www.quote.com**
Security APL Quote Server	**http://www.secapl.com/cgi-bin/qs**
Stock and Commodity Quotes from Telenium	**http://www.telenium.ca**
Vancouver Stock Exchange Official Home Page	**http://www.vse.ca**

CHAPTER 18

The Valuation of Common Shares

In Chapter 17, it was noted that one purpose of financial analysis is to identify mispriced securities. Fundamental analysis was mentioned as one approach for conducting a search for such securities. With this approach, the security analyst makes estimates of such things as the firm's future earnings and dividends. If these estimates are substantially different from the average estimates of other analysts but are viewed as being more accurate, then the security is considered to be mispriced. If it is also felt that the market price of the security will adjust to reflect these more accurate estimates, then the analyst will issue either a buy or sell recommendation, depending upon the direction of the anticipated price adjustment. Based upon the capitalization of income method of valuation, dividend discount models have been frequently used by fundamental analysts as a means of identifying mispriced common stocks. This chapter will examine dividend discount models and show how they can be related to models based on price-earnings ratios.

CAPITALIZATION OF INCOME METHOD OF VALUATION

There are many ways to implement the fundamental analysis approach to identifying mispriced securities. A number of them are either directly or indirectly related to what is sometimes referred to as the **capitalization of income method of valuation.**[1] This method states that the true, or intrinsic, value of any asset is based on the cash flows that the investor expects to receive in the future from owning the asset. Since these cash flows are expected in the future, they are discounted to reflect the time value of money, with the **discount rate** reflecting not only the time value of money but also the riskiness of the cash flows.

Algebraically, the intrinsic value of the asset (V) is equal to the sum of the present values of the expected cash flows:

$$V = \frac{C_1}{(1+k)^1} + \frac{C_2}{(1+k)^2} + \frac{C_3}{(1+k)^3} + \cdots = \sum_{t=1}^{\infty} \frac{C_t}{(1+k)^t} \tag{18.1}$$

where C_t denotes the expected cash flow associated with the asset at time t and k is the appropriate discount rate for cash flows of this degree risk. In this equation, the discount

[1]The appendix describes a model used by some fundamental analysts for identifying mispriced common stocks that is not directly related to the capitalization of income method of valuation. For a description of the typical financial characteristics of a stock market "winner," see Marc R. Reinganum, "The Anatomy of a Stock Market Winner," *Financial Analysts Journal* 44, no. 2 (March/April 1988): 16–28.

rate is assumed to be the same for all periods. Since the symbol ∞ above the summation sign in the equation denotes infinity, all expected cash flows, from immediately after making the investment until infinity, are discounted at the same rate in determining V.[2]

Net Present Value

For the sake of convenience, let the current moment in time be denoted by zero, or $t = 0$. If the cost of purchasing an asset at $t = 0$ is P, then its **net present value** (NPV) is equal to the difference between its intrinsic value and cost, or

$$\text{NPV} = V - P = \left[\sum_{t=1}^{\infty} \frac{C_t}{(1+k)^t}\right] - P. \tag{18.2}$$

The NPV calculation shown here is conceptually the same as the NPV calculation made for capital budgeting decisions that has long been advocated in introductory finance textbooks. Capital budgeting decisions involve deciding whether or not a given investment project should be undertaken (for example, whether to buy a new machine). In such decisions, the focal point is the NPV of the project. Specifically, an investment project will likely be viewed favourably if its NPV is positive and unfavourably if its NPV is negative. For a simple project involving a cash outflow now (at $t = 0$) and expected cash inflows in the future, a positive NPV means that the present value of all the expected cash inflows is greater than the cost of making the investment. Conversely, a negative NPV means that the present value of all the expected cash inflows is less than the cost of making the investment.

The same views about NPV apply when financial assets (such as a common share), instead of real assets (such as a new machine), are being considered for purchase. That is, a financial asset is viewed favourably and said to be underpriced, or undervalued, if NPV > 0. Conversely, a financial asset is viewed unfavourably and said to be overpriced, or overvalued, if NPV < 0. From equation (18.2), this is equivalent to stating that a financial asset is underpriced if $V > P$:

$$\sum_{t=1}^{\infty} \frac{C_t}{(1+k)^t} > P. \tag{18.3}$$

Conversely, the asset is overvalued if $V < P$:

$$\sum_{t=1}^{\infty} \frac{C_t}{(1+k)^t} < P. \tag{18.4}$$

Internal Rate of Return

Another way of making capital budgeting decisions that is similar to NPV involves calculating the **internal rate of return** (IRR) associated with the investment project. With IRR, the NPV in equation (18.2) is set equal to zero and the discount rate becomes the unknown that must be calculated. That is, the IRR for a given investment is the discount rate that makes the net present value of the investment equal to zero. Algebraically, the

[2] Sometimes the expected cash flows after some time period will be equal to zero, meaning that the summation only needs to be carried out to that point. Even if they are never equal to zero, in many cases the denominator in equation (18.1) will become so large as t gets large (for example, if t is 40 or more for a discount rate of 15%) that the present value of all expected cash flows past an arbitrary time in the future will be roughly zero and can be safely ignored. In addition, the discount rate may vary from period to period. It is assumed constant here for ease of exposition.

procedure involves solving the following equation for the internal rate of return, denoted by k^*:

$$0 = \sum_{t=1}^{\infty} \frac{C_t}{(1 + k^*)^t} - P \tag{18.5}$$

Equivalently, equation (18.5) can be rewritten as

$$P = \sum_{t=1}^{\infty} \frac{C_t}{(1 + k^*)^t}. \tag{18.6}$$

The decision rule for IRR involves comparing the project's IRR, denoted by k^*, with the required rate of return for an investment of similar risk (denoted by k). Specifically, the investment would be viewed favourably if $k^* > k$ and unfavourably if $k^* < k$. As with NPV, the same decision rule applies if either a real asset or a financial asset is being considered for possible investment.[3]

► An Application to Common Shares

This chapter is concerned with using the capitalization of income method to determine the intrinsic value of common shares. Since the cash flows associated with an investment in any particular common share are the dividends that are expected to be paid in the future, the models suggested by this method of valuation are often known as **dividend discount models** (DDMs).[4] Accordingly, D_t will be used instead of C_t to denote the expected cash flow in period t associated with a particular share of common stock, resulting in the following restatement of equation (18.1):

$$\begin{aligned} V &= \frac{D_1}{(1 + k)^1} + \frac{D_2}{(1 + k)^2} + \frac{D_3}{(1 + k)^3} + \cdots \\ &= \sum_{t=1}^{\infty} \frac{D_t}{(1 + k)^t}. \end{aligned} \tag{18.7}$$

Usually the focus of DDMs is on determining the true, or intrinsic, value of one share of a particular company's common stock, even if larger-size purchases are being contemplated. This is because it is usually believed that larger-size purchases can be made at a cost that is a simple multiple of the cost of one share (for example, the cost of 1000 shares is usually assumed to be 1000 times the cost of one share). Thus, the numerator in DDMs is the cash dividends per share that are expected in the future.

---

[3] With complex cash flows (such as a mix of positive and negative cash flows), the IRR method can be misleading. However, this is not a problem when it is applied to securities such as stocks and bonds. For a discussion of potential problems in other contexts, see Richard A. Brealey and Stewart C. Myers, *Principles of Corporate Finance* (New York: McGraw-Hill, 1991), Chapter 5.

[4] Since the focus of DDMs is on predicting dividends, there is a particular situation where using DDMs to value common shares is exceptionally difficult. This is the situation where the firm has not paid dividends on its shares in the recent past, which results in a complete lack of a historical record on which to base a prediction of dividends. Examples include valuing the shares of a firm being sold to the public for the first time (known as an initial public offering, or ipo) and valuing the shares of a firm that has not paid dividends recently (perhaps the firm has never paid dividends, or perhaps it has suspended paying them). A more extensive discussion of DDMs is contained in the entire November-December 1985 issue of the *Financial Analysts Journal*. For articles that describe some of the current applications of DDMs, see Barbara Donnelly, "The Dividend Discount Model Comes into Its Own," *Institutional Investor* 19, no. 3 (March 1985): 77–82, and Kent Hickman and Glen H. Petry, "A Comparison of Stock Price Predictions Using Court Accepted Formulas, Dividend Discount, and P/E Models," *Financial Management* 19, no. 2 (Summer 1990): 76–87.

However, there is a complication in using equation (18.7) to determine the intrinsic value of a share of common stock. In particular, in order to use this equation the investor must forecast *all* future dividends. Since common shares do not have a fixed lifetime, this suggests that an infinitely long stream of dividends must be forecast. While this may seem to be an impossible task, with the addition of certain assumptions, the equation can be made tractable (that is, usable).

These assumptions centre around dividend growth rates. That is, the dividend per share at any time t can be viewed as being equal to the dividend per share at time $t - 1$ times a dividend growth rate of g_t :

$$D_t = D_{t-1}(1 + g_t) \tag{18.8}$$

or, equivalently,

$$\frac{D_t - D_{t-1}}{D_{t-1}} = g_t. \tag{18.9}$$

For example, if the dividend per share expected at $t = 2$ is \$4 and the dividend per share expected at $t = 3$ is \$4.20, then $g_3 = (\$4.20 - \$4)/\$4 = 5\%$.

The different types of tractable DDMs are presented next. Each reflects a different set of assumptions about dividend growth rates. The discussion begins with the simplest case, the zero-growth model.

THE ZERO-GROWTH MODEL

One assumption that could be made about future dividends is that they will remain at a fixed dollar amount. That is, the dollar amount of dividends per share that were paid over the past year (D_0) will also be paid over the next year (D_1), the year after that (D_2), the year after that (D_3), and so on. That is,

$$D_0 = D_1 = D_2 = D_3 = \ldots$$

This is equivalent to assuming that all the dividend growth rates are zero, since if $g_t = 0$, then $D_t = D_{t-1}$ in equation (18.8). Accordingly, this model is often referred to as the **zero-growth** (or no-growth) **model**.

Net Present Value

The impact of this assumption on equation (18.7) can be analyzed by noting what happens when D_t is replaced by D_0 in the numerator:

$$V = \sum_{t=1}^{\infty} \frac{D_0}{(1 + k)^t}. \tag{18.10}$$

Fortunately, equation (18.10) can be simplified by noting that D_0 is a fixed dollar amount, which means it can be written outside the summation sign:

$$V = D_0 \left[\sum_{t=1}^{\infty} \frac{1}{(1 + k)^t} \right]. \tag{18.11}$$

The next step involves using a property of infinite series from mathematics. If $k > 0$, then it can be shown that

$$\sum_{t=1}^{\infty} \frac{1}{(1 + k)^t} = \frac{1}{k}. \tag{18.12}$$

Applying this property to equation (18.11) results in the following formula for the zero-growth model:

$$V = \frac{D_0}{k_0} \tag{18.13}$$

Since $D_0 = D_1$, equation (18.13) is sometimes written as

$$V = \frac{D_1}{k}. \tag{18.14}$$

As an example of how this DDM can be used, assume that the Zinc Company is expected to pay cash dividends amounting to \$8 per share into the indefinite future and has a required rate of return of 10%. Using either equation (18.13) or equation (18.14), it can be seen that the value of a share of Zinc stock is equal to \$8/.10 = \$80. With a current stock price of \$65 per share, equation (18.2) would suggest that the NPV per share is \$80 – \$65 = \$15. Equivalently, since V = \$80 > P = \$65, the stock is underpriced by \$15 per share and would be a candidate for purchase.

Internal Rate of Return

Equation (18.13) can be reformulated to solve for the IRR on an investment in a zero-growth security. First, the current price of the security is substituted for V; second, k^* is substituted for k. Doing so results in

$$P = \frac{D_0}{k^*}$$

which can be rewritten as

$$k^* = \frac{D_0}{P} \tag{18.15a}$$

$$= \frac{D_1}{P}. \tag{18.15b}$$

Applying this formula to the shares of Zinc indicates that k^* = \$8/\$65 = 12.3%. Since the IRR from an investment in Zinc exceeds the required rate of return on Zinc (12.3% > 10%), this method also indicates that Zinc is underpriced.[5]

An Application

The zero-growth model may seem quite restrictive. After all, it does not seem reasonable to assume a given stock will pay a fixed dollar-size dividend forever. While such a criticism has validity for common stock valuation, there is one particular situation where this model is quite useful. Specifically, whenever the intrinsic value of a preferred share is to be determined, this DDM is often appropriate. It is appropriate because most preferred shares are nonparticipating, meaning they pay a fixed dollar-size dividend that will not be changed as earnings-per-share changes. Furthermore, it can be expected to be paid forever, since preferred shares do not have a fixed lifetime.[6]

---

[5] A share of common stock has a positive NPV if and only if it has an IRR greater than its required rate of return. Thus, there can never be inconsistent signals given by the two approaches. That is, there will never be a situation where one approach indicates a share is underpriced and the other approach indicates it is overpriced. This is true not only for the zero-growth model but for all DDMs.

[6] The formula for valuing *consols* (these are bonds that make regular coupon payments but have no maturity date) is identical to equation (18.13), where the numerator now represents the annual coupon payment. Because

THE CONSTANT-GROWTH MODEL

The next type of DDM to be considered is one that assumes dividends grow from period to period at the same rate forever, and which is therefore known as the **constant-growth model.**[7] Specifically, the dividends per share that were paid over the previous year (D_0) are expected to grow at a given rate g, so that the dividends expected over the next year (D_1) are expected to be equal to $D_0(1 + g)$. Dividends the year after that are again expected to grow by the rate g, meaning that $D_2 = D_1(1 + g)$. Since $D_1 = D_0(1 + g)$, this is equivalent to assuming that $D_2 = D_0(1 + g)^2$ and, in general,

$$D_t = D_{t-1}(1 + g) \tag{18.16a}$$

$$= D_0(1 + g)^t. \tag{18.16b}$$

Net Present Value

The impact of this assumption on equation (18.7) can be analyzed by noting what happens when D_t is replaced by $D_0(1 + g)^t$ in the numerator:

$$V = \sum_{t=1}^{\infty} \frac{D_0(1 + g)^t}{(1 + k)^t}. \tag{18.17}$$

Fortunately, equation (18.17) can be simplified by noting that D_0 is a given dollar amount, which means it can be written outside the summation sign:

$$V = D_0 \left[\sum_{t=1}^{\infty} \frac{(1 + g)^t}{(1 + k)^t} \right]. \tag{18.18}$$

The next step involves using a property of infinite series from mathematics. If $k > g$, then it can be shown that

$$\sum_{t=1}^{\infty} \frac{(1 + g)^t}{(1 + k)^t} = \frac{1 + g}{k - g}. \tag{18.19}$$

Substituting equation (18.19) into equation (18.18) results in the valuation formula for the constant-growth model:

$$V = D_0 \left[\frac{1 + g}{k - g} \right]. \tag{18.20}$$

Sometimes equation (18.20) is rewritten as

$$V = \frac{D_1}{k - g} \tag{18.21}$$

since $D_1 = D_0(1 + g)$.

---

it has been found that the price behaviour of high-grade preferred shares is very similar to that of bonds, it is not surprising that the zero-growth model can be used to value high-grade preferred stocks. See John S. Bildersee, "Some Aspects of the Performance of Non-Convertible Preferred Stocks," *Journal of Finance* 28, no. 5 (December 1973): 1187–1201; and Enrico J. Ferreira, Michael F. Spivey, and Charles E. Edwards, "Pricing New-Issue and Seasoned Preferred Stock: A Comparison of Valuation Models," *Financial Management* 21, no. 2 (Summer 1992): 52–62.

[7] For an extension of this model which introduces capital gains taxes, see Raymond Chiang and Ricardo J. Rodriguez, "Personal Taxes, Holding Period, and the Variation of Growth Stocks," *Journal of Economics and Business* 42, no. 4 (November 1990): 303–309.

An Example

As an example of how this DDM can be used, assume that during the past year the Copper Company paid dividends amounting to \$1.80 per share. The forecast is that dividends on Copper shares will increase by 5% per year into the indefinite future. Thus, dividends over the next year are expected to equal \$1.80(1 + .05) = \$1.89. Using equation (16.20) and assuming the required rate of return of 11%, it can be seen that the value of a share of Copper stock is equal to \$1.80[(1 + .05)/(.11 – .05)] = \$1.89/(.11 – .05) = \$31.50. With a current stock price of \$40 per share, equation (18.2) would suggest that the NPV per share is \$31.50 – \$40 = –\$8.50. Equivalently, since V = \$31.50 < P = \$40, the stock is overpriced by \$8.50 per share and would be a candidate for sale if currently owned.

Internal Rate of Return

Equation (18.20) can be reformulated to solve for the internal rate of return on an investment in a constant growth security. First, the current price of the security is substituted for V and then k^* is substituted for k. Doing so results in

$$P = D_0\left[\frac{1+g}{k^*-g}\right] \tag{18.22}$$

which can be rewritten as

$$k^* = \frac{D_0(1+g)}{P} + g \tag{18.23a}$$

$$= \frac{D_1}{P} + g. \tag{18.23b}$$

An Example

Applying this formula to the shares of Copper indicates that k^* = [\$1.80(1+.05)/\$40]+.05 = [\$1.89/\$40] + .05 = 9.725%. Since the required rate of return on Copper exceeds the IRR from an investment in Copper (11% > 9.725%), this method also indicates that Copper is overpriced.

Relationship to the Zero-Growth Model

The zero-growth model of the previous section can be shown to be a special case of the constant-growth model. In particular, if the growth rate g is assumed to be 0, then dividends will be a fixed dollar amount forever, which is the same as saying that there will be zero growth. Letting $g = 0$ in equations (18.20) and (18.23a) results in two equations that are identical to (18.13) and (18.15a), respectively.

While assuming constant growth may seem less restrictive than assuming no growth, it may still be unrealistic in many cases. However, as will be shown next, the constant-growth model is important because it is embedded in the multiple-growth model.

THE MULTIPLE-GROWTH MODEL

The most general DDM for valuing common stocks is the **multiple-growth model**. With this model, the focus is on a time in the future after which dividends are expected to grow at a constant rate g. Although the investor is still concerned with forecasting dividends, these dividends do not need to have any specific pattern until this time, after which they will be assumed to have the specific pattern of constant growth. If this time is denoted by T, then dividends D_1, D_2, D_3, ..., D_T will be forecast separately by the investor (the investor also forecasts when this time T will occur). Thereafter, dividends are assumed to grow by a constant rate g that the investor must also forecast, meaning that

$$D_{T+1} = D_T(1 + g)$$
$$D_{T+2} = D_{T+1}(1 + g) = D_T(1 + g)^2$$
$$D_{T+3} = D_{T+2}(1 + g) = D_T(1 + g)^3$$

and so on. Figure 18.1 presents a time line of dividends and growth rates associated with the multiple-growth model.

▶ Net Present Value

In determining the value of a share of common stock with the multiple-growth model, the present value of the forecasted stream of dividends must be determined. This can be done by dividing the stream into two parts, finding the present value of each part, and then adding these two present values together.

The first part consists of finding the present value of all the forecasted dividends up to and including T. Denoting this present value by V_{T-}, it is equal to

$$V_{T-} = \sum_{t=1}^{T} \frac{D_t}{(1 + k)^t}. \tag{18.24}$$

The second part consists of finding the present value of all the forecasted dividends after T and involves the application of the constant-growth model. The application begins by imagining that the investor is not at time zero ($t = 0$) but is at time T ($t = T$) and has not changed his or her forecast of dividends for the shares. This means that next period's dividend, D_{T+1}, and all those thereafter are expected to grow at the rate g. Thus, the investor would be viewing the stock as having a constant growth rate, and its value *at time T* (V_T) could be determined with the constant-growth model of equation (18.21):

$$V_T = D_{T+1}\left[\frac{1}{k - g}\right]. \tag{18.25}$$

One way to view V_T is that it represents a lump sum that is just as desirable as the stream of dividends after T. That is, an investor would find a lump sum of cash equal to V_T, to be received at T, to be equally desirable to the stream of dividends D_{T+1}, D_{T+2}, D_{T+3}, and so on. Now, given that the investor is at time zero ($t = 0$), not at T, the present value at $t = 0$ of the lump sum V_T must be determined. This is done by discounting it for T periods at the rate k, resulting in the following formula for finding the present value at time zero for all dividends after T, denoted by V_{T+}:

$$\begin{aligned} V_{T+} &= V_T\left[\frac{1}{(1 + k)^T}\right] \\ &= \frac{D_{T+1}}{(k - g)(1 + k)^T}. \end{aligned} \tag{18.26}$$

Having found the present value of all dividends up to and including T with equation (18.24) and the present value of all dividends after T with equation (18.26), the value of a share can be determined by summing these two amounts:

$$
\begin{aligned}
V &= V_{T-} + V_{T+} \\
&= \sum_{t=1}^{T} \frac{D_t}{(1+k)^t} + \frac{D_{T+1}}{(k-g)(1+k)^T}.
\end{aligned}
\tag{18.27}
$$

Figure 18.1 illustrates the valuation procedure for the multiple-growth DDM that is given in equation (18.27).

An Example

As an example of how this DDM can be used, assume that during the past year the Magnesium Company paid dividends amounting to \$.75 per share. Over the next year Magnesium is expected to pay dividends of \$2 per share. Thus, $g_1 = (D_1 - D_0)/D_0 = (\$2 - \$.75)/\$.75 = 167\%$. The year after that dividends are expected to amount to \$3 per share, indicating that $g_2 = (D_2 - D_1)/D_1 = (\$3 - \$2)/\$2 = 50\%$. At this time, the forecast is that dividends will grow by 10% per year into the indefinite future, indicating that $T = 2$ and $g = 10\%$. Consequently, $D_{T+1} = D_3 = \$3(1 + .10) = \$3.30$.

Given a required rate of return on Magnesium shares of 15%, the value of V_{T-} and V_{T+} can be calculated, respectively, as follows:

$$
\begin{aligned}
V_{T-} &= \frac{\$2}{(1+.15)^1} + \frac{\$3}{(1+.15)^2} \\
&= \$4.01
\end{aligned}
$$

$$
\begin{aligned}
V_{T+} &= \frac{\$3.30}{(.15-.10)(1+.15)^2} \\
&= \$49.91
\end{aligned}
$$

Figure 18.1

Time line for multiple growth model.

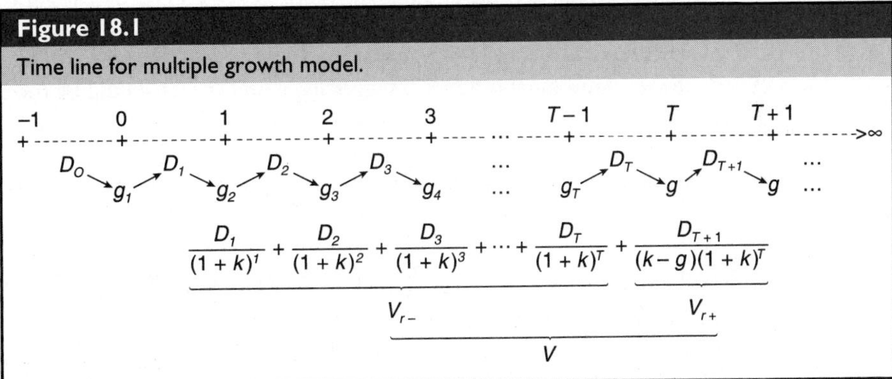

Summing V_{T-} and V_{T+} results in a value for V of \$4.01 + \$49.91 = \$53.92. With a current stock price of \$55 per share, Magnesium appears to be fairly priced. That is, since V and P are nearly of equal size, Magnesium is not mispriced.

Internal Rate of Return

The zero-growth and constant-growth models had equations for V that could be reformulated in order to solve for the internal rate of return on an investment in a share.

Unfortunately, a convenient expression similar to equations (18.15a), (18.15b), (18.23a), and (18.23b) is not available for the multiple-growth model. This can be seen by noting that the expression for IRR is derived by substituting P for V and k^* for k in equation (18.27):

$$P = \sum_{t=1}^{T} \frac{D_t}{(1+k^*)^t} + \frac{D_{T+1}}{(k^* - g)(1+k^*)^T}. \tag{18.28}$$

This equation cannot be rewritten with k^* isolated on the left-hand side, meaning that a closed-form expression for IRR does not exist for the multiple-growth model.

However, all is not lost. It is still possible to calculate the IRR for an investment in a share conforming to the multiple-growth model by using an "educated" trial-and-error method. The basis for this method is the observation that the right-hand side of equation (18.28) is simply equal to the present value of the dividend stream, where k^* is used as the discount rate. Hence, the larger the value of k^*, the smaller the value of the right-hand side of equation (18.28). The trial-and-error method proceeds by initially using an estimate for k^*. If the resulting value on the right-hand side of equation (18.28) is larger than P, then a larger estimate of k^* is tried. Conversely, if the resulting value is smaller than P, then a smaller estimate of k^* is tried. Continuing this search process, the investor can hone in on the value of k^* that makes the right-hand side equal P on the left-hand side. Fortunately, it is a relatively simple matter to program a computer to conduct the search for k^* in equation (18.28). Most spreadsheets include a function that does so automatically.

An Example

Applying equation (18.28) to the Magnesium Company results in

$$\$55 = \frac{\$2}{(1+k^*)^1} + \frac{\$3}{(1+k^*)^2} + \frac{\$3.30}{(k^* - .10)(1+k^*)^2}. \tag{18.29}$$

Initially a rate of 14% may be used in attempting to solve this equation for k^*. Inserting 14% for k^* in the right-hand side of equation (18.29) results in a value of \$67.54. Earlier 15% was used in determining V and resulted in a value of \$53.92. This means that k^* must have a value between 14% and 15%, since \$55 is between \$67.54 and \$53.92. If 14.5% is tried next, the resulting value is \$59.97, suggesting a higher rate should be tried. If 14.8% and 14.9% are subsequently tried, the respective results are \$56.18 and \$55.03. Since \$55.03 is the closest to P, the IRR associated with an investment in Magnesium is 14.9%. Given a required return of 15% and an IRR of approximately that amount, the stock of Magnesium appears to be fairly priced.

► Relationship to the Constant-Growth Model

The constant-growth model can be shown to be a special case of the multiple-growth model. In particular, if the time when constant growth is assumed to begin is set equal to zero, then

$$V_{T-} = \sum_{t=1}^{T} \frac{D_t}{(1+k)^t} = 0$$

and

$$V_{T+} = \frac{D_{T+1}}{(k-g)(1+k)^T} = \frac{D_1}{k-g}$$

since $T = 0$ and $(1 + k)^0 = 1$. Given that the multiple-growth model states that $V = V_{T-} + V_{T+}$, setting $T = 0$ results in $V = D_1/(k - g)$, a formula that is equivalent to the formula for the constant-growth model.

Two-Stage and Three-Stage Models

Two dividend discount models that are sometimes used are the two-stage and the three-stage models.[8] The two-stage model assumes a constant growth rate (g_1) exists only until some time T, when a different growth rate (g_2) is assumed to begin and continue thereafter. The three-stage model assumes a constant growth rate (g_1) exists only until some time T_1, when a second growth rate is assumed to begin and last until a later time T_2, when a third growth rate is assumed to begin and last thereafter. By letting V_{T+} denote the present value of all dividends after the last growth rate has begun and V_{T-} denote the present value of all the preceding dividends, it can be seen that these models are just special cases of the multiple-growth model.

In applying the capitalization of income method of valuation to common shares, it might seem appropriate to assume that they will be sold at some point in the future. In this case, the expected cash flows would consist of the dividends up to that point as well as the expected selling price. Since dividends after the selling date would be ignored, the use of a dividend discount model may seem to be improper. However, as is shown next, this is not so.

VALUATION BASED ON A FINITE HOLDING PERIOD

The capitalization of income method of valuation involves discounting all dividends that are expected in the future. Since the simplified models of zero growth, constant growth, and multiple growth are based on this method, they too involve a future stream of dividends. Upon reflection, it may seem that such models are relevant only for an investor who plans to hold a stock forever, since such an investor would expect to receive this stream of future dividends.

But what about an investor who plans to sell the shares in a year?[9] In such a situation, the cash flows that the investor expects to receive from purchasing a share of the stock are equal to the dividend expected one year from now (for ease of exposition, it is assumed that common shares pay dividends annually) and the expected selling price of the shares. Thus,

---

[8] For a discussion of these models, see Russell J. Fuller and Chi-Cheng Hsia, "A Simplified Common Stock Valuation Model," *Financial Analysts Journal* 40, no. 5 (September/October 1984): 49–56; Eric H. Sorensen and David A. Williamson, "Some Evidence on the Value of Dividend Discount Models," *Financial Analysts Journal* 41, no. 6 (November/December 1985): 60–69; Richard W. Taylor, "A Three-Phase Quarterly Dividend Discount Model," *Financial Analysts Journal* 44, no. 5 (September/October 1988): 79–80, and "A Three-Phase Quarterly Earnings Model," *Financial Analysts Journal* 45, no. 5 (September/October 1989): 79; and Michael S. Rozeff, "The Three-Phase Dividend Discount Model and the ROPE Model," *Journal of Portfolio Management* 16, no. 2 (Winter 1990): 36–42.

[9] The analysis is similar if it is assumed that the investor plans to sell the stock after some other length of time, such as six months or two years.

it would seem appropriate to determine the intrinsic value of the shares to the investor by discounting these two cash flows at the required rate of return as follows:

$$
\begin{aligned}
V &= \frac{D_1 + P_1}{(1 + k)} \\
&= \frac{D_1}{1 + k} + \frac{P_1}{1 + k}
\end{aligned}
\tag{18.30}
$$

where D_1 and P_1 are the expected dividend and selling price at $t = 1$, respectively.

In order to use equation (18.30), the expected price of a share at $t = 1$ must be estimated. The simplest approach assumes that the selling price will be based on the dividends that are expected to be paid after the selling date, $t = 1$. Thus, the expected selling price at $t = 1$ is

$$
\begin{aligned}
P_1 &= \frac{D_2}{(1 + k)^1} + \frac{D_3}{(1 + k)^2} + \frac{D_4}{(1 + k)^3} + \cdots \\
&= \sum_{t=2}^{\infty} \frac{D_t}{(1 + k)_{t-1}}.
\end{aligned}
\tag{18.31}
$$

Substituting equation (18.31) for P_1 in the right-hand side of equation (18.30) results in

$$
\begin{aligned}
V &= \frac{D_1}{1 + k} + \left[\frac{D_2}{(1 + k)^1} + \frac{D_3}{(1 + k)^2} + \frac{D_4}{(1 + k)^3} + \cdots\right]\left[\frac{1}{1 + k}\right] \\
&= \frac{D_1}{(1 + k)^1} + \frac{D_2}{(1 + k)^2} + \frac{D_3}{(1 + k)^3} + \frac{D_4}{(1 + k)^4} + \cdots \\
&= \sum_{t=1}^{\infty} \frac{D_t}{(1 + k)^t}
\end{aligned}
$$

which is exactly the same as equation (18.7). Thus, valuing a share of common stock by discounting its dividends up to some point in the future and its expected selling price at that time is equivalent to valuing a share by discounting all future dividends. Simply stated, the two are equivalent because the expected selling price is itself based on dividends to be paid after the selling date. Thus, equation (18.7)—as well as the zero-growth, constant-growth, and multiple-growth models that are based on it—is appropriate for determining the intrinsic value of a share of common stock regardless of the length of the investor's planned holding period.

An Example

As an example, reconsider the common shares of the Copper Company. Over the past year it was noted that Copper paid dividends of \$1.80 per share, with the forecast that the dividends would grow by 5% per year forever. This means that dividends over the next two years (D_1 and D_2) are forecast to be \$1.80(1 + .05) = \$1.89 and \$1.89(1 + .05) = \$1.985, respectively. If the investor plans to sell the shares after one year, the selling price can be estimated by noting that at $t = 1$, the forecast of dividends for the forthcoming year would be D_2, or \$1.985. Thus, the anticipated selling price at $t = 1$, denoted by P_1, would be equal to \$1.985/(.11 – .05) = \$33.08. Accordingly, the intrinsic value of Copper to such an investor would be equal to the present value of the expected cash flows, which are D_1 = \$1.89 and P_1 = \$33.08. Using equation (18.30) and assuming a required rate of 11%, this value is equal to (\$1.89 + \$33.08)/(1 + .11) = \$31.50. Note that this is the same amount that was calculated earlier when all the dividends from now to infinity were discounted using the constant-growth model: $V = D_1/(k - g) = \$1.89/(.11 - .05) = \$31.50$.

MODELS BASED ON PRICE-EARNINGS RATIOS

Despite the inherent sensibility of DDMs, many security analysts use a much simpler procedure to value common shares. First, a stock's earnings per share over the forthcoming year (E_1) are estimated, and then the analyst (or someone else) will estimate a "normal" **price-earnings ratio** for the stock. The product of these two numbers gives the estimated future price (P_1). Using this value, together with estimated dividends to be paid during the period (D_1) and current price (P), the estimated return on the stock over the period can be determined:

$$\text{Expected return} = \frac{(P_1 - P) + D_1}{P} \tag{18.32}$$

where

$$P_1 = (P_1/E_1) \times E_1$$

Some security analysts expand this procedure, estimating earnings per share and price-earnings ratios for optimistic, most likely, and pessimistic scenarios to produce a rudimentary probability distribution of a security's return. Other analysts determine whether a share is underpriced or overpriced by comparing its actual price-earnings ratio with its normal price-earnings ratio, as is shown next.[10]

In order to make this comparison, equation (18.7) must be rearranged and some new variables must be introduced. To begin, it should be noted that earnings per share (E_t) are related to dividends per share (D_t) by the firm's **payout ratio** (p_t):

$$D_t = p_t E_t. \tag{18.33}$$

Note that if an analyst has forecast earnings per share and payout ratios, then he or she has implicitly forecast dividends.

Equation (18.33) can be used to restate the various DDMs so as to focus on what the share's price-earnings ratio should be instead of on its intrinsic value. In order to do so, $p_t E_t$ is substituted for D_t in the right-hand side of equation (18.7), resulting in a general formula for determining a stock's intrinsic value that involves discounting earnings:

$$\begin{aligned} V &= \frac{D_1}{(1+k)^1} + \frac{D_2}{(1+k)^2} + \frac{D_3}{(1+k)^3} + \cdots \\ &= \frac{p_1 E_1}{(1+k)^1} + \frac{p_2 E_2}{(1+k)^2} + \frac{p_3 E_3}{(1+k)^3} + \cdots \\ &= \sum_{t=1}^{\infty} \frac{p_t E_t}{(1+k)^t}. \end{aligned} \tag{18.34}$$

10 Alternatively, some analysts focus on the **earnings-price ratio**, which is the reciprocal of the price-earnings ratio. Accordingly, the formulas for a share's normal earnings-price ratio can be found by simply taking the reciprocal of the forthcoming formulas for determining its normal price-earnings ratio. In cases where earnings are close to zero, the earnings-price ratio is computationally preferred by analysts to the price-earnings ratio. This is because it approaches zero in such a situation, whereas the price-earnings ratio approaches infinity.

Earlier, it was noted that dividends in adjacent time periods could be viewed as being "linked" to each other by a dividend growth rate, g_t. Similarly, earnings per share in any year t can be linked to earnings per share in the previous year $t-1$ by a growth rate in earnings per share, g_{et}:

$$E_t = E_{t-1}(1 + g_{et}). \tag{18.35}$$

This implies that

$$E_1 = E_0(1 + g_{e1})$$
$$E_2 = E_1(1 + g_{e2}) = E_0(1 + g_{e1})(1 + g_{e2})$$
$$E_3 = E_2(1 + g_{e3}) = E_0(1 + g_{e1})(1 + g_{e2})(1 + g_{e3})$$

and so on, where E_0 is the actual level of earnings per share over the past year, E_1 is the expected level of earnings per share over the forthcoming year, E_2 is the expected level of earnings per share for the year after E_1, and E_3 is the expected level of earnings per share for the year after E_2.

These equations relating expected future earnings per share to E_0 can be substituted into equation (18.34), resulting in

$$V = \frac{p_1[E_0(1 + g_{e1})]}{(1 + k)^1} + \frac{p_2[E_0(1 + g_{e1})(1 + g_{e2})]}{(1 + k)^2} + \frac{p_3[E_0(1 + g_{e1})(1 + g_{e2})(1 + g_{e3})]}{(1 + k)^3} + \cdots \tag{18.36}$$

Since V is the intrinsic value of a share of stock, it represents what the share should be selling for if it were fairly priced. It follows that V/E_0 represents what the price-earnings ratio should be for the share if it were fairly priced; it is sometimes referred to as the share's normal price-earnings ratio. Dividing both sides of equation (18.36) by E_0 and simplifying results in the formula for determining the normal price-earnings ratio:

$$\frac{V}{E_o} = \frac{p_1[(1 + g_{e1})]}{(1 + k)^1} + \frac{p_2[(1 + g_{e1})(1 + g_{e2})]}{(1 + k)^2} + \frac{p_3[(1 + g_{e1})(1 + g_{e2})(1 + g_{e3})]}{(1 + k)^3} + \cdots \tag{18.37}$$

This shows that, other things being equal, a share's normal price-earnings ratio will be *higher*:

1. The *greater* the expected payout ratios ($p_1, p_2, p_3, \ldots$),
2. The *greater* the expected growth rates in earnings per share ($g_{e1}, g_{e2}, g_{e3}, \ldots$), and
3. The *smaller* the required rate of return (k).

The qualifying phrase "other things being equal" should not be overlooked. For example, a firm cannot increase the value of its shares by simply planning on having greater payouts. This will increase $p_1, p_2, p_3, \ldots$ but will decrease the expected growth rates in earnings per share $g_{e1}, g_{e2}, g_{e3}, \ldots$. Assuming the firm's investment policy is not altered, the effects of the reduced growth in earnings per share will just offset the effects of the increased payouts, leaving value per share unchanged.

Earlier, it was noted that a share was viewed as being underpriced if $V > P$ and overpriced if $V < P$. Since dividing both sides of an inequality by a positive constant will not change the direction of the inequality, a share can be viewed as being underpriced if $V/E_0 > P/E_0$ and overpriced if $V/E_0 < P/E_0$. Thus, a share will be underpriced if its normal price-earnings ratio is greater than its actual price-earnings ratio and overpriced if its normal price-earnings ratio is less than its actual price-earnings ratio.

Unfortunately, equation (18.37) is intractable, meaning it cannot be used to estimate the normal price-earnings ratio for any share. However, simplifying assumptions can be made that result in tractable formulas for estimating normal price-earnings ratios. These assumptions, along with the formulas, parallel those made previously regarding dividends and are discussed next.

▶ The Zero-Growth Model

The zero-growth model assumed that dividends per share remained at a fixed dollar amount forever. This is equivalent to assuming that earnings per share remain at a fixed dollar amount forever, with the firm maintaining a 100% payout ratio. It is assumed to be 100% because if a lesser amount were paid out, it would mean that the firm was retaining part of its earnings. These retained earnings would be put to some use and would thus be expected to increase future earnings per share, and consequently dividends per share.

Accordingly, the zero-growth model assumes $p_t = 1$ for all time periods and $E_0 = E_1 = E_2 = E_3$ and so on. This means that $D_0 = E_0 = D_1 = E_1 = D_2 = E_2$ and so on, allowing valuation equation (18.13) to be restated as

$$V = \frac{E_0}{k}. \tag{18.38}$$

Dividing equation (18.38) by E_0 results in the formula for the normal price-earnings ratio for a stock having zero growth:

$$\frac{V}{E_0} = \frac{1}{k}. \tag{18.39}$$

An Example

Earlier, it was assumed that the Zinc Company was a zero-growth firm paying dividends of \$8 per share, selling for \$65 a share, and having a required rate of return of 10%. Since Zinc is a zero-growth company, this means that it has a 100% payout ratio, which, in turn, means that $E_0 = \$8$. At this point, equation (18.38) can be used to note that a normal price-earnings ratio for Zinc is $1/.10 = 10$. Since Zinc has an actual price-earnings ratio of $\$65/\$8 = 8.1$ and since $V/E_0 = 10 > P/E_0 = 8.1$, Zinc shares are underpriced.

▶ The Constant-Growth Model

Earlier, it was noted that dividends in adjacent time periods could be viewed as being connected to each other by a dividend growth rate, g_t. Similarly, it was noted that earnings per share can be connected by an earnings growth rate, g_{et}. The constant-growth model assumes that the growth rate in dividends per share will be the same throughout the future. An equivalent assumption is that earnings per share will grow at a constant rate (g_e) throughout the future, with the payout ratio remaining at a constant level (p). This means that

$$E_1 = E_0(1 + g_e)$$
$$E_2 = E_1(1 + g_e) = E_0(1 + g_e)(1 + g_e)$$
$$E_3 = E_2(1 + g_e) = E_0(1 + g_e)(1 + g_e)(1 + g_e)$$

and so on. In general, earnings in year t can be connected to E_0 as follows:

$$E_t = E_0(1 + g_e)^t. \tag{18.40}$$

Substituting equation (18.40) into the numerator of equation (18.34) and recognizing that $p_t = p$ results in the following:

$$V = \sum_{t=1}^{\infty} \frac{pE_0(1 + g_e)^t}{(1 + k)^t}$$

$$= pE_0 \left[\sum_{t=1}^{\infty} \frac{(1 + g_e)^t}{(1 + k)^t} \right]. \tag{18.41}$$

The same mathematical property of infinite series given in equation (18.19) can be applied to equation (18.41), resulting in

$$V = pE_0 \left[\frac{1 + g_e}{k - g_e} \right]. \tag{18.42}$$

It can be noted that the earnings-based constant-growth model has a numerator identical to the numerator of the dividend-based constant-growth model, since $pE_0 = D_0$. Furthermore, the denominators of the two models are identical if the growth rates in earnings and dividends are the same (that is, if $g_e = g$). Examining the assumptions of the models reveals that these growth rates must be equal. This can be seen by recalling that constant earnings growth means

$$E_t = E_{t-1}(1 + g_e).$$

When both sides of this equation are multiplied by the constant payout ratio, the result is

$$pE_t = pE_{t-1}(1 + g_e).$$

Since $pE_t = D_t$ and $pE_{t-1} = D_{t-1}$, this equation reduces to:

$$D_t = D_{t-1}(1 + g_e)$$

which indicates that dividends in any period $t - 1$ will grow by the earnings growth rate, g_e. Since the dividend-based constant-growth model assumed dividends in any period $t - 1$ would grow by the dividend growth rate g, it can be seen that the two growth rates must be equal for the two models to be equivalent.

Equation (18.42) can be restated by dividing each side by E_0, resulting in the following formula for determining the normal price-earnings ratio for a stock with constant growth:

$$\frac{V}{E_0} = p \left[\frac{1 + g_e}{k - g_e} \right]. \tag{18.43}$$

An Example

Earlier, it was assumed that the Copper Company had paid dividends of \$1.80 per share over the past year, with a forecast that dividends would grow by 5% per year forever. Furthermore, it was assumed that the required rate of return on Copper was 11%, and the current stock price was \$40 per share. Now, assuming E_0 was \$2.70, it can be seen that the payout ratio was equal to \$1.80/\$2.70 = 66²⁄₃%. This means that the normal price-earnings ratio for Copper, according to equation (18.43), is equal to .6667[(1 + .05)/(.11 − .05)] = 11.67.

Since this is less than Copper's actual price-earnings ratio of $40/$2.70 = 14.81, it follows that the shares of Copper Company are overpriced.

The Multiple-Growth Model

Earlier it was noted that the most general DDM is the multiple-growth model, where dividends are allowed to grow at varying rates until some point in time T, after which they are assumed to grow at a constant rate. In this situation the present value of all the dividends is found by adding the present value of all dividends up to and including T, denoted by V_{T-}, and the present value of all dividends after T, denoted by V_{T+}:

$$V = V_{T-} + V_{T+}$$
$$= \sum_{t=1}^{T} \frac{D_t}{(1+k)^t} + \frac{D_{T+1}}{(k-g)(1+k)^T}. \quad (18.27)$$

In general, earnings per share in any period t can be expressed as being equal to E_0 times the product of all the earnings growth rates from time zero to time t:

$$E_t = E_0(1 + g_e 1)(1 + g_e 2) \cdots (1 + g_e t). \quad (18.44)$$

Because dividends per share in any period t are equal to the payout ratio for that period times the earnings per share, it follows from equation (18.44) that

$$D_t = p_t E_t$$
$$= p_t E_0(1 + g_{e1})(1 + g_{e2}) \cdots (1 + g_{et}). \quad (18.45)$$

Replacing the numerator in equation (18.37) with the right-hand side of equation (18.45) and then dividing both sides by E_0 gives the following formula for determining a share's "normal" price-earnings ratio with the multiple-growth model:

$$\frac{V}{E_0} = \frac{p_1(1 + g_{e1})}{(1+k)^1} + \frac{p_2(1 + g_{e1})(1 + g_{e2})}{(1+k)^2} + \cdots$$
$$+ \frac{p_T(1 + g_{e1})(1 + g_{e2}) \cdots (1 + g_{eT})}{(1+k)^T}$$
$$+ \frac{p(1 + g_{e1})(1 + g_{e2}) \cdots (1 + g_{eT})(1+g)}{(k-g)(1+k)^T}. \quad (18.46)$$

An Example

Consider the Magnesium Company again. Its share price is currently $55, and per share earnings and dividends over the past year were $3 and $.75, respectively. For the next two years, forecast earnings and dividends, along with the earnings growth rates and payout ratios, are:

$$D_1 = \$2.00 \qquad E_1 = \$5.00 \qquad g_{e1} = 67\% \qquad p_1 = 40\%$$
$$D_2 = \$3.00 \qquad E_2 = \$6.00 \qquad g_{e2} = 20\% \qquad p_2 = 50\%.$$

Constant growth in dividends and earnings of 10% per year is forecast to begin at $T = 2$, which means that $D_3 = \$3.30$, $E_3 = \$6.60$, $g = 10\%$, and $p = 50\%$. Given a required return of 15%, equation (18.46) can be used as follows to estimate a "normal" price-earnings ratio for Magnesium:

$$\frac{V}{E_O} = \frac{.40(1+.67)}{(1+.15)^1} + \frac{.50(1+.67)(1+.20)}{(1+.15)^2} + \frac{.50(1+.67)(1+.20)(1+.10)}{(.15-.10)(1+.15)^2}$$
$$= .58 = .76 + 16.67$$
$$= 18.01.$$

Because the actual price-earnings ratio of 18.33 (= \$55/\$3) is close to the "normal" ratio of 18.01, the shares of the Magnesium Company can be viewed as fairly priced.

SOURCES OF EARNINGS GROWTH

So far, no explanation has been given as to why earnings or dividends can be expected to grow in the future. One explanation uses the constant-growth model. Assuming that no new capital is obtained externally and no shares are repurchased (meaning the number of shares outstanding does not increase or decrease), the portion of earnings not paid to shareholders as dividends will be used to pay for the firm's new investments. Given that p_t denotes the payout ratio in year t, then $(1-p_t)$ is equal to the portion of earnings not paid out, known as the **retention ratio**. Furthermore, the firm's new investments, stated on a per-share basis and denoted by I_t , will be

$$I_t = (1-p_t)E_t. \tag{18.47}$$

If these new investments have an average return on equity of r_t in period t and every year thereafter, they will add r_tI_t to earnings per share in year $t+1$ and every year thereafter. If all previous investments also produce perpetual earnings at a constant rate of return, next year's earnings will equal this year's earnings plus the new earnings resulting from this year's new investments:

$$\begin{aligned} E_{t+1} &= E_t + r_tI_t \\ &= E_t + r_t(1-p_t)E_t \\ &= E_t[1 + r_t(1-p_t)]. \end{aligned} \tag{18.48}$$

Because it was shown earlier that the growth rate in earnings per share is

$$E_t = E_{t-1}(1+g_{et}) \tag{18.35}$$

it follows that

$$E_{t+1} = E_t(1+g_{et+1}) \tag{18.49}$$

A comparison of equations (18.48) and (18.49) indicates that

$$g_{et+1} = r_t(1-p_t). \tag{18.50}$$

If the growth rate in earnings per share (g_{et+1}) is to be constant over time, then the average return on equity for new investments (r_t) and payout ratio (p_t) must also be constant over time. In this situation, equation (18.50) can be simplified by removing the time subscripts:

$$g_e = r(1-p). \tag{18.51a}$$

Since the growth rate in dividends per share (g) is equal to the growth rate in earnings per share (g_e), this equation can be rewritten as

$$g = r(1 - p). \tag{18.51b}$$

From this equation it can be seen that the growth rate g depends on (1) the proportion of earnings that is retained $(1 - p)$, and (2) the average return on equity for the earnings that are retained (r).

The constant-growth valuation formula given in equation (18.20) can be modified by replacing g with the expression on the right-hand side of equation (18.51b), resulting in

$$\begin{aligned} V &= D_0\left(\frac{1+g}{k-g}\right) \\ &= D_0\left[\frac{1+r(1-p)}{k-r(1-p)}\right] \\ &= D_1\left[\frac{1}{k-r(1-p)}\right] \end{aligned} \tag{18.52}$$

In terms of price-earnings ratios, the formula in equation (18.43) becomes

$$\begin{aligned} \frac{V}{E_0} &= p\left(\frac{1+g_e}{k-g_e}\right) \\ &= p\left[\frac{1+r(1-p)}{k-r(1-p)}\right] \end{aligned} \tag{18.53}$$

Under these assumptions, a share's value, and hence its price, should be greater, the greater its average return on equity for new investments, other things being equal.

An Example

Continuing with the Copper Company, recall that $E_0 = \$2.70$ and $p = 66^2/_3\%$. This means that $33^1/_3\%$ of earnings per share over the past year were retained and reinvested, an amount equal to $.3333 \times \$2.70 = \$.90$. The earnings per share in the forthcoming year (E_1) are expected to be $\$2.70(1 + .05) = \$2.835$, since the growth rate (g) for Copper is 5%. The source of the increase in earnings per share of $\$2.835 - \$2.70 = \$.135$ is the \$.90 per share that was reinvested at $t = 0$. The average return on equity for new investments (r) is 15%, since $\$.135/\$.90 = 15\%$. That is, the reinvested earnings of \$.90 per share can be viewed as having generated an annual increase in earnings per share of \$.135. This increase will occur not only at $t = 1$ but also at $t = 2$, $t = 3$, and so on. Equivalently, a \$.90 investment at $t = 0$ will generate a perpetual annual cash inflow of \$.135 beginning at $t = 1$.

Expected dividends at $t = 1$ can be calculated by multiplying the expected payout ratio (p) of $66^2/_3\%$ times the expected earnings per share (E_1) of \$2.835, or $.6667 \times \$2.835 = \$1.89$. It can also be calculated by multiplying 1 plus the growth rate (g) of 5% times the past amount of dividends per share (D_0) of \$1.80, or $1.05 \times \$1.80 = \$1.89$. It can be seen that the growth rate in dividends per share of 5% is equal to the product of the retention rate ($33^1/_3\%$) and the average return on equity for new investments (15%), an amount equal to $.3333 \times .15 = 5\%$.

Two years from now ($t = 2$), earnings per share are anticipated to be $\$2.835 \times (1 + .05) = \$2.977$, a further increase of $\$2.977 - \$2.835 = \$.142$ that is due to the retention and reinvestment of $.3333 \times \$2.835 = \$.945$ per share at $t = 1$. This expected increase in

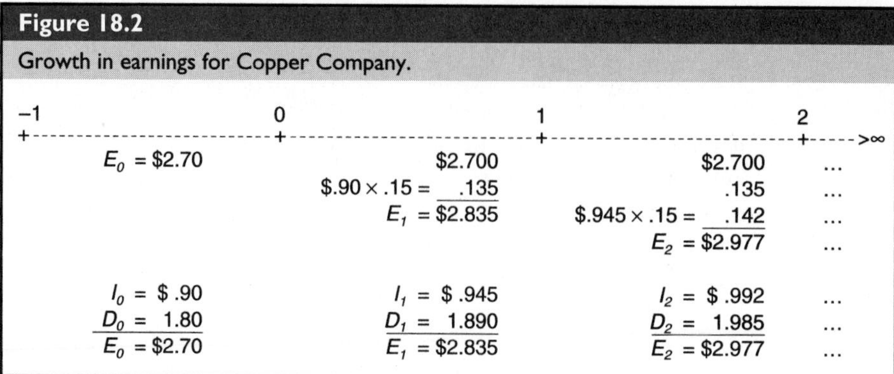
Figure 18.2
Growth in earnings for Copper Company.

earnings per share of $.142 is the result of earning 15% on the reinvested $.945, since .15 × $.945 = $.142.

The expected earnings per share at $t = 2$ have three components. The first is the earnings attributable to the assets held at $t = 0$, an amount equal to $2.70. The second is the earnings attributable to the reinvestment of $.90 at $t = 0$, earning $.135. The third is the earnings attributable to the reinvestment of $.945 at $t = 1$, earning $.142. These three components, when summed, equal $E_2 = \$2.70 + \$.135 + \$.142 = \$2.977$.

Dividends at $t = 2$ are expected to be 5% larger than at $t = 1$, or 1.05 × $1.89 = $1.985 per share. This amount corresponds to the amount calculated by multiplying the payout ratio times the expected earnings per share at $t = 2$, or .6667 × $2.977 = $1.985. Figure 18.2 summarizes the example.

A THREE-STAGE DDM

As this chapter's Institutional Issues section discusses, the three-stage DDM is the most widely applied form of the general multiple-growth DDM. Consider analyzing the ABC Company.

Making Forecasts

Over the past year, ABC has had earnings per share of $1.67 and dividends per share of $40. After carefully studying ABC, a security analyst has made the following forecasts of earnings per share and dividends per share for the next five years.

$$E_1 = \$2.67 \qquad E_2 = \$4.00 \qquad E_3 = \$6.00 \qquad E_4 = \$8.00 \qquad E_5 = \$10.00$$

$$D_2 = \$.60 \qquad D_2 = \$1.60 \qquad D_3 = \$2.40 \qquad D_4 = \$3.20 \qquad D_5 = \$5.00.$$

These forecasts imply the following payout ratios and earnings-per-share growth rates:

$$p_1 = 22\% \qquad p_2 = 40\% \qquad p_3 = 40\% \qquad p_4 = 40\% \qquad p_5 = 50\%$$

$$g_{e1} = 60\% \qquad g_{e2} = 50\% \qquad g_{e3} = 50\% \qquad g_{e4} = 33\% \qquad g_{e5} = 25\%.$$

Furthermore, the analyst believes that ABC will enter a transition stage at the end of the fifth year (that is, the sixth year will be the first year of the transition stage and that the transition stage will last three years. Earnings per share and the payout ratio for year 6 are forecast to be E_6 = \$11.90 and p_6 = 55%. Thus g_{e6} = (\$11.90 – \$10.00)/\$10.00 = 19% and D_6 = .55 × \$11.90 = \$6.55.

The last stage, known as the maturity stage, is forecast to have an earnings-per-share growth rate of 4% and a payout ratio of 70%. Now, it was shown in equation (18.51b) that with the constant-growth model, $g = r(1 - p)$, where r is the average return on equity for new investment and p is the payout ratio. Given that the maturity stage has constant growth, this equation can be reformulated and used to determine r:

$$r = g/(1 - p).$$

Thus, r for ABC has an implied value of 4%/(100% – 70%) = 13.33%, which is assumed to be consistent with the long-run growth forecasts for similar companies.

At this point there are only two missing pieces of information that are needed to determine the value of ABC—the earnings-per-share growth rates and the payout ratios for the transition stage. Taking earnings per share first, it has been forecast that g_{e6} = 19% and g_{e9} = 4%. One method of determining how 19% will "decay" to 4% is to note that there are three years between the sixth and ninth years, and 15% between 19% and 4%. A "linear decay" rate is determined by noting that 15%/3 years = 5% per year. This rate of 5% is deducted from 19% to get g_{e7}, resulting in (19% – 5% =)14%. Then it would be deducted from 14% to get g_{e8}, resulting in (14% – 5% =)9%. As a check it can be noted that (9% – 5% =)4% is the value that was forecast for g_{e9}.

A similar procedure can be used to determine how the payout ratio of 55% in year 6 will grow to 70% in year 9. The "linear growth" rate will be (70% – 55%)/3 years = 15%/3 years = 5% per year, indicating that p_7 = (55% + 5% =)60% and p_8 = (60% + 5% =)65%. Again, a check indicates that (65% + 5% =)70% is the value that was forecast for p_9.

With these forecasts of earnings-per-share growth rates and payout ratios in hand, forecasts of dividends per share can now be made:

$$\begin{aligned} D_7 &= p_7E_7 \\ &= p_7E_6(1 + g_{e7}) \\ &= .60 \times \$11.90 \times (1 = .14) \\ &= .60 \times \$13.57 \\ &= \$8.14 \end{aligned}$$

$$\begin{aligned} D_8 &= p_8E_8 \\ &= p_8E_6(1 + g_{e7})(1 + g_{e8}) \\ &= .65 \times \$11.90 \times (1 + .14) \times (1 + .09) \\ &= .65 \times \$14.79 \\ &= \$9.61 \end{aligned}$$

INSTITUTIONAL ISSUES

Applying Dividend Discount Models

Over the last 30 years, dividend discount models (DDMs) have achieved broad acceptance among professional common stock investors. Although few investment managers rely solely on DDMs to select stocks, many have integrated DDMs into their security valuation procedures.

The reasons for the popularity of DDMs are twofold. First, DDMs are based on a simple, widely understood concept: the fair value of any security should equal the discounted value of the cash flows expected to be produced by that security. Second, the basic inputs for DDMs are standard outputs for many large investment management firms—that is, these firms employ security analysts who are responsible for projecting corporate earnings.

Valuing common stocks with a DDM technically requires an estimate of future dividends over an infinite time horizon. Given that accurately forecasting dividends three years from today, let alone 20 years in the future, is a difficult proposition, how do investment firms actually go about implementing DDMs?

One approach is to use constant or two-stage dividend growth models, as described in the text. However, although such models are relatively easy to apply, institutional investors typically view the assumed dividend growth assumptions as overly simplistic. Instead, these investors generally prefer three-stage models, believing that they provide the best combination of realism and ease of application.

Whereas many variations of the three-stage DDM exist, in general, the model is based on the assumption that companies evolve through three stages during their lifetimes. (Figure 18.3 portrays these stages.)

1. **Growth stage:** Characterized by rapidly expanding sales, high profit margins, and abnormally high growth in earnings per share. Because of highly profitable expected investment opportunities, the payout ratio is low. Competitors are attracted by the unusually high earnings, leading to a decline in the growth rate.

Figure 18.3

The three stages of the multiple-growth model.

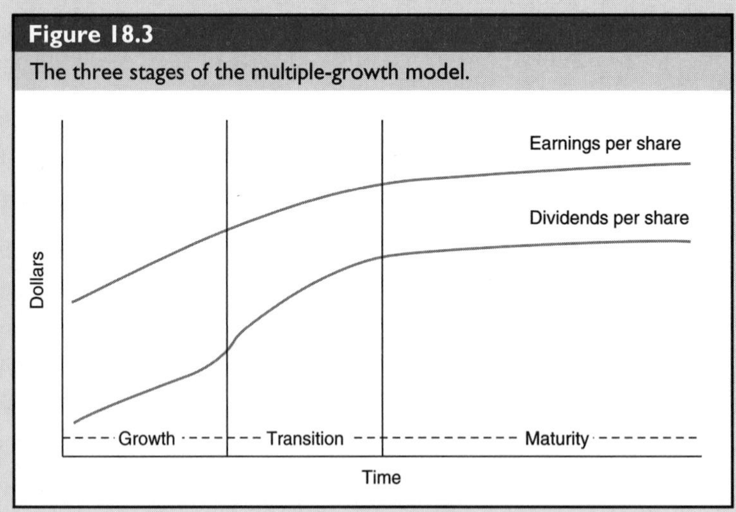

SOURCE: Adapted from Carmine J. Grigoli, "Demystifying Dividend Discount Models," *Merrill Lynch Quantitative Research*, April 1982.

2. **Transition stage:** In later years, increased competition reduces profit margins and earnings growth slows. With fewer new investment opportunities, the company begins to pay out a larger percentage of earnings.
3. **Maturity (steady-state) stage:** Eventually the company reaches a position where its new investment opportunities offer, on average, only slightly attractive returns on equity. At that time its earnings growth rate, payout ratio, and return on equity stabilize for the remainder of its life.

The forecasting process of the three-stage DDM involves specifying earnings and dividend growth rates in each of the three stages. Although one cannot expect a security analyst to be omniscient in his or her growth forecast for a particular company, one can hope that the forecast pattern of growth — in terms of magnitude and duration — resembles that actually realized by the company, particularly in the short run.

Investment firms attempt to structure their DDMs to make maximum use of their analysts' forecasting capabilities. Thus, the models emphasize specific forecasts in the near term, when it is realistic to expect security analysts to project earnings and dividends more accurately. Conversely, the models emphasize more general forecasts over the longer term, when distinctions between companies' growth rates become less discernible. Typically, analysts are required to supply the following for their assigned companies:

1. expected annual earnings and dividends for the next several years;
2. after these specific annual forecasts end, earnings growth and the payout ratio forecasts until the end of the growth stage;
3. the number of years until the transition stage is reached;
4. the duration (in years) of the transition stage — that is, once abnormally high growth ends, the number of years until the maturity stage is reached.

Most three-stage DDMs assume that during the transition stage, earnings growth declines and payout ratios rise linearly to the maturity-stage steady-state levels. (For example, if the transition stage is ten years long, earnings growth at the maturity stage is 5% per year, and earnings growth at the end of the growth stage is 25%, then earnings growth will decline 2% in each year of the transition stage.) Finally, most three-stage DDMs make standard assumptions that all companies in the maturity stage have the same growth rates, payout ratios, and returns on equity.

With analysts' inputs, plus an appropriate required rate of return for each security, all the necessary information for the three-stage DDM is available. The last step involves merely calculating the discounted value of the estimated dividends to determine the stock's "fair" value.

The seeming simplicity of the three-stage DDM should not lead one to believe that it is without its implementation problems. Investment firms must strive to achieve consistency across their analysts' forecasts. The long-term nature of the estimates involved, the substantial training required to make even short-term earnings forecasts accurately, and the coordination of a number of analysts covering many companies severely complicate the problem. Considerable discipline is required if the DDM valuations generated by a firm's analysts are to be sufficiently comparable and reliable to guide investment decisions. Despite these complexities, if successfully implemented, DDMs can combine the creative insights of security analysts with the rigour and discipline of quantitative investment techniques.

$$
\begin{aligned}
D_9 &= p_9 E_9 \\
&= p_9 E_6(1 + g_{e7})(1 + g_{e8})(1 + g_{e9}) \\
&= .70 \times \$11.90 \times (1 + .14) \times (1 + .09) \times (1 + .04) \\
&= .70 \times \$15.38 \\
&= \$10.76.
\end{aligned}
$$

Estimating the Intrinsic Value

Given a required rate of return on ABC of 12.4%, all the necessary inputs for the multiple-growth model have been determined. It is now possible to estimate ABC's intrinsic (or fair) value. To begin, it can be seen that $T = 8$, indicating that V_{T-} involves determining the present value of D_1 through D_8:

$$
\begin{aligned}
V_{T-} &= \left[\frac{\$.60}{(1 + .124)^1}\right] + \left[\frac{\$1.60}{(1 + .124)^2}\right] + \left[\frac{\$2.40}{(1 + .124)^3}\right] \\
&+ \left[\frac{\$3.20}{(1 + .124)^4}\right] + \left[\frac{\$5.00}{(1 + .124)^5}\right] + \left[\frac{\$6.55}{(1 + .124)^6}\right] \\
&+ \left[\frac{\$8.14}{(1 + .124)^7}\right] + \left[\frac{\$9.61}{(1 + .124)^8}\right] \\
&= \$18.89.
\end{aligned}
$$

Then V_{T+} can be determined using D_9:

$$
\begin{aligned}
V_{T+} &= \frac{\$10.76}{(.124 - .04)(1 + .124)^8} \\
&= \$50.28.
\end{aligned}
$$

Combining V_{T-} and V_{T+} results in the intrinsic value of ABC:

$$
\begin{aligned}
V &= V_{T-} + V_{T+} \\
&= \$18.89 + \$50.28 \\
&= \$69.17.
\end{aligned}
$$

Given a current market price for ABC of \$50, it can be seen that its stock is underpriced by (\$69.17 – \$50 =)\$19.17 per share. Equivalently, it can be noted that the actual price-earnings ratio for ABC is (\$50/\$1.67 =)29.9 but that a "normal" price-earnings ratio would be higher, equal to (\$69.17/\$1.67 =)41.4, again indicating that ABC is underpriced.

Implied Returns

As shown in the previous example, once the analyst has made certain forecasts, it is relatively easy to determine a company's expected dividends for each year up through the first year of the maturity stage. Then the present value of these predicted dividends can be calculate for a given required rate of return. However, many investment firms use a computerized trial-and-error procedure to determine the discount rate, which equates the present value of the stock's expected dividends with its current price. Sometimes this long-run internal rate of return is referred to as the security's **implied return**. In the case of ABC its implied return is 14.8%.

The Security Market Line

After implied returns have been estimated for a number of stocks, the associated beta for each stock can be estimated. Then, for all the stocks analyzed, this information can be plotted on a graph that has implied returns on the vertical axis and estimated betas on the horizontal axis.

There are several methods for estimating the security market line (SML).[11] One method involves determining a line of best fit for this graph by using a statistical procedure known as simple regression (described in Chapter 17). That is, the values of an intercept term and a slope term are determined from the data, thereby indicating the location of the straight line that best describes the relationship between implied returns and betas.[12]

Figure 18.4 provides an example of an estimated SML. In this case, the SML has been determined to have an intercept of 8% and a slope of 4%, indicating that, in general, securities with higher betas are expected to have higher implied returns in the forthcoming period. Depending on the sizes of the implied returns, such lines can have steeper or flatter slopes or even negative slopes.

The second method of estimating the SML involves calculating the implied return for a portfolio of common stocks. This is done by taking a value-weighted average of the implied returns of the stocks in the portfolio, with the resulting return being an estimate of the implied return on the market portfolio. Given this return and a beta of 1, the market portfolio can be plotted on a graph having implied returns on the vertical axis and betas on the horizontal axis. Next, the risk-free rate, having a beta of 0, can be plotted on the same graph. Finally, the SML is determined by simply connecting these two points with a straight line.

Either of these SMLs can be used to determine the required return on a stock. However, they will probably result in different numbers, since the two lines will probably have different intercepts and slopes. For example, note that in the first method the SML may not go through the risk-free rate, whereas the second method forces the SML to go through this rate.

Figure 18.4

A security market line estimated from implied returns.

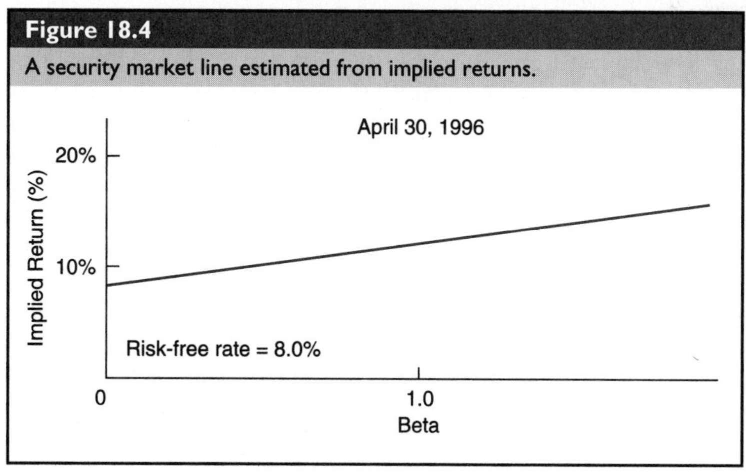

[11] There are numerous methods besides those described here. Some of them are based on more complicated versions of the CAPM, whereas others are based on the APT (discussed in Chapter 12).

[12] There are ways of forcing the intercept of the line to go through the risk-free rate in order to agree with the implications of the traditional CAPM.

Required Returns and Alphas

Once a security's beta has been estimated, its required return can be determined from the estimated SML. For example, the equation for the SML on April 30, 1996 (shown in Figure 18.4), is:

$$k_i = 8 + 4\beta_i.$$

Thus, if ABC has an estimated beta of 1.1 at the end of April 1996, then it would have a required return equal to 8 + (4 × 1.1) = 12.4%.

Once the required return on a stock has been determined, the difference between its implied return (from the dividend discount model) and this required return can be calculated. This difference can then be viewed as an estimate of the stock's *alpha* and represents "... the degree to which a stock is mispriced. Positive alphas indicate undervalued securities and negative alphas indicate overvalued securities."[13] In the case of ABC, its implied and required returns at the end of April 1996 were 14.8% and 12.4%, respectively. Thus, its estimated alpha is 14.8% – 12.4% = 2.4%. Since this is a positive number, ABC can be viewed as being underpriced.

The Implied Return on the Stock Market

Another product of this analysis is that the implied return for the portfolio of shares can be compared with expected returns on bonds. Specifically, the difference between the stock and bond returns can be used as an input for recommendations concerning asset allocation between stocks and bonds. That is, it can be used to form recommendations regarding what percentage of an investor's money should go into stocks and what percentage should go into bonds. Typically, the greater the implied return on stocks relative to bonds, the larger the percentage of the investor's money that should be placed in common shares.

DIVIDEND DISCOUNT MODELS AND EXPECTED RETURNS

The procedures described here are similar to those employed by a number of brokerage firms and portfolio managers.[14] A security's implied return, obtained from a dividend discount model, is often treated as an expected return, which in turn can be divided into two components — the security's required return and alpha. However, the expected return on a stock over a given holding period may differ from its DDM-based implied rate, k^*. A simple set of examples will indicate why this difference can exist.

Assume that a security analyst predicts that a stock will pay a dividend of $1.10 per share per year forever. On the other hand, the consensus opinion of "the market" (most other investors) is that the dividend will equal $1.00 per year forever. This suggests that the analyst's prediction is a deviant, or nonconsensus, prediction.

Assume that both the analyst and other investors agree that the required rate of return for a stock of this type is 10%. Using the formula for the zero-growth model, the value of a

---

[13] Carmine J. Grigoli, "Common Stock Valuation," Merrill Lynch Quantitative Analysis, May/June 1984. A subsequent procedure divides the estimated alpha by an estimate of the security's unique risk (that is, nonmarket or unsystematic risk) to obtain a standardized alpha. Then, based on the magnitude of the standardized alpha, the security is classified into one of ten standardized alpha deciles. See also Marshall E. Blume, "The Use of 'Alphas' to Improve Performance," *Journal of Portfolio Management* 11, no. 1 (Fall 1984): 86–92.

[14] An example of a similar procedure that has been used by Wells Fargo Investment Advisors is described by George Foster in *Financial Statement Analysis* (Englewood Cliffs, N.J.: Prentice Hall, 1986):428–30.

Table 18.1

Alpha and the Convergence of Predications.

	Expected Amount of Convergence		
	0%	100%	50%
	(A)	(B)	(C)
Dividend predictions D_2			
Consensus of other investors	1.10	1.10	1.05
Analyst	1.10	1.10	1.10
Expected stock price P_1	10.00	11.00	10.50
Expected return:			
Dividend yield D_1/P	11%	11%	11%
Capital gain $(P_1 - P)/P$	0	10	5
Total expected return	11%	21%	16%
Less required return	10	10	10
Alpha	1%	11%	6%

NOTE: P_1 is equal to the consensus dividend prediction at $t = 1$ divided by the required return of 10%. The example assumes that the current stock price P is $10, and dividends are forecast by the consensus at $t = 0$ to remain constant at $1.00 per share, whereas the analyst forecasts the dividends at $t = 0$ to remain constant at $1.10 per share.

share is $D_1/.10 = 10D_1$, meaning that a share should sell for ten times its expected dividend. Since other investors expect to receive $1.00 per year, the stock has a current price (P) of $10 per share. The analyst feels the stock has a value of $1.10/.10 = $11 and thus feels it is underpriced by $11 – $10 = $1 per share.

Rate of Convergence of Investors' Predictions

In this situation the implied return according to the analyst is $1.10/$10 = 11%. If the analyst buys a share now with a plan to sell it a year later, what rate of return might the analyst expect to earn? The answer depends on what assumption is made regarding the *rate of convergence of investors' predictions* — that is, the expected market reaction to the mispricing that the analyst believes currently exists.

The cases shown in Table 18.1 are based on an assumption that the analyst is confident that his or her forecast of future dividends is correct. That is, in all of the cases, the analyst expects that at the end of the year, the stock will pay the predicted dividend of $1.10.

No Convergence

In column (A), it is assumed that other investors will regard the higher dividend as a fluke and steadfastly refuse to alter their projections of subsequent dividends from their initial estimate of $1.00. As a result, the security's price at $t = 1$ can be expected to remain at $10 (= $1.00/.10). In this case the analyst's total return is expected to be at 11% (= $1.10/$10), which will be attributed entirely to dividends as no capital gains are expected.

The 11% expected return can also be viewed as consisting of the required return of 10% plus an alpha of 1% that is equal to the portion of the dividend unanticipated by other investors, $.10/$10. Accordingly, if it is assumed that there will be no convergence of predictions, the expected return would be set at the implied rate of 11% and the alpha would be set at 1%.

Complete Convergence

Column (B) shows a very different situation. Here it is assumed that the other investors will recognize their error and completely revise their predictions. At the end of the year, it is expected that they too will predict future dividends of $1.10 per year thereafter; thus, the stock is expected to be selling for $1.10/.10 = $11 at t = 1. Under these conditions, the analyst can expect to achieve a total return of 21% by selling the stock at the end of the year for $11, obtaining $1.10/$10 = 11% in dividend yield and $1/$10 = 10% in capital gains.

The 10% expected capital gains result directly from the expected repricing of the security because of the complete convergence of predictions. In this case the fruits of the analyst's superior prediction are expected to be obtained all in one year. Instead of 1% "extra" per year forever, as in column (A), the analyst expects to obtain $.10/$10 = 1% in extra dividend yield plus $1/$10 = 10% in capital gains this year. By continuing to hold the stock in subsequent years, the analyst would expect to earn only the required return of 10% over those years. Accordingly, the expected return is 21% and the alpha is 11% when it is assumed that there is complete convergence of predictions.

Partial Convergence

Column (C) shows an intermediate case. Here, the predictions of the other investors are expected to converge only halfway toward those of the analyst (that is, from $1.00 to $1.05 instead of to $1.10). Total return in the first year is expected to be 16%, consisting of $1.10/$10 = 11% in dividend yield plus $.50/$10 = 5% in capital gains.

Since the stock is expected to be selling for $1.05/.10 = $10.50 at t = 1, the analyst will still feel that it is underpriced at t = 1 because it will have an intrinsic value of $1.10/.10 = $11 at that time. To obtain the remainder of the "extra return" owing to this underpricing, the stock would have to be held past t = 1. Accordingly, the expected return would be set at 16% and the alpha would be set at 6% when it is assumed that there is halfway convergence of predictions.

In general, a security's expected return and alpha will be larger, the faster the assumed rate of convergence of predictions.[15] Many investors use the implied rate (that is, the internal rate of return k^*) as a surrogate for a relatively short-term (for example, one year) expected return, as in column (A). In doing so, they are assuming that the dividend forecast is completely accurate, but that there is no convergence. Alternatively, investors could assume that there is some degree of convergence, thereby raising their estimate of the security's expected return. Indeed, investors could further alter their estimate of the security's expected return by assuming that the security analyst's deviant prediction is less than perfectly accurate, as will be seen next.[16]

---

[15] In a perfectly efficient market (in the semistrong-form sense), these analysts would sometimes be right and sometimes be wrong, so that on balance their predictions would be of no value. In such a situation, the expected return for any security would be its required return and the alpha would be zero.

[16] As an example of how to estimate alpha if it is assumed that the analyst has less than perfect forecasting ability and there is less than 100% convergence, reconsider the example given in Table 18.1. First, assume that the forecast accuracy of the security analyst is 60%. Remembering that the analyst's forecast of D_1 is $1.10, but the consensus forecast is $1.00, then 60% accuracy means that the forecast that should be used is $1.00 + .60 × ($1.10 – $1.00) = $1.06. Second, assume that there will be 50% convergence. This means that the security's price at t = 1 is expected to be [$1.00 + .50 × ($1.06 – $1.00)]/.10 = $10.30. Hence the expected return under 60% forecast accuracy and 50% convergence is [($10.30 – $10) + $1.06]/$10 = 13.6%, which translates into an alpha of (13.6% – 10% =)3.6%.

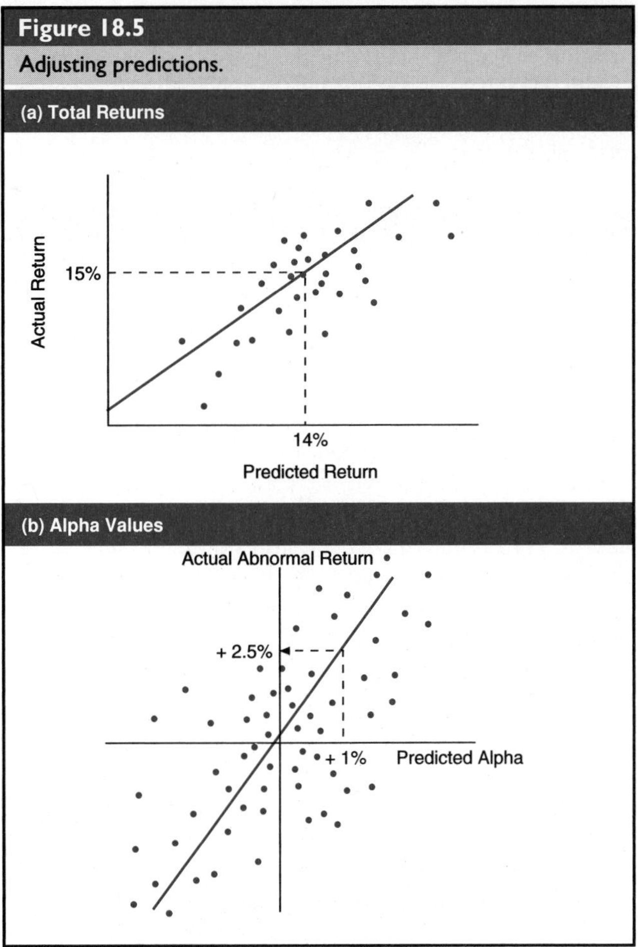

Figure 18.5
Adjusting predictions.

Predicted Versus Actual Returns

An alternative approach does not simply use outputs from a model "as is," but *adjusts* them, based on relationships between previous predictions and actual outcomes. Figure 18.5 provides examples.

Each point in Figure 18.5(a) plots *predicted return* on the stock market as a whole (on the horizontal axis) and the subsequent *actual return* for that period (on the vertical axis). The line of best fit (determined by simple regression) through the points indicates the general relationship between prediction and outcome. If the current prediction is 14%, history suggests that an estimate of 15% would be superior.

Each point in Figure 18.5(b) plots a predicted alpha value for a security (on the horizontal axis) and the subsequent abnormal return for that period (on the vertical axis). Such a diagram can be made for a given security, or for all the securities that a particular analyst makes predictions about, or for all the securities that the investment firm makes predictions about. Again a line of best fit can be drawn through the points. In this case, if the current prediction of a security's alpha is +1%, this relationship suggests that an "adjusted" estimate of +2.5% would be superior.

An important by-product of this type of analysis is the measure of correlation between predicted and actual outcomes, indicating the nearness of the points to the line. This **information coefficient** (IC) can serve as a measure of predictive accuracy. If it is too small to be significantly different from zero in a statistical sense, the value of the predictions is subject to considerable question.[17]

SUMMARY

1. The capitalization of income method of valuation states that the intrinsic value of any asset is equal to the sum of the discounted cash flows investors expect to receive from that asset.
2. Dividend discount models (DDMs) are a specific application of the capitalization of income method of valuation to common shares.
3. To use a DDM, the investor must implicitly or explicitly supply a forecast of all future dividends expected to be generated by a security.
4. Investors typically make certain simplifying assumptions about the growth of common stock dividends. For example, a common share's dividends may be assumed to exhibit zero growth or growth at a constant rate. More complex assumptions may allow for multiple growth rates over time.
5. Instead of applying DDMs, many security analysts use a simpler method of security valuation that involves estimating a share's "normal" price-earnings ratio and comparing it with the share's actual price-earnings ratio.
6. The growth rate in a firm's earnings and dividends depends on its earnings retention rate and its average return on equity for new investments.
7. Determining whether a security is mispriced using a DDM can be done in one of two ways. First, the discounted value of expected dividends can be compared with the share's current price. Second, the discount rate that equates the share's current price to the present value of forecast dividends can be compared with the required return for stocks of similar risk.
8. The rate of return that an analyst with accurate non-consensus dividend forecasts can expect to earn depends on the rate of convergence of other investors' predictions to the predictions of the analyst.

APPENDIX A

THE GRAHAM-REA MODEL

In 1934, a book that was to become the cornerstone of fundamental analysis was published by Benjamin Graham and David L. Dodd. This book, entitled *Security Analysis*, argued that

---

[17] It has been argued that a value of .15 for an IC is indicative of good performance with regard to stock forecasting, and that several different forecasters have recorded ICs of this magnitude (a value of zero would be expected in a perfectly efficient market). See Keith P. Ambachtsheer, "Profit Potential in an 'Almost Efficient' Market," *Journal of Portfolio Management* 1, no. 1 (Fall 1974): 84–87, and "Where Are the Customers' Alphas?" *Journal of Portfolio Management* 4, no. 1 (Fall 1977): 52–56; Keith P. Ambachtsheer and James L. Farrell, Jr., "Can Active Management Add Value?" *Financial Analysts Journal* 35, no. 6 (November/December 1979): 39–47; and S. D. Hodges and R. A. Brealey, "Portfolio Selection in a Dynamic and Uncertain World," *Financial Analysts Journal* 29, no. 2 (March/April 1973): 50–65.

the future earnings power of the firm was the most important determinant of a stock's value.[18] However, in 1974, Graham himself repudiated the book and the principles contained in it.[19] Instead of following his old approach, Graham, along with James Rea, developed a new approach to identifying underpriced common stocks.[20] The reason for his change in attitude was his belief that the stock market was becoming increasingly efficient, and that only smaller and smaller pockets of inefficiencies remained. Because Graham and Rea believed that these inefficiencies tended to be present in the shares of certain identifiable firms, they developed a set of criteria to spot such stocks.

The Graham-Rea approach can be applied mechanically, as it involves examining the current financial statements of the firm under consideration and relating certain items from these statements to the firm's current stock price and the current yield on triple-A bonds. Ten questions that can be answered with a simple "yes" or "no" are involved. Table 18.2 lists them, indicating that the first five questions deal with "rewards" and the second five questions deal with "risks." The idea behind these questions is to identify stocks that have the highest reward-to-risk ratio. In order for a stock to be recommended for purchase by Graham and Rea, it need not provide a "yes" answer to all of the questions.

The simplest way to use the questions is to first remove all stocks that do not provide a "yes" answer to question 6. Then, of the remaining stocks, remove those that do not provide a "yes" answer to either question 1 or question 3 or question 5. The stocks that are left are candidates for purchase.

In determining when to sell, the Graham-Rea approach says that the investor should sell as soon as the stock has risen 50% or two years have passed since the stock was purchased, whichever occurs first. However, if neither of these two sell signals has occurred and the stock either stops paying dividends or no longer generates the appropriate "yes" answers to the questions, then it should be sold immediately.

How well has the Graham-Rea approach to investing worked? In a study of this approach which focused on New York Stock Exchange and American Stock Exchange securities, three observations were particularly interesting.[21] First, since the approach was publicized it was found that the number of stocks that provided the appropriate "yes" answers declined dramatically. (For example, in 1980 only five securities had "yes" answers to questions 1 and 6.) Second, the historical record suggests that positive abnormal returns would have been earned had this approach been used subsequent to its publication. Third, because many of the firms recommended for purchase were small firms, it is possible that all that this

---

[18] Graham and Dodd also argued that each dollar of dividends is worth four times as much as each dollar of retained earnings. Subsequent examination of market data indicates that their argument has no support. See J. Ronald Hoffmeister and Edward A. Dyl, "Dividends and Share Value: Graham and Dodd Revisited," *Financial Analysts Journal* 41, no. 3 (May/June 1985): 77–78; and Lewis D. Johnson, "Dividends and Share Value: Graham and Dodd Revisited, Again," *Financial Analysts Journal* 41, no. 5 (September/October 1985): 79–80. For the most recent edition of the book, see Sidney Cottle, Roger F. Murray, and Frank E. Block, *Graham and Dodd's Security Analysis*, 5th ed. (New York: McGraw-Hill, 1988). For a brief discussion of their approach to investing, see Roger F. Murray, "Graham and Dodd: A Durable Discipline," *Financial Analysts Journal* 40, no. 5 (September/October 1984): 18–23.

[19] See "A Conversation with Benjamin Graham," *Financial Analysts Journal* 32, no. 5 (September/October 1976): 20–23.

[20] For a description of this approach, see Paul Blustein, "Ben Graham's Last Will and Testament," *Forbes* (August 1, 1977): 43–45; and James B. Rea, "Remembering Benjamin Graham — Teacher and Friend," *Journal of Portfolio Management* 3, no. 4 (Summer 1977): 66–72.

[21] Henry R. Oppenheimer, "A Test of Ben Graham's Stock Selection Criteria," *Financial Analysts Journal* 40, no. 5 (September/October 1984): 68–74.

Table 18.2

Graham-Rea Stock Selection Questions.

A. Rewards

1. Is the price-earnings ratio less than one-half the reciprocal of the triple-A bond yield? (For example, if the current triple-A rate is 12%, then the reciprocal is 1/.12 = $8\frac{1}{3}$, and half of that is $4\frac{1}{6}$. Thus, for a stock to provide a "yes" answer to this question, its price-earnings ratio must be less than $4\frac{1}{6}$.)

2. Is the price-earnings ratio less than 40% of the highest "average" price-earnings ratio of the last five years? (Here, the "average" price-earnings ratio for a stock for a given year is the average stock price for the year divided by the earnings per share for that year.)

3. Is the dividend yield at least $\frac{2}{3}$ of the triple-A bond yield?

4. Is the stock price below $\frac{2}{3}$ of the tangible book value per share? (Here tangible book value per share is simply total assets less total debt, with the difference divided by the number of shares outstanding.)

5. Is the stock price below $\frac{2}{3}$ of the net current asset value per share? (Here net current asset value per share is current assets less total debt, with the difference divided by the number of shares outstanding.)

B. Risks

6. Is the debt-to-equity ratio less than one? (Here the debt-to-equity ratio is simply total debt divided by total equity as shown on the balance sheet.)

7. Is the current ratio greater than two? (Here the current ratio is current assets divided by current liabilities.)

8. Is total debt less than twice the net current asset value? (Here net current asset value is current assets less total debt.)

9. Has the earnings-per-share growth rate of the last ten years averaged at least 7% per year? (If the earnings per share over the last year is denoted E_0 and the earnings per share over the year ending ten years ago is denoted E_{-10}, then the growth rate is the value of g that solves the equation $E_0 = E_{-10}(1 + g)^{10}$. To provide a "yes" answer to this question, g must be at least 7%.)

10. Over the time period examined in question 9, have eight or more of the annual growth rates in earnings per share been equal to –5% or more? (Here the ten annual growth rates in earnings per share would be calculated and then examined to see that no more than two of them were less than –5%.)

SOURCE: Adapted from Paul Blustein, "Ben Graham's Last Will and Testament," *Forbes* (August 1, 1977): 43–45; and James B. Rea, "Remembering Benjamin Graham—Teacher and Friend," *Journal of Portfolio Management* 3, no. 4 (Summer 1977): 66–72.

approach does is capture the size effect (that is, the small-firm effect that was discussed in the appendix to Chapter 17). However, the study found that even after adjusting for the size effect, the approach would still have earned positive abnormal returns since its publication.[22]

[22] A subsequent study focused on only one of the ten Graham-Rea questions, number 5 in Table 18.2. It found that portfolios consisting of securities that had "yes" answers to this question would have earned above-market returns. See Henry R. Oppenheimer, "Ben Graham's Net Current Asset Values: A Performance Update," *Financial Analysts Journal* 42, no. 6 (November/December 1986): 40–47.

In closing, it should be noted that a number of professional portfolio managers currently follow the Graham-Rea approach to investing. Examples include the Rea-Graham Fund, LMH Fund, Sequoia Fund, and Pacific Partners Fund.

QUESTIONS AND PROBLEMS

1. Consider five annual cash flows (the first occurring one year from today):

Year	Cash Flow
1	\$5
2	\$6
3	\$7
4	\$8
5	\$9

   Given a discount rate of 10%, what is the present value of this stream of cash flows?
2. Amy Cohen is considering buying a machine to produce baseballs. The machine costs \$10 000. With the machine, Amy expects to produce and sell 1 000 baseballs per year for \$3 per baseball, net of all costs. The machine's life is five years (with no salvage value). Based on these assumptions and an 8% discount rate, what is the net present value of Amy's investment?
3. Hugh Collins has invested in a project that promised to pay \$100, \$200, and \$300, respectively, at the end of the next three years. If Hugh paid \$513.04 for this investment, what is the project's internal rate of return?
4. Afton Product currently pays a dividend of \$4 per share on its common stock.
   a. If Afton Products plans to increase its dividend at a rate of 5% per year indefinitely, what will be the dividend per share in 10 years?
   b. If Afton Products' dividend per share is expected to be \$5.87 per share at the end of five years, at what annual rate is the dividend expected to grow?
5. Hammond Pipes has issued preferred stock that pays \$12 per share. The dividend is fixed and the stock has no expiration date. What is the intrinsic value of Hammond preferred shares, assuming a discount rate of 15%?
6. Milton Information Services currently pays a dividend of \$4 per share on its common stock. The dividend is expected to grow at 4% per year forever. Stocks with similar risk currently are priced to provide a 12% expected return. What is the intrinsic value of Milton stock?
7. Spring Valley Bedding stock currently sells for \$53 per share. The stock's dividend is expected to grow at 6% per year indefinitely. Spring Valley just paid a dividend of \$3 per share. Given this information, calculate the stock's internal rate of return.
8. Select a stock whose name begins with the first letter of your last name. From the *Value Line Investment Survey, Canadian Edition*, find the average annual compounded growth rate in the stock's dividend over the last five years. Assume that this growth rate will continue indefinitely. Also from the same *Value Line Investment Survey* find the beta of the stock. Using the current risk-free rate (90-day Treasury bills as found in the *Globe & Mail*) and a 6% expected market risk premium, calculate the SML and the required return on the stock. Finally, using the dividend growth rate and the required return,

calculate the intrinsic value of the stock. (*Note*: If the data for your stock is incompatible with the constant-growth DDM, select another stock.) Compare this intrinsic value to the latest closing price for the stock. Is the stock underpriced or overpriced? What potential problems are involved with this approach to making investment decisions?

9. The constant-growth model is an overly simplistic means of valuing most corporations' stocks. However, a number of market analysts believe that it is a useful means of estimating a fair value for the stock market as a whole. Why might the constant-growth DDM be a more reasonable valuation tool for the market in aggregate than for individual stocks?

10. This year Monona Air Cleaners Inc. will pay a dividend on its stock of $6 per share. The following year the dividend is expected to be the same, increasing to $7 the year after. From that point on, the dividend is expected to grow at 4% per year indefinitely. Stocks with similar risk are currently priced to provide a 10% expected return. What is the intrinsic value of Monona stock?

11. Knapp Carpet recently paid an annual dividend on its stock of $2 per share. The dividend is expected to grow at $1 per share for the next four years. Thereafter the dividend is expected to grow at 5% per year indefinitely. The required return on stocks with similar risk is 12%. What is the intrinsic value of Knapp stock?

12. Chief Medical Inc. is s little-known producer of heart pacemakers. The earnings and dividend growth prospects of the company are disputed by analysts. Albert Bender is forecasting 5% growth in dividends indefinitely. However, his brother John is predicting a 20% growth in dividends, but only for the next three years, after which the growth rate is expected to decline to 4% for the indefinite future. Chief dividends per share are currently $3. Stocks with similar risk are currently priced to provide a 14% expected return.

a. What is the intrinsic value of Chief stock according to Albert?

b. What is the intrinsic value of Chief stock according to John?

c. Assume that Chief stock now sells for $39 3/4 per share. If the stock is fairly priced at the present time, what is the implied perpetual dividend growth rate? What is the implied P/E (price-earnings ratio) on next year's earnings, based on this perpetual dividend growth assumption and assuming a 25% payout ratio?

13. Elk Mound Candy Company currently pays a dividend of $3 per share. That dividend is expected to grow at a 6% rate indefinitely. Stocks with similar risk provide a 10% expected return. Calculate the intrinsic value of Elk Mound stock today using an interim computation based on the sale of the stock at its expected intrinsic value three years from now.

14. How would an increase in the perceived riskiness of a common stock's future cash flows affect its price-earnings ratio? Explain intuitively and mathematically.

15. Roberts Roofing currently earns $4 per share. Its return on equity is 20% and it retains 50% of its earnings (both figures are expected to be maintained indefinitely). Stocks of similar risk are priced to return 15%. What is the intrinsic value of Roberts' stock?

16. Osseo Operations recently paid an annual dividend of $4 per share. Earnings for the same year were $8 per share. The required return on stocks with similar risk is 11%. Dividends are expected to grow 6% per year indefinitely. Calculate Osseo's "normal" price-earnings ratio.

17. Reedsburg Associates is currently paying a dividend of $2 per share on earnings of $4 per share. Its stock is selling for $200 per share. Stocks of similar risk are priced to return

15%. What kind of return on equity could explain investors' willingness to pay a price equal to 50 times earnings on this stock?

18. Rochelle Corp. is expected to pay out 40% of its earnings and to earn an average of 15% per year on its incremental reinvestment earnings forever. Stocks with similar risk are currently priced to provide a 12% expected return. By what percentage can Rochelle's earnings be expected to grow each year? What is an appropriate price-earnings multiple for the stock? What portion of the return on Rochelle stock is expected to come from capital gains?
19. A three-stage DDM has become a very popular common stock valuation model. It is used by a number of institutional investors and brokerage firms. What advantages does it offer relative to a simple constant-growth DDM? Despite its increased sophistication compared to the constant-growth DDM, what disadvantages does it still retain?
20. What explanations can you offer for the fact that the SML shown in Figure 18.4 is so flat?
21. Fay Thomas, a financial analyst, once remarked: "Even if your dividend estimates and discount rate assumption are correct, dividend discount models identify stocks that will produce positive risk-adjusted returns only if other investors eventually come to agree with the DDM's valuation conclusions." Is this statement correct? Why?
22. Some people assert that a "true" growth company is one whose dividends grow at a rate greater than its required rate of return. Why is the constant-growth DDM incapable of valuing such a "true" growth stock?

CFA Exam Questions

23. The constant-growth dividend discount model can be used for both the valuation of companies and the estimation of the long-term total return of a stock.

$$\begin{aligned} \textit{Assume}: \ \$20 &= \text{the price of a stock today,} \\ 8\% &= \text{the expected growth rate of dividends,} \\ \$0.60 &= \text{the annual dividend one year forward.} \end{aligned}$$

    a. Using only the above data, compute the expected long-term total return on the stock using the constant-growth dividend discount model. Show calculations.
    b. Briefly discuss three disadvantages of the constant-growth dividend discount model in its application to investment analysis.

24. As a firm operating in a mature industry, Arbot Industries is expected to maintain a constant dividend payout ratio and constant growth rate of earnings for the foreseeable future. Earnings were $4.50 per share in the recently completed fiscal year. The dividend payout ratio has been a constant 55% in recent years and is expected to remain so. Arbot's return on equity (ROE) is expected to remain at 10% in the future, and you require an 11% return on stock.

    a. Using the constant-growth dividend discount model, calculate the current value of Arbot common stock. Show your calculations.

    After an aggressive acquisition and marketing program, it now appears that Arbot's earnings per share and ROE will grow rapidly over the next two years. You are aware that the dividend discount model can be useful in estimating the value of common stock even when the assumption of constant growth does not apply.

    b. Calculate the current value of Arbot's common stock, using the dividend discount model, assuming that Arbot's dividend will grow at a 15% rate for the next two years, returning in the third year to the historical growth rate and continuing to grow at the historical rate for the foreseeable future. Show your calculations.

KEY TERMS

capitalization of income method of valuation
discount rate
net present value
internal rate of return (IRR)
dividend discount model (DDM)
zero-growth model
constant-growth model
multiple-growth model
price-earnings ratio
earnings-price ratio
payout ratio
retention ratio
implied return
information coefficient (IC)

REFERENCES

1. The foundation for dividend discount models was laid out in:

   John Burr Williams, *The Theory of Investment Value* (Amsterdam: North-Holland Publishing, 1964). The original edition was published in 1938.

2. The constant-growth and multiple-growth models were subsequently developed by, respectively:

   M. J. Gordon, "Dividends, Earnings, and Stock Prices," *Review of Economics and Statistics* 41, no. 2 (May 1959): 99–105.

   Nicholas Molodovsky, Catherine May, and Sherman Chottiner, "Common Stock Validation: Principles, Tables and Application," *Financial Analysts Journal* 21, no. 2 (March/April 1965): 104–123.

3. For more on DDMs, see the entire November/December 1985 issue of the *Financial Analysts Journal.* Some of the problems involved in using dividend discount models are discussed in:

   Richard O. Michaud and Paul L. Davis, "Valuation Model Bias and the Scale Structure of Dividend Discount Returns," *Journal of Finance* 38, no. 2 (May 1982): 563–573.

   Adam K. Gehr, Jr., "A Bias in Dividend Discount Models," *Financial Analysts Journal* 48, no. 1 (January/February 1992): 75–80.

4. For more on how to measure and use P/E ratios, see:

   John Markese, "Will the Real P/E Please Stand Up?" *AAII Journal* 11, no. 9 (October 1989): 32–34.

   Robert J. Angell and Alonzo Redman, "How to Judge a P/E? Examine the Expected Growth Rate," *AAII Journal* 12, no. 3 (March 1990): 16–17.

   John Baijkowski, "Price-Earnings Ratios and Fundamental Stock Valuation," *AAII Journal* 13, no. 6 (July 1991): 33–36.

5. For an interesting note on why Japanese P/E ratios appear to be overstated, see:

   Harold Bierman, Jr., "Price/Earnings Ratios Restructured for Japan," *Financial Analysts Journal* 47, no. 2 (March/April 1991): 91–92.

6. For an article that ties DDMs, P/E ratios, and Graham and Dodd together, see:

John Baijkowski, "From Theory to Reality: Applying the Valuation Models," *AAII Journal* 15, no. 1 (January 1993): 34–37.

7. The issue of market volatility has been studied by utilizing dividend discount models. In essence, these studies compare the actual levels of various stock market indices with their intrinsic values, calculated by determining the present value of rational forecasts of subsequent dividends paid on the stocks in the indices. The main observation is that the actual levels fluctuate far more over time than the intrinsic values. A conclusion that some people draw from these studies is that there is excess volatility in stock prices and hence markets are not efficient. This hotly debated topic was introduced in:

   Stephen F. LeRoy and Richard D. Porter, "The Present-Value Relation: Tests Based on Implied Variance Bounds," *Econometrica* 49, no. 3 (May 1981): 555–574.

   Robert J. Shiller, "Do Stock Prices Move Too Much to Be Justified by Subsequent Changes in Dividends?" *American Economic Review* 71, no. 3 (June 1981): 421–436.

8. For more on market volatility, see:

   Robert J. Shiller, "Theories of Aggregate Stock Price Movements," *Journal of Portfolio Management* 10, no. 2 (Winter 1984): 23–37.

   Robert J. Shiller, *Market Volatility* (Cambridge, MA: MIT Press, 1989).

   Stephen F. LeRoy, "Efficient Capital Markets and Martingales," *Journal of Economic Literature* 27, no. 4 (December 1989): 1583–1621.

   Stephen F. LeRoy, "Capital Market Efficiency: An Update," Federal Reserve Bank of San Francisco *Economic Review* (Spring 1990): 29–40.

   Lucy F. Ackert and Brian F. Smith, "Stock Price Volatility, Ordinary Dividends, and Other Cash Flows to Shareholders," *Journal of Finance* 48, no. 4 (September 1993): 1147–1160.

9. For a Canadian perspective on the dividend discount model, see:

   L. Ackert and J. Schnabel, "The Dividend Discount Model: A Victim of the Tumultuous Eighties?" *Canadian Investment Review* VI, no. 3 (Fall 1993).

CHAPTER 19

Earnings

Chapter 18 discussed how the intrinsic value of a share of common stock can be determined by discounting expected dividends per share at a rate of return that is appropriate for a security of similar risk. Alternatively, the implied return on a share of common stock can be determined by finding the discount rate that makes the present value of all the expected dividends equal to the current market price of the stock. In either case, a forecast of dividends per share is necessary. Because dividends per share are equal to earnings per share times a payout ratio, dividends can be forecast by forecasting earnings per share and payout ratios. Currently there are numerous methods that are used by security analysts for forecasting either earnings or dividends. This chapter presents a discussion of some of the important features of dividends and earnings that the analyst must be aware of in making such forecasts. It begins with a discussion of the relationship among earnings, dividends, and investment.

STOCK VALUATION BASED ON EARNINGS

A continual controversy in the investment community concerns the relevance of dividends versus earnings as the underlying source of value of common shares. Clearly, earnings are important to shareholders because earnings provide the cash flow necessary for paying dividends. However, dividends are also important because dividends are what shareholders actually receive from the firm, and they are the focus of the dividend discount models discussed in Chapter 18. Indeed, if management increased the proportion of earnings per share paid out as dividends, they could make their shareholders wealthier, suggesting that the **dividend decision** (deciding on the amount of dividends to pay) is a very important one.

Considerable light was shed on this controversy in 1961 when Merton Miller and Franco Modigliani published a seminal paper arguing that the underlying source of value of common shares was earnings, not dividends. An implication of this conclusion is that the dividend decision is relatively unimportant to the shareholders, as it will not affect the value of their investment in the firm.

In the course of a year, a firm generates revenues and incurs costs. With cash accounting, the difference between revenues and costs would be termed *cash flow*. With accrual accounting, used by almost all firms, both revenues and costs are likely to include estimates made by accountants of the values of non-cash items. Items such as depreciation charges are deducted from cash flow to obtain earnings. Moreover, each year some amount is invested in the business. Of the total (gross) investment, a portion will be equal in value to the estimated depreciation of various real assets (such as machines and buildings); the rest is new (net) investment.

The dollar amount of new investment each year should be based on the investment opportunities that are available to the firm, and they should be unaffected by the dollar amount of dividends that are to be paid out. In particular, any investment opportunity whose net present value (NPV) is positive should be undertaken. This means that the future prospects of the firm can be described by a stream of expected earnings ($E_1, E_2, E_3, \ldots$) and the expected net investment required to produce such earnings ($I_1, I_2, I_3, \ldots$). Taking these two streams as given, it can be shown that management can set the total dollar amount of current dividends (D_0) at any level without making the current shareholders either better or worse off.[1] This will be done next, with the focus on earnings and how they can be used to pay for new investments and dividends.

Earnings, Dividends, and Investment

Figure 19.1(a) shows one way that the firm can use total earnings for the current year (E_0). In this situation, new investment (I_0) is financed out of earnings, and the firm uses the remainder of the earnings to pay dividends (D_0) to its shareholders. For example, if the Plum Company has just earned \$5000 and has new investments it would like to make that cost \$3000, then Plum could pay for these investments out of earnings and declare a dividend of \$2000.

Issuing Shares

Whereas earnings are exactly equal to dividends and investment ($E_0 = D_0 + I_0$) in Figure 19.1(a), this need not be the case. In the situation shown in Figure 19.1(b), earnings are less than dividends and investment ($E_0 < D_0 + I_0$). Because the amount of investment has been determined by the number of positive NPV projects available to the firm, the reason for this inequality is that the firm has decided to pay its current shareholders a higher dividend than was paid in Figure 19.1(a). However, in order for higher dividends to be paid,

Figure 19.1

Earnings, dividends, and investment.

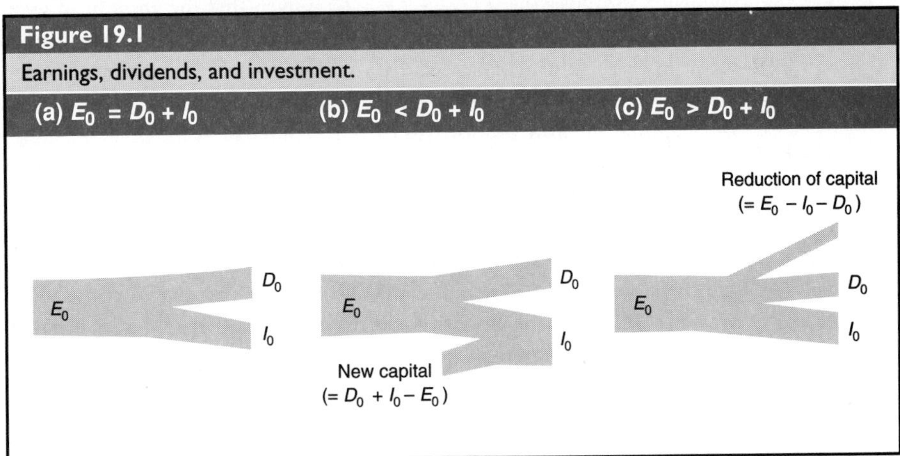

[1] In Chapter 18, D_0 denoted the per-share dividends that had been paid over the past year. Now D_0 is used to denote the aggregate amount of dividends that is about to be paid. Similarly, the quantities of earnings (E_t) and new investment (I_t) are measured for the firm on an aggregate basis, not a per-share basis. Note that dividends cannot be set at an arbitrarily high value relative to earnings (for example, earnings of \$10 million and dividends of \$100 million), because the firm would then find it practically impossible to obtain the necessary funds to pay the dividends.

additional funds must be obtained from outside the firm. This is accomplished by a new sale of common shares (it is assumed that the flotation costs associated with a new sale of common shares are negligible).

The reason the funds are obtained through a new sale of common shares instead of through a new sale of debt is a desire to avoid the confounding effects of a change in the firm's debt-equity ratio. That is, if debt financing is to be allowed, then two things would be changing at the same time—the amount of the dividend and the debt-equity ratio for the firm. As a result, if shareholders appear to be made better off by a change in the amount of the dividend, their betterment may actually be due to a change in the debt-equity ratio. By prohibiting debt financing, the debt-equity ratio will remain constant, and only the amount of the dividend will be allowed to change. That is, each additional dollar in equity funds raised by issuing new shares is offset by a dollar in dividend payments. Thus if shareholders appear to be better off, it has to be due to the change in the amount of the dividend, because everything else (specifically, the amount of investment and the debt-equity ratio) has remained fixed.

Note that if investment is financed out of earnings, as in Figure 19.1(a), then it has been financed with equity obtained internally. In Figure 19.1(b), investment has also been financed with equity, but here some of the equity has been obtained externally. As a result, the debt-equity ratio for the firm is the same in both situations.

In the case of Plum, instead of paying dividends amounting to \$2000, the firm could decide to pay dividends amounting to \$3000. Because investment is equal to \$3000, Plum will have a cash outflow of \$3000 + \$3000 = \$6000, with earnings amounting to only \$5000. This means that Plum will have to sell \$6000 – \$5000 = \$1000 of new common shares.

Repurchasing Shares

In Figure 19.1(c), the situation is reversed from 19.1(b) as earnings are now greater than dividends and investment ($E_0 > D_0 + I_0$). Given that the amount of investment has been determined by the number of positive NPV projects available to the firm, the reason for this inequality is that the firm has decided to pay its shareholders a lower dividend than was paid in Figure 19.1(a). In paying this smaller dividend, the firm will be left with excess cash. It is assumed that the firm will use this cash to repurchase some of its outstanding shares in the marketplace (and that the transaction costs associated with such repurchases are negligible).

The reason for this assumption is the desire to keep the situation comparable to the two earlier ones. Allowing the firm to keep the excess cash would be tantamount to letting the firm invest the cash, an investment decision that was not made in the two earlier cases and therefore does not have a positive NPV (remember that I_0 consists of all positive NPV projects). Allowing the firm to keep the excess cash would also mean that the firm has made a decision to lower its debt-equity ratio. This is because retention of the excess cash would increase the amount of equity for the firm, thereby decreasing the amount of debt outstanding relative to the amount of equity.

Continuing with the Plum Company, dividends could be set at \$1000 instead of \$2000 or \$3000. In this case, the firm would have a cash outflow for dividends and investment amounting to \$1000 + \$3000 = \$4000. With earnings of \$5000, this means that there would be \$5000 – \$4000 = \$1000 of cash left for the firm to use to repurchase its own stock.

The Dividend Decision

The firm has a decision to make regarding the size of its current dividends. The amount of current earnings E_0 and the amount of new investment I_0 have been determined. What is left to be decided is the amount of dividends, D_0. They can be set equal to earnings less investment as in Figure 19.1(a), or greater than this amount as in Figure 19.1(b), or less than this amount, as in Figure 19.1(c). The question that remains to be answered is: Will one of these three levels of dividends make the current shareholders better off than the other two? That is, which level of dividends—\$1000, \$2000, or \$3000—will make the current shareholders better off?

The simplest way to answer this question is to consider a shareholder who presently holds 1% of the common share of the firm and is determined to maintain this percentage ownership in the future.[2] If the firm follows a dividend policy as shown in Figure 19.1(a), the shareholder's current dividends will equal $.01D_0$ or, equivalently, $.01(E_0 - I_0)$. Similarly, the shareholder's future dividends will be equal to $.01D_t$ or, equivalently, $.01(E_t - I_t)$.

If the firm follows a dividend policy as shown in Figure 19.1(b), however, the shareholder must invest additional funds in the firm's common shares in order to avoid a diminished proportional ownership position in the firm. Why? Because in this situation the firm must raise funds by selling additional shares in order to pay for the larger cash dividends. As $E_0 < D_0 + I_0$, the total amount of funds that the firm needs to raise is the amount F_0 such that

$$E_0 + F_0 = D_0 + I_0 \tag{19.1}$$

or

$$F_0 = D_0 + I_0 - E_0. \tag{19.2}$$

The amount of the additional investment that the shareholder needs to make in order to maintain a 1% position in the firm is $.01F_0$, which from equation (19.2) is equal to $.01(D_0 + I_0 - E_0)$. Because the shareholder receives 1% of the dividends, the net amount the shareholder receives at time zero is equal to $.01D_0 - .01F_0$, or

$$.01D_0 - .01(D_0 + I_0 - E_0) = .01E_0 - .01I_0. \tag{19.3}$$

Interestingly, the net amount the shareholder receives, $.01E_0 - .01I_0$, is the same as in the first situation. This is because the amount of the extra cash dividend received is exactly offset by the amount the shareholder needs to spend to maintain his or her ownership position in the firm.

If the firm follows a dividend policy as shown in Figure 19.1(c), then the firm will repurchase shares. Accordingly, the shareholder must sell some shares back to the firm in order to avoid having an increased ownership position in the firm. As $E_0 > D_0 + I_0$, the total amount of funds that the firm will spend on repurchasing its own shares is the amount R_0 such that

$$E_0 = D_0 + I_0 + R_0 \tag{19.4}$$

or

$$R_0 = E_0 - D_0 - I_0. \tag{19.5}$$

[2]The use of such a shareholder is for ease of exposition. The same answer would be obtained if other types of shareholders (such as those who are not interested in maintaining a constant proportional ownership position in the firm in the future) are considered.

The number of shares that the shareholder needs to sell back to the firm to maintain a 1% position in the firm is $.01R_0$, which from equation (19.5) is equal to $.01(E_0 - D_0 - I_0)$. Because the shareholder receives 1% of the dividends, the net amount the shareholder receives at time zero is equal to $.01D_0 + .01R_0$, or

$$.01D_0 + .01(E_0 - D_0 - I_0) = .01E_0 - .01I_0. \tag{19.6}$$

Again this net amount, $.01E_0 - .01I_0$, is the same as in the first situation. That is, in the third situation, the smaller amount of the cash dividend received by the shareholder is exactly made up for by the amount of cash received from the repurchase of shares by the firm.

Thus, no matter what the firm's dividend policy, a shareholder choosing to maintain a constant proportional ownership will be able to spend the same amount of money on consumption at time zero. This amount will be equal to the proportion times the quantity $E_0 - I_0$. Furthermore, this will also be true in the future. That is, in any year t the shareholder will be able to spend on consumption an amount that is equal to the proportion times the quantity $E_t - I_t$.

► Earnings Determine Market Value

In determining the value of 1% of the current shares outstanding, remember that the firm is about to declare and pay current dividends. Regardless of the magnitude of these dividends, the shareholder will only be able to spend on consumption an amount equal to $.01(E_0 - I_0)$. Furthermore, the shareholder will be able to spend on consumption an amount equal to $.01(E_t - I_t)$ in any future year t. Discounting these expected amounts by a (constant) rate k reveals that the value (V) of 1% of the current shares outstanding will be

$$.01V = \frac{.01(E_0 - I_0)}{(1+k)^0} + \frac{.01(E_1 - I_1)}{(1+k)^1} + \frac{.01(E_2 - I_2)}{(1+k)^2} + \ldots$$

Multiplying both sides of this equation by 100 results in the following expression for the total market value of all shares outstanding:

$$V = \frac{(E_0 - I_0)}{(1+k)^0} + \frac{(E_1 - I_1)}{(1+k)^1} + \frac{(E_2 - I_2)}{(1+k)^2} + \ldots \tag{19.7}$$

Equation (19.7) shows that the aggregate market value of equity is equal to the present value of expected earnings net of investment. Note how the size of the dividends does not enter into the formula. This indicates that the market value of the stock is *independent* of the dividend decision made by the firm, meaning that the dividend decision is irrelevant to stock valuation. Instead, the market value of the firm is related to the earnings prospects of the firm, along with the required amounts of new investment needed to produce those earnings.[3]

---

[3] It has been argued that if the tax rate on dividends is greater than the tax rate on capital gains, then shareholders will earn more on an after-tax basis if the firm has a relatively low payout ratio. An additional benefit to shareholders if the firm has a low payout ratio is that capital gains taxes are paid only when the shares are sold, and can therefore be deferred. Thus, it appears that shareholders will be better off if the firm has a relatively low payout ratio. For a more detailed discussion of the issue, along with the relevant citations, see pp. 128–135 of Gordon J. Alexander and Jack Clark Francis, *Portfolio Analysis* (Englewood Cliffs, NJ: Prentice Hall, 1986). Also see James S. Ang, David W. Blackwell, and William L. Megginson, "The Effect of Taxes on the Relative Valuation of Dividends and Capital Gains: Evidence from Dual-Class British Investment Trusts," *Journal of Finance* 46, no. 1 (March 1991): 383–399.

Dividend Discount Models

In Chapter 18 it was shown that the value of a share of common stock was equal to the present value of all dividends expected in the future. Hence it is tempting to believe that, contrary to the assertion above, the market value of a firm's shares is *dependent* on the dividend decision. However, it turns out that there is nothing inconsistent between valuation being based on dividend discount models and the irrelevancy of the dividend decision.

The dividend irrelevancy argument suggests that if the firm decides to increase its current dividend, then new shares will need to be sold. This, in turn, suggests that future dividends will be smaller because the aggregate amount of dividends will have to be divided among an increased number of shares outstanding. Ultimately, the current shareholders will be neither better off nor worse off, as the increased current dividend will be exactly offset by the decreased future dividends. Conversely, if the firm decides to decrease its current dividend, then shares will be repurchased and future dividends will be increased due to the fewer shares outstanding. Ultimately, the decreased current dividend will be exactly offset by the increased future dividends, again leaving current shareholders neither better off nor worse off.

An Example

All this can be illustrated with the earlier example of the Plum Company. Because Plum currently has reported earnings of \$5000 and investments totalling \$3000, if dividends amounting to \$2000 were paid, then the shareholder owning 1% of the firm would receive cash amounting to .01 × \$2000 = \$20.

Alternatively, if dividends amounting to \$3000 were paid, then Plum would have to raise \$1000 from the sale of new common shares. The shareholder would receive .01 × \$3000 = \$30 in dividends, but would have to pay .01 × \$1000 = \$10 to purchase 1% of the new shares, thereby maintaining his or her 1% ownership position. Consequently, the net cash flow to the shareholder would be \$30 – \$10 = \$20, the same amount as in the previous situation.

Lastly, if dividends amounting to \$1000 were paid, then Plum would have cash amounting to \$1000 to use to repurchase common shares. The shareholder, desirous of maintaining a 1% position, would thus sell shares amounting to .01 × \$1000 = \$10. As a result, the shareholder would have a cash inflow totalling \$10 + \$10 = \$20, again the same amount as in the two previous situations.

Under all three situations, the 1% shareholder would receive the same cash flow at the present time (\$20) and have the same claim on the future earnings of Plum. That is, in all three cases, the shareholder would still own 1% of Plum and would therefore receive the same amount of dividends in the future. Accordingly, the 1% shareholder (and all the others) would be neither better off nor worse off if Plum pays a dividend amounting to \$1000, \$2000, or \$3000. In summary, the dividend decision is a non-event—whatever the level of dividends, current shareholders will be neither better off nor worse off. This result is sometimes referred to as the "dividend irrelevancy theorem."

DETERMINANTS OF DIVIDENDS

Few firms attempt to maintain a constant ratio of dividends to current earnings because doing so would result in a fluctuating dollar amount of dividends. The reason the dividends would fluctuate is that earnings on a year-to-year basis are likely to be quite variable. Instead,

Table 19.1

Earnings and Dividend Changes.[a]

Earnings Changes			Percentage of Cases in Which Firms		
Current Year	*Previous Year*	*Percentage of Cases*	*Increased Dividends*	*Did Not Change Dividends*	*Decreased Dividends*
+		59.3%	65.8%	13.9%	20.3%
−		40.7	42.8	17.9	39.5
+	+	33.4	74.8	11.4	13.8
+	−	25.9	54.1	17.2	28.7
−	+	24.7	49.7	16.9	33.4
−	−	16.0	31.8	19.4	48.8

[a] Based on 392 firms during the period 1946–1964.

SOURCE: Eugene F. Fama and Harvey Babiak, "Dividend Policy: An Empirical Analysis." *Journal of the American Statistical Association* 63. no. 324 (December 1968): 1134.

firms attempt to maintain a desired ratio of dividends to earnings over some relatively long period, meaning that there is a target payout ratio of dividends to long-run or sustainable earnings. As a result, dividends are usually kept at a constant dollar amount and are increased only when management is confident that it will be relatively easy to keep paying this increased amount in the future.[4] Nonetheless, larger earnings are likely to be accompanied by some sort of increase in dividends, as Table 19.1 shows.

Changes in Earnings and Dividends

The first two lines of Table 19.1 indicate that 59.3% of the time the earnings of the firms examined rose, and the remaining 40.7% of the time earnings fell. The majority of the times when current earnings rose, firms increased their current dividends. However, whenever current earnings fell, firms would increase their current dividends as frequently as they would decrease their current dividends (note that, roughly speaking, 42.8% ≅ 39.5%).

The next two lines of the table suggest that firms are more likely to increase current dividends if they have had two consecutive years of rising earnings than if they have had falling and then rising earnings (74.8% > 54.1%). The last two lines of the table suggest that firms are more likely to decrease current dividends if they have had two consecutive years of falling earnings than if they have had rising and then falling earnings (48.8% > 33.4%). Overall, the table shows that firms in general are more likely to increase dividends than to decrease them.

The Lintner Model

A formal representation of the kind of behaviour implied by a constant long-run target payout ratio begins by assuming that the goal of the firm is to pay out p^* (for example,

[4] In addition to a regular dividend, sometimes a firm will declare a "special" or "extra" dividend, usually at year-end. By calling it a special dividend, the firm is conveying a message to its shareholders that such a dividend is a one-time event.

$p^* = 60\%$) of long-run earnings. If this target ratio were maintained every year, total dividends paid in year t would be

$$D_t^* = p^* E_t \tag{19.8}$$

where D_t^* denotes the target amount for dividends to be paid in year t and E_t is the amount of earnings in year t. The difference between target dividends in year t and the previous year's actual dividends is determined by subtracting D_{t-1} from both sides of equation (19.8), resulting in

$$D_t^* - D_{t-1} = p^* E_t - D_{t-1}. \tag{19.9}$$

Although firms would like to change their dividends from D_{t-1} to D_t^*, few (if any) firms would actually change their dividends by this amount. Instead, the actual change in dividends will be a proportion of the desired change:

$$D_t - D_{t-1} = a(D_t^* - D_{t-1}) \tag{19.10}$$

where a is a "speed of adjustment" coefficient, a number between zero and one.

For example, if a firm has just earned \$5 million (E_t = \$5 million) and has a target payout ratio of 60%, then it would like to pay dividends amounting to $.6 \times$ \$5 million = \$3 million. Assuming that it paid dividends of \$2 million last year, this represents an increase of \$3 million – \$2 million = \$1 million. However, if $a = 50\%$, then the firm will actually increase the dividends by $.5 \times$ \$1 million = \$500 000. Thus actual dividends will be equal to \$2 million + \$500 000 = \$2.5 million, an amount equal to last year's dividends plus the change in dividends from last year to this year.

This model can be summarized by substituting $p^* E_t$ for D_t^* in equation (19.10) and then solving the resulting expression for D_t:

$$D_t = ap^* E_t + (1 - a)D_{t-1}. \tag{19.11}$$

Equation (19.11) indicates that the amount of current dividends is based on the amount of current earnings and the amount of the last year's dividends.[5] In the previous example, $a = 50\%$, $p^* = 60\%$, E_t = \$5 million, and D_{t-1} = \$2 million. Thus actual dividends D_t would be equal to ($.5 \times .6 \times$ \$5 million) + $(1 - .5) \times$ \$2 million = \$2.5 million.

By subtracting D_{t-1} from both sides of equation (19.11), it can be seen that the change in dividends is equal to

$$D_t - D_{t-1} = ap^* E_t - aD_{t-1}. \tag{19.12}$$

When written in this form, the model suggests that the size of the *change* in dividends will be positively related to the current amount of earnings (because ap^* is a positive number) and negatively related to the amount of the previous period's dividends (since $-aD_{t-1}$ is a negative number). Thus, the larger current earnings are, the larger the change in dividends, but the larger the previous period's dividends, the smaller the change in dividends.

---

[5] Looking backward in time, it can be shown that current dividends D_t are a linear function of past earnings $Et - 1$, E_{t-2}, E_{t-3}, and so on. More specifically, it can be shown that:

$$D_t = ap^*[(1-a)^0 E_{t-0} + (1-a)^1 E_{t-1} + (1-a)^2 E_{t-2} + (1-a)^3 E_{t-3} + \ldots].$$

Because the quantity $(1 - a)$ is a positive fraction (for example, 1/3), when it is raised to a power it becomes smaller in value, with larger powers resulting in values closer to zero. Thus, current dividends depend more on recent past earnings than on distant past earnings, and the equation can be approximated by using an arbitrary number of past earnings (the accuracy of the approximation depends on the number used).

Test Results

Statistical analysis has been used to test how well this model describes the way a sample of firms set the amount of their dividends. Table 19.2 summarizes some of the values obtained in one such study. The average firm had a target payout ratio of 59.1% and adjusted dividends 26.9% of the way toward its target each year. However, most firms' dividends varied substantially from the pattern implied by their targets and adjustment factors. Somewhat less than half (42%) of the annual variance in the typical firm's dividends could be explained in this manner. This means that the model, although explaining a portion of the changes in dividends that occurred, leaves a substantial portion unexplained.

Table 19.2

Target Payout Ratios and Speed of Dividend Adjustment Factors.[a]

Speed of Adjustment Coefficient		Target Payout Ratio		Percentage of Variance Explained	
Value	*Percentage of Firms with Smaller Value*	*Value*	*Percentage of Firms with Smaller Value*	*Value*	*Percentage of Firms with Smaller Value*
.104	10%	.401	10%	11%	10%
.182	30	.525	30	32	30
.251	50	.584	50	42	50
.339	70	.660	70	54	70
.470	90	.779	90	72	90
average .269		average .591		average 42	

[a] Based on 298 firms during the period 1946–1968.

SOURCE: Eugene F. Fama, "The Empirical Relationship Between the Dividend and Investment Decisions of Firms," *American Economic Review* 64, no. 3 (June 1974): 310.

The results from a comparable Canadian study of 40 companies in the manufacturing sector from 1947 to 1970 are shown in Table 19.3. In this case, however, current dividends were regressed against cash flow (rather than earnings) and the dividend paid in the prior period. The average target payout ratio and speed of adjustment coefficient were 0.316 and 0.379 respectively. The cash flow model used here appears to describe the firms' dividend behaviour better than the earnings model used in the US in that it explains about 77% of the variance of the typical firm's dividend compared with 42%. The behaviour of a few Canadian firms, however, does not conform well to this model in that these firms have low speed of adjustment coefficients, implying that they make little or no adjustment to their dividends in response to changes in cash flow.

THE INFORMATION CONTENT OF DIVIDENDS

It is reasonable to believe that management has more information about the future earnings of the firm than does the public (including its own shareholders). This situation of **asymmetric**

Table 19.3

Target Payout Ratios and Speed of Dividend Adjustment Factors for 40 Canadian Firms, 1947–1970.

Speed of Adjustment Coefficient		Target Payout Ratio		Percentage of Variance Explained	
Value	*Percentage of Firms with Smaller Value*	*Value*	*Percentage of Firms with Smaller Value*	*Value*	*Percentage of Firms with Smaller Value*
.204	25%	.244	25%	72%	25%
.324	50	.313	50	85	50
.506	75	.374	75	93	75
average .379		average .316		average 77	

SOURCE: J-P. D. Chateau, "La Politique de distribution de dividends des sociétés: une étude microéconométrique," *Canadian Journal of Economics* 9, no. 2 (1976): 255–77.

information suggests that managers will seek to convey the information to the public if they have an incentive to do so. Assuming that they have such an incentive, one way of doing so is by announcing a change in the amount of the firm's dividends. When used in this manner, dividend announcements are said to be a signaling device.[6]

Signaling

A relatively simple view of dividend changes is that an announced increase in dividends is a signal that management has increased its assessment of the firm's future earnings. The announced increase in dividends is therefore good news and will, in turn, cause investors to raise their expectations regarding the firm's future earnings. Conversely, an announced decrease in dividends is a signal that management has decreased its assessment of the firm's future earnings. The announced decrease in dividends is therefore bad news and will, in turn, cause investors to lower their expectations regarding the firm's future earnings. An implication is that an announced increase in dividends will cause the firm's share price to rise, and an announced decrease will cause it to fall.

This simple model of dividend changes can be thought of as a special case of the model given in equation (19.12), where the speed of adjustment, a, is zero. With this model, the expected change in dividends, $D_t - D_{t-1}$, is zero, suggesting that a simple increase in dividends will be viewed as good news. Conversely, a simple decrease in dividends will be viewed as bad news.

[6] Other signaling devices include changes in the firm's capital structure (for example, announcing an issuance of debt with the proceeds being used to repurchase stock). It has been argued that in order for the signal to be useful to the public, (1) management must have an incentive to send a truthful signal; (2) the signal cannot be imitated by competitors in different financial positions; and (3) there cannot be a cheaper means of conveying the same information. See Stephen A. Ross, "The Determination of Financial Structure: The Incentive Signalling Approach," *Bell Journal of Economics* 8, no. 1 (Spring 1977): 23–40.

One way of testing to see if dividend changes do indeed convey information to the public is to see how share prices react to announcements of changes in dividends. However, care must be exercised in conducting such a study because the firm's announcement of dividends is often made at the same time as the firm announces its earnings. Thus, when such announcements are made at the same time, any price change in the firm's common shares may be attributable to either (or both) announcements.

One study attempted to avoid this problem of contamination by looking only at cases where the announcement of earnings was at least 11 trading days apart from the announcement of dividends. Figure 19.2 provides an illustration of the average abnormal return associated with a firm's dividend announcement for those firms that announced their dividends 11 or more days after they announced their earnings (similar results were obtained when the authors examined those cases where dividend announcements preceded earnings announcements).

In those cases where firms announced an increase in their dividends, there is a significant positive reaction in their share prices. Conversely, in those cases where firms announced a decrease in their dividends, there is a significant negative reaction in their share prices. These findings strongly support the **information content of dividends hypothesis**, where dividend announcements are asserted to contain inside information about the firm's future prospects.

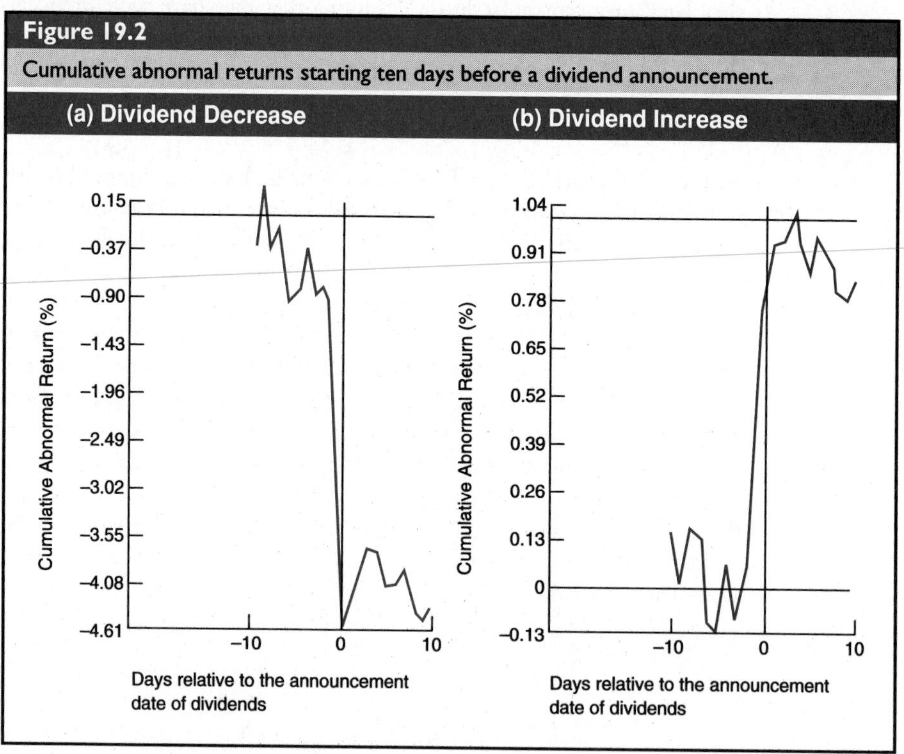

Figure 19.2

Cumulative abnormal returns starting ten days before a dividend announcement.

SOURCE: Joseph Aharony and Itzhak Swary, "Quarterly Dividend and Earnings Announcements and Stockholders' Returns: An Empirical Analysis," *Journal of Finance* 35, no. 1 (March 1980): 8.

Figure 19.3

Cumulative abnormal returns starting twenty-four months before a dividend announcement.

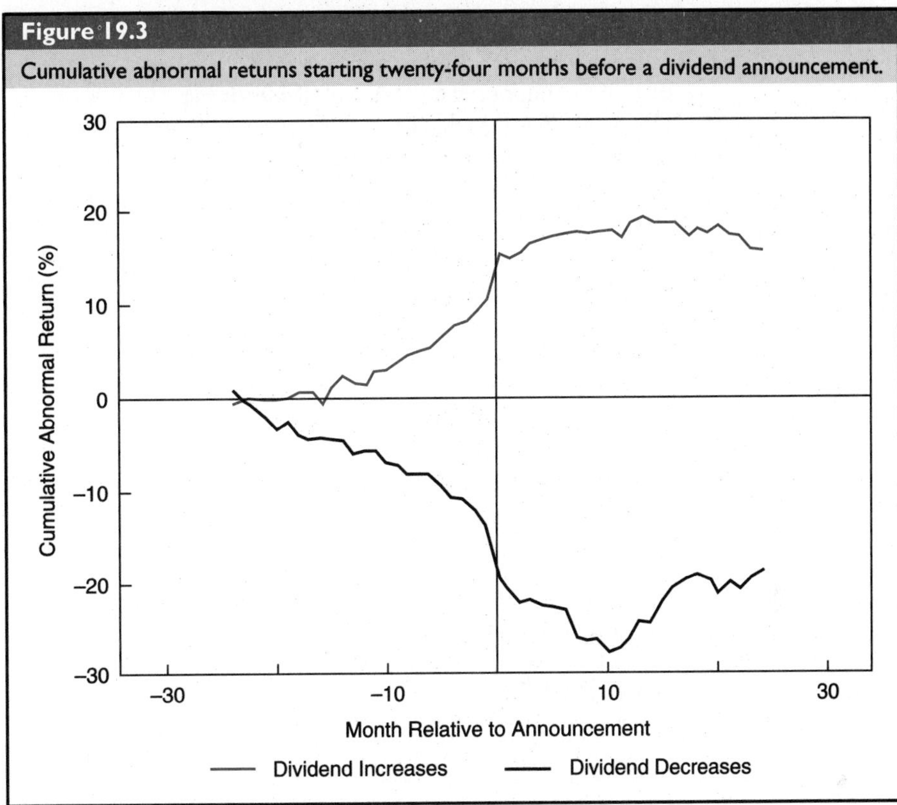

SOURCE: Adapted from G. Charest, "Returns to Dividend Changing Stocks on the Toronto Stock Exchange," *Journal of Business Administration* 12, no. 1 (Fall 1980): 7–8.

A study by Charest, that was not free of possible contamination by earnings announcements, found that dividend changes in Canada are anticipated by the market several months in advance of the announcement, as shown in Figure 19.3.[7] Here also dividend increases (decreases) are accompanied by positive (negative) reactions in the stock prices. These findings are also consistent with the information content of dividends hypothesis.

It should be noted that dividends being used as a signal is not inconsistent with the dividend irrelevancy argument of Miller and Modigliani that was made earlier. In particular, shareholders will be neither better nor worse off if the *level* of dividends, relative to earnings, is high or low. *Changes* in dividends may, however, be important because they convey information to the public about the future earnings prospects for the firm.

Dividend Initiations and Omissions

One study looked at the relationship between dividend changes and past, current, and future changes in earnings.[8] Specifically, it focused on the most dramatic dividend announcements

---

[7] G. Charest, "Returns to Dividend Changing Stocks on the Toronto Stock Exchange," *Journal of Business Administration* 12, no. 1 (Fall 1980): 1–18.

[8] Paul M. Healy and Krishna G. Palepu, "Earnings Information Conveyed by Dividend Initiations and Omissions," *Journal of Financial Economics* 21, no. 2 (September 1988): 149–175.

possible—dividend initiations and omissions—because the information being conveyed in these announcements is clearly unambiguous.

That is, if the information content of dividends hypothesis is correct, then firms that start to pay dividends for the first time in at least ten years must be signaling that they believe that earnings have recently increased to a permanently higher level, and that earnings may increase even more in the near future. The question to be addressed is this: have firms actually experienced notably higher earnings around the time of such initiations and afterward?

Conversely, firms that have paid dividends for at least ten years and that suddenly stop paying any dividends must believe that their earnings have recently decreased to a permanently lower level, and that earnings may decrease even more in the future. For them the question is this: have firms actually experienced notably lower earnings around the time of such omissions and afterward?

The answer supported the information content of dividends hypothesis. Specifically, the study found that earnings tended to increase for at least one year leading up to dividend initiations and to decrease for up to two years leading up to dividend omissions. Furthermore, earnings continued to increase for at least one year after initiations and to decrease for one year after omissions, and such changes appear to be permanent. Interestingly, the larger the change in the firm's share price when the dividend initiation or omission is announced, the larger the change in the firm's earnings in both the year of the announcement and the year thereafter. Thus, it seems that dividends do indeed convey information about earnings.

► Dividends and Losses

In a similar vein to dividend initiations and omissions, it is interesting to examine situations where firms that have had a string of at least ten years of positive earnings and dividend payments suddenly experience negative earnings. In particular, do dividends in such a situation convey information about future earnings?

One study examined this situation by looking at firms that had at least one year of negative earnings during the 1980–1985 period but previously had at least ten consecutive years of positive earnings and dividend payments; 167 firms ("loss" firms) were uncovered meeting these criteria.[9] A comparison sample of 440 firms ("non-loss" firms) that had positive earnings during the 1980–1985 period as well as during a previous ten-year period was also formed.

Approximately half the "loss" firms reduced or omitted their dividends in the four subsequent quarters after the fiscal year-end of the loss. In comparison, fewer than 1% of the "non-loss" firms either reduced or omitted their dividends during the six-year period of 1980–1985. Further examination revealed that:

1. The "loss" firms that did not reduce their dividends were more likely to have unusual income items, indicating that their earnings problems were more likely to be temporary.
2. The "loss" firms that reduced their dividends had deeper losses than the "loss" firms that did not reduce their dividends.

---

[9] Harry DeAngelo, Linda DeAngelo, and Douglas J. Skinner, "Dividends and Losses," *Journal of Finance* 47, no. 5 (December 1992): 1837–1863. Also see Harry DeAngelo and Linda DeAngelo, "Dividend Policy and Financial Distress: An Empirical Investigation of Troubled NYSE Firms," *Journal of Finance* 45, no. 5 (December 1990): 1415–1431.

3. The "loss" firms that reduced their dividends were much more likely to have negative earnings in the next two years than the nonreducing "loss" firms.

Hence, knowing what happened to dividends for a "loss" firm tends to make it easier to predict its future earnings, thereby indicating that dividends have information content when a firm suddenly has negative earnings.

ACCOUNTING EARNINGS VERSUS ECONOMIC EARNINGS

Because the prediction of earnings is of critical importance in security analysis and investment research, a review of what is known about earnings and the relationship between earnings and security prices is essential. At a fundamental level, consideration of the concept of "earnings" itself is needed. Specifically, just what is meant by "earnings" to those who produce the figures, and how does this affect the valuation process?

Accounting Earnings

A firm's accountants operate under constraints and guidelines imposed by regulatory authorities and professional organizations such as the Ontario Securities Commission (OSC) and the Canadian Institute of Chartered Accountants (CICA). In cooperation with management, the accountants produce, on a quarterly basis, a set of financial statements for the firm that ends with a figure for the firm's **accounting earnings** (also known as the firm's reported earnings). In a broad sense, such earnings represent the difference between revenues and expenses, including the expenses associated with non-equity sources of funds (such as debt). This difference, the "total earnings available for common stock," is divided by the number of shares outstanding to calculate **earnings per share** (EPS). It may also be divided by the book value per share to calculate the **return on equity** (ROE).

A basic principle of accounting makes the book value of a firm's equity at the end of a period (such as a quarter or a year) equal to (1) its value at the end of the previous period, plus (2) the portion of accounting earnings for the period that is retained by the firm (here it is assumed that there has been no change in the number of shares outstanding during the period). Letting B_t denote the book value of the equity of the firm at the end of period t, E_t^a denote the accounting earnings for period t, and D_t denote the dividends paid during period t, this relationship can be expressed algebraically as

$$B_t = B_{t-1} + E_t^a - D_t \tag{19.13}$$

From equation (19.13), it can be seen that accounting earnings equal the change in book value of equity plus dividends paid:

$$E_t^a = B_t - B_{t-1} + D_t \tag{19.14}$$

Economic Earnings

Economic earnings (E_t^e) may be defined as the amount that would be obtained in equation (19.14) if the change in the book value of the firm equalled the change in the **economic value of the firm**:

$$E_t^e = V_t - V_{t-1} + D_t \tag{19.15}$$

Figure 19.4

Ratio of price to book value: Standard & Poor's Industrial Stock Index, 1946–1992.

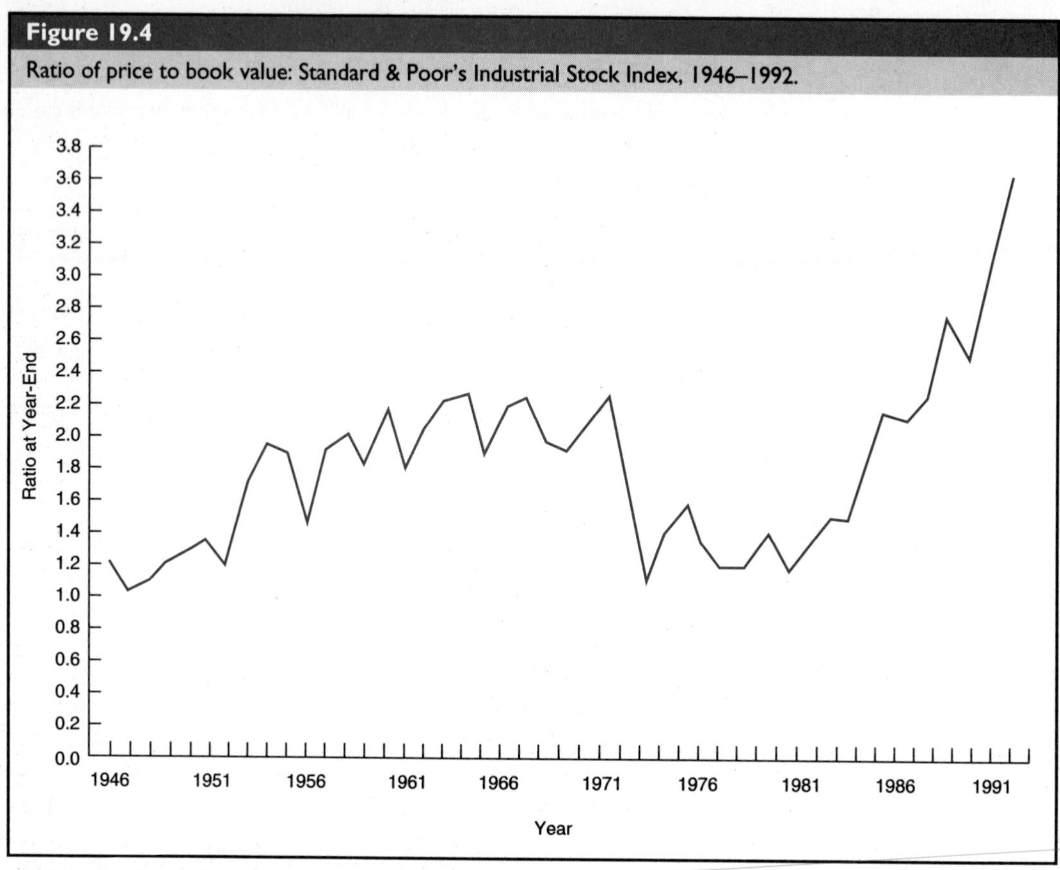

SOURCE: Standard & Poor's Statistical Service, various issues.

Here the change in the economic value of the firm during period t, $V_t - V_{t-1}$, is defined as the change in the market value of the firm's common shares (assuming that there is no change in the market value of the firm's other securities).[10]

It is easy to show that reported book values and market values (that is, economic values) of stocks are often considerably different. Figure 19.4 shows the ratio of (1) the year-end market price per share for Standard & Poor's Industrial Stock Index, to (2) the corresponding year-end book value per share. It can be seen that the ratio is typically greater than 1.0 and has fluctuated considerably from year to year.

Figure 19.5 plots book values (horizontal axis) and market values (vertical axis) for the stocks in the Dow Jones Industrial Average. If investors viewed market and book values as essentially equivalent, the points would plot along a 45-degree line (that is, a line with a

---

[10] Sir John R. Hicks, winner in 1972 of the Nobel Prize in Economics, defined the weekly economic income of an individual as "the maximum value which he can consume during a week and still be as well off at the end of the week as he was at the beginning" (*Value and Capital*, London: Oxford University Press, 1946, p. 172). The definition of the economic earnings of a firm that is given in equation (19.15) can be viewed as an extension of Hicks's definition for an individual.

Figure 19.5

Market and book values, stocks in Dow Jones Industrial Average, year-end 1992.

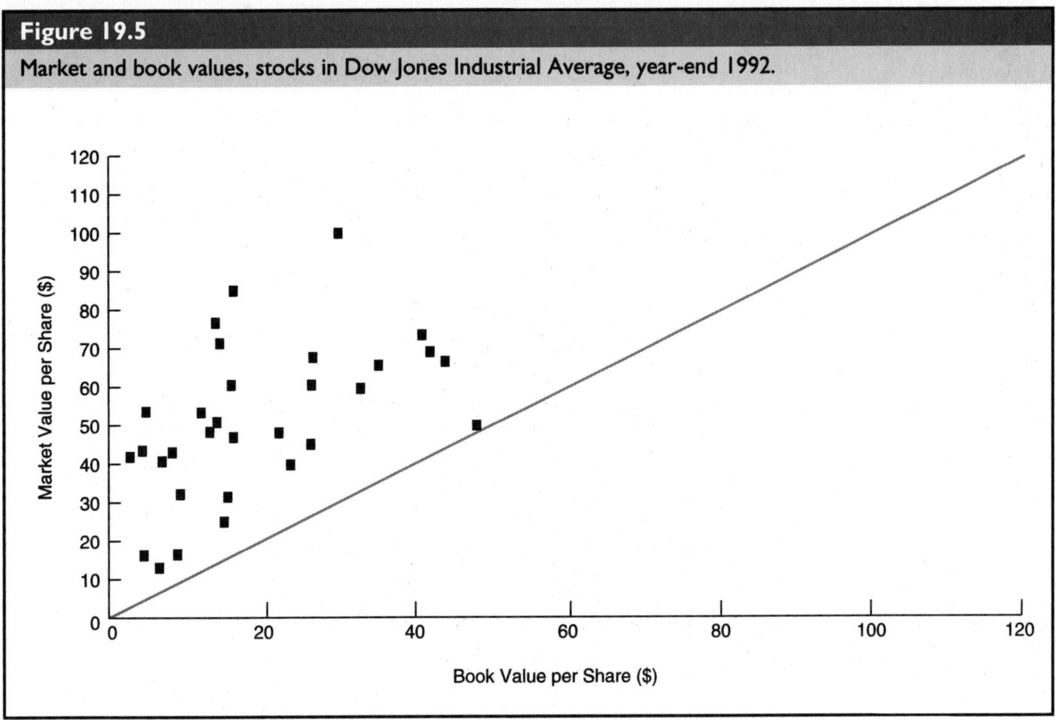

slope of 1) that emanates from the origin. However, as the extensive scatter of the points indicates, market values diverge from book values by different amounts for different stocks.

Both Figure 19.4 and Figure 19.5 indicate that there can be sizeable differences between market and book values. Because equations (19.14) and (19.15) show that accounting and economic earnings will be equal only if market and book values are equal, the evidence thus suggests that accounting and economic earnings differ by varying amounts for different firms.

It is sometimes contended that investors estimate the value of a firm's common stock by directly applying a formula to the firm's current and past accounting earnings.[11] Such a belief may tempt a firm's managers to try to "manage" such earnings in order to make a firm appear more valuable than it is, thereby fooling investors, at least temporarily. This is permissible since the **generally accepted accounting principles** (GAAP) set by the regulatory authorities (such as CICA) allow a large amount of discretion in how certain items are accounted for (examples include methods for depreciation and inventory valuation). As a result, management may pressure accountants to use those principles that maximize the level of reported earnings, or that result in a high growth rate of reported earnings, or that

[11] Two assertions that have been made in regard to what investors look at when valuing shares are known as the *mechanistic hypothesis* and the *myopic hypothesis*. The former asserts that investors look only at reported earnings, and the latter asserts that investors look only at the short-term future. Both these assertions seem to be invalid when data are analyzed. For an in-depth discussion, see George Foster, *Financial Statement Analysis* (Englewood Cliffs, NJ: Prentice Hall, 1986), pp. 443–445.

"smooth" earnings by reducing the year-to-year variability of earnings around a growth rate.[12] Some of these activities can be continued only for a limited number of years; others can go on indefinitely.

To obtain a truly independent estimate of value, analysts must dissect reported earnings. In doing so, they should not be fooled by any accounting illusions, meaning that they should ignore any manipulations that may have been made by the accountants at management's request.[13] Anyone who estimates value by applying a formula (no matter how complex) to reported earnings is not producing an estimate that is completely free from all possible manipulations by management. This is not to say that reported earnings are irrelevant for security valuation. Instead, they should be viewed as one source of information about the future prospects of a firm.

PRICE-EARNINGS RATIOS

Chapter 18 discussed how dividend discount models could be used to determine if stocks were either underpriced or overpriced. One means of making this determination was to compare the actual price-earnings ratio for a firm with what the security analyst had determined it should be. In view of this use of price-earnings ratios, some evidence on the behaviour of overall earnings, prices, and price-earnings ratios will now be presented.

► The Historical Record

Figure 19.6(a) presents a plot of the year-end price-earnings ratios for the Standard & Poor's 500. It can be seen from this plot that the variation in the ratio on a year-to-year basis is considerable, suggesting that investors do not simply apply a standard multiple to earnings in order to determine an appropriate value.

Figure 19.6(b) presents a plot of earnings per share (the lower jagged line) and price (the upper jagged line) for the Standard & Poor's 500.[14] Both lines generally move upward to the right, showing a general trend for both earnings per share and prices to increase over time. However, the two lines are not parallel. This means that earnings per share and prices do not move together in a lockstep manner, an observation that is also apparent in Figure 19.6(a).

Figure 19.7 presents a similar plot of price-earnings ratios for the TSE 300. This also shows a wide variation from year to year, particularly early in 1992 when the ratio rises sharply. The commentary included with the graph suggests one possible explanation for the variability. The large extraordinary writedowns reflect an adjustment of the accounts

---

[12] For a discussion of a number of related issues, see Ross Watts, "Does It Pay to Manipulate EPS?" in *Issues in Corporate Finance* (New York: Stern Stewart Putnam & Macklis, 1983).

[13] There is evidence that investors in publicly held firms are not fooled by such manipulations. See, for example, John R. M. Hand and Patricia Hughes, "The Motives and Consequences of Debt-Equity Swaps and Defeasances: More Evidence That It Does Not Pay to Manipulate Earnings," *Journal of Applied Corporate Finance* 3, no. 3 (Fall 1990): 77–81.

[14] The vertical axis of this figure actually measures the logarithm of earnings per share and of the price index. In this type of diagram, a given vertical distance represents the same percentage change, no matter where it appears. If prices, for example, changed by the same percentage every year (like \$10 to \$20 to \$40 to \$80), then the plot of log prices would be a straight line sloping upward to the right whereas the plot of prices would curve upward.

Figure 19.6

Price-earnings, and price-earnings ratios, standard & Poor's 500, year-end, 1951–1992.

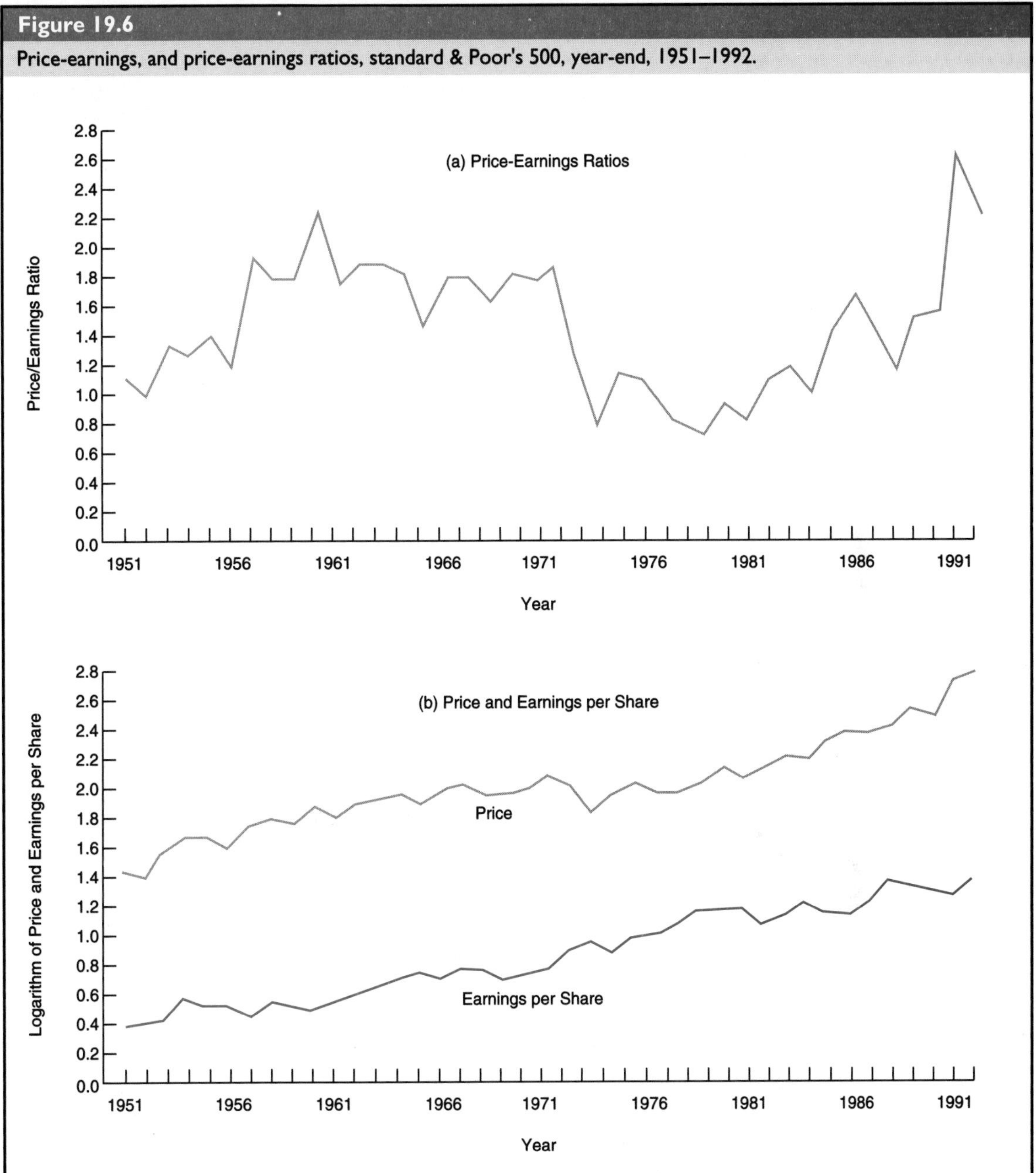

SOURCE: Standard & Poor's *Statistical Service*, various issues.

to reflect the fact that firms paid too much for assets in the 1980s or did not exercise due diligence in the control of operations. These high P/E ratios are, therefore, transitory.

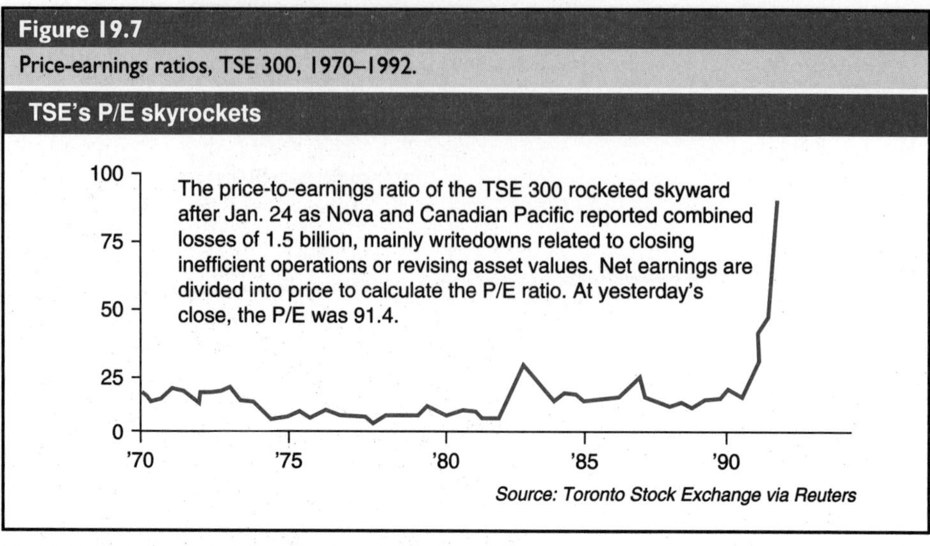
TSE's P/E skyrockets
100
75
50
25
0
The price-to-earnings ratio of the TSE 300 rocketed skyward after Jan. 24 as Nova and Canadian Pacific reported combined losses of 1.5 billion, mainly writedowns related to closing inefficient operations or revising asset values. Net earnings are divided into price to calculate the P/E ratio. At yesterday's close, the P/E was 91.4.
'70
'75
'80
'85
'90
Source: Toronto Stock Exchange via Reuters

Figure 19.7
Price-earnings ratios, TSE 300, 1970–1992.

SOURCE: *The Globe and Mail: Report on Business* (February 7, 1992).

The average P/E of those firms with positive earnings is 15, a figure that is in line with the historical record.

Permanent and Transitory Components of Earnings

When individual common stocks are analyzed, they too show considerable variation in their price-earnings ratios over time. Furthermore, their ratios are quite different from each other at any point in time. One possible explanation notes that reported earnings can be viewed as having two components. The *permanent component* is the component that is likely to be repeated in the future, whereas the *transitory component* is not likely to be repeated.

Earlier, it was argued that the intrinsic value of a share depends on the firm's future earnings prospects. This suggests that changes in a share's intrinsic value, and in turn its price, will be correlated with changes in the permanent component of its earnings but not with changes in the transitory component. If the transitory component is positive, then the price-earnings ratio would be relatively low due to a relatively large number in the denominator. Conversely, if the transitory component is negative, then the price-earnings ratio would be relatively high due to a relatively small number in the denominator.

As an example, consider a firm whose current share price is \$30. Its permanent component of earnings per share over the past year is \$4, and its transitory component is \$1, resulting in reported earnings of \$4 + \$1 = \$5 and a price-earnings ratio of \$30/\$5 = 6. Remember that the stock's current price is based on its future prospects, which are in turn based on the permanent component of earnings per share over the past year. Thus, if the firm had the same permanent component of \$4 but had a transitory component of –\$1 instead of +\$1, the stock would still have a current price of \$30 per share. However, its reported earnings would have been \$4 – \$1 = \$3 and its price-earnings ratio would have been \$30/\$3 = 10.

The permanent component of earnings will change over time, causing investors to revise their forecasts. This will lead to a change in a firm's share price and, in turn, its price-earnings ratio. However, changes in the transitory component will have an even greater effect on the

Figure 19.8

Price-earnings ratios over time for two groups of stocks.

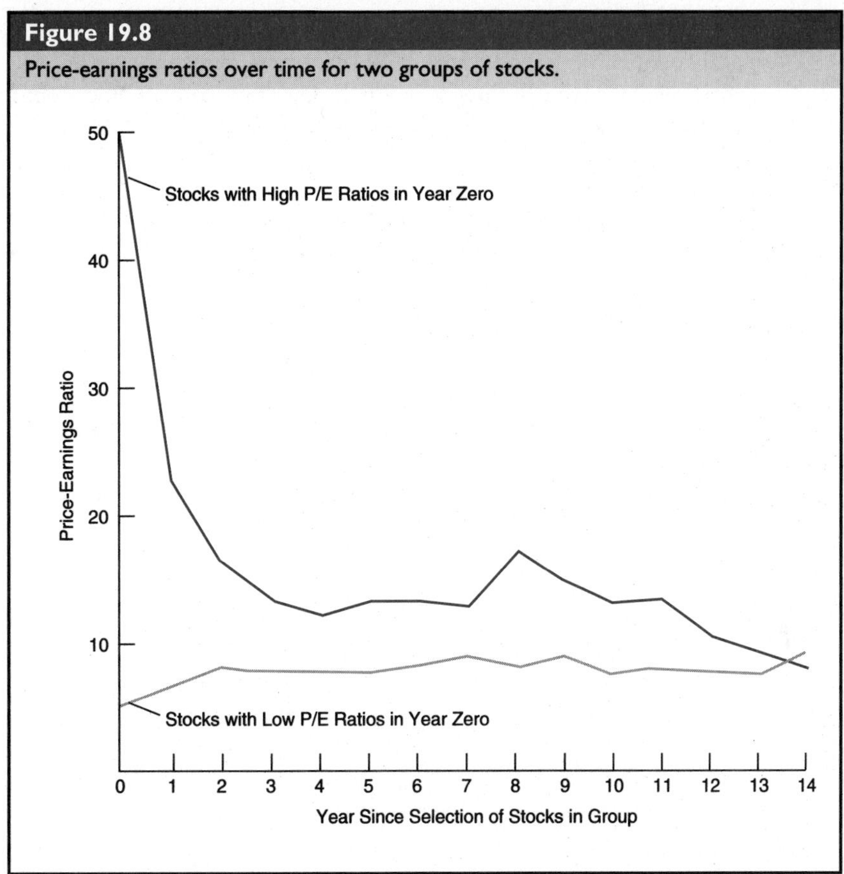

SOURCE: William Beaver and Dale Morse, "What Determines Price-Earnings Ratios?" *Financial Analysts Journal* 34, no. 4 (July/August 1978): 68.

price-earnings ratio because this component will sometimes be positive and sometimes be negative. As a result, a firm's price-earnings ratio will be variable over time, as was shown in Figure 19.6(a) for the S&P 500. This also means that at any point in time, the transitory component of earnings for a group of firms will have varying sizes, some being positive and some being negative. As a result, at any point in time, firms will have a range of different price-earnings ratios.

If this were a complete explanation for the considerable variation in price-earnings ratios over time and across firms, then most of the variation in a firm's price-earnings ratio would itself be transitory. That is, the ratio would vary over time around some average value. However, the evidence suggests that this is not the case. Figure 19.8 shows the behaviour over time of price-earnings ratios for two groups of stocks. The first group includes stocks with high price-earnings ratios at the beginning of the period (that is, during a portfolio formation period). The other group includes stocks with low price-earnings ratios at the beginning of the period.

Over time, the price-earnings ratios tend to revert to an average ratio for the market as a whole. The changes are substantial in the first two years, owing undoubtedly to the influence of transitory components of earnings. That is, those stocks in the high price-earnings ratio group apparently had, on average, a negative transitory component in their earnings in the portfolio formation period. (Remember that such a component would tend to give a stock a high ratio.) Conversely, those stocks in the low price-earnings ratio group apparently had, on average, a positive transitory component. (Remember that such a component would tend to give a stock a low ratio.) Over future periods, each group of stocks would tend to have an equal number of stocks with positive and negative transitory components, resulting in an average transitory component for each group of roughly zero.

However, Figure 19.8 shows that the two groups of stocks have different price-earnings ratios for many years after the portfolio formation period. Three explanations can be offered for this persistent difference.

1. Appropriate discount rates (that is, required returns) differ because of differences in security attributes. For two firms with the same current and expected future earnings, the firm with the lower discount rate will have a higher share price and hence a higher price-earnings ratio.
2. There may be permanent differences between economic and reported earnings due to the use of different accounting methods. As mentioned earlier, there is evidence that the market sees through such differences in reported earnings.
3. There may be persistent differences in the forecasts of long-term permanent earnings growth rates by security analysts. That is, firms with high price-earnings ratios may have high forecast long-term permanent earnings growth rates and hence relatively high prices. Conversely, firms with low price-earnings ratios may have low forecast long-term permanent earnings growth rates and hence relatively low prices.[15] If such forecasts persist over time, then firms with high price-earnings ratios would tend to continue having high ratios over time, while firms with low ratios would tend to continue having low ratios over time. Evidence suggests that indeed this is the case.

RELATIVE GROWTH RATES OF FIRMS' EARNINGS

Because security analysis typically involves forecasting earnings per share, it is useful to examine the historical record to see how earnings per share have changed over time. An interesting question about growth rates in firm earnings over time focuses on growth stocks. The very idea of a growth stock suggests that growth in some firms' earnings will exceed the average growth of all firms' earnings in most years, while other firms' earnings will grow less than the average.

Earnings Growth Rates

The results of a study of the earnings growth rates for 610 industrial companies from 1950 to 1964 are shown in Table 19.4. In every year, each firm's earnings were compared with its earnings in the previous year and the percentage change calculated. The year was counted as "good" for the firm if its percentage change was in the top half of the changes for all firms that year, and "bad" if it was in the bottom half. If some firms tend to experience

[15] This suggests that firms will have high price-earnings ratios if they have either negative transitory current earnings or high forecasted long-term permanent earnings, or both. The converse holds for firms with low price-earnings ratios.

Table 19.4

Earnings Growth Rates.[a]

Length of Run	*Actual Number of Good Runs*	*Actual Number of Bad Runs*	*Number of Good or Bad Runs Expected if the Odds Each Year Were 50–50 Regardless of Past Performance*
1	1152	1102	1068
2	562	590	534
3	266	300	267
4	114	120	133
5	55	63	67
6	24	20	33
7	23	12	17
8	5	6	8
9	3	3	4
10	6	0	2
11	2	0	1
12	1	0	1
13	0	0	0
14	0	1	0

[a] Based on 610 firms during the period 1950–1964.

SOURCE: Richard A. Brealey, *An Introduction to Risk and Return from Common Stocks* (Cambridge, MA: MIT Press, 1983), p. 89.

above-average earnings growth rates, then fairly long runs of good years should occur for these firms. Conversely, if some firms tend to experience below-average earnings growth rates, then they should have fairly long runs of bad years.

The middle two columns of Table 19.4 indicate the actual number of runs of various lengths. The right-hand column shows the number that would be expected if there were a 50–50 chance of either a good year or a bad year. The three columns are remarkably similar. Above-average earnings growth in the past does not appear to indicate above-average growth in the future; and below-average growth in the past does not appear to indicate below-average growth in the future. Flipping a coin seems to be as reliable a predictor of future growth as looking at past growth rates.

A study using longer time periods for measuring growth reached generally similar conclusions.[16] For each of 323 companies with positive earnings in each year from 1946 through 1965, average growth rates were computed for (1) the period from 1946 through

[16] John Lintner and Robert Glauber, "Higgledy Piggledy Growth in America," in James Lorie and Richard Brealey, eds., *Modern Developments in Investment Management* (Hinsdale, IL: Dryden Press, 1978). However, a more recent study came to a different conclusion concerning the predictability of earnings changes. This study divided a large number of companies into five groups based on their earnings-to-price (E/P) ratios, and found that lower E/P stock groups exhibited consistently higher long-term earnings growth rates. See Russell J. Fuller, Lex C. Huberts, and Michael Levinson, "It's Not Higgledy-Piggledy Growth!" *Journal of Portfolio Management* 18, no. 2 (Winter 1992): 38–45. Also see H. Bradlee Perry, "Analyzing Growth Stocks: What's a Good Growth Rate?", *AAII Journal* 13, no. 9 (October 1991): 7–10.

1955 and (2) the period from 1956 through 1965. Differences among firms' earnings growth rates in the first period accounted for less than 1% of the variation in the differences among their earnings growth rates in the second period.

Annual Earnings

The results of these and other studies suggest that *annual reported earnings* follow what is known in statistics as a **random walk model**. That is, annual earnings for the forthcoming year (E_t) can be thought of as being equal to annual earnings over the past year (E_{t-1}) plus a random error term. (Remember that a random error term can be thought of as a roulette wheel where the numbers on the wheel are distributed around zero.) Accordingly, next year's earnings can be described by the following statistical model:

$$E_t = E_{t-1} + \epsilon_t \tag{19.16}$$

where ϵ_t is the random error term. With this model, the estimate of next year's earnings is simply the past year's earnings, E_{t-1}. Another way of viewing a random walk model for earnings is that the change in earnings is independent and identically distributed:

$$E_t - E_{t-1} + \epsilon_t. \tag{19.17}$$

This means that the change in earnings, $E_t - E_{t-1}$, is unrelated to past changes in earnings and can be thought of as a spin from a roulette wheel that is perhaps unique to the firm but, more importantly, is used year after year. Because the expected outcome from a spin of the roulette wheel is zero, the expected change in earnings is zero. This implies that the expected level of earnings is equal to the past year's earnings, as was suggested earlier.[17]

Quarterly Earnings

In terms of *quarterly reported earnings*, consideration must be given to the fact that there is typically a seasonal component to a firm's earnings (for example, many firms have high earnings during the quarter that includes Christmas). As a result, a slightly different model appears to be best for forecasting purposes. This model forecasts the growth in earnings for the forthcoming quarter relative to the same quarter one year ago, a quantity denoted $QE_t - QE_{t-4}$. It does so by relating this growth to the growth during the most recent quarter relative to the comparable quarter one year before it, $QE_{t-1} - QE_{t-5}$. Formally, the model for the "seasonally differenced series" of quarterly earnings is known as an *autoregressive model of order one*, and is as follows:

$$QE_t - QE_{t-4} = a(QE_{t-1} - QE_{t-5}) + b + e_t \tag{19.18}$$

where a and b are constants and e_t is a random error term.

---

[17] Some people [for example, Jane Ou and Stephen H. Penman, "Financial Statement Analysis and the Prediction of Stock Returns," *Journal of Accounting and Economics* 11, no. 4 (November 1989): 295–329] think that a "random walk with drift" model as follows is more accurate:

$$E_t - E_{t-1} = \delta + \epsilon_t$$

where δ is a positive constant that represents the "drift" term. With this model, the expected change in earnings is equal to δ. Note how the random walk model given in equation (19.17) is a special case where $\delta = 0$.

Alternatively, the model can be rewritten by moving the term QE_{t-4} to the right-hand side:

$$QE_t = QE_{t-4} + a(QE_{t-1} - QE_{t-5}) + b + e_t. \quad (19.19)$$

By estimating the constants a and b, this model can be used to forecast quarterly earnings.[18]

For example, assuming estimates for a and b of .4 and .05, respectively, the forecast of a firm's earnings for the next quarter would be equal to $QE_{t-4} + .4(QE_{t-1} - QE_{t-5}) + \$.05$. Thus, if a firm had earnings per share for the last quarter $(t - 1)$ of \$3, for four quarters before now $(t-4)$ of \$2, and for five quarters before now $(t-5)$ of \$2.60, then its forecasted earnings for the forthcoming quarter would be equal to \$2 + .4(\$3 – \$2.60) + \$.05 = \$2.21. Note how the forecast consists of three components—a component equal to last quarter's earnings (\$2); a component that considers the year-to-year quarterly growth in earnings (.4[\$3 – \$2.60] = \$.16); and a component that is a constant (\$.05).[19]

CO-MOVEMENT OF EARNINGS

Past changes in security prices are of limited value for the prediction of future changes. And past changes in the overall level of the market are of limited help in the prediction of future market moves. However, security price changes are related to concurrent changes in the prices of the market portfolio and, to a lesser extent, an "industry" portfolio.[20] Although the strength of these relationships differs among securities, historical data can generally be utilized to help estimate the relative future strengths of the relationships for different securities. For example, the relationship between a security's returns and market returns has been referred to as the security's *beta* and can be estimated by examining historical returns. Similarly, the industry that a security belongs to can be determined and a portfolio of stocks in that industry constructed. Then the historical returns on the security can be compared to this portfolio, and an industry beta can be estimated.

It has been argued that security prices are determined by economic earnings, and that security price movements are related to movements in market and industry prices. Thus, an interesting issue is whether or not movements in the economic earnings of a firm are related to movements in the economic earnings of the market and industry portfolios. Such an issue has been explored by looking at accounting earnings and assuming that they are correlated with economic earnings.

---

[18] This model can also be used to forecast annual earnings by working forward one quarter at a time and then adding up the forecasts for the forthcoming four quarters. Doing so would result in a forecast of annual earnings (E_t) equal to $E_{t-1} + c(QE_{t-1} - QE_{t-5}) + d$, where $c = a^1 + a^2 + a^3 + a^4$ and $d = 4b + 3ab + 2a^2b + a^3b$. Note that the random walk model is a special case where a and b are equal to zero, thereby making c and d equal to zero.

[19] It has been argued that an improvement can be made in this model by either (1) adding to the right-hand side the term $c(QE_{t-4} - QE_{t-8})$ where c is a constant or (2) by multiplying the constant b term by the random error term that occurred four quarters ago now (e_{t-4}). See P. A. Griffin, "The Time-Series Behaviour of Quarterly Earnings: Preliminary Evidence," *Journal of Accounting Research* 15, no. 1 (Spring 1977): 71–83; Lawrence D. Brown and Michael S. Rozeff, "Univariate Time-Series Models of Quarterly Accounting Earnings per Share: A Proposed Model," *Journal of Accounting Research* 17, no. 1 (Spring 1979): 179–189; and Allen W. Bathke, Jr. and Kenneth S. Lorek, "The Relationship Between Time Series Models and the Security Market's Expectations of Quarterly Earnings," *Accounting Review* 59, no. 2 (April 1984): 163–176.

[20] Although the definition of what constitutes an "industry" differs from one study to another, various authors have found that security price movements can be attributed not only to market price movements but also to industry price movements. See Alexander and Francis, *Portfolio Analysis*, pp. 195–196, for a description of these studies and the relevant citations.

Table 19.5

The Proportion of the Variation of a Firm's Earnings Attributable to Market-wide and Industry-wide Earnings Changes.

	Proportion Attributable to	
Industy	*Market-wide Earnings Changes*	*Additional Influence of Changes in Industry-wide Earnings*
Aircraft	11%	5%
Autos	48	11
Beer	11	7
Cement	6	32
Chemicals	41	8
Cosmetics	5	6
Department stores	30	37
Drugs	14	7
Electricals	24	8
Food	10	10
Machinery	19	16
Nonferrous metals	26	25
Office machinery	14	6
Oil	13	49
Paper	27	28
Rubber	26	48
Steel	32	21
Supermarkets	6	33
Textiles and clothing	25	29
Tobacco	8	19
All firms	21	21

SOURCE: Richard Brealey, "Some Implications of the Comovement of American Company Earnings," *Applied Economics* 3, no. 3 (September 1971): 187.

Table 19.5 shows that such relationships do exist. Earnings reported by 217 corporations from 1948 through 1966 were compared first with the earnings for Standard & Poor's 425-stock index (which served as a surrogate for marketwide earnings) and then with the average earnings of all firms in the same industry. The proportion of each firm's earnings variations that could be attributed to each of these factors was determined. The results shown in the table are the average proportions for all the firms in each industry.

The results differ notably from one industry to another, with the marketwide factor ranging between 5% and 48% and the industry factor ranging from 5% to 49%. The bottom row of the table shows the values obtained by averaging over all 217 corporations. Changes in market-wide earnings accounted for 21% of the variation in the earnings of the typical firm, and changes in the earnings of firms in its industry accounted for another 21%.

Earlier, it was mentioned that a security's beta (sometimes known as its **market beta**) is a measure of how the price of the security will co-vary with the price of the market portfolio.

Similarly, a security's **accounting beta** is a measure of how the accounting earnings of the security will co-vary with the accounting earnings of the market portfolio. If security prices are related to earnings, then it seems reasonable to expect market betas to be related to accounting betas. Studies that have examined this issue have found that market and accounting betas are significantly correlated, with accounting betas explaining between 20% and 40% of the variation that is observed in market betas.

EARNINGS ANNOUNCEMENTS AND PRICE CHANGES

A number of studies have shown large price changes for stocks of companies that report earnings that differ substantially from consensus expectations. One study looked at three groups of 50 stocks.[21] The first group consisted of the 50 stocks listed on the New York Stock Exchange (NYSE) that experienced the greatest price rise during 1970. The second group consisted of 50 stocks chosen randomly from all those listed on the NYSE during 1970. The third group consisted of the 50 stocks listed on the NYSE that experienced the greatest price decline during 1970. As shown in Figure 19.9, the median changes in the prices of the shares in the top, random, and bottom groups were 48.4%, –3.2%, and –56.7%, respectively.

Next, the study looked at the actual change in earnings per share from 1969 to 1970 for each stock in each group. As shown in Figure 19.9, the median changes in earnings per share for the top, random, and bottom groups were 21.4%, –10.5%, and –83.0%, respectively.

Lastly, the study determined the forecasted change in earnings per share at the beginning of 1970 for each stock in each group. This was done by using the predictions contained in Standard & Poor's *Earnings Forecaster*, where estimates made by a number of investment research organizations are reported. The median forecasted changes in earnings per share for the top, random, and bottom groups are shown in Figure 19.9 to be 7.7%, 5.8%, and 15.3%, respectively.

Interestingly, the forecasts of earnings per share hardly correspond to the price movements of the shares. In fact, the earnings of the stocks in the bottom group were expected to increase more than the earnings of the stocks in the top group (15.3%, compared with 7.7%). However, the prediction for the bottom group was disastrously wrong, with a median earnings-per-share decline of 83.0%. And, as Figure 19.9 shows, prices definitely followed suit. Overall, it appears that unexpected changes in earnings do indeed affect security prices.[22]

But do earnings surprises affect prices before or after their announcement? In a completely efficient market, such information would be reflected in prices as soon as it had been disseminated to a few major market participants. The reaction of security prices around the time of earnings announcements has been examined by a number of authors and will be discussed next.

---

[21] Victor Niederhoffer and Patrick J. Regan, "Earnings Changes, Analysts' Forecasts, and Stock Prices," *Financial Analysts Journal* 28, no. 3 (May–June 1972): 65–71. It should be noted that the entire June/September 1992 issue of the *Journal of Accounting and Economics* is devoted to an examination of how share prices are related to earnings and other financial statement information.

[22] Another study using data from 1980 and 1981 reached similar conclusions. That is, the top 50 stocks had forecasted and actual earnings growth rates of 14.3% and 31.3%, respectively. For the bottom 50 stocks the respective rates were 17.4% and –10.3%. See Gary A. Benesh and Pamela P. Peterson, "On the Relation Between Earnings Changes, Analysts' Forecasts and Stock Price Fluctuations," *Financial Analysts Journal* 42, no. 6 (November/December 1986): 29–39, 55.

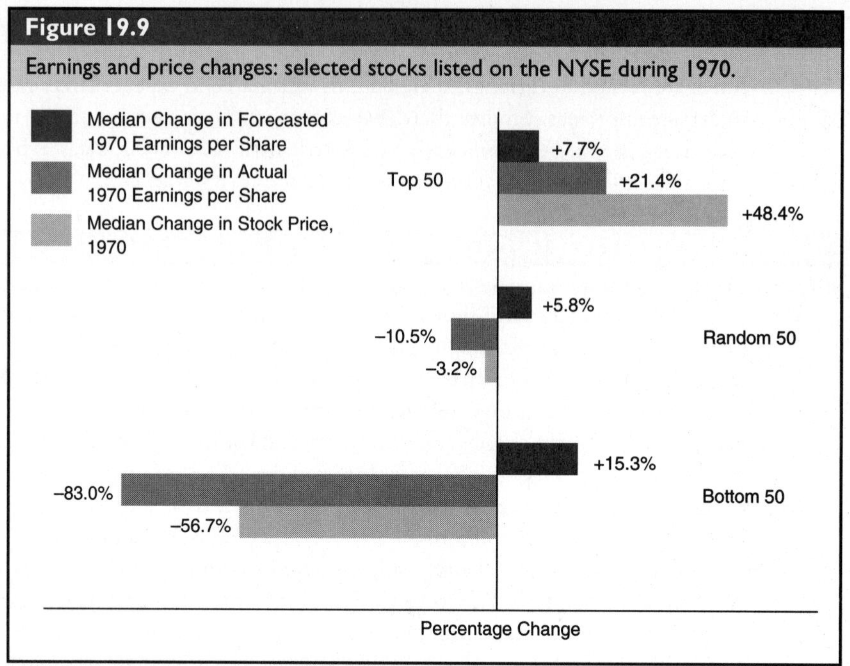

Figure 19.9

Earnings and price changes: selected stocks listed on the NYSE during 1970.

SOURCE: Victor Niederhoffer and Patrick J. Regan, "Earnings Changes, Analysts' Forecasts, and Stock Prices," *Financial Analysts Journal* 28, no. 3 (May/June 1972): 67.

Deviations from Time-Series Models of Earnings

A comprehensive study involving 2053 firms from 1974 through 1981 provided evidence concerning the speed of response of security prices to earnings announcements.[23] For each company, an expected earnings figure was computed for each quarter by using the model of the time-series behaviour of earnings shown in equation (19.19). With this model, the expected earnings for a firm during period t was equal to $QE_{t-4} + a(QE_{t-1} - QE_{t-5}) + b$. For example, the earnings expected for the firm in the second quarter of 1996 would equal (1) the firm's earnings in the second quarter of 1995, plus (2) the change in earnings from the first quarter of 1995 to the first quarter of 1996 times the parameter a, plus (3) the parameter b. The values of a and b would be determined by analysis of the behaviour of earnings prior to the second quarter of 1996.

Given actual earnings and an estimate of expected earnings, a forecast error (FE_t) can be computed for the firm:

$$FE_t = QE_t - \overline{QE}_t \qquad (19.20)$$

where QE_t are the actual earnings for quarter t and QE_t are the expected earnings for quarter t, forecast at time $t - 1$. Simply stated, equation (19.20) indicates that the forecast error for a quarter is the difference between actual earnings for that quarter and expected earnings.

---

[23] George Foster, Chris Olsen, and Terry Shevlin, "Earnings Releases, Anomalies, and the Behaviour of Security Returns," *Accounting Review*, 59, no. 4 (October 1984): 574–603. For a related paper, see Roger Kormendi and Robert Lipe, "Earnings Innovations, Earnings Persistence, and Stock Returns," *Journal of Business* 60, no. 3 (July 1987): 323–345.

The forecast error provides a measure of the "surprise" in the quarterly earnings announcement, but it fails to differentiate between stocks for which large forecast errors are routine and those for which they are rare. The important surprises are those associated with forecast errors that are large by historical standards. To account for this, a forecast error can be related to previous errors to obtain a measure of **standardized unexpected earnings** (SUE):

$$\text{SUE}_t = \frac{FE_t}{\sigma_{FE_t}} \tag{19.21}$$

where σ_{FE_t} is the standard deviation of forecast errors over the twenty quarterly earnings of the firm prior to t. (That is, forecast errors were determined for each one of the 20 quarters before t, then the standard deviation for this set of 20 errors was estimated.)

For example, a firm with a forecast of earnings per share of \$3 that subsequently reports actual earnings of \$5 will have a forecast error of \$5 – \$3 = \$2. That is, the earnings announcement will "surprise" people by \$2. Now, if the standard deviation of past errors is \$.80, this surprise will be notable, as the standardized unexpected earnings (SUE) equal \$2/\$.80 = 2.50.[24] However, if the standard deviation is \$4, then this surprise will be minor, because SUE will equal (\$2/\$4 =).50. Thus, a large positive value for SUE would indicate that the earnings announcement contained significant good news, whereas a large negative SUE would indicate that the earnings announcement contained significant bad news.

In the study, the SUEs associated with all the earnings announcements for all the sampled firms were ranked from smallest to largest. Then they were divided into ten equal-sized groups based on the ranking. Group 1 consisted of those announcements resulting in the most negative SUEs, and group 10 consisted of those with the most positive SUEs.

After forming these ten groups, the stock returns for each firm in each group were measured for the period from 60 days before its earnings announcement through 60 days after its announcement. Figure 19.10 shows the **abnormal return** for the average firm in each of the ten groups for three different time periods.

Figure 19.10(a) shows the average abnormal return for the period from 60 days before the earnings announcement through the day the announcement appeared in the *Wall Street Journal.* This period is denoted (–60, 0).

Figure 19.10(b) shows the average abnormal return for the two-day period consisting of the day before the announcement appeared in the *Wall Street Journal* and the day the announcement appeared, a period that is denoted (–1, 0). Because day 0 is the day the announcement appeared in the *Wall Street Journal*, day –1 is the day the announcement was made to the public. If this announcement was made after trading hours on day –1, investors would not have been able to buy or sell the stock until the next day, day 0. If the announcement was made during trading hours on day –1, then investors could have acted on that day. Due to the inability to pinpoint the hour of the announcement, the return over the two-day period was examined to see the immediate impact of the announcement on the price of the security.

Figure 19.10(c) shows the average abnormal return for the period from the day after the announcement through 60 days after the announcement, a period that is denoted (1, 60).

---

[24] Assume that a firm's earnings are normally distributed and that this distribution remains unchanged over time. Accordingly, 67% of the actual earnings should fall within one standard deviation of the firm's expected earnings. Equivalently, 67% of the SUEs should be less than 1.0. Similarly, 95% of the SUEs should be less than 2.0.

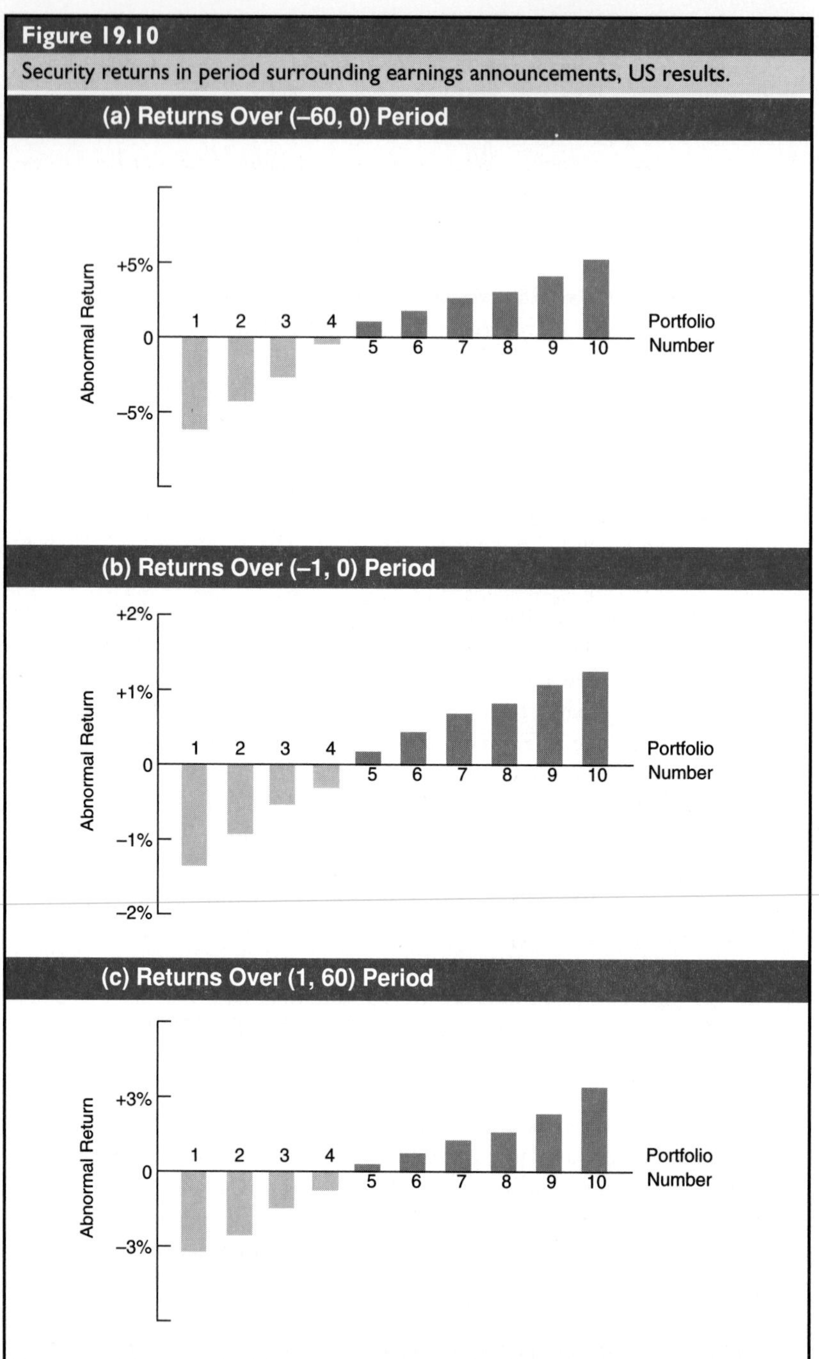

SOURCE: George Foster, Chris Olsen, and Terry Shevlin, "Earnings Releases, Anomalies, and the Behaviour of Security Returns," *Accounting Review* 59, no. 4 (October 1984): 587.

Figure 19.10(a) shows that prices of firms that announced unexpectedly high earnings (such as SUE group 10) tended to increase *prior* to the announcement (day 0), suggesting that information relevant to the earnings announcement was becoming available to the market prior to the actual announcement. Conversely, prices of firms that announced unexpectedly low earnings (such as SUE group 1) tended to decrease *prior* to the announcement, undoubtedly for the same reason. In general, there seems to be a strong direct correspondence between the size of the unexpected earnings and the size of the abnormal return. Note that if an investor knew what the earnings were going to be 60 days before the announcement, then he or she could exploit this information by either buying the stock (if the firm was going to announce unexpected large earnings), or short selling the stock (if the firm was going to announce unexpected low earnings). However, because investors typically do not have prior access to earnings, such exploitation is generally impossible. Thus, the existence of abnormal returns prior to the announcement date does not necessarily indicate some sort of market inefficiency.

Figure 19.10(b) shows that the larger the size of the unexpected earnings, the larger the price movement during the two-day period surrounding the announcement. For example, firms in SUE group 1 had an abnormal return of 11.34%, while those in SUE group 10 had an abnormal return of 1.26%. As in (a), there is a direct relationship between the size of the unexpected earnings and the abnormal stock return.[25] Thus, it appears that the market reacted in a predictable fashion, pushing up the share prices of those firms announcing good news and pushing down the share prices of those firms announcing bad news.

As shown in (c), the changes in share prices after the announcement dates are quite remarkable in that they appear to suggest a market inefficiency. Prices of shares of firms announcing unexpectedly high earnings tended to increase for many days *after* the announcement (the average abnormal return over the 60-day period after the announcement was 3.23% for SUE group 10). Conversely, the prices of firms announcing unexpectedly low earnings tended to decrease for many days *after* the announcement (the average abnormal return over the 60-day period subsequent to the announcement was 13.08% for SUE group 1).

As was noted in (a) and (b), there seems to be a strong direct correspondence between the size of the unexpected earnings and the size of the abnormal return. This observation suggests that an investor could make abnormal returns by simply looking at quarterly earnings announcements and, based on the magnitude and sign of the unexpected component, acting appropriately. That is, if the firm announced earnings that were notably above expectations, the investor should subsequently purchase some of the firm's shares. In contrast, if the announced earnings were notably below expectations, the investor should subsequently sell any holdings and perhaps even short-sell the firm's shares. Announcements of earnings that were reasonably close to expectations would not motivate either a buy or a sell order.

---

[25] Studies have shown that earnings announcements containing good news are often made earlier than expected, while those containing bad news are often made later than expected. These studies also show that the "timeliness" (defined as the difference between the actual announcement date and the expected announcement date) affects the size of the abnormal return. Interestingly, around the time of earnings announcements there appears to be both increased trading volume and increased variability in security returns. See George Foster, *Financial Statement Analysis* (Englewood Cliffs, NJ: Prentice Hall, 1986): 377–386; and V. V. Chari, Ravi Jagannathan, and Aharon Ofer, "Seasonalities in Security Returns: The Case of Earnings Announcements," *Journal of Financial Economics* 21, no. 1 (May 1988): 101–121.

Figure 19.11

Security returns in period surrounding earnings announcements, Canadian results.

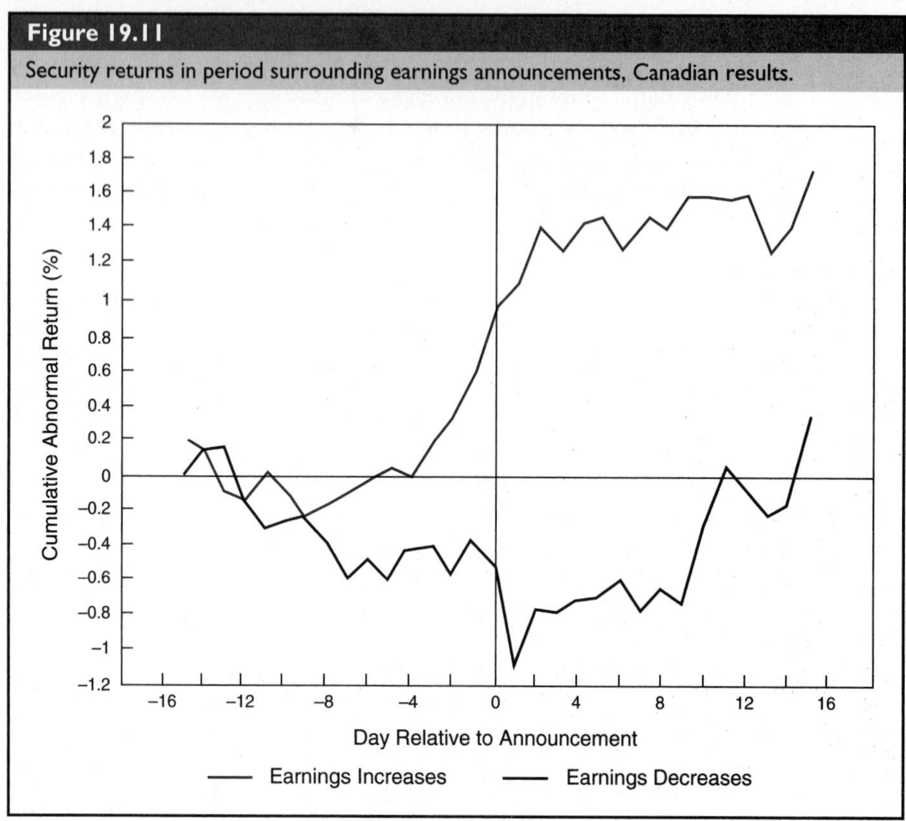

SOURCE: Adapted from J. Desrochers, "Bénefice annuel et réaction boursière au Canada," *Finéco* I, no. I (automne 1991): 72.

Accordingly, the "post-earnings-announcement drift" can be viewed as an empirical anomaly that is inconsistent with the notion of semistrong efficient markets.[26]

Figure 19.11 shows the TSE's reaction to earnings announcements for 400 earnings increases and 300 earnings decreases over the 1980–84 period.[27] A simple no-change forecasting model was used to determine the magnitude of the earnings' "surprises." Positive (negative) and significant forecast errors were observed following earnings increases (decreases). The upward drift following the announcement of the increases suggests that some inefficiencies may exist in the Canadian market. Whether or not these can be profitably exploited remains a moot question.

---

[26] One article argues that the post-earnings-announcement drift should be listed with the set of empirical regularities described in the appendix to Chapter 17. See Charles P. Jones and Bruce Bublitz, "The CAPM and Equity Return Regularities: An Extension," *Financial Analysts Journal* 43, no. 3 (May/June 1987): 77–79.

[27] J. Desrochers, "Bénéfice annuel et réaction boursière au Canada," *Finéco*, 1, no. 1 (automne 1991): 61–80.

Unexpected Earnings and Abnormal Returns

One plausible explanation for the abnormal returns associated with large SUEs concerns the cost of information transfer. "New news" must reach a large number of investors before the appropriate new equilibrium price can be completely established. Although large institutional investors can obtain news quickly, it may take some time before it reaches smaller institutional investors and individuals. Thus, after an earnings announcement there can be a period of abnormal price movement that is related in sign and magnitude to the nature of the announcement.

Alternatively, perhaps the measurement of "abnormal" returns has been in error. In making such a measurement, a determination of what is a "normal" return must be made. Such a determination is not straightforward but instead is fraught with difficulty. This means that the estimated abnormal returns could actually be due to measurement errors, leaving open the possibility that a more accurate measure of "normal return" would have resulted in no significant abnormal returns.

Nevertheless, there appear to be striking differences in subsequent stock returns for firms with different SUEs. Although the magnitudes of the return differences may be too small to warrant extensive trading, they do suggest the consideration of such things as SUE values and forecast revisions when money must be invested or a portion of an existing portfolio must be liquidated.

Security Analysts' Forecasts of Future Earnings

In using only the historical record of past earnings to forecast future earnings, it was mentioned earlier that an autoregressive model of order one, as shown in equation (19.19), seemed to work about as well as any other model. However, security analysts do not restrict themselves to just past earnings when developing their forecasts. Instead, they look at many different pieces of information. This raises several interesting questions. How well can analysts forecast earnings? And do their forecasts incorporate information other than that contained in past earnings? The results of two studies that provide some answers to these questions are shown in Tables 19.6 and 19.7.

Table 19.6

Accuracy of Mechanical and Judgmental Earnings Forecasts.

Earnings Forecast Error as a Percentage of Actual Earnings	Percentage of Forecasts with a Smaller Error	
	Mechanical Model	*Analysts' Forecasts*
5%	15.0%	18.0%
10	26.5	32.0
25	54.5	63.5
50	81.0	86.5
75	87.5	90.5
100	89.5	92.0

SOURCE: Lawrence D. Brown and Michael S. Rozeff, "The Superiority of Analyst Forecasts as Measures of Expectations: Evidence from Earnings," *Journal of Finance* 33, no. 1 (March 1978): 7–8.

Table 19.7

Forecast Accuracy of Time-Series Models and Security Models.

	Days before Annual Announcement Date			
Model	*240*	*180*	*120*	*60*
Random walk	$.963	$.781	$.620	$.363
Autoregressive	.975	.780	.592	.350
Average analyst	.747	.645	.516	.395
Current analyst	.742	.610	.468	.342

SOURCE: Adapted from Patricia C. O'Brien, "Analysts' Forecasts as Earnings Expectations," *Journal of Accounting and Economics* 10, no. 1 (January 1988): Table 4.

Forecasts of Analysts

In one study, illustrated in Table 19.6, two sets of forecasts were examined for the quarterly earnings of 50 firms over the period from 1971 through 1975.[28] The first set was obtained by applying sophisticated mechanical models, such as the autoregressive model of equation (19.19), to each firm's previous earnings history. The second set was obtained from the earnings forecasts of security analysts as reported in the *Value Line Investment Survey*.[29] The results suggest that the analysts outperformed the mechanical model. For example, 63.5% of the analysts' forecasts were within 25% of the actual earnings values, while only 54.4% of the forecasts made via mechanical models came as close. Analysts appear to base their forecasts on both past earnings and other information, and the latter appears to help.

In another study, forecasts of annual earnings made by security analysts approximately 240, 180, 120, and 60 days before the announcement date of actual earnings were examined.[30] Typically these days correspond to dates in each of the year's fiscal quarters before the announcement date. Hence, 240 days falls roughly between last year's earnings announcement and this year's first quarter earnings announcement, 180 days falls roughly between the first quarter and second quarter earnings announcement, and so on. These forecasts, made over the period from 1975 to 1982 by analysts at between 50 and 130 brokerage firms, were obtained from the Institutional Brokers Estimate System (I/B/E/S) database developed by the brokerage firm of Lynch, Jones, & Ryan.

Table 19.7 presents a comparison of the accuracy of four forecasts. The first forecast, denoted RW, is the annual forecast generated by using a model like the random walk model of equation (19.16). The second, denoted AR, is the annual forecast produced by using an autoregressive model like the one shown in equation (19.19). The third is the average forecast published by I/B/E/S, and the fourth is the single most current individual forecast published by I/B/E/S.

---

28 Lawrence D. Brown and Michael S. Rozeff, "The Superiority of Analyst Forecasts as Measures of Expectations: Evidence from Earnings," *Journal of Finance* 33, no. 1 (March 1978): 1–16.

29 Value Line also ranks stocks in terms of their relative attractiveness as investments. For a discussion of the usefulness of the Value Line rankings, see the appendix.

30 Patricia C. O'Brien, "Analysts' Forecasts as Earnings Expectations," *Journal of Accounting and Economics* 10, no. 1 (January 1988): 53–83.

Consensus Earnings Expectations

Reference is frequently made in the financial press to "market" or "consensus" expectations. We may read that the "market" expects inflation to remain stable or that the "market" expects the Bank of Canada to raise interest rates. Given that the market is the amalgam of a large, diverse group of investors, how does anyone determine what the market really expects?

Of course, the most important market expectations are established and published daily—that is, the expected values of corporate assets as reflected in security prices. But what about market expectations regarding economic and financial variables that underlie security prices? In general, these expectations are reported anecdotally, perhaps through interviews with prominent investors or through a variety of surveys.

Investing based on such ambiguous information is problematic. Abnormal returns can be earned only by staking out positions based on expectations contrary to those of the market. Superior investors will consistently identify securities for which market expectations are somehow in error. But unless these investors can correctly interpret the market's expectations, they will not know whether their expectations are significantly different from those of the market.

As the text discusses, earnings expectations are the most important determinant of common share prices. If an investor can identify companies for which the market is under- or overestimating future earnings, the investor can appropriately buy and sell these stocks to produce portfolio returns superior to those of the market on a risk-adjusted basis.

Many organizations publish earnings estimates, including Standard & Poor's, Value Line, and brokerage houses. However, individually these estimates do not represent market expectations; they are merely the opinions of specific analysts. What is needed is a way to collect the earnings estimates of many analysts following a particular company. That need has been satisfied for over 20 years by a firm called Institutional Brokers Estimate System, or I/B/E/S.

While I/B/E/S is not the only company collecting earnings expectations data (Zacks Investment Research is a prominent competitor), it was the first and it remains the leader in the field. I/B/E/S was formed in 1971. Its initial objectives were modest—to collect timely earnings estimates from brokerage firms on several hundred large, well-followed companies. These estimates were then compiled and the distributions of earnings estimates (high, low, median, measure of dispersion) were periodically reported to subscribers.

For example, suppose that an institutional investment firm was estimating earnings next year of \$2.50 per share for XYZ company and \$3.30 per share for ABC company. Through I/B/E/S, the institutional investor might find that the consensus earnings estimates for XYZ and ABC were currently \$1.50 and \$3.50, respectively. Further, the coefficient of variation (standard deviation divided by mean—a measure of the estimates' relative dispersion) was 0.20 for XYZ and 0.80 for ABC. If the institutional investor has confidence in its own estimates, then it should expect XYZ stock to perform relatively well. The market's earnings expectations are tight around the \$1.50 level, which is \$1.00 less than the investor's estimate. If the market comes to realize that \$2.50 is the actual level of XYZ earnings, it will likely bid the company's share price up.

ABC shares are much less attractive. The institutional investor's estimate is less than the consensus by \$0.20, so it might wish to sell ABC out of its portfolio if it owned the stock or perhaps even short sell the stock. However, the relatively high dispersion of estimates around the median indicates that the market's expectations are not firm. If ABC's earnings actually come

INSTITUTIONAL ISSUES (continued)

in at \$3.30, the result may not be a particularly unpleasant surprise to the market, and therefore may have little impact on ABC's stock price.

The advantages of using consensus earnings expectations in common stock analysis quickly caught on among institutional investors. Today, I/B/E/S receives, compiles, and distributes earnings estimates from over 6000 equity analysts in nearly 600 research departments in over 33 countries. Although by far the most intense analyst earnings coverage is for US companies, the contributing I/B/E/S analysts now cover over 13 000 companies in 39 equity markets around the world. Even companies in emerging equity markets such as the People's Republic of China, Sri Lanka, and Chile have attracted institutional analysts' coverage and have been included in the I/B/E/S service.

I/B/E/S collects earnings estimates in a number of ways, including faxes, diskettes, telephone calls, and printed reports. Many research firms now provide I/B/E/S with data directly by computer. Upon receipt of analysts' earnings estimates, I/B/E/S staffers perform several quality checks to ensure the integrity of the data. At that point, the estimates are entered into the firm's database. Summary consensus numbers are updated daily and made available to I/B/E/S subscribers.

The original I/B/E/S reports were simply printed books containing summary data on individual company earnings estimates. Although the original printed format is still available, I/B/E/S now provides data through a variety of electronic vendors. For example, I/B/E/S data can be accessed through an optical disk data delivery system that can easily bring earnings expectation data into an electronic spreadsheet for detailed analysis.

Customers can now receive I/B/E/S data diced and sliced in a number of ways. The firm makes available to subscribers analyst-by-analyst data, daily alerts of analyst changes, and custom-designed reports. The firm also provides commentaries and analyses of market trends that it discerns from the earnings estimate data.

The systematic collection of earnings estimates is an excellent example of the forces that have been increasing the efficiency of security markets. Before I/B/E/S collected such data, consensus earnings estimates were difficult to obtain and highly ambiguous. Now those estimates are rigorously quantified and widely distributed, decreasing the likelihood of investors acting on incomplete or erroneous information.

Forecast accuracy for a particular model and firm is measured by absolute forecast error, or

$$FE = |A - F|. \tag{19.22}$$

where F denotes the forecast and A denotes the subsequent actual earnings of the firm.

There are several interesting observations to be made from Table 19.7. First, as the announcement date gets closer, all of the forecasting models become more accurate. This is hardly surprising, because more information is available as the announcement date gets closer. Second, for long horizons both the average and most current forecasts are more accurate than either of the time-series models. Third, the current forecast is more accurate than any of the other models. However, subsequent examination of the forecasts indicates that the average forecast was more accurate than the most current forecast, provided that none of the individual forecasts used to determine the average was "stale" (that is, more than roughly a week old). This is because such averaging reduces the forecast error by having individual forecast errors offset each other (that is, positive errors will offset negative errors, resulting in a smaller error for the average forecast).

Another interesting observation that has been uncovered about security analysts' forecasts is that they tend to be too optimistic, meaning that they tend to have an upward bias (more on this shortly). Hence most of the typical analysts' revisions are downward. One interpretation of this observation is that many of the analysts work for brokerage firms and thus find it in their employers' best interest (and thus their own) to avoid antagonizing any corporation that is or might become an investment banking client.[31]

All-American Analysts

The monthly publication *Institutional Investor* announces each October its "All-American" Research Team by querying 2000 money managers.[32] These managers are asked to evaluate security analysts on the basis of (1) stock recommendations, (2) earnings forecasts, (3) written reports, and (4) overall performance. From these evaluations, analysts are selected for the Team (there is a First Team, a Second Team, a Third Team, and Runners-up) in over 60 industries as well as in such areas as portfolio strategy, quantitative analysis, economics, and market timing.

One study looked at the relative forecasting ability of All-American and non-All-American industry analysts for the fiscal years 1981–1985. Each EPS forecast of an All-American was matched with a forecast by a non-All-American for the same firm, where each forecast was made an identical number of days before the fiscal year-end. Forecast accuracy was measured by using equation (19.22). Table 19.8(a) indicates that the average forecast error for All-Americans was $.95, while non-All-Americans had an error of $.98. Hence, All-American EPS forecasts were more accurate by approximately $.03 per share.

Also examined in the study were the records of analysts in the three-year period before they became All-Americans ("future" All-Americans) and the records of All-Americans in the three-year period before they lost their exalted status and became non-All-Americans ("former" All-Americans).[33] This was done as follows.

1. The track records of future All-Americans were matched with analysts who were and remained non-All-Americans. Table 19.8(b) indicates that future All-Americans were only slightly more accurate {by [($.00 + $.01 + $.02)/3 =]$.01 per share, on average} than non-All-Americans in the three-year period before they became All-Americans.
2. The track records of former All-Americans were matched with All-Americans who maintained their Team membership ("remaining" All-Americans). Table 19.8(c) indicates that former All-Americans were less accurate than the remaining All-Americans by between $.04 and $.02 per share in the three-year period before removal.

---

31 The observation that analysts (1) tend to be too optimistic in their EPS forecasts, (2) tend to revise these forecasts downward, and (3) issue far more buy than sell recommendations has been documented in several places. See, for example, John C. Groth, Wilbur G. Lewellen, Gary Schlarbaum, and Ronald C. Lease, "An Analysis of Brokerage House Recommendations," *Financial Analysts Journal* 35, no. 1 (January/February 1979): 32–40; and Werner F. De Bondt and Richard H. Thaler, "Do Security Analysts Overreact?" *American Economic Review* 80, no. 2 (May 1990): 52–57. For a counterview, see Michael P. Keane and David E. Runkle, "Are Analysts' Forecasts Rational?", unpublished paper, November 1992, Federal Reserve Bank of Minneapolis.

32 The discussion that follows draws from Scott E. Stickel, "Reputation and Performance Among Security Analysts," *Journal of Finance* 47, no. 5 (December 1992): 1811–1836.

33 The study also found that the median number of firms analyzed by All-Americans and non-All-Americans was 14 and 8, respectively, and that All-Americans revised their forecasts within a given fiscal year on average every 86 days whereas non-All-Americans revised them every 93 days.

Table 19.8

EPS Forecast Accuracy of All-American and Non-All-American Analysts.

	Average Absolute Forecast Error[a]		
(a) While on Team:	*Non-All-Americans*	*All-Americans*	*Difference*
	\$.98	\$.95	\$.03
	(3.7%)	(3.6%)	(.1%)
(b) Before Gaining Membership:	*Non-All-Americans*	*Future All-Americans*	*Difference*
One Year Before	\$.97	\$.97	\$.00
	(3.1%)	(3.1%)	(.0%)
Two Years Before	.95	.94	.01
	(3.2%)	(3.2%)	(.0%)
Three Years Before	.96	.94	.02
	(3.5%)	(3.5%)	(.0%)
(c) Before Losing Membership:	*Former All-Americans*	*Remaining All-Americans*	*Difference*
One Year Before	\$1.03	\$1.01	\$.02
	(3.8%)	(3.7%)	(.1%)
Two Years Before	.91	.88	.03
	(3.3%)	(3.3%)	(.0%)
Three Years Before	.91	.87	.04
	(2.8%)	(2.7%)	(.1%)

[a] The numbers shown in parentheses below the average absolute forecast error represent the average of the percentage absolute forecast errors where the percentage is calculated as $|A - F|/A$ where A = actual and F = forecast.

SOURCE: Scott E. Stickel, "Reputation and Performance Among Security Analysts," *Journal of Finance* 47, no. 5 (December 1992): 1818, 1819, 1821.

Given the nearly indistinguishable differences in earnings forecasting performance between All-Americans and non-All-Americans, the reasons for Team membership appear to be explained by other factors, such as high-quality company research or good personal relationships with money managers.

The study also documented the existence of forecast bias. This bias was measured by the average forecast error, where the forecast error for a given analyst is

$$FE = A - F. \tag{19.23}$$

As before, F denotes the forecast and A denotes the subsequent actual earnings of the firm. Note how equation (19.23) is identical to equation (19.22), except that absolute values are no longer used. The average forecast error for All-Americans was \$ – .73 per share (or 2.9% of the actual EPS). For non-All-Americans the comparable figure was \$ – .74 (or 3.0%). Given that the average FE was negative, this means that both types of analysts tended to overestimate the level of EPS. As mentioned earlier, this is clear evidence of both All-Americans' and non-All-Americans' being too optimistic in forecasting EPS.

Management Forecasts of Future Earnings

Often management itself will make a forecast of next year's earnings for the firm. Generally, the forecasts of security analysts are not as accurate as the forecasts of management when both sets of forecasts are made about the same time, as shown in Table 19.8.[34] Here, average security analysts' forecasts, as reported weekly by Zacks Investment Research's Icarus Service, were compared with corresponding management forecasts.[35] The objective was to see who was the more accurate forecaster. To do this, forecast errors (FE) were calculated for both sets of forecasts as

$$FE = |(F - A)/A| \tag{19.24}$$

where F is the earnings forecast and A is the actual earnings subsequently reported by the firm. Hence, an earnings forecast of \$3 per share that subsequently turned out to be \$4 would have $FE = |(\$3 - \$4)/\$4| = .25$ or 25%.

Letting $t = 0$ denote the date that the management forecast is released, analysts' forecasts were collected weekly from 12 weeks before to 12 weeks after $t = 0$. As Table 19.9 shows at the bottom, the average forecast error for management was .150. Analyst forecast errors ranged from .224 at week −12 (meaning 12 weeks prior to the date of the management forecast) to .124 at week +12. Hence, as was shown in Table 19.7, analysts' forecasts became more accurate the closer they were to the date the actual earnings were announced, because the size of the average forecast error decreases fairly steadily from $t = -12$ to $t = +12$.

Most important, however, is the observation that management forecasts were more accurate than analyst forecasts from $t = -12$ to $t = +8$ (the difference was found to be statistically significant through $t = +4$). That is, forecasts issued by analysts before, coincident to, or up to four months after management's forecast were less accurate. This observation is not surprising up to $t = 0$, as management has private information about the firm that is not available to the analysts. However, it is surprising that management forecasts were superior from $t = +1$ through $t = +4$ because it suggests that analysts could improve their accuracy simply by using management's previously released forecast. After $t = +4$, the analysts' forecasts were more accurate (the difference was statistically significant beginning nine weeks after the release date of the management forecast—a finding that is not surprising, because the analysts probably had access to more timely information upon which to base their forecasts).

Sources of Errors in Forecasting

As security analysts' forecasts are not perfect, it is interesting to consider the major source of their errors. One study examined the I/B/E/S database and attempted to break down the forecast errors into three components: (1) errors that could be traced to misjudgments about the economy; (2) errors that could be traced to misjudgments about the firm's particular industry; and (3) errors that were purely due to misjudgments about the firm.[36]

---

[34] John M. Hassell and Robert H. Jennings, "Relative Forecast Accuracy and the Timing of Earnings Forecast Announcements," *Accounting Review* 61, no. 1 (January 1986): 58–75.

[35] Similar to I/B/E/S, Zacks Investment Research provides weekly summaries of earnings forecasts for over 2000 firms that are provided by analysts at roughly 50 brokerage firms. While Zacks dates forecasts by the date of issuance by the analysts' employers, I/B/E/S dates forecasts by when they receive them.

[36] Edwin J. Elton, Martin J. Gruber, and Mustafa N. Gultekin, "Professional Expectations: Accuracy and Diagnosis of Errors," *Journal of Financial and Quantitative Analysis* 19, no. 4 (December 1984): 351–363.

Table 19.9

Security Analyst and Management Forecast Errors.

Week	*Average Analyst Forecast Error*	*Average Analyst Forecast Error– Average Management Forecast Error*[a]
−12	.224	.074
−11	.222	.072
−10	.221	.071
−9	.221	.071
−8	.214	.064
−7	.221	.071
−6	.222	.072
−5	.216	.066
−4	• .210	.060
−3	.208	.058
−2	.211	.061
−1	.209	.059
0	.195	.045
+1	.186	.036
+2	.177	.027
+3	.174	.024
+4	.171	.021
+5	.166	.016
+6	.160	.010
+7	.153	.003
+8	.150	.000
+9	.141	−.009
+10	.133	−.017
+11	.129	−.021
+12	.124	−.026

[a] The size of the average management forecast error was .150.

SOURCE: Adapted from John M. Hassell and Robert H. Jennings, "Relative Forecast Accuracy and the Timing of Earnings Forecast Announcements," *Accounting Review* 61, no. 1 (January 1986): Tables 2 and 3.

The results indicated the following: less than 3% of the typical error was due to a misjudgment about the economy; roughly 30% of the typical error was due to a misjudgment about the industry; and over 65% of the typical error was due to a misjudgment about the firm.

SUMMARY

1. Assuming that a firm undertakes positive NPV projects and maintains a constant debt-equity ratio, shareholders will be indifferent to the level of dividends.
2. If dividends and new investment are greater than earnings, the firm may issue new equity. If dividends and new investment are less than earnings, the firm may repurchase

equity. In either case, a shareholder maintaining constant proportional ownership will be able to spend the same amount on consumption, regardless of the level of dividends.

3. Earnings, not dividends, are the source of a firm's value.
4. Few firms attempt to maintain a constant ratio of dividends to current earnings. It is often assumed that firms establish a long-run payout ratio and adjust current actual dividends based on the difference between current target dividends and the last period's actual dividends.
5. Corporate management often uses dividend changes as a signaling device, raising or lowering dividends based on its assessment of the firm's future earnings.
6. A firm has considerable discretion in calculating its accounting earnings. These accounting earnings may differ substantially from the firm's economic earnings. Similarly, a firm's book value may differ considerably from its market value.
7. Earnings can be divided into permanent and transitory components. A firm's intrinsic value will be based on the permanent component of earnings. The transitory component is a significant factor in short-run changes in a firm's price-earnings ratio.
8. There is a positive relationship between accounting betas and market betas. Firms whose earnings co-vary more with market-wide earnings are likely to have higher market betas.
9. Stocks with the highest returns typically have earnings that are substantially greater than expected, whereas those with the lowest returns have earnings substantially below expectations.
10. Share prices tend to correctly anticipate earnings announcements by moving in the appropriate direction beforehand.
11. Share prices tend to react correctly but not fully to earnings announcements immediately afterward.
12. Share prices continue to move in a direction similar to their initial reaction for several months afterward. This phenomenon is known as post-earnings-announcement drift.
13. Analysts appear to forecast earnings better than sophisticated mechanical models.
14. Analysts tend to overestimate when forecasting earnings per share.
15. Management earnings forecasts are generally more accurate than analysts' forecasts.

APPENDIX A

VALUE LINE RANKINGS

It has been observed that investors can use the information contained in either a quarterly earnings announcement or a revision of an earnings forecast by security analysts to make abnormal returns. Another source of information that may be useful to investors is the *Value Line Investment Survey* (published weekly by Value Line, Inc., New York, for $525 per year), which is reputed to be the largest stock investment advisory service in North America.[37]

Each week, every one of approximately 1700 stocks is assigned one of five possible ranks by Value Line. By design, the categories include the same number of stocks each week, as follows:

[37] Value Line also has a service called *VALUE/SCREEN III* (formerly called *VALUE/SCREEN Plus*) that involves software and periodic updates of their rankings as well as other data. An annual subscription costs $325 for quarterly updates (available only by mail), $465 for monthly updates by mail, $495 for monthly electronic updates, and $1995 for weekly updates (available only electronically).

Rank	Number of Stocks
1 (highest)	100
2 (above average)	300
3 (average)	900
4 (below average)	300
5 (lowest)	100

Many factors go into the ranking procedure. Not surprisingly, the exact details have not been revealed. However, the key elements are all based on publicly available information:[38]

1. the most recent year's earnings and average stock price, relative to the comparable values for the previous ten years, and the stock's average price over the preceding ten weeks relative to that of the preceding 52 weeks;
2. a price momentum element that is based on the stock's current price-earnings ratio relative to that of the market, compared with the average of the corresponding figures over the last five years;
3. an earnings momentum element that is based on the most recent quarter's earnings relative to the amount reported four quarters earlier;
4. an earnings "surprise" element where the most recent quarter's earnings are compared with the amount forecast by Value Line's security analysts.

A test of the resulting rankings showed them to be of some value.[39] Beginning on November 26, 1965, five portfolios were formed (on paper). The first included all stocks ranked "1" at that time, in equal dollar values; the second included all stocks ranked "2" and so on. After six months each portfolio was altered as necessary to again include equal dollar values of all stocks with the appropriate ranks at that time. The procedure was continued until February 3, 1978, when the last set of portfolios was formed. Then, each portfolio's actual rate of return was measured and adjustments for risk were made to determine "abnormal" returns.

The results, shown in Table 19.10, indicate that both the actual and abnormal returns are perfectly ordered with the rankings of the securities in the portfolios. More in-depth analysis indicated that most of the abnormal returns occurred in the 13-week period subsequent to the formation date. Interestingly, this study shows that the only notable abnormal return is for the securities with a ranking of 5. This suggests that an investor should sell (or even short sell) any securities that have such a ranking.

This study also looked at those securities whose rank had been changed by Value Line. Roughly 70 to 80 securities change ranks each week, evenly split between those being upgraded and those being downgraded. Almost all the changes are of one rank (seldom does a security jump two ranks — for example, from 1 to 3, or vice versa).

---

[38] For details, see Arnold Bernhard, "Investing in Common Stocks with the Aid of the Value Line Rankings and other Criteria of Stock Value," Arnold Bernhard, New York, 1975.

[39] Thomas E. Copeland and David Mayers, "The Value Line Enigma (1965–1978): A Case Study of Performance Evaluation Issues," *Journal of Financial Economics* 10, no. 3 (November 1982): 289–321.

Table 19.10					
Performance of Portfolios Formed on the Basis of Value Line Rankings.					
	Ranking				
	1	2	3	4	5
Actual return over subsequent 26 weeks	7.38%	6.51%	4.10%	2.70%	.37%
Abnormal return over subsequent 26 weeks	.33%	.35%	−.57%	−1.12%	−3.05%

SOURCE: Thomas E. Copeland and David Mayers, "The Value Line Enigma (1965–1978): A Case Study of Performance Evaluation Issues," *Journal of Financial Economics* 10, no. 3 (November 1982): 298, 301.

Focusing the analysis on the time of the change in rank, it was determined that, on average, securities whose rank had been upgraded earned an abnormal return of .77% in the subsequent 13 weeks. Conversely, those securities whose rank had been downgraded earned an abnormal return of 11.42% in the subsequent 13 weeks. Overall, most of the adjustment in the share prices of these securities was found to be concentrated in the two-week period subsequent to the publication of the change in rank.[40]

These results do not suggest that Value Line provides a guaranteed formula for outstanding portfolio performance. No transaction costs were charged in the calculations, and turnover was high.[41] Thus, it might not be possible to earn abnormal returns by continually using Value Line rankings when these costs are taken into consideration. But the results do suggest that, when initially investing in stocks, Value Line rankings may prove useful.[42] It can be conjectured that Value Line rankings "work" primarily because they use quarterly earnings in both the earnings momentum and surprise elements that go into the Value Line ranking procedure.[43] After all, it has been noted that there are abnormal price movements subsequent to the announcement of quarterly earnings.

To summarize, the results suggest that there is a two-part puzzle associated with Value Line ranks. First, Value Line appears to have superior forecasting ability that is based on public information. Second, the market takes time to adjust to the Value Line rankings. Both of these observations are puzzling because they are inconsistent with the notion of efficient

---

[40] A later study found that most of the adjustment actually was in the three-day period after the change. The most notable price movement was associated with those shares being upgraded from 2 to 1. Other notable but less sizeable price movements were associated with upgrades from 3 to 2, and downgrades from 1 to 2 and 2 to 3. See Scott E. Stickel, "The Effect of Value Line Investment Survey Rank Changes on Common Stock Prices," *Journal of Financial Economics* 14, no. 1 (March 1985): 121–143.

[41] A discussion of transaction costs is contained in Copeland and Mayers, "The Value Line Enigma," pp. 319–320; and Clark Holloway, "A Note on Testing an Aggressive Investment Strategy Using Value Line Ranks," *Journal of Finance* 36, no. 3 (June 1981): 711–719.

[42] Value Line also provides a measure of the risk of individual securities that is known as Safety Rank. This risk measure was found to be more highly correlated with subsequent returns than either beta or standard deviation, suggesting that it is a more useful measure of risk. See Russell J. Fuller and G. Wenchi Wong, "Traditional versus Theoretical Risk Measures," *Financial Analysts Journal* 44, no. 2 (March/April 1988): 52–57, 67.

[43] One speculation is that the rankings are simply capturing the size effect by giving higher ranks to smaller firms (the size effect is discussed in the appendix to Chapter 17). However, tests suggest that this is not true. See Gur Huberman and Shmuel Kandel, "Value Line Rank and Firm Size," *Journal of Business* 60, no. 4 (October 1987): 577–589.

markets.[44] To further complicate matters, one study found that most rank changes occur shortly after earnings announcements are made. Subsequent investigation revealed that Value Line's superior performance was attributable to the "post-earnings-announcement drift." Hence the two anomalies appear to be related.[45]

QUESTIONS AND PROBLEMS

1. For a given level of earnings (E), net new investment (I), and dividends (D), explain why a firm must issue new stock if $E < D + I$ and it desires to maintain a constant debt-equity ratio. Similarly, why must it repurchase shares if $E > D + I$ and it desires to maintain a constant debt-equity ratio?
2. Merrillan Motors had earnings of $8 million last year. It made $5 million of investments in projects with positive net present values. Asra Singh owns 20% of the firm's common shares. Assume that Asra desires no change in proportional ownership of Merrillan and the firm wishes to maintain a constant debt-equity ratio. What will be Asra's action in response to:
   a. Merrillan's paying out dividends of $5 million?
   b. Merrillan's paying out dividends of $1 million?
   c. Merrillan's paying out dividends of $3 million?
3. Why is an individual shareholder indifferent between the firm retaining $1 of earnings or paying out the $1 of earnings as a dividend, assuming that the firm and the shareholder maintain a constant debt-equity ratio and a constant proportional ownership position, respectively?
4. If the dividend decision is irrelevant to the valuation of a firm, then aren't dividend discount models irrelevant to valuing common shares? Why?
5. Patrick Cooney, a confused investment student, commented, "I understand the irrelevance of the dividend decision to the value of the firm. As a result, I calculate the value of a firm's shares based on the present value of the firm's expected earnings per share." Is Patrick correct? Why?
6. Why do most corporations not maintain a constant payout ratio? What payout strategy do most firms pursue?
7. Hixton Farms has a target payout ratio of 50%. Dividends paid last year amounted to $10 million. Its earnings were $20 million. Hixton's "speed of adjustment" factor for dividends is 60%. Calculate its dividend payments over the next five years if its earnings display the path shown at the top of the next page.
   Draw a graph of Hixton's actual dividends paid versus the desired dividend payments over this five-year period.
8. Rockton Plastics has made changes to its dividends over the last 14 years. Based on a target payout ratio of 30%, according to the Lintner Model the firm would have preferred to make a different set of dividend changes. Both the actual and preferred dividend changes are shown in the second table on the next page. What "speed of adjustment" factor is

---

[44] For an argument on why these observations do not violate market efficiency, see Gur Huberman and Shmuel Kandel, "Market Efficiency and Value Line's Record," *Journal of Business* 63, no. 2 (April 1990): 187–216.

[45] See John Affleck-Graves and Richard R. Mendenhall, "The Relation Between the Value Line Enigma and Post-Earnings-Announcement Drift," *Journal of Financial Economics* 31, no. 1 (February 1992): 75–96.

Year	Earnings
1	$30 million
2	35 million
3	30 million
4	25 million
5	30 million

Year	Actual Change in Dividends	Preferred Change in Dividends
1	$–0.28	$–0.47
2	–0.09	–0.16
3	–0.05	–0.08
4	–0.01	–0.02
5	0.01	0.02
6	0.04	0.07
7	0.01	0.01
8	0.03	0.05
9	0.03	0.05
10	0.01	0.02
11	0.04	0.07
12	0.03	0.06
13	0.03	0.05

implied by these two dividend change series? (Use of a computer regression program, such as one provided with an electronic spreadsheet, is recommended.)

9. How are dividends used as a signaling device by corporate management? To the extent that dividends are a signaling device, how are dividend changes related to share prices?

10. Discuss why there generally does not exist a one-to-one relationship between corporations' book values and their market values.

11. The price per share of the Dells Deli Corporation is less than its book value. Does this indicate that those who now hold the firm's shares have lost money in the past? Does it indicate that they are likely to lose money in the future? Does it indicate that the Dells Deli should not undertake any further capital investment? Explain your answers.

12. Why might a steady trend in a firm's reported earnings from year to year suggest that the figures do not represent the firm's economic earnings?

13. Reported earnings typically differ, sometimes considerably, from economic earnings. Nevertheless, it is often argued that reported earnings are intended simply to provide a "source of information" to investors about the value of the firm. If so, might there not be many alternative accounting procedures of equal use to investors? How might one go about evaluating the usefulness of such procedures?

14. Distinguish between permanent and transitory earnings. Would you expect companies across industries to differ in terms of the relative importance of transitory earnings to total earnings? Explain.

15. Price-earnings ratios for individual companies vary over time and across firms. Discuss some of the possible reasons for this variability.

16. Why would you expect a security's market beta to be highly correlated with its accounting beta?

17. Harry Clift once wrote in a market newsletter that, "I focus my research on consensus earnings forecasts. Those companies that the consensus believes will produce the largest earnings increases next year are most likely to produce the best returns." Is Harry's opinion consistent with empirical evidence? Explain why or why not.

18. Calculate the relationship between the following series of quarterly earnings using an autoregressive model of order one (use of a computer regression program is recommended). What is your forecast for earnings in Quarter 21?

Quarter	*Earnings*	*Quarter*	*Earnings*
1	$4.00	11	$4.25
2	4.10	12	4.49
3	3.95	13	4.59
4	4.20	14	4.58
5	4.30	15	4.39
6	4.29	16	4.63
7	4.11	17	4.73
8	4.35	18	4.72
9	4.44	19	4.54
10	4.43	20	4.78

19. Oakdale Orchards has produced the following earnings over the last nine quarters:

Quarter	*Earnings per Share*
1	$2.00
2	1.95
3	2.05
4	2.10
5	2.40
6	2.24
7	2.67
8	2.84
9	2.64

The expected earnings for the current quarter are based on the equation $QE_t = QE_{t-4} + .75(QE_{t-1} - QE_{t-5})$. Calculate the standardized unexpected earnings in each of the last four quarters, given a standard deviation of $0.35.

20. Why might the price of a stock react only partially to an "earnings surprise" on the first day or two after the earnings announcement?
21. (Appendix Question) The Value Line ranking system has long shown a consistent ability to produce positive risk-adjusted returns. These results have been particularly disconcerting for efficient-market proponents. Why?

Key Terms

dividend decision
asymmetric information
information content of dividends hypothesis
accounting earnings
earnings per share (EPS)
return on equity (ROE)
economic earnings
economic value of the firm
generally accepted accounting principles (GAAP)
random walk model
market beta
accounting beta
standardized unexpected earnings (SUE)
abnormal return

References

1. The seminal paper on dividend policy that established both the "dividend irrelevancy theorem" and the notion that earnings are the basis for the market value of the firm was written by two Nobel laureates in economics:

   Merton H. Miller and Franco Modigliani, "Dividend Policy, Growth, and the Valuation of Shares," *Journal of Business* 34, no. 4 (October 1961): 411–433.

2. The Lintner Model of dividend behaviour and some studies that empirically tested it are found in:

   John Lintner, "Distribution of Incomes of Corporations Among Dividends, Retained Earnings, and Taxes," *American Economic Review* 46, no. 2 (May 1956): 97–113.

   John A. Brittain, *Corporate Dividend Policy* (Washington, DC: The Brookings Institution, 1966).

   Eugene F. Fama and Harvey Babiak, "Dividend Policy: An Empirical Analysis," *Journal of the American Statistical Association* 63, no. 324 (December 1968): 1132–1161.

   Eugene F. Fama, "The Empirical Relationship Between the Dividend and Investment Decisions of Firms," *American Economic Review* 64, no. 3 (June 1974): 304–318.

   Terry A. Marsh and Robert C. Merton, "Dividend Behavior for the Aggregate Stock Market," *Journal of Business* 60, no. 1 (January 1987): 1–40.

3. The determinants of recent dividend behaviour appear to be similar to those in the Lintner Model from the 1950s, according to:

   H. Kent Baker, Gail E. Farrelly, and Richard B. Edelman, "A Survey of Management Views on Dividend Policy," *Financial Management* 14, no. 3 (Autumn 1985): 78–84.

4. A summary of the literature on signaling can be found in:

Thomas E. Copeland and J. Fred Weston, *Financial Theory and Corporate Policy* (Reading, MA: Addison-Wesley, 1988), pp. 501–507, 584–588.

5. The information content of dividends hypothesis, closely linked to the signaling literature, has been the subject of much research. Some of the more important papers are:

R. Richardson Pettit, "Dividend Announcements, Security Performance, and Capital Market Efficiency," *Journal of Finance* 27, no. 5 (December 1972): 993–1007.

Ross Watts, "The Information Content of Dividends," *Journal of Business* 46, no. 2 (April 1973): 191–211.

Joseph Aharony and Itzak Swary, "Quarterly Dividend and Earnings Announcements and Stockholders' Returns: An Empirical Analysis," *Journal of Finance* 35, no. 1 (March 1980): 1–12.

Clarence C. Y. Kwan, "Efficient Market Tests of the Informational Content of Dividend Announcements: Critique and Extension," *Journal of Financial and Quantitative Analysis* 16, no. 2 (June 1981): 193–206.

Paul Asquith and David W. Mullins, Jr., "The Impact of Initiating Dividend Payments on Shareholders' Wealth," *Journal of Business* 56, no. 1 (January 1983): 77–96.

James A. Brickley, "Shareholder Wealth, Information Signaling and the Specially Designated Dividend: An Empirical Study," *Journal of Financial Economics* 12, no. 2 (August 1983): 187–209.

J. Randall Woolridge, "Dividend Changes and Stock Prices," *Journal of Finance* 38, no. 5 (December 1983): 1607–1615.

Terry E. Dielman and Henry R. Oppenheimer, "An Examination of Investor Behavior During Periods of Large Dividend Changes," *Journal of Financial and Quantitative Analysis* 19, no. 2 (June 1984): 197–216.

Paul M. Healy and Krishna G. Palepu, "Earnings Information Conveyed by Dividend Initiations and Omissions," *Journal of Financial Economics* 21, no. 2 (September 1988): 149–175.

P. C. Venkatesh, "The Impact of Dividend Initiation on the Information Content of Earnings Announcements and Returns Volatility," *Journal of Business* 62, no. 2 (April 1989): 175–197.

Larry H. P. Lang and Robert H. Litzenberger, "Dividend Announcements: Cash Flow Signalling vs. Free Cash Flow Hypothesis," *Journal of Financial Economics* 24, no. 1 (September 1989): 181–191.

Harry DeAngelo, Linda DeAngelo, and Douglas J. Skinner, "Dividends and Losses," *Journal of Finance* 47, no. 5 (December 1992): 1837–1863.

Keith M. Howe, Jia He, and G. Wenchi Kao, "One-Time Cash Flow Announcements and Free Cash-Flow Theory: Share Repurchases and Special Dividends," *Journal of Finance* 47, no. 5 (December 1992): 1963–1975.

6. The relationship between economic and accounting earnings is discussed in:

   Fischer Black, "The Magic in Earnings: Economic Earnings versus Accounting Earnings," *Financial Analysts Journal* 36, no. 6 (November/December 1980): 19–24.

7. For a study on the timing of dividend announcements as well as a listing of other studies concerning dividend announcements, see:

   Avner Kalay and Uri Loewenstein, "The Informational Content of the Timing of Dividend Announcements," *Journal of Financial Economics* 16, no. 3 (July 1986): 373–388.

   Aharon R. Ofer and Daniel R. Siegel, "Corporate Financial Policy, Information, and Market Expectations: An Empirical Investigation of Dividends," *Journal of Finance* 42, no. 4 (September 1987): 889–911.

8. For a review of the literature dealing with dividends, see:

   James S. Ang, *Do Dividends Matter? A Review of Corporate Dividend Theories and Evidence*, Monograph Series in Finance and Economics #1987–2, New York University Salomon Center, Leonard N. Stern School of Business.

9. For a discussion of price-earnings ratios, see:

   William Beaver and Dale Morse, "What Determines Price-Earnings Ratios?" *Financial Analysts Journal* 34, no. 4 (July/August 1978): 65–76.

   William H. Beaver, *Financial Reporting: An Accounting Revolution* (Englewood Cliffs, NJ: Prentice Hall, 1981), Chapters 4 and 5.

   George Foster, *Financial Statement Analysis* (Englewood Cliffs, NJ: Prentice Hall, 1986), pp. 437–442.

   Paul Zarowin, "What Determines Earnings-Price Ratios: Revisited," *Journal of Accounting, Auditing, and Finance* 5, no. 3 (Summer 1990): 439–454.

   Peter D. Easton and Trevor S. Harris, "Earnings as an Explanatory Variable for Returns," *Journal of Accounting Research* 29, no. 1 (Spring 1991): 19–36.

10. Time-series models of annual and quarterly earnings per share are discussed in:

    George Foster, "Quarterly Accounting Data: Time-Series Properties and Predictive-Ability Results," *Accounting Review* 52, no. 1 (January 1977): 1–21.

    George Foster, *Financial Statement Analysis* (Englewood Cliffs, NJ: Prentice Hall, 1986), Chapter 7.

    Ross L. Watts and Jerold L. Zimmerman, *Positive Accounting Theory* (Englewood Cliffs, NJ: Prentice Hall, 1986), Chapter 6.

11. The relationship between market betas and accounting betas has been explored by:

    Ray Ball and Philip Brown, "Portfolio Theory and Accounting," *Journal of Accounting Research* 7, no. 2 (Autumn 1969): 300–323.

    William Beaver and James Manegold, "The Association Between Market-Determined and Accounting-Determined Measures of Systematic Risk: Some Further Evidence," *Journal of Financial and Quantitative Analysis* 10, no. 2 (June 1975): 231–284.

12. The relationship between earnings announcements and share prices has been documented in many studies. See the following as well as their citations:

Ray Ball and Philip Brown, "An Empirical Evaluation of Accounting Income Numbers," *Journal of Accounting Research* 6, no. 2 (Autumn 1968): 159–178.

William H. Beaver, "The Information Content of Annual Earnings Announcements," *Empirical Research in Accounting: Selected Studies*, Supplement to *Journal of Accounting Research* 6 (1968): 67–92.

Leonard Zacks, "EPS Forecasts—Accuracy Is Not Enough," *Financial Analysts Journal* 35, no. 2 (March/April 1979): 53–55.

Dale Morse, "Price and Trading Volume Reaction Surrounding Earnings Announcements: A Closer Examination," *Journal of Accounting Research* 19, no. 2 (Autumn 1981): 374–383.

James M. Patell and Mark A. Wolfson, "The *Ex Ante* and *Ex Post* Effects of Quarterly Earnings Announcements Reflected in Stock and Option Prices," *Journal of Accounting Research* 19, no. 2 (Autumn 1981): 434–458.

Richard J. Rendleman, Jr., Charles P. Jones, and Henry A. Latane, "Empirical Anomalies Based on Unexpected Earnings and the Importance of Risk Adjustments," *Journal of Financial Economics* 10, no. 3 (November 1982): 269–287.

James M. Patell and Mark A. Wolfson, "The Intraday Speed of Adjustment of Stock Prices to Earnings and Dividend Announcements," *Journal of Financial Economics* 13, no. 2 (June 1984): 223–252.

George Foster, Chris Olsen, and Terry Shevlin, "Earnings Releases, Anomalies, and the Behavior of Security Returns," *Accounting Review* 59, no. 4 (October 1984): 574–603.

Catherine S. Woodruff and A. J. Senchack, Jr., "Intradaily Price-Volume Adjustments of NYSE Stocks to Unexpected Earnings," *Journal of Finance* 43, no. 2 (June 1988): 467–491.

The entire issue of the *Journal of Accounting and Economics* 15, no. 2/3 (June/September 1992).

13. Some of the studies that have examined possible explanations for the "post-earnings-announcement drift" in share prices are:

Richard J. Rendleman, Jr., Charles P. Jones, and Henry A. Latane, "Further Insight into the Standardized Unexpected Earnings Anomaly: Size and Serial Correlation Effects," *Financial Review* 22, no. 1 (February 1987): 131–144.

Victor L. Bernard and Jacob K. Thomas, "Post-Earnings-Announcement Drift: Delayed Price Response or Risk Premium?" *Journal of Accounting Research* 27 (Supplement 1989): 1–36.

Robert N. Freeman and Senyo Tse, "The Multiperiod Information Content of Accounting Earnings: Confirmations and Contradictions of Previous Earnings Reports," *Journal of Accounting Research* 27 (Supplement 1989): 49–79.

Victor L. Bernard and Jacob K. Thomas, "Evidence That Stock Prices Do Not Fully Reflect the Implications of Current Earnings for Future Earnings," *Journal of Accounting and Economics* 13, no. 4 (December 1990): 305–340.

Richard R. Mendenhall, "Evidence on the Possible Underweighting of Earnings-Related Information," *Journal of Accounting Research* 29, no. 1 (Spring 1991): 170–179.

Ray Ball, "The Earnings-Price Anomaly," *Journal of Accounting and Economics* 15, no. 2/3 (June/September 1992): 319–345.

Jeffrey S. Abarbanell and Victor L. Bernard, "Tests of Analysts' Overreaction/Underreaction to Earnings Information as an Explanation for Anomalous Stock Price Behavior," *Journal of Finance* 47, no. 3 (July 1992): 1181–1207.

14. There have been numerous studies concerning the earnings forecasts made by security analysts and management. Some of the studies are:

Lawrence D. Brown and Michael S. Rozeff, "The Superiority of Analyst Forecasts as Measures of Expectations: Evidence from Earnings," *Journal of Finance* 33, no. 1 (March 1978): 1–16.

Lawrence D. Brown and Michael S. Rozeff, "Analysts Can Forecast Accurately!", *Journal of Portfolio Management* 6, no. 3 (Spring 1980): 31–34.

John G. Cragg and Burton G. Malkiel, *Expectations and the Structure of Share Prices* (Chicago: University of Chicago Press, 1982), particularly pp. 85–86 and 165.

Dan Givoly and Josef Lakonishok, "Properties of Analysts' Forecasts of Earnings: A Review and Analysis of the Research," *Journal of Accounting Literature* 3 (Spring 1984): 117–152.

Dan Givoly and Josef Lakonishok, "The Quality of Analysts' Forecasts of Earnings," *Financial Analysts Journal* 40, no. 5 (September/October 1984): 40–47.

Philip Brown, George Foster, and Eric Noreen, *Security Analyst Multi-Year Earnings Forecasts and the Capital Markets* (Sarasota, FL: American Accounting Association, 1985).

John M. Hassell and Robert H. Jennings, "Relative Forecast Accuracy and the Timing of Earnings Forecast Announcements," *Accounting Review* 61, no. 1 (January 1986): 58–75.

Gary A. Benesh and Pamela P. Peterson, "On the Relation Between Earnings Changes, Analysts' Forecasts and Stock Price Fluctuations," *Financial Analysts Journal* 42, no. 6 (November/December 1986): 29–39, 55.

Lawrence D. Brown, Robert L. Hagerman, Paul A. Griffin, and Mark Zmijewski, "Security Analyst Superiority Relative to Univariate Time-Series Models in Forecasting Quarterly Earnings," *Journal of Accounting and Economics* 9, no. 1 (April 1987): 61–87.

Robert Conroy and Robert Harris, "Consensus Forecasts of Corporate Earnings: Analysts' Forecasts and Time-Series Methods," *Management Science* 33, no. 6 (June 1987): 725–738.

Lawrence D. Brown, Robert L. Hagerman, Paul A. Griffin, and Mark Zmijewski, "An Evaluation of Alternative Proxies for the Market's Assessment of Unexpected Earnings," *Journal of Accounting and Economics* 9, no. 2 (July 1987): 159–193.

Patricia C. O'Brien, "Analysts' Forecasts as Earnings Expectations," *Journal of Accounting and Economics* 10, no. 1 (January 1988): 53–83.

Werner F. De Bondt and Richard H. Thaler, "Do Security Analysts Overreact?" *American Economic Review* 80, no. 2 (May 1990): 52–57.

Lawrence D. Brown and Kwon-Jung Kim, "Timely Aggregate Analyst Forecasts as Better Proxies for Market Earnings Expectations," *Journal of Accounting Research* 29, no. 2 (Autumn 1991): 382–385.

Ashiq Ali, April Klein, and James Rosenfeld, "Analysts' Use of Information about Permanent and Transitory Earnings Components in Forecasting Annual EPS," *Accounting Review* 67, no. 1 (January 1992): 183–198.

Scott E. Stickel, "Reputation and Performance Among Security Analysts," *Journal of Finance* 47, no. 5 (December 1992): 1811–1836.

15. For a description of the analyst forecasts published by Value Line, I/B/E/S, and others, see:

Donna R. Philbrick and William E. Ricks, "Using Value Line and IBES Analyst Forecasts in Accounting Research," *Journal of Accounting Research* 29, no. 2 (Autumn 1991): 397–417.

John Markese, "The Role of Earnings Forecasts in Stock Price Behavior," *AAII Journal* 14, no. 4 (April 1992): 30–32.

16. As the footnotes to the appendix show, the Value Line Investment Survey has been intensively scrutinized. Those who would like to learn more about Value Line can purchase the following software manual and user's guide directly from Value Line.

Value Line, Inc., *VALUE/SCREEN Plus* (Englewood Cliffs, NJ: Prentice Hall, 1990).

Gerald P. Madden, *Investment Analysis with VALUE/SCREEN Plus* (Englewood Cliffs, NJ: Prentice Hall, 1991).

17. For a Canadian perspective on the topics covered in this chapter, see:

N. Betts and L. Johnson, "The Determinants of the P/E Ratio: Theory and Evidence," *Proceedings*, Administrative Sciences Association of Canada Conference, Lake Louise, June 1993.

S. Hennessey, "Using Tests of the Rationality of Canadian Analysts' Earnings Forecasts," *Proceedings*, Administrative Sciences Association of Canada Conference, Lake Louise, June 1993.

J. Bourgeois and J. Lussier, "P/Es and Performance in the Canadian Market," *Canadian Investment Review* VII, no. 1 (Spring 1994).

S. Hennessey, "Using Analysts' Revised Forecasts as a Stock Selection Tool," *Canadian Investment Review* VIII, no. 4 (Winter 1995/96).

CHAPTER 20

Options

In the world of investments, an **option** is a type of contract between two people where one person grants the other person the right to buy a specific asset at a specific price within a specific time period. Alternatively, the contract may grant the other person the right to sell a specific asset at a specific price within a specific time period. The person who has received the right, and thus has a decision to make, is known as the option buyer because he or she must pay for this right. The person who has sold the right, and thus must respond to the buyer's decision, is known as the option writer.

The variety of contracts containing an option feature is enormous. Even within the domain of publicly traded securities, many types can be found. Traditionally only certain instruments are referred to as options; the others, though similar in nature, are designated differently. This chapter presents an introduction to the institutional features of option contracts, along with some basics regarding how they are valued in the marketplace.

TYPES OF OPTION CONTRACTS

The two most basic types of option contracts are known as calls and puts. Currently such contracts are traded on many exchanges around the world. Furthermore, many of these contracts are created privately (that is, "off exchange" or "over the counter"), typically involving financial institutions or investment banking firms and their clients. A brief introduction to calls and puts follows.

► Call Options

The most common type of option contract is the **call option** for stocks. It gives the buyer the right to buy ("call away") a specific number of shares of a specific company from the option writer at a specific purchase price at any time up to and including a specific date. Note how the contract specifies four items:

1. the company whose shares can be bought;
2. the number of shares that can be bought;
3. the purchase price for those shares, known as the **exercise price** (or striking price);
4. the date when the right to buy expires, known as the **expiration date.**

An Example

Consider a simple hypothetical example where investors B and W are thinking about signing a call option contract. This contract will allow B to buy 100 shares of Widget from W for $50 per share at any time during the next six months. Currently Widget is selling for $45 per share on an organized exchange. Investor B, the potential option buyer, believes that the price of Widget's common shares will rise substantially over the next six months. Investor W, the potential option writer, has a different opinion about Widget, believing that its stock price will not rise above \$50 over this time period.

Will investor W be willing to sign this contract without receiving something in return from investor B? No. W is running a risk by signing the contract and would demand compensation for doing so. The risk is that Widget's share price will subsequently rise above \$50 per share, in which case W will have to buy the shares at that price and then turn them over to B for only \$50 per share. Perhaps the shares will rise to \$60, costing W \$6000 = \$60 × 100 shares to buy the stock. Then W will give the 100 shares to B and receive in return \$5000 = \$50 × 100 shares. Consequently W will have lost \$6000 – \$5000 = \$1000.

The point is that the buyer of a call option will have to pay the writer something in order to get the writer to sign the contract. The amount paid is known as the **premium,** although *option price* is a more appropriate term. In the example, perhaps the premium is \$3 per share, meaning that investor B will pay \$300 (= \$3 × 100 shares) to investor W in order to induce W to sign the contract. Because investor B expects Widget's share price to rise in the future, he or she would expect to make money by purchasing shares of Widget at \$45 per share. The attraction of purchasing call options instead of shares is that investor B can apply a high degree of leverage, since only \$3 per share needs to be spent in order to purchase the option.

At some point in time after investors B and W have signed the call option contract, investor W might like to get out of the contract. But breaching the contract is illegal, so how can this be done? Investor W could buy the contract back from investor B for a negotiated amount of money and then destroy the document. If Widget rises in one month to \$55 per share, perhaps the amount will be \$7 per share or, in total, \$7 × 100 shares = \$700. In this case, W will have lost \$300 – \$700 = \$400 and B will have made \$400. Alternatively, if Widget falls to \$40 per share, perhaps the amount will be \$.50 per share or, in total, \$.50 × 100 shares = \$50, in which case W will have made \$300 – \$50 = \$250 and B will have lost \$250.

Another way that W can get out of the contract is to find someone else to take his or her position in the contract (assuming that the contract has a provision that allows this to be done). For example, if Widget has risen to \$55 per share after one month, perhaps investor W will find an investor, denoted WW, who is willing to become the option writer if W will pay him or her \$7 per share (or \$700 in total). Assuming that they both agree, the contract will be amended so that WW is now the option writer, with W no longer being a party in the contract.

What if investor B subsequently wants to get out of the contract? In this case, B could look and see if someone is willing to pay an agreeable sum of money in order to possess the right to buy Widget stock under the terms of the contract—that is, B could attempt to sell the contract to someone else. In this situation, perhaps investor B will find another investor, denoted BB, who is willing to pay B \$7 per share (or \$700 in total) in return for the right to buy Widget under the terms of the call option contract. Provided that B is agreeable, the call option contract will be sold to BB and amended, making BB the option buyer.

In this example, both of the original parties, W and B, have "closed out" (or "offset" or "unwound") their positions and are no longer involved in the call option contract. However, the example suggests that the original writer and buyer must meet face to face in order to draw up the terms of the contract. It also suggests that if either the original writer or buyer wants to get out of the contract, then he or she must reach an agreeable price with the other original party or, alternatively, find a third investor to whom he or she can transfer the position in the contract. Thus, it would appear that dealing in options involves a great deal of effort.

Role of Exchanges

Fortunately this is not the case in Canada and the United States because of the introduction of *standardized contracts* and the maintenance of a relatively liquid marketplace by organized exchanges for listed options.[1] The Canadian Derivatives Clearing Corp. (CDCC), formerly known as Trans-Canada Options, Inc., a company that is jointly owned by the Montreal Exchange and the Toronto and Vancouver Stock Exchanges greatly facilitates trading in these options. (The Options Clearing Corporation (OCC) performs the same function in the United States.) It maintains a computer system that keeps track of all of these options by recording the position of each investor in each one. Although the mechanics are rather complex, the principles are simple enough. As soon as a buyer and a writer decide to trade a particular option contract and the buyer pays the agreed-upon premium, the CDCC steps in, becoming the effective writer as far as the buyer is concerned and the effective buyer as far as the writer is concerned. Thus, at this time all direct links between original buyer and writer are severed. If a buyer chooses to exercise an option, the CDCC will randomly choose a writer who has not closed his or her position and assign the exercise notice accordingly. The CDCC also guarantees delivery of stock if the writer is unable to come up with the shares.

The CDCC makes it possible for buyers and writers to "close out" their positions at any time. If a buyer subsequently becomes a writer of the same contract, meaning that the buyer later "sells" the contract to someone else, the CDCC computer will note the offsetting positions in this investor's account and will simply cancel both entries. Consider an investor who buys a contract on Monday and then sells it on Tuesday. The computer will note that the investor's net position is zero and will remove both entries. The second trade is a **closing sale** because it serves to close out the investor's position from the earlier trade. Closing sales thus allow buyers to sell options rather than exercise them.

A similar procedure allows a writer to pay to be relieved of the potential obligation to deliver stock. Consider an investor who writes a contract on Wednesday and buys an identical one on Thursday. The latter is a **closing purchase** and, analogous to a closing sale, serves to close out the investor's position from the earlier trade.

► Stock-Split and Dividend Protection

Call options are protected against stock splits and stock dividends on the underlying stock. In the example where the option was on 100 shares of Widget stock with an exercise price of $50, a two-for-one stock split would cause the contract to be altered so that it was for 200 shares at $25 per share. The reason for this protection has to do with the effect that stock splits and stock dividends have on the share price of the firm. Since either of these events will cause the share price to fall below what it otherwise would have been, without adjustment

[1] Prior to 1973 in the US and 1975 in Canada, options were traded over the counter through the efforts of dealers and brokers in a relatively illiquid market. These dealers and brokers brought buyers and writers together, arranged terms, helped with the paperwork, and charged fees for their efforts.

they would work to the disadvantage of the call option buyer and to the advantage of the call option writer.

In terms of cash dividends, there is no protection for listed call options.[2] That is, the exercise price and the number of shares are unaffected by the payment of cash dividends. For example, the terms of the Widget call option would remain the same if Widget declared and paid a $4 per share cash dividend.

Put Options

A second type of option contract for stocks is the **put option.** It gives the buyer the right to sell ("put away") a specific number of shares of a specific company to the option writer at a specific selling price at any time up to and including a specific date. Note how the contract specifies four items that are analogous to those for call options:

1. the company whose shares can be sold;
2. the number of shares that can be sold;
3. the selling price for those shares, known as the exercise price (or striking price);
4. the date when the right to sell expires, known as the expiration date.

An Example

Consider an example where investors B and W are thinking about signing a put option contract. This contract will allow B to sell 100 shares of XYZ Company to W for $30 per share at any time during the next six months. Currently XYZ is selling for $35 per share on an organized exchange. Investor B, the potential option buyer, believes that the price of XYZ's common shares will fall substantially over the next six months. Investor W, the potential option writer, has a different opinion about XYZ, believing that its share price will not fall below $30 over this time period.

As with the call option on Widget, investor W would be running a risk by signing the contract and would demand compensation for doing so. The risk is that XYZ's share price will subsequently fall below $30 per share, in which case W will have to buy the shares at $30 per share from B when they are not worth that much in the marketplace. Perhaps XYZ will fall to $20, costing W $30 × 100 shares = $3000 to buy shares that are worth only $20 × 100 shares = $2000. Consequently W would have lost $3000 – $2000 = $1000. In this case B would make $1000, purchasing XYZ in the marketplace for $2000 and then selling the shares to W for $3000.

As with a call option, the buyer of a put option will have to pay the writer an amount of money known as a premium in order to get the writer to sign the contract and assume this risk. Also as with call options, the buyer and writer may "close out" (or "offset" or "unwind") their positions at any time by simply entering an offsetting transaction. As with calls, this is easily done for listed put options in Canada because these contracts are standardized.

Again, the CDCC facilitates trading in listed puts, as these options exist only in the memory of its computer system. As with calls, as soon as a buyer and a writer decide to trade a particular put option contract and the buyer pays the agreed-upon premium, the CDCC steps in, becoming the effective writer as far as the buyer is concerned and the effective buyer as far as the writer is concerned. If a buyer chooses to exercise an option, the CDCC

[2] However, there is protection for any cash dividend that is formally designated a "return of capital." Furthermore, options that are traded over the counter typically are protected from any type of cash dividend. In both cases the protection is in the form of a reduction in the exercise price.

Figure 20.1

Options expiry cycles.

OPTION EXPIRIES AVAILABLE – LISTED BY CYCLE AND BY MONTH

CYCLE 5(1)	JAN	FEB	MAR	APR	MAY	JUN	JUL	AUG	SEP	OCT	NOV	DEC
	JAN	FEB	MAR	APR	MAY	JUN	JUL	AUG	SEP	OCT	NOV	DEC
	FEB	MAR	APR	MAY	JUN	JUL	AUG	SEP	OCT	NOV	DEC	JAN
	APR	APR	JUL	JUL	JUL	OCT	OCT	OCT	JAN	JAN	JAN	APR
	JUL	JUL	OCT	OCT	OCT	JAN	JAN	JAN	APR	APR	APR	JUL

CYCLE 5(2)	JAN	FEB	MAR	APR	MAY	JUN	JUL	AUG	SEP	OCT	NOV	DEC
	JAN	FEB	MAR	APR	MAY	JUN	JUL	AUG	SEP	OCT	NOV	DEC
	FEB	MAR	APR	MAY	JUN	JUL	AUG	SEP	OCT	NOV	DEC	JAN
	MAY	MAY	MAY	AUG	AUG	AUG	NOV	NOV	NOV	FEB	FEB	FEB
	AUG	AUG	AUG	NOV	NOV	NOV	FEB	FEB	FEB	MAY	MAY	MAY

CYCLE 5(3)	JAN	FEB	MAR	APR	MAY	JUN	JUL	AUG	SEP	OCT	NOV	DEC
	JAN	FEB	MAR	APR	MAY	JUN	JUL	AUG	SEP	OCT	NOV	DEC
	FEB	MAR	APR	MAY	JUN	JUL	AUG	SEP	OCT	NOV	DEC	JAN
	MAR	JUN	JUN	JUN	SEP	SEP	SEP	DEC	DEC	DEC	MAR	MAR
	JUN	SEP	SEP	SEP	DEC	DEC	DEC	MAR	MAR	MAR	JUN	JUN

HOW TO USE THIS CHART: Look up the cycle and the month, e.g. Canadian Pacific is a Cycle 5(2). In March the options available are March, April, May and August. After the March expiry, move to the April column, March has been deleted, and November added on.

The Toronto Futures Exchange

The Exchange TORONTO STOCK

SOURCE: Reprinted by permission of the Toronto Stock Exchange, Derivative Markets Division.

will randomly choose a writer who has not closed his or her position and assign the exercise notice accordingly. The CDCC also guarantees delivery of the exercise price if the writer is unable to come up with the necessary cash.

Like calls, puts are protected against stock splits and stock dividends on the underlying stock. In the example where the option was on 100 shares of XYZ with an exercise price of \$30, a two-for-one stock split would cause the contract to be altered so that it was for 200 shares at \$15 per share. In terms of cash dividends, there is no protection for listed puts.

OPTION TRADING IN CANADA

Before January 1992, TSE traded options were introduced on a nine-month cycle (as is done in US markets). Beginning in January 1992, a new set of options on a given stock begin trading on the TSE every month. Figure 20.1 shows the available expiry dates listed by cycle and by month. Each underlying stock is assigned to a given cycle and options are introduced according to the schedule shown. For example, in January, options on Canadian Pacific (a cycle 5(2) stock) will be introduced with an August expiry such that contracts

Table 20.1

Exercise Price Intervals for New Options for Different Prices of the Underlying Stock.

Stock Price	*Exercise Price Interval*
Less than $20	$1.00
$20 to $30	$1.00 or $2.50 (optional)
$30 to $75	$2.50
Over $75	$5.00

SOURCE: Information provided by Derivatives Markets, Marketing, Toronto Stock Exchange, January 1996.

with January, February, May, and August expiries will be available. In February, contracts expiring in March will be introduced to replace the January options that expired and so on. The object is to maintain contracts with expiry in the two near months and two more distant months in existence at all times. The maximum term to expiry is eight months. The exercise prices of the new options are determined using the schedule shown in Table 20.1 and the proviso that their prices should bracket the current market price.

For example, if in January Canadian Pacific is selling for $18.50, then the two August call options introduced have exercise prices of $18 and $19; similarly, the two August put options have exercise prices of $18 and $19. Exchange officials acting in conjunction with the market makers have some latitude in setting the price and introduction date of additional options on a volatile stock.

The exchange also offers long-lived options that are known as *Long-term Equity Participation Securities* or **LEAPS**. These may be either calls or puts with a maximum of two years to expiration when issued. All LEAPS expire in January and become part of the regular option class at nine months or less to expiry.

An option remains listed until its expiry date. Listed options on common stocks generally expire on the Saturday after the third Friday of the specified month. Index options (to be discussed later) expire on the third Friday of the month. Trading ends on the last business day prior to the expiry date.

► Trading Activity

The bulk of options trading in Canada takes place on the Toronto Stock Exchange.[3] Figure 20.2 shows a portion of the daily listing of the trading activity of Trans Canada Options. The first row for each company shows the name of the company, the closing price of its shares and the option volume (Opt Vol). The option volume is the total number of contracts of all series of options on that stock which traded during the previous trading day. Indented below the name are the expiry month and exercise price (P for put, otherwise call) for each series followed by the bid and ask prices for each series, the last recorded premium, the number of contracts traded, and the open interest. The open interest is the number of contracts outstanding in that series. For example, on January 4, 1996 Alcan Aluminum common stock closed at $43 3/8. The prices for the last trades of Alcan January and April

[3] In the US option trading activity is rather more extensive than in Canada with common stock options traded on the Chicago Board Options Exchange (CBOE) and on the American, Pacific, Philadelphia, and New York Stock Exchanges. For a detailed description of how options are created and traded in the US, see Chapter 3 of John C. Cox and Mark Rubinstein, *Options Markets* (Englewood Cliffs, N.J.: Prentice Hall, 1985).

Figure 20.2

Listed options quotations (excerpts).

Canadian Equity Options

Trans Canada Options Inc. has changed its name to Canadian Derivatives Clearing Corp.

Trading yesterday in Canadian equity options on the Toronto, Montreal, and Vancouver exchanges by the Canadian Derivatives Clearing Corp. P is a Put.

Five most active option classes

	Volume	Op Int
TSE 35	1795	13700
Corel	1638	10336
Royal Oak	1000	9224
Inco	722	7877
Diamond Fi	554	13055

Stock Series		Close Bid	Close Ask	Last	Total Vol Vol	Tot Op Int Op Int
AXL		**$**			**40**	**308**
Jan96	$13	1.15	1.35	1.55	20	0
	$14	0.40	0.50	0.55	20	25
Abitibi-Price		**$20¾**			**221**	**8393**
Feb96	$22	0.75	0.85	0.95	30	93
Mar96	$18	3.45	3.70	3.70	30	151
	$20	2.15	2.40	2.40	10	148
	$22	1.25	1.40	1.35	15	656
	$24	0.55	0.65	0.75	70	632
Jun96	$18	4.25	4.50	4.65	15	36
	$18 p	1.05	1.30	1.05	30	213
	$20	3.25	3.50	3.40	9	69
	$20 p	2.05	2.30	1.90	10	45
	$22 p	3.15	3.40	3.00	2	12
Agnico Eagl		**$18½**			**85**	**489**
Jan96	$18	0.65	0.90	0.45	10	13
Feb96	$18	1.00	1.25	1.00	15	15
Jun96	$19	1.40	1.65	1.30	60	60
Air Canada		**$4.75**			**395**	**27973**
Jan96	$5	0.10	0.15	0.10	90	3830
Feb96	$5	0.20	0.25	0.20	10	10
	$5 p	0.30	0.45	0.30	10	10
Apr96	$5	0.30	0.40	0.40	55	1262
	$5 p	0.40	0.50	0.50	20	502
Jul96	$5	0.55	0.65	0.60	125	996
	$5 p	0.45	0.55	0.45	20	210
	$6	0.30	0.35	0.35	65	759
Alberta Enr		**$22¼**			**70**	**719**
Jun96	$21 p	0.70	0.85	0.75	20	30
	$23	1.25	1.40	1.25	50	45
Alcan		**$43⅜**			**185**	**9130**
Jan96	$35	8¼	8½	8¼	10	82
	$40	3.30	3.55	3.10	5	193
	$42½	1.30	1.45	1.30	10	346
	$45	0.25	0.35	0.35	20	1712
Feb96	$42½	2.00	2.25	2.00	35	139
	$45	0.90	1.05	0.80	60	71
Apr96	$42½p	1.80	1.95	2.10	10	77
Jul96	$40	5½	5¾	5¾	30	91
	$45 p	3.55	3.80	3.70	5	10
BCE Inc		**$47¾**			**42**	**22932**
Feb96	$45	2.95	3.15	3.10	12	1850
	$50	0.10	0.20	0.25	20	30
May96	$47½	1.40	1.60	1.40	3	884
Aug96	$45	3.45	3.70	3.50	2	17
	$50	0.75	0.95	0.90	5	20
Bank Mtl		**$32**			**104**	**7775**
Jan96	$26	5⅝	6	5¾	8	118
	$28	3.70	3.95	3.85	20	503
	$30	1.70	1.95	2.05	11	786
Apr96	$31	1.30	1.50	1.50	20	626
	$32	0.80	1.00	1.00	5	55
Jul96	$30	2.50	2.75	2.85	10	41
Jan97	$26	6½	7	6¾	10	144
	$28	4.80	5¼	5⅛	20	342
Bank of NS		**$30¾**			**235**	**12962**
Jan96	$25	5⅞	5⅝	5½	76	946
	$29	1.65	2.05	2.00	10	2429
	$30	0.90	0.95	0.90	64	2466
Feb96	$31	0.60	0.65	0.55	20	347
Jul96	$31	1.35	1.60	1.40	10	174
Jan97	$25	5¾	6⅛	6	10	181
Jan98	$25	6¾	7⅛	7½	25	127
	$30	3.80	4.20	4.00	10	43
	$30 p	2.20	2.50	2.30	10	19
Barrick Gld		**$37¾**			**510**	**32153**
Jan96	$35	2.75	2.95	2.95	40	5550
	$37½	0.80	0.95	0.90	40	3393
	$40	0.15	0.30	0.20	100	3004
	$40 p	2.25	2.45	2.45	10	90
Feb96	$37½p	1.05	1.25	1.25	5	25
	$40	0.45	0.65	0.45	6	6
Apr96	$32½	6	6¼	5⅞	5	62
	$35	4.00	4.20	4.00	4	2252
	$35 p	0.70	0.90	0.90	20	2138
	$37½	2.40	2.60	2.55	50	824
	$37½p	1.60	1.80	1.90	10	121
	$40	1.30	1.50	1.45	80	250
	$40 p	2.95	3.15	3.10	15	85
Jul96	$37½	3.40	3.60	3.40	75	89
	$37½p	2.10	2.30	2.15	5	3035
	$40	2.25	2.45	2.25	30	182
	$40 p	3.40	3.60	3.65	5	111
Jan97	$35 p	1.80	2.10	1.80	10	333
BioChem Ph		**$53¼**			**192**	**23931**
Jan96	$44	9½	9⅞	8⅜	3	296
	$50	4.15	4.40	2.55	50	201
	$50 p	0.80	0.95	1.55	30	129
	$52	2.85	3.10	2.00	20	96
	$52 p	1.50	1.70	2.00	10	67
	$54 p	2.45	2.70	3.55	10	114
Feb96	$46 p	1.00	1.20	1.50	10	30
	$50 p	2.10	2.35	2.60	5	40
	$52 p	3.00	3.25	4.10	6	31
	$54 p	3.90	4.15	3.70	8	19
Mar96	$48 p	2.35	2.60	2.75	3	6
	$56	3.95	4.20	3.40	10	168
Jun96	$46	12	12⅜	10⅞	3	30
	$46 p	3.40	3.65	3.90	5	5
	$50	9⅞	10¼	9½	5	5
Jan97	$24 p	0.25	0.75	0.50	10	90
	$30 p	0.80	1.30	1.25	4	188
Biomira		**$4.90**			**113**	**1701**
Mar96	$5	0.50	0.70	0.60	60	408
	$5 p	0.45	0.65	0.40	30	92
Jun96	$5 p	0.65	0.85	0.70	20	60
	$6	0.55	0.70	0.70	3	235
Bomb		**$18⅛**			**377**	**10300**
Jan96	$12	6	6⅜	6½	34	360
	$14	4.05	4.30	4.50	10	158
	$16	2.05	2.30	2.50	25	238
	$16½	1.55	1.80	2.00	13	109
	$17	1.05	1.30	1.05	80	378
	$18	0.30	0.55	0.65	10	416
Apr96	$19	0.85	0.90	0.85	50	50
Jul96	$18	1.50	1.75	1.75	10	151
	$18 p	0.85	1.10	0.80	10	40
	$19	1.25	1.30	1.30	69	77
Jan97	$9	9¾	10¼	10¼	30	108
	$16	3.80	4.30	4.25	6	120
	$17	3.40	3.65	3.40	30	262
Cambior		**$15⅞**			**160**	**3909**
Jan96	$13	2.70	2.95	2.85	20	34
	$14	1.70	1.90	1.80	20	56
	$16 p	0.45	0.70	0.50	30	180
Feb96	$15	1.10	1.35	1.35	30	86
	$16 p	0.65	0.90	0.80	20	110
Jan97	$14 p	0.60	1.10	0.70	20	46
	$16 p	1.30	1.80	1.40	20	70
Cameco		**$51½**			**24**	**544**
May96	$44 p	1.05	1.25	1.10	15	15
	$46	8¼	8⅝	8⅝	9	40
Cdn Bd 2001		**$113.40**			**20**	**227**
Jan96	$113p	0.25	0.50	0.30	20	20
Cdn Bd 2021		**$124.80**			**33**	**566**
Jan96	$124	1.25	1.50	1.70	4	6
	$126	0.30	0.55	0.70	4	22
Feb96	$122	3.20	3.45	3.95	10	12
	$126p	2.25	2.50	2.10	15	16
Cdn Bd 2011		**$114.65**			**86**	**759**
Jan96	$114	0.85	1.10	1.50	2	48
Feb96	$112p	0.35	0.40	0.25	20	40
	$114	1.55	1.80	2.35	4	20
	$116	0.65	0.90	1.00	4	11
Mar96	$112	3.20	3.45	3.05	37	88
Jun96	$112p	1.30	1.55	1.20	15	15
	$116	1.80	1.95	2.20	4	4
CIBC		**$41⅝**			**30**	**2909**
Jan96	$35	6⅜	6⅝	6½	20	100
	$40 p	0.05	0.25	0.20	5	6
Mar96	$42½	0.85	1.10	1.25	5	40
Cdn Occide		**$46¼**			**10**	**1545**
May96	$45 p	0.95	1.20	1.15	10	10
Cdn Pacific		**$25**			**24**	**3123**
Jan96	$20	4.80	5	4.90	10	95
	$22	2.85	3.10	3.10	4	14
	$25	0.35	0.45	0.35	10	933
Corel		**$14⅞**			**1638**	**10336**
Jan96	$15	0.65	0.90	1.05	35	20
	$15 p	0.60	0.85	0.55	20	20
	$17½p	2.50	2.75	1.75	90	85
	$20	0.05	0.15	0.05	183	898
	$20 p	5	5½	4.40	233	448
	$22½p	7½	8	6⅞	115	238
Feb96	$15 p	0.90	1.05	0.90	80	65
	$17½	0.55	0.60	0.60	80	75
	$17½p	2.75	3.10	1.80	30	300
	$20	0.15	0.35	0.40	15	365
	$20 p	5	5½	4.05	10	35
	$22½p	7⅜	7⅞	6⅜	25	0
Apr96	$15	2.00	2.40	2.10	57	32
	$15 p	1.45	1.70	1.50	60	60
	$17½	1.30	1.40	1.35	34	63
	$17½p	3.25	3.35	2.70	5	647
	$20	0.70	0.90	0.75	112	717
	$20 p	5¼	5¾	4.70	31	354
	$22½	0.35	0.45	0.45	96	673
	$25	0.10	0.25	0.10	3	489
Jul96	$15	3.10	3.35	3.25	50	55
	$15 p	1.70	1.95	1.65	20	20
	$17½	2.05	2.30	2.05	91	93
	$17½p	3.40	3.80	3.15	60	150
	$20	1.40	1.60	1.55	53	191
	$22½	0.80	0.90	0.85	50	127
Cott		**$8**			**530**	**8846**
Jan96	$8	0.25	0.40	0.30	5	213
Feb96	$6	2.05	2.30	2.05	40	46
	$8	0.55	0.70	0.60	20	30
	$8 p	0.55	0.70	0.55	30	50
	$9	0.20	0.35	0.25	50	120
	$10	0.15	0.20	0.15	20	40
Mar96	$8 p	0.70	0.85	0.75	20	185
Jun96	$8 p	1.00	1.15	1.20	10	40
	$10	0.55	0.65	0.60	70	80
Delrina Exch		**$26½**			**47**	**595**
Mar96	$20 p	3.45	3.95	3.50	20	112
	$22½	0.15	0.65	0.40	15	101
Jun96	$17½p	1.75	2.25	1.75	10	12
	$22½	0.85	1.35	1.30	2	10
Diamond Fi		**$27½**			**554**	**13055**
Jan96	$25	2.60	3.00	3.00	60	199
	$26	1.95	2.15	1.95	60	703
	$27	1.40	1.50	1.50	88	1714
	$28	0.90	1.00	0.90	52	47
Feb96	$26 p	1.00	1.25	0.85	25	25
	$27	2.30	2.65	2.85	125	706
Mar96	$20	7⅝	8⅛	8¼	30	375
	$25	4.00	4.40	4.25	10	1688
	$26	3.25	3.65	3.50	10	520
	$27	2.70	3.10	2.70	4	295
Jun96	$25	5¼	5¾	5¾	10	551
	$26 p	2.25	2.60	2.10	3	13
	$28	3.60	3.85	3.85	77	77
Dofasco Inc		**$18⅛**			**106**	**2555**
Mar96	$16	2.40	2.65	2.45	20	70
	$18	0.90	1.00	0.85	76	190
	$18 p	0.75	1.00	0.90	10	275
Domtar		**$11¼**			**50**	**3384**
Feb96	$11	0.65	0.90	0.80	10	226
	$12	0.25	0.50	0.55	30	94
May96	$12	0.65	0.90	0.90	10	301
Echo Bay		**$15⅜**			**55**	**1829**
Jan96	$15	0.45	0.55	0.55	10	402
Apr96	$15	1.25	1.45	1.25	10	422
Jul96	$14	2.30	2.55	2.50	25	48
	$16	1.25	1.45	1.25	10	63
Gandalf		**$20½**			**434**	**4491**
Jan96	$18	2.90	3.10	2.20	20	33
	$20	1.70	1.85	1.35	30	28
	$20 p	1.00	1.15	1.25	90	189
	$22½	0.65	0.80	0.50	30	169
	$22½p	2.50	2.70	3.00	15	143
	$25	0.20	0.35	0.20	2	230
	$25 p	4.55	4.75	5½	16	175
Feb96	$20	2.65	2.85	2.20	4	4
	$20 p	2.00	2.20	2.60	8	20
	$22½	1.70	1.85	1.50	7	35
	$22½p	3.50	3.70	4.10	15	10
Apr96	$13 p	0.60	0.75	0.90	30	37
	$18 p	2.30	2.50	2.85	20	47
	$22½	3.25	3.45	3.40	50	75
	$25	2.50	2.70	1.90	10	126
	$27½	1.95	2.10	1.80	20	334
Jul96	$17	6⅞	7¼	6½	1	129
	$20	5⅝	6	4.95	1	210
	$20 p	4.50	4.70	4.95	21	83
	$25	4.00	4.20	3.65	29	80
	$27½	3.40	3.60	3.05	15	240
Gulf Cda		**$5¾**			**32**	**970**
Jun96	$6	0.40	0.65	0.50	2	2
	$7	0.08	0.35	0.20	30	30
Renaissanc		**$34¾**			**10**	**379**
May96	$35	2.05	2.30	2.10	10	10
Repap		**$6½**			**90**	**6331**
May96	$7	0.75	0.85	0.90	20	260
	$8	0.40	0.60	0.60	10	165
Aug96	$6	1.50	1.70	1.55	20	20
	$7	1.05	1.25	1.05	30	100
	$7 p	1.00	1.20	1.05	10	60
Rgr Cm		**$15¼**			**80**	**6506**
Jan96	$14	1.70	1.95	1.70	15	60
	$15	0.85	1.10	0.95	10	1982
Feb96	$16	0.50	0.75	0.55	30	20
Apr96	$15	1.50	1.75	1.70	20	40
	$16	1.10	1.20	1.15	5	506
Royal Bank		**$32⅛**			**263**	**9184**
Jan96	$25	6⅞	7⅜	7	45	254
	$30	2.05	2.20	1.95	80	2105
	$31	1.00	1.15	1.10	20	379
Apr96	$31 p	0.50	0.75	0.55	30	74
	$32½	1.00	1.10	1.05	25	639
Jul96	$29	3.60	4.00	3.75	30	0
	$32	1.75	2.00	1.70	7	118
	$33	1.25	1.50	1.25	16	101
Jan98	$25	8⅞	9⅜	9	10	55
Royal Oak		**$5½**			**1000**	**9224**
Jan96	$5	0.35	0.45	0.40	420	670
Feb96	$6	0.05	0.15	0.10	70	70
Mar96	$5	0.55	0.70	0.55	400	3351
Jun96	$5	0.80	0.95	0.85	50	491
	$6	0.35	0.45	0.40	60	774
Seagram		**$48¾**			**22**	**5952**
Apr96	$50	2.20	2.70	2.25	2	164
Jul96	$47½p	2.05	2.30	2.10	20	75
Stelco		**$6⅛**			**50**	**5542**
May96	$6	0.50	0.65	0.55	50	125
Stone-Consol		**$19**			**90**	**541**
Apr96	$17	2.20	2.70	2.45	20	5
	$18	1.55	1.80	1.80	40	10
Jul96	$16	3.45	3.95	3.90	30	15
TSE 100		**$292.55**			**13**	**157**
Jan96	$290	4.15	4.60	5¾	9	12
Jun96	$290	11¼	12¼	13⅜	4	12
TSE 35		**$253.89**			**1795**	**13700**
Jan96	$240	14¼	14¾	14	5	41
	$242½	11⅞	12⅜	11⅞	5	45
	$245	9⅝	10⅛	11½	5	184
	$245p	0.25	0.45	0.50	14	483
	$247½p	0.50	0.70	0.70	20	94
	$250	5¼	5¾	6	22	915
	$250p	0.95	1.15	1.20	220	534
	$252½	3.65	4.05	3.55	74	2038
	$252½p	1.80	2.00	2.00	283	730
	$255	2.35	2.55	2.55	225	1175
	$255p	2.80	3.10	3.10	40	414
	$257½	1.25	1.45	1.70	130	130
	$260	0.65	0.85	0.85	50	63
	$260p	6	6½	6¼	40	130
Feb96	$250p	2.40	2.60	2.55	9	17
	$252½	5¾	6¼	6	3	3
	$252½p	3.25	3.55	3.75	200	290
	$255p	4.15	4.55	4.15	5	10
	$260	2.40	2.50	2.35	46	62
Mar96	$245	12⅛	12⅝	12¼	289	768
	$245p	2.10	2.30	1.65	16	189
	$250	8½	9	8⅜	15	373
	$250p	3.40	3.70	3.45	15	65
	$255	5⅝	6⅛	5¾	19	438
	$260	3.30	3.60	3.35	35	51
	$260p	8⅛	8⅝	8⅞	10	300
TVX Gold		**$10½**			**433**	**4940**
Jan96	$9	1.45	1.65	1.55	10	148
	$10	0.55	0.60	0.60	220	2370
	$11 p	0.55	0.70	0.70	12	32
Feb96	$9	1.45	1.65	1.45	1	2
	$11	0.25	0.35	0.35	10	100
Apr96	$10	1.05	1.15	1.05	10	511
	$11	0.55	0.65	0.55	60	199
	$12	0.30	0.40	0.30	10	10
Jul96	$9 p	0.30	0.40	0.30	30	30
	$10	1.35	1.50	1.35	20	119
	$10 p	0.65	0.80	0.75	40	70
	$11 p	1.05	1.25	1.05	10	16
Talisman		**$29¼**			**10**	**629**
Jun96	$30	1.80	2.05	1.80	10	111
Teck		**$27½**			**20**	**140**
Aug96	$25 p	0.60	0.85	0.55	20	20
Tee-Comm		**$15⅛**			**90**	**5345**
Jan96	$17	0.10	0.25	0.25	10	258
Feb96	$16	0.95	1.10	0.95	20	103
Apr96	$17	1.55	1.70	1.65	30	179
	$18	1.20	1.35	1.50	10	92
	$19	0.95	1.10	0.85	10	348
Jul96	$16	3.30	3.45	3.40	10	271
Telus		**$16¼**			**37**	**1379**
Jun96	$16	0.75	0.95	0.75	7	65
Sep96	$16	0.90	1.10	0.90	30	30
TIPS		**$25.50**			**13**	**618**
Mar96	$22½	3.25	3.35	3.35	3	0
	$25½	0.65	0.75	0.85	10	110
TD Bank		**$24¾**			**109**	**3639**
Jan96	$20	4.55	5	4.55	16	74
	$25	0.25	0.35	0.25	30	585
Apr96	$23	2.15	2.40	2.25	20	122
	$24	1.55	1.70	1.65	5	121
	$25	1.00	1.25	1.05	30	211
Jan97	$25	1.70	2.20	2.00	4	181
Jan98	$30	0.85	1.35	0.90	4	4
TransAlta		**$14¾**			**60**	**1549**
Sep96	$15	0.40	0.50	0.40	60	73
TCPL		**$19⅛**			**122**	**5210**
Feb96	$18	1.15	1.30	1.45	20	54
	$19	0.45	0.60	0.55	62	1630
May96	$19	0.80	0.95	1.10	10	503
Jan98	$16	3.70	3.90	4.15	30	380
Transcontl		**$**			**64**	**3123**
Jan97	$16	3.45	3.65	3.80	40	290
	$18	2.00	2.20	2.25	4	388
	$20 p	1.35	1.55	1.50	20	125
WBB		**$**			**25**	**973**
Jan98	$15	6⅛	6⅝	6⅝	15	103
	$18 p	1.85	2.00	2.00	10	29
WCA		**$**			**60**	**341**
Jan96	$9 p	1.70	2.10	1.75	20	30
Jan98	$8	1.20	1.60	1.25	20	40
	$8 p	0.80	1.20	0.85	20	40
WCJ		**$**			**10**	**288**
Jan98	$18	2.40	2.90	2.55	10	14
WLV		**$**			**20**	**109**
Jan98	$14	2.15	2.65	2.30	20	52
Total contract volume				**14153**		
Total open interest				**438112**		

SOURCE: Reprinted with permission of *The Globe and Mail: Report on Business*, (January 4, 1996).

call options (with an exercise price of $45 per share) were $0.35 and $0.80, respectively. Similarly, the price for the last trades of Alcan July put options (with an exercise price of $45) that stop trading on the third Friday of July was $3.70. The bid and ask prices were $3.55 and $3.80 respectively. If on a particular day some options are not traded there will be no record.

The last entries show the total volume (the number of contracts traded) and total open interest (the number of contracts outstanding) for calls and puts. The first entries of Figure 20.2 indicate the five "most active" options.

► Trading on Exchanges

Investors may place the same kinds of orders for options as for stocks — market, limit, and stop orders (these were discussed in Chapter 2). However, the way the orders for options are executed on the exchanges is, in some ways, different from the way that orders for stocks are executed.

As mentioned in Chapter 2, trading on stock exchanges centres around market-makers. On the options trading floor of the TSE there are are also market-makers known as **specialists**. They serve two functions, acting as both dealers and brokers. As dealers, they set the bid and asked prices and keep an inventory of the options (and the underlying stocks) that are assigned to them. They buy into and sell from that inventory as required to maintain a market. As brokers, they keep the limit order book and execute the orders in it as market prices move up and down. There are also **competitive option traders** (COTs), who trade solely for their own account, hoping to buy low and sell high, and *floor traders*, who handle orders from the public.

Orders may be executed either by means of an auction at the trading post with "open outcry," (meaning that the auction is conducted orally) or entered electronically through the *Market Order System of Trading* (MOST). Option trading is, therefore, a hybrid system in the process of evolving towards full automation. The MOST system guarantees a complete fill at the current bid or offer price for every market and tradeable limit order for 10 contracts or less, and provides immediate price confirmation electronically. In addition, MOST orders are transmitted to the floor. If a price that is better than the current bid or ask is available from a trader on the floor then a delayed but improved fill will be confirmed.

More than one specialist may be assigned to the options on a given stock (a few have as many as four). The specialists have the choice of maintaining either an open or a closed limit order book that, unlike the stock exchange limit order book, has manual entries. The information in an open book is available to all market participants, whereas that in a closed book is known only to the specialists. Specialists must provide a minimum guaranteed fill (MGF) that is generally ten contracts, but some offer an MGF as large as 25 contracts. In addition, they must ensure that the maximum spread between the bid and ask prices of options on a particular stock is not exceeded. A typical schedule is shown in Table 20.2.

Table 20.2

Maximum Spread Between Bid and Ask Prices for Option Contracts.

Option Price	*Maximum Spread*[a]
under $2.00	$0.25
over $2.00	$0.50

[a] For LEAPS and index options, maximum spreads are double these shown.

In North America all options are traded in continuous markets, meaning that orders can be executed any time the exchanges are open. Trading in options, however, is frequently far from continuous. In the financial press, it is not unusual to find prices for various options that appear to be out of line with one another or with the price of the underlying stock. It should be remembered that each listed price is that of the last trade recorded in the day and that these trades may have taken place at different times. Observed price disparities may simply reflect trading that occurred before and after major news, rather than concurrent values at which arbitrage trades could have been made.

Commissions

Whereas a commission must be paid to a stockbroker whenever an option is either written, bought, or sold, the size of the commission has been reduced substantially since options began to be traded on organized exchanges in 1973. Furthermore, this commission is typically smaller than the commission that would be paid if the underlying stock had been purchased instead of the option. This is probably due to the facts that clearing and settling are easier with options than with stocks (with options there are no share certificates that have to change hands with every trade) and that the order size is smaller (the total dollar amount paid for the option is much less than the total dollar amount of the underlying stock).

However, the investor should be aware that exercising an option will typically result in the buyer's having to pay a commission equivalent to the commission that would be incurred if the stock itself were being bought or sold.

MARGIN

In contrast to a stock buyer, a call or put buyer is not allowed to use margin. The option buyer is required to pay 100% of the option's purchase price. The buyer of an option, however, would like some assurance that the writer can deliver as required if the option is exercised. Specifically, the buyer of a call option would like some guarantee that the writer is capable of delivering the requisite shares, and the buyer of a put option would like some guarantee that the writer is capable of delivering the necessary cash. Since all option contracts are with Canadian Derivatives Clearing Corp., Inc., the CDCC is also concerned about the ability of the writer to fulfill the terms of the contract.

To relieve the CDCC of this concern, margin requirements have been set by the exchanges where the options are traded. However, brokerage firms, since they are ultimately liable to the CDCC for the actions of their clients, are allowed to impose stricter requirements if they wish.

If a call is exercised, shares are delivered by the writer in exchange for the exercise price. If a put is exercised, cash is delivered in exchange for shares. In either case, the cost to the option writer is the difference between the exercise price and the stock's market value at the time of exercise. Since the CDCC is at risk if the writer is unable to bear this cost, it is not surprising that the CDCC has a system in place that protects itself. This system is known as **margin**, and it is similar in some ways to the notion of margin associated with short sales of stocks (discussed in Chapter 2).

Before proceeding further some terminology must be defined. A call option is said to be **at the money** if the underlying stock has a market price roughly equal to the call's exercise price. If the stock's market price is below the exercise price, the call is said to be **out of the money**, and if the market price is above the exercise price, the call is said to be **in the money**.

Occasionally finer gradations are invoked, and one hears of "near the money," "deep in the money," "far out of the money," and so on.

Calls

In a situation known as **covered call writing**, where the writer of a call owns the underlying stock, the writer does not need to provide any cash margin. If the option is out of the money, then the premium paid by the buyer is given to the writer but the writer's shares are kept in escrow by the brokerage firm.[4] Thus, if the buyer chooses to exercise the option, the requisite shares are at hand for delivery. If the option expires or if the writer enters a closing purchase, then the writer will have access to the shares. If, however, the share price moves up so that the option goes into the money, the writer will be required to add the difference between the share and exercise prices to the margin account.

In situations known as **naked call writing**, where the writer of the option does not own the underlying stock, the margin requirements are slightly more complicated. Specifically, the amount that must be maintained in the margin account is the sum of three components: (1) the option premium; (2) 25% of the market value of the underlying stock; and (3) an amount equal to the share price less the exercise price. If the option is out of the money then the third figure will be negative. At no time, however, must the margin fall below the option premium plus 5% of the value of the stock. The amount required is the larger of these two calculations.

As an example of the margin required for naked call writing, consider an investor who writes a February 42 1/2 call contract and receives, through his broker, a premium of $0.20 per share. If the underlying share is selling for $39 1/2, then the margin is calculated as follows:

Margin:

Option premium = $0.20 × 100 shares =	$ 20.00
25% of market value of stock	
= .25 × $39.5 × 100 shares =	$987.50
Stock price less exercise price	
= (39.5 – 42.5) × 100 =	–$300.00
Sum = $20 + 987.50 – 300 =	$707.50
Check:	
option premium plus 5% of value of stock =	$217.50

Therefore the amount required is $707.50.

Another investor, however, may have written a February 35 call on the same stock receiving a premium of $4.45. This writer will have to provide the following margin:

[4] The option writer may have purchased the shares on margin and, therefore, have borrowed 70% of the value of the stock from the broker.

Actual Margin:

Option premium = $4.45× 100 shares =	$445.00
25% of market value of stock	
= .25 × $39.5 × 100 shares =	$987.50
Stock price less exercise price	
= (39.5 – 35) × 100 =	$450.00
Sum = $445 + 987.50 + 450 =	$1882.50
Check:	
option premium plus 5% of value of stock =	$642.50

Therefore the amount required is $1882.50.

In the first case, the writer need only add $687.50 to the margin account, as the premium received is part of the total. In the second case, however, the writer must provide $1437.50 of new money and can expect a margin call if the share price rises further. The minimum margin will only apply to options that are "deep out of the money."

Puts

For puts, the margin requirements are similar. If the brokerage account of the writer of a put contains cash (or other securities) amounting to the exercise price of the put, then no margin is required. Furthermore, the writer can remove from the account an amount of cash that is equal to the premium received, since the account will still have collateral that is equal in value to the exercise price.

If, however, the brokerage account of a put writer does not contain cash (or securities), then the process is known as **naked put writing**. The amount of margin required for such a writer is calculated in a manner similar to that for the writer of a naked call option. That is, the put writer must provide margin equal to the option premium plus 25% of the market value of the underlying stock plus the difference between the exercise price and the share price. For out-of-the-money puts, the third amount will be negative and will reduce the margin requirement. The minimum margin will again be equal to the sum of the option premium and 5% of the market price of the underlying security.

It should be noted that these are minimum maintenance margin requirements and that any adverse movement in the share price will result in a margin call. Furthermore, the calculation of margin requirements becomes much more complex when the individual is engaged in various investment activities (such as simultaneously buying and writing different put and call options as well as buying some common stocks on margin while short selling others).

INSTITUTIONAL ISSUES

A Derivatives Debacle

By Karen Howlett and John Partridge

May 9, 1992 was a day for celebration at Ukrainian (Fort William) Credit Union Ltd., as it opened its new head office in a former Bank of Montreal branch at the corner of Victoria Ave. East and Simpson St. in Thunder Bay.

Clad in striking, off-white stone with the bank's coat of arms still carved above the imposing front entrance, the 55-year-old building was much grander than the humble shopfront a couple of blocks north on Simpson where the credit union had opened its doors in 1949.

"It was a beautiful, nice opening," recalls Peter Michailishin, 76, a Ukrainian immigrant who was one of the tiny credit union's founding fathers and also one of the officers who approved the purchase of the building for $135 000.

But for the past 18 months, 303 Victoria has again stood empty, its tall steel gates locked shut, and the link between Bank of Montreal and Ukrainian Fort William has come back to haunt them both.

The credit union has gone bust and provincial regulators, in a lawsuit, are blaming the bank's investment dealer subsidiary, Nesbitt Burns Inc., for the debacle. Nesbitt denies it was responsible for the credit union's demise.

In the grand scheme of things, the dollars involved are insignificant. At its peak, the tiny financial co-operative had assets of about $10-million and only about 1300 members drawn from Thunder Bay's 20 000-strong Ukrainian population.

As well, Deposit Insurance Corp. of Ontario (DICO), the provincial agency that protects credit union deposits of up to $60 000, said none of the members lost money, even though the credit union ended up $2-million in the red.

But what has made the case one of international interest is that Nesbitt, the country's biggest investment dealer, stands accused of being involved in the first known Canadian fatality in the booming but volatile world of international derivatives trading.

Derivatives. The D-word. The often complex and sometimes risky financial contracts at the heart of such calamities as the bankruptcy of California's Orange County, the demise of Barings PLC — Britain's oldest merchant bank — and the massive lawsuit by US consumer products giant Procter & Gamble against Bankers Trust of New York.

The lawsuit contends that what sank Ukrainian Fort William was aggressive investing in options on millions of dollars worth of Government of Canada bonds over a 21-month period beginning in October, 1992.

The program was designed and sold not just to Ukrainian Fort William but to about half a dozen other credit unions in the area by Walter Zanewycz, a young broker at Nesbitt's local branch, who has strong family connections in the Ukrainian community. Although Ukrainian Fort William was the only one of the players that collapsed, two others were damaged heavily and are being managed by the deposit insurer.

Now Nesbitt, Mr. Zanewycz, 32, and his manager Gregory Pilot, 43, have become the target of an $8-million lawsuit by the deposit insurer, acting in its role as Ukrainian Fort William's major creditor.

DICO has accused Mr. Zanewycz, his manager, and their employer of having enriched themselves through fat commissions and margin-account interest charges by irresponsibly selling an unsophisticated buyer investments that it did not understand and never should have bought.

But DICO also has alleged that others played a role in the collapse. In a separate but related suit, it is seeking $8-million in damages from the credit union's former manager, Roman

Kozyra, and five of its nine former directors. It alleges that they failed to act in Ukrainian Fort William's best interests and to exercise sufficient care, diligence and skill in in running its affairs.

Neither they nor Nesbitt have yet filed statements of defence, and Mr. Kozyra and his co-defendants refuse to comment on the case.

However, for their part, officials at Nesbitt's Toronto head office are promising a vigorous fight against the allegations. They insist that everything about how they handled their end of the derivatives deals with Ukrainian Fort William was entirely appropriate.

There is also a school of thought among directors from other Thunder Bay credit unions that bought derivatives from Nesbitt that DICO caused the collapse of Ukrainian Fort William and the heavy losses elsewhere by forcing them to unwind the options contracts before they matured.

Who is to blame for Ukrainian Fort William's demise is a matter that will take months, maybe even years, for the courts to decide.

How did a tiny credit union come to risk depositors' money on derivatives? How many companies are in way over their heads, gambling with highly sophisticated instruments they don't fully grasp?

The essence of the lawsuit against Nesbitt deals with a brokerage firm's responsibility to ensure that its clients understand what they are buying. This burden is taking on a heightened importance as complex and potentially risky trading instruments, such as derivatives, become increasingly popular.

The credit union's board, made up of retired businessmen, a lawyer, and other volunteers with little in the way of financial background, placed its complete trust in Nesbitt to act in its best interests, the lawsuit alleges. However, the brokerage let it down, the suit contends, by embarking on a strategy that produced big profits for itself but big losses for Ukrainian Fort William.

Based on documents filed in the courts so far, as well as interviews with many players familiar with the drama, *The Globe and Mail* has pieced together events leading up to Ukrainian Fort William's collapse.

Walter Zanewycz had been in the investment business for only about three years back in 1991. Despite his inexperience, he had a keen sense that derivatives were the way of the future.

In the past few years, deivatives have become big moneyspinners for many big brokerages and banks, so Mr. Zanewycz set about finding potential customers in Thunder Bay.

He attended a board meeting of the credit union's board in early 1991, where he told the directors he had the expertise to buy and sell options contracts.

They were impressed with his apparent savvy.

The statement of claim alleges that he told directors that the options trades were designed as a hedge against interest rate fluctuations and would be low-risk investments that would provide the credit union with a stable rate of return.

These types of derivatives are relatively unsophisticated by Bay Street standards, but to a credit union that for years had invested its cash in Treasury bills, they marked an exotic departure.

Shortly after Mr. Zanewycz had done his first options trade for the credit union in October 1992, he attended another board meeting.

There, he assured directors that under his guidance, the credit union would reap significant gains trading these instruments. He described himself as a "leading expert" in derivatives, according to the statement of claim.

Some of the directors were so much in the dark, they confused these options with Canada Savings Bonds, while others expressed concern over what the credit union was getting itself into.

But Nesbitt's rising star succeeded in convincing most of the directors that he knew what he was doing.

He also had a big fan at the credit union — Roman Kózyra.

Mr. Kozyra, now 41, was a son of one of the credit union's other founders and brother to one of its directors.

Armed with a degree in Economics and a one-year graduate diploma in business administration from Thunder Bay's Lakehead University, he also added the Canadian Securities Course somewhere along the road. Mr. Kozyra took over the manager's job at the credit union in his mid-20s.

Mr. Kozyra boasted to Ukrainian Fort William members in the 1993 annual report that at a time when the economy remained in a slump and many financial institutions were struggling, it was flourishing.

The credit union was able to generate a profit and pay dividends to its members by adopting a "pro-active approach" to interest rate risk, he wrote. "Careful evaluation of economic trends has allows us to implement sophisticated hedging strategies that both enhance returns and protect against market volatility."

This involved having the credit union buy and sell options on Government of Canada bonds, with Nesbitt orchestrating the trades.

Buying options gave the credit union the right, but not the obligation, to buy or sell bonds at a specific price and date. Selling options meant that some time down the road, the credit union could be called upon by the person on the other side of the trade to buy or sell the bonds at potentially unfavourable prices that could force the credit union to incur large losses.

The credit union was hoping that it was betting the right way on interest rate movements. When the strategy worked at first, Mr. Zanewycz made handsome commissions and Mr. Kozyra was the toast of Thunder Bay's credit union sector.

Other managers came under pressure from their members to replicate Ukrainian Fort William's performance, while some who initially resisted eventually went along for the ride. Before long, Mr. Zanewycz was doing options trades for about half a dozen other credit unions in Thunder Bay and communities further north, including West Fort William Credit Union, which, with assets of $45-million, was the biggest in the area.

Initially, the credit unions made money from Mr. Zanewycz's hedging strategies. Mr. Kozyra said in Ukrainian Fort William's 1993 annual report that assets had grown 16 percent "notwithstanding the general weakness in the economy."

But that was to be his final message to members. The credit union's fortunes began to reverse in February, 1994, when interest rates started rising after more than three years of near continuous decline. The higher rates sharply reduced bond prices and put the credit union ino the red.

When bond prices started falling, the credit union had to pump more money into the margin account that Nesbitt had opened for it because it was forced to sell the bonds at a lower price than it had originally agreed to pay at the time it entered the contract.

The statement of claim says that what made the risk so high for Ukrainian Fort William is that it began to do "naked" transactions — that is, it was selling options contracts without owning the underlying bonds.

Players close to the credit union contend that DICO's statement of claim, which includes a list of all the options trades between October 1992, and June 1994, does not provide a complete picture of the hedging strategies Mr. Zanewycz and Nesbitt helped to orchestrate. This, they contend, is because it does not include any information from the credit union's balance sheet, which might indicate it was using the options as a legitimate hedge against its loans.

But Andy Poprawa, DICO's president, says his agency saw "no apparent relationship" between the options trades and the balance sheet.

Along the way, Nesbitt made several margin calls and the credit union was able to meet them until one day in June, 1994. "Nesbitt called up and said, 'okay guys, you're going to have to buy the bonds.' "

But Ukrainian Fort William didn't have the funds. Mr. Kozyra got on the phone to Credit Union Central of Ontario — which acts as central banker for the province's more than 380 credit unions — and asked to draw down the credit union's line of credit. But CUC refused to grant the credit unless Ukrainian Fort William agreed to let DICO come in and manage its affairs, said CUC chief executive officer Jonathan Guss.

Mr. Guss alleged that the line of credit Ukrainian Fort William had set up at Nesbitt to handle its margin trading was unauthorized under CUC rules. These require all members to get permission before opening such lines at other financial institutions, he said in an interview.

At that point, it was game over for Ukrainian Fort William. CUC called DICO, which agreed to extend a loan that allowed the credit union to meet the margin call. At the same time, DICO officials took over management of the credit union, replaced Mr. Kozyra and the directors and seized the assets.

In December, DICO closed the options contracts, leaving Ukrainian Fort William with losses of $2-million, enough to more than wipe out the $500 000 in capital it had slowly built up over 45 years in business.

The tiny credit union founded by immigrant farmhands, labourers, carpenters and railway workers, who joined together to provide a credit co-operative for the city's flourishing Ukrainian-Canadian community, closed its doors in June, 1994.

Over the past few years, dozens of credit unions in Ontario have been forced to close. In every case, DICO has come to the rescue and, in the process, it has rung up a deficit of $75-million.

But the demise of Ukrainian Fort William marks the first time the agency has taken an investment dealer to court — and the first time it has had to deal with the fallout from derivatives.

DICO officials are calling it a landmark case and that is why they spent well over a year in research and preparation before issuing statements of claim against Nesbitt and the former directors in December. "The information we have compelled us to take action," said Bill Foster, vice-president of supervision and asset management. "This is not something you do lightly."

In the wake of the wave of trouble in Thunder Bay, DICO and CUC have found their rules and powers lacking and have moved to strengthen them.

One well-placed source said the Ontario Ministry of Finance, which is responsible for regulating the credit unions in the province, first became aware of the derivatives activities in Thunder Bay in August, 1993. But at that point, the transactions were for hedging purposes only and the bonds were in place to cover any call, the source said.

"Then some of them decided to go off and play silly games in the yard."

But by the time DICO started taking a hard look at these trades in early 1994, triggered by a panicked call from the new manager of West Fort William Credit Union who did not understand the derivatives investments her predecessor had made, most of the damage had been done.

SOURCE: Reprinted with permission of *The Globe and Mail: Report on Business* (January 13, 1996).

TAXATION OF OPTION PROFITS AND LOSSES

Revenue Canada's rules regarding the reporting of gains and losses incurred through options trading are not crystal clear, especially when dealing with naked option writing. As indicated in Chapter 10, the investor has the option of declaring that his or her investment gains or losses should be treated as either income or capital gains or losses as long as this is done consistently through time. Interpretation Bulletin 479R section 25 states that gains or losses incurred from either holding (buying) options or writing covered calls should be reported on the same account as the investor's transactions in shares. Writing naked calls, however, is different. Section 25 (c) states "the gain or loss realized by the writer of naked options is normally on income account. However, the Department will accept reporting of gains and losses on capital account provided the practice is followed consistently from year to year." Commissions paid are added to purchase prices and subtracted from selling prices in determining the amount of the capital gains or losses. Any frequent trader in options is subject to the risk of being deemed to be a "sophisticated or professional investor" and, therefore, required to report gains and losses as income.

Example 1

Consider a call option buyer. If the call is exercised, the buyer is considered to have bought the shares for a total cost equal to the exercise price plus the premium paid for the option itself (plus commissions). When the stock is subsequently sold, the difference between this cost and the selling price (less commissions) is the buyer's capital gain or loss. If the option expires out of the money (i.e., without being either closed out or exercised) then the cost of the option is treated as either a deduction from income or a capital loss depending on the investor's normal practice. If the call buyer later sells the option instead of exercising it, the gain or loss is the difference between the buying and selling prices (less commissions).

Example 2

Consider the writer of a call option. If the call is exercised, the writer is considered to have sold the shares for a total value equal to the exercise price plus the premium received for the option (less commissions). The difference between this value and the price paid when the stock was purchased (plus commissions) is the amount of the gain or loss incurred by the writer. If the call writer later buys the option, thereby closing out his or her position, the difference between the premium that was received when the option was written and the premium that was paid to close out the position (less commissions) is the amount of the gain or loss. However, if the option expires unexercised, then the writer will have a gain equal to the amount of the premium received (less commissions).

Example 3

The treatment of puts is similar. If the put expires unexercised, then the buyer has a loss and the writer has a gain equal to the premium on the put (adjusted for commissions). If a closing transaction is entered, then the difference between the buying and selling prices (adjusted for commissions) is the amount of the gain or loss. If the put is exercised, then the buyer has a gain equal to the exercise price less the amount paid for both the stock and the put (less commissions). The writer who receives the stock is treated as having made a stock purchase for an amount equal to the exercise price less the premium received on the put (less commissions).

These and other rules give rise to a number of strategies that take tax consequences into account. For example, consider an investor who owns a stock whose market price has risen dramatically. If the investor now sells it, a capital gain is incurred. However, if instead, the investor buys a January put and holds off selling the stock until the turn of the year, the capital gain is not realized until the following year, so no taxes need be paid in the current year. The gain on the stock will have been protected by the use of the put. In January, the investor can decide to either exercise the put or sell the stock, realizing the gain at that time, thus deferring tax payments for a year.

VALUATION OF OPTIONS

Valuation at Expiration

The value of an option is related to the value of the underlying security in a manner that is most easily seen just prior to expiration (which for simplicity will be referred to as "at expiration"). Figure 20.3(a) relates the value of a call option with an exercise price of $100 to the price of the underlying stock at expiration. If the stock price is below $100, the option will be worthless when it expires. If the price is above $100, the option can be exercised for $100 to obtain a security with a greater value, resulting in a net gain to the option buyer that will equal the difference between the security's market price and the $100 exercise price. However, there is no need for the option buyer to actually exercise the option. Instead, the option writer can simply pay the buyer the difference between the security price and the $100 exercise price, thereby allowing both parties to avoid the inconvenience of exercise. This is commonly done for listed options (by using the services of the CDCC), although a minority of investors choose to exercise their options, possibly for tax purposes.

Figure 20.3(b) shows the value at expiration of a put option with an exercise price of $100. If the stock price is above $100, the option will be worthless when it expires. If the price is below $100, the option can be exercised to obtain $100 for stock having a lower value, resulting in a net gain to the option buyer that will equal the difference between the $100 exercise price and the stock's market price. As with a call option, neither the put option buyer nor the writer need actually deal in the stock. Instead, the writer of any put option that is worth exercising at expiration can simply pay the buyer of the option the difference between the stock price and the $100 exercise price.

In both panels of Figure 20.3, the lines indicating the value of a call and a put at expiration can also be interpreted to be the value of a call or a put *at the moment the option is exercised*, no matter when that occurs during the life of the option. In particular, for calls the kinked line connecting points 0, E, and Z is known as the **intrinsic value** of the call. Similarly, for puts the kinked line connecting points Z, E, and $200 is known as the intrinsic value of the put.

The kinked lines representing the intrinsic values of calls and puts such as those shown in Figure 20.3 can be expressed as IV_c and IV_p, respectively, as follows:

$$IV_c = \max\{0, P_s - E\} \tag{20.1a}$$

$$IV_p = \max\{0, E - P_s\} \tag{20.1b}$$

where P_s denotes the market price of the underlying stock and E denotes the exercise price of the option. (Here max means to use the larger of the two values in braces.)

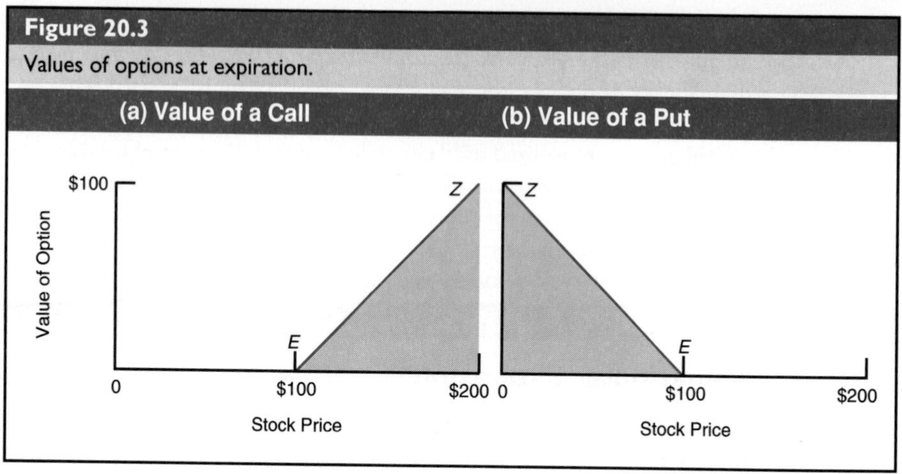

Consider the call option in Figure 20.3(a). Its intrinsic value, according to equation (20.1a), is max{0, P_s–$100} because its exercise price is $100. Note that for any market price of the stock that is below $100, such as $50, its intrinsic value is max{0, $50 – $100} = 0. Hence $IV_c = 0$ in such situations. Next imagine that the market price of the stock is above $100, for example, $150. In this situation its intrinsic value is max{0, $150 – $100} = $50. Hence $IV_c = P_s - E$. Thus, the kinked intrinsic value line has its kink at E, as it has two components that meet there: a horizontal line going through the origin out to the value E, and then a 45–degree line (and therefore having a slope of 1) going northeast from E. Similar analysis reveals that the kinked intrinsic value line for the put also has its kink at E, as shown in Figure 20.3(b).

Calls and puts will not sell for less than their intrinsic values, owing to the actions of shrewd investors. If an option sold for less than its intrinsic value, then such investors could instantaneously make riskless profits. For example, if the stock price was $150 and the call was selling for $40, which is $10 less than its intrinsic value of $50, then these investors would simultaneously buy these calls, exercise them, and sell the shares received from the writers. In doing so they would spend $140 on each call and exercise price and get $150 in return for each share sold, resulting in a net riskless profit of $10 per call. As a consequence, the call will not sell for less than $50 if the stock price is $150.

Profits and Losses on Calls and Puts

Figure 20.3 shows the values of call and put options at expiration. However, in order to determine profits and losses from buying or writing these options, the premiums involved must be taken into consideration.[5] Figure 20.4 does this for investors who engage in some of the more complicated option strategies. Each strategy assumes that the underlying stock is selling for $100 at the time an option is initially bought or written. It is also assumed that closing transactions are made just prior to the expiration date for the option being considered. Outcomes are shown for each of ten strategies. Because the profit obtained by

[5] Because the premium is paid by the buyer to the writer at the time the option is created, its value should be compounded to the expiration date using an appropriate rate of interest when calculating profits and losses.

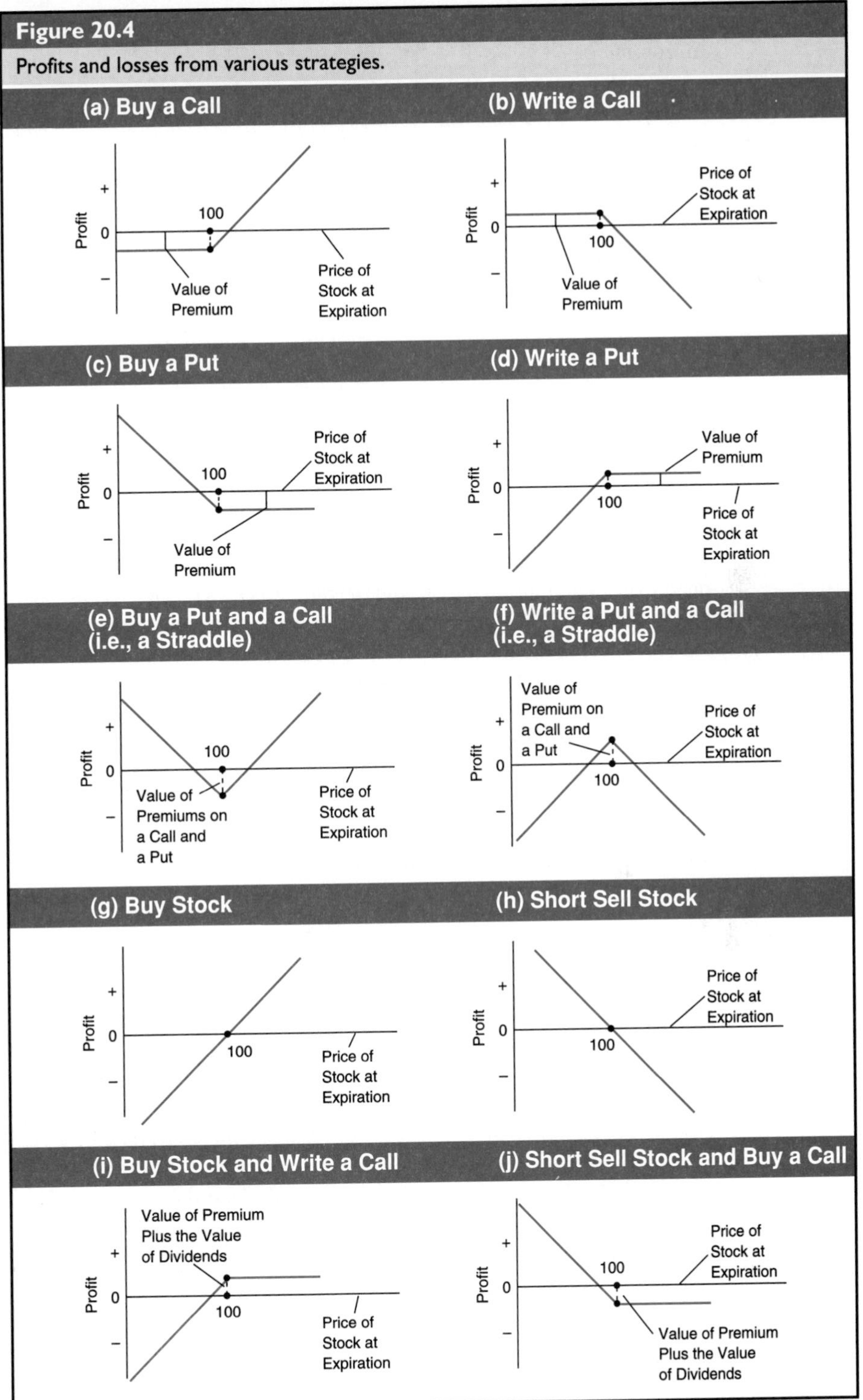

Figure 20.4
Profits and losses from various strategies.
(a) Buy a Call
Profit
+
0
-
100
Value of Premium
Price of Stock at Expiration
(b) Write a Call
Profit
+
0
-
100
Value of Premium
Price of Stock at Expiration
(c) Buy a Put
Profit
+
0
-
100
Value of Premium
Price of Stock at Expiration
(d) Write a Put
Profit
+
0
-
100
Value of Premium
Price of Stock at Expiration
(e) Buy a Put and a Call (i.e., a Straddle)
Profit
+
0
-
100
Value of Premiums on a Call and a Put
Price of Stock at Expiration
(f) Write a Put and a Call (i.e., a Straddle)
Profit
+
0
-
100
Value of Premium on a Call and a Put
Price of Stock at Expiration
(g) Buy Stock
Profit
+
0
-
100
Price of Stock at Expiration
(h) Short Sell Stock
Profit
+
0
-
100
Price of Stock at Expiration
(i) Buy Stock and Write a Call
Profit
+
0
-
100
Value of Premium Plus the Value of Dividends
Price of Stock at Expiration
(j) Short Sell Stock and Buy a Call
Profit
+
0
-
100
Value of Premium Plus the Value of Dividends
Price of Stock at Expiration

a buyer is the writer's loss and vice versa, each diagram in the figure has a corresponding mirror image.

Panels (a) and (b) in Figure 20.4 show the profits and losses associated with buying and writing a call, respectively. Similarly, panels (c) and (d) show the profits and losses associated with buying and writing a put, respectively.

Consider panels (a) and (c) first. The kinked lines representing profits and losses in these two panels are simply graphs of the intrinsic value equations, equations (20.1a) and (20.1b), shown in Figure 20.3, less the premiums on the options. Thus, they are graphs of the following equations:

$$\begin{aligned} \pi_c &= \text{IV}_c - P_c \\ &= \max\{0, P_s - E\} - P_c \\ &= \max\{-P_c, P_s - E - P_c\} \end{aligned} \tag{20.2a}$$

$$\begin{aligned} \pi_p &= \text{IV}_p - P_p \\ &= \max\{0, E - P_s\} - P_p \\ &= \max\{-P_p, E - P_s - P_p\} \end{aligned} \tag{20.2b}$$

where π_c and π_p denote the profits associated with buying a call and a put, and P_c and P_p denote the premiums on the call and the put, respectively. This means that the kinked profit line for the call is simply the same kinked line for the intrinsic value but lowered by an amount equal to the call premium P_c. Similarly, the kinked profit line for the put is simply the kinked intrinsic value line for the put, lowered by an amount equal to the put premium P_p.

If the premium on the call and put options shown in Figure 20.3 were \$5, then their profit lines would be graphs of the following two equations:

$$\begin{aligned} \pi_c &= \max\{-\$5, P_s - \$100 - \$5\} \\ &= \max\{-\$5, P_s - \$105\} \\ \pi_p &= \max\{-\$5, \$100 - P_s - \$5\} \\ &= \max\{-\$5, \$95 - P_s\} \end{aligned}$$

Therefore the kinked line for the call would be a horizontal line intersecting the vertical axis at –\$5, and it would have a kink at a stock price of \$100, where it would turn upward to intersect the horizontal axis at \$105. This indicates that the call buyer would not make a profit unless the stock price was above the breakeven point of \$105 at expiration. Each dollar that the stock price is above \$105 represents an additional dollar of profit. (Hence a price of \$108 would represent a profit of \$3, since the call buyer pays a premium of \$5 and an exercise price of \$100 to procure a share of stock that is worth \$108.)

Similarly, the kinked line for the put would be a downward-sloping line that would have a kink at a stock price of \$100 after intersecting the horizontal axis at \$95. At the kink the line would become horizontal so that if this part of the line were extended leftward to the vertical axis, it would intersect it at –\$5. This indicates that the put buyer would not make a profit unless the stock price was below the breakeven point of \$95 at expiration. Each dollar that the stock price is below \$95 represents an additional dollar of profit. (Hence, a price of \$92 would represent a profit of \$3, since the put buyer pays a premium of \$5 and gives up a share of stock worth \$92 in order to receive \$100 in return.)

Panels (b) and (d) of Figure 20.4 are mirror images of panels (a) and (c), respectively. This is because options are zero-sum games, where the profits to one party occur at the expense of the other party. Hence, if the stock price is at $108 so that the call buyer has a $3 profit, then the call writer has a $3 loss (because the writer receives the $5 premium and $100 exercise price but must give up a share of stock worth $108). Similarly, if the put buyer has a $3 profit, then the put writer has a loss of $3.

Profits and Losses from Some Option Strategies

Panels (e) and (f) of Figure 20.4 illustrate a more complicated options strategy known as a **straddle.** This strategy involves buying (or writing) both a call and a put on the same stock, with the options having the same exercise price and expiration date.[6] Note how panel (e) can be derived by adding the profits and losses shown in panels (a) and (c), whereas panel (f) can be derived by adding the profits and losses shown in panels (b) and (d). It can also be seen that panels (e) and (f) are mirror images of each other, again reflecting the fact that the profits to buyers equal the losses to writers and vice versa.

Panel (g) of Figure 20.4 shows the profit or loss made by an investor who avoids options entirely but buys a share of the underlying stock (at $100) at the same time that others buy or write options and sells the stock when the options expire. Assuming that no dividends are paid in the interim, the relationship is that shown by the solid line.[7] Similarly, panel (h) shows the profit or loss obtained by an investor who short sells the stock at the initial date and then buys it back at the expiration date.

Panel (i) of Figure 20.4 shows the results obtained by an investor who buys one share of stock and simultaneously writes a call on it. These results can be derived by adding the profits and losses shown in panels (b) and (g). As mentioned earlier, such an investor is said to have written a fully covered option. In contrast, the writer who does not hold the underlying stock, depicted in panel (b), is said to have written a naked option.

Panel (j) of Figure 20.4 shows the results obtained by an investor who short sells one share of stock and simultaneously buys a call option, and it can be derived by adding the profits and losses in panels (a) and (h). Note that this panel is the mirror image of panel (i).

Comparison of the diagrams in Figure 20.4 suggests that similar results can be obtained via alternative strategies. Panels (c) and (j) are similar, as are (d) and (i). Neither the premiums involved nor the initial investments required need be equal in every case. Nonetheless, the similarity of the results obtained with different "packages" of securities suggests that the total market values of the packages will be similar.

Having discussed the value of options (and option-based strategies) when they expire, it is appropriate to discuss next the value of options before they expire. Specifically, what is the fair (or true) value of an option today if it expires at some future date? The binomial option pricing model can be used to answer such a question. It is presented next.

---

[6] Strips and straps are option strategies similar to a straddle. The former involves combining two puts with one call, and the latter involves combining two calls with one put. Another kind of strategy is known as a spread, where one call is bought while another is written on the same underlying security. Specifically, a price spread involves two calls having the same expiration date but different exercise prices. A time spread involves two calls having the same exercise price but different expiration dates.

[7] If there are dividends, they should be expressed as a compounded value at the expiration date associated with the options (as they would have been previously received) and added to the line, thereby shifting it upward.

THE BINOMIAL OPTION PRICING MODEL

The binomial option pricing model (BOPM) can be used to estimate the fair value of a call or put option. It is best presented through an example in which it is assumed that the options are **European options**, meaning that they can be exercised only on their expiration dates. In addition, it is assumed that the underlying stock does not pay any dividends during the life of the option. It should be noted that the model can be modified to value **American options**, which are options that can be exercised any time during their life and can also be used to value options on stocks that pay dividends during the life of the option.

Call Options

Assume that the price of Widget stock today ($t = 0$) is \$100, and that after one year ($t = T$) its stock will be selling for either \$125 or \$80, meaning that the stock will either rise by 25% or fall by 20% over the year. In addition, the annual risk-free rate is 8% compounded continuously. Investors are assumed to be able to either lend (by purchasing these 8% bonds) or borrow (by short-selling the bonds) at this rate.

Now consider a call option on Widget that has an exercise price of \$100 and an expiration date of one year from now. This means that on the expiration date the call will have a value of either \$25 (if Widget is at \$125) or \$0 (if Widget is at \$80). Panel (a) of Figure 20.5 illustrates the situation by use of a "price tree." It can be seen from this tree why this is called a binomial model, as there are only two branches that represent prices at the expiration date.

Figure 20.5

Binomial model of prices for Widget.

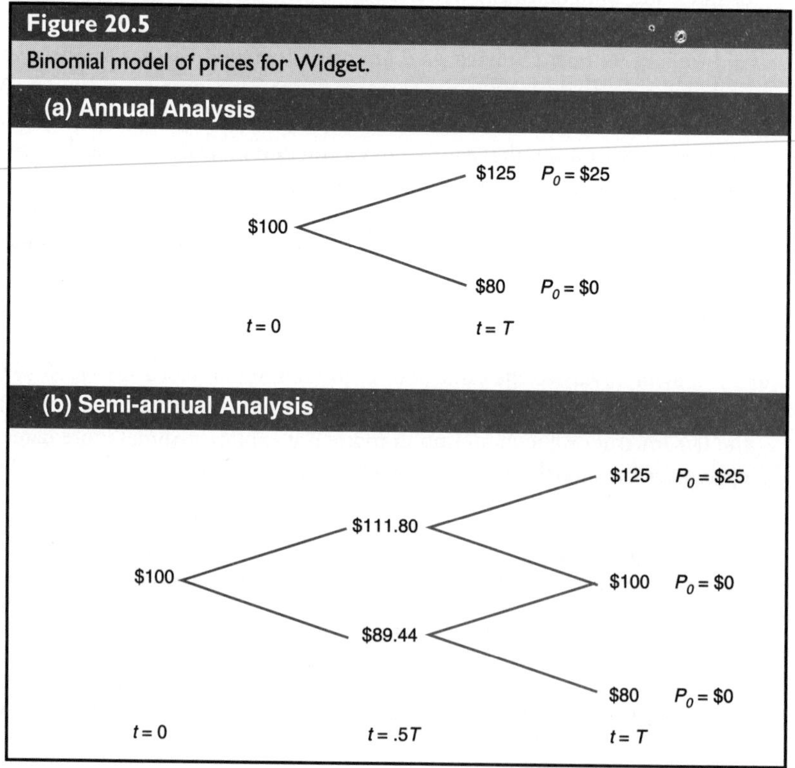

Valuation

What is a fair value for the call at time 0? The binomial option pricing model is designed to answer this question.

There are three investments that are of interest here: the share, the option, and a risk-free bond. The prices and payoffs for the share are known. It is also known that $100 invested in a risk-free bond will grow to approximately $108.33 given interest that is continuously compounded at an annual rate of 8%.[8] Finally, the end-of-period payoffs associated with the option are known. What is to be determined is a fair selling price for the option for now.

The key to understanding the situation is the observation that there are two possible future *states of nature*. The share's price may go up or down. For simplicity, these two states are called the "up state" and the "down state," respectively. This essential information is summarized as follows:

Security	*Payoff in Up State*	*Payoff in Down State*	*Current Price*
Share	$125.00	$80.00	$100.00
Bond	$108.33	$108.33	$100.00
Call	$25.00	$0.00	???

Note that at this juncture the current price of the call is unknown.

Replicating Portfolios

Although the Widget call option may seem exotic, its characteristics can in fact be replicated with an appropriate combination of the Widget stock and the risk-free bond. Moreover, the cost of this *replicating portfolio* constitutes the fair value of the option. Why? Because otherwise there would be an *arbitrage opportunity*—an investor could buy the cheaper of the two alternatives and sell the more expensive one, thereby achieving a guaranteed profit. (Just how this is done will be shown shortly.)

The composition of a portfolio that will precisely replicate the payoffs of the Widget call option needs to be determined. Consider a portfolio with N_s shares of Widget stock and N_b risk-free bonds. In the up state such a portfolio will have a payoff of $\$125N_s + \$108.33N_b$, whereas in the down state it will have a payoff of $\$80N_s + \$108.33N_b$. The call option is worth $25 in the up state. Thus N_s and N_b need to have values so that

$$\$125N_s + \$108.33N_b = \$25 \tag{20.3a}$$

On the other hand, the call option is worthless in the down state. Thus, N_s and N_b need to have values so that

$$\$80N_s + \$108.33N_b = \$0 \tag{20.3b}$$

These two linear equations, (20.3a) and (20.3b), have two unknowns and can easily be solved. Subtracting the second equation from the first gives

$$(\$125 - \$80)N_s = \$25 \tag{20.3c}$$

[8] In general, $1 will grow to $\$1e^{RT}$ at the end of T periods if it is continuously compounded at a rate of R. Here e represents the base of the natural logarithm, which is equal to approximately 2.71828. For a more detailed discussion, see Chapter 5.

so that N_s equals .5556. Substituting this value in either equation (20.3a) or equation (20.3b) gives the remainder of the solution, $N_b = -.4103$.

What does this mean in financial terms? It means that an investor can replicate the payoffs from the call by *short selling* \$41.03 of the risk-free bonds (note that investing −.4103 in \$100 bonds is equivalent to short selling \$41.03 of the bonds or borrowing \$41.03 at the risk-free rate) and *purchasing* .5556 shares of Widget stock. This is indeed the case, as can be seen here:

Portfolio Component	*Payoff in Up State*	*Payoff in Down State*
Share investment	.5556 × \$125	.5556 × \$80
	= \$69.45	= \$44.45
Loan repayment	−\$41.03 × 1.0833	−\$41.03 × 1.0833
	= −\$44.45	= −\$44.45
Net payoff	\$25.00	\$0.00

Because the replicating portfolio provides the same payoffs as the call, only its cost needs to be calculated in order to find the fair value of the option. To obtain the portfolio, \$55.56 must be spent to purchase .5556 shares of Widget stock (at \$100 per share). However, \$41.03 of this amount is provided by the proceeds from the short sale of the bond. Thus, only \$55.56 − \$41.03 = \$14.53 of the investor's own funds must be spent. Accordingly, this is the fair value of the call option.

More generally, the value of the call option will be

$$V_o = N_s P_s + N_b P_b \qquad (20.4)$$

where V_o represents the value of the option, P_s is the price of the stock, P_b is the price of a risk-free bond, and N_s and N_b are the number of shares and risk-free bonds required to replicate the option's payoffs.

Overpricing

To show that equilibrium will be attained if the call is selling for \$14.53, consider what a shrewd investor would do if the call were selling for either more or less than this amount. Imagine that the call is selling for \$20, so it is overpriced. In this case the investor would consider writing one call, buying .5556 shares, and borrowing \$41.03. The net cash flow when this is done (that is, at $t = 0$) would be \$20 − (.5556 × \$100) + \$41.03 = \$5.47, indicating that the investor has a net cash inflow. At the end of the year (that is, at $t = T$) the investor's net cash flow will be as shown at the top of the next page. Because the net aggregate value is zero regardless of the ending stock price, the investor has no risk of loss from this strategy. Thus, the investor currently has a means for generating free cash as long as the call is priced at \$20, since the investment strategy does not require any cash from the investor later on. This cannot represent equilibrium, as anyone can get free cash by investing similarly.

Portfolio Component	*Payoff in Up State*	*Payoff in Down State*
Written call	–$25.00	$0.00
Share investment	.5556 × $125 = $69.45	.5556 × $80 = $44.45
Loan repayment	–$41.03 × 1.0833 = –$44.45	–$41.03 × 1.0833 = –$44.45
Net payoff	$0.00	$0.00

Underpricing

Next, imagine that the call is selling for $10 instead of $20, so it is underpriced. In this case the investor would consider buying one call, short selling .5556 shares, and investing $41.03 at the risk-free rate. The net cash flow when this is done (that is, at $t = 0$) would be $-\$10 + (.5556 \times \$100) - \$41.03 = \$4.53$, indicating that the investor has a net cash inflow. At the end of the year (that is, at $t = T$) the investor's net cash flow will be as follows:

Portfolio Component	*Payoff in Up State*	*Payoff in Down State*
Call investment	$25.00	$0.00
Repay shorted share	–.5556 × $125 = –$69.45	–.5556 × $80 = –$44.45
Risk-free investment	$41.03 × 1.0833 = $44.45	$41.03 × 1.0833 = $44.45
Net payoff	$0.00	$0.00

Once again, the net aggregate value is zero regardless of the ending stock price, indicating that the investor has no risk of loss from this strategy. Hence, the investor currently has a means for generating free cash as long as the call is priced at $10. This cannot represent equilibrium, however, as anyone can get free cash by investing similarly.

The Hedge Ratio

To replicate the Widget call option, imagine borrowing $41.03 and purchasing .5556 shares of Widget stock. Now, consider the effect of a change in the price of the stock tomorrow (not a year from now) on the value of the replicating portfolio. Because .5556 shares of stock are included in the portfolio, the value of the portfolio will change by $.5556 for every $1 change in the price of Widget stock. But because the call option and the portfolio should sell for the same price, it follows that the price of the call should also change by $.5556 for every $1 change in the price of the stock. This relationship is defined as the option's **hedge ratio.** It is equal to the value of N_s that was determined in equation (20.3c).

In the case of the Widget call option, the hedge ratio was equal to .5556, which equals the value of (\$25–\$0)/(\$125–\$80). Note that the numerator equals the difference between the option's payoffs in the up and down states, and the denominator equals the difference between the stock's payoffs in the two states. More generally, in the binomial model:

$$h = \frac{P_{ou} - P_{od}}{P_{su} - P_{sd}} \tag{20.5}$$

where P represents the end-of-period price and the subscripts indicate the instrument (o for option, s for stock) and the state of nature (u for up, d for down).

To replicate a call option in a binomial world, h shares of stock [where h represents the hedge ratio determined by using equation (20.5)] must be purchased. Simultaneously, an amount must be risklessly borrowed by short selling bonds; this amount is equal to

$$B = PV(hP_{sd} - P_{od}) \tag{20.6}$$

where PV refers to taking the present value of the figure calculated in the following parentheses. (Note that the figure in parentheses is the value of the bond at the end of the period.)[9]

To summarize, the value of a call option is given to be

$$V_o = hP_s - B \tag{20.7}$$

where h and B are the hedge ratio and the current value of a short bond position in a portfolio that replicates the payoffs of the call, and they are calculated by using equations (20.5) and (20.6).

More Than Two Prices

At this juncture it is reasonable to wonder about the accuracy of the BOPM if it is based on an assumption that the price of Widget shares can assume only one of two values at the end of a year. Realistically, Widget shares can assume any one of a great number of prices at year-end. It turns out that this is not a problem, as the model can be extended in a straightforward manner.

In the case of Widget, divide the year into two six-month periods. In the first period, assume that Widget can go up to \$111.80 (an 11.80% increase) or down to \$89.44 (a 10.56% decrease). For the second six-month period, the price of Widget can again go either up by 11.80% or down by 10.56%. Hence, the price of Widget will follow one of the paths of the price tree shown in panel (b) of Figure 20.5 over the forthcoming year. Widget can now assume one of three prices at year-end: \$125, \$100, or \$80. The associated value of the call option is also given in the figure for each of these stock prices.

How can the value of the Widget call option at time 0 be calculated from the information given in the figure? The answer is remarkably simple. The problem is broken down into three parts, each of which is solved in a manner similar to that shown earlier when panel (a) was discussed. The three parts must be approached sequentially by working backward in time.

First, imagine that six months have passed and the price of Widget stock is \$111.80. What is the value of the call option at this node in the price tree? The hedge ratio h is

[9] Equations (20.5) and (20.6) can be derived by solving the set of equations (20.3a) and (20.3b) using symbols instead of numbers.

calculated to be ($25 – $0)/($125 – $100) = 1.0, and the amount of the borrowing B is calculated to be (1 × $100 – $0)/1.0408 = $96.08. (The 8% risk-free rate compounded continuously corresponds to a discrete discount rate of 4.08% for the six-month period.) Using equation (20.7), the value of the call is determined to be 1 × $111.80 – $96.08 = $15.72.

Second, again imagine that six months have passed but the price of Widget is $89.44. While equations (20.5), (20.6), and (20.7) could be used to determine the value of the call at this node in the price tree, intuition gives the answer more quickly: the call has to be selling for $0. This is because in six months the price of Widget will be either $100 or $80, and regardless of which it is, the call will still be worthless. That is, investors will realize that the call will be worthless at the end of the year if the stock price is at $89.44 after six months, and hence they will be unwilling to pay anything for the call option.

Third, imagine that no time has elapsed, so that it is time 0. In this case the price tree can be simplified to

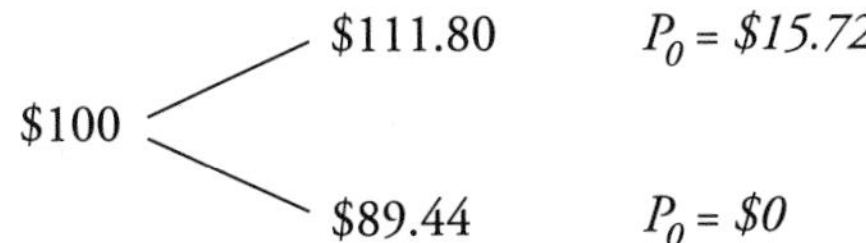

Applying equations (20.5) and (20.6) indicates that the hedge ratio h is equal to .7030 [= ($15.72 – $0)/($111.80 – $89.44)] and the amount of borrowing B is equal to $60.41 [= (.7030 × $89.44 – $0)/1.0408]. Applying equation (20.7) results in a value for the call at t = 0 of $9.89 (= .7030 × $100 – $60.41).

There is no need to stop here. Instead of analyzing two six-month periods, four quarterly periods can be analyzed, or 12 monthly periods. Note that the number of year-end stock prices for Widget is equal to one more than the number of periods in a year. Hence, when annual periods were used in panel (a) of Figure 20.5, there were two year-end prices, and when semiannual prices were used, there were three year-end prices. It follows that if quarterly or monthly periods had been used, there would have been 5 or 13 year-end prices, respectively.

▶ Put Options

Can the BOPM be used to value puts? Because the formulas cover any set of payoffs, they can be applied directly. Consider Widget once again from an annual perspective, where the put option has an exercise price of $100 and an expiration date of one year. Its price tree will be

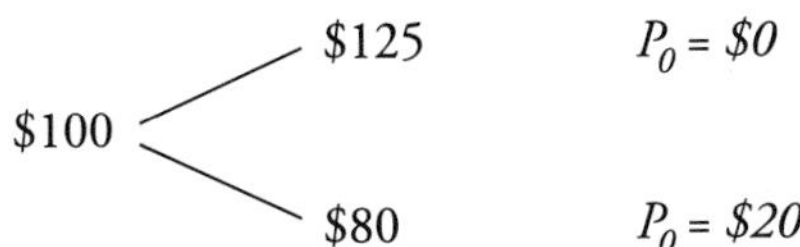

Applying equation (20.5) gives the hedge ratio for the put option as ($0–$20)/($125–$80) = –.4444. Note that this is a negative number, indicating that a rise in the price of the stock will lower the price of the put.

Applying equation (20.6) shows that B equals –$51.28, which is the present value of the year-end value of –$55.55. Because these are negative numbers, they denote the amount of bonds to be purchased (that is, the negative value of a short position should be interpreted as the value of a long position).

To replicate the put option, then, one *sells short* .4444 shares of Widget and *lends* (that is, invests in the risk-free bond) \$51.28. As the short sale will generate \$44.44 while the bond purchase will cost \$51.28, the net cost of the replicating portfolio will be (\$51.28–\$44.44 =) \$6.84. Accordingly, this is the fair value of the put.

This is the same value that is obtained when equation (20.7) is used: $-.4444 \times \$100 - (-\$51.28) = \$6.84$, where $h = .4444$, $B = -\$51.28$, and $P_s = \$100$. Hence equations (20.5), (20.6), and (20.7) can be used to value not only calls but also puts. Furthermore, the procedure for extending the valuation of puts to the situation where there is more than one period between now and the expiration date is analogous to the one that was given for calls.

Put-Call Parity

Earlier it was shown that the call on Widget had a hedge ratio of .5556. Note that $.5556 - 1 = -.4444$, the hedge ratio for the put. This is not a coincidence. The hedge ratios of a European put and call having the same exercise price and expiration date are related in the following manner:

$$h_c - 1 = h_p \tag{20.8}$$

where h_c and h_p denote the hedge ratios for the call and the put, respectively.

Of even greater interest is the relationship between the market prices of a call and a put on a given stock that have the same exercise price and expiration date. Again consider the example involving Widget options that have an exercise price of \$100 and an expiration date of one year. Two investment strategies need to be compared. Strategy *A* involves buying a put and a share of stock. (This strategy is sometimes known as a "protective put" or a "married put.") Strategy *B* involves buying a call and investing an amount of money in the risk-free asset that is equal to the present value of the exercise price.

At the expiration date the values of these two investment strategies can be calculated under two scenarios: the price of Widget being below its exercise price of \$100, and the price of Widget being above its exercise price. (The case where it is exactly equal to its exercise price can be added to either scenario without affecting the results.) Table 20.3 does this. Note that if the stock of Widget is selling for less than the \$100 exercise price on the expiration date, both strategies have a payoff of \$100 in cash. Alternatively, if the price of Widget stock is above \$100, both strategies result in the investor having possession of a share of stock that is worth more than \$100. Hence, because both strategies have the same payoffs, they must cost the same amount in equilibrium:

$$P_p + P_s = P_c + E/e^{RT} \tag{20.9}$$

where P_p and P_c denote the current market prices of the put and the call, respectively.

This equation represents what is known as **put-call parity**. In Table 20.3 it can be seen that the cost of each strategy is \$106.84, just as was suggested previously by the calculations using equations (20.5), (20.6), and (20.7).

Table 20.3

Put-Call Parity Involving Widget.

Strategy	*Initial Cost*	*Value at Expiration Date* $P_s < E = \$100$	*Value at Expiration Date* $E = \$100 > P_s$
A: Buy put Buy share of stock	$P_p + P_s$ = \$6.84 + \$100 = \$106.84	Exercise put, get \$100	Throw away put, have stock worth P_s
B: Buy call Invest present value of E in risk-free asset	$P_c + E/e^{RT}$ = \$14.53 + \$92.31 = \$106.84	Throw away call, get \$100 from risk-free asset	Exercise call, get stock worth P_s

THE BLACK-SCHOLES MODEL FOR CALL OPTIONS

Consider what would happen with the binomial option pricing model if the number of periods before the expiration date were allowed to increase. For example, with Widget's option for which the expiration date was a year in the future, there could be a price tree with periods for each one of the approximately 250 trading days in a year. Hence there would be 251 possible year-end prices for Widget stock. Needless to say, the fair value of any call associated with such a tree is found by using a computer to quickly perform calculations such as those shown earlier for Widget. If the number of periods was even larger, with each one representing a specific hour of each trading day, then there would be about $7 \times 250 = 1750$ hourly periods (and 1751 possible year-end prices). Note that the number of periods in a year gets larger as the length of each period gets shorter. In the limit there will be an infinite number of infinitely small periods (and, consequently, an infinite number of possible year-end prices). In this situation the BOPM given in equation (20.7) reduces to the Black-Scholes model, so named in honour of its originators.[10]

► Limitations on Its Use

At first this model might seem to have limited use, because almost all options in North America are American options that can be exercised at any time up to their expiration date whereas the Black-Scholes model applies only to European options. Furthermore, strictly speaking, the model is applicable only to options on stocks that will not pay any dividends over the life of the option. However, most of the common stocks on which options are written do in fact pay dividends.

The first drawback of the Black-Scholes model — that it is only applicable to European options — can be dispensed with rather easily when the option is a call and the underlying stock does not pay dividends. This is because it can be shown that it is unwise for an investor holding an American call option on a non-dividend-paying stock to exercise it

---

10 Fischer Black and Myron Scholes, "The Pricing of Options and Corporate Liabilities," *Journal of Political Economy* 81, no. 3 (May/June 1973): 637–654. Also see Fischer Black, "How We Came Up with the Option Formula," *Journal of Portfolio Management* 15, no. 2 (Winter 1989): 4–8, and "How to Use the Holes in Black-Scholes," *Journal of Applied Corporate Finance* 1, no. 4 (Winter 1989): 67–73.

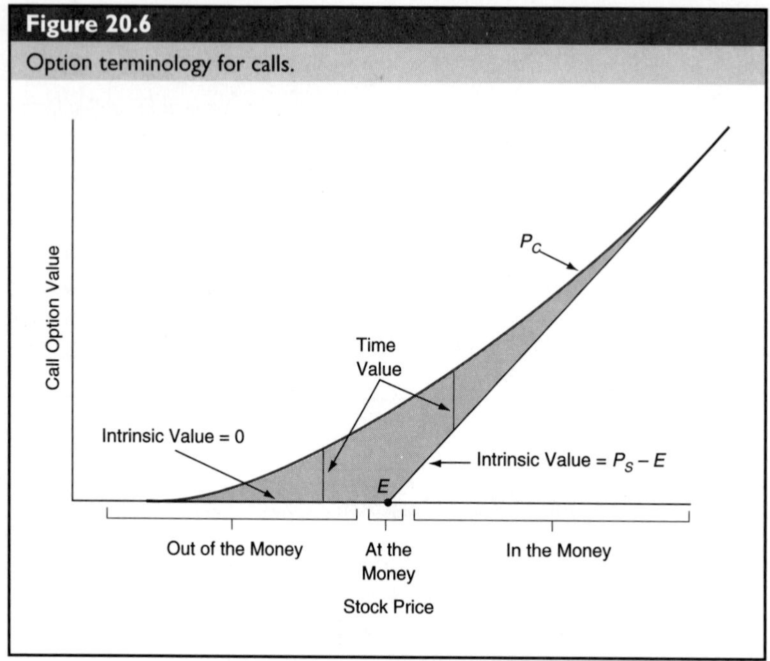

Figure 20.6

Option terminology for calls.

prior to maturity.[11] As there is no reason for exercising such an option prior to maturity, the opportunity to do so is worthless. Consequently there will be no difference in the values of an American and a European call option. In turn, this means that the Black-Scholes model can be used to estimate the fair value of American call options on non-dividend-paying stocks. The reason for this can be seen in Figure 20.6.

As mentioned earlier, the value of an option if it were exercised immediately is known as its intrinsic value. This value is equal to zero if the option is out of the money. However, it is equal to the difference between the stock price and the exercise price if the option is in the money. The excess of the option's price over its intrinsic value is the option's **time value** (or time premium). The time value of a call option at expiration is zero, but is positive before then. Note that a call option's premium is simply the sum of its intrinsic and time values.

An investor considering exercising a call option on a non-dividend-paying stock prior to its expiration date will always find it cheaper to sell the call option and purchase the stock in the marketplace. This is because exercising the call will result in the investor's losing the time value of the option (hence the expression that call options are "worth more alive than dead").

For example, consider a stock that has a current price of $110. If this stock has a call option with an exercise price of $100 that is selling for $14, then the intrinsic and time values of this option are $110 – $100 = $10 and $14 – $10 = $4, respectively. An investor who owns one of these calls could exercise it by spending an additional $100. However, it would be cheaper for the investor to get the share of stock by selling the call option and

[11] See Robert C. Merton, "Theory of Rational Option Pricing," *Bell Journal of Economics and Management Science* 4, no. 1 (Spring 1973): 141–183.

buying the share of stock in the marketplace, because the additional cost would be only $110 − $14 = $96.

The second drawback of the Black-Scholes model—that it is only applicable to non-dividend-paying stocks—cannot be easily dismissed, as many call options are written on stocks that will pay dividends over the life of the option. Some procedures have been suggested for amending this formula to value call options on such stocks.[12]

► The Formula

In the absence of taxes and transaction costs, the fair value of a call option can be estimated by using the valuation formula developed by Black and Scholes. It has been widely used by those who deal with options to search for situations where the market price of an option differs substantially from its fair value. A call option that is found to be selling for substantially less than its Black-Scholes value is a candidate for purchase, whereas one that is found to be selling for substantially more is a candidate for writing. The Black-Scholes formula for estimating the fair value of a call option V_c is

$$V_c = N(d_1)P_s - \frac{E}{e^{RT}}N(d_2) \tag{20.10}$$

where:

$$d_1 = \frac{\ln(P_s/E) + (R + .5\sigma^2)T}{\sigma\sqrt{T}} \tag{20.11}$$

$$d_2 = \frac{\ln(P_s/E) + (R - .5\sigma^2)T}{\sigma\sqrt{T}} \tag{20.12a}$$

$$= d_1 - \sigma\sqrt{T} \tag{20.12b}$$

and where: P_s = current market price of the underlying stock,
E = exercise price of the option,
R = continuously compounded risk-free rate of return expressed on an annual basis,
T = time remaining before expiration, expressed as a fraction of a year,
σ = risk of the underlying common stock, measured by the standard deviation of the continuously compounded annual rate of return on the stock.

Note that E/e^{RT} is the present value of the exercise price where a continuous discount rate is used. The quantity $\ln(P_s/E)$ is the natural logarithm of P_s/E. Finally, $N(d_1)$ and $N(d_2)$ denote the probabilities that outcomes of less than d_1 and d_2, respectively, will occur in a normal distribution that has a mean of 0 and a standard deviation of 1.

Table 20.4 provides values of $N(d_1)$ for various levels of d_1.[13] Only this table and a pocket calculator are needed in order to use the Black-Scholes formula for valuing a call option. It should be noted that with this formula the interest rate R and the stock volatility σ are assumed to be constant over the life of the option. (More recently people have developed

---

[12] These procedures are reviewed in the options textbooks cited at the end of the chapter.

[13] Table 20.4 is an abbreviated version of a standard cumulative normal distribution table. More detailed versions can be found in most statistics textbooks.

Table 20.4

Values of $N(d)$ for Selected Values of d.

d	N(d)	d	N(d)	d	N(d)
		−1.00	.1587	1.00	.8413
−2.95	.0016	−.95	.1711	1.05	.8531
−2.90	.0019	−.90	.1841	1.10	.8643
−2.85	.0022	−.85	.1977	1.15	.8749
−2.80	.0026	−.80	.2119	1.20	.8849
−2.75	.0030	−.75	.2266	1.25	.8944
−2.70	.0035	−.70	.2420	1.30	.9032
−2.65	.0040	−.65	.2578	1.35	.9115
−2.60	.0047	−.60	.2743	1.40	.9192
−2.55	.0054	−.55	.2912	1.45	.9265
−2.50	.0062	−.50	.3085	1.50	.9332
−2.45	.0071	−.45	.3264	1.55	.9394
−2.40	.0082	−.40	.3446	1.60	.9452
−2.35	.0094	−.35	.3632	1.65	.9505
−2.30	.0107	−.30	.3821	1.70	.9554
−2.25	.0122	−.25	.4013	1.75	.9599
−2.20	.0139	−.20	.4207	1.80	.9641
−2.15	.0158	−.15	.4404	1.85	.9678
−2.10	.0179	−.10	.4602	1.90	.9713
−2.05	.0202	−.05	.4801	1.95	.9744
−2.00	.0228	.00	.5000	2.00	.9773
−1.95	.0256	.05	.5199	2.05	.9798
−1.90	.0287	.10	.5398	2.10	.9821
−1.85	.0322	.15	.5596	2.15	.9842
−1.80	.0359	.20	.5793	2.20	.9861
−1.75	.0401	.25	.5987	2.25	.9878
−1.70	.0446	.30	.6179	2.30	.9893
−1.65	.0495	.35	.6368	2.35	.9906
−1.60	.0548	.40	.6554	2.40	.9918
−1.55	.0606	.45	.6736	2.45	.9929
−1.50	.0668	.50	.6915	2.50	.9938
−1.45	.0735	.55	.7088	2.55	.9946
−1.40	.0808	.60	.7257	2.60	.9953
−1.35	.0885	.65	.7422	2.65	.9960
−1.30	.0968	.70	.7580	2.70	.9965
−1.25	.1057	.75	.7734	2.75	.9970
−1.20	.1151	.80	.7881	2.80	.9974
−1.15	.1251	.85	.8023	2.85	.9978
−1.10	.1357	.90	.8159	2.90	.9981
−1.05	.1469	.95	.8289	2.95	.9984

formulas where these assumptions have been relaxed.) For example, consider a call option that expires in three months and has an exercise price of \$40 (thus $T = .25$ and $E = 40$). Furthermore, the current price and the risk of the underlying common stock are \$36 and

50%, respectively, whereas the risk-free rate is 5% (thus $P_s = 36$, $R = .05$, and $\sigma = .50$). Solving equations (20.11) and (20.12b) provides the following values for d_1 and d_2:

$$d_1 = \frac{\ln(36/40) + [.05 + .5(.50)^2].25}{.50\sqrt{.25}} = -.25$$

$$d_2 = -.25 - .50\sqrt{.25} = -.50.$$

Now Table 20.4 can be used to find the corresponding values of $N(d_1)$ and $N(d_2)$:

$$N(d_1) = N(-.25) = .4013$$

$$N(d_2) = N(-.50) = .3085.$$

Finally, equation (20.10) can be used to estimate the fair value of this call option:

$$V_c = (.4013 \times \$36) - \left(\frac{\$40}{e^{.05 \times .25}} \times .3085\right)$$

$$= \$14.45 - \$12.19 = \$2.26.$$

If this call option is currently selling for \$5, the investor should consider writing some of them. This is because they are overpriced (according to the Black-Scholes model), suggesting that their price will fall in the near future. Thus, the writer would receive a premium of \$5 and would expect to be able to enter a closing buy order later for a lower price, making a profit on the difference. Conversely, if the call option were selling for \$1, the investor should consider buying some of them. This is because they are underpriced and can be expected to rise in value in the future.

► Comparison to BOPM

At this juncture the BOPM formula given in equation (20.7) where V_0 is now denoted V_c can be compared with the Black-Scholes option pricing formula given in equation (20.10):

$$V_c = hP_s - B \tag{20.7}$$

$$V_c = N(d_1)P_s - \frac{E}{e^{RT}}N(d_2). \tag{20.10}$$

In comparing the two equations, the quantity $N(d_1)$ in equation (20.10) can be seen to correspond to h in equation (20.7). Remembering that h is the hedge ratio, the quantity $N(d_1)$ in the Black-Scholes formula can be interpreted in a similar manner. That is, it corresponds to the number of shares that an investor would need to purchase in executing an investment strategy that was designed to have the same payoffs as a call option. Similarly, the quantity $EN(d_2)/e^{RT}$ corresponds to B, the amount of money that the investor borrows as the other part of the strategy. This means that the quantity $EN(d_2)$ corresponds to the face amount of the loan, because it is the amount that must be paid back to the lender at time T, the expiration date. Hence e^{RT} is the present value (or discount) factor, indicating that the interest rate on the loan is R per period and that the loan is for T periods. Thus, the seemingly complex Black-Scholes formula can be seen to have an intuitive interpretation. It simply involves calculating the cost of a buy-stock-and-borrow-money investment strategy that has the same payoffs at T as a call option.

In the example, $N(d_1)$ was equal to .4013 and $EN(d_2)/e^{RT}$ was equal to \$12.19. Hence, an investment strategy that involves buying .4013 shares and borrowing \$12.19 at time 0 will have payoffs exactly equal to those associated with buying the call.[14] Because this strategy costs \$2.26, it follows that in equilibrium the market price of the call must also be \$2.26.

Static Analysis

Close scrutiny of the Black-Scholes formula reveals some interesting features of European call option pricing. In particular, the fair value of a call option is dependent on five inputs—the market price of the common stock P_s, the exercise price of the option E, the length of time until the expiration date T, the risk-free rate R, and the risk of the common stock σ. What happens to the fair value of a call option when one of these inputs is changed while the other four remain the same?

1. The higher the price of the underlying stock P_s, the higher the value of the call option.
2. The higher the exercise price E, the lower the value of the call option.
3. The longer the time to the expiration date T, the higher the value of the call option.
4. The higher the risk-free rate R, the higher the value of the call option.
5. The greater the risk σ of the common stock, the higher the value of the call option.

Of these five factors, the first three (P_s, E, and T) are readily determined. The fourth factor, the risk-free rate R, is often estimated by using the yield-to-maturity on a Treasury bill having a maturity date close to the expiration date of the option. The fifth factor, the risk of the underlying stock σ, is not readily observed; consequently various methods for estimating it have been proposed. Two of these methods will be presented next.

Estimating a Stock's Risk from Historical Prices

One method for estimating the risk of the underlying common stock associated with a call option involves analyzing historical prices of the stock. Initially a set of $n + 1$ market prices on the underlying stock must be obtained from either financial publications such as the *Globe and Mail* or a computer database. These prices are then used to calculate a set of n continuously compounded returns as follows:

$$r_t = \ln\left(\frac{P_{st}}{P_{st-1}}\right) \tag{20.13}$$

where P_{st} and P_{st-1} denote the market price of the underlying stock at times t and $t - 1$, respectively. Here, ln denotes taking the natural logarithm of the quantity P_{st}/P_{st-1}, which thus results in a continuously compounded return.

For example, the set of market prices for the stock might consist of the closing price at the end of each of 53 weeks. If the price at the end of one week was \$105 and the price at the end of the next week was \$107, then the return for that week r_t will be equal to $\ln(107/105) = 1.886\%$. Similar calculations will result in a set of 52 weekly returns.

[14] It should be pointed out that the investment strategy is more complicated than it might appear because the number of shares that are to be held will change over time as the share price changes and the expiration date gets closer. Similarly, the amount of the loan will change over time. Hence, it is a *dynamic strategy*.

Having calculated a set of n returns on the stock, the next step involves using them to estimate the stock's average return:

$$r_{av} = \frac{1}{n}\sum_{t=1}^{n} r_t. \tag{20.14}$$

The average return is then used in estimating the per-period variance — that is, the square of the per-period standard deviation:

$$s^2 = \frac{1}{n-1}\sum_{t=1}^{n}(r_t - r_{av})^2. \tag{20.15}$$

This is called the per-period variance because its size is dependent on the length of time over which each return is measured. In the example, weekly returns were calculated and would lead to the estimation of a weekly variance. Alternatively, daily returns could have been used, leading to a daily variance that would be of smaller magnitude than the weekly variance. However, what is needed is not a weekly or daily variance, but an annual variance. This is obtained by multiplying the per-period variance by the number of periods in a year. Thus an estimated weekly variance would be multiplied by 52 in order to estimate the annual variance σ^2 (that is, $\sigma^2 = 52s^2$).[15]

Alternative methods of estimating a stock's total risk exist. One such method involves subjectively estimating the probabilities of possible future stock prices. Another method involves combining the historical and subjective risk estimates.

For any estimate of future uncertainty, historical data are likely to prove more helpful than definitive. And because recent data may prove more helpful than older data, some analysts study daily price changes over the most recent 6 to 12 months, sometimes giving more weight to more recent data than to earlier ones. Others take into account the price histories of related stocks and the possibility that a stock whose price has recently decreased may be more risky in the future than it was in the past. Still others make explicit subjective estimates of the future, taking into account changes in uncertainty concerning the economy in general as well as uncertainty in specific industries and in stocks.

In some cases an analyst's estimate of a stock's risk over the next three months may differ from that for the following three months, leading to the use of different values of σ for call options on the same stock that have different expiration dates.

THE MARKET CONSENSUS OF A STOCK'S RISK

Another way to estimate a stock's risk is based on the assumption that a currently outstanding call option is fairly priced in the marketplace. Because this means that $P_c = V_c$, the current market price of the call P_c can be entered on the left-hand side of equation (20.10) in place of the fair value of the call V_c. Next all the other factors except for σ are entered on the right-hand side, and a value for σ, the only unknown variable, is found that satisfies the

---

[15] If daily data are used, it is best to multiply the daily variance by 250 instead of 365 because there are about 250 trading days in a year. See Mark Kritzman, "About Estimating Volatility: Part I," *Financial Analysts Journal* 47, no. 4 (July/August 1991): 22–25; and "About Estimating Volatility: Part II," *Financial Analysts Journal* 47, no. 5 (September/October 1991): 10–11. For a method of estimating σ that uses high, low, opening, and closing prices as well as trading volume, see Mark B. Garman and Michael J. Klass, "On the Estimation of Security Price Volatilities from Historical Data," *Journal of Business* 53, no. 1 (January 1980): 67–78.

equation. The solution for σ can be interpreted as representing a consensus opinion in the marketplace on the size of the stock's risk, and it is sometimes known as the stock's **implicit** (or implied) **volatility**.[16]

For example, assume that the risk-free rate is 6%, and that a six-month call option with an exercise price of $40 sells for $4 when the price of the underlying stock is $36. Different estimates of σ can be "plugged into" the right-hand side of equation (20.10) until a value of $4 for this side of the equation is obtained. In this example an estimated value of .40 (that is, 40%) for σ will result in a number for the right-hand side of equation (20.10) that is equal to $4, the current market price of the call option that is on the left-hand side.

The procedure can be modified by applying it to several call options on the same stock. For example, σ can be estimated for each of several call options on the same stock that have different exercise prices but the same expiration date. Then the resulting estimates for σ can be averaged and, in turn, used to determine the fair value of another call option on the same stock having yet another exercise price but a similar expiration date.

In the example, σ can be estimated not only for a six-month option having an exercise price of $40, but also for six-month options having exercise prices of $35 and $45. Then the three estimates of σ can be averaged to produce a "best estimate" of σ that is used to value a six-month $50 option on the same stock.

Alternatively, the procedure can be modified by averaging the estimates for σ associated with each of several expiration dates. In the example, σ can be estimated not only for a six-month option having an exercise price of $40 but also for a three-month and a nine-month option that each have an exercise price of $40. The three estimates of σ can be averaged to produce a best estimate of σ that will subsequently be used to determine the fair value of a one-month $40 option on the same stock.

There are other ways of using a set of estimates of σ that correspond to different call options on the same stock. Perhaps σ will be estimated for a set of calls having different expiration prices and different exercise prices, and then averaged. Perhaps σ will be estimated from historical returns using equation (20.15), with the resulting figure averaged with one or more estimates of the stock's implicit volatility. Although the evidence is still unclear, it appears that methods based on calculating implicit volatility are better than methods based on historical returns.[17] It should be remembered, however, that all of these methods assume that volatility remains constant over the life of the option—an assumption that can be challenged.

► More on Hedge Ratios

The slope of the Black-Scholes value curve at any point represents the expected change in the value of the option per dollar change in the price of the underlying common stock. This amount corresponds to the hedge ratio of the call option and is equal to $N(d_1)$ in equation (20.10). As can be seen in Figure 20.6 (assuming that the market price of the call is equal to its Black-Scholes value), the slope (that is, the hedge ratio) of the curve is always positive.

---

[16] Alternatively, equation (20.10) could be solved for the interest rate R; doing so gives an estimate of the *implied interest rate.* See Menachem Brenner and Dan Galai, "Implied Interest Rates," *Journal of Business* 59, no. 3 (July 1986): 493–507.

[17] For a further discussion of these methods, see any of the options textbooks cited at the end of the chapter, or see Menachem Brenner and Marti Subrahmanyam, "A Simple Formula to Compute the Implied Standard Deviation," *Financial Analysts Journal* 44, no. 5 (September/October 1988): 80–83.

Note that if the stock has a relatively low market price, the slope will be near zero. For higher stock prices the slope increases and ultimately approaches a value of 1 for relatively high prices.

Because the hedge ratio is typically less than 1, a $1 increase in the stock price will typically result in an increase in a call option's value of less than $1. However, the percentage change in the value of the call option will generally be much greater than the percentage change in the price of the stock. It is this relationship that leads people to say that options offer high leverage.

The reason for referring to the slope of the Black-Scholes value curve as the hedge ratio is that a "hedge" portfolio, meaning a nearly risk-free portfolio, can be formed by simultaneously writing one call option and purchasing a number of shares equal to the hedge ratio, $N(d_1)$. For example, assume that the hedge ratio is .5, indicating that the hedge portfolio consists of writing one call and buying .5 shares of stock. Now if the stock price rises by $1, the value of the call option will rise by approximately $.50. This means that the hedge portfolio would lose approximately $.50 on the written call option but gain $.50 from the rise in the stock's price. Conversely, a $1 decrease in the stock's price would result in a $.50 gain on the written call option but a loss of $.50 on the half-share of stock. Overall, it can be seen that the hedge portfolio will neither gain nor lose value when the price of the underlying common stock changes by a relatively small amount.[18]

Even if the Black-Scholes model is valid and all the inputs have been correctly specified, it should be noted that risk is not permanently eliminated in the hedge portfolio when the portfolio is first formed (or, for that matter, at any time). This is because the hedge ratio will change as the stock price changes and as the life of the option decreases with the passage of time. In order to eliminate risk from the hedge portfolio, the investor will have to alter its composition continuously. Altering it less often will reduce but not completely eliminate risk.

► Adjustments for Dividends

Thus far, the issue of dividend payments on the underlying stock during the life of an option has been avoided. Other things being equal, the greater the amount of the dividends to be paid during the life of a call option, the lower the value of the call option. This is because the greater the dividend that a firm declares, the lower its stock price will be. Since options are not "dividend protected," this lower stock price will result in a lower value for the call option.

Moreover, it may pay to exercise an American call option just prior to an ex-dividend date. Earlier it was mentioned that in the absence of dividends, an American call option would be worth at least as much "alive" (not exercised) as "dead" (exercised). When dividends are involved, however, the situation may be different. This is shown in Figure 20.7.

The call option's value if exercised immediately, referred to as the option's "intrinsic value," lies along the lower boundary $0EZ$. If allowed to live, the option's value will lie along the higher Black-Scholes curve, as shown in the figure. Imagine that the stock is currently priced at P_{s1} and is about to go ex-dividend for the last time prior to the option's expiration. Afterward it can be expected to sell for a lower price, P_{s2}. The Black-Scholes formula can be used to estimate the option's value if it remains "alive" just after the ex-dividend date. In

---

[18] This explanation of a hedge ratio follows from the BOPM-based interpretation of the Black-Scholes formula that was given earlier. That is, if a call's payoffs can be duplicated by buying shares and borrowing at the risk-free rate, it follows that buying shares and writing a call will duplicate investing in the risk-free asset.

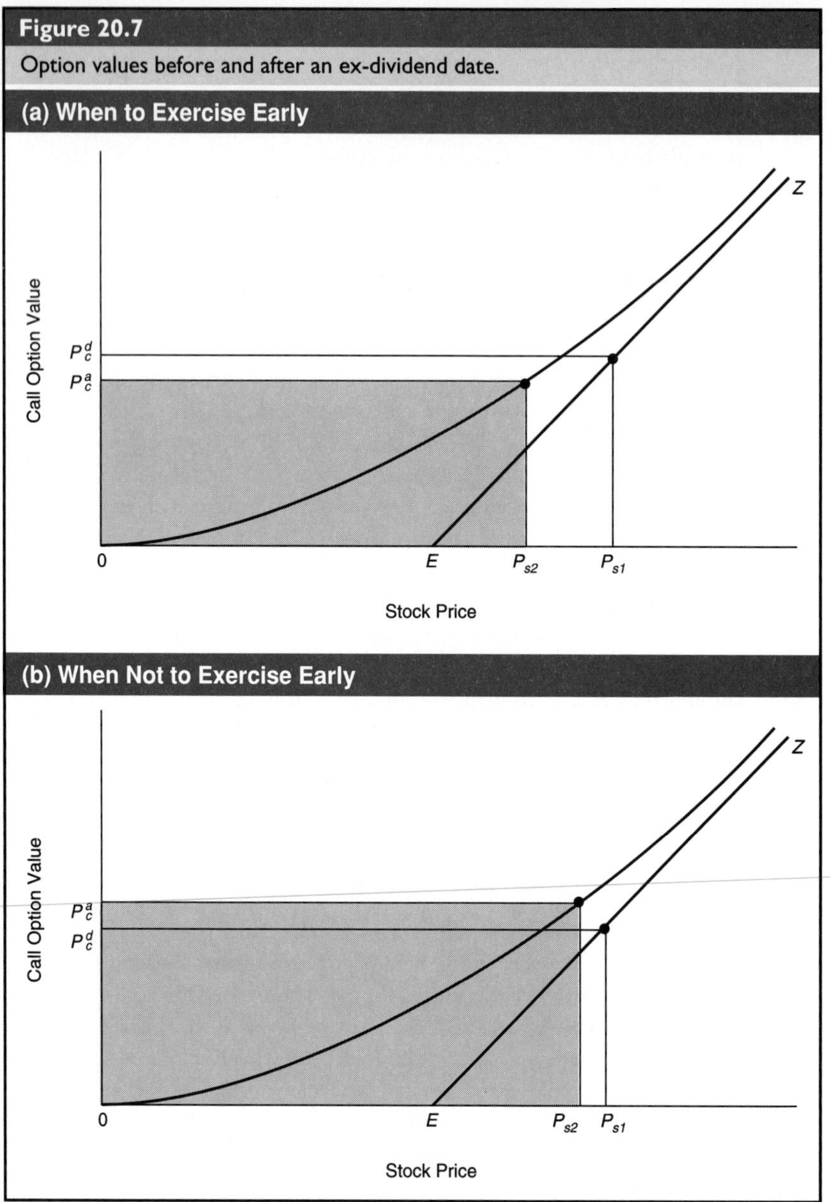

Figure 20.7, this alive value is P_c^a. If instead the option is exercised just before the ex-dividend date while the stock price is still P_{s1}, the investor will obtain the "dead" value (that is, the intrinsic value) of P_c^d. If P_c^d is greater than P_c^a, as is the case in panel (a), the option should be exercised now, just before the ex-dividend date; if P_c^d is less than P_c^a, as is the case in panel (b), the option should not be exercised. Hence, for a call option on a dividend-paying stock, the possibility of early exercise must be taken into consideration.[19]

[19] See footnote 12.

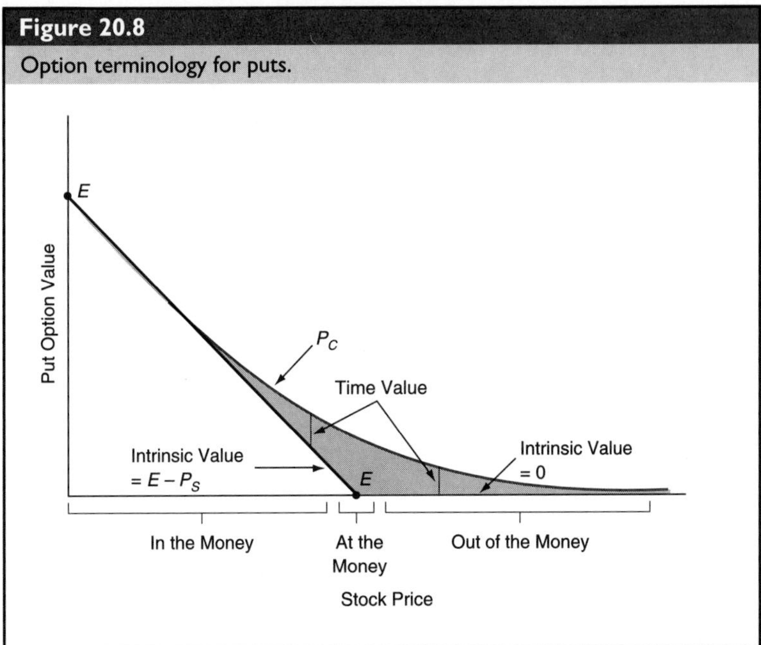

Figure 20.8
Option terminology for puts.

THE VALUATION OF PUT OPTIONS

Similar to a call option, a put option is said to be at the money if the underlying stock has a market price roughly equal to the put's exercise price. However, the terms "out of the money" and "in the money" have, in one sense, *opposite meanings* for puts and calls. In particular, a put option is out of the money if the underlying stock has a market price above the exercise price and is in the money if the market price is below the exercise price. Figure 20.8 provides an illustration of how these terms apply to a put option.

As mentioned earlier, the value of either a call or a put, if it were exercised immediately, is known as its intrinsic value. This value is equal to zero if the option is out of the money, and is equal to the difference between the stock price and the exercise price if the stock is in the money. Thus in another sense, the terms "out of the money" and "in the money" have *similar meanings* for puts and calls.

The excess of the price of a call or a put over this intrinsic value is the option's time value (or time premium). As shown for calls and puts in panels (a) and (b) of Figure 20.3, respectively, the time value is 0 at expiration. However, Figures 20.6 and 20.8 show that the time value is generally positive before expiration. Note that an option's premium is simply the sum of its intrinsic value and its time value.

► Put-Call Parity

Consider a put and a call on the same underlying stock that have the same exercise price and expiration date. It was shown in equation (20.9) that their market prices should be related, with the nature of the relationship known as put-call parity. This relationship, however, is valid only for European options on non-dividend-paying stocks.

Equation (20.9) can be rearranged to estimate the value of European put options:

$$P_p = P_c + \frac{E}{e^{RT}} - P_s \tag{20.16}$$

Thus, the value of a put can be estimated by using either the BOPM or the Black-Scholes formula to estimate the value of a matching call option, then adding an amount equal to the present value of the exercise price to this estimate, and finally subtracting from this sum an amount that is equal to the current market price of the underlying common stock.

For example, consider a put option that expires in three months and has an exercise price of \$40, while the current market price and the risk of the underlying common stock are \$36 and 50%, respectively. Assuming that the risk-free rate is 5%, it was shown earlier that the Black-Scholes estimate of the value for a matching call option was \$2.26. Because the 5% risk-free rate is a continuously compounded rate, the present value of the exercise price is equal to \$39.50 [= $\$40/(e^{.05\times.25})$]. At this point, since it has been determined that $P_c = \$2.26$, $E/e^{RT} = \$39.50$, and $P_s = \$36$, equation (20.16) can be used to estimate the value of the put option as \$2.26 + \$39.50 – \$36 = \$5.76.

Alternatively, the Black-Scholes formula for estimating the value of a call given in equation (20.10) can be substituted for P_c in equation (20.16). After simplifying, the equation can be used directly for estimating the value of a put:

$$P_p = \frac{E}{e^{RT}}N(-d_2) - P_s N(-d_1) \tag{20.17}$$

where d_1 and d_2 are given in equations (20.11) and (20.12a), respectively.

In the previous example, $d_1 = -.25$ and $d_2 = -.50$; thus $N(-d_1) = N(.25) = .5987$ and $N(-d_2) = N(.50) = .6915$. Applying equation (20.17), the value of this put can be estimated directly:

$$\begin{aligned} P_p &= \left(\frac{\$40}{e^{.05\times.25}} \times .6915\right) - (\$36 \times .5987) \\ &= \$27.31 - \$21.55 = \$5.76 \end{aligned}$$

which is the same estimated value as indicated earlier when equation (20.16) was used.

Static Analysis

Close scrutiny of the put-call parity equation reveals some interesting features of European put option pricing. In particular, the value of a put option is dependent on the values of the same five inputs used for call valuation—the market price of the common stock P_s, the exercise price of the option E, the length of time until the expiration date T, the risk-free rate R, and the risk of the common stock σ. What happens to the value of a put option when one of these inputs is changed while the other four remain the same?

1. The higher the price of the underlying stock P_s, the lower the value of the put option.
2. The higher the exercise price E, the higher the value of the put option.
3. Generally, the longer the time to the expiration date T, the higher the value of the put option.
4. The higher the risk-free rate R, the lower the value of the put option.
5. The greater the risk σ of the common stock, the higher the value of the put option.

The relationships for the underlying stock price P_s, exercise price E, and risk-free rate R are in the opposite direction from those shown earlier for call options, while the relationships for the time to the expiration date T and risk σ are in the same direction. It should be noted that exceptions can occur with T when the put is deep in the money. In such a situation a longer time to expiration could actually decrease the value of the put.

Early Exercise and Dividends

Equations (20.16) and (20.17) apply to a European put on a stock that will not pay dividends prior to the option's expiration. As with call options, complications arise when it is recognized that most put options are American, meaning that they can be exercised before expiration, and that often dividends on the underlying common stock will be paid before the expiration date.

Consider first the ability to exercise a put option at any time up to its expiration date. Earlier it was shown that if there were no dividends on the underlying stock, then a call option was worth more "alive" than "dead," meaning that call options should not be exercised prior to expiration. Such an argument does *not* hold for put options.

Specifically, if a put option is in the money, meaning that the market price of the stock is less than the exercise price, then the investor may want to exercise the put option. In doing so, the investor will receive an additional amount of cash equal to $E - P_s$. In turn, this cash can be invested at the risk-free rate to earn money over the remaining life of the option. Because these earnings may be greater than any additional profits received by the investor if the put option were held, it may be advantageous to exercise the put early and thereby receive the earnings.

An example can be used to illustrate the point. Consider a put option on Widget that has a year left until its expiration date. The exercise price on the put is $100, and the annual risk-free rate is 10%. Imagine that the stock price of Widget is now at $5 per share, having recently plunged in value. If an investor owned such a deep-in-the-money option, it would be in his or her best interest to exercise it immediately. The logic is as follows.

The intrinsic value of the put is currently $100 – $5 = $95, indicating that if the put is exercised immediately, the buyer will receive $95. That is, the buyer will spend $5 to buy a share of Widget and then turn the share and the put over to the writer in return for the exercise price of $100. The net cash inflow to the put buyer of $95 could be invested in the risk-free asset so that in one year it would be worth $95 × 1.10 = $104.50. Alternatively, if the put is held, what is the best that the buyer can hope to earn at year-end? If the stock price of Widget drops to $0, the buyer will receive $100 at expiration from the put writer. Clearly the buyer would be better off exercising the put now instead of holding onto it. Hence, early exercise is merited in such a situation.

What will happen to the market price of the put in such a situation? In equilibrium it will be equal to the put's intrinsic value $E - P_s$ (in this instance, $95). Hence, the put's time premium would be zero, because nobody would pay more than the intrinsic value for the put, knowing that they could get a better return by investing in the risk-free asset. In addition, nobody would be willing to sell a put for less than its intrinsic value because this would open up the opportunity for immediately earning risk-free profits by purchasing the put and exercising it right away. Therefore, the only price that the put could sell for would be its intrinsic value.

Consider next the impact of dividends on put valuation. Previously it was shown that the owner of a call may find it optimal to exercise just *before* an ex-dividend date, as doing so allowed the investor to receive the forthcoming dividends on the stock. With respect to a put, the owner may find it optimal to exercise just *after* the ex-dividend date, as the corresponding drop in the stock price will cause the value of the put to rise.[20]

INDEX OPTIONS

Not all options are written on individual issues of common stock. In recent years many new options have been created that have as an underlying asset something other than the stock of a particular company. One of them — index options — is discussed here. The appendix discusses others, while the next chapter discusses what are known as futures options.

Cash Settlement

A call option on Inco stock is a relatively simple instrument. Upon exercise, the call buyer literally calls away 100 shares of Inco stock. The call writer is expected to physically deliver the shares. In practice, both the buyer and the writer may find it advantageous to close their positions in order to avoid the costs associated with the physical transfer of shares. In this event the buyer may expect a gain (and the seller a loss) approximately equal to the difference between the current market price of the security and the option's exercise price.

It would be entirely feasible to use only a "cash settlement" procedure upon expiration for any option contract. Here, the writer would be required to pay the buyer an amount equal to the difference between the current price of the security and the call option's exercise price (provided that the current price is larger than the exercise price). Similarly for puts, the writer could be expected to pay the buyer an amount equal to the difference between the option's exercise price and the current market price (provided that the exercise price is larger than the current price).

Although listed options on individual securities retain the obligation to "deliver," the realization that cash settlement can serve as a substitute has allowed the creation of index options.

The Contract

An index option is based on the level of an index of stock prices and thus allows investors to take positions in the market that the index represents. Some indices are designed to reflect movements in the stock market, broadly construed. Other "specialized" indices are intended to capture changes in the fortunes of particular industries or sectors. Some of the indices are highly specialized, consisting of only a few stocks. Others are broadly representative of major portions of the stock market. Roughly one-half are European and the other half are American. Generally, the options expire within a few months, but a few (the LEAPs, shown in the lower right part of Figure 20.9) expire in over a year.[21]

---

[20] See Robert Geske and Kuldeep Shastri, "The Early Exercise of American Puts," *Journal of Banking and Finance* 9, no. 2 (June 1985): 207–219, and footnote 12.

[21] A rather unusual kind of index option, referred to as a "warrant," has appeared recently on the American Stock Exchange. Usually the underlying asset is a foreign stock market index. Daily trading activity in these warrants is reported in the AMEX's stock tables, listed in the appropriate alphabetical place under the name of the issuer (such as under *S* for Salomon Brothers). Put warrants give the owner the right to "sell the index" at a stated exercise price, while call warrants give the owner the right to "buy the index" at a stated exercise price. Note that the warrants are only as good as the credit quality of the issuer, since the warrant owner might be left with an option that cannot

In Canada the only index options traded are those based on the Toronto 35 Index that was designed by the TSE in 1987 specifically for trading derivative securities (i.e., predominantly options and futures). These are European options that can only be exercised on the expiry date — the third Friday of the expiry month. The companies included in this index are among the largest listed firms with the most heavily traded issues on the TSE. Trading details for these options, identified as TSE 35 Index, are included with other CDCC options in Figure 20.2.

Contracts for index options are not stated in terms of numbers of shares. Instead, the size of a contract is determined as the product of the level of the index and a multiplier specified by the exchange on which the option is traded. The premium (price) of an index option times the applicable multiplier indicates the total amount paid.

For example, on May 10, 1996 the call option on the TSE 35 Index with an exercise price of $265 (when the index was at $267.89) that expires in June had an indicated premium of $5.55. Since the multiplier for TSE 35 option contracts is 100, an investor has to pay $555.00 (5.55 × 100) (plus a commission) for this contract.

Subsequently, the investor could either exercise or sell the contract for its cash settlement value. Suppose that, at the end of May the TSE 35 is at 280, then the investor could exercise the call and receive its intrinsic value of [(280 – 265) × 100 =] $1500. Alternatively, the investor could simply sell the contract on the exchange and could expect to receive an amount greater than $1500 because it would sell for a price that is equal to the sum of its intrinsic value and its time value (see Figure 20.6).

A related contract is the *Toronto 35 Index Participation Option* (TIP Options). TIPs, (described in Chapter 15) are in effect units of a fund, managed by the TSE, that mimics the TSE 35 Index. These units and their related options are traded on the exchange. The price of a TIP unit is approximately $^1/_{10}$ of the value of the index. These options are treated in the same way as ordinary stock options and their trading details are shown in Figure 20.2 under TSE 35 Tips.

► Flex Options

In an effort to counteract the growing off-exchange market for customized call and put options in the US, the Chicago Board Options Exchange (CBOE) has recently started to list "flexible option contracts," called "flex options" for short. These contracts are on indices, and they allow an investor (typically an institution) to specify the exercise price and expiration date. Once the investor places the order, it is executed on the CBOE, where someone else takes the other side of the contract. Because the OCC is in the middle between the buyer and the writer, there is little risk of default on the contract. This is an advantage to these customized options, since options created off-exchange (say between investors A and B) are only as good as the creditworthiness of the parties themselves. (The possibility that the writer of one of these off-exchange options may default on his or her obligations is referred to as **counterparty risk.**)

---

be exercised if the issuer goes bankrupt. For a discussion of how the possibility of default by the writer affects the prices of such options, see Herb Johnson and Rene Stulz, "The Pricing of Options with Default Risk," *Journal of Finance* 42, no. 2 (June 1987): 267–280.

PORTFOLIO INSURANCE

In the mid-1980s one of the more popular uses of options, procuring **portfolio insurance**, was developed. Consider an investor who holds a highly diversified portfolio. This investor would like to be able to benefit from any upward movements that may subsequently occur in the stock market but would also like to be protected from any downward movements.[22] There are, in principle, at least three ways this might be accomplished.[23]

Purchase an Insurance Policy

One alternative is to sign a contract with an insurance company. For example, assume that the portfolio is currently worth \$100 000. The insurance company might agree to cover any loss in value over some specified period, such as over the forthcoming year. At the end of the year, if the portfolio value was \$95 000, the insurance company would pay the investor \$5000. On the other hand, if the value was \$105 000, the insurance company would pay nothing.

Figure 20.9(a) illustrates this situation. The horizontal axis measures the value of the portfolio at year-end. The 45-degree line $0BC$ shows the value of the uninsured portfolio, while the kinked line ABC shows the value of the insured portfolio. As the figure shows, if the portfolio value at the end of the year is more than \$100 000, then the insured portfolio will be worth the same amount as the uninsured portfolio. However, if the portfolio value is less than \$100 000, then the insured portfolio is worth more, with the vertical difference between $0B$ and AB representing the size of the payment made to the investor by the insurance company.

Unfortunately, insurance companies rarely sign contracts of this sort. However, this is not the only alternative. Instead of dealing with an insurance company, the investor could consider purchasing a put option.

Purchase a Protective Put

Assume that a put option is available on a stock market index that closely resembles the investor's portfolio. The kinked line ADE in Figure 20.9(b) shows the value to a buyer of such a put at the expiration date, where the put has an exercise price of \$100 000 (note how it corresponds to part (b) in Figure 20.3). Line $0BC$ is the value of the portfolio on the expiration date, assuming that the put was not purchased.

What would happen to an investor who (1) held the portfolio and (2) purchased this put? Figure 20.9(c) shows the answer. The value of the portfolio (ABC) is simply the sum of the values $0BC$ and ADE shown in Figure 20.9(b). Not surprisingly, it is precisely the same as the kinked line ABC in Figure 20.9(a).

In this case the purchase of a put provides protection against declines in portfolio value. In this role it is termed a protective put (or "married put"). In practice, stock indices may not closely correspond with an investor's portfolio. Thus, the purchase of a put on a stock index

---

[22] In an efficient market, investors with "average" attitudes toward risk should not purchase portfolio insurance. Those who are especially averse to "downside risk" (relative to "upside potential") may find it useful to buy insurance. The key is the nature of the investor's attitudes toward risk and return. See Hayne E. Leland, "Who Should Buy Portfolio Insurance?" *Journal of Finance* 35, no. 2 (May 1980): 581–594.

[23] Some people would argue that the use of stop orders represents a fourth way.

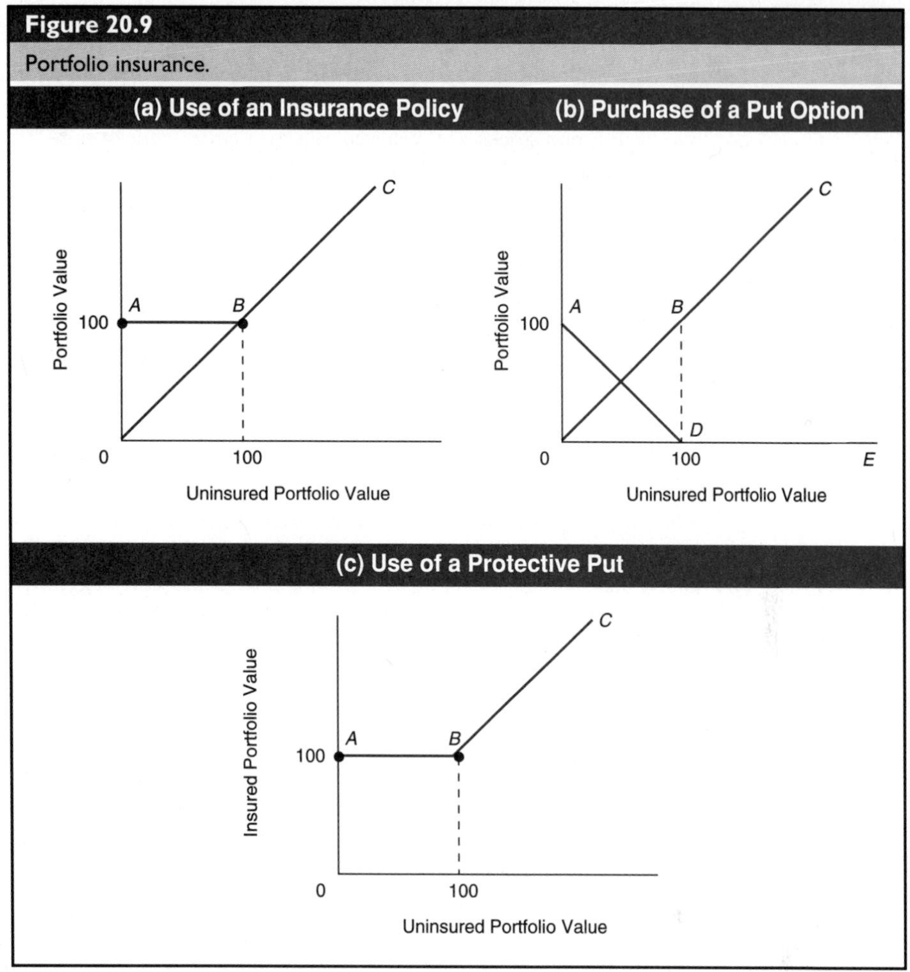

Figure 20.9
Portfolio insurance.

may provide only imperfect insurance. In a graph such as that shown in Figure 20.9(c), the resulting curve would be somewhat fuzzy owing to the possible divergence of values of the portfolio and the index. For example, the portfolio may decline in value by $25 000 whereas the index declines only by $10 000. In this case the portfolio would be insured for only $10 000/$25 000 = 40% of its decline in value.

What if neither explicit insurance nor an appropriate put were available? Can something still be done to insure the portfolio's value against market declines? Yes, if the allocation of funds between the portfolio and a riskless security can be altered frequently enough (and at reasonable cost). This type of portfolio insurance involves the creation of a **synthetic put**, and its application involves the use of a dynamic strategy for asset allocation, which will be discussed next.

► Create a Synthetic Put

Insuring a portfolio by creating a synthetic put can most easily be described with an example.[24] Assume that the investor has $100 000 and is considering the purchase of a portfolio of common stocks. It is believed that the market value of this portfolio will either increase to $125 000 or decrease to $80 000 in six months. If it does increase to $125 000, then it will end up being worth either $156 250 or $100 000 after another six months. Alternatively, if it decreases to $80 000, then it will subsequently end up being worth either $100 000 or $64 000. Each one of these possible "states of nature" is indicated by a letter in Figure 20.10(a), with the current state being denoted as state *A*.

Figure 20.10(a) also shows two sets of terminal portfolio values (that is, portfolio values after 12 months) on the assumption that the common stock portfolio is purchased. The first set gives the values of the portfolio if it is uninsured. The second shows the desired portfolio values—that is, the values of an insured portfolio. In this example the investor wants to be certain that the ending portfolio is worth at least $100 000, while also being able to earn the returns associated with state *D*, should that state occur.[25]

What should the investor do initially in order to be certain of this? Clearly, the investor cannot simply purchase the portfolio of stocks because the portfolio could be worth only $64 000 if state *G* occurs. However, the investor could consider purchasing portfolio insurance—that is, creating a synthetic put—by investing in both the stock portfolio and risk-free bonds.

The way this is done is to imagine that six months have passed and that state *B* has occurred. In this situation, how might one be certain to have $156 250 if the final state is *D* and $100 000 if the state is *E*? The answer is simple—if state *B* occurs, make sure that the portfolio at that point is worth $125 000. Thus, an initial investment strategy is required that will provide $125 000 if the six-month state turns out to be state *B*.

It is also possible that after the first six months state *C* will occur. In this situation, how might one be certain to have $100 000 regardless of the final state? Assuming that risk-free bonds return 5% (compounded discretely) per six months, the investor should purchase $95 238 ($100 000/1.05) of these bonds if state *C* occurs. This means that an initial investment strategy is required that will provide $95 238 if the six-month state turns out to be state *C*.

Figure 20.10(b) shows the investments and the amounts required in situations *B* and *C*. It remains only to determine an appropriate initial set of investments (at point *A*).

An amount of $1 invested in the common stock portfolio at *A* will grow to $1.25 after six months if the state at that time is *B*. More generally, s invested in the common stock portfolio at *A* will grow to $1.25s$ if the six-month state is *B*. Similarly, b invested in bonds

---

[24] For an exposition, see Mark Rubinstein and Hayne E. Leland, "Replicating Options with Positions in Stock and Cash," *Financial Analysts Journal* 37, no. 4 (July/August 1981): 63–72; Mark Rubinstein, "Alternative Paths to Portfolio Insurance," *Financial Analysts Journal* 41, no. 4 (July/August 1985): 42–52; Robert Ferguson, "How to Beat the S&P 500 (Without Losing Sleep)," *Financial Analysts Journal* 42, no. 2 (March/April 1986): 37–46; and Thomas J. O'Brien, "The Mechanics of Portfolio Insurance," *Journal of Portfolio Management* 14, no. 3 (Spring 1988): 40–47.

[25] In this example, portfolio insurance is sought for a one-year horizon with a floor of 0% (meaning that the investor does not want to lose any of the initial investment over the next 12 months). Other horizons and floors, such as a two-year horizon with a floor of –15% (meaning that the investor does not want to lose more than 5% of the initial investment over the next 24 months), are possible. Note the parallel to the discussion of the BOPM, which provides a theoretical basis for the development of portfolio insurance.

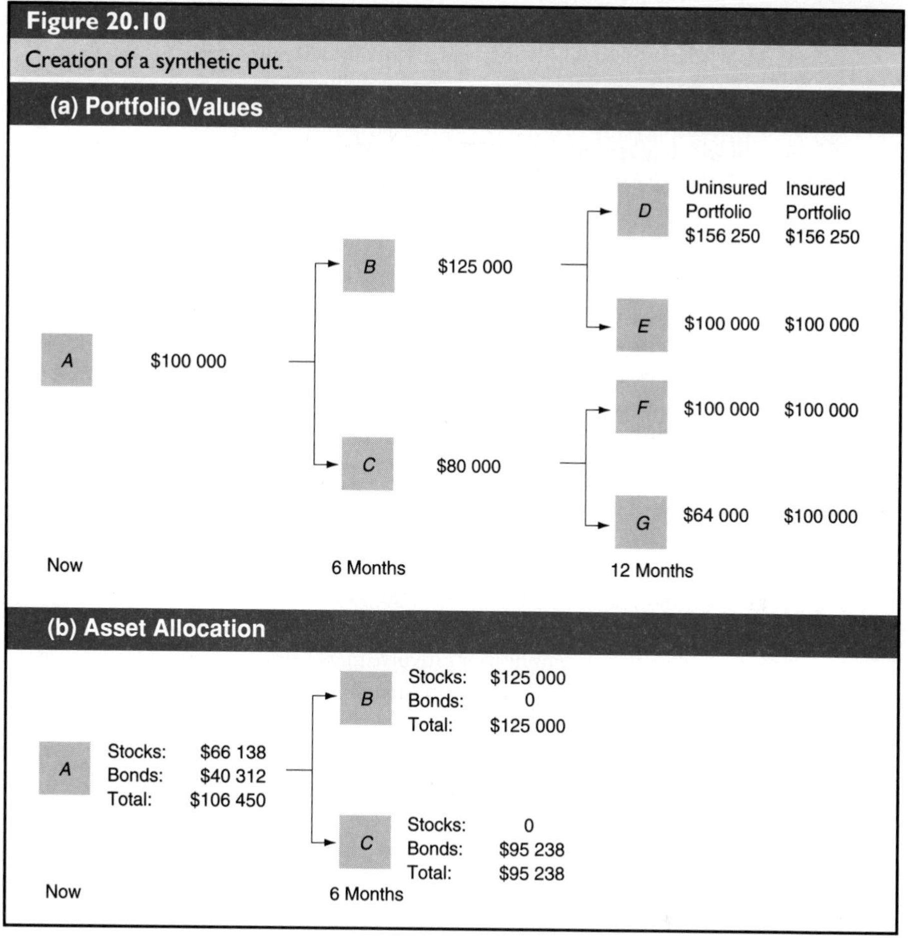

Figure 20.10

Creation of a synthetic put.

at A will grow to $1.05b$ after six months. Thus, a set of initial investments that will provide \$125 000 if state B occurs can be found by solving the following equation for s and b:

$$1.25s + 1.05b = \$125\,000. \tag{20.18}$$

If the six-month state is C, then s invested in the common stock portfolio will be worth $.8s$, while b invested in bonds will be worth $1.05b$. Thus a set of initial investments that will provide \$95 238 if state C occurs can be found by solving the following equation for s and b:

$$.8s + 1.05b = \$95\,238. \tag{20.19}$$

Solutions for s and b can now be found because there are two equations and two unknowns. The solution, shown in Figure 20.10(b), is that the investor should initially put \$66 138 in common stocks and \$40 312 in bonds (that is, s = \$66 138 and b = \$40 312), for a total initial investment of (\$66 138 + \$40 312 =) \$106 450.

Making this initial investment is equivalent to investing \$100 000 in the common stock portfolio and buying a protective put option (or an insurance policy) for \$6450. Indeed, this analysis could be used to determine the appropriate price for such an option or insurance policy. Equivalently, the actions of the investor have resulted in the creation of a synthetic put where the stocks being held are the underlying asset.

By design, this initial investment will provide precisely the desired ending values, but only if the "mix" is altered as values change. The goal is achieved by using a *dynamic strategy* in which investments are bought and sold at intermediate points, depending on the returns of the underlying assets.

In the example, if state B occurs, the stocks will be worth \$66 138 × 1.25 = \$82 672, and the bonds will be worth \$40 312 × 1.05 = \$42 328, for an aggregate value of \$125 000. In this situation the \$42 328 of bonds would be sold and the proceeds used to make an additional investment in the common stock portfolio so that the investor is entirely invested in common stocks for the last six months.

However, if state C occurs, the stocks will be worth \$66 138 × .8 = \$52 910, and the bonds will be worth \$40 312 × 1.05 = \$42 328, for an aggregate value of \$95 238. In this situation the \$52 910 of stocks would be sold and the proceeds used to make an additional investment in the risk-free bonds for the last six months.

Thus, more money is invested in common stocks if the initial portfolio rises in value, with the money obtained by selling bonds. However, if the initial portfolio falls in value, more money is invested in bonds, with the money obtained by selling stocks. In this example, the percentage invested in stocks is initially \$66 138/\$106 450 = 62.13% and subsequently goes to either 100% (if stocks go up) or 0% (if stocks go down).

More realistic applications involve many time intervals within the one-year period, with smaller stock price movements in each interval. Consequently there would be more changes in the mix of stocks and bonds after each interval, but the changes would be of smaller magnitude. Nevertheless, the essential nature of the strategy would be the same:

When stock prices rise, sell some bonds and buy more stocks.

When stock prices fall, sell some stocks and buy more bonds.

Computers are often used to monitor stock price movements of investors who have obtained portfolio insurance in this manner. When these movements are of sufficient magnitude, the computer is used to place the requisite buy and sell orders electronically. Because much of this monitoring and ordering is programmed into a computer, portfolio insurance is often referred to as a form of **program trading**.[26]

If there are only two states of nature in each interval, and reallocation is possible after every interval, and there are no transaction costs, then the values associated with any desired "insured portfolio" can be replicated exactly with a dynamic strategy. In practice, however, the results are likely to be only approximately equal. First, there are transaction costs associated with buying and selling securities for the dynamic strategy.[27] Second, if an interval is defined as a length of time over which only two alternative states may occur, then the amount of time to an interval may be so short that reallocation is impossible after each interval.

In practice, arbitrary rules are applied to avoid frequent revisions and the associated transaction costs while being reasonably certain of providing the portfolio with the desired

[26] The next chapter discusses another form of program trading that is known as index arbitrage.

[27] There is another dynamic strategy for insuring the portfolio that is often preferred because it has smaller transaction costs. It involves index futures, which are a type of financial contract that is discussed in the next chapter. For a survey of dynamic trading strategies, see Robert R. Trippi and Richard B. Harriff, "Dynamic Asset Allocation Rules: Survey and Synthesis," *Journal of Portfolio Management* 17, no. 4 (Summer 1991): 19–26.

level of insurance.[28] Unfortunately, these arbitrary rules did not work very well on Black Monday and Terrible Tuesday (October 19–20, 1987). During these two days stock prices moved downward so fast that reallocation could not be performed in a timely fashion, resulting in a situation where portfolio insurance did not provide the anticipated protection. As a result, some people believe that dynamic strategies will be used less frequently in the future, and that puts will be used more often.[29]

SUMMARY

1. An option is a contract between two investors that grants one investor the right (but not the obligation) to sell to or buy from the other investor a specific asset at a specific price within a specific time period.
2. A call option for a stock gives the buyer the right to buy a specific number of shares of a specific company from the option writer at a specific purchase price at any time up to and including a specific date.
3. A put option for a stock gives the buyer the right to sell a specific number of shares of a specific company to the option writer at a specific selling price at any time up to and including a specific date.
4. Option trading is facilitated by standardized contracts traded on organized exchanges. These exchanges employ the services of a clearing corporation, which maintains records of all trades and acts as a buyer from all option writers and a writer to all option buyers.
5. Option writers are required to deposit margin to ensure performance of their obligations. The amount and form of the margin will depend on the particular option strategy involved.
6. The intrinsic value of a call option equals the difference between the stock's price and the option's exercise price, if this difference is positive. Otherwise the option's intrinsic value is zero.
7. The intrinsic value of a put option equals the difference between its exercise price and the stock's price, if this difference is positive. Otherwise, the option's intrinsic value is zero.
8. Calls and puts will not sell for less than their intrinsic values. However, they may sell for more than their intrinsic values owing to their time values.
9. The binomial option pricing model can be used to determine the fair value of an option based on the assumption that the underlying asset will attain one of two possible known prices at the end of each of a finite number of periods, given its price at the start of each period.

---

[28] For a discussion of transaction costs, see John E. Gilster, Jr., and William Lee, "The Effects of Transactions Costs and Different Borrowing and Lending Rates on the Option Pricing Model: A Note," *Journal of Finance* 39, no. 4 (September 1984): 1215–1222; Hayne E. Leland, "Option Pricing and Replication with Transactions Costs," *Journal of Finance* 40, no. 5 (December 1985): 1283–1301; Fischer Black and Robert Jones, "Simplifying Portfolio Insurance," *Journal of Portfolio Management* 14, no. 1 (Fall 1987): 48–51; and Phelim P. Boyle and Ton Yorst, "Option Replication in Discrete Time with Transactions Costs," *Journal of Finance* 47, no. 1 (March 1992): 271–293.

[29] See Mark Rubinstein, "Portfolio Insurance and the Market Crash," *Financial Analysts Journal* 44, no. 1 (January/February 1988): 38–47. For a discussion of various types of dynamic strategies, see André F. Perold and William F. Sharpe, "Dynamic Strategies for Asset Allocation," *Financial Analysts Journal* 44, no. 1 (January/February 1988): 16–27; and Philip H. Dybvig, "Inefficient Dynamic Portfolio Strategies or How to Throw Away a Million Dollars in the Stock Market," *Review of Financial Studies* 1, no. 1 (Spring 1988): 67–88.

10. An option's hedge ratio indicates the change in the option's value resulting from a one-dollar change in the value of the underlying asset.
11. The Black-Scholes option valuation model shows that the fair value of an option is determined by five factors: the market price of the stock, the exercise price, the life of the option, the risk-free rate, and the risk of the common stock. It assumes that the risk-free rate and common stock risk are constant over the option's life.
12. Put-call parity states that buying both a put option on a stock and a share of the stock will produce the same payoff as buying both a call option on the stock and a risk-free bond (assuming that both options have the same exercise price and expiration date).
13. In addition to put and call options on individual common stocks, options on other assets are traded, such as options on stock indices, debt instruments, and foreign currency.
14. Synthetic options can be created by holding the underlying asset and a risk-free asset in relative amounts that vary with the market price of the underlying asset.

APPENDIX A

SECURITIES WITH OPTIONLIKE FEATURES

Many securities have features that are similar to stock options, particularly call options. In some cases the optionlike features are explicit. Examples include options on stock market indices (discussed earlier in the chapter), debt instruments, and foreign currencies.[30] These options let investors take positions based on their forecasts of movements of the stock market, interest rates, and foreign exchange rates. In other cases more subtle optionlike features are involved. This appendix discusses some of these securities.

WARRANTS

A stock purchase warrant (or, more simply, a warrant) is a call option issued by the firm whose stock serves as the underlying security.[31] At the time of issue, a warrant usually has a longer time to expiration (for example, five or more years) than a typical call option. Some perpetual warrants, with no expiration date, have also been issued. Generally, warrants may be exercised before expiration — that is, they are like American call options — but some require an initial waiting period.

The exercise price may be fixed, or it may change during the life of the warrant, usually increasing in steps. The initial exercise price is typically set to exceed the market price of the underlying security at the time the warrant is issued, often by a substantial amount.

At the time of issue, one warrant typically entitles the holder to purchase one share of stock for the appropriate exercise price. However, most warrants are protected against stock

---

[30] See the textbooks cited at the end of the chapter for more on these types of options. For more on foreign exchange options, see Ian Giddy, "The Foreign Exchange Option as a Hedging Tool," *Midland Corporate Finance Journal* 1, no. 3 (Fall 1983): 32–42; Niso Abauf, "Foreign Exchange Options: The Leading Hedge," *Midland Corporate Finance Journal* 5, no. 2 (Summer 1987): 51–58; and Mark Kritzman, "About Option Replication," *Financial Analysts Journal* 48, no. 1 (January/February 1992): 21–23.

[31] These warrants should not be confused with the put warrants and call warrants on foreign stock market indices that were discussed in footnote 21. Those warrants are issued by some entity such as a brokerage firm. These warrants are issued by the firm whose shares can be purchased by the owner of the warrant.

splits and stock dividends. This means that any warrant with such protection will enable the investor to buy more or less than one share at an altered exercise price if a stock dividend or stock split is declared. For example, a two-for-one stock split would allow the warrant holder to purchase two shares at one-half the original exercise price, whereas a one-for-two reverse stock split would allow the warrant holder to purchase one-half share at twice the original exercise price.

Warrants may be distributed to shareholders in lieu of a stock or cash dividend or sold directly as a new security issue. Alternatively, warrants may be issued in order to "sweeten" an offering of some other kind of security. For example, a bond may be sold by the firm with warrants attached to it. In some cases, the warrants are nondetachable, except upon exercise. This means that if an investor wants to sell one of the bonds, the warrants must be either exercised or sold with the bond. In other cases the warrants are detachable, meaning that after the initial sale of the bonds an investor may sell either the bonds or the warrants (or both).

Terms associated with a warrant are contained in a warrant agreement, which serves the same function as an indenture for a bond issue. In this agreement the scope of the warrant holder's protection is defined (for example, the treatment of warrants in the event of a merger). It may also specify certain restrictions on corporate behaviour.

Some warrants that are issued with bonds have an additional attribute. Although they may be detached and exercised by paying cash to the corporation, an alternative method of payment is provided. This alternative allows bonds from the initial issue to be used in lieu of cash to pay the exercise price, with the bonds being valued at par for this purpose.

One difference between warrants and call options is the limitation on the amount of warrants that are outstanding. A specific number of warrants of a particular type will be issued. The total generally cannot be increased, and typically will be reduced as the warrants are exercised. In contrast, a call option can be created whenever two people wish to create one. Thus, the number outstanding is not fixed. Exercise of a call option on its stock has no more effect on a corporation than a transaction in its stock on the secondary market. However, the exercise of a warrant does have an effect. In particular, it leaves the corporation with more cash, fewer warrants outstanding, and more stock outstanding.

Warrants are traded on major stock exchanges and on the over-the-counter market. Quotations for those with active markets are provided in the financial press in the sections devoted primarily to stocks.

RIGHTS

A right is similar to a warrant in that it also is like a call option issued by the firm whose stock serves as the underlying security. Rights, also known as subscription warrants, are issued to give existing shareholders their preemptive right to subscribe to a new issue of common stock before the general public is given an opportunity. Each share receives one right. A stated number of rights plus cash equal to a specified subscription price are required in order to obtain one new share. To ensure the sale of the new stock, the subscription price is usually set below the stock's market price at the time the rights are issued. This does not mean that new subscribers get a bargain, as they must pay old shareholders for the required number of rights, which become valuable as a result.

Rights generally have short lives (from two to ten weeks when issued) and may be freely traded prior to exercise. Up to a specified date, old shares of the stock trade *cum rights*, meaning that the buyer of the stock is entitled to receive the rights when issued. Afterward the stock trades *ex rights* at a correspondingly lower price. Rights for popular issues of stock are sometimes traded on exchanges; others are available in the over-the-counter market. Often trading begins prior to actual availability, with the rights sold for delivery on a *when-issued* basis.

A right is, in effect, a warrant, although one with a rather short time before expiration. It also differs with regard to exercise price, which is typically set above the stock's market price at issuance for a warrant and below it for a right. Because of their short lives, rights need not be protected against stock splits and stock dividends. Otherwise they have all the attributes of a warrant and can be valued in a similar manner.[32]

BOND CALL PROVISIONS

Many firms issue bonds with call provisions that allow the firm to repurchase the bonds before maturity, usually at a price above par value. This amounts to the simultaneous sale of a straight bond and purchase of a call option that is paid by the corporation in the form of a relatively lower selling price for the bond. The writer of the option is the bond purchaser.

Bond call provisions usually can be exercised only after some specified date (for example, five years after issue). Moreover, the exercise price, known as the call premium, may be different for different exercise dates (typically shrinking in size the longer the bond is outstanding). The implicit call option associated with such a bond is thus both longer lived and more complex than those traded on the listed option markets.[33]

CONVERTIBLE SECURITIES

A particularly popular financial instrument is a security that can be converted into a different security of the same firm under certain conditions. The typical case involves a bond or a preferred share convertible into shares of the firm's common stock, with a stated number of shares received for each bond or preferred share. Usually no cash is involved: the old security is simply traded in, and the appropriate number of new securities is issued in return. Convertible preferred shares are issued from time to time, but like other preferred shares, tax effects make them attractive primarily to corporate investors. For other investors many issues of convertible bonds are more attractive.

If a \$1000 par-value bond can be converted into 20 common shares, the *conversion ratio* is 20. Alternatively, the *conversion price* may be said to be \$1000/20 = \$50, because \$50 of the bond's par value must be given up to obtain one common share. Neither the conversion ratio nor the conversion price is affected by changes in a bond's market value.

Conversion ratios are typically set so that conversion will not prove attractive unless the stock price increases substantially from its value at the time the convertible security was first issued. This is similar to the general practice used in setting exercise prices for warrants.

A convertible bond's *conversion value*, obtained by multiplying the conversion ratio by the stock's current market price, is the value that would be obtained by conversion; it is

---

[32] Rights are also discussed in Chapter 17. Valuation of rights is relatively simple if it is assumed that there is no chance that they will end up being out of the money on the expiration date and the time value of money is ignored (meaning that the risk-free rate is assumed to be zero).

[33] Bond call provisions are also discussed in Chapters 14 and 15.

the bond's current "value as stock." The *conversion premium* is the amount by which the bond's current market price exceeds its conversion value, expressed as a percent of the latter. A related amount is the convertible's *investment value.* This value is an estimate—based on the convertible's maturity date, coupon rate, and credit rating—of the amount for which the bond might sell if it were not convertible. Equivalently, it is the convertible's "value as a straight bond."

Consider a $1000 par-value bond convertible into 20 shares of stock. If the market price of the shares is $60 per share, then the conversion value of the bond is $60 × 20 = $1200. If the current market price of the convertible bond is $1300, then its conversion premium is $1300 – $1200 = $100. Its investment value might be estimated to be, say, $950, meaning that the bond would sell for this much if it did not provide the investor with the option of convertibility.

Convertible securities of great complexity can be found in the marketplace. Some may be converted only after an initial waiting period. Some may be converted up to the bond's maturity date; others, only for a stated, shorter period. Some have different conversion ratios for different years. A few can be converted into packages of two or more different securities; others require the additional payment of cash upon conversion.

Convertible bonds are usually protected against stock splits and stock dividends via adjustments in the conversion ratio. For example, a bond with an initial conversion ratio of 20 could be adjusted to have a ratio of 22 following a 10% stock dividend. Protection against cash dividends is not generally provided, but some indentures require that the holders of convertible bonds be notified prior to payment of cash dividends so that they may convert before the resultant fall in the stock's market price.

Convertible securities often contain a call provision, which may be used by the corporation to force conversion when the stock's market price is sufficiently high to make the value of the shares obtained on conversion exceed the call price of the bond. For example, if the conversion value of the bond is $1200 (the bond is convertible into 20 shares of stock that are currently selling for $60 per share) and the call price is $1100, the firm can force conversion by calling the bond. This is because a bondholder faces two choices when the call is received—either convert and receive 20 shares collectively worth $1200 or receive cash of $1100—and should choose the shares because they have a higher value.

A convertible bond is, for practical purposes, a bond with nondetachable warrants plus the restriction that *only* the bond is usable (at par) to pay the exercise price. If the bond were not callable, the value of this package would equal the value of a straight non-callable bond (that is, the estimated investment value) plus that of the warrants. However, most convertible bonds are callable and thus involve a double option: the holder has an option to convert the bond to shares, and the issuing corporation has an option to buy the bond back from the investors.

QUESTIONS AND PROBLEMS

1. Why have organized options exchanges been so important to the growth in options trading?
2. How do organized options exchanges permit option buyers and writers to open and close positions without having to contact one another directly?
3. Consider the following stocks selling for the prices listed at the top of the next page:

Stock	Current Price
A	$ 26
B	$ 73
C	$215

Specify the likely exercise prices that will be set for newly created options on these stocks.

4. From the latest two consecutive issues of the *Globe and Mail Report on Business*, find the price of the Nor Tel call option with the nearest expiration date and the exercise price closest to the current price of Nor Tel stock. What is the premium on the call option? What has been the percentage change in the option's price from the previous day? From another part of the *Report*, calculate the percentage change in the price of Nor Tel stock from the previous day. Compare this number to the option's percentage price change.
5. Polly Wolfe has written a September 45 naked call option on Albion software stock. When the option was written, the stock sold for $42 per share. The option premium was $2.75. Calculate how much margin Polly had to deposit upon writing the call.
6. Donald Troy wrote a March 75 naked put option on Lodi Mines stock. When the option was written, the stock sold for $80 per share. The option premium was $.30. How much margin did Donald have to deposit?
7. Draw a profit-loss graph for the following option strategies:
   a. Buy a put, $2 premium, $70 exercise price.
   b. Write a call, $3 premium, $40 exercise price.
   c. Buy a stock for $80 and buy a put on the same stock, $1 premium, $70 exercise price.
8. Elizabeth Stroud had only a few hours left to decide whether to exercise a call option on Carson Company stock. The call option has an exercise price of $54. Elizabeth originally purchased the call six months ago for $400 (or $4 per share).
   a. For what range of stock prices should Elizabeth exercise the call on the last day of the call's life?
   b. For what range of stock prices would Elizabeth realize a net loss (including the premium paid for the call)?
   c. If Elizabeth had purchased a put instead of a call, how would your answers to parts (a) and (b) change?
9. On November 18, three call options on Eden Prairie Associates stock, all expiring in December, sold for the following prices:

Exercise Price	Option Price
$50	$7 1/2
$60	$3
$70	$1 1/2

Fred Marberry is considering a "butterfly spread" that involves the following positions:
Buy 1 call at $50 exercise price.
Sell (write) 2 calls at $60 exercise price.
Buy 1 call at $70 exercise price.

a. What would be the values at expiration of Fred's spread if Eden Prairie Associates' stock price is below \$50? Between \$50 and \$60? Between \$60 and \$70? Above \$70?

b. What dollar investment would be required of Fred to establish the spread?

10. What is the time value of an option? Why does an option's time value decline as the option approaches expiration?

11. Shorewood Systems stock currently sells for \$50 per share. One year from today the stock will be worth either \$58.09 or \$43.04. The continuously compounded risk-free rate is 5.13% for one year. Based on the binomial option pricing model, what is the fair value for a call option on Shorewood stock with one year to expiration and a \$50 exercise price?

12. Hopkins Pharmaceuticals stock is currently priced at \$40 per share. Six months from now its price will be either \$44.21 or \$36.19. If the price rises to \$44.21, then six months later the price will be either \$48.86 or \$40. If, however, the price initially falls to \$36.19, then six months later the price will be either \$40 or \$32.75. The risk-free rate (continuously compounded) is 3.05% over each six-month period. Using the binomial option pricing model, what is the fair value of a one-year call option on Hopkins stock?

13. Given the information below, calculate the three-month call option price that is consistent with the Black-Scholes model:

$$P_s = \$47, \qquad E = \$45, \qquad R = .05, \qquad \sigma = .40.$$

14. If the premium on a call option has recently declined, does this indicate that the option is a better buy than it was previously? Why?

15. List the variables needed to estimate the value of a call option. Describe how a change in the value of these variables affects the value of a call option.

16. Calculate the hedge ratio of a call option for a stock with a current price of \$40, an exercise price of \$45, a standard deviation of 34%, and a time to expiration of six months, given a risk-free return of 7% per annum.

17. Using the Black-Scholes model, calculate the implicit volatility of a stock with a three-month call option currently selling for \$8.54 and:

$$P_s = \$83, \qquad E = \$80, \qquad R = .05.$$

18. Amir Gutman owns 20 000 shares of Merrimac Monitoring Equipment stock. This stock makes up the bulk of Amir's wealth. Concerned about the stock's near-term prospects, Amir wishes to fully hedge the risk of the stock. Given a hedge ratio of .37 and a premium of \$2.50 for the near Merrimac put option, how many put options should Amir buy?

19. A six-month call option with an exercise price of \$40 is selling for \$5. The current price of the stock is \$41.25. The hedge ratio of the option is .65.

a. What percentage change in the option's price is likely to accompany a 1% change in the stock's price?

b. If the beta of the stock is 1.10, what is the beta of the option? (*Hint:* Recall what the beta of a stock implies about the relationship between the stock's price and that of the market.)

20. The fair value of a three-month call option on Portage Industries stock is \$1.50. The exercise price of the call option is \$30. The risk-free rate is 5%, and the stock price of Portage is currently \$28 per share. What is the fair value of a three-month put option on Portage stock with the same exercise price as the call option?

21. Given the following information, calculate the three-month put option price that is consistent with the Black-Scholes model:

$$P_s = \$32, \qquad E = \$45, \qquad R = .06, \qquad \sigma = .35.$$

22. Explain why call options on non-dividend-paying stocks are "worth more alive than dead."
23. In February George Gardner sold a September 55 call on Dane Corporation stock for \$4.375 per share and simultaneously bought a September 55 put on the same stock for \$6 per share. At the time, Treasury bills coming due in September were priced to yield 12.6%, and Dane stock sold for \$53 per share.
    a. What value would put-call parity suggest was appropriate for the Dane put?
    b. Dane was expected to make three dividend payments between February and September. Could that account for the discrepancy between your answer to part (a) and the actual price of the put? Why or why not?
    c. If Dane stock were to fall to a very low value before September, might it pay for George to exercise the put? Why?
24. Why does a stock index option sell at a lower price than the cost of a portfolio of options on the constituent stocks (assuming that the index call option and the portfolio of call options control the same dollar value of stocks)?
25. Distinguish between portfolio insurance implemented through a protective put and through dynamic asset allocation.
26. (Appendix Question) What is the primary advantage to an investor of a warrant compared to a call option?
27. (Appendix Question) Wheeling Corp. has a 10% subordinated convertible debenture outstanding, maturing in 8 years. The bond's face value is \$1000. It currently sells for 99 of par. The bond is convertible into 15 shares of common stock. The company's common stock currently sells for \$50 per share. Nonconvertible bonds of similar risk have a yield of 12%.
    a. What is the bond's conversion value?
    b. What is the bond's conversion premium?
    c. What is the bond's investment value?

KEY TERMS

option
call option
exercise price
expiration date
premium
closing sale
closing purchase
put option
LEAPS
specialists
competitive option trader (COT)
margin
covered call writing
naked call writing
naked put writing
intrinsic value
straddle
European option
American option
hedge ratio
put-call parity
time value
implicit volatility
counterparty risk
portfolio insurance
synthetic put
program trading

REFERENCES

1. Investment strategies involving options are discussed in many papers. Here are three of the most notable ones:

   Robert C. Merton, Myron S. Scholes, and Mathew L. Gladstein, "The Returns and Risk of Alternative Call Option Portfolio Investment Strategies," *Journal of Business* 51, no. 1 (April 1978): 183–242.

   Robert C. Merton, Myron S. Scholes, and Mathew L. Gladstein, "The Returns and Risk of Alternative Put-Option Portfolio Investment Strategies," *Journal of Business* 55, no. 1 (January 1982): 1–55.

   Aimee Gerberg Ronn and Ehud I. Ronn, "The Box Spread Arbitrage Conditions: Theory, Tests, and Investment Strategies," *Review of Financial Studies* 2, no. 1 (1989): 91–107.

2. The binomial option pricing model was initially developed in:

   William F. Sharpe, *Investments* (Englewood Cliffs, NJ: Prentice Hall, 1978), Chapter 14.

3. A short while later the following two papers expanded upon Sharpe's model:

   John C. Cox, Stephen A. Ross, and Mark Rubinstein, "Option Pricing: A Simplified Approach," *Journal of Financial Economics* 7, no. 3 (September 1979): 229–263.

   Richard J. Rendleman, Jr., and Brit J. Bartter, "Two-State Option Pricing," *Journal of Finance* 34, no. 5 (December 1979): 1093–1110.

4. For more on the theory of binomial models, see:

   Daniel B. Nelson and Krishna Ramaswamy, "Simple Binomial Processes as Diffusion Approximations in Financial Models," *Review of Financial Studies* 3, no. 3 (1990): 393–430.

5. Two seminal papers on option pricing are:

   Robert C. Merton, "Theory of Rational Option Pricing," *Bell Journal of Economics and Management Science* 4, no. 1 (Spring 1973): 141–183.

   Fischer Black and Myron Scholes, "The Pricing of Options and Corporate Liabilities," *Journal of Political Economy* 81, no. 3 (May/June 1973): 637–654.

6. The Black-Scholes option pricing model assumes that the risk-free rate is constant over the life of the option. For three interesting papers that relax this assumption, see:

   Ramon Rabinovitch, "Pricing Stock and Bond Options When the Default-Free Rate Is Stochastic," *Journal of Financial and Quantitative Analysis* 24, no. 4 (December 1989): 447–457.

   Stuart M. Turnbull and Frank Milne, "A Simple Approach to Interest-Rate Option Pricing," *Review of Financial Studies* 4, no. 1 (1991): 87–121.

   Jason Z. Wei, "Valuing American Equity Options with a Stochastic Interest Rate: A Note," *Journal of Financial Engineering* 2, no. 2 (June 1993): 195–206.

7. The Black-Scholes model also assumes that the volatility of the underlying asset is constant over the life of the option. For papers that relax this assumption, see:

   John Hull and Alan White, "The Pricing of Options on Assets with Stochastic Volatilities," *Journal of Finance* 42, no. 2 (June 1987): 281–300.

Herb Johnson and David Shanno, "Option Pricing When the Variance Is Changing," *Journal of Financial and Quantitative Analysis* 22, no. 2 (June 1987): 143–151.

Louis O. Scott, "Option Pricing When the Variance Changes Randomly: Theory, Estimation, and an Application," *Journal of Financial and Quantitative Analysis* 22, no. 4 (December 1987): 419–438.

James B. Wiggins, "Option Values Under Stochastic Volatility: Theory and Empirical Estimates," *Journal of Financial Economics* 19, no. 2 (December 1987): 351–372.

Marc Chesney and Louis Scott, "Pricing European Currency Options: A Comparison of the Modified Black-Scholes Model and a Random Variance Model," *Journal of Financial and Quantitative Analysis* 24, no. 3 (September 1989): 267–284.

Thomas J. Finucane, "Black-Scholes Approximations of Call Option Prices with Stochastic Volatilities: A Note," *Journal of Financial and Quantitative Analysis* 24, no. 4 (December 1989): 527–532.

Steven L. Heston, "A Closed-Form Solution for Options in Stochastic Volatility with Applications to Bond and Currency Options," *Review of Financial Studies* 6, no. 2 (1993): 327–343.

8. Portfolio insurance has received much attention. In addition to the citations given in the chapter, see:

M. J. Brennan and R. Solanki, "Optimal Portfolio Insurance," *Journal of Financial and Quantitative Analysis* 16, no. 3 (September 1981): 279–300.

Ethan S. Etzioni, "Rebalance Disciplines for Portfolio Insurance," *Journal of Portfolio Management* 13, no. 1 (Fall 1986): 59–62.

Richard J. Rendelman, Jr., and Richard McEnally, "Assessing the Costs of Portfolio Insurance," *Financial Analysts Journal* 43, no. 3 (May/June 1987): 27–37.

C. B. Garcia and F. J. Gould, "An Empirical Study of Portfolio Insurance," *Financial Analysts Journal* 43, no. 4 (July/August 1987): 44–54.

Robert Ferguson, "A Comparison of the Mean-Variance and Long-Term Return Characteristics of Three Investment Strategies," *Financial Analysts Journal* 43, no. 4 (July/August 1987): 55–66.

Fischer Black and Robert Jones, "Simplifying Portfolio Insurance," *Journal of Portfolio Management* 14, no. 1 (Fall 1987): 48–51.

Yu Zhu and Robert C. Kavee, "Performance of Portfolio Insurance Strategies," *Journal of Portfolio Management* 14, no. 3 (Spring 1988): 48–54.

Fischer Black and Robert Jones, "Simplifying Portfolio Insurance for Corporate Pension Plans," *Journal of Portfolio Management* 14, no. 4 (Summer 1988): 33–37.

Thomas J. O'Brien, *How Option Replicating Portfolio Insurance Works: Expanded Details*, Monograph Series in Finance and Economics #1988–4, New York University Salomon Center, Leonard N. Stern School of Business.

Erol Hakanoglu, Robert Kopprasch, and Emmanuel Roman, "Constant Proportion Portfolio Insurance for Fixed-Income Investment," *Journal of Portfolio Management* 15, no. 4 (Summer 1989): 58–66.

Michael J. Brennan and Eduardo Schwartz, "Portfolio Insurance and Financial Market Equilibrium," *Journal of Business* 62, no. 4 (October 1989): 455–472.

Sanford J. Grossman and Jean-Luc Vila, "Portfolio Insurance in Complete Markets: A Note," *Journal of Business* 62, no. 4 (October 1989): 473–476.

Robert R. Trippi and Richard B. Harriff, "Dynamic Asset Allocation Rules: Survey and Synthesis," *Journal of Portfolio Management* 17, no. 4 (Summer 1991): 19–26.

Charles J. Jacklin, Allan W. Kleidon, and Paul Pfleiderer, "Underestimation of Portfolio Insurance and the Crash of October 1987," *Review of Financial Studies* 5, no. 1 (1992): 35–63.

9. A great deal has been written on warrants and convertibles. For an introduction to this literature, see:

Richard A. Brealey and Stewart C. Myers, *Principles of Corporate Finance* (New York: McGraw-Hill, 1991), Chapter 22.

10. Many textbooks are devoted exclusively to options or have options as one of their primary subjects. Most cover everything discussed in this chapter, but in more detail and with a more complete list of citations. Here are a few:

Robert A. Jarrow and Andrew Rudd, *Option Pricing* (Homewood, IL: Richard D. Irwin, 1983).

John C. Cox and Mark Rubinstein, *Options Markets* (Englewood Cliffs, NJ: Prentice Hall, 1985).

Richard M. Bookstaber, *Option Pricing and Investment Strategies* (Chicago: Probus Publishing, 1987).

Peter Ritchken, *Options: Theory, Strategy, and Applications* (Glenview, IL: Scott, Foresman, 1987).

Don M. Chance, *An Introduction to Options and Futures* (Fort Worth, TX: The Dryden Press, 1991).

Robert W. Kolb, *Options: An Introduction* (Miami, FL: Kolb Publishing, 1991).

Alan L. Tucker, *Financial Futures, Options, and Swaps* (St. Paul, MN: West Publishing, 1991).

David A. Dubofsky, *Options and Financial Futures* (New York: McGraw-Hill, 1992).

John C. Hull, *Options, Futures, and Other Derivative Securities* (Englewood Cliffs, NJ: Prentice Hall, 1993).

Hans R. Stoll and Robert E. Whaley, *Futures and Options* (Cincinnati, OH: South-Western Publishing, 1993).

11. A useful software package and manual for valuing options is:

Stuart M. Turnbull, *Option Valuation* (Toronto: Holt, Rinehart and Winston of Canada, 1987).

12. For a Canadian perspective on the topics covered in this chapter, see:

P. Halpern and S. Turnbull, "Empirical Tests on Boundary Conditions for Toronto Stock Exchange Options," *Journal of Finance* 40, no. 3 (June 1985).

A. Mandron, "Some Empirical Evidence about Canadian Stock Options, Part I: Valuation; Part II: Market Structure," *Canadian Journal of Administrative Sciences* 5, no. 2 (June 1988).

L. Gagnon, "Empirical Investigation of the Canadian Government Bond Option Market," *Canadian Journal of Administrative Sciences* 11, no. 1 (March 1994).

CHAPTER 21

Futures

Consider a contract that involves the delivery of some specific asset by a seller to a buyer at an agreed-upon future date. While such a contract also specifies the purchase price, the asset is not to be paid for until the delivery date. However, the buyer and the seller will both be requested to make a security deposit at the time the contract is signed. The reason for this deposit is to protect each person from experiencing any losses, should the other person renege on the contract. Hence, the size of the deposit is checked daily to see that it provides sufficient protection. If it is insufficient, it will have to be increased. If it is more than sufficient, the excess can be withdrawn.

These contracts are often referred to as **futures** (short for futures contract), and in the United States they involve assets such as agricultural goods (for example, wheat), natural resources (for example, copper), foreign currencies (for example, Swiss francs), fixed-income securities (for example, Treasury bonds), and market indices (for example, the Standard & Poor's 500).[1] As with options, standardization of the terms in these contracts makes it relatively easy for anyone to create and subsequently trade the contracts.

Futures contracts are available on exchanges in Canada on agricultural products (cereals), bankers' acceptances, long Canada Bonds and the Toronto 35 index. Canadian investors can readily trade futures contracts on other commodities on US exchanges. The Canadian business press provides price quotations for contracts traded in both countries.

HEDGERS AND SPECULATORS

There are two types of people who deal in futures (and options) — speculators and hedgers. **Speculators** buy and sell futures for the sole purpose of making a profit by closing out their positions at a price that is better than the the initial price (or so they hope). Such people neither produce nor use the asset in the ordinary course of business. In contrast, **hedgers** buy and sell futures to offset an otherwise risky position in the spot market. In the ordinary course of business, they either produce or use the asset.

► Example of Hedging

For example, consider wheat futures. A farmer might note today that the market price for a wheat futures contract with delivery around harvest time is $105 per tonne, a price that is high enough to ensure a profitable year. Although the farmer could sell wheat futures today,

---

[1] The term *commodity futures* is often used to refer to futures on agricultural goods and natural resources. The term *financial futures* is typically used in reference to futures on financial instruments such as Treasury bonds, foreign currencies, and stock market indices.

alternatively the farmer could wait until harvest and sell the wheat on the spot market at that time.[2] However, waiting until harvest entails risk because the spot price of wheat could fall by then, perhaps to $85 per tonne, which would bring financial ruin to the farmer. In contrast, selling wheat futures today will allow the farmer to "lock in" a $105-per-tonne selling price. Doing so would remove an element of risk from the farmer's primary business of growing wheat. Thus, a farmer who sells futures is known as a hedger or, more specifically, a **short hedger**.

Perhaps the buyer of the farmer's futures contract is a baker who uses wheat in making bread. Currently the baker has enough wheat in inventory to last until harvest season. In anticipation of the need to replenish the inventory at that time, the baker could buy a wheat futures contract today at $105 per tonne. Alternatively, the baker could simply wait until the inventory runs low and then buy wheat in the spot market. However, there is a chance that the spot price will be $125 per tonne at that time. Should this happen, the baker would have to raise the selling price of bread and perhaps lose sales in doing so. Alternatively, by purchasing wheat futures, the baker can "lock in" a $105 per tonne purchase price, thereby removing an element of risk from the bread business. Thus, a baker who buys futures is also known as a hedger or, more specifically, a **long hedger**.

► Example of Speculating

The farmer and the baker can be compared with a speculator—a person who buys and sells wheat futures, based on the forecast price of wheat, in the pursuit of relatively short-term profits. As mentioned earlier, such a person neither produces nor uses the asset in the ordinary course of business.

A speculator who thinks that the price of wheat is going to rise substantially will buy wheat futures. Later this person will enter a **reversing trade** by selling wheat futures. If the forecast was accurate, a profit will have been made on an increase in the wheat futures price.

For example, consider a speculator expecting at least a $20 per tonne rise in the spot price of wheat. Whereas this person could buy wheat, store it, and hope to sell it later at the anticipated higher price, it would be easier and more profitable to buy a wheat futures contract today at $105 per tonne. Later, assuming that the spot price of wheat rises by $20, the speculator would enter a reversing trade by selling the wheat futures contract for perhaps $125 per tonne. (A $20 rise in the spot price of wheat will cause the futures price to rise by about $20.) Thus the speculator will make a profit of $20 per tonne, or $400 in total, because these contracts are for 20 tonnes.[3] As will be shown later, the speculator might need to make a security deposit of $100 at the time the wheat futures contract is bought. As this is returned when the reversing trade is made, the speculator's rate of return is quite high (400%) relative to the percentage rise in the price of wheat (19%).

Alternatively, if a speculator forecasts a substantial price decline, then initially wheat futures would be sold. Later, the person would enter a reversing trade by purchasing wheat futures. Assuming that the forecast was accurate, a profit will be made on the decrease in the wheat futures price.

---

[2] The **spot market** involves the immediate exchange of an asset for cash. The purchase price of the asset is known as its **spot price**.

[3] Prices quoted in the business press refer to 20-tonne contracts (a *job lot*) although a board lot is generally 100 tonnes.

THE FUTURES CONTRACT

Futures contracts are standardized in terms of delivery as well as the type of asset that can be delivered. For example, *The Winnipeg Commodity Exchange* (WCE) specifies the following requirements for its wheat contracts:

1. The seller agrees to deliver 20 tonnes of No. 3 CWRS wheat at the agreed-upon price. Alternatively, three other grades can be delivered at $5.00 per tonne discounts from the agreed-upon price. In any case, the seller is allowed to decide which grade shall be delivered.
2. The grain will be delivered by registered warehouse receipts issued by approved warehouses in Thunder Bay, Ontario.
3. Delivery will take place during the contract month, with the seller allowed to decide the actual date. Delivery must be completed by the last business day of the contract month. Alternative delivery points are permitted for some cereals, but delivery at these must be completed by the eighth business day before the end of the contract month.
4. Upon delivery of the warehouse receipt from the seller to the buyer, the latter will pay the former the agreed-upon price in cash.

After an organized exchange has set all the terms of a futures contract except for its price, the exchange will authorize trading in the contract.[4] Buyers and sellers (or their representatives) meet at a specific place on the floor of the exchange and try to agree on a price at which to trade. If they succeed, one or more contracts will be created, with all the standard terms plus an additional one — the price involved. Prices are normally stated on a per-unit basis. Thus, if a buyer and seller agree to a price of $105 per tonne for a contract of 20 tonnes of wheat, the amount of money involved is $2100.

Figure 21.1 shows a set of daily quotations of the prices at which commodity futures contracts were traded on the Winnipeg Exchange and the total volume of sales for each type of contract. Such listings of active futures markets are published regularly in the financial press, with each item for delivery having a heading that indicates the number of units per contract (e.g., 20 metric tons for oats) and the terms on which prices are stated (dollars per ton).

Below the heading for the asset are certain details for each type of contract. In Figure 21.1, for example, there are seven different futures contracts for canola, having different delivery dates that are shown in the third column. The first two columns show the *seasonal high (SeaHi)* and the *seasonal low (SeaLow)* that are the highest and lowest prices recorded during the lifetime of the contract. In the fourth, fifth, sixth, and seventh columns are the *open*, denoting the price at which the first transaction was made; the *high* and *low*, representing the highest and lowest prices recorded during the preceeding trading day; and the *settle*, a price (for example, the average of the high and low prices) that is representative of trades executed during the "closing period" designated by the exchange (for example, the last two minutes of trading). The eighth and ninth columns show the *change* from the

[4] For a relatively complete description of the terms for many exchange-traded futures contracts, see the *Commodity Trading Manual* (Chicago Board of Trade, 1985); Robert W. Kolb, *Understanding Futures Markets* (Glenview, Ill.: Scott, Foresman and Company, 1988); and the extensive literature published by The Winnipeg Commodity Exchange. The first two of these books also contain descriptions of various futures exchanges.

Figure 21.1

Quotations for commodity futures contracts.

Winnipeg Commodity Exchange

Futures

SeaHi	SeaLow	Mth.	Open	High	Low	Settle	Chg.	Opint
CANOLA 20 tonnes, can $/tonne								
436.9	383.0	Jan96	424.0	426.5	423.9	426.0	+1.2	837
440.5	390.0	Mar96	432.0	432.0	428.5	429.1	−2.4	22740
449.9	408.0	Jun96	438.5	438.5	435.0	435.2	−2.2	9060
448.0	410.3	Aug96	437.0	437.0	437.0	437.0	−5.0	519
405.0	359.3	Sep96	396.0	398.0	396.0	396.0	−1.9	4882
402.3	361.0	Nov96	394.0	396.5	394.0	394.5	−1.5	4427
408.0	371.5	Jan97	396.0	397.5	394.7	394.7	−2.9	1044
Est sales			Prv Sales	Prv Open Int				Chg.
			4520	43509				
FLAXSEED 20 tonnes, can $/tonne								
352.0	291.9	Mar96	346.0	346.0	343.5	344.5	−1.5	4368
353.9	318.0	May96	348.0	348.0	345.8	346.3	−1.7	1129
355.9	326.5	Jul96	348.5	348.7	348.3	348.5	−1.0	191
Est sales			Prv Sales	Prv Open Int				Chg.
			381	5688				
OATS 20 tonnes, can $/tonne								
231.0	130.0	Mar96				228.0		280
227.5	141.0	May96				230.0		254
		Jul96				231.0		
191.0	175.0	Oct96				176.2		5
Est sales			Prv Sales	Prv Open Int				Chg.
			0	539				
WESTERN BARLEY 20 tonnes,can $/tonne								
188.9	114.5	Feb96	181.5	181.9	181.0	181.0	−1.5	3983
193.0	119.0	May96	189.0	189.0	187.7	187.8	−0.8	6213
180.0	136.5	Aug96	175.7	176.3	175.4	176.0	+0.3	1352
163.5	142.0	Nov96	164.5	164.8	163.5	163.5	+0.2	1291
166.0	155.5	Feb97	167.0	167.0	167.0	167.0	+1.0	140
Est sales			Prv Sales	Prv Open Int				Chg.
			1330	12979				+25
WHEAT 20 tonnes, can $/tonne								
214.7	139.6	Mar96	209.9	210.5	208.5	209.5	−0.4	4353
211.5	155.1	May96	207.0	207.4	206.3	206.5	−0.4	3065
Est sales			Prv Sales	Prv Open Int				Chg.
			245	8381				−20

SOURCE: Reprinted with permission of the *Globe and Mail* (January 11, 1996).

previous day's settlement price and the **open interest** (the number of outstanding contracts) on the previous day.

For each futures contract, information is summarized below the figures for the last delivery date and indicates the estimated and previous sales (that is, the number of contracts traded on that day and on the previous trading day) as well as the total open interest in those contracts on the previous day and the change in total open interest from the previous day (in the case of canola, these summary figures are below the January 1997 delivery date figures).

Futures Markets

The futures contracts shown in Figure 21.1 were traded on The Winnipeg Commodity Exchange, the only one of its kind in Canada.

In the United States, futures contracts are traded on various organized exchanges, notably the Chicago Board of Trade (CBT), currently the largest futures exchange in the world.

The method of trading futures on organized exchanges is similar in some ways and different in other ways from the way that stocks and options are traded. Like stocks and options, customers can place market, limit, and stop orders. Furthermore, once an order is transmitted to an exchange floor, it must be taken to a designated spot for execution by a member of the exchange, just as is done for stocks and options. This spot is known as a "pit" because of its shape, which is circular with a set of interior descending steps on which members stand. What transpires in the pit is what distinguishes trading in futures from trading in stocks and options.

First of all, there are no specialists or market-makers on futures exchanges. Trading is carried out by floor brokers, who may trade for their own personal account in an attempt to make profits by buying low and selling high, or for the firm they work for, or they may execute customers' orders. In doing so, they (or their phone clerks) each keep a file of any stop or limit orders that cannot be immediately executed. All orders are treated equally on the floor regardless of where they originate. Floor brokers are in some ways similar to market-makers, since a floor broker may have an inventory of futures contracts and may act as a dealer. However, unlike a market-maker, a floor broker is not required to do so.

Second, all futures orders must be announced by "open outcry," meaning that any member wishing to buy or sell any futures contract must verbally announce the order and a price at which the member is willing to trade. By doing so, the order is exposed to everyone in the pit, thereby enabling an auction to take place that will lead to the order being filled at the best possible price.

► The Clearinghouse

Each futures exchange has an associated clearinghouse that becomes the "seller's buyer" and the "buyer's seller" as soon as a trade is concluded. The procedure is similar to that used for options, which is not surprising, since the first market in listed options was set up by people associated with a futures exchange (specifically, the Chicago Board Options Exchange was set up by the Chicago Board of Trade). In Winnipeg the clearing house is Winnipeg Commodity Clearing Ltd.

In order to understand how a clearinghouse operates, consider the futures market for wheat. Assume that on the first day of trading in July wheat, buyer B agrees to purchase 20 tonnes (one contract) from seller S for $105 per tonne (actually, what happens is that a floor broker working for B's brokerage firm and a floor broker working for S's brokerage firm meet in the wheat pit and agree on a price). In this situation, B believes that the price of wheat is going to rise, whereas S believes it is going to fall.

After B and S reach their agreement, the clearinghouse will immediately step in and break the transaction apart. That is, B and S no longer deal directly with each other. Now it is the obligation of the clearinghouse to deliver the wheat to B and to accept delivery from S. At this point, there is an open interest of one contract (20 tonnes) in July wheat, since only one contract exists at this time (technically, there are two, since the clearinghouse has separate contracts with B and S). Figure 21.2 summarizes the creation of this contract.

It is important to realize that if nothing else is done at this point, the clearinghouse is in a potentially risky position. For example, if the price of wheat rises to $125 per tonne by July, what happens if S does not deliver the wheat? The clearinghouse would have to buy the wheat on the spot market for $2500 (20 × $125) and then deliver it to B. Because the clearinghouse will receive the selling price of $2100 (20 × $105) from B in return, it will

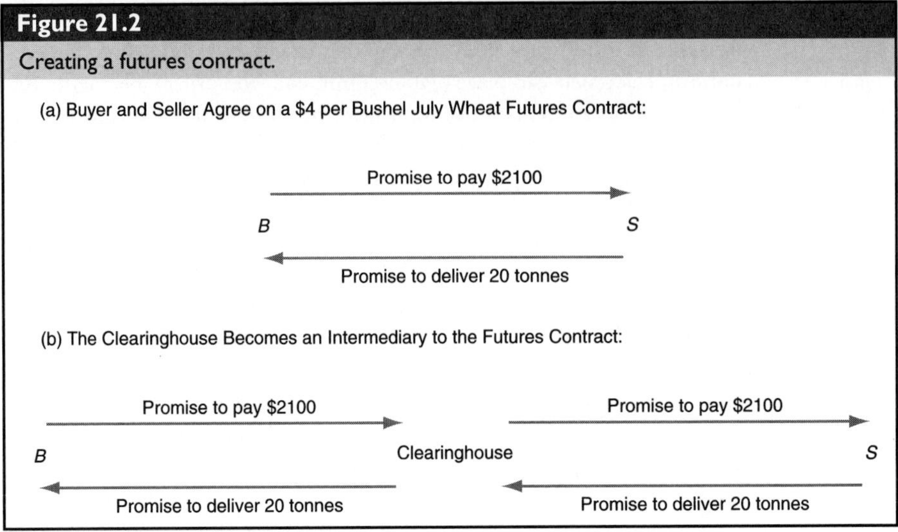

Figure 21.2
Creating a futures contract.

have lost $400. Although the clearinghouse has a claim on S for the $400, it faces protracted legal battles in trying to recover this amount and may end up with little or nothing from S.

Alternatively, if the price of wheat falls to $85 per tonne by July, then B will be paying $2100 for delivery of wheat that is only worth $1700 (10 × $85) on the spot market. What happens if B refuses to make payment? In this case, the clearinghouse will not deliver the wheat that it received from S. Instead, it will have to sell the wheat for $1700 on the spot market. Since the clearinghouse paid $2100 for the wheat, it has lost $400. Again, although the clearinghouse has a claim on B for the $400, it may end up with little or nothing from B.

The procedures that protect the clearinghouse from such potential losses involve having brokers (1) impose initial margin requirements on both buyers and sellers; (2) mark to market the accounts of buyers and sellers every day; and (3) impose daily maintenance margin requirements on both buyers and sellers.

Initial Margin

In order to buy and sell futures, an investor must open a commodity account with a brokerage firm. This type of account must be kept separate from other accounts (such as a cash account or a margin account) that the investor might have. Whenever a futures contract is signed, both the buyer and seller are required to post initial margin. That is, both the buyer and seller are required to make security deposits that are intended to guarantee that they will in fact be able to fulfill their obligations; accordingly, initial margin is often referred to as **performance margin**. The amount of this margin is roughly 5% to 15% of the total purchase price of the futures contract. In Winnipeg, however, it is stated as a given dollar amount regardless of the purchase price, $100 for speculators and $70 for hedgers per 20 tonne contract.[5]

[5] Since Black Monday and Terrible Tuesday (October 19–20, 1987), a number of people have advocated an increase in the size of the initial margin deposit for certain futures contracts (particularly stock index futures, which will be discussed later). The levels of initial and maintenance margins are set by each exchange, with brokers being allowed to set them higher. Typically, higher amounts of margin are required on futures contracts that have greater price volatility, since the clearinghouse faces larger potential losses on such contracts.

For example, a July wheat futures contract for 20 tonnes at $105 per bushel would have a total purchase price of $2100 (20 × $105). With a 5% initial margin requirement, buyer B and seller S (both speculators) would each have to make a deposit of $100 (approximately .05 × $21 000). This deposit can be made in the form of cash, cash equivalents (such as Treasury bills), or a bank line of credit and forms the equity in the account on the first day.

Although initial margin provides some protection to the clearinghouse, it does not provide complete protection. As indicated earlier, if the price of wheat rises to $125 per tonne by July, the clearinghouse faces a potential loss of $400, only $100 of which can be quickly recovered due to the margin deposit. This is where the use of marking to market, coupled with a maintenance margin requirement, provides the requisite amount of additional protection.

► Marking to Market

In order to understand marking to market, the previous example, where B and S were, respectively, a buyer and a seller of a 20-tonne wheat futures contract at $105 per tonne, is continued. Assume now that on the second day of trading the settle price of July wheat is $106 per tonne. In this situation, S has lost $20 due to the rise in the price of wheat from $105 to $106 per tonne, whereas B has made $20. Thus, the equity in the account of S is reduced by $20 and the equity in the account of B is increased by $20. Since the initial equity was equal to the initial margin requirement of $100, this means that S has equity of $80, and B has equity of $120. This process of adjusting the equity in an investor's commodity account in order to reflect the change in the settle price of the futures contract is known as **marking to market**. It should also be noted that each day, as part of the marking-to-market process, the clearinghouse replaces each existing futures contract with a new one that has the settle price as reported in the financial press as the purchase price in the new contract.

In general, the equity in either a buyer's or seller's commodity account is the sum of (1) the initial margin deposit and (2) the sum of all daily gains, less losses, on open positions in futures. Since the amount of the gains (less losses) changes every day, the amount of equity changes every day.

In the example, if the settle price of the July wheat futures contract had fallen to $103.5 per tonne the day after rising to $106, then B would have lost $50 (20 × ($106 – $103.50)), whereas S would have made $50 on that day. When their accounts are marked to market at the end of the day, the equity in B's account would have dropped from $120 to $70, and S's equity would have risen from $80 to $130.

► Maintenance Margin

Another key concept is the requirement of maintenance margin. According to this requirement, the investor must keep the commodity account's equity equal to or greater than a certain percentage of the amount deposited as initial margin. In Winnipeg this percentage is 70% for speculators and 100% for hedgers; therefore, the speculator must have equity equal to or greater than 70% of the initial margin. If this requirement is not met, the investor will receive a margin call from his or her broker. This call is a request for an additional deposit of cash (nothing else can be deposited for this purpose) to bring the equity up to the initial margin level. If the investor does not (or cannot) respond, then the broker will close out the investor's position by entering a reversing trade in the investor's account.

For example, reconsider investors B and S who had, respectively, bought and sold a July wheat futures contract at $105 per tonne; each investor had made a deposit of $100 in order to meet the initial margin requirement. The next day, the price of the wheat futures contract rose to $107 per tonne, or $2140. Thus, B's equity had increased to $140, whereas S's equity had decreased to $60. With the maintenance margin requirement set at 70% of initial margin, both B and S are required to have equity of at least $70 (.70 × $100) in their accounts every day. Since the actual level of equity for B clearly exceeds this amount, B does not need to do anything. Indeed, B may withdraw an amount of cash equal to the amount by which the equity exceeds the initial margin; in this example, B can withdraw $40.

However, S is undermargined and will be asked to make a cash deposit of at least $40, since this would increase the equity from $60 to $100, the level of the initial margin. In the event that S refuses to make this deposit, the broker will enter a reversing trade for S by purchasing a July wheat futures contract. The result is that S will simply receive an amount of money approximately equal to the account's equity, $60, and the account will be closed. Since S initially deposited $100, this represents a personal loss of $40.

► Reversing Trades

Suppose that on the next day, B finds that people are paying $108 per tonne for July wheat. This represents an additional profit to B of $1.00 per tonne, since the price was $107 the previous day. If B believes that the price of July wheat will not go any higher, then B might sell a July wheat futures contract for $108 to someone else. In this situation, B has made a reversing trade, since B now has offsetting positions with respect to July wheat (equivalently, B is said to have unwound, or closed out, his or her position in July wheat).

At this point, the benefit to B of having a clearinghouse involved can be seen. Nominally, B is obligated to deliver 20 tonnes of wheat to the clearinghouse in July, which is in turn obligated to deliver it back to B. This situation occurs because B is involved in two July wheat contracts, one as a seller and one as a buyer. However, the clearinghouse will note that B has offsetting positions in July wheat and will immediately cancel both of them. Furthermore, once the reversing trade had been made, B will be able to withdraw the initial margin of $100 as well as the $60 (20 × ($108 – $105)) profit that has been made.

In effect, a futures contract is replaced every day by (1) adjusting the equity in the investor's commodity account and (2) drawing up a new contract that has a purchase price equal to the current settle price. This daily marking-to-market procedure, coupled with margin requirements, results in the clearinghouse always having a security deposit of sufficient size to protect it from losses due to the actions of the individual investors.[6]

These rather complex arrangements make it possible for futures traders to think in very simple terms. In the example, B bought a contract of July wheat at $105 and sold it two days later for $108, making a profit of $3 per tonne. If S, having initially sold a contract of July wheat at $105, later made a reversing trade for $107, then S's position can also be thought of in simple terms—specifically, S sold July wheat for $105 and later bought it back for $107, suffering a loss of $2 per tonne in the process.

---

[6] Actually, only brokerage firms belong to a clearinghouse, and it is *their* accounts that are settled by the clearinghouse at the end of every day. Each brokerage firm acts in turn as a clearinghouse for its own clients. For more information on clearing procedures, see Chapter 4 of the *Commodity Trading Manual.*

► Futures Positions

In the previous example, B was the person who initially bought a July wheat futures contract. Accordingly, B now has a long position and is said to be long one contract of July wheat. In contrast, S, having initially sold a July wheat futures contract, has a short position and is said to be short one contract of July wheat.

The process of marking to market every day means that changes in the settle price are realized as soon as they occur. When the settle price rises, those with long positions realize profits equal to the change and those who are short realize losses. When the settle price falls, those with long positions realize losses, whereas those with short positions realize profits. In either event, total profits always equal total losses. Thus, either the buyer gains and the seller loses, or the seller gains and the buyer loses because both parties are involved in a "zero-sum game" (as was also the case with buyers and writers of options, discussed in Chapter 20).

► Taxation

Earlier, it was mentioned that there are two types of people who deal in futures — speculators and hedgers. These two types of investors are treated differently by Revenue Canada.

A speculator in futures (whether long or short) is considered to have a capital asset for tax purposes. When the position is closed out, the resultant profit or loss is treated as a capital gain or loss, and is taxed accordingly. That is, net gains are taxed at 75% of the individual's ordinary income tax rate, and net losses are carried back to previous years as described in Chapter 13.

In contrast, as a hedger deals in futures as part of a normal business activity, the resulting profits or losses are viewed as ordinary income or losses for the business, and taxed accordingly.

► Open Interest

When trading is first allowed in a contract, there is no open interest, since no contracts are outstanding. Subsequently, as people begin to make transactions, the open interest grows. At any time, open interest equals the amount that those with short positions (the sellers) are currently obligated to deliver. It also equals the amount that those with long positions (the buyers) are obligated to receive.

Open interest figures are typically shown with futures prices in the financial press. For example, Figure 21.1 indicates that on January 11, 1996, a total of 22 740 contracts in March 1996 canola were outstanding on The Winnipeg Commodity Exchange (WCE). Note the substantial differences in the open interest figures for the other canola contracts on the WCE that day. This is quite typical of agricultural commodities around the world. Figure 21.3 shows why. Open interest in a wheat contract on the Chicago Board of Trade is shown for every month from the preceding January until the contract expired at the end of the delivery month, December. From January until the end of September, more trades were generally made to open new positions than to reverse old ones, and open interest continued to increase. As the delivery month came closer, reversing trades began to outnumber those intended to open new positions, and the open interest began to decline. The amount remaining at the beginning of December was the maximum number of bushels of wheat that could have been delivered against futures contracts at that time, but most of these contracts were also settled by reversing trades instead of delivery.

Figure 21.3

Open interest, December 1978, Chicago Board of Trade wheat contract: January 3, 1978 through December 28, 1978.

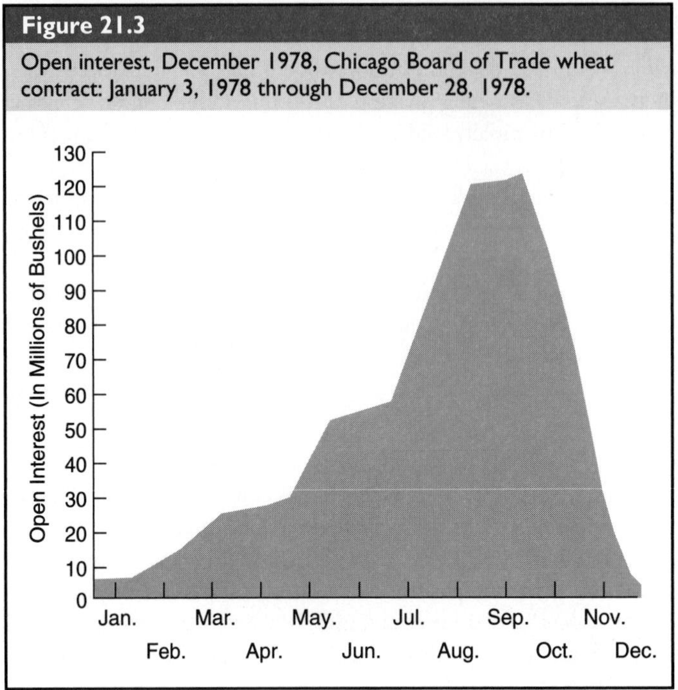

Relatively few futures positions — less than 3% of the total — end in actual delivery of the asset involved.[7] However, the fact that delivery is a possibility makes a contract's value in the delivery month differ only slightly, if at all, from the spot price (that is, the current market price) of the asset.

If not reversed, most futures contracts require delivery of the corresponding asset. Notable exceptions are market index futures, since they do not require delivery of the set of securities comprising the corresponding index. Instead, an amount proportional to the difference between the level of the index and the purchase price is to be paid *in cash* on the delivery date. Nevertheless, as with other types of futures, most positions in market index futures are closed out with reversing trades prior to the date at which delivery (in cash) is required.

► Price Limits

The by-laws of the WCE place dollar limits on the extent to which futures prices are allowed to vary from day to day. These price limits on futures are imposed so that traders who might overreact to major news are protected from voluntarily entering into agreements under such conditions. For example, if July wheat contracts had closed at $105 on the previous day and the daily price limit was $5, then only contracts for July wheat at prices in the range from $100 to $110 would be allowed. If news during the day led traders to consider $115 a reasonable price for the contract, they would have to (1) trade privately, foregoing the advantages offered by the exchange; or (2) trade on the exchange at the limit price of $110;

---

[7] Merrill Lynch, Pierce, Fenner & Smith, Inc., *Speculating on Inflation: Futures Trading in Interest Rates, Foreign Currencies and Precious Metals*, July 1979.

or (3) wait until the next day, when the range of acceptable prices would be from $105 to $115.

One negative result of this "limit move" up to $110 or down to $100 is that all traders may choose option 3 and, therefore, no July wheat contracts will be traded on that day. This is because nobody will want to sell these wheat contracts for a below-market price of $110, preferring to wait until the next day when the range of acceptable prices is raised. Indeed, if the news is important enough (such as hail storms in Saskatchewan, which destroy the wheat crop and dramatically increase the price of wheat futures), the daily limit moves could prevent trading from taking place for several days. In an attempt to avoid this situation the WCE has ruled that when two of the three nearest contracts close at the normal limit (up or down) then the daily price limit is immediately expanded by 50% and remains there for the next three days. If after three days trading at the expanded limit continues then the expanded limit remains in force until two of the three nearest contracts close within the expanded limit.

Interestingly, initial margins are usually set at an amount that is roughly equal to the price limit times the size of the contract. In the case of wheat having a $5 price limit and a contract for 20 tonnes, the initial margin is $100 ($5 × 20). Thus, if the price of wheat moves the limit against the investor, no more than the initial margin of $100 will be lost on the day of the adverse limit move. In a sense, the price limit protects the investor from losing more than $100 on that day. However, it is possible that the investor cannot enter a reversing trade after prices have reached the limit, meaning that much larger losses could be incurred later.

BASIS

The difference between the current spot price on an asset (that is, the price of the asset for immediate delivery) and the corresponding futures price (that is, the purchase price stated in the futures contract) is known as the **basis** for the futures:

$$\text{Basis} = \text{current spot price} - \text{futures price}. \qquad (21.1)$$

A person with a short position in a futures contract and a long position in the deliverable asset (meaning that he or she owns the asset) will profit if the basis is positive and widens (or is negative and narrows). This is because the futures price will be falling or the spot price will be rising (or both). A falling futures price benefits those who are short futures, and a rising spot price benefits those who own the asset. Using the same type of reasoning, it can be shown that this person will lose if the basis is positive and narrows (or is negative and widens).

Speculating on the Basis

As an example, consider the situation previously discussed where the July futures price of wheat was $105 per tonne and the contract was for 20 tonnes. Assuming that the current spot price of wheat is $115 per tonne, the basis is +$10(= 115 – 105). Now imagine that the basis widens by $5 to +$15 owing to the futures price falling to $102 and the spot price rising to $117. (Note that other combinations of price movements could cause the $5 widening of the basis.) A person who has a short position in one futures contract and a long position of 20 tonnes of wheat will make a profit of $5 × 20 tonnes = $100. This is because he or she gains on both the short position in the futures contract (owing to the \$3 fall in the futures price) and the long position in the asset (owing to the \$2 rise in its spot price).

However, if the basis narrows by \$5 to +\$5, then the person will have a loss of \$5 × 20 tonnes = \$100. Perhaps the narrowing resulted from both (1) a \$3 rise in the futures price to \$108, causing a \$60 loss on the person's short position, and (2) a \$2 fall in the spot price to \$113, causing a \$40 loss on his or her long position.

Note that if the \$10 basis was negative because the spot price was \$95 and it subsequently widened by \$5 to –\$15, then the person would have a loss of \$5 × 20 tonnes = \$100. However, if it narrowed by \$5 to –\$5, then he or she would have a gain of \$100. Hence, the person gains if the basis is positive and widens or is negative and narrows, but he or she loses if the basis is positive and narrows or is negative and widens:

	Long in Spot Market, Short in Futures Market	
	Positive Basis	*Negative Basis*
Basis widens	Gain	Loss
Basis narrows	Loss	Gain

Conversely, a person with a long position in a futures contract and a short position in the deliverable asset (meaning that he or she has borrowed the asset and sold it, and now has an obligation to buy the asset in order to repay the loan or has contracted to purchase it at a fixed price) will profit if the basis is positive and narrows (or is negative and widens). However, a loss would be incurred if a positive basis widened (or a negative basis narrowed).

	Short in Spot Market, Long in Futures Market	
	Positive Basis	*Negative Basis*
Basis widens	Loss	Gain
Basis narrows	Gain	Loss

The risk that the basis will narrow or widen, causing gains or losses to these people, is known as **basis risk**. The only type of uncertainty they face concerns the difference between the spot price of the deliverable asset and the price of the futures contract. Such a person is said to be **speculating on the basis**.[8]

Spreads

It is quite possible to take a long position in a futures contract and a short position in another futures contract in the same asset, but with a different delivery date. The person who does

[8] Typically, the basis narrows over time until it equals zero on the delivery date. For more on the relationship between spot and futures prices as reflected in the basis, see the *Commodity Trading Manual*, Chapter 8. It should be noted that sometimes basis is defined as the futures price less the current spot price—the reverse of what is shown in equation (21.1).

this is speculating on changes in the difference between the prices of the two contracts, a difference that constitutes the "basis" for these particular positions.

Others attempt to profit from temporary imbalances among the prices of futures contracts on different but related assets. For example, one might take a long position in soybeans along with a short position in an item produced from soybeans, such as soybean meal. Another possibility involves a position in wheat with an offsetting position in corn, which serves as a substitute for wheat in many applications.

Such people are known as *spreaders*, and, like those who speculate on the basis, they reduce or eliminate the risk associated with general price moves. Instead, they take on the risk associated with changes in price *differences* in the hope that superior knowledge will enable them to consistently make profits from such changes.

RETURNS ON FUTURES

During the period from 1950 through 1976, a portfolio made up of positions in 23 different commodity futures contracts was compared with a diversified portfolio of common stocks.[9] The average rates of return and risk level of the two portfolios were found to be of similar magnitude:

Portfolio	*Average Annual Return*	*Standard Deviation*
Futures	13.83%	22.43%
Common stocks	13.05%	18.95%

Given these results, an investor might view the two alternatives as equally desirable. Better yet, during the period from 1950 to 1976, a combination of the two portfolios was found to be more desirable than either portfolio by itself. This resulted from the fact that the returns of the commodity futures and stock portfolios were negatively correlated, suggesting that the return on a combined portfolio would have had considerably less variation than on either portfolio separately. Specifically, the correlation coefficient was –.24, resulting in the following standard deviations for portfolios with different combinations:

Percentage in Stocks	*Percentage in Futures*	*Standard Deviation*	*Average Annual Return*
0%	100%	22.43%	13.83%
20	80	17.43	13.67
40	60	13.77	13.52
60	40	12.68	13.36
80	20	14.74	13.21
100%	0	18.95	13.05

[9] The futures contracts consisted of agricultural goods and natural resources. See Zvi Bodie and Victor Rosansky, "Risk and Return in Commodity Futures," *Financial Analysts Journal* 36, no. 3 (May/June 1980): 27–39. Similar conclusions were reached when the period from 1978 to 1981 was examined. See Cheng F. Lee, Raymond M. Leuthold, and Jean E. Cordier, "The Stock Market and the Commodity Futures Market: Diversification and Arbitrage Potential," *Financial Analysts Journal* 41, no. 4 (July/August 1985): 53–60.

Whereas there was little difference in the average returns of the various portfolios, there was a noticeable difference in their risks. In particular, the portfolio with 60% in stocks and 40% in futures seems to have had much less risk than the others.

Also of interest was the observation that commodity futures have been at least a partial hedge against inflation. During the period from 1950 to 1976, the returns on the portfolio of 23 futures were positively correlated with changes in the Consumer Price Index, having a correlation coefficient of .58. In contrast, the returns on the portfolio of common stocks were negatively correlated with changes in the Consumer Price Index, having a correlation coefficient of −.43. (See the accompanying *Institutional Issues* section for a further discussion of commodity futures returns.)

At this point it is appropriate to discuss the pricing of futures contracts. Specifically, what is the relationship between the futures price and investors' expectations of what the spot price will be on the delivery date? And what is the relationship between the futures price and the current spot price of the deliverable asset? The next two sections explore these relationships and provide some answers to the questions.

FUTURES PRICES AND EXPECTED SPOT PRICES

Certainty

If future spot prices could be predicted with certainty, there would be no reason for anyone to be either a buyer or a seller of a futures contract. To understand why, imagine what a futures contract would look like in a world of certainty. First, the purchase price of the futures contract would simply equal the (perfectly predictable) expected spot price on the delivery date. This means that neither buyers nor sellers would be able to make profits from the existence of futures. Second, the purchase price would not change as the delivery date got closer.[10] Finally, no margin would be necessary because there would not be any unexpected "adverse" price movements.

Uncertainty

While it is useful to know something about the way in which futures prices and expected spot prices are related to each other in a world of certainty where forecasting is done with complete accuracy, the real world is uncertain. Given this, how are futures prices related to expected spot prices? While there are several possible explanations, no definitive answer has been provided.

Expectations Hypothesis

One possible explanation is given by the **expectations hypothesis**: the current purchase price of a futures contract equals the consensus expectation of the spot price on the delivery date. In symbols:

$$P_f = \overline{P}_s$$

[10] These first two points do not mean that the current spot price will not change as time passes. For futures involving a seasonal commodity (such as wheat), the spot price will sometimes be greater than and sometimes be less than the futures price during the life of the contract. Furthermore, sometimes a futures contract involving a more distant delivery date will sell for more than one with a nearer delivery date, whereas at other times it will sell for less.

where P_f is the current purchase price of the futures contract and $\overline{P}_s$ is the expected spot price of the asset on the delivery date. Thus, if a July wheat futures contract is currently selling for $105 per tonne, then it can be inferred that the consensus opinion is that in July the spot price of wheat will be $105.

If the expectations hypothesis is correct, a speculator should not expect to either win or lose from a position in the futures market, be it long or short. Neglecting margin requirements, a speculator who takes a long position in futures agrees to pay P_f at the delivery date for an asset that is expected to be worth $\overline{P}_s$ at that time. Thus the long speculator's expected profit is $\overline{P}_s - P_f$, which equals zero. Conversely, a speculator with a short position will have sold an asset at a price of P_f and will expect to enter a reversing trade at $\overline{P}_s$ on the delivery date. Thus, the short speculator's expected profit is $P_f - \overline{P}_s$, which also equals zero.

The expectations hypothesis is often defended on the grounds that speculators are indifferent to risk and are thus happy to accommodate hedgers without any compensation in the form of the risk premium. The reason for their indifference has to do with the belief that the impact of a specific futures position on the risk of a diversified portfolio that includes many types of assets will be very small. As a result, speculators holding diversified portfolios may be willing to take over some risk from hedgers with little (if any) compensation in the form of a risk premium.

Figure 21.4 shows the pattern of futures prices implied by the expectations hypothesis, given that the expected spot price $\overline{P}_s$ does not change during the life of the contract.

Figure 21.4

Price of a futures contract through time when the spot price expected at the time of delivery does not change.

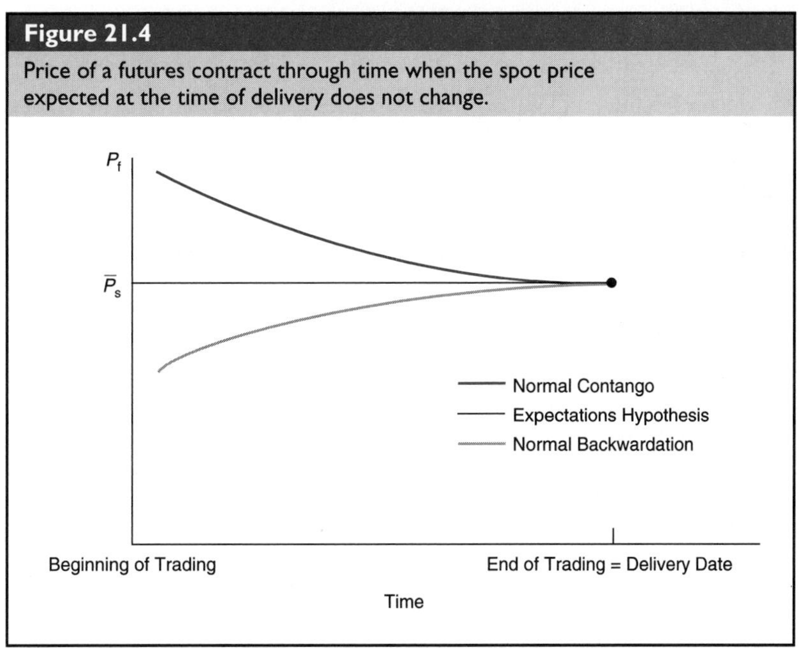

Normal Backwardation

The famous economist John Maynard Keynes felt that the expectations hypothesis did not correctly explain futures prices.[11] He argued that, on balance, hedgers will want to be short in futures, and therefore they will have to entice the speculators to be long in futures. Because there are risks associated with being long, Keynes hypothesized that the hedgers would have to entice the speculators by making the expected return from a long position greater than the risk-free rate. This requires the futures price to be less than the expected spot price:

$$P_f < \overline{P}_s.$$

Thus, a speculator who bought a futures contract at a price P_f would expect to be able to sell it on (or near) the delivery date at a higher price $\overline{P}_s$. This relationship between the futures price and the expected spot price has been referred to as **normal backwardation** and implies that the price of a futures contract can be expected to rise during its life, as shown in Figure 21.4.

Normal Contango

A contrary hypothesis holds that, on balance, hedgers will want to be long in futures and therefore they will have to entice speculators to be short in futures. Because there are risks associated with being short, it can be hypothesized that the hedgers will have to entice the speculators by making the expected return from a short position greater than the risk-free rate. This requires the futures price to be greater than the expected spot price:

$$P_f > \overline{P}_s.$$

Thus, a speculator who short sold a futures contract at a price P_f would expect to be able to buy it back on (or near) the delivery date at a lower price, $\overline{P}_s$. This relationship between the futures price and the expected spot price has been referred to as **normal contango** and implies that the price of a futures contract can be expected to fall during its life, as shown in Figure 21.4.[12]

FUTURES PRICES AND CURRENT SPOT PRICES

The previous section discussed the relationship between the futures price associated with an asset and the expected spot price of the asset on the delivery date given in the futures contract. What about the relationship between the futures price and the current spot price of the asset? In general, they will be different, but is there some explanation for why these prices are different? Is there some model that can be used to forecast how the size of the difference will change over time? This section attempts to answer these questions.[13]

---

[11] J. M. Keynes, *Treatise on Money*, vol. 2 (London: Macmillan, 1930), pp. 142–144.

[12] There are other hypotheses regarding the relationship between futures prices and expected spot prices. See, for example, Paul H. Cootner, "Speculation and Hedging," Stanford University, *Food Research Institute Studies*, Supplement, 1967.

[13] This section and the next one borrow from Kenneth R. French, "Pricing Financial Futures Contracts: An Introduction," *Journal of Applied Corporate Finance* 1, no. 4 (Winter 1989): 59–66. It ignores the apparently minor effect that daily marking to market has on the futures price that is stated in futures contracts (see p. 65 and footnotes 5 and 6 in French's paper).

INSTITUTIONAL ISSUES

Commodity Futures: The Selling of an Asset Class

When institutional investors discuss investments in futures, we can safely assume that they are referring to *financial futures*—that is, futures contracts on, for example, stock market indices or Treasury bonds. Commodity futures, on the other hand, play only an insignificant role in institutional investors' portfolios.

Given the history of the futures markets, this situation might seem somewhat surprising. After all, financial futures are mere fledglings compared to commodity futures. The oldest futures exchange, the Chicago Board of Trade, was organized in 1848 for the sole purpose of trading futures contracts on agricultural commodities. The first financial futures contracts (a futures contract on foreign currencies) were established in 1972. The most popular financial futures contracts today, S&P 500 futures, were not created until 1981.

The dollar volume of trading in financial futures contracts now far exceeds the trading volume in commodity futures. Traditional users of commodity futures contracts have not become less enamored with those products. Rather, directly and indirectly institutional investors have helped create a gigantic market for financial futures.

The question then is not why institutional investors have become extensively involved in financial futures. The application of financial futures to the activities of institutional investors, in terms of both hedging and speculating, are obvious. More intriguing is why institutional investors have not entered the commodity futures market in any substantial way.

Institutional investors, particularly pension funds, in recent years have expanded the range of asset types (or classes) in which they invest. Whereas once they restricted themselves to domestic common stocks, high-grade bonds, and cash equivalents, institutional investors now own foreign securities, junk bonds, real estate, and oil and gas wells, to mention just a few. With some notable exceptions, however, institutional investors have been unwilling to add commodity futures to their asset class toolboxes.

Financial services providers have recognized the tremendous profit potential if institutional investors could be enticed to invest in commodities. If those investors chose to place just 2% to 3% of their immense wealth in commodities, the accompanying fees to brokers and money managers would easily run into the hundreds of millions of dollars.

How to convince institutional investors to trade in commodities? One potential means is to help publicize the risk-reward opportunities historically offered by investments in commodities. Institutional investors have generally shown a reluctance to become involved in investments lacking a quantifiable track record. By developing an index of a diversified investment in commodity futures, institutional investors would have performance data that could be compared against the results of investments in other asset classes. Furthermore, institutional investors would be able to construct simulated past portfolios that included commodity futures, thus emphasizing the diversification benefits of this asset class.

Beyond the industrywide benefit of stimulating institutional investor interest in commodity futures, a unique benefit accrues to the creator of an investable commodity futures index. If that index were to become widely accepted, the creator would have a considerable advantage in designing and trading products based on that index. That advantage could translate into significant revenue.

In 1991 Goldman Sachs, the large New York brokerage firm, with considerable fanfare introduced its own commodity futures index. Other organizations had previously developed such indices. Goldman Sachs, however, directly targeted institutional investors by designing its index to be more truly reflective of the commodity futures investment opportunities available to large investors. Furthermore, Goldman Sachs developed detailed simulated performance data for the index extending back to 1970.

The Goldman Sachs Commodities Index (GSCI) is composed of "near" futures commodity contract prices for which active liquid markets exist. ("Near" refers to the contract in a given commodity with the shortest time remaining until delivery.) This liquidity requirement allows large investors to replicate the index by buying its individual components. Weights in the index are based on world production of the respective commodities. Thus, the most economically important commodities receive the most weight in the index.

Currently, 18 commodities constitute the index, which is dominated by various energy, livestock, and grain futures (with weights of roughly 50%, 25%, and 15%, respectively). Historically the composition of the index has changed over time as new commodity futures contracts were created or met the GSCI liquidity requirements. In the 1970s the livestock and grain futures made up most of the index. Energy-related futures did not begin trading until 1983 and were not added to the index until 1987.

The reported historical performance of the GSCI has been impressive in terms of both return and risk. Ibbotson Associates reports the following returns, standard deviations, and correlations for the GSCI and comparative asset classes over the period of 1970 through the first quarter of 1992:

	Annual Return	*Annual Standard Deviation*	*Correlation with GSCI*
GSCI	14.8%	18.3	1.00
US stocks	11.5	16.2	–.42
Foreign stocks	13.1	17.6	–.27
US long-term bonds	9.0	11.5	–.32
US Treasury bills	7.5	0.8	–.20
US inflation	6.0	1.4	.26

The GSCI has produced returns exceeding those of US and foreign stocks while offering only slightly more variability. Also impressive has been the GSCI's negative correlation with other asset classes and its positive correlation with inflation. The conclusions one draws from this data are that commodities offer equitylike returns, are excellent portfolio diversifiers, and are a good inflation hedge.

How Goldman Sachs has calculated the GSCI returns has generated some controversy. Those returns have three components: the spot return, the Treasury-bill return, and the roll yield. The first two components are straightforward. The spot yield is how much the price of the underlying commodity changes. The Treasury-bill yield is the interest earned if the investor were to post as collateral the full dollar value (that is, the notional principal) of the investment in the commodities at the time of the futures contract purchase.

The roll yield is more complicated. It represents the change in the futures price over the life of the contract. If futures are priced according to normal backwardation (discussed in this chapter), then futures prices are expected to rise toward the spot price of the commodity over time. Therefore, the process of "rolling" over expiring futures will be profitable on average.

Which is the correct explanation of the relationship between futures and expected spot prices: the expectations hypothesis, normal backwardation, or normal contango? As historically about one-third of the GSCI's return has come from roll yield, this question is more than academic. Goldman Sachs argues that the markets for commodities that are normally consumed as they are produced (such as energy or livestock) are typically subject to backwardation. Only if this will be the case in the future can a positive roll yield for the GSCI (and the resulting high GSCI total returns) be expected to persist.

Equally problematic is whether institutional investors can be expected to increase their investments in commodities. Current indications are

INSTITUTIONAL ISSUES (continued)

that institutions are beginning to dip their toes in commodity futures through accounts called *managed futures*. In these accounts money managers actively take long and short positions in commodity and financial futures. The accounts gain only if their managers are adept at anticipating the direction of various futures price changes. Over $2 billion is now invested in managed futures accounts. Are these investments the harbingers of increased institutional activity, or a mere passing fancy? The jury is still out.

Introducing the Problem

Consider the owner of a circa 1910 Honus Wagner baseball card who is getting ready to sell the card. The owner knows that the current market price of the card is $100 000 because there are very few (reputedly fewer than five) of these cards available. (One actually sold for $451 000 in 1990.) Furthermore, an investor has offered to buy it but wants to pay for it a year from now. The buyer is willing to take delivery of the card then and wants to sign the contract for sale today. More specifically, he or she would like to sign a futures contract with the owner in which the delivery date is one year from now.

No Costs or Benefits of Ownership

What price should the owner ask for in the futures contract? Assume that there is no risk that either party will default on the contract, and that there are no benefits (such as from showing the card) or costs (such as insurance) associated with owning the card. Given that the current one-year interest rate is 4%, the owner could sell the card today on the spot market for $100 000, put the proceeds in the bank to earn 4%, and have $104 000 in one year. Hence the owner would not be willing to sign the futures contract for any futures price that is less than $104 000. The buyer, on the other hand, is unwilling to pay more than $104 000 because he or she could pay $100 000 now and get the card immediately but forgo $4000 of interest that would have been earned had the $100 000 been left in the bank where it earned 4%. Since the seller wants to receive at least $104 000 and the buyer will pay no more than $104 000, they will settle at a futures price of $104 000.

To generalize, let P_s denote the current spot price of the asset (in this case, $100 000) and I the dollar amount of interest corresponding to the period of time from the present to the delivery date (in this case, $4000). If P_f denotes the futures price, then

$$P_f = P_s + I. \tag{21.2}$$

This equation shows that the futures price will be greater than the spot price by the amount of the interest that the owner forgoes by holding onto the asset, provided that there are no costs or benefits associated with ownership.

Benefits from Ownership

To add a complication to the model, imagine that a baseball card exhibition will be held in 12 months, just before the delivery date. The exhibitor is willing to pay the card owner $1000 in order to have the card displayed at the exhibition. How will this benefit of ownership affect the futures price?

As mentioned earlier, if the owner sells the card now, then he or she will receive \$100 000 immediately, which could be invested right away and be worth \$104 000 in 12 months. Alternatively, the owner could hold on to the card and receive the \$1000 exhibitor fee as well as the futures price. Hence, the futures price must be at least \$103 000 in order for the owner to be as well off financially by selling the card by means of a futures contract as by selling it immediately in the spot market. On the other side, the buyer will accept a futures price of no more than \$103 000. This is because he or she could buy the card on the spot market for \$100 000, thereby forgoing \$4000 of interest but receiving the \$1000 exhibitor fee. Consequently, the futures price will be \$103 000, as this is the only price that is agreeable to both buyer and seller. What if the exhibition were to be held in six months instead of one year? In that case the owner of the card would receive the \$1000 exhibitor fee in six months and would be able to invest it risklessly at 2% for the remaining six months until the delivery date. Thus, the \$1000 in six months is equivalent to \$1020 in 12 months, and the futures price would be \$100 000 + \$4000 – \$1020 = \$102 980.

Let B denote the value of the benefits of ownership (sometimes known as the convenience yield of the asset) as of the delivery date (in this case, \$1020). When such benefits are present, the futures price can be calculated as

$$P_f = P_s + I - B. \tag{21.3}$$

This equation shows that the futures price can be greater or lower than the spot price, depending on whether the net amount of interest forgone less benefits received is positive or negative and provided that there are no costs associated with ownership of the asset.

► Costs of Ownership

What if the owner of the baseball card decides that it must be insured at an annual cost of \$100? How will this affect the futures price? The easiest way to think of such costs of ownership as insurance and storage is to view them as the opposite of benefits of ownership. Because the benefits of ownership result in cash inflows to the owner, the costs of ownership result in cash outflows. Hence the previously calculated futures price of \$102 980 would have to be increased by the \$100 cost of insurance to \$103 080. If C denotes the costs of ownership (in this example, \$100), then the futures price will be

$$P_f = P_s + I - B + C. \tag{21.4}$$

The total value of interest less benefits received plus cost of ownership, $I - B + C$, is known as the **cost of carry** associated with the futures contract. Note that the futures price can be greater or lower than the spot price, depending upon whether the cost of carry is positive or negative.

It has now been shown how the futures price will be related to the current spot price. But is this compatible with the earlier discussion of the relationship between the futures price and the expected future spot price? It is. By adjusting production and consumption over time, producers and consumers of a good can bring about an appropriate relationship between the current price and the price expected in the future. The price of a futures contract will reflect both this relationship and that implied by the current price plus the cost of carry.

FINANCIAL FUTURES

Until the 1970s, futures contracts were limited to those on agricultural goods and natural resources. Since then, financial futures based on foreign currencies, fixed-income securities, and market indices have been introduced on major exchanges. Indeed, in terms of trading volume, they are now far more important than both the underlying assets and traditional futures contracts. Unlike other types of futures that permit delivery any time during a given month, most financial futures have a specific delivery date. (The exceptions involve some fixed-income futures.)

► Foreign Currency Futures

Anyone who has crossed a national border knows that there is an active spot market for foreign currency, and that the rate at which one currency can be exchanged for another varies over time. At any particular point in time, however, all such rates must be in conformance or else a riskless profit-making situation may arise. For example, it is usually possible to exchange US dollars for British pounds, then exchange the British pounds for French francs, and, finally, exchange the French francs for US dollars. If all three exchange rates were not in line, an investor might end up with more dollars at the end of this chain of transactions than at the beginning. Such an opportunity would attract large amounts of money, placing pressure on exchange rates and rapidly restoring balance. Although transaction costs and certain exchange restrictions might limit the ability of people to exploit such imbalances among exchange rates, they would nevertheless force the rates into being closely aligned.

The familiar market in foreign currency, operated by banks, travel agents, and others, is in effect a spot market, because both the agreement on terms and the actual exchange of currencies occur at the same time. There are also markets for agreements involving the future delivery of foreign currency.

The largest such market is operated by banks and specialized brokers that maintain close communications with each other throughout the world. Corporations, institutions, and some individuals deal in this market via large banks. Substantial amounts of money are involved, and every agreement is negotiated separately. Typical rates are quoted daily in the financial press, as shown in Figure 21.5. This network of large institutions is generally termed the *market for forward exchange* because there is no marking to market. Furthermore, because the contracts are not standardized, no organized secondary market for them exists. However, there is a market that deals in standardized futures contracts for foreign currency.[14] Procedures are similar to those used for commodity futures.

For example, one of the currency futures contracts traded on the International Monetary Market (IMM) of the Chicago Mercantile Exchange requires the seller to deliver 12 500 000 Japanese yen to the buyer on a specific date for a number of US dollars agreed upon in

---

[14] The prices of foreign currency forward and futures contracts appear to be quite similar. See Bradford Cornell and Marc Reinganum, "Forward and Futures Prices: Evidence from the Foreign Exchange Market," *Journal of Finance* 36, no. 5 (December 1981): 1035–1045. Their findings are challenged by Michael A. Polakoff and Paul C. Grier, "A Comparison of Foreign Exchange Forward and Futures Prices," *Journal of Banking and Finance* 15, no. 6 (December 1991): 1057–1079, but supported by Carolyn W. Chang and Jack S. K. Chang, "Forward and Futures Prices: Evidence From the Foreign Exchange Markets," *Journal of Finance* 45, no. 4 (September 1990): 1333–1336. See Kenneth R. French, "A Comparison of Futures and Forward Prices," *Journal of Financial Economics* 12, no. 3 (November 1983): 311–342 for a discussion of the difficulties encountered when testing to see whether the prices of forward and futures contracts are similar.

Figure 21.5

Quotations for foreign exchange rates.

Foreign Exchange

Cross Rates

	Canadian dollar	U.S. dollar	British pound	German mark	Japanese yen	Swiss franc	French franc	Dutch guilder	Italian lira
Canada dollar	—	1.3652	2.1202	0.9520	0.013220	1.1840	0.2791	0.8522	0.000861
U.S. dollar	0.7325	—	1.5530	0.6973	0.009684	0.8673	0.2044	0.6242	0.000631
British pound	0.4717	0.6439	—	0.4490	0.006235	0.5584	0.1316	0.4019	0.000406
German mark	1.0504	1.4340	2.2271	—	0.013887	1.2437	0.2932	0.8952	0.000904
Japanese yen	75.64	103.27	160.38	72.01	—	89.56	21.11	64.46	0.065129
Swiss franc	0.8446	1.1530	1.7907	0.8041	0.011166	—	0.2357	0.7198	0.000727
French franc	3.5829	4.8914	7.5966	3.4110	0.047367	4.2422	—	3.0534	0.003085
Dutch guilder	1.1734	1.6020	2.4879	1.1171	0.015513	1.3893	0.3275	—	0.001010
Italian lira	1161.44	1585.60	2462.49	1105.69	15.354239	1375.15	324.16	989.78	—

Mid-market rates in Toronto at noon, Dec. 29, 1995. Prepared by the Bank of Montreal Treasury Group.

		$1 U.S. in Cdn.$ =	$1 Cdn. in U.S.$ =
U.S./Canada spot		1.3652	0.7325
1 month forward		1.3653	0.7324
2 months forward		1.3654	0.7324
3 months forward		1.3654	0.7324
6 months forward		1.3663	0.7319
12 months forward		1.3700	0.7299
3 years forward		1.3952	0.7167
5 years forward		1.4342	0.6973
7 years forward		1.4877	0.6722
10 years forward		1.5877	0.6298
Canadian dollar	High	1.3273	0.7534
in 1995:	Low	1.4267	0.7009
	Average	1.3726	0.7285

Country	Currency	Cdn. $ per unit	U.S. $ per unit
Britain	Pound	2.1202	1.5530
1 month forward		2.1187	1.5518
2 months forward		2.1175	1.5508
3 months forward		2.1160	1.5497
6 months forward		2.1129	1.5464
12 months forward		2.1086	1.5391
Germany	Mark	0.9520	0.6973
1 month forward		0.9537	0.6985
3 months forward		0.9565	0.7005
6 months forward		0.9614	0.7037
12 months forward		0.9717	0.7093
Japan	Yen	0.013220	0.009684
1 month forward		0.013281	0.009728
3 months forward		0.013393	0.009809
6 months forward		0.013566	0.009929
12 months forward		0.013909	0.010153
Algeria	Dinar	0.0263	0.0192
Antigua, Grenada and St. Lucia	E.C.Dollar	0.5066	0.3711
Argentina	Peso	1.36520	1.00000
Australia	Dollar	1.0156	0.7439
Austria	Schilling	0.13530	0.09911
Bahamas	Dollar	1.3652	1.0000
Barbados	Dollar	0.6860	0.5025
Belgium	Franc	0.04634	0.03394
Bermuda	Dollar	1.3652	1.0000
Brazil	Real	1.4079	1.0312
Bulgaria	Lev	0.0193	0.0141
Chile	Peso	0.003353	0.002456
China	Renminbi	0.1641	0.1202
Cyprus	Pound	2.9939	2.1930
Czech Rep	Koruna	0.0513	0.0376
Denmark	Krone	0.2457	0.1800
Egypt	Pound	0.4027	0.2950
Fiji	Dollar	0.9552	0.6997
Finland	Markka	0.3143	0.2302
France	Franc	0.2791	0.2044
Greece	Drachma	0.00576	0.00422
Hong Kong	Dollar	0.1766	0.1293
Hungary	Forint	0.00998	0.00731
Iceland	Krona	0.02093	0.01533
India	Rupee	0.03886	0.02847
Indonesia	Rupiah	0.000592	0.000433
Ireland	Punt	2.1823	1.5985
Israel	N Shekel	0.4355	0.3190
Italy	Lira	0.000861	0.000631
Jamaica	Dollar	0.03740	0.02740
Jordan	Dinar	1.9255	1.4104
Lebanon	Pound	0.000855	0.000626
Luxembourg	Franc	0.04634	0.03394
Malaysia	Ringgit	0.5375	0.3937
Mexico	N Peso	0.1768	0.1295
Netherlands	Guilder	0.8522	0.6242
New Zealand	Dollar	0.8926	0.6538
Norway	Krone	0.2156	0.1579
Pakistan	Rupee	0.03992	0.02924
Philippines	Peso	0.05206	0.03813
Poland	Zloty	0.5532	0.4052
Portugal	Escudo	0.00914	0.00669
Romania	Leu	0.000513	0.000376
Russia	Ruble	0.000294	0.000216
Saudi Arabia	Riyal	0.3641	0.2667
Singapore	Dollar	0.9651	0.7070
Slovakia	Koruna	0.0460	0.0337
South Africa	Rand	0.3745	0.2743
South Korea	Won	0.001760	0.001289
Spain	Peseta	0.01125	0.00824
Sudan	Dinar	0.0165	0.0121
Sweden	Krona	0.2059	0.1508
Switzerland	Franc	1.1840	0.8673
Taiwan	Dollar	0.0504	0.0369
Thailand	Baht	0.0542	0.0397
Trinidad, Tobago	Dollar	0.2391	0.1751
Turkey	Lira	0.0000223	0.0000163
Venezuela	Bolivar	0.00472	0.00346
Zambia	Kwacha	0.001476	0.001081
European Currency Unit		1.7503	1.2821
Special Drawing Right		2.0294	1.4865

The U.S. dollar closed at $1.3640 in terms of Canadian funds, up $0.0025 from Thursday. The pound sterling closed at $2.1190, up $0.0148.

In New York, the Canadian dollar closed down $0.0014 at $0.7331 in terms of U.S. funds. The pound sterling was up $0.0080 to $1.5535.

SOURCE: Reprinted with permission of the *Globe and Mail* (December 30, 1995).

Figure 21.6

Quotations for foreign currency futures contracts.

–Lifetime– High	Low	Month	Open	— Daily — High	Low	Settle	Chg	Open Interest
Currency								
Australian Dollar (IMM)								
A$100,000, US$ per A$; 0.0001 = $10 per contract								
0.7617	0.7045	Mar96	0.7420	0.7423	0.7396	0.7401	−0.0019	5,361
Est. vol.	324			Prev. vol.	675		Prev. open int.	5,411
British Pound (IMM)								
62,500 pounds, US$ per pound; 0.0002 = $12.50 per contract								
1.6140	1.5160	Mar96	1.5444	1.5518	1.5406	1.5514	+0.0072	31,188
Est. vol.	4,962			Prev. vol.	12,071		Prev. open int.	31,222
Canadian Dollar (IMM)								
C$100,000, US$ per C$; 0.0001 = $10 per contract								
0.7580	0.6898	Mar96	0.7343	0.7350	0.7321	0.7331	−0.0014	23,804
0.7500	0.6905	June96	0.7335	0.7343	0.7320	0.7327	−0.0014	2,072
0.7490	0.7135	Sep96	...	...	0.7317	0.7318	−0.0013	663
0.7460	0.7130	Dec96	0.7300	0.7310	0.7300	0.7308	−0.0013	728
Est. vol.	2,851			Prev. vol.	2,366		Prev. open int.	27,346
French Franc (IMM)								
500,000 francs, US$ per franc; 0.0001 = $5 per contract								
0.2101	0.1943	Mar96	0.2045	0.2045	0.2045	0.2045	+0.0012	1,135
Est. vol.	1			Prev. vol.	8		Prev. open int.	1,214
German Mark (IMM)								
125,000 marks, US$ per mark; 0.0001 = $12.50 per contract								
0.7505	0.6449	Mar96	0.6974	0.7025	0.6966	0.6988	+0.0009	48,151
0.7315	0.6765	June96	0.7035	0.7057	0.7018	0.7018	+0.0009	2,868
0.7332	0.6795	Sep96	...	...	...	0.7046	+0.0009	1,089
Est. vol.	10,963			Prev. vol.	14,148		Prev. open int.	52,119
Japanese Yen (IMM)								
12.5 million yen, US$ per yen (scaled .00); 0.0001 = $12.50 per contract								
1.2990	0.9771	Mar96	0.9851	0.9851	0.9771	0.9773	−0.0072	64,041
1.3143	0.9886	June96	0.9945	0.9945	0.9886	0.9890	−0.0075	2,024
1.2136	1.0001	Sep96	1.0005	1.0005	1.0001	1.0001	−0.0081	293
Est. vol.	8,153			Prev. vol.	9,850		Prev. open int.	66,441
Mexican Peso (IMM)								
500,000 new pesos, US$ per peso; 0.000025 = $12.50 per contract								
0.1417	0.1028	Mar96	0.1200	0.1207	0.1198	0.1198	−0.0004	9,709
0.1340	0.0902	June96	0.1115	0.1116	0.1112	0.1112	−0.0003	3,485
0.1270	0.0841	Sep96	...	...	...	0.1040	...	684
0.1000	0.0970	Dec96	...	...	...	0.0990	...	153
Est. vol.	369			Prev. vol.	1,135		Prev. open int.	14,031
Swiss Franc (IMM)								
125,000 francs, US$ per franc; 0.0001 = $12.50 per contract								
0.9220	0.8220	Mar96	0.8720	0.8769	0.8713	0.8731	+0.0007	33,638
0.9120	0.8288	June96	0.8827	0.8842	0.8806	0.8809	+0.0007	961
Est. vol.	4,419			Prev. vol.	7,514		Prev. open int.	34,702
U.S. Dollar Index (FINEX)								
1000 x index points and US cents; 0.01 = $10 per contract								
87.69	80.80	Mar96	84.80	84.87	84.58	84.83	−0.02	5,243
				Prev. vol.	681		Prev. open int.	5,283

SOURCE: Reprinted with permission of the *Financial Post* (December 30, 1995).

advance. Only the price of the transaction (expressed in both dollars per yen and yen per dollar) is negotiated by the parties involved; all other terms are standard. Clearing procedures allow positions to be covered by reversing trades, and few contracts result in the actual delivery of foreign currency. As shown in Figure 21.6, prices and volumes for such contracts are quoted daily in the financial press along with those for other futures.

Markets for foreign currency futures attract both hedgers and speculators. Hedgers wish to reduce or possibly eliminate the risk associated with planned future transfers of funds from one country to another.

An Example

For example, a US importer might know on December 29, 1995, that he or she will have to make a payment of 50 million yen to a Japanese exporter in June 1996. The current exchange rate is \$.009683 per yen (or, equivalently, 103.27 yen per dollar), so the anticipated dollar size of the payment is $\$.009683 \times 50\ 000\ 000 = \$484\ 150$. The risk the importer faces by simply waiting until June to make this payment is that the exchange rate will change in an unfavourable manner—perhaps rising to \$.0105 per yen, in which case the dollar cost to the importer will have risen to \$.0105 × 50 000 000 = \$525 000. The importer can hedge this risk by purchasing four June futures contracts for yen. The settlement price on December 29, 1995 for these contracts was \$.009890, meaning that the dollar cost of one contract is \$.009890 × 50 000 000 = \$494 500. Thus, the importer can remove the risk of the yen's appreciating by more than \$.000207 against the dollar before the payment date by purchasing the four yen futures contracts.

A Canadian firm needing to hedge future Japanese yen liability would have to proceed differently because yen/CAD futures contracts do not exist. One way to set up such a hedge would be to buy an over-the-counter six-month forward contract. These contracts can be negotiated through the firm's bank at a price close to that quoted in the financial press (see Figure 21-5). Alternatively, the firm could arrange a cross-hedge by simultaneously buying yen/USD contracts and selling CAD/USD contracts. The optimal way to proceed would, of course, depend on the relative costs of the two approaches.

Speculators are attracted to the foreign currency futures market when they believe that the current price of the futures contract is substantially different from what they expect the spot rate to be on the delivery date.

For example, a speculator might believe that the price of the June futures contract for Japanese yen is too high. Perhaps a speculator might believe that when June comes around, the exchange rate will be \$.0095 per yen (or, equivalently, 111.11 yen per dollar). By selling (that is, short selling) a June futures contract for yen, the speculator will be selling yen for \$.009890, the settlement price on December 19, 1995. At the time delivery has to be made, the speculator believes that yen can be bought on the spot market for \$.0095, thereby allowing a profit to be made on the difference between the selling and buying prices.[15] Specifically, the speculator expects to be able to make a profit of (\$.009890–\$.0095) × 12 500 000) = \$4875 per futures contract.

Pricing

Futures contracts involving foreign currencies are priced according to the notion of **interest-rate parity**, which is merely a special application of the model of futures pricing given in equation (21.4).

Imagine that it is December 1995 and you are planning to invest some money for one year. You could simply invest in a one-year US risk-free security and then receive the principal and interest a year later in the form of US dollars. Alternatively, you could exchange the dollars for German marks and use the marks to buy a one-year German risk-free security. In addition, you would short sell the requisite number of one-year German mark futures contracts so that a year later, when you receive the principal and interest in the form of German marks, you know exactly how many US dollars you would receive for them.

Both of these strategies—investing in US risk-free securities or investing in German risk-free securities—have no risk associated with them in that you know exactly how many US dollars they will yield after one year. If the German strategy had a higher return per dollar invested, Americans would not buy the US risk-free securities because they could

[15] Actually, the typical speculator will plan to realize this profit by entering a reversing trade instead of buying yen on the spot market and then making delivery. Similarly, the previously mentioned hedging importer will typically plan to enter a reversing trade.

earn the same amount for a smaller investment by buying the German risk-free securities. Similarly, if the US strategy had a higher return per dollar invested, Germans would not buy the German risk-free securities because they could earn the same amount for a smaller investment by buying US dollars in the spot market, purchasing US risk-free securities, and buying a one-year German mark futures contract. As a consequence, in equilibrium the two strategies must have the same cost if they have the same dollar payoffs.

Consider what would happen per dollar invested. The strategy of investing \$1 in a US risk-free security that has a return of R_{US} will provide a cash inflow of $\$1(1 + R_{US})$ after one year. The strategy of investing \$1 in a German risk-free security that has a return of R_G, where the current spot rate of exchange is P_s and the futures price is P_f, will provide a dollar cash inflow of $(\$1/P_s)(1 + R_G)P_f$ after one year. (Here both P_s and P_f are stated in dollars per mark.) Given that these two strategies cost the same (\$1), their payoffs must be equal:

$$\$1(1 + R_{US}) = \left(\frac{\$1}{P_s}\right)(1 + R_G)P_f. \tag{21.5}$$

Hence, the futures price of the mark can be determined by rewriting equation (21.5) as the interest-rate parity equation:

$$P_f = P_s\left(\frac{1 + R_{US}}{1 + R_G}\right). \tag{21.6}$$

Thus if the current spot rate of exchange for the German mark is \$.6973, and the US and German one-year risk-free rates are 4% and 5%, respectively, then the one-year futures price of the mark will be $\$.6973 \times 1.04/1.05 = \$.6907$.

In relation to equation (21.4), the cost of carry is $\$.6907 - .6973 = -\$.0066 = .6907 - .6973$. In the case of foreign currency, the costs of ownership C are zero. However, the net benefits of ownership $I - B$ amount to the $-\$.0066$ cost of carry. More generally, the cost of carry will equal

$$\text{Carry} = P_s\left(\frac{R_{US} - R_G}{1 + R_G}\right) \tag{21.7}$$

for foreign currency futures, where R–G now denotes the risk-free rate in the foreign currency under consideration. From equation (21.7) it can be seen that because carry = $I - B$, it follows that

$$I = \frac{P_s R_{US}}{1 + R_G} \tag{21.8a}$$

$$B = \frac{P_s R_G}{1 + R_G} \tag{21.8b}$$

Hence, in the example I, the amount of interest forgone by the owner by selling marks in the futures market instead of the spot market equals $\$.6973 \times .04/1.05 = \$.0266$, whereas B, the benefit of owning marks instead of selling them, equals $.6973 \times .05/1.05 = \$.0332$. Consequently, the cost of carry equals $.0266 - .0332 = -\$.0066$, as shown earlier.

Equation (21.4) indicates that the futures price will be less than the current spot price when the cost of carry is negative. This will occur when the US risk-free rate is less than the foreign risk-free rate, because the numerator on the right-hand side of equation (21.7) will be negative whereas the denominator is positive in such a situation. Conversely, the futures price will be greater than the current spot price when the cost of carry is positive, which will occur when the US risk-free rate is greater than the foreign risk-free rate. Hence, the reason why futures prices are different from spot prices is that risk-free interest rates between countries are different.

Interest-Rate Futures

Futures involving fixed-income securities are often referred to as interest-rate futures because their prices are greatly influenced by the current and forecast interest rates. More specifically, their pricing can be related to the term structure of interest rates, which in turn is related to the concept of forward rates.[16]

An Example

Just how the pricing of interest-rate futures is related to the concept of forward rates can be illustrated with an example. Consider the futures market for US 90-day Treasury bills. As Figure 21.7 indicates, on December 29, 1995, any purchaser of a futures contract calling for delivery in June 1996 of $1 000 000 face value of 90-day US Treasury bills (maturing in September 1996) would have paid a settlement price of 95.36. More precisely, the seller of the contract was obligated to deliver Treasury bills to the buyer in June 1996 for an amount that would make the interest rate on the Treasury bills, stated on an annualized discount basis, equal to 4.64% per year.[17] Thus on December 29, 1995, the forward rate on 90-day Treasury bills to be delivered in June 1996 was 4.64%.

As with commodity futures, neither the buyers nor the sellers of such contracts are obligated to maintain their positions until the delivery date. Reversing trades can be made at any time, and relatively few contracts result in actual delivery.

Figure 21.7 shows that on December 29, 1995, the structure of 90-day forward rates was downward sloping, ranging from 4.87% for March 1996 delivery to 4.59% for September 1996 delivery. Under the unbiased expectations hypothesis (discussed in Chapter 5), these forward rates can be interpreted to represent what investors, on average, think that spot rates will be in the future. Specifically, the 4.64% forward rate on 90-day Treasury bills to be delivered in June 1996 can be taken as an indication that on December 29, 1995, investors, on average, expected the interest rate on 90-day Treasury bills to be equal to 4.64% in June 1996. Because the interest rate that is available on December 29, 1995 on 90-day Treasury bills for immediate delivery is approximately 4.87%, it can be seen that investors, on average, expected interest rates to fall in the near future.

Actively traded interest-rate futures involve underlying securities ranging from short term (such as 90-day Treasury bills) to intermediate term (such as 10-year Treasury notes) to long term (such as 20-year Treasury bonds). Prices are generally stated in terms of percentages of par values for the corresponding securities. Yields-to-maturity (or discounts) associated with the settlement prices are also given.[18]

Pricing

In general, pricing of interest rate futures contracts involves applying the cost-of-carry model given in equation (21.4). As an example, consider a 90-day Treasury bill futures contract

---

[16] See Chapter 5 for a discussion of term structure and forward rates.

[17] The use of annualized discount-based yields introduces some errors into the analysis that are ignored here. See French, "Pricing Financial Futures Contracts," p. 62.

[18] For some interest-rate futures there is flexibility in just what the seller has to deliver, known as the *quality option*. Sometimes there is also some flexibility regarding when an intention to deliver must be announced, known as the *wild card option*.

Figure 21.7

Quotations for interest rate futures contracts.

–Lifetime–				— Daily —				Open
High	Low	Month	Open	High	Low	Settle	Chg	interest
Interest Rate								
Canadian Govt. Bonds 5 Year (ME)								
$100,000, points of 100%; 0.01 = $10 per contract								
108.57	106.18	Mar96	108.57	108.57	108.42	108.50	+0.10	2,105
Vol.	66			Prev. vol.	0		Prev. open int.	2,105
Canadian Govt. Bonds 10 Year (ME)								
$100,000, points of 100%; 0.01 = $10 per contract								
112.20	106.02	Mar96	112.15	112.20	111.90	112.15	+0.15	15,308
Vol.	260			Prev. vol.	572		Prev. open int.	15,308
Canadian 1 Month Bankers' Acceptance (ME)								
$3,000,000, points of 100%; 0.01 = $25 per contract								
Vol.	0			Prev. vol.	0		Prev. open int.	0
Canadian 3 Month Bankers' Acceptance (ME)								
$1,000,000, points of 100%; 0.01 = $25 per contract								
94.42	89.91	Mar96	94.38	94.42	94.36	94.39	−0.01	30,317
94.38	89.82	June96	94.38	94.38	94.33	94.34	−0.02	20,243
94.36	90.17	Sep96	94.32	94.36	94.30	94.31	−0.02	9,488
94.19	90.20	Dec96	94.15	94.18	94.15	94.16	+0.01	4,864
94.02	91.98	Mar97	93.97	94.02	93.97	94.02	+0.05	1,692
93.89	91.82	June97	...	...	...	93.89	+0.05	838
93.75	92.34	Sep97	...	...	...	93.75	+0.05	462
93.60	93.32	Dec97	...	...	...	93.60	+0.05	120
Vol.	2,831			Prev. vol.	3,296		Prev. open int.	68,024
Eurodollars (IMM)								
US$1,000,000, points of 100%; 0.01 = $25 per contract								
94.56	94.28	Jan96	94.44	94.45	94.42	94.44	...	32,142
94.63	94.46	Feb96	94.58	94.59	94.55	94.58	...	11,573
95.10	91.20	Mar96	94.67	94.69	94.63	94.68	+0.02	445,782
94.95	91.59	June96	94.93	94.95	94.87	94.93	+0.01	388,586
95.01	91.61	Sep96	94.98	95.01	94.93	94.99	+0.01	248,446
94.94	91.57	Dec96	94.90	94.94	94.83	94.90	...	232,302
94.89	91.57	Mar97	94.87	94.89	94.81	94.88	+0.03	162,052
94.77	91.45	June97	94.75	94.77	94.70	94.76	+0.03	148,710
94.65	91.58	Sep97	94.62	94.65	94.58	94.64	+0.03	114,272
94.49	91.51	Dec97	94.48	94.49	94.42	94.49	+0.04	86,449
94.45	91.53	Mar98	94.43	94.45	94.38	94.45	+0.05	79,514
94.38	91.48	June98	94.34	94.37	94.30	94.36	+0.05	69,272
94.32	91.43	Sep98	94.26	94.29	94.23	94.29	+0.05	55,314
94.20	91.33	Dec98	94.15	94.17	94.11	94.17	+0.05	44,303
94.18	91.36	Mar99	94.14	94.16	94.09	94.16	+0.05	36,705
94.13	91.31	June99	94.08	94.10	94.03	94.10	+0.05	31,171
94.06	91.26	Sep99	94.02	94.04	93.97	94.04	+0.05	27,257
93.96	91.15	Dec99	93.93	93.95	93.88	93.94	+0.04	22,922
93.95	91.19	Mar00	93.93	93.95	93.89	93.94	+0.04	20,529
93.90	91.14	June00	93.87	93.89	93.84	93.88	+0.04	18,010
93.85	91.10	Sep00	93.83	93.85	93.79	93.84	+0.04	13,751
93.77	91.00	Dec00	93.74	93.76	93.71	93.75	+0.04	10,603
93.77	91.05	Mar01	93.74	93.76	93.72	93.75	+0.03	8,029
93.72	91.01	June01	93.71	93.72	93.68	93.71	+0.03	7,906
93.68	90.98	Sep01	93.67	93.68	93.64	93.67	+0.03	8,308
93.61	90.90	Dec01	93.57	93.61	93.57	93.60	+0.03	8,209
93.62	90.95	Mar02	93.60	93.62	93.60	93.61	+0.03	7,005
93.58	90.93	June02	93.56	93.58	93.55	93.57	+0.03	4,557
93.53	90.91	Sep02	93.51	93.53	93.51	93.52	+0.03	4,675
93.46	90.83	Dec02	93.44	93.46	93.43	93.45	+0.03	4,166
93.47	90.87	Mar03	93.46	93.47	93.45	93.46	+0.03	3,824
93.43	90.84	June03	93.42	93.43	93.40	93.42	+0.03	3,495
93.39	90.82	Sep03	93.38	93.39	93.36	93.38	+0.03	5,502
93.32	90.73	Dec03	93.31	93.32	93.29	93.31	+0.03	3,794
93.32	90.77	Mar04	93.32	93.32	93.30	93.32	+0.03	4,290
93.28	90.74	June04	93.28	93.28	93.26	93.28	+0.03	4,513
93.25	90.71	Sep04	93.25	93.25	93.23	93.25	+0.03	4,244
93.18	91.12	Dec04	93.18	93.18	93.16	93.17	+0.02	3,703
93.19	91.14	Mar05	93.16	93.19	93.16	93.18	+0.02	3,765
93.15	91.50	June05	93.14	93.15	93.13	93.13	+0.02	2,481
93.10	92.25	Sep05	93.10	93.10	93.08	93.08	+0.02	1,943
Est. vol.	224,628			Prev. vol.	192,641		Prev. open int.	2,394,095
Libor - 1 Month (IMM)								
US$3,000,000, points of 100%; 0.01 = $25 per contract								
94.74	91.93	Jan96	94.4000	94.4100	94.3900	94.4100	...	19,212
94.74	92.35	Feb96	94.5400	94.5600	94.5200	94.5500	...	15,640
94.73	93.04	Mar96	94.6300	94.6400	94.6200	94.6300	...	2,533
94.7900	93.33	Apr96	94.7200	94.7400	94.7200	94.7400	+0.0200	740
94.8400	93.92	May96	94.8100	94.8200	94.8100	94.8200	+0.0200	123
Est. vol.	3,937			Prev. vol.	2,858		Prev. open int.	38,415
U.S. Treasury Bills 3 Month (IMM)								
US$1,000,000, points of 100%; 0.01 = $25 per contract								
95.20	93.21	Mar96	95.1600	95.1600	95.1000	95.1300	...	7,371
95.3800	94.36	June96	95.3700	95.3800	95.3300	95.3600	...	4,241
95.4100	94.7900	Sep96	...	...	95.3800	95.4100	...	133
Est. vol.	876			Prev. vol.	1,556		Prev. open int.	11,745
U.S. Treasury Bonds 30 Year 8% (CBOT)								
US$100,000, points and 32nds of 100%; 1/32nd = $31.25 per contract								
121-20	93-13	Mar96	121-05	121-20	120-28	121-15	+0-11	367,778
121-07	93-00	June96	120-22	121-07	120-16	121-02	+0-11	17,190
120-21	92-20	Sep96	120-14	120-21	120-01	120-18	+0-11	5,871
120-04	92-10	Dec96	119-26	120-04	119-20	120-02	+0-12	491
119-21	98-25	Mar97	119-12	119-21	119-06	119-20	+0-12	1,323
				Prev. vol.	87,829		Prev. open int.	392,692
U.S. Treasury Notes 2 Year (CBOT)								
US$200,000, points and 32nds of 100%; 1/32nd = $31.25 per contract								
104-27	103-12	Mar96	104-24	104-27	104-24	104-27	+0-02	17,017
				Prev. vol.	801		Prev. open int.	17,141
U.S. Treasury Notes 5 Year (CBOT)								
US$100,000, points and 32nds of 100%; 1/32nd ~ $62.50 per contract								
110-13	105-18	Mar96	110-06	110-13	110-02	110-13	+0-06	139,906
110-05	107-29	June96	110-04	110-05	109-29	110-05	+0-06	10,745
110-05	108-29	Sep96	...	...	...	110-05	+0-06	3,781
				Prev. vol.	17,862		Prev. open int.	154,432
U.S. Treasury Notes 10 Year (CBOT)								
US$100,000, points and 32nds of 100%; 1/32nd = $31.25 per contract								
114-22	98-18	Mar96	114-10	114-22	114-06	114-19	+0-09	214,900
114-01	102-09	June96	113-30	114-01	113-20	113-31	+0-09	18,165
114-01	107-04	Sep96	...	...	...	114-01	+0-09	300
				Prev. vol.	24,337		Prev. open int.	233,415

SOURCE: Reprinted with permission of *The Financial Post* (December 30, 1995).

that calls for delivery in six months. Note that nine-month Treasury bills will be equivalent to 90-day Treasury bills after six months have passed. Hence, they could be delivered as the underlying assets in 90-day Treasury bill futures contracts where the delivery date is six months from now. What futures price is fair for these contracts?

Assume that the current market price of a nine-month Treasury bill is $95.24, providing a yield of 5% ($4.76/$95.24) over the nine months. (This yield and those that follow are not annualized.) If an owner sold this security now, he or she would be able to risklessly earn 3% on the proceeds over the next six months. This means that the owner should not short sell a futures contract calling for delivery in six months of a 90-day Treasury bill, where the price to be received is less than $98.10 ($95.24 × 1.03). For example, if the price of the futures contract was $97, then the owner would be making only 1.85% on his or her initial investment of $95.24 over the subsequent six months. This is less than the 3% that could be earned by selling the nine-month Treasury bill now and investing in a six-month Treasury bill.

Conversely, the buyer should not agree to a price that is more than \$98.10. This is because the buyer could buy the nine-month Treasury bill in the spot market today for \$95.24 and receive \$100 in nine months, or the buyer could risklessly invest the \$95.24 for six months at 3% and then use the \$98.10 proceeds to pay the futures price for a 90-day Treasury bill that pays \$100 at maturity. If the futures price were greater than \$98.10 then the buyer would have to invest more than \$95.24 today. For example, if the futures price was \$99, then \$96.12 (= \$99/1.03) would have to be invested today, so that the principal plus 3% interest for six months would be sufficient to pay the futures price (\$99) after six months. In such a situation, nobody would choose to be long in the futures contract, because he or she would be better off buying a nine-month Treasury bill in the spot market for \$95.24 instead of investing more at 3% for six months in order to be able to pay the futures price upon delivery of the Treasury bill. Consequently, the futures price must be \$98.10, because this is the only price that is acceptable to both parties to the futures contract.

Generalizing, the futures price P_f must equal the spot price P_s plus the forgone interest I, just as shown in equation (21.2), because the benefits B and costs of ownership C are zero with such assets. Equivalently, letting R denote the risk-free interest rate that exists on Treasuries that mature on the delivery date, the futures price is

$$P_f = P_s(1 + R). \tag{21.9}$$

The futures price will be greater than the spot price as long as the risk-free rate R is positive. Similarly, note that the cost of carry equals

$$\text{Carry} = P_s R \tag{21.10}$$

because both B and C are equal to zero. In this example, carry = \$2.86 (\$95.24 × .03). Note that the difference between the futures price of \$98.10 and the spot price of \$95.24 also equals \$2.86.

Market Index Futures

Figure 21.8 shows a set of quotations for futures contracts on a variety of market indices. Each of these contracts involves the payment of *cash* on the delivery date of an amount equal to a *multiplier* times the difference between (1) the value of the index at the close of the last trading day of the contract and (2) the purchase price of the futures contract. If the index is above the futures price, those with short positions pay those with long positions. If the index is below the futures price, those with long positions pay those with short positions.

In practice, a clearinghouse is used, and all contracts are marked to market every day. In a sense, the delivery day differs from other days in only one respect—all open positions are marked to market for the last time and then closed. Cash settlement provides results similar to those associated with the delivery of all the securities in the index. It avoids the effort and transaction costs associated with (1) the purchase of securities by people who have taken short futures positions; (2) the delivery of these securities to people who have taken long futures positions; and (3) the subsequent sale of the securities by those who receive them.

Major Contracts

Three major stock market index futures are quoted in Figure 21.8, with the most popular one in terms of both trading volume and open interest based on the Standard & Poor's 500 (S&P

Figure 21.8

Quotations for index futures contracts.

–Lifetime– High	Low	Month	Open	— Daily — High	Low	Settle	Chg	Open interest
Indexes								
Commodity Research Bureau (NYFE)								
500 x index points; 0.05 pt. = $25 per contract								
243.30	232.50	Mar96	237.60	237.95	236.00	237.10	–0.85	1,128
241.70	232.50	May96	234.65	234.65	234.00	234.15	–1.10	423
240.00	232.25	July96	233.05	233.05	232.25	232.40	–1.10	328
Est. vol.	358			Prev. vol.	302		Prev. open int.	1,879
Major Market Index (IMM)								
US$500 x index points; 0.05 pt. = $25 per contract								
551.00	502.10	Jan96	534.70	536.00	534.20	536.00	+1.00	278
Est. vol.	1			Prev. vol.	0		Prev. open int.	290
Municipal Bond Index (CBOT)								
US$1,000 x index points; 1/32 pt. = $31.25 per contract								
121-10	110-20	Mar96	120-28	121-04	120-15	121-01	+0-10	14,823
				Prev. vol.	1,341		Prev. open int.	14,835
NIKKEI 225 Index (CME)								
$5 x index points; 5 pts. = $25 per contract								
20130	14605	Mar96	19910	20080	19910	20060	+90	27,543
20200	14655	June96	20100	20100	20060	20060	+50	264
Est. vol.	506			Prev. vol.	607		Prev. open int.	27,837
NYSE Composite Index (NYFE)								
500 x index points; 0.05 pt. = $25 per contract								
335.35	275.15	Mar96	330.40	330.90	329.25	330.30	+0.10	2,232
337.65	297.85	June96	333.30	333.30	333.05	333.05	+0.25	974
Est. vol.	1,671			Prev. vol.	1,570		Prev. open int.	3,262
S&P 500 Composite Index (CME)								
500 x index points; 0.05 = $25 per contract								
629.70	511.00	Mar96	617.50	619.50	616.20	618.45	+0.70	191,419
635.05	554.25	June96	624.20	624.90	621.70	624.05	+0.80	6,343
639.75	589.45	Sep96	628.50	629.30	626.50	628.75	+0.85	2,297
Est. vol.	51,699			Prev. vol.	33,563		Prev. open int.	200,101
Toronto 35 (TFE)								
500 x index points; 0.02 pt. = $10 per contract								
253.10	226.80	Mar96	249.10	250.30	248.90	250.30	+1.60	5,567
Vol.	110			Prev. vol.	164		Open int.	5,627
Toronto 100 (TFE)								
500 x index points; 0.02 pt. = $10 per contract								
Vol.	0			Prev. vol.	0		Open int.	99
Value Line Composite Index (KBOT)								
500 x index points; 0.05 pt. = $25 per contract								
580.70	498.55	Mar96	575.20	576.80	573.40	575.40	+0.90	1,426
				Prev. vol.	138		Prev. open int.	1,428

SOURCE: Reprinted with permission of *The Financial Post* (December 30, 1995).

500). This contract, along with one on the Nikkei 225 (a major Japanese index), are traded on the Index and Option Market Division of the Chicago Mercantile Exchange (CME). The other stock index futures use the New York Stock Exchange Composite Stock Index, traded at the New York Futures Exchange (NYFE). (There are also index futures contracts on the Major Market Index, which, when multiplied by five, closely resembles the Dow Jones Industrial Average; it is traded on the Chicago Board of Trade.)[19] In Canada futures contracts on the TSE 35 and the TSE 100 are traded on the Toronto Futures Exchange (TFE), a subsidiary of the TSE. Trading in the TSE 100 contracts is extremely thin.

For all contracts but the Nikkei 225 futures, the multiplier is $500; for the Nikkei 225, it is $5. Thus, the purchase of an S&P 500 contract when the index is 400 would cost $200 000 ($500 × 400). The subsequent sale of this contract when the index is 420 would result in proceeds of $500 × 420 = $210 000 and a profit of $210 000–$200 000 = $10 000.

[19] The NYFE is a subsidiary of the New York Stock Exchange. There are other market index futures available besides these four, such as the Value Line Average Stock Index (traded on the Kansas City Board of Trade).

Trading Volume

The volume of trading in futures contracts is very large. To assess its relative size, the number of contracts can be multiplied by the total dollar value represented by one contract. As shown in Figure 21.8, the estimated volume on December 29, 1995, for S&P 500 futures was 51 699 contracts. At a value of 617.50 for the lowest priced S&P 500 contract, the total dollar value is about $16 billion (51 699 × 617.50 × $500). In comparison, the average daily dollar value of all trades of shares on the New York Stock Exchange during 1993 was about $10 billion per day — less than the dollar size of the S&P futures on December 29, 1995. This is not unusual. On many days the dollar value involved in trades of S&P 500 futures exceeds that of all trades of individual stocks.

The situation is quite different on the TFE, as interest in futures has not developed in Canada to the extent that it has in the US. On December 29, 1995 about 110 index futures traded, representing a total dollar volume of about $14 million or about 0.1% of the US trading value and 20% of the average daily value of TSE equity trades.

Hedging

What accounts for the popularity of market index futures in general and the S&P 500 in particular? Simply stated, they provide relatively inexpensive and highly liquid positions similar to those obtained with diversified stock portfolios.

For example, instead of purchasing 500 stocks in anticipation of a market advance, one can invest an equivalent amount of money in Treasury bills and take a long position in S&P 500 futures. Alternatively, instead of trying to take short positions in 500 stocks in anticipation of a market decline, one can take a short position in S&P 500 futures, using Treasury bills as margin.

Market index futures also allow broker-dealers to hedge the market risk associated with the temporary positions they often take in the course of their business.[20] This hedging ultimately benefits investors by providing them with greater liquidity than they would have otherwise. For example, consider an investor who wants to sell a large block of shares. In this situation a broker-dealer might agree to purchase the shares immediately at an agreed-upon price, and then spend time "lining up" buyers. In the interim, however, economic news might cause the market to fall, and with it the price of the shares. This would cause the broker-dealer to experience a loss, because the broker-dealer owns the shares during the period between purchasing it from the investor and lining up the ultimate buyers. One traditional way that broker-dealers protect themselves (at least partially) from this risk is to pay the investor a relatively low price for the stock. However, the broker-dealer can now hedge this risk (at least partially) by short selling S&P 500 futures at the time the stock is bought from the investor and reversing this position when the ultimate buyers are found.

Conversely, when an investor wants to buy a large block of shares, a broker-dealer might agree to provide it at a certain price and then go about the task of lining up sellers. In the interim, however, economic news might cause the market to rise, and with it the price of the shares. This would cause the broker-dealer to experience a loss, because the price that will have to be paid to the sellers might end up being greater than the price agreed to with the investor. Traditionally, broker-dealers protect themselves from such risk by charging the

---

[20] Similarly, interest-rate futures are often used by financial institutions to hedge interest-rate risk to which they may be exposed — that is, when a large movement in interest rates would cause a large loss, these institutions will seek protection by either buying or selling interest-rate futures.

investor a relatively high price for the shares. However, a broker-dealer can now hedge this risk (at least partially) by going long in S&P 500 futures at the time the investor agrees to buy the shares and then reversing this position when the shares are ultimately bought.

Given competition among broker-dealers, the existence of S&P 500 futures will lead them to provide higher bid prices and lower asked prices. This reduced bid-ask spread means that the existence of S&P 500 futures has provided the associated spot market for stocks with greater liquidity.

It should be pointed out that the use of S&P 500 futures in such situations does not remove all risk from the position of the broker-dealer. All that it removes is market risk, because these futures contracts involve a broad market index, not an individual stock. Thus, it is possible for the broker-dealer to experience a loss even if an appropriate position has been taken in futures. Specifically, the individual stock with which the broker-dealer is involved may move up or down in price while the S&P 500 is stable, or the S&P 500 may move up or down while the individual stock is stable. In either case, the broker-dealer who has hedged with S&P 500 futures may still experience a loss. The possibility of this happening is substantial when the broker-dealer has little diversification, with the greatest possibility associated with a one-stock portfolio.

Index Arbitrage

When stock index futures were first proposed, a number of people predicted that at long last there would be an indicator of investors' expectations about the future course of the stock market. It was said that the market price of such a futures contract would indicate the consensus opinion of investors concerning the future level of the associated index. In times of optimism, the futures price might be much higher than the current level of the market, whereas in times of pessimism, the futures price might be much lower.

Such predictions have since been found to be quite off the mark. This is because the price of a futures contract on an asset will not diverge by more than the cost of carry from the spot price of the asset. Should a relatively large divergence occur, clever investors known as *arbitrageurs* will make trades designed to capture riskless (that is, "arbitrage") profits.

The presence of arbitrageurs has an effect on the pricing of stock index futures. Their actions will force the price of a stock index futures contract to stay close to an "appropriate" relationship with the current level of the associated index. To find out just what is meant by appropriate, consider a hypothetical example where today is a day in June when the TSE 35 is at 200 and a December TSE 35 futures contract is selling for 210. The following investment strategies can be compared:

1. Purchase the stocks in the TSE 35, hold them until December and then sell them on the delivery date of the December TSE 35 contract.
2. Purchase a December TSE 35 futures contract along with Treasury bills that mature in December. Hold the futures contract until the delivery date in December.

Strategy 1 would cost \$200 (in "index terms") at the outset. In return, it would provide the investor with (1) an amount of money equal to the value of the TSE 35 on the delivery date and (2) dividends on those stocks that went ex-dividend prior to the delivery date. That is, by denoting the level the TSE 35 will have on the delivery date as P_d and assuming the dividend yield over the six-month time period from June to December is 3%, the investor following strategy 1 will receive in December an amount that is equal to P_d + \$6 (that is, P_d + (.03 × \$200)).[21]

Assume that \$200 is invested in Treasury bills in strategy 2. Since Treasury bills can be used as margin on futures, the total cost of strategy 2 is \$200, which is the same as the cost of strategy 1. In return, strategy 2 would provide the investor with (1) an amount of money equal to the difference between the value of the TSE 35 and \$210 on the delivery date and (2) the face value of the Treasury bills on the delivery date. That is, assuming that the yield on the Treasury bills is 5%, the investor following strategy 2 will receive in December an amount that is equal to P_d (that is, (P_d – \$210) + (1.05 × \$200)).

By design, both strategies require the same initial outlay. Furthermore, both strategies are subject to precisely the same uncertainty, the unknown level of the TSE 35 on the future delivery date, denoted by P_d. However, the inflows are not equal, indicating that an opportunity exists for **index arbitrage.**[22]

In this example, index arbitrage would cause an investor to go long on strategy 1 and short on strategy 2 because strategy 1 has a higher payoff than strategy 2 (note that $P_d + \$6 > P_d$). Going long on strategy 1 means that the investor is to do exactly what was indicated earlier—purchase the stocks in the TSE 35 and hold them until the December delivery date. Going short on strategy 2 means doing exactly the opposite. The investor shorts (that is, sells) a December TSE 35 futures contract and sells Treasury bills that mature in December. The net cash outflow of going long on strategy 1 and short on strategy 2 is zero—the \$200 spent buying the stocks in going long on strategy 1 was obtained by selling \$200 worth of December Treasury bills when going short on strategy 2. The margin necessary for being short on the future contract is met by having purchased the underlying stocks. Thus, no additional cash needs to be committed in order to engage in index arbitrage—owning Treasury bills that mature in December is sufficient.

Having gone long on strategy 1 and short on strategy 2, what is the investor's position on the delivery date in December? First, the investor bought the individual stocks in the TSE 35 at \$200 and assured himself of a selling price of \$210 by being short the TSE 35 futures contract. Thus, the investor has made \$10 from being long on the individual stocks and short on the futures on the index. Second, the investor has received dividends totalling \$6 (.03 × \$200) from owning the stocks from June to December. Third, by selling, in June, \$200 of December Treasury bills the investor has foregone the \$10 (.05 × \$200) on them. Overall, the investor has increased the dollar return by \$6 (\$10 + \$6 – \$10). Furthermore, this increase is certain, meaning it will be received regardless of what happens to the level of the TSE 35. Thus, by going long on strategy 1 and short on strategy 2, the investor will not have increased the risk of his or her portfolio but will have increased the dollar return.

Earlier, it was mentioned that an investor going long on strategy 1 would receive cash of P_d + \$6 in December, whereas an investor going long on strategy 2 would receive cash of

---

[21] The 3% dividend yield is actually the accumulated December value of the dividends divided by the purchase price of the stocks. Hence, the dividends might be received in three months and amount to 2.93% of the purchase price of the index. Putting them in a risk-free asset that returns 2.47% for the last three months results in a yield of 3%, or \$3, in December.

[22] Index arbitrage is one of two major forms of program trading. The other form, known as portfolio insurance, was discussed in the previous chapter. For a discussion and example of how futures can be used to procure portfolio insurance, see Stephen R. King and Eli M. Remolona, "The Pricing and Hedging of Market Index Deposits," Federal Reserve Bank of New York *Quarterly Review* 12, no. 2 (Summer 1987): 9–20; or Thomas J. O'Brien, *How Option Replicating Portfolio Insurance Works: Expanded Details*, Monograph Series in Finance and Economics no. 1988–4, New York University Salomon Center, Leonard N. Stern School of Business.

P_d. From these figures it can be seen that going long on strategy 1 and short on strategy 2 will provide a net dollar return of \$6 (that is, $(P_d + \$6) - P_d$). However, if enough investors do this, the opportunity for making the \$6 riskless profit will disappear. This is because (1) going long on the individual stocks will push the prices of these stocks up, thereby raising the level of the TSE 35 above 200; and (2) going short on the TSE 35 futures will reduce the price of the futures below 210. These two adjustments will continue until it is no longer profitable to go long on strategy 1 and short on strategy 2.

What if the price of the TSE 35 December futures contract were \$190 instead of \$210? The dollar return from being long on strategy 1 is still equal to $P_d + \$6$. However, the dollar return from being long on strategy 2 will be different. Purchasing Treasury bills and the futures contract will provide the investor with a dollar return in December of $P_d + \$20$ (that is, $(P_d - \$190) + (1.05 \times \$200)$). Since these two inflows are not equal, again there is an opportunity for index arbitrage. However, it would involve the investor going short on strategy 1 and long on strategy 2. This is because strategy 1 now has a lower payoff than strategy 2 (note that $P_d + \$6 < P_d + \$20$). By doing this, the investor will, without risk, earn \$14 (that is, $(P_d + \$20) - (P_d + \$6)$). Furthermore, being short the individual stocks and long the futures will reduce the level of the TSE 35 below 200 and raise the price of the futures above 190.

In the example, the interest rate was 5%, the dividend yield was 3%, and the current level of the TSE 35 was 200. This means that the difference between the TSE 35 December futures contract and the current level of the TSE 35 should be $(.05 - .03) \times 200 = 4$. Equivalently, the equilibrium price of the futures contract when the TSE 35 is 200 would be 204. Note that when three of the six months have passed, the interest rate and dividend yield will be 2.5% (5%/2) and 1.5% (3%/2), respectively. Thus, the difference should be about $(.025 - .015) \times 200 = 2$, assuming the TSE 35 is still at 200 at that time.

In equilibrium, because these two strategies cost the same to implement, prices will adjust so that their net cash inflows are equal. Letting y denote the dividend yield on the stocks in the index, P_f the current price of the futures contract on the index, and P_s the current spot price of the index (that is, P_s denotes the current level of the index), the net cash inflow from strategy 1 is

$$P_d + yP_s.$$

Letting R denote the interest rate on Treasury bills, the net cash inflow from strategy 2 is

$$(P_d - P_f) + [(1 + R) \times P_s].$$

Setting these two inflows equal to each other results in

$$P_d + yP_s = (P_d - P_f) + [(1 + R) \times P_s]. \tag{21.11}$$

Simplifying this equation results in

$$P_f - P_s = (R - y)P_s \tag{21.12}$$

or

$$P_f = P_s + RP_s - yP_s. \tag{21.13}$$

Equation (21.12) indicates that the difference between the price of the futures contract and the current level of the index should depend only on (1) the current level of the index P_s, and (2) the difference between the interest rate on Treasury bills and the dividend yield on the index $R - y$. As the delivery date nears, the difference between the interest rate and the dividend yield diminishes, converging to zero on the delivery date. Thus as the delivery date approaches, the futures price P_f should converge to the current spot price P_s.

Equation (21.13) shows that index futures are priced according to the cost-of-carry model given earlier in equation (21.4), where the costs of ownership C are zero. Here the interest forgone by ownership I is equal to RP_s, whereas the benefit of ownership B is the dividend yield yP_s. Hence, the cost of carry is

$$\text{Carry} = RP_s - yP_s \tag{21.14}$$

which will be positive as long as the risk-free interest rate R is greater than the dividend yield on the index y—a situation that exists nearly all the time.

In practice, the situation is not this simple for a number of reasons. Positions in futures, stocks, and Treasury bills involve transaction costs.[23] This means that arbitrage will not take place unless the difference diverges far enough from the amount shown in equation (21.12) to warrant incurring such costs. The futures price, and hence the difference, can be expected to move within a band around the "theoretical value," with the width of the band determined by the costs of those who can engage in transactions most efficiently. To add to the complexity, both the dividend yield and the relevant interest rate on Treasury bills are subject to some uncertainty. Neither the amounts of dividends to be declared nor their timing can be specified completely in advance. Furthermore, because futures positions must be marked to market daily, the amount of cash required for strategy 2 may have to be varied via additional borrowing (if short this strategy) or lending (if long this strategy). Also, on occasion market prices may be reported with a substantial time lag, making the current level and the futures price of the index appear to be out of line when they actually are not. Thus, an investor may enter into the transactions necessary for index arbitrage when actual prices are in equilibrium, thereby incurring useless transaction costs. Nevertheless, index arbitrage is still actively pursued, most notably by brokerage firms.

Stock index futures are also used extensively by other professional money managers. As a result, prices of such contracts are likely to track their underlying indices very closely, taking into account both dividends and current interest rates. It is unlikely that a private investor will be able to exploit "mispricing" of such a contract by engaging in index arbitrage. Nevertheless, stock index futures can provide inexpensive ways to take positions in the stock market or to hedge portions of the risk associated with other positions. Furthermore, their use can lower transaction costs by reducing the size of the bid-ask spread in individual securities, thereby benefiting investors who may never take direct positions in futures contracts.

The 35 underlying stocks in the TSE 35, a "mutual" fund consisting of these stocks in the form of TIPs, options on TIPs, TSE 35 options, and TSE 35 futures contracts can all be traded and, therefore, it is possible to arbitrage freely between all six of these securities. One therefore expects these six securities to be fairly priced at most times.

The existence of index arbitrage permits the use of stock index futures as a substitute for holding the underlying stocks. The substitution of a futures position for a stock portfolio has led to the development of synthetic index funds. These allow a foreign investor to gain access to Canadian equity markets without hiring either research and portfolio management

[23] People involved in index arbitrage need to be able to quickly make a large number of transactions in individual stocks. In order to do this, they often have their computers send in their orders through the MOST system (discussed in Chapter 3). For a discussion of some of the complications involved in successfully executing index arbitrage strategies, see David M. Modest, "On the Pricing of Stock Index Futures," *Journal of Portfolio Management* 10, no. 4 (Summer 1984): 51–57.

Figure 21.9

Terminal values of positions in calls and futures.

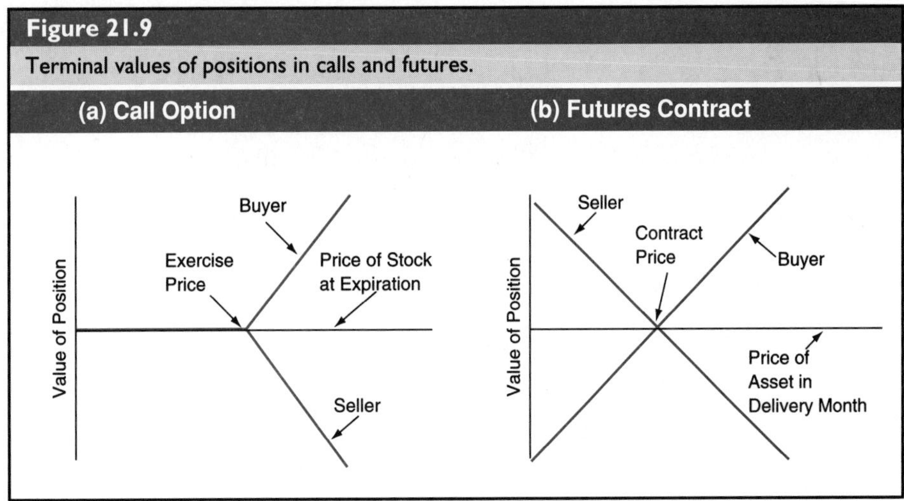

services or an investment counsellor, by creating a synthetic Toronto 35 index fund using futures contracts. The earlier example illustrated the equivalence of a TSE 35 stock position and a combination of TSE 35 futures contracts and Treasury bills; therefore, the investor can replicate the return on the index with minimal transactions costs and management fees.

FUTURES VERSUS OPTIONS

People occasionally make the mistake of confusing a futures contract with an options contract.[24] With an options contract there is the possibility that both parties involved will have nothing to do at the end of the life of the contract. In particular, if the option is "out of the money" on the expiration date, then the options contract will be worthless and can be thrown away. However, with a futures contract, both parties involved must do something at the end of the life of the contract. The parties are obligated to complete the transaction, either by a reversing trade or by actual delivery.

Figure 21.9 contrasts the situation faced by the buyer and the seller of a call option with the situation faced by the buyer and the seller of a futures contract. Specifically, terminal values for buyers and sellers are shown at the last possible moment—the expiration date for the option and the delivery date for the futures contract.

As shown in panel (a), no matter what the price of the underlying stock, an option buyer cannot lose and an option seller cannot gain on the expiration date. Option buyers compensate sellers for putting themselves in this position by paying them a premium when the contract is signed.

The situation is quite different with a futures contract. As shown in panel (b), the buyer may gain or lose, depending on the price of the asset in the delivery month. Whatever the buyer gains or loses, an exactly offsetting loss or gain will be registered by the seller. The higher the contract price (that is, the price of the futures contract when the buyer purchased

[24] Adding to the confusion is the existence of a contract known as a futures option, which is an option that has a futures contract instead of a stock as its underlying asset. Futures options are discussed in more detail in the Appendix.

INSTITUTIONAL ISSUES

Transportable Alpha

Years ago trustees of the $1 billion General Mills pension fund adopted a disciplined approach to allocating assets among various broad categories. This was accomplished by establishing specific long-run allocation targets: 60% to common stocks and 40% to fixed-income securities. The trustees believe that this *policy asset allocation* provides an optimal balance of expected return and risk, given their collective tolerance for possible adverse outcomes. The trustees expect the fund's staff, which handles the fund's day-to-day investment operations, to stick closely to this policy asset allocation. In turn, the staff follows a procedure of reducing exposure to the asset category that has appreciated in relative value and increasing exposure to the asset category that has depreciated in relative value.

To manage the pension fund's assets, the staff had retained what the trustees considered to be a superior group of domestic common stock managers. Over a ten-year period, those managers, in aggregate, had outperformed the S&P 500 by 1.5% annually (after all fees and expenses)—an exceptional amount by the standards of the investment management business. The trustees and staff expected such superior performance to continue in the future.

More recently, the trustees found themselves facing a dilemma: they would have liked to have assigned more than 60% of the fund's assets to the common stock managers. However, the trustees were also committed to the discipline of their asset allocation process. Could the trustees have their proverbial cake and eat it too? The answer was "Yes," through a concept called *transportable alpha.*

Consider three strategies through which General Mills could have maintained its policy asset allocation, yet taken advantage of its common stock managers' skills. Each strategy involves allocating more than 60% of the pension fund's assets to the common stock managers, while simultaneously reducing the pension fund's common stock exposure and increasing its fixed-income exposure in order to comply with the fund's asset allocation targets.

1. *Long-short strategy*. The managers, in aggregate, purchase long positions in stocks as they typically would with their assigned assets. However, they also short sell stocks (see Chapter 2) equal in value to the pension fund's overweighting of domestic equity assets. The cash generated by these short sales is used to buy fixed-income securities that are held as margin, but nevertheless provide returns through interest income and price changes. The particular long-short transactions result from the managers' investment research, which identifies under- and overpriced securities.
2. *Futures strategy*. The managers purchase long stock positions with their assigned assets. At the same time the pension fund's staff sells futures contracts on a stock market index and buys futures contracts on Treasury bonds in sufficient amounts to compensate for the over- and underweighting of common stocks and fixed-income securities.
3. *Swap strategy*. The managers purchase long stock positions with their assigned assets. Through a financial intermediary (such as a bank or a broker) the pension fund "swaps" (exchanges) with another institutional investor the return on a common stock index in order to receive the return on a fixed-income index. These swaps (see Chapter 24) are based on dollar amounts equal to the over and underweightings of the common stocks and fixed-income securities.

In general, these strategies can be characterized as allowing the pension fund to earn (1) the total return generated by a 40% allocation to fixed-income securities, (2) the total return produced by a 60% allocation to common stocks (that is, the normal plus abnormal returns of the common stock managers), and (3) the abnormal returns earned by the common stock managers associated with the allocation in excess of 60% to common stocks. The common stock managers' abnormal returns (known as *alphas*) are effectively "transported" to the fixed-income asset category.

In the final analysis, General Mills chose to implement the second strategy. The pension fund's staff believed that listed futures contracts provided the cheapest and administratively least cumbersome means of carrying out its alpha transport program. Nevertheless, the ability to customize the other strategies to specific situations may make those strategies attractive at times to certain institutional investors.

These strategies highlight fundamental changes in the financial markets that began in the 1980s and have rapidly gathered momentum in the 1990s. Through the development of derivative financial instruments (options, futures, and swaps) and the technological advancements in communications and computing power, financial markets have become highly integrated and fungible. Investors are increasingly able to exploit perceived profit opportunities and simultaneously maintain desired risk positions.

Pacific Investment Management Company (PIMCO) provides another example of the transportable alpha concept. PIMCO is one of the largest fixed-income managers in the world, with assets under management exceeding $60 billion. Over the years, the firm has produced an enviable track record, earning positive risk-adjusted returns under a variety of fixed-income investment assignments.

Since 1986, PIMCO has transported its fixed-income management skills to the US stock market through a product called StocksPlus. PIMCO's process is simple. The firm purchases S&P 500 futures contracts equal to a specified *notional* principal. (A notional principal is the market exposure of the futures contracts — that is, the number of contracts purchased times the contracts' price times the contract multiplier.) At the same time PIMCO sets aside cash reserves equal to the notional principal. The cash reserves serve as collateral for the futures contracts.

As the text discusses, futures prices are set by investors predicated on the assumption that they can hold a combination of futures contracts and the risk-free asset. PIMCO uses its investment skills to create a short-term fixed-income portfolio that has substantially outperformed 90-day Treasury bills with little incremental risk. As a result, the firm's combination of S&P 500 futures contracts and short-term fixed-income investments has consistently exceeded the returns on the S&P 500.

PIMCO uses a variety of cash management strategies to add value relative to a portfolio of 90-day Treasury bills. The firm takes advantage of the most consistently upward portion of the yield curve — that is, maturities between zero days and one year. As the StocksPlus strategy needs liquidity from only a small portion of its fixed-income portfolio to meet margin requirements, PIMCO extends roughly one-half of its portfolio to maturities past 90 days. Further, the firm accepts some credit risk by purchasing non-government securities such as commercial paper. PIMCO also takes advantage of certain securities that offer little credit risk, but relatively high yields. At times these securities have included short-term tranches of collateralized mortgage obligations, floating-rate notes, and foreign government short-term securities (with currency risk fully hedged).

Transportable alpha involves investors capturing inefficiencies in certain markets, while maintaining desired exposure to markets beyond those in which the superior performance is earned. Transportable alpha is not a free lunch. Investors must pay commissions on their trades in stocks, options, futures, and swaps either directly or through bid-ask spreads. Real-world frictions such as collateral requirements and even custodial accounting difficulties still complicate the smooth implementation of the alpha transport strategies. Further, investors must take active

INSTITUTIONAL ISSUES (continued)

management risk in order to earn their alphas. For example, General Mills's common stock managers, in aggregate, may underperform the stock market, or PIMCO's short-term portfolio may underperform 90-day Treasury bills. However, institutional investors applying thetransportable alpha concept believe that their active management investment strategies possess sufficiently positive expected returns to more than compensate for the additional risk assumed.

it from the seller), the greater the likelihood that the buyer will lose and the seller will gain. The lower the contract price, the greater the likelihood that the seller will lose and the buyer will gain.

SYNTHETIC FUTURES

For some assets, futures contracts are unavailable, but both put and call options are available. In such cases, an investor can create a **synthetic futures contract**.

The clearest example involves European options on common stocks. As shown in the previous chapter, the *purchase* of a European call option and the *sale* of a European put option at the same exercise price and with the same expiration date will provide a value at expiration that will be related, dollar for dollar, to the stock price at that time. This is shown in Figure 21.10.

Panel (a) shows the payoff associated with the purchase of a call at an exercise price E, whereas panel (b) shows the payoff associated with the sale of a put at the same exercise price. The results obtained by taking *both* positions are shown by the solid line in panel (c).

Depending on the prices (that is, premiums) of the call and the put, this strategy may initially either require a net outflow of cash or provide a net inflow. For comparability with the purchase of a futures contract, this cash flow may be offset with borrowing or lending as required to bring the net investment to zero. The dashed line in panel (c) shows a case in which the call option costs more than is provided by the sale of the put option. The difference is borrowed, requiring the loan repayment shown in the figure. The dashed line thus indicates the net end-of-period payoffs for a strategy requiring no initial outlay. Because these payoffs are equivalent to the payoffs from a futures contract with a contract price equal to F, a synthetic futures contract has been created.

In practice, the equivalence is not perfect. Most listed options are American, not European, raising the possibility that the buyer of the put will exercise it prior to maturity. Moreover, the synthetic future is not marked to market on a daily basis. Despite these differences, the existence of well-functioning markets for call and put options will enable investors to create arrangements similar to futures on the underlying asset synthetically.

Figure 21.10

Creating a synthetic futures contract.

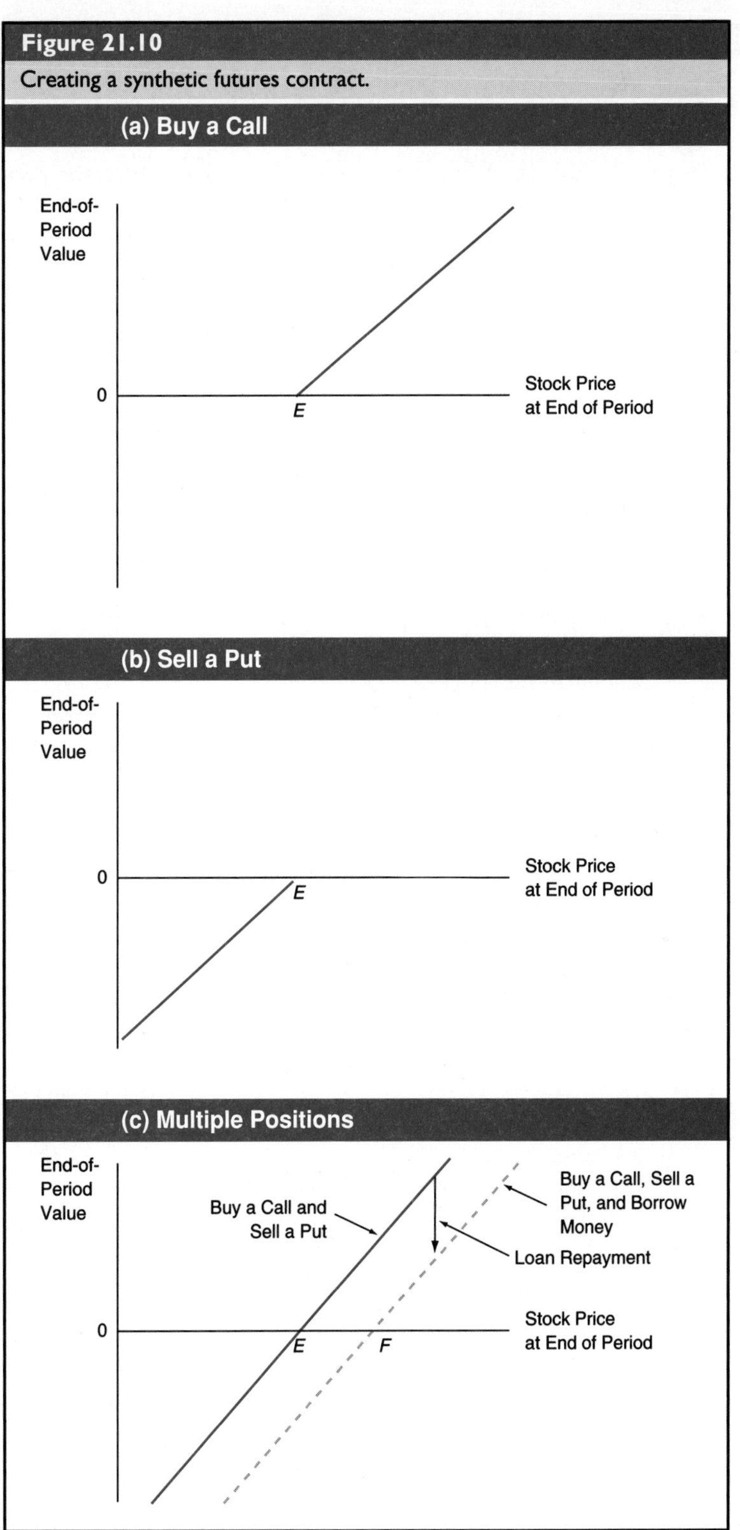

SUMMARY

1. A futures contract involves the delivery of a specific type of asset at a specific location at a given future date.
2. People who buy and sell futures can be classified as either hedgers or speculators. Hedgers transact in futures primarily to reduce risk, because these people either produce or use the asset in their ordinary course of business. Speculators transact in futures in pursuit of relatively short-term profits.
3. Futures are bought and sold on organized exchanges. Futures are standardized in terms of the type of asset, time of delivery, and place of delivery.
4. Each futures exchange has an associated clearinghouse that becomes the "seller's buyer" and the "buyer's seller" as soon as the trade is concluded.
5. A futures investor is required to deposit initial margin in order to guarantee fulfillment of his or her obligations.
6. A futures investor's account is marked to market daily, with the equity in the investor's account adjusted to reflect the change in the futures contract's settlement price.
7. A futures investor must maintain his or her account's equity equal to or greater than a certain percentage of the amount deposited as initial margin. If this requirement is not met, the investor will be requested to deposit variation margin in the account.
8. The basis for futures is the difference between the current spot price of the asset and the corresponding futures price.
9. There are three possible relationships between the current futures price and the expected spot price: the expectations hypothesis (futures price equal to expected spot price), normal backwardation (futures price less than expected spot price), and normal contango (futures price greater than expected spot price).
10. The current futures price should equal the current spot price plus the cost of carry. The cost of carry equals (1) the amount of interest that the owner forgoes by holding onto the asset less (2) the benefits of owning the asset plus (3) the costs of owning the asset.
11. If the price of a futures contract becomes too far removed from the current spot price of the asset plus the cost of carry, arbitrageurs will enter into transactions that generate riskless profits from the perceived price discrepancy. Their actions will cause prices to adjust until the opportunity to make such profits disappears.

APPENDIX A

FUTURES OPTIONS

The previous chapter described options, while this chapter has described futures. Interestingly, there are contracts currently in existence that are known as **futures options** (or options on futures). As might be expected, these contracts are, in a sense, combinations of futures and options contracts. In particular, a futures option is an option in which the underlying asset is a specific futures contract, with the expiration date on the option being shortly after the delivery date on the futures contract.[25] Figure 21.11 provides a set of

[25] The near-simultaneous quarterly expiration of (1) options on individual stocks and market indices, (2) futures on market indices, and (3) options on market index futures has been referred to as the **triple witching hour**. When it occurs, the stock market is allegedly roiled, particularly in the latter part of the day. See Hans R.

quotations on some of the more frequently traded ones. As the figure shows, there are both put and call options on futures. Thus, an investor can be either a buyer or a writer of either a put or a call option on a futures contract.[26] Five futures options are traded on Canadian exchanges: commodity contracts (barley, canola, feedwheet and flaxseed) trade on the WCE, and a bond futures contract trades on the Montreal exchange.

CALL OPTIONS ON FUTURES CONTRACTS

If a call option on a futures contract is exercised, then the writer must deliver the appropriate futures contract to the buyer — that is, the writer must assume a short position in the futures contract while the buyer assumes the long position. For example, consider the buyer of a call option on May barley futures where the exercise price is 155 (that is, \$155) per tonne. Because the futures contract is for 20 tonnes, the total exercise price is 20 × 155 = \$3100. If the buyer purchased this option at the settle price on December 28, 1995, which is given in Figure 21.11, then the buyer would have paid the writer a premium of 30.60 (that is, \$30.60) per tonne, or \$612 (20 × 30.60) in total.

Now, if the buyer subsequently decides to exercise this option, then the writer of this option must deliver a May barley futures contract to the buyer. Furthermore, this futures contract will be fully marked to market at the time it is delivered. In the example, assume that the option is exercised in February when May barley futures are selling for \$205 per tonne. The call writer must then provide the call buyer with a May barley futures contract that has a delivery price of \$155, which has been marked to market. This can be accomplished in two steps. First, the writer must purchase a May barley futures contract and deliver it to the call buyer. Because the cost of the futures will be \$205 per tonne (the current market price of May barley futures), this is costless to the call writer. Second, the futures contract that has been delivered must be marked to market, which is done by having the call writer pay the call buyer an amount of cash equal to \$50 (205 – 155) per tonne, or 50 × 20 = \$1000 in aggregate. Thus the call writer has lost \$388 (\$1000 – 612) while the call buyer has made an equivalent amount.

Whereas this example has shown what happens when the call is exercised, it should be noted that most futures options are not exercised. Instead, just as with most options and futures, buyers and writers of futures options typically make reversing trades before the expiration date.

PUT OPTIONS ON FUTURES CONTRACTS

If a put option on a futures contract is exercised, then the writer must accept delivery of the appropriate futures contract from the buyer — that is, the writer must assume a long

Stoll and Robert E. Whaley, "Program Trading and Expiration Day Effects," *Financial Analysts Journal* 43, no. 2 (March/April 1987): 16–28; Arnold Kling, "How the Stock Market Can Learn to Live with Index Futures and Options," *Financial Analysts Journal* 43, no. 5 (September/October 1987): 33–39; and G. J. Santoni, "Has Programmed Trading Made Stock Prices More Volatile?" *Federal Reserve Bank of St. Louis Review* 69, no. 5 (May 1987): 18–29.

[26] For more on futures options, see Chapter 12 of the *Commodity Trading Manual*. For a computer program that can be used to determine the "true" value of these complex contracts, see Chapter 8 of Stuart M. Turnbull, *Option Valuation* (Holt, Rinehart and Winston of Canada, 1987).

Figure 21.11

Quotations for futures options contracts.

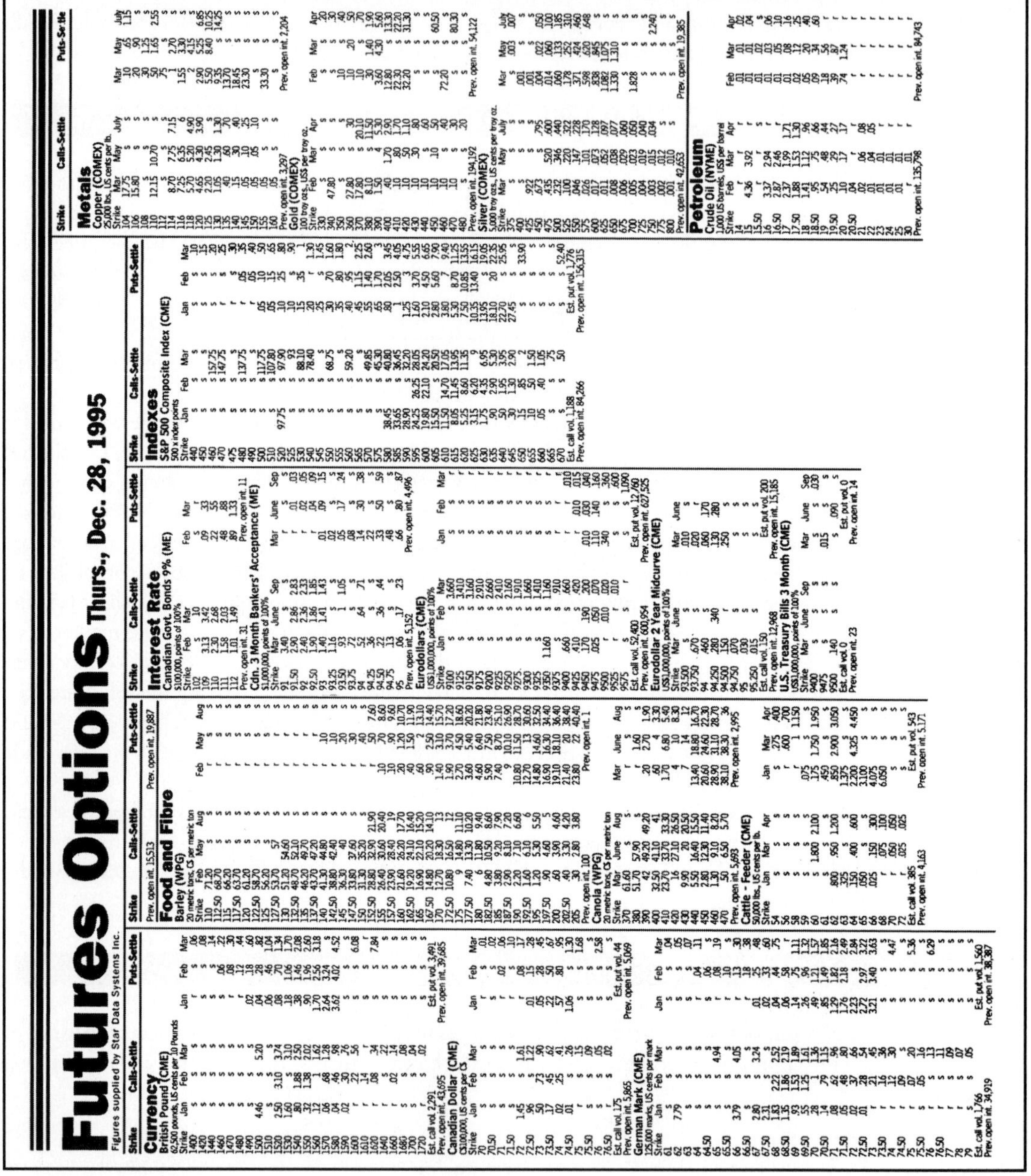

Futures Options Thurs., Dec. 28, 1995

Figures supplied by Star Data Systems Inc.

Currency

British Pound (CME)

62,500 pounds, US cents per 10 Pounds

Strike	Calls-Settle Jan	Calls-Settle Feb	Calls-Settle Mar	Puts-Settle Jan	Puts-Settle Feb	Puts-Settle Mar
1400	s	s	s	r	s	.06
1420	s	s	s	s	s	.08
1440	s	s	s	s	s	.14
1460	s	s	s	s	.06	.22
1470	s	s	s	r	.08	.30
1480	s	s	s	r	.12	.44
1490	s	s	s	.02	.18	.60
1500	4.46	s	5.20	.04	.28	.82
1510	s	s	s	.06	.46	1.04
1520	2.50	3.10	3.74	.08	.70	1.34
1530	1.60	s	3.10	.18	1.06	1.70
1540	.80	1.88	2.50	.38	1.46	2.08
1550	.32	1.38	2.02	.90	1.96	2.60
1560	.12	1	1.62	1.70	2.56	3.18
1570	.06	.68	1.28	2.64	3.24	s
1580	.04	.46	.98	3.62	4.02	4.52
1590	.02	.30	.76	s	s	s
1600	r	.22	.56	s	s	6.08
1610	r	.14	r	s	s	r
1620	r	.08	.34	s	s	7.84
1640	r	s	.22	s	s	s
1660	r	.02	.14	s	s	s
1680	s	s	.08	s	s	s
1700	s	s	.04	s	s	s
1720	r	s	.02	s	s	s

Est. call vol. 2,291 — Est. put vol. 3,491

Prev. open int. 43,695 — Prev. open int. 39,685

Canadian Dollar (CME)

C$100,000, US cents per C$

Strike	Calls-Settle Jan	Calls-Settle Feb	Calls-Settle Mar	Puts-Settle Jan	Puts-Settle Feb	Puts-Settle Mar
70	s	s	s	r	s	.01
70.50	s	s	s	s	s	.02
71	s	s	s	r	.02	.06
71.50	s	s	s	r	s	.10
72	1.45	s	1.61	r	.08	.17
72.50	.96	s	1.22	.01	.15	.28
73	.50	.73	.90	.05	.28	.45
73.50	.17	.45	.62	.22	.50	.67
74	.02	.25	.41	.57	.80	.95
74.50	.01	s	.26	1.06	s	1.30
75	r	s	.15	s	s	1.68
75.50	s	s	.09	s	s	s
76	s	s	.05	s	s	2.58
76.50	r	s	.02	s	s	s

Est. call vol. 175 — Est. put vol. 44

Prev. open int. 5,865 — Prev. open int. 5,069

German Mark (CME)

125,000 marks, US cents per mark

Strike	Calls-Settle Jan	Calls-Settle Feb	Calls-Settle Mar	Puts-Settle Jan	Puts-Settle Feb	Puts-Settle Mar
61	s	s	s	s	s	.04
62	7.79	s	s	s	s	.05
63	s	s	s	s	s	.07
64	s	s	s	r	.04	.11
64.50	s	s	s	s	.06	s
65	s	s	4.94	r	.08	.19
65.50	s	s	s	r	.10	s
66	3.79	s	4.05	r	.13	.30
66.50	s	s	s	r	.18	.38
67	2.80	s	3.24	.01	.25	.48
67.50	2.31	s	s	.02	.33	.60
68	1.83	2.22	2.52	.04	.44	.75
68.50	1.35	1.86	2.19	.06	.58	r
69	.93	1.53	1.89	.14	.75	1.11
69.50	.55	1.25	1.61	.26	.96	1.32
70	.28	1	1.36	.49	1.21	1.57
70.50	.14	.79	1.15	.85	1.49	1.85
71	.08	.62	.96	1.29	1.82	2.16
71.50	.05	.48	.80	1.76	2.18	2.49
72	.02	.37	.66	2.23	s	2.84
72.50	.01	.28	.54	2.72	2.97	3.22
73	r	.21	.45	3.21	3.40	3.63
73.50	r	.16	.36	s	s	s
74	r	.12	.30	s	s	4.47
74.50	r	.09	s	s	s	s
75	r	.07	.20	s	s	5.36
75.50	s	.05	.16	s	s	s
76	r	s	.13	s	s	6.29
76.50	r	s	.11	s	s	s
77	r	s	.09	s	s	s
78	r	s	.07	s	s	s
79	s	s	.05	s	s	s

Est. call vol. 1,766 — Est. put vol. 1,560

Prev. open int. 34,919 — Prev. open int. 38,387

Prev. open int. 15,513 — Prev. open int. 19,887

Food and Fibre

Barley (WPG)

20 metric tons, C$ per metric ton

Strike	Calls-Settle Feb	Calls-Settle May	Calls-Settle Aug	Puts-Settle Feb	Puts-Settle May	Puts-Settle Aug
110	71.20	s	s	r	s	s
112.50	68.70	s	s	r	s	s
115	66.20	s	s	r	s	s
117.50	63.70	s	s	r	s	s
120	61.20	s	s	r	s	s
122.50	58.70	s	s	r	s	s
125	56.20	s	s	r	s	s
127.50	53.70	57	s	r	r	s
130	51.20	54.60	s	r	r	s
132.50	48.70	52.10	s	r	r	s
135	46.20	49.70	s	r	r	s
137.50	43.70	47.20	s	r	r	s
140	41.30	44.80	s	r	.10	s
142.50	38.80	42.40	s	r	.10	s
145	36.30	40	s	r	.20	s
147.50	33.80	37.60	s	r	.30	s
150	31.30	35.20	s	r	.40	s
152.50	28.80	32.90	21.90	r	.50	7.60
155	26.40	30.60	20.40	.10	.70	8.60
157.50	23.90	28.40	19	.10	.90	9.60
160	21.60	26.20	17.70	.20	1.20	10.70
162.50	19.20	24.10	16.40	.40	1.50	11.90
165	16.90	22.10	15.20	.60	2	13.10
167.50	14.80	20.20	14.10	.90	2.50	14.40
170	12.70	18.30	13	1.40	3.10	15.70
172.50	10.80	16.50	12	1.90	3.70	17.20
175	9	14.80	11.10	2.70	4.50	18.60
177.50	7.40	13.30	10.20	3.60	5.40	20.20
180	6	11.80	9.40	4.60	6.40	21.80
182.50	4.80	10.50	8.60	5.90	7.50	23.40
185	3.80	9.20	7.90	7.40	8.70	25.10
187.50	2.90	8.10	7.20	9	10.10	26.90
190	2.20	7.10	6.60	10.80	11.50	28.70
192.50	1.60	6.10	6	12.70	13	30.60
195	1.20	5.30	5.50	14.80	14.60	32.50
197.50	.90	4.60	5	16.90	16.30	34.40
200	.60	3.90	4.60	19.10	18.10	36.40
202.50	.40	3.30	4.20	21.40	20	38.40
205	.30	2.80	3.80	23.80	22	40.40

Prev. open int. 100 — Prev. open int. 1

Canola (WPG)

20 metric tons, C$ per metric ton

Strike	Calls-Settle Mar	Calls-Settle June	Calls-Settle Aug	Puts-Settle Mar	Puts-Settle June	Puts-Settle Aug
370	61.60	s	s	r	s	s
380	51.70	57.90	s	r	1.60	s
390	42	49.20	49.20	.20	2.70	1.90
400	32.50	41.10	41	.60	4	3.30
410	23.70	33.70	33.30	1.70	6.80	5.40
420	16	27.10	26.50	4	10	8.30
430	9.90	20	20.50	7	14	12
440	5.50	16.40	15.50	13.40	18.80	16.70
450	2.80	12.30	11.40	20.60	24.60	22.30
460	1.30	9.10	8.20	28.90	31.10	28.70
470	.50	6.50	5.70	38.10	38.30	36

Prev. open int. 5,693 — Prev. open int. 2,995

Cattle - Feeder (CME)

50,000 lbs., US cents per lb.

Strike	Calls-Settle Jan	Calls-Settle Mar	Calls-Settle Apr	Puts-Settle Jan	Puts-Settle Mar	Puts-Settle Apr
54	s	s	s	s	.275	.400
56	s	s	s	r	.600	.700
58	s	s	s	r	1	1.150
59	s	s	s	.075	s	s
60	s	1.800	2.100	.175	1.750	1.950
61	s	s	s	.450	s	s
62	.800	.950	1.200	.850	2.900	3.050
63	.325	s	s	1.375	s	s
64	.150	.400	.600	2.200	4.325	4.450
65	.050	s	s	3.100	s	s
66	.025	.150	.300	4.075	s	s
68	r	.075	.100	6.050	s	s
70	r	.050	.050	s	s	s
72	r	.025	.025	s	s	s

Est. call vol. 385 — Est. put vol. 543

Prev. open int. 4,163 — Prev. open int. 5,171

Interest Rate

Canadian Govt. Bonds 9% (ME)

$100,000, points of 100%

Strike	Calls-Settle Feb	Calls-Settle Mar	Puts-Settle Feb	Puts-Settle Mar
102	s	10	s	r
109	3.13	3.42	.09	.33
110	2.30	2.68	.22	.55
111	1.58	2.03	.48	.88
112	1.01	1.49	.89	1.33

Prev. open int. 31 — Prev. open int. 11

Cdn. 3 Month Bankers' Acceptance (ME)

$1,000,000, points of 100%

Strike	Calls-Settle Mar	Calls-Settle June	Calls-Settle Sep	Puts-Settle Mar	Puts-Settle June	Puts-Settle Sep
91	3.40	s	s	r	s	s
91.50	2.90	2.86	2.83	r	.01	.03
92	2.40	2.36	2.33	r	.02	.05
92.50	1.90	1.86	1.85	r	.04	.09
93	1.40	1.41	1.43	.01	.09	.15
93.25	1.16	s	s	.02	s	s
93.50	.93	1	1.05	.05	.17	.24
93.75	.72	s	s	.08	s	s
94	.52	.64	.71	.14	.30	.38
94.25	.36	s	s	.22	s	s
94.50	.22	.36	.44	.33	.50	.59
94.75	.13	s	s	.48	s	s
95	.06	.17	.23	.66	.80	.87

Prev. open int. 5,152 — Prev. open int. 4,496

Eurodollars (CME)

US$1,000,000, points of 100%

Strike	Calls-Settle Jan	Calls-Settle Feb	Calls-Settle Mar	Puts-Settle Jan	Puts-Settle Feb	Puts-Settle Mar
9100	s	s	3.660	s	s	r
9125	s	s	3.410	s	s	r
9150	s	s	3.160	s	s	r
9175	s	s	2.910	s	s	r
9200	s	s	2.660	s	s	r
9225	s	s	2.410	s	s	r
9250	s	s	2.160	s	s	r
9275.	s	s	1.910	s	s	r
9300	s	s	1.660	s	s	r
9325	s	s	1.410	s	s	r
9350	1.160	s	1.160	s	s	r
9375	s	s	.910	r	r	r
9400	.660	s	.660	r	r	.010
9425	.410	s	.420	r	.010	.015
9450	.170	.190	.200	.010	.030	.040
9475	.025	.050	.070	.110	.140	.160
9500	r	.010	.020	.340	s	.360
9525	r	r	.010	s	s	.600
9575	s	s	r	s	s	1.090

Est. call vol. 52,400 — Est. put vol. 12,760

Prev. open int. 600,954 — Prev. open int. 627,525

Eurodollar 2 Year Midcurve (CME)

US$1,000,000, points of 100%

Strike	Calls-Settle Mar	Calls-Settle June	Puts-Settle Mar	Puts-Settle June
93.500	s	s	.010	s
93.750	.670	s	.020	r
94	.460	s	.060	.170
94.250	.280	.340	.130	.280
94.500	.150	r	.250	s
94.750	.070	s	s	s
95	.030	s	s	s
95.250	.015	s	s	s

Est. call vol. 150 — Est. put vol. 200

Prev. open int. 12,968 — Prev. open int. 15,185

U.S. Treasury Bills 3 Month (CME)

US$1,000,000, points of 100%

Strike	Calls-Settle Mar	Calls-Settle June	Calls-Settle Sep	Puts-Settle Mar	Puts-Settle June	Puts-Settle Sep
9400	s	s	s	s	s	.030
9475	s	s	s	.015	s	s
9500	.140	s	s	s	.090	s

Est. call vol. 0 — Est. put vol. 0

Prev. open int. 23 — Prev. open int. 14

Indexes

S&P 500 Composite Index (CME)

500 x index points

Strike	Calls-Settle Jan	Calls-Settle Feb	Calls-Settle Mar	Puts-Settle Jan	Puts-Settle Feb	Puts-Settle Mar
440	s	s	s	s	s	.10
450	s	s	s	s	s	.15
460	s	s	157.75	s	s	.20
470	s	s	147.75	r	s	.25
475	s	s	s	r	s	.30
480	s	s	137.75	r	.05	.35
490	s	s	s	r	.05	.40
500	s	s	117.75	.05	.10	.50
510	s	s	107.80	.05	.15	.65
520	97.75	s	97.90	.10	.25	.80
525	s	s	93	.10	s	.90
530	s	s	88.10	.15	.35	1
540	s	s	78.40	.20	r	1.30
545	s	s	s	.25	s	1.45
550	s	s	68.75	.30	.70	1.60
555	s	s	s	.35	.80	1.80
560	s	s	59.20	.40	.95	2.
565	s	s	s	.45	1.15	2.25
570	s	s	49.85	.55	1.40	2.60
575	s	s	45.30	.65	1.70	3
580	38.45	s	40.80	.80	2.05	3.45
585	33.65	s	36.45	1	2.50	4.05
590	28.90	s	32.20	1.25	3	4.75
595	24.25	26.25	28.05	1.60	3.70	5.55
600	19.80	22.10	24.20	2.10	4.50	6.65
605	15.50	s	20.50	2.80	5.60	7.90
610	11.50	14.70	17.05	3.80	7	9.40
615	8.05	11.45	13.95	5.30	8.70	11.25
620	5.25	8.60	11.35	7.50	10.85	13.55
625	3.15	6.20	9	10.35	13.40	16.15
630	1.75	4.35	6.95	13.95	s	19.05
635	.90	2.90	5.30	18.10	20	22.35
640	.50	1.95	3.95	22.70	s	25.95
645	.30	1.30	2.90	27.45	s	s
650	.15	.85	2	s	s	33.90
655	.10	.50	1.50	s	s	s
660	.05	.40	1.05	s	s	s
665	s	s	.75	s	s	s
670	s	s	.50	s	s	52.40

Est. call vol. 1,188 — Est. put vol. 1,776

Prev. open int. 84,266 — Prev. open int. 156,315

Metals

Copper (COMEX)

25,000 lbs., US cents per lb.

Strike	Calls-Settle Mar	Calls-Settle May	Calls-Settle July	Puts-Settle Mar	Puts-Settle May	Puts-Settle July
104	17.75	s	s	.10	.65	1.15
106	15.80	s	s	.20	.90	s
108	s	s	s	.30	1.25	s
110	12.15	10.70	s	.50	1.65	2.55
112	s	s	s	.75	s	s
114	8.70	7.75	7.15	1	2.70	s
116	7.25	6.35	6	1.55	3.30	s
118	5.70	5.20	4.90	2	4.15	s
120	4.65	4.30	3.90	2.90	5.25	6.85
125	2.20	2.45	s	5.50	8.40	10.25
130	1.05	1.30	1.30	9.35	s	14.25
135	.40	.60	.70	13.70	s	s
140	.15	.30	.40	18.45	s	s
145	.05	.10	.25	23.30	s	s
150	.05	.05	.10	s	s	s
155	.05	s	s	33.30	s	s
160	.05	s	s	s	s	s

Prev. open int. 3,297 — Prev. open int. 2,204

Gold (COMEX)

100 troy ozs., US$ per troy oz.

Strike	Calls-Settle Feb	Calls-Settle Mar	Calls-Settle Apr	Puts-Settle Feb	Puts-Settle Mar	Puts-Settle Apr
330	s	s	s	s	s	.20
340	47.80	s	s	s	s	.30
350	s	s	s	.10	s	.40
360	27.80	s	30	.10	.20	.50
370	17.80	s	20.10	.10	s	.70
380	8.10	s	11.50	.30	1.40	1.90
390	1.50	4	5.30	3.60	4.30	5.60
400	.40	1.70	2.90	12.80	s	13.30
410	.10	.80	1.70	22.30	s	22.20
420	.10	.50	1.10	32.20	s	31.30
430	.10	.30	.80	s	s	s
440	.10	s	.60	s	s	s
450	.10	.10	.50	s	s	60.50
460	.10	s	.40	72.20	s	s
470	.10	s	.30	s	s	80.30
480	s	s	.20	s	s	s

Prev. open int. 194,192 — Prev. open int. 54,122

Silver (COMEX)

5,000 troy ozs., US cents per troy oz.

Strike	Calls-Settle Mar	Calls-Settle May	Calls-Settle July	Puts-Settle Mar	Puts-Settle May	Puts-Settle July
375	s	s	s	s	.003	.007
400	s	s	s	.001	s	s
425	.922	s	s	.001	s	s
450	.673	s	.795	.004	.022	.050
475	.435	.520	.600	.014	.060	.100
500	.232	.346	.440	.060	.133	.185
525	.100	.220	.322	.178	.252	.310
550	.046	.147	.228	.371	.424	.460
575	.026	.101	.170	.598	.620	.648
600	.017	.073	.128	.838	.845	s
625	.011	.052	.097	1.082	1.075	s
650	.008	.038	.077	1.330	1.310	s
675	.006	.029	.060	s	s	s
700	.005	.023	.050	1.828	s	s
725	.004	.019	.040	s	s	s
750	.003	.015	.034	s	s	2.240
775	.002	.012	s	s	s	s
800	.001	.010	s	s	s	s

Prev. open int. 42,653 — Prev. open int. 19,385

Petroleum

Crude Oil (NYME)

1,000 US barrels, US$ per barrel

Strike	Calls-Settle Feb	Calls-Settle Mar	Calls-Settle Apr	Puts-Settle Feb	Puts-Settle Mar	Puts-Settle Apr
14	r	r	r	.01	.01	.02
15	4.36	3.92	r	.01	.01	.04
15.50	r	r	s	.01	.02	s
16	3.37	2.94	r	.01	.03	.06
16.50	2.87	2.46	r	.01	.05	.10
17	2.37	1.99	1.71	.01	.08	.16
17.50	1.88	1.53	1.30	.02	.12	.25
18	1.41	1.12	.96	.05	.20	.40
18.50	.95	.75	.66	.09	.34	.60
19	.54	.48	.44	.18	.56	r
19.50	.25	.29	.27	.39	.87	r
20	.10	.17	.17	.74	1.24	r
20.50	.04	r	r	r	r	r
21	.02	.06	.08	r	r	r
22	.01	.04	.05	r	r	r
23	.01	.01	r	r	r	r
24	.01	.01	r	r	r	r
25	.01	.01	r	r	r	r
30	r	.01	r	r	r	r

Prev. open int. 135,798 — Prev. open int. 84,743

SOURCE: Reprinted with permission of *The Financial Post* (December 29, 1995).

position in the futures contract while the buyer assumes the short position. For example, consider the buyer of a put option on May barley where the exercise price is 155, meaning $155 per tonne or $3100 in total because the futures contract is for 20 tonnes. If the buyer purchased this put at the settlement price on December 28, 1995, as shown in Figure 21.11, then the buyer would have paid the writer a premium of .70 per tonne, or $14 (20 × .70) in total.

Now, if the buyer subsequently decides to exercise this option, then the writer of this option must accept delivery of a May barley futures contract from the buyer. Furthermore, this futures contract must be fully marked to market at the time it is delivered. In the example, assume that the option is exercised in April when May barley futures are selling for 105 per tonne. What happens in April is that the put buyer will become the seller of a May barley futures contract where the purchase price is $105 per tonne. That is, when this contract is marked to market, the put writer must pay the put buyer an amount of cash equal to $50 (155 – 105) per tonne, or $1000 (50 × 20) in aggregate. Thus, the put writer has lost $986 ($1000 – $14), whereas the put buyer has made an equivalent amount.

Again, it should be kept in mind that most put options on futures are not exercised. Instead, these option buyers and writers typically enter reversing trades sometime before the expiration date.

In summary, the positions of futures options buyers and writers in the futures contracts upon exercise by the buyer are as follows:

	Buyer	*Seller*
Call	Long	Short
Put	Short	Long

As mentioned earlier, neither a writer nor a buyer needs to maintain his or her position. Both are free to enter into offsetting trades at any time, even after the buyer has exercised the option (but then the offsetting trade would be made in the futures market).

COMPARISON WITH FUTURES

At this point it is worthwhile to think about the distinctions between futures and futures options. In doing so, consider an investor who is contemplating *buying* a futures contract. If this contract is purchased, the investor can potentially make or lose a great deal of money. In particular, if the price of the asset rises substantially, then so will the price of the futures, and the investor will have made a sizeable profit. In contrast, if the price of the asset drops substantially, then the investor will have lost a sizeable amount of money.

In comparison, if the investor had bought a futures call option on the asset, then the investor would also make a sizeable profit if the price of the asset rose substantially. Unlike futures, however, if the price of the asset dropped, then the investor need not worry about incurring a sizeable loss. Instead, only the premium (the price paid to buy the futures option) would be lost. This does not mean that purchasing a futures call option is "better" than purchasing a futures contract. Why? Because the protection on the downside that an investor gets from buying a futures call option is paid for in the form of the premium. This premium would not be present if the investor had bought a futures contract instead.

Consider next an investor who is contemplating *selling* a futures contract. In doing so, the investor can potentially make a great deal of money if the price of the asset declines substantially. However, if the price of the asset rises substantially, then the investor will have lost a sizeable amount of money.

In comparison, the investor could buy a futures put option on the asset. The investor would make a sizeable profit if the price of the asset declined substantially. Unlike futures, however, if the price of the asset rose, then the investor need not worry about incurring a sizeable loss. Instead, only the premium would be lost. Again, this does not mean that purchasing a futures put option is "better" than selling a futures contract.

COMPARISON WITH OPTIONS

Having established that futures options can exist if futures already exist, one may wonder why futures options exist if options already exist. For example, there are futures options and options on Japanese yen (as well as futures on Japanese yen). The commonly given reason why futures options exist in such a situation is that it is easier to make or take delivery of a futures contract on the asset, as required by the futures options contract, than to make or take delivery in the asset itself, as required by the options contract. That is, the deliverable asset in the case of the Japanese yen futures option contract is a futures contract in Japanese yen, which is more easily delivered than Japanese yen, as required for the options contract.

In addition, there is sometimes more timely price information on the deliverable asset for the futures option contract (namely, price information on the futures contract) than on the deliverable asset for the options contract (namely, price information in the spot market).

For these reasons (although they are not compelling for certain contracts), futures, futures options, and options can exist simultaneously with the same underlying asset.

QUESTIONS AND PROBLEMS

1. Distinguish between a speculator and a hedger. Give an example of a short hedger and a long hedger.
2. Using the latest *Financial Post*, for the near futures contracts in corn, orange juice, and gasoline, calculate the percentage change in the settlement price from the previous day. Find the open interest in these contracts. Into how many units of the commodities do these open-interest figures translate?
3. How do organized futures exchanges ensure that the obligations incurred as various parties enter into futures contracts are ultimately satisfied?
4. What is the purpose of initial and maintenance margins? How does marking to market affect the amount of funds held in the futures investor's margin account?
5. Lloyd Wolf sells ten June 5000-bushel corn futures at $2 per bushel. Lloyd deposits $5000 in performance margin. If the price of corn rises to $2.20 per bushel, how much equity is in Lloyd's margin account? What if corn falls to $1.80 per bushel?
6. Mai-Lin Chu has just bought four September 20 tonne canola futures contracts at $449 per tonne. The initial margin requirement is 3%. The maintenance margin requirement is 80% of the initial margin requirement.
   a. How many dollars in initial margin must Mai-Lin put up?
   b. If the September price of canola rises to $475, how much equity is in Mai-Lin's commodity account?

c. If the September price of canola falls to $436, how much equity is in Mai-Lin's commodity account? Will Mai-Lin receive a margin call?

7. How does a futures contract differ from a forward contract?
8. Do exchange-imposed price limits protect futures traders from losses that would result in the absence of such limits? Explain.
9. Cora Withrow is long a stock market futures contract and short a diversified portfolio of stocks. Would Cora prefer the basis to widen or to narrow? Why?
10. A publication used by farmers such as Mordecai Brown provides diagrams of the typical annual patterns of cash prices for a number of seasonal commodities. Should Mordecai expect that the price of a futures contract will follow the same pattern? Why?
11. In the market for a particular agricultural or natural resource commodity, what kind of market forces might lead to normal backwardation or normal contango?
12. Consider a futures contract on mangoes that calls for the delivery of 2000 pounds of the fruit three months from now. The spot price of mangoes is $2 per pound. It costs $.10 per pound to store mangoes for three months. What should be the price of this futures contract?
13. Barb Lynn owns a famous Renoir painting that has a current market value of $5 000 000. It costs Barb $200 000 annually to insure the painting, payable at the start of the year. Barb is able to loan the painting to a local art gallery for $300 000 per year, paid at the end of the year. Barb is considering selling the painting under a futures contract arrangement that calls for delivery one year from today. If the one-year risk-free rate is 5%, what is the fair value of the futures contract?
14. Tom Turner is planning a trip in six months to Germany, where he plans to purchase a BMW for 80 000 deutsche marks (DM). Using a recent *Globe and Mail,* calculate how much the purchase would cost in US dollars at the current exchange rate. Given the recent settlement price of a six-month DM futures contract, how much would Tom have to pay to hedge the cost of the BMW purchase?
15. Assume that the exchange rate between British pounds and US dollars is currently $1.80 per pound. If the six-month risk-free rate is 3% in the United States and 3.5% in Great Britain, what should the six-month futures price of US dollars in British pounds be? Why is the futures exchange rate greater or less than the current spot exchange rate?
16. The one-year futures price of the Utopian currency darmas is $2.03 per darma. The interest forgone by selling darmas in the futures market instead of the spot market is $.0591. The benefit of owning darmas instead of selling them is $.0788. If the Canadian one-year risk-free rate is 3%, according to interest rate parity, what should be the Utopian one-year risk-free rate?
17. What should be the price of a three-month 90-day Treasury bill futures contract if the spot price of a six-month Treasury bill is currently $98 and the three-month risk-free rate is 1%?
18. Stella Paravano believes that the spread between long-term and short-term interest rates is going to narrow in the next few months but does not know in which direction interest rates in general will move. What financial futures position would permit Stella to profit from this forecast if it is correct?
19. Suzy Markotic bought five TSE 35 December futures contracts at 310. If the TSE 35 index rises to 318, what is Suzy's dollar profit?
20. Why does hedging a common stock portfolio using stock index futures work best if the portfolio being hedged is very similar to the underlying stock index of the futures contract?

21. Assume that the TSE 35 currently has a value of 200 (in "index" terms). The dividend yield on the underlying stocks in the index is expected to be 4% over the next six months. New-issue six-month Treasury bills now sell for a six-month yield of 6%.
   a. What is the theoretical value of a six-month futures contract on the TSE 35?
   b. What potential problems are inherent in this calculation?
22. In December 19X1 Jill Hamner bought a January 19X2 gold futures contract on the New York Commodity Exchange for $487.50 per ounce. Simultaneously, Jill sold an October 19X3 contract for $614.80. At the time, yields on Treasury notes with 1.75 years to maturity were 10.50%. Will this transaction be profitable for Jill? What factors are relevant to making this calculation?
23. In each of the following situations, discuss how Luc Sanio might use stock index futures to protect a well-diversified stock portfolio:
   a. Luc expects to receive a sizeable bonus cheque next month and would like to invest in stocks, believing that current stock market prices are extremely attractive (but realizing they may not remain so for long).
   b. Luc expects the stock market to decline dramatically very soon and realizes that selling a stock portfolio quickly would result in significant transaction costs.
   c. Luc has a large, unrealized gain and for tax purposes would like to defer the gain until the next tax year, which is several weeks away.
24. Does the fair value of a stock index futures contract depend on investors' expectations about the future value of the underlying stock index? Why?
25. Slava Swacina, a futures investor who has lost considerable sums in futures investments, said, "Even though I don't directly borrow to invest in futures, the performance of my investments acts as if I were highly leveraged." Is Slava correct? Why?
26. (Appendix Question) Distinguish between futures contracts and options on futures contracts.
27. (Appendix Question) Maya Swander buys a call option on a March 5000-bushel soybean futures contract. The call costs $.50 per bushel and has an exercise price of $5.25 per bushel. If Maya exercises the option in February at a price of $5.55 per bushel, what is Maya's return on investment in the option?

CFA Exam Questions

28. Robert Chen, CFA, is reviewing the characteristics of derivative securities and their use in portfolios.
   a. Chen is considering the addition of either a short position in stock index futures or a long position in stock index options to an existing well-diversified portfolio of equity securities. Contrast the way in which each of these two alternatives would affect the risk and return of the resulting combined portfolios.
   b. Four factors affect the value of a futures contract on a stock index. Three of these factors are: the current price of the stock index, the time remaining until the contract maturity (delivery) date, and the dividends on the stock index. Identify the fourth factor and explain how and why changes in this factor affect the value of the futures contract.
   c. Six factors affect the value of call options on stocks. Three of these factors are: the current price of the stock, the time remaining until the option expires, and the dividend on the stock. Identify the other three factors and explain how and why changes in each of these three factors affect the value of call options.

29. The foundation's grant-making and investment policy issues have been finalized. Receipt of the expected $45 million Franklin cash gift will not occur for 90 days, yet the committee believes current stock and bond prices are unusually attractive and wishes to take advantage of this perceived opportunity.

a. Briefly describe two strategies which utilize derivative financial instruments and could be implemented to take advantage of the committee's market expectations.

b. Evaluate whether or not it is appropriate for the foundation to undertake a derivatives-based hedge to bridge the expected 90-day time gap, considering both positive and negative factors.

KEY TERMS

futures
speculators
hedgers
short hedger
long hedger
reversing trade
spot market
spot price
open interest
performance margin
marking to market
basis
basis risk
speculating on the basis
expectations hypothesis
normal backwardation
normal contango
cost of carry
interest-rate parity
index arbitrage
synthetic futures contract
futures options
triple witching hour

REFERENCES

1. Many books either are devoted exclusively to futures or have futures as one of their primary subjects. Most cover everything discussed in this chapter in more detail and with a more complete list of citations. Here are a few:

Stephen Figlewski, *Hedging with Financial Futures for Institutional Investors* (Cambridge, MA: Ballinger, 1986).

Edward W. Schwarz, Joanne M. Hill, and Thomas Schneeweis, *Financial Futures* (Homewood, IL: Richard D. Irwin, 1986).

Commodity Trading Manual (Chicago: Chicago Board of Trade, 1989).

Darrell Duffie, *Futures Markets* (Englewood Cliffs, NJ: Prentice Hall, 1989).

Daniel R. Siegel and Diane F. Siegel, *Futures Markets* (Hinsdale, IL: Dryden Press, 1990).

Don M. Chance, *An Introduction to Options & Futures* (Fort Worth, TX: Dryden Press, 1991).

Alan L. Tucker, *Financial Futures, Options, & Swaps* (St. Paul, MN: West, 1991).

David A. Dubofsky, *Options and Financial Futures* (New York: McGraw-Hill, 1992).

John C. Hull, *Options, Futures, and Other Derivative Securities* (Englewood Cliffs, NJ: Prentice Hall, 1993).

Hans R. Stoll and Robert E. Whaley, *Futures and Options* (Cincinnati, OH: South-Western, 1993).

Robert T. Daigler, *Financial Futures and Markets: Concepts and Strategies* (New York: HarperCollins, 1994).

Robert W. Kolb, *Understanding Futures Markets* (Miami, FL: Kolb, 1994).

2. For a discussion of the market structure of futures exchanges, see:

Sanford J. Grossman and Merton H. Miller, "Liquidity and Market Structure," *Journal of Finance* 43, no. 3 (July 1988): 617–633.

Michael J. Fishman and Francis A. Longstaff, "Dual Trading in Futures Markets," *Journal of Finance* 47, no. 2 (June 1992): 643–671.

3. For a more complete discussion of margin and marking to market, see:

Robert W. Kolb, Gerald D. Gay, and William C. Hunter, "Liquidity Requirements for Financial Futures Investments," *Financial Analysts Journal* 41, no. 3 (May/June 1985): 60–68.

Don M. Chance, *The Effect of Margins on the Volatility of Stock and Derivative Markets: A Review of the Evidence*, Monograph Series in Finance and Economics no. 1990–2, New York University Salomon Center, Leonard N. Stern School of Business.

Ann Kremer, "Clarifying Marking to Market," *Journal of Financial Education* 20 (November 1991): 17–25.

4. The concepts of spreads and basis are discussed in:

Martin L. Leibowitz, *The Analysis of Value and Volatility in Financial Futures*, Monograph Series in Finance and Economics no. 1981–3, New York University Salomon Center, Leonard N. Stern School of Business.

5. Foreign currency markets are discussed in:

J. Orlin Grabbe, *International Financial Markets* (New York: Elsevier Science, 1991), Part II.

6. Interest-rate futures were shown to be useful in immunizing bond portfolios by:

Robert W. Kolb and Gerald D. Gay, "Immunizing Bond Portfolios with Interest Rate Futures," *Financial Management* 11, no. 2 (Summer 1982): 81–89.

Jess B. Yawitz and William J. Marshall, "The Use of Futures in Immunized Portfolios," *Journal of Portfolio Management* 11, no. 2 (Spring 1985): 51–58.

7. Using futures to hedge bond portfolios is discussed in:

Richard Bookstaber and David P. Jacob, "The Composite Hedge: Controlling the Credit Risk of High-Yield Bonds," *Financial Analysts Journal* 42, no. 2 (March/April 1986): 25–35.

Robin Grieves, "Hedging Corporate Bond Portfolios," *Journal of Portfolio Management* 12, no. 4 (Summer 1986): 23–25.

8. Stock index futures and their relationship to the market crash in October 1987 have been heavily researched. Some of the papers are:

Paula A. Tosini, "Stock Index Futures and Stock Market Activity in October 1987," *Financial Analysts Journal* 44, no. 1 (January/February 1988): 28–37.

F. J. Gould, "Stock Index Futures: The Arbitrage Cycle and Portfolio Insurance," *Financial Analysts Journal* 44, no. 1 (January/February 1988): 48–62.

Lawrence Harris, "The October 1987 S&P 500 Stock-Futures Basis," *Journal of Finance* 44, no. 1 (March 1989): 77–99.

Marshall E. Blume, A. Craig MacKinlay, and Bruce Terker, "Order Imbalances and Stock Price Movements on October 19 and 20, 1987," *Journal of Finance* 44, no. 4 (September 1989): 827–848.

Lawrence Harris, "S&P 500 Cash Stock Price Volatilities," *Journal of Finance* 44, no. 5 (December 1989): 1155–1175.

Hans R. Stoll and Robert E. Whaley, "The Dynamics of Stock Index and Stock Index Futures Returns," *Journal of Financial and Quantitative Analysis* 25, no. 4 (December 1990): 441–468.

Kolak Chan, K. C. Chan, and G. Andrew Karolyi, "Intraday Volatility in the Stock Index and Stock Index Futures Markets," *Review of Financial Studies* 4, no. 4 (1991): 657–684.

Avanidhar Subrahmanyam, "A Theory of Trading in Stock Index Futures," *Review of Financial Studies* 4, no. 1 (1991): 17–51.

Kolak Chan, "A Further Analysis of the Lead-Lag Relationship Between the Cash Market and Stock Index Futures Market," *Review of Financial Studies* 5, no. 1 (1992): 123–152.

9. Papers on index arbitrage and program trading include:

A. Craig MacKinlay and Krishna Ramaswamy, "Index-Futures Arbitrage and the Behavior of Stock Index Futures Prices," *Review of Financial Studies* 1, no. 2 (Summer 1988): 137–158.

Michael J. Brennan and Eduardo S. Schwartz, "Arbitrage in Stock Index Futures," *Journal of Business* 63, no. 1, part 2 (January 1990): S7–S31.

Hans R. Stoll and Robert E. Whaley, "Program Trading and Individual Stock Returns: Ingredients of the Triple-Witching Brew," *Journal of Business* 63, no. 1, part 2 (January 1990): S165–S192.

Gary L. Gastineau, "A Short History of Program Trading," *Financial Analysts Journal* 47, no. 5 (September/October 1991): 4–7.

10. Forward and futures prices were shown to be equal when interest rates are constant over time in:

John C. Cox, Jonathan E. Ingersoll, and Stephen A. Ross, "The Relation Between Forward Prices and Futures Prices," *Journal of Financial Economics* 9, no. 4 (December 1981): 321–346.

11. The performance of commodity funds, which are investment companies that speculate in futures, has not been attractive, according to:

Edwin J. Elton, Martin J. Gruber, and Joel C. Rentzler, "Professionally Managed, Publicly Traded Commodity Funds," *Journal of Business* 60, no. 2 (April 1987): 175–199.

12. The relationships among futures, options, and futures options are discussed in:

Clifford W. Smith, Jr., Charles W. Smithson, and D. Sykes Wilford, "Managing Financial Risk," *Journal of Applied Corporate Finance* 1, no. 4 (Winter 1989): 27–48.

Clifford W. Smith, Jr., Charles W. Smithson, and D. Sykes Wilford, *Managing Financial Risk* (New York: Harper & Row, 1990).

13. The seminal paper on the pricing of futures options is:

Fischer Black, "The Pricing of Commodity Contracts," *Journal of Financial Economics* 3, nos. 1/2 (January/March 1976): 167–179.

14. For a thought-provoking book that covers futures markets, among other subjects, see:

Merton H. Miller, *Financial Innovations and Market Volatility* (Cambridge, MA: Blackwell, 1991).

15. For a Canadian perspective on the topics covered in this chapter, see:

J. E. Hore, "Trading on Canadian Futures Markets" (Toronto, Ont.: The Canadian Securities Institute, 1989).

N. T. Khoury and P. Yourougou, "Price Discovery Performance and Maturity Effects in the Canadian Feed Wheat Market," *Review of Futures Markets* 8, no. 3 (1989).

C. A. Carter and R. M. A. Lyons, "Hedging Canadian Grains and Oilseeds" (Winnipeg, Man.: The Winnipeg Commodity Exchange, 1991).

N. T. Khoury and P. Yourougou, "The Informational Content of the Basis: Evidence from Canadian Barley, Oats and Canola Futures Markets" *Review of Futures Markets* 11, no. 1 (1991).

INTERNET RESOURCES

The following investment information sources can be accessed at these Internet addresses:

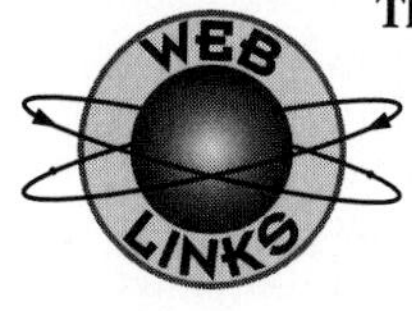

Royal Bank Currency and Credit Market Daily
http://www.RoyalBank.COM/english/fin/fin_daily/index.html
Stock and Commodity Quotes from Telenium
http://www.telenium.ca
Universal Currency Converter
http://www.xe.net/xenon/currency.html

CHAPTER **22**

Investment Companies

Investment companies are a type of financial intermediary. They obtain money from investors and use it to purchase financial assets such as stocks and bonds. In return, the investors receive certain rights regarding the financial assets the company has bought and any earnings that it may make. In the simplest and most common situation, the investment company has only one type of investor — shareholders. These shareholders directly own the investment company and thus indirectly own the financial assets that the company itself owns.

For an individual, there are two advantages to investing in such companies instead of investing directly in the financial assets these companies own: economies of scale and professional management. In describing these benefits, consider an individual with moderate financial resources who wishes to invest in the stock market. In terms of economies of scale, the individual could buy stocks in odd lots and thus have a diversified portfolio. However, the brokerage commissions on odd-lot transactions are relatively high. Alternatively, the individual could purchase round lots, but would only be able to afford a few different securities. Unfortunately, the individual would then be giving up the benefits of owning a well-diversified portfolio, in which declines in some securities would more likely be offset by gains in others.

In order to receive the benefits of diversification and substantially reduced brokerage commissions, the individual could invest in the shares of an investment company. Economies of scale make it possible for an investment company to provide diversification at a lower cost per dollar of investment than would be incurred by a small individual investor.

In terms of professional management, the individual investing directly in the stock market would have to go through all the details of investing, including making all buying and selling decisions and keeping records of all transactions for tax purposes. In doing so, the individual would have to be continually on the lookout for mispriced securities in an attempt to find undervalued ones for purchase, while selling any that were found to be overvalued. Simultaneously, the individual would have to keep track of the overall risk level of the portfolio so that it did not deviate from some desired level. However, by purchasing shares of an investment company, the individual can turn over all of these details to a professional money manager.

Many of these managers hope to identify areas of mispricing in the market, exploit them, and share the resultant abnormal gains with investors by charging them for a portion of the gains. However, it appears that they typically cannot find enough mispriced situations to recoup more than the additional costs they have incurred, costs that take the form of increased management fees and transaction costs due to the continual buying and selling of securities. Nevertheless, other potential advantages to be gained from investing in an investment company may still outweigh any disadvantages, particularly for smaller investors.

Investment companies differ in many ways, and classification is difficult. Common practice is followed here; the term is restricted to those financial intermediaries that do not obtain money from depositors. Thus, the traditional operations of trust companies and banks, for example, are excluded. However, the process of deregulation is rapidly breaking down previous barriers so that the future may very well bring even more competition for traditional investment companies.

NET ASSET VALUE

An important concept in understanding how investment companies operate is **net asset value** (NAV). Given that an investment company has assets consisting of various securities, it is generally quite easy to determine the market value of all the assets held by the investment company at the end of each business day. For example, an investment company that holds various common stocks traded on The Toronto Stock Exchange could easily find out what the closing prices of those stocks were at the end of the day and then simply multiply these prices by the number of shares that it owns. After adding up these figures, the investment company would subtract any liabilities that it had outstanding. Dividing the resulting difference by the number of outstanding shares of the investment company produces its net asset value.

Equivalently, an investment company's net asset value at the end of day t, NAV_t, can be determined by using the following equation:

$$NAV_t = \frac{MVA_t - LIAB_t}{NSO_t} \tag{22.1}$$

where MVA_t, $LIAB_t$, and NSO_t denote the market value of the investment company's assets, the dollar amount of the investment company's liabilities, and the number of shares the investment company has outstanding, respectively, as of the end of day t.

As an example, consider an investment company with 4 000 000 shares outstanding whose assets consisted of common stocks with an aggregate market value of $102 000 000 and whose liabilities amounted to $2 000 000 as of November 15. This company would report a net asset value on that date of ($102 000 000 – $2 000 000)/4 000 000 = $25 per share. This amount will change every day, as the values of either MVA_t, $LIAB_t$, and NSO_t (or of some combination of the three) will typically change daily.

Investors should note that calculating NAV_t can be difficult if some of the assets do not trade frequently. In such situations, estimates of their fair market value must be used. Referring to the previous example, what if on November 16 there were 3 800 000 shares outstanding, the liabilities were $2 200 000, but the common shares had not been traded on any market since November 15? In this situation MVA_t is often calculated by using the last bid prices for the stocks on November 16, which in the example is assumed to result in a value for MVA_t of $101 000 000.[1] Hence, the net asset value on November 16 is ($101 000 000 – $2 200 000)/3 800 000 = $26.

[1] As mentioned in Chapter 3, dealers in securities generally quote both bid and asked prices. The bid price is the amount the dealer will pay for a security; the asked price is the amount an investor must pay to purchase the security from the dealer.

MAJOR TYPES OF INVESTMENT COMPANIES

The *Investment Funds Institute of Canada* classifies **managed investment companies** as either 1. closed-end investment companies or 2. open-end investment companies or investment funds. Managed investment companies, whether incorporated or unincorporated, have a board of directors or a board of trustees to oversee the operation of the company. The board commonly hires a firm — the investment manager — to manage the company's assets for an annual fee that is typically based (at least in part) on the total market value of the assets. These management companies may be independent firms, investment advisors, firms associated with brokerage firms, or insurance companies. Often the management company is the business entity (for example, a subsidiary of a brokerage firm) that started and promoted the investment company. One management company may have contracts to manage a number of investment companies, each of which is a separate entity with its own board of directors or board of trustees.

Annual management fees average about 1.5% (they range from 0.25% to 2.8%) of the market value of the investment company's total assets, with the percentage decreasing as the assets increase. Some funds provide "incentive compensation," where the better the fund's investment performance, the higher the fee paid to the management company.

In addition to the fee paid by an investment company to its management company, there are administrative and custodial expenses. These services are usually arranged by the investment manager, but the costs are charged to the investment company. For the typical investment company, such annual expenses are roughly 0.50% of the market value of its total assets. The term "management fees" tends to be used rather loosely; it includes administrative and custodial expenses in some cases and not in others. In order to compare costs on a uniform basis, the industry has defined the **management expense ratio** to be the total costs divided by the average net monthly assets for the year. The total costs include all fees paid by the fund (to the investment company and any third parties) except brokerage fees.

► Closed-End Investment Companies

Closed-end investment companies (or closed-end funds) are not very popular in Canada. These companies issue a specific number of shares at their inception. The number remains unchanged until such time as additional shares are issued. Their shares are traded either on an organized exchange or in the over-the-counter market. Thus, an investor who wants to buy or sell shares of a closed-end fund simply places an order with a broker, just as if he or she wanted to buy or sell shares of BCE.

Most closed-end funds have unlimited lives. Dividends and interest received and any net capital gains realized by a closed-end fund are paid out to its shareholders. However, most funds allow (and encourage) the reinvestment of such payments. The fund keeps the money and sends the investor additional shares based on the net asset value per share at that time. For example, consider a closed-end fund that has just declared a dividend of $1 per share. If its net asset value were $15 per share, a holder of 30 shares would have a choice of receiving either $30 (= 30 × $1) or 2 shares ($30/$15).

Being a corporation, closed-end funds can issue new shares not only through reinvestment plans but also with public stock offerings. However, this is done infrequently, and the fund's capital structure is closed most of the time.

Although it is seldom done, most closed-end funds can repurchase their own shares in the open market. If a fund's market price falls substantially below net asset value, a repurchase will increase the fund's net asset value per share. For example, if net asset value were $20 per share at a time when the fund's shares could be purchased in the open market (say, on the Toronto Stock Exchange) for $16 per share, the managers of the fund could sell $20 worth of securities from the fund's portfolio, buy back one of the fund's outstanding shares, and have $4 left over. If the $4 were used to buy securities for the fund, the net asset value per share would increase, with the size of the increase depending, in addition to the number of shares repurchased and their repurchase price, on the number of remaining shares.

Provided that the closed-end funds are listed on an exchange or traded actively in the over-the-counter market their market prices are published daily in the financial press. However, their net asset values are only published weekly, based on closing market prices for securities in their portfolios as of the previous Friday. Figure 22.1 provides an example. Both the net asset value and the market value based on either the closing or bid price at which the fund's shares traded on the day in question are shown. The final column indicates the percentage difference between each fund's share price and its net asset value. If this difference is positive (meaning the share price is greater than the NAV), the fund's shares are said to be selling at a premium. Conversely, if this difference is negative (meaning the share price is less than the NAV), the fund's shares are said to be selling at a discount. For example, Figure 22.1 indicates that the First Australia Prime Income fund was selling at a discount, while the Canadian World fund was selling for a premium.

▸ Open-End Investment Companies

An investment company that stands ready at all times to purchase its own shares at or near their net asset value is termed an **open-end investment company** (or investment trust or open-end fund). These include both incorporated companies or unincorporated trusts.[2] Most of these companies, commonly known as *mutual funds*, also offer new shares or units

Figure 22.1

Listing of closed-end funds.

Closed End Funds

	NAVPS	Market value per share	Discount(-) premium(+)
BGR Precious Metals	17.59	13.63	-22.54%
Canada Trust Income Inv. (Sep)	8.99	8.63	-4.06%
Canadian General Investments	43.03	30.38	-29.41%
Canadian World Fund	4.98	3.50	-29.72%
Central Fund of Canada	6.57	6.00	-8.68%
China Opportunities Fund	9.69	8.63	-10.99%
Diversified Mthly Incm	14.92	14.75	-1.14%
Dynamic Israel Growth	7.80	6.63	-15.06%
Economic Investment Tr.	91.63	62.50	-31.79%
First Australia Prime Income	13.04	13.38	2.57%
First Mercantile Currency	15.85	13.38	-15.62%
Health Care & Biotech.	11.04	6.75	-38.86%
MPG Investment (Oct)	10.38	7.13	-51.36%
New Altamira Value	12.28	11.75	-4.32%
Old Canada Investments (Oct)	3.56	3.00	-15.73%
Templeton Emerg Mkts App	14.21	11.75	-17.31%
Third Canadian Gen Invt.	13.56	12.25	-9.66%
United Corporations	48.52	34.75	-28.38%

All funds valued weekly on Dec 28 except as noted.

SOURCE: Reprinted by permission of *The Financial Post* (December 30, 1995).

[2] For practical purposes, except for some tax considerations that will be discussed subsequently, the differences between the two are negligible.

to the public for a price at or near their net asset values on demand. When mutual fund shareholders want to sell their shares, they usually receive an amount equal to the fund's net asset value times the number of shares sold.

Some open-end companies, known as **no-load funds**, sell their shares at a price equal to net asset value. Others, known as **load funds**, offer shares through brokers or other selling organizations, thereby adding a percentage **load charge** to the net asset value. These funds charge either a front-end load, a back-end load or, in some cases, the investor can choose between the two. With the first type, a percentage of the money contributed to the fund is deducted before it is invested. With the second type, a percentage of the proceeds from redemption is deducted before the investor receives the money. For example, a fund that charges a 5% front-end load receives $1000 from an investor and will deduct $50 immediately leaving $950 to purchase the fund's units at the current net asset value. While this is described as a 5% load charge it is, in fact, equal to 5.3% ($50/$950) of the amount ultimately invested. The same fund may give the investor the option to select a 6% back-end load instead of the front-end load. In this case, an investor who redeems $1000 worth of units will receive $940 in cash.

There have been dramatic changes in the structure of the industry in Canada over the last ten years. In 1982, load funds represented 84% of all funds. By 1993 this figure had dropped to 57%. Over the same period the typical front-end load charge fell from about 9% to under 3%.[3] Currently, the largest fund group in Canada charges a non-negotiable 2.5% front-end load or 3% back-end load on equity funds, and less on fixed income funds.

Not surprisingly, the performance of non-load funds as a whole does not differ in any notable way from that of load funds. The load charge, which goes to the selling organization, represents the cost of education and persuasion. No-load funds do not employ sales people and are generally purchased directly from the financial institution that manages them.

Figure 22.2 shows a portion of the quotations for mutual funds provided in the financial press daily.[4] Following the name is a brief description of the loading fees charged, the eligibility for RRSP investment, the method of distributing (i.e. selling) the fund and the net asset value, based on closing prices for the fund's securities on the day in question. The final column indicates the difference (in dollars) between the day's net asset value per share and that computed at the close of the previous trading day.

Figure 22.3 shows the weekly quotations that appear for a special type of mutual fund known as a money market fund. Such funds invest in short-term, fixed-income securities such as Treasury bills, commercial paper, and bank term deposits. Next to the name of such a fund is shown a brief description of the way the fund is sold, the current annualized yield, and the compounded annual yield (known as the effective yield), with the final column showing the change in the yield from the previous day. Not shown, but an important factor in deciding in which money market fund to invest, is the degree of safety (that is, default risk) associated with the assets held by each fund.

A number of institutions similar to investment companies exist. The next section describes some of the more important types of securities they offer.

---

[3] Earl Bederman, Competition and Change in the Individual Investment Market: A Study Conducted for The Investment Funds Institute of Canada, mimeo (Toronto: Investor Economics, Inc., October 1994).

[4] Funds are listed under a name in boldface type. This is the name of the common investment management company that is associated with those funds.

Figure 22.2

Listings of mutual funds (excerpts).

Canadian Mutual Funds

Recent prices of investment funds supplied by Fundata Canada Inc. at 5:45 p.m. Jan. 11. Prices reported by funds are the net asset value per share or unit last calculated and are for information purposes only. Confirmation of price should be obtained from the fund. Chg—penny change from last valuation; D—distributed by fund sponsor; G—redemption charge; I—distributed by independent dealers; L—sales charge; N—no sales charge; O—optional front-end or redemption charge; R—eligible for RRSPs; Z—not available for sale; m—minimum purchase of $150,000; u—U.S. currency; x—ex—dividend; (n)—not a member of IFIC; (Date following fund denotes last valuation).

Fund	Load	RSP	Dist	Val	Chg
ABC FUNDS					
mFully-Mgd 12/29	N	R	D	7.18	—
mFund-Value 12/29	N	R	D	9.84	—
ACADIA INVESTMENT FUNDS					
Balanced 01/10	N	R		10.49	-.06
Bond 01/10	N	R		10.47	-.03
Mortgage 01/10	N	R		10.00	unch
ADMAX REGENT GROUP					
A.Amer Perf 12/29	O		I	6.56	—
A.Amer Sel Gth	O		I	5.06	+.00
A.Asset All	O	R	I	12.31	-.01
A.Cdn Perf	O	R	I	6.58	+.02
A.Cdn Sel Gth	O	R	I	5.17	-.00
A.Glo Hlth	O		I	9.23	+.13
R.Dragon 888	O		I	7.13	+.02
R.Europa	O		I	10.32	-.06
R.Intl	O		I	6.02	+.00
R.Korea	O		I	11.35	-.05
R.Nippon	O		I	11.94	-.14
R.Tiger	O		I	11.67	-.05
R.World Inc	O	R	I	12.12	+.01
AGF GROUP C$ SERIES A					
Amer Grth	L		I	12.49	+.17
Asian Grth	L		I	15.85	+.19
Cdn Bond	L	R	I	5.27	unch
Cdn Equity	L	R	I	12.02	unch
Cdn Resources	L	R	I	15.88	-.04
China Focus	L		I	7.44	+.05
Euro Growth	L		I	9.40	-.03
Germany	L		I	19.91	-.08
Glo GovtBond	L		I	10.82	+.03
Grth & Income	L	R	I	15.51	-.05
Grth Equity	L	R	I	20.42	+.06
High Income	L	R	I	9.96	+.02
Intl ST Income	L		I	10.77	unch
Japan	L		I	5.20	-.05
Resource Cap	L	R	I	7.69	-.12
Special	L		I	10.46	+.20
Strategic Inc	L	R	I	9.93	+.02
US Income	L		I	10.66	+.01
World Equity	L		I	6.32	+.01

Fund	Load	RSP	Dist	Val	Chg
Small Cap 01/04	N	R	D	22.17	—
BNP (CANADA) FUNDS					
xBond 01/10	N	R	D	10.58	-.06
Equity 12/31	N	R	D	29.58	—
BPI CAPITAL MANAGEMENT					
Amer Equ Valu	O		I	6.78	+.02
Amer Small Co	O		I	21.93	+.04
Cdn Balanced	O	R	I	4.83	unch
Cdn Bond	O	R	I	5.13	+.04
Cdn Equ Value	O	R	I	7.29	+.01
Cdn Resource	O	R	I	19.62	+.24
Cdn Small Co	O	R	I	9.30	unch
Glo Bal RSP	O	R	I	14.53	unch
Glo Equity	O		I	17.55	-.10
Glo RSP Bond	O	R	I	10.94	+.03
Glo Real Estate	O		I	10.31	-.04
Glo Small Co	O		I	15.67	-.02
Income	O	R	I	9.94	unch
Intl Equity	O		I	7.33	-.06
N.A. Bal RSP	O	R	I	5.77	+.03
BULLOCK GROUP					
American A 01/10	L		I	21.71	—
American B 01/10	G		I	21.70	—
American C 01/10	N		I	21.69	—
American D 01/10	O		I	22.03	—
uAmr A US$ 01/10	L		I	15.91	—
uAmr D US$ 01/10	O		I	16.14	—
AsianDyn A 01/10	L		I	10.76	—
AsianDyn B 01/10	G		I	10.66	—
AsianDyn C 01/10	N		I	10.67	—
AssetStrat A 01/10	L	R	I	12.61	—
AssetStrat B 01/10	G	R	I	12.53	—
AssetStrat C 01/10	N	R	I	12.52	—
AssetStrat D 01/10	O	R	I	12.66	—
CIF 01/10	O	R	I	7.91	—
EmergMkts A 01/10	L		I	9.89	—
EmergMkts B 01/10	G		I	9.84	—
EmergMkts C 01/10	N		I	9.92	—
EuroEntrprs A 01/10	L		I	11.51	—
EuroEntrprs B 01/10	G		I	11.48	—
EuroEntrprs C 01/10	N		I	11.50	—
GloblBond A 01/10	L		I	10.48	—
GloblBond B 01/10	G		I	10.45	—
GloblBond C 01/10	N		I	10.46	—
Growth A 01/10	L	R	I	4.11	—
Growth B 01/10	G	R	I	4.08	—
Growth C 01/10	N	R	I	4.08	—
Growth D 01/10	O	R	I	4.11	—
OptimaxUS A 01/10	L		I	11.61	—
OptimaxUS B 01/10	G		I	11.48	—
OptimaxUS C 01/10	N		I	11.56	—
CALDWELL SECURITIES					
Associate 01/04	G	R	I	6.23	—
International 01/04	G		I	5.49	—
CALPA(n)					
Gyro Bond	N	R		10.33	-.01
Gyro Equity	N	R		12.10	+.03
CAMAF(n)					
Camaf 01/05	N	R	D	11.39	—
CANADA TRUST					
Ev AmeriGth	N	R	D	10.38	+.08
Ev AsiaGth	N	R	D	10.04	+.03
Ev Balanced	N	R	D	14.97	+.05
Ev Bond	N	R	D	11.61	+.04

Fund	Load	RSP	Dist	Val	Chg
uEm MktsBd US$	O		I	6.88	+.02
uEm MktsPtl US$	O		I	9.25	+.06
uEuro Gth US$	O		I	11.52	-.03
uFar East US$	O		I	19.27	+.14
uGth Amer US$	O		I	14.66	+.23
uIntl Ptl US$	O		I	13.12	+.05
uJapan Gth US$	O		I	7.32	-.06
uLatin Amer US$	O		I	4.81	+.05
uN.A.Inc US$	O		I	6.57	unch
uRSP GloBd US$	O	R	I	6.92	+.01
uSm CapAm US$	O		I	8.39	+.08
FIRST HERITAGE FUND(n)					
1st Heritage 01/10	O	R	I	5.74	+.03
FONDS DE-CROIS SELECT(n)					
mCrois Select 12/29	N			114.64	—
FRIEDBERG COMMODITY(n)					
Double Gold 01/10	L	R	D	3.26	+.03
Prec Metals 01/10	G		Z	10.21	+.13
GBC FUNDS(n)					
Bond	N	R	I	11.14	-.08
Canada	N	R	I	14.44	-.07
Internat'l	N		I	10.44	+.03
N.A. Growth	N		I	6.98	-.11
GENERAL TRUST					
Balanced 01/05	N	R	D	12.15	—
Bond 01/05	N	R	D	10.82	—
Cdn Equity 01/05	N	R	D	29.68	—
Growth 01/05	N	R	D	16.51	—
Internat'l 01/05	N		D	17.08	—
MMF 01/05	N	R	D	10.12	—
Mortgage 01/05	N	R	D	11.14	—
US Equity 01/05	N		D	26.62	—
GLOBAL STRATEGY					
Asia	O		I	7.31	+.07
Bond	O	R	I	6.12	+.01
Canada Grth	O	R	I	19.43	+.03
Cdn Small Cap	O	R	I	11.54	unch
Divr Americas	O	R	I	10.78	+.02
Divr Asia	O	R	I	5.81	+.05
Divr Bond	O	R	I	11.10	+.01
Divr Europe	O	R	I	17.83	-.09
Divr Fn Bond	O	R	I	14.05	+.01
Divr Gold Plus	O	R	I	9.30	-.09
Divr Growth	O	R	I	10.99	+.01
Divr Japan Plus	O	R	I	5.13	-.01
Divr LatinAmer	O	R	I	4.70	+.04
Divr ST Inc	O	R	I	9.78	unch
Divr World Equ	O	R	I	9.74	+.02
Europe Plus	O		I	12.00	-.04
Fn Bond C$	O		I	14.74	+.01
uFn Bond US$	O		I	10.80	+.01
Income Plus	O	R	I	18.38	+.04
Japan	O		I	13.48	-.08
Latin America	O		I	5.66	+.04
Real Estate	O		I	7.89	-.01
US Equity C$	O		I	12.20	+.15
uUS Equity US$	O		I	8.94	+.11
US Growth C$	O		I	14.89	+.03
uUS Growth US$	O		I	10.91	+.02
World Balanced	O		I	10.85	+.02
World Bond	O		I	10.80	+.01
World EmergCo	O		I	15.07	+.09
World Equity	O		I	19.71	+.04

YEAR-END DATA

A summary of 1995 closing prices and 1995 distributions for Canadian mutual funds will appear on Saturday, Jan. 13.

The next monthly Report on Mutual Funds comes out Thursday, Jan. 18, and a 15-Year Review of Mutual Funds appears Thursday, Feb. 1.

Fund	Load	RSP	Dist	Val	Chg
MACKENZIE UNIVERSAL US$					
uAmericas	O		I	7.17	+.07
uCdn Growth	O		I	8.41	-.01
uCdn Resource	O		I	7.32	-.05
uEuro Opportun	O		I	4.84	+.02
uFar East	O		I	3.59	+.04
uGrowth	O		I	3.96	-.00
uJapan	O		I	3.16	-.03
uUS Emerg Gth	O		I	7.12	+.13
uWld AssetAll	O		I	4.10	-.01
uWld BalRRSP	O		Z	3.53	+.00
uWld Emerg	O		I	3.34	+.00
uWld Equity	O		I	6.77	-.02
uWld IncRRSP	O		Z	3.70	-.00
uWld PreMet	O		I	4.56	-.06
uWld TactBond	O		I	4.16	+.01
MACKENZ STAR PORTFOLIO C$					
For Bal Gro&Inc	O		I	57.07	-.03
For Max Equ Gro	O		I	51.24	+.16
For MaxLTrm Gro	O		I	56.44	+.04
Inv Bal Gro&Inc	O		I	56.01	+.01
Inv ConsInc&Gro	O		I	59.36	+.04
Inv LongTrm Gro	O		I	56.62	+.08
Inv MaxLTrm Gro	O		I	56.69	+.13
Reg Bal Gro&Inc	O	R	I	55.89	+.02
Reg ConsInc&Gro	O	R	I	58.35	-.01
Reg LongTrm Gro	O	R	I	56.64	+.04
Reg Max Equ Gro	O	R	I	51.18	+.12
Reg MaxLTrm Gro	O	R	I	57.71	+.16
MACKENZ STAR PORTFOLIO US$					
uFor Bal Gro&Inc	O		I	58.78	-.04
uFor Max Equ Gro	O		I	51.20	+.15
uFor MaxLTrm Gro	O		I	57.09	+.03
MANAGED INVESTMENTS LTD.(n)					
Global 01/10	N		I	11.24	-.13
Wealth 01/05	N	R	I	10.69	—
MANULIFE CABOT FUNDS					
Blue Chip	N	R	D	11.96	-.03
Cdn Equity	N	R	D	12.10	-.04
Cdn Growth	N	R	D	9.53	+.06
Divrs Bond	N	R	D	9.90	+.02
Emerg Growth	N	R	D	9.72	+.06
Global Equ	N		D	11.40	+.03
MARATHON EQUITY FUND					
MarathonEqu	N	R	I	10.81	+.00
MARLBOROUGH(n)					

Fund	Load	RSP	Dist	Val	Chg
ROYAL MUTUAL FUNDS					
Asian Growth	N		D	12.40	+.09
Balanced	N	R	D	7.69	+.01
Cdn Growth	N	R	D	15.02	-.01
Cdn Small Cap	N	R	D	13.82	-.06
Energy	N	R	D	12.09	-.17
Euro Growth	N		D	12.83	-.02
Intl Equity	N		D	14.71	-.04
Japanese	N		D	15.70	-.09
Latin American	N		D	9.77	+.02
Life Sci & Tech	N		D	9.98	+.29
Prec Metals	N	R	D	25.17	-.44
Zweig Global	N		D	10.20	+.01
Zweig Gth C$	N		D	16.17	+.06
uZweig Gth US$	N		D	11.84	+.04
ROYAL: ROYAL TRUST GROUP					
Adv Balanced 01/10	N	R	D	13.60	—
Adv Growth 01/10	N	R	D	14.33	—
Adv Income 01/09	N	R	D	12.30	—
American C$ 01/10	N		D	12.19	—
uAmerican US$ 01/10	N		D	8.93	—
Bond 01/10	N	R	D	10.34	—
Cdn Stock 01/10	N	R	D	15.73	—
Gth & Inc 01/10	N	R	D	10.37	—
Intl Bond 01/10	N	R	D	12.73	—
Mortgage 01/10	N	R	D	10.71	—
Real Estate 12/29	N	R	D	8.50	—
ROYAL: ROYFUND GROUP					
Bond	N	R	D	5.63	+.02
Cdn Equity	N	R	D	29.26	-.02
Dividend	N	R	D	12.82	+.05
Intl Income	N	R	D	11.30	+.02
Mortgage	N	R	D	11.25	+.01
U.S. Equity	N		D	17.41	+.31
SAGIT GROUP					
Cam Amer Gro C$	O		I	4.79	+.21
uCam Amer Gro US$	O		I	3.51	+.16
Cam Americas C$	O		I	9.94	+.11
uCam Americas US$	O		I	7.29	+.09
Cam Balanced	O	R	I	7.47	+.05
Cam China C$	O		I	5.69	+.22
uCam China US$	O		I	4.17	+.16
Cam Global C$	O		I	6.91	+.10
uCam Global US$	O		I	5.07	+.06
Cam Growth	O	R	I	8.35	+.03
Cam Pacific C$	O		I	5.06	+.10

Fund	Load	RSP	Dist	Val	Chg
uGrowth US$	O		I	6.33	+.01
Intl Bal C$	O		I	5.39	-.01
uIntl Bal US$	O		I	3.95	-.01
Intl Stock C$	O		I	10.77	-.02
uIntl Stock US$	O		I	7.89	-.02
TOP 50 GROUP					
TP50 Cdn Equ 01/10	L	R	D	10.78	-.10
TP50 T-B/Bnd 01/10	L	R	D	4.75	-.02
TP50 US Equ 01/10	L		D	10.46	-.14
TOTAL RETURN					
Total Return 01/10	N		D	4.49	+.03
TRADEX					
Bond 01/05	N	R		9.65	—
Emerg Mkts 01/05	N			10.81	—
Equity 01/05	N	R		10.11	—
TRIMARK GROUP					
Advantage Bond	O	R	I	5.64	+.01
Canadian Bond	O	R	I	5.50	+.01
Government Inc	O	R	I	5.04	unch
Indo-Pacific C$	O		I	5.45	+.02
uIndo-Pacific US$	O		I	4.00	+.02
RSP Equity	G	R	I	8.04	+.02
Sel Balanced	O	R	I	7.57	+.03
Sel Cdn Growth	O	R	I	7.49	+.02
Sel Growth C$	O		I	10.99	+.04
uSel Growth US$	O		I	8.06	+.04
The Americas C$	O		I	5.73	+.06
uThe Americas US$	O		I	4.20	+.05
Trimark C$	L		I	20.94	+.06
uTrimark US$	L		I	15.35	+.05
Trimark Cdn	L	R	I	16.85	+.03
Trimark Inc Gth	L	R	I	7.24	+.02
20/20 FUNDS INC C$					
Aggr Growth	O		I	13.77	+.44
American	O		I	15.20	+.06
Asia Pacific	O		I	12.32	+.03
Cdn Asset A	O	R	I	4.44	unch
Cdn Growth	O	R	I	16.59	-.06
Dividend	O	R	I	13.84	+.03
Emerg Mkts	O		I	4.13	+.01
Euro AA	O		I	5.59	unch
For RSP Bond	O	R	I	4.90	unch
Income	O	R	I	9.53	+.03
India	O		I	2.53	unch
Intl Value	O		I	22.44	-.03
Latin Amer	O		I	4.23	+.06

Fund	Load	RSP	Dist	Val	Chg
Bonds 01/05	L	R	D	58.00	—
Diversified 01/05	L	R	D	21.04	—
Ecoflex A 01/05	G	R	D	15.22	—
Ecoflex B 01/05	G	R	D	12.33	—
Ecoflex D 01/05	G	R	D	13.79	—
Ecoflex H 01/05	G	R	D	11.90	—
Ecoflex M 01/05	G	R	D	12.22	—
MMF 01/05	L	R	D	12.22	—
Mortgages 01/05	L	R	D	53.77	—
Stocks 01/05	L	R	D	106.06	—
LONDON LIFE(n)					
Bond 01/10	G	R	D	154.28	-1.44
Cdn Equity 01/10	G	R	D	210.48	-.64
Diversified 01/10	G	R	D	120.03	-.54
MMF 01/10	G	R	D	17.45	+.00
Mortgage 01/10	G	R	D	116.06	+.01
US Equity 01/10	G		D	17.44	-.19
MANULIFE FINANCIAL(n)					
VistaAmerStk 1 01/05	L		I	12.24	—
VistaAmerStk 2 01/05	G		I	12.16	—
VistaBond 1 01/05	L	R	I	18.35	—
VistaBond 2 01/05	G	R	I	17.49	—
VistaCapG 1 01/05	L	R	I	17.23	—
VistaCapG 2 01/05	G	R	I	16.41	—
VistaDivrs 1 01/05	L	R	I	16.53	—
VistaDivrs 2 01/05	G	R	I	15.73	—
VistaEqu 1 01/05	L	R	I	15.58	—
VistaEqu 2 01/05	G	R	I	14.81	—
VistaGloBond 1 01/05	L		I	10.86	—
VistaGloBond 2 01/05	G		I	10.78	—
VistaGloEqu 1 01/05	L		I	10.96	—
VistaGloEqu 2 01/05	G		I	10.90	—
VistaSTS 1 01/05	L	R	I	15.99	—
VistaSTS 2 01/05	G	R	I	15.22	—
MARITIME LIFE(n)					
Amer GIF 01/10	N		I	118.92	-1.74
Balanced 01/10	N	R	I	19.65	-.12
Bond 01/10	N	R	I	17.76	+.01
Cdn Equity 01/10	N	R	I	11.51	-.11
Div Income 01/10	N	R	I	11.18	-.04
Global Equities 01/10	N		I	10.34	-.09
Growth 01/10	N	R	I	19.74	-.16
MMF 01/10	N	R	I	29.78	+.00
Pacific Basin 01/10	N		I	94.31	-.88
S&P 500 01/10	N	R	I	13.24	-.14
METLIFE MVP(n)					
Balanced 01/04	G	R	D	16.89	—
Bond 01/04	G	R	D	19.67	—
Equity 01/04	G	R	D	13.97	—
Growth 01/04	G	R	D	15.67	—
U.S. Equity 01/04	G		D	14.21	—
NATIONAL LIFE OF CANADA(n)					
Balanced 01/05	G	R	D	15.25	—
Equities 01/05	G	R	D	329.17	—
Fixed Inc 01/05	G	R	D	189.82	—
Global Equ 01/05	G		D	12.54	—
MMF 01/05	G	R	D	12.64	—
NN FINANCIAL(n)					
Balanced 01/10	G	R	I	11.75	—
Bond 01/10	G	R	I	9.90	—
Can-Am 01/10	G	R	I	10.19	—
Can-Asian 01/10	G	R	I	9.97	—

SOURCE: Reprinted by permission of the *Globe and Mail* (January 12, 1996).

Figure 22.3

Listing of money market funds (excerpts).

MONEY MARKET FUNDS

Cur—current yield (actual return over past 7 days, annualized); Eff—effective yield. Effective yield includes compounding. Yields will vary; Chg—change from previous yield.

Fund	Dist	Cur	Eff	Chg
ACADIA INVESTMENT FUNDS				
MMF 01/10		4.97	5.09	–.08
ADMAX REGENT GROUP				
A.Cash Prf	I	4.68	4.79	–.03
AGF MANAGEMENT				
SrAMMF	I	5.07	5.20	+.01
SrBMMF	I	4.53	4.63	unch
SrCMMF	I	5.07	5.20	unch
uUS MMF	I	4.53	4.63	–.01
AIC GROUP				
MMF	I	5.04	5.17	+.03
AMI PRIVATE CAPITAL				
MMF	D	5.24	5.38	unch
ATLAS ASSET MGT: ATLAS				
uAm MMF	I	4.59	4.69	–.01
MMF	I	4.98	5.10	–.00
T-Bill	I	4.92	5.04	–.02
BANK OF MONTREAL				
FC MMF	D	5.36	5.51	+.11
FC T-Bill	D	5.07	5.20	–.02
BEUTEL GOODMAN(n)				
MMF	I	5.99	6.17	unch
BNP (CANADA) FUNDS				
MMF 12/31	D	3.47	3.53	—
BPI CAPITAL MANAGEMENT				
T-Bill	I	5.70	5.86	+.01
CANADA TRUST				
Ev MMF	D	4.67	4.78	unch
CAPSTONE GROUP(n)				
Cash	I	4.81	4.93	–.02
CI MUTUAL FUNDS C$				
MMF	I	5.32	5.46	–.01
CI MUTUAL FUNDS U$				
uU$ MMF	I	5.12	5.25	–01
CIBC FUNDS				
Cdn TBill	D	4.74	4.85	unch
MMF	D	4.83	4.95	+.01
mPrem TBill	D	5.25	5.39	+.01
uUS MMF	D	4.28	4.37	–.01
CONCORDE				
MMF 01/10	I	5.17	5.30	+.03
DESJARDINS FUNDS				
MMF 01/10	D	5.01	5.13	+ 00
DYNAMIC GROUP				
Dyn MMF	I	5.00	5.12	unch
ELLIOTT & PAGE				
EP Mon	I	5.26	5.40	–.01
T-Bill	I	4.36	4.45	–.01
ETHICAL FUNDS				
MMF	I	5.41	5.56	–.03
FICADRE FUNDS				
MMF 01/10	D	5.24	5.38	–.06
FIDELITY INVESTMENTS C$				
CdnST	I	4.63	4.74	–.01
FIDELITY INVESTMENTS U$				
uUS MMF	I	4.49	4.59	–.01
GBC FUNDS(n)				
MMF	I	4.92	5.04	–.50
GLOBAL STRATEGY				
T-Bill	I	4.83	4.95	unch

SOURCE: Reprinted by permission of the *Globe and Mail* (January 12, 1996).

SIMILAR TYPES OF INVESTMENTS

Fixed and Deferred Annuities

A **fixed annuity** is a contract in which a life insurance company promises to pay the investor a fixed dollar amount on a regular (generally monthly) basis. The size and number of these payments will depend on how much money the investor gives the insurance company and the size of an up-front fee (if any) that is charged. Also important are the investor's age and the annuity option that the investor chooses.

One option the investor may choose is a life annuity, where fixed dollar payments are provided regularly until the investor's death. Another option is a joint and last survivor annuity, where fixed dollar payments of a lesser amount continue on a regular basis until both the investor and spouse have died. A third option is a period certain annuity (or fixed period annuity), where fixed dollar payments are made on a regular basis for a prespecified number of years (perhaps 5, 10, 15, or 20); if the investor dies before then, subsequent payments are made to the investor's beneficiary. A fourth option, known as a life annuity with a period certain, is a combination of the first and third options. With this option, the investor receives regular fixed dollar payments until death. However, if death should occur before some prespecified number of years have elapsed, then payments will continue until that number of years has elapsed.

Some plan sponsors offer a **variable annuity** where the size of the regular payments is not prespecified but depends directly on the performance of an investment portfolio managed by the institution.

The previous discussion described an immediate annuity, where the investor purchases a fixed annuity with a single payment. However, the investor also has the option of making a single payment and acquiring a **deferred annuity** that starts making periodic payments on a specified future date based on the principal and accumulated investment returns. A variant on this is a **guaranteed investment annuity** which gives the investor the option of receiving either periodic payments or a lump sum at maturity.

Pooled Funds

Trust and insurance companies invest money for individuals and organizations. Trust companies manage personal trust funds; both trust and insurance companies manage individual retirement funds. Any such fund can be invested on an individual basis, with specific securities selected and held in a separate account. This is often done for large accounts. To capture economies of scale, small accounts are often pooled, allowing joint participation in one or more large pools of securities.

The vehicle utilized in this process is the **pooled fund**. In form (but not in law), it is similar to an open-end mutual fund. The securities in the fund are valued periodically, and total value divided by current number of units determines net asset value per unit. On any valuation date, money from an account may be used to purchase units at this value. Alternatively, units purchased at an earlier date may be redeemed at the current net asset value.

A trust or insurance company may offer several pooled funds. One fund may hold only short-term money market instruments, whereas another holds long-term bonds, and yet another holds common stocks. A pooled fund investing in mortgages may also be offered, as may one investing in real property.[5] When a menu of this sort is available, money from a given trust or retirement account can be invested in two or more pooled funds.

Real Estate Investment Trusts

Real estate investment trusts (REITs) are plentiful in the US, but less so in Canada. These are a useful vehicle for the individual investor to use to invest in real estate. Although not classified as investment companies for legal purposes, REITs are similar to closed-end funds in that they serve as a conduit for earnings on certain types of investments, passing them on to their shareholders and avoiding corporate taxation.

REITs must invest primarily in real estate or loans secured by real estate. They can obtain funds by issuing shares, bonds, and even warrants. They can also borrow from banks, issue mortgages on some or all of their property, and issue commercial paper. Like other managed investment companies, REITs hire a management firm for a fee, usually about 1% per year of the value of the assets.

The shares of Canadian REITs are listed on the TSE; therefore, price and volume quotations are provided regularly in the financial press. Because the assets held by these trusts are generally quite illiquid, it is difficult to calculate NAVs on a regular basis. Consequently it is hard to tell whether they sell at a premium or at a discount from NAV.

[5] Pooled funds are referred to as commingled funds in the US. Due to the illiquidity of the assets, the sponsor of real property commingled funds may reserve the right to limit the redemption of units, either temporarily or until sale of the underlying property. For an analysis of the performance of such funds, see Mike Miles and Arthur Esty, "How Well Do Commingled Real Estate Funds Perform?" *Journal of Portfolio Management* 8, no. 2 (Winter 1982): 62–68.

Most REITs are highly leveraged. A typical trust might have debt amounting to 70% of its total assets. Consequently, any decline in the value of the property held by such a trust will generally cause a greater percentage decline in the market value of its common stock. Furthermore, adverse changes in the relationship between the interest paid on a trust's short-term debt and that earned on the trust's assets will also result in declines in the market value of the trust's common stock — and may even lead to default and bankruptcy, as happened to many in the recession of 1973–74. Nevertheless, REITs are a desirable investment for many individuals due to their unique investment policies and typically high leverage. However, only a portion of an individual's portfolio should usually consist of such securities.

LABOUR-SPONSORED INVESTMENT FUNDS

Labour-sponsored investment funds are investment funds sponsored by a labour union with the objective of investing in small and startup businesses. Although sponsored by a labour union these funds are generally run by professional money managers (for a fee).[6] The attraction these funds hold for some investors is that a 15% federal tax credit is granted on a maximum yearly investment of $3500 that is matched by a corresponding tax credit in many provinces. The investor, however, must hold the units for at least eight years or return the tax credit. An unattractive feature is that these funds invest in extremely illiquid securities, so it is difficult to calculate NAVs and hence fund performance. Furthermore, the eight-year required holding period is a deterrent to some investors.

REGULATION AND INVESTMENT POLICIES

The regulation of mutual funds is currently in flux. A major report prepared for the Ontario Securities Commission recommends sweeping changes to the way in which mutual funds should be regulated.[7] Many of the recommendations are controversial, so it is not easy to predict the direction that new legislation will take.

As of January 1996, investment funds are subject to provincial regulation under the appropriate Securities Act augmented by a number of national policies that have been agreed to by all provinces, but particularly National Policy No. 39, Mutual Funds.

Mutual funds can only be sold with a prospectus that describes (among other items) the fund's investment policies, discloses the fees and expenses, and particularly any incentive fees payable to the investment managers. Management expense ratios and financial statements for five prior years must also be included.

The regulations can influence a mutual fund's investment policy. For example, a mutual fund that wishes to become a qualified investment for registered retirement savings plans must limit the proportion of its funds that it invests in foreign securities to a maximum of 20%. It is important, therefore, to understand the constraints imposed by legislation.

---

[6] The labour union also collects a fee for the use of its name.

[7] Glorianne Stromberg, *Regulatory Strategies for the Mid-'90s: Recommendations for Regulating Mutual Funds in Canada* (Toronto: Ontario Securities Commission, January 1995).

► Regulation of Mutual Funds

National Policy No. 39 imposes certain restrictions on both the investments that a mutual fund may undertake and the practices that it follows. The salient sections of National Policy No. 39 are: section 2.04 covering investment restrictions, section 2.05 describing investment practices, and section 2.07 outlining permitted transactions in derivatives. The following is a summary of the key points in these sections:

1. *Diversification:* no mutual fund may invest in such a manner that more than 10% of its portfolio consists of the securities of one issuer.
2. *Control:* a mutual fund may not own more than 10% of the shares of any other issuer, nor may a fund buy shares for the purpose of exercising control of a company.
3. *Illiquid assets:* assets that are not subject to regular arms-length valuation (e.g., by being traded on an exchange) are generally not permitted or at least restricted. Examples include real estate, fine art, and commodities. Permissible illiquid assets are restricted to a maximum of 10% of the value of the portfolio (these include private placements, mortgages (except a mortgage fund) and OTC options acquired for non-hedging purposes)[8]
4. *Derivatives:* trades in derivatives are not regulated as long as they are made in order to hedge a position. Funds may write covered calls and puts providing they either own the underlying asset or have a sufficient cash balance to cover the ensuing obligations.[9]
5. *Ownership of other funds:* investments in other funds are closely regulated and duplication of management fees and sales charges is prohibited.
6. *Borrowing:* funds may only borrow up to 5% of the portfolio value to meet unusually heavy redemption requests.
7. *Lending:* funds may not lend either cash or securities, except by buying debt obligations such as bonds.
8. *Margin transactions:* these are prohibited.
9. *Short sales:* these are prohibited.
10. *Guarantees:* funds may not guarantee another party's securities or obligations.
11. *Connected party dealings:* mutual funds owned by a brokerage house may not invest in securities underwritten or distributed by the owner for 60 days following the end of public distribution. (This rule is relaxed if the brokerage distributes no more than 5% of the shares.)
12. *Underwriting:* funds may not underwrite any securities.

National Policy No. 39 also provides for a 60-day "cooling off" period during which a buyer of mutual funds under a purchase plan is entitled to a full refund including 100% of any sales commission if he or she wishes to cancel the contract.

---

[8] An illiquid investment is defined as one that cannot be readily disposed of in its customary marketplace or where regular quotations are not regularly published. Examples of illiquid investments are limited partnership interests not traded on an exchange and securities of private companies.

[9] The use of currency forward and futures contracts is permitted, providing that these are used to hedge the portfolio against adverse foreign currency fluctuations.

Investment Policies

Different investment companies follow different investment policies. Some companies are designed as substitutes for their shareholders' entire portfolio; others expect their shareholders to own other securities. Some restrict their domain or selection methods severely; others give their managers wide latitude. Many engage in highly active management, making substantial portfolio changes designed to exploit their perceived superior investment predictions. However, others are more passive, concentrating instead on tailoring a portfolio to serve the interests of a particular clientele.

The Investment Funds Institute of Canada identifies five generic types of funds that are distinguished by broad differences in their investment policies. These are:

1. Fixed income funds (bond funds)
2. Balanced funds
3. Common stock or growth funds
4. Specialty funds
5. Fixed trusts[10]

Most funds fall into one of the first three categories. However, funds in the fourth category have become significant. Specialty funds include mortgage funds, money market funds, dividend funds, option income funds, real estate funds, and global funds.

Some mutual funds develop their own investment policies that complement the generic styles described above. For example, a family of ethical funds may include an ethical growth fund, an ethical balanced fund, or an ethical bond fund. International and global funds should probably be considered as a separate generic category, as there is an added element of risk (foreign exchange) associated with the investments. Asset allocation services are also investment vehicles that have their own investment objectives, management, and fees.

Categorization of a specific fund can be difficult, but broad classes can be identified. As mentioned earlier, money market funds hold short-term (typically less than one year) fixed-income instruments such as bank certificates of deposit, commercial paper, and Treasury bills. These open-end funds make it possible for small investors to move in and out of the short-term market. The fund manager will charge an annual fee for this service, usually between 0.25% and 1% of the average value of total assets. There are usually no load charges, and investors may add money to, or remove money from, their accounts at almost any time.

Bond funds invest in fixed-income securities. Some go farther, specifying that particular types will be emphasized. There are corporate bond funds, government bond funds (Canadian and/or US), global bond funds, and so on. A few funds concentrate on holding preferred shares or both bonds and preferred shares in their portfolios. These funds aim to provide the investor with price stability and income.

Many funds consider themselves managers for the bulk of the investment assets of their clients. Those that hold both equity and fixed-income securities particularly fit this description and are referred to as balanced funds. These funds seek to "combine capital growth (gains) with income and price stability."[11] Some of these funds hold relatively constant

---

[10] All the capital of a fixed trust is invested in specific securities on a long-term basis. As new capital is introduced it is invested in the same securities in the same proportions. This policy minimizes transaction and management costs but reduces flexibility. Fixed trusts have been declining in number as a larger variety of funds have been introduced.

[11] The Investment Funds Institute of Canada, *The Canadian Investment Funds Course*, Toronto, 1991.

mixes of bonds, preferred shares, convertible bonds, and equities; others alter the proportions periodically in attempts to "time the market." Option-income funds are a type of balanced fund that invests primarily in high-dividend-paying common stocks, while controlling risk by writing call options on these stocks. (Call options are discussed in Chapter 20.)

The largest group of investment funds are common stock or growth funds, of which a large variety exist. A diversified common stock fund invests most of its assets in common stocks, although some short-term money market instruments are often held to accommodate irregular cash flows or to engage in market timing. The majority of common stock funds have as their objective either growth or combined long-term growth and income.[12] Two factors appear to be involved in these objectives: the relative importance of dividend income versus capital gains and the overall level of risk to be taken. Since high-dividend portfolios are generally less risky than those with low dividends, relatively few major conflicts arise.

Some specialized investment companies concentrate on the securities of firms in a particular *industry* or *sector*. For example, there are resource funds, real estate funds, small capitalization stock funds, and gold funds. Others provide a convenient means for holding the securities of firms in a particular *country* or *region*, such as Global Strategy Japan or Latin America funds. There are also investment companies that invest even more widely internationally, purchasing stocks from a variety of different countries. International funds are those investing in non-Canadian securities, while global funds invest in both Canadian and non-Canadian securities.

An index fund attempts to provide results similar or identical to those computed for a specified market index. For example, the *Green Line Canadian Index Fund*, a no-load open-end investment fund, provides a vehicle for small investors who wish to obtain results similar to those of TSE 300-stock index. Despite continuing evidence that indexing outperforms most managers (after deducting fees) the number of index funds in Canada remains small.

MUTUAL FUND ACCOUNTS

▸ Accumulation Plans

Although an investor can purchase shares in a fund and receive all distributions in cash, this is only one of many possible arrangements. Mutual funds offer plans of several types to satisfy investors' desires for different patterns of contributions and withdrawals over time. Accumulation plans are designed for those who do not want to receive any income or capital gains distributions over some period of time. The simplest procedure involves automatic reinvestment of these distributions, where the shareholder elects to receive additional shares in the fund instead of cash. As with other plans, this often involves fractional shares, but since most accounts are maintained via computerized records, this poses no problem.

Voluntary accumulation plans allow an investor to add to an account as desired, subject only to some minimum amount that must be invested each time. Alternatively, a fixed dollar amount may be invested at periodic intervals — in some cases via automatic bank transfers.

Contractual accumulation plans call for a fixed amount to be contributed at regular intervals (usually monthly) over a relatively long period (often five or more years). Sales charges may or may not be lower than those applicable to a voluntary accumulation plan. The investor is not legally bound to make all the payments, but since a large proportion of

---

[12] The statement of a fund's objectives can be obtained from its prospectus that must be available to all prospective buyers. Sometimes picturesque terminology, such as "maximum capital gain" or "aggressive growth," is used to describe the objectives, making the official statement of investment objectives less than lucid.

early contributions typically goes toward sales charges, commitment to a contractual plan should not be considered if cancellation is at all likely.

National Policy No. 39 places limits on the load charges for contractual plans. Specifically, no more than 50% of the first year's contribution may be allocated to sales charges (that is, at least half must be invested in fund shares). Moreover, if a 50% "front-end" load charge is assessed in the first year, then the sales charges in subsequent years must be such that the total sales charges over the life of the plan do not exceed 12% of the total contributions. A few funds offer insurance with their contractual accumulation plans. This insurance provides the remaining contributions if the investor dies or is disabled before all the contracted payments have been made. The premium for such insurance is, in effect, added to the sales charge.

► Registered Retirement Savings Plans

Accumulation of untaxed funds for retirement may be accomplished via a Registered Retirement Savings Plan (RRSP). These were discussed in some detail in Chapter 13. Mutual funds that hold more than 10% of their assets in foreign securities are not eligible for inclusion in RRSP accounts. RRSP accounts are trusteed and maintained by a financial institution such as a bank or trust company. The simplest procedure is to invest the funds in either demand or term deposits or in eligible mutual funds managed by the institution. An alternative is to establish a *self-directed* RRSP that allows the contributor to invest in a wider variety of eligible securities and mutual funds. Institutions generally charge a modest annual fee (typically $100) for providing custodial and book-keeping services for self-directed plans.

► Exchange Privileges

It is increasingly common to find several investment companies operating as a "family of funds." An investor may purchase shares in more than one of the funds under common management and also may switch money from one fund to another. (Sales charges for switching between funds in the same company are typically lower than those applicable to switching between different companies and in some cases transfers between a family of funds managed by the same company may be made without charge.) A single account is usually maintained, with all contributions, withdrawals, and tax information included in one statement. The investor then has the opportunity to make timing decisions (for example, switching money from one fund to another when the latter is believed to be underpriced).

► Withdrawal Plans

Many mutual funds offer voluntary withdrawal plans. The investor instructs the fund to pay out periodically (for example, monthly) either a fixed amount or a specified percentage of the account's value, thereby decreasing the number of shares that the investor owns.

MUTUAL FUND PERFORMANCE

Mutual funds need to compute and publicize their net asset values daily. Since their income and capital gain distributions are also publicized, they are ideal candidates for studies of the performance of professionally managed portfolios. Thus, it is hardly surprising that mutual funds have frequently been the subject of extensive study in the US. Ironically, despite the importance of mutual funds in RRSP investments, only a limited number of Canadian studies (to be discussed in a later section) have been undertaken.

► Calculating Returns

In studies of performance, the rate of return on a mutual fund for period t is calculated by adding the change in net asset value to the amount of income and capital gains distributions made during the period, denoted I_t and G_t, respectively, and dividing this total by the net asset value at the beginning of the period:

$$r_t = \frac{(\text{NAV}_t - \text{NAV}_{t-1}) + I_t + G_t}{\text{NAV}_{t-1}} \tag{22.2}$$

For example, a mutual fund that had a net asset value of \$10 at the beginning of month t and made income and capital gain distributions of, respectively, \$.05 and \$.04 per share during the month, and then ended the month with a net asset value of \$10.03 would have a monthly return of

$$r_t = \frac{(\$10.03 - \$10.00) + \$.05 + \$.04}{\$10.00}$$
$$= 1.20\%.$$

It should be noted that returns calculated in this manner can be used to evaluate the performance of the portfolio manager of a mutual fund, since it indicates the results of the manager's investment decisions. However, it does not necessarily indicate the return earned by the shareholders in the fund, since there may have been a load charge involved. In the example, perhaps the investor paid \$10.50 at the beginning of the month for one share of this fund, with \$.50 being a front-end load. If this were the case, the investor's return for this month could be calculated using equation (20.2), where NAV_{t-1} would be \$10.50, not \$10.00:

$$r_t = \frac{(\$10.03 - \$10.50) + \$.05 + \$.04}{\$10.50}$$
$$= -3.62\%.$$

Thus, the return for the investor who bought one share at the beginning of the month and paid a \$.50 per share load charge at that time would be –3.62%. However, the portfolio manager was only given \$10.00 per share to invest, since the load charge was given to those people that were responsible for getting the investor to buy the share. Accordingly, the portfolio manager should be evaluated on the basis of the return provided on the \$10.00, which in this example was 1.20%.

Recently, data on professionally managed pension funds and bank commingled funds have become available. The performance of the managers of such funds appears to be similar to that of mutual fund managers: they do reasonably well tailoring portfolios to meet clients' objectives, but few seem to be able to consistently "beat the market." Although the following sections deal only with US mutual funds, many of the results apply to other investment companies, both in the United States and in other countries.[13] A more detailed discussion

---

[13] For evidence on funds outside the United States see, for example, Jess H. Chua and Richard S. Woodward, "Gains from Market Timing," Monograph Series in Finance and Economics 1986-2, Salomon Brothers Center for the Study of Financial Institutions, Graduate School of Business Administration, New York University; Andre L. Farber, "Performance of Internationally Diversified Mutual Funds," in *International Capital Markets*, eds. Edwin J. Elton and Martin J. Gruber (Amsterdam: North-Holland Publishing Company, 1975): 298–309; Michael A. Firth, "The Investment Performance of Unit Trusts in the Period 1965–75," *Journal of Money, Credit and Banking* 9, no. 4 (November 1977): 597–604; James R. F. Guy, "The Performance of the British Investment Trust Industry," *Journal of Finance* 33, no. 2 (May 1978): 443–55, and "An Examination of the Effects of International Diversification from the British Viewpoint on Both Hypothetical and Real Portfolios," *Journal of Finance* 33, no. 5 (December

of certain risk-adjusted measures of performance and their application to mutual funds is deferred to Chapter 25.

Risk Control

One of the functions that a mutual fund can perform for its investors is the maintenance of a particular risk posture. Formal statements of objectives provide some idea of a fund's intended posture, but often the wording is vague. Nevertheless, there appears to be a general relationship between portfolio risk and stated objectives.

Figure 22.4 summarizes information on the standard deviations of monthly excess returns over a ten-year period for funds with similar objectives, using classifications assigned by Wiesenberger Investment Companies Service's annual *Investment Companies* at the beginning of the period. In particular, the monthly returns for each one of 123 mutual funds were calculated using equation (22.2). Then, using these 120 monthly returns, the standard deviation was calculated for each one of the funds. Each bar in the figure plots the range of values of the standard deviations for funds having the same objective, with the average standard deviation being shown by a square near the middle of the bar. It can be seen that generally, the lower the amount of promised risk, the lower the amount of actual risk (a similar looking figure resulted when beta was used). However, the overlapping of some of the bars indicates that some funds with conservative objectives took on more risk than others with less conservative objectives.

Figure 22.4

Risk versus fund objectives: 123 mutual funds, 1960–1969.

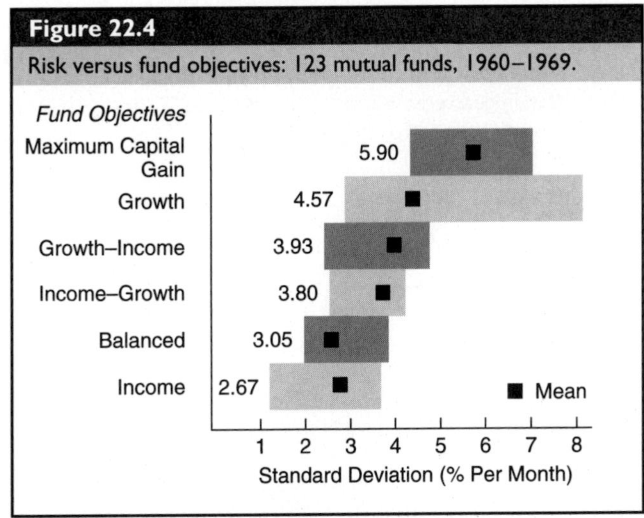

SOURCE: John G. McDonald, "Objectives and Performance of Mutual Funds, 1960–1969," *Journal of Financial and Quantitative Analysis* 9, no. 3 (June 1974): 316.

1978): 1425–38; John G. McDonald, "French Mutual Fund Performance: Evaluation of Internationally Diversified Portfolios," *Journal of Finance* 28, no. 5 (December 1973): 1161–80; Juan A. Palacios, "The Stock Market in Spain: Tests of Efficiency and Capital Market Theory," in *International Capital Markets*, eds. Edwin J. Elton and Martin J. Gruber (Amsterdam: North-Holland Publishing Company, 1975): 114–49; and R. S. Woodward, "The Performance of UK Investment Trusts as Internationally Diversified Portfolios Over the Period 1968 to 1977," *Journal of Banking and Finance* 7, no. 3 (September 1983): 417–26.

Diversification

An important task for any investment manager is the provision of an appropriate degree of portfolio diversification. The correct amount depends on the proportion of client's funds managed and on the likelihood that superior abnormal returns can be obtained by sacrificing diversification. Since most mutual funds are intended to be a major component of a shareholder's portfolio, it is reasonable to expect them to be substantially diversified.

Figure 22.5 shows that many are. Quarterly excess returns over a five-year period were computed for 100 funds and compared with corresponding values for Standard & Poor's 500-stock index. For each fund a value of R^2, the coefficient of determination, was computed. This indicates the proportion of the variation in a fund's excess returns that can be attributed to variations in excess returns on the index. As the figure shows, approximately 90% of the quarter-by-quarter variation in a typical fund's excess return was associated with swings in the value of the S&P 500 during this period, with values ranging from 66% to 98%. Lower correlations have been observed for funds that invest internationally or in sectors (such as gold funds that invest in gold mining shares).[14]

Average Return

One way to evaluate the general performance of mutual funds is to compare their average return with that of a suitable market index of comparable securities. Data that allow investors to perform these comparisons is reported monthly in *The Globe and Mail: Report on Mutual*

Figure 22.5

Proportion of variation in quarterly returns attributable to market fluctuations: 100 mutual funds, 1970–1974.

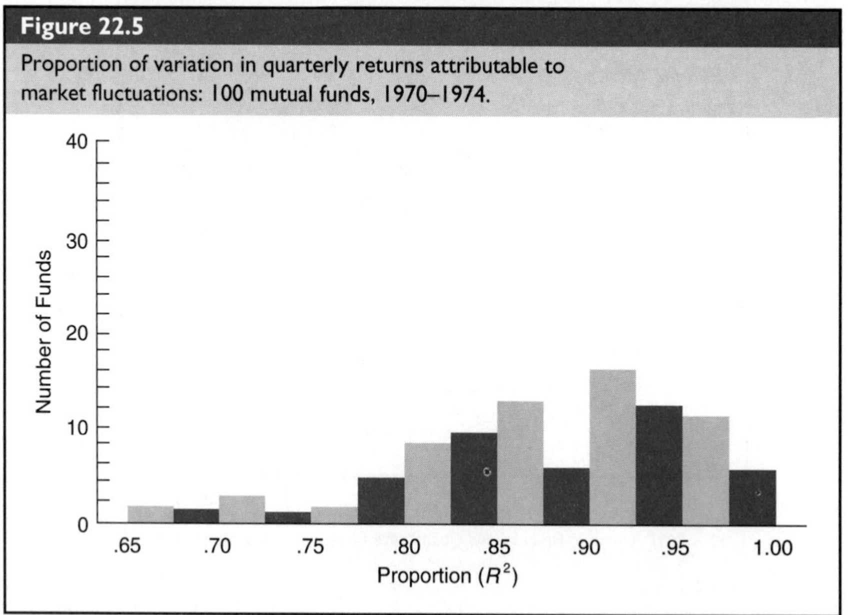

SOURCE: Merrill Lynch, Pierce, Fenner & Smith, Inc., *Investment Performance Analysis, Comparative Survey, 1970–1974.*

[14] See John Bogle, *Bogle on Mutual Funds* (Burr Ridge, Ill: Richard D. Irwin, 1994).

Figure 22.6

Mutual fund performance data (excerpts).

How to read the tables

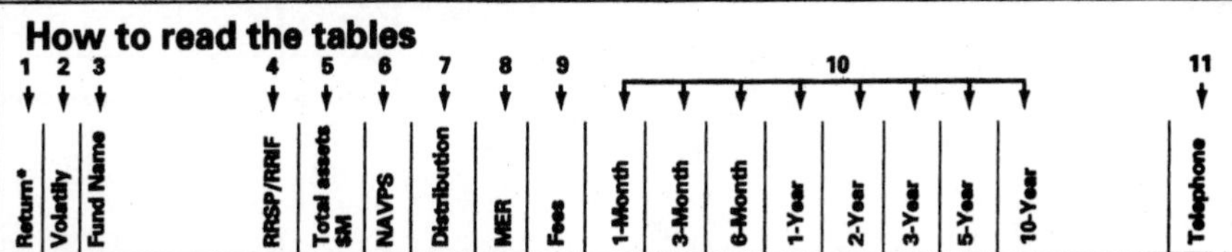

1. Return - * to *****. Funds are ranked on their 3-year average annual compound return. In each category, the top 5% earn five stars, 20% earn four stars. About 25% of the funds fall into each of the remaining ranks.
2. Volatility - The variation in a fund's monthly rate of return, the standard deviation, is used to rank the volatility of funds in a category from Hi (high) to Av (average) to Lo (low). Funds are ranked only against others in the same category. Volatility is ranked on funds' 3-year average annual compound return.
3. Fund Name - The name of the managing company is in brackets if it is different from the fund name. "C" indicates the fund is closed to new investors. "R" indicates investor restrictions.
4. RRSP/RRIF - R=100% eligible. F = eligible as foreign content. N = ineligible.
5. Total assets - In millions of dollars.
6. NAVPS - Net asset value per share as of the end of the previous month.
7. Distribution - Payout of income, capital gains or return of capital over the month.
8. MER - A fund's management fees and expenses, expressed as a percentage of assets, is the management-expense ratio. An "m" indicates the ratio represents the management fee only. Management-expense ratios are deducted before fund performance is calculated.
9. Fees - N = no sales fees. F= front-end load. D = deferred load. O = optional. B = both, usually a front-end and back-end fee but sometimes a redemption fee and a deferred load.
10. Performance - Represents the total return under one year, or the average annual returns, with reinvestment of distributions. All returns date back to the end of the previous month. All returns are shown after the deduction of management fees and expenses. Also, all returns, except for some U.S. money market funds, are shown in Canadian dollars. **Bold face** indicates above average returns.
11. Telephone - Numbers to reach the customer service departments.

To comment or make suggestions about our Mutual Fund Tables, please call 416-585-5500.
You can also reach us by E-mail at investing@globeandmail.ca

Results are for the month ended Dec. 31

Benchmarks

Index	Total return 1 mo.	3 mo.	6 mo.	1 yr.	Average annual compound return 2 yrs.	3 yrs.	5 yrs.	10 yrs.
Canada Savings Bonds Rate	0.4	1.4	2.9	6.4	6.0	5.9	7.0	8.2
CPI - All Items(est.)	0.1	0.2	0.4	2.0	1.1	1.3	2.0	3.2
Midland Walwyn Canadian Bond	1.1	5.4	8.1	19.2	5.7	9.3	·	-
Midland Walwyn Canadian Equity	1.8	3.5	3.9	10.6	3.9	14.1	·	
Midland Walwyn Global Bond	1.9	4.4	6.0	12.3	2.8	6.7	·	
Midland Walwyn International Equity	2.3	2.3	4.7	8.5	5.1	17.1	·	
Midland Walwyn U.S. Equity	1.1	4.0	10.9	27.3	14.7	15.6	·	
Morgan Stanley - Europe	3.7	4.8	7.2	18.8	13.6	20.5	15.8	**14.2**
Morgan Stanley - EAFE	4.5	5.4	7.8	8.5	11.4	19.8	13.3	13.7
Morgan Stanley - Japan	5.6	6.5	9.1	-1.9	12.4	18.3	9.3	12.5
Morgan Stanley - World Index	3.4	6.2	10.1	18.0	14.9	19.2	16.0	13.4
Morgan Stanley - Emerging Markets	4.9	-0.1	-2.7	-7.8	4.9	18.2	26.3	
Nesbitt Burns Cdn Small-Cap Index	3.3	3.0	5.1	13.9	2.0	15.6	13.6	
Russell 100 Growth Index	0.7	4.5	4.6	13.0	4.2	11.2	8.5	
Russell 100 Value Index	1.6	5.1	5.7	15.4	10.2	17.4	12.0	
Russell 300 Growth Index	1.1	4.7	5.1	14.1	4.0	11.5	9.0	
Russell 300 Value Index	1.7	4.6	5.4	14.6	9.3	17.6	12.1	
S&P 500 Total Return Index	2.2	7.8	13.8	33.9	19.9	18.1	20.4	**14.6**
Salomon Brothers World Gov't Bond	1.5	4.2	1.1	15.7	12.0	14.0	14.7	**11.9**
ScotiaMcLeod Universe Bond Total Return	1.2	5.7	8.8	20.7	7.5	10.9	12.8	**11.3**
TSE300 Total Return	1.4	4.7	5.3	14.5	6.9	14.9	10.8	8.3
5-Year GIC	0.5	1.7	3.3	8.4			9.7	**9.6**
91 Day Treasury Bill	0.5	1.8	3.6	7.6	6.5	6.1	7.1	**8.8**

Note: All Benchmarks are expressed in Canadian dollars
Source: Datastream, ScotiaMcLeod, Frank Russell Canada, Morgan Stanley Capital Int'l

Figure 22.6 (continued)

Mutual fund performance data (excerpts).

Canadian Equity Funds

Funds in which the primary objective is long-term capital appreciation.
These funds invest mainly in Canadian common shares but their investment content may vary given certain market conditions.

Return	Volatility	Fund Name	RRSP/RRIF	Total Assets ($M)	NAVPS	Distributions	MER	Fees	1-Month	3-Month	6-Month	1-Year	2-Year	3-Year	5-Year	10-Year	Telephone
★	AV-	Admax Canadian Performance Fund	R	14.9	6.52	0.066	2.67	O	0.9	4.0	5.4	12.0	3.1	10.4	7.8	·	800-667-2369
★	LO	Admax Canadian Select Growth Fund	R	12.1	5.17		2.63	O	-2.3	-1.5	-0.7	7.2	2.1	4.5	2.7	·	800-667-2369
★★★★	AV	All-Canadian CapitalFund	R	13.4	11.19	0.964	2.00	F	-0.1	-3.1	-3.3	3.1	6.6	15.0	9.0	7.1	905-648-2026
★★★★	AV	All-Canadian Compound(C)	R	13.0	14.65	1.380	0.00	N	-0.2	-3.0	-3.2	3.0	6.4	14.9	8.9	7.1	905-648-2025
NA		All-Canadian ConsumerFund	R	1.2	3.33	0.024	2.00	F	0.4	-0.2	-2.8	1.0	3.9	·	·	·	905-648-2025
★★★★	AV+	Altafund Investment Corp.	R	118.9	17.44	0.240	2.39	N	3.8	2.1	2.8	11.4	4.0	15.1	·	·	800-263-2824
★★★	AV+	Altamira Capital Growth Fund	R	171.6	14.33	0.010	2.02	N	-0.3	1.5	1.2	9.1	6.2	13.8	13.6	9.0	800-263-2824
★★★★	AV+	Altamira Equity Fund	R	2004.0	29.24	2.130	2.32	N	1.5	4.5	5.0	14.8	8.0	19.6	24.6	·	800-263-2824
NA	·	Altamira North American Recovery	R	65.5	10.76	0.650	2.33	N	0.0	-1.3	-3.5	1.3	-0.2	·	·	·	800-263-2824
★	LO	Associate Investors Ltd.	R	7.4	7.58	0.090	2.06	N	1.3	3.1	5.1	10.8	3.7	10.0	7.6	6.4	416-864-1120
★	LO	Atlas Canadian Large Cap Growth	R	15.3	12.78		2.73	N	0.6	3.0	3.7	12.5	6.1	9.5	6.9	5.3	800-567-4525
NA	·	Atlas Canadian Large Cap Value Fund	R	3.1	10.86	0.033	2.67	N	0.8	2.6	2.8	8.9	·	·	·	·	800-567-4525
★★★★★	HI	ABC Fundamental Value Fund(R)	R	155.4	9.84	0.259	2.00	N	0.2	0.6	3.8	11.1	7.0	36.4	26.6	·	416-365-9696
★	AV-	AGF Canadian Equity Fund 'A'	R	132.2	11.86		2.52	F	1.8	4.0	5.0	12.1	1.3	10.2	8.4	5.0	800-520-0620
NA	·	AGF Canadian Equity Fund 'B'	R	454.9	11.78		2.50m	D	1.8	3.9	4.8	11.6	·	·	·	·	800-520-0620
NA	·	AGF Canadian Equity Fund 'C'(R)	R	8.9	11.80		2.50m	N	1.8	3.9	4.8	11.5	·	·	·	·	800-520-0620
★★★★	AV+	AGF Growth Equity Fund Ltd. 'A'	R	170.2	20.07		2.43	F	3.5	2.4	5.0	14.3	-0.6	17.8	17.4	9.1	800-520-0620
NA	·	AGF Growth Equity Fund Ltd. 'B'	R	359.7	19.94		2.50m	D	3.5	2.3	4.7	13.7	·	·	·	·	800-520-0620
NA	·	AGF Growth Equity Fund Ltd. 'C'(R)	R	7.7	19.96		2.50m	N	3.4	2.3	4.6	13.5	·	·	·	·	800-520-0620
★★★★★	AV+	AIC Advantage Fund	R	281.3	27.60		2.70	O	5.4	11.7	12.5	30.7	6.9	23.5	23.5	12.3	800-263-2144
NA	·	AIC Diversified Canada Fund	R	13.5	12.62		2.75	O	4.2	7.8	10.1	26.2	·	·	·	·	800-263-2144
★★	LO	AMI Private Capital Equity	R	2.1	13.69	0.246	1.75	N	1.3	5.1	4.1	12.7	5.3	11.9	7.9	·	416-865-1985
NA	·	APEX Equity Growth Fund(R)	R	16.3	5.03	0.013	1.99	O	1.1	3.3	3.6	13.0	6.0	·	·	·	604-737-9107
NA	·	Batirente - Section Actions(R)	R	·	·		1.61	N	·	·	·	·	·	·	·	·	514-288-7545
★★★	AV	Beutel Goodman Canadian Equity	R	21.4	12.70	0.156	2.28	N	1.8	4.4	2.3	8.3	7.3	12.8	7.4	·	800-461-4551
★★★★	LO	Bissett Canadian Equity Fund(R)	R	14.0	23.53	0.271	1.34	N	0.9	3.2	5.8	16.4	6.6	14.9	13.4	9.8	403-266-4664
★	AV-	BNP (Canada) Equity Fund	R	6.2	29.58	3.930	3.25	N	0.9	3.8	4.4	14.1	5.7	10.0	·	·	514-285-7597
★	AV-	BPI Canadian Equity Value Fund	R	186.4	7.20		2.69	O	0.0	2.0	6.8	14.4	1.9	8.7	9.9	·	800-937-5146
NA	·	BPI Canadian Opportunities RSP Fund(R)	R	11.5	19.97	0.070	2.25m	O	8.1	11.1	·	·	·	·	·	·	800-937-5146
NA	·	C.I. Canadian Growth Fund	R	853.2	6.50	0.490	2.40	O	0.0	3.3	2.9	11.5	5.8	·	·	·	800-563-5181
★★★★	AV+	C.I. Sector Canadian Fund	F	48.3	5.80		0.03	O	0.0	3.2	2.6	10.9	5.5	19.1	9.7	·	800-563-5181
★	HI	Cambridge Growth Fund (Sagit)	R	67.3	8.19	0.053	2.71	O	6.2	1.8	2.7	2.7	-10.1	9.3	8.7	10.4	800-663-1003
★★	AV-	Canada Life Canadian Equity S-9	R	341.0	121.59		2.00	R	0.7	2.9	5.1	13.6	4.8	11.0	10.4	7.8	800-387-4447
★	AV-	Canada Trust Everest Stock Fund	R	604.4	15.13	0.152	1.85	N	0.3	1.6	1.1	9.1	0.9	10.4	10.5	·	800-668-8888
★	LO	Canadian Investment Fund (Bullock)	R	44.6	7.90	0.021	2.25	O	2.1	6.3	6.3	15.7	6.8	10.2	6.7	5.0	800-363-0260
NA	·	Canadian Protected Fund(R)	R	·	·		2.10	R	·	·	·	·	·	·	·	·	416-960-4890
★	LO	Chou RRSP Fund	R	1.0	11.94	0.300	2.44	F	0.2	3.2	12.1	19.0	3.2	7.1	7.0	·	416-299-6740
★★★	AV	Clean Environment Equity Fund(R)	R	31.0	7.47	0.010	2.60	O	2.5	0.3	6.6	21.5	2.4	13.7	·	·	800-461-4570
★★	AV	Co-operators Canadian Equity Fund(R)	R	5.2	139.70		2.07	N	1.7	1.8	1.5	9.3	4.5	11.9	·	·	800-667-8164
★	LO	Colonia Equity Fund	R	9.6	11.90		2.00	D	-0.0	3.7	1.4	11.3	-0.2	5.7	·	·	800-461-1086
★★	LO	Concorde Croissance(R)	R	18.9	6.58	0.135	2.10	O	2.4	3.7	5.9	17.1	7.7	11.9	·	·	800-363-0598
★	AV-	Confed Equity Fund	R	34.0	18.77		2.00	N	1.0	3.2	2.2	8.6	4.5	10.2	9.8	6.4	800-267-5001
★★	AV-	Confed Life B	R	34.0	19.95		0.96	F	1.1	3.4	2.8	9.8	5.4	11.2	11.0	7.5	800-267-5001
★★★	AV	Cornerstone Cdn Growth (N Am Tr)	R	51.5	5.98	0.606	2.06	N	1.5	8.3	10.5	21.2	8.9	13.3	12.6	·	416-362-7214
★★★	AV+	Cote 100 Amerique REER(R)	R	13.0	18.05		1.36	N	5.7	6.0	5.5	25.4	3.3	12.9	·	·	514-461-2826
NA	·	Cote 100 EXP(R)	R	8.0	12.83		2.08	N	2.5	3.9	5.9	26.0	·	·	·	·	514-461-2826
★★★★★	LO	Cundill Security Fund(C)	R	16.7	16.34	1.741	2.00	F	1.5	-1.3	0.0	10.5	12.3	20.8	9.2	6.8	800-663-0156
★★	AV	CAMAF(Cdn-Anaest)	R	33.7	11.07		1.85	N	1.9	4.9	5.8	13.2	4.2	10.8	7.3	7.0	800-267-4713
★★	LO	CCPE Growth Fund R(R)	R	34.0	82.23		1.35	N	0.4	3.9	2.9	12.6	7.2	10.7	8.2	·	416-229-4515
★★★	AV	CDA Common Stock Fund(R)	R	57.2	25.62		0.95m	N	1.2	3.1	4.5	11.2	4.1	12.3	10.2	9.3	800-561-9401
★	AV	CIBC Canadian Equity Fund	R	331.8	11.92	0.150	2.26	N	0.5	3.0	0.9	7.7	-0.1	7.9	4.2	·	800-465-3863
★★	AV-	Dolphin Growth Fund	R	5.3	6.47	3.110	2.00	F	1.8	4.5	2.8	10.4	5.0	11.5	10.2	7.3	800-263-2860
★★★★★	HI	Dynamic Canadian Growth Fund	R	356.4	10.23	0.058	2.66	O	1.7	-0.4	1.0	4.2	-2.2	24.1	23.3	9.9	800-268-8186
★★★	AV+	Dynamic Fund of Canada	R	196.4	16.03	0.205	2.49	O	1.7	1.0	2.2	5.0	-3.6	12.5	11.7	9.1	800-268-8186
★★★★	AV+	Elliott & Page Equity Fund	R	173.7	11.69	1.052	1.97	O	1.8	8.4	11.1	22.4	9.8	16.5	15.3	·	800-363-6647
★	LO	Empire Elite Equity Fund 5	R	269.5	96.62		2.57	D	1.2	4.9	6.7	14.5	4.4	10.4	11.2	6.5	613-548-1881
★★★	AV-	Empire Equity Growth Fund 3(R)	R	14.3	23.10		1.28	F	1.4	5.1	7.2	14.8	4.3	13.4	12.4	10.0	613-548-1881
★★	AV-	Empire Premier Equity Fund 1	R	178.4	81.52		1.54	F	1.1	4.7	6.4	14.2	5.1	11.9	10.9	8.7	613-548-1881
★★	LO	Equitable Life Canadian Stock Fund	R	19.5	10.57		2.25	D	0.8	4.6	2.7	11.1	6.8	11.1	·	·	519-886-5210
★★★	LO	Equitable Life Seg. Common Stock	R	17.6	13.73		1.04	F	1.5	5.2	4.3	14.9	9.8	13.9	10.6	7.2	519-886-5210
★★★	LO	Ethical Growth Fund(R)	R	190.5	8.43		2.24	O	0.9	4.8	6.7	17.5	7.5	13.7	9.3	·	800-267-5019
★★★	AV	Ferique Equity Fund(R)	R	81.7	35.73	0.145	0.57	N	1.5	4.9	4.6	13.7	7.5	12.5	11.0	8.9	800-461-61[illegible]
★★	AV+	Fidelity Capital Builder Fund	R	590.3	18.96		2.61	O	3.0	5.2	6.3	15.1	3.2	10.5	9.7	·	800-263-4077
★★★	AV	First Canadian Equity Index	R	200.0	13.52	0.029	1.51	N	1.3	4.2	4.5	12.5	5.0	12.4	8.7	·	416-927-6000
NA	·	First Cdn. Growth Fund	R	80.0	11.18	0.002	2.26	N	1.0	3.7	4.0	12.0	2.9	·	·	·	416-927-6000
★	AV	Fonds de Professionnels Cdn. Equity(R)	R	64.6	14.68	0.444	0.75	N	1.5	4.8	5.8	15.9	5.1	10.2	7.8	·	514-350-5050
★★	AV	Fonds Desjardins Actions(R)	R	64.0	22.24	0.344	1.98	N	1.3	4.7	3.9	11.8	4.8	11.3	8.0	·	800-361-2680
NA	·	Fonds Desjardins Croissance(R)	R	5.4	10.14		1.80m	N	0.8	2.1	3.8	10.5	·	·	·	·	800-361-2680
★	AV	Fonds Desjardins Environnement(R)	R	12.4	12.00	0.286	1.98	N	1.3	3.1	2.6	12.6	5.0	9.8	6.8	·	800-361-2680
★★	LO	Fonds Ficadre Actions	R	6.3	8.23	0.310	2.75	R	1.3	2.9	4.8	17.1	4.8	11.9	8.9	·	800-667-7648
NA	·	G.T. Global Canada Worldwide RSP	R	43.6	5.66		2.70	O	1.1	5.0	8.8	13.1	·	·	·	·	800-588-4880
★★	AV	General Trust of Canada Cdn Equity(R)	R	26.8	29.04	1.818	1.88	N	2.1	5.1	6.4	16.8	6.3	11.2	7.9	5.3	514-871-7530

Funds. A sample of the data provided is shown in Figure 22.6. Funds are grouped into categories according to the type of securities they predominantly invest in. As well as reporting one-month, three-month, six-month and one-year total returns (including reinvestment of distributions) these tables provide 2-, 3-, 5-, and 10-year compound rates of return and a ranking of the one-month return volatility against other funds in the same category. Similar data are also provided for an extensive list of national and international **benchmark portfolios**. All mutual funds are placed in one of the following asset categories:

1. Canadian equity funds
2. Canadian small-to-mid cap equity funds
3. International equity funds
4. US equity funds
5. European equity funds
6. Asian and Pacific Rim funds
7. Latin American and emerging market funds
8. Precious metal and resource funds
9. Sector equity funds
10. Canadian balanced funds
11. US and international balanced funds
12. Canadian bond funds
13. International bond funds
14. Mortgage funds
15. Money market funds
16. International money market funds

Many US studies have compared the performance of investment companies that invest primarily in common stocks with the performance of a *benchmark portfolio* that consisted of a combination of (1) a market index, such as Standard & Poor's 500-stock index, and (2) a risk-free asset, such as Treasury bills. Each particular combination was chosen so that the benchmark portfolio had a risk level that was equal to that of the investment company. Thus, an investment company that had a beta of 0.80 would be compared with a benchmark portfolio that had 80% invested in the market index and 20% invested in the risk-free asset.[15]

One way of determining whether or not a mutual fund has beaten the market is to subtract the average return on the benchmark portfolio from the average return of the mutual fund. This amount is known as the fund's ***ex post*** **alpha**, denoted α_p:

$$\alpha_p = ar_p - ar_{bp} \tag{22.3}$$

where ar_p is the average return on portfolio p and ar_{bp} is the average return on the benchmark portfolio associated with portfolio p. Note that if $\alpha_p > 0$, then the portfolio will have performed well because it will have had positive risk-adjusted returns. Conversely, if $\alpha_p < 0$, then the portfolio will have had inferior returns.

---

[15] Alternatively, the benchmark portfolio may be based on the investment company's standard deviation relative to that of a market index, such as the S&P 500. For example, if the investment company's standard deviation has been 60% of the index's standard deviation, then the mix should consist of 60% invested in the market index and 40% invested in the risk-free asset. The results from evaluating mutual fund performance when using beta as the measure of risk seems to be very similar to the results when standard deviation is used. See, for example, Hany A. Shawky, "An Update on Mutual Funds: Better Grades," *Journal of Portfolio Management* 8, no. 2 (Winter 1982): 29–34.

INSTITUTIONAL ISSUES

Management Fees, Operating Expenses and Brokerage Costs

If the old saw that you get exactly what you pay for were true in the mutual fund arena, costs might not matter. But the fact is that the reverse is true: the more you pay, the less you earn.[16]

-John Bogle

Over the past decade mutual funds have been the fastest growing segment of the financial services sector. At the end of 1985 there were 155 funds offered in Canada with a total of $10.2 billion under management. By the end of 1995 these figures had grown to 916 funds with $146.2 billion under management, representing impressive average compound growth rates of 19.4% and 30.5% respectively. With an average management fee of 1.5%, the $146.2 billion would yield total fee revenues of about $2.2 billion, suggesting that mutual fund management had become big business in Canada. It is interesting, therefore, to examine the cost structure of mutual funds in a little more detail.

Funds typically incur two kinds of expenses: direct costs (i.e., management fees and operating expenses) are reported regularly in the financial press (see Figure 22.6, column marked MER, for Management Expense Ratio). Transactions costs, however, are only partly measurable. While brokerage costs can be identified, implicit costs such as the effect of bid-ask spreads and the price impacts of trading are hard to calculate and are rarely estimated. In Canada, brokerage costs are recorded only in the detailed annual financial statements of the fund and are not included in the calculation of the MER.

Management fees can vary quite dramatically even between funds that appear to have similar investment objectives. The table below shows both management fees and MERs for sets of no-load funds sponsored by two Canadian chartered banks. The data were taken from year-end financial reports for 1994.

MANAGEMENT FEES. There are six major reasons for differences in management fees between funds. We will look at each in turn.

	TD Green Line		Royal Trust	
Type of Fund	*Fees*	*MERs*	*Fees*	*MERs*
Cdn. Money Market	0.55%	0.72%	0.93%	1.14%
US Money Market	0.98	1.16	0.93	1.08
Cdn. Fixed Income	0.82	1.04	1.14	1.34
Cdn. Mortgage	0.92	1.62	1.30	2.23
Cdn. Index	0.79	1.02	N/A	N/A
Cdn. Equity	1.93	2.12	1.63	2.14
US Index	0.43	0.67	N/A	N/A
US Equity	N/A	N/A	1.57	1.92
International Bond	1.75	2.00	1.40	1.72
Intl. & Global Equity	2.12	2.41	1.87	2.78
Specialty	2.05	2.33	1.64	2.23

[16] John Bogle, *Bogle on Mutual Funds: New Perspectives for the Intelligent Investor* (New York: Dell Publishing, 1994), p. 208.

1. **The asset mix**. Different asset mixes require different levels of management activity. In the case of money market and index funds, the assets and asset mix are predetermined. Therefore, little management effort is required for research, security analysis, and selection. As a result fees are generally low. Actively managed equity and international funds require constant monitoring and frequent analysis of markets and securities and, therefore, command higher fees.
2. **Investment practices**. Two funds that ostensibly invest primarily in the same type of assets may, in fact, differ noticeably in their investment practices. Whereas one fund will restrict its investments to the primary asset class (say mortgages), the other may include a 10 or 20% equity component to try to improve performance. This increases both research and brokerage costs. In the same vein, a global bond and equity fund may add investment in currency derivatives unrelated to any hedging strategy (in other words, a currency gamble). Such a move involves added expenses for derivative expertise that may have to be obtained from outside advisors — and thus, added transactions costs.
3. **Average unitholder account size**. When the average size of the unitholder accounts is small, the fund incurs more administrative costs to process statements, tax returns, and other unitholder communications. To control these costs many funds establish a minimum investment requirement. One of the fund groups with the lowest MERs has established an investment minimum of $25 000.
4. **Distribution system**. A fund that employs an in-house sales force and that charges a loading fee has a different management structure from a no-load fund that distributes its product through existing institutions like banks or trust companies. In general, load funds charge higher management fees than no-load funds because there is less sales administration involved in the latter. No-load funds, however, must sometimes pay minor trailer fees (commissions) to the institutions that distribute the units to the public.

   The type of load can also affect the management fees of load funds. For example, the average fees for the Class A units (front-end load) of four typical load funds in 1994 were 1.70% while the fees for the Class B units (back-end load) of the same funds were 1.99%. This is because the load fee is not received by the fund from the investor until redemption occurs.
5. **Economies of scale**. There are economies of scale in the provision of management services to mutual funds, particularly in the case of money market and index funds. In these cases an increase in the size of the fund involves nothing more than purchasing more of the same assets. Even actively managed funds show a less than proportional increase in management cost with increase in size as long as there is no change in asset mix. Economies of scale partially explain why management fees for US mutual funds are lower than those typically found in Canada. Earl Bederman, in "Competition and Change in the Individual Investment Market: A Study Conducted for The Investment Funds Institute of Canada" (Toronto: Investor Economics, Inc., October 1994), reports that, in 1993, average MERs for no-load international equity funds in Canada were 28.4% higher than those in the US (1.90% versus 1.48%) while the US funds were, on average, 278% larger than the corresponding Canadian ones. At the same time average Canadian MERs for deferred load international equity funds were 3% lower than those in the US, the average size of the funds being essentially equal. This suggests that management fees should be calculated on a sliding scale such that they decrease as the fund size increases. The TD Green Line US Index Fund actually does this.

The quoted management fees start at 0.5% for the first $25 million in assets and decline to 0.25% for asset values in excess of $100 million.

6. **Use of outside managers**. In most instances, the fund sponsor also acts as the investment manager, but in the case of specialized funds the sponsor may employ an outside specialist or an advisor to assist in the management of the investments. Outside managers/advisors are frequently associated with international and global funds and other specialized types such as science and technology or precious metal funds. This can result in a double set of management fees being paid to operate the fund.

The fact that management fees are based on a percentage of asset values should be a cause for unitholders to be concerned. Although such a scheme is intended to reward better performance—all other things being equal, the higher the fund value (i.e., the performance) the higher the fee—it can also encourage artificial inflation of the value of the fund. Valuation is based on continual recalculation of the fair market value of the assets held. Therefore, it is appropriate for mutual funds to invest only in assets that are themselves subject to continual revaluation in a liquid market. National Policy No. 39 recognizes the difficulties associated with thinly traded or illiquid assets and regulates the proportion of these that each fund can hold. For example, holdings of private placements or over-the-counter options are restricted to 10% of the value of the portfolio. Many mutual funds do hold some proportion of these assets in their portfolios, whose valuation, involving some degree of subjectivity, may be optimistic. Related party transactions, such as the negotiated purchase of an asset from a related company, can also involve a valuation of assets that differs from an objective market price.

OPERATING EXPENSES. Operating costs used in the calculation of MERs are defined as all costs associated with the operation of the fund (record keeping, custodial fees, audit, etc.) but excluding goods and services tax and brokerage commissions. The last two are costs an individual investor would have to incur when managing his or her own portfolio. The MER, then, reflects the additional costs an investor incurs by virtue of purchasing mutual fund units.

BROKERAGE COSTS. It is clear that MERs do not tell the whole story. Brokerage costs can have a significant effect on a fund's performance. The following table shows an analysis of the

	1994		1993	
	$	%	$	%
Management fee	33.42	2.00	25.08	2.00
Operating expenses	5.43	0.32	4.62	0.37
MER-related expenses	38.85	2.32	29.70	2.37
Taxes	2.72	0.16	2.08	0.17
Brokerage costs	19.00	1.14	25.65	2.05
Non-MER costs	21.72	1.30	27.73	2.22
Total costs	60.57	3.62	57.43	4.59
Portfolio turnover rate	2.4×		3.4×	

INSTITUTIONAL ISSUES (continued)

total management costs (in millions of dollars and percent of average assets) incurred by the Altamira Equity Fund in 1993 and 1994, using data obtained from the 1994 annual report.

The table shows that although the MER changed little from year to year the total costs changed significantly as a result of the change in brokerage costs. The two main factors that influence brokerage costs are portfolio turnover and soft-dollar transactions. A passively managed portfolio, like an index fund, will trade relatively infrequently and, therefore, incur lower transactions costs than an actively managed portfolio that is traded frequently in the expectation of exploiting undervalued (or disposing of overvalued) securities. The fund management can elect to execute their trades by using either a full-service broker or a discount broker. If they use the former the commission includes research and other services, including in some cases back-office operations (for example, record keeping, custodial and even filing services). The effect of this is to remove a number of management expenses from the income statement where they are likely to be noticed and from the reported MER that an investor uses to assess fund performance. Furthermore, funds that are sponsored by brokerage houses may incur higher transactions costs through "churning" the portfolio to feed additional commission income back to the sponsor.

What does the investor get as a result of paying management fees, operating expenses and brokerage costs? Unfortunately, few Canadian studies address this question. A number of US studies, however, shed some interesting light on the issue and lead to the following general conclusions. (References for these studies can be found at the end of the chapter.)

1. Large funds perform no better, other things being equal, than smaller funds, where size is measured by the dollar value of the fund's total assets.
2. Funds with load charges performed no better, other things being equal, than those with no load charges. Because of the load charge, investors in no-load funds did better than those in load funds.
3. Funds with higher **portfolio turnover rates** had lower levels of performance, other things being equal. (A fund's turnover rate is the ratio of the smaller of purchases or sales during a time period divided by the average total asset value during the period, and, therefore, is a measure of the amount of trading executed during the period.)

One reasonable explanation for these conclusions is that, in an efficient market, higher expense ratios and more frequent portfolio revisions will cause a fund to incur higher costs that cannot be consistently offset by the higher returns obtained by trading mispriced securities. Furthermore, whereas revisions to a fund's portfolio may be necessary in order to maintain a specified risk level or dividend yield, the evidence indicates that revisions intended to exploit supposed market inefficiencies generally prove to be unprofitable.

Figure 22.7(a) shows the distribution of *ex post* alpha values for 70 mutual funds, based on monthly returns beginning in 1955 and going through 1964. The average value was .09% per year, suggesting that the typical fund provided approximately the same return as a market-based passive fund with a constant beta equal to the fund's average beta. Of the 70 funds, 40 had positive *ex post* alphas and 30 had negative *ex post* alphas.

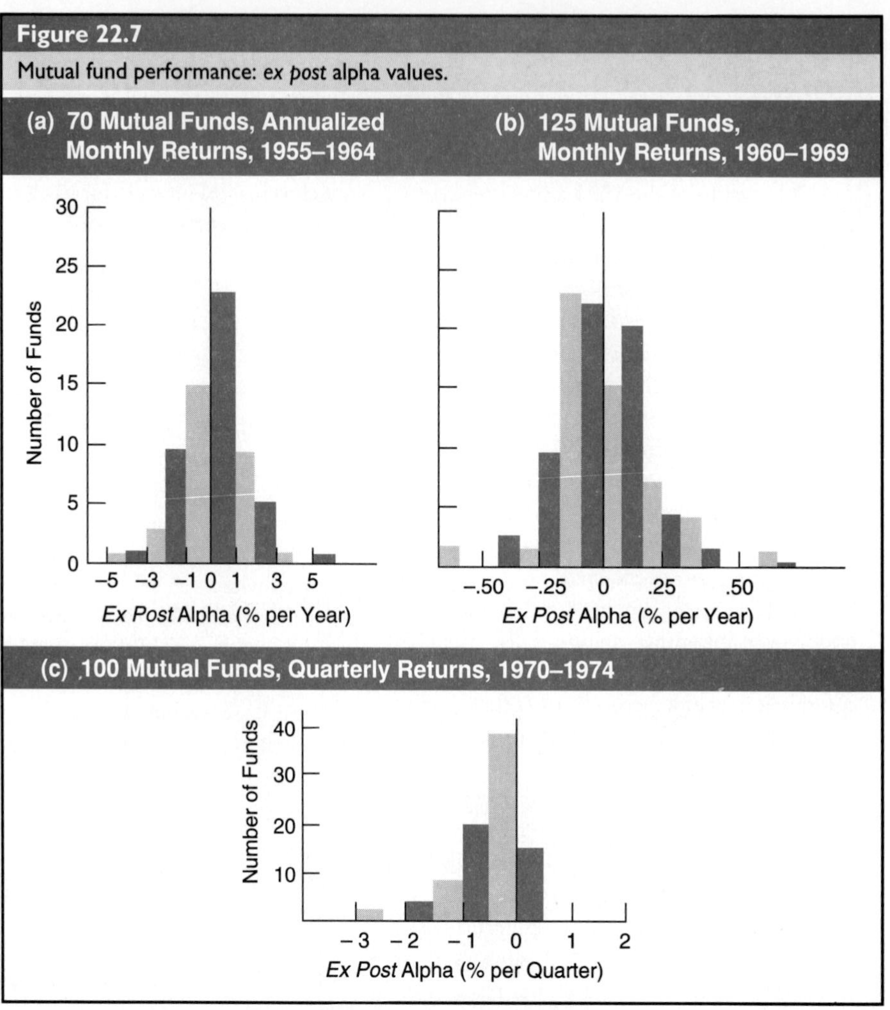

SOURCE: (a) Adapted from Norman E. Mains, "Risk, the Pricing of Capital Assets, and the Evaluation of Investment Portfolios: Comment," *Journal of Business* 50, no. 3 (July 1977): 378–80; (b) United States Securities and Exchange Commission, *Institutional Investor Study Report*, March 10, 1971 (Washington DC: US Governmental Printing Office); (c) Merrill Lynch, Pierce, Fenner & Smith, Inc., *Investment Performance Analysis, Comparative Survey, 1970–1974.*

Different time periods give slightly different results. Figure 22.7(b) shows the distribution of *ex post* alphas based on monthly returns for 125 funds beginning in 1960 and going through 1969. The average alpha was .05% per month, or about .60% per year. During this period, the typical fund outperformed a passive fund of similar risk by slightly more than .50% per year, and slightly more than half (53%) of the funds had positive *ex post* alphas.

Figure 22.7(c) provides a third example. It shows returns for 100 funds based on quarterly returns beginning in 1970 and going through 1974. The average *ex post* alpha was –.50% per quarter, or approximately –2.00% per year, and only 20 of the funds had positive alphas.

Although not shown in the figure, two more recent studies of mutual funds that invest in common stocks reached similar conclusions. In the first study, annual returns for 143 mutual funds from 1965 through 1984 were examined. The average *ex post* alpha was –.88% per year, and only 44 of the funds had positive alphas. The second study, using monthly returns from April 1979 through March 1989, found the average *ex post* alpha value to be equal to –.062% per month (or –.74% per year), with only 115 out of 257 funds having positive alphas.[17]

These results suggest that the average mutual fund has not significantly outperformed an equal-risk passive alternative over any extended period.[18] This is not too surprising. After all, the market's performance is itself an average of the performance of all investors. If, on the average, mutual funds had beaten the market, then some other group of investors would have lost to the market. With the substantial amount of professional management in today's stock market, it is difficult to think of a likely group of victims.

► Market Timing

To achieve superior portfolio performance, an investor must either select securities that outperform others of comparable risk or switch from risk class to risk class at appropriate times. The latter strategy is often called market timing or asset allocation (discussed more fully in Chapter 24). The idea is to hold a high-beta portfolio prior to market rises and a low-beta portfolio prior to market declines. An all-equity fund can change its beta by switching among stocks that have different betas. That is, a high-beta portfolio can be achieved by holding high-beta securities, and a low-beta portfolio can be achieved by holding low-beta securities. Although a balanced fund can also do this, it can change its beta in another manner — namely, by altering the relative proportions it has invested in stocks and bonds. Typically, the more a balanced fund has invested in stocks, the higher its beta.

Successful market timing will eventually be reflected in a positive ex post alpha that is based on long-term performance. Overall performance may also be separated into one part attributed to security selection and another part attributed to market timing.

In a US study of the performance of 57 mutual funds over the period from 1953 through 1962, only one was found with a record suggesting any significant ability to time the market.[19] A later study of the performance of 116 funds from February 1968 through June 1980 found that only three funds had significant timing ability over the entire period, with only one fund having a record indicating significant market timing ability in both the

---

[17] Edwin J. Elton, Martin J. Gruber, Sanjiv Das, and Matthew Hlavka, "Efficiency with Costly Information: A Reinterpretation of Evidence from Managed Portfolios," *Review of Financial Studies* 6, no. 1 (1993): 1–22; and Ravi Shukla and Charles Trzcinka, "Performance Measurement of Managed Portfolios," *Financial Markets, Institutions and Instruments* 1, no. 4 (1992).

[18] Similar conclusions can be drawn regarding pension and endowment funds. See Eugene F. Fama, "Efficient Capital Markets: II," *Journal of Finance* 46, no. 5 (December 1991): 1575–1617, particularly pp. 1605–1607, and the Lakonishok, Schleifer, and Vishny study cited in footnote 30.

[19] Jack L. Treynor and Kay Mazuy, "Can Mutual Funds Outguess the Market?" *Harvard Business Review* 44, no. 4 (July-August 1966): 131–36.

first and the second half of the period.[20] Furthermore, a recent study of 257 funds from April 1979 through March 1989 indicates that the average fund had negative timing ability.[21] This suggests that the average fund might have been better off if its timing activities had been the exact opposite of what was actually done.

Such results are not surprising. If many funds were consistently successful at market timing, they would have shown up in the previously mentioned tests for superior overall performance unless they were consistently engaging in inferior security selection that offset their superior timing ability. However, such a situation seems highly improbable. More likely, investment managers find it as difficult to time the market as to select underpriced securities. Such is the lot of an investor in a highly efficient market.

► Performance of Canadian Mutual Funds

Canadian studies of mutual fund performance are not plentiful. An early study, using Jensen's methodology, examined the performance of 19 Canadian mutual funds over the period 1960 to 1974.[22] The average beta for these funds was only 0.79 with a maximum of 0.99 and a minimum of 0.54, indicating that these funds are quite conservatively managed. The average R-squared was only 0.52 with a maximum of 0.69 and a minimum of 0.24 that suggests that these funds were not well diversified and had significant levels of unsystematic risk. None of the funds showed superior performance and, even after allowing for management and administration costs, underperformed the TSE index which was used as a benchmark portfolio.

Dhingra attempted to determine whether *ex post* systematic risk levels of mutual funds were consistent with their stated investment objectives. Data on 88 mutual funds whose stated objectives could be identified were collected for the period 1966 to 1975. These funds fell into two categories — growth funds or income funds. In general, growth funds generated higher returns and exhibited higher betas than income funds suggesting that the funds are generally managed in a style consistent with their stated objectives. This conclusion is borne out by a later study of 71 mutual funds over the 1980 to 1989 time period which found that performance was not consistent from year to year but that management style was.[23]

Do mutual funds provide protection against inflation? This was the question addressed by Calvet and Lefoll. Using Jensen's measure of performance on a sample of 17 mutual funds from 1966 to 1979 they concluded that Canadian funds perform no better than the market

---

[20] Roy D. Henriksson, "Market Timing and Mutual Fund Performance: An Empirical Investigation," *Journal of Business* 57, no. 1, pt. 1 (January 1984): 73–96. Similar results suggesting that mutual fund managers have no special ability to time the market is provided by Stanley J. Kon, "The Market-Timing Performance of Mutual Fund Managers," *Journal of Business* 56, no. 3 (July 1983): 323–47; Eric C. Chang and Wilbur G. Lewellen, "Market Timing and Mutual Fund Investment Performance," *Journal of Business* 57, no. 1, pt. 1 (January 1984): 57–72; and Chua and Woodward, "Gains from Stock Market Timing." op. cit.

[21] Shukla and Trzcinka, "Performance Measurement of Managed Portfolios."

[22] D. Grant, "Investment Performance of Canadian Mutual Funds: 1960–1974," *Journal of Business Administration* 8, no. 1 (Fall 1976): 1–9.

[23] H. L. Dhingra, "Portfolio Volatility Adjustment by Canadian Mutual Funds, *Journal of Business Finance and Accounting* 5, no.4 (Winter 1978): 305–33. J. McLaughlin and N. Bossen, "The Historical Performance of Canadian Investment Managers: Predictors of Future Performance?" *Canadian Investment Review* III, no.1 (Spring 1990): 87–91.

after risk adjustment and provide no better inflation protection. The fund alphas and betas were remarkably similar in both real and nominal terms.[24]

Two studies examine the potential gains from market timing in Canada.[25] The first uses simulations to obtain estimates of the gains to be obtained from less than perfect forecasts of future market conditions. With perfect hindsight, after including modest transactions costs, a fund manager who switches between common stocks and T-bills can expect a return of about 4% more and a standard deviation of about 5% less than buying and holding a market index. With less than perfect foresight the manager must achieve an accuracy of 80% in forecasting both bull and bear markets in order to outperform a buy and hold strategy. This is probably beyond the reach of most managers.

The second compares two different approaches to market timing. One, referred to as a *swing fund* (SW) approach, requires the manager to shift funds between asset classes in response to new forecasts about economic conditions. The other approach, referred to as **tactical asset allocation** (TAA), relies on the derivative securities market to implement shifts between asset classes. A comparison of eight TAA simulation models with six SF managers showed that six of the TAA models and three SF managers showed statistically significant market timing ability. On average the TAA "managers" outperformed the SF managers in market timing ability, although both added value to the portfolios.

▸ Bond Mutual Funds

All of the results reported so far focus on mutual funds that have at least a large part of their assets invested in common stocks. But what about bond mutual funds? Is their performance similar to that of stock funds? One study looked at a sample of 41 bond funds over the period from 1979 through 1988.[26]

Using a variety of models to produce benchmark returns, the average *ex post* alpha valued ranged from –.023% to –.069% per month. Furthermore, regardless of the model, at least two-thirds of the funds had negative alphas. Expanding the sample to cover 223 bond funds over the period 1987 to 1991 produced similar results. It was determined that there was an inverse relationship between the size of a fund's expense ratio and its performance — that is, higher expenses tended to be associated with worse performance. In summary it appears that the results regarding stock funds are also applicable to bond funds.

▸ Persistence of Performance

Even if the average mutual fund displays no ability to select underpriced securities or time the market, it is still possible that a few of the funds do have such abilities. If so, they should continually generate higher returns and rank at or near the top of their peer groups over consecutive, non-overlapping evaluation periods.

---

[24] A. L. Calvet and J. Lefoll, "Performance and Systematic Risk Stability of Canadian Mutual Funds under Inflation," *Journal of Business Finance and Accounting* 8, no.2 (Summer 1981): 279–89.

[25] J. H. Chua, R. S. Woodward and E. C. To, "Potential Gains from Stock Market Timing in Canada," *Financial Analysts Journal* 43 (September-October 1987): 50–6;E. J. Weigel and J. H. Ilkiw, "Market Timing Skills in Canada: An Assessment," *Canadian Investment Review* IV, no.1 (Spring 1991): 19–28.

[26] Christopher R. Blake, Edwin J. Elton, and Martin J. Gruber, "The Performance of Bond Mutual Funds," *Journal of Business* 66, no. 3 (July 1993): 371–403.

Table 22.1

Consecutive-Period Returns for Mutual Funds, 1974–1988.

	Subsequent Average Excess Quarterly Rate of Return							
	Group Number (1 = Worst; 8 = Best)							
Formation Period (# of Quarters)	*1*	*2*	*3*	*4*	*5*	*6*	*7*	*8*
One	1.42%	1.66%	1.84%	1.91%	2.11%	2.45%	2.41%	2.67%
Two	1.33	1.73	1.81	1.99	2.07	1.99	2.33	3.24
Four	.99	1.68	1.40	1.82	1.90	2.32	2.94	3.47
Eight	.69	1.05	1.40	1.76	1.59	2.24	2.11	2.80

SOURCE: Adapted from Darryll Hendricks, Jayendu Patel, and Richard Zeckhauser, "Hot Hands in Mutual Funds: Short-Run Persistence of Relative Performance, 1974–1988," *Journal of Finance* 48, no. 1 (March 1993): Table III, pp. 108–109.

Persistence of Returns

One study carefully examined the quarterly excess returns of 165 mutual funds from 1974 through 1988 in order to see whether funds with relatively high returns in one period tended to have relatively high returns in the next period.[27] These funds had invested primarily in common stocks with objectives of either growth, growth and income, or aggressive growth.

In the study each fund was placed in one of eight groups based on its excess return over the first quarter of 1974. Then the excess return of each group was measured for the second quarter of 1974 by averaging the excess returns of the funds in that group. The process was then repeated, except that funds were assigned to one of eight groups based on their quarterly excess returns for the second quarter of 1974, and then the average fund excess return for each group was calculated for the third quarter of 1974. This process was repeated through the fourth quarter of 1988, resulting in a set of quarterly excess returns for each group ranging from the second quarter of 1974 through the fourth quarter of 1988. At this point average excess quarterly returns for these eight groups were calculated over the entire period.

The top line of Table 22.1 displays the results. Mutual funds that were in the bottom one-eighth (group 1) had an average quarterly excess return of 1.42% in the quarter after they were ranked in the bottom. Conversely, mutual funds that ranked in the top one-eighth (group 8) had an average quarterly excess return of 2.67% in the quarter after their top ranking. Glancing at the other averages indicates that mutual funds that did better in one quarter were likely to do better in the next quarter.

The evidence presented in the next three lines of the table is even stronger. Consider the second line. Here funds were assigned to one of eight groups based on their excess returns over the previous two quarters, and then their excess returns were recorded over the next quarter. Note again how it appears that mutual funds that did better over two quarters were more likely to do better in the next quarter. The last two lines were similarly constructed, except that the assignment of the funds to groups was based on their excess returns over the previous four and eight months, respectively.

---

[27] Darryll Hendricks, Jayendu Patel, and Richard Zeckhauser, "Hot Hands in Mutual Funds: Short-Run Persistence of Relative Performance, 1974–1988," *Journal of Finance* 48, no. 1 (March 1993): 93–130.

Table 22.2

Consecutive-Period Rankings for Mutual Funds, 1976–1987

	Subsequent Period					
	One-Year		*Two-Year*		*Three-Year*	
	Winners	*Losers*	*Winners*	*Losers*	*Winners*	*Losers*
Initial Period:						
Winners	55.3%	44.7%	59.9%	40.1%	61.2%	38.8%
Losers	44.9	55.1	40.3	59.7	22.9	77.1

SOURCE: Adapted from William N. Goetzmann and Roger G. Ibbotson, "Do Winners Repeat?" *Journal of Portfolio Management* 20, no. 2 (Winter 1994): Exhibits 1, 8, and 11, pp. 11, 13 and 17.

Of particular interest is the extreme difference in the sizes of the average excess returns in groups 1 and 8. For formation periods of at least four quarters, the difference is more than 2% per quarter, with the largest difference for four quarters. This suggest that an investor should be concerned with short-term relative performance, avoiding mutual funds that are in the bottom octile, while seeking those that are in the top octile (or two), based on the funds' returns over the past four quarters. Similar results were obtained when various risk-adjusted measures of performance, such as *ex post* alphas, were used. However, it is important to remember that these results are based on averages, and that individual funds can differ significantly from these averages. In other words, there are no assurances that top performing funds will continue to perform well.

Persistence of Rankings

Another study looked at the performance rankings of broad-based equity funds in consecutive time periods.[28] For each year beginning in 1976 each mutual fund in a sample of 258 was labelled either "winner" or "loser" based on whether its return was in the top or bottom half. This continued through 1988, by which time the sample had grown to 728 funds. Then fund labels were compared to see what labels the winners or losers received in adjacent years. The results are shown in Table 22.2.

If there is persistence in performance, then substantially more than half the winners in year t should be winners in year $t + 1$ (and substantially less than half should be losers). Similarly, substantially more than half of the losers should remain losers in the next year. The table shows that this is what happened. Over 55% of the winners remained winners and losers remained losers. Even more dramatic results were obtained as adjacent two-year and three-year periods were examined, when about 60% of the winners remained winners in the next period. As for losers, over two-year periods about 60% of them remained losers and over three years over 70% of them remained losers. These results were confirmed when using subgroups of funds and risk-adjusted measures of performance. However, it should again be noted that about 40% of the three-year winners turned into losers over the next three years, indicating that there is plenty of uncertainty about good performance continuing into the future.

---

[28] William N. Goetzmann and Roger G. Ibbotson, "Do Winners Repeat?" *Journal of Portfolio Management* 20, no. 2 (Winter 1994): 9–18. For a discussion of rankings in general, see John Markese, "Mutual Fund Rankings: What Accounts for Differences?" *AAII Journal* 15, no. 4 (April 1993): 31–33.

Instead of looking at above-average funds, another study looked at only the best performing funds.[29] Specifically, for each year beginning in 1982 the top 20 funds were identified based on their annual returns that year. Then their rank was determined for the next year based on their annual return then, and the process was repeated through 1992. The average rank of the top 20 funds in the year after being so honoured was 284th out of 681, which is only slightly above the median. Furthermore, the top 20 funds based on their returns over the 1972–1982 period had ten-year average returns over the subsequent decade that resulted in their having a slightly above-median average rank of 142nd out of 309. Lastly, the equity funds on the *Forbes* Honor Role (prepared since 1974 and analyzed through 1992, and similar to the top 20) had average annual returns in the year after being so honoured of 13.0%, whereas the average equity fund had an average return of 12.8%.

The results from these three studies indicate that there is a mild degree of persistence of performance among mutual funds.[30] Investors still face a good deal of risk if they purchase a fund that recently was a top performer. Clearly, past performance is not a strong predictor (let alone a guarantee) of future performance.

EVALUATING MUTUAL FUNDS

Along with the rapid growth in money invested in mutual funds in recent years has come a corresponding increase in the number and diversity of mutual funds offered to investors. Not surprisingly then, various organizations have created businesses devoted to evaluating mutual funds. One of the most prominent of these organizations is Morningstar, Inc., located in Chicago. Besides providing a wealth of information on a given fund, it also provides an in-depth analysis of past returns.

The best way to understand the breadth of Morningstar's mutual fund evaluations is to consider an analysis of a specific fund. An example involving the Fidelity Magellan Fund, an equity fund, is shown in Figure 22.8 and explained next. Where different, a description of the analysis is also given for a fixed-income fund.

Performance/Risk Analysis

In the left column of Figure 22.8 is a section with the heading *Performance/Risk*. Displayed here are the average returns earned by the fund over various time periods ending February 28, 1994, and ranging from the past three months to the past 15 years. These returns are calculated net of operating expenses and distribution fees, although load charges are ignored. Thus, the average returns reflect what an investor would have earned after having bought the fund's shares. Next to each average return is an indication of how it compares with the average return on the S&P 500 over the same time period. For fixed-income funds the S&P 500 is replaced by the Lehman Brothers Aggregate Bond Index.

---

[29] John C. Bogle, *Bogle on Mutual Funds*, Chapter 4. Also see John C. Bogle, "Selecting Equity Mutual Funds," *Journal of Portfolio Management* 18, no. 2 (Winter 1992): 94–100.

[30] Persistence of performance was also observed in the study of bond mutual funds cited in footnote 23, and in a study of pension funds. See Josef Lakonishok, Andrei Shleifer, and Robert W. Vishny, "The Structure and Performance of the Money Management Industry," *Brookings Papers on Economic Activity: Microeconomics 1992*, pp. 339–379. It should be noted that all of these studies finding persistence have been challenged by others on methodological grounds.

Figure 22.8

Performance and risk analysis of the Magellan Fund (excerpts).

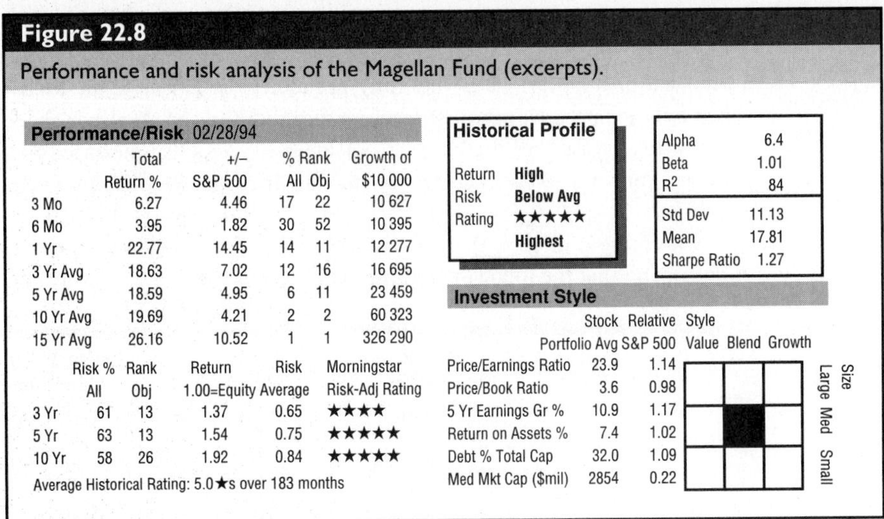

Performance/Risk 02/28/94

	Total Return %	+/– S&P 500	% Rank All	% Rank Obj	Growth of $10 000
3 Mo	6.27	4.46	17	22	10 627
6 Mo	3.95	1.82	30	52	10 395
1 Yr	22.77	14.45	14	11	12 277
3 Yr Avg	18.63	7.02	12	16	16 695
5 Yr Avg	18.59	4.95	6	11	23 459
10 Yr Avg	19.69	4.21	2	2	60 323
15 Yr Avg	26.16	10.52	1	1	326 290

	Risk % Rank All	Risk % Rank Obj	Return	Risk 1.00=Equity Average	Morningstar Risk-Adj Rating
3 Yr	61	13	1.37	0.65	★★★★
5 Yr	63	13	1.54	0.75	★★★★★
10 Yr	58	26	1.92	0.84	★★★★★

Average Historical Rating: 5.0★s over 183 months

Historical Profile

Return	**High**
Risk	**Below Avg**
Rating	★★★★★ **Highest**

Alpha	6.4
Beta	1.01
R^2	84
Std Dev	11.13
Mean	17.81
Sharpe Ratio	1.27

Investment Style

	Stock Portfolio Avg	Relative S&P 500
Price/Earnings Ratio	23.9	1.14
Price/Book Ratio	3.6	0.98
5 Yr Earnings Gr %	10.9	1.17
Return on Assets %	7.4	1.02
Debt % Total Cap	32.0	1.09
Med Mkt Cap ($mil)	2854	0.22

SOURCE: Excerpts from *Morningstar Mutual Funds*. A comprehensive publication covering 1310 mutual funds. Morningstar, Inc. 225 W. Wacker Dr., Chicago IL. 60606. March 18, 1994, p. 154.

In the third and fourth columns from the left are the percentile ranks of the fund's average return relative to all mutual funds and relative to those categorized as having a similar stated investment objective. Here a rank of 1 places a fund at the top and a rank of 100 places a fund at the bottom. The fifth column shows to what amount a $10 000 dollar investment in the fund would have grown over the applicable time period (ignoring taxes and load charges).

Over the three months ending February 28, 1994, Magellan had a return of 6.27%, which was 4.46% better than the S&P 500. This return caused the fund to be ranked at about the 20th percentile against both all funds (17th percentile) and those funds having a similar objective (22nd percentile). Furthermore, over the past 15 years it can be seen that the Magellan Fund did substantially better than the S&P 500, placing it in the first percentile overall and in its category. Note how a $10 000 investment in the Magellan Fund that was made on February 28, 1979, would have grown to $326 290 on February 28, 1994, 15 years later.

Ratings

In the lower part of the *Performance/Risk* section of Figure 22.8 are two columns under *Risk % Rank*, as well as individual columns for *Return, Risk, Average*, and *Morningstar Risk-Adj Rating*. The two columns labelled *Return* and *Risk Average* need to be explained first. Here it is easiest to focus on the three-year row, as the other two rows are straightforward extensions of it. First, the average return for Magellan and all other portfolios having similar objectives are determined for the past three years. Here, the actual net return is adjusted for any load charges that the fund levies on investors. Second, the average three-year returns for all of the similar funds are averaged. Third, Magellan's average return is divided by this overall average. Hence, a return measure of greater than 1 means that the fund did better than average, whereas a return measure of less than 1 indicates that the fund did worse than average. In Magellan's case the return measure of 1.37 indicates that its average return was 37% better than the overall average.

For the *Risk Average* entry, the appropriate monthly Treasury bill return is subtracted from each of the previous 36 monthly net returns to calculate the fund's excess returns. Then only the negative excess returns are summed and the absolute value is divided by 36 to provide a measure of the fund's downside risk. (This risk measure is similar to the risk measure known as *mean shortfall,* which was discussed in Chapter 7's *Institutional Issues* section.)

For example, imagine that this risk measure is calculated over six months instead of 36 months, and that the following returns are observed:

Month	*Fund Return*	*T-bill Return*	*Fund Return less T-bill Return*
1	4.0%	.5%	3.5%
2	−2.0	.5	−2.5
3	.4	.6	−.2
4	5.0	.6	4.4
5	−3.0	.6	−3.6
6	1.0	.7	.3

The three negative excess returns of −2.5%, −.2%, and −3.6% sum to −6.3%. Dividing this sum by 6, the total number of months, results in a downside risk measure of 1.05 (6.3/6).

Downside risk measures are calculated by Morningstar for all similar funds, and an overall average for these funds is determined. Then the fund's downside risk measure is divided by this overall measure; the resulting number is Morningstar's measure of the fund's relative risk. In the case of Magellan, it is .65, indicating that it had 35% less downside risk that the average similar fund over the three-year period.

Under the heading *Risk % Rank* the percentile rankings are found for the fund's downside risk measure against all funds (*All*) and the set of similar funds (*Obj*). Here a percentile rank of 1 indicates that the fund had the least risk, whereas a rank of 100 indicates that the fund had the most risk. In the case of Magellan, its ranks of 61 and 13 over three years indicate that it had more risk than 61% of all the other funds and 13% of the other funds having a comparable objective.

Morningstar's rating system has five categories, as follows:

Stars	*Percentile*	*Return Category*	*Risk Category*
*****	1–10	Highest or High	Lowest or Low
****	11–32.5	Above Average	Below Average
***	33.5–67.5	Average	Average
**	68.5–90	Below Average	Above Average
*	91–100	Lowest or Low	Highest or High

Hence, the percentile rank, based on the set of funds with similar objectives, determines how many stars the fund is given and the category in which it is placed.[31]

The *Morningstar Risk-Adj Rating* is determined by subtracting the fund's downside risk measure from its return measure. In the case of Magellan, its three-year risk-adjusted measure is 1.37 – .65 = .72. This measure is also determined for all the other funds having similar objectives, and then percentile ranks are determined. In the case of Magellan, it ranked somewhere between 11 and 32.5, causing it to receive a four-star rating.

► Historical Profile

Summary performance measures are contained in the *Historical Profile* box in the centre of Figure 22.8. Consider the return measure first. Here, the previously described return measures for three, five, and ten years are averaged using weights of 20%, 30%, and 50% to arrive at a weighted-average return. After doing this for each of the other funds that have similar objectives, the fund is given a percentile rank and then a rating, as indicated before. In the case of Magellan, its percentile rank was somewhere between 1 and 10, giving it a *high* ranking. Similar weighted-average calculations are done for the fund's downside risk measure and risk-adjusted measure, resulting in Magellan's receiving a *below average* risk rating and a five-star *highest* risk-adjusted rating.

At the bottom of the Performance/Risk section is an indication of the *Average Historical Rating* that is based on the *Rating* in the *Historical Profile* section for all of the months that Morningstar has rated the fund. In the case of Magellan, its average overall rating over the past 183 months is five stars — the highest rating category.

► MPT Statistics

In the upper right part of Figure 22.8 is the section that Morningstar refers to as *MPT Statistics*, for Modern Portfolio Theory. The top part provides values for *Alpha*, *Beta*, and R^2. They correspond to the statistics related to a portfolio's *ex post* characteristic line, which is a regression model like the market model that was discussed in Chapter 8.[32] The only difference between the two is that the *ex post* characteristic line uses excess returns instead of returns. Hence, Morningstar regresses the previous 36 monthly excess returns on the mutual fund (that is, the fund's net returns less the corresponding Treasury bill rates) on the previous 36 monthly excess returns on the S&P 500 (that is, the index's returns less the corresponding Treasury bill rates). As a result the fund's *ex post* alpha *(Alpha)* and beta *(Beta)* are estimated. Similarly, R^2 is the coefficient of determination (multiplied by 100) that is determined when the 36 excess returns of the fund are compared with those of the of the S&P 500.

The statistics show that Magellan had a beta of 1.01, similar to that of the S&P 500. Its *ex post* alpha of 6.4% indicates that it did much better than the market on a beta-adjusted basis over the last 36 months. The R^2 of 84 means that roughly 84% of the variation in the excess returns of the fund could be attributed to variations in the excess returns on the S&P 500.

---

31 Similar ratings are provided in *The Individual Investor's Guide to No-Load Mutual Funds* (Chicago: American Association of Individual Investors, 1994).

32 The *ex post* characteristic line is discussed more fully in Chapter 25.

The second part of this section provides values for *Std Dev*, *Mean*, and *Sharpe Ratio*. These three values are also based on the previous 36 monthly rates of return on the fund. *Std Dev* and *Mean* are the standard deviation and the average return (annualized) for the portfolio, which for Magellan are 11.13% and 17.81%, respectively. The *Sharpe Ratio*, discussed more fully in Chapter 25, gives a risk-adjusted measure of performance. Here Morningstar takes the fund's excess return over the previous 12 months and divides it by the fund's standard deviation over the previous 36 months. Hence, it is the ratio to risk, which for Magellan equals 1.27.

► Investment Style

This section appears in the lower centre part of Figure 22.8. On the left are six descriptive measures of the average stock held by the fund using the most recently available data. For example, the average *Price/Earnings Ratio* of the stocks held in the Magellan Fund was 23.9 as of February 28, 1994. This number is divided by the average price-earnings ratio of the stocks in the S&P 500, indicating a value of 1.14, or 14% greater than the average ratio in the index. Similarly, the average *Price/Book Ratio* of the stocks held by Magellan was 3.6, or 2% less than the average price-book ratio of the stocks held in the S&P 500. Both of these ratios are weighted averages, where the weight for each security is based on the relative proportion of the fund that is invested in the security. With the exception of the fourth measure, the other measures are also weighted averages of measures of the securities in the fund:

1. *5-Year Earnings-Growth Rate* (%). This measures the average of the securities' five-year earnings-growth rate. Stocks with negative earnings are not included in calculating the average.
2. *Return on Assets* (%). This measures the average of the securities' ratios of earnings after taxes to total assets.
3. *Debt as a Percent of Total Capitalization*. This measures the average of the securities' ratios of long-term debt to total assets.
4. *Median Market Capitalization* (in million dollars). This measures the stock market capitalization of the median security.

The values of these measures are also divided by their respective values for the S&P 500, thereby allowing a quick comparison of how the securities in the fund stack up against the securities in this index.

In the case of a fund that invests in fixed-income securities, all six of these measures are replaced by measures such as average maturity, credit quality, and coupon rate. As mentioned, the Lehman Brothers Aggregate Bond Index replaces the S&P 500 as a standard for comparison.

Also in this part of Figure 22.8 is a 3×3 matrix, which Morningstar calls a *style box*. The two extreme columns represent the investment styles of value and growth, with the middle column representing a mixture of the two. A fund's style is determined by summing the fund's price-earnings ratio and price-book ratio, where both are expressed relative to the S&P 500. Note that this sum for the S&P 500 itself is 2.00 (since each ratio is, by definition, equal to 1.00). Morningstar has decided that if the sum for a fund is less than 1.75, then the fund follows a *value style*. This is because the fund has invested in stocks that collectively have relatively low valuation ratios and hence are viewed as value stocks. On the other hand, if the sum is greater than 2.25, then the fund is deemed to follow a *growth style* because it has invested in stocks with relatively high valuation ratios. Sums between 1.75 and 2.25 indicate that the fund follows a *blended style*, investing in stocks that in aggregate have no distinct style.

In the case of Magellan, its sum is 1.14 + .98 = 2.12, indicating that it follows a blended style. As the value of this sum for the S&P 500 itself is 2.00, the Magellan Fund tends to purchase stocks that have price-earnings and price-book ratios that on average are only slightly higher than the valuation ratios of stocks in the S&P 500.

The three rows of the style box are based on the size of the stocks held by the fund, where size is measured by the median market capitalization figure for the fund. If this figure is less than $1 billion, the fund is deemed to be *small*, and if it is greater than $5 billion, then the fund is deemed to be *large*. A figure between $1 billion and $5 billion—as is the case with Magellan, whose holdings have a median size of $2.854 billion—results in the fund being categorized as *medium*.

In Chapter 17 it was mentioned that stocks can be classified along the two dimensions of value-growth and size. Now it can be seen that investment companies can be similarly classified. Morningstar does this by use of the style box, thereby allowing investors to quickly understand a fund's investment strategy. Nine combinations of the three levels of value-growth and size are possible. Morningstar indicates its classification of a fund by darkening one of the nine sections of the style box. In the case of Magellan the centre box is darkened, indicating that its investment strategy involves purchases of both value and growth stocks without concentrating on either large or small ones.

In the case of fixed-income funds, the columns of the style box are based on the average maturity (soon to be changed to duration) of the securities in the fund, and hence the style box focuses on the fund's interest rate sensitivity. The column headings are *Short Term* (if the average maturity is less than four years), *Intermediate Term* (if the average is between four and ten years), and *Long Term* (if the average is greater than ten years). The rows are based on the average credit quality of the securities in the fund, and hence measure default risk. The row headings are *High* (if the average bond rating is at least AA), *Average* (if the average is between BBB and AA), and *Low* (if the average is less than BBB).

► Caveats

Morningstar's performance measures are useful in giving an investor a quick reading of how a mutual fund has performed in the past relative to other funds. However, several things should be kept in mind.

1. Comparisons are made with the S&P 500 for all equity funds, but this index may not be appropriate for certain funds. For example, a fund that invests primarily in securities listed on NASDAQ might more appropriately be compared with an over-the-counter index.
2. As will be discussed in Chapter 24, portfolio managers can attempt to earn abnormal returns by trying to buy underpriced securities and then profit from their subsequent abnormal price appreciation, or by shifting funds out of the stock market just before it goes down and then back into the stock market just before it rises, or both. Morningstar's performance measures do not indicate which approach the fund is using in its quest for abnormal returns.
3. The use of peer group comparisons to evaluate performance has several serious conceptual and practical shortcomings. For example, the set of similar funds may not be entirely appropriate (even though they may be the best match that Morningstar

can provide), causing the ratings to be misleading. One fund may be restricted to buying just NYSE-listed common stock whereas another is free to purchase stocks that are listed on the NYSE, AMEX, or NASDAQ. Furthermore, similar funds may differ considerably in the amount of risk that they take on. Finally, *survivorship bias* (the tendency for poorly performing funds to go out of business and hence leave the peer group) hampers comparisons with similar funds.

CLOSED-END FUND PREMIUMS AND DISCOUNTS

Several studies have shown that the performance of diversified closed-end investment company managers in the United States is similar to that of open-end investment company managers.[33] When returns are measured by changes in net asset values (plus all distributions), closed-end investment companies appear to be neither better nor worse than open-end ones. Again, there is little evidence that portfolio managers can either select underpriced securities or time the market successfully.

However, there is more to be said about closed-end funds. An investor can purchase an open-end fund's shares for their net asset value (plus any required load charge) and sell them later at the subsequent net asset value. Except for any load charges, the performance of the *management* of such a fund, based on net asset values, corresponds exactly to the returns provided to the *shareholders*. This is not the case for closed-end investment companies, since investors buy and sell shares of investment companies at prices determined on the open (secondary) market. Although some companies have share prices that are above their net asset values (such shares are said to sell at a premium), many have share prices below their net asset values (such shares are said to sell at a discount). Canadian closed-end mutual funds exhibit the same divergence between net asset value and share price as shown in Figure 22.1.

The fact that the price of a closed-end investment company differs from its net asset value, with the magnitude of the difference varying from time to time, introduces an added source of risk and potential return to investors. By purchasing shares at a discount, an investor may be able to earn more than just the change in the company's net asset value. Even if the company's discount remains constant, the effective dividend yield will be greater than that of an otherwise similar no-load, open-end investment company, since the purchase price will be less. If the discount is substantial when the shares are purchased, it may subsequently narrow, and the return will be even greater.[34] On the other hand, if the discount increases, the investor's overall return may be less than that of an otherwise comparable open-end investment company.

Some of the risk associated with varying discounts can be reduced by holding a portfolio of shares in several closed-end investment companies. Discounts on different companies move together, but not perfectly. For example, past data suggest that the standard deviation

---

[33] See, for example, William F. Sharpe and Howard B. Sosin, "Closed-End Investment Companies in the United States: Risk and Return," *Proceedings*, 1974 Meeting of the European Finance Association, ed. B. Jacquillat (Amsterdam: North-Holland Publishing Co., 1975); Antonio Vives, "Analysis of Forecasting Ability of Closed-End Fund's Management," (working paper, Carnegie-Mellon University, September 1975) and "Discounts and Premiums on Closed-End Funds: A Theoretical and Empirical Analysis," Ph.D. diss., Carnegie-Mellon University, 1975.

[34] There is some evidence that discounts narrow during "down markets" and widen during "up markets." See R. Malcolm Richards, Donald R. Fraser, and John C. Groth, "Premiums, Discounts, and the Volatility of Closed-End Mutual Funds," *Financial Review* (Fall 1979): 26–33, and "The Attractions of Closed-End Bond Funds," *Journal of Portfolio Management* 8, no. 2 (Winter 1982): 56–61.

of the percentage change in the ratio of market price to net asset value for a portfolio of 10 to 12 closed-end investment companies is likely to be approximately half that of a typical investment in the shares of a single closed-end investment company.[35]

Open-Ending Closed-End Funds

Explaining the puzzling behaviour of prices of closed-end investment companies is a challenge for anyone who believes that capital markets are highly efficient. For anyone not firmly committed to such a view, the purchase of shares of closed-end investment companies at prices sufficiently below net asset values may provide an opportunity for superior returns.[36] One way of realizing superior returns is for the closed-end investment company to convert to an open-end one.[37] By doing so, the discount on the shares would have to disappear because conversion would result in the investment company's offering its shareholders the right to redeem their shares for their net asset value.

TAXATION OF INVESTMENT FUNDS

Investment funds can be either incorporated or unincorporated. The former are regulated by either the federal or provincial corporations act, depending on the jurisdiction in which it is chartered. The latter are subject to the appropriate provincial securities act and national policies agreed to by all provinces. They are taxed differently.

Incorporated Investment Funds

Incorporated funds are taxed as Canadian corporations at a 25% tax rate if they meet certain conditions. In order to qualify for this rate, 85% of their gross revenues must be derived from Canadian sources; interest may only account for 25% of their gross income; *and* at least 85% of taxable income must be distributed to shareholders as dividends. Failure to meet these three conditions results in tax being assessed at a regular corporate tax rate of about 45%. Dividends received by unit holders are treated as bona fide dividends from Canadian corporations and, therefore, are eligible for the dividend tax credit even though the fund's income may have been derived from interest income or dividends from foreign corporations. Furthermore, dividends received by the fund from tax-paying Canadian corporations are not subject to tax.

A fund that meets the necessary conditions and is largely invested in equities should not face a significant tax bill.

---

35 Sharpe and Sosin, "Closed-End Investment Companies in the United States."

36 Burton G. Malkiel advocated such an investment strategy in the 1973, 1975, and 1981 editions of *A Random Walk Down Wall Street* (New York: W. W. Norton), but not in the 1985 and 1990 editions. The basis for his initial advocacy can be found in two studies: Burton Malkiel, "The Valuation of Closed-End Investment Company Shares," *Journal of Finance* 32, no. 3 (June 1977): 847-859; and Rex Thompson, "The Information Content of Discounts and Premiums on Closed-End Fund Shares," *Journal of Financial Economics*, 6, no. 2/3 (June/September 1978): 151–186.

37 For an analysis of the "open-ending" of closed-end investment companies, see Greggory a. Brauer, " 'Open-Ending' Closed-End Funds," *Journal of Financial Economics*, 13, no. 4 (December 1984): 491–507.

Unincorporated Investment Funds

These funds are not subject to tax. The fund's income, net of expenses, is flowed through to the individual unit holder and taxed in his or her hands. Thus, unit holders have to pay taxes on their proportionate share of the interest income, dividends, and realized capital gains received by the fund. Dividends from taxable Canadian corporations qualify for the dividend tax credit and capital gains are taxed at 75% of the regular rate. The fund's expenses are also flowed through to the investor and may be allocated to income in the most advantageous way. In general, expenses will first be allocated to foreign income, followed by interest income, then either dividends or capital gains depending on the investor's situation.

The total tax payable on income derived from an incorporated fund is very similar to that from an unincorporated fund. Incorporation is perhaps slightly advantageous in that it allows the fund a small measure of flexibility because it can retain for reinvestment up to 15% of its income.

SUMMARY

1. Investment companies are financial intermediaries that obtain money from investors and use it to purchase financial assets.
2. Investment companies offer investors the advantages of economics of scale and professional management.
3. The net asset value of an investment company is the difference between the market value of its assets and its liabilities divided by the number of outstanding shares.
4. The operating expense ratio of an investment company represents the annual percentage of total assets that are spent in operating the fund. Typically these expenses consist of fees paid to the management company as well as administrative and other operating expenses.
5. The two major types of investment companies are closed-end investment companies and open-end investment companies.
6. Closed-end investment companies issue an initial number of shares to capitalize the fund. After that, new shares are rarely issued (or repurchased). Closed-end investment company shares trade on organized exchanges or on the over-the-counter market at prices determined by the market.
7. Open-end investment companies have a variable capitalization, standing ready to issue new shares or repurchase existing shares at prices based on their net asset values.
8. Different investment companies follow different investment policies. These polices determine such characteristics as the asset classes in which the investment companies invest, the degree of active management (if any), and the emphasis on income as opposed to capital appreciation.
9. Owing to data availability, mutual funds have been the subject of many performance studies. The results show that, on average, mutual funds consistently maintain risk postures in line with their stated investment policies. However, the typical fund has not been able to produce superior rates of return consistently.
10. There is some evidence that the superior results of top performing mutual funds persist over time. However, this evidence is not strong, indicating that many top performers subsequently become either mediocre or below average performers.

11. Closed-end investment companies typically sell at premiums to their net asset values at their initial offerings. Later they typically sell at discounts to their net asset values, which vary over time. Explaining why investors buy initial public offerings of closed-end investment companies and why the discounts of these companies vary over time are puzzles for efficient market proponents.

QUESTIONS AND PROBLEMS

1. The Neptune Value Fund has sold 15 000 shares to investors. Currently the fund has accrued investment management fee obligations of $50 000. The fund's portfolio is shown below. Calculate the fund's net asset value.

Stock	*Shares*	*Price/Share*
A	50 000	$ 10
B	20 000	7
C	35 000	30
D	10 000	100

2. Bill Schulter, a veteran mutual fund investor, argued: "I can compute the monthly rate of return on a mutual fund by calculating the percentage change in the fund's NAV from the beginning to the end of the month (assuming no distributions to shareholders)." Is Bill correct? Why?
3. The X Fund, a closed-end investment company, has a portfolio of assets worth $500 million. It has liabilities of $2 million. It also has $40 million shares outstanding.
   a. What is the fund's NAV?
   b. If the fund trades at an 8% discount from its NAV, what is the market price of the fund's shares?
4. Distinguish between closed-end and open-end investment companies?
5. Why do some mutual funds have load charges whereas others do not? Why are investors willing to pay load charges?
6. Assume that you placed a $1000 investment with a mutual fund that charged an 8.5% load. Management and other fees charged by the fund total 1.10% per annum. Ignoring other costs, over five years, what annual return would the fund have to produce to equal the value that your initial investment would have earned in a savings account paying 5% interest? (Assume annual compounding of income and no taxes.)
7. In recent years so-called "families of funds" that offer a wide range of investment policies through narrowly focused mutual funds have become popular. Discuss why these funds have achieved such popularity.
8. There are literally thousands of mutual funds available for purchase. Describe what criteria you might use in selecting from among these many funds.
9. At the beginning of the year, the Saturn Fund's NAV was $18.50. At the end of the year its NAV was $16.90. At year-end the fund paid out $1.25 in income and capital gains. What was the return to an investor in the Saturn Fund during the year?

10. Over the last three years, the Pluto Fund produced the following per-share financial results. Calculate the annual returns on an investment in the Pluto Fund over this period.

	Year 1	Year 2	Year 3
NAV at Beginning of Year	$13.89	$14.40	$15.95
NAV at End of Year	14.40	15.95	15.20
Income Distribution	0.29	0.33	0.36
Capital Gains Distribution	0.12	0.25	0.05

11. Analysis of mutual fund performance has been extensive. What does the evidence indicate about the ability of mutual fund managers, as a group, to produce positive abnormal returns consistently?
12. Lesley Pike is attempting to select a superior-performing mutual fund. Based on the evidence presented in the text, discuss how much importance Lesley should attach to the past performance of mutual funds in making decisions.
13. Why do the stated percentage load charges of mutual funds not fully reflect the percentage costs of these sales fees?
14. Distinguish between a common stock fund and a balanced fund. In particular, compare their expected return and risk characteristics.
15. If most investment managers appear unable to "beat the market" on a risk-adjusted basis, should an investor still consider investing in investment companies? Why?
16. Consider three individuals: a young, well-educated woman just beginning a career with high expected future earnings; a middle-aged man with a young family who has a secure job but modest expected future earnings growth; a widow in her seventies, living comfortably but not richly off a pension. Referring to the *Globe and Mail: Report on Mutual Funds*, prescribe and explain an investment strategy for these persons involving investments in the various funds listed. (Feel free to introduce other assumptions regarding such things as the individuals' risk tolerances and consumption preferences.)
17. Assuming that certain conditions are satisfied, an investment company does not have to pay federal tax on the income it earns. Why?
18. Why do the market prices of closed-end investment company shares represent a "mystery" to proponents of market efficiency?

KEY TERMS

investment company
net asset value (NAV)
managed investment company
management expense ratio
closed-end investment company
open-end investment company
no-load fund
load fund
load charge
fixed annuity
variable annuity
deferred annuity
guaranteed investment annuity
pooled fund
real estate investment trust (REIT)
labour-sponsored investment fund
benchmark portfolio
portfolio turnover rate
ex-post alpha
tactical asset allocation (TAA)

REFERENCES

1. Good reference sources for information on investment companies are:

   William J. Baumol, Stephen M. Goldfeld, Lilli A. Gordon, and Michael F. Koehn, *The Economics of Mutual Fund Markets: Competition Versus Regulation* (Boston: Kluwer Academic Publishers, 1990).

   Investment Companies Yearbook 1993 (to order, write: CDA Investment Technologies, Inc., 1355 Piccard Drive, Rockville, MD 20850).

   1993 Mutual Fund Fact Book (to order, write: Investment Company Institute, P.O. Box 66140, Washington, DC 20035-6140).

   John C. Bogle, *Bogle on Mutual Funds* (Burr Ridge, IL: Richard D. Irwin, 1994).

   The Individual Investor's Guide to No-Load Mutual Funds (to order, write: American Association of Individual Investors, 625 North Michigan Avenue, Research Department, Chicago, IL 60611).

   Morningstar Mutual Funds (to order this biweekly publication, write: Morningstar, Inc., 225 West Wacker Drive, Chicago, IL 60606).

2. Although annual management fees of investment companies are usually a given percentage of the market value of the assets under management, performance-based fees are allowed. In addition to the January/February 1987 issue of the *Financial Analysts Journal*, which is devoted to this topic, see:

   Laura T. Starks, "Performance Incentive Fees: An Agency Theoretic Approach," *Journal of Financial and Quantitative Analysis* 22, no. 1 (March 1987): 17–32.

   Mark Grinblatt and Sheridan Titman, "How Clients Can Win the Gaming Game," *Journal of Portfolio Management* 13, no. 4 (Summer 1987): 14–23.

   Joseph H. Golec, "Do Mutual Fund Managers Who Use Incentive Compensation Outperform Those Who Don't?" *Financial Analysts Journal* 44, no. 6 (November/December 1988): 75–78.

   Mark Grinblatt and Sheridan Titman, "Adverse Risk Incentives and the Design of Performance-Based Contracts," *Management Science* 35, no. 7 (July 1989): 807–822.

   Jeffery V. Bailey, "Some Thoughts on Performance-Based Fees," *Financial Analysts Journal* 46, no. 4 (July/August 1990): 31–40.

   Philip Halpern and Isabelle I. Fowler, "Investment Management Fees and Determinants of Pricing Structure in the Industry," *Journal of Portfolio Management* 17, no. 2 (Winter 1991): 74–79.

3. Closed-end investment companies known as "country funds" have been examined by:

   Catherine Bonser-Neal, Greggory Brauer, Robert Neal, and Simon Wheatley, "International Investment Restrictions and Closed-End Country Fund Prices," *Journal of Finance* 45, no. 2 (June 1990): 523–547.

   Gordon Johnson, Thomas Schneeweis, and William Dinning, "Closed-End Country Funds: Exchange Rate and Investment Risk," *Financial Analysts Journal* 49, no. 6 (November/December 1993): 74–82.

4. For evidence on the performance of funds outside of North America, see:

John G. McDonald, "French Mutual Fund Performance: Evaluation of Internationally Diversified Portfolios," *Journal of Finance* 28, no. 5 (December 1973): 1161–1180.

Juan A. Palacios, "The Stock Market in Spain: Tests of Efficiency and Capital Market Theory," in *International Capital Markets*, eds. Edwin J. Elton and Martin J. Gruber (Amsterdam: North-Holland Publishing, 1975): 114–149.

André L. Farber, "Performance of Internationally Diversified Mutual Funds," in *International Capital Markets*, eds. Edwin J. Elton and Martin J. Gruber (Amsterdam: North-Holland Publishing, 1975): 298–309.

Michael A. Firth, "The Investment Performance of Unit Trusts in the Period 1965–75," *Journal of Money, Credit and Banking* 9, no. 4 (November 1977): 597–604.

James R. F. Guy, "The Performance of The British Investment Trust Industry," *Journal of Finance* 33, no. 2 (May 1978): 443–455.

———, "An Examination of the Effects of International Diversification from the British Viewpoint on Both Hypothetical and Real Portfolios," *Journal of Finance* 33, no. 5 (December 1978): 1425–1438.

R. S. Woodward, "The Performance of UK Investment Trusts as Internationally Diversified Portfolios Over the Period 1968 to 1977," *Journal of Banking and Finance* 7, no. 3 (September 1983): 417–426.

Jess H. Chua and Richard S. Woodward, *Gains from Market Timing*, Monograph Series in Finance and Economics 1986–2, New York University Salomon Center, Leonard N. Stern School of Business.

Robert E. Cumby and Jack D. Glen, "Evaluating the Performance of International Mutual Funds," *Journal of Finance* 45, no. 2 (June 1990): 497–521.

Cheol S. Eun, Richard Kolodny, and Bruce G. Resnick, "US-Based International Mutual Funds: A Performance Evaluation," *Journal of Portfolio Management* 17, no. 3 (Spring 1991): 88–94.

A. Black, P. Fraser, and D. Power, "UK Unit Trust Performance 1980–1989: A Passive Time-Varying Approach," *Journal of Banking and Finance* 16, no. 5 (September 1992): 1015–1033.

5. Studies of mutual fund performance are discussed and cited in:

Gordon J. Alexander and Jack Clark Francis, *Portfolio Analysis* (Englewood Cliffs, NJ: Prentice Hall, 1986), Chapter 13.

Mark Grinblatt and Sheridan Titman, "Mutual Fund Performance: An Analysis of Quarterly Portfolio Holdings," *Journal of Business* 62, no. 3 (July 1989): 393–416.

Edwin J. Elton and Martin J. Gruber, *Modern Portfolio Theory and Investment Analysis* (New York: John Wiley & Sons, 1991), Chapter 22.

Ravi Shukla and Charles Trzcinka, "Performance Measurement of Managed Portfolios," *Financial Markets, Institutions & Instruments* 1, no. 4 (1992).

Edwin J. Elton, Martin J. Gruber, Sanjiv Das, and Matthew Hlavka, "Efficiency with Costly Information: A Reinterpretation of Evidence from Managed Portfolios," *Review of Financial Studies* 6, no. 1 (1993): 1–22.

Richard A. Ippolito, "On Studies of Mutual Fund Performance," *Financial Analysts Journal* 49, no. 1 (January/February 1993): 42–50.

Christopher R. Blake, Edwin J. Elton, and Martin J. Gruber, "The Performance of Bond Mutual Funds," *Journal of Business* 66, no. 3 (July 1993): 371–403.

6. The finding of inferior performance by mutual funds is contested in:

Bruce N. Lehmann and David M. Modest, "Mutual Fund Performance Evaluation: A Comparison of Benchmarks and Benchmark Comparisons," *Journal of Finance* 42, no. 2 (June 1987): 233–265.

Richard A. Ippolito, "Efficiency with Costly Information: A Study of Mutual Fund Performance," *Quarterly Journal of Economics* 104, no. 1 (February 1989): 1–23.

Mark Grinblatt and Sheridan Titman, "Mutual Fund Performance: An Analysis of Quarterly Portfolio Holdings," *Journal of Business* 63, no. 2 (July 1989): 393–415.

Cheng F. Lee and Shafiqur Rahman, "Market Timing, Selectivity, and Mutual Fund Performance: An Empirical Investigation," *Journal of Business* 63, no. 2 (April 1990): 261–278.

Cheng F. Lee and Shafiqur Rahman, "New Evidence on Timing and Security Selection Skill of Mutual Fund Managers," *Journal of Portfolio Management* 17, no. 2 (Winter 1991): 80–83.

7. The persistence of performance of mutual funds is examined in:

John C. Bogle, "Selecting Equity Mutual Funds," *Journal of Portfolio Management* 18, no. 2 (Winter 1992): 94–100.

Mark Grinblatt and Sheridan Titman, "The Persistence of Mutual Fund Performance," *Journal of Finance* 47, no. 5 (December 1992): 1977–1984.

Darryll Hendricks, Jayendu Patel, and Richard Zeckhauser, "Hot Hands in Mutual Funds: Short-Run Persistence of Relative Performance, 1974–1988," *Journal of Finance* 48, no. 1 (March 1993): 93–130.

William N. Goetzmann and Roger G. Ibbotson, "Do Winners Repeat?" *Journal of Portfolio Management* 20, no. 2 (Winter 1994): 9–18.

John Bogle, *Bogle on Mutual Funds* (Burr Ridge, IL: Richard D. Irwin, 1994), Chapter 4.

8. *Survivorship bias* refers to the problems incurred in mutual fund studies due to the fact that unskilled portfolio managers are usually fired while the skilled ones stay around. These problems are examined in:

Stephen J. Brown, William Goetzmann, Roger G. Ibbotson, and Stephen A. Ross, "Survivorship Bias in Performance Studies," *Review of Financial Studies* 5, no. 4 (1992): 553–580.

9. For a discussion and extensive set of references regarding closed-end funds, see, along with the citations given in the chapter, the following papers:

Rex Thompson, "The Information Content of Discounts and Premiums on Closed-End Fund Shares," *Journal of Financial Economics* 6, no. 2/3 (June/September 1978): 151–186.

Greggory A. Brauer, "Closed-End Fund Shares' Abnormal Returns and the Information Content of Discounts and Premiums," *Journal of Finance* 43, no. 1 (March 1988): 113–127.

J. Bradford DeLong and Andrei Shleifer, "Closed-End Fund Discounts," *Journal of Portfolio Management* 18, no. 2 (Winter 1992): 46–53.

10. Open-ending of closed-end investment companies is discussed in:

Greggory A. Brauer, "'Open-Ending' Closed-End Funds," *Journal of Financial Economics* 13, no. 4 (December 1984): 491–507.

James A. Brickley and James S. Schallheim, "Lifting the Lid on Closed-End Investment Companies: A Case of Abnormal Returns," *Journal of Financial and Quantitative Analysis* 20, no. 1 (March 1985): 107–117.

CHAPTER 23

Financial Analysis

In a broad sense, financial analysis involves determining the levels of risk and expected return of individual financial assets as well as groups of financial assets. For example, financial analysis involves both individual common stocks, such as Stelco; groups of common stocks, such as the steel industry; or, on an even larger basis, the stock market itself. In this case, financial analysis would result in a decision regarding how to split the investor's money between the stock and bond markets as well as a decision regarding whether to buy or sell steel stocks in general and Stelco in particular.

An alternative definition of financial analysis is more pragmatic: Financial analysis is what financial analysts do. *The Financial Analyst's Handbook*[1] defines the term *financial analyst* as synonymous with security analyst or investment analyst—"one who analyzes securities and makes recommendations thereon."[2] Using this definition, financial analysis can be viewed as the activity of providing inputs to the portfolio management process. This chapter (as well as Chapters 18 and 19) have such a view in discussing the financial analysis of common stocks. Chapter 24 subsequently discusses how financial analysis can be used by **portfolio managers**, also known as investment managers.

PROFESSIONAL ORGANIZATIONS

In Canada and the United States, those who belong to a local society of financial analysts automatically belong to an umbrella organization known as the Financial Analysts Federation. Among other things, membership brings with it a subscription to the *Financial Analysts Journal*, a major source of information on basic research done by other analysts and by members of the academic community. In 1993, there were about 24 000 members of the AIMR.

In 1962 the Institute of Chartered Financial Analysts (ICFA) was formed by the Financial Analysts Federation (the precursor to the AIMR) to award the professional designation of Chartered Financial Analyst (CFA). In 1993 over 19 000 analysts held the CFA designation. The CFA program is designed to establish a common set of investment knowledge and ethical standards for the various types of investment professionals. The ICFA attempts to accomplish the first objective by requiring that prospective CFAs pass a series of three exams and attain several years of investment experience. It attempts to achieve the

[1] Sumner N. Levine, ed., *Financial Analyst's Handbook I* (Homewood, Ill.: Dow Jones-Irwin, 1975).

[2] William C. Norby, "Overview of Financial Analysis," in Levine, *Financial Analyst's Handbook I*, 3.

second objective by disseminating and enforcing a set of professional conduct guidelines. (The CFA program is discussed further in this chapter's *Institutional Issues* section.)[3]

Societies of financial analysts have been formed around the world. For example, the European Federation of Financial Analysts draws its membership from ten European countries. Other societies are located in countries such as Australia, Japan, and Brazil.

REASONS FOR FINANCIAL ANALYSIS

There are two primary reasons for engaging in financial analysis. The first reason is to try to determine certain characteristics of securities; the second reason is to attempt to identify mispriced securities.[4]

These reasons are discussed next.

Determining Security Characteristics

According to modern portfolio theory, a financial analyst will want to estimate a security's future beta and unique risk, since these are needed to determine the risk (measured by standard deviation) of a portfolio. Perhaps the analyst may also want to estimate the dividend yield of a security over the next year in order to determine its suitability for portfolios in which dividend yield is relevant (owing to, for instance, legal restrictions). Careful analysis of such things as a company's dividend policy and likely future cash flows may lead to better estimates than can be obtained by simply extrapolating last year's dividend yield.

In many cases it may be desirable to know something about the sources of a security's risk and return. If a portfolio is being managed for a person who is in the oil business, one might want to minimize the sensitivity of the portfolio's return to changes in oil prices. This is because it is likely that if oil prices are in a decline, then the person's income from the oil business will also be in a decline. If the portfolio were sensitive to oil prices (which would be the case if it contained a substantial investment in oil stocks), then it too would be in a decline in value, thereby reinforcing the deterioration of the person's financial position.[5]

Attempting to Identify Mispriced Securities

A search for a mispriced security typically involves the use of **fundamental analysis**. In essence, this entails searching for a security in which the financial analyst's estimates of such things as the firm's future earnings and dividends:

1. differ substantially from consensus (that is, average) estimates of others,
2. are viewed as being closer to the correct values than the consensus estimates, and
3. are not currently reflected in the security's market price.

---

[3] To obtain more information about becoming a CFA, contact the Toronto Society of Financial Analysts, 390 Bay Street, Toronto, Ontario, M5H 9Z9; the telephone number is (416) 366–5755. A useful annual publication of the Institute is *The CFA Candidate Study and Examination Program Review.*

[4] Some would add a third reason for conducting financial analysis: monitoring the firm's management in order to prevent managers from consuming an excessive amount of perquisites and failing to make appropriate decisions to the detriment of the firm's shareholders. See Michael C. Jensen and William H. Meckling, "Theory of the Firm: Managerial Behavior, Agency Costs and Ownership Structure," *Journal of Financial Economics* 3, no. 4 (October 1976): 305–360.

[5] For a discussion regarding portfolio selection by an investor who has earned income (for example, from wages or from running a business), see Edward M. Miller, "Portfolio Selection in a Fluctuating Economy," *Financial Analysts Journal* 34, no. 3 (May/June 1978): 77–83.

INSTITUTIONAL ISSUES

The Chartered Financial Analyst Program

The investment profession encompasses a wide range of activities. Investment bankers, brokers, portfolio managers, traders, security analysts, salespeople, consultants, and pension fund administrators all fall under the rubric of investment professionals. These individuals, and the organizations for which they work, directly or indirectly affect the financial well-being of millions of people.

The Chartered Financial Analyst (CFA) program was born of a need to bring a common set of investment management concepts and standards of professional conduct to the diverse membership of the investment industry. From its modest beginnings in 1963, when 268 professionals were effectively "grandfathered" as chartered members, the CFA program has grown to a worldwide organization, with approximately 19 000 CFA charters awarded and more than 18 000 candidates currently enrolled. Although the CFA charter is far from a prerequisite for employment in the investment industry, many organizations are encouraging or even requiring new employees to participate in the CFA program.

From its inception, the Institute of Chartered Financial Analysts (ICFA), which administers the CFA program, has pursued three explicit objectives:

1. To compile a comprehensive set of currently accepted concepts and techniques relevant to the investment decision-making process (the CFA "Body of Knowledge").
2. To establish a uniform set of ethical standards to guide the activities of investment professionals.
3. To ensure that CFA charterholders have demonstrated satisfactory understanding of the Body of Knowledge and that they adhere to the established ethical standards.

Of course, like any other professional certification organization, the ICFA has multiple motives for promoting the CFA designation. By setting difficult hurdles for prospective members to clear, the CFA certification process enhances the monetary value of the charter to existing holders. Further, by demonstrating a responsible and comprehensive education and ethics program, the ICFA helps the investment industry ward off onerous government regulation and provides the industry with wider latitude to police itself.

To enroll in the CFA program, an individual must hold a bachelor's degree (or equivalent work experience), provide three acceptable character references, and pay the required registration fee. Once accepted into the program, to earn the CFA designation a candidate must pass three exams, possess three years of investment-related work experience, be a member of (or have applied to) a constituent financial analyst society, demonstrate a high level of professional conduct, and abide by the Code of Ethics and Standards of Practice of the Association for Investment Management and Research.

The CFA course of study and examinations are the cornerstone of the CFA certification process. Candidates must pass three six-hour exams. The ICFA administers these exams once a year in June at 140 locations, primarily in the United States and Canada. As candidates may take only one exam per year, a minimum of three years is required to complete the examination sequence.

The ICFA specifies a set of review materials and assigned readings for candidates to use in preparation for the exams. The study program has evolved over the years as new concepts have been introduced into the exams. The ICFA estimates that candidates average 200 hours per exam in individual study time. Many candidates also participate in independently sponsored study groups.

INSTITUTIONAL ISSUES (continued)

The CFA examinations were designed in a progressive format. The exam levels became increasingly comprehensive, building on previous levels. The CFA curriculum underwent a major change in 1993, which will be phased in over three years. When it was fully implemented in 1995, the exams were divided into four major subject areas and several subtopics within each major subject:

1. Ethical and professional standards:
   a. Applicable laws and regulations
   b. Professional standards of practice
   c. Ethical conduct and professional obligations
   d. International ethical and professional considerations
2. Tools for inputs for investment valuation and management:
   a. Quantitative methods and statistics
   b. Macroeconomics
   c. Microeconomics
   d. Financial statements and accounting
3. Investment (asset) evaluation:
   a. Overview of the valuation process
   b. Applying economic analysis in investment valuation
   c. Applying industry analysis in investment valuation
   d. Applying company analysis in investment valuation
   e. Equity securities
   f. Fixed-income securities
   g. Other investments
   h. Derivative securities
4. Portfolio management:
   a. Capital market theory
   b. Portfolio policies
   c. Expectational factors
   d. Asset allocation
   e. Fixed-income portfolio management
   f. Equity portfolio management
   g. Real estate portfolio management
   h. Specialized asset portfolio management
   i. Implementing the investment process
   j. Performance measurement

The CFA exams are rigorous and difficult. A high number of the candidates fail at least one exam, although exams can be retaken. In 1993, a total of 12 809 candidates sat for the exams. Only 55%, 56%, and 76% of the candidates taking the first, second, and third exams, respectively, passed.

The CFA program experienced tremendous growth in the 1980s. The number of candidates sitting for the exams has increased over sevenfold since 1980. Given this past success, where does the CFA program go from here?

Clearly, the ICFA desires to continue to enhance the prestige and uniqueness of its CFA certification. In recent years, however, the ICFA has also begun to strongly emphasize the continuing education aspect of its mission. Technological obsolescence is a serious problem in the rapidly changing investment industry. (For example, organized financial futures markets—see Chapter 21—did not even exist in 1980). Many professionals who received the CFA designation just a decade ago might find it difficult to pass an exam now. Current charterholders are encouraged (although not yet required) to participate in a self-administered continuing education program.

The ICFA also sees a role for itself globally. With the investment industry becoming increasingly international in scope, the ICFA has moved to administer its program abroad. It has also begun to join forces with analyst societies in other countries to develop means of jointly recognizing one another's certification programs.

Two rather different approaches may be taken in the search for mispriced securities using fundamental analysis. The first approach involves valuation, where an attempt is made to determine the appropriate "intrinsic" or "true" value for a security. After making this determination, the intrinsic value is compared with the security's current market price. If the market price is substantially greater than the intrinsic value, the security is said to be overpriced, or overvalued. If the market price is substantially less than the intrinsic value, the security is said to be underpriced, or undervalued. Instead of comparing price with value, the analyst sometimes estimates a security's expected return over a specified period, given its current market price and intrinsic value. This estimate is then compared with the "appropriate" return for securities with similar attributes.

Determining a security's intrinsic value may be done in great detail, using estimates of all major factors (for example, gross national product of the economy, industry sales, firm sales and expenses, and capitalization rates). Alternatively, a shortcut may be taken where, for example, an estimate of earnings per share may be multiplied by a "justified," or "normal," price-earnings ratio to determine the intrinsic value of a share of common stock. (To avoid complications arising when seeking the intrinsic value of a share that has negative earnings per share, some analysts estimate sales per share and multiply this figure by a "normal" price-sales ratio).

A second approach has the analyst estimate only one or two financial variables and then compare these estimates directly with consensus estimates. For example, next year's earnings per share for a stock may be estimated. If the analyst's estimate substantially exceeds the consensus of other analysts' estimates, the stock may be considered an attractive investment. This is because the analyst expects the actual earnings to provide a happy surprise for the market when announced. In turn, there will be an increase in the share's price at that time, resulting in the investor receiving a greater-than-normal return. Conversely, when an analyst's estimate of earnings per share is substantially below that of the other analysts, then the analyst expects the market will receive an unhappy surprise. The resulting decrease in the share's price will lead to a smaller-than-normal return.

At an aggregate level, an analyst may be more optimistic about the economy than the consensus of other analysts. This would suggest that a larger-than-normal investment in stocks be taken, offset perhaps by a smaller-than-normal investment in fixed-income securities. Conversely, a relatively pessimistic view would suggest a smaller-than-normal investment in stocks, offset perhaps by a larger-than-normal investment in fixed-income securities.

Alternatively, the analyst might agree with the consensus view on both the economy and the individual characteristics of specific securities but feel that the consensus view of the prospects for a certain group of securities in a particular industry is in error. In such a case, a larger-than-normal investment may be made in stocks from an industry having prospects about which the analyst feels relatively optimistic. Conversely, a smaller-than-normal investment would be made in stocks from an industry about which the analyst feels relatively pessimistic.

The use of fundamental analysis to identify mispriced common stocks and fixed-income securities was discussed in previous chapters. This chapter will introduce the method of technical analysis and compare it to fundamental analysis.

► Beating the Market

Many books and articles have been written that allegedly show how financial analysis can be used to beat the market, meaning they purport to show how to make abnormally high returns by investing in the stock market. In order to evaluate such systems, an understanding of what "the market" is and how to measure its performance is in order.

Market Indices

What did the market do yesterday? How much would an unmanaged common stock portfolio have returned last year? Such questions are often answered by examining the performance of a **market index**. Figure 23.1 displays many indices that are commonly discussed. These indices differ from one another with respect to (1) the securities included in the index and (2) the method employed in calculating the value of the index.

In order to understand how some of the most popular indices are computed, consider a simple example where the market index is based on two stocks, referred to as A and B. At the end of day 0, their closing prices are, respectively, \$10 and \$20 per share. Furthermore, at this time A has 1500 shares outstanding and B has 2000 shares outstanding.

There are three weighting methods that are often used in computing a market index. The first method, involving **price weighting**, begins by summing the prices of the shares that are included in the index and ends by dividing this sum by a constant (the divisor). If the index includes only stocks A and B and was started on day 0, the divisor would be equal to the number of stocks in the average, 2. Thus, on day 0 the index would have a value of (10 + 20)/2 = 15. The divisor is adjusted thereafter whenever there is a stock split in order to avoid giving misleading indications of the market's direction.[6]

For example, assume that on day 1, B splits 2-for-1 and closes at \$11 per share, while A closes at \$13. In this situation, it is clear that the market has risen, since both stocks have a higher price than on day 0 after adjusting B for the split. If nothing were done in computing the index, its value on day 1 would be (13 + 11)/2 = 12, a drop of 20% = (12 – 15)/15 from day 0 that falsely suggests the market went down on day 1. In reality, the market went up to [13 + (11 × 2)]/2 = 17.5, a gain of 16.67% = (17.5 – 15)/15.

A stock split is accounted for in a price-weighted index by adjusting the divisor whenever a split takes place. In the example, the divisor is adjusted by examining the index on day 1, the day of the split. More specifically, the following equation would be solved for the unknown divisor d:

$$\frac{13 + 11}{d} = 17.5. \tag{23.1}$$

The value of d that solves this equation is 1.37. The new divisor will continue in use after day $t + 1$ until there is another split, when it will again be recalculated.

If the index begins at a given level, such as 100 on day 0, then updating it is straightforward. First, the percentage change in average price is calculated. In the example, this was determined to be 16.67%. Second, this percentage is multiplied by the previous day's index value in order to determine the change in the index. Continuing with the

---

[6] The divisor is also adjusted whenever the composition of the stocks in the index changes (meaning whenever one stock is substituted for another).

Figure 23.1

North American stock market indices published daily in *The Financial Post.*

North American Indexes

52W high	52W low	Index	Yield %	P/E	High	Low	Close	Net change	% change
Toronto Stock Exchange									
4752.80	3983.34	TSE 300	2.29	13.69	4689.32	4675.27	4689.10	+4.94	+0.1
5278.76	3789.91	Metals & Minerals	1.69	14.69	4845.47	4812.50	4844.99	+23.53	+0.5
5531.06	3903.86	Integrated Mines	1.90	13.49	4906.68	4862.24	4906.68	+34.63	+0.7
2897.54	1930.50	Mining	0.89	22.04	2802.92	2774.80	2774.80	−9.30	−0.3
11371.22	8410.94	Gold & Precious Mnrl	0.68	55.55	10336.22	10280.78	10328.38	−14.00	−0.1
4736.99	3811.38	Oil & Gas	1.03	32.89	4736.99	4719.83	4735.16	+10.50	+0.2
4882.62	4119.66	Integrated Oils	2.81	16.62	4882.62	4844.49	4882.62	+44.73	+0.9
4787.51	3783.44	Oil & Gas Producers	0.41	51.66	4781.06	4764.62	4778.55	−1.52	nil
831.52	606.54	Oil & Gas Services	1.84	13.86	831.52	818.41	831.52	+8.50	+1.0
5410.21	4186.34	Paper & Forest Prods	1.84	6.78	4273.03	4249.89	4264.24	−10.63	−0.2
8521.68	6274.05	Consumer Products	1.96	6.04	8142.71	8096.86	8132.94	+1.69	nil
5629.96	4793.48	Food Processing	3.91	20.61	5179.73	5095.44	5179.73	+84.29	+1.7
14177.18	10282.33	Tobacco	3.75	11.32	13931.43	13678.48	13856.57	−138.10	−1.0
13217.97	8836.11	Distilleries	1.74	3.59	11762.56	11702.59	11702.59	−59.97	−0.5
5683.62	4093.82	Breweries, Beverages	2.49	46.00	4558.93	4499.27	4536.66	+38.22	+0.8
1595.26	1191.28	Household Goods	1.44	55.97	1413.93	1390.04	1412.12	+8.87	+0.6
1223.37	474.44	Biotchnlgy Phrmctcls	0.11	n.a.	1223.37	1189.81	1223.37	+29.04	+2.4
3269.55	2619.71	Industrial Products	1.49	12.05	3200.21	3186.80	3189.48	−9.31	−0.3
1177.80	923.24	Steels	2.55	6.77	1001.16	986.60	1001.16	+13.36	+1.4
3908.01	3027.37	Fabricating & Engr	0.94	14.21	3481.64	3451.89	3455.96	−25.68	−0.7
32230.83	20292.38	Transportation Equip	1.12	29.17	31980.99	31545.80	31980.99	+244.90	+0.8
9089.07	6269.22	Technology-Hardware	0.65	27.44	8766.59	8686.25	8688.31	−112.95	−1.3
4784.18	3883.26	Building Materials	1.72	18.73	4137.82	4097.85	4130.50	+22.52	+0.5
5113.11	3988.84	Chemicals & Fertlzrs	1.82	7.61	4959.71	4925.84	4935.64	+1.37	nil
1907.62	1433.75	Business Services	4.95	6.52	1826.72	1809.41	1809.41	−8.66	−0.5
1927.59	1140.94	Technology Software	n.a.	29.03	1680.30	1662.91	1673.72	+10.45	+0.6
10739.99	7248.83	Autos & Parts	1.79	11.95	10016.30	9884.08	9884.08	−114.09	−1.1
2128.29	1647.50	Real Estate	1.24	n.a.	1676.24	1665.28	1676.24	+5.19	+0.3
5317.02	4273.77	Transn & Envrnmtl	0.97	21.36	4973.89	4933.55	4962.43	+6.41	+0.1
3961.06	3510.71	Pipelines	5.65	12.11	3924.05	3897.24	3910.39	+11.39	+0.3
3535.27	3167.71	Utilities	5.32	16.48	3524.17	3506.83	3524.17	+15.33	+0.4
3369.29	3019.04	Telephone Utilities	5.11	18.62	3352.90	3337.02	3352.90	+14.25	+0.4
3832.45	3338.48	Gas & Electric Utils	6.09	11.67	3832.45	3803.05	3829.37	+18.04	+0.5
8430.88	7465.54	Communs & Media	1.99	46.00	8430.88	8354.81	8430.88	+69.87	+0.8
5822.69	3834.16	Broadcasting	1.48	25.96	5649.72	5611.76	5642.95	+31.19	+0.6
22187.77	14555.73	Cable & Entmt	0.34	n.a.	17769.05	17506.29	17725.26	+213.06	+1.2
8823.90	7530.90	Publishing & Prtg	2.83	18.01	8823.90	8727.58	8823.90	+63.48	+0.7
4242.88	3435.57	Merchandising	1.90	14.83	3763.01	3725.92	3758.39	+36.50	+1.0
5973.00	4785.63	Wholesale Distrs	1.38	10.69	5072.93	4968.77	5072.93	+104.16	+2.1
7794.57	5938.59	Food Stores	1.43	13.46	7773.87	7744.44	7744.44	−29.43	−0.4
1210.90	815.09	Department Stores	4.54	12.41	843.58	830.70	843.58	+12.88	+1.6
1571.90	1229.23	Specialty Stores	3.15	19.71	1375.98	1355.50	1369.68	+7.88	+0.6
68186.45	46965.57	Hospitality	0.69	17.59	51866.98	50806.84	51812.78	+1218.62	+2.4
3678.27	2938.05	Financial Services	3.94	9.66	3654.26	3641.86	3654.26	−6.61	−0.2
4109.38	3282.46	Banks & Trusts	4.09	9.23	4069.18	4052.62	4069.18	−6.52	−0.2
7395.22	5207.46	Investment Companies	2.15	20.63	7244.15	7180.62	7200.61	−46.51	−0.6
3825.41	2811.69	Insurance	2.19	11.59	3801.68	3771.25	3776.45	−25.23	−0.7
1176.67	955.87	Financial Mgmt Cos	4.45	10.87	1141.05	1129.23	1141.05	+3.55	+0.3
5560.69	4402.69	Conglomerates	2.08	23.46	5421.89	5370.74	5421.89	+29.46	+0.5
280.99	239.00	TSE 200	1.36	18.12	280.86	279.50	280.82	+0.71	+0.3
290.41	241.58	TSE 100	2.50	12.97	285.05	284.05	284.97	+0.20	+0.1
301.30	232.60	Resource	1.37	20.01	280.96	280.07	280.89	+0.33	+0.1
321.71	262.39	Industrial	1.70	12.68	316.53	314.65	315.53	−0.47	−0.1
277.01	233.42	Interest Sensitive	4.65	11.15	276.66	275.26	276.66	+0.22	+0.1
289.58	234.67	Consumer	2.11	8.17	275.31	273.50	275.05	+0.85	+0.3
251.51	209.79	Toronto 35	2.82	12.52	247.65	246.60	247.34	−0.27	−0.1
Financial Post									
112.37	96.30	Unweighted	1.87	16.43			111.90	+0.42	+0.4
264.71	227.47	All-Canadian Junior	1.87	27.44			262.17	+1.75	+0.7
Montreal Exchange									
2344.69	1948.39	Market Portfolio			2307.78	2299.70	2307.78	−1.54	−0.1
2862.13	2277.85	Banking			2847.31	2830.38	2847.31	−2.12	−0.1
3334.95	2514.24	Forest Products			2618.46	2588.06	2596.74	−2.17	−0.1
2340.07	1836.67	Industrial Products			2302.32	2282.70	2282.70	−21.13	−0.9
3298.48	2479.94	Mining & Minerals			2968.51	2955.72	2968.51	+1.28	nil
1762.19	1447.76	Oil & Gas			1754.65	1744.10	1753.90	+7.92	+0.5
1993.97	1806.53	Utilities			1992.73	1977.94	1992.73	+9.86	+0.5
Vancouver Stock Exchange									
876.84	690.00	Composite			778.91	774.68	777.49	−0.98	−0.1
720.37	624.22	Commercial & Industrial			697.57	686.45	691.25	−6.32	−0.9
1414.04	1073.34	Resource			1259.96	1239.82	1243.79	−15.65	−1.2
692.96	528.81	Venture			602.78	598.57	602.28	+2.68	+0.4
Alberta Stock Exchange									
1456.89	1029.32	Combined Value			1444.05	1436.80	1443.58	+1.86	+0.1
Dow Jones									
5266.69	3794.40	Industrials			5132.65	5062.21	5095.80	−10.12	−0.2
2105.19	1426.39	Transportation			1974.30	1935.79	1953.49	−5.98	−0.3
226.03	179.67	Utilities			226.03	222.47	224.57	+0.70	+0.3
1749.01	1261.54	Composite			1694.80	1667.95	1680.94	−2.84	−0.2
New York Stock Exchange									
331.73	249.86	Composite			328.92	327.40	328.35	+0.22	+0.1
418.51	316.26	Industrials			412.48	410.49	411.69	+0.16	nil
310.88	219.58	Transportation			300.66	298.35	299.93	+1.04	+0.3
252.65	196.88	Utilities			252.65	251.35	252.40	+0.53	+0.2
279.51	195.50	Financial			273.99	272.88	273.53	+0.18	+0.1
Standard & Poor's									
622.88	457.20	500 Composite			615.50	612.40	614.12	−0.41	−0.1
733.57	544.35	400 Industrials			720.62	716.92	718.90	−0.77	−0.1
492.57	336.54	Transportation			476.47	471.94	475.15	+2.50	+0.5
63.80	41.28	Financial			62.08	61.76	61.91	−0.05	−0.1
202.34	149.57	Utilities			202.34	201.18	201.98	+0.32	+0.2
598.35	425.87	100 Stocks			586.66	584.15	585.17	−1.09	−0.2
American Stock Exchange									
550.94	397.39	Major Market			535.60	533.04	533.96	−1.69	−0.3
553.96	429.27	Average			544.60	542.38	544.52	−0.18	nil
Nasdaq									
1084.02	740.44	Composite			1048.16	1039.47	1042.22	−5.91	−0.6
1004.22	740.26	Industrials			955.26	949.86	954.20	−1.13	−0.1
1280.75	915.20	Insurance			1272.99	1265.13	1271.20	+2.32	+0.2
1008.43	688.79	Banks			1008.43	1004.33	1007.08	+1.53	+0.2
1242.51	852.92	Financial			1238.00	1233.91	1234.50	−1.20	−0.1
848.30	647.90	Transportation			814.82	808.66	811.57	−2.95	−0.4
214.91	152.47	Telecomms			206.79	204.85	206.79	+0.39	+0.2
Value Line									
571.20	448.26	Arithmetic			567.35	565.26	566.94	−0.14	nil

SOURCE: Reprinted by permission of *The Financial Post* (December 29, 1995).

example, the index level on day 0 was 100, so the change from day 0 to day 1 would be 16.67% × 100 = 16.67, resulting in a level on day 1 of 116.67.[7]

The *Dow Jones Industrial Average*, one of the most widely followed indices, is this type of index. It involves the prices of 30 stocks that generally represent large-size firms.[8] Other Dow Jones Averages, for example one involving 20 transportation stocks and another involving 15 utility stocks, are similarly calculated. Furthermore, Dow Jones calculates stock market indices for each of several countries as well as an Asia/Pacific index and two World Indices, one with and one without the United States. Levels of several of these Dow Jones Averages are reported in many US daily newspapers. Historical data on the Averages, including quarterly dividends and earnings figures, are published from time to time in *Barron's* and other periodicals.[9]

A second weighting method is known as **value weighting** (or capitalization weighting). With this method, the prices of the shares of the stocks in the index are multiplied by their respective numbers of shares outstanding and then added up in order to arrive at a figure equal to the aggregate market value for that day. This figure is then divided by the corresponding figure for the day the index was started, with the resulting value being multiplied by an arbitrarily set beginning index value.

Continuing with the example, assume that the start-up day for the index is day 0 and that the index is assigned a beginning value of 100. First, note that the aggregate market value on day 0 is equal to (\$10 × 1500) + (\$20 × 2000) = \$55 000. Next, note that the aggregate market value on day 1 is equal to (\$13 × 1500) + (\$11 × 4000) = \$63 500. Dividing \$63 500 by \$55 000 and then multiplying the result by 100 gives the index value for day 1 of (\$63 500/\$55 000) × 100 = 115.45. Thus, the market would be reported as having risen by 15.45% = (115.45 – 100)/100 from day 0 to day 1.

The Standard & Poor's 500, widely used by institutional investors, is a value-weighted average of 500 large-sized stocks. Standard & Poor's also computes value-weighted indices for industrial, transportation, utility, and financial stocks. Furthermore, a variety of industry indices are also calculated. Values for all indices, along with quarterly data on dividends, earnings, and sales, may be found in Standard & Poor's *Analysts' Handbook* (annual), *Trade and Securities Statistics* (annual), and *Analysts' Handbook Supplement* (monthly). The Vancouver Stock Exchange index is a value-weighted index of those companies that trade at least 50% of their volume on the VSE.

More comprehensive value-weighted indices for US stocks are also computed. The New York Stock Exchange publishes a composite index of all stocks listed on that exchange, as well as four subindices (industrials, utilities, transportation, and finance). The American Stock Exchange computes an index of its stocks. The National Association of Securities Dealers (NASD), using its automated quotation service (NASDAQ), computes indices based on the market value of approximately 5000 over-the-counter stocks; in addition to a composite

---

[7] This is equivalent to dividing the average price on day 1 (17.5) by the average price on the beginning date (15) and then multiplying the result by the index's level on the beginning day (100). Mathematically the formula is $I_t = IO \times AP_t / AP_0$ where AP_t denotes the average price on day t and I_t denotes the index level on day t.

[8] The Montreal Exchange index is calculated in this manner. The Montreal *Market Portfolio Index* consists of 25 of the largest publicly held corporations in Canada.

[9] Some bond market indices are also calculated in this manner. For example, the *Dow Jones 20-Bond Index* is computed by averaging the price of ten utility and ten industrial bonds. For more on bond indices, see Chapter 25 and John Markese, "The Complexities of Bond Market Indicators," *AAII Journal* 14, no. 9 (October 1992): 34–36.

index, NASD calculates indices for six categories representing industrials, banks, insurance, other finance, transportation, and utilities. NASD also publishes four indices that are based on just those stocks in their National Market System (the previously mentioned NASD indices are based on both NMS and non-NMS stocks).[10]

The TSE 300 is a modified value-weighted index. The number of shares in all control blocks (representing more than 20% of outstanding shares) is subtracted from the number of shares outstanding to determine an adjusted market value. The following are the criteria for inclusion in the TSE 300: an adjusted market value of greater than \$3 million, an annual trading volume of at least 25 000 shares, and trading value greater than \$1 million per year. The 300 stocks with the largest adjusted market value that meet the above criteria are included in the index. The TSE 35 is also a modified value-weighted index that includes 35 of Canada's larger publicly-listed corporations that are among the more heavily traded issues on the TSE. In order to prevent one stock from dominating this index the maximum weight assigned to any stock is 10%.

The values of the TSE 300 (and its associated sub-indices), the TSE 35, the Montreal Exchange, Vancouver Stock Exchange and various US indices are published daily in *The Financial Post* (as shown in Figure 23.1).

Both the TSE 300 and the TSE 35 are calculated in two forms — a price index and a total return index. The former follows the procedure described above and represents aggregate price movements. The total return index includes reinvested dividend payments on each of the stocks as well as capital gains.

The third method of weighting in known as **equal weighting**. This index is computed daily by multiplying the level of the index on the previous day by the arithmetic mean of the daily **price relatives** (today's price divided by yesterday's price) of the relevant stocks in the index. For example, the value of the index consisting of A and B on day 1 would be calculated by first determining the price relatives to be equal to $13/10 = 1.3$ for A and $(11 \times 2)/20 = 1.1$ for B. Note how an adjustment was made in calculating the price relative for B due to its stock split. All that was required was to multiply the post-split price of 11 by 2, the split ratio.

Once the price relatives have been determined, then their arithmetic mean would be calculated as

$$(1.3 + 1.1)/2 = 1.20.$$

If the value of the index on day 0 was 100, then the value on day 1 would be reported as $100 \times 1.20 = 120$, an increase of 20% $(1.20 - 1)$. (When the index is created, its value on that day can be set at any arbitrary starting value, such as 100.) The Value Line Composite (Arithmetic) Index, based on 1635 stocks, is prepared in this manner.

One popular index that does not involve price weighting, value weighting, or equal weighting is the *Value Line Composite Average*. This index is computed daily by multiplying the previous day's index by the geometric mean of the daily price relatives (today's price divided by yesterday's price) of the relevant stocks in the index. For example, the value of

---

[10] The broadest value-weighted index is calculated by Wilshire Associates. Their index, known as the Wilshire 5000 Equity Index, is based on all stocks listed on the New York and American Stock exchanges plus those "actively traded over-the-counter." The Russell 1000, 2000, and 3000 are also broad value-weighted indices, covering roughly the largest 1000 stocks; the next 2000; and the sum of the two. In terms of international indices, *Morgan Stanley Capital International Perspective* publishes value-weighted indices using various combinations of 1371 stocks from 19 different countries, resulting in a "world market index." These and other international indices are discussed in Chapter 26 (see Figure 26.2).

the index consisting of stocks A and B on day 1 would be calculated by first determining the price relatives to be equal to (13/10) = 1.3 for A and (11 × 2)/20 = 1.1 for B. Then the geometric mean would be calculated as[11]

$$(1.3 \times 1.1)^{1/2} = 1.1958.$$

If the value of the index on day 0 was 120, then the value on day 1 would be reported as 120 × 1.1958 = 143.496, an increase of 1.1958 – 1 = 19.58%. In the case of the Value Line index, the initial value was set at 100 on June 30, 1961, and has been updated ever since then in this manner.[12]

In summary, four types of indices have been presented; various people use these indices when they refer to how the market has done. However, the indices can give notably different answers. In the example shown here, the market was calculated to have risen by either 16.67%, 15.45%, 20%, or 19.58%, depending on the index used. In practice, most professional money managers use either the TSE 300 or the S&P 500 as the barometer (depending on the market in which they are trading) since they have a fairly wide base and weight larger companies more heavily than smaller companies, thereby representing more closely the performance of the average dollar invested in the market.

Conveying Advice on Beating the Market

It is interesting to ponder whether or not advice on how to beat the market will remain useful after becoming public. It seems logical that any such prescription that has been in print for long is not likely to allow the investor to beat the market without fail. Even if an approach has worked in the past (and because someone asserts it has worked does not mean that it has), as more and more investors apply it, prices will be driven to levels at which the approach will not work in the future. Any system designed to beat the market, once known to more than a few people, carries the seeds of its own destruction.

There are two reasons for not including advice on "guaranteed" ways to beat the market in this book. First, to do so would make a successful system public and hence unsuccessful. Second, the authors know of no such system. Some apparent anomalies and possible inefficiencies have been described previously. But any book that purports to open the door to the *certainty* of making abnormally high returns for those who follow its advice should be regarded with the greatest skepticism.

This does not mean that financial analysis is useless. Although individuals should be skeptical when others tell them how to use financial analysis to beat the market, individuals can try to *understand* the market with the use of financial analysis.

► Financial Analysis and Market Efficiency

The concept of an efficient market (discussed in Chapter 4) may appear to be based on a paradox. Financial analysts carefully analyze the prospects for companies, industries, and the economy in the search for mispriced securities. If an undervalued security is found, for example, then it will be purchased. However, the act of purchasing the security will tend to push its price upward toward its intrinsic value, thereby making it no longer undervalued.

---

[11] In order to determine the geometric mean for N stocks, multiply their price relatives and then take the Nth root of the resulting product.

[12] Value Line also has indices for industrials, rails, and utilities that are similarly computed and updated. Before March 1986 the Montreal Exchange index was also a geometric index.

That is, financial analysis tends to result in security prices that reflect intrinsic values, which is equivalent to saying that financial analysis tends to make markets efficient. But if this is the case, why would anyone perform financial analysis in an attempt to identify mispriced securities?

There are two responses to this question. First, there are costs associated with performing financial analysis. This means that financial analysis may not be conducted on all securities all the time. As a result, the prices of all securities will not reflect intrinsic values all the time. Pockets of opportunity may occasionally arise, thereby opening the possibility for added benefits from financial analysis. This suggests that people should engage in financial analysis only to the point at which the added benefits cover the added costs.[13] Ultimately, in a highly competitive market, prices would be close enough to intrinsic values to make it worthwhile for only the most skillful analysts to search for mispriced securities. Thus, the market would be nearly, but not perfectly, efficient. Skilled investors will be able to earn abnormally high gross returns, but after the costs of gathering and processing information and then making the requisite trades are taken into consideration, they will end up with a net return that is not abnormal.[14]

The other response to the question focuses on the first reason given earlier for engaging in financial analysis: to determine certain characteristics of securities. This reason is appropriate even in a perfectly efficient market. Since investors differ in their circumstances (consider the person in the oil business, discussed earlier), portfolios should be "tailored" to accommodate such differences. Successful performance of this task generally requires estimation of certain characteristics of securities, thereby justifying the use of financial analysis.

► Needed Skills

To understand and estimate the risk and return of individual securities as well as groups of securities (such as industries), financial markets and the principles of valuation must be understood. Much of the material required for such an understanding can be found in this book. But, as Figure 23.1 indicates, even more is required. Future prospects must be estimated and interrelationships assessed. This requires the skills of an economist and an understanding of industrial organization. To process relevant historical data, some command of quantitative methods is needed, along with an understanding of the nuances of accounting.

This book cannot provide all the material necessary to becoming a successful financial analyst. Books on accounting, economics, industrial organization, and quantitative methods are required. Instead, some techniques used by financial analysts are discussed, along with some of the pitfalls involved. In addition, sources of investment information are presented.

---

[13] If the added benefits exceeded the added costs, then it would be profitable to perform more financial analysis because the incremental benefits from doing so would cover the associated costs. If, on the other hand, the added costs exceeded the added benefits, then it would be profitable to cut back on the amount of financial analysis because costs would be reduced by an amount greater than benefits.

[14] For an interesting argument on why the existence of trading costs results in some investors' performing financial analysis in an efficient market, see Sanford J. Grossman, "On the Efficiency of Competitive Stock Markets Where Traders Have Diverse Information," *Journal of Finance* 31, no. 2 (May 1976): 573–585; Sanford J. Grossman and Joseph E. Stiglitz, "On the Impossibility of Informationally Efficient Markets," *American Economic Review* 70, no. 3 (June 1980): 393–408; and Bradford Cornell and Richard Roll, "Strategies for Pairwise Competitions in Markets and Organizations," *Bell Journal of Economics* 12, no. 1 (Spring 1981): 201–213.

EVALUATING INVESTMENT SYSTEMS

Many statements have been made in the past asserting that some mechanical investment system, using only available historical data and a set of objective analytical procedures, can provide results superior to those obtained with a **passive investment system**. (A passive investment system involves simply buying and holding a well-diversified portfolio of stocks over a performance evaluation period; the return on a market index is often used as a substitute for such a portfolio.) Some mechanical systems simply provide predictions of how the market will behave; others prescribe a complete set of instructions for investing in individual securities. All of them present impressive statistics based on tests using data from some past evaluation period.

Consider as examples the following four statements:

> ...switch from bonds to stocks after the growth rate of the money supply has risen for two months; switch from stocks to bonds after the growth rate of the money supply has been below its most recent peak for 15 months. Historically, such a policy would have produced over twice the return obtained by simply holding stocks.
>
> ...this simple formula predicted over 95% of the quarterly variation in Standard & Poor's 500-stock index over the period studied.
>
> ...A portfolio of the 25 stocks with the greatest historical relative strength would have outperformed a portfolio of the 25 stocks with the smallest relative strength in 8 months out of 12.
>
> ...This completely objective stock selection procedure, which can be performed without error on a microcomputer, would have outperformed 80% of the professionally managed portfolios during the period in question.

Statements such as these four have been made in the past and will undoubtedly continue to be made in the future. Advocates of such mechanical investment systems may sincerely believe they have found the path to instant affluence. However, their proofs often rest on shaky ground. When evaluating any system, it is imperative that several possible errors be avoided.

► Failure to Adjust for Risk

Any investment system that results in the selection of high-beta stocks is likely to produce above-average returns in bull markets and below-average returns in bear markets. Since the stock market over the long term has trended upward, on balance such a system will tend to produce above-average returns over the long run. However, an evaluation of the performance of any investment system should involve not only measuring the resulting average return but also determining the amount of risk incurred. Then the average return from a passive investment system of similar risk can be computed for comparison. Techniques for making such comparisons are presented in Chapter 25.

► Failure to Consider Transaction Costs

Systems that rely on constant trading may produce *gross* returns that exceed those of a passive investment strategy of comparable risk. But this is not an accurate evaluation of a system's performance because transaction costs should be considered in measuring returns. *Net* returns are calculated by adding transaction costs to the purchase price of an investment and deducting them from the investment's selling price.

For example, if 100 shares of a stock are purchased at $19 per share with a transaction cost of $100, then the cost of the investment is (100 × $19) + $100 = $2000. If the stock is subsequently sold for $23 per share, with another $100 transaction cost, then the proceeds from the sale are (100 × $23) – $100 = $2200. As a result, the net return is ($2200 – $2000)/$2000 = 10%, whereas the gross return is ($2300 – $1900)/$1900 = 21.05%, a substantial difference.

Failure to Consider Dividends

When the performance of a mechanical system is compared with that of a passive investment system, dividends (and interest payments) are often ignored. This may seriously bias the results. For example, a system may be advocated that, in effect, selects low-yield stocks. The prices of such stocks should increase at a faster rate than those of high-yield stocks with the same amount of risk. This is because a stock's return consists of both dividends and capital appreciation. If two stocks have the same risk, they should have the same return, meaning that the stock with a smaller yield will have a larger capital appreciation. Thus, if just capital appreciation is examined, a system that selects low-yield stocks would tend to show a more rapid rate of capital appreciation than a passive investment strategy involving a well-diversified portfolio consisting of both low-yield and high-yield stocks. Consequently, when yields of systems differ significantly from average yields, it is important to examine returns, not the rate of capital appreciation.

Non-operational Systems

Although obvious, it still must be mentioned: to be useful, a system must not require information about the future. For example, many systems require action after some time series of values (such as a stock's price per share) has reached a peak or trough. But it is rarely apparent until well afterwards that in fact a peak or trough has been reached. Therefore such a system is non-operational.

A similar situation arises when an equation is estimated from a set of data. For example, a system might assume that there is a relationship between the money supply at time $t - 1$ and share prices at time t. The general relationship might be

$$\bar{I}_t = a + bM_{t-1} \tag{23.2}$$

where $\bar{I}_t$ is the predicted level of the TSE 300 at time t, M_{t-1} is the level of the money supply at time t - 1, and a and b are constants. In this system, the level of the TSE 300 one period from now can be predicted from the current level of the money supply.

To make such a system operational, specific numerical values for a and b are needed. These numbers might be estimated by examining monthly data over a ten-year period from 1986 through 1995, which means that these numbers would be known only after 1995. However, some people might test the predictive ability of the equation over the same ten-year period of 1986 to 1995 using these numbers. In doing so, they fail to realize that the system would not have been operational with these numbers for this test period, since the numbers were determined after the test period. A true test of the predictive ability of this or any system must involve an estimation period that is earlier than the test period. That is, the test period must use out-of-sample data, as is discussed shortly.

Spurious Fits

Using a set of data from a past period, it is not too difficult to discover a system that works quite well when tested on the same data.[15] In spite of the previously mentioned criticism that such a system would not have been operational during the test period, some investors might still be tempted to use it if it worked well enough in retrospect. However, there is another criticism that can be made about such a system.

Imagine that equation (23.2) did not appear to work well. If so, then the following equation could be tried:

$$\bar{I}_t = a + bM_{t-1} + cM_{t-2} \tag{23.3}$$

where M_{t-2} is the level of the money supply at time $t - 2$ and c is a constant. If equation (23.3) does not seem to work well, more variables and constants could be tried. Ultimately, an equation could be found that appears to work quite well. However, this does not mean that it would be useful to the investor. If 100 seemingly irrelevant systems are tried with a set of data, due to the laws of probability one of them is likely to give results that are "statistically significant at the 1% level." This should not cause undue excitement, since it would not have any notable predictive power.

For example, share prices in the United States have been shown to be correlated with both sunspot activity and with the length of skirts. Few would associate causal relationships in these instances. Instead, these correlations are likely to have been *spurious*, meaning they probably were coincidental. Without solid reasons to believe that a relationship is due to underlying forces, it would be unwise to predict its continuation in the future.

Comparisons with Easily Beaten Systems

Often an investment system is said to explain a large part of the variation in some stock index. Figure 23.2 shows the quarterly level of the S&P 500 over a ten-year period (the solid curve) and the levels predicted by a system based on historic levels of the money supply (the dotted curve). The two sets of values appear to be quite similar.

This is not very impressive. An extremely simple set of predictions, shown by the dashed curve, is even better. This procedure predicts that each quarter's index will equal that of the preceding quarter:

$$\overline{SP}_t = \overline{SP}_{t-1}. \tag{23.4}$$

Any system that is purported to be able to beat the market must predict percentage price changes (or returns), not price levels, because such changes (or returns) determine profits and losses. Thus, a good test is the extent to which predicted changes conform to actual changes. Figure 23.3 shows the percentage price change predicted by the system analyzed in Figure 23.2, along with the corresponding actual change for each quarter. The relationship is, at best, tenuous.

Reliance on Misleading Visual Comparisons

Occasionally the proponent of a system will produce a graph that plots both the level of an indicator intended to predict market moves and the levels of the market itself. Visual

[15] This is sometimes known as "data snooping." See Andrew W. Lo and A. Craig MacKinlay, "Data-Snooping Biases in Tests of Financial Pricing Models," *Review of Financial Studies* 3, no. 3 (1990): 431–467; and Fischer Black, "Beta and Return," *Journal of Portfolio Management* 20, no. 1 (Fall 1993): 8–18.

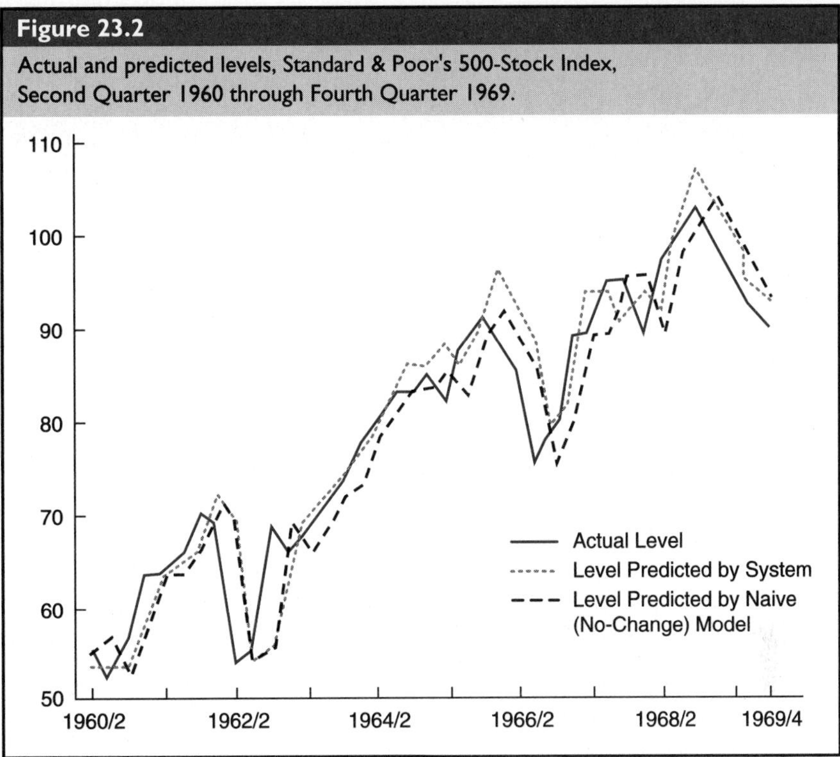

SOURCE: Kenneth E. Homa and Dwight M. Jaffee, "The Supply of Money and Common Stock Prices," *Journal of Finance* 26, no. 5 (December 1971): 1052.

comparison of the two curves may suggest that the indicator does indeed predict changes in the market. However, the eye cannot easily differentiate between a situation in which changes in a market "predictor" *lead* the market and one in which the changes *lag* behind the market. This is a crucial distinction because only a leading indicator can bring superior investment performance.

Ex Post Selection Bias

Many studies describe a stock-selection system that has outperformed standard stock market indices. Some of these systems avoid the errors considered thus far, but another error may be involved. To facilitate computer-based analysis, a standard set of data might have been employed. For example, an investigator might use a database prepared in 1995 with share price data relating to the period from 1984 through 1994. The stocks included in the database might have been chosen because they existed and were important in 1995 (for example, they might have been considered important because they were listed on the TSE in 1995). An investment system based on analysis of this database is liable to reflect ***ex post*** **selection bias** (or survivorship bias). That is, the system discovered in 1995 was based on an analysis of those stocks that were certain to be alive, well, and important in 1984. Accordingly, it should have done well over the period from 1984 to 1994. Studies of this type implicitly commit an error described earlier—they require information not available

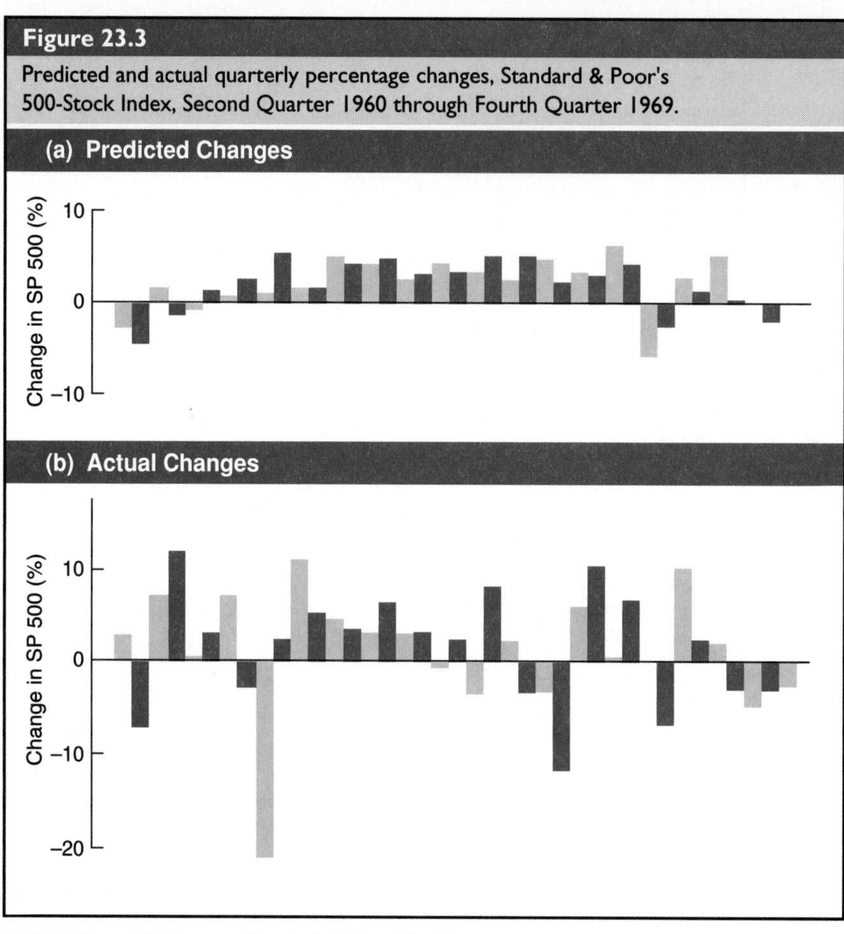

SOURCE: Kenneth E. Homa and Dwight M. Jaffee, "The Supply of Money and Common Stock Prices," *Journal of Finance* 26, no. 5 (December 1971): 1052.

in advance. In particular, they assume that it was known in 1984 which stocks would be still listed in 1994.[16]

Failure to Use Out-of-Sample Data

Can any evidence concerning a system's ability to beat the market be persuasive? Probably not to those who believe absolutely in market efficiency. But there are appropriate tests that can be undertaken.

The search for a system should be conducted using one set of data, and the test of the system's predictive ability should be performed using an entirely different set of data. The latter set of data is sometimes known as **out-of-sample data** (or a holdout sample). To be complete, such a test should involve the (simulated) management of a portfolio and be designed so that each investment decision is based solely on information available at

[16] For a discussion of how *ex post* selection bias influences studies of the performance of mutual funds, see Stephen J. Brown, William Goetzmann, Roger G. Ibbotson, and Stephen A. Ross, "Survivorship Bias in Performance Studies," *Review of Financial Studies* 5, no. 4 (1992): 553–580.

the time the decision is made. Finally, the performance of the system should be measured in the way one would measure the performance of any investment manager (discussed in Chapter 25). This involves, among other things, attempting to determine the probability that the investment results were due to chance rather than skill.

Figure 23.4 shows the performance of one system using out-of-sample data. Values forecast by three predictive systems for quarterly percentage changes in the S&P 500 are shown, along with the subsequent actual changes. Each of the predictive systems worked extremely well with past data. The same cannot be said for their predictions using out-of-sample data.

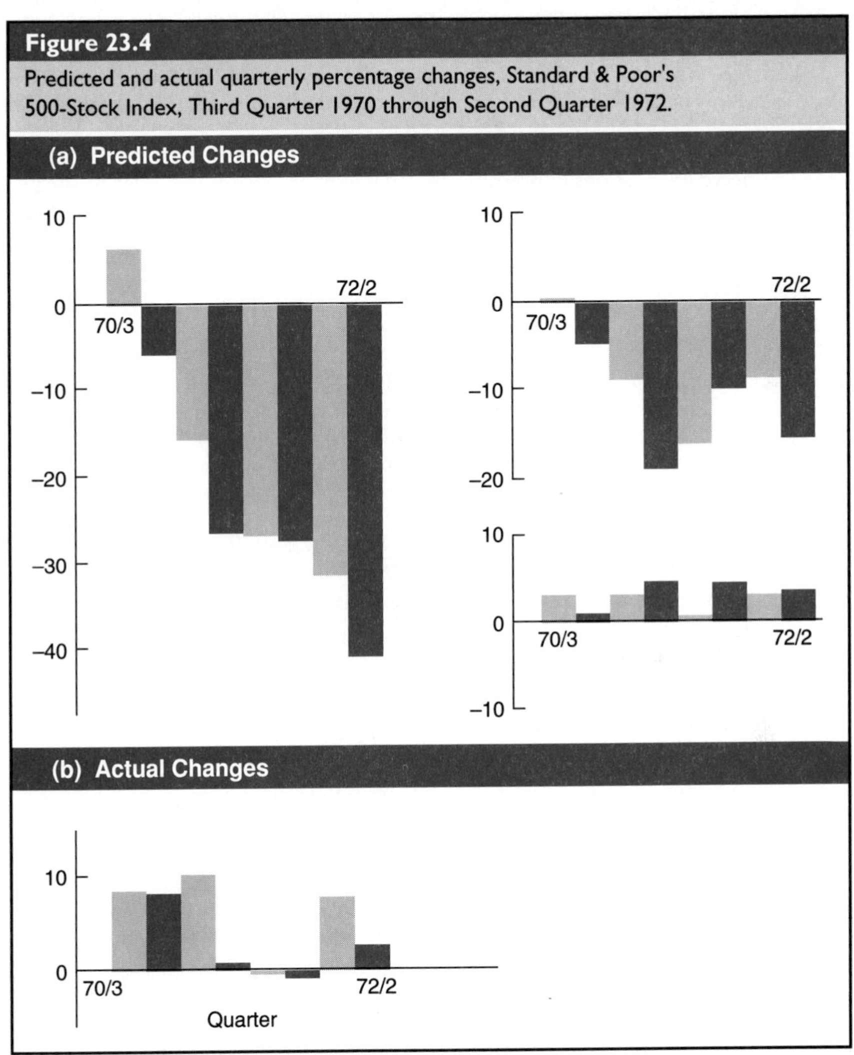

SOURCE: James E. Pesando, "The Supply of Money and Common Stock Prices: Further Observations on the Econometric Evidence," *Journal of Finance* 29, no. 3 (June 1974): 916.

TECHNICAL ANALYSIS

One of the major divisions in the ranks of financial analysts is between those using fundamental analysis (known as fundamental analysts, or fundamentalists) and those using **technical analysis** (known as technical analysts, or technicians). The fundamentalist tends to look forward; the technician, backward. The fundamentalist is concerned with such things as future earnings and dividends, whereas the technician thinks little (if at all) about such things.

> Technical analysis is the study of the internal stock exchange information as such. The word "technical" implies a study of the market itself and not of those external factors which are reflected in the market . . . [A]ll the relevant factors, whatever they may be, can be reduced to the volume of the stock exchange transactions and the level of share prices; or more generally, to the sum of the statistical information produced by the market.[17]

The technician usually attempts to predict short-term price movements and thus makes recommendations concerning the *timing* of purchases and sales of specific stocks, groups of stocks (such as industries) or of stocks in general. It is sometimes said that fundamental analysis is designed to answer the question What? and technical analysis to answer the question When?

The concept of technical analysis is completely at odds with the notion of efficient markets:

> . . . the methodology of technical analysis . . . rests upon the assumption that history tends to repeat itself in the stock exchange. If a certain pattern of activity has in the past produced certain results nine times out of ten, one can assume a strong likelihood of the same outcome whenever this pattern appears in the future. *It should be emphasized, however, that a large part of the methodology of technical analysis lacks a strictly logical explanation.*[18]

Thus, technicians assert that the study of past patterns of things such as prices and volumes allows the investor to identify accurately times when certain specific stocks (or groups of stocks, or the market in general) are either overpriced or underpriced. Most (but not all) technical analysts rely on charts of stock prices and trading volumes. The appendix describes some of the more frequently used ones.

Early studies found little evidence showing technical analysis to be useful in enabling investors to "beat the market."[19] Many "proofs" of this ability were offered, but most committed at least one of the errors described earlier. However, several recent studies have indicated that technical analysis may be useful to investors.[20] The evidence presented in these studies can be divided into two groups based on the strategies involved. The first group,

---

[17] Felix Rosenfeld, ed., *The Evaluation of Ordinary Shares*, a summary of the proceedings of the Eighth Congress of the European Federation of Financial Analysts Societies (Paris: Dunod, 1975): 297.

[18] Rosenfeld, *The Evaluation of Ordinary Shares*, pp. 297–298. For an argument that technical analysis can be of value in an efficient market, see David P. Brown and Robert H. Jennings, "On Technical Analysis," *Review of Financial Analysis* 2, no. 4 (1989): 527–551. Also see Jack L. Treynor and Robert Ferguson, "In Defense of Technical Analysis," *Journal of Finance* 40, no. 3 (July 1985): 757–773; and Lawrence Blume, David Easley, and Maureen O'Hara, "Market Statistics and Technical Analysis: The Role of Volume," *Journal of Finance* 49, no. 1 (March 1994): 153–181.

[19] See, for example, Eugene F. Fama, "Efficient Capital Markets: A Review of Theory and Empirical Work," *Journal of Finance* 25, no. 2 (May 1970): 383–417.

[20] See, for example, Eugene F. Fama, "Efficient Capital Markets: II," *Journal of Finance* 46, no. 5 (December 1991): 1575–1617.

consisting of momentum and contrarian strategies, simply examines the returns on stocks over a time period that just ended in order to identify candidates for purchase and sale. The second group, consisting of moving average and trading range breakout strategies, makes such an identification based on the relationship of a security's price over a relatively short time period that just ended to its price over a relatively longer time period.

► Momentum and Contrarian Strategies

Consider ranking a group of stocks based on the size of their returns over some time period that just ended. *Momentum investors* seek out for purchase those stocks that have recently risen significantly in price on the belief that they will continue to rise due to an upward shift in their demand curves. Conversely, those stocks that have recently fallen significantly in price are sold on the belief that their demand curves have shifted downward.

Investors who call themselves *contrarians* do just the opposite of what most other investors are doing in the market: they buy stocks that other have shunned and think of as losers and they sell stocks that others have feverishly pursued and think of as winners. They do so in the belief that investors tend to overreact to news. That is, stocks that have plunged in price because of some recent piece of bad news (such as recently announced weak earnings) are thought to have fallen too far in price. Such stocks are viewed as being ready for a price rebound, as investors realize that they have overreacted to the bad news associated with the stock and subsequently drive the price upward toward the stock's fundamental value.

Similarly, stocks that have risen rapidly in price due to some recent piece of good news (such as recently announced strong earnings) are thought to have risen too far in price. These stocks are viewed as being ready for a price drop, as investors realize that they have overreacted to the good news associated with the stock and subsequently drive the price downward toward the stock's fundamental value. Researchers have tested strategies of this type. Their overall test design is discussed first, followed by the results.

The Test Design

Consider the following investment strategy:

1. Identify those stocks that have been listed on either the NYSE or AMEX (or just the NYSE). This focuses the technician's attention on established stocks.
2. Rank these stocks based on the size of their returns over a just-ending time period, referred to as the portfolio "formation period."
3. Assign some of those stocks that have the lowest average return in the formation period to the "loser" portfolio and some of those stocks that have the highest average return in this period to the "winner" portfolio.
4. Determine the returns on the winner and loser portfolios over a just-starting subsequent time period, referred to as the portfolio "test period."
5. Repeat the analysis all over again, starting with step 1, but moving forward one time period. Stop after several repetitions.
6. Determine the abnormal returns on the winner portfolio by subtracting the returns on a benchmark portfolio having a comparable level of risk (see Chapter 22); calculate the average of these abnormal returns. Similarly, determine the average abnormal returns on the loser portfolio.

If a momentum strategy works, then the winner portfolio should have a positive average abnormal return and the loser portfolio a negative one. Furthermore, the difference in their abnormal returns should be significantly positive. Conversely, if a contrarian strategy works, then the loser portfolio should have a positive abnormal return and the winner portfolio a negative one. and the difference should be significantly negative.

However, if stocks are priced efficiently, then their past price behaviour is useless in terms of its predictive value. Neither momentum nor contrarian strategies should "work"—winner portfolios should perform no differently from loser portfolios. Both portfolios should have average abnormal returns of approximately zero. Even more important, *the difference in these returns should be approximately zero.*

► Test Results

Table 23.1 presents the test results. In part A, portfolios were formed based on their returns during the past week. All stocks with an above-average return were put into a loser portfolio. Then the returns on these two portfolios were tracked for the next week. When this was done repeatedly week by week from 1962 through 1986, it was found that there were marked differences in the annualized average abnormal returns on the two portfolios. Specifically, the returns were nearly −25% for the winner and 90% for the losers, with a difference of −115%. *This difference (as well as the differences in the other parts of the table) was found to be statistically significantly different from zero.* Note that a similar but not as extreme observation is apparent in part B, where the time frame is one month instead of a week.[21] Overall, this evidence indicates that contrarian strategies hold promise. Interestingly, the correction for the overreaction is asymmetric in part A because the losers rebound by a much larger percentage than the winners fall. This suggests that contrarians should concentrate more on identifying losers than on winners if they are going to focus on weekly returns.

In part C of Table 23.1, portfolios were formed based on their returns over the past six months. The 10% of stocks with the highest returns were put in the winner portfolio whereas the 10% with the lowest returns were put in the loser portfolio. Tracking their returns over the next six months revealed significant differences. In complete contrast to parts A and B, now the winners have a much higher average abnormal return than the losers, suggesting that momentum strategies have promise. Stocks that shot up in price over six months continued to go up during the next six months, whereas those that plunged over six months continued their plunge. Although not quite as strong, similar results were observed when the top 10% and bottom 10% were identified based on a full year's returns, as shown in part D.[22]

---

[21] There are other studies that present evidence that is consistent with these results. See Barr Rosenberg, Kenneth Reid, and Ronald Lanstein, "Persuasive Evidence of Market Inefficiency," *Journal of Portfolio Management* 11, no. 3 (Spring 1985): 9–16; John S. Howe, "Evidence on Stock Market Overreaction," *Financial Analysts Journal* 42, no. 4 (July/August 1986): 74–77; and Andrew W. Lo and A. Craig MacKinlay, "When Are Contrarian Profits Due to Stock Market Overreaction?" *Review of Financial Studies* 3, no. 2 (1990): 175–205.

[22] One explanation for these results that has been offered is that investors underreact to quarterly earnings announcements. See Chapter 19, particularly section 8.1, and Victor L. Bernard, Jacob K. Thomas, and Jeffrey S. Abarbanell, "How Sophisticated Is the Market in Interpreting Earnings News?" *Journal of Applied Corporate Finance* 6, no. 2 (Summer 1993): 54–63. Another related observation involved buying the ten highest dividend-yielding stocks in the Dow Jones Industrial Average (DJIA) and holding them for one year, at which point the portfolio was revised accordingly for another year. From 1973 through 1992 this strategy outperformed the DJIA by 5.15% per year, on average. See Dale L. Domian, David A. Louton, and Irene M. Seahawk, "The Dow Dividend Strategy: How it Works — and Why," *AAII Journal* 16, no. 4 (May 1994): 7–10.

Table 23.1

Returns from Momentum and Contrarian Strategies.

Length of Portfolio Formation and Test Periods	Annualized Abnormal Returns: *Winner Portfolio*	*Loser Portfolio*	*Winner Return less Loser Return*
A. Weekly, 1962–1986:			
Top 50% and bottom 50% of NYSE and AMEX stocks	–24.9%	89.8%	–114.7%
B. Monthly, 1929–1982:			
Top 10% and bottom 10% of all NYSE and AMEX stocks	–11.6%	12.1%	–23.7%
C. Semiannually, 1962–1989:			
Top 10% and bottom 10% of all NYSE and AMEX stocks	8.7%	–3.5%	12.2%
D. Annually, 1929–1982:			
Top 10% and bottom 10% of all NYSE and AMEX stocks[a]	5.0%	–6.1%	11.1%
E. Three years, 1926–1982:			
Top 35 and bottom 35 NYSE stocks	–1.7%	6.5%	–8.2%
F. Five years, 1926–1982:			
Top 50 and bottom 50 NYSE stocks	–2.4%	7.2%	–9.6%

[a] Abnormal returns were measured over one month subsequent to the portfolio formation date.

SOURCE: Adapted from:
A. Bruce N. Lehmann, "Fads, Martingales, and Market Efficiency," *Quarterly Journal of Economics* 105, no. 1 (February 1990): 16.
B. Narasimhan Jegadeesh, "Evidence of Predictable Behavior of Security Returns," *Journal of Finance* 45, no. 3 (July 1990): 890–891.
C. Narasimhan Jegadeesh and Sheridan Titman, "Returns to Buying Winners and Selling Losers: Implications for Stock Market Efficiency," *Journal of Finance* 48, no. 1 (March 1993): 79.
D. Narasimhan Jegadeesh, "Evidence of Predictable Behavior of Security Returns," *Journal of Finance* 45, no. 3 (July 1990): 890–891.
E. Werner F. M. De Bondt and Richard Thaler, "Does the Stock Market Overreact?" *Journal of Finance* 40, no. 3 (July 1985): 799.
F. Werner F. M. De Bondt and Richard Thaler, "Further Evidence on Investor Overreaction and Stock Market Seasonality," *Journal of Finance* 42, no. 3 (July 1987): 561.

Oddly, parts E and F show that the momentum strategy would not have worked if the winner and loser portfolios were formed based on three-year or five-year stock returns. (It should be noted that there are subtle differences in how the portfolios in parts E and F were formed.) Instead, the contrarian strategy appears to have worked once again. Note that the average annual abnormal return in part E on the loser portfolio was +6.5%. Conversely, the average annual abnormal return on the winner portfolio was –1.7%, resulting in a significant difference of 8.2%. Part F shows that similar results were obtained when portfolios were formed based on returns over the previous five years.[23] As in part A, the correction for the

[23] A puzzling observation associated with part F was that 5% of the 7.2% abnormal return for the loser portfolio was earned during the Januaries that occurred during the test period. Conversely, –.8% of the –2.4% abnormal return for the winners was earned during Januaries. Hence, the January anomaly (discussed in the appendix to Chapter 17) appears to somehow be intertwined with the long-term contrarian strategy.

overreaction is asymmetric in that losers rebound by a much larger percentage than the winners fall.

In summary, there does appear to be some merit to the contrarian strategy for both very short (a week or month) and very long (three to five years) time periods. Surprisingly, for intermediate periods such as six months and one year, an exact opposite strategy—momentum—seems to have merit. Unfortunately, both strategies involve a high degree of turnover, as portfolios are reconstituted frequently—particularly for the weekly contrarian strategy. As the strategies would incur substantial transaction costs, it remains to be seen whether they are profitable after such costs are fully accounted for.[24]

It should be noted that other studies have examined contrarian strategies and have been unable to confirm the usefulness of such strategies. In two of these studies it was argued that the benchmark portfolio returns were incorrectly determined. This means that the abnormal returns were not calculated correctly because by definition they are equal to the difference between the returns on the portfolio and its benchmark. In a third study, the alleged cause of the overreaction—security analysis underpredicting earnings on losers and overpredicting earnings on winners—was contested. As fourth study suggested that the size effect (discussed in the appendix to Chapter 17) was largely responsible for the results because losers tend to be smaller than winners. Lastly, a fifth study argued that incorrect prices were used when the costs of buying and selling stocks were determined in arriving at the results reflected in parts E and F of Table 23.1. However, these studies have, in turn, been contested in a sixth study. Specifically, after taking the objections into consideration it was found that losers outperform winners by 5% to 10% per year, with the difference being the largest when only small firms were classified into winners and losers.[25]

Adding to the puzzle is the behaviour of Canadian stocks. For one-year test periods the results were similar to those in the United States in that a momentum strategy seemed to work (as in part D of Table 23.1). For three-year and five-year test periods, neither a momentum nor a contrarian strategy worked (unlike parts E and F of Table 23.1).[26]

---

[24] Apparently significant returns can be earned from the weekly strategy if transaction costs are small (such as for large institutional investors). However, larger transaction costs result in negative net returns. See Bruce N. Lehmann, "Fads, Martingales, and Market Efficiency," *Quarterly Journal of Economics* 105, no. 1 (February 1990): 1–28. For an argument that Lehmann has underestimated the size of transaction costs, see Jennifer Conrad, Mustafa N. Gultekin, and Gautam Kaul, "Profitability of Short-Term Contrarian Portfolio Strategies," unpublished paper, The University of Michigan, 1991.

[25] The six studies are, respectively, K. C. Chan, "On Contrarian Investment Strategy," *Journal of Business* 61, no. 2 (April 1988): 147–163; Ray Ball and S. P. Kothari, "Nonstationary Expected Returns: Implications for Tests of Market Efficiency and Serial Correlations in Returns," *Journal of Financial Economics* 25, no. 1 (November 1989): 51–74; April Klein, "A Direct Test of the Cognitive Bias Theory of Share Price Reversals," *Journal of Accounting and Economics* 13, no. 2 (July 1990): 155–166; Paul Zarowin, "Size, Seasonality, and Stock Market Overreaction," *Journal of Quantitative Analysis* 25, no. 1 (March 1990): 113–125; Jennifer Conrad and Gautam Kaul, "Long-Term Overreaction or Biases in Computed Returns?" *Journal of Finance* 48, no. 1 (March 1993): 39–63; and Navin Chopra, Josef Lakonishok, and Jay R. Ritter, "Measuring Abnormal Performance: Do Stocks Overreact?" *Journal of Financial Economics* 31, no. 2 (April 1992): 235–268.

[26] See Lawrence Kryzanowski and Hao Zhang, "The Contrarian Investment Strategy Does Not Work in Canadian Markets," *Journal of Financial and Quantitative Analysis* 27, no. 3 (September 1992): 383–395.

► Moving Average and Trading Range Breakout Strategies

Consider the following investment strategy:

1. Calculate the average closing price of a given stock over the last 200 trading days.
2. Take today's closing price and divide it by the 200-day average to form a short-to-long price ratio.
3. If the ratio is greater than one, this is a buy signal that indicates that the stock is to be bought tomorrow. If the ratio is less than one, this is a sell signal that indicates that the stock is to be sold tomorrow.
4. Tomorrow after closing, repeat the above process.
5. At the end of a test period, calculate the average daily return during both the "buy" days and the "sell" days.

If the stock market is efficient, the average return during the buy days should be approximately the same as the average return during the sell days. That is, *the difference in their returns should be approximately zero*. However, technical analysis might have merit if they are significantly different.

A study examined this strategy using daily data from 1897 to 1986, a total of over 25 000 trading days. However, the daily closing level of the Dow Jones Industrial Average (DJIA) was used instead of daily closing prices for individual stocks. As shown in part A of Table 23.2, this strategy resulted in markedly different returns on buy and sell days. In particular, the annualized average return on buy days was 10.7%, whereas the return on sell days was –6.1%. *The difference of 16.8% was statistically significantly different from zero (as were the differences in the other parts of the table).*

Because this strategy classifies every day as either a buy day or a sell day, thereby allowing a given stock to be bought on consecutive days, it is referred to as a variable-length moving average strategy. However, it can result in many trades over the course of a year, as an investor using it could be "whipsawed" into buying and selling repeatedly. In order to reduce the frequency of changing positions from buying to selling, or selling to buying, the strategy can be modified as follows to become a fixed-length moving average strategy. Buy signals are now generated only when the ratio *changes* from less than one to greater than one, and sell signals are generated only when the ratio *changes* from greater than one to less than one. Furthermore, when a buy signal is generated, the stock is bought the next day and then held for ten days. Similarly, when a sell signal is generated, the stock is sold and not bought for ten days. In either case, when the ten days are over, the investor starts looking again for a buy or sell signal. Whereas the variable-length strategy classified every day as either a buy or sell day, there can be days that are not classified as either buy or sell with the fixed-length strategy.

Part A of Table 23.2 shows that the fixed-length moving average strategy performed similarly to the variable length one. The annualized average return on buy days was 13.8% and on sell days was –4.8%, resulting in a significant difference of 18.6%. On average there were about 1.3 and 1.7 buy and sell signals per year, respectively.

The trading range breakout strategy is similar to the fixed-length moving average strategy. Here the high and low prices over the past 200 trading days are noted. A buy signal is generated on a given day only when that day's closing price is greater than the high, provided that the previous day's closing price was less than the high. Conversely, a sell signal arises when the closing price moves from being above the low on one day to being below the low on the next day. When a buy signal is generated, the stock is bought the next day and

Table 23.2

Returns from Moving Average and Trading Range Breakout Strategies.

	Annualized Average Returns		
	Buy Signal	*Sell Signal*	*Buy Return Less Sell Return*
A. Moving average tests:			
Variable length	10.7%	–6.1%	16.8%
Fixed length	13.8	–4.8	18.6
B. Trading range breakout tests:	11.8%	–5.8%	17.6%

SOURCE: Adapted from William Brock, Josef Lakonishok, and Blake LeBaron, "Simple Technical Trading Rules and the Stochastic Properties of Stock Returns," *Journal of Finance* 47, no. 5 (December 1992): 1739, 1741, 1742. Based on one-day short and 200-day long periods during 1897 to 1986 with no filter, annualized assuming that there are 260 trading days in a year and 26 ten-day trading periods in a year.

then held for ten days. Similarly, when a sell signal is generated, the stock is sold and not bought for ten days. In either case, when the ten days are over, the investor starts looking again for a buy or sell signal.

Part B of Table 23.2 shows that the trading range breakout strategy performed similarly to the two moving average strategies. The annualized average returns on buy days was 11.8% and on sell days was –5.8%, with a significant difference of 17.6%. On average there were about 5.2 and 2.0 buy and sell signals per year, respectively.

► The Bottom Line

The four strategies reported in Tables 23.1 and 23.2 have been rigorously tested, avoiding the pitfalls mentioned earlier. Furthermore, although not reported, slight variations among the strategies had only a minor effect on their results. However, the usefulness of such technical strategies remains an open question subject to much debate. Despite appearing to be profitable, even after considering transaction costs, it is quite possible that a more complete consideration of these costs (including such things as the impact of bid-ask spreads) will reveal that they are incapable of generating abnormal profits. Hence, evaluating investment systems will not always provide unambiguous answers on their potential usefulness. Furthermore, it has been speculated that the commonplace usage of computerized trading programs designed to implement technical strategies will ultimately eliminate any potential such strategies have for generating abnormal profits.[27] Nevertheless, the apparent success of these strategies offers a challenge to those who contend that the stock market is highly efficient.

FUNDAMENTAL ANALYSIS

The rest of this chapter is concerned with the principles of fundamental analysis of common stocks. Although technical analysis is used by many investors, fundamental analysis is far more prevalent. Furthermore, unlike technical analysis, it is an essential activity if capital markets are to be efficient.

[27] Lehmann, "Fads, Martingales, and Market Efficiency," p. 26.

Top-Down versus Bottom-Up Forecasting

Fundamental analysts forecast, among other things, future levels of the economy's gross national product, future sales and earnings for a number of industries, and future sales and earnings for an even larger number of firms. Eventually such forecasts are converted to estimates of expected returns of specific stocks and, perhaps, certain industries and the stock market itself. In some cases the conversion is made explicitly. For example, an estimate of next year's earnings per share for a firm may be multiplied by a projected price-earnings ratio in order to estimate the expected price of the firm's shares a year hence, thereby allowing a forecast of the expected return to be made. In other cases the conversion is implicit. For example, stocks with projected earnings exceeding consensus estimates may be placed on an "approved" list.

Some investment organizations that employ financial analysts follow a sequential **top-down approach** to forecasting. With this approach, the financial analysts first make forecasts for the economy, then for industries, and finally for companies. The industry forecasts are based on the forecasts for the economy and, in turn, the company forecasts are based on the forecasts for both its industry and the economy.

Other investment organizations begin with estimates of the prospects for companies and then build to estimates of the prospects for industries and ultimately the economy. Such a **bottom-up approach** may unknowingly involve inconsistent assumptions. For example, one analyst may use one forecast of foreign exchange rates in projecting the foreign sales of company A, whereas another analyst may use a different forecast in projecting the foreign sales of company B. Top-down systems are less susceptible to this danger, since all the analysts in the organization would use the same forecast of exchange rates.

In practice, a combination of the two approaches is often employed. For example, forecasts are made for the economy in a top-down manner. These forecasts then provide a setting within which financial analysts make bottom-up forecasts for individual companies. The sum of the individual forecasts should be consistent with the original economy-wide forecast.[28] If not, the process is repeated (perhaps with additional controls) to ensure consistency.

Probabilistic Forecasting

Explicit **probabilistic forecasting** often focuses on economy-wide forecasts, since uncertainty at this level is of the greatest importance in determining the risk and expected return of a well-diversified portfolio. A few alternative economic scenarios may be forecast, along with their respective probability of occurrence. Then accompanying projections are made of the prospects for industries, companies, and share prices. Such an exercise provides an idea of the likely sensitivities of different stocks to surprises concerning the economy. By assigning probabilities to the different scenarios, risks may also be estimated.

---

[28] Input-output analysis is sometimes used to ensure consistency between various industries and the economy in aggregate. This type of analysis is based on the notion that the output of certain industries (for example, the steel industry) is the input for certain other industries (for example, the household appliance industry).

Econometric Models

An **econometric model** is a statistical model that provides a means of forecasting the levels of certain variables, known as **endogenous variables**. In order to make these forecasts, the model relies on assumptions that have been made in regard to the levels of certain other variables, known as **exogenous variables**. For example, the level of next year's car sales may be specified by an econometric model to be related to next year's level of gross domestic product and interest rates. The values of next year's gross domestic product and interest rates, the exogenous variables, must be provided in order to forecast next year's car sales, the endogenous variable.

The model may be extremely complex or it may be a simple formula that can be used with a desk calculator. In any event, it should involve a blend of economics and statistics, where economics is used to suggest the forms of relevant relationships and statistical procedures are applied to historical data to estimate the exact nature of the relationships involved.

Some investment organizations utilize large-scale econometric models to translate predictions about such factors as the federal budget, expected consumer spending, and planned business investment into predictions of future levels of gross national product, inflation, and unemployment. Several firms and nonprofit organizations maintain such models, selling either the forecasts or the computer program itself to investment organizations, corporate planners, public agencies, and others.

The developers of large-scale models usually provide several "standard" predictions, based on different sets of assumptions about the exogenous variables; some also assign probabilities to the alternative predictions. In some cases, users can substitute their own sets of assumptions and subsequently examine the resulting predictions.

Large-scale econometric models of this type employ many equations that describe many important relationships. Although estimates of the magnitudes of such relationships are obtained from historical data, these estimates may or may not enable the model to work well in the future. When predictions turn out to be poor, it is sometimes said that there have been structural changes in the underlying economic relationships. However, the failure may be due to the influence of factors omitted from the model. In any event, inaccurate predictions require changes in either the size of the estimates or the basic form of the econometric model, or even both. Rare indeed is the user who does not fine-tune (or completely overhaul) such a model, from time to time in light of further experience.

Financial Statement Analysis

For some, the image of a typical financial analyst is that of a gnome, fully equipped with green eyeshade, poring over financial statements in a back room. Though the physical description is rarely accurate, it is true that many analysts do study financial statements in an attempt to predict the future.

A company's financial statements can be regarded as the output of a model of the firm—a model designed by management, the company's accountants, and (indirectly) the tax authorities. Different companies use different models, meaning they treat similar events in different ways. One reason this is possible is because generally accepted accounting principles (GAAP), as established by the Canadian Institute of Chartered Accountants (CICA), allow a certain degree of latitude in how to account for various events. Examples include the method of depreciating assets (straight-line or accelerated) and the method of valuing inventory.

To understand a company fully and to compare it with others that use different accounting procedures, the financial analyst must be a financial detective, looking for clues in footnotes and the accompanying text that discuss how the financial statements were prepared. Those who take bottom-line figures such as earnings per share on faith may be more surprised by future developments than those who try to look behind the accounting veil.

The ultimate goal of the fundamental analyst is to determine the values of the outstanding claims on a firm's income (claimants include the firm's bondholders and shareholders). The firm's income must first be projected; then the possible distributions of that income among the claimants must be considered, with relevant probabilities assessed.

In practice, shortcut procedures are often used. Many analysts focus on reported accounting figures, even though such numbers may not adequately reflect true economic values. In addition, simple measures are often used to assess complex relationships. For example, some analysts attempt to estimate the probability that short-term creditors will be paid in full and on time by examining the ratio of liquid assets to the amount of short-term debt. Similarly, the probability that interest will be paid to bondholders in a timely fashion is often estimated by examining the ratio of earnings before interest and taxes to the periodic amount of such interest payments. Often the prospects for a firm's common stock are estimated by examining the ratio of earnings after taxes to the book value of equity.

Ratio Analysis

The use of ratios such as these to facilitate predicting the future is widespread. Some ratios use items from the same financial statement (either a particular balance sheet or income statement), whereas others use items from two different statements. Still other ratios use items from two or more statements of the same type but of different years (for example, this year's balance sheet and last year's balance sheet), or incorporate data on market values.

Ratios may be used in several ways. Some analysts apply absolute standards, on the grounds that a substandard ratio indicates a potential weakness that merits further analysis. Other analysts compare a company's ratios to those of the "average" firm in the same industry in order to detect differences that may need further consideration. Yet others analyze trends in a company's ratios over time, hoping it will help them predict future changes. Still others combine ratios with technical analysis in order to arrive at investment decisions.

Another use of ratios is illustrated in Figure 23.5. In this figure, each ratio is equal to the product of the two ratios on its right-hand side, with one exception. The exception is the turnover ratio (sales/assets), whose reciprocal (assets/sales) equals the sum of the reciprocals of the four ratios on its right-hand side. Given the interrelationships among the ratios, it can be seen that once the future values of these ratios are forecast, then an implied forecast for the price of the firm's shares can be computed. The difficulty with such an approach, however, is in accurately predicting the future values of the ratios.

Ratio analysis can be very sophisticated, but it can also be overly simplistic. Routine extrapolation of a present ratio (or its recent trend) may produce a poor estimate of its future value. (For example, there is no reason for a firm to maintain a constant ratio of inventory to sales). Moreover, a series of simple projections may produce inconsistent financial statements. For example, projections of ratios imply predictions of the levels of various balance sheet items. However, it may be that when these levels are looked at altogether, the resulting balance sheet does not balance.

Spreadsheets

To project future financial statements, the model should include the relationships among the items on such statements and outside factors. Traditional ratio analysis does this, but

Figure 23.5

The use of predicted ratios to compute predicted price.

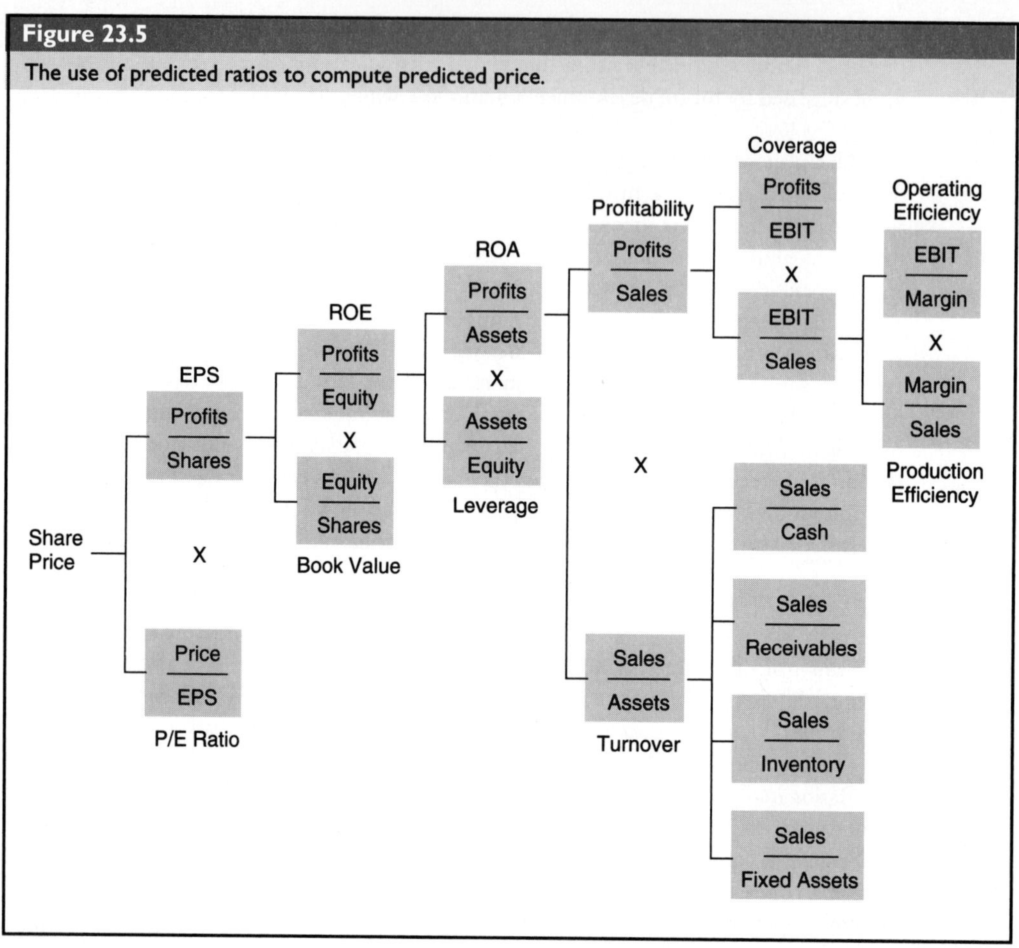

SOURCE: Samuel E. Stewart, Jr., "Corporate Forecasting," in Sumner N. Levine, ed., *Financial Analyst's Handbook I* (Homewood Il: Dow Jones & Company, Inc., 1975): 912.

somewhat crudely. A much better procedure uses microcomputers and a type of software known as spreadsheets.[29]

Basically, a spreadsheet is an arrangement of information in rows and columns. Each cell on a traditional (paper) spreadsheet typically contains a number or a label. Some of the numbers (for example, sales) are entered directly; others (for example, earnings before interest and taxes) are computed from the numbers in other cells.

An electronic spreadsheet simulates a traditional spreadsheet on a computer screen. There are, however, notable differences. Most importantly, cells can contain formulas. For example, the cell for earnings before interest and taxes (EBIT) could contain the formula for calculating the value as well as the value produced by the formula. Normally, only the value would be displayed, giving an outward appearance similar to that of a traditional spreadsheet. However, any change in the number in the cell for sales would immediately

[29] Lotus Development Corporation has been one of the leading developers of such software. Their products Lotus 1-2-3, Excel and Quattro Pro have been top sellers.

change the value of EBIT, since the formula for EBIT would contain the value for sales as an input. This feature of electronic spreadsheets allows the user to rapidly explore the implications of changes in key assumptions (such as prices, quantities, and costs) on various balance sheet and income statement items. Accordingly, exploration of this sort is often known as *sensitivity analysis*, or *what-if analysis*.

In summary, financial statement analysis can help an analyst understand what a company is, where it may be going, what factors affect it, and how these factors affect it. If others are doing such analysis and doing it well, it will be difficult to find mispriced securities in this manner. But it should be possible to more accurately identify firms likely to go bankrupt, firms with higher or lower betas, firms with greater or lesser sensitivities to major factors, and so forth. Increased understanding of such aspects may well provide ample rewards.

ANALYSTS' RECOMMENDATIONS AND SHARE PRICES

When a security analyst decides that a stock is mispriced and informs certain clients of this, some of the clients may act on the information. As they do so, the price of the security may be affected. As news of the analyst's recommendation spreads, more investors may act, and the price may react even more. At some point, the analyst's information will be "fully reflected" in the security's price.

If the analyst decides a stock is underpriced and clients subsequently purchase it, the share's price will tend to rise. Conversely, if the analyst decides a stock is overpriced and clients subsequently sell it, the share's price will tend to decline. If the analyst's views were well founded, no subsequent counterreaction in the share's price would be expected. Otherwise, the price is likely to return to its prerecommendation level at some later time.

An interesting example of the impact of analysts' recommendations is provided by the behaviour of prices of stocks mentioned in the "Heard on the Street" column of the *Wall Street Journal*, which periodically summarizes recent stock recommendations. An analyst's opinion is typically published in "Heard on the Street" after it is first given to clients. The analyst's view is thus "somewhat public" for several days before publication, but when the column appears the opinion becomes "very public," since it then reaches a substantially larger audience.

Panel (a) of Figure 23.6 summarizes the price reactions of about 597 stocks that received positive opinions in "Heard on the Street" during 1970 and 1971. Panel (b) summarizes the reactions of about 188 stocks that received negative opinions during the same time period. In each panel, the vertical axis plots the average cumulative abnormal return — that is, the average return, adjusted for normal reactions to overall market moves. The horizontal axes indicate trading days relative to the date of publication of the recommendation, going from 20 days before to 20 days after publication.

As shown in the two parts, the publication of such a recommendation does typically affect a share's price.[30] After adjusting for market moves, on the publication date the price of

[30] Similar observations have been made in regard to the recommendations made by major brokerage houses. See John C. Groth, Wilbur G. Lewellen, Gary G. Schlarbaum, and Ronald C. Lease, "An Analysis of Brokerage House Securities Recommendations," *Financial Analysts Journal* 35, no. 1 (January/February 1979): 32–40; and Philip Heitner, "Isn't It Time to Measure Analysts' Track Records?" *Financial Analysts Journal* 47, no. 3 (May/June 1991): 5–6. For a comment on the first study, see the Letter to the Editor in the May/June issue by Clinton M. Bidwell, with a responding Letter to the Editor in the July/August 1980 issue by Wilbur G. Lewellen. Also see footnote 1 in Chapter 24.

Figure 23.6

Effect on stock prices of stock recommendations in "Heard on the Street": 1970 and 1971.

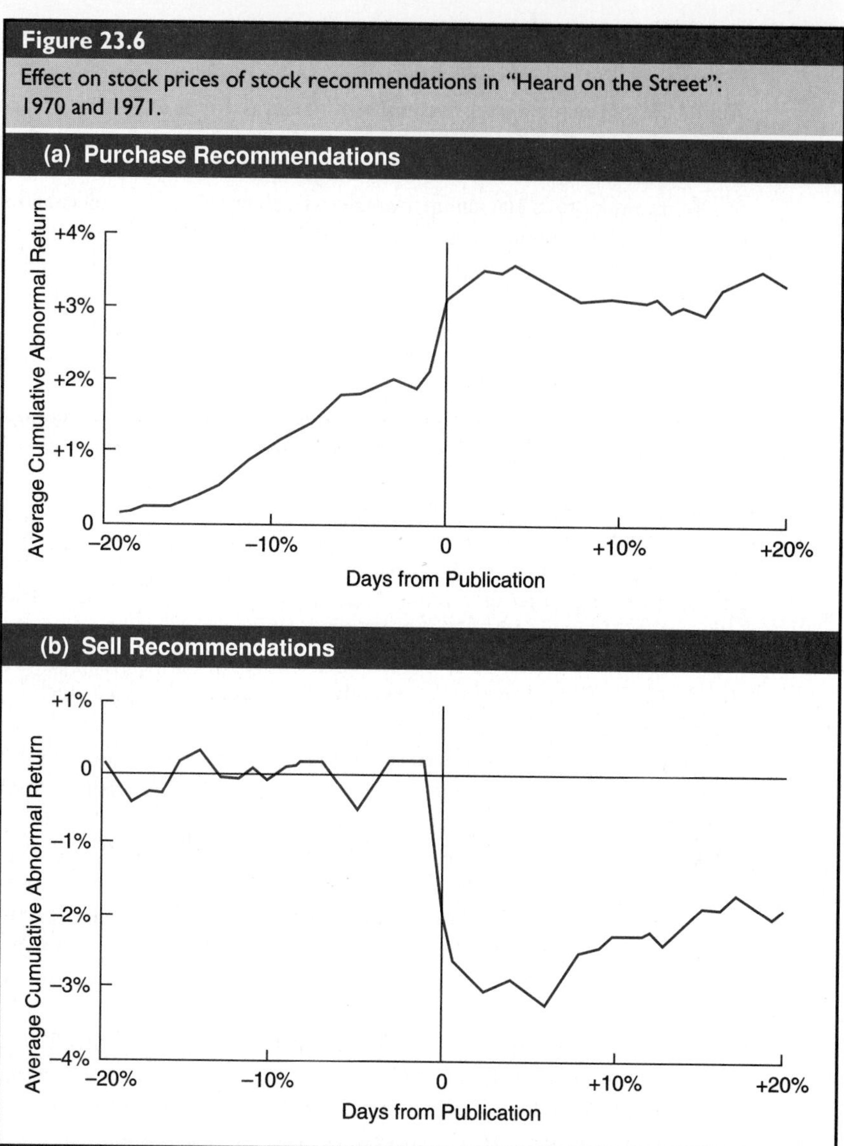

SOURCE: Peter Lloyd Davies and Michael Canes, "Stock Prices and the Publication of Second-Hand Information," *Journal of Business* 51, no. 1 (January 1978): 52.

the shares recommended for purchase rose .923%, whereas that of the shares recommended for sale fell 2.374%. Furthermore, after making such adjustments, 70% of the 597 stocks recommended for purchase rose on the date of publication, and 90% of the 188 stocks recommended for sale fell on the date of publication.

The roughly horizontal lines after day 0 in both parts show that both types of recommendations appeared to contain information. This is because the horizontal lines indicate that there was no significant counterreaction in the 20 days after either a buy or sell recommendation was made.[31]

The upward moves in panel (a) prior to day 0 suggest prior purchases of the stocks have been made by clients of the analysts. An alternative explanation is that analysts simply recommended purchases of stocks that had recently risen in price. Note, however, that panel (b) is quite different: there is no distinct pattern prior to the date of publication of a sell recommendation. This suggests that the analysts did not tend to recommend the sale of securities that had recently fallen in price.[32]

A study of the recommendations made by a regional Canadian investment service company obtained similar results.[33] This company published lists of *recommended, speculative*, and *representative* stocks. The recommended lists consisted of stocks the firm's investment committee recommended for purchase, the speculative list contained stocks regarded as risky and the representative list consisted of stocks that either had been recently dropped from the recommended list or had been evaluated by a new analyst for the first time. The stocks on the representative list were interpreted to be those an investor should hold if they were already owned, but were not encouraged to buy. The firm provided these lists for both Canadian and US stocks. Figure 23.7 presents a comparison of the cumulative abnormal returns for the combined Canadian and US stocks on the recommended and representative lists over the period September 1977 through February 1981 and covered 221 recommendations. This shows that substantial returns could be achieved by following the buy recommendations. The firm was successful in outperforming both the TSE 300 in a bull market with their Canadian recommendations and the S&P 500 with their US recommendations. Stocks on the speculative list showed negative, but not statistically significant, abnormal returns. Representative stocks showed no abnormal returns.

ANALYST FOLLOWING AND STOCK RETURNS

An interesting issue involves the relationship between the amount of attention devoted by analysts to individual stocks and the price behaviour of those stocks. Do stocks that are

---

[31] The "Dartboard" column, appearing monthly in the *Wall Street Journal*, contains one buy recommendation from each of four security analysts. In the two-day period after publication these stocks have an abnormal return of just over 4% and their trading volume is roughly double the normal amount. However, unlike the recommendations in the "Heard on the Street" column, over the next 25 trading days these stocks drop in price, losing about half their 4% gain. See Brad M. Barber and Douglas Loeffler, "The 'Dartboard' Column: Second-Hand Information and Price Pressure," *Journal of Financial and Quantitative Analysis* 28, no. 2 (June 1993): 273–284.

[32] Two more recent studies made similar observations. Both also noted unusually high returns for two days prior to a buy recommendation and unusually low returns for two days prior to a sell recommendation. According to one of the studies, trading volume was unusually high prior to both types of recommendations, leaving open the possibility that some investors traded on advance notice of the contents of the column. See Pu Liu, Stanley D. Smith, and Azmat A. Syed, "Stock Price Reactions to *The Wall Street Journal*'s Securities Recommendations," *Journal of Financial and Quantitative Analysis* 25, no. 3 (September 1990): 399–410, and Messod D. Beneish, "Stock Prices and the Dissemination of Analysts' Recommendations," *Journal of Business* 64, no. 3 (July 1991): 393–416. Interestingly, a former author of the "Heard on the Street" column, R. Foster Winans, was convicted of fraud and theft in 1985 for leaking the contents of his column to four brokers and subsequently sharing in the associated trading profits.

[33] J. Bjerring, J. Lakonishok and T. Vermaelen, "Stock Prices and Analysts' Recommendations," *Journal of Finance* 38, no. 1 (March 1983):187–204. A similar study over a later time period (March 1983 through December 1985) found that following Canadian analysts' recommendations provided substantial gains; see L. Brown, G. Richardson and C. Trzcinka, "Strong-Form Efficiency on the Toronto Stock Exchange: An Examination of Analyst Price Forecasts," *Contemporary Accounting Research* 7, no. 2 (Spring 1991): 323–46.

Figure 23.7

Cumulative abnormal returns from a broker's recommended list compared with the representative list, US and Canadian stocks.

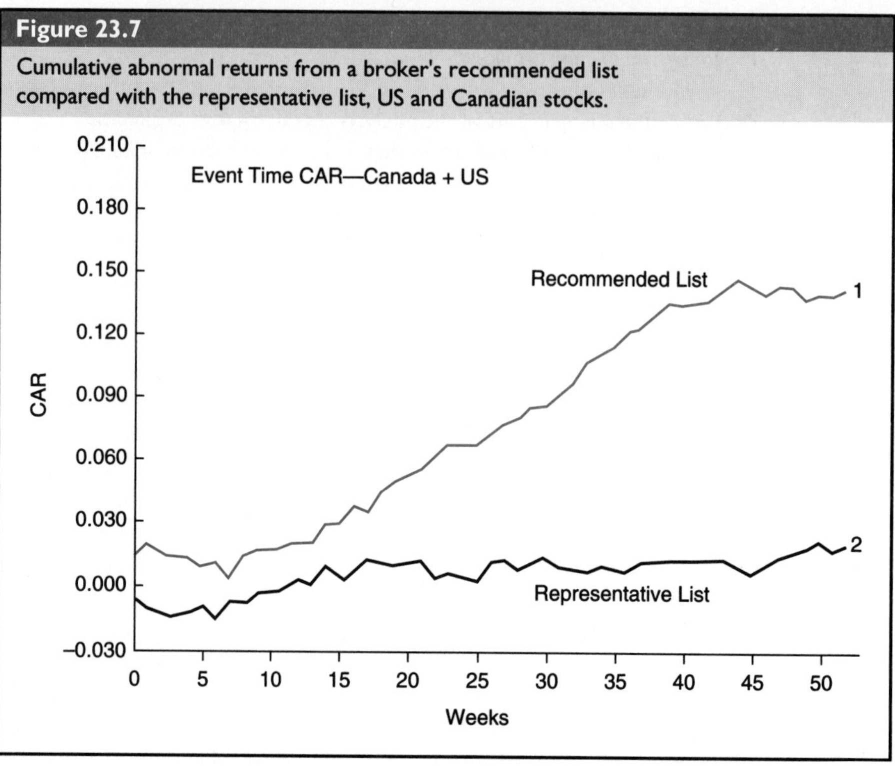

SOURCE: J. Bjerring, J. Lakonishok and T. Vermaelen, "Stock Prices and Financial Analysts' Recommendations," *Journal of Finance* 38, no. 1 (March 1983): 198.

intensively followed have significantly different returns from those stocks that are relatively neglected by analysts? One study examined all stocks in the S&P 500 for the period from 1970 to 1979 in order to answer such a question. Table 23.3 summarizes the results.

Column (1) shows that the stocks followed by the largest number of analysts had the lowest average returns. However, the stocks followed by the fewest analysts had the highest average returns, thereby suggesting the presence of a **neglected firm effect**.

Table 23.3

Analyst Following and Stock Returns.

Amount of Following	*All Stocks (1)*	*Small Firms (2)*	*Medium Firms (3)*	*Large Firms (4)*
High	7.5%	5.0%	7.4%	8.4%
Moderate	11.8%	13.2%	11.0	10.2%
Low	15.4	15.8	13.9%	15.3
Low-high	7.9%	10.8%	6.5%	6.9%
Average return	11.0	13.5	10.7	9.8

SOURCE: Adapted from Avner Arbel and Paul Strebel, "Pay Attention to Neglected Firms!" *Journal of Portfolio Management* 9, no. 2 (Winter 1983): 39.

It is possible that this effect is simply a reflection of the size effect, as the average return on small-sized firms has been shown to be larger than the average return on larger firms.[34] The reason for this possibility is that the number of analysts following a stock is generally related to the size of the underlying firm. However, columns (2), (3), and (4) show that this is not simply another manifestation of the size effect.[35] It can be seen that the neglected firm effect exists for all firm sizes. Furthermore, it is most pronounced for small firms—note that the difference between the high and low categories is largest in column (2).

What are the implications of the neglected firm effect? First, it could be that the higher average return associated with neglected firms is a reward for investing in securities that have less available information. Second, because the neglected firm effect exists across all sizes of firms, large institutional investors that are prohibited from investing in small firms can still take advantage of this effect, as it also exists from medium and large firms (although it is notably less significant). Finally, whether or not such a simple rule will be useful in the future is open to debate. Why? If investors increase their purchases of neglected firms, then such firms will no longer be neglected and hence will no longer provide abnormally high returns.

SOURCES OF INVESTMENT INFORMATION

Since information affects the values of investments, the serious financial analyst must be well informed. There is a staggering array of such investment information, some of it published on paper (hard copy) and some of it appearing in computer-readable form.

▶ Publications

Space precludes a detailed listing of publications relating to investing; however, a selected bibliography of general sources of investment information is presented below. Nothing can substitute for a careful perusal of these (and other) publications, and no attempt is made here to describe each one.

A serious investor should, at the very least, read *The Globe and Mail: Report on Business* and/or *The Financial Post* plus the *Wall Street Journal* and *The Financial Times* (London). These provide extensive statistical data, financial news, analysis, and even a bit of humour. Other daily newspapers contain financial information, but much less than those listed above.

A useful source of daily stock price and volume figures is the *Toronto Stock Exchange Daily Record*. Historical data and analyses for a number of Canadian and foreign stocks can be found in the *Value Line Investment Survey: Canadian Edition*. Adjusted betas are also shown for the individual stocks in the *Survey*.[36] *The Toronto Stock Exchange Monthly Review* also contains a wealth of historical information.

In addition to providing bond quality ratings, the bond rating service companies produce other useful information. For example, *Canadian Bond Rating Service* provides ratings, on a quarterly basis, for bonds and debentures, commercial paper, asset-backed

---

34 See the appendix to Chapter 17 for a discussion of the size effect.

35 The presence of the size effect can be seen by noting that the average return for small firms of 13.5% is much larger than the average return for medium and large firms of 10.7% and 9.8%, respectively.

36 These estimates for common stocks appear to be useful in helping the US investor beat the market. See the appendix to Chapter 19.

securities, mortgage-backed securities, provincial and municipal government bonds, crown corporations, Eurobonds, preferred shares and investment funds as well as industry and individual company financial analyses.

Publications of major security analysts' societies include the *Financial Analysts Journal* (US); *Analyse Financière* (France); and *The Investment Analyst* (United Kingdom). Academic journals that emphasize various aspects of investing include the *Journal of Business*, the *Journal of Finance*, the *Journal of Financial and Quantitative Analysis*, the *Journal of Financial Economics*, the *Review of Financial Studies*, the *Canadian Journal of Administrative Sciences*, *Finéco*, and the proceedings of the *Administrative Sciences Association of Canada: Finance Division*.

Anyone interested in the management of money for institutional or corporate investors (especially pension funds) should read the *Canadian Investment Review* and the *Journal of Portfolio Management*, which publish the views of both practitioners and academicians. Periodicals aimed at institutional investors and money managers are *Benefits Canada*, *Canadian Business* and the *Investor's Digest*.

A company's annual report provides useful information, which can be supplemented by information filed with the *Ontario Securities Commission* and published in their weekly *Bulletin*.

Sources of macroeconomic data such as monetary aggregates (like the money supply) and other monetary items are the monthly *Bank of Canada Review* and the *Bank of Canada Weekly Financial Statistics*. The C. D. Howe Institute and the Economic Council of Canada provide analysis of economic conditions and forecasts on a periodic basis.

The Conference Board of Canada and Data Resources of Canada publish quarterly macroeconomic forecasts based on economic indicators. **Leading indicators** have been found to signal future changes in the economy, whereas **lagging indicators** change after the economy has done so; **coincident indicators** change simultaneously with the economy. Data on national income and production along with industry information is published regularly by Statistics Canada.

► Computer-Readable Data

The rapid increase in the use of microcomputers by those who invest money for others as well as by those who invest for themselves has led to a major expansion in the availability of computer-readable investment data.

Large amounts of financial and economic data, such as common stock prices and financial statements, are provided on magnetic tapes that are made available to investors for a fee by Standard & Poor's Canadian Compustat Services, Infoglobe, *The Financial Post* Corporate Database, Micromedia and Value Line, Inc. These databases are also available on a dial-up basis via time-shared computer services and on disks for use in microcomputers.

Dial-up services are also provided by *Telerate*, *Bloomberg*, *Interactive Data Corporation*, and others. Each service is designed so that users of microcomputers can download prices and other data into their own machines easily and inexpensively. Often the data are in spreadsheet format, readily available for analysis using programs such as Lotus 1-2-3.

Databases containing prices, fundamental information, and predictions made by brokerage houses and others are provided on compact disks by Standard and Poor's Corporation.

SUMMARY

1. Financial analysts are investment professionals who evaluate securities and then make investment recommendations. Those recommendations may be used by professional money managers (portfolio managers) or by certain clients of the analysts.
2. There are two primary reasons for engaging in financial analysis: to determine certain characteristics of securities and to attempt to identify mispriced securities.
3. To understand and estimate the risks and returns of individual securities as well as groups of securities, both financial markets and the principles of security valuation must be understood.
4. Market indices are portfolios of securities designed to represent the performance of an entire asset class (for example, stocks or bonds) or a specific segment of an asset class.
5. Market indices are typically computed on the basis of either price-weighting, value-weighting, or equal-weighting the component securities.
6. Many investors claim to have identified investment systems that can outperform a passive investment system. Frequently, however, the investors testing these systems commit fundamental errors that invalidate their results.
7. Technical analysis involves short-term predictions of security price movements based on past patterns of prices and trading volumes. Fundamental analysis concerns estimates of the basic determinants of security values, such as future sales, expenses, and earnings for firms.
8. Many financial analysts focus their research efforts on analyzing company financial statements. Such research permits an analyst to better understand a company's business operations, its plans for future growth, what factors affect its profitability, and how those factors affect its profitability.

APPENDIX A

TECHNICAL ANALYSIS

As mentioned earlier, most (but not all) technical analysts rely on charts of stock prices and trading volumes. Virtually all employ colourful, and sometimes even mystical, terminology. For example, a significant price rise on relatively large trading volume might be described as an *accumulation*, where the stock is allegedly moving from "weak hands" to "strong hands." This is because a rising stock price on large trading volume is viewed as a situation where demand is stronger than supply. In contrast, a significant price decline on relatively large trading volume may be described as a distribution, where the stock is allegedly moving from "strong hands" to "weak hands." This is because a declining stock price on large trading volume is viewed as a situation where supply is stronger than demand. In both situations, relatively large trading volume might be considered a sign of sustainable change in the stock's price, while relatively small trading volume indicates a transitory change.

What if there is a period when a stock's price does not move significantly? If the stock's price movements are within a narrow band, the stock is said to be in a *consolidation phase*. A price level that a stock has difficulty rising above is known as a *resistance level*, and a price level that a stock does not seem to fall below is known as a *support level*.

Such statements may sound meaningful, but an efficient market proponent would argue that they fail to pass the test of simple logic. First, changes in a stock's price occur when the consensus opinion concerning its value changes. This means that large volume associated with a price change only reflects a substantial difference of opinion concerning the impact of new information on the stock's value; small volume reflects smaller differences of opinion. Second, if price or volume data could be used to predict future short-term price movements, investors would rush to exploit such information, moving prices rapidly enough to make the information useless. However, as shown in Tables 23.1 and 23.2, some evidence suggest that there may be some technical trading rules that have merit. Whether they will be useful after transaction costs are fully taken into account is difficult to determine. Even if they do pass muster with respect to transaction costs, it is uncertain whether they will be useful in the future.

CHARTS

Chartists (technicians who rely on chart formations) nonetheless believe that certain patterns carry great significance, although they often disagree among themselves on the significance of a pattern or even on the existence of a pattern. Before displaying some hypothetical examples of patterns, it should be noted that there are three basic types of charts used. They are known as bar charts, line charts, and point and figure charts.

For a *bar chart* the horizontal axis is a time line, with the vertical axis measuring a particular stock's price. Corresponding to a given day on the horizontal axis will be a vertical line, the top and bottom of which represent the high and low price for that stock on that day. Somewhere on this vertical line will be a small horizontal line representing the closing price for that day. As an example, consider the following hypothetical stock, whose trading background over the last five days is as follows:

Day	High Price	Low Price	Closing Price	Volume
$t-5$	11	9	10	200
$t-4$	12	9	11	300
$t-3$	13	12	12	400
$t-2$	11	10	11	200
$t-1$	14	11	12	500

Panel (a) of Figure 23.8 presents a bar chart for this stock, whereas panel (b) indicates how such a bar chart of prices can be augmented by adding trading volume at the bottom.

Figure 23.9 (a) shows a bar chart exhibiting a pattern that is known as "head and shoulders." As time passed, the stock's price initially rose, hit a peak at A, and then fell to a bottom at B. Recovering from this fall, it went up to an even higher peak at C, but then fell again to a bottom at D. Next it rose to a peak at E that was not as high as the previous peak, C, and then started to fall. As soon as the price went down past its previous low, D, immediately a forecast was made that the stock was going to plunge much lower (if the stock had not reached a level equal to D, no such forecast would have been made).

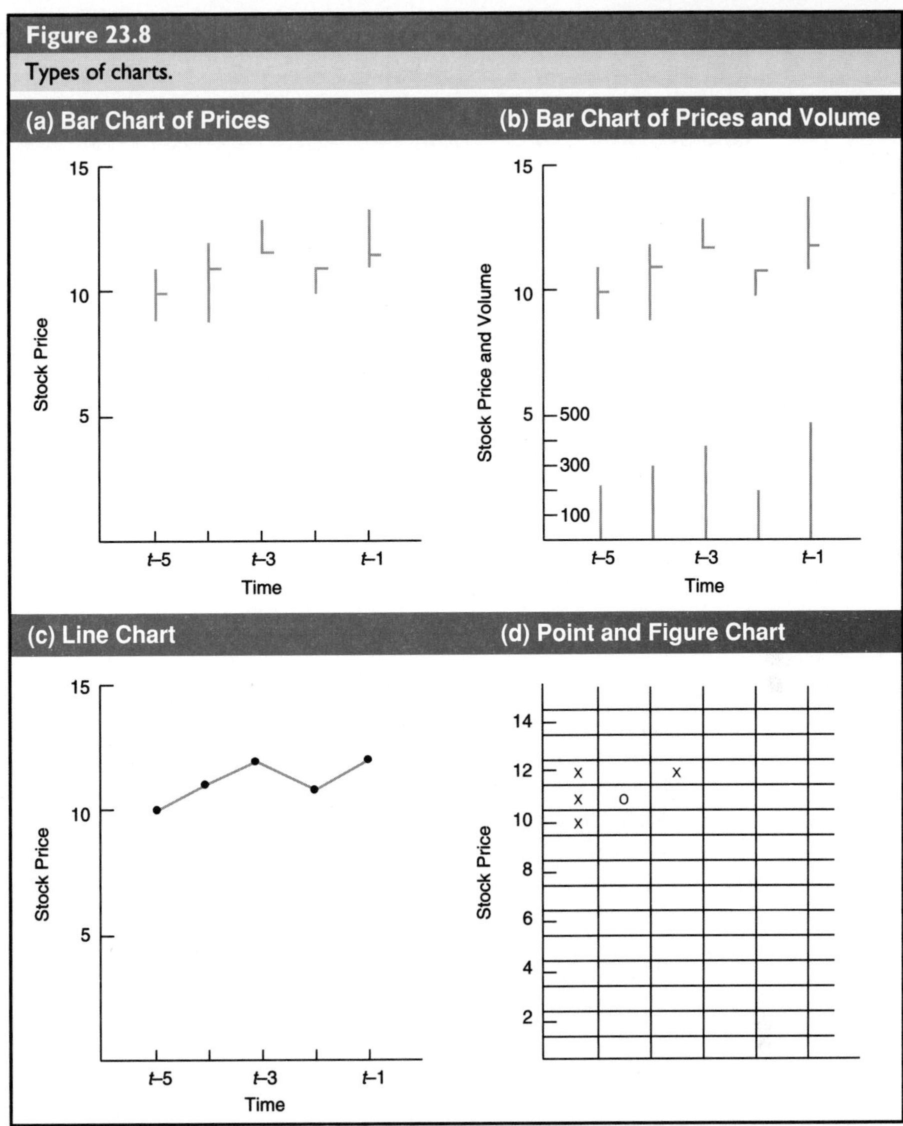

Figure 23.8

Types of charts.

Figure 23.9 (b) shows a bar chart pattern known as "inverted head and shoulders," which results in a forecast that the stock is going to quickly rise by a substantial amount.[37]

For a *line chart*, the axes are the same as with a bar chart. However, only closing prices are presented, and they are connected to each other successively with straight lines, as illustrated in panel (c) of Figure 23.8. Although it is not shown, line charts are also frequently augmented with volume data in a manner identical to bar charts.

---

[37] For details on many kinds of patterns, see Alan R. Shaw, "Technical Analyst's," in Levine, *Financial Analyst's Handbook* I, pp. 944–988; Chapter 8 in Jerome B. Cohen, Edward D. Zinbarg, and Arthur Zeikel, *Investment Analysis and Portfolio Management* (Homewood, IL: Richard D. Irwin, 1987); and Richard L. Evans, "Chart Basics Using Bars, Point & Figure and Candlesticks," *AAII Journal* 15, no. 4 (April 1993): 24–28.

Figure 23.9

Bar chart patterns.

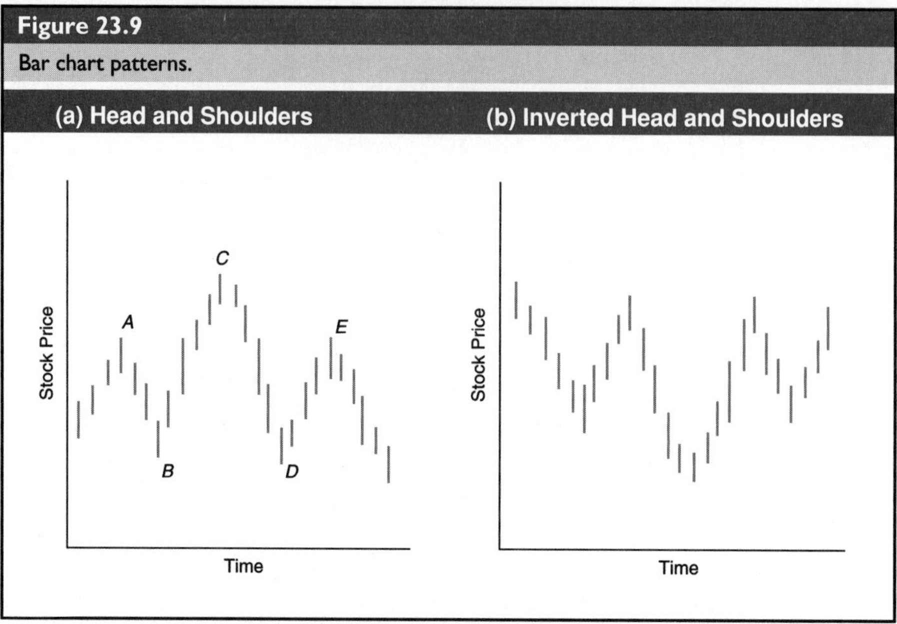

Details for construction of *point and figure charts* vary, but the idea is to plot closing prices that form a trend in a single column, moving to the next column only when the trend is reversed. For example, closing prices might be rounded to the nearest dollar and the chart begun by plotting a beginning rounded price on a certain day. As long as the (rounded) price does not change, nothing is done. When a different price is recorded, it is plotted on the chart. A price higher than the initial price is indicated with an X, with any gaps between the prices also marked with an X. A price below the initial price is marked with an O in a similar fashion. Then when a price that is different from the last one is recorded, it is plotted in the same column only if it is in the same direction.

For example, if the first different price is above the beginning price, this price is plotted above the beginning one. Then, if a price is recorded that is above the second one, it is plotted in the same column, but if it is below the second one, then it is plotted in a new column to the right of the first column. Continuing, as long as new prices are in the same direction, they are plotted in the same column. Whenever there is a reversal, a new column is started. Panel (d) of Figure 23.8 presents a point and figure chart for the same hypothetical stock used in the other panels.

Point and figure enthusiasts look for all sorts of patterns in their charts. As with all chartist techniques, the idea is to recognize a pattern early enough to profit from one's ability to foresee the future course of prices — a neat trick, if one can do it.

MOVING AVERAGES

Many other procedures are used by technicians. Some construct moving averages to try to detect "intermediate" and "long-term" trends. Here a set number of the most recent closing prices on a security are averaged each day. (For example, daily closing prices over the previous 200 days may be used.) This means that each day, the oldest price is replaced with the most recent price in the set of closing prices that will be averaged. Frequently a line chart of these moving averages is plotted, along with a line chart of daily closing prices. Each day the charts are updated and then examined for trends to see if there is a buy or sell signal present somewhere.

Alternatively, a long-term moving average may be compared with a short-term moving average (the distinction between the two averages is that the long-term average uses a substantially larger set of closing prices in its calculations than the short-term average). When the short-term average crosses the long-term average, a "signal" is said to have been given. The action recommended will depend on such things as whether the averages have been rising or falling, as well as the direction from which the short-term average crossed the long-term average (it may have been below and now is above, or it may have been above and now is below). A moving average trading rule was used to generate the returns shown in part A of Table 23.2.

RELATIVE STRENGTH MEASURES

Another procedure used by technicians involves measuring what they call relative strength. For example, a stock's price may be divided by a price index of its industry each day to indicate the stock's movement relative to its industry. Similarly, an industry index may be divided by a market index to indicate the industry's movement relative to the market, or a stock's price may be divided by a market index to indicate a stock's movement relative to the market. The idea here is to examine changes in these relative strength measures with the hope of finding a pattern that can be used to accurately predict the future.

The momentum trading rules used in preparing Table 23.1 were based on the notion of relative strength in its simplest form. Stock returns over a just-ended holding period were calculated and then portfolios of winners and losers were formed. When this was done using semi-annual or annual returns, the momentum trading rules seemed to have merit.

Some procedures of technical analysts focus on relationships among different indexes. For example, the Dow Theory requires that a pattern in the Dow Jones Industrial Average be "confirmed" by a certain movement in the Dow Jones Railroad (now Transportation) Average before action be taken.[38] Another example involves computing the difference between the number of issues advancing and the number declining each day. A chart of the differences cumulated over time, known as the *advance-decline line*, may then be compared with a market index such as the Dow Jones Industrial Average.

CONTRARY OPINION

Many technical procedures are based on the idea of contrary opinion. The idea here is to determine the consensus opinion and then do the opposite. Two examples that were discussed earlier involved (1) buying stocks that had recently dropped in price and selling stocks that had recently risen in price, and (2) buying stocks with low P/E ratios and selling stocks with high P/E ratios. For a third example, one might see whether the "odd-lotters" (those with trade orders involving less than 100 shares) are buying, and then sell any holdings

[38] For more on the Dow Theory, see Richard L. Evans, "Dow's Theory and the Averages: Relevant . . . or Relics?" *AAII Journal* 15, no. 1 (January 1993): 27–29.

of these stocks. If "the little investor is usually wrong," this will be a procedure that is usually right. However, the basic premise about the little investor has yet to be factually established.

The widespread availability of personal computers and "dial-up" services with data on stock prices and volumes has made it possible for individual investors to engage in technical analysis in the privacy of their own homes. Producers of software have been quick to provide programs to perform such analysis, complete with multicoloured graphs. Nevertheless, the number of investors using fundamental analysis is much larger than the number using technical analysis.

TECHNICAL ANALYSIS IN OTHER MARKETS

The use of charts to forecast the future and to find undervalued securities is not confined to the stock market. Figures 23.10 and 23.11 show charts prepared for an institutional fixed-income investor, and include the analyst's interpretation of the trends that are presented. The chart in Figure 23.10 could be used (together with other information) in the preparation of an interest rate forecast, while Figure 23.11 identifies a pricing imbalance between US Treasury bonds (maturities over 10 years) and US Treasury Notes (maturities from one to ten years).

Figure 23.10

Moving average price chart for 90-day Euro-dollar charts March '92 futures.

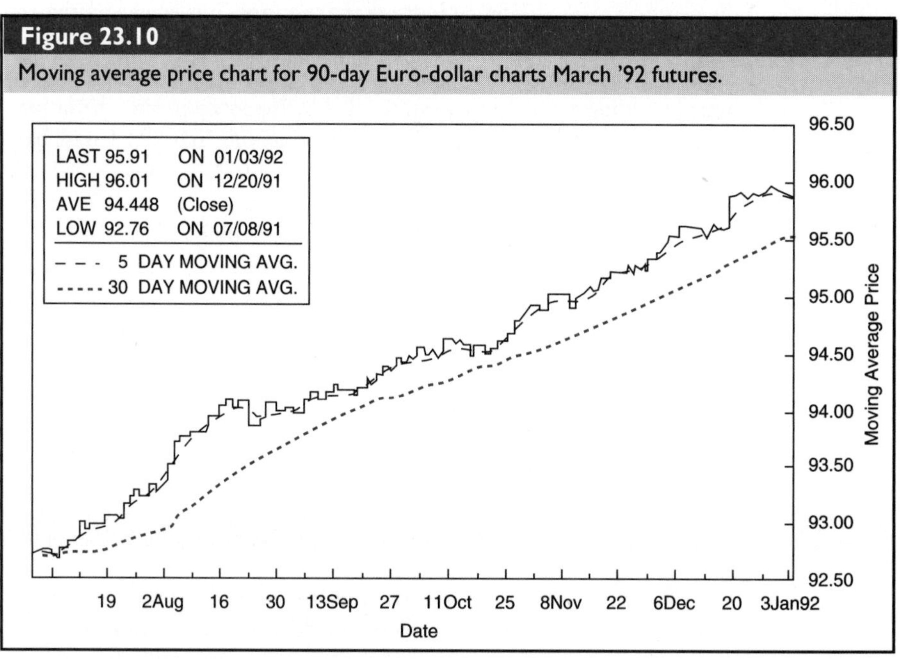

SOURCE: The Canada Life Assurance Company, January 1992.

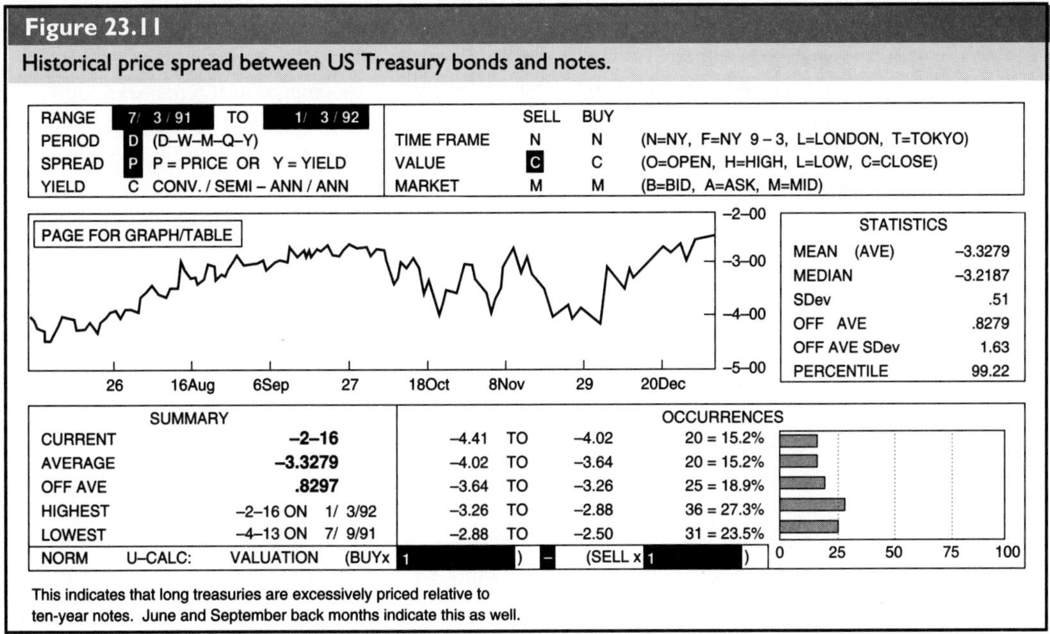

Figure 23.11

Historical price spread between US Treasury bonds and notes.

SOURCE: The Canada Life Assurance Company, January 1992.

QUESTIONS AND PROBLEMS

1. Using a recent *Globe and Mail*, find the closing value of the TSE 35 Index. On the same date, find the closing prices of the TSE's component stocks. (The names of those stocks and their weights are listed monthly in the Toronto Stock Exchange *Review*.) Calculate the value of the TSE 35's divisor.
2. Consider a price-weighted market index composed of two securities A and B, with prices of \$16 and \$30, respectively. The index divisor is currently 2.0. Calculate the value of the divisor when:
   a. Stock A issues a 5% stock dividend.
   b. Stock B undergoes a 3-for-1 stock split.
   c. Stock A undergoes a 4-for-1 stock split.
3. It is argued that the TSE 300 is a better indicator than the TSE 35 of the performance of the entire Canadian stock market. Explain the reasoning behind this contention.
4. Assume that the market is composed of the following three securities:

Security	*Current Price*	*Shares Outstanding*
A	\$20	20 000
B	35	40 000
C	30	40 000

   a. What is the aggregate value of the market?

b. If security C's price increases by 20%, what is the percentage change in the market's aggregate value?

c. If security B splits 2-for-1, what is the percentage change in the market's aggregate value?

5. Consider three stocks, X, Y, and Z, with the following closing prices on two particular dates:

Stock	*Date 1*	*Date 2*
X	$16	$22
Y	5	4
Z	24	30

On date 1 there are 100 shares of stock X, 200 shares of stock Y, and 100 shares of stock Z outstanding.

a. Construct a price-weighted market index using the three stocks, X, Y, and Z. What is the index's value on date 1?

b. What is the price-weighted index's value on date 2?

c. Assume that, on date 2, stock X splits 4-for-1. What is the price-weighted index's value on that date?

d. Construct a value-weighted index using the three stocks. Assign the value-weighted index a value of 100 on date 1. What is the index's value on date 2?

6. According to Ferris Fain, "The success of a stock market index depends on its ability to measure the performance of stocks not included in the index." Explain what Ferris means.

7. Consider an equal-weighted market index composed of three securities. The market prices of those securities on three dates are shown below.

	Market Prices		
Security	*Date 1*	*Date 2*	*Date 3*
A	$50	$55	$60
B	30	28	30
C	70	75	73

a. What is the return on the index from date 1 to date 2?

b. What is the return on the index from date 2 to date 3?

8. Consider a market index based on three securities and their associated prices on three dates.

	Market Prices		
Security	*Date 1*	*Date 2*	*Date 3*
L	$20	$23	$30
M	27	30	31
N	40	35	29

If the index's value is 200 on date 1, calculate its value on date 2 and date 3 if the index return is computed on a geometric mean basis.

9. What types of stocks or industries will an equal-weighted market index emphasize relative to a value-weighted market index?
10. List and describe several possible uses of security market indices.
11. If security markets are highly efficient, what role is there for financial analysts?
12. Compare the price reaction to the purchase of stocks that have been identified with a system that previously has been able to "beat the market" with the reactions to (a) the accurate prediction of rainfall and (b) the accurate prediction of the locations of enemy submarines.
13. Listed below are several test results from studies of mechanical investment systems. For each test result, identify the primary research error committed, and comment as to why the error is applicable to the study.
    a. A portfolio managed using a filter rule (that is, buying a stock after it has appreciated in price by x%, holding the stock until its price has depreciated by x%, then selling the stock) outperforms a broad market index when the filter is very small (that is, when x is small).
    b. An investment system estimated over the 1970 and 1980 time period indicates that the system outperformed a broad market index in the latter half of the period.
    c. A portfolio composed of stocks of highly cyclical industrial companies outperforms a broad market index.
    d. Buying and selling Canadian stocks based on a measure of liberal and conservative voting patterns in Great Britain produces returns that outperform a broad Canadian market index.
    e. The price performance of a portfolio of ipo (that is, initial public offering) high-technology stocks outperforms a broad market index.
14. Ezra Falk, a portfolio manager for a large pension fund, is fond of saying "Buy low, sell high." Why is the system suggested by Ezra not operational?
15. Despite the arguments and evidence of efficient markets proponents, many investors pay attention to technical analysis in some form. Speculate as to why these investors use this kind of investment research.
16. Distinguish between "top-down" and "bottom-up" approaches to financial forecasting. What are the primary advantages and disadvantages of each approach?
17. Last year both Hudson Homes and Baldwin Construction earned $1 million in net income. Both companies have assets of $10 million. However, Hudson generated a return on equity of 11.1% whereas Baldwin produced a return on equity of 20.0%. What can explain the differences in return on equity between the two companies?
18. Last fiscal year, Afton Machinery had the following financial statement data:

Sales/Assets	2.10
Profits/EBIT	0.65
EBIT/Sales	0.10
Assets/Equity	3.00

Calculate Afton's return on assets and return on equity.

19. Augusta Ironworks reported the following fiscal year-end financial data (stated in 000's).

Assets	$1500
Liabilities	$900
Shareholders' equity	$600
Net income	$200
Dividends per share	$0.50
Stock price	$30
Shares outstanding	100

Given this information, calculate Augusta's:
a. Price-earnings ratio
b. Book value per share
c. Price-book ratio
d. Dividend yield
e. Payout ratio

20. Is it true that, when comparing the reported earnings of corporations, "a dollar is a dollar"?
21. (Appendix Question) Technical analysis is predicated on stock prices moving in repetitive patterns. What would one have to believe about the timing of the receipt of information by financial markets' participants in order to believe in the existence of such patterns?
22. (Appendix Question) The closing, high, and low prices for Fort McCoy Packaging stock over a ten-day interval are shown below. Construct a bar chart for Fort McCoy Packaging stock over this period of time.

	Fort McCoy Packaging		
Day	*Closing Price*	*High*	*Low*
1	20	21	19
2	20.10	20.10	18
3	21	22	20.50
4	21.05	22.90	21.05
5	21	23.10	20
6	21.75	22	20.75
7	22	23.50	20.05
8	20.05	22	19.10
9	19.05	21.50	19
10	18.10	21.90	17.05

23. (Appendix Question) Calculate the relative strength of Fort McCoy Packaging stock versus the TSE 35 over the ten-day period referred to in Problem 22, given the following closing prices for the TSE 35.

	Day									
	1	*2*	*3*	*4*	*5*	*6*	*7*	*8*	*9*	*10*
TSE 35 Closing Price	300	302	306	310	320	315	330	325	325	330

CFA Exam Question

24. The duPont formula defines the net return on shareholders' equity as a function of the following components:
- operating margin,
- asset turnover,
- interest burden,
- financial leverage, and
- income tax rate.

Using only the data in the table shown below:

a. Calculate each of the five components listed above for 1985 and 1989, and calculate the return on equity (ROE) for 1985 and 1989, using all of the five components. Show calculations.

b. Briefly discuss the impact of the changes in asset turnover and financial leverage on the change in ROE from 1985 to 1989.

	1985	*1989*
Income Statement Data		
Revenues	$542	$979
Operating income	38	76
Depreciation and amortization	3	9
Interest expense	3	0
Pre-tax income	32	67
Income taxes	13	37
Net income after tax	19	30
Balance Sheet Data		
Fixed assets	$41	$70
Total assets	245	291
Working capital	123	157
Total debt	16	0
Total shareholders' equity	159	220

Key Terms

portfolio manager
fundamental analysis
market index
price weighting
value weighting
equal weighting
price relatives
passive investment system
ex post selection bias
out-of-sample data
technical analysis
top-down forecasting
bottom-up forecasting
probabilistic forecasting
econometric model
endogenous variable
exogenous variable
neglected firm effect
leading indicator
lagging indicator
coincident indicators
chartists

References

1. For a discussion of contrarian investment strategies, see the references in footnotes 21 and 25 and:

   David Dremen, *Contrarian Investment Strategies* (New York: Random House, 1979).

   Werner F. M. DeBondt and Richard Thaler, "Does the Stock Market Overreact?" *Journal of Finance* 40, no. 3 (July 1985): 793–805.

   Werner F. M. DeBondt and Richard Thaler, "Further Evidence on Investor Overreaction and Stock Market Seasonality," *Journal of Finance* 42, no. 3 (July 1987): 557–581.

   Paul Zarowin, "Short-Run Market Overreaction: Size and Seasonality Effects," *Journal of Portfolio Management* 15, no. 3 (Spring 1989): 26–29.

   Paul Zarowin, "Does the Stock Market Overreact to Corporate Earnings Information?" *Journal of Finance* 44, no. 5 (December 1989): 1385–1399.

   Bruce N. Lehmann, "Fads, Martingales, and Market Efficiency," *Quarterly Journal of Economics* 105, no. 1 (February 1990): 1–28.

   Narasimhan Jegadeesh, "Evidence of Predictable Behavior of Security Returns," *Journal of Finance* 45, no. 3 (July 1990): 881–898.

   Jennifer Conrad, Mustafa N. Gultekin, and Gautam Kaul, "Profitability of Short-Term Contrarian Portfolio Strategies," unpublished paper, The University of Michigan, 1991.

   Victor L. Bernard, Jacob K. Thomas, and Jeffrey S. Abarbanell, "How Sophisticated Is the Market in Interpreting Earnings News?" *Journal of Applied Corporate Finance* 6, no. 2 (Summer 1993): 54–63.

2. Closely related to the issue of contrarian investment strategies is the issue of how stock price levels in one period are related to stock price levels in a subsequent period. This issue, like the usefulness of contrarian strategies, has been open to debate. Two of the earliest papers and two recent ones that contradict them are:

   Eugene F. Fama and Kenneth R. French, "Permanent and Temporary Components of Stock Prices," *Journal of Political Economy* 96, no. 2 (April 1988): 246–273.

   James M. Poterba and Lawrence H. Summers, "Mean Reversion in Stock Prices: Evidence and Implications," *Journal of Financial Economics* 22, no. 1 (October 1988): 27–59.

Myung Jig Kim, Charles R. Nelson, and Richard Startz, "Mean Reversion in Stock Prices? A Reappraisal of the Empirical Evidence," *Review of Economic Studies* 58, no. 3 (May 1991): 515–528.

Grant McQueen, "Long-Horizon Mean-Reverting Stock Prices Revisited," *Journal of Financial and Quantitative Analysis* 27, no. 1 (March 1992): 1–18.

3. Momentum strategies are discussed in:
   Narasimhan Jegadeesh and Sheridan Titman, "Returns to Buying Winners and Selling Losers: Implications for Stock Market Efficiency," *Journal of Finance* 48, no. 1 (March 1993): 65–91.

4. Moving average and trading range breakout strategies are discussed in:

   William Brock, Joseph Lakonishok, and Blake LeBaron, "Simple Technical Trading Rules and the Stochastic Properties of Stock Returns," *Journal of Finance* 47, no. 5 (December 1992): 1731–1764.

5. The reaction of stock prices to the publication of analysts' recommendations is discussed in:

   John C. Groth, Wilbur G. Lewellen, Gary G. Schlarbaum, and Ronald C. Lease, "An Analysis of Brokerage House Securities Recommendations," *Financial Analysts Journal* 35, no. 1 (January/February 1979): 32–40.

   James H. Bjerring, Josef Lakonishok, and Theo Vermaelen, "Stock Prices and Financial Analysts' Recommendations," *Journal of Finance* 38, no. 1 (March 1983): 187–204.

   Philip Heitner, "Isn't It Time to Measure Analysts' Track Records?" *Financial Analysts Journal* 47, no. 3 (May/June 1991): 5–6.

   Brad M. Barber and Douglas Loeffler, "The 'Dartboard' Column: Second-Hand Information and Price Pressure," *Journal of Financial and Quantitative Analysis* 28, no. 2 (June 1993): 273–284.

6. The reactions of stock prices to recommendations published in the "Heard on the Street" column in the *Wall Street Journal* are discussed in:

   Peter Lloyd-Davies and Michael Canes, "Stock Prices and the Publication of Second-Hand Information," *Journal of Business* 51, no. 1 (January 1978): 43–56.

   Pu Liu, Stanley D. Smith, and Azmat A. Syed, "Stock Price Reactions to *The Wall Street Journal's* Securities Recommendations," *Journal of Financial and Quantitative Analysis* 25, no. 3 (September 1990): 399–410.

   Messod Beneish, "Stock Prices and the Dissemination of Analysts' Recommendations," *Journal of Business* 64, no. 3 (July 1991): 393–416.

   The "Heard on the Street" column also sometimes discusses takeover rumours. For an analysis of the effects these rumours have on stock prices, see John Pound and Richard Zeckhauser, "Clearly Heard on the Street: The Effect of Takeover Rumors on Stock Prices," *Journal of Business* 63, no. 3 (July 1990): 291–308.

7. For a discussion of the neglected firm effect, see:

   Avner Arbel and Paul Strebel, "Pay Attention to Neglected Firms!" *Journal of Portfolio Management* 9, no. 2 (Winter 1983): 37–42.

Avner Arbel, Steven Carvel, and Paul Strebel, "Giraffes, Institutions, and Neglected Firms," *Financial Analysts Journal* 39, no. 3 (May/June 1983): 57–63.

8. Leading books on technical analysis, financial statement analysis, and fundamental analysis are, respectively:

Robert D. Edwards and John Magee, *Technical Analysis of Stock Trends* (Boston: John Magee, 1966).

George Foster, *Financial Statement Analysis* (Englewood Cliffs, NJ: Prentice Hall, 1986).

Sidney Cottle, Roger Murray, and Frank Block, *Graham and Dodd's Security Analysis* (New York: McGraw-Hill, 1988).

9. Information sources for investing are described in:

Maria Crawford Scott and John Bajkowski, "Sources of Information for the Simplified Approach to Valuation," *AAII Journal* 16, no. 3 (April 1994): 29–32.

John Markese, "Picking Common Stocks: What Seems to Work, At Least Sometimes," *AAII Journal* 16, no. 5 (June 1994): 24–27.

10. For a Canadian perspective on the topics covered in this chapter, see:

S. Foerster, A. Prihar and J. Schmitz, "Price Momentum Models and How they Beat the Canadian Equity Markets," *Canadian Investment Review* VII, no. 4 (Winter 1994–95).

Internet Resources

The following investment information sources can be accessed at these Internet addresses:

Altamira Investment Services	**http://www.altamira.com**
Annual Report Source	**http://www.annualreport/CyberPlex/ARS/AnnualreportSource.html**
Canadian Financial Network	**http://www.canadianfinance.com**
Canadian Investment Discussion Group	**USENET: misc.invest.canada**
InvestNet Canada	**http://islandnet.com/invest**
Quote.Com Financial Market Data	**http://www.quote.com**
Security APL Quote Server	**http://www.secapl.com/cgi-bin/qs**
Stock and Commodity Quotes from Telenium	**http://www.telenium.ca**
Vancouver Stock Exchange Official Home Page	**http://www.vse.ca**

CHAPTER 24

Investment Management

Investment management, also known as portfolio management, is the process by which money is managed. It may (1) be active or passive, (2) use explicit or implicit procedures, and (3) be relatively controlled or uncontrolled. The trend is toward highly controlled operations consistent with the notion that capital markets are relatively efficient. However, approaches vary, and many different investment styles can be found. This chapter will discuss investment management, and in doing so it will present various types of investment styles.

TRADITIONAL INVESTMENT MANAGEMENT ORGANIZATIONS

Few people or organizations like to be called "traditional." However, some investment management organizations follow procedures that have changed little from those that were popular decades ago, and thus deserve the title. Figure 24.1 shows the major characteristics of a traditional investment management organization.

Projections concerning the economy and the money and capital markets are made by economists, technicians, fundamentalists, or other market experts within or outside the organization. The projected economic environment is communicated via briefings and written reports—usually in a rather implicit and qualitative manner—to the organization's **security analysts**. Each analyst is responsible for a group of securities, often those in one or more industries (in some organizations, analysts are called industry specialists). Often a group of analysts report to a senior analyst responsible for a sector of the economy or market.

The analysts, often drawing heavily on reports of others (for example, "street analysts" in brokerage houses), make predictions about the securities for which they are responsible. In a sense, such predictions are conditional on the assumed economic and market environments, although the relationship is typically quite loose.

Analysts' predictions seldom specify an expected rate of return or the time over which predicted performance will take place. Instead, an analyst's feelings about a security may be summarized by assigning it one of five codes, where a 1 represents a buy and a 5 represents a sell, as indicated in Figure 24.1.[1] (Some organizations reverse the numbers, so that a 5 is a buy and a 1 is a sell; some European organizations favour five codes that are denoted +, 0+, 0, 0–, and –; some organizations have long-term lists as well as short-term lists.)

[1] One study found that a firm's stock price tended to move upward when analysts upgraded its coding, and downward when analysts downgraded its coding. See Edwin J. Elton, Martin J. Gruber, and Seth Grossman, "Discrete Expectational Data and Portfolio Performance," *Journal of Finance* 41, no. 3 (July 1986): 699–713, and Chapter 23.

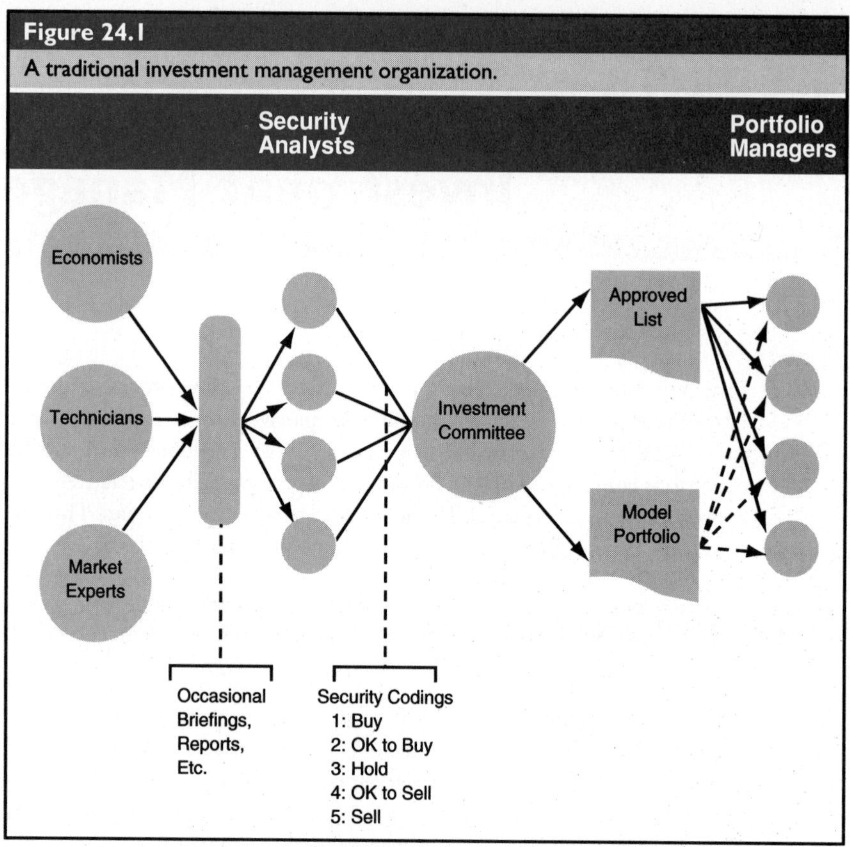

Figure 24.1
A traditional investment management organization.

These security codings and various written reports constitute the information formally transmitted to an **investment committee**, which typically includes the senior management of the organization. In addition, analysts occasionally brief the investment committee on their feelings about various securities. The investment committee's primary formal output is often an **approved** (or authorized) **list**, which consists of the securities deemed worthy of accumulation in a given portfolio. The rules of the organization typically specify that any security on the list may be bought, whereas those not on the list should be either held or sold, barring special circumstances.

The presence or absence of a security on the approved list constitutes the major information transmitted explicitly from the investment committee to a **portfolio manager**. In some organizations, senior management supervises a "model portfolio" (for example, a bank's major commingled equity fund), the composition of which indicates to portfolio managers the relative intensity of senior management's feelings regarding different securities.

In many ways, this description is a caricature of an investment organization—even one run along traditional lines. Nevertheless, most of these attributes can be observed in practice in one form or another.

In recent years, specialty investment firms have gained considerable popularity. As opposed to traditional investment firms that invest in a broad spectrum of securities, these organizations concentrate their investment efforts on a particular asset class, such as stocks or bonds. They often specialize even further, focusing on a narrow segment of a particular asset class, such as the stocks of small start-up companies.

Although these specialty investment firms may follow many of the security analysis procedures of the traditional investment organizations, they usually employ few security analysts. Often the portfolio managers serve as analysts. Furthermore, their decision-making processes are typically more streamlined, often avoiding investment committee structures entirely, thereby permitting portfolio managers considerable discretion to research securities and construct portfolios. Whether this less hierarchical approach to investing actually produces superior results is open to question.

INVESTMENT MANAGEMENT FUNCTIONS

In Chapter 1 a five-step procedure was outlined for making investment decisions. These steps can all be viewed as functions of investment management, and they must be undertaken for each client whose money is being managed. They are as follows:

1. *Set investment policy*—identify the client's investment objectives, particularly as regards his or her attitude toward the trade-off between expected return and risk.
2. *Perform security analysis*—scrutinize individual securities or groups of securities in order to identify mispriced situations.
3. *Construct a portfolio*—identify specific securities in which to invest, along with the proportion of investable wealth to be put into each security.
4. *Revise the portfolio*—determine which securities in the current portfolio are to be sold and which securities are to be purchased to replace them.
5. *Evaluate the performance of the portfolio*—determine the actual performance of a portfolio in terms of risk and return, and compare the performance with that of an appropriate "benchmark" portfolio.

The remainder of this chapter deals with how an investment management organization could perform the first four functions; the next chapter deals with the fifth function.

SETTING INVESTMENT POLICY

An investment manager who is in charge of a client's entire portfolio must be concerned with the client's risk-return preferences. Investors who use more than one manager can select one to help in this important phase, or they may employ the services of a consultant or financial planner. In any event, one of the key characteristics that differentiates clients from one another concerns their investment objectives. According to modern portfolio theory, these objectives are reflected in the client's attitude toward risk and expected return. As mentioned in Chapter 7, specifying indifference curves is one method of describing these objectives. However, determining a client's indifference curves is not a simple task. In practice, it is often done in an indirect and approximate fashion by estimating the client's level of **risk tolerance**, defined as the largest amount of risk that the client is willing to accept for a given increase in expected return.

Estimating Risk Tolerance

The starting point in making such an estimation is to provide the client with a set of risks and expected returns for different combinations of two hypothetical portfolios. For example,

Table 24.1

Combinations of Stock and Risk-free Treasury Bill Portfolios.

Proportion In				
Stocks	*Bills*	*Expected Return*	*Standard Deviation*	*Implied Level of Risk Tolerance*
0%	100%	7.50%	0.0%	0
10	90	7.95	1.5	10
20	80	8.40	3.0	20
30	70	8.85	4.5	30
40	60	9.30	6.0	40
50	50	9.75	7.5	50
60	40	10.20	9.0	60
70	30	10.65	10.5	70
80	20	11.10	12.0	80
90	10	11.55	13.5	90
100	0	12.00	15.0	100
110	−10	12.45	16.5	110
120	−20	12.90	18.0	120
130	−30	13.35	19.5	130
140	−40	13.80	21.0	140
150	−50	14.25	22.5	150
.	.	.	.	.
.	.	.	.	.
.	.	.	.	.

imagine that the client is told that the expected return on a stock portfolio is 12%, while the return on a risk-free portfolio consisting of Treasury bills is 7.5% (that is, $\overline{r}_S = 12\%$ and $r_F = 7.5\%$). Similarly, the client is told that the standard deviation on the stock portfolio is 15%, while the standard deviation on the risk-free portfolio is, by definition, 0.0% (that is, $\sigma_S = 15\%$ and $\sigma_F = 0.0\%$).[2] Additionally, the client is told that all combinations of these two portfolios lie on a straight line that connects them. (This is because the covariance between these two portfolios is 0.0, meaning that $\sigma_{SF} = 0.0$.) Some combinations of these two portfolios are shown in Table 24.1.

Note that the investor is being presented with the efficient set that arises when there is a set of stocks and a risk-free borrowing and lending rate. As shown in Chapter 9, this efficient set is linear, meaning that it is a straight line that emanates at the risk-free rate and goes through a tangency portfolio that consists of a certain combination of securities. (In this case those securities are common stocks.) Hence, negative percentages in Treasury bills (shown at the bottom of Table 24.1) represent risk-free borrowing in order to purchase greater amounts of stocks.

[2] This example is taken from William F. Sharpe, *Asset Allocation Tools* (Redwood City, CA: Scientific Press, 1987), p. 38.

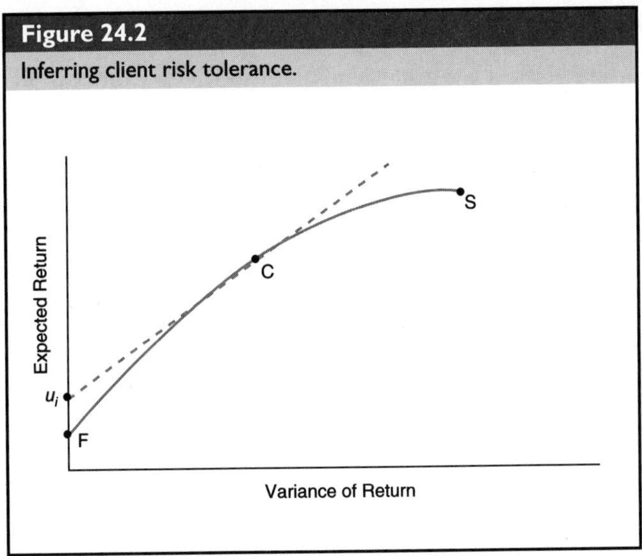

Figure 24.2
Inferring client risk tolerance.

At this point, the client is asked to identify the combination that appears to be most desirable, in terms of expected return and standard deviation. Asking the investor to identify the most desirable combination is equivalent to asking the investor to locate where one of his or her indifference curves is tangent to the linear efficient set, as this point will represent the most desirable portfolio.[3]

After the client has selected the best stock/Treasury bill mix, what can be said about his or her risk tolerance? One would, of course, like to identify all the indifference curves that represent a client's attitude toward risk and expected return. However, in practice a more modest goal is usually adopted—to obtain a reasonable representation of the shape of such curves in the region of risk and expected return within which the client's optimal choices will most likely fall.

The points in Figure 24.2 plot the alternative mixes presented to the client that were given in Table 24.1. Curve *FCS* shows the risk-return characteristics of all possible mixes, and point *C* identifies the attributes of the mix chosen by the client. In this figure expected return is measured on the vertical axis and *variance* on the horizontal axis. Although the combinations available to the client plot on a straight line when standard deviation is measured on the horizontal axis, the combinations plot on a concave curve when variance is used (as in this figure).

Assuming that all the possible mixes had been presented to the client and point *C* had been chosen, it could be inferred that the slope of the client's indifference curve going through *C* is precisely equal to that of curve *FCS* at this point. As mentioned earlier, this follows from the observation that the portfolio on the efficient set that a client identifies as being the "best" corresponds to the one where the client's indifference curves are just tangent to the efficient set.

---

[3] If such a decision is made on behalf of the client (for example, by a trustee for one or more beneficiaries), the task is much more difficult, but a decision is still required.

Constant Risk Tolerance

In principle, the choice of a mix provides information about the slope of an indifference curve at only one point. To go beyond this, an assumption must be made about the general shape of the client's indifference curves. An assumption commonly made is that the client has constant risk tolerance over a range of alternative portfolios in the neighbourhood of the point originally chosen. Figure 24.3 shows the nature of this assumption. As indicated in panel (a), indifference curves in a diagram with *variance* on the horizontal axis are *linear* when it is assumed that the client has constant risk tolerance. This means that the equation for an indifference curve of such an investor is equivalent to the equation for a straight line where the variable on the horizontal axis is variance (σ_P^2) and the variable on the vertical axis is expected return ($\bar{r}_P$). Given that the equation of a straight line takes the form of $Y = a + bX$, where a is the vertical intercept and b is the slope, the equation for an indifference curve can be written as

$$\bar{r}_P = a + b\sigma_P^2$$

or

$$\bar{r}_P = u_i + \frac{1}{\tau}\sigma_P^2 \tag{24.1}$$

where u_i is the vertical intercept for indifference curve i and the slope of the indifference curve is $1/\tau$.[4] Note how any two indifference curves for a client differ from one another by only the value of the vertical intercept. This is because the indifference curves are parallel, meaning that they have the same slope, $1/\tau$.

Figure 24.3(b) plots the same indifference curves in a more familiar manner—with *standard deviation* on the horizontal axis. Note that the curves have the conventional shape—they indicate that the investor requires more return to compensate for an additional unit of standard deviation as the risk of the portfolio increases. That is, the curves are *convex* when standard deviation is measured on the horizontal axis.

In order to estimate the client's level of risk tolerance τ, it was mentioned that the slope of the indifference curves, $1/\tau$, would be set equal to the slope of the efficient set at the location of the portfolio that was selected, denoted portfolio C. Doing so results in the following formula for estimating τ:

$$\tau = \frac{2[(\bar{r}_C - r_F)\sigma_S^2]}{(\bar{r}_S - r_F)^2} \tag{24.2}$$

where $\bar{r}_C$ denotes the expected return of the portfolio that the client selected, $\bar{r}_S$ and r_F denote the expected return of the stock portfolio and risk-free rate, respectively, and σ_S^2 denotes the variance of the stock portfolio. (A detailed presentation of how this formula was derived is presented in the appendix.)

In the example, the client was given a choice between S, F, and various combinations of S and F where $\bar{r}_S = 12\%$, $r_F = 7.5\%$, and $\sigma_S^2 = 15^2 = 225$. Now, by using equation (24.2),

[4] Normally risk tolerance τ is expressed as units of variance per unit of expected return. However, the reciprocal of risk tolerance $1/\tau$ appears in equation (24.1). This is necessitated by having risk on the horizontal axis in Figure 24.3.

Figure 24.3

Constant risk tolerance.

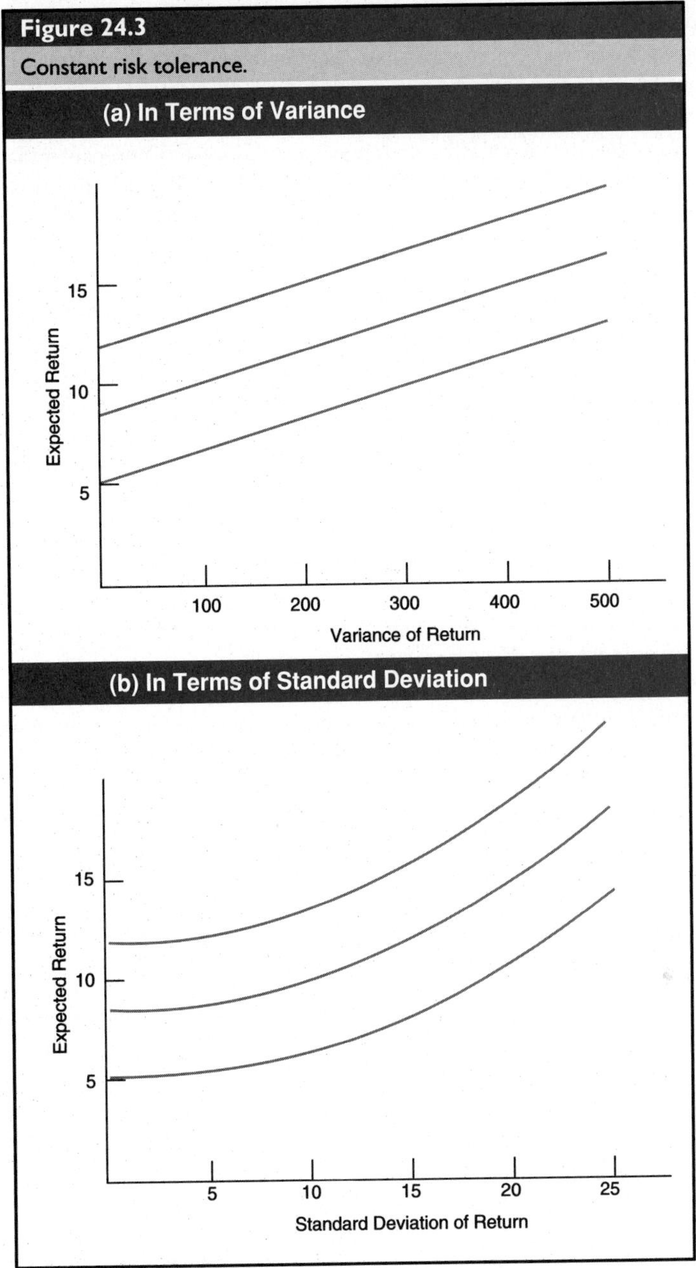

the level of risk tolerance τ inferred from the choice of portfolio C can be determined to equal

$$\tau = \frac{2[(\bar{r}_C - 7.5)225]}{(12 - 7.5)^2} \tag{24.3}$$
$$= 22.22\bar{r}_C - 166.67.$$

Assuming the choice of a portfolio consisting of a 50% investment in stocks and a 50% investment in risk-free Treasury bills, the client in this example has chosen a portfolio C with an expected return of 9.75%. Accordingly, equation (24.3) can be used to determine the value of τ for this client, resulting in an estimated level of τ equal to $(22.22 \times 9.75) - 166.67 = 50$. This means that the client will accept up to an additional 50 units of variance in order to receive an extra 1% in expected return. Thus, the client's indifference curves are estimated to have the form of

$$\overline{r}_P = u_i + \frac{1}{50}\sigma_P^2. \tag{24.4}$$

Table 24.1 shows the inferred level of risk tolerance τ if a different portfolio had been chosen by the client. These levels were determined by substituting the appropriate values for $\overline{r}_C$ into the right-hand side of equation (24.3) and then solving for τ. First, note that the level of risk tolerance is the same as the percentage invested in the stock portfolio associated with C. That is, equation (24.3) can be rewritten as $\tau = 100X_S$, where X_S is the proportion invested in the stock portfolio associated with C. It can be shown that this will always be the case when $\overline{r}_S - r_F = 4.5\%$ and $\sigma_S = 15\%$. Other estimates would give different expressions for τ, but the relationship between X_S and τ would still be linear.

Second, note how the level of risk tolerance is lower if the selected portfolio is more conservative (that is, when the selected level of expected return and standard deviation is lower). Thus, more conservative risk-averse clients will have lower levels of risk tolerance than less conservative risk-averse clients.

Having estimated the client's indifference curves, recall from Chapter 7 that the objective of investment management is to identify the portfolio that lies on the indifference curve furthest to the northwest because such a portfolio will offer the investor the level of expected return and risk that is preferable to all the other portfolios. This is equivalent to identifying the portfolio that lies on the indifference curve that has the highest vertical intercept, u_i. This can be seen graphically in Figures 24.3(a) and 24.3(b), where the indifference curves have been extended to the vertical axis.

Certainty Equivalent Return

The term u_i can be thought of as the **certainty equivalent return** for any portfolio that lies on indifference curve i.[5] Thus portfolio C in Figure 24.2 is as desirable for this particular client as a hypothetical portfolio with an expected return of u_i and no risk—that is, one providing a return of u_i with certainty. When viewed in this manner, the job of the portfolio manager is to identify the portfolio with the highest certainty equivalent return.

Equation (24.1) can be rewritten so that the certainty equivalent return u_i appears on the left-hand side. Doing so results in

$$u_i = \overline{r}_P - \frac{1}{\tau}\sigma_P^2. \tag{24.5}$$

This equation shows that the certainty equivalent return can be thought of as a risk-adjusted expected return because a risk penalty that depends on both the portfolio's variance and the

[5] The term u_i is also known as the expected utility of indifference curve i. It represents the level of satisfaction associated with all portfolios plotting on indifference curve i. For more about utility theory, indifference curves, and certainty equivalent returns, see Mark Kritzman, "... About Utility," *Financial Analysts Journal* 48, no. 3 (May/June 1992): 17–20.

client's risk tolerance must be subtracted from the portfolio's expected return in determining u_i.

In the example, the investor selected the portfolio with $\bar{r}_P = 9.75\%$ and $\sigma_P^2 = 56.25 (= 7.5^2)$. Thus, the certainty equivalent return for this portfolio is $9.75 - (56.25/50) = 8.625\%$. Equivalently, the risk penalty for the portfolio that was selected was $56.25/50 = 1.125\%$. If the certainty equivalent return for any other portfolio shown in Table 24.1 is calculated, it will have a lower value. For example, the 80/20 portfolio has a certainty equivalent return of $11.1 - (144/50) = 8.22\%$. Thus, the goal of investment management can be thought of as identifying the portfolio that has the maximum value of $\bar{r}_P - (\sigma_P^2/\tau)$, because it will provide the client with the maximum certainty equivalent return.

SECURITY ANALYSIS AND PORTFOLIO CONSTRUCTION

Passive and Active Management

Within the investment industry, a distinction is often made between **passive management**—holding securities for relatively long periods with small and infrequent changes—and **active management**. Passive managers generally act as if the security markets are relatively efficient. Put somewhat differently, their decisions are consistent with the acceptance of consensus estimates of risk and return. The portfolios they hold may be surrogates for the market portfolio that are known as **index funds**, or they may be portfolios that are tailored to suit clients with preferences and circumstances that differ from those of the average investor.[6] In either case, passive portfolio managers do not try to outperform their designated benchmark.

For example, a passive manager might only have to choose the appropriate mixture of Treasury bills and an index fund that is a surrogate for the market portfolio. The best mixture would depend on the shape and location of the client's indifference curves. Figure 24.4 provides an illustration.

Point F plots the risk-free return offered by Treasury bills, and point M plots the risk and expected return of the surrogate market portfolio, using consensus forecasts. Mixtures of the two investments plot along line FM. The client's attitude toward risk and return is shown by the set of indifference curves, and the optimal mixture lies at the point O^* where an indifference curve is tangent to line FM. In this example, the best mixture uses both Treasury bills and the surrogate market portfolio. In other situations, the surrogate market portfolio might be "levered up" by borrowing (that is, money might be borrowed and added to the client's own investable funds, with the total being used to purchase the surrogate market portfolio).

When management is passive, the overall mixture is altered only when (1) the client's preferences change; (2) the risk-free rate changes; or (3) the consensus forecast about the risk and return of the benchmark portfolio changes. The manager must continue to monitor the last two variables and keep in touch with the client concerning the first one. No additional activity is required.

Active managers believe that from time to time there are mispriced securities or groups of securities. They do not act as if they believe that security markets are efficient. Put somewhat

[6] An example of a tailored portfolio would be one consisting of stocks with high dividend yields. Such a portfolio might be purchased for a corporate investor because 100% of all dividends received by a corporate investor are exempt from corporate income tax.

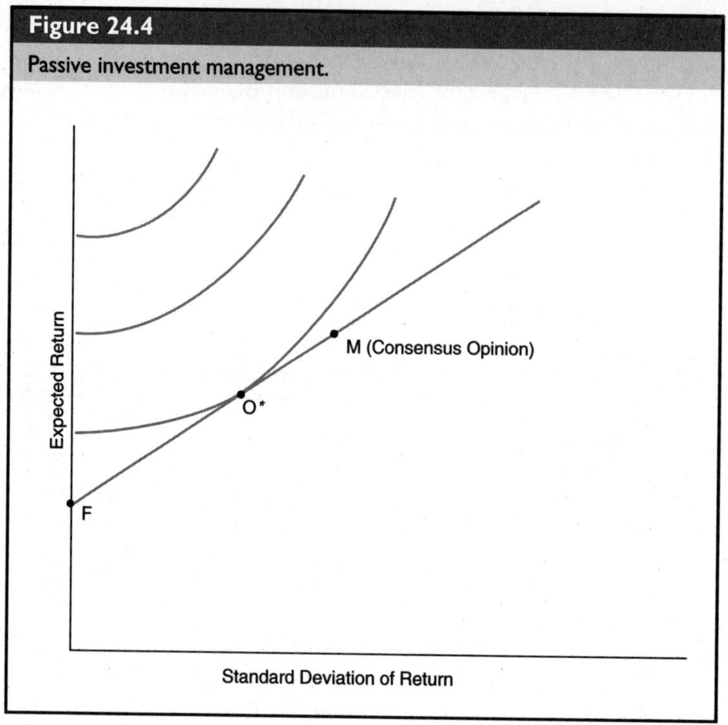

Figure 24.4

Passive investment management.

differently, they use deviant predictions: their forecasts of risks and expected returns differ from consensus opinions. Whereas some managers may be more bullish than average about a security, others may be more bearish. The former will hold "more-than-normal" proportions of the security, while the latter will hold "less-than-normal" proportions.

Assuming that there is no tailoring, it is useful to think of a portfolio as having two components: (1) a benchmark portfolio (actually, a surrogate for it); and (2) deviations designed to take advantage of security mispricing. For example, a portfolio can be broken down as follows:

Name of Security (Col. 1)	*Proportion in Actual Portfolio (Col. 2)*	*Proportion in Market Portfolio (Col. 3)*	*Active Position (Col. 4)*
S1	.30	.45	−.15
S2	.20	.25	−.05
S3	.50	.30	+.20
	1.00	1.00	.00

The second column shows the actual proportions in the actively managed portfolio. The third column indicates the percentages in a benchmark portfolio, which in this case is represented by a surrogate market portfolio—the holdings that might be best for an average client in a perfectly efficient market. The **active positions** can be represented by the differences between the proportions in the actual and benchmark portfolios. Such differences arise because active managers disagree with the consensus forecast about expected returns or risks. When expressed as differences of this sort, the actual portfolio can be viewed as an investment in the benchmark portfolio with a series of *bets* being placed on certain securities (such as S3) and against certain other securities (such as S1 and S2). Note how the bets are "balanced" in that the amount of the negative bets exactly counters the amount of the positive bets.

▶ Security Selection, Asset Allocation, and Market Timing

Security Selection

In principle, the investment manager should make forecasts of expected returns, standard deviations, and covariances for all available securities. This will allow an efficient set to be generated, upon which the indifference curves of the client can be plotted. Having done this, the investment manager should invest in those securities that form the optimal portfolio (that is, the portfolio indicated by the point where an indifference curve is tangent to the efficient set) for the client in question. Such a one-stage **security selection** process is illustrated in Figure 24.5(a).

In practice, this is rarely (if ever) done. Excessive costs would be incurred to obtain detailed forecasts of the expected returns, standard deviations, and covariances for all the individual securities under consideration. Instead, the decision on which securities to purchase is made in two or more stages.

Figure 24.5(b) illustrates a two-stage procedure where the investment manager has decided to consider investing in common stocks and corporate bonds for a client. In this case, the expected returns, standard deviations, and covariances are forecast for all common stocks under consideration. Then, based on just these common stocks, the efficient set is formed and the optimal stock portfolio identified. Next, the same analysis is performed for all corporate bonds under consideration, resulting in the identification of the optimal bond portfolio. The security selection process used in each of these two **asset classes** can be described as being myopic. That is, covariances between the individual common stocks and corporate bonds have not been considered in the identification of the two optimal portfolios.

Although this example has only two asset classes—stocks and bonds—it should be noted that the number of asset classes can be relatively large. Other asset classes that are often used are money market securities ("cash"), foreign stocks, foreign bonds, and real estate.

Asset Allocation

The second stage of the process divides the client's funds among two asset class portfolios, and is known as **asset allocation**.[7] In this stage, forecasts of the expected return and standard deviation are needed for both the optimal stock portfolio and the optimal bond portfolio, along with the covariance between the two portfolios. This will allow the expected return and standard deviation to be determined for all combinations of these two portfolios. Finally, after generating the efficient set from these combinations, the indifference curves of the client can be used to determine which portfolio should be chosen.

[7] For evidence suggesting that asset allocation is the most important decision an investor has to make, see Gary P. Brinson, L. Randolph Hood, and Gilbert L. Beebower, "Determinants of Portfolio Performance," *Financial Analysts Journal* 42, no. 4 (July/August 1986): 39–44; and Gary P. Brinson, Brian D. Singer, and Gilbert L. Beebower, "Determinants of Portfolio Performance II: An Update," *Financial Analysts Journal* 47, no. 3 (May/June 1991): 40–48.

INSTITUTIONAL ISSUES

The Active Versus Passive Debate

The debate between proponents of active and passive management has raged for over two decades, with little resolution in sight. At stake are billions of dollars in investment management fees, professional reputations, and, some would argue, even the efficient functioning of our capital markets.

As the text describes, passive management involves a long-term, buy-and-hold approach to investing. The investor selects an appropriate target and buys a portfolio designed to closely track the performance of that target. Once the portfolio is purchased, little additional trading occurs, beyond reinvestment of income or minor rebalancings necessary to accurately track the target. Because the selected target is usually (although not necessarily) a broad, diversified market index, passive management is commonly referred to as "indexation," and the passive portfolios are called "index funds."

Active management involves a systematic effort to exceed the performance of a selected target. A wide array of active management investment approaches exists, far too many to summarize in this space. Nevertheless, all active management entails the search for mispriced securities, or mispriced groups of securities. Accurately identifying and adroitly purchasing or selling these mispriced securities provides the active investor with the potential to outperform the passive investor.

Passive management is a relative newcomer to the investment industry. Prior to the mid 1960s, it was axiomatic that investors should search for mispriced stocks. Some investment strategies had passive overtones, such as buying "solid, blue-chip" companies for the "long term." Nevertheless, even these strategies implied an attempt to outperform some nebulously specified market target. The concepts of broad diversification and passive management were, for practical purposes, nonexistent.

Attitudes changed in the 1960s with the popularization of Markowitz's portfolio selection concepts (see Chapter 8), the introduction of the efficient market hypothesis (see Chapter 4), the emphasis on "the market portfolio" derived from the Capital Asset Pricing Model (see Chapter 10), and various academic studies proclaiming the futility of active management. Many investors, especially large institutional investors, began to question the wisdom of actively managing all of their assets. The first domestic common stock index fund was introduced in 1971. By the end of the decade, roughly $100 million was being invested in index funds. Today, hundreds of billions of dollars are invested in domestic and international stock and bond index funds. Even individual investors have become enamoured with index funds. Passively managed portfolios are some of the fastest growing products offered by many large mutual fund organizations.

Proponents of active management argue that capital markets are inefficient enough to justify the search for mispriced securities. They may disagree on the degree of the markets' inefficiencies. Technical analysts (see Chapter 23), for example, tend to view markets as dominated by emotionally driven and predictable investors, thereby creating numerous profit opportunities for the creative and disciplined investor. Conversely, managers who use highly quantitative investment tools often view profit opportunities as smaller and less persistent. Nevertheless, all active managers possess a fundamental belief in the existence of consistently exploitable security mispricings. As evidence they frequently point to the stellar track records of certain successful managers and various studies identifying market inefficiencies (see the appendix to Chapter 17 that discusses empirical regularities).

Some active management proponents also introduce into the active-passive debate what amounts to a moralistic appeal. They contend that investors virtually have an obligation to seek out mispriced securities, because their actions help remove these mispricings and thereby lead to a more efficient allocation of capital. Moreover, some proponents derisively contend that passive management implies settling for mediocre, or average, performance.

Proponents of passive management do not deny that exploitable profit opportunities exist or that some managers have established impressive performance results. Rather, they contend that the capital markets are efficient enough to prevent all but a few with inside information from consistently being able to earn abnormal profits. They point out that examples of past successes are more likely the result of luck rather than skill. If 1000 people flip a coin ten times, the odds are that one of them will flip all heads. In the investment industry, this person is crowned a brilliant money manager.

Passive management proponents also argue that the expected returns from active management are actually less than those for passive management. The fees charged by active managers are typically much higher than those levied by passive managers. (The difference averages anywhere from 0.30% to 1.00% of the managers' assets under management.) Further, passively managed portfolios usually experience very small transaction costs, whereas, depending on the amount of trading involved, active management transaction costs can be quite high. Thus, it is argued that passive managers will outperform active managers because of cost differences. Passive management thus entails settling for superior, as opposed to mediocre, results.

The active-passive debate will never be totally resolved. The random "noise" inherent in investment performance tends to drown out any systematic evidence of investment management skill on the part of active managers. Subjective issues therefore dominate the discussion, and as a result neither side can convince the other of the correctness of its viewpoint.

Despite the rapid growth in passively managed assets, most domestic and international stock and bond portfolios remain actively managed. Many large institutional investors, such as pension funds, have taken a middle ground on the matter, hiring both passive and active managers. In a crude way, this strategy may be a reasonable response to the unresolved active-passive debate. Clearly, all assets cannot be passively managed—who would be left to maintain security prices at "fair" value levels? On the other hand, investors with above-average investment skills are clearly in the minority of the group currently offering their services to investors.

Some people refer to two types of asset allocation. *Strategic asset allocation* refers to how a portfolio's funds would be divided, given the portfolio manager's long-term forecasts of expected returns, variances, and covariances, whereas *tactical asset allocation* refers to how these funds are to be divided at any particular moment, given the investor's short-term forecasts. Hence, the former reflects what the portfolio manager would do for the long term and the latter reflects what he or she would do under current market conditions.

For example, the first stage might have indicated that the investor should hold the proportions of stocks S1, S2, and S3 given earlier (that is, the optimal stock portfolio has proportions of .30, .20, and .50, respectively). Similarly, the first stage might have indicated that the investor should hold a proportion of .35 in bond B1 and .65 in bond B2. Then, under tactical asset allocation, the second stage might indicate that the client's funds should be split so that 60% goes into stocks and 40% into bonds because of current market conditions (whereas under strategic asset allocation these percentages might have been 70% and 30%, respectively). This translates into individual investments of the following magnitudes:

Stocks:		
S1	.60 × .30 =	.18
S2	.60 × .20 =	.12
S3	.60 × .50 =	.30
Bonds:		
B1	.40 × .35 =	.14
B2	.40 × .65 =	.26
		1.00

The two-stage process just discussed can be extended by introducing groups (sometimes referred to as sectors). Figure 24.5(c) illustrates a three-stage process. In the first stage, known as security selection, the investment manager would exercise discretion in identifying groups of securities in each asset class. Then having identified the groups, the investment manager would determine the optimal portfolio for each one. For example, within the asset class of common stocks, it could be that the investment manager has identified all industrial stocks as the first group, all utility stocks as the second group, and all transportation stocks as the third group. Within the asset class of bonds, groups of long-term, intermediate-term, and short-term bonds have been identified. Then, the investment manager would proceed to identify six optimal portfolios, one for each group of securities.

In the second stage, known as **group selection** (or group rotation), the investment manager determines the appropriate combination of the groups within each asset class. For example, the manager may have decided that the appropriate combination is 70% industrials, 10% utilities, and 20% transportation stocks. Similarly, the manager may have decided that the appropriate combination of bonds is 100% in long-term, with nothing in either intermediate-term or short-term bonds. Thus, in this stage the manager will determine the composition of an optimal stock portfolio and an optimal bond portfolio but will not know how much to allocate to each one.

The third and final stage makes this allocation and, as noted previously, is referred to as asset allocation. It is performed in a manner that is identical to the second stage of the two- stage procedure illustrated in Figure 24.5(b).

Active or passive management may be used in any stage. For example, *active bets* might be placed on individual securities, but with funds allocated across asset classes based on consensus long-term forecasts of expected returns for such classes. That is, the investment manager may decide to stick to a long-term mix of 75% stocks and 25% bonds. However, the choice of individual stocks and bonds in which to invest will change with time, based on the manager's forecasts.

Alternatively, passive portfolios of individual securities might be constructed, with deviant predictions of asset class returns used to allocate funds actively among the asset classes. For example, the investment manager may decide to always hold common stocks in the same relative proportions they have in the TSE 300, which is often used as a surrogate for the Canadian stock market portfolio. However, the proportion of funds invested in the TSE 300 will change at the start of every period, based on the overall prognosis for the stock and bond markets. Thus, during one period the manager may have as much as 100% of the client's funds in stocks, on the strong belief that the stock market is going to rise rapidly in the near future. Conversely, during another period the manager may have as much as 100% of the client's funds in bonds, in the strong belief that the stock market will soon crash dramatically.

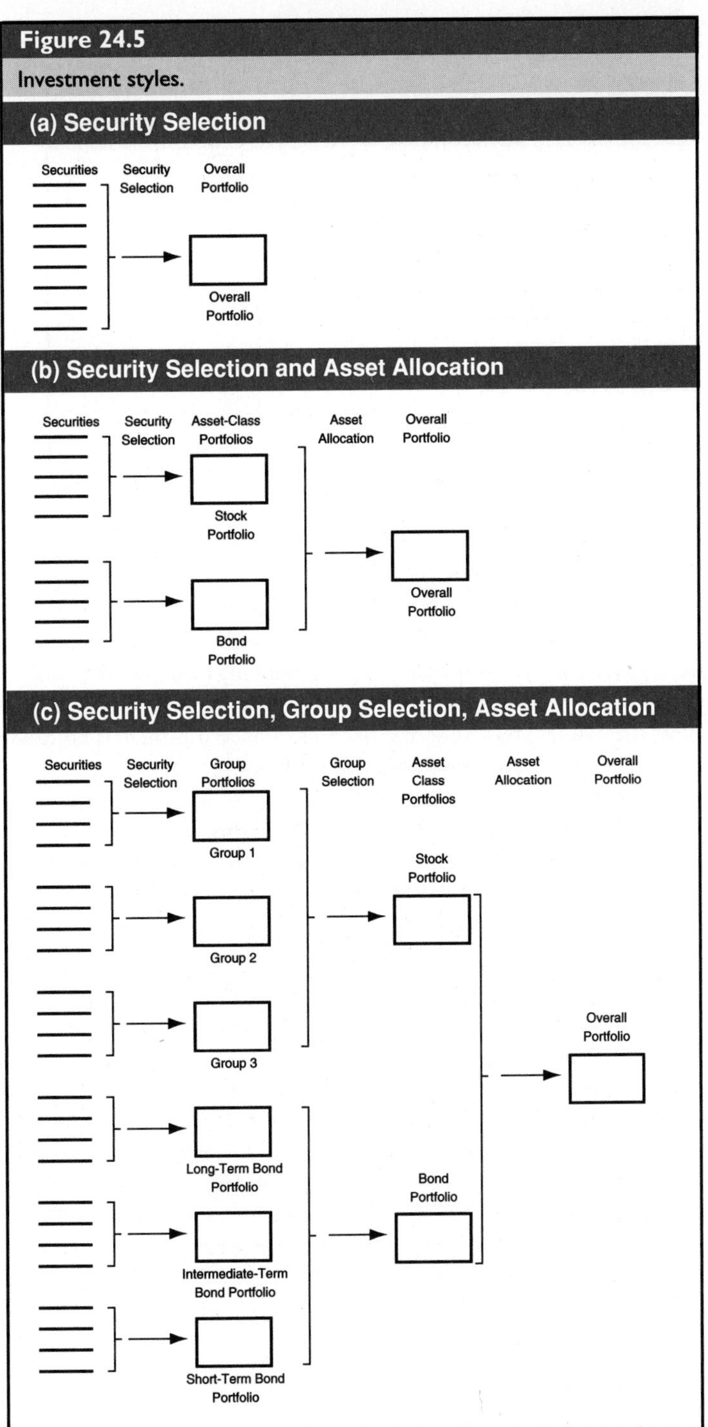

Figure 24.5

Investment styles.

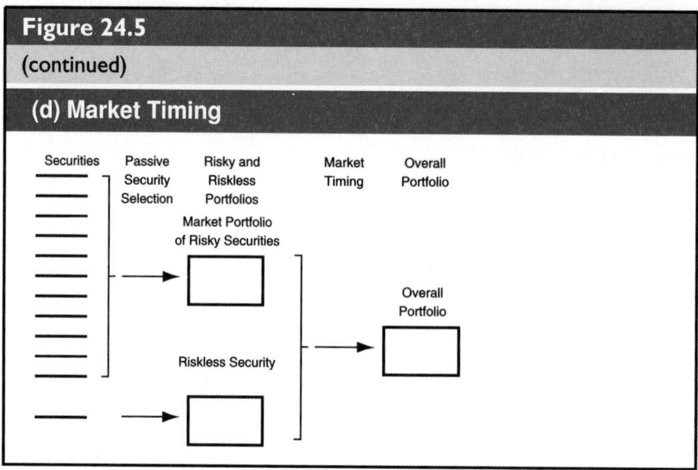

Market Timing

Figure 24.5(d) portrays a manager following an investment style that is known as **market timing**. The only active decision concerns the appropriate allocation of funds between a surrogate market portfolio (usually consisting of either stocks or long-term bonds) and a risk-free asset, such as Treasury bills. An investment organization following this style changes its mixture of risky and risk-free assets based on its own forecasts of the risk and expected return of "the market" relative to the risk-free rate, even if there is no change in consensus forecasts or the client's attitude toward risk and return.

Investment organizations that engage in the type of management where active bets are placed on individual securities are said to have a *security selection style*. Those that engage in the type of management where active bets are placed on asset classes are said to have an *asset allocation style*, with market timing being one specific example. Lastly, investment organizations that place active bets on certain groups of securities are said to employ a *group rotation style*. Some organizations use relatively pure **investment styles**, meaning that they use basically just one of the three styles previously mentioned. Others employ various combinations, making it difficult to classify them into neat categories.

Although these styles have been described in terms of modern portfolio theory, it should be pointed out that other procedures could be used to implement them. For example, with modern portfolio theory an optimal stock portfolio (as in Figure 24.5(b)) is identified by use of forecast expected returns, standard deviations, and covariances in conjunction with indifference curves. Once it is identified, the portfolio manager will have determined the appropriate relative investments in individual common stocks. However, such an identification could be made using some other procedure. Often it is done on a much less formal and more qualitative basis.

► International Investing

An interesting extension of the previous discussion of investment styles involves international investing. Consider security selection first. This style, when applied internationally, would involve determining the efficient set associated with a number of stocks found around the world. Alternatively, a security selection style could be combined with an asset allocation style. Here, for example, the portfolio manager could first determine the optimal portfolios associated with just Japanese stocks, just Canadian stocks, and just German stocks. Then, using these optimal portfolios, the manager would decide how much to allocate to each one of the three countries.

Imagine that the optimal Japanese portfolio consisted of two stocks, J_1 and J_2, in proportions of 70% and 30%, respectively, and half of the portfolio's funds were to be devoted to Japanese stocks. As a result, $.50 \times 70\% = 35\%$ and $.50 \times 30\% = 15\%$ of the portfolio would be invested in J_1 and J_2, respectively. Similar calculations could be done for the sets of Canadian and German stocks.

Procedures analogous to those previously described could be followed for the security selection, group rotation, asset allocation, and market timing styles in an international setting. However, the issue of foreign currency risk adds a complicating element to this comparison.[8]

PORTFOLIO REVISION

With the passage of time, a previously purchased portfolio that is currently held will often be viewed as suboptimal by the investment manager, meaning that the portfolio is no longer viewed as the best one for the client. This is because either the client's attitude toward risk and return is thought to have changed or, more likely, the manager's forecasts have changed. In response, the manager could identify a new optimal portfolio and then make the necessary revisions to the current portfolio so that subsequently the new optimal portfolio will be held. However, this is not as straightforward as it might seem at first because transaction costs will have to be paid when any revisions are made. Such costs must be compared with the perceived benefits associated with the revision in order to determine what course of action to take.

▶ Cost-Benefit Analysis

Transaction costs were discussed in Chapter 3. They include brokerage commissions, price impacts, and bid-ask spreads. Because of these costs, a security would have to increase in value by a certain amount just to pay these costs and leave the investor neither better nor worse off. This necessary increase in value may exceed 1% for many securities and can range as high as 5% to 10% or more for others, particularly small-size stocks.

The existence of transaction costs greatly complicates the life of any investment manager, and the more active the manager, the greater the complications. The hoped-for advantage of any revision must be weighed against the cost of making that revision. That is, a revision can be viewed as bringing certain kinds of benefits—either it will increase the expected return of the portfolio, or it will reduce the standard deviation of the portfolio, or it will do both. To be weighed against these benefits are the transaction costs that will be incurred if the revision is made. As a result, some of the revisions in the holdings of individual securities that the manager may initially want to make will be dropped from consideration because of the transaction costs involved. The goal of the manager is to identify the set of

[8] An intriguing description of how to use equilibrium models (like the CAPM, discussed in Chapter 10) and portfolio optimizers (see the *Institutional Issues* section in Chapter 8 for more on portfolio optimizers) to make asset allocation decisions in a global setting is presented in Fischer Black and Robert Litterman, "Global Portfolio Optimization," *Financial Analysts Journal* 48, no. 5 (September/October 1992): 28–43. Black and Litterman's model includes foreign currencies as one of the assets; see Chapter 26 for a discussion of foreign currencies and their risks.

individual revisions that collectively maximizes the improvement, after transaction costs, in the risk-return characteristics of the current portfolio.

In order to identify the appropriate set of individual revisions, sophisticated procedures (for example, quadratic programming) are required to compare the relevant costs and benefits. Fortunately, improvements in procedures and dramatic decreases in computing costs have made such approaches economically feasible for many investment managers.

In some situations investors may find it economically more attractive to revise their portfolios by transacting in entire asset classes instead of individual securities. Buying or selling futures contracts (see Chapter 21) on stock market indices or Treasury bonds is one such approach. A potentially more flexible strategy makes use of the swaps market.

Swaps

Consider a situation where a portfolio manager wants to make major changes in the proportions of funds that are invested in different asset classes. He or she recognizes that substantial transaction costs will be incurred if the traditional method of selling certain securities and replacing them with others is used to make these changes. Indeed, these costs can be so large that most of the changes, if conducted in this manner, should not be made. One relatively new method that has become very popular in allowing such changes to be made at relatively low transaction costs involves the use of swaps.[9]

While the unique features of swaps can become quite complicated, their general nature is quite simple. Such "plain-vanilla" swaps are contracts that typically involve two parties (in the language of swaps they are referred to as *counterparties*) exchanging sets of cash flows over a predetermined period of time.[10] Two types of swaps—equity and interest rate—are considered here.

Equity Swaps

With an **equity swap**, one counterparty agrees to pay a second counterparty a stream of variable cash payments that is based on the rate of return of an agreed-upon stock market index. In return, the second counterparty agrees to pay the first counterparty a stream of fixed cash payments that is based on current interest rates. Both sets of payments are to be made for a given time period and are based on a certain percentage (the percentage is variable for one counterparty and fixed for the other) of an underlying *notional principal.* Through an equity swap the first counterparty has, in essence, sold stocks and bought bonds while the second counterparty has sold bonds and bought stocks. Both of them have effectively restructured their portfolios without having to pay any transaction costs, other than a relatively small fee to a **swap bank** (usually a commercial or investment bank) that set up the contract.

Consider the example that is shown in Figure 24.6(a). Ms. Bright, a pension fund manager, thinks that the stock market is going to move upward sharply in the next three years. In contrast, Mr. Gloom, who also runs a pension fund, thinks that the stock market is likely to move downward in the next three years. Ms. Bright is considering selling $100 million of bonds and investing the proceeds in common stocks whereas Mr. Gloom is thinking of

---

[9] The discussion of swaps here should not be confused with the discussion of bond swaps in Chapter 16.

[10] For a discussion of many of the complicating features present in swaps, see Robert H. Litzenberger, "Swaps: Plain and Fanciful," *Journal of Finance* 47, no. 3 (July 1992): 831–850. He reports that at that time the amount of outstanding interest rate and currency swaps was estimated to be about $3 trillion, with over two-thirds of them being of the "plain vanilla" variety, and that the first major swap took place in 1981.

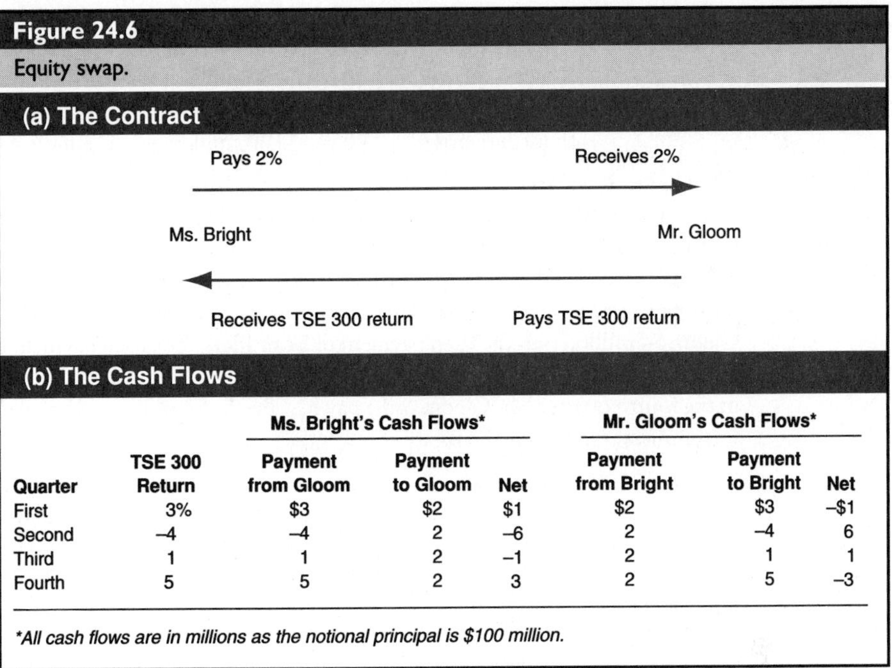

(b) The Cash Flows

		Ms. Bright's Cash Flows*			Mr. Gloom's Cash Flows*		
Quarter	TSE 300 Return	Payment from Gloom	Payment to Gloom	Net	Payment from Bright	Payment to Bright	Net
First	3%	$3	$2	$1	$2	$3	–$1
Second	–4	–4	2	–6	2	–4	6
Third	1	1	2	–1	2	1	1
Fourth	5	5	2	3	2	5	–3

**All cash flows are in millions as the notional principal is $100 million.*

Figure 24.6
Equity swap.

selling $100 million of common stocks and using the proceeds to purchase bonds. However, both portfolio managers realize that such changes will involve the payment of substantial transaction costs. Consequently, both of them contact a swap bank.

The swap bank sets up the following contract for Ms. Bright and Mr. Gloom. Shortly after the end of each quarter Mr. Gloom is to pay Ms. Bright an amount that is equal to the rate of return on the TSE 300 for the quarter times the notional principal. At the same time, Ms. Bright is to pay Mr. Gloom an amount that is equal to 2% of the notional principal. Both Ms. Bright and Mr. Gloom agree that the notional principal will be equal to $100 million, and that the contract will last for three years. Each pay the swap bank a fee for setting up the contract.[11]

Imagine that the quarterly rates of return on the TSE 300 during the first year of the swap contract are equal to 3%, –4%, 1%, and 5%, as shown in Figure 24.6(b). While Ms. Bright must pay $2 million (.02 × $100 million) to Mr. Gloom each quarter, in return Mr. Gloom must pay Ms. Bright the following amounts:

---

[11] Swaps can be compared to a series of forward contracts (forward contracts were discussed in Chapter 5). In this case, Ms. Bright has a swap position equivalent to having long positions in a series of equity forward contracts, whereas Mr. Gloom has short positions in these contracts. Consider the swap contract's first quarterly payment. Imagine that instead of the swap contract Ms. Bright had taken a long position in a forward contract. In general, forward contracts involve the exchange of a stated amount of cash for a given asset at a specified future date. Here Ms. Bright has agreed to pay $2 million one quarter later for delivery of an asset that can be thought of as shares in a TSE 300 index fund (the number of shares will be determined on the delivery date, and will be equal to $100 million times the quarterly return on the TSE 300, divided by the fund's net asset value at the end of the quarter).

First quarter:	.03 × \$100 million = \$3 million
Second quarter:	–.04 × \$100 million = –4 million
Third quarter:	.01 × \$100 million = 1 million
Fourth quarter:	.05 × \$100 million = 5 million

Hence, it appears that in the first quarter Ms. Bright pays \$2 million to Mr. Gloom and in return Mr. Gloom pays \$3 million to Ms. Bright. However, the way the contract is structured, only the net amount is paid—in this case, Mr. Gloom will pay \$1 million (\$3 million – \$2 million) to Ms. Bright. In the second quarter it appears that Mr. Gloom must pay –\$4 million to Ms. Bright. The minus sign means that Ms. Bright must pay Mr. Gloom \$4 million plus the fixed payment of \$2 million, for a total payment of \$6 million. In the third period, Ms. Bright must pay Mr. Gloom \$1 million (\$2 million – \$1 million), and in the fourth quarter Mr. Gloom must pay Ms. Bright \$3 million (\$5 million – \$2 million). In summary, the net payments are

First quarter:	Mr. Gloom pays \$1 million to Ms. Bright
Second quarter:	Ms. Bright pays \$6 million to Mr. Gloom
Third quarter:	Ms. Bright pays \$1 million to Mr. Gloom
Fourth quarter:	Mr. Gloom pays \$3 million to Ms. Bright

These amounts reflect what would have happened (roughly) if Mr. Gloom had sold stocks and bought bonds and Ms. Bright had sold bonds and bought stocks, and both incurred relatively low transaction costs. Consider the first quarter. If Mr. Gloom had sold the stocks and replaced them with 2% bonds, he would have earned \$2 million. Instead, he kept the stocks and earned \$3 million on them (remember that the TSE 300 went up 3%) but had to pay Ms. Bright a net amount of \$1 million, leaving him with \$2 million, the same amount.

There are many ways that equity swaps can be modified. For example, a foreign stock market index such as the Nikkei 225 could be used instead of the TSE 300. This would allow one counterparty to achieve the benefits of international diversification more cheaply. Alternatively, the swap could involve two stock market indices, such as a large stock index like the TSE 300 and a small stock index like the *Financial Post* All-Canadian Junior Index. There are many other variations, limited only by investors' imaginations and their ability to periodically determine the value of the swaps.

Interest Rate Swaps

With an **interest rate swap**, one counterparty agrees to pay a second party a stream of cash payments whose size is reset regularly based on the current level of a highly visible interest rate. A popular one is the London Interbank Offered Rate (LIBOR), which is an interest rate set daily in London that applies to loans made among large international banks. In return, the second counterparty agrees to pay the first counterparty a stream of fixed-size cash payments that is based on the level of interest rates in existence at the time the contract is signed. Like equity swaps, both sets of payments are to be made for a certain number of years and are based on a certain percentage of an underlying notional principal. (The percentage is variable—or "floating"—for one counterparty and fixed for the other.) Through the interest rate swap the first counterparty has, in essence, sold short-term fixed-income securities and bought long-term bonds while the second counterparty has sold these bonds and bought the short-term fixed-income securities. Both of them have effectively restructured their

Figure 24.7

Interest rate swap.

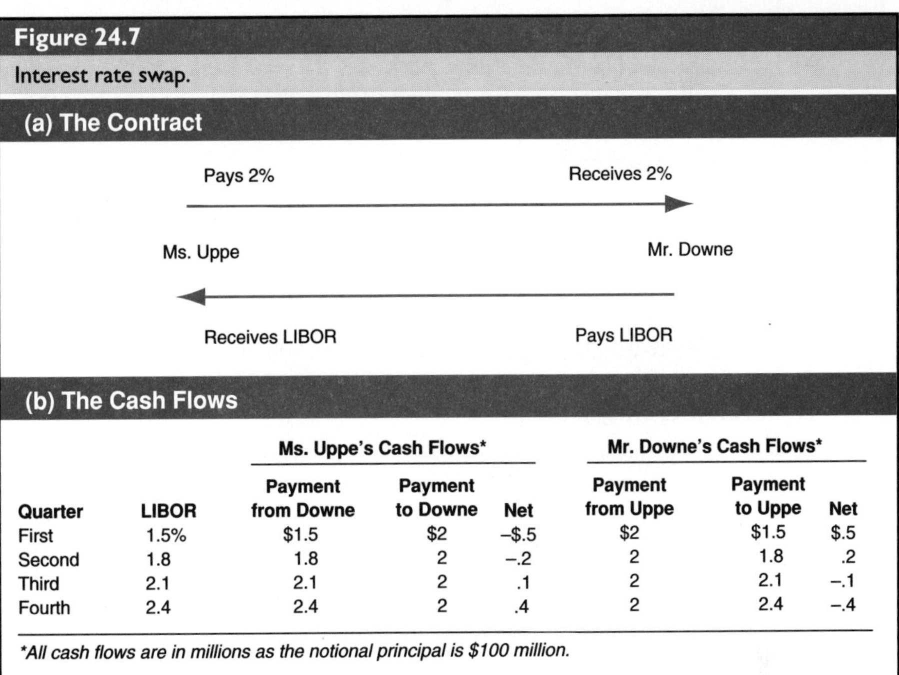

		Ms. Uppe's Cash Flows*			Mr. Downe's Cash Flows*		
Quarter	LIBOR	Payment from Downe	Payment to Downe	Net	Payment from Uppe	Payment to Uppe	Net
First	1.5%	$1.5	$2	–$.5	$2	$1.5	$.5
Second	1.8	1.8	2	–.2	2	1.8	.2
Third	2.1	2.1	2	.1	2	2.1	–.1
Fourth	2.4	2.4	2	.4	2	2.4	–.4

**All cash flows are in millions as the notional principal is $100 million.*

portfolios without having to pay any transaction costs other than a relatively small fee to a swap bank that set up the contract.

Consider the example that is shown in Figure 24.7(a). Ms. Uppe, a fixed-income mutual fund manager, thinks that interest rates are going to move upward in the near future. In contrast, Mr. Downe, who also runs a fixed-income mutual fund, thinks that interest rates are likely to move downward. Consequently, Ms. Uppe is considering selling $100 million of long-term bonds and investing the proceeds in money market securities, whereas Mr. Downe is thinking of selling $100 million of money market securities and using the proceeds to purchase long-term bonds.[12] As with the case of an equity swap, both of them contact a swap bank to help them make such changes without the payment of substantial transaction costs.[13]

The swap bank sets up the following contract for the two of them. Shortly after the end of each quarter Mr. Downe is to pay Ms. Uppe an amount that is equal to the end-of-quarter three-month LIBOR times the notional principal. At the same time, Ms. Uppe is to pay Mr. Downe an amount that is equal to 2% of the notional principal. Both Ms. Uppe and

[12] By convention, the counterparty that makes the fixed payments (Ms. Uppe) is known as the *swap buyer*, and the counterparty that makes the variable payments (Mr. Downe) is known as the *swap seller*. Hence, the swap buyer "pays fixed and receives floating," and the swap seller "pays floating and receives fixed."

[13] In this case, Ms. Uppe has a swap position equivalent to having long positions in a series of money market forward contracts, whereas Mr. Downe has short positions in these contracts. For example, the first quarterly payment is identical to what would happen if Ms. Uppe signed a forward contract agreeing to pay $2 million in exchange for the delivery of shares in a money market mutual fund (the number of shares will be determined on the delivery date, and will be equal to $100 million times the LIBOR, divided by the fund's net asset value at the end of the quarter). See footnote 11.

Mr. Downe agree that the notional principal will be equal to $100 million, and that the contract will last for five years. Each pays the swap bank a fee for setting up the contract.

Imagine that the three-month LIBOR at the beginning of each of the next four quarters equals, successively, 1.5%, 1.8%, 2.1%, and 2.4%. This means that the following amounts are to be paid by Mr. Downe to Ms. Uppe:

First quarter:	.015 × $100 million =	$1.5 million
Second quarter:	.018 × $100 million =	1.8 million
Third quarter:	.021 × $100 million =	2.1 million
Fourth quarter:	.024 × $100 million =	2.4 million

In return, Ms. Uppe must pay .02 × $100 million = $2 million to Mr. Downe each quarter. Since the payments from Ms. Uppe and Mr. Downe are netted against each other, the net payments are

First quarter:	Ms. Uppe pays $.5 million to Mr. Downe
Second quarter:	Ms. Uppe pays $.2 million to Mr. Downe
Third quarter:	Mr. Downe pays $.1 million to Ms. Uppe
Fourth quarter:	Mr. Downe pays $.4 million to Ms. Uppe

These amounts reflect what would have happened (roughly) if Ms. Uppe had sold bonds and bought money market securities and Mr. Downe had sold money market securities and bought bonds, and both incurred relatively low transaction costs. Consider the first quarter. If Ms. Uppe had sold the bonds and replaced them with money market securities yielding roughly LIBOR, she would have earned $1.5 million in interest. Instead, she kept the bonds and earned $2 million on them but had to pay Mr. Downe a net amount of $.5 million, leaving her with $1.5 million, the same amount.

As with equity swaps, there are many variations on this plain-vanilla type of interest rate swap. For example, the notional principal could change over time, or one variable-rate stream of cash flows based on one interest rate (such as LIBOR) could be swapped for a variable rate stream of cash flows based on another interest rate (such as Treasury bills). In addition, there can be caps or floors or collars on the size of the variable payments.

Swaps Market

The swaps market is an unregulated market in that no governmental agency has oversight responsibilities. As a consequence, there has been a high degree of innovation in the types of swap contracts that have been created.[14] Furthermore, there is privacy for all parties involved,

---

[14] One interesting innovation is the *swaption*, a contract that combines an option (usually European) with an interest rate swap (or some other kind of swap). Call swaptions involve the right to "pay fixed and receive floating" and put swaptions involve the right to "pay floating and receive fixed." The notional principal, fixed rate, source of the floating rate, and swap life are all set when the swaption is created, as is the life of the swaption itself. If the owner of either type of swaption decides to exercise the option, then the writer (usually a swap bank) must become the other counterparty to the swap. In return for this right, the owner pays the writer a premium. Owners of calls will exercise their options if interest rates rise because then the fixed payment cash outflows will be less than the floating rate cash inflows. Conversely, put owners will exercise their options if interest rates fall. See David R. Smith, "A Simple Method for Pricing Interest Rate Swaptions," *Financial Analysts Journal* 47, no. 3 (May/June 1991): 72–76.

as no reporting requirements exist other than those imposed by accountants. In addition, it means that anyone involved in a swap must be concerned with counterparty risk. That is, each counterparty to a swap must pay close attention to the creditworthiness of the other counterparty in order to reduce the risk that the other counterparty will default in making his or her required payments under the terms of the contract.

At the heart of the swaps market are swap banks, which facilitate the creation of swaps for their clients, and will often take the other side of the contract if another counterparty is not available at the moment. In such situations they are acting as *swap dealers*, and they will use various kinds of techniques (such as taking positions in futures or contacting other swap banks) to hedge their exposure to financial risk. In such a situation no fee is typically charged to the counterparty. Instead, the terms of the swap are set in the swap dealer's favour, thereby allowing the dealer to make a profit after hedging his or her position.

What happens if at some point during the life of the swap one counterparty wants to get out of the contract? In such a situation the counterparty has a choice of contacting either the other counterparty or a swap bank. In the first case, it is possible that the swap contract can be cancelled if a mutually acceptable cash payment is made from one counterparty to the other. In the interest rate swap example, if interest rates have risen high enough (as in the third and fourth quarter), then Ms. Uppe will be in a favourable position because the swap's net cash flows will be going from Mr. Downe to her. Hence, regardless of who wants to get out of the swap, Ms. Uppe would want to be compensated for the loss of the anticipated future cash flows. This means that Mr. Downe would give her a lump sum payment when the contract is cancelled.

Similarly, if a swap bank is contacted, then either it will assume the counterparty's position in the contract or it will search for someone else to do so. (Note that the counterparty that wants to get out of the contract can conduct such a search without using a swap bank.) In the previous example, if Ms. Uppe wants to get out of the contract, then the swap bank will pay her a lump sum. Conversely, if Mr. Downe wants to get out, then he will have to pay a lump sum to the swap bank. In either case, the contract remains in force afterward for the other counterparty.

It is also possible that the swap bank will arrange for the party that wants to get out to agree to a second swap contract that effectively cancels the first one. For example, if after one year Ms. Uppe wants to get out of the contract where she "pays fixed and receives floating," then the swap bank could construct a four-year swap where she "pays floating and receives fixed" for the same amount of notional principal. With the first contract she pays 2% and receives LIBOR, and with the second contract she will pay LIBOR and receive 2.3%. Note that the fixed rate is higher with the second contract (2.3% > 2%) as interest rates have risen since the first contract was signed. Now Ms. Uppe both receives and pays LIBOR, so those two cash streams effectively cancel each other out. She also pays 2% and receives 2.3%, meaning that, on balance, she receives .3%, or \$300 000 (= .003 × \$100 million). Thus, for the next four years she will receive \$300 000 quarterly.

MANAGER-CLIENT RELATIONS

The larger the amount of money managed, the more communication there is likely to be between investment manager and client. Not surprisingly, corporate, union, and government officials responsible for pension funds spend a great deal of time with those who manage their money. Such officials also concern themselves with a number of questions: who should manage the money, how should it be managed, and how should the managers be instructed and constrained?

Many aspects of manager-client relations can be characterized as responses to a difference of opinion concerning the manager's ability to make "good bets." Often clients will divide their funds among two or more managers. This type of **split-funding** is used by most pension funds. Two reasons are given. First, it allows the employment of managers with different skills or different styles. Second, the impact of erroneous "bets" can be reduced by diversifying across different managers because the managers are the "bettors." However, if a client were to broadly diversify across managers without regard to the managers' investment abilities, the overall portfolio would likely produce results similar to those of the market portfolio. Thus, excessive use of split-funding is like explicitly investing in a passive fund, but at considerably greater cost to the client, owing to the expenses associated with transaction costs and fees charged by the investment managers.

Whether or not split-funding is used, a client who feels that a manager is "betting" too much would like to simply reduce the size of the "bets." For example, the client might ask a manager to diverge only half as much as he or she normally would from passive proportions of individual securities. Thus, if the manager decides that the optimal proportion in stock S1 is 30% and the market proportion is 45%, this would mean that the manager would ultimately invest only a proportion equal to $(30\% + 45\%)/2 = 37.5\%$. However, there is no simple way to monitor compliance. In the example, the manager could buy 30% of S1 and state that he or she originally wanted to invest 45% in it but settled for 30%, even though truthfully he or she originally wanted 30%. Instead, a simpler approach is often employed: limits are placed on the holdings in any single security.[15]

Institutional investors (for example, pension and endowment funds) often use more than one investment manager and provide each with a set of objectives and a set of constraints on allowed divergences from specified target positions.[16] Individual investors who employ investment managers tend to give such instructions implicitly, if at all. This may reflect less sophistication, a less formal relationship with the manager, or the fact that the management fee for a small account is not large enough to cover the cost of dealing with a series of client-specific objectives and constraints.

---

[15] There are other kinds of limits frequently imposed on the manager, such as limits on the holdings of bonds versus stocks, or on the amount invested in a single industry.

[16] Sometimes these objectives and constraints are stated vaguely; in other cases they are specified precisely.

INSTITUTIONAL ISSUES

Manager Structuring

Administrators of pension and endowment funds might be surprised to find themselves referred to as investment engineers. Yet these particular institutional investors (who are often called "plan sponsors") face the complex problem of efficiently allocating their assets among various investment managers so as to best achieve their stated investment objectives. The disciplined process through which this manager "structuring" problem can best be resolved is analogous to an engineer designing a building or a machine.

When plan sponsors choose to invest in a particular asset class, especially a well-defined and liquid one such as the common stock market, they typically choose a market index to characterize the expected return and risk opportunities of the asset class and to serve as a benchmark against which to evaluate the subsequent performance of their investments. In this context, the selected market index is called an *asset class target*. For example, a plan sponsor might specify the TSE 300 and the ScotiaMcLeod Index as the asset class targets for its Canadian common stock and fixed-income investments, respectively. In a sense these market indices represent the portfolios that the plan sponsors would own if all of their investments in these asset classes were passively managed.

Plan sponsors rarely opt to conduct all of their investments in an asset class on a strictly passive basis. Instead, they typically hire a number of active investment managers (possibly in addition to using an index fund). In aggregate, these active managers are expected to exceed the performance of the asset class target on a risk-adjusted basis.

For various reasons most active investment managers pursue distinct investment styles, focusing their efforts in particular niches of the marketplace. For example, some common stock managers concentrate on small capitalization growth stocks, whereas some bond managers invest only in mortgage-backed securities.

Just as an investment manager will diversify within a portfolio to avoid unintended risks, a plan sponsor will diversify across investment managers. This manager diversification reduces the possibility that one manager's mistakes will seriously harm the plan sponsor's total portfolio. Further, it avoids the risk that the total portfolio will be excessively exposed to the results of a specific investment style. In particular, it is this "diversification of style" that underlies the plan sponsor's investment engineering problem.

The goal of efficient style diversification is to be *style neutral* relative to the asset class target. That is, in aggregate, the investment styles of a plan sponsor's managers should exhibit exposures to factors of risk and return (see Chapter 11) similar to those of the asset class target.

Suppose that a plan sponsor decision-maker, who had selected the TSE 300 as the asset class target for his or her Canadian common stock investments, were to hire only investment managers that invested in large capitalization, high-dividend-yield stocks. The aggregate of the managers' investment styles would display investment characteristics quite different from those of the TSE 300. For example, relative to the TSE 300, the aggregate manager style would heavily emphasize utility stocks, which pay high dividends, and deemphasize technology stocks, which pay small dividends or none.

In some periods, such as during an economic downturn, these large high-yield stocks would perform well relative to the TSE 300. In other periods, they might perform relatively poorly. This relative performance difference would occur regardless of whether the large capitalization, high-yield managers were good or bad stock pickers within their area of expertise. The aggregate style of these managers does not "fit" with the asset class target. Therefore the risk that the aggregate manager style will perform differently from the asset class target is known as *misfit risk*. Style diversification seeks to limit misfit risk.

Unfortunately, simply hiring many active managers with differing investment styles is not a cost-effective means of controlling misfit risk. Investment skill is a rare commodity. A plan sponsor decision-maker may not be able to identify what he or she believes to be skillful managers in sufficient quantity to provide a diverse group of investment styles. As the costs of active management are much higher than those of passive management, a strategy of hiring a large number of active managers with different investment styles within an asset category is likely to produce nothing more than an expensive index fund.

Plan sponsors would prefer to allocate their assets only to those managers whom they believe can perform best relative to the managers' investment styles, without concern for how those investment styles in aggregate compare to the asset class target. How can plan sponsors accommodate this preference and at the same time control misfit risk? That is the essence of the investment engineering problem.

Consider a plan sponsor who has identified certain managers that he or she believes will be the strongest risk-adjusted performers. Upon examining the managers' aggregate investment style, the plan sponsor finds that it heavily emphasizes smaller companies and companies expected to produce high relative earnings growth. The plan sponsor has selected the TSE 300 as the asset class target, which tends to be dominated by large, mature companies. Thus, considerable misfit risk exists.

The plan sponsor could reduce this misfit risk by also investing in a specially designed, passively managed portfolio. This portfolio, called a *completeness fund*, would hold long positions in securities underrepresented by the managers' aggregate investment style relative to the asset class target. Conversely, it would contain short positions in overrepresented securities. In our example, the completeness fund would purchase large capitalization, low-growth stocks and sell short smaller, high-growth stocks.

Properly constructed, the completeness fund will eliminate misfit risk and create a style-neutral total portfolio. If the active managers exceed the performance of their respective investment style benchmarks, then the total portfolio will outperform the asset class target.

Complicating the issue is the fact that the active managers' investment styles may have non-zero covariances with one another. If so, various allocations among them will produce different levels of misfit risk. Moreover, the plan sponsor may have more confidence in some managers than in others, and therefore wish to allocate more funds to the former than to the latter. These active manager allocation decisions directly affect the aggregate manager investment style and thus the composition of the completeness fund.

Determining desired allocations to the active managers and the composition of the resulting completeness fund requires a disciplined, quantitative approach. Further, the problem is dynamic, with the appropriate solution shifting over time as the investment characteristics of securities evolve and plan sponsors' estimates of the relative skills of their current and prospective managers change. The task of manager structuring is truly one of investment engineering.

SUMMARY

1. Investment decisions are made through a five-step procedure: (1) set investment policy; (2) perform security analysis; (3) construct a portfolio; (4) revise the portfolio; and (5) evaluate the performance of the portfolio.
2. To set investment policy, an investor should specify his or her risk tolerance—that is, the maximum amount of additional risk that the investor will accept for a given increase in expected return.
3. One means of establishing an investor's risk tolerance is for the investor to identify the most desirable portfolio from a set of portfolios. Once this identification has been made, the slope of the investor's indifference curve, and hence the investor's attitude toward risk and expected return, can be established.
4. Passive management rests on the belief that markets are efficient and typically involves investing in an index fund. Active management, conversely, involves a belief that mispriced situations occur and can be identified with reasonable consistency.
5. There are many forms of active management. They can involve security selection, group selection, asset allocation, and market timing.
6. Portfolio revision involves both realizing that the currently held portfolio is not optimal and specifying another portfolio to hold with superior risk-return characteristics. The investor must balance the costs of moving to the new portfolio against the benefits of the revision.
7. Swaps often provide a low-cost method of restructuring a portfolio's funds across various asset classes.

APPENDIX A

DETERMINING THE RISK TOLERANCE OF AN INVESTOR

The purpose of this appendix is to derive in some detail the formula for determining the risk tolerance τ of an investor. As mentioned earlier, the equation for an indifference curve of an investor having constant risk tolerance is of the form:

$$\bar{r}_P = u_i + \frac{1}{\tau}\sigma_P^2 \tag{24.1}$$

where u_i and $1/\tau$ are the vertical intercept and slope for indifference curve i when variance is measured on the horizontal axis. As the equation shows, an indifference curve will be a straight line because u_i and $1/\tau$ are constants (thus the equation is of the general form $Y = a + bX$, which is a straight line). Furthermore, any two indifference curves for an investor will have the same slope $(1/\tau)$ but will have different vertical intercepts (u_i).

In order to estimate the investor's level of risk tolerance τ, it was mentioned that the slope of the indifference curve, $1/\tau$, would be set equal to the slope of the efficient set at the location of the portfolio that was selected, denoted portfolio C. This is because the indifference curve is tangent to the efficient set at this point, so the two must have the same slope. Thus the slope of the efficient set at point C must be determined in order to estimate τ.

Let X_S denote the proportion invested in the stock portfolio S and $(1 - X_S)$ denote the proportion invested in a risk-free Treasury bill portfolio F. Now the expected return of any portfolio consisting of S and F is simply

$$\overline{r}_P = X_S\overline{r}_S + (1 - X_S)r_F \tag{24.6}$$

where $\overline{r}_S$ and r_F are the expected return of the stock portfolio and the risk-free rate, respectively. This equation can be solved for X_S, resulting in

$$X_S = \frac{\overline{r}_P - r_F}{\overline{r}_S - r_F}. \tag{24.7}$$

The equation for the variance of portfolio P is equal to

$$\sigma_P^2 = X_S^2\sigma_S^2 + (1 - X_S)^2\sigma_F^2 + 2X_S(1 - X_S)\sigma_{SF} \tag{24.8}$$

where σ_S^2 and σ_F^2 are the variances of the stock and risk-free portfolios, respectively, and σ_{SF} is the covariance between these two portfolios. However, because F is the risk-free portfolio, by definition, σ_F^2 and σ_{SF} are equal to zero. Thus, equation (24.8) reduces to

$$\sigma_P^2 = X_S^2\sigma_S^2. \tag{24.9}$$

Next, the right-hand side of equation (24.7) can be substituted for X_S in equation (24.9), resulting in

$$\sigma_P^2 = \frac{(\overline{r}_P - r_F)^2}{(\overline{r}_S - r_F)^2}\sigma_S^2. \tag{24.10}$$

This equation can be viewed as describing the functional relationship between the expected return and variance of any portfolio P that can be formed by combining the stock portfolio S and the risk-free portfolio F. That is, for a particular S and F, it gives the variance for a portfolio consisting of S and F with expected return $\overline{r}_P$. Equivalently, it represents the slope of the curved line in Figure 24.2 that connects S and F. Using calculus, the slope of this line can be shown to be equal to[17]

$$\text{Slope} = \frac{(\overline{r}_S - r_F)^2}{2[(\overline{r}_P - r_F)\sigma_S^2]}. \tag{24.11}$$

The next step in estimating the slope of the client's indifference curves is to note that the portfolio on the curve connecting S and F that is of concern is the tangency portfolio C. Thus, the slope of the curve at C is determined by substituting $\overline{r}_C$ for $\overline{r}_P$ in equation (24.11) and equating this value with the slope of the indifference curves, $1/\tau$. Doing this results in the following equation:

$$\frac{1}{\tau} = \frac{(\overline{r}_S - r_F)^2}{2[(\overline{r}_C - r_F)\sigma_S^2]}. \tag{24.12}$$

Finally, equation (24.12) can be solved for τ:

$$\tau = \frac{2[(\overline{r}_C - r_F)\sigma_S^2]}{(\overline{r}_S - r_F)^2} \tag{24.13}$$

---

[17] Note that the slope of this line, $d\overline{r}_P/d\sigma_P^2$, is equal to $1/(d\sigma_P^2/d\overline{r}_P)$. Thus the slope can be determined by taking the derivative of σ_P^2 with respect to $\overline{r}_P$ in equation (24.10) and then inverting the resulting expression.

Note that this is the same formula that was given earlier in equation (24.2) for estimating τ, given the client's choice of portfolio C.[18]

After substituting $\overline{r}_C$ for $\overline{r}_P$, equation (24.7) can be rewritten as

$$(\overline{r}_S - \overline{r}_F)X_S = \overline{r}_C - r_F. \tag{24.14}$$

Thus, $(\overline{r}_S - r_F)X_S$ can be substituted for $\overline{r}_C - r_F$ in the numerator of equation (24.13). Doing so and simplifying results in

$$\tau = \frac{2[X_S\sigma_S^2]}{(\overline{r}_S - r_F)}. \tag{24.15}$$

In the example given earlier in the chapter, $\sigma_S = 15\%$ and $\overline{r}_S - r_F = 4.5\%$. Substituting these values into equation (24.15) and simplifying results in

$$\begin{aligned}\tau &= \frac{2[X_S \times 15^2]}{4.5} \\ &= 100X_S\end{aligned} \tag{24.16}$$

as was previously mentioned and illustrated in Table 24.1.

QUESTIONS AND PROBLEMS

1. Describe the functioning of a "traditional" investment management organization. Much of the decision-making in these organizations is "qualitative" in nature. What types of "quantitative" decision-making techniques might be introduced?
2. Technological changes have decreased the cost and increased the speed of information dissemination in security markets. Why might one suspect that firms following a "traditional" approach to investment management would find it increasingly difficult to generate "positive alphas" (that is, to identify and acquire underpriced securities) in this environment?
3. Consider Table 24.1. If your investment advisor presented you with this data, which stock/Treasury bill combination would you choose? Describe your thought process in making this choice.
4. Why is it difficult to specify the risk-return preferences of investment management clients? Why are these problems particularly acute in the case of institutional investor clients (for example, pension and endowment funds)?
5. Consider a portfolio whose asset mix can vary between stocks and Treasury bills. Given the historical returns on these two assets that is provided in Chapter 1, describe the distribution of possible portfolio returns as the proportion of the portfolio invested in stocks increases and that invested in Treasury bills decreases. What causes the distribution to change as the asset mix changes?
6. Explain the meaning of the slope of an investor's indifference curve at any particular point. For a "typical" risk-averse investor, describe how the investor's risk-return trade-off changes at different points along one of his or her indifference curves.
7. Assume that the expected return on stocks is 12%, the standard deviation of stocks is 18%, and the risk-free rate is 5%. Given this information, an investor selects a

[18] Risk tolerance, along with a procedure for estimating the value of τ, is presented in William F. Sharpe, *Asset Allocation Tools* (Redwood City, CA: Scientific Press, 1987), pp. 33–39.

portfolio comprised of a 70% allocation to stocks and a 30% allocation to the risk-free asset. According to the derivation of risk tolerance found in equation (24.2), what risk tolerance is indicated by this choice?

8. Buzz Arlett, a portfolio manager for an investment management firm, has estimated the following risk-return characteristics for the stock and bond markets.

	Expected Return	*Standard Deviation*
Stocks	18.0%	22.0%
Bonds	10.0	5.0

The correlation between stocks and bonds is estimated to be 0.50.

Using these estimates, Buzz ran a number of simulations, tracing out the implications of different bond/stock mixes for the financial situation of Arnold Beck, a client. After much thought, Arnold indicated that, of the mixes considered, the most desirable was the allocation of 60% to stocks and 40% to bonds. Given this information, calculate Arnold's risk tolerance. [Hint: To solve this problem algebraically, write equation (24.5) using the 60/40 stock/bond allocation. Do the same for a 61/39 allocation. Finally, set these two formulas equal to each other and solve for the risk tolerance.] Is this answer likely to represent Arnold's risk tolerance over all possible stock/bond allocations?

9. Should an "overpriced" stock definitely be excluded from an investor's portfolio? Why?
10. Studies that simulate the value of an investment portfolio under alternative mixes of stocks and bonds invariably demonstrate that higher stock allocations produce higher returns, particularly as the holding period increases. If you as an investor have a time horizon that is reasonably long, say over ten years, and you have no current income needs, could you justify holding any bonds in your portfolio?
11. Assume a risk-free return of 7%, an expected stock return of 18%, and a standard deviation of 21%. Under these conditions, if Maria Gomez chooses a 40% stock, 60% risk-free portfolio, what is Maria's risk tolerance? In words, describe what this value means.
12. Louise Cousineau can earn a risk-free return of 6%. Louise expects the stock market to return 15% and exhibit a standard deviation of 20%. If Louise chooses a portfolio of 60% stocks and 40% risk-free asset, calculate Louise's certainty equivalent return.
13. The portfolio manager's job can be defined as identifying the portfolio with the highest certainty equivalent return. Explain.
14. Despite its obvious simplicity and potential benefits, common stock passive management is a relatively "new" investment tool. Yet in the last 20 years, assets under passive management have grown from essentially zero to hundreds of billions of dollars. What are some possible reasons for the tremendous growth in passive management?
15. It is often argued (especially by active managers) that passive management implies settling for "mediocre" performance. Is this statement necessarily true? Why?
16. Gavin Crowther, an astute investor, once commented, "With the stock market composed of about 6000 actively traded securities, I view my portfolio as about 5950 short positions and 50 long positions." Explain what Gavin means.

17. Why is the "one-stage" approach to security selection theoretically superior to the "two-stage" approach? Why is the "two-stage" approach preferred by most investment managers?
18. Why should investment portfolios, even those that are passively managed, be periodically revised? What factors weigh against making such revisions?
19. A typical money management firm, particularly one specializing in stocks or bonds, invests in essentially the same portfolio for all of its clients, regardless of the clients' individual risk-return preferences. Speculate as to why money managers often operate in this manner. What can clients do to ensure that their portfolios reflect their own specific risk-return preferences?
20. Many investment management clients split their assets among a number of managers. Two rationales for this approach have been described as "diversification of judgment" and "diversification of style." Explain the meaning of these two terms.

CFA Exam Questions

21. Advisor 1: "Long-term asset allocation should be determined using an efficient frontier. Returns, risks (standard deviations), and correlations can be determined for each asset class from historical data. After calculating the efficient frontier for various allocations, you should select the asset mix on the efficient frontier that best meets your fund's risk tolerance."

    Advisor 2: "History gives no guide to the future. For example, everybody agrees that bond risk has increased above historical levels as a result of financial deregulation. A far better approach to long-term asset allocation is to use your best judgment about expected returns on the various asset classes, based on current market conditions. You should rely on your experience to determine the best asset mix and avoid being influenced by computer printouts."

    Advisor 1 Rebuttal: "Current market conditions are not likely to persist into the future and are not appropriate for long-term asset allocation decisions. Moreover, your use of judgment and experience can be influenced by biases and emotions and is not as rigorous a method as my efficient frontier approach."

    Evaluate the strengths and weaknesses of each of the two approaches presented above. Recommend and justify an alternative process for asset allocation that draws from the strengths of each approach and corrects their weaknesses.
22. Colinos Associates is an investment management firm utilizing a very rigorous and disciplined asset allocation methodology as a key element of its investment approach. Twice a year, three or four economic scenarios are developed, based on the judgment of Colinos' most senior people. Probabilities are then assigned to the scenarios; return forecasts for stocks, bonds, and cash equivalents (the only asset types used by the firm) are generated; and expected values are computed for each asset category. These expected values are then combined with historical standard deviations and covariances to produce forecasts of results from various combinations of the three asset classes.

    From this range of possible outcomes, senior staff selects what it regards as the best asset combinations, defined as those combinations promising the highest three-year returns with a 90% probability of achieving a pre-set minimum annual return requirement. These optimal allocations (sample output in the following table) are then presented to all clients for discussion and implementation. The process is repeated in roughly six months' time, when new allocations are developed.

Minimum Annual Required Return (90% Probability	Anticipated 3-Year Compound Annual Return	Recommended Asset Allocation		
		Cash	Bonds	Stocks
–6%	12.0%	10%	30%	60%
–4	11.0	20	40	40
–2	10.0	30	40	30
0	9.0	50	30	20
2	8.5	60	30	10
4	8.0	70	20	10
6	7.5	80	15	5

a. Discuss the strengths and weaknesses of Colinos' asset allocation approach.
b. Recommend and justify an alternative asset allocation approach for wealthy individuals.

KEY TERMS

security analyst
investment committee
approved list
portfolio manager
risk tolerance
certainty equivalent return
passive management
active management
index fund
active position
security selection
asset classes
asset allocation
group selection
market timing
investment styles
equity swap
swap bank
interest rate swap
split-funding

REFERENCES

1. Investment management is discussed in:

William F. Sharpe, "Decentralized Investment Management," *Journal of Finance* 36, no. 2 (May 1981): 217–234.

Jeffery V. Bailey and Robert D. Arnott, "Cluster Analysis and Manager Selection," *Financial Analysts Journal* 42, no. 6 (November/December 1986): 20–28.

Richard A. Brealey, "Portfolio Theory versus Portfolio Practice," *Journal of Portfolio Management* 16, no. 4 (Summer 1990): 6–10.

William F. Sharpe, "The Arithmetic of Active Management," *Financial Analysts Journal* 47, no. 1 (January/February 1991): 7–9.

Robert H. Jeffrey, "Do Clients Need So Many Portfolio Managers?" *Journal of Portfolio Management* 18, no. 1 (Fall 1991): 13–19.

C. B. Garcia and F. J. Gould, "Some Observations on Active Manager Performance and Passive Indexing," *Financial Analysts Journal* 47, no. 6 (November/December 1991): 11–13.

2. Investment management for an individual investor is discussed in:

Burton G. Malkiel, *A Random Walk Down Wall Street* (New York: W. W. Norton, 1990), particularly Chapter 11.

3. Assessment of investor risk tolerance is discussed in:

Gail Farrelly and Dean LeBaron, "Assessing Risk Tolerance Levels: A Prerequisite for Personalizing and Managing Portfolios," *Financial Analysts Journal* 45, no. 1 (January/February 1989): 14–16.

W. V. Harlow and Keith C. Brown, "Understanding and Assessing Financial Risk Tolerance: A Biological Perspective," *Financial Analysts Journal* 46, no. 6 (November/December 1990): 50–62.

William B. Riley, Jr., and K. Victor Chow, "Asset Allocation and Individual Risk Aversion," *Financial Analysts Journal* 48, no. 6 (November/December 1992): 32–37.

4. An extensive discussion of risk tolerance is included in:

William F. Sharpe, *Asset Allocation Tools* (Redwood City, CA: Scientific Press, 1987), Chapter 2.

William F. Sharpe, "Integrated Asset Allocation," *Financial Analysts Journal* 43, no. 5 (September/October 1987): 25–32.

5. Market timing, asset allocation, and investment styles are discussed in the previous article and in:

Keith P. Ambachtsheer, "Portfolio Theory and the Security Analyst," *Financial Analysts Journal* 28, no. 6 (November/December 1972): 53–57.

Jack L. Treynor and Fischer Black, "How to Use Security Analysis to Improve Portfolio Selection," *Journal of Business* 46, no. 1 (January 1973): 66–86.

William F. Sharpe, "Likely Gains From Market Timing," *Financial Analysts Journal* 31, no. 2 (March/April 1975): 60–69.

———, "Major Investment Styles," *Journal of Portfolio Management* 4, no. 2 (Winter 1978): 68–74.

Keith P. Ambachtsheer and James L. Farrell, Jr., "Can Active Management Add Value?" *Financial Analysts Journal* 35, no. 6 (November/December 1979): 39–47.

Robert D. Arnott and James N. von Germeten, "Systematic Asset Allocation," *Financial Analysts Journal* 39, no. 6 (November/December 1983): 31–38.

Jess H. Chua and Richard S. Woodard, *Gains From Market Timing*, Monograph Series in Finance and Economics #1986–2, New York University Salomon Center, Leonard N. Stern School of Business.

Richard A. Brealey, "How to Combine Active Management with Index Funds," *Journal of Portfolio Management* 12, no. 2 (Winter 1986): 4–10.

André F. Perold and William F. Sharpe, "Dynamic Strategies for Asset Allocation," *Financial Analysts Journal* 44, no. 1 (January/February 1988): 16–27.

William F. Sharpe, "Asset Allocation," in *Managing Investment Portfolio: A Dynamic Process*, eds. John L. Maginn and Donald L. Tuttle (Boston, MA: Warren, Gorham & Lamont, 1990), Chapter 7.

David E. Tierney and Kenneth Winston, "Defining and Using Dynamic Completeness Funds to Enhance Total Fund Efficiency," *Financial Analysts Journal* 46, no. 4 (July/August 1990): 49–54.

Craig B. Wainscott, "The Stock-Bond Correlation and its Implications for Asset Allocation," *Financial Analysts Journal* 46, no. 4 (July/August 1990): 55–60, 79.

John Markese, "All Eggs in One Basket, or A Basket for Each Egg?" *AAII Journal* 12, no. 7 (August 1990): 31–33.

David E. Tierney and Kenneth Winston, "Using Generic Benchmarks to Present Manager Styles," *Journal of Portfolio Management* 17, no. 4 (Summer 1991): 33–36.

P. R. Chandy and William Reichenstein, "Timing Strategies and the Risk of Missing Bull Markets," *AAII Journal* 13, no. 7 (August 1991): 17–19.

William F. Sharpe, "Asset Allocation: Management Style and Performance Measurement," *Journal of Portfolio Management* 18, no. 2 (Winter 1992): 7–19.

P. R. Chandy and William Reichenstein, "Stock Market Timing: A Modest Proposal," *AAII Journal* 14, no. 4 (April 1992): 7–10.

Mark Hulbert, "Market Timing Strategies: Taxes are a Drag," *AAII Journal* 14, no. 7 (August 1992): 18–20.

Maria Crawford Scott, "Asset Allocation Among the Three Major Categories," *AAII Journal* 15, no. 4 (April 1993): 13–16.

Mark Hulbert, "Bond Market Timing: Even More Tough Than Timing the Stock Market," *AAII Journal* 16, no. 3 (April 1994): 11–13.

Joseph B. Ludwig, "The Market Timing Approach: A Guide to the Various Strategies," *AAII Journal* 16, no. 4 (May 1994): 11–14.

6. Investing in an international context is discussed in Chapter 26 (see the references listed there) and in:

Robert D. Arnott and Roy D. Henriksson, "A Disciplined Approach to Global Asset Allocation," *Financial Analysts Journal* 45, no. 2 (March/April 1989): 17–28.

Bruno Solnik, *International Investments* (Reading, MA: Addison-Wesley, 1991), particularly Chapter 5.

Fischer Black and Robert Litterman, "Global Portfolio Optimization," *Financial Analysts Journal* 48, no. 5 (September/October 1992): 28–43.

Carlo Capaul, Ian Rowley, and William F. Sharpe, "International Value and Growth Stock Returns," *Financial Analysts Journal* 49, no. 1 (January/February 1993): 27–36.

7. For a discussion of portfolio revision procedures, see:

Gordon J. Alexander and Jack Clark Francis, *Portfolio Analysis* (Englewood Cliffs, NJ: Prentice Hall, 1986), 221–228.

William F. Sharpe, *Asset Allocation Tools* (Redwood City, CA: Scientific Press, 1987), 65–68.

8. Swaps are discussed in many of the textbooks on options and futures listed in the references for Chapters 20 and 21. Also see the following and their lists of references:

Clifford W. Smith, Jr., Charles W. Smithson, and D. Sykes Wilford, *Managing Financial Risk* (New York: Harper & Row, 1990), Chapters 9–12.

Robert H. Litzenberger, "Swaps: Plain and Fanciful," *Journal of Finance* 47, no. 3 (July 1992): 831–850.

John F. Marshall and Vipul K. Bansal, *Financial Engineering* (Miami, FL: Kolb Publishing, 1993), Chapters 13, 23–24.

John F. Marshall and Kenneth R. Kapner, *The Swaps Market* (Miami, FL: Kolb Publishing, 1993).

Frank J. Fabozzi, Franco Modigliani, and Michael G. Ferri, *Foundations of Financial Markets and Institutions* (Englewood Cliffs, NJ: Prentice Hall, 1994), Chapter 29.

Robert W. Kolb, *Futures, Options, and Swaps* (Miami, FL: Kolb Publishing, 1994), Chapters 18–19.

9. For a Canadian perspective on the topics covered in this chapter, see:

J. A. Knowles and W. R. Waters, "Professional Portfolio Management: Is 'Style' Substance?" *Canadian Investment Review* II, no. 2 (Fall 1989).

R. Auger and D. Parisien, "Understanding Asset Allocation," *Canadian Investment Review* IV, no. 1 (Spring 1991).

P. Potvin, "Passive Management, the TSE 300 and the Toronto 35 Stock Indexes," *Canadian Investment Review* V, no. 1 (Spring 1992).

H. Marmer, "Investment Style and Its Impact on Canadian Equity Returns," *Canadian Investment Review* VIII, no. 1 (Spring 1995).

P. Williams, "Special Report: The CIR Roundtable, Shaking Down the Devil: Meeting the Derivatives Challenge Head On," *Canadian Investment Review* VIII no. 2 (Summer 1995).

P. Brodeur and S. Wiseman, "A Style Allocation Is a Powerful Tool for Managing Risk," *Canadian Investment Review* VIII, no. 3 (Fall 1995).

CHAPTER 25

Portfolio Performance Evaluation

An investor who has been paying someone actively to manage his or her portfolio has every right to insist on knowing what sort of performance was obtained. Such information can be used to alter either the constraints placed on the manager, the investment objectives given to the manager, or the amount of money allocated to the manager. Perhaps more importantly, by evaluating performance in specified ways, a client can forcefully communicate his or her interests to the investment manager and, in all likelihood, affect the way in which his or her portfolio is managed. Moreover, an investment manager, by evaluating his or her own performance, can identify sources of strength or weakness. Thus, although the previous chapter indicated portfolio performance evaluation was the last stage of the investment management process, it can also be viewed as simply part of a continuing operation.

Superior performance in the past may have been due to good luck, in which case such performance should not be expected to continue in the future. On the other hand, superior performance in the past may have been due to the actions of a highly skilled investment manager (and support staff). Conversely, inferior performance in the past may have been the result of bad luck, but it may also have been due to excessive turnover, high management fees, or other costs associated with an unskilled investment manager. This suggests that the first task in performance evaluation is to try to determine whether past performance was superior or inferior. Once this task is done, the second task is to try to determine whether such performance was due to skill or luck. Unfortunately, there are difficulties associated with carrying out both of these tasks. Accordingly, this chapter presents not only certain methods that have been advocated and used for evaluating portfolio performance but also a discussion of the difficulties encountered with their use.

MEASURES OF RETURN

Frequently portfolio performance is evaluated over a time interval of at least four years, with returns measured for a number of periods within the interval — typically monthly or quarterly. This provides a fairly adequate sample size for statistical evaluation (for example, if returns are measured quarterly for four years, there will be 16 observations). Sometimes, however, a shorter time interval must be used in order to avoid examining returns earned under a different investment manager. The examples to follow will involve 16 quarterly observations for tractability. In practice, one would prefer monthly observations if only four years were to be analyzed.

In the simplest situation, where the client neither deposits nor withdraws money from the portfolio during a time period, calculation of the portfolio's return is straightforward.

All that is required is that the market value of the portfolio be known at two points in time — the beginning and the end of the period.

In general, the market value of a portfolio at a point in time is determined by adding the market values of all the securities held at that particular time. For example, the value of a common stock portfolio at the beginning of a period is calculated by (1) noting the market price per share of each stock held in the portfolio at that time, (2) multiplying each of these share prices by the corresponding number of shares held, and (3) adding the resulting products. This sum will equal the market value of the portfolio at the beginning of the period. The market value of the portfolio at the end of the period is calculated in the same way, only using end-of-period prices and shares.

With the beginning and ending portfolio values in hand, the return on the portfolio can be calculated by subtracting the beginning value (V_b) from the ending value (V_e) and then dividing the difference by the beginning value:

$$r_p = \frac{V_e - V_b}{V_b}. \tag{25.1}$$

For example, if a portfolio has a market value of $40 million at the beginning of a quarter and a market value of $46 million at the end of the quarter, then the return on this portfolio for the quarter is ($46 million – $40 million)/$40 million = 15%.

Measurement of portfolio returns is complicated by the fact that the client may either add or withdraw money from the portfolio. This means that the percentage change in the market value of the portfolio during a period may not be an accurate measurement of the portfolio's return during that period.

For example, consider a portfolio that at the beginning of a quarter has a market value of $100 million. Just before the end of the quarter the client deposits $5 million with the investment manager, and, subsequently, at the end of the quarter the market value of the portfolio is $103 million. If the quarterly return was measured without consideration of the $5 million deposit, the reported return would be ($103 million – $100 million)/$100 million = 3%. However, this would be incorrect, since $5 million of the ending $103 million market value was not due to the investment actions of the manager. Consideration of the deposit would suggest that a more accurate measure of the quarterly return would be [($103 million – $5 million) – $100 million]/$100 million = –2%.

Identification of exactly *when* any deposits or withdrawals occur is important in accurately measuring portfolio returns. If a deposit or withdrawal occurs just *before* the end of the period, then the return on the portfolio should be calculated by adjusting the ending market value of the portfolio. In the case of a deposit, the ending value should be reduced by the dollar amount (as was done in the previous example); in the case of a withdrawal, the ending value should be increased by the dollar amount.

If a deposit or withdrawal occurs just *after* the start of the period, then the return on the portfolio should be calculated by adjusting the beginning market value of the portfolio. In the case of a deposit, the beginning value should be increased by the dollar amount; in the case of a withdrawal, the beginning value should be decreased by the dollar amount. For example, if the $5 million deposit in the earlier example had been received just after the start of the quarter, the return for the quarter should be calculated as [$103 million – ($100 million + $5 million)]/($100 million + $5 million) = –1.90%.

Dollar-Weighted Returns

Difficulties are encountered when deposits or withdrawals occur sometime *between* the beginning and end of the period. One method that has been used for calculating a portfolio's return in this situation results in the portfolio's **dollar-weighted return** (or internal rate of return). For example, if the \$5 million deposit in the earlier example was made in the middle of the quarter, the dollar-weighted return would be calculated by solving the following equation for r:

$$\$100 \text{ million} = \frac{-\$5 \text{ million}}{(1+r)} + \frac{\$103 \text{ million}}{(1+r)^2}. \tag{25.2}$$

The solution to this equation, $r = -.98\%$, is a semiquarterly rate of return. It can be converted into a quarterly rate of return by adding 1 to it, squaring this value, and then subtracting 1 from the square, resulting in a quarterly return of $[1 + (-.0098)]^2 - 1 = -1.95\%$.[1]

Time-Weighted Returns

Alternatively, the **time-weighted return** on a portfolio can be calculated when there are cash flows occurring between the beginning and end of the period. This method involves using the market value of the portfolio just before each cash flow occurs. In the earlier example, assume that in the middle of the quarter the portfolio had a market value of \$96 million, so that right after the \$5 million deposit the market value was \$96 million + \$5 million = \$101 million. In this case, the return for the first half of the quarter would be (\$96 million – \$100 million)/\$100 million = –4%; the return for the second half of the quarter would be (\$103 million – \$101 million)/\$101 million = 1.98%. Next, these two semiquarterly returns can be combined to give a quarterly return by adding 1 to each return, multiplying the sums, and then subtracting 1 from the product. In the example, this procedure results in a quarterly return of $[(1 - .04)(1 + .0198)] - 1 = -2.1\%$.

Comparing Dollar-Weighted and Time-Weighted Returns

Which method is preferable for calculating the return on a portfolio? In the example given here, the dollar-weighted return was –1.95%, whereas the time-weighted return was –2.1%, suggesting the difference between the two methods may not be very important. Although this may be true in certain situations, examples can be given to show that such differences can be quite large and that the time-weighted return method is preferable.

Consider a hypothetical portfolio that starts a quarter with a market value of \$50 million. In the middle of the quarter, it has fallen to a market value of \$25 million, at which point the client deposits \$25 million with the investment manager. At the end of the quarter the portfolio has a market value of \$100 million. The semiquarterly dollar-weighted return for this portfolio is equal to the value of r in the following equation:

$$\$50 \text{ million} = \frac{-\$25 \text{ million}}{(1+r)} + \frac{\$100 \text{ million}}{(1+r)^2}. \tag{25.3}$$

Solving this equation for r results in a value of 18.6%, which in turn equals a quarterly dollar-weighted return of $(1.186)^2 - 1 = 40.66\%$. However, its quarterly time-weighted

[1] This procedure provides a quarterly return with "quarterly compounding." Alternatively, the semiquarterly return could be doubled, resulting in a quarterly return with "semiquarterly compounding" of $-.98\% \times 2 = -1.96\%$.

return is 0%, since its return for the first half of the quarter was –50% and its return for the second half of the quarter was 100% (note that $(1 - .5)(1 + 1) - 1 = 0\%$).

Comparing these two returns—40.66% and 0%—indicates a sizeable difference exists. However, the time-weighted return figure of 0% is more meaningful for performance evaluation than the dollar-weighted return figure of 40.66%. To understand why, consider the return over the entire quarter on each dollar that was in the portfolio at the start of the quarter. Each dollar lost half of its value over the first half of the quarter, but then the remaining half-dollar doubled its value over the second half. Consequently, a dollar at the beginning was worth a dollar at the end, suggesting a return of 0% on the portfolio is a more accurate measure of the investment manager's performance than the 40.66% figure.

In general, the dollar-weighted return method of measuring a portfolio's return for purposes of evaluation is regarded as inappropriate. The reason behind this view is that the return is strongly influenced by the size and timing of the cash flows (namely, deposits and withdrawals) over which the investment manager has no control. In the example, the dollar-weighted return was 40.66% because the client fortuitously made a big deposit just before the portfolio appreciated rapidly in value. Thus, the 40.66% return figure is due at least partly to the actions of the client, not the manager.

▶ Annualizing Returns

The previous discussion has focused on calculating quarterly returns. Such returns may be added or multiplied to obtain an annual measure of return. For example, if the return in the first, second, third, and fourth quarters of a given year are denoted by r_1, r_2, r_3, and r_4, respectively, then the annual return could be calculated by adding the four figures:

$$\text{Annual return} = r_1 + r_2 + r_3 + r_4. \tag{25.4}$$

Alternatively, the annual return could be calculated by adding 1 to each quarterly return, then multiplying the four figures, and finally subtracting 1 from the resulting product:

$$\text{Annual return} = [(1 + r_1)(1 + r_2)(1 + r_3)(1 + r_4)] - 1. \tag{25.5}$$

This return is more accurate because it reflects the value that $1 would have at the end of the year if it were invested at the beginning of the year and grew *with compounding* at the rate of r_1 for the first quarter, r_2 for the second quarter, r_3 for the third quarter, and r_4 for the fourth quarter. That is, it assumes reinvestment of both the dollar and any earnings at the end of each quarter.

MAKING RELEVANT COMPARISONS

The essential idea behind performance evaluation is to compare the returns obtained by the investment manager through active management with the returns that could have been obtained for the client if one or more appropriate alternative portfolios had been chosen for investment. The reason for this comparison is straightforward—performance should be evaluated on a relative basis, not on an absolute basis.

As an example, consider a client who is told that his or her portfolio, invested in common stocks and of average risk, had a return of 20% last year. Does this suggest superior or inferior performance? If the stock market went up by 10% last year, then it suggests superior performance and is good news. However, if the stock market went up by 30% last year, then it suggests inferior performance and is bad news. In order to infer whether the manager's performance is superior or inferior, the returns on similar portfolios that are either actively or passively managed are needed for comparison.

Such comparison portfolios are often referred to as **benchmark portfolios**. In selecting them, the client should be certain they are relevant, feasible, and known in advance, meaning they should represent alternative portfolios that could have been chosen for investment instead of the portfolio being evaluated. That is, the benchmark should reflect the objectives of the client. Hence, if the objective is to earn superior returns by investing in small stocks, then the TSE 35 would be an inappropriate benchmark. Instead, an index like the *Financial Post* All-Canadian Junior Index may be more suitable. *Return* is a key aspect of performance, of course, but some way must be found to account for the portfolio's exposure to *risk*. The choice of benchmark portfolios may be restricted to portfolios perceived to have similar levels of risk, thereby permitting a direct comparison of returns.

Figure 25.1 illustrates such a comparison for a hypothetical common stock (or "equity") portfolio referred to as Fund 07632. In this figure, Fund 07632's performance for each year is represented by a diamond. The hypothetical comparison portfolios are other common stock portfolios that are represented by the box surrounding the diamond (such a representation

Figure 25.1

Comparing returns of equity portfolios.

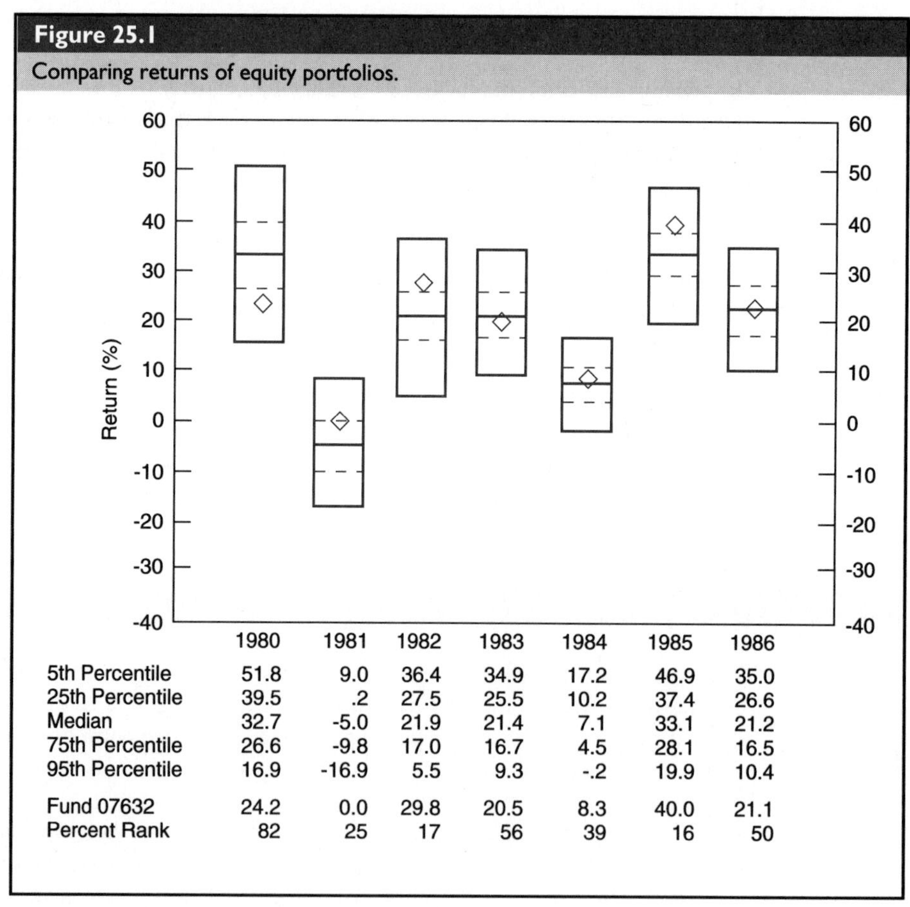

	1980	1981	1982	1983	1984	1985	1986
5th Percentile	51.8	9.0	36.4	34.9	17.2	46.9	35.0
25th Percentile	39.5	.2	27.5	25.5	10.2	37.4	26.6
Median	32.7	-5.0	21.9	21.4	7.1	33.1	21.2
75th Percentile	26.6	-9.8	17.0	16.7	4.5	28.1	16.5
95th Percentile	16.9	-16.9	5.5	9.3	-.2	19.9	10.4
Fund 07632	24.2	0.0	29.8	20.5	8.3	40.0	21.1
Percent Rank	82	25	17	56	39	16	50

SOURCE: Adapted from SEI, *Funds Evaluation Service.*

Custom Benchmark Portfolios

Investment management has become increasingly specialized in recent years. Managers have chosen not only to concentrate on specific asset classes (for example, stocks or bonds), but within those asset classes they have further focused their efforts on certain types of securities. This specialization has been particularly prevalent among domestic common stock managers. For example, some managers specialize in small, emerging growth stocks. Others select only from certain industries, such as health care. These specializations have come to be known as "investment styles." Investment styles have significant ramifications for the evaluation of investment manager performance.

Investment management can be viewed as a fishing contest. Each angler has his or her own fishing hole (investment style). No one fishing hole is assumed to be any better than another, although from year to year the sizes and quantity of fish fluctuate independently in each hole. The anglers attempt to catch the largest fish from their fishing holes. How should institutional investor clients evaluate the proficiency of these anglers based on their catches? It would make little sense to directly compare the anglers' respective catches. If Angler A's fishing hole was extremely well-stocked this year and Angler B's was not, Angler B would be at a tremendous disadvantage. More appropriately, clients would like to compare what each angler caught against the opportunities available in their respective fishing holes. In other words, the clients should want to take into account the impact of managers' investment styles on their performance.

Investment styles tend to dominate the performance of investment managers within a particular asset class. For example, suppose that the domestic common stock market was split along two dimensions similar to those discussed in Chapter 17: market capitalization (share price times shares outstanding) and growth prospects. In 1991, for example, the best-performing group comprised large, high-growth stocks, which returned 45.0%. Conversely, small, low-growth stocks returned 19.0%, a difference of 26 percentage points. Differences among investment styles of similar magnitudes can be found in other years. These differences are typically large enough so that no investment manager can hope to consistently overcome the performance effect of his or her investment style. Therefore, to evaluate a manager's investment skill, how the manager has performed relative to his or her investment style should be considered explicitly.

One means of dealing with this issue is to develop a comparison portfolio that specifically represents the manager's investment style. This comparison portfolio is referred to as a *custom benchmark portfolio*. The custom benchmark contains the types of securities from which the manager typically selects. Further, these securities are weighted in the custom benchmark in a manner similar to weights typically assigned by the manager. Moreover, the custom benchmark displays portfolio characteristics (for example, price-earnings ratios, earnings growth rates, and market capitalizations) consistent with the manager's actual portfolio.

Consider a manager whose investment style entails investing in large-capitalization, high-dividend-yield stocks. In building portfolios, the manager follows certain rules, some explicitly, others implicitly. For example, the manager does not buy stocks with less than $500 million in market capitalization. All stocks in the manager's portfolio must display at least a 5% dividend yield. The manager assigns each stock an equal weight in the portfolio. Further, to avoid overconcentrations, no industry may constitute more than 10% of the portfolio's market value.

A custom benchmark can be designed to reflect these characteristics of the manager's investment style. The custom benchmark might

INSTITUTIONAL ISSUES (continued)

be composed of 300 stocks, as opposed to the manager's portfolio, which might contain only 30 stocks. The manager, in effect, has selected the 30 stocks that he or she thinks will perform the best. An evaluation of the manager's performance over time will be based on how these 30 stocks perform relative to the 300 stocks.

This performance evaluation process takes advantage of a powerful paired-comparison test. Given a group of stocks, can the manager consistently identify the best-performing issues? The question is simple and the results easy to interpret. No special risk-adjusted performance measures are required. It the custom benchmark has been properly constructed, it exhibits a risk level consistent with that exhibited on average by the manager.

The primary drawback of custom benchmarks is the effort required to design them. Each manager's investment style has unique aspects, and not all of them are as explicit as those of the large-capitalization, high-yield manager discussed above. Typically, identifying those unique aspects involves examining past portfolios and engaging in lengthy discussions with the manager.

Recently a number of analysts have adopted a method in which a benchmark made up of combinations of standard indices is constructed based on statistical analysis of a manager's past returns. The use of this procedure, known as *style analysis*, can in many cases provide some of the advantages of custom benchmark portfolios at a fraction of the cost, time, and effort. (For details on this approach, see the references listed at the end of the chapter.)

Custom benchmarks, whether derived via detailed analyses or using style analysis, can provide effective performance evaluations. Moreover, they have uses outside of performance evaluation. For example, as discussed in Chapter 24's *Institutional Issues* section, clients who hire more than one investment manager can use custom benchmarks to examine how various investment styles fit together into an aggregate portfolio. This type of analysis permits a client to better understand and control the investment risks present in the client's total portfolio.

is known as a *box plot* or a *floating bar chart*). The top and bottom lines of the box indicate the returns of the 5th and 95th percentile comparison portfolios, respectively. Similarly, the top and bottom dashed lines represent the 25th and 75th percentiles, respectively. The solid line in the middle represents the median (that is, the 50th percentile) portfolio. Note that this particular evaluation technique presumes that the comparison portfolios exhibit risk similar to Fund 07632 and that they represent feasible alternatives for Fund 07632's owner. Failing to meet these conditions (as is often the case in such peer group comparisons) will generally invalidate the performance evaluation.

Alternatively, risk may be explicitly measured so that a single measure of performance taking both return and risk into account can be employed. This will allow benchmark portfolios of varying degrees of risk to be compared with the portfolio being evaluated.

RISK-ADJUSTED MEASURES OF PERFORMANCE FOR EQUITY PORTFOLIOS

Having measured the periodic returns for a portfolio during an evaluation interval (for example, quarterly returns for a four-year evaluation interval), the next step is to determine if these returns represent superior or inferior performance. In order to do this, an estimate of the portfolio's risk level during the evaluation interval is needed. For equity portfolios, two kinds of risk can be estimated—the portfolio's market (or systematic) risk, measured by its beta, and the portfolio's total risk, measured by its standard deviation. It is important to analyze risk appropriately. The key issue here is determining the impact of the portfolio on the client's overall level of risk. If the client has many other assets, then the market risk of the portfolio provides the relevant measure of the portfolio's impact on the client's overall level of risk. If, however, the portfolio provides the client's sole support, then its total risk is the relevant measure of risk. Risk-adjusted performance evaluation is generally based on one of these two viewpoints, taking either market risk or total risk into consideration.

Assume there are T time periods in the evaluation interval (for example, $T = 16$ when there are four years of quarterly data) and let r_{pt} denote the return on the portfolio during period t. The average return on the portfolio, denoted by ar_p, is simply

$$ar_p = \frac{\sum_{t=1}^{T} r_{pt}}{T}. \tag{25.6}$$

Having calculated ar_p, the *ex post* (that is, after the fact) standard deviation can be calculated as

$$\sigma_p = \left[\frac{\sum_{t=1}^{T} (r_{pt} - ar_p)^2}{T - 1}\right]^{1/2} \tag{25.7}$$

This estimate of the portfolio's standard deviation can be used as an indication of the amount of total risk that the portfolio had during the evaluation interval.[2] It can be compared directly with the standard deviations of other portfolios, as illustrated in Figure 25.2. (This figure is to be interpreted in the same manner as Figure 25.1.)

The returns of a portfolio may also be compared with those of a substitute for the market portfolio, such as the TSE 300, in order to determine the portfolio's *ex post* beta during the evaluation interval. Denoting the *excess return* on the portfolio during period t by $er_{pt} = r_{pt} - r_{ft}$, the return on the TSE 300 (or some other market substitute) during

[2] Sometimes the excess return for a portfolio, which is equal to its return minus the risk-free rate $(r_{pt} - r_{ft})$, is used instead of r_{pt} in equation (25.6) to determine the average excess return (denoted by aer_p). Then, the summation in the numerator of equation (25.6) is carried out using $[(r_{pt} - r_{ft}) - aer_p]^2$ instead of $(r_{pt} - ar_p)^2$. The resulting number is the standard deviation of excess returns, which is sometimes used as an estimate of the total risk of the portfolio. Typically, the two standard deviations are quite similar in numerical value.

Figure 25.2

Comparing standard deviations of equity portfolios.

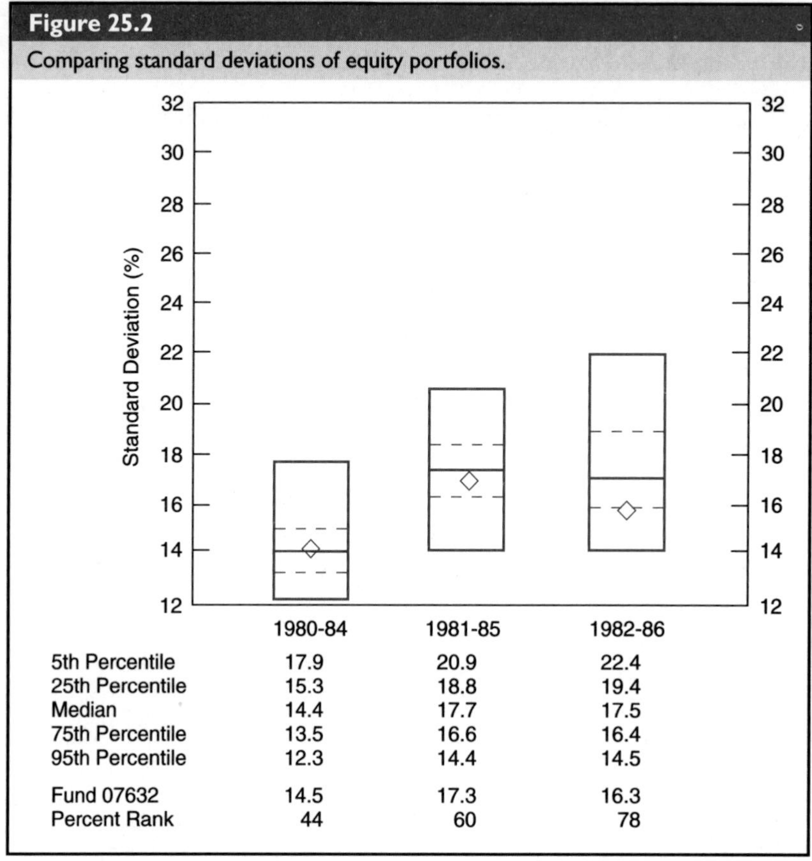

	1980-84	1981-85	1982-86
5th Percentile	17.9	20.9	22.4
25th Percentile	15.3	18.8	19.4
Median	14.4	17.7	17.5
75th Percentile	13.5	16.6	16.4
95th Percentile	12.3	14.4	14.5
Fund 07632	14.5	17.3	16.3
Percent Rank	44	60	78

SOURCE: Adapted from SEI, *Funds Evaluation Service.*

period t by r_{Mt}, and the excess return on the TSE 300 during period t by $er_{Mt} = r_{Mt} - r_{ft}$, this beta can be estimated as follows:

$$\beta_p = \frac{\left(\sum_{t=1}^{T} er_{Mt} er_{pt}\right) - \left(\sum_{t=1}^{T} er_{pt} \sum_{t=1}^{T} er_{Mt}\right)}{\left(T\sum_{t=1}^{T} er_{Mt}^2\right) - \left(\sum_{t=1}^{T} er_{Mt}\right)^2}. \tag{25.8}$$

This estimate of the portfolio's beta can be used as an indication of the amount of market risk that the portfolio had during the evaluation interval.[3] It can be compared directly with the betas of other portfolios, as illustrated in Figure 25.3.

Although a portfolio's return and a measure of its risk can be compared individually with those of other portfolios, as in Figures 25.1 through 25.3, it is often not clear how the

[3] Equation (25.8) corresponds to the formula for estimating the slope term in a simple regression model where the independent variable is er_{Mt} and the dependent variable is er_{pt}. Sometimes returns are used in equation (23.7), where er_{Mt} is replaced by r_{Mt} and er_{pt} is replaced by r_{pt}. In this situation, the beta corresponds to the slope term in the *market model* for the portfolio. Typically, the two betas are quite similar in numerical value.

Figure 25.3
Comparing betas of equity portfolios.

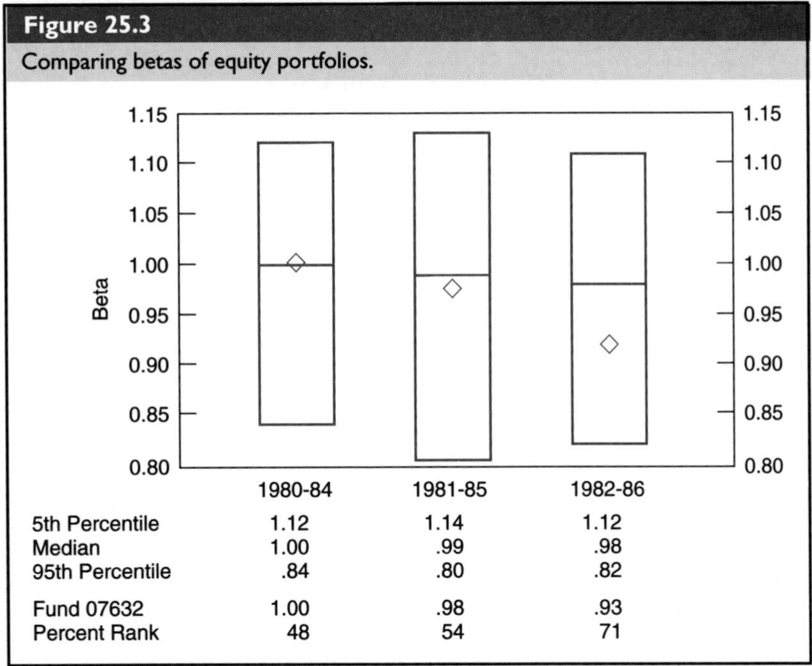

SOURCE: Adapted from SEI, *Funds Evaluation Service.*

portfolio performed on a risk-adjusted basis relative to these other portfolios. For the fund shown in the figures, the average percent rank for the portfolio's return over the five years ending in 1986 is $(17 + 56 + 39 + 16 + 50)/5 = 36\%$. Over the same period, its standard deviation put it in the 78th percent rank. Assuming the client is concerned with total risk, how does he or she interpret these percent ranks? In the case of the return, the portfolio was slightly above average; in terms of standard deviation, it was less risky than approximately three-fourths of the other portfolios. Overall, this suggests that the portfolio did better on a risk-adjusted basis than the others, but it does not give the client a clear and precise sense of how much better.

Such a sense can be conveyed by certain CAPM-based measures of portfolio performance. Each one of these measures provides an estimate of a portfolio's risk-adjusted performance, thereby allowing the client to see how the portfolio performed relative to other portfolios as well as the market. They are presented next.

Ex Post Characteristic Lines

Over an evaluation interval, an *ex post security market line* (SML) can be estimated by determining the average risk-free rate and market return:

$$ar_f = \frac{\sum_{t=1}^{T} r_{ft}}{T} \tag{25.9}$$

$$ar_M = \frac{\sum_{t=1}^{T} r_{Mt}}{T} \tag{25.10}$$

Once these averages have been calculated, the *ex post* SML is simply the equation of the line going through the points $(0, ar_f)$ and $(1, ar_M)$:

$$ar_p^e = ar_f + (ar_M - ar_f)\beta_p. \tag{25.11}$$

Equivalently, the equilibrium average return during this interval of time for a portfolio with a beta of β_p would simply be equal to $ar_f + (ar_M - ar_f)\beta_p$. Accordingly, ar_p^e can be used as the benchmark return for a portfolio with a beta of β_p.

Panel (2) of Table 25.1 presents an example by using the quarterly returns for the TSE 300 over a 16-quarter time interval, along with corresponding returns on 91-day Treasury bills. Using equations (25.9) and (25.10), the average risk-free return and market return were, respectively, 2.39% and 3.05%. Inserting these values into equation (25.11), the *ex post* SML for this time interval was

$$\begin{aligned} ar_p^e &= 2.39\% + (3.05\% - 2.39\%)\beta_p \\ &= 2.39\% + 0.66\%\beta_p. \end{aligned} \tag{25.12}$$

Table 25.1

The *Ex Post* Characteristic Line for the First Fund.

a. Return Data

Quarter	*Treasury Bill Return*	*First Fund*		*TSE 300*	
		Return	*Excess Return*	*Return*	*Excess Return*
1	2.64%	3.94%	1.30%	5.84%	3.20%
2	2.20	1.27	−0.93	2.02	−0.18
3	2.07	−4.89	−6.96	−2.74	−4.81
4	2.08	7.01	4.93	3.74	1.66
5	1.82	16.59	14.77	22.70	20.88
6	2.00	−0.57	−2.57	0.68	−1.32
7	2.26	8.78	6.52	4.94	2.68
8	1.95	−29.44	−31.39	−18.33	−20.28
9	2.09	10.13	8.04	5.65	3.56
10	2.21	1.50	−0.71	4.72	2.51
11	2.32	−3.91	6.23	−3.64	−5.96
12	2.60	7.90	5.30	4.20	1.60
13	2.80	12.03	9.23	6.47	3.67
14	3.09	3.53	0.44	6.15	3.06
15	3.02	10.80	7.78	5.72	2.70
16	3.04	1.89	−1.15	1.58	−1.46

b. Calculations[a]

Quarter	First Fund Excess Returns = Y (1)	TSE 300 Excess Returns = X (2)	Y^2 (3)	X^2 (4)	$Y \times X$ (5)
1	1.30	3.2	10.24	1.695204	4.1664
2	–0.93	–0.18	0.0324	0.871235	0.168012
3	–6.96	–4.81	23.1361	48.40402	33.46461
4	4.93	1.66	2.7556	24.30292	8.183468
5	14.77	20.88	435.9744	218.1056	308.3641
6	–2.57	–1.32	1.7424	6.623416	3.397152
7	6.52	2.68	7.1824	42.54170	17.48003
8	–31.39	–20.28	411.2784	985.3572	636.5973
9	8.04	3.56	12.6736	64.71880	28.63948
10	–0.71	2.51	6.3001	0.503674	–1.78134
11	–6.23	–5.96	35.5216	38.84779	37.14748
12	5.30	1.6	2.56	28.11120	8.4832
13	9.23	3.67	13.4689	85.10247	33.85611
14	0.44	3.06	9.3636	0.193424	1.345788
15	7.78	2.7	7.29	60.48172	20.9979
16	–1.15	–1.46	2.1316	1.317444	1.675788
	$\Sigma Y = 8.37$	$\Sigma X = 11.51$	$\Sigma Y^2 = 981.65$	$\Sigma X^2 = 1607.2$	$\Sigma XY = 1142.2$

1. Beta:

$$\frac{(T \times \Sigma XY) - (\Sigma Y \times \Sigma X)}{(T \times \Sigma X^2) - (\Sigma X)^2} = \frac{(16 \times 1142.19) - (11.51 \times 8.37)}{(16 \times 981.65) - (11.51)^2} = 1.16$$

2. Alpha:

$$\frac{\Sigma Y}{T} - \left(\text{Beta} \times \frac{\Sigma X}{T}\right) = \frac{8.37}{16} - \left(1.16 \times \frac{11.51}{16}\right) = -0.31\%$$

3. Standard deviation of random error term:

$$\left[\frac{\Sigma Y^2 - (\text{alpha} \times \Sigma Y) - (\text{Beta} \times \Sigma XY)}{T-2}\right]^{1/2}$$

$$= \left[\frac{1607.18 - (-0.31 \times 8.37) - (1.16 \times 1142.19)}{16-2}\right]^{1/2} = 4.49\%$$

4. Standard error of beta:

$$\frac{\text{Standard deviation of random error term}}{[\Sigma X^2 - (\Sigma X)^2/T^{1/2}} = \frac{4.49}{[981.65 - (11.51)^2/16]^{1/2}} = .14$$

5. Standard error of alpha:

$$\frac{\text{Standard deviation of random error term}}{[T - (\Sigma X)^2/\Sigma X^2]^{1/2}} = \frac{4.49}{[16 - (11.51)^2/981.65]^{1/2}} = 1.12$$

6. Correlation coefficient:

$$\frac{(T \times \Sigma XY) - (\Sigma Y \times \Sigma X)}{[(T \times \Sigma Y^2) - (\Sigma Y)^2] \times [(T \times \Sigma X^2) - (\Sigma X)^2]^{1/2}}$$

$$= \frac{(16 \times 1142.19) - (11.51 \times 8.37)}{[(16 \times 1607.18) - (8.37)^2] \times [(16 \times 981.65) - (11.51)^2]^{1/2}} = .91$$

7. Coefficient of determination:

$$(\text{Correlation coefficient})^2 = (.91)^2 = .83$$

8. Coefficient of nondetermination:

$$1 - \text{coefficient of determination} = 1 - .83 = .17$$

---

[a] All summations are to be carried out over t, where t goes from 1 to T (in this example, $t = 1, \ldots, 16$).

Thus, after estimating a portfolio's *ex post* beta and entering this value on the right-hand side of equation (25.12), a benchmark return for the portfolio can be determined. For example, a portfolio with a beta of .8 would have a benchmark return of 2.39% + (0.66% × .8) = 2.92%. Figure 25.4 presents a graph of the *ex post* SML given by equation (25.12).

If the average return on a portfolio was ar_p, calculated as shown in equation (25.6), then one measure of its risk-adjusted performance would be the difference between its average return and the return on its corresponding benchmark. This difference is generally referred to as the portfolio's ***ex post*** **alpha** (or differential return) and is denoted by α_p(see Chapter 22):

$$\alpha_p = ar_p - ar_p^e. \tag{22.3}$$

A positive value of α_p for a portfolio would indicate that the portfolio had an average return greater than the benchmark return, suggesting its performance was superior. On the other hand, a negative value of α_p would indicate that the portfolio had an average return less than the benchmark return, suggesting its performance was inferior.[4]

By substituting the right-hand side of equation (25.11) for ar_p^e in equation (22.3), it can be seen that a portfolio's *ex post* alpha based on the *ex post* SML is equal to:

$$\alpha_p = ar_p - [ar_f + (ar_M - ar_f)\beta_p]. \tag{25.13}$$

After determining the values for α_p and β_p for a portfolio, the ***ex post*** **characteristic line** for the portfolio can be written as

$$r_p - r_f = \alpha_p + \beta_p(r_M - r_f). \tag{25.14}$$

The characteristic line is similar to the market model except that the portfolio's returns and the market index's returns are expressed in excess of the risk-free return. Graphically, this is the equation of a straight line, where $r_M - r_f$ is measured on the horizontal axis and $r_p - r_f$ is measured on the vertical axis. Furthermore, the line has a vertical intercept of α_p and a slope of β_p.

As an example, consider the performance of the hypothetical portfolio "First Fund," indicated in panel (2) of Table 25.1 for the evaluation interval. During this interval, the First

---

[4] This measure of performance is sometimes known as the *Jensen coefficient* because it was developed by Michael C. Jensen in "The Performance of Mutual Funds in the Period 1945 -1964," *Journal of Finance* 23, no. 2 (May 1968): 389–416.

Figure 25.4
Performance evaluation using the *ex post* SML.

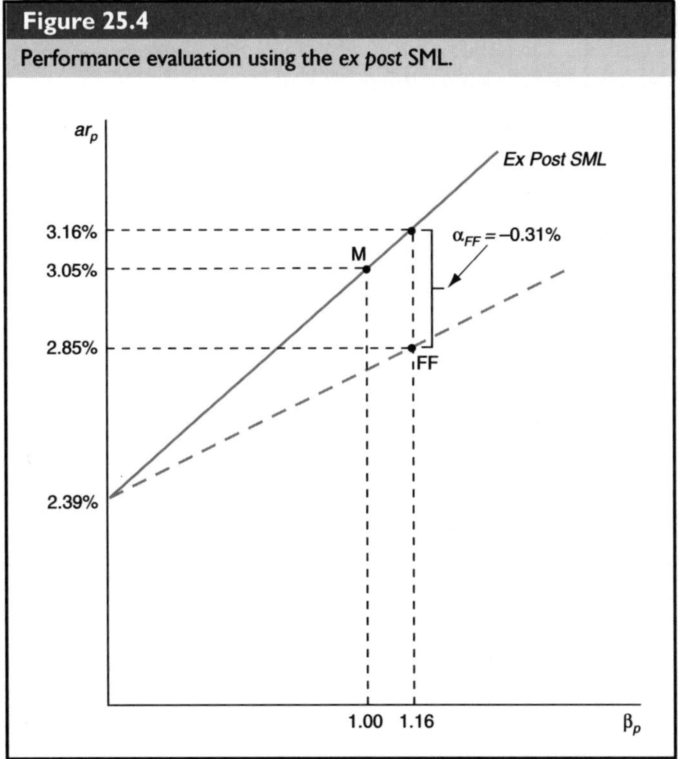

Fund had an average quarterly return of 2.85%. Using equation (25.8), it can be shown that First Fund had a beta of 1.16. Having an average beta over the 16 quarters that is greater than the market portfolio's beta of 1 indicates that First Fund was relatively aggressive (if it were less than 1, it would have been defensive).

Given these values for its beta and average return, the location of First Fund in Figure 25.4 is represented by the point having coordinates of (1.16, 2.85%), denoted by *FF*. The exact vertical distance from *FF* to the *ex post* SML can be calculated by using equation (25.13):

$$\begin{aligned}\alpha_p &= ar_p - [ar_f + (ar_M - ar_f)\beta_p]\\ &= 2.85\% - [2.39\% + (3.05\% - 2.39\%)1.16]\\ &= -0.31\%.\end{aligned}$$

Since *FF* lies below the *ex post* SML, its *ex post* alpha is negative, and its performance would be viewed as inferior.[5] Using equation (25.14), the *ex post* characteristic line for First Fund would be

$$r_p - r_f = -0.31\% + 1.16(r_M - r_f).$$

[5] Alternatively, if *FF*'s average return had been 4%, then its coordinates would have been (1.16, 4.00%), placing it above the *ex post* SML. In this situation, *FF*'s *ex post* alpha would have been 0.84%, and its performance would have been viewed as superior.

Figure 25.4 provides an illustration of this line.[6]

The method of determining a portfolio's *ex post* alpha, beta, and characteristic line suggests the use of a five-step procedure:

1. Determine the periodic rates of return for the portfolio and market index over the time interval, as well as the corresponding risk-free rates.
2. Determine the average market return and risk-free rate by using the formulas in equations (25.9) and (25.10).
3. Determine the portfolio's *ex post* beta by using the formula in equation (25.8).
4. Determine the portfolio's *ex post* alpha by using the formula given in equation (25.13).
5. Insert these values for alpha and beta in equation (25.14) in order to determine the portfolio's *ex post* characteristic line.

However, there is a simpler method for determining a portfolio's *ex post* alpha, beta, and characteristic line that also provides a number of other pieces of information relating to the portfolio's performance. This method involves the use of **simple linear regression** and corresponds to the method presented in Chapters 8 and 17 for estimating the market model line for an individual security.

With this method, the excess return on portfolio p in a given period t is viewed as having three components. The first component is the portfolio's alpha, the second component is a risk premium equal to the excess return on the market times the portfolio's beta, and the third component is a random error term.[7] These three components can be seen on the right-hand side of the following equation:

$$r_{pt} - r_{ft} = \alpha_p + \beta_p(r_{Mt} - r_{ft}) + \epsilon_{pt}. \tag{25.15}$$

Since α_p and β_p are assumed to be constant during the evaluation interval, equation (25.15) can be viewed as a regression equation. Accordingly, there are certain standard formulas for estimating α_p, β_p, and a number of other statistical parameters associated with the regression equation.

Panel (b) of Table 25.1 presents these formulas, with First Fund being used as an example. As can be seen, the formulas indicate that First Fund's *ex post* alpha and beta were equal to –0.31% and 1.16, respectively. These values are the same as those arising when equations (25.8) and (25.13) were used earlier. Indeed, they will always result in the same values.

Figure 25.5 presents a scatter diagram of the excess returns on First Fund and the TSE 300. Based on equation (25.15), the regression equation for First Fund is

$$r_{FF} - r_f = -0.31\% + 1.16(r_M - r_f) + \epsilon_{FF} \tag{25.16}$$

---

[6] An alternative measure of performance involves dividing the *ex post* alpha by an estimate of the *ex post* unique (or unsystematic) risk of the portfolio. This measure, known as the ***appraisal ratio***, would be equal to –0.31%/4.48% = –0.07 for First Fund. Comparisons can be made with the value of the appraisal ratio for the market portfolio (its value is defined to be 0) and other portfolios. Note that a positive value indicates superior performance and that the larger the value, the better the performance. See Jack L. Treynor and Fischer Black, "How to Use Security Analysis to Improve Portfolio Selection," *Journal of Business* 46, no. 1 (January 1973): 66–86.

[7] The random error term can be viewed as a number that arises from a spin of a roulette wheel, where the numbers on the wheel are symmetrically distributed around zero. That is, the expected outcome from a spin of the roulette wheel is zero; the standard deviation associated with the wheel is denoted by $\sigma\epsilon_p$.

where –0.31% and 1.16 are the estimated *ex post* alpha and beta for First Fund. As mentioned earlier, also shown in the figure is the *ex post* characteristic line for First Fund, a line that is derived by the use of simple linear regression:

$$r_{FF} - r_f = -0.31\% + 1.16(r_M - r_f). \tag{25.17}$$

The vertical distance between each point in the scatter diagram and the regression line represents an estimate of the size of the random error term for the corresponding quarter. The exact distance can be found by rewriting equation (25.16) as

$$\epsilon_{FF} = (r_{FF} - r_f) - [-0.31\% + 1.16(r_M - r_f)]. \tag{25.18}$$

For example, in the twelfth quarter, the excess return on First Fund and the TSE 300 were 5.30% and 1.60%, respectively. The value of ϵ_{FF} for that quarter can be calculated by using equation (25.18) as follows:

$$\begin{aligned}\epsilon_{FF} &= 5.30 - (-0.31 = 1.16 \times 1.60) \\ &= 3.75\%.\end{aligned}$$

The values of ϵ_{FF} can be calculated similarly for the other 15 quarters of the evaluation interval. The standard deviation of the resulting set of 16 numbers is an estimate of the standard deviation of the random error term (also known as the residual standard deviation), and is shown in panel (b) of Table 25.1 to be equal to 4.48%. This number can be viewed as an estimate of the *ex post* unique (or unsystematic or nonmarket) risk of First Fund.

The regression line for First Fund that is shown in Figure 25.5 is the line of best fit for the scatter diagram. What is meant by "best fit?" Given that a straight line is defined by its intercept and slope, there are no other values for alpha and beta that will define a straight line that fits the scatter diagram any better than this one. In simple regression, best fit means that there is no line that could be drawn such that the resulting standard deviation of the random error term is smaller than the one of best fit.

It should be pointed out that a portfolio's "true" *ex post* beta cannot be observed. All that can be done is to estimate its value. Thus, even if a portfolio's true beta remained the same forever, its estimated value, obtained in the manner illustrated in Table 25.1 and Figure 25.5, would still change from time to time because of errors (known as sampling errors) in estimating it. For example, if a different set of 16 quarters were examined, the resulting estimated beta for First Fund would almost certainly be different from 1.13.

The standard error of beta shown in Table 25.1 indicates the extent of such estimation errors. Given a number of necessary assumptions (for example, the true beta did not change during the estimation period), the chances are roughly two out of three that the true beta is within one standard error, plus or minus, of the estimated beta. Thus, First Fund's true beta is likely to be between the values of 1.16 – 0.14 = 1.02 and 1.16 + 0.14 = 1.30. Similarly, the value for standard error of alpha provides an indication of the magnitude of the possible sampling error that has been made in estimating it.

The value for the correlation coefficient provides an indication of how closely the excess returns on First Fund were associated with the excess returns on the TSE 300. Since its range is between –1 and +1, the value for First Fund of 0.91 indicates a strong positive relationship between First Fund and the TSE 300. That is, larger excess returns for First Fund seem to have been closely associated with larger excess returns on the TSE 300.

The coefficient of determination represents the proportion of variation in the excess return on First Fund that is related to the variation in the excess return on the TSE 300.

Figure 25.5

Ex post characteristic line for First Fund.

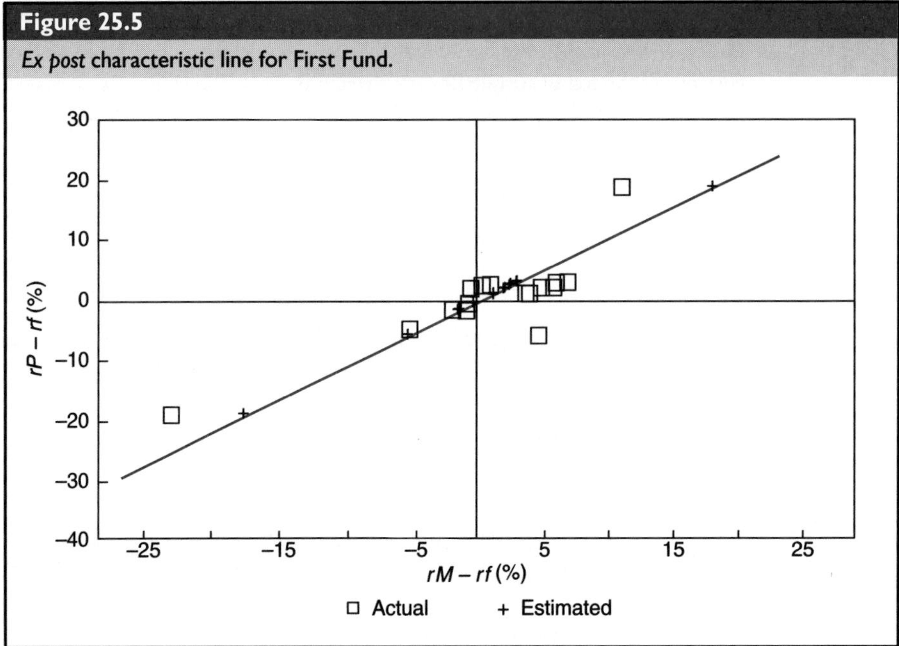

That is, it shows how much of the movement in First Fund's excess returns can be explained by movements in the excess returns on the TSE 300. With a value of 0.83, it can be seen that 83% of the movement in the excess return on First Fund over the 16 quarters can be attributed to movement in the excess return on the TSE 300.

Since the coefficient of nondetermination is 1 minus the coefficient of determination, it represents the proportion of movement in the excess return on First Fund that is not due to movement in the excess return on the TSE 300. Thus, 17% of the movement in First Fund cannot be attributed to movement in the TSE 300.

Although Table 25.1 shows the formulas for calculating all these values, it should be pointed out that there are many different software packages that can carry out all these calculations in a fraction of a second. The only substantive effort involves gathering all the return data shown in panel (a) of Table 25.1 and then entering the information into a computer.

The Reward-to-Volatility Ratio

Closely related to the differential return measure of portfolio performance is a measure known as the **reward-to-volatility ratio**.[8] This measure, denoted RVOL_p, also uses the *ex post* security market line to form a benchmark for performance evaluation. The calculation of the reward-to-volatility ratio for a portfolio involves dividing its average excess return by its market risk:

$$\text{RVOL}_p = \frac{ar_p - ar_f}{\beta_p}. \tag{25.19}$$

[8] This measure of performance is sometimes known as the *Treynor ratio* because it was developed by Jack L. Treynor in "How to Rate Management of Investment Funds," *Harvard Business Review* 43, no. 1 (January-February 1965): 63–75.

Here, the beta of the portfolio can be determined using the formula in equation (25.8).

Continuing with the example of First Fund, it was noted earlier that its average return for the evaluation interval was 2.85 and the average Treasury bill rate was 2.39%. Thus, the average excess return for First Fund was 2.85% – 2.39% = 0.46% and, given a beta of 1.16, its reward-to-volatility ratio was 0.46%/1.16 = 0.40%.

The reward-to-volatility ratio corresponds to the slope of a line originating at the average risk-free rate and going through the point (β_p, ar_p). This can be seen by noting that the slope of a line is easily determined if two points on the line are known — it is simply the vertical distance between the two points (rise) divided by the horizontal distance between the two points (run). In this case, the vertical distance is $ar_p - ar_f$ and the horizontal distance is $\beta_p - 0 = \beta_p$, so the slope is $(ar_p - ar_f)/\beta_p$; this corresponds to the formula for RVOL_p given in equation (25.19). Note that the value being measured on the horizontal axis is β_p and the value being measured on the vertical axis is ar_p, suggesting that the line can be drawn on the same diagram as the *ex post* SML.

In the First Fund example, remember that the *ex post* SML was shown by the solid line in Figure 25.4. Also appearing in this figure was the point denoted by *FF*, corresponding to $(\beta_p, ar_p) = (1.16, 2.85\%)$ for First Fund. The line in this figure with dots and dashes originates from the point $(0, ar_f) = (0, 2.39\%)$, goes through *FF*, and has a slope of $(2.85\% - 2.39\%)/1.16 = 0.40\%$, which corresponds to the value noted earlier for RVOL_p.

The benchmark for comparison with this measure of performance is the slope of the *ex post* SML. Since this line goes through the points $(0, ar_f)$ and $(1, ar_M)$, its slope is simply $(ar_M - ar_f)/(1-0) = (ar_M - ar_f)$. If RVOL_p is greater than this value, the portfolio lies above the *ex post* SML, indicating it has outperformed the market. Alternatively, if RVOL_p is less than this value, the portfolio lies below the *ex post* SML, indicating it has not performed as well as the market.

In the case of First Fund, the benchmark is $(ar_M - ar_f) = (3.05\% - 2.39\%) = 0.66\%$. Since RVOL_p for First Fund is less than the benchmark $(0.40\% < 0.66\%)$, according to this measure of portfolio performance, First Fund did not perform as well as the market.

In comparing the two measures of performance that are based on the *ex post* SML, α_p and RVOL_p, it should be noted that they *always* give the same assessment of a portfolio's performance relative to the market portfolio. That is, if one measure indicates the portfolio outperformed the market, so will the other. Similarly, if one measure indicates the portfolio did not perform as well as the market, the other measure will show the same thing. This can be seen by noting that any portfolio with a positive *ex post* alpha (an indication of superior performance) lies *above* the *ex post* SML and thus must have a slope *greater* than the slope of the *ex post* SML (also an indication of superior performance). Similarly, any portfolio with a negative *ex post* alpha (an indication of inferior performance) lies *below* the *ex post* SML and thus must have a slope *less* than the slope of the *ex post* SML (also an indication of inferior performance).

However, it should be noted that it is possible for the two measures to *rank* portfolios differently on the basis of performance simply because the calculations are different. For example, if Second Fund had a beta of 1.5 and an average return of 3.00%, its *ex post* alpha would be $3.00\% - [2.39\% + (3.05\% - 2.39\%)1.5] = -0.38\%$. Thus, its performance appears to be worse than First Fund, since it has a smaller *ex post* alpha $(-0.38\% < -0.31\%)$. However, its reward-to-volatility ratio of $0.41\% = (3.00\% - 2.39\%)/1.5$ is larger than the reward-to-volatility of 0.40% for First Fund, suggesting its performance was better than that of First Fund.

▶ The Reward-to-Variability Ratio

Both measures of risk-adjusted performance described so far, *ex post* alpha (that is, differential return) and the reward-to-volatility ratio, use benchmarks that are based on the *ex post* SML. Accordingly, they measure returns relative to the market risk of the portfolio. In contrast, the **reward-to-variability ratio** is a measure of risk-adjusted performance that uses a benchmark based on the *ex post* Capital Market Line (CML).[9] This means that it measures returns relative to the total risk of the portfolio, where total risk is the standard deviation of portfolio returns.

In order to use the reward-to-variability ratio (RVAR_p), the location of the *ex post* CML must be determined. This line goes through two points on a graph where average return is measured on the vertical axis and standard deviation is measured on the horizontal axis. The first point is the vertical intercept of the line and corresponds to the average risk-free rate during the evaluation interval. The second point corresponds to the location of the market portfolio, meaning its coordinates are the average return and standard deviation of return for the market portfolio during the evaluation interval, or $(\sum_M, ar_M)$. Since the *ex post* CML goes through these two points, its slope can readily be calculated as the vertical distance between the two points divided by the horizontal distance between the two points, or $(ar_M - ar_f)/(\sum_M - 0) = (ar_M - ar_f)/\sum_M$. Given a vertical intercept of ar_f, the equation of this line is

$$ar_p^e = \frac{ar_f + ar_M - ar_f}{\sigma_M}\sigma_p. \tag{25.20}$$

In the example shown in Table 25.1, the average return and standard deviation for the TSE 300, calculated using equations (25.5) and (25.6), were 3.05% and 7.83%, respectively. Since the average return on Treasury bills was 2.39%, the *ex post* CML for 1986 to 1989 was

$$\begin{aligned} ar_p^e &= 2.39\% + \frac{3.05\% - 2.39\%}{7.83\%}\sigma_p \\ &= 2.23\% + 0.084\sigma_p. \end{aligned} \tag{25.21}$$

Figure 25.6 presents a graph of this line.

Having determined the location of the *ex post* CML, the average return and standard deviation of the portfolio being evaluated can be determined next by using equations (25.5) and (25.6). With these values in hand, the portfolio can be located on the same graph as the *ex post* CML. In the case of First Fund, its average return and standard deviation were 2.85% and 10.10%, respectively. Thus, in Figure 25.6 its location corresponds to the point having coordinates (10.1%, 2.85%), which is denoted by *FF*.

The calculation of the reward-to-variability ratio (RVAR_p) is analogous to the calculation of the reward-to-volatility ratio (RVOL_p) described earlier. Specifically, RVOL_p involves dividing the portfolio's average excess return by its beta, whereas RVAR_p involves dividing the portfolio's average excess return by its standard deviation:

$$\text{RVAR}_p = \frac{ar_p - ar_f}{\sigma_p}. \tag{25.22}$$

Note that RVAR_p corresponds to the slope of a line originating at the average risk-free rate and going through a point having coordinates of (σ_p, ar_p). This can be seen by noting that

---

[9] This measure of performance is sometimes known as the *Sharpe ratio* because it was developed by William F. Sharpe in "Mutual Fund Performance," *Journal of Business* 39, no. 1 (January 1966): 119–38.

Figure 25.6

Performance evaluation using the *ex post* CML.

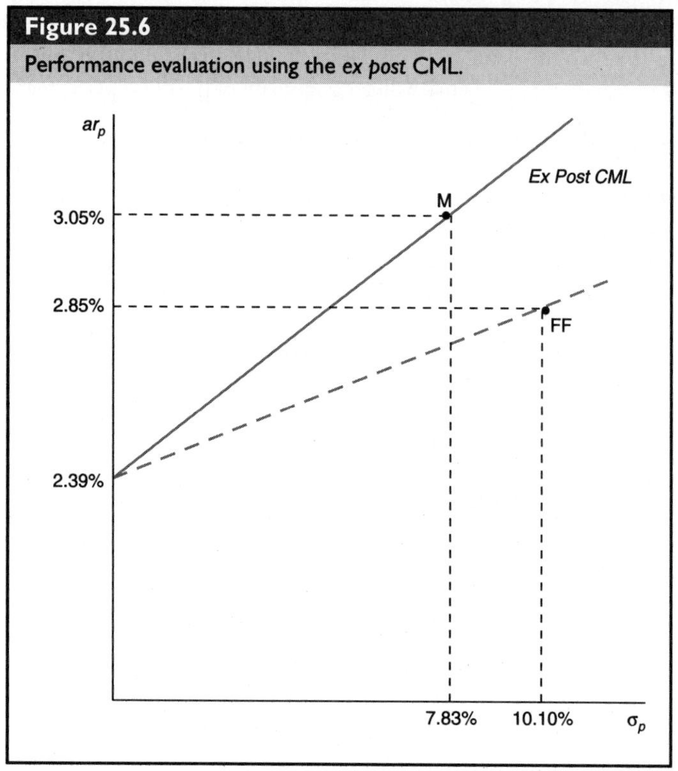

the slope of this line is simply the vertical distance between the two points divided by the horizontal distance between the two points, or $(ar_p - ar_f)/(\sigma_p - 0) = (ar_p - ar_f)/\sigma_p$, which corresponds to the formula for $RVAR_p$ given in equation (25.22). Since the value being measured on the horizontal axis is σ_p and the value being measured on the vertical axis is ar_p, the line can be drawn on the same diagram as the *ex post* CML.

In the First Fund example, recall that the *ex post* CML was shown by the upper line in Figure 25.6. Also appearing in this figure was the point denoted by *FF*, corresponding to (σ_p, ar_p) = (10.1%, 2.85%) for First Fund. The bottom line in this figure originates from the point $(0, ar_f)$ = (0, 2.39%) and goes through *FF*; the slope of this line is simply (2.85% – 2.39%)/10.1% = 0.046.

Since the *ex post* CML represents various combinations of risk-free lending or borrowing with investing in the market portfolio, it can be used to provide a benchmark for the reward-to-variability ratio in a manner similar to the SML-based benchmark for the reward-to-volatility ratio. As noted earlier, the slope of the *ex post* CML is $(ar_M - ar_f)/\sigma_M$. If $RVAR_p$ is greater than this value, the portfolio lies above the *ex post* CML, indicating it has outperformed the market. Alternatively, if $RVAR_p$ is less than this value, the portfolio lies below the *ex post* CML, indicating it has not performed as well as the market.[10]

---

[10] There is a second measure of portfolio performance that is based on the *ex post* CML. This measure, called the ***ex post* total risk alpha**, is simply the vertical distance the portfolio lies above or below the *ex post* CML. It is similar to the measure referred to earlier as *ex post* alpha (or differential return), except that it is based on a different risk measure (total risk instead of market risk) and uses a different benchmark (the *ex post* CML instead of the *ex post* SML).

In the case of First Fund, the benchmark is (3.05% – 2.39%)/7.83% = 0.084. Since $RVAR_p$ is less than the benchmark (0.046 < 0.084), First Fund did not perform as well as the market, according to this risk-adjusted measure of portfolio performance.

Comparing the Risk-Adjusted Measures of Performance

The measures of performance that are based on the *ex post* SML, α_p, and $RVOL_p$, can be compared with the measure of performance that is based on the *ex post* CML, $RVAR_p$. Focusing on $RVOL_p$ (the comparison also applies to α_p), it should be noted that in certain situations, $RVOL_p$ and $RVAR_p$ can give different assessments of a portfolio's performance relative to the market portfolio.

In particular, if $RVOL_p$ indicates the portfolio outperformed the market, it is possible for $RVAR_p$ to indicate the portfolio did not perform as well as the market. The reason for this is that the portfolio may have a relatively large amount of unique risk. Such risk would not be a factor in determining the value of $RVOL_p$ for the portfolio, since only *market risk* is in the denominator. However, such risk would be included in the denominator of $RVAR_p$ for the portfolio, since this measure is based on *total risk* (that is, both market and unique risk). Thus, a portfolio with a low amount of market risk could have a high amount of total risk, resulting in a relatively high $RVOL_p$ (due to the low amount of market risk) and a low $RVAR_p$ (due to the high amount of total risk). Accordingly, $RVOL_p$ could indicate the portfolio outperformed the market, while at the same time $RVAR_p$ may indicate it did not perform as well as the market.[11]

As an example, consider Third Fund, which had an average return of 3.0%, a beta of .8, and a standard deviation of 18%. Accordingly, $RVOL_{TF}$ = (3.0%–2.39%)/.8 = 0.76%, indicating that Third Fund outperformed the market portfolio, since the benchmark is (3.05% – 2.39%)/1.0 = 0.66%. However, $RVAR_{TF}$ = (3.0% – 2.39%)/18% = 0.034, indicating that Third Fund did not perform as well as the market portfolio, since the benchmark is (3.05% – 2.39%)/7.83% = 0.084. The reason for the difference can be seen by noting Third Fund's low beta relative to the market (.8 < 1.0) but high standard deviation relative to the market (18% > 7.39%). This suggests that Third Fund had a relatively high level of unique risk.

It also follows that it is possible for $RVOL_p$ and $RVAR_p$ to rank two or more portfolios differently on the basis of their performance. This is because these two measures of risk-adjusted performance use different types of risk.

Continuing the example, First Fund had an average return of 1.85%, a beta of 1.16, and a standard deviation of 10.1%. Thus, $RVOL_{FF}$ = (2.85% – 2.39%)/1.16 = 0.40%, which is less than $RVOL_{TF}$ = (3.0% – 2.39%)/0.8 = 0.76%, thereby indicating that First Fund ranked lower than Third Fund. However, $RVAR_{FF}$ = (2.85% – 2.39%)/10.1% = 0.046, which is greater than $RVAR_{TF}$ = 0.034, thereby indicating that First Fund ranked higher than Third Fund.

Did Third Fund do better or worse than the market on a risk-adjusted basis? And did Third Fund perform better or worse than First Fund? The answer to these two questions lies in identifying the appropriate measure of risk for the client. If the client has many other

[11] Since the market portfolio does not have any unique risk, it can be shown that if $RVOL_p$ indicates a portfolio did not perform as well as the market, then $RVAR_p$ must also indicate that the portfolio did not perform as well as the market. This is because a portfolio with a relatively high amount of market risk will also have a relatively high amount of total risk.

assets, then beta is the relevant measure of risk, and performance should be based on $RVOL_p$. To such a client, Third Fund should be viewed as a superior performer relative to both the market and First Fund. However, if the client has few other assets, then standard deviation is the relevant measure of risk, and performance should be based on $RVAR_p$. To such a client, Third Fund should be viewed as an inferior performer relative to both the market and First Fund.

MARKET TIMING

A successful market timer positions a portfolio to have a relatively high beta during a market rise and a relatively low beta during a market decline. This is because, as noted earlier, the expected return on a portfolio is a linear function of its beta:

$$\bar{r}_p = \alpha_p + r_f + (\bar{r}_M - r_f)\beta_p. \tag{25.23}$$

This means that the market timer will want to have a high-beta portfolio when he or she expects the market to have a higher return than the risk-free rate because such a portfolio will have a higher expected return than a low-beta portfolio. Conversely, the market timer will want to have a low-beta portfolio when he or she expects the market to have a lower return than the risk-free rate, as it will have a higher expected return than a high-beta portfolio. Simply put, the market timer will want to:

1. Hold a high-beta portfolio when $\bar{r}_M > r_f$, and
2. Hold a low-beta portfolio when $\bar{r}_M < r_f$.

If the timer is accurate in his or her forecasts of the expected return on the market, then his or her portfolio will outperform a benchmark portfolio that has a constant beta equal to the average beta of the timer's portfolio.

For example, if the market timer successfully set the portfolio beta at 0 when $\bar{r}_M < r_f$ and at 2 when $\bar{r}_M > r_f$, the return on the portfolio would be higher than the return on a portfolio having a beta constantly equal to 1. Unfortunately, if the market timer alters the portfolio's beta in ways unrelated to subsequent market moves (for example, sometimes setting the beta equal to zero when $\bar{r}_M > r_f$ and equal to two when $\bar{r}_M < r_f$), then the timer's portfolio will not perform as well as a constant beta portfolio.

To "time the market," either the average beta of the stocks held in the portfolio can be changed or the relative amounts invested in the risk-free asset and stocks can be altered. For example, to increase the beta of a portfolio, low-beta stocks could be sold, with the proceeds used to purchase high-beta stocks. Alternatively, Treasury bills in the portfolio could be sold (or the amount of borrowing increased), with the resulting proceeds invested in stocks.

In Figure 25.7, the excess returns of two hypothetical portfolios are measured on the vertical axis, while those of a market index are on the horizontal axis. Straight lines, fit via standard regression methods, reveal positive *ex post* alpha values in each case. However, the scatter diagrams tell a different story. Panel (a) seems to indicate that the relationship between the portfolio's excess returns and the market's excess returns was linear, since the points cluster close to the regression line. This suggests that the portfolio consisted of securities in a manner such that the beta of the portfolio was roughly the same at all times. Since the *ex post* alpha

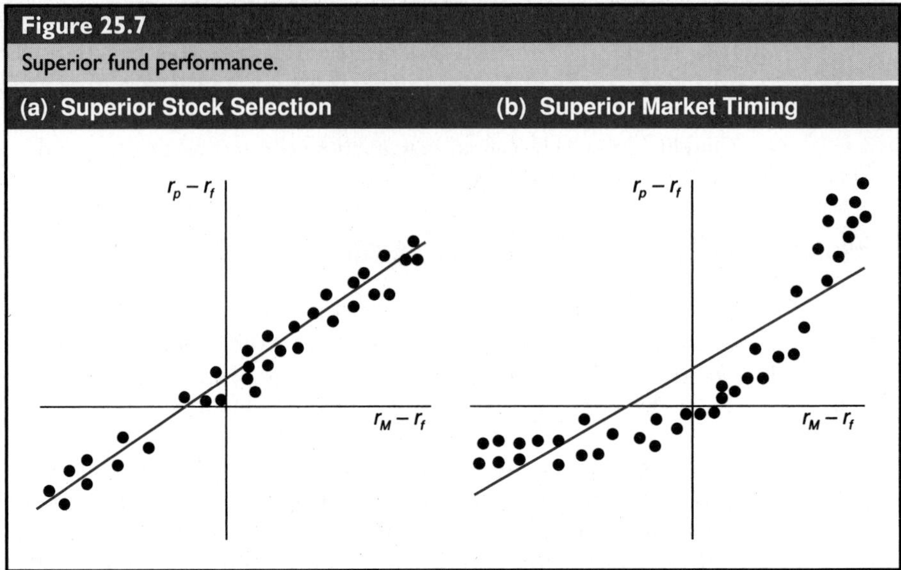

Figure 25.7
Superior fund performance.

was positive, it appears that the investment manager successfully identified and invested in some underpriced securities.

The scatter diagram for the portfolio shown in panel (b) seems to indicate the relationship between this portfolio's excess returns and the market's excess returns was not linear, since the points in the middle lie below the regression line and those at the ends lie above the regression line. This suggests that the portfolio consisted of high-beta securities during periods when the market return was high and low-beta securities during periods when the market return was low. Upon examination, it appears that the portfolio has a positive *ex post* alpha due to successful market timing by the investment manager.

Quadratic Regression

To measure the ability of an investment manager to time the market successfully, something more complex than a straight line can be fit to scatter diagrams such as those shown in Figure 25.7. One procedure fits a curve, where statistical methods are used to estimate the parameters a, b, and c in the following *quadratic regression equation*:

$$r_{pt} - r_{ft} = a + b(r_{Mt} - r_{ft}) + c[(r_{Mt} - r_{ft})^2] + \epsilon_{pt} \quad (25.24)$$

where ϵ_{pt} is the random error term.

The *ex post characteristic curve* shown in Figure 25.8(a) is simply the following quadratic function, where the values of a, b, and c for the portfolio have been estimated by standard regression methods:

$$r_{pt} - r_{ft} = a + b(r_{Mt} - r_{ft}) + c[(r_{Mt} - r_{ft})^2]. \quad (25.25)$$

If the estimated value of c is positive [as it is for the portfolio depicted in Figure 25.8(a)], the curve would become less steep as one moves to the left. This would indicate that the portfolio manager successfully timed the market. Note that this equation corresponds to the equation for the *ex post* characteristic line if c is equal to zero; in such a situation, a and b would correspond to the portfolio's *ex post* alpha and beta, respectively.

Figure 25.8

Ex post characteristic curve and lines.

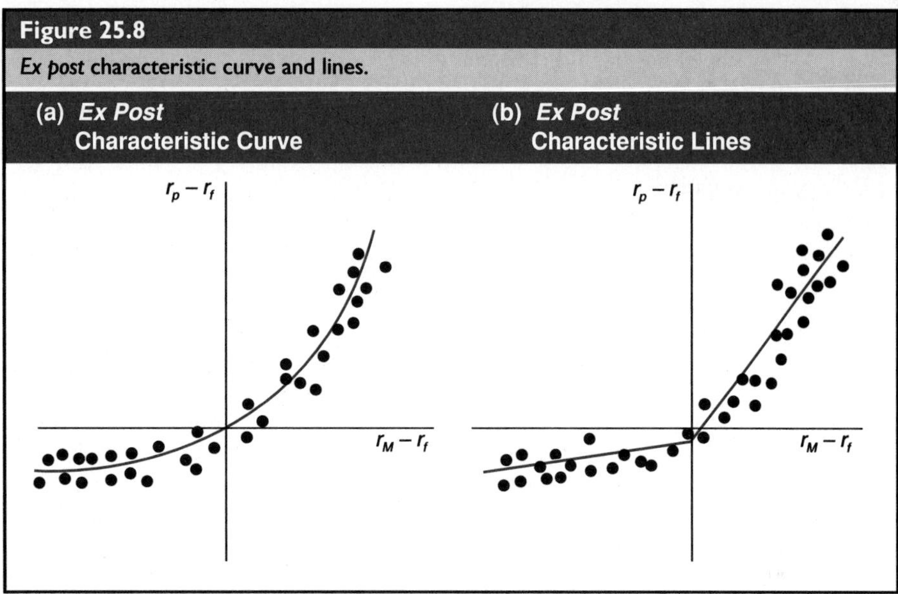

Dummy Variable Regression

An alternative procedure fits two *ex post* characteristic lines to the scatter diagram, as shown in Figure 25.8(b). Periods when risky securities outperform risk-free securities (that is, when $r_{Mt} > r_{ft}$) can be termed *up markets*. Periods when risky securities do not perform as well as risk-free securities (that is, when $r_{Mt} < r_{ft}$) can be termed *down markets*. A successful market timer would select a high up-market beta and a low down-market beta. Graphically, the slope of the *ex post* characteristic line for positive excess market returns is greater than the slope of the *ex post* characteristic line for negative excess market returns.

To estimate such a relationship, standard regression methods can be used to estimate the parameters a, b, and c in the following *dummy variable regression equation*:

$$r_{pt} - r_{ft} = a + b(r_{Mt} - r_{ft}) + c[D_t(r_{Mt} - r_{ft})] + \epsilon_{pt}. \quad (25.26)$$

Here, ϵ_{pt} is the random error term and D_t is a dummy variable that is assigned a value of 0 for any time period t when $r_{Mt} > r_{ft}$ and a value of –1 for any time period t when $r_{Mt} < r_{ft}$. To see how this works, consider the effective equations for different values of $r_{Mt} - r_{ft}$:

Value of $r_{Mt} - r_{ft}$	*Equation*
> 0	$r_{pt} - r_{ft} = a + b(r_{Mt} - r_{ft}) + \epsilon_{pt}$
$= 0$	$r_{pt} - r_{ft} = a + \epsilon_{pt}$
< 0	$r_{pt} - r_{ft} = a + (b - c)(r_{Mt} - r_{ft}) + \epsilon_{pt}$

Note that the parameter b corresponds to the portfolio's up-market beta, whereas $(b - c)$ corresponds to the portfolio's down-market beta. Thus, the parameter c indicates the difference between the two betas and is positive for the successful market timer.

For the portfolio shown in Figure 25.8(b), the *ex post* characteristic line on the right side of the graph corresponds to the equation

$$r_{pt} - r_{ft} = a + b(r_{Mt} - r_{ft}) \tag{25.27a}$$

whereas the *ex post* characteristic line shown on the left side of the graph corresponds to the equation

$$r_{pt} - r_{ft} = a + (b - c)(r_{Mt} - r_{ft}). \tag{25.27b}$$

In this example, the investment manager has successfully engaged in market timing, since the slope of the line on the right side (that is, b) is greater than the slope of the line on the left side (that is, $b - c$).

In either regression equation (25.24) or (25.26), the value of the parameter a provides an estimate of the investment manager's ability to identify mispriced securities (that is, security selection), and the value of the parameter c provides an estimate of the manager's ability at market timing. The difference between the two equations is that the quadratic equation indicates the portfolio's beta fluctuated over many values, depending on the size of the market's excess returns. This can be seen graphically by noting that the slope of the quadratic curve is continually increasing when moving from left to right in Figure 25.8(a). On the other hand, the dummy variable equation indicates the portfolio's beta fluctuates between just two values, depending on whether r_M is less or greater than r_f. This can be seen graphically by noting that the slope of the equation increases from one value (that is, $b - c$) to a second value (that is, b) when moving from left to right in Figure 25.8(b).

As an example, consider again the First Fund. Table 25.2 presents the results from applying regression equations (25.24) and (25.26) to this portfolio for the 16 quarters along with the *ex post* characteristic line results. The results in the table provide evidence of some positive selectivity, but negative market timing ability by the portfolio manager. This can be seen by noting that the parameter a is negative in the simple regression but becomes positive when the effect of market timing is taken into account. The parameter c, however, is negative in both cases indicating that the manager tends to increase beta in down-markets and decrease it in up-markets.[12] The correlation is higher for both multiple regressions than for the *ex post* characteristic line. This is further evidence that negative market timing ability is present. Care should be taken in drawing conclusions from these regressions. An examination of Figure 25.5 suggests that three large outliers may be producing the results obtained.

CRITICISMS OF RISK-ADJUSTED PERFORMANCE MEASURES

The previously mentioned risk-adjusted measures of portfolio performance have been criticized on several grounds. Some of the major criticisms are described in this section.

---

[12] The size of parameter c (as well as the parameters a and b) should be judged relative to its standard error. In both equations shown here, it is quite large relative to the corresponding standard error. Most standard statistical textbooks have an introductory discussion of the regression procedures that are used here. See, for example, Peter Tryfos, *Business Statistics* (Toronto, Ont.: McGraw-Hill Ryerson, 1989).

Table 25.2

Market Timing Test Results for First Fund.

Parameter Being Estimated[a]	*Ex Post Characteristic Line*	*Quadratic Equation*	*Dummy Variable Equation*
a	−0.31%	1.10%	2.20%
	(1.13)	(0.82)	(1.01)
b	1.16	1.16	1.66
	(.14)	(0.096)	(0.16)
c	—	−0.02	−1.01
	—	(.005)	(0.26)
Correlation[b]	0.91	0.96	0.95

[a] Standard errors are shown in parentheses below the respective parameters.
[b] The correlation coefficient for the quadratic and dummy variable equations has been adjusted for the number of independent variables.

Use of a Market Surrogate

All the measures other than the reward-to-variability ratio require the identification of a market portfolio. This means that whatever surrogate is used, it can be criticized as being inadequate. Indeed, it has been shown that by making slight changes in the surrogate, the performance rankings of a set of portfolios can be completely reversed (that is, the top-ranked portfolio with one surrogate could be the bottom-ranked portfolio if a slightly different surrogate was used). However, it has been noted that when commonly used NYSE-based surrogates are involved, such as the Dow Jones Industrial Average, the S&P 500, and an index comparable to the New York Stock Exchange Composite, the performance rankings of common stock portfolios appear to be quite similar.[13]

A related criticism of using a market index such as the S&P 500 to determine the benchmark portfolio's return is that it is nearly impossible for an investor to form a portfolio whose returns replicate those on such an index over time. This is because transaction costs will be encountered in initially forming the portfolio, in restructuring the portfolio when stocks are replaced in the index, and in purchasing more shares of stocks when cash dividends are received.[14] Hence it has been argued that the returns on an index overstate the returns that a passive investor could earn, meaning that the returns on the benchmark portfolio are too high.[15]

---

[13] See Richard Roll, "Ambiguity When Performance Is Measured by the Security Market Line," *Journal of Finance* 33, no. 4 (September 1978): 1051–69; and David Peterson and Michael L. Rice, "A Note on Ambiguity in Portfolio Performance Measures," *Journal of Finance* 35, no. 5 (December 1980): 1251–56; and Heinz Zimmermann and Claudia Zogg-Wetter, "On Detecting Selection and Timing Ability: The Case of Stock Market Indexes," *Financial Analysts Journal* 48, no. 1 (January/February 1992): 80–83.

[14] The problem is much more severe when the index is equal-weighted, because periodically part of the holdings of those stocks that had risen the most would have to be sold and the proceeds invested in additional shares of those stocks that had risen the least in order to keep equal weights in each stock.

[15] With the existence of index funds and index futures (discussed in Chapter 21), this criticism has lost much of its validity.

Distinguishing Skill from Luck

A very long evaluation interval is needed in order to be able to obtain a measure of performance that can distinguish skill from luck on the part of the investment manager. That is, it would be useful to know if an apparently successful manager was skilled or just lucky, since skill can be expected to have a favourable impact on the portfolio's performance in the future, whereas luck cannot be expected to continue. Unfortunately, too many years' worth of experience is generally needed to make such a determination.[16]

Measuring the Risk-Free Rate

The use of Treasury bills for measuring the risk-free rate in determining benchmark portfolios based on either the *ex post* SML or CML can be criticized. Consider a benchmark portfolio that involves an investment in both Treasury bills and the market portfolio. Such a benchmark portfolio can be criticized for having too low a rate of return, making it easy for a portfolio to show superior performance. This is because Treasury bills may provide excessively low returns to compensate for their high degree of liquidity. If a higher risk-free rate (such as the commercial paper rate) is used, then any benchmark portfolio that lies between this risk-free rate and the market portfolio on either the *ex post* SML or CML will have a higher rate of return and thus represent a higher but more appropriate standard.

Next, consider a benchmark portfolio that involves levering a positive investment in the market portfolio by borrowing at the risk-free rate. Use of the Treasury bill rate can be criticized because realistic borrowing alternatives typically involve a higher rate and are thus less attractive. Accordingly, benchmarks that involve borrowing at the Treasury bill rate have too high a rate of return, making it difficult for a portfolio to show superior performance. If a higher risk-free borrowing rate (such as the call money rate plus a small premium) is used, then any benchmark portfolio involving risk-free borrowing will have a lower rate of return and thus represent a lower but more appropriate standard.

In summary, measures of portfolio performance based on either the *ex post* SML or CML and using Treasury bills to determine the risk-free rate are alleged to discriminate in favour of conservative portfolios and against aggressive ones.

Validity of the CAPM

The measures of portfolio performance that involve beta (namely, the *ex post* alpha and reward-to-volatility measures) are based on the CAPM, yet the CAPM may not be the correct asset pricing model. That is, perhaps assets are priced according to some other model. If so, the use of beta-based performance measures will be inappropriate.

Interestingly, a measure analogous to *ex post* alpha has been shown to be a meaningful gauge of performance if the arbitrage pricing theory's (APT) model of asset pricing is believed to be more appropriate.[17] In such a situation, the APT is used to estimate the benchmark

---

[16] See Dan W. French and Glenn V. Henderson, Jr., "How Well Does Performance Evaluation Perform?" *Journal of Portfolio Management* 11, no. 2 (Winter 1985): 15–18.

[17] Under APT (discussed in Chapter 12), there is another measure of portfolio performance that has even more theoretical justification than the APT-based *ex post* alpha. This measure is analogous to the CAPM-based "appraisal ratio" mentioned in footnote 6 and involves dividing the APT-based *ex post* alpha by the *ex post* standard deviation of the APT-based random error term. For details, see Gregory Connor and Robert A. Korajczyk, "Performance Measurement with the Arbitrage Pricing Theory: A New Framework for Analysis," *Journal of Financial Economics* 15, no. 3 (March 1986): 373–94; and Bruce N. Lehmann and David M. Modest, "Mutual Fund Performance

portfolio's return ar_{bp} that is used in equation (22.3) to calculate α_p. Furthermore, the reward-to-variability ratio is immune to this criticism, since it uses standard deviation as a measure of risk and does not rely on the validity of the CAPM or the APT or on the identification of a market portfolio.

Performance Attribution

The previously mentioned risk-adjusted measures of performance concentrate on the question of *how* a portfolio did relative to both a benchmark and a set of other portfolios. The use of quadratic and dummy variable regression is an attempt to evaluate separately the manager's ability at selectivity and timing. However, the client might want to know more about *why* the portfolio had a certain return over a particular time period. **Performance attribution** using a *factor model* is one method that has been used to try to make such a determination; an example is presented in the appendix.

BOND PORTFOLIO PERFORMANCE EVALUATION

The performance of portfolios consisting of bonds (and other types of fixed-income securities) is often evaluated by comparing their total returns (consisting of coupon payments plus capital gains or losses) with those of an index representing a comparable class of securities over some evaluation interval. Hence a portfolio that is invested in investment-grade long-term corporate bonds would be compared with an investment-grade long-term corporate bond index, a portfolio invested in mortgage-backed securities would be compared with a mortgage-backed security index and a junk bond fund would be compared with a "high-yield" index.

Bond Indices

Bond indices typically represent either the average yield-to-maturity or the average price on a portfolio of bonds that have certain similar characteristics. Figure 25.9 presents various bond indices that are published monthly by ScotiaMcLeod Inc. Average yield as well as price and total return indices are reported. This bulletin also includes information (not shown) about residential mortgages, mortgage-backed securities, money market instruments, Euro-Canadian bonds and Canadian Yankee bonds. Historical information is provided in ScotiaMcLeod's *Handbook of Canadian Debt Market Indices*, published annually.

Time Series and Cross-Sectional Comparisons

Figure 25.10 illustrates two ways of comparing the returns on a bond portfolio with those on a bond index over an evaluation interval. In panel (a), a time-series comparison is made, where the bond portfolio's quarterly returns over time during the evaluation interval are graphed along with those of the bond index. In panel (b), a cross-sectional comparison is made in a manner similar to the equity performance measures that were based on the *ex post* CML. Here, the bond portfolio's average return and standard deviation are graphed and compared with a line that goes through the average risk-free rate and the average return

---

Evaluation: A Comparison of Benchmarks and Benchmark Comparisons," *Journal of Finance* 42, no. 2 (June 1987): 233–65.

Figure 25.9

Bond indices published monthly by ScotiaMcLeod Inc.

CANADIAN BOND MARKET SECTOR PERFORMANCE

November 30, 1995

				Total Returns: Percentage Change															PC-Bond Ref #
	Avg. Yield	Price Index	Total Return Index	Last Month	Last 3 Months	Last 6 Months	Year to Date	Last 1 Year	Last 3 Years	Last 5 Years	Last 10 Years	Sector Weight	Macaulay Duration	Modified Duration	Value of 01	Average Coupon	Average Term	Con-vexity	Yld & Price / Yld & T.R.
SHORT TERM BOND INDEX (1-5) YEARS)																			
Canadas	6.41	99.21	253.74	1.69	4.27	6.18	14.21	13.92	8.79	10.29	9.87	70.10	2.71	2.63	2.80	8.07	3.10	0.10	25026/26026
Provincials	6.42	101.93	267.02	1.59	4.04	6.23	14.23	13.88	9.62	11.24	10.45	20.40	2.33	2.26	2.44	8.98	2.80	0.08	25027/26027
Municipals	6.61	100.33	278.30	1.77	4.45	6.60	14.98	14.68	10.09	11.62	10.91	0.90	2.79	2.70	3.04	10.27	3.30	0.10	25028/26028
All Governments	6.41	100.05	257.99	1.67	4.22	6.19	14.22	13.92	9.06	10.59	10.06	91.50	2.63	2.54	2.73	8.30	3.00	0.09	25034/26034
AA	6.71	104.32	262.26	1.61	4.23	6.27	14.97	14.69	9.78	11.12	N/A	4.00	2.33	2.25	2.47	9.43	2.70	0.07	25031/26031
A	6.66	104.46	268.90	1.68	4.19	6.39	14.19	13.93	10.17	11.45	N/A	3.60	2.50	2.42	2.65	9.37	3.00	0.09	25032/26032
BBB	7.49	111.34	300.37	1.79	4.99	7.21	17.81	17.70	13.11	13.18	N/A	0.90	2.81	2.71	3.04	10.79	3.40	0.10	25033/26033
All Corporates	6.77	105.18	268.90	1.67	4.30	6.41	14.94	14.69	10.21	11.36	10.52	8.50	2.45	2.37	2.61	9.55	2.90	0.08	25029/26029
Overall	6.44	100.36	258.81	1.67	4.23	6.21	14.29	13.99	9.15	10.65	10.09	100.00	2.61	2.53	2.72	8.40	3.00	0.09	25035/26035
MID TERM BOND INDEX (5-10 YEARS)																			
Canadas	7.02	111.07	281.02	2.77	6.29	7.84	19.97	20.56	10.72	12.83	11.11	59.80	5.51	5.32	6.06	8.97	7.30	0.37	25011/26011
Provincials	7.16	113.39	294.21	2.72	6.22	8.38	20.64	20.94	12.10	13.78	11.58	28.40	4.83	4.66	5.25	9.48	7.20	0.30	25012/26012
Municipals	7.12	110.91	303.05	2.65	5.96	8.11	20.08	20.17	12.20	13.93	11.89	1.10	4.35	4.20	5.07	11.01	6.10	0.23	25013/26013
All Governments	7.07	111.85	286.17	2.75	6.26	8.02	20.18	20.68	11.23	13.19	11.29	89.20	5.28	5.10	5.79	9.15	7.20	0.35	25014/26014
AA	7.38	112.03	291.91	2.76	6.21	8.09	20.36	20.84	11.85	13.79	11.56	5.30	5.41	5.22	5.84	9.23	7.30	0.37	25016/26016
A	7.48	111.45	292.79	2.82	6.49	8.87	21.78	22.42	12.62	13.63	11.55	5.20	5.03	4.85	5.41	9.46	7.50	0.33	25017/26017
BBB	7.83	119.98	329.64	2.28	5.74	7.47	20.80	21.68	17.97	16.35	12.79	0.30	4.61	4.43	4.86	9.43	6.00	0.26	25018/26018
All Corporates	7.44	112.83	294.82	2.76	6.30	8.35	20.91	21.47	12.49	13.91	11.64	10.80	5.21	5.02	5.60	9.35	7.40	0.34	25019/26019
Overall	7.11	111.94	287.36	2.75	6.27	8.05	20.26	20.75	11.37	13.27	11.34	100.00	5.27	5.09	5.77	9.17	7.20	0.35	25020/26020
LONG TERM BOND INDEX (1O+ YEARS)																			
Canadas	7.48	120.42	308.43	4.06	8.90	10.20	24.36	25.91	12.38	14.63	12.21	59.00	9.49	9.15	0.18	9.51	19.30	1.34	25001/26001
Provincials	7.94	119.41	324.33	4.20	9.24	11.51	26.41	27.61	14.30	15.85	12.76	26.30	9.27	8.91	0.40	9.57	20.60	1.32	25002/26002
Municipals	7.86	119.76	332.02	3.81	8.58	11.35	25.71	27.03	14.15	16.01	12.99	2.60	8.45	8.13	9.36	9.46	15.10	0.98	25003/26003
All Governments	7.63	120.16	314.18	4.09	8.99	10.62	24.99	26.43	13.07	15.07	12.41	87.80	9.40	9.05	0.89	9.53	19.60	1.33	25004/26004
AA	7.94	119.64	319.21	3.97	8.76	10.52	24.63	25.88	13.58	15.80	12.61	2.90	8.93	8.58	0.04	9.75	19.90	1.24	25006/26006
A	8.18	122.87	330.73	3.95	8.93	10.62	24.66	25.84	14.36	16.63	12.94	8.90	8.68	8.34	0.00	10.24	19.40	1.16	25007/26007
BBB	9.16	123.16	353.63	8.08	12.96	15.84	35.55	37.42	21.12	18.42	13.73	0.30	8.04	7.69	8.63	10.39	15.90	0.92	25008/26008
All Corporates	8.15	118.77	318.85	4.04	8.93	10.68	24.86	26.09	14.03	15.99	12.57	12.20	8.73	8.39	9.98	10.13	19.40	1.17	25009/26009
Overall	7.69	120.20	315.10	4.09	8.99	10.63	24.98	26.39	13.20	15.19	12.45	100.00	9.31	8.97	0.78	9.60	19.60	1.31	25010/26010
HIGH YIELD BOND INDEX (COMPOSITE)																			
Real Estate	9.58	108.77	119.75	1.96	5.37	9.54	19.75	N/A	N/A	N/A	N/A	28.50	2.83	2.70	2.87	10.89	3.40	0.10	
Industrial	8.07	109.89	120.21	3.06	6.22	9.28	20.21	N/A	N/A	N/A	N/A	8.15	3.47	3.33	3.58	10.32	4.40	0.18	
Resources	8.19	112.46	123.18	3.74	7.38	9.83	23.18	N/A	N/A	N/A	N/A	32.34	4.99	4.79	5.39	10.89	8.30	0.42	
Retail	7.43	108.12	118.03	1.79	5.00	7.16	18.03	N/A	N/A	N/A	N/A	15.40	3.15	3.04	3.41	10.60	3.90	0.13	
Other	9.07	117.92	128.88	3.06	7.68	15.66	28.88	N/A	N/A	N/A	N/A	15.61	6.08	5.81	6.10	9.80	11.20	0.58	
Overall	8.60	111.29	121.95	2.77	6.38	10.12	21.95	N/A	N/A	N/A	N/A	100.00	4.14	3.96	4.33	10.63	6.40	0.29	

SOURCE: Melanie Moore, *Debt Market Indices*, ScotiaMcLeod Inc. (November 30, 1995).

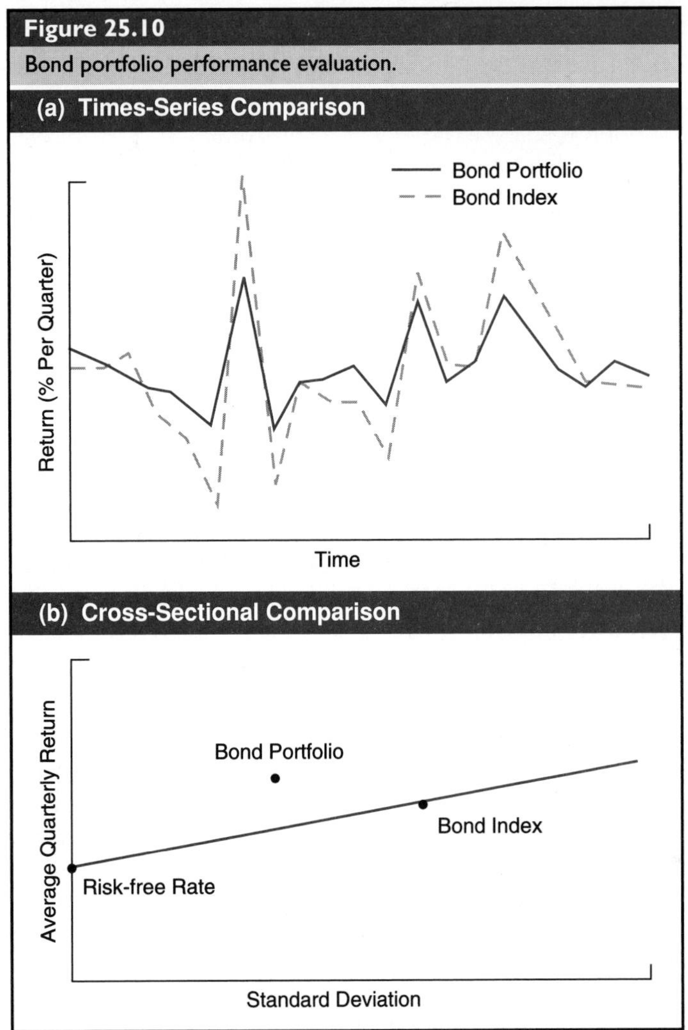

Figure 25.10

Bond portfolio performance evaluation.

and standard deviation of the bond index (instead of an equity index), based on quarterly returns during the evaluation interval.

A variation of this procedure involves estimating the bond portfolio's *ex post* alpha by using the *ex post* characteristic line approach described earlier. That is, a figure similar to Figure 25.5 would be prepared, but now the excess returns on a bond portfolio would be measured on the vertical axis and the excess returns on a bond index would be measured on the horizontal axis.[18] The returns on the Scotia-McLeod overall total return bond index, which is an index of government and corporate investment-grade bonds can be used as the market index. Alternatively, the returns on a bond index that most closely fits with the

[18] In the US, this method is used by Morningstar, Inc. in evaluating bond mutual fund performance. It is also used by Christopher R. Blake, Edwin J. Elton, and Martin J. Gruber in "The Performace of Bond Mutual Funds," *Journal of Business* 66, no. 3 (July 1993): 371–403. These authors also used multiple regression where the excess returns on more that one bond index were the explanatory variables.

investment objectives and policies of the portfolio under scrutiny should be used. In either case, an *ex post* alpha would be calculated and used as a measure of portfolio performance.

Bond Market Line

A different approach involves the use of a *bond market line*.[19] Assume that the performance of a bond portfolio is to be evaluated over a given quarter (or year, as this approach can be used for a longer period). There are five steps to this approach:

1. Calculate the quarterly return for the portfolio, along with its average duration for the quarter (this could be calculated by averaging the portfolio's duration at the beginning and end of the quarter), and plot the portfolio on a graph that measures return on the vertical axis and duration on the horizontal axis. (Duration is discussed in Chapter 16.)
2. Calculate the return and average duration for a broadly representative bond index for the same quarter, and plot the index on the same graph.
3. Determine the 90-day Treasury bill rate at the beginning of the quarter, and plot it on the same graph (because the Treasury bill is a pure discount security, its duration is the same as its term-to-maturity—90 days, or roughly .25 years).
4. Construct the bond market line by drawing a straight line connecting the Treasury bill and bond index.
5. Determine whether the portfolio plots above or below this line, and measure its performance by its distance from this line.

With this approach the bond market line is used to determine the benchmark in evaluating the performance of the bond portfolio. If the portfolio lies above the bond market line, as in Figure 25.11, it outperformed the benchmark (the benchmark portfolio lies on the bond market line directly below the portfolio) and its performance would be viewed as superior. Conversely, if the portfolio lies below the bond market line, it underperformed the benchmark (the benchmark portfolio lies on the bond market line directly above the portfolio) and its performance is viewed as inferior. Hence, equation (22.3) is being used to calculate the bond portfolio's *ex post* alpha, with the bond market line being used to determine the return on the benchmark portfolio, ar_{bp}.[20]

Other bond portfolios and indices can also be shown on the graph to give more information on the relative performance of the portfolio being evaluated. In Figure 25.11, one federal government bond index and three corporate bond indices are shown, in addition to the overall bond index published by Merrill Lynch. Their *ex post* alphas can be compared to the bond portfolio's *ex post* alpha. Furthermore, the bond portfolio's *ex post* alpha can be used to determine its rank among a group of bond portfolios.

---

[19] See Wayne H. Wagner and Dennis A. Tito, "Definitive New Measures of Bond Performance and Risk," *Pension World* 13, no. 5 (May 1977): 10–12; and "Is Your Bond Manager Skillful?" *Pension World* 13, no. 6 (June 1977): 9–13. Bond portfolio performance evaluation is also discussed in Peter O. Dietz and Jeannette R. Kirschman, "Evaluating Portfolio Performance," Chapter 14 in *Managing Investment Portfolios: A Dynamic Process*, eds. John L. Maginn and Donald L. Tuttle (Boston, MA: Warren, Gorham & Lamont, 1990).

[20] Using the bond market line as a benchmark in this manner is similar to using the SML as a benchmark in evaluating the performance of stock portfolios.

Figure 25.11

Bond market line.

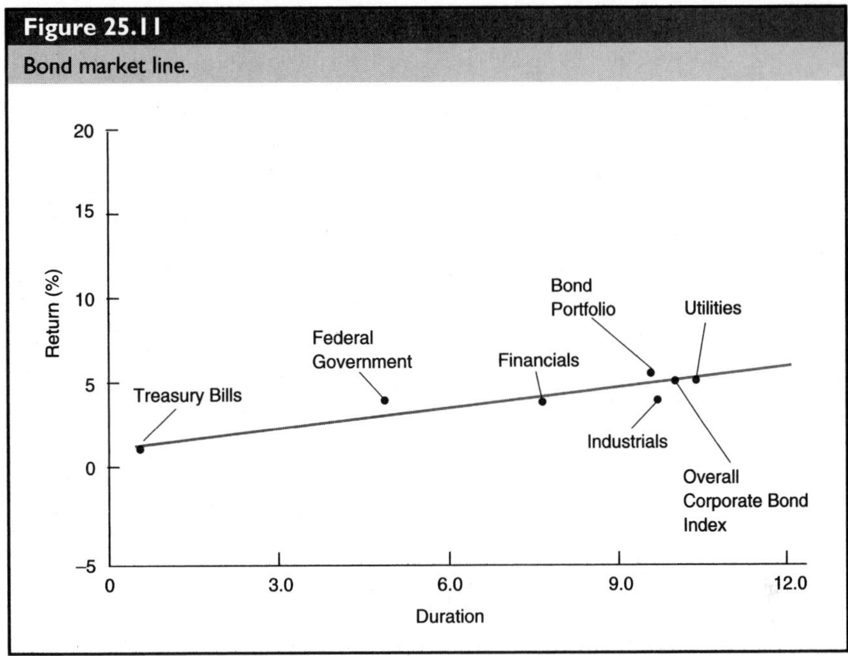

SOURCE: Adapted from Wayne H. Wagner and Dennis A Tito, "Definitive New Measures of Bond Performance and Risk," *Pension World* 13, no. 5 (May 1977): 12.

SUMMARY

1. Performance measurement is an integral part of the investment management process. It is a feedback and control mechanism that can make the investment management process more effective.
2. In evaluating performance, there are two major tasks: determining whether the performance is superior or inferior, and determining whether the performance is due to luck or skill.
3. Without intra-period contributions or withdrawals, measurement of periodic portfolio returns is simple: the difference between ending and beginning portfolio values divided by beginning portfolio value.
4. Intra-period cash flows complicate the calculation of periodic portfolio returns. Two methods have been developed to calculate returns when these cash flows occur: dollar-weighted and time-weighted returns.
5. The dollar-weighted return is influenced by the size and timing of cash flows, whereas the time-weighted return is not. As a result, the time-weighted return is generally the preferred method when evaluating portfolio performance.
6. The essential idea behind performance evaluation is to compare an actively managed portfolio's returns against the returns of an alternative benchmark portfolio. An appropriate benchmark should be relevant and feasible, and it should exhibit risk similar to that of the actively managed portfolio.
7. Risk-adjusted performance measures involve both a portfolio's *ex post* return and its *ex post* risk.

8. *Ex post* alpha (differential return) and the reward-to-volatility ratio compare a portfolio's excess return to the portfolio's systematic risk. The reward-to-variability ratio compares a portfolio's excess return to the portfolio's total risk.
9. Successful market timers will hold portfolios with relatively high betas during market rises and relatively low betas during market declines. Quadratic regression and dummy variable regression are two methods designed to measure market timing performance.
10. Risk-adjusted measures of performance have been criticized for using a market surrogate instead of the "true" market portfolio; being unable to statistically distinguish luck from skill except over very long periods of time; using an inappropriate risk-free rate; and relying on the validity of the CAPM.

APPENDIX A

PERFORMANCE ATTRIBUTION

With performance attribution, an attempt is made to ascertain why an equity portfolio had a given return over a particular time period. One procedure for making such a determination involves assuming security returns are related to a number of pre-specified factors as well as to sector-factors.[21] For example, there may be a beta factor, a size factor, and two sector-factors that indicate whether or not a stock is an industrial. With such a model, the returns for a set of stocks during a given time period are related to these factors and sector-factors in the following manner:

$$r_i = \beta_i F_1 + s_i F_2 + c_{i1} SF_1 + c_{i2} SF_2 + \epsilon_i. \tag{25.28}$$

Here, each stock has four attributes—β_i, s_i, c_{i1}, and c_{i2}. The attributes β_i and s_i are, respectively, the beta and firm size of stock i in a given time period, and c_{i1} and c_{i2} are sector-factor attributes that have values of 1 and 0, respectively, if stock i is an industrial firm and values of 0 and 1 if stock i is not an industrial firm. (For example, it may be a utility or transportation company such as Canadian Utilities or PWA.)

The factors and sector-factors F_1, F_2, SF_1, and SF_2 are parameters that can be estimated using a statistical technique known as multiple regression. For example, the returns for 500 firms for 1994 could be calculated. Then, the betas for each stock could be estimated using 16 quarters of returns ending with the last quarter of 1993 (by using the *ex-post* characteristic line equation given earlier). The firm size for each stock could be measured by taking the market price per share as of December 31, 1993, multiplying it by the number of shares outstanding at that time, and then taking the logarithm of the product (expressed in billions). Lastly, each firm can be classified as either an industrial or nonindustrial, resulting in a value of 0 or 1 assigned to c_{i1} and c_{i2}. This will give four columns of 500 numbers representing security attributes—one column with the betas for each stock, one column for the firm sizes of each stock, and two columns of 0s and 1s corresponding to whether the firms are industrials or nonindustrials —upon which will be "regressed" the column of returns for the 500 stocks during 1994.

---

[21] For a discussion of factor models, see Chapter 11 and William F. Sharpe, "Factors in New York Stock Exchange Security Returns, 1931–1979," *Journal of Portfolio Management* 8, no. 4 (Summer 1982): 5–18.

Suppose the resulting regression resulted in estimated values for F_1, F_2, SF_1, and SF_2 of 1.20, –.40, 10.00, and 9.00, respectively. Then, equation (25.28) for 1994 would be

$$r_i = 1.20\beta_i - .40s_i + 10.00c_{i1} + 9.00c_{i2} + \epsilon_i. \tag{25.29}$$

Since the estimated value of F_1 (1.20) is positive, 1994 was a year where high beta stocks tended to outperform low beta stocks. Furthermore, since the estimated value of F_2 (–.40) is negative, the year 1994 was one where the stocks of small firms tended to outperform the stocks of large firms. With an estimated value for SF_1 that is greater than the estimated value for SF_2 ($10.00 > 9.00$), 1994 also appears to have been a year when industrials tended to outperform nonindustrials.

Equation (25.29) can be used to analyze the 1994 return on a stock. Consider, for example, a hypothetical industrial stock that had a return of 12.13%, a beta of .8, and size of 4.00 (its market value was \$54.6 billion, so s_i = natural logarithm of 54.6 = ln(54.6) = 4.00). According to equation (25.29), the "normal" return on such a stock is $(1.20 \times .8) - (.40 \times 4.00) + (10.00 \times 1) + (9.00 \times 0) = 9.36\%$. Thus, for this stock, its "nonfactor return" (ϵ_i) for 1994 was $12.13\% - 9.36\% = 2.77\%$, suggesting this particular stock did relatively well in comparison with other stocks having comparable attributes.

Similar analysis can be conducted on a portfolio's return for 1994. Consider a hypothetical portfolio that had a return of 10.03% in 1994. Upon close examination, it has been determined that this portfolio had an average beta of 1.3 and an average size of 3.2 (that is, the average value of s_i for all the stocks held was 3.2). Furthermore, 67% of the stocks in the portfolio were industrials and 33% were nonindustrials. According to equation (23.29), the normal return on such a portfolio is $(1.20 \times 1.30) - (.40 \times 3.20) + (10.00 \times .67) + (9.00 \times .33) = 9.95\%$. Since the nonfactor return on this portfolio was $10.03\% - 9.95\% = .08\%$, this portfolio shows little evidence of successful security selection.

Such absolute performance evaluation with a factor model is interesting, but in many cases comparative performance is more relevant. A manager may do poorly in a bad market. But if he or she provides a higher return than would have been obtained otherwise, the client is clearly better off. With comparative performance, the overall return of a portfolio is compared with that of one or more other portfolios or market indices in order to determine the *differences* in the returns. Then the sources of the differences can be determined with **comparative performance attribution**.

Assume that the i in equation (25.28) refers to the portfolio under evaluation. Letting j refer to the return on a portfolio (or market index) to which it is to be compared, the difference in their returns is simply $r_i - r_j$. Using equation (25.28), this difference can be expressed as

$$\begin{aligned} r_i - r_j = &(\beta_i F_1 + s_i F_2 + c_{i1} SF_1 + c_{i2} SF_2 + \epsilon_i) \\ &- (\beta_j F_1 + s_j F_2 + c_{j1} SF_1 + c_{j2} SF_2 + \epsilon_j). \end{aligned} \tag{25.30}$$

Gathering similar terms, this equation can be rewritten as

$$\begin{aligned} r_i - r_j = &F_1(\beta_i - \beta_j) + F_2(s_i - s_j) \\ &+ SF_1(c_{i1} - c_{j1}) + SF_2(c_{i2} - c_{j2}) + (\epsilon_i - \epsilon_j). \end{aligned} \tag{25.31}$$

Each of the first four terms represents a differential effect equal to the product of (1) the difference in the attributes of the two portfolios and (2) the actual value of the related factor. The last term in the equation indicates the difference in the nonfactor returns of the two portfolios.

Table 25.3

Comparative Performance Attribution.

	Attribute				
	Portfolio i (*a*)	*Portfolio j* (*b*)	*Difference* (*c*) = (*a*) − (*b*)	*Factor* (*d*)	*Differential Effect* (*e*) = (*c*) × (*d*)
a. Factors:					
Common factors					
Beta	1.30	1.50	−.20	1.20	− .24%
Size	3.20	1.40	1.80	−.40	− .72%
Sector-factors					
Industrials	.67	.80	−.13	10.00	−1.30%
Nonindustrials	.33	.20	.13	9.00	1.17%
					−1.09%

	Returns		
	Portfolio i (*a*)	*Portfolio j* (*b*)	*Difference* (*c*) = (*a*) − (*b*)
b. Returns:			
Factor return	9.95%	11.04%	−1.09%
Nonfactor return	.08%	.17%	− .09%
Total return	10.03%	11.21%	−1.18%

Table 25.3 provides an example where portfolio i is the one mentioned earlier that had a return in 1994 of 10.03%. It is being compared with a benchmark portfolio that had a return in 1994 of 11.21%. This benchmark portfolio had a beta of 1.50, and the average size of the firms whose stocks it held was 1.40. Furthermore, 80% of the portfolio's funds were invested in industrials, with the remaining 20% being invested in nonindustrials. Using equation (25.29), the normal return on such a portfolio in 1994 was $(1.20 \times 1.50) - (.40 \times 1.40) + (10.00 \times .80) + (9.00 \times .20) = 11.04\%$, indicating the portfolio had a nonfactor return of 11.21% – 11.04% = .17%.

A direct comparison of the two portfolios reveals a difference in returns of $r_i - r_j =$ 10.03% – 11.21% = –1.18%. That is, portfolio i performed worse than the benchmark by 1.18%. Security selection played a small role, since the nonfactor returns were both quite low (.08% for portfolio i and .17% for the benchmark). On balance, sector selection lowered returns for portfolio i relative to the benchmark slightly—the sum of the values in the last column for the two sector-factors was –0.13%. In portfolio i, industrials were underweighted relative to the benchmark, while nonindustrials were overweighted. A successful "sector picker" would have placed bets on (that is, overweighted) the sector with a relatively high factor value (industrials) and placed bets against (that is, underweighted) the sector with a relatively low factor value (nonindustrials), leading to a net positive *sector bet effect.*

In 1994, the investment manager for portfolio i was not as successful a sector picker relative to the benchmark.

The major sources of the relatively lower performance of portfolio i were those associated with common factors. The manager had lower-beta stocks than those in the benchmark during a period when high-beta stocks tended to do better than low-beta stocks. That is, the manager placed a bet against high-beta stocks in favour of low-beta stocks and lost. He or she also had invested in stocks that were larger than those in the benchmark during a period when larger stocks tended to do poorly. That is, the manager placed a bet against smaller firms in favour of larger firms and lost. Both differences lowered returns relative to the benchmark, with the size bet being more detrimental than the beta bet.

QUESTIONS AND PROBLEMS

1. Craig Patrick owns a portfolio of three stocks. Craig's holdings and the prices of the stocks at the end of Year 1 and Year 2 are shown below. Assuming no contributions, withdrawals, or dividends paid, what is the return on Craig's portfolio in Year 2?

Stock	Shares Owned	Year 1 Price	Year 2 Price
A	100	$10	$15
B	300	5	4
C	250	12	14

2. Why do cash inflows and outflows between the beginning and end of a performance evaluation period complicate the measurement of portfolio returns?
3. At the beginning of the year, Lorne Grossman's portfolio was worth $39 000. At year-end, Lorne received a gift of $4000, which was invested in the portfolio. The portfolio's value at year-end was $42 000. What was the return on Lorne's portfolio during the year?
4. New Lisbon Laundry's pension fund was worth $30 million at the end of Year 1. On the first day of Year 2 the firm made a $2 million contribution to the fund. At the end of Year 2, the pension fund was valued at $38 million. What was the return on the New Lisbon pension fund during Year 2?
5. At the beginning of the year, Connie Daily's portfolio was worth $9000. At the end of each of the next four quarters, Connie received a gift of $500, which was invested in the portfolio. At the end of each quarter, Connie's portfolio was worth, respectively, $9800, $10 800, $11 200, and $12 000. What was the time-weighted rate of return on Connie's portfolio during the year?
6. Dave Das's portfolio is worth $12 000 at the beginning of a 30-day month. On day 10 of the month, Dave received a contribution to the portfolio of $800. At the end of the month, Dave's portfolio is worth $13 977.71. What was the dollar-weighted return on Dave's portfolio for the month?

7. Ginger Beaumont began the year with a portfolio valued at $10 000 and made a contribution to and a withdrawal from this portfolio over the next three months. Information regarding amounts and dates of these cash flows and the portfolio's market value at various dates is shown below.

Date	Contribution (+) or Withdrawal (–)	Portfolio Value
12/31	$ 0	$10 000
1/31	+956	9 000
2/28	–659	12 000
3/31	0	13 000

a. Calculate the dollar-weighted return for the three-month period. (Hint: Unless you have a suitable calculator, you will have to use trial and error to find the dollar-weighted return. To begin, the monthly dollar-weighted return is less than 10%.)
b. Calculate the time-weighted return for the three-month period.
c. Why is the time-weighted return of the quarter less than the dollar-weighted return in this particular period?

8. Distinguish between time-weighted and dollar-weighted rates of return. Under what performance measurement circumstances might the dollar-weighted return be preferred to the time-weighted?

9. Oscar DeMaestri's portfolio is valued at $22 000 at the beginning of a 31-day month. During the month, Oscar withdrew $1500 from the portfolio on day 12 and contributed $600 on day 21. At month-end, the portfolio was worth $21 769.60. What was Oscar's dollar-weighted return for the month?

10. At the beginning of a 30-day month, Lindsay Dickerson owned a portfolio valued at $5000. On day 10, Lindsay's portfolio was worth $7300 after a $2000 contribution had been made on that day. At the end of the month, the portfolio was worth $9690.18. Calculate both the time-weighted and dollar-weighted returns on Lindsay's portfolio for the month. Why do the two returns differ so substantially?

11. Why does performance evaluation require an appropriate benchmark in order to be meaningful? How would you define the term *appropriate* in this context?

12. It is common practice for performance evaluation services to compare the returns on a common stock portfolio to a distribution of returns obtained from a large sample of other common stock portfolios. What potential problems are involved in this sort of analysis?

13. Janice Dillhoefer owns a portfolio that over the last five years has produced a 16.8% annual return. During that time the portfolio produced a 1.10 beta. Further, the risk-free return and market return averaged 7.4% and 15.2% per year, respectively. What was the *ex post* alpha on Janice's portfolio over this time period? Draw the *ex post* SML and the position of Janice's portfolio.

14. The performance of the Venus Fund, a common stock mutual fund, compared with that of the TSE 300 over a ten-year period, is as follows:

	Venus Fund	TSE 300
Average quarterly excess return	0.6%	0.5%
Standard deviation of quarterly excess returns	9.9%	6.6%
Beta	1.10	1.00

John Vance is considering investing in either the Venus Fund or another mutual fund whose objective is to track the performance of the TSE 300. Which fund would you recommend that John select, assuming that your decision is based solely on past performance? Justify your answer using various measures of risk-adjusted performance.

15. Why is the reward-to-variability ratio a more appropriate measure of performance than the *ex post* alpha if the portfolio being assessed represents the entire wealth of the portfolio's owner?

16. Can the *ex post* alpha, the reward-to-volatility ratio, and the reward-to-variability ratio give conflicting answers to the question of whether a particular portfolio has outperformed a market index on a risk-adjusted basis? If so, which of these measures can conflict with the others, and why can this conflict occur?

17. Does a portfolio's *ex post* alpha measure gains and losses due to security selection, market timing, or both? Explain.

18. Assume that broad stock market indices, such as the TSE 300, are not good surrogates for the "true" market portfolio. What potential problems does this cause for performance evaluation using the *ex post* alpha measure?

19. You are given the following historical performance information on the capital markets and the Jupiter Fund, a common stock mutual fund.

Year	Jupiter Fund Beta	Return on Jupiter Fund	Return on Market Index	Return on Treasury Bills
1	0.90	−2.99%	−8.50%	6.58%
2	0.95	0.63	4.01	6.53
3	0.95	22.01	14.30	4.39
4	1.00	24.08	18.98	3.84
5	1.00	−22.46	−14.66	6.93
6	0.90	−25.12	−26.47	8.00
7	0.80	29.72	37.20	5.80
8	0.75	22.15	23.84	5.08
9	0.80	0.48	−7.18	5.12
10	0.85	6.85	6.56	7.18

a. Compute the Jupiter Fund's average beta over the ten-year period. What investment percentages in the market index and Treasury bills are required in order to produce a beta equal to the fund's average beta?

b. Compute the year-by-year returns that would have been earned on a portfolio invested in the market index and Treasury bills in the proportions calculated in part (a).

c. Compute the year-by-year returns that would have been earned on a portfolio invested in the market index and Treasury bills in the proportions needed to match Jupiter's beta year by year. (Note: These proportions will change yearly as the fund's beta changes yearly.)

d. One measure of a fund's market timing ability is the average difference between (1) what the fund would have earned annually by investing in the market index and Treasury bills so that the year-by-year beta equals the fund's actual year-by-year beta, and (2) what the fund would have earned annually by investing in the market index and Treasury bills so that the year-by-year beta equals the fund's average beta. Given your previous calculations, evaluate the market timing ability of Jupiter's manager.

e. One measure of a fund's security selection ability is the average difference between (1) the fund's annual returns and (2) what the fund would have earned annually by investing in the market index and Treasury bills so that the year-by-year beta equals the fund's actual year-by-year beta. Calculate Jupiter's average return and then, using your previous calculations, evaluate the security selection ability of Jupiter's manager.

20. Consider the following annual returns produced by a MiniFund, a mutual fund investing in small stocks:

1971	16.50%	1976	57.38%	1981	13.88%	1986	6.85%
1972	4.43	1977	25.38	1982	28.01	1987	−9.30
1973	−30.90	1978	23.46	1983	39.67	1988	22.87
1974	−19.95	1979	43.46	1984	−6.67	1989	10.18
1975	52.82	1980	39.88	1985	24.66	1990	−21.56

Referring to Table 1.1, use the Treasury bill returns as the risk-free return and the common stock returns as the market return, and calculate the following risk-adjusted return measures for the small stock mutual fund:

a. *ex post* alpha

b. reward-to-volatility ratio

c. reward-to-variability ratio.

Comment on the mutual fund's risk-adjusted performance. What problems are associated with using a large capitalization index such as the TSE 300 (the source of the common stock returns) as the benchmark in evaluating this small company mutual fund?

21. In an article in *Journal of Finance* (March 1983), Jess Chua and Richard Woodward investigated the investment skill of the legendary economist John Maynard Keynes. A portfolio managed by Keynes had the returns shown at the top of the following page. Chua and Woodward concluded that Keynes demonstrated superior investment abilities. They did not, however, distinguish between his market timing and security selection skills. Using the quadratic regression and dummy variable techniques, evaluate Keynes's market timing skills. (Hint: Use of a regression package found in a standard personal computer spreadsheet program is highly recommended.)

	Keynes's Return	Market Return	Risk-free Return
1928	–3.4%	7.9%	4.2
1929	0.8	6.6	5.3
1930	–32.4	–20.3	2.5
1931	–24.6	–25.0	3.6
1932	44.8	–5.8	1.6
1933	35.1	21.5	0.6
1934	33.1	–0.7	0.7
1935	44.3	5.3	0.6
1936	56.0	10.2	0.6
1937	8.5	–0.5	0.6
1938	–40.1	–16.1	0.6
1939	12.9	–7.2	1.3
1940	–15.6	–12.9	1.0
1941	33.5	12.5	1.0
1942	–0.9	0.8	1.0
1943	53.9	15.6	1.0
1944	14.5	5.4	1.0
1945	14.6	0.8	1.0

22. Discuss the potential drawbacks of evaluating bond portfolio performance by using a bond market line.
23. (Appendix Question) What is the purpose of performance attribution? What types of problems can hinder performance attribution?
24. (Appendix Question) Assume that security returns are explained by a sector-factor model. Eugene Stephens has been asked to develop a performance attribution report analyzing the returns on portfolio A versus those of a market index for the latest year, and he has collected the following information:

	Portfolio A	Market Index	Sector-Factor Values
Return	12.50%	5.50%	—
Beta	1.10	1.00	–0.50
Size	1.30	6.00	–0.60
% Industrial	40%	80%	8.00
% Nonindustrial	60%	20%	16.00

Unfortunately, Eugene is confused by the subject of performance attribution. Carry out the analysis for him.

CFA Exam Question

25. As a corporate treasurer, you are responsible for evaluating prospective investment managers for your company's pension fund. You have interviewed three managers,

examined their reported investment performances, and identified clear-cut differences in their investment approaches.

Manager A has developed a very appealing and apparently successful investment process based on extensive research and back-testing but she has not yet managed money using this process.

Manager B has been investing relatively small amounts of money over only the past two years, producing what appears to be extraordinary investment performance. His process is based on exploiting what he believes to be a market inefficiency (or anomaly) to produce superior returns.

Manager C is a global investment counsellor who emphasizes active selection of stocks and bonds across the major world markets. He has a long track record and uses a well-established and widely accepted process for selecting securities.

a. Discuss the usefulness of historical investment performance in evaluating investment managers.

b. For each of the three managers, identify and discuss the two most important factors that you would consider in assessing the manager's performance.

KEY TERMS

dollar-weighted return
time-weighted return
benchmark portfolio
ex post alpha
ex post characteristic line
simple linear regression
reward-to-volatility ratio
reward-to-variability ratio
performance attribution
comparative performance attribution

REFERENCES

1. The use of portfolio benchmarks for performance evaluation is discussed in:

Richard Roll, "Performance Evaluation and Benchmark Errors (I)," Journal of Portfolio Management 6, no. 4 (Summer 1980): 5–12.

———, "Performance Evaluation and Benchmark Errors (II)," *Journal of Portfolio Management* 7, no. 2 (Winter 1981): 17–22.

Gary P. Brinson, Jeffrey J. Diermeier, and Gary G. Schlarbaum, "A Composite Portfolio Benchmark for Pension Plans," *Financial Analysts Journal* 42, no. 2 (March/April 1986): 15–24.

Mark P. Kritzman, "How to Build a Normal Portfolio in Three Easy Steps," *Journal of Portfolio Management* 13, no. 4 (Summer 1987): 21–23.

Jeffery V. Bailey, Thomas M. Richards, and David E. Tierney, "Benchmark Portfolios and the Manager/Plan Sponsor Relationship," *Journal of Corporate Finance* 4, no. 4 (Winter 1988): 25–32.

Arjun Divecha and Richard C. Grinold, "Normal Portfolios: Issues for Sponsors, Managers, and Consultants," *Financial Analysts Journal* 45, no. 2 (March/April 1989): 7–13.

Edward P. Rennie and Thomas J. Cowhey, "The Successful Use of Benchmark Portfolios: A Case Study," *Financial Analysts Journal* 46, no. 5 (September/October 1990): 18–26.

Jeffery V. Bailey, "Are Manager Universes Acceptable Performance Benchmarks?" *Journal of Portfolio Management* 18, no. 3 (Spring 1992): 9–13.

———, "Evaluating Benchmark Quality," *Financial Analysts Journal* 48, no. 3 (May/June 1992): 33–39.

T. Daniel Coggin, Frank J. Fabozzi and Shafiqur Rahman, "The Investment Performance of US Equity Pension Fund Managers: An Empirical Investigation," *Journal of Finance* 48, no. 3 (July 1993): 1039–1055.

2. The three measures of risk-adjusted performance were initially developed in:

Jack L. Treynor, "How to Rate Management of Investment Funds," *Harvard Business Review* 43, no. 1 (January/February 1965): 63–75.

William F. Sharpe, "Mutual Fund Performance," *Journal of Business* 39, no. 1 (January 1966): 119–138.

Michael C. Jensen, "The Performance of Mutual Funds in the Period 1945–1964," *Journal of Finance* 23, no. 2 (May 1968): 389–416.

———, "Risk, the Pricing of Capital Assets, and the Evaluation of Investment Portfolios," *Journal of Business* 42, no. 2 (April 1969): 167–185.

3. More sophisticated measures of portfolio performance that also measure market timing ability were initially developed by:

Jack L. Treynor and Kay K. Mazuy, "Can Mutual Funds Outguess the Market?" *Harvard Business Review* 44, no. 4 (July/August 1966): 131–136.

Robert C. Merton, "On Market Timing and Investment Performance I: An Equilibrium Theory of Value for Market Forecasts," *Journal of Business* 54, no. 3 (July 1981): 363–406.

Roy D. Henriksson and Robert C. Merton, "On Market Timing and Investment Performance II: Statistical Procedures for Evaluating Forecasting Skill," *Journal of Business* 54, no. 4 (October 1981): 513–533.

4. There have been many criticisms leveled at the various measures of portfolio performance that are presented in this chapter. One of the most formidable critiques was:

Richard Roll, "Ambiguity When Performance Is Measured by the Security Market Line," *Journal of Finance* 33, no. 4 (September 1978): 1051–1069.

5. APT-based measures of portfolio performance have been developed by:

Gregory Connor and Robert Korajczyk, "Performance Measurement with the Arbitrage Pricing Theory: A New Framework for Analysis," *Journal of Financial Economics* 15, no. 3 (March 1986): 373–394.

Bruce N. Lehmann and David M. Modest, "Mutual Fund Performance Evaluation: A Comparison of Benchmarks and Benchmark Comparisons," *Journal of Finance* 42, no. 2 (June 1987): 233–265.

Nai-Fu Chen, Thomas E. Copeland, and David Mayers, "A Comparison of Single and Multifactor Portfolio Performance Methodologies," *Journal of Financial and Quantitative Analysis* 22, no. 4 (December 1987): 401–417.

6. Some recent developments in measuring portfolio performance are discussed in:

Stanley J. Kon, "The Market-Timing Performance of Mutual Fund Managers," *Journal of Business* 56, no. 3 (July 1983): 323–347.

Anat R. Admati and Stephen A. Ross, "Measuring Investment Performance in a Rational Expectations Equilibrium Model," *Journal of Business* 58, no. 1 (January 1985): 1–26.

Philip H. Dybvig and Stephen A. Ross, "Differential Information and Performance Measurement Using a Security Market Line," *Journal of Finance* 40, no. 2 (June 1985): 383–399.

———, "The Analytics of Performance Measurement Using a Security Market Line," *Journal of Finance* 40, no. 2 (June 1985): 401–416.

Mark Kritzman, "How to Detect Skill in Management Performance," *Journal of Portfolio Management* 12, no. 2 (Winter 1986): 16–20.

Ravi Jagannathan and Robert A. Korajczyk, "Assessing the Market Timing Performance of Managed Portfolios," *Journal of Business* 59, no. 2, pt. 1 (April 1986): 217–235.

Anat R. Admati, Sudipto Bhattacharya, Paul Pfleiderer, and Stephen A. Ross, "On Timing and Selectivity," *Journal of Finance* 41, no. 3 (July 1986): 715–730.

Gary P. Brinson, L. Randolph Hood, and Gilbert L. Beebower, "Determinants of Portfolio Performance," *Financial Analysts Journal* 42, no. 4 (July/August 1986): 39–44.

William Breen, Ravi Jagannathan, and Aharon R. Ofer, "Correcting for Heteroscedasticity in Tests for Market Timing Ability," *Journal of Business* 59, no. 4, pt. 1 (October 1986): 585–598.

Robert E. Cumby and David M. Modest, "Testing for Market Timing Ability: A Framework for Forecast Evaluation," *Journal of Financial Economics* 19, no. 1 (September 1987): 169–189.

Larry J. Lockwood and K. Rao Kadiyala, "Measuring Investment Performance with a Stochastic Parameter Regression Model," *Journal of Banking and Finance* 12, no. 3 (September 1988): 457–467.

Alex Kane and Gary Marks, "Performance Evaluation of Market Timers: Theory and Evidence," *Journal of Financial and Quantitative Analysis* 23, no. 4 (December 1988): 425–435.

Mark Grinblatt and Sheridan Titman, "Portfolio Performance Evaluation: Old Issues and New Insights," *Review of Financial Studies* 2, no. 3 (1989): 393–421.

Cheng-few Lee and Shafiqur Rahman, "Market Timing, Selectivity, and Mutual Fund Performance: An Empirical Investigation," *Journal of Business* 63, no. 2 (April 1990): 261–278.

Michel Gendron and Christian Genest, "Performance Measurement Under Asymmetric Information and Investment Constraints," *Journal of Finance* 45, no. 5 (December 1990): 1655–1661.

Cheng-few Lee and Shafiqur Rahman, "New Evidence of Timing and Security Selection Skill of Mutual Fund Managers," *Journal of Portfolio Management* 17, no. 2 (Winter 1991): 80–83.

Gary P. Brinson, Brian D. Singer, and Gilbert L. Beebower, "Determinants of Portfolio Performance II: An Update," *Financial Analysts Journal* 47, no. 3 (May/June 1991): 40–48.

Chris R. Hensel, D. Don Ezra, and John H. Ilkiw, "The Importance of the Asset Allocation Decision," *Financial Analysts Journal* 47, no. 4 (July/August 1991): 65–72.

Eric J. Weigel, "The Performance of Tactical Asset Allocation," *Financial Analysts Journal* 47, no. 5 (September/October 1991): 63–70.

G. L. Beebower and A. P. Varikooty, "Measuring Market Timing Strategies," *Financial Analysts Journal* 47, no. 6 (November/December 1991): 78–84, 92.

L. R. Glosten and R. Jagannathan, "A Contingent Claim Approach to Performance Evaluation," *Journal of Empirical Finance* 1, no. 2 (January 1994): 133–160.

7. An alternative approach to portfolio performance evaluation that is called style analysis is described in:

William F. Sharpe, "Determining a Fund's Effective Asset Mix," *Investment Management Review* (December 1988): 59–69.

———, "Asset Allocation: Management Style and Performance Measurement," *Journal of Portfolio Management* 18, no. 2 (Winter 1992): 7–19.

8. Some other major articles on portfolio performance evaluation are listed in:

Gordon J. Alexander and Jack Clark Francis, *Portfolio Analysis* (Englewood Cliffs, NJ: Prentice Hall, 1986), Chapter 13.

Ravi Shukla and Charles Trzcinka, "Performance Measurement of Managed Portfolios," *Financial Markets, Institutions & Instruments* 1, no. 4 (1992).

9. Bond portfolio performance evaluation is discussed in:

Wayne H. Wagner and Dennis A. Tito, "Definitive New Measures of Bond Performance and Risk," *Pension World* 13, no. 5 (May 1977): 10–12.

———, "Is Your Bond Manager Skillful?" *Pension World* 13, no. 6 (June 1977): 9–13.

Peter O. Dietz, H. Russell Fogler, and Donald J. Hardy, "The Challenge of Analyzing Bond Portfolio Returns," *Journal of Portfolio Management* 6, no. 3 (Spring 1980): 53–58.

Mark Kritzman, "Can Bond Managers Perform Consistently?" *Journal of Portfolio Management* 9, no. 4 (Summer 1983): 54–56.

Robert N. Anthony, "How to Measure Fixed-Income Performance Correctly," *Journal of Portfolio Management* 11, no. 2 (Winter 1985): 61–65.

Peter O. Dietz and Jeannette R. Kirschman, "Evaluation Portfolio Performance," Chapter 14 in *Managing Investment Portfolios: A Dynamic Process*, eds. John L. Maginn and Donald L. Tuttle (Boston, MA: Warren, Gorham & Lamont, 1990).

Ronald N. Kahn, "Bond Performance Analysis: A Multi-Factor Approach," *Journal of Portfolio Management* 18, no. 1 (Fall 1991): 40–47.

Christopher R. Blake, Edwin J. Elton, and Martin J. Gruber in "The Performance of Bond Mutual Funds," *Journal of Business* 66, no. 3 (July 1993): 371–403.

10. Performance attribution was initially developed and then expanded in:

Eugene F. Fama, "Components of Investment Performance," *Journal of Finance* 27, no. 3 (June 1972): 551–567.

H. Russel Fogler, "Common Stock Management in the 1990s," *Journal of Portfolio Management* 16, no. 2 (Winter 1990): 26–35.

Ernest M. Ankrim, "Risk-Adjusted Performance Attribution," *Financial Analysts Journal* 48, no. 2 (March/April 1991): 74–82.

Peter J. Higgs and Stephen Goode, "Target Active Returns and Attribution Analysis," *Financial Analysts Journal* 49, no. 3 (May/June 1993): 77–80.

11. For a Canadian perspective on the topics covered in this chapter, see:

J. McLaughlin and N. Bossen, "The Historical Performance of Canadian Investment Managers: Predictor of Future Performance," *Canadian Investment Review* III, no. 1 (Spring 1990).

T. Appelt, "Active Management: What Is the Right Performance Benchmark?" *Canadian Investment Review* V, no. 1 (Spring 1992).

B. Curwood, "Solving the Mysteries of Performance Measurement," *Canadian Investment Review* VII, no. 1 (Spring 1994).

CHAPTER **26**

Extended Diversification

One of the major themes of modern portfolio theory concerns the merits of diversification: in an efficient capital market, sensible investment strategies will include holdings of many different assets. Previous chapters have considered traditional securities, such as stocks and bonds, and some less traditional ones, such as options and futures. However, an investor should also consider holding foreign securities and tangible assets.

This chapter will discuss these two aspects of diversification, and then turn to a less lofty subject: betting on sporting events. As indicated in previous chapters, active investment management can be considered a form of betting. Now this rather subtle form of wagering that is handled by security brokers and dealers will be compared and contrasted with the more explicit form handled by people at racetracks and "bookmakers."

INTERNATIONAL INVESTMENT

If the world were under one political jurisdiction, with one currency and complete freedom of trade, then "the market portfolio" could be thought of as including all securities in the world, each in proportion to its market value. In such a situation, limiting one's investments to securities representing firms located in only one part of the world would most likely result in a relatively low rate of return per unit of risk. After all, few people would advocate that Albertans own only securities issued by Alberta firms. And in a world without political boundaries, few people would advocate that Canadians own only securities issued by Canadian firms.

Unfortunately, there are political boundaries, different currencies, and restrictions on trade and currency exchange. Such irritants diminish, but do not destroy, the advantages to be gained from international investment.

► The Total Investable Capital Market Portfolio

Figure 26.1 provides a 1993 year-end estimate of the size of the total investable capital market portfolio in the world, which can be thought of as representing the set of investments that are available to Canadian portfolio managers. Many problems are encountered in the construction of such a portfolio. It is almost impossible to adequately represent *all* security

Figure 26.1

Total investable capital market portfolio, year-end 1993.[a]

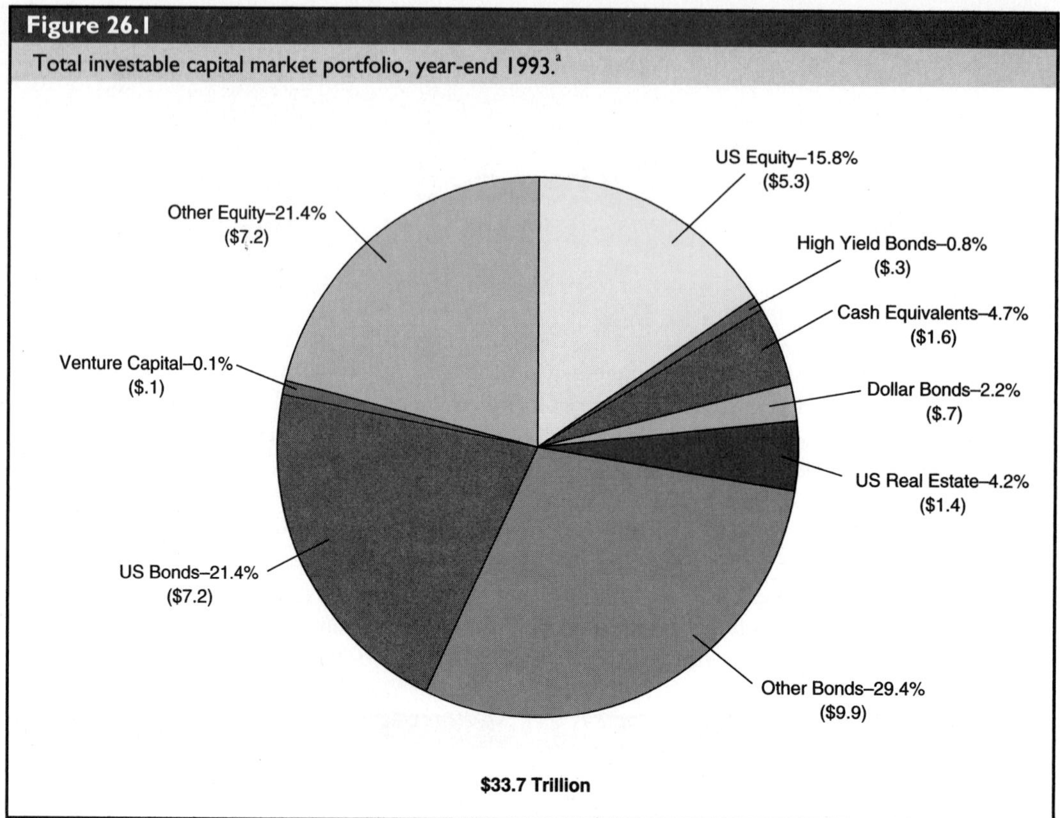

[a] Preliminary, figures measured in trillions of US dollars.

SOURCE: Provided by Brinson Partners, Inc. (Chicago, 1994).

markets, as undoubtedly certain classes of assets have been omitted (such as foreign real estate) and double counting is involved in that some firms own parts of other firms.[1]

The figure indicates that non-US bond and equity markets amount to $7.2 + $.7 + $9.9 = $17.8 trillion, and comprise about one-half the value of the entire $33.7-trillion portfolio (there are three foreign categories— *Other Equity, Other Bonds*, and *Dollar Bonds*; the latter are foreign and Eurobonds denominated in US dollars). Also of interest is the observation that fixed-income securities amount to $7.2 + $9.9 + $.7 + $1.6 + $.3 = $19.7 trillion, and make up nearly 60% of the portfolio's value.[2] About one-half of this total is non-US fixed-income securities. Similarly, about 60% of the $12.6 trillion ($5.3 + $7.2 + $.1) equity market consists of non-US stocks.

[1] For a discussion of the difficulties in measuring the size of the world portfolio along with an estimate of its size at year-end 1984, see Roger G. Ibbotson, Laurence B. Siegel, and Kathryn S. Love, "World Wealth: Market Values and Returns," *Journal of Portfolio Management* 12, no. 1 (Fall 1985): 4–23.

[2] A more detailed study of bonds estimated their global value to be $11 trillion at the end of 1989. Of this total, $6.3 trillion was government debt, $2.4 trillion was local corporate debt, $1 trillion was "crossborder" debt (that is, foreign bonds and Eurobonds), and $1.3 trillion was "other domestic" debt. See Roger G. Ibbotson and Laurence B. Siegel, "The World Bond Market: Market Values, Yields, and Returns," *Journal of Fixed Income* 1, no. 1 (June 1991): 90–99.

A more detailed breakdown of the stock market capitalization at the end of December 1995 in the countries followed by *Morgan Stanley Capital International Perspective* is provided in column (2) of Table 26.1. The largest market for common stocks is the United States, followed by Japan. In total, these two countries make up 64.2% of the total. A distant third is the United Kingdom, and then notably behind the United Kingdom come Germany and France. These five countries represent 81.4% of the total. It will be shown next how Morgan Stanley calculates international stock market indices involving these countries.

Table 26.1

Stock Market Capitalization, December 1995.

Country (1)	Market Capitalization *Dollars*[a] (2)	Market Capitalization *Percentage* (3)	*GDP Weight* (4)
Austria	$ 22.6	0.2%	1.1%
Belgium	60.2	0.7	1.1
Denmark	41.7	0.5	0.7
Finland	27.3	0.3	0.4
France	330.6	3.6	6.7
Germany	360.3	3.9	10.3
Ireland	14.7	0.2	0.2
Italy	117.2	1.3	5.0
Netherlands	211.1	2.3	1.7
Norway	24.2	0.3	0.6
Spain	94.5	1.0	2.4
Sweden	106.7	1.2	1.1
Switzerland	312.5	3.4	1.4
UK	887.5	9.6	5.1
Total Europe	$2611.0	28.3%	37.8%
Australia	134.7	1.5	1.6
Hong Kong	162.7	1.8	0.6
Japan	2152.9	23.4	23.1
Malaysia	115.2	1.2	0.3
New Zealand	20.8	0.2	0.2
Singapore	61.5	0.7	0.3
Total Pacific	$2647.8	28.7%	26.3%
Canada	200.5	2.2	2.4
USA	3759.7	40.8	33.4
Total North America	$3960.2	43.0%	35.8%
Total World	$9219.0	100.0%	100.0%

[a] Measured in billions of US dollars.

SOURCE: Adapted from MCSI, *Morgan Stanley Capital International: EAFE and World Perspective*, January 1996, p. 8.

International Equity Indices

In most countries, there are indices of overall stock values and of the values of stocks within various industry or economic sectors. Such indices can be used for assessing "market moves" within the country and, more importantly, for comparative performance measurement. Important indices include the Financial Times-Stock Exchange 100 Index (often referred to as FT-SE, or the "footsie") for the London Stock Exchange; the Nikkei 225 Average for the Tokyo Stock Exchange; the Paris Bourse's CAC 40 and the DAX Index for the Frankfurt Stock Exchange. These and other indices from both developed and emerging markets are reported daily in *The Globe and Mail: Report on Business* as shown in Figure 26.2(a). Figure 26.2(b) shows the extensive daily coverage given to US indices in the *Report on Business*. With the advent of 24-hour trading across different exchanges worldwide and greater international brokerage representation for investors, the financial press also reports prices for a selected sample of individual companies traded on 14 different overseas markets.[3]

On the international level, the indices produced by *Morgan Stanley Capital International Perspective* are also widely used for such purposes.[4] Each index is based on a valued-weighted portfolio of stocks (using total shares outstanding) in a particular country. Nearly all of these stocks can be purchased by foreigners. Values for each of 22 national indices (plus an index of South African gold mining companies) are given in both the local currency and in US dollars based on exchange rates at the time. Approximately 1500 stocks are currently included, representing about 60% of the aggregate market value of the 22 covered equity markets.[5] The countries involved are listed in Table 26.1.

The individual country indices are combined into various regional indices. Furthermore, all of the country indices are also used to compute two "World" indices that involve different sets of weights. These weights are based on market capitalization (thus producing a value-weighted index) and gross domestic product (GDP), and are shown in columns (3) and (4) of Table 26.1. Compared with the market capitalization weights, the United States, Japan, and the United Kingdom have lower GDP weights but Germany, France, and Italy have notably larger ones.

Morgan Stanley also calculates the "Europe, Australia, Far East: (EAFE) index, which is widely used as a benchmark when evaluating the performance of international portfolio managers. The index excludes the United States, Canada, and South Africa and is currently based on the stock performance in the remaining 20 countries listed in Table 26.1. Three of the Morgan Stanley composite indices published weekly in the *Globe and Mail*, and shown in panel (c) of Figure 26.2, are The World Index, the EAFE, and the Emerging Markets Index.

In recent years several countries have instituted organized stock exchanges or highly active over-the-counter stock markets. In general, these countries have in common a relatively

---

[3] For a discussion of European stock markets, see Gabriel Hawawini, *European Equity Markets: Price Behavior and Efficiency*, Monograph Series in Finance and Economics #1984–4/5, New York University Salomon Center, Leonard N. Stern School of Business. Also see Victor A. Canto, "Everything You Always Wanted to Know About the European Monetary System, the ECU and ERM, But Didn't Know Who to Ask," *Financial Analysts Journal* 47, no. 6 (November/December 1991): 22–25.

[4] For a discussion of the Morgan Stanley indices, see Campbell R. Harvey, "The World Price of Covariance Risk," *Journal of Finance* 46, no. 1 (March 1991): 111–157.

[5] For more on these and other indices, see Chapter 5 in Bruno Solnik, *International Investments* (Reading, MA: Addison-Wesley, 1991); and John Markese, "An Investor's Guide to the International Marketplace," *AAII Journal* 14, no. 7 (August 1992): 29–32.

Figure 26.2

International equity indices and benchmarks.

(a)

Stock Indexes

	Yesterday	Previous	1995/96 high	1995/96 low
Amsterdam AEX	500.89	503.61	503.61	388.33
Brussels	1624.87	1611.96	1624.87	1271.53
Frankfurt DAX	2349.66	2323.48	2349.66	1910.96
Hong Kong	10427.20	10466.67	10573.90	6967.93
London FT 30	2738.7	2750.5	2750.5	2238.3
FT-SE 100	3700.3	3720.6	3720.6	2954.2
Mexico City	2957.46	3002.10	3011.05	1447.52
Milan	9445	9435	10911	8804
Paris CAC-40	1916.29	1916.56	2017.27	1721.14
Sydney All ord	2262.8	2274.9	2274.9	1823.3
Tokyo	20652.08	20563.58	20669.03	14507.17
Zurich SMI	3361.5	3368.1	3395.8	2426.6

Emerging Markets

	Close	Chg		Close	Chg
Bangkok	1349.16	−15.30	**Kuala Lumpur**	1050.75	−3.79
Bombay	3001.03	−2.16	**Madrid**	327.24	−0.58
Buenos Aires	546.88	−11.68	**Manila**	2681.76	−13.87
Caracas	2018.21	+2.68	**Santiago**	5791.47	−12.87
China World	944.04	−24.25	**Sao Paulo**	46538	−8.72
Istanbul	39998.93	+153.21	**Seoul**	881.99	+15.18
Jakarta	530.81	−2.29	**Singapore**	2373.60	−12.27
Johannesburg	6628	+25	**Taipei**	4911.99	−22.87

(b)

U.S. Indexes

New York Stock Exchange

52-week high	52-week low	Index	Open	High	Low	Close	Chg	% Chg	Vol (100s)
5216.47	3832.08	DJ Industrials	5187.21	5225.50	5163.36	5197.68	+16.25	+0.3	110944
2092.11	1492.06	DJ Transport	1992.00	1999.42	1975.26	1986.02	−10.29	−0.5	16216
228.62	183.23	DJ Utilities	227.92	229.46	227.01	228.62			12612
1735.81	1289.09	DJ 65 Composite	1711.42	1721.90	1701.59	1712.34	+0.13	+0.0	139772
109.77	93.56	DJ 20 Bond	105.30	105.30	105.29	105.29	−0.17	−0.2	
598.35	347.56	S&P 100	589.16	591.09	589.16	591.09	+1.96	+0.3	
220.73	135.12	S&P 400 MidCap	215.08	215.33	214.94	215.33	+0.25	+0.1	
624.57	611.94	S&P 500	616.71	618.47	616.60	618.46	+1.75	+0.3	
62.68	60.22	S&P Financial	60.81	60.91	60.76	60.90	+0.09	+0.2	
731.56	716.71	S&P Industrial	723.33	726.00	723.23	726.21	+2.88	+0.4	
491.36	467.71	S&P Transport	482.09	483.05	481.21	481.86	−0.23	−0.0	
207.04	199.32	S&P Utilities	205.45	205.59	204.62	204.74	−0.71	−0.3	

New York

Index	High	Low	Close	Chg	% Chg
NYSE Composite	331.26	330.01	331.26	+1.08	+0.3
NYSE Financial	271.79	271.27	271.78	+0.30	+0.1
NYSE Industrial	416.37	414.27	416.37	+1.97	+0.5
NYSE Transport	305.04	304.09	304.48	+0.36	+0.1
NYSE Utilities	256.63	255.62	256.06	−0.57	−0.2

Nasdaq

Index	High	Low	Close	Chg	% Chg
Nasdaq composite	1035.90	1031.28	1032.37	−1.10	−0.1
NNM Composite	463.34	461.26	461.77	−0.51	−0.1
NNM Industrial	386.74	385.16	385.82	−0.63	−0.2

American

Index	High	Low	Close	Chg	% Chg
Amex markt valu	546.37	543.88	546.35	+2.43	+0.5
Biotech	134.93	132.51	134.84	+1.43	+1.1
Institutional	641.75	639.25	641.74	+2.11	+0.3
Japan Index	209.14	209.14	209.14	−1.03	−0.5
Major market	546.13	543.52	545.98	+2.05	+0.4
Oil and gas	331.84	329.24	331.69	+2.45	+0.7

New York Odd Lots

Odd-lot trades made Friday through the New York Stock Exchange:

Customer purchases..... 1,411,422 Short sales 95,830

Other sales .... 1,717,155 Total sales... 1,812,985

(c)

This Week In Numbers

	This week	Change in a week	Change in a year
TSE 300	4839.74	+2.7%	+16.6%
Best group: Gold & silver	11365.40	+9.1%	+29.8%
Worst group: Real estate & const.	1694.39	-0.2%	-19.6%
Toronto 35	255.75	+2.9%	+16.8%
TSE 100	294.72	+2.9%	+16.8%
TSE 200	287.30	+1.5%	+15.5%
Dow Jones industrial average	5181.43	+1.3%	+34.0%
Standard & Poor's 500	616.71	+0.1%	+33.9%
Morgan Stanley world index ($U.S.)	742.30	+1.1%	+21.4%
–World ex U.S. and Canada (EAFE)	1156.50	+1.8%	+13.7%
–Emerging Markets	478.30	+4.5%	-0.3%
Gold ($U.S. an ounce)	395.80	+2.1%	+6.6%

SOURCE: Reprinted with permission of the *Globe and Mail* (January 6–10, 1996).

low (compared to Western countries) level of per capita gross domestic product, improved political and economic stability, a currency convertible into Western countries' currencies (or at least some means for foreigners to repatriate income and capital gains), and most important, securities available for investment by foreigners. Such countries have what are referred to as **emerging markets**.

Investments in emerging market stocks have proven attractive to a number of institutional investors, who in many cases have invested directly in those securities, or when that is not possible, through regional funds (such as a Latin American Fund; see Chapter 22). Because many emerging market economies are undergoing rapid growth, and because their stock markets are not highly developed and therefore are less efficient, there is considerable opportunity for relatively high returns from emerging market investments. However, there is also a relatively high level of risk involved.

Morgan Stanley Capital International defines 21 countries as emerging markets: India, Indonesia, South Korea, Malaysia, Pakistan, the Philippines, Sri Lanka, Taiwan, Thailand, Argentina, Brazil, Chile, Columbia, Mexico, Peru, Venezuela, Greece, Israel, Jordan, Portugal, and Turkey. The publish stock market indices for each of these countries as well as three regional stock market indices (Asia; Latin America; Europe and Middle East) and an overall emerging markets index.[6] Also popular are the International Financial Corporation (IFC) Emerging Market Indexes and the IFC Investable Indexes. The latter are based on stocks that can be held by foreigners, and hence are often the indices of choice for international investors.

► Risk and Return from Foreign Investing

Investing in a foreign security involves all the risks associated with investing in a domestic security plus some additional ones. The investor expects to receive cash flows in the future

[6] For more on emerging markets, see Vihang Errunza, "Emerging Markets: A New Opportunity for Improving Global Portfolio Performance," *Financial Analysts Journal* 39, no. 5 (September/October 1983): 51–58; Vihang Errunza and Etienne Losq, "How Risky are Emerging Markets? Myths and Perceptions Versus Theory and Evidence," *Journal of Portfolio Management* 14, no. 1 (Fall 1987): 62–67; and Vihang Errunza and Prasad Padmanabhan, "Further Evidence on the Benefits of Portfolio Investments in Emerging Markets," *Financial Analysts Journal* 44, no. 4 (July/August 1988): 76–78.

from the foreign security. However, these cash flows will be in a foreign currency and thus will be of relatively little use to the investor if they cannot be converted into the investor's domestic currency. The additional risks associated with foreign investing result from uncertainties associated with converting these foreign cash flows into domestic currency. They are known as **political risk** and **exchange** (or currency) **risk**.[7]

Political risk refers to uncertainty about the *ability* of an investor to convert the foreign currency into domestic currency. Specifically, a foreign government might restrict, tax, or completely prohibit the exchange of one currency for another. Because such policies change from time to time, the ability of an investor to repatriate foreign cash flows may be subject to some uncertainty. There may even be a possibility of complete expropriation, making political risk very large.

Exchange risk refers to uncertainty about the *rate* at which a foreign currency can be exchanged for the investor's domestic currency in the future. That is, at the time a foreign security is bought, the rate at which future foreign cash flows can be converted into domestic currency is uncertain, and it is this uncertainty that is known as exchange risk.

Hedging Exchange Risk

To an extent, exchange risk can be reduced by hedging in the forward (or futures) market for foreign currency. In the case of default-free fixed-income securities, it may be possible to completely eliminate such risk in this way. For example, assume that a one-year pure discount bond paying 1000 British pounds at maturity can be purchased for 925 British pounds. Furthermore, assume that a forward contract can be signed where the investor will receive $2110.50 for delivering 1000 British pounds a year from now. In this situation, the rate of return *in British pounds* on this security is (1000 – 925)/925 = 8.11%.

If the current (that is, spot) exchange rate were $2.1673 per pound, then the cost of this bond to a Canadian investor would be 925 × $2.1673 = $2004.75. Thus, the rate of return *in Canadian dollars* on this British security would be ($2110.50 – $2004.75)/$2004.75 = 5.27%. Except for political risk, this is a certain return, since exchange risk has been completely removed by hedging with a forward contract.

Unfortunately, it is not possible to hedge completely the exchange risk associated with risky investments. Forward contracts can be made to cover expected cash flows, but if the actual cash flows are larger or smaller than expected, then some of the foreign currency may have to be exchanged at the spot rate prevailing at the time that the cash is received. Since future spot rates usually cannot be predicted with complete certainty, this will affect overall risk. As a practical matter, this "unhedgeable" risk is likely to be small. Nevertheless, the cost of hedging foreign investments may exceed the benefit (see the *Institutional Issues* section, "Currency Risk: To Hedge or Not to Hedge").

Foreign and Domestic Returns

Changes in exchange rates can cause major differences between the returns obtained by domestic investors and the returns obtained by unhedged foreign investors.

Consider a Canadian investor and a Swiss investor, both of whom purchase shares of a Swiss company whose stock is traded only in Switzerland. Let the price of the shares in Swiss

---

[7] The effects these types of risk have on asset pricing has been considered by a number of people. For a discussion and list of references, see Chapter 1 and 5 in Solnik, *International Investments*.

francs be P_0 at the beginning of a period and P_1 at the end of the period. The **domestic return**, denoted by r_d, is

$$r_d = \frac{P_1 - P_0}{P_0}. \tag{26.1}$$

For example, if $P_0 = 10$ Swiss francs and $P_1 = 12$ Swiss francs, then $r_d = (12–10)/10 = 20\%$.

For the Swiss investor, r_d is the stock's return. Not so for the Canadian investor. Assume that at the beginning of the period the price (in dollars) of one Swiss franc is $0.8481. Denoting this exchange rate (that is, the exchange rate at the beginning of the period) by X_0, the cost of a share to the Canadian investor will be X_0P_0. In the example, this cost will be $\$0.8481 \times 10 = \$8.48$.

Now, assume that the exchange rate rises to $0.8905 per Swiss franc at the end of the period. Denoting this by X_1, the ending value of a share for the Canadian investor will be X_1P_1. In the example, this value will be $\$.8905 \times 12 = \$10.69$.

The **foreign return** (that is, the return to a foreign investor), denoted by r_f, is

$$r_f = \frac{X_1P_1 - X_0P_0}{X_0P_0}. \tag{26.2}$$

In the example, the foreign investor (a Canadian) would have earned a return of $r_f = (\$10.69 - \$8.48)/\$8.48 = 26\%$ on an investment in the Swiss firm's stock.

In effect, the Canadian has made *two* investments: (1) an investment in a Swiss stock and (2) an investment in the Swiss franc. Accordingly, the overall return to the Canadian can be decomposed into a return on the investment in the Swiss stock and a return on an investment in the Swiss franc. This can be illustrated by considering a Canadian who had purchased a Swiss franc at the beginning of the period. If the Canadian subsequently sold the franc at the end of the period, the return on foreign currency, denoted by r_c, would be

$$r_c = \frac{X_1 - X_0}{X_0}. \tag{26.3}$$

In the example, $r_c = (\$0.8905 - \$0.8481)/\$0.8481 = 5\%$.

From equations (26.1), (26.2), and (26.3), it can be shown that

$$1 + r_f = (1 + r_d)(1 + r_c) \tag{26.4}$$

which can be rewritten as

$$r_f = r_d + r_c + r_d r_c. \tag{26.5}$$

In the example, equation (26.5) reveals that $r_f = .20 + .05 + (.20 \times .05) = 26\%$.

The last term in this equation ($r_d r_c$) will generally be smaller than the two preceding ones, since it equals their product and both are generally less than 1.0. Thus, equation (26.5) can be restated as an approximation:

$$r_f \approx r_d + r_c. \tag{26.6}$$

It can now be seen that the return on a foreign security (r_f) can be decomposed into two parts, representing the domestic return on the security (r_d) and the return on foreign currency (r_c). In the example, the precise value for r_f was shown earlier to be 26%; use of the approximation indicates its value to be equal to $.20 + .05 = 25\%$. Thus, the approximation is in error by 1%, a relatively small amount.

Expected Returns

Equation (26.6) leads directly to the proposition that the expected return on a foreign security will approximately equal the expected domestic return plus the expected return on foreign currency:

$$\bar{r}_f \approx \bar{r}_d + \bar{r}_c. \tag{26.7}$$

It might be tempting for an investor to purchase a foreign security that has a high expected return in its host country, $\bar{r}_d$, on the belief that this means the security will have a high expected return to the foreign investor, $\bar{r}_f$. However, equation (26.7) reveals this logic to be flawed. Just because a foreign security has a high value for $\bar{r}_d$ does not mean that it has a high value for $\bar{r}_f$, since $\bar{r}_c$ can be negative. This can be shown by considering the case of bonds.

The expected domestic returns of bonds in countries with high expected inflation rates will typically be high. However, a foreign investor in a country with a lower expected inflation rate should expect a *negative* return on foreign currency, as his or her currency can be expected to *appreciate* relative to that of the country with the higher expected inflation rate. In evaluating the expected return on the foreign security, there is thus good news (a high expected domestic return, $\bar{r}_d$) and bad news (a negative expected return on foreign currency, $\bar{r}_c$). On balance, the expected foreign return $\bar{r}_f$ might not be as exceptional as first thought when just $\bar{r}_d$ was considered. Indeed, if markets were completely integrated, it would be reasonable to expect the values of $\bar{r}_d$ and $\bar{r}_c$ to sum to an amount $\bar{r}_f$ that is equal to the expected return on an equivalent bond in the investor's own country.

Columns (2) and (3) of Table 26.2 indicate what average excess returns (that is, returns over the London Interbank Offered Rate, an estimate of the risk-free rate) were for the stocks and bonds of six countries as well as the United States for the 200-month period ending August 1991. These averages were measured from the perspective of a US investor, and hence represent the historical average value of r_f. The table indicates that while the stock and bond averages for the six countries are very similar to the US averages, there are some notable differences among individual countries. For both stocks and bonds, the Canadian market had an average return that was much lower than the US average, while the UK and Japanese averages were notably higher.[8]

Foreign and Domestic Risks

Having seen in equation (26.7) that the expected return on a foreign security consists of two components, it is appropriate that the risk of the foreign security be evaluated next. As before, consider a Canadian investor and a Swiss investor who have purchased shares of a Swiss company. The domestic variance, denoted by σ_d^2, is the risk that the Swiss investor faces with respect to the Swiss stock. Correspondingly, the foreign variance, denoted by σ_f^2, is the risk that the Canadian investor faces with respect to the Swiss stock. Based on equation (26.6), it can be shown that the foreign variance consists of three components:

$$\sigma_f^2 = \sigma_d^2 + \sigma_c^2 + 2\rho_{dc}\sigma_d\sigma_c \tag{26.8}$$

[8] In a study of monthly stock returns from February 1970 through May 1989 using the Morgan Stanley indices, it was found that the return on Japanese stocks was inexplicably high. See Harvey, "The World Price of Covariance Risk."

Table 26.2

Security Returns, January 1975–August 1991.[a]

Excess Returns and Standard Deviations:

	Average Excess Returns		Standard Deviation	
Country (*1*)	*Stocks* (*2*)	*Bonds* (*3*)	*Stocks* (*4*)	*Bonds* (*5*)
Australia	4.5%	–.8%	21.9%	5.5%
Canada	.9	–1.5	18.3	7.8
France	4.8	–.1	22.2	4.5
Germany	4.7	.9	18.3	4.5
Japan	7.3	2.1	17.8	6.5
UK	8.6	1.2	24.7	9.9
US	5.2	–.3	16.1	6.8
Average (ex. US)	5.1%	.3%	20.5%	6.4%
Average	5.1	.2	19.9	6.5

[a] Results are given from US investor perspective and are in excess of the London Interbank Offered Rate (LIBOR).

SOURCE: Adapted from Fischer Black and Robert Litterman, "Global Portfolio Optimization," *Financial Analysts Journal* 48, no. 5 (September/October 1992): 30–31.

where σ_c^2 is the variance associated with the currency return to a Canadian from investing in Swiss francs and later exchanging them for Canadian dollars, and ρ_{dc} is the correlation coefficient between the returns on the Swiss stock and the return on Swiss francs.

For example, assume that the domestic variance is 225 (meaning that the domestic standard deviation, σ_d, is $\sqrt{225} = 15\%$) and the currency variance is 25 (meaning the currency standard deviation, σ_c, is $\sqrt{25} = 5\%$). If $\rho_{dc} = 0$, then equation (26.8) indicates that the foreign variance is 225 + 25 = 250. Accordingly, the foreign standard deviation is $\sqrt{250} = 15.8\%$, which is only slightly greater than the domestic standard deviation of 15%.

Equation (26.8) reveals that the smaller the correlation between returns on a foreign currency and returns on a foreign investment, the smaller will be the foreign variance.[9] One study that used data from 17 countries over the period from January 1971 through December 1980 found an average correlation of .034, which is effectively, zero.[10] Thus, it appears that the correlation is sufficiently small that the foreign variance typically will be near, but not less than, the sum of the domestic and currency variances.[11] However, it should be remembered that this is an *average figure*, and that there can be individual situations where the correlation is not approximately zero (such as the United States and Canada).

---

[9] The importance of accurately estimating the correlations between asset and currency returns in determining whether or not to hedge a portfolio is stressed in Victor S. Filatov and Peter Rappoport, "Is Complete Hedging Optimal for International Bond Portfolios?" *Financial Analysts Journal* 48, no. 4 (July/August 1992): 37–47.

[10] Bruno Solnik and Eric Nemeth, "Asset Returns and Currency Fluctuations: A Time Series Analysis," paper presented at the second tagung, Geld Banken und Versicherungen, Universitat Karlsruhe, December 1982.

[11] Since standard deviation is the square root of variance, this means that the foreign standard deviation will typically be substantially less than the sum of the domestic and currency standard deviations.

Columns (3) and (4) of Table 26.2 provide the standard deviations of the excess returns for six foreign countries along with the United States from the perspective of a US investor. Hence, it provides estimates of the value of σ_f for the 200-month period ending in August 1991. The six-country average standard deviation for both stocks and bonds is similar to the respective US values, with the United Kingdom having notably larger values for both stocks and bonds.

Table 26.3 provides evidence on the relative magnitudes of the three types of risk. Standard deviations of monthly values over the period from December 1970 through December 1980 are shown for domestic risk (corresponding to σ_d), currency risk (corresponding to σ_c), and foreign risk (corresponding to σ_f), where the latter two types of risk have been measured from the perspective of a US investor. The last column represents the ratio of foreign risk to domestic risk. Thus, a ratio greater than 1 can be taken as an indication that the risk to a US investor is greater than the risk to a domestic investor. Indeed, with the exception of Hong Kong stocks, all the ratios are greater than 1, suggesting that fluctuations in currency exchange rates increased the risk a US investor would have faced in buying foreign securities.

The importance of currency risk can easily be exaggerated. Calculations such as those in Table 26.3 assume that investors purchase only domestic goods and services and thus convert all proceeds from foreign investments into their own currency before engaging in any spending for consumption purposes. But most people buy foreign goods and many buy foreign services as well (for example, as tourists). The cheaper another country's currency relative to one's own, the more attractive purchases of its goods and services will be. Other things being equal, it may make sense to invest more in countries whose products and scenery are admired, for the effective currency risk is likely to be smaller there than elsewhere. Furthermore, the riskiness of real returns may be less than that of nominal returns if the exchange rate movements are related to inflation differentials.

► The Implications for Canadian Investors

In a global perspective, Canadian markets are small (the equity market represents about 2.5% of global equity capitalization) and heavily concentrated in cyclical resource industries. International investment, therefore, offers Canadian investors an opportunity to increase return and reduce risk through extended diversification. A revealing study demonstrates the advantages of global diversification by examining the effects of adding foreign stocks to a diversified Canadian portfolio.[12] The S&P 500 and EAFE indices were used as proxies for two different kinds of diversified foreign portfolios. The study looked at the addition of these foreign portfolios (both hedged and unhedged) to a domestic portfolio. Hedging was accomplished by buying the appropriate forward contracts. Table 26.4 shows the correlation coefficients between the foreign portfolios (hedged and unhedged) and three classes of Canadian securities.

---

[12] Robert Auger and Denis Parisien, "The Risks and Rewards of Global Investing," *Canadian Investment Review* II, no.1 (Spring 1989): 25–30.

Table 26.3

Risks for Domestic and US Investors Based on Historic Values, December 1970–December 1980.

	Domestic Risk (1)	*Currency Risk (2)*	*Foreign Risk (3)*	*Foreign Domestic Risk (4)*
Stocks				
Australia	24.62%	9.15%	27.15%	1.10
Belgium	13.28	11.02	18.76	1.41
Canada	18.92	4.16	20.29	1.07
Denmark	15.41	10.28	17.65	1.15
France	22.00	10.24	25.81	1.17
Germany	13.87	11.87	18.39	1.33
Hong Kong	47.95	5.63	45.80	.96
Italy	24.21	8.58	26.15	1.08
Japan	16.39	10.42	19.55	1.19
Netherlands	16.37	10.97	18.91	1.16
Norway	28.61	8.89	29.92	1.05
Singapore	35.82	6.52	36.03	1.01
Spain	16.71	9.10	20.26	1.21
Sweden	15.05	8.89	18.06	1.20
Switzerland	16.80	14.67	21.40	1.27
United Kingdom	28.94	8.84	31.61	1.09
United States	16.00	.00	16.00	1.00
Bonds				
Canada	6.16	4.16	7.93	1.29
France	4.39	10.24	11.80	2.69
Germany	6.91	11.87	14.35	2.08
Japan	6.53	10.42	14.36	2.20
Netherlands	7.16	10.97	13.61	1.90
Switzerland	4.33	14.67	15.33	3.54
United Kingdom	12.30	8.84	16.29	1.32
United States	8.96	.00	8.96	1.00

SOURCE: Adapted from Bruno Solnik and Bernard Noetzlin, "Optimal International Asset Allocation," *Journal of Portfolio Management* 9, no. 1 (Fall 1982): 13.

The correlations between the EAFE portfolios and the Canadian securities are much lower than the correlations between the S&P 500 and the Canadian securities, indicating that the EAFE provides useful diversification opportunities. Table 26.5 shows the risk and return relationships for all the investments considered.

Table 26.4

Correlation Coefficients for Domestic and Foreign Returns, 1973–1987.

	TSE 300	*Cdn. Paper*	*Cdn. Bonds*	*Hedged S&P 500*	*Unhedged S&P 500*	*Hedged EAFE*	*Unhedged EAFE*
TSE 300	1.0	–0.2	0.2	0.7	0.7	0.5	0.4
Cdn. Paper		1.0	0.0	0.0	0.0	–0.1	–0.3
Cdn. Bonds			1.0	0.5	0.5	0.3	0.3
Hedged S&P 500				1.0	1.0	0.8	0.6
Unhedged S&P 500					1.0	0.8	0.6
Hedged EAFE						1.0	0.8
Unhedged EAFE							1.0

SOURCE: Robert Auger and Denis Parisien, "The Risks and Rewards of Global Investing," *Canadian Investment Review* II, no.1 (Spring 1989): 27.

Table 26.5

Domestic and Foreign Investments: Annualized Average Returns and Standard Deviations, 1973–1987.

Period	*TSE 300*	*Unhedged EAFE*	*Local EAFE*	*Hedged EAFE*	*Unhedged S&P 500*	*Local S&P 500*	*Hedged S&P 500*	*Cdn. Paper*	*Cdn. Bonds*
1973–1987									
Return	11.0	17.7	12.0	16.0	11.8	9.8	10.7	10.8	9.7
Std dev.	22.2	27.2	17.3	19.3	17.8	18.0	18.5	1.2	14.5
1973–1987									
Return	1.6	4.6	–0.2	0.2	1.7	–0.2	0.8	8.6	7.2
Std.dev.	12.4	21.6	18.0	19.5	18.8	18.2	19.2	1.7	8.5
1978–1982									
Return	18.3	14.5	13.8	20.8	16.8	14.0	14.5	14.0	8.1
Std. dev.	26.1	18.6	7.9	7.6	12.4	12.8	12.3	4.1	13.9
1983–1987									
Return	13.8	36.2	23.7	29.0	17.5	16.4	17.7	9.9	13.9
Std. dev.	20.4	27.1	11.6	12.4	14.4	15.5	16.0	1.5	14.9

SOURCE: Robert Auger and Denis Parisien, "The Risks and Rewards of Global Investing," *Canadian Investment Review* II, no.1 (Spring 1989): 26.

The differences between the columns listed as unhedged and local in this table provide an indication of the degree of foreign exchange risk present. As can be seen, foreign exchange risk varies significantly in different time periods. The hedged EAFE portfolio provides the most attractive risk-return combination of any investment considered. Table 26.6 shows the results of implementing three optimal investment strategies based on different levels of risk tolerance.

Table 26.6

Optimal Investment Strategies, 1973–1987.

Level of risk tolerance:	*Lower*	⟶	*Higher*
Portfolio weightings (%):			
Canadian paper	15	15	5
Bonds	45	35	35
TSE 300	25	25	25
Hedged S&P 500	0	0	0
Unhedged S&P 500	0	0	0
Hedged EAFE	15	25	18
Unhedged EAFE	0	0	17
Average rate of return (%)	11.2	11.8	12.6
Standard deviation	11.2	11.6	13.9

SOURCE: Robert Auger and Denis Parisien, "The Risks and Rewards of Global Investing," *Canadian Investment Review* II, no.1 (Spring 1989): 28.

All three of these portfolios outperform a portfolio consisting of 100% Canadian stocks. These optimal portfolios exclude US stocks as these do not provide as attractive diversification as does the EAFE index. A prospective investment strategy was also investigated in which an expected return was assigned to each asset class and the optimal portfolios reconstructed. The results were similar to those shown in Table 26.6. The authors report that, for a large institutional investor, hedging can be accomplished at a cost of 0.1 to 0.15% per annum of the value of the portfolio. They conclude that "Foreign investments have a natural place in Canadian investment portfolios, even in conservative ones. They permit an increase in stock exposure without any increase in risk."

Auger and Parisien's results suggest that there is a substantial degree of integration of Canadian and US stock markets. The empirical evidence is mixed. Jorion and Schwartz, using data from 1968 to 1982, concluded that there were sufficient rigidities in the financial system that the two markets were effectively segmented, even for interlisted stocks. A more recent study finds that the two markets show evidence of segmentation in the five-year period 1977 to 1982, but that there is strong evidence of integration in a later period, 1982 to 1986.[13]

---

[13] P. Jorion and E. S. Schwartz, "Integration versus Segmentation in the Canadian Stock Market," *Journal of Finance* 41, no. 4 (Sept 1988): 897–914; U. R. Mittoo, "Additional Evidence on the Integration of the Canadian and US Stock Markets," Department of Accounting and Finance Working Paper, University of Manitoba, October 1991. Further evidence of the benefits of international diversification for Canadian investors is provided in Harry S. Marmer, "International Investing: A New Canadian Perspective," *Canadian Investment Review* IV, no.1 (Spring 1991): 47–53.

INSTITUTIONAL ISSUES

Currency Risk: To Hedge or Not to Hedge

Investors in securities denominated in currencies other than those of their home country incur a risk not borne by their domestic investor counterparts: currency risk. For investors in foreign assets, currency risk is the variability in portfolio returns caused by fluctuations in the rate at which foreign currencies can be converted into their home currency. Whether investors in foreign securities should attempt to minimize currency risk in their portfolios has become a topic of considerable controversy in recent years. Among institutional investors, the issue has taken on increased importance as these investors have expanded their foreign investments.

As the text describes, the return on an investor's foreign portfolio can be divided into two components: a domestic (also called local) return and a currency (also called foreign exchange) return. Likewise, foreign portfolio risk can be decomposed into domestic risk, currency risk, and any possible interaction between the two. Most studies indicate that currency risk can increase total portfolio risk by anywhere from 15% to 100% of the underlying domestic risk.

Investors have a choice of whether to bear currency risk. Through a variety of techniques, currency risk can be "hedged" and almost eliminated. The most popular means of hedging currency risk is to purchase units of the investor's home currency in the forward market equal to the value of the foreign investment. For example, consider an investor holding 1000 shares of a Japanese company selling for 4000 yen per share. He or she can purchase dollars for delivery six months from today at a rate of 125 yen per dollar. The forward market is quite similar to the futures market—see Chapter 21. Both forward and futures contracts involve a promise to deliver something of value on a specified future date at a currently agreed-upon price. The forward market, however, does not involve a standardized contract traded on an organized exchange with a third-party clearinghouse that ensures that contracts are honoured. Moreover, forward contracts, unlike futures contracts, are not "marked to market" daily. By purchasing \$32 000 for delivery six months from today to be paid for with 4 million yen, the investor insulates himself or herself from changes in the exchange rate between the yen and the dollar over the next six months.

Despite the availability of effective hedging tools, why do many investors in foreign securities choose not to hedge their currency risks and instead remain exposed to exchange rate fluctuations? Considered next are the primary arguments in support of and in opposition to currency risk hedging.

Proponents of hedging currency risk contend that a no-hedge policy violates one of the basic laws of modern portfolio theory: only accept risks for which adequate compensation is expected to be earned. They view currencies as having zero expected returns. That is, in a world in which capital is free to flow across borders, there is no reason to expect the value of foreign currencies to move systematically in one direction relative to an investor's home currency. However, exchange rates do fluctuate, generating additional risk for an investor in foreign securities. Proponents view currency risk as uncompensated and believe that risk-averse investors should seek to minimize it. Investors who do not hedge would seem to be passing up an opportunity to reduce portfolio risk while not diminishing portfolio returns. Proponents point out that the reduction in portfolio variability gained by hedging currency risk can be substantial.

Opponents of currency hedging generally concede that forgoing hedging means accepting additional uncompensated risks. (However, there is a school of thought that contends that currency risk should be systematically rewarded by the market.) Nevertheless, they believe that market "frictions" cause the costs of currency hedging to outweigh the risk reduction benefits. That is, significant expenses are likely to be incurred by an investor managing currency risk. Currency dealers must be compensated for facilitating hedging transactions. Custodian banks must be paid for record keeping. Investment managers charge fees for maintaining the hedge. Estimates of the total cost of hedging typically range from .25% to .50% per year of the value of the hedged assets, enough to convince opponents that currency risk hedging may not be cost-effective.

In addition, some hedging opponents have questioned the wisdom of hedging for an investor who spends a high percentage of his or her income on goods produced abroad. Suppose the value of foreign currencies declines relative to the investor's home currency (thereby negatively affecting the investor's foreign portfolio returns, other things being equal). The declining relative value of the foreign currencies also reduces the effective cost of foreign-produced goods to the investor. In a sense the investor's own consumption basket serves as a hedge against currency risk in his or her portfolio.

In the final analysis, an investor's optimal currency hedge will depend on a number of factors, including the following:

1. correlations between currencies,
2. correlations between domestic returns and currency returns,
3. the cost of hedging,
4. the portions of the investor's portfolio allocated to foreign securities,
5. the variability of foreign asset returns,
6. the variability of currency returns,
7. the investor's consumption basket,
8. the investor's level of risk aversion, and
9. the premium earned (if any) for holding foreign currencies.

These factors are difficult to quantify, making it hard to build a strong case for or against currency hedging. Moreover, as investors differ in both their financial circumstances and their beliefs about the characteristics of currencies and security markets, it is not surprising that everything from zero hedges to fully hedged positions is observed.

► Multinational Firms

Firms operating in many countries provide international diversification at the corporate level. One might expect that investment in the stocks of such **multinational firms** could serve as a good substitute for investment in stocks of foreign ("national") firms.

A number of studies have shown that this may not be the case. In one, returns on portfolios of stocks of multinational firms headquartered in each of nine countries were calculated for the period from April 1966 through June 1974. Then each portfolio's returns were compared with the returns on the market index for the country of its headquarters. The middle column in Table 26.7 shows the proportion of each portfolio's variance that can be attributed to movements in its corresponding "domestic" market index. Finally, each portfolio's returns were compared with the returns on market indices in all nine countries. The final column in Table 26.7 shows the proportion of each portfolio's variance that can be attributed to movements in its domestic market index as well as in the foreign market indices.

Table 26.7

Proportions of Returns on Stocks on Multinational Firms Explained by Stock Market Indices.

Headquarters Country of Multinational Firms	Proportion of Variance in Returns Explained by	
	Domestic Market Index	*Domestic and Other Market Indices*
Belgium	45%	58%
France	45	62
Germany	65	74
Italy	47	51
Netherlands	50	63
Sweden	42	50
Switzerland	52	75
United Kingdom	44	49
United States	29	31

SOURCE: Adapted from Bertrand Jacquillat and Bruno Solnik, "Multinationals Are Poor Tools for Diversification," *Journal of Portfolio Management* 4, no. 2 (Winter 1978): 10.

Yalawar examined the diversification efficiency of Canadian multinationals and concluded that those firms whose operations were predominantly outside the US provided some limited diversification opportunities.[14] His sample, however, consisted of only 32 firms with operations outside the US, of which 10 were predominantly in the UK, a market also significantly correlated with Canada's.

During the period covered in Table 26.7, only 2% (31% – 29%) of the variance of the returns for multinational firms based in the US could be attributed to foreign market indices. This suggests that US-headquartered multinationals were a poor substitute for direct investment in foreign stocks by US investors.[15] The situation was somewhat better for non-US multinationals, since the differences in the percentages shown in the two columns were greater than 2%. One possible explanation for this is that non-US multinationals have more extensive foreign operations than US multinationals.

International Listings

The common stocks of many firms are traded not only on the major stock exchange in their home country but also on an exchange in a foreign country. Therefore, foreign investors no

[14] Firms with predominantly US operations provided little diversification. See Y. Yalawar, "Are Common Stocks of Canadian Multinationals Good Tools for International Diversification?" Proceedings, Administrative Sciences Association of Canada Conference, Saskatoon, 1979.

[15] However, a study of US multinationals found that the percentage of a firm's sales that were overseas varied directly with a measure of how sensitive the firm's stock price was to an index of the dollar's value. That is, the greater the percentage, the larger the positive effect of dollar depreciations on the firm's profits and hence on its stock returns. Accordingly, investing in US firms that have a large percentage of their sales overseas may be beneficial. See Philippe Jorion, "The Exchange-Rate Exposure of US Multinationals," *Journal of Business* 63, no. 3 (July 1990): 331–345; and "The Pricing of Exchange Rate Risk in the Stock Market," *Journal of Financial and Quantitative Analysis* 26, no. 3 (September 1991): 363–376.

longer have to engage in foreign currency transactions when buying and selling the firm's stock. It is also possible that foreign investors can escape certain taxes and regulations to which they would be subject if the security had been bought in the firm's home country.

There are two ways in which foreign securities can be traded in the United States. Either shares are interlisted on two (or more) exchanges, one in the US and the other in the home market, or American depository receipts are used.

As of November 30, 1995 there were 198 Canadian issues representing 183 companies interlisted on US exchanges reported in the *TSE Monthly Review*. Of the 198 issues, 38 traded on the NYSE, 41 on the ASE, 104 on NASDAQ, and 15 on unidentified exchanges. These stocks provide US investors with a direct and easy means of participating in the Canadian market, thereby achieving a degree of additional diversification. There are also 47 foreign firms listed on the TSE. These are mainly US corporations and a handful of British companies. Access to international diversification through interlisted companies is, therefore, limited for Canadian investors. A number of Canadian brokers, however, are represented on foreign exchanges and can trade there on their customers' behalf. For smaller investors a number of regional, international, and global funds are available from various financial institutions (see Chapter 22).

Foreign securities can also be traded in the United States through **American depository receipts** (ADRs).[16] ADRs are financial assets that are issued by US banks and represent indirect ownership of a certain number of shares of a specific foreign firm that are held on deposit in a bank in the firm's home country. The advantage of ADRs over direct ownership is that the investor need not worry about the delivery of the share certificates or converting dividend payments from a foreign currency into dollars. The depository bank automatically does the conversion for the investor and also forwards all financial reports from the firm; the investor pays the bank a relatively small fee for these services.

At the end of 1993 the common shares of 108 companies out of a total of 159 foreign companies traded as ADRs on the New York Stock Exchange, whereas the shares of only 97 companies out of 303 foreign firms traded as ADRs on the NASDAQ system. This disparity was due in large part to the 104 Canadian issues that were all interlisted on NASDAQ.

One study examined the diversification implications of investing in ADRs and found that such securities were of notable benefit to US investors.[17] Specifically, a sample of 45 ADRs was examined and compared with a sample of 45 US securities over the period from 1973 to 1983. Using an index based on all NYSE-listed stocks, the betas of the ADRs had an average value of .26, which was much lower than the average beta of 1.01 for the US securities. Furthermore, the correlation of the ADRs' returns with those of the NYSE market portfolio averaged .33, whereas US securities had a notably higher average correlation of .53.

---

[16] The London Stock Exchange began trading many of these ADRs simultaneously in August 1987, with prices being quoted in US dollars.

[17] Dennis T. Officer and J. Ronald Hoffmeister, "ADRs: A Substitute for the Real Thing?" *Journal of Portfolio Management* 13, no. 2 (Winter 1987): 61–65. See also Leonard Rosenthal, "An Empirical Test of the Efficiency of the ADR Market," *Journal of Banking and Finance* 7, no. 1 (March 1983): 17–29.

Given these two observations, it is not surprising that portfolios formed from US securities and ADRs had much lower standard deviations than portfolios consisting of just US securities. For example, portfolios consisting of 10 US securities had an average monthly standard deviation of 5.50%, whereas a 10-security portfolio split evenly between US securities and ADRs had an average monthly standard deviation of 4.41%. Thus, in contrast to investing in multinationals, it seems that investing in ADRs brings significant risk reduction. ADRs offer Canadian investors a viable method for investing the shares of foreign companies since few of these are listed on Canadian exchanges.

► Correlations Between Markets

If all economies were tied together completely, stock markets in different countries would move together, and little advantage could be gained through international diversification. However this is not the case. Table 26.8 shows the correlations of returns on diversified portfolios of equities and bonds of various countries with the returns on indexes of Canadian equities and bonds. Two general conclusions can be drawn:

1. With the exception of the United States and Hong Kong, the correlations of foreign equities with Canadian equities are less than 0.7 and only four others are greater than 0.5.[18] These figures, taken along with the results shown in Table 26.5 that indicate that foreign equities can outperform the TSE 300, suggest that there are potential diversification advantages for Canadian equity investors.
2. With the exception of the United States, the correlations of foreign bonds with Canadian bonds are less than 0.3 and in five cases they are negative. These figures, taken along with the results shown in Table 26.2 that indicate that foreign bonds can outperform the Canadian bonds, suggest that there are potential diversification advantages for Canadian bond investors.

Further evidence of the potential advantages of international diversification for Canadian investors is given by the data presented in Table 26.8, which shows the correlation between the TSE 300 index and its major sub-indices with five important international equity markets. With the possible exception of the UK, all countries' correlations are extremely low.

The bottom line is that international diversification is beneficial. Investors may either increase their expected return without increasing risk or decrease their risk without decreasing their expected return by judiciously adding foreign securities to their portfolios.[19]

---

[18] Another study of 349 stocks in 11 countries revealed an average intercountry correlation coefficient of .234 for the period from January 1973 to December 1983. See D. Chinhyung Cho, Cheol S. Eun, and Lemma W. Senbet, "International Arbitrage Pricing Theory: An Empirical Investigation," *Journal of Finance* 41, no. 2 (June 1986): 313–329. In addition, the correlations between emerging markets and the United States have historically been near zero; see the references given in footnote 6. For a multi-period approach that indicates the benefits from international diversification, particularly for highly risk-averse investors, see Robert R. Grauer and Nils H. Hakansson, "Gains from International Diversification: 1968–85 Returns on Portfolios of Stocks and Bonds," *Journal of Finance* 42, no. 3 (July 1987): 721–739. Although the correlation between Canadian and foreign stock markets is frequently much less than one, the actual values are highly dependent on the time period studied.

[19] Unfortunately, a recent study has found that the benefits from international diversification are lessened just when these benefits are most needed by investors. Specifically, the low correlations between market returns appear to increase when markets become more volatile. See Patrick Odier and Bruno Solnik, "Lessons for International Asset Allocation," *Financial Analysts Journal* 49, no. 2 (March/April 1993): 63–77.

Table 26.8

Correlations of Returns on Foreign Equity and Bond Portfolios with Returns on Canadian Equity and Bond Indices, 1960–1980[a]

Country	*Equities*	*Bonds*
Austria	0.239	0.244
Belgium	0.623	0.159
Denmark	0.341	–0.010
France	0.441	0.010
Germany	–0.037	0.179
Italy	0.269	–0.225
Netherlands	0.554	0.211
Norway	0.469	n/a
Spain	0.260	–0.102
Sweden	0.312	0.264
Switzerland	0.350	0.037
Hong Kong	0.791	n/a
Japan	0.231	–0.172
Singapore	0.598	n/a
Australia	0.577	n/a
United States	0.710	0.632

[a] All figures are US dollar adjusted total returns

SOURCE: Roger G. Ibbotson, Richard C. Carr and Anthony W. Robinson, "International Bond and Equity Portfolios," *Financial Analysis Journal* 38, no. 4 (July/August 1982): 61–83.

TANGIBLE ASSETS

In the first half of the 1970s, marketable securities such as stocks and bonds provided returns that were relatively disappointing, especially after adjusting for inflation. And, as shown in Chapter 13, neither bonds nor stocks have served as good hedges against unanticipated inflation in recent years. Overall, tangible assets have been better hedges against inflation. One example, real estate, was shown in Chapter 13 to have been an attractive inflation hedge in recent years.[20] Other examples, such as collectible assets and precious metals (like gold and silver), provide various degrees of protection against inflation.

► Collectible Assets

Not surprisingly, disenchantment with returns on marketable securities has led some investors to examine a host of tangible assets that are normally considered only by collectors. Table 26.10 shows the average returns over three five-year periods for several different kinds of collectible assets (often simply referred to as *collectibles*).

[20] While not a tangible asset, commodity futures were shown in Chapter 21 to have also been an attractive inflation hedge.

Table 26.9

Co-Movement of TSE Sub-Indexes and Foreign Markets. (R-Squared between returns, all in CDN$.)

	United Kingdom	*Hong Kong*	*West Germany*	*Japan*	*France*
Metals	0.25	0.13	0.00	0.11	0.23
Gold and precious metals	0.19	0.14	0.01	0.08	0.09
Oil and gas	0.18	0.19	0.00	0.02	0.03
Forest Products	0.51	0.10	0.01	0.28	0.42
Consumer	0.51	0.12	0.14	0.15	0.44
Steel	0.36	0.04	0.00	0.11	0.16
Real Estate	0.14	0.05	0.03	0.19	0.20
Transportation	0.28	0.17	0.00	0.12	0.16
Pipelines	0.01	0.07	0.05	0.04	0.00
Utilities	0.04	0.03	0.01	0.00	0.02
Communications	0.22	0.05	0.08	0.09	0.36
Retail	0.30	0.03	0.18	0.05	0.28
Banks	0.01	0.07	0.12	0.07	0.13
Financial	0.07	0.08	0.14	0.01	0.19
Management	0.20	0.19	0.04	0.20	0.32
TSE 300	0.44	0.20	0.05	0.08	0.28

SOURCE: Evan Schulman, "The 'Global Village' Securities Market: Will Canada be a Participant.... or a Bystander?" *Canadian Investment Review* II, no. 2 (Fall 1989): 63.

Some of the returns shown in the table are quite high. However, none of the collectible assets provided consistently high results over all three periods. This is not surprising because if one (or more) had provided consistently high returns, many investors would have been attracted to it and bid its price up to a level where high returns would no longer have been possible. Indeed, more recent studies or prints and paintings have concluded that their risk and return characteristics make them relatively unattractive investments for risk-averse investors.[21]

In a sense, a collectible asset often provides income to the owner in the form of consumption. For example, an investor can admire a Rembrandt, sit on a Chippendale, play a Stradivarius, and drive a Morgan. Value received in this manner is not subject to income taxation and is thus likely to be especially attractive for those in high tax brackets. However, the value of such consumption depends strongly on one's preferences.

---

[21] See James E. Pesando, "Art as an Investment: The Market for Modern Prints," *American Economic Review* 83, no. 5 (December 1993): 1075–1089. See also William N. Goetzmann, "Accounting for Taste: Art and the Financial Markets Over Three Centuries," *American Economic Review* 83, no. 5 (December 1993): 1370–1376.

Foreign's Outer Limits

By Keith Ambachtsheer

In 1990, the Canadian pension investment community celebrated the success of its long and arduous campaign to raise the 10% foreign property rule. The results are evident today. The ceiling on foreign investing by pension funds and RRSPs has finally risen to 20%, the final stop in a five-year program of annual 2% rises in the foreign property cap. With the limit now at its maximum, this is an appropriate time to pose the question: where do we go from here?

It is instructive to recap what has happened [since the rule change.] First, the 1990–1993 performance of the MSCI World Index measured in Canadian dollars was 6.7% annualized versus 5.7% for the TSE 300. Actually, the foreign content of Canadian funds outperformed the TSE 300 by considerably more than 1% per annum in most cases. The 6.7% annualized return of the MSCI World Index hides the countervailing effects of a very strong US stock market and a very weak Japanese stock market over the 1990–1993 period. Most Canadian foreign content was in US stocks, very little of it was in Japan. This history confirms that the long and arduous pension investment community campaign to raise the limit potentially has paid dividends for Canadians already.

Fortunately, in many cases, that potential was realized at least in part. For example, in a sample of 72 Canadian pension funds aggregating to $169 billion monitored by Cost Effectiveness Measurement Inc., the median pension fund had a 9.9% weighting in foreign stocks at the beginning of 1991. That weighting had moved to 15.1% by the beginning of 1993. There is every indication that foreign investing activity has continued vigorously in both pension funds and RRSPs since that time.

Philosophically, there is no justifiable basis for placing any limitation on foreign investing by pension funds. Pension fund fiduciaries are legally obliged to seek out investment policies which best serve the interests of pension plan stakeholders. Pension investment legislation now enshrines the notion that prudence must be judged from a portfolio perspective (and by extension, a balance sheet perspective), and not from an individual investment perspective. Two remaining material investment constraints in pension legislation relate to a) maximum exposure to the securities of any one issuer (10%), and b) maximum exposure to direct investments in energy and real estate (25%). These limitations, however, are not inconsistent with the notion of portfolio prudence.

The same cannot be said for the 20% ceiling on foreign investing. This ceiling effectively requires 80% of a Canadian pension fund to be in the securities of a capital market which constitutes only 3% of the global capital market. Further, the Canadian capital market is not a simple mini-replica of the global capital market. Its equity market is still heavily skewed towards resources and financial services stocks. Its debt market is increasingly skewed towards public sector issuers with declining quality ratings on their bonds. Further, that declining debt quality spills over to produce a declining currency. In short, the 20% ceiling on foreign investing may well be hampering many Canadian pension fund fiduciaries in discharging their fiduciary obligations under Canadian pension law.

A counter argument that foreign exposure can be legally extended beyond 20% through the use of derivatives falls short on at least three counts. First, this approach still forces an underlying investment in Canadian securities which may be unattractively priced. Second, it may expose Canadian pension plans to hard-to-assess counter party risks. Third, it prevents

INSTITUTIONAL ISSUES (continued)

Canadian pension funds from participating in individual foreign investment opportunities which may be attractively priced.

Meanwhile, the principle that free markets in goods, services, and capital maximize economic welfare has never been more universally accepted than today. So strong is that evidence that even people with histories of uttering interventionist rhetoric (names like Paul Martin in Canada and Bill Clinton in the United States come to mind) praise the free-markets-are-best principle. In a world that accepts the principle of free markets producing the greatest good for the most people, there should be no room for a rule which prevents some $400 billion of Canadian retirement savings from achieving the best possible balance between risk and reward.

To its dismay, the pension investment community learned back in 1985 that logic alone does not change foreign property limits. That was the year it first went to Ottawa with irrefutable logic supporting the complete removal of the 10% limit which existed at that time. It took four more years of hard (and expensive!) lobbying to get not a removal, but a 10% increase in the ceiling, phased over a four-year period. So where do we go from here [...] as a practical matter? We propose an initial two-step process:

1. Put Ottawa on notice that it is the view of Canada's pension investment community that a 20% limitation on foreign investing in pension funds and RRSPs is not in the interest of Canadians. Propose the continuation of annual 2% per annum increments in the ceiling, with another review scheduled for 1999, when the ceiling reaches 30% of total assets.
2. If necessary, be prepared to present a research study which demonstrates clearly, once again, that while the limitation causes harm to Canadian pension funds and their millions of beneficiaries even at a 20% level, it continues to benefit no one.

Hopefully, these two steps will be sufficient to accomplish the modest goal of simply continuing the process of slow liberation initiated four years ago. However, if things look bleak after this initial two-step process, the industry will have to decide if it has the stomach for another protracted and expensive battle. May it not come to that again.

SOURCE: Canadian Investment Review VII, no. 1 (Spring 1994): 47–48. Reprinted with permission of the Canadian Investment Review.

Table 26.10

Annual Returns on Collectible Assets, Five-Year Periods Ending June 1.

	1969–1974	*1974–1979*	*1979–1984*
Chinese ceramics	31.1%	–3.1%	15.7%
Coins	9.5	32.4	11.3
Diamonds	11.6	13.6	6.1
Old masters	7.3	17.3	1.5
US stamps	14.1	24.9	9.8

SOURCE: Based on data in R. S. Salomon, Jr., and Mallory J. Lennox, "Financial Assets —A Temporary Setback," *Stock Research Investment Policy*, Salomon Brothers, Inc., June 8, 1984.

If markets are efficient, collectible assets will be priced so those who enjoy them most will find it desirable to hold them in greater-than-market-value proportions, whereas those who enjoy them least will find it desirable to hold them in less-than-market-value proportions (and, in many cases, not at all).

Institutional funds and investment pools have been organized to hold paintings, stamps, coins, and other collectible assets. Such arrangements are subject to serious question if they involve locking such objects in vaults where they cannot be seen by those who derive pleasure from this sort of consumption. On the other hand, if the items are rented to others, the only loss may be that associated with the transfer of a portion of the consumption value to the government in the form of a tax on income.

Investors in collectibles should be aware of two types of risk that are especially notable. The first is that the bid-ask spread is often very large. Thus, an investor must see a large price increase just to recoup the spread and break even. The second is that collectibles are subject to fads. (This risk has been referred to as stylistic risk.)[22] For example, Chinese ceramics may be actively sought by many investors today, leading to high prices and big returns for earlier purchasers. However, they may fall out of favour later on and plunge in value. Unlike financial assets, there is no such thing as a fair value for collectibles that can act as a kind of anchor for the market price.

Gold

In the United States, private holdings of gold bullion were illegal before the 1970s. There have been no Canadian restrictions on private holdings of gold since the end of World War II. In other countries, investment in gold has long been a tradition. According to one estimate, at the end of 1984 gold represented over 6% of the world market wealth portfolio.[23]

Table 26.11 contrasts a US investor's returns from gold with the returns from US equities over the period from 1960 through 1984. Gold is clearly a risky investment, but in this period, at least, it also provided high average returns. For any single investment, risk and return are only parts of the story: correlations of an asset's return with the returns on other assets are also relevant. In the period covered in Table 26.11, gold price changes were

Table 26.11

Characteristics of Gold and US Equity Returns, 1960–1984.

	Average Annual Return		*Standard Deviation of Annual Return*
US equities	10.20%		16.89%
Gold	12.62		29.87
Correlation: Gold and US equities		–.09	
Gold and inflation		.63	

SOURCE: Adapted from Roger G. Ibbotson, Laurence B. Siegel, and Kathryn S. Love, "World Wealth: Market Values and Returns," *Journal of Portfolio Management* 12, no. 1 (Fall 1985): 17, 21.

[22] The term *stylistic risk* was coined by William N. Goetzmann in "Accounting for Taste," p. 1371.

[23] Ibbotson, Siegel, and Love, "World Wealth: Market Values and Returns," p. 9.

slightly negatively correlated with stock returns. Similar results have been obtained for other periods. Gold thus appears to be an effective diversifying asset for an equity investor. Table 26.11 also shows that gold prices were highly correlated with the rate of inflation in the United States, as measured by changes in the Consumer Price Index. This is consistent with gold's traditional role as a hedge against inflation, since higher inflation generally brings higher gold prices. It should be noted, however, that an international study that examined the inflation hedging properties of gold for investors in six countries — Canada, Germany, Japan, Switzerland, UK, and US — demonstrated that only for US investors was it an effective vehicle.[24]

Investors interested in gold need not restrict themselves to bullion. Other possibilities range from stocks of gold mining companies to gold futures to gold coins and commemoratives. Furthermore, there are other types of precious metals, such as silver and platinum, that investors may want to consider.

SPORTS BETTING

Throughout the world, large amounts of money are wagered on the outcomes of sporting events. In the United States and Canada, betting on horse races is generally conducted legally at race tracks and via legal off-track betting establishments in some jurisdictions. In addition, illegal bookmakers accept bets on horse races. Bets on other events — most notably professional football games — are made legally in Nevada and illegally with bookmakers almost everywhere, including Canada.

There are some interesting parallels between betting and investing in securities. Both involve an initial outlay of cash and an outcome that, being uncertain, can be thought of as a random variable. For both betting and investing, an individual must have some sort of strategy in deciding where to put his or her money — after all, there are a large number of sporting events (as well as securities) to choose from. Furthermore, these strategies can be thought of as being either fundamental or technical in nature. In the case of fundamental strategies, an investor or bettor looks at the underlying strength of the firm or team or horse that is being evaluated, whereas in the case of a technical strategy, only past performance is of concern. Both of these strategies are typically based on publicly available information; thus, the historical performance of investors and bettors can be examined in order to see if the respective financial markets and "sports markets" are semistrong-form efficient. To begin the discussion, a parallel will be made between a security dealer and a bookmaker.

A security dealer typically wishes to operate with, on average, a small inventory of securities so as to have relatively little exposure to loss through security price fluctuations. To do this, the dealer usually sets a bid price and an asked price that will bring roughly an equal number of orders for purchases and sales in a given time period (say, a week's time). The bid-ask spread represents the dealer's profit margin and part of the investor's transaction costs.

---

[24] J. Chua and R. S. Woodward, "Gold as an Inflation Hedge: A Comparative Study of Six Major Industrial Countries," *Journal of Business Finance and Accounting* 9, no.2 (March 1982): 191–7. For a view against investing in gold, see James B. Cloonan, "Goodbye Gold: It's Now Just Another Commodity," *AAII Journal* 14, no. 9 (October 1992): 25–26.

INSTITUTIONAL ISSUES

Alternative Investments

Institutional investors have long acknowledged the wisdom of holding well-diversified portfolios. For many years, however, they focused their investments almost exclusively on Canadian common stocks, bonds, and short-term securities. The spectrum of investable asset categories extends well beyond these three (for example, see the discussion of the world capital market portfolio in this chapter). Thus, for a considerable time institutional investors overlooked fertile opportunities to reduce their portfolios' risks and perhaps even enhance returns as well.

That myopia receded in the 1980s. Institutional investors began to take significant positions in international stocks and bonds. Furthermore, they made sizeable commitments to a variety of asset categories commonly grouped under the rubric *alternative investments*.

Although there is no precise definition of the term, in practice institutional investors consider alternative investments to be virtually any type of asset not actively traded in the public markets. In terms of their relative importance in institutional investors' portfolios, the most prominent types of alternative investments are:

- *Venture capital*, which involves investments in young companies, ranging from start-up firms to developed businesses preparing to initially offer their stock in the public market.
- *Resource investments*, which involve primarily holdings of properties producing or expected to produce crude oil and natural gas. In recent years, timber properties have gained in relative importance as a resource investment.
- *Leveraged buy-outs*, which involve acquisitions of existing companies using large amounts of debt and little equity to finance the deal. Typically, these companies are restructured, with various divisions sold off to retire debt and other divisions consolidated or otherwise altered to improve efficiency for later reissuance of equity in the public market.
- *Real estate*, which involves investments in income-producing physical structures, including retail shopping centres, office buildings, apartments, and commercial warehouses.

Each type of alternative investment exhibits its own distinct risk and return characteristics. As a result, treating them as one monolithic category leads to faulty analysis. Yet each of these asset types has several similar features:

- Illiquidity
- Difficulty in determining current market values
- Limited historical return and risk data
- Extensive investment analysis required.

The primary distinguishing characteristic of alternative investments is their illiquidity. Institutional investors typically participate in alternative investments through a limited partnership structure (although sometimes direct investments are made with the issuing entity). In a limited partnership, a general partner (or partners) negotiates a deal with the issuing entity. The general partner then solicits limited partners to provide the financing for the deal. The general partners exercise complete control over the investment, while limited partners absorb the risk of failure and share any profits with the general partners.

With rare exceptions, limited partnerships are not registered with the Securities and Exchange Commission. Thus, the limited partners cannot freely trade their ownership interests in the public market. Some secondary markets for limited partnership interests have begun to form, but their volume is extremely small. Essentially, institutional investors participating in alternative investments must be prepared to hold those investments until they expire.

For similar reasons, little pricing data is available for alternative investments. General

INSTITUTIONAL ISSUES (continued)

partners periodically (at most quarterly, often annually) supply estimates for a partnership's current market value. Limited partners, however, have few practical means of independently verifying those prices.

Because of the relative newness of alternative investments and the paucity of market prices, virtually no historical return and risk data on these investments is available. Such questions as, "How can the standard deviation of my existing portfolio be expected to change if I place 10% of my funds in venture capital?" are essentially unanswerable. Thus, when making portfolio allocation decisions, institutional investors must rely on highly subjective estimates of alternative investments' expected returns, standard deviations, and correlations with other asset categories.

Finally, alternative investments require considerable analysis on the part of institutional investors. Information on potential investments is not readily available. Investors must carefully study partnership agreements, consider the management fees and other operating costs, and investigate the capabilities of the general partners. Unlike common stocks and bonds, investors cannot rely on the market to provide efficient pricing. Although these less efficient markets present many potential pitfalls, conversely they offer the opportunity for relatively high returns.

Each of the alternative investment categories described previously has seen dramatic highs and lows over the last 20 years. For all these categories, the high-water marks of performance were attained in the late 1970s and early 1980s, followed soon after by disappointing results. Venture capital returns declined in the poor market for small capitalization stocks in the mid and late 1980s. Real estate suffered staggering losses in the late 1980s. Oil and gas prices plummeted in the mid-1980s and have yet to rebound significantly. Leveraged buyout deals fell in terms of volume and profitability after the most obvious targets were purchased in the 1980s. Perhaps not coincidentally, these performance downturns occurred in a period of declining inflation, whereas the best performance took place during a period of relatively high inflation.

Despite this recent unimpressive track record, the diversification argument remains intact for alternative investments. Over the last two decades, returns on alternative investments have exhibited low or even negative correlations with those of the stock and bond markets. Given the historically high returns provided by these traditional investments, perhaps one should not be surprised or even dissatisfied with the recent results. At some point in the future, alternative investments will almost certainly again offer attractive returns relative to traditional investments and reward the patient, well-diversified investor.

Similarly, in sports betting the bookmaker acts as dealer and wishes to have relatively little "inventory" (exposure to loss). Two major methods are employed to achieve this: *spread betting* and *odds betting*. The former is used for bets on games such as football and baseball and the latter for bets on contests such as horse races and presidential elections.

► Spread Betting

In order to understand spread betting, consider a hypothetical professional football game between the San Francisco 49ers and the Minnesota Vikings. It is widely felt that the 49ers are likely to win. Thus, the bookmaker establishes a spread, perhaps deciding that the 49ers are "favoured by 7 points." This means that the final score will, in effect, be modified by subtracting 7 points from the 49ers score and then paying those who bet on the "winner" using that adjusted score. People who bet on San Francisco believe that the team will "cover the spread"; those who bet on Minnesota believe that Minnesota will "beat the spread." If the final score is 28-20 in favour of San Francisco, then after adjusting for the spread the score is 21-20 in favour of San Francisco, and those betting on San Francisco will have won. However, if the final score is 24–20 in favour of San Francisco, then the adjusted score will be 17–20 in favour of Minnesota, and those betting on Minnesota to beat the spread will have won.[25]

The point spread serves as an equilibrating mechanism. Other things being equal, the greater the spread, the smaller will be the amount bet on San Francisco and the larger the amount bet on Minnesota. At some level the "books will be balanced," meaning an equal amount has been bet on both teams. Given local prejudices, this may be accomplished by San Francisco bookmakers "laying off" excess money bet on the 49ers with Minnesota bookmakers who have excess money bet on the Vikings.

The bookmaker makes a living with a range that corresponds to the security dealer's bid-ask spread. Typically, the bettor puts up $11 for a $10 bet, meaning a winner will receive $10 (plus his or her initial $11 bet, if paid in advance), whereas a loser is out the initial $11 bet. If the books are balanced, the bookmaker will pay out $21 for every $22 taken in. For example, if there is one $11 bet on San Francisco and one $11 bet on Minnesota, the books are balanced. Then, whichever team wins, the bookmaker will pay out $21 of the $22 that has been bet.

While bookmakers generally set point spreads to balance their books, in an efficient market such spreads would provide good estimates of the expected differences in points scored (and, by and large, the evidence is consistent with market efficiency).

► Odds Betting

A goal of many bookmakers is to be reasonably certain that after the contest is over, less money will be paid out than is received. Therefore, if they are successful, the average return to bettors will be negative. To do this, terms must be set so that bets on underdogs are attractive. Spreads are one way; odds are another.

An example from horse racing illustrates the procedure. Assume that Black Socks is favoured to win the sixth race at Woodbine, while the other seven horses are considered inferior but of roughly equal speed. If the payoff per dollar bet were the same for all eight horses, most of the bets would be placed on the favourite. To spread the betting over the contenders, a larger amount must be paid per dollar bet if a long shot is bet on and subsequently wins.

Assume that the odds are set at 7-to-1 for each of the seven slow horses. This means that if $1 is bet on one of them and the horse wins, the bettor will receive $8 (the original $1 that was bet plus $7 in winnings). Assume also that the odds on Black Socks are set at 5-to-3, so that every $3 bet on the favourite will return $8 (the original $3 that was bet plus $5 in winnings) if the horse wins. Now imagine that the amounts bet, given these odds, are as shown in Table 26.11. The total pool, or *handle* (that is, the total amount bet), is $1000, but no matter which horse wins the race, only $800 will be paid out. The remaining $200

---

[25] In the event of a tie in the adjusted score, the money that was bet is returned to both sides.

Table 26.12

Odds, Amounts Bet, and Payouts for a Horse Race.

Horse	Amount Bet	Odds	Amount Paid Out If Horse Wins
# 1 (favourite)	$ 300	5-to-3	$800
2	100	7-to-1	800
3	100	7-to-1	800
4	100	7-to-1	800
5	100	7-to-1	800
6	100	7-to-1	800
7	100	7-to-1	800
8	100	7-to-1	800
Total amount bet =	$1000		

is for the track, the government, and the bookmaker and is known as the *take*. Note that the average return to the bettors is –200/1000 = –20% because of the take.

Although the numbers in Table 26.11 seem contrived, they do represent the kind of situation achieved automatically by parimutuel betting. In this form of wagering (used at most horse racetracks), the actual odds for a horse are determined *after all betting has finished* by subtracting the take (typically about 20%) and the amount bet on the horse from the handle and then dividing this amount by the amount bet on that horse.[26] For example, in the case of Black Socks (horse number 1), the odds are ($1000 – $200 – $300)/$300 = $500/$300 = 5/3, as shown in the table. It should be noted that the dealer is always assured of receiving a fixed percentage (20%) for "transaction costs" with this procedure.

Betting on horses is a negative-sum game: owing to transaction costs, the amount paid out is less than the amount paid in. Consequently, the expected return on the average bet will be negative. Since it is difficult to justify such activity on the basis of hedging, a bettor either (1) believes that he or she is a superior predictor, (2) is willing to pay in this manner for entertainment, or (3) prefers risk. All three aspects play a role in the sports betting market. One attribute that makes betting on sports entertaining is the suspension of the bettor's usual mind-set and the taking of risks with relatively small amounts of money. In such an environment and with limited exposure, even a conservative investor may take pleasure in acting like a riverboat gambler.

Evidence consistent with risk preference of this sort has been found in many analyses of the expected returns from bets on horses with different probabilities of winning races. Figure 26.3 summarizes a number of such studies. The horizontal axis indicates closing odds (on a logarithmic scale). Favourites plot at the left end of the scale and extreme long shots at the right end. The vertical axis indicates average returns. All are negative, but the returns on favourites are considerably better than those on long shots. "Investors" at the track are apparently willing to give up some expected return to get more risk—in this domain they appear to prefer risk.

---

[26] This applies only to bets that a horse will win the race. More complex procedures are used for place (second or better) and show (third or better) bets. In addition, the actual payoff is usually rounded down to the nearest multiple of $.10 per $2 bet, for instance.

Figure 26.3

Average return versus odds in horse race betting.

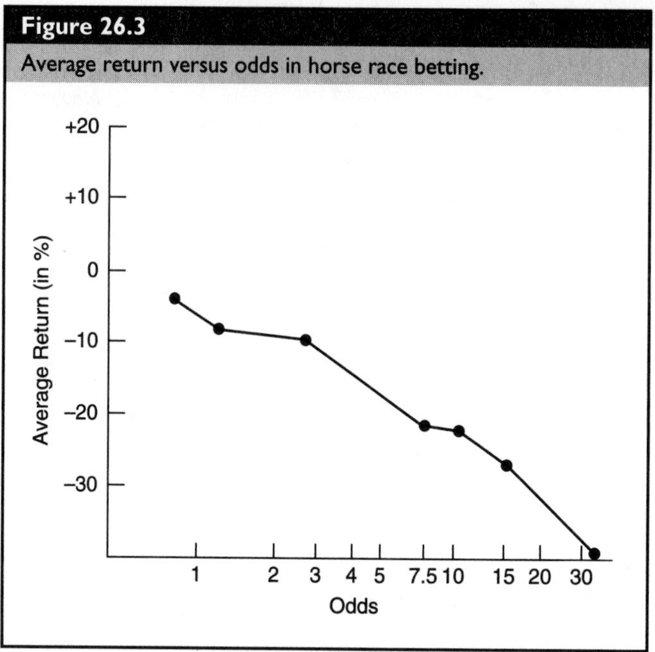

SOURCE: Wayne W. Snyder, "Horse Racing: Testing the Efficient Markets Model," *Journal of Finance* 33, no. 4 (September 1978): 1113.

The Efficiency of Horse Race Betting

Investors in stocks can avail themselves of the results of financial analysis, both fundamental and technical. However, the high degree of efficiency of the stock market diminishes the value of such information for a single investor, since much of it is already reflected in security prices.

A similar situation prevails in the market for horse race betting. Fundamental analyses of such factors as the abilities of horses and trainers and the effects of weather abound, as do technical analyses of trends, reversals, and other changes in "form." If the market is efficient, public information provided by such analysts (*handicappers*) will be reflected in prices (*closing odds*).

In one test that examined the bets placed at Belmont Race Track in New York State, the odds at the track appeared to reflect the information contained in published picks by 14 handicappers. However, this did not seem to be the case in the less "professional" (and higher-transaction-cost) off-track betting market — a fact that may give some solace to those who invest in small and little-followed stocks.[27]

---

[27] Stephen Figlewski, "Subjective Information and Market Efficiency in a Betting Market," *Journal of Political Economy* 87, no. 1 (February 1979): 75–88. It should be noted that there is some evidence that information is better reflected in the win pool than in the show and place pools. For details of a "system" designed to exploit such discrepancies, see Donald B. Hausch, William T. Ziemba, and Mark Rubenstein, "Efficiency of the Market for Racetrack Betting," *Management Science* 27, no. 12 (December 1981): 1435–52; and Peter Asch, Burton G. Malkiel, and Richard E. Quandt, "Market Efficiency in Racetrack Betting," *Journal of Business* 57, no. 2 (April 1984): 165–75; and "Market Efficiency in Racetrack Betting: Further Evidence and a Correction," *Journal of Business* 59, no. 1 (January 1986): 157–60.

SUMMARY

1. Investing in foreign security involves all the risks associated with investing in a domestic security, plus political and exchange (currency) risks associated with converting foreign cash flows into domestic currency.
2. The return on a foreign security can be decomposed into a domestic return and a return on the currency in which the security is denominated.
3. The standard deviation of return on a foreign security is a function of the security's domestic return standard deviation, the foreign currency return standard deviation, and the correlation between the two returns.
4. Exchange risk can be reduced by hedging in the forward or futures market for foreign currency.
5. Investments in multinational firms offer investors only limited diversification benefits. Interlisted securities and ADRs, however, offer significant diversification opportunities for Canadian investors.
6. Overall, tangible assets have been better hedges against unanticipated inflation than stocks or bonds.
7. Sports betting and security investing exhibit interesting parallels. For example, both involve an initial outlay of cash and generally uncertain outcomes. Further, publicly available information appears to be quickly impounded into both betting spreads and odds as well as security prices.

QUESTIONS AND PROBLEMS

1. What types of political risks are relevant only for foreign investors? What types are relevant for both foreign and domestic investors? To what extent and in what manner would you expect the current prices of securities in a particular country to reflect these types of political risk?
2. Using a recent *Globe and Mail*, find the exchange rate between German marks, British pounds, and Canadian dollars. Lloyd Luttrell, a British citizen, is planning a trip to Germany and has budgeted expenses of 30 pounds per day. At current exchange rates, into how many dollars and marks does 30 pounds translate?
3. Why would an investor wish to hedge the currency risk in a portfolio of foreign securities? What considerations are relevant to making the decision whether to hedge?
4. How might a US citizen or company use currency futures to hedge against exchange-rate risk? How would a Canadian citizen proceed in the same situation?
5. Willy McAvoy, a Canadian citizen, holds a portfolio of French common stocks. Last year the portfolio produced an 8% return, denominated in French francs. Over that year the franc appreciated 20% against the Canadian dollar. What was Willy's return measure in Canadian dollars?
6. Terry Speaker bought a Japanese stock one year ago when it sold for 280 yen per share and the exchange rate was $0.008 per yen. The stock now sells for 350 yen and the exchange rate is $0.010 per yen. The stock paid no dividends over the year. What was Terry's rate of return on this stock? What would be the rate of return on the stock to a Japanese investor?

7. Why is international diversification attractive to an investor like Johann Statz, who already has a well-diversified portfolio?
8. Owen Carroll owns a portfolio composed of Canadian stocks and bonds. Interested in further diversifying the portfolio, Owen decides to add investments in US common stocks. Owen's broker, Slick Castleman, voices the opinion that the US securities would not be particularly effective risk-reducing investments. Discuss the logic behind Slick's opinion.
9. Patsy Veach, a Canadian citizen, estimates that a diversified portfolio of German common stocks has a standard deviation of 24%. Patsy also estimates that the standard deviation of the Canadian and German currency return is 7%. Finally, Patsy estimates the correlation between the dollar-mark currency return and the German stock market return to be 0.20. Given this information, what should Patsy conclude is the standard deviation for a Canadian investor investing solely in the German stock market?
10. When a Canadian citizen like Sam Jolly is attempting to estimate the expected return and standard deviation for a foreign security, what factors, in addition to those recognized in domestic security analysis, should he consider?
11. Lin Liu, a Canadian citizen, is considering investing in both Canadian and Zanistan common stock index funds. Lin estimates the following market characteristics:

Cdn. market expected return	20%
Cdn. market standard deviation	18%
Zanistan market expected return	30%
Zanistan market standard deviation	30%
Cdn.-Zanistan expected currency return	0%
Cdn.-Zanistan currency return standard deviation	10%
Zanistan domestic return and Cdn.-Zanistan currency return correlation	0.15

Further, Lin estimates that the Canadian and Zanistan markets are uncorrelated, as is the Canadian market return (or the Zanistan market return) and the Canadian-Zanistan currency exchange rate. Given that Lin is planning to hold a portfolio 60% invested in the Canadian index fund and 40% invested in the Zanistan index fund, what is the expected return and standard deviation of Lin's portfolio?
12. Eva Langevin wants the diversification benefits of international investments but does not want to own foreign securities directly. Would investing in domestically headquartered multinational corporations and ADRs be effective substitutes for Eva? Explain.
13. Discuss why mutual funds are a particularly cost-effective means for small investors to own foreign securities.
14. Is a low correlation between the price movements of two countries' market indices a sufficient condition to ensure that a portfolio containing securities of both countries dominates a portfolio containing only domestic securities?
15. What practical difficulties prevent collectible assets from playing a major role in most investors' portfolios?
16. Hal Chase, a neophyte sports gambler, was heard to remark, "The bookmakers took a terrible beating this week because 80% of the underdogs beat the point spread." Does this seem plausible? Why?
17. In the third race at Canterbury Downs, the handle is $25 000. The track's take is 15%. If $2000 is bet on Harvest Harry to win, what are the parimutuel betting odds on the horse?

18. Pick of handicappers such as Don Hansen generally do not add directly to the information reflected in the odds given at the track. Does this mean that Don and the other handicappers cannot pick winners? Does this mean that their picks are of no value? What aspects of security markets are comparable to the position of track handicappers?

CFA Exam Questions

19. Robert Devlin and Neil Parish are portfolio managers at the Broward Investment Group. At their regular Monday strategy meeting, the topic of adding international bonds to one of their portfolios came up. The portfolio, a pension account for a US client, was currently 90% invested in US Treasury bonds, and 10% invested in 10-year Canadian government bonds. Devlin suggested buying a position in 10-year German government bonds, while Parish argued for a position in 10-year Australian government bonds.
    a. Briefly discuss the three major issues that Devlin and Parish should address in their analysis of the return prospects for German and Australian bonds relative to those of US bonds.

    Having made no changes to the original portfolio, Devlin and Parish hold a subsequent strategy meeting and decide to add positions in the government bonds of Japan, United Kingdom, France, Germany, and Australia.

    b. Identify and discuss two reasons for adding a broader mix of international bonds to the pension portfolio.
20. Advisor 1: "A currency cannot consistently appreciate or depreciate relative to an investor's local currency, since some local or global economic adjustment must eventually redress the currency change. Therefore, having currency exposure in a portfolio increases risk but does not increase long-term expected returns. Since you are not compensated for taking currency risk, you should always hedge a portfolio's currency exposure back to your local currency."

    Advisor 2: "I completely disagree, except as to the implication that economic changes are related to currency changes. Because economic changes affect international stocks, bonds, and currencies, as well as domestic stocks and bonds in ways that often offset each other, currency exposure improves diversification in a portfolio. Portfolios should never hedge their currency exposures; otherwise, they would be less diversified."

    Advisor 1 Rebuttal: "I have evidence which would appear to refute your claim of improved diversification resulting from currency exposure. My studies of hedged and unhedged international bond portfolios show very little difference between either their risks or returns over the past ten years."

    Evaluate the strengths and weaknesses of each of the two approaches presented above. Recommend and justify an alternative currency strategy that draws from the strengths of each approach and corrects their weaknesses.

Key Terms

emerging markets
political risk
exchange risk
domestic return
foreign return
multinational firms
American depository receipts (ADRs)

REFERENCES

1. Two books devoted to understanding international financial markets and investing are:

   J. Orlin Grabbe, *International Financial Markets* (New York: Elsevier Science, 1991).

   Bruno Solnik, *International Investments* (Reading, MA: Addison-Wesley, 1991).

2. Foreign stock market indices are studied in:

   Campbell R. Harvey, "The World Price of Covariance Risk," *Journal of Finance* 46, no. 1 (March 1991): 111–157.

   Richard Roll, "Industrial Structure and the Comparative Behavior of International Stock Market Indices," *Journal of Finance* 47, no. 1 (March 1992): 3–41.

3. Investing internationally in bonds has been recently studied by:

   Kenneth Cholerton, Pierre Pieraerts, and Bruno Solnik, "Why Invest in Foreign Currency Bonds?" *Journal of Portfolio Management* 12, no. 4 (Summer 1986): 4–8.

   Haim Levy and Zvi Lerman, "The Benefits of International Diversification of Bonds," *Financial Analysts Journal* 44, no. 5 (September/October 1988): 56–64.

   Paul Burik and Richard M. Ennis, "Foreign Bonds in Diversified Portfolios: A Limited Advantage," *Financial Analysts Journal* 46, no. 2 (March/April 1990): 31–40.

   Roger G. Ibbotson and Laurence B. Siegel, "The World Bond Market: Market Values, Yields, and Returns," *Journal of Fixed Income* 1, no. 1 (June 1991): 90–99.

   Victor S. Filatov, Kevin M. Murphy, Peter M. Rappoport, and Russell Church, "Foreign Bonds in Diversified Portfolios: A Significant Advantage," *Financial Analysts Journal* 47, no. 4 (July/August 1991): 26–32.

   Mark Fox, "Different Ways to Slice the Optimization Cake," *Financial Analysts Journal* 47, no. 4 (July/August 1991): 32–36.

   Richard M. Ennis and Paul Burik, "A Response from Burik and Ennis," *Financial Analysts Journal* 47, no. 4 (July/August 1991): 37

   Fischer Black and Robert Litterman, "Asset Allocation: Combining Investors Views with Market Equilibrium," *Journal of Fixed Income* 1, no. 2 (September 1991): 7–19.

   Shmuel Hauser and Azriel Levy, "Effect of Exchange Rate and Interest Rate Risk on International Fixed-Income Portfolios," *Journal of Economics and Business* 43, no. 4 (November 1991): 375–388.

   Mark R. Eaker and Dwight M. Grant, "Currency Risk Management in International Fixed-Income Portfolios," *Journal of Fixed Income* 1, no. 3 (December 1991): 31–37.

   Steven Dym, "Global and Local Components of Foreign Bond Risk," *Financial Analysts Journal* 48, no. 2 (March/April 1992): 83–91.

   John Markese, "Foreign Bond Funds: What Are You Buying Into?" *AAII Journal* 14, no. 10 (November 1992): 28–31.

   Kent G. Becker, Joseph E. Finnerty, and Kenneth J. Kopecky, "Economic News and Intraday Volatility in International Bond Markets," *Financial Analysts Journal* 49, no. 3 (May/June 1993): 81–86, 65.

Richard M. Levich and Lee R. Thomas, "The Merits of Active Currency Risk Management: Evidence from International Bond Portfolios," *Financial Analysts Journal* 49, no. 5 (September/October 1993): 63–70.

4. Investing internationally in stocks has also been studied recently by:

Jeff Madura and Wallace Reiff, "A Hedge Strategy for International Portfolios," *Journal of Portfolio Management* 12, no. 1 (Fall 1985): 70–74.

Lee R. Thomas III, "Currency Risks in International Equity Portfolios," *Financial Analysts Journal* 44, no. 2 (March/April 1988): 68–71.

Fischer Black, "Universal Hedging: Optimizing Currency Risk and Reward in International Equity Portfolios," *Financial Analysts Journal* 45, no. 4 (July/August 1989): 16–22.

Warren Bailey and Rene M. Stulz, "Benefits of International Diversification: The Case of Pacific Basin Stock Markets," *Journal of Portfolio Management* 16, no. 4 (Summer 1990): 57–61.

Mark R. Eaker and Dwight Grant, "Currency Hedging Strategies for Internationally Diversified Equity Portfolios," *Journal of Portfolio Management* 17, no. 1 (Fall 1990): 30–32.

John E. Hunter and T. Daniel Coggin, "An Analysis of the Diversification Benefit from International Equity Investment," *Journal of Portfolio Management* 17, no. 1 (Fall 1990): 33–36.

Martin L. Leibowitz and Stanley Kogelman, "Return Enhancement from 'Foreign' Assets: A New Approach to the Risk Return Trade-off," *Journal of Portfolio Management* 17, no. 4 (Summer 1991): 5–13.

Mark Eaker, Dwight Grant, and Nelson Woodard, "International Diversification and Hedging: A Japanese and US Perspective," *Journal of Economics and Business* 43, no. 4 (November 1991): 363–374.

5. Many of the previously cited papers include a discussion of hedging foreign exchange risk. For a description, see:

Andre F. Perold and Evan C. Schulman, "The Free Lunch in Currency Hedging: Implications for Investment Policy and Performance Standards," *Financial Analysts Journal* 44, no. 3 (May/June 1988): 45–50.

Fischer Black, "Equilibrium Exchange Rate Hedging," *Journal of Finance* 45, no. 3 (July 1990): 899–907.

Stephen L. Nesbitt, "Currency Hedging Rules for Plan Sponsors," *Financial Analysts Journal* 47, no. 2 (March/April 1991): 73–81.

Ira G. Kawaller, "Managing the Currency Risk of Non-Dollar Portfolios," *Financial Analysts Journal* 47, no. 3 (May/June 1991): 62–64.

Evi Kaplanis and Stephen M. Schaefer, "Exchange Risk and International Diversification in Bond and Equity Portfolios," *Journal of Economics and Business* 43, no. 4 (November 1991): 287–307.

Michael Adler and Bhaskar Prasad, "On Universal Currency Hedges," *Journal of Financial and Quantitative Analysis* 27, no. 1 (March 1992): 19–38.

Mark Kritzman, "...About Currencies," *Financial Analysts Journal* 48, no. 2 (March/April 1992): 27–30.

Mark Kritzman, "The Minimum-Risk Currency Hedge Ratio and Foreign Asset Exposure," *Financial Analysts Journal* 49, no. 5 (September/October 1993): 77–79.

Ira G. Kawaller, "Foreign Exchange Hedge Management Tools: A Way to Enhance Performance," *Financial Analysts Journal* 49, no. 5 (September/October 1993): 79–80.

Jack Glen and Philippe Jorion, "Currency Hedging for International Portfolios," *Journal of Finance* 48, no. 5 (December 1993): 1865–1886.

John Markese, "How Currency Exchange Rates Can Affect Your International Returns," *AAII Journal* 16, no. 2 (February 1994): 29–31.

6. International asset allocation has been studied by:

Philippe Jorion, "Asset Allocation with Hedged and Unhedged Foreign Stocks and Bonds," *Journal of Portfolio Management* 15, no. 4 (Summer 1989): 49–54.

Fischer Black and Robert Litterman, "Global Portfolio Optimization," *Financial Analysts Journal* 48, no. 5 (September/October 1992): 28–43.

Patrick Odier and Bruno Solnik, "Lessons for International Asset Allocation," *Financial Analysts Journal* 49, no. 2 (March/April 1993): 63–77.

Bruno Solnik, "The Performance of International Asset Allocation Strategies Using Conditional Information," *Journal of Empirical Finance* 1, no. 1 (June 1993): 33–55.

7. The evaluation of the performance of professionally managed portfolios that invest internationally is the subject of:

Robert E. Cumby and Jack D. Glen, "Evaluating the Performance of International Mutual Funds," *Journal of Finance* 45, no. 2 (June 1990): 497–521.

Cheol S. Eun, Richard Kolodny, and Bruce G. Resnick, "US-Based International Mutual Funds: A Performance Evaluation," *Journal of Portfolio Management* 17, no. 3 (Spring 1991): 88–94.

8. For an interesting paper that examines the market crash of October 1987 from a worldwide perspective, and three subsequent related papers, see:

Richard Roll, "The International Crash of October 1987," *Financial Analysts Journal* 44, no. 5 (September/October 1988): 19–35.

Mervyn A. King and Sushil Wadhwani, "Transmission of Volatility Between Stock Markets," *Review of Financial Studies* 3, no. 1 (1990): 5–33.

Yasushi Hamao, Ronald W. Masulis, and Victor Ng, "Correlations in Price Changes and Volatility Across International Stock Markets," *Review of Financial Studies* 3, no. 2 (1990): 281–307.

C. Sherman Cheung and Clarence C. Y. Kwan, "A Note on the Transmission of Public Information Across International Stock Markets," *Journal of Banking and Finance* 16, no. 4 (August 1992): 831–837.

9. In addition to the references provided in footnote 6, emerging markets are also discussed in:

W. Scott Bauman, "Investment Research Analysis in an Emerging Market: Singapore and Malaysia," *Financial Analysts Journal* 45, no. 12 (November/December 1989): 60–67.

Jarrod W. Wilcox, "Global Investing in Emerging Markets," *Financial Analysts Journal* 48, no. 1 (January/February 1992): 15–19.

Warren Bailey and Joseph Lim, "Evaluating the Diversification Benefits of the New Country Funds," *Journal of Portfolio Management* 18, no. 3 (Spring 1992): 74–80.

Arjun B. Divecha, Jamie Drach, and Dan Stefek, "Emerging Markets: A Quantitative Perspective," *Journal of Portfolio Management* 18, no. 1 (Fall 1992): 41–50.

10. Discussions of international and global factor models can be found in:

Richard Grinold, Andrew Rudd, and Dan Stefek, "Global Factors: Fact or Fiction?" *Journal of Portfolio Management* 15, no. 1 (Fall 1989): 79–88.

Martin Drummen and Heinz Zimmerman, "The Structure of European Stock Returns," *Financial Analysts Journal* 48, no. 7 (July/August 1992): 15–26.

11. For some general thoughts on investing in collectibles and three studies of collectibles (stamps, prints, and paintings), see:

Burton G. Malkiel, *A Random Walk Down Wall Street* (New York: W. W. Norton, 1990), pp. 304–309.

William M. Taylor, "The Estimation of Quality-Adjusted Auction Returns with Varying Transaction Intervals," *Journal of Financial and Quantitative Analysis* 27, no. 1 (March 1992): 131–142.

James E. Pesando, "Art as an Investment: The Market for Modern Prints," *American Economic Review* 83, no. 5 (December 1993): 1075–1089.

William N. Goetzmann, "Accounting for Taste: Art and the Financial Markets Over Three Centuries," *American Economic Review* 83, no. 5 (December 1993): 1370–1376.

12. Sports betting is discussed in:

Colin Camerer, "Does the Basketball Market Believe in Hot Hands?" *American Economic Review* 79, no. 5 (December 1989): 1257–1261.

Joseph Golec and Maurry Tamarkin, "The Degree of Inefficiency in the Football Betting Market," *Journal of Financial Economics* 30, no. 2 (December 1991): 311–323.

William O. Brown and Raymond D. Sauer, "Does the Basketball Market Believe in Hot Hands? Comment," *American Economic Review* 83, no. 5 (December 1993): 1377–1386.

Linda M. Woodland and Bill M. Woodland, "Market Efficiency and the Favorite-Longshot Bias: The Baseball Betting Market," *Journal of Finance* 49, no. 1 (March 1994): 268–280.

13. For a Canadian perspective on the topics covered in this chapter, see:

T. Zouikin, "Is International Investing Losing its Lustre?" *Canadian Investment Review* V, no. 2 (Winter 1992).

H. Chrisman, J-M Suret et K. Belkacem, "Avantages et Limites de la Diversification Internationale: Le Point de Vue Canadien," *Finéco* 2, no. 2 (2ᵉ semestre 1992).

V. Lacroix, "Risk and Reward in Emerging Markets," *Canadian Investment Review* VII, no. 2 (Summer 1994).

J. McDonald and M. Cheung, "Optimizing Exposure to Foreign Securities," *Canadian Investment Review* VII, no. 2 (Summer 1994).

M. Gilroy, "Is There a Role for Foreign Bonds in the Canadian Investment Portfolio?" *Canadian Investment Review* VIII, no. 2 (Summer1995).

E. Peters, B. Clarke and P. Rathjens, "Taking a Portfolio Global on the Wings of Tactical Asset Allocation," *Canadian Investment Review* VIII, no. 3 (Fall 1995).

INTERNET RESOURCES

The following investment information sources can be accessed at these Internet addresses:

Royal Bank Currency and Credit Market Daily	**http://www.RoyalBank.COM/english/fin/fin_daily/index.html**
Universal Currency Converter	**http://www.xe.net/xenon/currency.html**

Glossary

Abnormal Return The return earned on a financial asset in excess of that required to compensate for the risk of the asset.

Account Executive A representative of a brokerage firm whose primary responsibility is servicing the accounts of individual investors.

Accounting Beta A relative measure of the sensitivity of a firm's accounting earnings to changes in the accounting earnings of the market portfolio.

Accounting Earnings (Alternatively, **Reported Earnings**.) A firm's revenues less its expenses. Equivalently, the change in the firm's book value of the equity plus dividends paid to shareholders.

Accrued Interest Interest earned, but not yet paid.

Active Management A form of investment management which involves buying and selling financial assets with the objective of earning positive risk-adjusted returns.

Active Position The difference between the percentage of an investor's portfolio invested in a particular financial asset and the percentage of a benchmark portfolio invested in that same asset.

Actual Margin The equity in an investor's margin account expressed as a percentage of the account's total market value (for margin purchases) or total debt (for short sales).

Adjusted Beta An estimate of a security's future beta, derived initially from historical data, but modified by the assumption that the security's "true" beta has a tendency over time to move toward the market average of 1.0.

Adverse Selection A problem in pricing insurance in that those with above-average risk are more likely to purchase insurance than those with below-average risk.

Aggressive Stocks Stocks that have betas greater than one.

Alpha The difference between a security's expected return and its equilibrium expected return.

Alternative Minimum Tax A Revenue Canada requirement that taxpayers with substantial tax-deductible items add back many of the deductions to their regular taxable income. A tax rate of 17% is applied to this adjusted taxable income. If the resulting tax is higher than the individual's normally-calculated tax, then the alternative tax must be paid.

American Depository Receipts (ADRs) Financial assets issued by US banks that represent indirect ownership of a certain number of shares of a non-US firm. ADRs are held on deposit in a bank in the firm's home country.

American Option An option that can be exercised any time through its expiration date.

Annual Percentage Rate (APR) With respect to a loan, the APR is the yield-to-maturity of the loan computed using the most frequent time between payments as the compounding interval.

Anomaly An empirical regularity that is not predicted by any known asset pricing model.

Approved List A list of securities that an investment organization deems worthy of inclusion in a given portfolio.

Arbitrage The simultaneous purchase and sale of the same, or essentially similar, security in two different markets for advantageously different prices.

Arbitrage Pricing Theory An equilibrium model of asset pricing which states that the expected return on a security is a linear function of the security's sensitivity to various common factors.

Arbitrage Portfolio A portfolio that requires no investment, has no sensitivity to any factor, and has a positive expected return. More strictly, a portfolio that provides inflows in some circumstances and requires no outflows under any circumstances.

Arbitrageur A person who engages in arbitrage.

Ask (or Asked) Price The price at which a market-maker is willing to sell a specified quantity of a particular security.

Asset Allocation The process of determining the optimal division of an investor's portfolio among available asset classes.

Asset Class A broadly defined generic group of financial assets, such as stocks or bonds.

Asymmetric Information A situation in which one party has more information than another party.

At the Money Option An option whose exercise price is roughly equal to the market price of its underlying asset.

Attribute See Factor Loading.

Average Return on Investment The total income earned from an investment in an asset, expressed as a percentage of the total investment in the asset.

Average Tax Rate The amount of taxes paid expressed as a percentage of the total income subject to tax.

Back-End Load See **Redemption Fee**.

Bank Discount Basis A method of calculating the interest rate on a fixed-income security that uses the principal of the security as the security's cost.

Bankers' Acceptance A type of money market instrument. It is a promissory note issued by a corporation, with a stated maturity date, that is endorsed by a bank. The bank, by endorsing the note, assumes the obligation that may subsequently be traded.

Basis The difference between the spot price of an asset and the futures price of the same asset.

Basis Point 1/100th of 1%.

Basis Risk The risk to a futures investor of the basis widening or narrowing.

Bearer Bond A bond with attached coupons that represent the right to receive interest payments. The owner submits each coupon on its specified date to receive payment. Ownership is transferred by the seller endorsing the bond over to the buyer.

Benchmark Portfolio A portfolio, of equivalent risk, against which the performance of an investor's holdings can be compared for the purpose of determining investment skill. A benchmark portfolio represents a relevant and feasible alternative to the investor's actual portfolio and, in particular, is similar in terms of risk exposure.

Best-Efforts Underwriting A security underwriting in which the members of the investment banking group serve as agents instead of dealers, agreeing only to obtain for the issuer the best price that the market will pay for the security.

Beta Coefficient (Alternatively, **Market Beta**.) A relative measure of the sensitivity of an asset's return to changes in the return on the market portfolio. Mathematically, the beta coefficient of a security is the security's covariance with the market portfolio divided by the variance of the market portfolio.

Bid-Ask Spread The difference between the price that a market-maker is willing to pay for a security and the price at which the market-maker is willing to sell the same security.

Bidder In the context of a corporate takeover, the firm making a tender offer to the target firm.

Bid Price The price at which a market-maker is willing to purchase a specified quantity of a particular security.

Block House A brokerage firm with the financial capacity and the trading expertise to deal in block trades.

Block Trade A large order (usually 10 000 shares or more) to buy or sell a security.

Board List The standard unit of trading, generally 100 shares.

Bond Ratings An indicator of the creditworthiness of specific bond issues. These ratings provide an indication of a bond issuer's likelihood of default.

Bond Swap A form of active bond management which entails the replacement of bonds in a portfolio with other bonds so as to enhance the yield of the portfolio.

Book Value of the Equity The sum of the cumulative retained earnings and other balance sheet entries classified under shareholders' equity such as common stock and capital contributed in excess of par value.

Book Value per Share A corporation's book value of the equity divided by the number of its common shares outstanding.

Bottom-Up Forecasting A sequential approach to security analysis which entails first making forecasts for individual companies, then for industries, and finally for the economy. Each level of forecasts is conditional on the previous level of forecasts made.

Broker An agent, or middleman, who facilitates the buying and selling of securities for investors.

Call Market A security market in which trading is allowed only at certain specified times. At those times, persons interested in trading a particular security are physically brought together and a market clearing price is established.

Call Money Rate The interest rate paid by brokerage firms to banks on loans used to finance margin purchases by the brokerage firm's customers.

Call Option A contract that gives the buyer the right to buy a specific number of shares of a company from the option writer at a specific purchase price during a specific time period.

Call Premium The difference between the call price of a bond and the par value of the bond.

Call Price The price that an issuer must pay bondholders when an issue is retired prior to its stated maturity date.

Call Provision A provision in some bond indentures that permits an issuer to retire some or all of the bonds in a particular bond issue prior to the bonds' stated maturity date.

Canadian Investor Protection Fund (CIPF) An industry maintained fund that insures investors' accounts against loss due to the failure of a brokerage firm.

Capital Asset Pricing Model (CAPM) An equilibrium model of asset pricing which states that the expected return in a security is a positive linear function of the security's sensitivity to changes in the market portfolio's return.

Capital Gain (or Loss) The difference between the current market value of an asset and the original cost of the asset, with the cost adjusted for any improvement or depreciation in the asset.

Capital Market Line The set of portfolios obtainable by combining the market portfolio with risk-free borrowing or lending. Assuming homogeneous expectations and perfect markets, the Capital Market Line represents the efficient set.

Capital Markets Financial markets in which financial assets with a term-to-maturity of typically more than one year are traded.

Capitalization of Income Method Valuation An approach to valuing financial assets. It is based on the concept that the "true" or intrinsic value of a financial asset is equal to the discounted value of future cash flows generated by that asset.

Capitalization-Weighted Market Index See **Value-Weighted Market Index.**

Cash Account An account maintained by an investor with a brokerage firm in which deposits (cash and the proceeds from security sales) must fully cover withdrawals (cash and the costs of security purchases).

Cash Matching A form of immunization which involves the purchase of bonds that generate a stream of cash inflows identical in amount and timing to a set of expected cash outflows over a given period of time.

Certainty Equivalent Return For a particular risky investment, the return on a risk-free investment which makes the investor indifferent between the risky and risk-free investments.

Certificate of Deposit A form of time deposit issued by banks and other financial institutions.

Certificate of Incorporation See **Charter.**

Characteristic Line A simple linear regression model expressing the relationship between the excess return on a security and the excess return on the market portfolio.

Charter (Alternatively, **Certificate of Incorporation.**) A document issued by a state to a corporation that specifies the rights and obligations of the corporation's shareholders.

Chartist A technical analyst who primarily relies on stock price and volume charts when evaluating securities.

Clearing Corporations A cooperative venture between banks, brokerage firms, and other financial intermediaries, which maintains records of transactions made by member firms during a trading day. At the end of the trading day, the clearing corporation calculates net amounts of securities and cash to be delivered among the members, permitting each member to settle once with the clearing corporation.

Close See **Closing price.**

Closed-End Investment Company (Alternatively, **Closed-End Mutual Fund.**) A managed investment company, with an unlimited life, that does not stand ready to purchase its own shares from its owners and rarely issues new shares beyond its initial offering.

Closing Price (Alternatively, **Close.**) The price at which the last trade of the day took place in a particular stock.

Closing Purchase The purchase of an option contract by an investor that is designed to offset, and thereby cancel, the previous sale of the same option contract by the investor.

Closing Sale The sale of an option contract by an investor that is designed to offset, and thereby cancel, the previous purchase of the same option contract by the investor.

Coefficient of Determination (Alternatively, **R-squared.**) In the context of a simple linear regression, the proportion of the variation in the dependent variable that is related to variation in (that is, "explained by") the independent variable.

Coefficient of Nondetermination In the context of a simple linear regression, the proportion of the variation in the dependent variable that is not related to variation in (that is, not "explained by") the independent variable. Equivalently, one minus the coefficient of determination.

Coincident Indicators Economic variables which have been found to change at the same time that the economy is changing.

Collateral Trust Bond A bond that is backed by other financial assets.

Commercial Paper A type of money instrument. It represents unsecured promissory notes of large, financially sound corporations.

Commingled Fund An investment fund, offered by a bank or insurance company, which is similar to a mutual fund in that investors are permitted to purchase and redeem units that represent ownership in a pool of securities.

Commission The fee an investor pays to a brokerage firm for services rendered in the trading of securities.

Commodity Fund An investment company that speculates in futures.

Common Factor A factor which affects the return on virtually all securities to a certain extent.

Common Shares Legal representation of an equity (or ownership) position in a corporation.

Comparative Performance Attribution Comparing the performance of a portfolio with that of one or more other portfolios (or market indices) in order to determine the sources of the differences in their returns.

Competitive Bidding With respect to selecting an underwriter, the process of an issuer soliciting bids on the underwriting and choosing the underwriter offering the best overall terms.

Complete Market A market where there are enough unique securities so that for any given contingency an investor can construct a portfolio that will produce a payoff if that contingency occurs.

Compounding The payment of interest on interest.

Computer-Assisted Trading System (CATS) A computer system for trading stocks on the Toronto Stock Exchange that involves a computer file containing a publicly accessible limit order book.

Constant Growth Model A type of dividend discount model in which dividends are assumed to exhibit a constant growth rate.

Consumer Price Index A cost-of-living index which is representative of the goods and services purchased by Canadian consumers.

Contingent Deferred Sales Charge See **Redemption Fee.**

Contingent Immunization A form of bond management that entails both passive and active elements. Under contingent immunization, as long as "favourable" results are obtained, the bond portfolio is actively managed. However, if "unfavourable" results occur, then the portfolio is immediately immunized.

Continuous Market A security market in which trades may occur at any time during business hours.

Contrarian An investor who has opinions opposite those of most other investors, leading to actions such as buying recent losers and selling recent winners.

Convertible Bond A bond which may, at the holder's option, be exchanged for other securities, often common stock.

Convexity The tendency for bond prices to change asymmetrically relative to yield changes. Typically, for a given yield change, a bond will rise in price more if the yield change is negative than it will fall in price if the yield change is positive.

Corner Portfolio An efficient portfolio possessing the property that, if combined with any adjacent corner portfolio, will produce another efficient portfolio.

Correlation Coefficient A statistical measure similar to covariance, in that it measures the degree of mutual variation between two random variables. The correlation coefficient rescales covariance to facilitate comparison among pairs of random variables. The correlation coefficient is bounded by the values –1 and +1.

Cost of Carry The differential between the futures and spot prices of a particular asset. It equals the interest forgone less the benefits plus the costs of ownership.

Cost-of-Living Index A collection of goods and services, and their associated prices, designed to reflect changes over time in the cost of making normal consumption expenditures.

Counterparty Risk The risk posed by the possibility that the person or organization with which an investor has entered into a financial arrangements may fail to make required payments.

Coupon Payments The periodic payment of interest on a bond.

Coupon Rate The annual dollar amount of coupon payments made by a bond expressed as a percentage of the bond's par value.

Coupon Stripping The process of separating and selling the individual cash flows of Treasury notes or bonds.

Covariance A statistical measure of the relationship between two random variables. It measures the extent of mutual variation between two random variables.

Covered Call Writing The process of writing a call option on an asset owned by the option writer.

Crown Jewel Defence A strategy used by corporations to ward off hostile takeovers. The strategy entails the target company selling off its most attractive assets to make itself less attractive to the acquiring firm.

Cumulative Dividends A common feature of preferred stock which requires that the issuing corporation pay all previously unpaid preferred stock dividends before any common stock dividends may be paid.

Cumulative Voting System In the context of a corporation, a method of voting in which a shareholder is permitted to give any one candidate for the board of directors a maximum number of votes equal to the number of shares owned by that shareholder times the number of directors being elected.

Currency Risk See **Exchange Risk.**

Current Yield The annual dollar amount of coupon payments made by a bond expressed as a percentage of the bond's current market price.

Date of Record The date, established quarterly by a corporation's board of directors, on which the shareholders of record are determined for the purpose of paying a cash or stock dividend.

Day-of-the-Week Effect (Alternatively, **Weekend Effect.**) An empirical regularity whereby stock returns appear to be lower on Mondays as opposed to other days of the week.

Day Order A trading order which the broker will attempt to fill only during the day in which it was entered.

Dealer A person who trades in financial assets for his or her own account and maintains an inventory of particular securities. The dealer buys for and sells from this inventory, profiting from the difference in the buying and selling prices.

Dealer's Spread The bid-asked spread quoted by a security dealer.

Debenture A bond that is not secured by specific property.

Debit Balance The dollar amount borrowed from a broker as the result of a margin purchase.

Debt Refunding The issuance of new debt for the purpose of paying off currently maturing debt.

Dedicated Portfolio A portfolio of bonds that provides its owner with cash inflows that are matched against a specific stream of cash outflows.

Deep Discount Bond A bond whose coupon interest rate is considerably below those of other bonds which otherwise possess similar attributes. Hence, these bonds sell at prices significantly below the other bonds.

Default Premium The difference between the promised and expected yield-to-maturity on a bond arising from the possibility that the bond issuer might default on the bond.

Defensive Stocks Stocks that have betas less than one.

Delisting The process of removing a security's eligibility for trading on an organized security exchange.

Delta See **Hedge Ratio.**

Demand Deposit A chequing account at a financial institution.

Demand-to-Buy Schedule A description of the quantities of a security that an investor is prepared to purchase at alternative prices.

Demand-to-Hold Schedule A description of the quantities of a security an investor desires to maintain in his or her portfolio at alternative prices.

Designated Market-Maker (Also known as a **Registered Trader with responsibilty for a stock**.) A dealer who continuously provides bid and ask prices at which he or she is willing to trade a specified number of shares any time an order is entered for which no other counter-party is available.

Differential Return A portfolio's *ex post* alpha where the CAPM is used to estimate the return on the benchmark portfolio.

Discount Broker An organization that offers a limited range of brokerage services and charges fees substantially below those of brokerage firms that provide a full range of services.

Discount Factor The present value of one dollar to be received from a security in a specified number of years.

Discount Rate The interest rate used in calculating the present value of future cash flows. The discount rate reflects not only the time value of money, but also the riskiness of the cash flows.

Discounting The process of calculating the present value of a given stream of cash flows.

Discretionary Order A trading order that permits the broker to set the specifications for the order.

Disintermediation A pattern of funds flow whereby investors withdraw funds from financial intermediaries, such as banks and savings and loans, because market interest rates exceed the maximum interest rates that these organizations are permitted to pay. The investors reinvest their funds in financial assets that pay interest rates not subject to ceilings.

Diversification The process of adding securities to a portfolio in order to reduce the portfolio's unique risk and, thereby, the portfolio's total risk.

Dividend Decision The process of determining the amount of dividends that a corporation will pay its shareholders.

Dividend Discount Model The term used for the capitalization of income method of valuation as applied to common shares. All variants of dividend discount models assume that the intrinsic value of a share of common stock is equal to the discounted value of the dividends forecast to be paid on the shares.

Dividend Tax Credit A credit applicable to the tax payable on dividend income that lowers the effective tax rate.

Dividend Yield The current annualized dividend paid on a share of common stock, expressed as a percentage of the current market price of the corporation's common stock.

Dividends Cash payments made to shareholders by the corporation.

Dollar-Weighted Return A method of measuring the performance of a portfolio over a particular period of time. It is the discount rate which makes the present value of cash flows into and out of the portfolio, as well as the portfolio's ending value, equal to the portfolio's beginning value.

Domestic Return The return on an investment in a foreign financial asset, excluding the impact of exchange rate changes.

Double Auction Bidding among both buyers and sellers for a security that may occur when the market-maker's bid-ask spread is large enough to permit sales at one or more prices within the spread.

Duration A measure of the average maturity of the stream of payments generated by a financial asset. Mathematically, duration is the weighted average of the lengths of time until the asset's remaining payments are made. The weights in this calculation are the proportion of the asset's total present value of the respective cash flows.

Earnings per Share A corporation's accounting earnings divided by the number of its common shares outstanding.

Earnings-Price Ratio The reciprocal of the price-earnings ratio.

Econometric Model A statistical model designed to explain and forecast certain economic phenomena.

Economic Earnings The change in the economic value of the firm plus dividends paid to shareholders.

Economic Value of the Firm The aggregate market value of all securities issued by the firm.

Efficient Market A market for securities in which every security's price equals its investment value at all times, implying that a set of information is fully and immediately reflected in market prices.

Efficient Portfolio A portfolio within the feasible set which offers investors both maximum expected return for varying levels of risk and minimum risk for varying levels of expected return.

Efficient Set (Frontier) The set of efficient portfolios.

Efficient Set Theorem The proposition that investors will choose their portfolios only from the set of efficient portfolios.

Electronic Book See **Limit Order Book**.

Emerging Markets Financial markets in countries that have a relatively low level of per capita gross domestic product, improved political and economic stability, a currency that is convertible into Western countries' currencies, and securities available for investment by foreigners.

Empirical Regularities Differences in returns on securities that occur with regularity from period to period.

Endogenous Variable In the context of an econometric model, an economic variable which represents the economic phenomena explained by the model.

Equal-Weighted Market Index A market index in which all the component securities contribute equally to the value of the index, regardless of the various attributes of those securities.

Equilibrium Expected Return The expected return on a security assuming that the security is correctly priced by the market. This "fair" return is determined by an appropriate asset pricing model.

Equipment Obligation (Alternatively, **Equipment Trust Certificate.**) A bond which is backed by specific pieces of equipment that, if necessary, can be readily sold and delivered to a new owner.

Equipment Trust Certificate See **Equipment Obligation.**

Equity Premium The difference between the expected rate of return on common stocks and the risk-free return.

Equity Swap A contract between two counterparties where one pays the other a fixed stream of cash flows and in return receives a varying stream whose cash flows are regularly reset based on the performance of a given stock market index.

Equivalent Yield The annualized yield-to-maturity on a fixed-income security sold on a discount basis.

Eurobond A bond that is offered outside of the country of the borrower and usually outside of the country in whose currency the security is denominated.

Eurodollar Certificate of Deposit A certificate of deposit denominated in US dollars and issued by banks domiciled outside North America.

Eurodollar Deposit A US dollar-denominated time deposit held in a bank domiciled outside North America.

European Option An option that can only be exercised on its expiration date.

Ex Ante Before the fact; future.

Ex-Distribution Date The date on which ownership of stock is determined for purposes of paying stock dividends or issuing new shares due to stock splits. Owners purchasing shares before the ex-distribution date receive the new shares in question. Owners purchasing shares on or after the ex-distribution date are not entitled to the new shares.

Ex-Dividend Date The date on which ownership of stock is determined for purposes of paying dividends. Owners purchasing shares before the ex-dividend date receive the dividend in question. Owners purchasing shares on or after the ex-dividend date are not entitled to the dividend.

Ex Post After the fact; historical.

***Ex Post* Alpha** A portfolio's alpha calculated on an *ex post* basis. Mathematically, over an evaluation interval, it is the difference between the average return on the portfolio and the average return on the benchmark portfolio.

***Ex Post* Selection Bias** In the context of constructing a security valuation model, the use of securities that have performed well and the avoidance of securities that have performed poorly, thus making the model appear more effective than it truly is.

Ex-Rights Date The date on which ownership of stock is determined for purposes of granting rights to purchase new stock in a rights offering. Owners purchasing shares before the ex-rights date receive the rights in question. Owners purchasing shares on or after the ex-rights date are not entitled to the rights.

Excess Return The difference between the return on a security and the return on a risk-free asset.

Exchange Risk (Alternatively, **Currency Risk.**) The uncertainty in the return on a foreign financial asset due to unpredictability regarding the rate at which the foreign currency can be exchanged into the investor's own currency.

Exercise Price (Alternatively, **Striking Price.**) In the case of a call option, the price at which an option buyer may purchase the underlying asset from the option writer. In the case of a put option, the price at which an option buyer may sell the underlying asset to the option writer.

Exit Fee See **Redemption Fee.**

Exogenous Variables In the context of an econometric model, an economic variable taken as given and used in the model to explain the model's endogenous variables.

Expectations Hypothesis A hypothesis that the futures price of an asset is equal to the expected spot price of the asset on the delivery date of the futures contract.

Expected Rate of Inflation That portion of inflation experienced over a given period of time that was anticipated by investors.

Expected Return The return on a security (or portfolio) over a holding period that an investor anticipates receiving.

Expected Return Vector A column of numbers that correspond to the expected returns for a set of securities.

Expected Value See **Mean.**

Expected Yield-to-Maturity The yield-to-maturity on a bond calculated as a weighted average of all possible yields that the bond might produce under different scenarios of default or late payments, where the weights are the probabilities of each scenario occurring.

Expiration Date The date on which the right to buy or sell a security under an option contract ceases.

Face Value See **Principal.**

Factor (Alternatively, **Index.**) An aspect of the investment environment which influences the returns of financial assets. To the extent that a factor influences a significant number of financial assets, it is termed common or pervasive.

Factor Beta A relative measure of the mutual variation of a particular common factor with the return on the market portfolio. Mathematically, a factor beta is the covariance of the factor with the market portfolio, divided by the variance of the market portfolio.

Factor Loading (Alternatively, **Attribute** or **Sensitivity.**) A measure of the responsiveness of a security's returns to a particular common factor.

Factor Model (Alternatively, **Index Model.**) A return generating process which attributes the return on a security to the security's sensitivity to the movements of various common factors.

Factor Risk That part of a security's total risk which is related to moves in various common factors and, hence, cannot be diversified away.

Factor Risk Premium The expected return over and above the risk-free rate on a portfolio that has unit sensitivity to a particular factor and zero sensitivity to all other factors.

Fail to Deliver A situation in which a seller's broker is unable to deliver the traded security to the buyer's broker on or before the required settlement date.

Fallen Angel A junk bond that was of investment grade when originally issued.

Feasible Set (Alternatively, **Opportunity Set**.) The set of all portfolios that can be formed from the group of securities being considered by an investor.

Fill-or-Kill Order A trading order which is cancelled if the broker is unable to execute it immediately.

Financial Analyst (Alternatively, **Security Analyst** or **Investment Analyst**.) An individual who analyzes financial assets in order to determine the investment characteristics of those assets and to identify mispricings among those assets.

Financial Asset See **Security**.

Financial Institution See **Financial Intermediary**.

Financial Intermediary (Alternatively, **Financial Institution.**) An organization that issues financial claims against itself and uses the proceeds of the issuance primarily to purchase financial assets issued by corporations, government entities, and other financial intermediaries.

Financial Investment An investment in financial assets.

Financial Leverage The use of debt to fund a portion of an investment.

Financial Market (Alternatively, **Security Market**.) A mechanism designed to facilitate the exchange of financial assets by bringing buyers and sellers of securities together.

Firm Commitment An arrangement between underwriters and a security issuer whereby the underwriters agree to purchase, at the offering price, all of the issue not bought by the public.

Fixed Annuity A series of payments of a fixed and equal amount.

Floating Rate (Alternatively, **Variable Rate**.) A rate of interest on a financial asset that may vary over the life of the asset, depending on changes in a specified indicator of current market interest rates.

Floor Trader An employee of a member firm who may execute trades on the floor of an exchange. See also **Order Trader** and **Registered Trader**.

Foreign Return The return on an investment in a foreign financial asset, including the impact of exchange rate changes.

Forward Rate The interest rate that links the current spot interest rate over one holding period to the current spot interest rate over a long holding period. Equivalently, the interest rate agreed to at a point in time where the loan will be made at a future date.

Fourth Market A US secondary security market in which investors (typically, financial institutions) trade securities directly with each other, bypassing the brokers and dealers on organized security exchanges and the over-the-counter market.

Fundamental Analysis A form of security analysis which seeks to determine the intrinsic value of securities based on underlying economic factors. These intrinsic values are compared to current market prices to estimate current levels of mispricing.

Futures (Future Contract) An agreement between two people under which the seller promises to deliver a specific asset on a specific future date to the buyer for a predetermined price to be paid on the delivery date.

Future Option (Alternatively, **Options on Futures**.) An option contract for which the deliverable asset is a specific futures contract.

Generally Accepted Accounting Principles (GAAP) Accounting rules established by recognized authorities, such as the Canadian Institute of Chartered Accountants (CICA).

Geometric Mean Return The compounded per-period average rate of return on a financial asset over a specified time interval.

Good-Till-Cancelled Order See **Open Order.**

Greenmail An offer by the management of a corporation that is the target of a hostile takeover to repurchase its shares from the hostile bidder at an above-market price.

Group In the context of a specific asset class, a collection of financial assets that have common distinguishing financial characteristics.

Group Selection A component of the security selection process involving the identification of desirable combinations of groups within an asset class.

Growth Stock A stock that has experienced or is expected to experience rapidly increasing earnings per share, and is often characterized as having low earnings-to-price and book-value-to-market-value ratios.

Guaranteed Bond A bond issued by one corporation but backed by another corporation.

Hedge Ratio (Alternatively, **Delta.**) The expected change in the value of an option per dollar change in the market price of the underlying asset.

Hedger An investor in futures contracts whose primary objective is to offset an otherwise risky position.

Historical Beta An estimate of a security's beta, derived solely from historical returns. Equivalently, the slope of the *ex post* characteristic line.

Holding Period The length of time over which an investor is assumed to invest a given sum of money.

Holding-Period Return The rate of return on an investment over a given holding period.

Holdout Sample See **Out-of-Sample Data.**

Homogeneous Expectations A situation in which all investors possess the same perceptions with regard to the expected returns, standard deviations, and covariances of securities.

Horizon Analysis A form of active bond management where a single holding period is selected for analysis and possible yield structures at the end of the period are considered. Bonds with the most attractive expected returns under the alternative yield structures are selected for the portfolio.

Hypothecation Agreement A legal arrangement between a brokerage firm and an investor that permits the brokerage firm to pledge the investor's securities as collateral for bank loans, provided the securities were purchased through the investor's margin account.

Idiosyncratic Risk See **Nonfactor Risk.**

Immunization A bond portfolio management technique that permits an investor to meet a promised stream of cash outflows with a high degree of certainty.

Implied (or **Implicit) Volatility** The risk of an asset derived from an options valuation model, assuming that an option on the asset is fairly priced by the market.

Implied Return See **Internal Rate of Return.**

In the Money Option In the case of a call (put) option, an option whose exercise price is less than (greater than) the market price of its underlying asset.

Income Bond A bond for which the size of the interest payments varies, based on the income of the issuer.

Indenture A legal document formally describing the terms of the legal relationship between a bond issuer and bondholders.

Index See **Factor.**

Index Arbitrage An investment strategy that involves buying a stock index futures contract and selling the individual stocks in the index or vice versa. The strategy is designed to take advantage of a mispricing between the stock index futures contract and the underlying stocks.

Index Fund A passively managed investment in a diversified portfolio of financial assets designed to mimic the investment performance of a specific market index.

Index Model See **Factor Model.**

Indifference Curve All combinations of portfolios, considered in terms of expected returns and risk, that provide an investor with an equal amount of satisfaction.

Inefficient Portfolio A portfolio that does not satisfy the criteria of an efficient portfolio and, hence, does not lie on the efficient set.

Inflation The rate of change in a price index over a certain period of time. Equivalently, the percentage change in the purchasing power of a unit of currency over a certain period of time.

Inflation Hedge An asset which preserves the value of its purchasing power over time despite changes in the price level.

Information Coefficient The correlation co-efficient between a security analyst's predicted returns and subsequent actual returns that is used to measure the accuracy of the analyst's predictions.

Information Content of Dividends Hypothesis The proposition that dividend announcements contain inside information about a corporation's future prospects.

Initial Margin Requirement The minimum percentage of a margin purchase (or short sale) price that must come from the investor's own funds.

Initial Public Offering (IPO) (Alternatively, **Unseasoned Offering.**) The first offering of the shares of a company to the public.

Initial Wealth The value of an investor's portfolio at the beginning of a holding period.

Insider Narrowly defined, shareholders, officers, and directors of a corporation who own a "significant" proportion of a corporation's stock. More broadly defined, anyone who has access to information that is both "materially" related to the value of a corporation's securities and is unavailable to the general public.

Instinet Acronym for Institutional Network. A computerized communications system that provides price quotations and order execution for fourth market participants.

Interest-Rate Parity An explanation for why spot and futures exchange rates differ. It asserts that such differences result from different interest rates in the two countries.

Interest Rate Risk The uncertainty in the return on a fixed-income security caused by unanticipated fluctuations in value of the asset due to changes in interest rates.

Interest Rate Swap A contract between two counterparties where one pays the other a fixed stream of cash flows and in return receives a varying stream whose cash flows are regularly reset based on the level of a given interest rate.

Intermarket Spread Swap A type of bond swap where an investor moves out of one market segment and into another because the investor believes that one segment is significantly underpriced relative to the other.

Internal Rate of Return (Alternatively, **Implied Return.**) The discount rate that equates the present value of future cash flows expected to be received from a particular investment to the cost of that investment.

Intrinsic Value of an Option The value of an option if it were exercised immediately. Equivalently, the market price of the asset upon which a call option is written less the exercise price of the option (or the exercise price less the market price of the asset in the case of a put option).

Investment The sacrifice of certain present value for (possibly uncertain) future value.

Investment Advisor An individual or organization that provides investment advice to investors.

Investment Analyst See **Financial Analyst**.

Investment Banker (Alternatively, **Underwriter**.) An organization that acts as an intermediary between issuers and the ultimate purchasers of securities in the primary security market.

Investment Banking The process of analyzing and selecting a means of procuring financing on behalf of an issuer of securities.

Investment Committee Within a traditional investment organization, a group of senior management responsible for establishing the organization's broad investment strategy.

Investment Company A type of financial intermediary which obtains money from investors and uses that money to purchase financial assets. In return, the investors receive shares in the investment company, and thus indirectly own a proportion of the financial assets that the company itself owns.

Investment Environment The financial structure in which investors operate, consisting of the kinds of marketable securities available for purchase or sale and the process by which these securities are bought and sold.

Investment Grade Bonds Bonds which possess bond ratings that permit them to be purchased by the vast majority of institutional investors, particularly regulated financial institutions. Usually, investment grade bonds have a BBB (Dominion Bond Rating Service), B++ (Canadian Bond Rating Service) or higher bond rating.

Investment Policy A component of the investment process that involves determining an investor's objectives and amount of the funds available to invest.

Investment Process The set of procedures by which an investor decides what marketable securities to invest in, how extensive those investments should be, and when the investments should be made.

Investment Style The method an investor uses to take active positions in certain types of securities.

Investment Value The present value of a security's future prospects as estimated by well-informed market participants.

January Effect An empirical regularity whereby stock returns appear to be higher in January as opposed to other months of the year.

Junk Bonds See **Speculative Grade Bonds**.

Lagging Indicators Economic variables which have been found to follow movements in the economy.

Lambda The expected return premium (above the risk-free rate of interest) per unit of sensitivity to a particular common factor.

Leading Indicators Economic variables which have been found to signal future changes in the economy.

Leveraged Buy Out A situation in which a private investment group, using substantial amounts of debt financing, buys all of the shares of a publicly held firm, thereby gaining complete control of the firm.

Limit Order A trading order which specifies a limit price at which the broker is to execute the order. The trade will be executed only if the broker can meet or better the limit price.

Limit Order Book (Alternatively, **Electronic Book**.) The records kept by the exchange identifying the limit, stop, and stop limit orders that brokers have entered for execution in a particular security. On the TSE the information in the electronic book is available to all participants.

Limit Order Trading System (LOTS) An automated system used on the TSE for recording and queueing limit orders by price as they arrive.

Limit Price The price specified when a limit order is placed with a broker, defining the maximum purchase price or minimum selling price at which the order can be executed.

Limited Liability An aspect of the corporate form of organization that prevents common shareholders from losing more than their investment if the corporation should default on its obligation.

Liquidity (Alternatively, **Marketability**.) The ability of investors to convert securities to cash at a price similar to the price of the previous trade in the security, assuming no significant new information has arrived since the previous trade. Equivalently, the ability to sell an asset quickly without having to make a substantial price concession.

Liquidity Preference (Premium) Theory An explanation of the term structure of interest rates. It holds that the term structure is a result of the preference of investors for short-term securities. Investors can only be induced to hold longer-term securities if they expect to receive a higher return.

Liquidity Premium The expected incremental return of longer-term securities over shorter-term securities that compensates investors for the greater interest rate risk entailed in holding longer-term securities.

Listed Security A security that is traded on an organized security exchange.

Load Charge A sales charge levied by a mutual fund when an investor buys its shares.

Load Fund A mutual fund that has a load charge.

Long Hedger A hedger who offsets risk by buying futures contracts.

Maintenance Margin Requirement The minimum actual margin that a brokerage firm will permit commodity futures investors to keep in their margin accounts.

Majority Voting System (Alternatively, **Straight Voting System**.) In the context of a corporation, a method of voting in which a shareholder is permitted to give any one candidate for the board of directors a maximum number of votes equal to the number of shares owned by that shareholder.

Managed Investment Company An investment company with a portfolio that may be altered at the discretion of the company's portfolio manager.

Management Expense Ratio The percentage of an investment company's assets that were used to pay for management fees, administrative expenses, and other operating expenses in a given year.

Management Buy Out A situation in which the existing management of a publicly owned firm, perhaps joined by an outside investment group, buys all the shares of the existing shareholders, thereby gaining complete control of the firm.

Margin Account An account maintained by an investor with a brokerage firm in which securities may be purchased by borrowing a portion of the purchase price from the brokerage firm, or may be sold short by borrowing the securities from the brokerage firm.

Margin Call A demand upon an investor by a brokerage firm to increase the equity in the investor's margin account. The margin call is initiated when the investor's actual margin falls below the margin requirement.

Margin Purchase The purchase of securities financed by borrowing a portion of the purchase price from a brokerage firm.

Marginal Return on Investment The additional income, expressed as a percentage, earned on each additional dollar invested in an asset.

Marginal Tax Rate The amount of taxes, expressed as a percentage, paid on each additional dollar of taxable income received.

Markdown The difference in prices between what an investor's broker receives and what the investor receives for a security sold in the over-the-counter market.

Marked (Marking) to the Market The process of calculating, on a daily basis, the actual margin in an investor's account. Equivalently, the daily process of adjusting the equity in an investor's account to reflect the daily changes in the market value of the account's assets and liabilities.

Market Beta See **Beta Coefficient**.

Market Capitalization The aggregate market value of a security, equal to the market price per unit of the security multiplied by the total number of outstanding units of the security.

Market Discount Bond A bond that sells at a price below its par value in the secondary market.

Market Discount Function The set of discount factors on all default-free bonds across the spectrum of terms-to-maturity.

Market Index A collection of securities whose prices are averaged to reflect the overall investment performance of a particular market for financial assets.

Market-Maker See **Designated Market-Maker**.

Market Model A simple linear model that expresses the relationship between the return on a security and the return on a market index.

Market Order A trading order which instructs the broker to buy or sell a security immediately at the best obtainable price.

Market Order System for Trading (MOST) An automated system on the TSE designed to fill small orders immediately at the bid or the ask with immediate confirmation.

Market Portfolio A portfolio consisting of an investment in all securities. The proportion invested in each security equals the percentage of the total market capitalization represented by the security.

Market Risk (Alternatively, **Systematic Risk**.) A part of a security's total risk that is related to moves in the market portfolio and, hence, cannot be diversified away.

Market Segmentation Theory An explanation of the term structure of interest rates. It holds that various investors and borrowers are restricted by law, preference, or custom to certain maturity ranges. Spot rates in each market segment are determined by supply and demand conditions there.

Market Timing A form of active management that entails shifting an investor's funds between a surrogate market portfolio and a risk-free asset, depending on the investor's perception of their near-term prospects.

Marketability See **Liquidity**.

Markup The difference in prices between what an investor pays and what the investor's broker pays for a security purchased in the over-the-counter market.

Maturity Date The date upon which a bond issuer repays investors the principal of the bond.

May Day The date (May 1, 1975) that the New York Stock Exchange ended its fixed-commission rate requirement and permitted member firms to negotiate commission rates with customers.

Mean (Alternatively, **Expected Value**.) A measure of central tendency of the probability distribution of a random variable that equals the weighted average of all possible outcomes using their probabilities as weights.

Median The outcome of a random variable where there is an equal probability of observing a value greater or less than it.

Member Corporation See **Member Firm**.

Member Firm (Alternatively, **Member Corporation** or **Member Organization**.) A brokerage firm with one or more memberships in an organized security exchange.

Member Organization See **Member Firm**.

Merger A form of corporate takeover in which two firms combine their operations and become one firm. Mergers are usually negotiated by the management of the two merging corporations.

Minimum Guaranteed Fill (MGF) The number of shares a designated market-maker stands ready to buy or sell in order to execute an order with no other counterparty.

Mispriced Security A security that is trading at a price substantially different from its intrinsic value.

Mode The outcome of a random variable that has the highest probability of occurring.

Money Market Deposit A short-term fixed income security.

Money Markets Financial markets in which financial assets with a term-to-maturity of typically one year or less are traded.

Moral Hazard A problem in pricing insurance where the likelihood of the insured event's occurring increases after insurance is purchased.

Mortgage Bond A bond which is secured by the pledge of specific property. In the event of default, bondholders are entitled to obtain the property in question and sell it to satisfy their claims on the issuer.

Multinational Firm A company whose business operations and financial investments extend across a number of countries.

Multiple Growth Model A type of dividend discount model in which dividends are assumed to grow at different rates over specifically defined time periods.

Municipal Bond A bond issued by a state or local unit of government.

Mutual Fund See **Open-end Investment Company**.

Naked Call Writing The process of writing a call option on a stock that the option writer does not own.

Naked Put Writing The process of writing a put option on a stock when the writer does not have the sufficient cash (or securities) in his or her brokerage account to purchase the stock.

National Association of Securities Dealers Automated Quotations (NASDAQ) An automated nationwide communications network operated by the National Association of Securities Dealers which connects dealers and brokers in the US over-the-counter market. NASDAQ provides current market-maker bid-ask price quotes to market participants.

Neglected Firm Effect An empirical observation that firms followed by relatively few security analysts have had abnormally high returns.

Net Asset Value The market value of an investment company's assets, less any liabilities, divided by the number of shares outstanding.

Net Present Value The present value of future cash flows expected to be received from a particular investment less the cost of that investment.

No Growth Model See **Zero Growth Model**.

No-Load Fund A mutual fund that does not have a load charge.

Nominal Return The percentage change in the value of an investment in a financial asset, where the beginning and ending values of the asset are not adjusted for inflation over the time of the investment.

Nonfactor Risk (Alternatively, **Idiosyncratic Risk**.) That part of a security's total risk which is not related to moves in various common factors and, hence, can be diversified away.

Nonmarket Risk See **Unique Risk**.

Nonsatiation A condition whereby investors are assumed to always prefer higher levels of terminal wealth to lower levels of terminal wealth.

Normal Backwardation An expected relationship between the futures price of an asset and the expected spot price of the asset on the delivery date of the contract. Normal backwardation states that the futures price will be less than the expected spot price.

Normal Contango An expected relationship between the futures price of an asset and the expected spot price of the asset on the delivery date of the contract. Normal contango states that the futures price will be greater than the expected spot price.

Normal Probability Distribution A symmetrical bell-shaped probability distribution, completely described by its mean and standard deviation.

Normative Economics A form of economic analysis which is prescriptive in nature, dealing with what "ought to be."

Odd Lot An amount of stock, less than a board lot, generally from 1 to 99 shares.

Ontario Securities Commission (OSC) A provincial agency that regulates the issuance of securities in the primary market and the trading of securities in the secondary market.

Open See **Opening Price**.

Open-End Investment Company (Alternatively, **Mutual Fund**.) A managed investment company, with an unlimited life, that stands ready at all times to purchase its shares from its owners and usually will continuously offer new shares to the public.

Open Interest The number of a particular futures contract outstanding at a particular point in time.

Open Order (Alternatively, **Good-Till-Cancelled Order**.) A trading order which remains in effect until it is either filled or cancelled by the investor.

Opening Price (Alternatively, **Open**.) The price at which the first trade of the day took place in a particular stock.

Opportunity Set See **Feasible Set**.

Optimal Portfolio The feasible portfolio that offers an investor the maximum level of satisfaction. This portfolio represents the tangency between the efficient set and an indifference curve of the investor.

Option A contract between two investors in which one investor grants the other the right to buy (or sell) a specific asset at a specific price within a specific time period.

Options on Futures See **Futures Option**.

Order Specification The investor's instructions to a broker regarding the particular characteristics of a trading order, including the name of the security's issuing firm, whether to buy or sell, order size, maximum time the order is to be outstanding, and the type of order to be used.

Order Trader A floor trader who may only trade client orders on the floor of an exchange.

Ordinary Least Squares See **Simple Linear Regression**.

Organized Exchange A central physical location where trading of securities is done under a set of rules and regulations.

Original Issue Discount Security A security which is issued with a coupon interest rate below prevailing market interest rates on similar securities and, thus, is originally sold at a discount from par value.

Out of the Money Option In the case of a call (put) option, an option whose exercise price is greater than (less than) the market price of its underlying asset.

Out-of-Sample Data (Alternatively, **Holdout Sample**.) In the context of constructing a security valuation model, information which is obtained from periods different from those used to estimate the valuation model.

Overmargined Account A margin account in which the actual margin has risen above the initial margin requirement.

Overpriced Security (Alternatively, **Overvalued Security**.) A security whose expected return is less than its equilibrium expected return. Equivalently, a security with a negative alpha.

Oversubscription Privilege The opportunity given shareholders who have exercised their rights in a rights offering to buy shares that were not purchased in the offering.

Over-the-Counter Market (OTC Market) A secondary market for securities distinct from an organized security exchange.

Overvalued Security See **Overpriced Security**.

Pac-Man Defence A strategy used by corporations to ward off hostile takeovers. The targeted company reverses the takeover effort and seeks to acquire the firm making the initial takeover attempt.

Par Value of Bond See **Principal**.

Par Value of Common Stock The nominal value of shares of common stock as legally carried on the books of a corporation.

Participating Bond A bond that promises to pay a stated rate of interest to its owner, but may also pay additional interest if the issuer's earnings exceed a specified level.

Participation Certificate A bond which represents an ownership interest in a pool of fixed-income securities. The holders of the certificates receive the interest and principal payments on the pooled securities in proportion to their ownership of the pool.

Passive Investment System (Alternatively, **Passive Management**.) The process of buying and holding a well-diversified portfolio.

Passive Management See **Passive Investment System**.

Payout Ratio The percentage of a firm's earnings paid to shareholders in the form of cash dividends.

Pegging The process by which investment bankers attempt to stabilize the price of an underwritten security in the secondary market for a period of time after the initial offering date.

Perfect Markets Security markets in which no impediments to investing exist. These impediments include such things as finite divisibility of securities, taxes, transactions costs, and costly information.

Performance Attribution The identification of sources of returns for a portfolio or security over a particular evaluation interval of time.

Performance Margin The initial margin that must be posted by a futures buyer or seller.

Poison Pill Defence A strategy used by corporations to ward off hostile takeovers. The targeted company gives its shareholders certain rights that can be exercised only in the event of a hostile takeover, and that, once exercised, will be extremely onerous to the acquirer.

Political Risk The uncertainty in the return on a foreign financial asset due to the possibility that the foreign government might take actions that are detrimental to the investor's financial interests.

Portfolio Construction (Alternatively, **Security Selection**.) A component of the investment process that involves identifying which assets to invest in and determining the proportion of funds to invest in each of the assets.

Portfolio Insurance An investment strategy designed to guarantee a minimum rate of return while allowing the investor to benefit substantially from the positive returns generated by an investment in a risky portfolio.

Portfolio Manager An individual who utilizes the information provided by financial analysts to construct a portfolio of financial assets.

Portfolio Performance Evaluation A component of the investment process involving periodic analysis of how a portfolio performed in terms of both returns earned and risk incurred.

Portfolio Revision A component of the investment process, involving periodically repeating the processes of setting investment policy, conducting security analysis, and constructing a portfolio.

Portfolio Turnover Rate A measure of how much buying and selling occurs in a portfolio over a given period of time.

Positive Economics A form of economic analysis that is descriptive in nature, dealing with "what is."

Preemptive Rights When a corporation plans an issuance of new common shares, the right of existing shareholders to purchase the new shares in proportion to the numbers of shares that they currently own.

Preferred Shares A hybrid form of security that has characteristics of both common shares and bonds.

Premium The price of an option contract.

Price-Earnings Ratio A corporation's current stock price divided by its earnings per share.

Price Impact The effect on the price of a security resulting from a trade in that security. Price impact is the result of several factors: size of the trade, demand for immediate liquidity, and presumed information of the individual or organization placing the order.

Price Relative The price of a security in one period divided by the price of that same security in a previous period.

Price-Weighted Market Index A market index in which the contribution of a security to the value of the index is a function of the security's current market price.

Primary Security Market The market in which securities are sold at the time of their initial issuance.

Principal (Alternatively, **Face Value** or **Par Value of Bond.**) The nominal value of a bond which is repaid to bondholders at the maturity date.

Private Placement The direct sale of a newly issued security to one or a small number of large institutional investors.

Probabilistic Forecasting A form of security analysis which begins with a series of economic scenarios, along with their respective probabilities of occurrence. Under each of these scenarios, accompanying projections are made as to the prospects for various industries, companies, and stock prices.

Probability Distribution A model describing the relative frequency of possible values that a random variable can assume.

Professional Money Manager An individual or organization that invests funds on behalf of others.

Program Trading The purchase or sale of a collection of securities as if the collection were one security. Program trades are predominantly employed in portfolio insurance and index arbitrage strategies.

Promised Yield-to-Maturity The yield-to-maturity on a bond calculated assuming that all promised cash flows are received on a full and timely basis.

Prospectus The official selling circular that must be given to purchasers of new securities registered with the provincial regulator. The prospectus provides information about the issuer's business, its financial condition, and the nature of the security being offered.

Proxy A power of attorney that authorizes a designated party to cast all of a shareholder's votes on any matter brought up at the corporation's annual meeting.

Proxy Fight An attempt by dissident shareholders to solicit proxies to vote against corporate incumbents.

Purchasing Group See **Syndicate.**

Purchasing-Power Risk The risk experienced by investors in financial assets due to uncertainty concerning the impact of inflation on the real returns produced by those financial assets.

Pure-Discount Security A fixed-income security that promises to make only one payment to its owner.

Pure Factor Play See **Pure Factor Portfolio.**

Pure Factor Portfolio A portfolio which possesses a unit sensitivity to one factor, no sensitivity to any other factor, and has zero nonfactor risk.

Pure Yield Pickup Swap A type of bond swap where an investor exchanges one bond for another to obtain a higher yield over the long term, with little attention paid to the near-term outlook for the bonds' respective market segments or the market as a whole.

Put-Call Parity The relationship between the market price on a put and a call that have the same exercise price, expiration date, and underlying stock.

Put Option A contract that gives the buyer the right to sell a specific number of shares of a company to the writer at a specific price within a specific time.

R-Squared See **Coefficient of Determination.**

Random Error Term The difference between the actual value of a random variable and the predicted value based on some model.

Random Variable A variable that takes on alternative values according to chance.

Random Walk (or **Random Walk Model)** In general, a situation in which changes in the value of a random variable are independent and identically distributed. When applied to common shares, it refers to a situation in which security price changes are independent and identically distributed, meaning that the size of a security's price change from one period to the next can be viewed as being determined by the spin of a roulette wheel.

Rate Anticipation Swap A type of bond swap where an investor exchanges bonds that are expected to perform relatively poorly for those that are expected to perform relatively well, given an anticipated movement in interest rates.

Rate of Return The percentage change in the value of an investment in a financial asset (or portfolio of financial assets) over a specified time period.

Real Estate Investment Trust (REIT) An investment fund, similar to an investment company, whose investment objective is to hold primarily real-estate-related assets, either through mortgages, construction and development loans, or equity interests.

Real Investment An investment involving some kind of tangible asset, such a land, equipment, or buildings.

Real Return The percentage change in the value of an investment in a financial asset, where the beginning and ending values of the asset are adjusted for inflation over the time of the investment.

Real Return Bond A Government of Canada bond whose coupon payments and face value are indexed to the Consumer Price Index, thereby providing investors with a known real return if held to maturity.

Realized Capital Gain (or **Loss)** A capital gain (or loss) on an asset that is recognized, for tax purposes, through the sale or exchange of the asset.

Red Herring A preliminary prospectus that provides much of the information in the final prospectus, but is not an offer to sell the security, nor does it display an actual offering price.

Redemption Fee (Alternatively, **Back-End Load** or **Contingent Deferred Sales Charge** or **Exit Fee**.) A fee levied by an investment company when an investor sells shares back to the investment company.

Regional Brokerage Firm An organization offering brokerage services that specializes in trading the securities of companies located in a particular region of the country.

Regional Exchange An organized exchange which specializes in trading the securities of companies located in a particular region of the country.

Registered Bond A bond for which the owner is registered with the issuer. The bondholder receives coupon payments directly from the issuer. Ownership changes require notification of the issuer.

Registered Representative See **Account Executive**.

Registered Trader A floor trader who may execute both client and the firm's orders on the floor of an exchange.

Registrar A designated agent of a corporation responsible for cancelling and issuing shares of stock in the corporation as these shares are issued or traded.

Registration A procedure, usually involving the filing of a prospectus with the relevant provincial regulator, that must be completed prior to initiating a public security offering.

Reinvestment-Rate Risk The uncertainty in the return on a fixed-income asset caused by unanticipated changes in the interest rate at which cash flows from the asset can be reinvested.

Repo Rate The rate of interest involved in a repurchase agreement.

Reported Earnings See **Accounting Earnings**.

Repurchase Agreement A type of money market instrument. It involves the sale of a financial asset from one investor to another. The investor selling the asset simultaneously agrees to repurchase it from the purchaser on a stated future date at a predetermined price, which is higher than the original transaction price.

Repurchase Offer An offer by the management of a corporation to buy back some of its own stock.

Residual Standard Deviation See **Standard Deviation of the Random Error Term**.

Restricted Stock Equity shares whose voting rights are in some way diminished or curtailed. Restricted voting shares each carry the requisite number of votes per share but the shareholder is not permitted to vote the full number of shares he or she owns. Subordinate voting shares are those with fewer votes per share than regular common shares and non-voting shares are those with no voting rights.

Retention Ratio The percentage of a firm's earnings that are not paid to shareholders, but instead are retained by the firm. Equivalently, one minus the payout ratio.

Return Generating Process A statistical model which describes how the returns on a security are produced.

Return on Equity The earnings per share of a firm divided by the firm's book value per share.

Reverse Stock Split A form of stock split whereby the number of shares is reduced and the par value per share is increased.

Reversing Trade The purchase or sale of a futures (or options) contract designed to offset, and thereby cancel, the previous sale or purchase of the same contract.

Reward-to-Variability Ratio (Sharpe Ratio) An *ex post* risk-adjusted measure of portfolio performance where risk is defined as the standard deviation of the portfolio's returns. Mathematically, over an evaluation interval, it is the excess return of a portfolio divided by the standard deviation of the portfolio's returns.

Reward-to-Volatility Ratio (Treynor Ratio) An *ex post* risk-adjusted measure of portfolio performance where risk is defined as the market risk of the portfolio. Mathematically, over an evaluation interval it is the excess return of portfolio divided by the beta of the portfolio.

Right An option issued to existing shareholders that permits them to buy a specified number of new shares at a designated subscription price. For each shareholder, this number is proportional to the number of existing shares currently owned by each shareholder.

Rights Offering The sale of new stock conducted by first offering the stock to existing shareholders in proportion to the number of shares owned by each shareholder.

Risk The uncertainty associated with the end-of-period value of an investment in an asset or portfolio of assets.

Risk-Adjusted Return The return on an asset or portfolio, modified to explicitly account for the risk to which the asset or portfolio is exposed.

Risk-Averse Investor An investor who prefers an investment with less risk over one with more risk, assuming that both investments offer the same expected return.

Risk-free Asset An asset whose return over a given holding period is certain and known at the beginning of the holding period.

Risk-free Borrowing The act of borrowing funds that are to be repaid with a known rate of interest.

Risk-free Lending (Investing) The act of investing in a risk-free asset.

Risk-Neutral Investor An investor who has no preference between investments with varying levels of risk, assuming that the investments offer the same expected return.

Risk Premium The difference between the expected yield-to-maturity of a risky bond and the expected yield-to-maturity of a similar default-free bond.

Risk-Seeking Investor An investor who prefers an investment with more risk over one with less risk, assuming that both investments offer the same expected return.

Risk Structure The set of yields-to-maturity across bonds that possess different degrees of default risk, but are similar with respect to other attributes.

Risk Tolerance The trade-off between risk and expected return demanded by a particular investor.

Round Lot An amount of stock generally equal to 100 shares or a multiple of 100 shares.

Savings Foregone consumption. The difference between current income and current consumption.

Seat The designation of membership in an organized exchange. By holding a seat, the member has the privilege of being able to execute trades using the facilities provided by the exchange.

Secondary Distribution A means of selling a block of stock where the shares are sold away from an organized exchange after the close of trading in a manner similar to the sale of new issues of common stock.

Secondary Security Market The market in which securities are traded that have been issued at some previous point in time.

Sector Factor A factor which affects the return on securities within a particular economic sector.

Securities and Exchange Commission (SEC) A US federal agency established by the Securities Exchange Act of 1934 that regulates the issuance of securities in the primary market and the trading of securities in the secondary market.

Security (Alternatively, **Financial Asset**.) A legal representation of the right to receive prospective future benefits under stated conditions.

Security Analysis A component of the investment process that involves determining the prospective future benefits of a security, the conditions under which such benefits will be received, and the likelihood of such conditions occurring.

Security Analyst See **Financial Analyst**.

Security Market See **Financial Market**.

Security Market Line Derived from the CAPM, a linear relationship between the expected returns on securities and the risk of those securities, with risk expressed as the security's beta (or equivalently, the security's covariance with the market portfolio).

Security Selection See **Portfolio Construction**.

Selectivity An aspect of security analysis that entails forecasting the price movements of individual securities.

Self-Regulation A method of governmental regulation where the rules and standards of conduct in security markets are set by firms that operate in these markets, subject to the oversight of various governmental agencies such as the OSC.

Selling Group A group of investment banking organizations who, as part of a security underwriting are responsible for selling the security.

Semistrong-Form Market Efficiency A level of market efficiency in which all relevant publicly available information is fully and immediately reflected in security prices.

Sensitivity See **Factor Loading**.

Separation Theorem A feature of the Capital Asset Pricing Model which states that the optimal combination of risky assets for an investor can be determined without any knowledge about the investor's preferences towards risk and return.

Serial Bond A bond issue with different portions of the issue maturing at different dates.

Settle Price (or **Settlement Price**) The representative price for a futures contract determined during the closing period of the futures exchange.

Settlement Date The date after a security has been traded, on which the buyer must deliver cash to the seller and the seller must deliver the security to the buyer.

Shelf Registration Under National Policy 44, issuers may register securities in advance of their issuance and sell these securities up to two years later.

Short Hedger A hedger who offsets risk by selling futures contracts.

Short Interest Position The number of shares of a given company that have been sold short and, as of a given date, the loans remain outstanding.

Short Sale The sale of a security that is not owned by an investor, but rather is borrowed from a broker. The investor eventually repays the broker in kind by purchasing the same security in a subsequent transaction.

Simple Linear Regression (Alternatively, **Ordinary Least Squares**.) A statistical model of the relationship between two random variables in which one variable is hypothesized to be linearly related to the other. This relationship is depicted by a regression line which is a straight line, "fitted" to pairs of values of the two variables, so that the sum of the squared random error terms is minimized.

Sinking Fund Periodic payments made by a bond issuer to reduce, in an orderly manner, the amount of outstanding principal on a bond issue over the life of the bond.

Size Effect (Alternatively, **Small Firm Effect**.) An empirical regularity whereby stock returns appear to differ consistently across the spectrum of market capitalization. Over extended periods of time, smaller capitalization stocks have outperformed larger capitalization stocks on a risk-adjusted basis.

Small Firm Effect See **Size Effect**.

Soft Dollars Brokerage commissions ostensibly paid for having a brokerage firm execute a trade and indirectly designated, in part, as payment for non-trade-related services rendered.

Special Offering or Bid A trade involving a large block of stock on an organized security exchange whereby a number of brokerage firms attempt to execute the order by soliciting offsetting orders from their customers.

Specialist A dealer who acts as a market maker on the New York Stock Exchange. The term is also used to describe the market makers on the Canadian options exchanges.

Speculative Grade Bonds (Also known in the US as **Junk Bonds.**) Bonds which are not investment grade bonds. Usually, speculative bonds have a BB (Dominion Bond Rating Service) or B+ (Canadian Bond Rating Service) or lower rating.

Speculator An investor in future contracts whose primary objective is to make a profit from buying and selling these contracts.

Split-Funding A situation in which an institutional investor divides its funds among two or more professional money managers.

Spot Market The market for an asset which involves the immediate exchange of the asset for cash.

Spot Price The purchase price of an asset in the spot market.

Spot Rate The annual yield-to-maturity on a pure-discount security.

Standard Deviation A measure of the dispersion of possible outcomes around the expected outcome of a random variable.

Standard Deviation of the Random Error Term (Alternatively, **Residual Standard Deviation.**) In the context of simple linear regression, a measure of the dispersion of possible outcomes of the random error term.

Standard Error of Alpha The standard deviation of a security's estimated alpha, as derived from the *ex post* characteristic line.

Standard Error of Beta The standard deviation of a security's estimated beta, as derived from the *ex post* characteristic line.

Standardized Unexpected Earnings The difference between a firm's actual earnings over a given period less an estimate of the firm's expected earnings, with this quantity divided by the standard deviation of the firm's previous earnings forecast errors.

Standby Agreement An arrangement between a security issuer and an underwriter as part of a rights offering. The underwriter agrees to purchase at a fixed price all securities not purchased by current stockholders.

State-Preference Method A method of valuing securities that is based on analyzing a security's payoffs in different states of the world (outcomes) and the probabilities of those states occurring.

Stochastic Process Risk In the context of immunization, the risk that the yield curve will shift in a way that prevents an immunized bond portfolio from producing its expected cash inflows.

Stock Dividend An accounting transaction that distributes stock to existing shareholders in proportion to the number of shares currently owned by the shareholders. A stock dividend entails a transfer from retained earnings to the capital stock account of a dollar amount that is equal to the market value of the distributed stock.

Stock Split Similar to a stock dividend, an accounting transaction that increases the amount of stock held by existing shareholders in proportion to the number of shares currently owned by shareholders. A stock split entails a reduction in the par value of the corporation's stock and the simultaneous exchange of a multiple number of new shares for each existing share.

Stop Loss Order See **Stop Order.**

Stop Order (Alternatively, **Stop Loss Order.**) A trading order that specifies a stop price. If the security's price reaches or passes the stop price, then a market order is created.

Stop Price The price specified by an investor when a stop order or a stop limit order is placed that defines the price at which the market order or limit order for the security is to become effective.

Straddle An options strategy which involves buying (or writing) both a call and a put on the same asset, with the options having the same exercise price and expiration date.

Straight Voting System See **Majority Voting System.**

Street Name An arrangement between an investor and a brokerage firm where the investor maintains an account in which the investor's securities are registered in the name of the brokerage firm.

Striking Price See **Exercise Price.**

Strong-Form Market Efficiency A level of market efficiency in which all relevant information, both public and private, is fully and immediately reflected in security prices.

Subordinated Debenture A debenture whose claims, in the event of bankruptcy, are junior to other bonds issued by the firm.

Subscription Price The price at which holders of rights are permitted to purchase shares of stock in a rights offering.

Substitution Swap A type of bond swap where an investor exchanges one bond with a lower yield for another with a higher yield, yet both bonds have essentially the same financial characteristics.

Supply-to-Sell Schedule A description of the quantities of a security that an investor is prepared to sell at alternative prices.

Sustainable Earnings The amount of earnings that a firm could pay out each year, with the result that the firm's future earnings neither increase nor decrease.

Swap Bank Typically a chartered or investment bank that sets up equity, interest rate, and other kinds of swaps between interested counterparties.

Syndicate (Alternatively, **Purchase Group.**) A group of investment banking organizations that, as part of a security underwriting, are responsible for purchasing the security from the issuer and reselling it to the public.

Synthetic Futures (Synthetic Futures Contract) The creation of a position equivalent to either the purchase of a futures contract by buying a call option and writing a put option on the asset or to the sale of a futures contract by buying a put option and writing a call option on the asset.

Synthetic Put A form of portfolio insurance that emulates the investment outcomes of a put option through the use of a dynamic asset allocation strategy.

Systematic Risk See **Market Risk**.

Takeover An action by an individual or firm to acquire controlling interest in a corporation.

Target Firm A firm that is the subject of a takeover attempt.

Technical Analysis A form of security analysis which attempts to forecast the movement in the prices of securities based primarily on historical price and volume trends in those securities.

Tender Offer A form of corporate takeover in which a firm or individual offers to buy some or all of the shares of a target firm at a stated price. This offer is publicly advertised and material describing the bid is mailed to the target's stockholders.

Term Bond A bond issued where all of the bonds mature on the same date.

Term Structure The set of yields-to-maturity across bonds that possess different terms-to-maturity, but are similar with respect to other attributes.

Term-to-Maturity The time remaining until a bond's maturity date.

Terminal Wealth The value of an investor's portfolio at the end of a holding period. Equivalently, the investor's initial wealth multiplied times one plus the rate of return earned on the investor's portfolio over the holding period.

Third Market A secondary security market where exchange-listed securities are traded over the counter.

Time Deposit A savings account at a financial institution.

Time Value (Premium) The excess of the market price of an option over its intrinsic value.

Time-Weighted Return A method of measuring the performance of a portfolio over a particular period of time. It is the cumulative compounded rate of return of the portfolio, calculated on each date that a cash flow moves into or out of the portfolio over the performance measurement period.

Timing An aspect of security analysis which entails forecasting the price movements of asset classes relative to one another.

Top-Down Forecasting A sequential approach to security analysis which entails first making forecasts for the economy, then for industries, and finally for individual companies. Each level of forecasts is conditional on the previous level of forecasts made.

Total Risk The standard deviation of the return on a security or a portfolio.

Trading Halt A temporary suspension in the trading of a security on an organized exchange.

Trading Post The physical location on the floor of an organized exchange where a market-maker in a particular stock is located and where all orders involving the stock may be taken for execution.

Transfer Agent A designated agent of a corporation, usually a bank, which administers the transfer of shares of a corporation's stock between old and new owners.

Treasury Bill A security issued by the Canadian Government with a maximum term-to-maturity of one year. Interest and principal are paid only at maturity.

Treasury Stock Common stock which has been issued by a corporation and then later purchased by the corporation in the open market or through a tender offer. This stock does not include voting rights or rights to receive dividends and is equivalent economically to unissued stock.

Triple Witching Hour The date when options on individual stocks and market indices, futures on market indices, and options on market index futures expire simultaneously.

Trustee An organization, usually a bank, which serves as the representative of bondholders. The trustee acts to protect the interests of bondholders and facilitates communication between them and the issuer.

Turn-of-the-Month Effect The observation that average stock returns have been abnormally high during a four-day period beginning on the last trading day of the month.

Unbiased Expectations Theory An explanation of the term structure of interest rates. It holds that a forward rate represents the average opinion of the expected future spot rate for the time period in question.

Underpriced Security (Alternatively, **Undervalued Security**.) A security whose expected return is greater than its equilibrium expected return. Equivalently, a security with a positive alpha.

Undervalued Security See **Underpriced Security**.

Underwriter See **Investment Banker**.

Underwriting The process by which investment bankers bring new securities to the primary security market.

Unexpected Rate of Inflation That portion of inflation experienced over a given period of time that was not anticipated by investors.

Unique Risk (Alternatively, **Non-Market Risk** or **Unsystematic Risk**.) That part of a security's total risk which is not related to moves in the market portfolio and, hence, can be diversified away.

Unrealized Capital Gain (or Loss) A capital gain (or loss) on an asset that has not yet been recognized for tax purposes through the sale or exchange of the asset.

Unseasoned Offering See **Initial Public Offering**.

Unsystematic Risk See **Unique Risk**.

Up-Tick A trade in a security made at a price higher than the price of the previous trade in that same security.

Value-Relative The holding period return for a security, plus one.

Value Stock Typically, a stock that has experienced relatively poor past price performance, or whose issuing company has experienced relatively poor past earnings results. It is often characterized as having high earnings-to-price and book-value-to-market-value ratios.

Value-Weighted Market Index (Alternatively, **Capitalization-Weighted Market Index**.) A market index in which the contribution of a security to the value of the index is a function of the security's market capitalization.

Variable Rate See **Floating Rate**.

Variance The squared value of the standard deviation.

Variance-Covariance Matrix A table which symmetrically arrays the covariances between a number of random variables. Variances of the random variables lie on the diagonal of the matrix, while covariances between the random variables lie above and below the diagonal.

Wash Sale The sale and subsequent purchase of a "substantially identical" security solely for the purpose of generating a tax deductible capital loss.

Weak-Form Market Efficiency A level of market efficiency in which all previous security price data is fully and immediately reflected in current security prices.

Weekend Effect See **Day-of-the-Week Effect**.

White Knight Another firm, favourably inclined toward a target firm's current management, which during the process of a hostile takeover of that corporation, agrees to make a better offer to the corporation's shareholders.

Yield The yield-to-maturity of a bond.

Yield Curve A visual representation of the term structure of interest rates.

Yield Spread The difference in the promised yields-to-maturity of two bonds.

Yield Structure The set of yields-to-maturity across bonds differing in terms of a number of attributes. These attributes include term-to-maturity, coupon rate, call provisions, tax status, marketability, and likelihood of default.

Yield-to-Call The yield-to-maturity of a callable bond calculated assuming that the bond is called at the earliest possible time.

Yield-to-Maturity For a particular fixed-income security, the single interest rate (with interest compounded at some specified interval) that, if paid by a bank on the amount invested in the security, would enable the investor to obtain all the payments made by that security. Equivalently, the discount rate that equates the present value of future cash flows from the security to the current market price of the security.

Zero Coupon Bond See **Pure-Discount Security**.

Zero Growth Model (Alternatively, **No Growth Model**.) A type of dividend discount model in which dividends are assumed to maintain a constant value in perpetuity.

Zero-Plus Tick A trade in a security made at a price equal to that of the previous trade in that security but higher than that of the last trade made in the security at a different price.

Solutions

Selected Solutions to End-of-Chapter Questions and Problems

Chapter 1

3. 18.2%
4. a. 30.0% b. –13.3% c. 4.0%
8. Small stock average return: 16.05%
   Small stock standard deviation: 24.79%
   Common stock average return: 12.48%
   Common stock standard deviation: 17.05%

Chapter 2

2. Five board lots and one 11-share odd lot
5. Total assets: $15 000
   Total liabilities: $6750
6. a. 62.5% b. 75.0% c. 57.1%
7. 40.0%
8. $9.23
9. $30 000
10. 17.1%
11. 74.0%, –26.0%
12. a. 56.0% b. –65.2% c. 36.7%, –30.0%
14. Total assets: $18 750
    Total liabilities: $12 500
15. a. 25.0% b. 72.6%
16. Actual margin: 39.5%
17. $53.57
19. –20.0%
20. a. –27.6% b. 43.6%
22. a. $5400 b. $5500
23. Total assets: $12 750
    Total liabilities: $7600

Chapter 3

13. Round trip transaction cost: 27.3%
    Return before transaction cost: 12.5%

Chapter 4

3. $30 100 shares
   $40 90 shares
   $50 80 shares
   $60 70 shares
   $70 60 shares

Chapter 5

1. a. 7.0% b. 9.0%
2. $939.26, $1066.23
3. a. 10.0% b. 9.8%
5. One-year spot rate: 7.5%
   Two-year spot rate: 4.0%
   Three-year spot rate: 2.8%
6. Three-year discount factor: .810
   Four-year discount factor: .731
   Five-year discount factor: .650
8. Forward rate from year one to year two: 6.0%
   Forward rate from year two to year three: 8.5%
   Forward rate from year three to year four: 8.5%
9. One-year spot rate: 10.0%
   Two-year spot rate: 9.8%
   Three-year spot rate: 9.5%
   Four-year spot rate: 9.2%
10. $994.45
11. a. One-year discount rate: .909
       Two-year discount rate: .819
       Three-year discount rate: .749
    b. Forward rate from today to one year. 10.0%
       Forward rate from year one to year two: 11.0%

Forward rate from year two or year three: 9.4%

c. $1470.20

12. a. 6.1% b. 6.2%
13. a. $39 916.80 b. $40 195.58
19. Yield on one-year pure-discount bond: 10.0%
    Yield on two-year pure-discount bond: 12.0%
20. $923.36

Chapter 6

1. a. $0.0067 b. $0.0040 d. $0.0330
2. 7.1%
9. b. $14.98
10. Expected return: 21.6%
11. $2.03
13. 6.7%
14. 10.2 years
15. a. .234 b. –30.5%
16. 16.3%

Chapter 7

11. 18.3%
12. 35.0%
13. Expected return: 8.5%
    Standard deviation: 10.1%
14. Expected return: 17.0%
    Standard deviation: 15.4%
17. Covariance: –52.1
    Correlation: –.98
18. Covariance: (*A*,*B*): .53
    Correlation: (*A*,*C*): .71
    Correlation: (*B*,*C*): .21
19. 11.6%
20. Expected return: 5.3%
    Standard deviation: 4.7%
23. a. 34.1% b. 25.0% c. 9.2%
24. a. 8.8% b. 4.7%
    c. Weight in security *A*: .556
       Weight in security *B*: .444

Chapter 8

7. Minimum standard deviation: 9.2%
   Maximum standard deviation: 23.3%
9. 12.3%
15. 1.03%
17. 19.7%
18. Portfolio 1 standard deviation: 25.0%
    Portfolio 2 standard deviation: 22.1%
21. 0.80
22. a. 1325 b. 152

Chapter 9

4. a. 17.0% b. 14.0% c. 12.5%
5. Risky portfolio weight: 1.46
6. a. 26.0% b. 18.0% c. 14.0%
7. 11.0%
14. b. Expected return: 9.0%
       Standard deviation: 10.2%
    c. Expected return: 8.0%
       Standard deviation: 7.7%

Chapter 10

10. $\bar{r}_p = 5.0\% + .39\sigma_p$
12. 15.8%
18. 1.03
19. 25.2%
20. c. Security *A* expected return: 9.4%
       Security *B* expected return: 10.8%
21. b. $\beta_1 = 1.50$
       $\beta_2 = 0.60$
23. $\beta_A = 0.74$
    $\beta_B = 1.17$

Chapter 11

6. 82% factor related, 18% nonfactor related
7. a. 1069.3 b. 43.8 c. 33.4%
8. a. 866.1 b. 35.5 c. 30.0%
9. 22.4%
10. Standard deviation of security *A*: 28.9%
    Standard deviation of security *B*: 26.3%
11. 22.5, 2.25, 0.225
13. 220, 20
15. Sensitivity to factor 1: 0.28
    Sensitivity to factor 2: 4.60
    Sensitivity to factor 3: 0.24
17. Expected return: 15.5%
    Standard deviation: 15.8%
19. Earnings yield factor value: .243%
    Book-price factor value: 4.286%
20. Security *A* standard deviation: 64.8%
    Security *B* standard deviation: 30.2%
    Covariance (*A*,*B*): 1936.5

Chapter 12

5. Weight of security *B*: –.10
   Weight of security *C*: –.10
9. 26.0%
11. r_f = 5.0%
13. 13.6%
14. a. b_{p1} = 0.0
       b_{p2} = 0.5
    b. b_{p1} = 0.0
       b_{p2} = 1.0
    c. 17.0%
    d. 7.0%
15. a. Weight of security *A*: –.043
       Weight of security *B*: –.019
       Weight of security *C*: .012
    b. 0.3%
20. a. β_A = 0.65
       β_B = 1.02
    b. Security *A* expected return: 9.9%
       Security *B* expected return: 12.1%
21. β_A = 2.08
    β_B = 1.56

Chapter 13

8. 5.26%, 5.55%
9. a. 6.90% b. 6.82% c. 6.74%
11. a. 15.6% b. 27.3% c. 42.9%
15. 4.35%
21. a. $9820
    b. 5.12% semi-annually or 10.5% annually

Chapter 14

1. 16.9%
2. a. 13.0% b. 13.6%
10. 12.8%
24. a. 14.9% b. 10.4%

Chapter 15

1. Bond's intrinsic value: $937.82
2. Bond's intrinsic value: $9358.16
3. a. $9366.03 b. 12.0%
4. Change in five-year bond's price: –7.6%
   Change in ten-year bond's price: –12.3%
6. 107 basis points
7. a. 9.0% b. 12.5%
8. 12.9%
9. Actual yield with 15% reinvestment: 9.7%
   Actual yield with 0% reinvestment: 8.0%
14. 7.6%

Chapter 16

1. $10 000.00, $8770.68, $12 316.36
2. Price of bond *A*: $10 912.50
   Price of bond *B*: $10 388.70
3. 5-year bond's price: $713.00
   10-year bond's price: $508.30
   20-year bond's price: $258.40
4. 4-year bond's price change: –11.7%
   15-year bond's price change: –24.6%
5. –7.2%, 8.0%
6. Proportion of 5-year bond's price increase due to change in present value of principal: 79.1%
   Proportion of 20-year bond's price increase due to change in present value of principal: 42.4%
7. 10% coupon bond's price increase: 14.1%
   8% coupon bond's price increase: 14.7%
8. 2.8 years
9. 2.7 years
11. 3.4 years
14. –.98%
21. Overall rate of return: 50.9%

Chapter 17

2. a. 750 001 b. 500 001 c. 1
8. a. 1 380 000, $34.78
   b. 1 600 000, $30.00
   c. 400 000, $120.00
9. a. 0.05 b. $0.476 c. $74.00
10. a. $6.00 b. $35 310.00
    c. $34 050.70 d. $34 050.70
13. 0.67
14. 1.04
15. a. 1.18 b. –0.05
    c. 1.45 d. 0.91
17. $308 million
18. a. 1.07 b. 1.39
20. 0.69

Chapter 18

1. $25.82
2. $1978.10
3. 7.0%
4. a. $6.52 b. 8.0%
5. $80.00

6. $52.00
7. 12.0%
10. $106.83
11. $70.44
12. a. $35.00 b. $46.34 c. 3.13
13. $73.03
15. $44.00
16. 10.60
17. 27.8%
18. 14.53

CHAPTER 19

2. a. Purchase $400 000 of new equity
   b. Sell $400 000 of existing equity
   c. No action
7. D_1 = $13.0 million
   D_2 = $15.7 million
   D_3 = $15.3 million
   D_4 = $13.6 million
   D_5 = $14.4 million
8. 0.60
18. $4.88
19. $SUE_6 = -0.03$
    $SUE_7 = +1.14$
    $SUE_8 = +0.77$
    $SUE_9 = -0.91$

CHAPTER 20

5. $815.00
6. $1130.00
11. $4.87
12. $3.28
13. $5.08
16. .41
17. .40
18. 216 contracts
19. a. 5.4% b. 5.94
20. $3.13
21. $11.48
23. a. $2.19
27. a. $750.00 b. $240.00 c. $900.66

CHAPTER 21

5. $15 000.00, $0.00
6. a. $1050.00 b. $3050.00 c. $50.00
12. $4200.00
13. $5 164 286.00
15. $1.79
16. 4.0%
17. $98.98
19. $20 000.00
21. a. 204
27. –40.0%

CHAPTER 22

1. $17.60
3. a. $12.45 b. $11.45
6. 8.0%
9. –1.9%
10. Year 1: 6.6%
    Year 2: 14.8%
    Year 3: –2.1%

CHAPTER 23

2. a. 1.967 b. 1.130 c. 1.478
4. a. $3 000 000 b. 8.0%
5. a. 15.0 b. 18.7 c. 18.7 d. 120.0
7. a. 3.5% b. 4.5%
8. 207.6, 215.3
18. ROA = 13.7%
    ROA = 41.1%
19. a. 15.0 b. $6.00 c. 5.0
    d. 1.7% e. 25.0%

CHAPTER 24

7. 64.8
8. 51.5
11. 32.1
12. 8.7%

CHAPTER 25

1. 12.7%
3. –2.6%
4. 18.8%
5. 10.5%
6. 9.4%
7. a. 26.0% b. 22.6%
9. 3.1%
10. 40.7%, 43.0%
13. 0.8%
14. 0.05, 0.55, 0.06
19. d. –0.51% e. 1.11%
20. 3.50, 8.24, 0.35

CHAPTER 26

5. 29.6%
6. 56.3%
9. 26.3%
11. 17.0%

Index

C

D

E

F

G

H

I

J

K

L

M

N

O

Q

R

S

U

V

W

Y

Z